THE POETICAL WORKS

OF

WORDSWORTH.

THE

COMPLETE WORKS

OF

WORDSWORTH

O sylvan Wye! Thou wanderer through the woods,
How often has my spirit turned to thee!
The Excursion

LONDON
FREDERICK WARNE & CO.

PUBLISHERS' PREFACE.

This present Edition of Wordsworth has been carefully revised, and numerous additions have been made to it. It now comprises all the Poet's best and finest poems (with his latest corrections), and is indeed complete, with the exception of "The Prelude," his last work, which was published after his death, and is not generally considered equal to his former poems.

If thou indeed derive thy light from Heaven,
Then, to the measure of that heaven-born light
Shine, Poet! in thy place, and be content,—
The stars pre-eminent in magnitude,
And they that from the zenith dart their beams,
(Visible though they be to half the earth,
Though half a sphere be conscious of their brightness)
Are yet of no diviner origin,
No purer essence, than the one that burns,
Like an untended watch-fire, on the ridge
Of some dark mountain; or than those which seem
Humbly to hang, like twinkling winter lamps
Among the branches of the leafless trees;
All are the undying offspring of one Sire
Then, to the measure of the light vouchsafed,
Shine Poet! in thy place, and be content

CONTENTS

Juvenile Poems.

Poems Referring to the Period of Childhood.

Poems Founded on the Affections.

Poems of the Fancy.

Poems of the Imagination

Miscellaneous Sonnets.

Memorials of a Tour in Scotland.

1803.

Memorials of a Tour in Scotland.

1814.

Poems on the Naming of Places.

Inscriptions.

Sonnets Dedicated to Liberty.

Memorials of a Tour on the Continent.

1820.

Ecclesiastical Sketches.

PART I.

FROM THE INTRODUCTION OF CHRISTIANITY INTO BRITAIN, TO THE CONSUMMATION OF THE PAPAL DOMINION.

PART II.

TO THE CLOSE OF THE TROUBLES IN THE REIGN OF CHARLES I.

PAGE

PART III.

FROM THE RESTORATION TO THE PRESENT TIMES.

The River Duddon.

A SERIES OF SONNETS.

Poems of Sentiment and Reflection.

Poems Referring to the Period of Old Age.

Epitaphs and Elegiac Poems

The Excursion.

POEMS COMPOSED DURING A TOUR IN SCOTLAND, AND ON THE ENGLISH BORDER, IN THE AUTUMN OF 1831.

Memorials of a Tour in Italy.

MEMOIR.

WILLIAM WORDSWORTH, the most distinguished philosophical poet that England has produced, was born at Cockermouth, in Cumberland, on the 7th of April, 1770.

The family of Wordsworth appears to have been of some little antiquity, as members of it are found settled at Pennistone, near Doncaster, so far back as the reign of Edward III., and the poet himself had in his possession an antique oak chest, or almery, of the reign of Henry VIII. (1525), on which was recorded, in curious carving, some generations of the family pedigree. But the branch from which he sprang was originally planted at Falthwaite, near Stainborough, and removed thence to Sockbridge, in Westmoreland, about the beginning of the last century.

The poet's father, who is said to have been a man of vigorous mental powers and of some eloquence, was an attorney, and held the appointment of law-agent to the Earl of Lonsdale. Ann Cookson, the poet's mother, was the daughter of a mercer of Penrith, and was descended, on her mother's side, from a very ancient family—the Crackanthorpes—who had been seated at Newbiggen Hall, in Westmoreland, for more than five hundred years. She appears to have been a woman of gentle and affectionate disposition, of much wisdom, high moral principle, and unaffected piety. She died when the poet was in his eighth year; so that, like Cowper, he had hardly listened to the language of maternal love when it was lost to him for ever. Henceforth he was confided to the care of strangers. But the impressions left upon his mind by his mother's tender treatment, and by the liberal and enlarged, yet gentle and confiding spirit in which she conducted the moral and mental training of his childhood, appear to have been deep and abiding, for he has embodied them in one or two passages of his poems, in lines as full of truthful feeling and tender pathos as any in the language.

The family consisted of five children—four sons and one daughter. The eldest son became an attorney and died in 1816; the third went to sea, became commander of the *Earl of Abergavenny*, East Indiaman, and perished by shipwreck off Weymouth in 1805. The youngest, Christopher, entered the Church, and became well known as Dr. Wordsworth,* author of a work entitled 'Ecclesiastical

* Two of Dr. Wordsworth's sons have become somewhat distinguished. One of them—Christopher Wordsworth, D.D. was, in 1869, made by Mr. Gladstone, Bishop of Lincoln. He

Biography," and for many years Master of Trinity College, Cambridge. Dorothy Wordsworth, the only daughter, and the constant companion of the poet down to the day of her death, was, like her mother, a woman of gentle and affectionate nature, but of exquisite sensibility, and of considerable literary and poetic power.

But the poet, it would appear, was the only one of the family about whose future welfare his mother was anxious. He, she is recorded to have said, would be remarkable either for good or for evil. "The cause of this was," he says, "that I was of a stiff, moody, and violent temper; so much so, that I remember going once into the attics of my grandfather's house at Penrith, upon some indignity having been put upon me, with the intention of destroying myself with one of the foils which I knew was kept there. I took the foil in hand—but my heart failed." Another and better destiny was in store for him.

He received the first rudiments of learning at a dame-school at Penrith, where he was often taken when a child to reside with his maternal grand-parents. And here he had for classmate a little girl, a few months younger than himself, named Mary Hutchinson, who, some thirty years afterwards, became sole mistress of his house and heart.

After having spent a year or two at school at Cockermouth, he was, in 1778, when in the ninth year of his age, sent to the endowed Grammar-school of Hawkshead, in Lancashire, where he remained till he was fourteen. And it was while here his first attempts at verse-making were made. One of the pieces he composed unmistakably presaged two of his most prominent mental characteristics. "It was," he says, "a long poem running upon my own adventures, and the scenery of the country in which I was brought up." These verses, he adds, were admired far more than they deserved, "for they were but a tame imitation of Pope's versification, and a little in his style." The days he spent at school here, he says, were amongst the happiest of his life, chiefly because he was at liberty to read whatever books he liked. "I read," he says, "all Fielding's works, 'Don Quixote,' 'Gil Blas,' 'Gulliver's Travels,' and the 'Tale of a Tub;' the two latter," he adds, "being much to my taste," a circumstance which may account for the remarkable strength and purity of his English style.

In 1783 his father died, leaving little fortune to his children, beyond some heavy claims for professional labour rendered to the Earl of Lonsdale, whose law-agent, as already mentioned, he was. But as this nobleman refused to recognise these claims, or to meet them in any way, they remained unpaid till his death in 1802. In the meantime, the poet, and his three brothers and his sister, were thrown upon the care of their two uncles—Richard Wordsworth and Christopher

wrote the poet's life, and was the author of various valuable works on religious, classical, historical, literary, and polemical subjects. The other—Charles Wordsworth, D.D., equally able and learned, and the author of the best and most popular Greek Grammar of the present day, and of a number of other works on religious and literary topics—is Bishop of St. Andrews in the Episcopal Church of Scotland. Christopher died 1885.

Crackanthorpe—who appear to have treated them with the greatest kindness and consideration.

In 1787 Wordsworth, when in his eighteenth year, was sent by his uncles to St. John's College, Cambridge, where he remained for four years. But his university career was neither pleasant to himself nor satisfactory to his friends. His early scholastic training does not appear to have been of a kind to enable him to pursue his university studies with the same prospect of success as was within reach of youths who had been reared at the great public schools; and he consequently felt inwardly dissatisfied and ill at ease, and spent his time in aimless projects and in desultory pursuits. Besides, in other respects, the cloistered silence and constraint of these classic shades seem to have been unsuited to his nature. They "froze the genial current of his soul," for the only poem composed while he was at Cambridge was the "Evening Walk," none of the imagery of which is derived from academic scenes. It certainly does appear, at first sight, somewhat singular, that a mind so meditative, so calmly philosophical, should have felt so ill at ease in this "garden of great intellects.' But the cause is clear. Hi. love of nature from childhood upwards was intense. "The sounding cataract, the tall rock, the mountain, and the deep and gloomy wood, their glorious colours and their glowing forms," haunted him like a passion; so that, amid these grand old halls, grey with age and rich in historic and intellectual renown—for centuries "the sacred nurseries of blooming youth"—his spirit pined for the freedom of its native hills and dales; and at every convenient opportunity he seems to have escaped from academic rule, and to have rambled at will, for months together, among his beloved lakes and mountains.

In the autumn of 1790, his last college vacation, he made, in the company of a fellow-collegian, Mr. Jones, afterwards a clergyman of the Church of England, a pedestrian tour through France and Switzerland to the north of Italy. "We went staff in hand," he says, "without knapsacks, and carrying each his needments tied up in a pocket-handkerchief, with about £20 apiece in our pockets." During this journey he seems to have become infected with the prevailing revolutionary fever, which had just then become epidemic in France; and he hailed the rising revolution with feelings of enthusiastic admiration, as a new era of liberty and happiness that was about to burst upon mankind.

"Bliss was it in that dawn to be *alive*;
But to be *young* was very heaven."

Few of the younger spirits of the time escaped the contagion—the poets especially, Burns, Byron, Coleridge, Southey, Campbell all felt the flame more or less intensely. The poem entitled "Descriptive Sketches" arose out of materials obtained during this ramble.

In January, 1791, he took his degree of B.A. and left Cambridge; and, after a few months' residence in London, he paid a visit to his friend Jones, at the house of his father in Wales, and with him made a pedestrian excursion among the magnificent mountains of North Wales.

About this time he was urged by some of his friends to enter the Church; but probably his republican sentiments, and the unsettled state of his mind, rendered him averse to such a step. In the meantime he resolved to visit France again.

The first thrilling scenes of the great revolutionary drama which was then enacting on the soil of France seem to have stirred his soul "like the sound of a trumpet." The flutter of the tricolor was for ever in his eyes, and the deep roll of the tocsin for ever in his ears, and he became too excited to remain a mere distant spectator. In November, 1791, therefore, he hurried across the little strip of silver sea that separated him from them, and spent the following year in the midst of them. He passed a few days at Paris, listened to the harangues in the National Assembly and at the Club of the Jacobins, picked up a stone as a relic from the ruins of the Bastille; and

> "Became a patriot—and his heart was all
> Given to the people; and his love was theirs."

From Paris he proceeded to Orleans; and, as he marched along the endless avenues of elms, and passed each vine-clad slope, it seemed, to his excited mind, as if

> "From every cot, he watchful bird
> Crowed with ear-piercing power till then unheard."

At Orleans he became acquainted with the republican General Beaupuis, whom he has described in glowing and affectionate terms as an ardent patriot, a brave soldier, and a wise and virtuous philosopher. On the banks of the Loire, and in the woods near Orleans, the enthusiastic and delighted pair took long and frequent walks, in which they talked in rapt and hopeful terms of an approaching "progeny of golden years" that were about to bless mankind. His friend ultimately fell—"fighting in supreme command"—in one of the many engagements which took place on the banks of the Loire.

In the spring of 1792 Wordsworth left Orleans for Blois, where he spent the summer. In the autumn he proceeded to Paris, which he reached while the blood of the massacres of September may be said to have still clung to the streets. Royalty had fallen, and was speedily to perish. The unfortunate king, and his still more unfortunate family, were in prison, and apart. France was a republic. And everywhere the general joy was being proclaimed amidst the roll of drums, the rattle of arms, and the shouts of maddened multitudes marching to the music of the *Marseillaise*. But clouds had already begun to gather. The first red drops had fallen—ominous precursors of the coming torrents that were to drench the soil with blood. Such were the libations poured out to so-called Liberty! The poet, says his nephew, visited the dungeon and the palace, and the Place du Carrousel, where

> "So late had lain
> The dead upon the dying heaped"

"He describes the awe which he felt by night in the high, dark, lonely chamber in which he lodged, when he thought of those scenes of carnage, until he seemed

> To hear a voice that cried,
> To the whole city, 'Sleep no more!'"

These scenes are said to have made so deep an impression on him, that for years afterwards they haunted him in his dreams!

Appalled by what he saw, and stung with disappointment that no great spirit had emerged to crush the impious leaders of "the atheist crew," he began to forebode the approach of the Reign of Terror. Yet, as if by some mysterious spell, he seemed fascinated by what he saw, and felt riveted to the fatal spot. Fortunately for him however, circumstances compelled him to return to England, and he reluctantly tore himself away. Had he remained but a little longer, he would, in all probability, have been swept away with the innumerable victims that perished in the excesses of that sanguinary period. He afterwards gratefully acknowledged that he had been rescued "by the gracious providence of Heaven" from a bloody and untimely end.

Yet, notwithstanding what he had witnessed, he clung for some years unfalteringly to his republican faith. Gradually, however, as he grew older, his political opinions changed, and he ultimately became "the constant advocate of a strong government, which should rigidly administer the institutions matured in a long course of ages, and only suffer them to be altered slowly and gradually according to the dictates of experience." In other words, he became a Conservative in politics. For this change in his political opinions, however, he was frequently and bitterly attacked. And there cannot be a doubt but that much of the hostility which greeted the literary efforts of his earlier years arose from the strong feelings engendered by a knowledge of this fact. For in those times party spirit ran so high, that the light in which a man's productions were regarded, whether in literature, science, or art, depended almost entirely on the special political bias of the party regarding them. In reference to this change, however, the poet, in his defence, said,—"I should think that I had lived to little purpose if my notions on the subject of government had undergone no modification. My youth must, in that case, have been without enthusiasm, and my manhood endued with small capability of profiting by *reflection*." His conservatism, he asserted, arose from reflection on the frightful excesses he had seen perpetrated on the soil of France in the sacred name of Liberty; and from indignation and abhorrence at the insane ambition and sanguinary and oppressive measures of the imperial despot who had sprung phœnix-like from the ashes of that Liberty whose coming had been so long and so hopefully looked for, and whose birth had been so universally and so enthusiastically welcomed, but whose existence, alas! had been at once so brief and so bloody.

In 1793 his first pieces appeared—"The Evening Walk" and "Descriptive Sketches." They attracted little public attention; but Coleridge, into whose hands they had fallen, thought highly of them, and asserted with some warmth that "seldom, if ever, was the emergence of an original poetic genius above the literary horizon more evidently announced."

For the next year or two Wordsworth wandered about, making various pedestrian excursions, accompanied by his sister Dorothy ; who, for the rest of his days, was to be the faithful and revered companion of his life and labours. And during this period he seems to have become gradually impressed with the belief that the vocation of the poet was the calling for which he had been born. But while he thought so, he was, for the time, compelled to look about for some other means of livelihood. He planned a monthly publication—*The Philanthropist*—which was to have been republican, but not revolutionary ; but it came to nothing He then tried to find employment in connexion with the metropolitan newspaper press; and while he was still in doubt as to whether he should succeed, the liberality of an amiable young friend, whose sick-bed he had attended, placed him for a time beyond all anxiety on this score. This generous friend—Raisley Calvert, son of a gentleman who was steward to the Duke of Norfolk—was so impressed with the belief that Wordsworth, if possessed of independent means, would benefit mankind by his writings, that he left him a legacy of £900 that he might devote himself to the vocation that was to be the sole business of his life. Upon the interest of this sum, £400 having been laid out in annuity, with £200 deducted from the principal, and £100, a legacy his sister had been left, and £100 more which he had for "The Lyrical Ballads," his sister and himself contrived to live for nearly eight years, at the end of which period Lord Lonsdale died, and his successor at once discharged the debt due to the Wordsworth family, which amounted to £8500. Of this sum £1800 apiece fell to his sister and himself, an amount which, for their moderate desires, amply sufficed to support them in comfort for many additional years.

In the autumn of 1795, Wordsworth and his sister were settled at Racedown Lodge, in Dorsetshire, where they industriously employed themselves in reading, writing, and gardening. Here he wrote his tragedy of "The Borderers," which he sent to Mr. Harris, who was then manager of Covent Garden Theatre ; but which that gentleman returned as unsuited for the stage. It appears to have been thrown aside, as it was not published till nearly fifty years afterwards (1842). Here, also, he first made the acquaintance of Coleridge, whom he described at that time as "a noticeable man, with large grey eyes," but "depressed by weight of musing fantasy." The two poets appear to have been so delighted with each other's society, that they became eager for closer intimacy. In July, 1797, therefore, Wordsworth and his sister removed to Alfoxden, a beautiful and romantic spot in the neighbourhood of Nether-Stowey, in Somersetshire, where Coleridge then resided. The house they occupied is described by Miss Wordsworth as charmingly situated on a slope within sight of the sea, and "in the midst of woods as wild as fancy ever painted." Here they remained for about a year—a period which the poet describes as a most pleasant and productive time of his life.

It was during his residence here, also, that the "Lyrical Ballads" originated. Their plan was the joint production of himself and Coleridge, and a distinct part in its execution was assigned to each. It had arisen out of the idea that a series of poems might be composed of two sorts. In the one the incidents and agents were to be in part supernatural; in the other, the subjects were to be chosen from ordinary life.

Accordingly, the supernatural or romantic section was assigned to Coleridge, while Wordsworth was "to give the charm of novelty to things of every day," and to awaken "the mind's attention to the lethargy of custom, and to direct it to the loveliness and the wonders of the world around us." In the autumn of 1798, therefore, the "Lyrical Ballads" were published in one volume, consisting of twenty-three poems ("The Ancient Mariner" and two others having been contributed by Coleridge), by Joseph Cottle, a bookseller of Bristol, who gave thirty guineas for the copyright.

The poems were published as a protest against the prevailing artificial literature of the period. The false and unnatural diction of that literature, its general inattention to the beauties of external nature, and its utter want of sympathy with the ordinary events and common feelings of mankind, the poet had long perceived and lamented; and he felt that he possessed the power of producing poetry in which these faults should not only be avoided, but in which he should "impart moral grandeur to poverty, and invest the objects of irrational and inanimate nature with a beauty and grace, of which, it seemed to him, they had long been stripped by a heartless and false taste pretending to the title of delicacy and refinement." But in this his first attempt to run full tilt against the popular taste, he was singularly unfortunate. The refined and sentimental school of verse, with its elegant and polished diction, had far too firm a hold of the public mind to be so easily overthrown. And the transition from such polish and refinement to the extreme simplicity, and, in many instances, childish nature, of the subjects of the "Lyrical Ballads," and the homely and colloquial style in which they were treated, was far too great either to escape censure or insure success. But although assailed on all hands by a storm of ridicule, they succeeded in creating a public for themselves; and the poet was, therefore, not without hope that he should ultimately succeed in freeing men's minds from the fetters of a false and pernicious system of ethics and of art, and in leading them into the freedom of the broad, clear light of day, where they might behold, with unveiled eyes, and face to face, the surpassing beauty and sublime grandeur of external nature; and where, while they gazed, chastened and subdued, they might feel "a sense sublime"—a pervading "presence,"—

> "Whose dwelling is the light of setting suns,
> And the round ocean, and the living air,
> And the blue sky, and in the mind of man!"

Strong in resolution, and firm in his faith in himself and in the future, he set out in September, 1798, accompanied by his sister and Coleridge, for Germany. At Hamburg the party separated—Coleridge going on to Ratzeburg, and Wordsworth and his sister proceeding to Goslar, in Hanover, a town situated at the foot of a cluster of mountains which form part of the Hartz forest, and where they spent the winter of 1798-99, the severest of the century. Here he wrote several of his most beautiful pieces, such as "Ruth," "Lucy Grey," "Nutting," and the blank-verse lines beginning "There was a boy," and "Wisdom and Spirit of the universe."

Here, also, he began his great blank-verse poem, "The Prelude," the subject of which was to be the growth of his mind and his personal history—"his travels, hopes, aspirations, disappointments, and distresses—his inward conflicts and perplexities."

During his absence from England, the sale of the "Lyrical Ballads," (the edition of which consisted of 500 copies,) had been so small, and the severity of the leading reviews so great, that his publisher thought their progress to oblivion seemed certain. And some idea may be formed of the *general* estimate in which they were held, when it is stated, that, when the publisher, shortly after their publication, gave up business, and transferred all his copyrights to Messrs. Longman and Co., of London, the copyright of the "Ballads" was valued at *nil*. The publisher therefore begged that it might be returned, which it was, and he presented it to the author.

In February, 1799, Wordsworth and his sister returned to England; and, at the end of the same year, he took up his abode, which was to be a life-long one, among the lakes and mountains of his native district, having settled, with his sister, in a small cottage, pleasantly situated in the midst of a plot of orchard ground, overlooking the lake of Grasmere. Here he remained for eight years.

About the close of 1800, the second volume of the "Lyrical Ballads" was published, along with a reprint of the first. For two editions of the two volumes, the poet received from Messrs. Longman & Co., of London, his publishers, the sum of £100. This time, their appearance excited even more intense hostility than at first, the critics almost to a man being against them. And this hostility was chiefly provoked by the preface prefixed to the second edition, in which the poet, with considerable power, sets forth and defends certain principles of poetry which he deemed the main articles of his philosophical and poetical creed. What these principles were, and whether true or false, need not now be discussed. As embodied in his works, with some few modifications of his maturer years, they have been so long before the world, and have formed the subject of so many elaborate and laudatory essays by some of the ablest intellects of the age, that, in their present popularity, we may almost be said to hear the judgment of posterity on them. But no amount of adverse criticism had the slightest effect upon the poet. He kept the noiseless tenor of his way, and continued to write and publish, regardless of the storm he raised.

In October, 1802, he bade a brief "Farewell!" to the "little nook of mountain ground," his residence at Grasmere, and set out for Penrith, in company with his sister, to bring home one who was to be his bride—the school companion of his boyish days—Mary Hutchinson—

"A perfect woman, nobly planned,
To warn, to comfort, and command;"

and to whose graces of person, charms of manner, and sweetness of temper, his poems pay warm and beautiful tributes. To this lady he now united himself in marriage.

In 1803, accompanied by his sister and Coleridge, he paid a visit to Scotland. Of this tour his sister kept a very interesting diary, from which it appears that he visited the house and grave of Burns, Loch Lomond, the Trosachs, the Pass of Killicrankie, and a host of other places hallowed by their sacred associations, celebrated for their beauty, famous in history, or renowned in tradition and song. And wherever he went his genius kindled and poured itself forth in consecrating and antistrophic song. On their return south, they met with Scott at Melrose, who conducted them to the abbey, pointed out its beauties, and related its history, and with whom they afterwards dined at the inn there, he being at that time travelling to the assizes at Jedburgh in his capacity of Sheriff of Selkirk. They seem to have been delighted with him, and long remembered the visit with pleasure.

Shortly after the poet's return home, he became acquainted with Sir George Beaumont, a descendant of the celebrated Elizabethan dramatist, in whom he found a generous and admiring friend, and at whose seat of Coleorton, in Leicestershire, he was a frequent and welcome guest.

In February, 1805, he sustained a severe shock in the loss of his brother, Captain Wordsworth, who went down in the *Abergavenny*, East Indiaman, off the coast of Weymouth. A man of warm and susceptible temperament, of pure and simple manners, and of remarkable literary taste and critical discernment, considering the calling he followed, his untimely death seems to have been one of the heaviest blows the poet ever experienced. In this year Scott visited Grasmere, and, in company with Wordsworth and Sir Humphry Davy, ascended to the top of Helvellyn. In this year, also, were composed "The Waggoner," the "Ode to Duty," and "The Happy Warrior;" and the autobiographical poem of "The Prelude" was finished, and consigned to the poet's desk for the next forty-five years.

Undeterred by the reception given to the two volumes of the "Lyrical Ballads," in 1807 he gave to the world two other volumes of poems, which had been composed since the publication of the second volume of the former. They consisted, in addition to some very fine ballads, and a number of the most beautiful of his smaller pieces, of "Miscellaneous Sonnets," "Sonnets Dedicated to Liberty," and the "Memorials of a Tour in Scotland." But the poet's persistency in his principles, and the evident vitality of his poetic powers, would seem to have provoked afresh the hostility of his critics; for no sooner had the poems appeared, than they were assailed with a fierceness of feeling and a licence of language wholly disproportioned to the faults condemned—which nothing could justify, and which few indeed would have had the courage to combat or the spirit to endure. But his opponents, says his nephew, "were irritated by the energy of that which they despised. Their own character for critical acumen seemed to be at stake; and they conspired to crush a reputation whose existence was a practical protest against their own literary principles and practice, and which doubtless appeared to them to be fraught with pernicious consequences to the dignity of English literature, and the progress of English intelligence." The effect of these ungenerous strictures in checking the sale of the poems was such, that no edition of them was required between 1807 and 1815.

But contempt and neglect were alike ineffectual. The poet lived and wrote as if he knew of neither. And, amidst all the hostility and obloquy which for years he endured, the just and discriminating estimate which he formed of his works, and the calm confidence with which he regarded its ultimate ratification both by his contemporaries and by posterity, are perhaps the most astonishing circumstances in his remarkable literary career. A few sentences from himself, therefore, on this subject, may be fitly quoted here. "I distinctly foresaw," he said, in writing to a friend, "what you and my other friends would have to encounter in defending me. But trouble not yourself about their present reception [his poems]; of what moment is that compared with what I trust is their destiny?—to console the afflicted; to add sunshine to daylight, by making the happy happier; to teach the young and the gracious of every age to see, to think, and feel, and therefore to become more actively and securely virtuous; this is their office, which I trust they will faithfully perform long after we are mouldered in our graves. I am well aware how far it would seem to many I overrate my own exertions when I speak in this way. I am not, however, afraid of such censure. . . . Let the poet first consult his own heart as I have done, and leave the rest to posterity. . . . There is scarcely one of my poems which does not aim to direct the attention to some moral sentiment, or to some general principle, or law of thought, or of our intellectual constitution." And in reference to the "Sonnets Dedicated to Liberty," he says, "I would boldly say at once that these sonnets, while they each fix the attention upon some important sentiment, separately considered, do, at the same time, collectively make a poem on the subject of civil liberty and national independence, which, either for simplicity of style or grandeur of moral sentiment, is, alas! likely to have few parallels in the poetry of the present day." . . . "But, the fact is," he says, "the English *public* are at this moment in the same state of mind with respect to my poems, if small things can be compared with great, as the French are in respect to Shakspeare, and not the French alone, but almost the whole Continent. I am condemned for the very thing for which I ought to have been praised, namely, that I have not written down to the level of superficial observers and unthinking minds Every great poet is a teacher. I wish either to be considered as a teacher, or as nothing." Again, he says, "Never forget what I believe was observed by Coleridge—that every great and original writer, in proportion as he is great or original, must himself create the taste by which he is to be relished; he must teach the art by which he is to be seen."

In the spring of 1808, the poet removed to Allan Bank, a new house which stood at the head of the lake of Grasmere, where he resided for three years. This period was perhaps the least prolific of his life in poetry, a circumstance which his nephew attributes to the many inconveniences of his new residence. "But, on the other hand," says the same authority, "the time of his sojourn here was rendered memorable by the production of two works in prose by two poets—the 'Essay on the Convention of Cintra,' by Wordsworth, and *The Friend*, by

Coleridge, who *dictated* it (for he did not write it with his own hand) under Wordsworth's roof."

Although the greater part of the poet's life was spent in comparative retirement, and in the contemplation of scenes and objects far removed from the turmoil and fierce contention of political strife, it would be a great mistake to suppose that he was an inattentive observer of public events. "Few persons," says his nephew, "though actually engaged in the great struggle of that period, felt more deeply than Wordsworth did in his peaceful retreat, for the calamities of European nations suffering at that time from the imbecility of their governments, and from the withering oppression of a prosperous despotism. His heart burned within him when he looked forth upon the contest; and impassioned words proceeded from him both in poetry and in prose. 'It would not,' he said himself in conversation, 'be easy to conceive with what a depth of feeling I entered into the struggle carried on by the Spaniards for their deliverance from the usurped power of the French. Many times have I gone from Allan Bank in Grasmere Vale, to the Raise-Gap, as it is called, so late as two o'clock in the morning, to meet the carrier bringing the newspaper from Keswick.'"

In his "Essay on the Convention of Cintra," the poet appears before the world as depressed in mind and indignant in spirit, because the war in the Peninsula had not been carried on by England against France with all the vigour that it might have been, and because, when it was, as he believed, in the power of England to have emancipated Spain and Portugal from the intolerable thraldom of French tyranny, she allowed the enemy to escape by a retreat similar to a triumph. Although lucidly conceived, and written in a strain of impassioned prose, and said to have been pronounced by Canning to be the most eloquent production that had appeared since the days of Burke, it yet fell almost still-born from the press, and attracted so very little attention, that there is scarcely any production of the century so difficult to be met with as this tract. As a specimen of the spirit and style of this little known but noble essay, a single extract may be given. In the following passage the poet contends for the supremacy of moral over physical power, and shows how the spirit of freedom, when actuated by pure passions and high actions, must always ultimately triumph over all the tools and implements of tyranny:—

"There is no middle course: two masters cannot be served:—Justice must either be enthroned above might, and the moral law take the place of the edicts of selfish passion; or the heart of the people, which alone can sustain the efforts of the people, will languish; their desires will not spread beyond the plough and the loom, the field and the fireside; the sword will appear to them an emblem of no promise; an instrument of no hope; an object of indifference, of disgust or fear. Was there ever—since the earliest actions of men which have been transmitted by affectionate tradition, or recorded by faithful history, or sung to the impassioned harp of poetry—was there ever a people who presented themselves to the reason and the imagination, as under more holy influences than the dwellers upon the Southern peninsula; as roused more instantaneously from a deadly sleep to a more hopeful wakefulness; as a mass fluctuating with one motion under the breath of a mightier wind; as breaking themselves up, and settling into several bodies, in more harmonious order; as reunited and embattled under a standard which was reared to the sun with more authentic assurance of final victory? . . . Let the fire, which is never wholly to be extinguished, break out afresh; let but the human creature be roused; whether he have lain headless and torpid in religious or civil slavery; have languished under a thraldom, domestic or foreign, or under both these alternately; or have drifted about, a helpless member of a clan of disjointed and feeble barbarians,—let him rise and act; and his domineering imagination, by which from childhood he has been betrayed, and the debasing affections which it has imposed upon him, will from that moment participate in the dignity of the newly-ennobled being whom they will now acknowledge for their master; and will further him in his progress, whatever be the object at which he aims. Still more inevitable and momentous are the results, when the individual knows that the fire which is reanimated in him is not less lively in the breasts of his associates; and sees the signs and testimonies of his own power, incorporated with those of a growing multitude, and not to be distinguished from them, accompany him wherever he moves. Hence those marvellous achievements which were performed by the first enthusiastic followers of Mohammed, and by other conquerors, who with their armies have swept large portions of the earth like a transitory wind, or have founded new religions or empires. But if the object contended for be worthy and truly great (as, in the instance of the Spaniards, we have seen that it is); if cruelties have been committed upon an ancient and venerable people, which shake the human frame with horror; if not alone the life which is sustained by the bread of the mouth, but that—without which there is no life—the life in the soul has been directly and mortally warred against; if reason has had abominations to endure in her inmost sanctuary; then does intense passion, consecrated by a sudden revelation of justice, give birth to those higher and better wonders which I have described; and exhibit true miracles to the eyes of men, and the noblest which can be seen. It may be added that,—as this union brings back to the right road the faculty of imagination, where it is prone to err and has gone furthest astray; as it corrects those qualities which are in their essence indifferent, and cleanses those affections which (not being inherent in the constitution of man, nor necessarily determined to their object), are more immediately dependent upon the imagination, and which may have received from it a thorough taint of dishonour;—so the domestic loves and sanctities which are in their nature less liable to be stained—so these, wherever they have flowed with a pure and placid stream, do instantly, under the same influence, put forth their strength as in a flood; and without being sullied or polluted, pursue—exultingly and with song—a course which leads the contemplative reason to the ocean of eternal love."

In 1810, he wrote the introduction to a folio volume of "Select Views in Cumberland, Westmoreland, and Lancashire," which, as a description of the beauty and magnificence of the lake scenery, of the inhabitants, their homesteads and their manner of living, of the most striking and characteristic features of each district, with instructions as to the best manner of seeing these, is reckoned the most accurate and interesting thing of the kind ever written.

In the spring of 1813, after one temporary change of residence, he took up his abode at Rydal Mount, about two miles distant from Grasmere, and here he continued to reside till the day of his death, thirty-seven years after. The house, which has since become so famous, is a two-storied, sober-hued, modest mansion, tinged with weather stains, mantled over here and there with roses, ivy, jessamine, and Virginia creeper, and stands on the sloping side of a rocky hill, with a southern aspect, overlooking the lake of Windermere, and commanding beautiful views of the romantic vale of the Rothay, and of the distant wood-fringed waters of the lake; while around the dark waters rise the gracefully-rounded, richly-wooded mountains—soft as the scenery of a still Dreamland; beautiful with cultured picturesqueness, as of the gardens of the Titans; clothed with the "infinite enchantment" of atmospheric effects ever varying and always lovely; and glowing—"in the light of setting suns"—with a glory of colour—orange, and bronze, purple and amethyst,—against the loftier and remoter peaks that rise in the far distance, faint and unsubstantial in the wide lapse of light, like high-piled cloud on cloud.

The poet's good fortune seems to have followed him to this beautiful abode; for he had hardly taken possession of it when he received the appointment of distributor of stamps in the county of Westmoreland—an office which added about £500 a year to his income, and the duties of which were discharged by a clerk, so that he was still left ample liberty to follow his literary pursuits. For this desirable appointment he was indebted to the influence of the Earl of Lonsdale, who had been for many years his constant and generous friend, and whose kindness on this occasion he gratefully acknowledged by dedicating "The Excursion" to him in a complimentary prefatory sonnet.

A second tour in Scotland early in 1814, in company with his wife and his sister, gave birth to a few poems, amongst which was "Yarrow Visited." And in the summer of the same year appeared his great poem, "The Excursion." It need scarcely be said, that, with the leading reviewers of the day, it fared no better than his former less ambitious attempts had done; and that, with hardly a single exception, and in the strongest terms of condemnation, they doomed it to oblivion! And it is a somewhat remarkable fact in literary history that a single edition of 500 copies of this poem satisfied the English public for a period of six years. Another edition, also confined to 500 copies, published in 1827, was found sufficient for the following seven years. But, notwithstanding these discouragements, the poet's equanimity was undisturbed. "Let the age continue to love its own darkness," he said, in a letter to Southey, "I shall continue to write, with, I trust, the light of Heaven upon me." "If 'The Excursion' is to be judged of by its best passages," says one of his admirers, "hardly any poem in the language is equal to it. Some of its scenes, extending to hundreds of lines, many smaller passages, and innumerable verses and phrases, are among the most exquisite things to which any poetic mind ever gave expression" "In power of intellect," says another, Hazlitt, "in lofty conception, in the depth of feeling, at once simple and sublime, which pervades every part of it, and which gives to every object an almost preternatural and preter-human interest, this work has seldom been surpassed!"

In 1815 appeared the "White Doe of Rylstone," a beautiful legendary poem, which the poet considered, in conception, the highest work he had ever produced. In the preceding and two following years were composed "Laodamia," "Dion," and the "Ode to Lycoris," in conception and expression the purest and most richly classic pieces he ever penned. The "Thanksgiving Ode," and a rhymed translation, in the style of Pope, of three books of the "Æneid," were produced in 1816.

In 1819, appeared "Peter Bell," which had been written nearly twenty years before, and which is really remarkable as having been more in request than any of his previous publications. An edition of 500 copies was printed in April, and another impression of it was required in the following month. "The Waggoner," which appeared at the same time, was not, however, so successful. To this year, also, belong the beautiful series of "Sonnets on the River Duddon."

In 1820, Wordsworth, accompanied by his wife and sister, made a tour of four months on the Continent, which gave birth to a volume of sonnets and other poems, published in 1822, under the title of "Memorials of a Tour on the Continent." In this year, too, a brief visit to his friend, Sir George Beaumont, at his seat of Coleorton, in Leicestershire, suggested the splendid series of "Ecclesiastical Sonnets."

During the next few years the poet appears to have done little else than travel about, either on special tours, or on visits to his friends, and in the autumn of 1831 he set off from Rydal Mount, in company with his daughter, to visit Sir Walter Scott before his departure, ruined in fortune, and weakened in body and mind, for Italy

They reached Abbotsford on Monday. "How sadly changed," says Wordsworth, "did I find him from the man I had seen so healthy, gay, and hopeful a few years before. The inmates and guests we found there were Sir Walter, Major Scott, Anne Scott, and Mr. and Mrs. Lockhart, Mr. Liddell, his lady and brother, Mr. Allan, the painter, and Mr. Laidlaw. In the evening Mr. and Mrs. Liddell sang, and Mrs. Lockhart chanted old ballads to her harp; and Mr. Allan, hanging over the back of a chair, told and acted old stories in a humorous way. With this exhibition and his daughter's singing, Sir Walter was much amused, and, indeed, were we all, as far as circumstances would allow. On Tuesday morning Sir Walter accompanied us to Newark Castle, on the Yarrow. . . . Of that excursion the verses, 'Yarrow Revisited,' are a memorial. . . On our return, in the afternoon, we had to cross the Tweed directly opposite Abbotsford. . . . A rich but sad light, of rather a purple than a golden hue, was spread over the Eildon Hills at that moment; and, thinking it probable that it might be the last time Sir Walter would cross the stream, I was not a little moved, and expressed some of my feelings in the following sonnet:—

"'A trouble, not of clouds or weeping rain,
Nor of the setting sun's pathetic light
Engendered, hangs o'er Eildon's triple height:
Spirits of Power, assembled there, complain
For kindred Power departing from their sight;
While Tweed, best pleased in chanting a blithe strain,
Saddens his voice again, and yet again.
Lift up your hearts, ye mourners! for the might
Of the whole world's good wishes with him goes;
Blessings and prayers in nobler retinue
Than sceptered king or laurelled conqueror knows.
Follow this wondrous Potentate! Be true,
Ye winds of ocean, and the midland sea,
Wafting your charge to soft Parthenope!'

On Thursday morning Sir Walter and I had a serious conversation, *tête-à-tête*, when he spoke with gratitude of the happy life, which, upon the whole, he had led. He had written in my daughter's album, before he came into the breakfast-room that morning, a few stanzas addressed to her; and while putting the book into her hand, in his own study, standing by his desk, he said to her, in my presence, 'I should not have done anything of this kind but for your father's sake; they are probably the last verses I shall ever write.' They showed how much his mind was impaired, not by the strain of thought, but by the execution, some of the lines being imperfect, and one stanza wanting corresponding rhymes." At noon on the same day the poets parted, and on Wordsworth expressing a hope that Sir Walter's health would be benefited by the climate of the country to which he was going, and by the interest he would take in the classic remembrances of Italy, he, with a flash of flitting recollection, but in a tone of deepest sadness, made answer in Wordsworth's own words—a quotation from "Yarrow Unvisited"—"When I am there, although 'tis fair, 'twill be *another* Yarrow."

This visit, and another, which he paid to Scotland in 1833, accompanied by his son, and Henry Crabb Robinson, Esq., furnished materials for a volume which he published in 1835, entitled, "Yarrow Revisited, and other Poems."

A five months' tour in Italy in the spring and summer of 1837 suggested several pieces, which appeared in 1842, in a volume entitled "Poems Chiefly of Early and Late Years." This was the last volume published during his lifetime.

About this time public feeling and critical opinion began to change, and the mists of prejudice, which had so long lowered over his greatness, and concealed or obscured it, gradually vanished. Henceforth, year by year, the fame of the Poet of the Lakes grew wider and wider; and long before his death he was acknowledged to be the greatest English poet of his age, and regarded with reverence as one of the purest and most blameless of English writers. Honours now flowed fast upon him, and the remaining years of his life were passed in the midst of that which should accompany old age—"as honour, love, obedience, troops of friends."

In the summer of 1839, amid the enthusiastic acclamations of the students, the University of Oxford honoured him with the degree of D.C.L. In 1842 he resigned the Government appointment he held in favour of his son, who had for some time acted as his deputy. A few months afterwards, he received, through Sir Robert Peel, a grant from the Crown of £300 a year. In 1843, on the death of his friend

Southey, he was offered, in flattering terms, the vacant Laureateship, which, after some hesitation, on account of his age, he accepted, on the assurance that it was to be entirely nominal and honorary. In 1844, Lord Jeffrey, perhaps the severest of his literary censors, in republishing his contributions to the *Edinburgh Review*, took occasion, in graceful and fitting terms, to acknowledge the poet's many and great merits.

In 1846, his brother, Christopher Wordsworth, D.D., died; and in the following year he sustained a still greater grief in the death of his accomplished and darling daughter, Dora (Mrs. Quillinan).

Two years afterwards, at Rydal Mount, on the 23rd of April, 1850, the poet himself passed peacefully away in the eightieth year of his age. His remains were laid near those of his children, in Grasmere Churchyard.

"His own prophecy," says his nephew, "in the lines to the daisy—

> "'Sweet flower! belike one day to have
> A place upon thy poet's grave,
> I welcome thee once more,'

is now fulfilled. He reposes, according to his own wish, beneath the green turf, among the dalesmen of Grasmere, under the sycamores and yews of a country churchyard, by the side of a beautiful stream, amid the mountains which he loved; and a solemn voice seems to breathe from his grave, which blends its tones in sweet and holy harmony with the accents of his poetry, speaking the language of humility and love, of adoration and faith, and preparing the soul, by a religious exercise of the kindly affections, and by a devout contemplation of natural beauty, for a translation to a purer, and nobler, and more glorious state of existence, and for a fruition of heavenly felicity."

In this brief and necessarily imperfect sketch, it would be impossible to enter at any length into the merits of Wordsworth's poetry. But a very fair estimate may be formed of the poet's artistic power, and of the pervading spirit of his poetry from the two following brief extracts. The first few justly-discriminating and happily-expressed sentences, descriptive of the higher characteristics of his poetry, are from the able and admirably drawn literary and poetical character of the poet by his friend Coleridge, in his *Biographia Literaria.* The second series, equally able, and quite as felicitously expressed, are from the pen of William Ellery Channing, and describe those simpler, but, for the popular mind, more attractive, characteristics which so touchingly and so powerfully appeal to the instincts and feelings of our common humanity

Wordsworth's poetry is marked by—"*First,* An austere purity of language, both grammatically and logically; in short, a perfect appropriateness of the words to the meaning. *Secondly,* A correspondent weight and sanity of the thoughts and sentiments won, not from books, but from the poet's own meditations. They are *fresh,* and have the dew upon them. Even throughout his smaller poems, there is not one which is not rendered valuable by some just and original reflection. *Thirdly*, The sinewy strength and originality of single lines and paragraphs, the frequent *curiosa felicitas* of his diction. *Fourthly*, The perfect truth of nature in his images and descriptions, as taken immediately from nature, and proving a long and genial intimacy with the very spirit which gives a physiognomic expression to all the works of nature. *Fifthly*, A meditative pathos, a union of deep and subtle thought with sensibility: a sympathy with man as man; the sympathy, indeed, of a contemplator rather than a fellow-sufferer and co-mate (*spectator, haud particeps*), but of a contemplator from whose view no difference of rank conceals the sameness of the nature; no injuries of wind or weather, or toil, or even of ignorance, wholly disguise the human face divine. *Last*, and pre-eminently, I challenge for this poet the gift of imagination in the highest and strictest sense of the word. In the play of *fancy*, Wordsworth, to my feelings, is always graceful, and sometimes recondite. The *likeness* is occasionally too strange, or demands too peculiar a point of view, or is such as appears the creature of predetermined research, rather than spontaneous presentation. Indeed, his fancy seldom displays itself as mere and unmodified fancy. But in imaginative power he stands nearest of all modern writers to Shakspeare and Milton, and yet in a mind perfectly unborrowed, and his own. To employ his own words, which are at once an instance and an illustration, he does indeed, to all thoughts and to all objects—

> 'Add the gleam,
> The light that never was on sea or land,
> The consecration and the poet's dream.'"

"The great poet of our times, Wordsworth—one of the few who are to live—has gone to common life, to the feelings of our universal nature, to the obscure and neglected portions of society, for beautiful and touching themes. Genius is not a creator, in the sense of fancying or feigning what does not exist. Its distinction is to discern more of truth than common minds. It sees under disguises and humble forms everlasting beauty. This it is the prerogative of Wordsworth to discern and reveal in the ordinary walks of life, in the common human heart. He has revealed the loveliness of the primitive feelings, of the universal affections of the human soul. The grand truth which pervades his poetry, is that the beautiful is not confined to the rare, the new, the distant—to scenery and modes of life open only to the few; but that it is poured forth profusely on the common earth and sky, that it gleams from the loneliest flower, that it lights up the humblest sphere, that the sweetest affections lodge in lowliest hearts, that there is sacredness, dignity, and loveliness in lives which few eyes rest on—that, even in the absence of all intellectual culture, the domestic relations can quietly nourish that disinterestedness which is the element of all greatness, and without which intellectual power is a splendid deformity. Wordsworth is the poet of humanity; he teaches reverence for our universal nature; he breaks down the factitious barriers between human hearts."

POEMS

BY

WILLIAM WORDSWORTH.

Juvenile Poems.

EXTRACT.

FROM THE CONCLUSION OF A POEM, COMPOSED UPON LEAVING SCHOOL.

DEAR native regions, I foretell,
From what I feel at this farewell,
That, wheresoe'er my steps shall tend,
And whensoe'er my course shall end,
If in that hour a single tie
Survive of local sympathy,
My soul will cast the backward view,
The longing look alone on you.

Thus, when the sun, prepared for rest,
Hath gained the precincts of the west
Though his departing radiance fail
To illuminate the hollow vale,
A lingering light he fondly throws
On the dear hills where first he rose.

AN EVENING WALK,

ADDRESSED TO A YOUNG LADY.

FAR from my dearest friend, 'tis mine to rove [pastoral cove;
Through bare gray dell, high wood, and
Where Derwent stops his course to hear the roar
That stuns the tremulous cliffs of high Lodore;
Where peace to Grasmere's lonely island leads, [meads,
To willowy hedgerows, and to emerald
Leads to her bridge, rude church, and cottaged grounds, [bounds;
Her rocky sheepwalk†, and her woodland
Where, deep embosomed, shy* Winander peeps [steeps;
'Mid clustering isles, and holly-sprinkled
Where twilight glens endear my Esthwaite's shore,
And memory of departed pleasures, more

Fair scenes! ere-while I taught, a happy child,
The echoes of your rocks my carols wild
Then did no ebb of cheerfulness demand
Sad tides of joy from Melancholy's hand,
In youth's keen eye the livelong day was bright,
The sun at morning, and the stars of night,
Alike, when heard the bittern's hollow bill,
Or the first woodcocks† roamed the moonlight hill.

In thoughtless gaiety I coursed the plain,
And hope itself was all I knew of pain
For then, even then, the little heart would beat [seat,
At times, while young Content forsook her
And wild Impatience, pointing upward, showed [summits glowed
Where, tipped with gold, the mountain-
Alas! the idle tale of man is found
Depicted in the dial's moral round,
Hope with Reflection blends her social rays
To gild the total tablet of his days,

* These lines are only applicable to the middle part of that lake

† In the beginning of winter these mountains are frequented by woodcocks, which in dark nights retire into the wood.

Yet still, the sport of some malignant power,
He knows but from its shade the present hour.

But why, ungrateful, dwell on idle pain?
To show what pleasures yet to me remain,
Say, will my friend with unreluctant ear,
The history of a poet's evening hear?

When, in the south, the wan noon, brooding still,
Breathed a pale steam around the glaring hill,
And shades of deep-embattled clouds were seen,
Spotting the northern cliffs, with lights between;
When, at the barren wall's unsheltered end,
Where long rails far into the lake extend,
Crowded the shortened herds, and beat the tides
With their quick tails, and lashed their speckled sides,
When school-boys stretched their length upon the green,
And round the humming elm, a glimmering scene!
In the brown park, in herds, the troubled deer
Shook the still-twinkling tail and glancing ear;
When horses in the sunburnt intake* stood,
And vainly eyed below the tempting flood,
Or tracked the passenger, in mute distress,
With forward neck the closing gate to press—
Then while I wandered where the huddling rill
Brightens with water-breaks the sombrous ghyll,†
As by enchantment, an obscure retreat
Opened at once, and stayed my devious feet.
While thick above the rill the branches close,
In rocky basin its wild waves repose,
Inverted shrubs, and moss of gloomy green,
Cling from the rocks, with pale wood-weeds between;
Save that aloft the subtle sunbeams shine
On withered briars that o'er the crags recline,
Sole light admitted here, a small cascade,
Illumes with sparkling foam the impervious shade;
Beyond, along the vista of the brook,
Where antique roots its bustling course o'erlook,
The eye reposes on a secret bridge‡
Half gray, half shagged with ivy to its ridge;
Whence hangs, in the cool shade, the listless swain
Lingering behind his disappearing wain.
—Did Sabine grace adorn my living line,
Blandusia's praise, wild stream, should yield to thine!
Never shall ruthless minister of death
'Mid thy soft glooms the glittering steel unsheath;
No goblets shall, for thee, be crowned with flowers,
No kid with piteous outcry thrill thy bowers;
The mystic shapes that by thy margin rove
A more benignant sacrifice approve;
A mind, that, in a calm angelic mood
Of happy wisdom, meditating good,
Beholds, of all from her high powers required,
Much done, and much designed, and more desired,—
Harmonious thoughts, a soul by truth refined,
Entire affection for all human-kind

Sweet rill, farewell! To-morrow's noon again
Shall hide me, wooing long thy wildwood strain;
But now the sun has gained his western road,
And eve's mild hour invites my steps abroad

While, near the midway cliff, the silvered kite
In many a whistling circle wheels her flight,
Slant watery lights, from parting clouds, apace
Travel along the precipice's base,
Cheering its naked waste of scattered stone,
By lichens gray, and scanty moss, o'ergrown;
Where scarce the foxglove peeps, or thistle's beard:
And restless stone-chat, all day long, is heard.

How pleasant, as the sun declines, to view
The spacious landscape change in form and hue!
Here, vanish, as in mist, before a flood
Of bright obscurity, hill, lawn, and wood;

* The word *intake* is local and signifies a mountain inclosure.

† Ghyll is also, I believe, a term confined to this country; ghyll and dingle have the same meaning.

‡ The reader who has made the tour of this country, will recognise, in this description, the features which characterize the lower waterfall in the grounds of Rydal.

There, objects, by the searching beams
betrayed,
Come forth, and here retire in purple
shade; [white,
Even the white stems of birch, the cottage
Soften their glare before the mellow light.
The skiffs, at anchor where with umbrage
wide [hide,
Yon chestnuts half the latticed boat-house
Shed from their sides, that face the sun's
slant beam, [lous stream
Strong flakes of radiance on the tremu-
Raised by yon travelling flock, a dusty
cloud [moving shroud;
Mounts from the road, and spreads its
The shepherd, all involved in wreaths of
fire, [lost entire.
Now shows a shadowy speck, and now is

Into a gradual calm the zephyrs sink:
A blue rim borders all the lake's still brink,
And now, on every side, the surface breaks
Into blue spots, and slowly lengthening
streaks; [bright
Here, plots of sparkling water tremble
With thousand thousand twinkling points
of light; [away,
There, waves that, hardly weltering, die
Tip their smooth ridges with a softer ray,
And now the universal tides repose,
And, brightly blue, the burnished mirror
glows,
Save where, along the shady western marge,
Coasts, with industrious oar, the charcoal
barge; [sleeps,
The sails are dropped, the poplar's foliage
And insects clothe, like dust, the glassy
deeps.

Their panniered train a group of potters
goad,
Winding from side to side up the steep road;
The peasant, from yon cliff of fearful edge
Shot, down the headlong path darts with
his sledge: [illume,
Bright beams the lonely mountain-horse
Feeding 'mid purple heath, "green rings,"*
and broom; [confounds,
While the sharp slope the slackened team
Downward the ponderous timber-wain re-
sounds;
In foamy breaks the rill, with merry song,
Dashed o'er the rough rock, lightly leaps
along;

From lonesome chapel at the mountain's
feet,
Three humble bells their rustic chime re-
peat, [boat;
Sounds from the water-side the hammered
And *blasted* quarry thunders, heard remote!

Even here, amid the sweep of endless
woods, [floods,
Blue pomp of lakes, high cliffs, and calling
Not undelightful are the simplest charms,
Found by the grassy door of mountain
farms.

Sweetly ferocious,† round his native
walks, [stalks;
Pride of his sister-wives, the monarch
Spur-clad his nervous feet, and firm his
tread;
A crest of purple tops his warrior head.
Bright sparks his black and rolling eye-ball
Afar, his tail he closes and unfurls, [hurls
On tiptoe reared, he strains his clarion
throat, [remote·
Threatened by faintly-answering farms
Again with his shrill voice the mountain
rings, [sound his wings!
While, flapped with conscious pride, re-

Brightening the cliffs between, where
sombrous pine
And yew-tree o'er the silver rocks recline;
I love to mark the quarry's moving trains,
Dwarf panniered steeds, and men, and
numerous wains:
How busy all the enormous hive within,
While Echo dallies with the various din!
Some (hardly heard their chisels' clinking
sound)
Toil, small as pigmies in the gulf profound,
Some, dim between the aerial cliffs de-
scried, [side:
O'erwalk the slender plank from side to
These, by the pale-blue rocks that ceaseless
ring,
Glad from their airy baskets hang and sing.

Hung o'er a cloud, above the steep that
rears [pears;
An edge all flame, the broadening sun ap-
A long blue bar its ægis orb divides,
And breaks the spreading of its golden
tides;

* "Vivid rings of green" – Greenwood's Poem on Shooting

† "Dolcemente feroce."—TASSO In this description of the cock, I remembered a spirited one of the same animal in the "L'Agriculture, ou, Les Géorgiques Françaises," of M Rossuet.

And now it touches on the purple steep
That flings his shadow on the pictured deep.
'Cross the calm lake's blue shades the cliffs
aspire [fire;"
With towers and woods a "prospect all on
The coves and secret hollows, through a
ray
Of fainter gold, a purple gleam betray;
The gilded turf invests with richer green
Each speck of lawn the broken rocks be-
tween; [illume,
Deep yellow beams the scattered stems
Far in the level forest's central gloom;
Waving his hat, the shepherd, from the
vale,
Directs his winding dog the cliffs to scale,
That, barking busy, 'mid the glittering
rocks, [flocks.
Hunts, where he points, the intercepted
Where oaks o'erhang the road the radiance
shoots [roots;
On tawny earth, wild weeds, and twisted
The Druid stones their lighted fane unfold,
And all the babbling brooks are liquid
gold;
Sunk to a curve, the day-star lessens still,
Gives one bright glance, and drops behind
the hill.*

In these secluded vales, if village fame,
Confirmed by silver hairs, belief may claim;
When up the hills, as now, retired the
light,
Strange apparitions mocked the gazer's
sight.

A desperate form appears, that spurs his
steed
Along the midway cliffs with violent speed;
Unhurt pursues his lengthened flight, while
all
Attend, at every stretch, his headlong fall.
Anon, in order mounts a gorgeous show
Of horsemen shadows moving to and fro;
At intervals imperial banners stream,
And now the van reflects the solar beam,
The rear through iron brown betrays a
sullen gleam; [they go,
Lost gradual,† o'er the heights in pomp
While silent stands the admiring crowd
below;

Till, save the lonely beacon, all is fled,
That tips with eve's last gleam his spiry
head.

Now, while the solemn evening
shadows sail, [vale;
On red slow-waving pinions, down the
And, fronting the bright west, yon oak
entwines [lines,
Its darkening boughs and leaves, in stronger
How pleasant near the tranquil lake to
stray
Where winds the road along a secret bay:
Along the "wild meandering shore" to
view
Obsequious grace the winding swan pursue:
He swells his lifted chest, and backward
flings [wings;
His bridling neck between his towering
In all the majesty of ease, divides,
And, glorying, looks around, the silent
tides;
On as he floats, the silvered waters glow,
Proud of the varying arch and moveless
form of snow. [loves,
While tender cares and mild domestic
With furtive watch pursue her as she
moves;
The female with a meeker charm succeeds,
And her brown little-ones around her
leads,
Nibbling the water lilies as they pass,
Or playing wanton with the floating grass.
She, in a mother's care, her beauty's pride
Forgets, unwearied watching every side;
She calls them near, and with affection
sweet
Alternately relieves their weary feet;
Alternately they mount her back, and rest
Close by her mantling wings' embraces
prest.

Long may ye float upon these floods
serene; [green,
Yours be these holms untrodden, still, and
Whose lofty shades fence off the blustering
gale,
Where breathes in peace the lily of the vale.
Yon isle, which feels not even the milk-
maid's feet, [more sweet,"
Yet hears her song, "by distance made
Yon isle conceals your home, your cottage
bower,
Fresh water-rushes strew the verdant floor;
Long grass and willows form the woven
wall,
And swings above the roof the poplar tall.

---

* From Thomson. See Scott's Critical Essays.

† See a description of an appearance of this kind in Clark's "Survey of the Lakes," accompanied by vouchers of its veracity that may amuse the reader.

Thence issuing often with unwieldy stalk,
With broad black feet ye crush your
flowery walk; [morn
Or, from the neighbouring water, hear at
The hound, the horse's tread, and mellow
horn; [rings,
Involve your serpent necks in changeful
Rolled wantonly between your slippery
wings,
Or, starting up with noise and rude delight,
Force half upon the wave your cumbrous
flight.

Fair swan! by all a mother's joys
caressed, [thee blessed;
Haply some wretch has eyed, and called
The whilst upon some sultry summer's day
She dragged her babes along this weary
way; [road
Or taught their limbs along the burning
A few short steps to totter with their load

I see her now, denied to lay her head,
On cold blue nights, in hut or straw-built
shed.
Turn to a silent smile their sleepy cry,
By pointing to a shooting star on high.
I hear, while in the forest depth, he sees
The moon's fixed gaze between the opening
trees,
In broken sounds her elder child demand,
And skyward lift, like one that prays, his
hand,
If, in that country, where he dwells afar,
His father views that good, that kindly star;
—Ah me! all light is mute amid the gloom,
The interlunar cavern, of the tomb.
—When low-hung clouds each star of
summer hide,
And fireless are the valleys far and wide,
Where the brook brawls along the painful
road, [broad,
Dark with bat-haunted ashes stretching
Oft has she taught them on her lap to play
Delighted, with the glow-worm's harmless
ray [the ground
Tossed light from hand to hand; while on
Small circles of green radiance gleam
around.

Oh! when the sleety showers her path
assail,
And roars between the hills the torrent gale;
No more her breath can thaw their fingers
cold, [fold;
Their frozen arms her neck no more can
Weak roof a cowering form two babes to
shield,
And faint the fire a dying heart can yield!

Press the sad kiss, fond mother! vainly
fears [tears;
Thy flooded cheek to wet them with its
No tears can chill them, and no bosom
warms, [arms.
Thy breast their death-bed, coffined in thine

Sweet are the sounds that mingle from
afar, [star,
Heard by calm lakes, as peeps the folding
Where the duck dabbles 'mid the rustling
sedge, [edge,
And feeding pike starts from the water's
Or the swan stirs the reeds, his neck and
bill
Wetting, that drip upon the water still;
And heron, as resounds the trodden shore,
Shoots upward, darting his long neck
before.

Now with religious awe, the farewell
light [night;
Blends with the solemn colouring of the
'Mid groves of clouds that crest the moun-
tain's brow, [shadows throw,
And round the west's proud lodge their
Like Una shining on her gloomy way,
The half-seen form of Twilight roams
astray, [small,
Shedding, through paly loopholes mild and
Gleams that upon the lake's still bosom
fall; [pale,
Soft o'er the surface creep those lustres
Tracking the fitful motions of the gale.
With restless interchange at once the bright
Wins on the shade, the shade upon the
light.
No favoured eye was e'er allowed to gaze
On lovelier spectacle in faery days;
When gentle spirits urged a sportive
chase,
Brushing with lucid wands the water's face;
While music, stealing round the glimmer-
ing deeps, [steeps.
Charmed the tall circle of the enchanted
—The lights are vanished from the watery
plains:
No wreck of all the pageantry remains.
Unheeded night has overcome the vales:
On the dark earth the baffled vision fails;
The latest lingerer of the forest train,
The lone black fir, forsakes the faded plain,
Last evening sight, the cottage smoke, no
more, [hoar;
Lost in the thickened darkness, glimmers
And, towering from the sullen dark-brown
mere, [appear,
Like a black wall, the mountain steeps

—Now o'er the soothed accordant heart we
feel
A sympathetic twilight slowly steal,
And ever, as we fondly muse, we find
The soft gloom deepening on the tranquil
mind.
Stay! pensive, sadly-pleasing visions, stay!
Ah no! as fades the vale, they fade away:
Yet still the tender, vacant gloom remains;
Still the cold cheek its shuddering tear
retains.

The bird, who ceased, with fading light,
to thread
Silent the hedge or streaming rivulet's bed,
From his gray re-appearing tower shall
soon
Salute with boding note the rising moon,
Frosting with hoary light the pearly ground,
And pouring deeper blue to ether's bound;
And pleased her solemn pomp of clouds to
fold
In robes of azure, fleecy-white, and gold.

See, o'er the eastern hill, where darkness
broods [woods;
O'er all its vanished dells, and lawns, and
Where but a mass of shade the sight can
trace,
She lifts in silence up her lovely face;
Above the gloomy valley flings her light,
Far to the western slopes with hamlets
white; [upland strew,
And gives, where woods the chequered
To the green corn of summer autumn's
hue.

Thus Hope, first pouring from her
blessed horn [own morn;
Her dawn, far lovelier than the moon's
Till higher mounted, strives in vain to cheer
The weary hills, impervious, blackening
near; [while
Yet does she still, undaunted, throw the
On darling spots remote her tempting
smile.

Even now she decks for me a distant
scene, [between)
(For dark and broad the gulf of time
Gilding that cottage with her fondest ray,
(Sole bourne, sole wish, sole object of my
way; [appear!
How fair its lawns and sheltering woods
How sweet its streamlet murmurs in mine
ear!) [rise,
Where we, my friend, to happy days shall
Till our small share of hardly-paining
sighs
(For sighs will ever trouble human breath)
Creep hushed into the tranquil breast of
death.

But now the clear-bright moon her zenith
gains,
And rimy without speck extend the plains;
The deepest dell the mountain's front dis-
plays, [rays;
Scarce hides a shadow from her searching
From the dark-blue faint silvery threads
divide
The hills, while gleams below the azure tide;
The scene is wakened, yet its peace unbroke,
By silvered wreaths of quiet charcoal smoke,
That, o'er the ruins of the fallen wood,
Steal down the hill, and spread along the
flood.

The song of mountain streams, unheard
by day, [way.
Now hardly heard, beguiles my homeward
All air is, as the sleeping water, still,
Listening the aërial music of the hill,
Broke only by the slow clock tolling deep,
Or shout that wakes the ferryman from
sleep,
Soon followed by his hollow-parting oar,
And echoed hoof approaching the far
shore; [borne,
Sound of closed gate, across the water
Hurrying the feeding hare through rustling
corn;
The tremulous sob of the complaining owl;
And at long intervals the mill-dog's howl;
The distant forge's swinging thump pro-
found;
Or yell, in the deep woods, of lonely
hound.

LINES

WRITTEN WHILE SAILING IN A BOAT AT EVENING.

How richly glows the water's breast
Before us, tinged with evening hues,
While, facing thus the crimson west,
The boat her silent course pursues!
And see how dark the backward stream!
A little moment past so smiling!
And still, perhaps, with faithless gleam,
Some other loiterers beguiling.

Such views the youthful bard allure;
But, heedless of the following gloom,
He deems their colours shall endure
Till peace go with him to the tomb.

And let him muse his fond deceit,
And what if he must die in sorrow !
Who would not cherish dreams so sweet,
Though grief and pain may come to-morrow ?

REMEMBRANCE OF COLLINS.

COMPOSED UPON THE THAMES, NEAR RICHMOND.

GLIDE gently, thus for ever glide,
O Thames ! that other bards may see
As lovely visions by thy side
As now, fair river ! come to me.
Oh, glide, fair stream, for ever so !
Thy quiet soul on all bestowing,
Till all our minds for ever flow,
As thy deep waters now are flowing.

Vain thought !—Yet be as now thou art,
That in thy waters may be seen
The image of a poet's heart—
How bright, how solemn, how serene !
Such as did once the poet bless,
Who murmuring here a later* ditty,
Could find no refuge from distress
But in the milder grief of pity.

Now let us, as we float along,
For *him* suspend the dashing oar,
And pray that never child of song
May know that poet's sorrows more.
How calm ! how still ! the only sound
The dripping of the oar suspended !
The evening darkness gathers round,
By virtue's holiest powers attended.

* Collins's Ode on the Death of Thomson ; the last written, I believe, of the poems which were published during his lifetime. This ode is also alluded to in the next stanza.

DESCRIPTIVE SKETCHES

TAKEN DURING A PEDESTRIAN TOUR AMONG THE ALPS.

WERE there, below, a spot of holy ground
Where from distress a refuge might be found,
And solitude prepare the soul for heaven ;
Sure, nature's God that spot to man had given,
Where falls the purple morning far and wide
In flakes of light upon the mountain side ;
Where with loud voice the power of water shakes
The leafy wood, or sleeps in quiet lakes.

Yet not unrecompensed the man shall roam,
Who at the call of summer quits his home,
And plods through some far realm o'er vale and height,
Though seeking only holiday delight ;
At least, not owning to himself an aim
To which the sage would give a prouder name.
No gains too cheaply earned his fancy cloy,
Though every passing zephyr whispers joy :
Brisk toil, alternating with ready ease,
Feeds the clear current of his sympathies.
For him sod-seats the cottage door adorn ;
And peeps the far-off spire, his evening bourn !
Dear is the forest frowning o'er his head,
And dear the velvet greensward to his tread :
Moves there a cloud o'er mid-day's flaming eye?
Upward he looks—" and calls it luxury ;"
Kind nature's charities his steps attend ;
In every babbling brook he finds a friend ;
While chastening thoughts of sweetest use, bestowed
By wisdom, moralize his pensive road.
Host of his welcome inn, the noon-tide bower,
To his spare meal he calls the passing poor ;
He views the sun uplift his golden fire,
Or sink, with heart alive like Memnon's lyre,†
Blesses the moon that comes with kindly ray,
To light him shaken by his rugged way ;
With bashful fear no cottage children steal
From him, a brother at the cottage meal ;
His humble looks no shy restraint impart,
Around him plays at will the virgin heart.
While unsuspended wheels the village dance,
The maidens eye him with inquiring glance,
Much wondering what sad stroke of crazing care
Or desperate love could lead a wanderer there.

Me, lured by hope her sorrows to remove,
A heart that could not much herself approve,

† The lyre of Memnon is reported to have emitted melancholy or cheerful tones, as it was touched by the sun's evening or morning rays.

O'er Gallia's wastes of corn dejected led,
Her road elms rustling high above my head,
Or through her truant pathways' native charms,
By secret villages and lonely farms,
To where the Alps ascending white in air,
Toy with the sun, and glitter from afar.

And now, emerging from the forest's gloom,
I heave a sigh at hoary Chartreuse' doom.
Where now is fled that power whose frown severe [fear?
Tamed sober reason till she crouched in
The cloister startles at the gleam of arms,
And blasphemy the shuddering fane alarms;
Nod the cloud-piercing pines their troubled heads ; [o'erspreads ;
Spires, rocks, and lawns, a browner night
Strong terror checks the female peasant's sighs, [eyes.
And start the astonished shades at female
That thundering tube the aged angler hears,
And swells the groaning torrent with his tears ; [jay,
From Bruno's forest screams the affrighted
And slow the insulted eagle wheels away.
The cross, with hideous laughter, demons mock,
By angels planted on the aërial rock.*
The "parting genius" sighs with hollow breath [Death.†
Along the mystic streams of Life and
Swelling the outcry dull, that long resounds
Portentous through her old woods' trackless bounds,
Vallombre,‡'mid her falling fanes, deplores,
For ever broke, the sabbath of her bowers.

More pleased. my foot the hidden margin roves
Of Como, bosomed deep in chestnut groves,
No meadows thrown between, the giddy steeps [deeps.
Tower, bare or sylvan, from the narrow
—To towns, whose shades of no rude sound complain, [wain,
To ringing team unknown and grating
To flat-roofed towns, that touch the water's bound,
Or lurk in woody sunless glens profound,
Or, from the bending rocks, obtrusive cling,
And o'er the whitened wave their shadows fling ·
The pathway leads, as round the steeps it twines,
And Silence loves its purple roof of vines ;
The viewless lingerer hence, at evening, sees [the trees ;
From rock-hewn steps the sail between
Or marks, 'mid opening cliffs, fair dark-eyed maids [glades,
Tend the small harvest of their garden
Or stops the solemn mountain-shades to view [and blue,
Stretch o'er the pictured mirror broad
Tracking the yellow sun from steep to steep,
As up the opposing hills with tortoise foot they creep.
Here, half a village shines, in gold arrayed,
Bright as the moon ; half hides itself in shade : [spire,
While, from amid the darkened roofs the
Restlessly flashing, seems to mount like fire ;
There, all unshaded, blazing forests throw
Rich golden verdure on the waves below.
Slow glides the sail along the illumined shore,
And steals into the shade the lazy oar ;
Soft bosoms breathe around contagious sighs,
And amorous music on the water dies.

How blest, delicious scene ! the eye that greets
Thy open beauties, or thy lone retreats ;
The unwearied sweep of wood thy cliffs that scales ;
The never-ending waters of thy vales ;
The cots, those dim religious groves embower,
Or, under rocks that from the water tower,
Insinuated, sprinkling all the shore ;
Each with its household boat beside the door, [droop,
Whose flaccid sails in forms fantastic
Brightening the gloom where thick the forests stoop ; [sky,
Thy torrents shooting from the clear-blue
Thy towns, that cleave, like swallows' nests, on high ; [descried
That glimmer hoar in eve's last light
Dim from the twilight water's shaggy side,
Whence lutes and voices down the enchanted woods [floods ;
Steal, and compose the oar-forgotten

* Alluding to crosses seen on the tops of the spiry rocks of Chartreuse, which have every appearance of being inaccessible.

† Names of rivers at the Chartreuse.

‡ Name of one of the valleys of the Chartreuse.

—Thy lake, 'mid smoking woods, that blue
and gray [morning's ray
Gleams, streaked or dappled, hid from
Slow travelling down the western hills, to
fold [gold,
Its green-tinged margin in a blaze of
From thickly-glittering spires, the matin
bell
Calling the woodman from his desert cell,
A summons to the sound of oars, that pass,
Spotting the steaming deeps, to early mass;
Slow swells the service, o'er the water
borne, [of morn
While fill each pause the ringing woods
Farewell those forms that in thy noontide
shade, [glade;
Rest, near their little plots of wheaten
Those charms that bind the soul in power-
less trance,
Lip-dewing song, and ringlet-tossing dance
Where sparkling eyes and breaking smiles
illume
The sylvan cabin's lute-enlivened gloom.
—Alas! the very murmur of the streams
Breathes o'er the failing soul voluptuous
dreams, [dwell
While slavery, forcing the sunk mind to
On joys that might disgrace the captive's
cell, [marge,
Her shameless timbrel shakes on Como's
And winds, from bay to bay, the vocal
barge.

Yet arts are thine that soothe the unquiet
heart,
And smiles to solitude and want impart.
I loved by silent cottage-doors to roam,
The far-off peasant's day-deserted home;
And once I pierced the mazes of a wood,
Where, far from public haunt, a cabin
stood;
There by the door a hoary-headed sire
Touched with his withered hand an ancient
lyre;
Beneath an old gray oak, as violets lie,
Stretched at his feet with steadfast up-
ward eye, [sound
His children's children joined the holy
—A hermit with his family around!

But let us hence, for fair Locarno smiles
Embowered in walnut slopes and citron
isles;
Or seek at eve the banks of Tusa's stream,*
While, 'mid dim towers and woods, her
waters gleam,
From the bright wave, in solemn gloom,
retire
The dull-red steeps, and, darkening, still
aspire,
To where afar rich orange lustres glow
Round undistinguished clouds, and rocks,
and snow,
Or, led where Via Mala's chasms confine
The indignant waters of the infant Rhine,
Hang o'er the abyss —the else impervious
gloom
His burning eyes with fearful light illume.

The Grison gipsy here her tent hath
placed,
Sole human tenant of the piny waste;
Her tawny skin, dark eyes, and glossy
locks, [rocks
Bend o'er the smoke that curls beneath the
The mind condemned, without reprieve, to
go [woe,
O'er life's long deserts with its charge of
With sad congratulation joins the train,
Where beasts and men together o'er the
plain
Move on—a mighty caravan of pain;
Hope, strength, and courage, social suffer-
ing brings, [and springs.
Freshening the waste of sand with shades
She, solitary, through the desert drear
Spontaneous wanders, hand in hand with
Fear.

A giant moan along the forest swells
Protracted, and the twilight storm fore-
tells,
And, ruining from the cliffs, their deafen-
ing load [abroad;
Tumbles,—the wildering thunder slips
On the high summits darkness comes and
goes, [snows;
Hiding their fiery clouds, their rocks, and
The torrent, traversed by the lustre
broad,
Starts like a horse beside the flashing
road,
In the roofed bridge,† at that terrific hour,
She seeks a shelter from the battering
shower. [ing wood
—Fierce comes the river down; the crash-
Gives way, and half its pines torment the
flood;

---

* The river along whose banks you descend in crossing the Alps by the Simplon Pass.

† Most of the bridges among the Alps are of wood and covered; these bridges have a heavy appearance, and rather injure the effect of the scenery in some places.

Fearful, beneath the water-spirits call,*
And the bridge vibrates, tottering to its
fall.

Heavy, and dull, and cloudy is the night;
No star supplies the comfort of its light,
Glimmer the dim-lit Alps, dilated round,
And one sole light shifts in the vale profound;
While opposite, the waning moon hangs still
And red, above the melancholy hill.
By the deep gloom appalled, the gipsy sighs, [eyes.
Stoops her sick head, and shuts her weary
She hears, upon the mountain-forest's brow, [below;
The death-dog, howling loud and long,
On viewless fingers counts the valley-clock,
Followed by drowsy crow of midnight cock.
The dry leaves stir as with a serpent's walk,
And, far beneath, banditti voices talk;
Behind her hill, the moon, all crimson, rides,
And his red eyes the slinking water hides
—Vexed by the darkness, from the piny gulf
Ascending, nearer howls the famished wolf,
While through the stillness scatters wild dismay [prey.
Her babe's small cry, that leads him to his

Now, passing Urseren's open vale serene,
Her quiet streams, and hills of downy green, [Terror's breath,
Plunge with the Reuss embrowned by
Where danger roofs the narrow walks of death; [dizzy height,
By floods, that, thundering from their
Swell more gigantic on the steadfast sight;
Black drizzling crags, that, beaten by the din,
Vibrate, as if a voice complained within,
Bare steeps, where Desolation stalks, afraid,
Unsteadfast, by a blasted yew upstayed;
By cells† whose image, 'trembling as he prays, [surveys;
Awe-struck, the kneeling peasant scarce
Loose-hanging rocks the day's blessed eye that hide,
And crosses‡ rear'd to death on every side,
Which with cold kiss Devotion planted near,
And, bending, watered with the human tear,
That faded silent from her upward eye,
Unmoved with each rude form of danger nigh,
Fixed on the anchor left by Him who saves
Alike in whelming snows and roaring waves.

On as we move, a softer prospect opes,
Calm huts, and lawns between, and sylvan slopes. [gale,
While mists, suspended on the expiring
Moveless o'erhang the deep secluded vale,
The beams of evening slipping soft between,
Gently illuminate a sober scene;
Winding its dark-green wood and emerald glade,
The still vale lengthens underneath the shade; [recede,
While in soft gloom the scattering bowers
Green dewy lights adorn the freshened mead,
On the low brown wood-huts § delighted sleep
Along the brightened gloom reposing deep.
While pastoral pipes and streams the landscape lull,
And bells of passing mules that tinkle dull,
In solemn shapes before the admiring eye
Dilated hang the misty pines on high,
Huge convent domes with pinnacles and towers, [showers.
And antique castles seen through drizzling

From such romantic dreams, my soul, awake!
Lo! Fear looks silent down on Uri's lake,
Where by the unpathwayed margin, still and dread, [tread.
Was never heard the plodding peasant's
Tower like a wall the naked rocks, or reach
Far o'er the secret water dark with beech;
More high, to where creation seems to end,
Shade above shade, the aerial pines ascend,
Yet with his infants man undaunted creeps
And hangs his small wood-cabin on the steeps.

---

* "Red came the river down and loud, and oft
The angry spirit of the water shriek'd."
—HOME'S *Douglas*.

† The Catholic religion prevails here; these cells are, as is well known, very common in Catholic countries, planted, like the Roman tombs, along the roadside.

‡ Crosses commemorative of the deaths of travellers by the fall of snow, and other accidents, are very common along this dreadful road.

§ The houses in the more retired Swiss valleys are all built of wood.

Where'er below amid the savage scene
Peeps out a little speck of smiling green,
A garden-plot the desert air perfumes,
'Mid the dark pines a little orchard blooms;
A zig-zag path from the domestic skiff,
Threading the painful crag, surmounts the
cliff. [know
—Before those hermit doors, that never
The face of traveller passing to and fro,
No peasant leans upon his pole, to tell
For whom at morning tolled the funeral
bell, [foregoes,
Their watch-dog ne'er his angry bark
Touched by the beggar's moan of human
woes; [shade
The grassy seat beneath their casement
The pilgrim's wistful eye hath never stayed.
—There, did the iron genius not disdain
The gentle power that haunts this myrtle
plain, [chide
There might the love-sick maiden sit, and
The insuperable rocks and severing tide;
There watch at eve her lover's sun-gilt sail
Approaching, and upbraid the tardy gale;
There list at midnight till is heard no more,
Below, the echo of his parting oar.

'Mid stormy vapours ever driving by,
Where ospreys, cormorants, and herons cry,
Hovering o'er rugged wastes too bleak to
rear [ear;
That common growth of earth, the foodful
Where the green apple shrivels on the spray,
And pines the unripened pear in summer's
kindliest ray;
Even here Content has fixed her smiling
reign
With Independence, child of high Disdain
Exulting, 'mid the winter of the skies,
Shy as the jealous chamois, Freedom flies,
And often grasps her sword, and often eyes;
Her crest a bough of winter's bleakest pine,
Strange weeds and Alpine plants her helm
entwine,
And, wildly-pausing, oft she hangs aghast,
While thrills the "Spartan fife," between
the blast.

'Tis storm; and hid in mist from hour to
hour, [pour;
All day the floods a deepening murmur
The sky is veiled, and every cheerful sight.
Dark is the region as with coming night;
But what a sudden burst of overpowering
light!
Triumphant on the bosom of the storm
Glances the fire-clad eagle's wheeling form;
Eastward, in long perspective glittering,
shine [recline;
The wood-crowned cliffs that o'er the lake
Wide o'er the Alps a hundred streams
unfold, [gold:
At once to pillars turned that flame with
Behind his sail the peasant strives to shun
The west that burns like one dilated sun,
Where in a mighty crucible expire
The mountains, glowing-hot, like coals of
fire.

But lo! the boatman, overawed, before
The pictured fane of Tell suspends his oar;
Confused the Marathonian tale appears,
While burn in his full eyes the glorious
tears. [days
And who that walks where men of ancient
Have wrought with godlike arm the deeds
of praise,
Feels not the spirit of the place control,
Exalt, and agitate his labouring soul?
Say, who, by thinking on Canadian hills,
Or wild Aosta lulled by Alpine rills,
On Zutphen's plain; or where, with softened
gaze, [veys;
The old gray stones the plaided chief sur-
Can guess the high resolve, the cherished
pain,
Of him whom passion rivets to the plain,
Where breathed the gale that caught
Wolfe's happiest sigh,
And the last sunbeam fell on Bayard's eye,
Where bleeding Sidney from the cup retired,
And glad Dundee in "faint huzzas" expired!

But now with other mind I stand alone
Upon the summit of this naked cone,
And watch, from peak to peak amid the sky
Small as a bird the chamois chaser fly,*
Through vacant worlds where nature never
gave
A brook to murmur or a bough to wave,
Which unsubstantial phantoms sacred
keep; [and motion sleep,
Through worlds where life, and sound,
Where silence still her death-like reign
extends, [rends
Save when the startling cliff unfrequent
In the deep snow the mighty ruin drowned,
Mocks the dull ear of time with deaf
abortive sound. [to height,
—'Tis his while wandering on, from height

* For most of the images in the next sixteen verses I am indebted to M Raymond's interesting observations annexed to his translation of Coxe's Tour in Switzerland.

To see a planet's pomp and steady light
In the least star of scarce-appearing night,
While the near moon, that coasts the vast profound
Wheels pale and silent her diminished round,
And far and wide the icy summits blaze,
Rejoicing in the glory of her rays:
To him the day-star glitters small and bright,
Shorn of its beams, insufferably white,
And he can look beyond the sun, and view
Those fast-receding depths of sable blue,
Flying till vision can no more pursue!
—At once bewildering mists around him close,
And cold and hunger are his least of woes;
The demon of the snow, with angry roar
Descending, shuts for aye his prison door.
Then with despair's whole weight his spirits sink,
No bread to feed him, and the snow his drink,
While, ere his eyes can close upon the day,
The eagle of the Alps o'ershades her prey.

Hence shall we turn where, heard with fear afar,
Thunders through echoing pines the head-long Aar?
Or rather stay to taste the mild delights
Of pensive Underwalden's * pastoral heights?

Is there who 'mid these awful wilds has seen
The native genii walk the mountain green?
Or heard, while other worlds their charms reveal,
Soft music from the aërial summit steal?
While o'er the desert, answering every close,
Rich steam of sweetest perfume comes and goes.
—And sure there is a secret power, that reigns
Here, where no trace of man the spot profanes,
Nought† but the herds that, pasturing upward, creep,
Hung dim-discovered from the dangerous steep,
Or summer hamlet, flat and bare, on high
Suspended, 'mid the quiet of the sky.
How still! no irreligious sound or sight
Rouses the soul from her severe delight.
An idle voice the Sabbath region fills
Of deep that calls to deep across the hills,
Broke only by the melancholy sound
Of drowsy bells for ever tinkling round;
Faint wail of eagle melting into blue
Beneath the cliffs, and pine-wood's steady *sugh*;‡
The solitary heifer's deepened low;
Or rumbling, heard remote, of falling snow;
Save that, the stranger seen below, the boy
Shouts from the echoing hills with savage joy.

When warm from myrtle bays and tranquil seas,
Comes on, to whisper hope, the vernal breeze,
When hums the mountain-bee in May's glad ear,
And emerald isles to spot the heights appear,
When shouts and lowing herds the valley fill,
And louder torrents stun the noontide hill,
When fragrant scents beneath the enchanted tread
Spring up, his choicest wealth around him spread,
The pastoral Swiss begins the cliffs to scale,
To silence leaving the deserted vale;
Mounts, where the verdure leads, from stage to stage,
And pastures on as in the Patriarchs' age:
O'er lofty heights serene and still they go,
And hear the rattling thunder far below;
They cross the chasmy torrent's foam-lit bed,
Rocked on the dizzy larch's narrow tread;
Or steal beneath loose mountains, half deterred,
That sigh and shudder to the lowing herd.
—I see him, up the midway cliff he creeps
To where a scanty knot of verdure peeps,
Thence down the steep a pile of grass he throws,
The fodder of his herds in winter snows.
Far different life to what tradition hoar
Transmits of days more blest in times of yore;
Then summer lengthened out his season bland,
And with rock-honey flowed the happy land.
Continual fountains welling cheered the waste,
And plants were wholesome, now of deadly taste.
Nor winter yet his frozen stores had piled;
Usurping where the fairest herbage smiled;
Nor hunger forced the herds from pastures bare
For scanty food the treacherous cliffs to dare.

* The people of this Canton are supposed to be of a more melancholy disposition than the other inhabitants of the Alps; this, if true, may proceed from their living more secluded.

† This picture is from the middle region of the Alps.

‡ *Sugh*, a Scotch word expressive of the sound of the wind through the trees.

Then the milk-thistle bade those herds de-
mand [hand
Three times a day the pail and welcome
But human vices have provoked the rod
Of angry nature to avenge her God.
Thus does the father to his sons relate,
On the lone mountain top, their changed
estate.
Still, nature, ever just, to him imparts
Joys only given to uncorrupted hearts.

'Tis morn: with gold the verdant moun-
tain glows, [rose.
More high, the snowy peaks with hues of
Far-stretched beneath the many-tinted hills
A mighty waste of mist the valley fills,
A solemn sea! whose vales and mountains
round
Stand motionless, to awful silence bound.
A gulf of gloomy blue, that opens wide
And bottomless, divides the midway tide.
Like leaning masts of stranded ships appear
The pines that near the coast their summits
rear; [shore
Of cabins, woods, and lawns a pleasant
Bounds calm and clear the chaos still and
hoar; [sound
Loud through that midway gulf ascending,
Unnumbered streams with hollow roar pro-
found. [of birds,
Mount through the nearer mist the chant
And talking voices, and the low of herds,
The bark of dogs, the drowsy tinkling bell,
And wild-wood mountain lutes of saddest
swell.
Think not, suspended from the cliff on high,
He looks below with undelighted eye.
—No vulgar joy is his, at eventide
Stretched on the scented mountain's purple
side.
For as the pleasures of his simple day
Beyond his native valley seldom stray,
Nought round its darling precincts can he
find
But brings some past enjoyment to his mind,
While Hope, that ceaseless leans on Plea-
sure's urn, [return.
Binds her wild wreaths, and whispers his

Once Man, entirely free, alone and wild.
Was blest as free—for he was nature's
child.
He, all superior but his God disdained,
Walked none restraining, and by none re-
strained, [taught,
Confessed no law but what his reason
Did all he wished, and wished but what he
ought.
As man in his primeval dower arrayed
The image of his glorious Sire displayed,
Even so, by vestal nature guarded here
The traces of primeval man appear
The native dignity no forms debase,
The eye sublime, and surly lion-grace.
The slave of none, of beasts alone the lord,
He marches with his flute, his book, and
sword; [pared
Well taught by that to feel his rights, pre-
With this "the blessings he enjoys to
guard."

And, as his native hills encircle ground
For many a wondrous victory renowned,
The work of freedom daring to oppose,
With few in arms,* innumerable foes,
When to those glorious fields his steps are
led, [dead.
An unknown power connects him with the
For images of other worlds are there;
Awful the light, and holy is the air
Uncertain through his fierce uncultured
soul [roll,
Like lighted tempests troubled transports
To viewless realms his spirit towers amain,
Beyond the senses and their little reign.

And oft, when passed that solemn vision
by, [high,
He holds with God himself communion
Where the dread peal of swelling torrents
fills
The sky-roofed temple of the eternal hills;
Or, when upon the mountain's silent brow
Reclined, he sees, above him and below,
Bright stars of ice and azure fields of
snow;
While needle peaks of granite shooting bare
Tremble in ever-varying tints of air:
—Great joy, by horror tamed, dilates his
heart, [impart.
And the near heavens their own delights
—When the sun bids the gorgeous scene
farewell,
Alps overlooking Alps their state up-swell;
Huge Pikes of Darkness named, of Fear
and Storms,†
Lift, all serene, their still, illumined forms,
In sea-like reach of prospect round him
spread,
Tinged like an angel's smile all rosy red.

---

* Alluding to several battles which the Swiss in very small numbers have gained over their oppressors, the house of Austria

† As Schreck-Horn, the pike of terror, Wetter-Horn, the pike of storms, &c &c.

When downward to his winter hut he goes, [grows;
Dear and more dear the lessening circle
That hut which from the hills his eye employs
So oft, the central point of all his joys.
And as a swift, by tender cares opprest,
Peeps often ere she darts into her nest,
So to the untrodden floor, where round him looks
His father, helpless as the babe he rocks,
Oft he descends to nurse the brother pair,
Till storm and driving ice blockade him there.
There, safely guarded by the woods behind,
He hears the chiding of the baffled wind,
Hears Winter, calling all his terrors round,
Rush down the living rocks with whirlwind sound.

Through nature's vale his homely pleasures glide
Unstained by envy, discontent, and pride;
The bound of all his vanity, to deck,
With one bright bell, a favourite heifer's neck; [feast,
Well-pleased upon some simple annual
Remembered half the year and hoped the rest,
If dairy produce from his inner hoard
Of thrice ten summers consecrate the board.
—Alas! in every clime a flying ray
Is all we have to cheer our wintry way.
But, ah! the unwilling mind may more than trace
The general sorrows of the human race:
The churlish gales, that unremitting blow
Cold from necessity's continual snow,
To those the gentle groups of bliss deny
That on the noonday bank of leisure lie.
Yet more;—compell'd by powers which only deign
That *solitary* man disturb their reign,
Powers that support a never-ceasing strife
With all the tender charities of life,
The father, as his sons of strength become
To pay the filial debt, for food to roam,
From his bare nest amid the storms of heaven [driven;
Drives, eagle-like, those sons as he was
His last dread pleasure watches to the plain—
And never, eagle-like, beholds again!

When the poor heart has all its joys resigned, [behind?
Why does their sad remembrance cleave
Lo! where through flat Batavia's willowy groves,
Or by the lazy Seine the exile roves;
Soft o'er the waters mournful measures swell, [cell;"
Unlocking tender thought's "memorial
Past pleasures are transformed to mortal pains, [veins,
While poison spreads along the listener's
Poison which not a frame of steel can brave, [grave.*
Bows his young head with sorrow to the

Gay lark of hope, thy silent song resume!
Fair smiling lights the purpled hills illume!
Soft gales and dews of life's delicious morn,
And thou, lost fragrance of the heart, return!
Soon flies the little joy to man allowed,
And grief before him travels like a cloud:
For come diseases on, and penury's rage,
Labour, and care, and pain, and dismal age,
Till, hope-deserted, long in vain his breath
Implores the dreadful untried sleep of death.

'Mid savage rocks, and seas of snow that shine
Between interminable tracts of pine,
A temple stands; which holds an awful shrine,
By an uncertain light revealed, that falls
On the mute image and the troubled walls:
Pale, dreadful faces round the shrine appear,
Abortive joy, and hope that works in fear;
While strives a secret power to hush the crowd, [rights aloud.
Pain's wild rebellious burst proclaims her

Oh! give not me that eye of hard disdain
That views undimmed Ensiedlen's wretched fane.† [ment meet,
'Mid muttering prayers all sounds of tor-
Dire clap of hands, distracted chafe of feet; [cry,
While, loud and dull, ascends the weeping
Surely in other thoughts contempt may die.
If the sad grave of human ignorance bear
One flower of hope—oh, pass and leave it there.

---

* The effect of the famous air called in French Ranz des Vaches upon the Swiss troops.

† This shrine is resorted to, from a hope of relief, by multitudes, from every corner of the Catholic world, labouring under mental or bodily afflictions.

The tall sun, tiptoe on an Alpine spire,
Flings o'er the wilderness a stream of fire;
Now let us meet the pilgrims ere the day
Close on the remnant of their weary way;
While they are drawing toward the sacred floor
Where the charmed worm of pain shall gnaw no more.
How gaily murmur and how sweetly taste
The fountains* reared for them amid the waste!
There some with tearful kiss each other greet,
And some, with reverence, wash their toil-worn feet.
Yes, I will see you when ye first behold
Those holy turrets tipped with evening gold,
In that glad moment when the hands are prest
In mute devotion on the thankful breast.

Last let us turn to where Châmouny shields
With rocks and gloomy woods her fertile fields;
Five streams of ice amid her cots descend,
And with wild flowers and blooming orchards blend.
A scene more fair than what the Grecian feigns
Of purple lights and ever-vernal plains;
Here lawns and shades by breezy rivulets fanned,
Here all the seasons revel hand in hand.
—Red stream the cottage-lights; the landscape fades,
Erroneous wavering 'mid the twilight shades.
Alone ascends that hill of matchless height,†
That holds no commerce with the summer night.
From age to age, amid his lonely bounds
The crash of ruin fitfully resounds;
Mysterious havoc! but serene his brow,
Where daylight lingers 'mid perpetual snow;
Glitter the stars above, and all is black below.

At such an hour I heaved a pensive sigh,
When roared the sullen Arve in anger by,
That not for thy reward, delicious vale!
Waves the ripe harvest in the autumnal gale;
That thou, the slave of slaves, art doomed to pine;
Hard lot!—for no Italian arts are thine,
To soothe or cheer, to soften or refine.

Beloved freedom! were it mine to stray,
With shrill winds roaring round my lonely way,
O'er the bleak sides of Cumbria's heath-clad moors,
Or where dank sea-weed lashes Scotland's shores,
To scent the sweets of Piedmont's breathing rose,
And orange gale that o'er Lugano blows;
In the wide range of many a varied round,
Fleet as my passage was, I still have found
That where despotic courts their gems display,
The lilies of domestic joy decay,
While the remotest hamlets blessings share
In thy dear presence known, and only there!
The casement's shed more luscious woodbine binds,
And to the door a neater pathway winds;
At early morn, the careful housewife, led
To cull her dinner from its garden bed,
Of weedless herbs a healthier prospect sees,
While hum with busier joy her happy bees;
In brighter rows her table wealth aspires,
And laugh with merrier blaze her evening fires;
Her infants' cheeks with fresher roses glow,
And wilder graces sport around their brow;
By clearer taper lit, a cleanlier board
Receives at supper hour her tempting hoard.
The chamber hearth with fresher boughs is spread,
And whiter is the hospitable bed.

And oh! fair France! though now along the shade
Where erst at will the gray-clad peasant strayed,
Gleam war's discordant vestments through the trees,
And the red banner fluctuates in the breeze;
Though martial songs have banished songs of love,
And nightingales forsake the village grove,
Scared by the fife and rumbling drum's alarms,
And the short thunder, and the flash of arms;
While, as night bids the startling uproar die,
Sole sound, the sourd‡ renews his mournful cry!
—Yet, hast thou found that freedom spreads her power
Beyond the cottage hearth, the cottage door:

---

* Rude fountains built and covered with sheds for the accommodation of the pilgrims, in their ascent of the mountain.

† It is only from the higher part of the valley of Châmouny that Mont Blanc is visible.

‡ An insect so called which emits a short, melancholy cry, heard at the close of the summer evenings on the banks of the Loire

All nature smiles, and owns beneath her eyes
Her fields peculiar, and peculiar skies.
Yes, as I roamed where Loiret's waters glide
Through rustling aspens heard from side to side,
When from October clouds a milder light
Fell, where the blue flood rippled into white,
Methought from every cot the watchful bird
Crowed with ear-piercing power till then unheard ; [muring streams,
Each clacking mill, that broke the mur-
Rocked the charmed thought in more delightful dreams ; [ing leaf
Chasing those long, long dreams, the fall-
Awoke a fainter pang of moral grief ;
The measured echo of the distant flail
Wound in more welcome cadence down the vale ;
A more majestic tide the water rolled,
And glowed the sun-gilt groves in richer gold. [raise
—Though Liberty shall soon, indignant,
Red on the hills his beacon's comet blaze ;
Bid from on high his lonely cannon sound,
And on ten thousand hearths his shout rebound ;
His 'larum-bell from village-tower to tower
Swing on the astonished ear its dull undying roar ;
Yet, yet rejoice, though pride's perverted ire
Rouse hell's own aid, and wrap thy hills in fire ! [birth,
Lo ! from the innocuous flames, a lovely
With its own virtues springs another earth :
Nature, as in her prime, her virgin reign
Begins, and love and truth compose her train ; [gaze,
While, with a pulseless hand, and steadfast
Unbreathing justice her still beam surveys.

Oh, give, great God, to freedom's waves to ride
Sublime o'er conquest, avarice, and pride,
To sweep where pleasure decks her guilty bowers, [bed towers.
And dark oppression builds her thick rib-
—Give them, beneath their breast while gladness springs, [wings ;
To brood the nations o'er with Nile-like
And grant that every sceptred child of clay,
Who cries, presumptuous, "Here their tides shall stay," [shore,
Swept in their anger from the affrighted
With all his creatures sink—to rise no more !

To-night, my friend, within this humble cot
Be the dead load of mortal ills forgot
In timely sleep ; and when at break of day,
On the tall peaks the glistening sunbeams play, [new,
With lighter heart our course we may re-
The first whose footsteps print the mountain dew.

LINES

Left upon a seat in a yew-tree, which stands near the Lake of Esthwaite, on a desolate part of the shore, commanding a beautiful prospect.

NAY, traveller ! rest. This lonely yew-tree stands
Far from all human dwelling : what if here
No sparkling rivulet spread the verdant herb ?
What if these barren boughs the bee not loves ? [waves,
Yet, if the wind breathe soft, the curling
That break against the shore, shall lull thy mind
By one soft impulse saved from vacancy.

Who he was
That piled these stones, and with the mossy sod [tree
First covered o'er, and taught this aged
With its dark arms to form a circling bower
I well remember.—He was one who owned
No common soul. In youth by science nursed,
And led by nature into a wild scene
Of lofty hopes, he to the world went forth
A favoured being, knowing no desire
Which genius did not hallow,—'gainst the taint [hate,
Of dissolute tongues, and jealousy, and
And scorn,—against all enemies prepared,
All but neglect. The world, for so it thought,
Owed him no service : wherefore he at once
With indignation turned himself away,
And with the food of pride sustained his soul [boughs
In solitude.—Stranger ! these gloomy
Had charms for him ; and here he loved to sit,
His only visitants a straggling sheep,
The stone-chat, or the glancing sand-piper :
And on these barren rocks, with fern and heath,

And juniper and thistle, sprinkled o'er,
Fixing his downcast eye, he many an hour
A morbid pleasure nourished, tracing here
An emblem of his own unfruitful life:
And, lifting up his head, he then would gaze
On the more distant scene,—how lovely 'tis
Thou seest,—and he would gaze till it became
Far lovelier, and his heart could not sustain
The beauty, still more beauteous! Nor, that time,
When nature had subdued him to herself,
Would he forget those beings, to whose minds,
Warm from the labours of benevolence,
The world, and human life, appeared a scene
Of kindred loveliness, then he would sigh
With mournful joy, to think that others felt
What he must never feel: and so, lost man!
On visionary views would fancy feed,
Till his eye streamed with tears. In this deep vale
He died,—this seat his only monument.

If thou be one whose heart the holy forms
Of young imagination have kept pure,
Stranger! henceforth be warned; and know that pride,
Howe'er disguised in its own majesty,
Is littleness; that he who feels contempt
For any living thing, hath faculties
Which he has never used; that thought with him
Is in its infancy. The man whose eye
Is ever on himself doth look on one,
The least of nature's works, one who might move
The wise man to that scorn which wisdom holds
Unlawful, ever. O be wiser, thou!
Instructed that true knowledge leads to love,
True dignity abides with him alone
Who, in the silent hour of inward thought,
Can still suspect, and still revere himself,
In lowliness of heart.

THE FEMALE VAGRANT.

My father was a good and pious man,
An honest man by honest parents bred,
And I believe that soon as I began
To lisp, he made me kneel beside my bed,
And in his hearing there my prayers I said:
And afterwards, by my good father taught,
I read, and loved the books in which I read;
For books in every neighbouring house I sought,
And nothing to my mind a sweeter pleasure brought.

Can I forget what charms did once adorn
My garden, stored with pease, and mint, and thyme,
And rose, and lily, for the Sabbath morn?
The Sabbath bells, and their delightful chime;
The gambols and wild freaks at shearing time;
My hen's rich nest through long grass scarce espied;
The cowslip-gathering in June's dewy prime;
The swans that, when I sought the water-side,
From far to meet me came, spreading their snowy pride?

The staff I yet remember which upbore
The bending body of my active sire:
His seat beneath the honeyed sycamore
Where the bees hummed, and chair by winter fire;
When market morning came, the neat attire
With which, though bent on haste, myself I decked;
My watchful dog, whose starts of furious ire,
When stranger passed, so often I have checked;
The redbreast known for years, which at my casement pecked.

The suns of twenty summers danced along,—
Ah! little marked how fast they rolled away:
But, through severe mischance, and cruel wrong,
My father's substance fell into decay;
We toiled and struggled—hoping for a day
When fortune should put on a kinder look:
But vain were wishes—efforts vain as they:
He from his old hereditary nook
Must part—the summons came—our final leave we took.

It was indeed a miserable hour
When from the last hill-top, my sire surveyed,
Peering above the trees, the steeple tower
That on his marriage day sweet music made!
Till then, he hoped his bones might there be laid,
Close by my mother in their native bowers.
Bidding me trust in God, he stood and prayed—
I could not pray:—through tears that fell in showers,
Glimmered our dear-loved home, alas! no longer ours.

There was a youth whom I had loved so
long,
That when I loved him not I cannot say.
'Mid the green mountains many a thought-
less song [May.
We two had sung, like gladsome birds in
When we began to tire of childish play,
We seemed still more and more to prize
each other ; [day ;
We talked of marriage and our marriage
And I in truth did love him like a brother,
For never could I hope to meet with such
another !

Two years were passed since to a distant
town
He had repaired to ply the artist's trade.
What tears of bitter grief till then un-
known ! [layed !
What tender vows our last sad kiss de-
To him we turned :—we had no other aid.
Like one revived upon his neck I wept,
And her whom he had loved in joy, he said,
He well could love in grief : his faith he
kept, [slept.
And in a quiet home once more my father

We lived in peace and comfort, and were
blest [plied.
With daily bread, by constant toil sup-
Three lovely infants lay upon my breast ;
And often viewing their sweet smiles, I
sighed, [died
And knew not why. My happy father
When sad distress reduced the children's
meal : [hide
Thrice happy ! that for him the grave did
The empty loom, cold hearth, and silent
wheel, [could not heal.
And tears that flowed for ills which patience

'Twas a hard change, an evil time was come,
We had no hope, and no relief could gain.
But soon, with proud parade, the noisy
drum [and pain.
Beat round, to sweep the streets of want
My husband's arms now only served to
strain
Me and his children hungering in his view ,
In such despair, my prayers and tears were
vain :
To join those miserable men, he flew ;
And now to the sea coast, with numbers
more, we drew.

There long were we neglected, and we
bore [weighed ,
Much sorrow, ere the fleet its anchor
Green fields before us, and our native shore,
We breathed a pestilential air that made
Ravage for which no knell was heard. We
prayed [nor knew
For our departure ; wished and wished—
'Mid that long sickness, and those hopes
delayed, [view ·
That happier days we never more must
The parting signal streamed, at last the
land withdrew.

But the calm summer season now was past.
On as we drove, the equinoctial deep
Ran mountains high before the howling
blast ; [sweep
And many perished in the whirlwind's
We gazed with terror on their gloomy
sleep, [ensue,
Untaught that soon such anguish must
Our hopes such harvest of affliction reap,
That we the mercy of the waves should
rue : [voted crew.
We reached the western world a poor de-

The pains and plagues that on our heads
came down,
Disease and famine, agony and fear,
In wood or wilderness, in camp or town,
It would thy brain unsettle even to hear.
All perished—all in one remorseless year,
Husband and children ! one by one, by
sword [tear
And ravenous plague, all perished ; every
Dried up, despairing, desolate, on board
A British ship I waked, as from a trance
restored.

Peaceful as some immeasurable plain
By the first beams of dawning light im-
prest, [main,
In the calm sunshine slept the glittering
The very ocean hath its hour of rest .
I, too, forgot the heavings of my breast.
Oh, me, how quiet sky and ocean were !
As quiet all within me. I was blest ·
And looked, and looked along the silent air,
Until it seemed to bring a joy to my
despair.

Ah ! how unlike those late terrific sleeps,
And groans, that rage of racking famine
spoke ! [heaps !
The unburied dead, that lay in festering
The breathing pestilence that rose like
smoke ! [broke !
The shriek that from the distant battle
The mine's dire earthquake, and the pallid
host

Driven by the bomb's incessant thunder-
stroke
To loathsome vaults, where heart-sick
anguish tossed, [lost !
Hope died, and fear itself in agony was

Some mighty gulf of separation past,
I seemed transported to another world —
A thought resigned with pain, when from
the mast
The impatient mariner the sail unfurled,
And whistling, called the wind that hardly
curled [of home
The silent sea. From the sweet thoughts
And from all hope I was for ever hurled
For me—farthest from earthly port to roam
Was best, could I but shun the spot where
man might come.

And oft I thought (my fancy was so strong)
That I, at last, a resting-place had found ;
"Here will I dwell," said I, "my whole
life long,
Roaming the illimitable waters round
Here will I live, of every friend disowned,
And end my days upon the ocean flood." —
To break my dream the vessel reached its
bound : [stood,
And homeless near a thousand homes I
And near a thousand tables pined, and
wanted food.

By grief enfeebled, was I turned adrift,
Helpless as sailor cast on desert rock ;
Nor morsel to my mouth that day did lift,
Nor dared my hand at any door to knock.
I lay where, with his drowsy mates, the cock
From the cross timber of an out-house hung :
Dismally tolled that night the city clock !
At morn my sick heart hunger scarcely
stung, [frame my tongue.
Nor to the beggar's language could I

So passed another day, and so the third :
Then did I try in vain the crowd's resort.
—In deep despair, by frightful wishes
stirred,
Near the sea-side I reached a ruined fort ,
There pains, which nature could no more
support, [fall,
With blindness linked, did on my vitals
And after many interruptions short
Of hideous sense, I sank, nor step could
crawl ; [recall
Unsought for was the help that did my life

Borne to an hospital, I lay with brain
Drowsy and weak, and shattered memory ;
I heard my neighbours in their beds, com-
plain
Of many things which never troubled me ;
Of feet still bustling round with busy glee ;
Of looks where common kindness had no
part :
Of service done with careless cruelty,
Fretting the fever round the languid heart ;
And groans, which, as they said, might
make a dead man start

These things just served to stir the torpid
sense,
Nor pain nor pity in my bosom raised.
With strength did memory return ; and,
thence
Dismissed, again on open day I gazed,
At houses, men, and common light amazed
The lanes I sought, and as the sun retired,
Came where beneath the trees a faggot
blazed ; [quired,
The travellers saw me weep, my fate in-
And gave me food,—and rest, more wel-
come, more desired.

They with their panniered asses semblance
made
Of potters wandering on from door to door :
But life of happier sort to me portrayed,
And other joys my fancy to allure ;
The bag-pipe dinning on the midnight
moor,
In barn uplighted, and companions boon
Well met from far with revelry secure,
Among the forest glades, when jocund
June [genial moon,
Rolled fast along the sky his warm and

But ill they suited me—those journeys dark
O'er moor and mountain, midnight theft
to hatch ! [bark,
To charm the surly house-dog's faithful
Or hang on tip-toe at the lifted latch,
The gloomy lantern, and the dim blue
match, [shrill,
The black disguise, the warning whistle
And ear still busy on its nightly watch,
Were not for me, brought up in nothing ill ;
Besides, on griefs so fresh my thoughts
were brooding still.

What could I do, unaided and unblest ?
My father ! gone was every friend of thine:
And kindred of dead husband are at best
Small help , and after marriage such as
mine,
With little kindness would to me incline,

Ill was I then for toil or service fit :
With tears whose course no effort could confine,
By the roadside forgetful would I sit
Whole hours, my idle arms in moping sorrow knit.

I led a wandering life among the fields :
Contentedly, yet sometimes self-accused,
I lived upon what casual bounty yields,
Now coldly given, now utterly refused.
The ground I for my bed have often used :
But, what afflicts my peace with keenest ruth
Is, that I have my inner self abused,
Foregone the home delight of constant truth
And clear and open soul, so prized in fearless youth.

Three years thus wandering, often have I viewed,
In tears, the sun towards that country tend
Where my poor heart lost all its fortitude :
And now across this moor my steps I bend
—Oh, tell me whither—for no earthly friend
Have I.—She ceased, and weeping turned away,
As if because her tale was at an end
She wept ; because she had no more to say
Of that perpetual weight which on her spirit lay.

Poems Referring to the Period of Childhood.

My heart leaps up when I behold
A rainbow in the sky :
So was it when my life began ;
So is it now I am a man :
So be it when I shall grow old,
Or let me die !
The child is father of the man ;
And I could wish my days to be
Bound each to each by natural piety.

TO A BUTTERFLY.

Stay near me—do not take thy flight !
A little longer stay in sight !
Much converse do I find in thee,
Historian of my infancy !
Float near me ; do not yet depart !
Dead times revive in thee :
Thou bring'st, gay creature as thou art !
A solemn image to my heart,
My father's family !

Oh ! pleasant, pleasant were the days,
The time, when, in our childish plays,
My sister Emmeline and I
Together chased the butterfly !
A very hunter did I rush
Upon the prey :—with leaps and springs
I followed on from brake to bush ;
But she, God love her ! feared to brush
The dust from off its wings.

FORESIGHT.

That is work of waste and ruin—
Do as Charles and I are doing !
Strawberry-blossoms, one and all,
We must spare them —here are many :
Look at it—the flower is small,
Small and low, though fair as any :
Do not touch it ! summers two
I am older, Anne, than you.

Pull the primrose, sister Anne !
Pull as many as you can.
—Here are daisies, take your fill ;
Pansies, and the cuckow flower :
Of the lofty daffodil
Make your bed, and make your bower
Fill your lap, and fill your bosom ;
Only spare the strawberry-blossom !

Primroses, the spring may love them :
Summer knows but little of them :
Violets, a barren kind,
Withered on the ground must lie ;
Daisies leave no fruit behind
When the pretty flowerets die ;
Pluck them, and another year
As many will be blowing here.

God has given a kindlier power
To the favoured strawberry-flower.
When the months of spring are fled
Hither let us bend our walk ;

Lurking berries, ripe and red,
Then will hang on every stalk,
Each within its leafy bower;
And for that promise spare the flower!

CHARACTERISTICS OF A CHILD THREE YEARS OLD.

Loving she is, and tractable, though wild;
And innocence hath privilege in her
To dignify arch looks and laughing eyes;
And feats of cunning; and the pretty round
Of trespasses, affected to provoke
Mock-chastisement and partnership in play.
And, as a faggot sparkles on the hearth,
Not less if unattended and alone
Than when both young and old sit gathered
And take delight in its activity, [round
Even so this happy creature of herself
Is all-sufficient; solitude to her
Is blithe society, who fills the air
With gladness and involuntary songs.
Light are her sallies as the tripping fawn's
Forth-startled from the fern where she lay couched;
Unthought of, unexpected, as the stir
Of the soft breeze ruffling the meadow flowers;
Or from before it chasing wantonly
The many-coloured images impressed
Upon the bosom of a placid lake

ADDRESS TO A CHILD DURING A BOISTEROUS WINTER EVENING.

BY A FEMALE FRIEND OF THE AUTHOR.

What way does the wind come? What way does he go?
He rides over the water and over the snow,
Through wood, and through vale; and o'er rocky height,
Which the goat cannot climb takes his sounding flight;
He tosses about in every bare tree,
As, if you look up, you plainly may see,
But how he will come and whither he goes
There's never a scholar in England knows.

He will suddenly stop in a cunning nook
And ring a sharp 'larum;—but if you should look, [snow
There's nothing to see but a cushion of
Round as a pillow and whiter than milk,
And softer than if it were covered with silk.
Sometimes he'll hide in the cave of a rock,
Then whistle as shrill as the buzzard cock;
—Yet seek him,—and what shall you find in the place?
Nothing but silence and empty space;
Save, in a corner a heap of dry leaves,
That he's left, for a bed, to beggars or thieves!

As soon as 'tis daylight, to-morrow, with me
You shall go to the orchard, and then you will see [rout,
That he has been there, and made a great
And cracked the branches, and strewn them about; [upright twig
Heaven grant that he spare but that one
That looked up at the sky so proud and big
All last summer, as well you know,
Studded with apples, a beautiful show!

Hark! over the roof he makes a pause,
And growls as if he would fix his claws
Right in the slates, and with a huge rattle
Drive them down like men in a battle;
—But let him range round; he does us no harm,
We build up the fire, we're snug and warm
Untouched by his breath see the candle shines bright,
And burns with a clear and steady light;
Books have we to read,—but that half-stifled knell—
Alas! 'tis the sound of the eight o'clock bell
—Come now, we'll to bed! and when we are there [we care?
He may work his own will and what shall
He may knock at the door,—we'll not let him in; [his din;
May drive at the windows,—we'll laugh at
Let him seek his own home wherever it be;
Here's a *cozie* warm house for Edward and me.

THE MOTHER'S RETURN.

BY THE SAME.

A month, sweet little ones, is passed
Since your dear mother went away,—
And she to-morrow will return;
To-morrow is the happy day.

Oh, blessed tidings! thought of joy!
The eldest heard with steady glee;
Silent he stood; then laughed amain.
And shouted, "Mother, come to me!"

Louder and louder did he shout,
With witless hope to bring her near;
"Nay, patience! patience, little boy!
Your tender mother cannot hear."

I told of hills, and far-off towns,
And long, long vales to travel through,—
He listens, puzzled, sore perplexed,
But he submits; what can he do?

No strife disturbs his sister's breast:
She wars not with the mystery
Of time and distance, night and day,
The bonds of our humanity.

Her joy is like an instinct, joy
Of kitten, bird, or summer fly;
She dances, runs without an aim,
She chatters in her ecstasy.

Her brother now takes up the note,
And echoes back his sister's glee,
They hug the infant in my arms,
As if to force his sympathy.

Then, settling into fond discourse,
We rested in the garden bower;
While sweetly shone the evening sun
In his departing hour.

We told o'er all that we had done,—
Our rambles by the swift brook's side
Far as the willow-skirted pool,
Where two fair swans together glide.

We talked of change, of winter gone,
Of green leaves on the hawthorn spray,
Of birds that build their nests and sing,
And "all since mother went away."

To her these tales they will repeat,
To her our new-born tribes will show,
The goslings green, the ass's colt,
The lambs that in the meadow go.

—But, see, the evening star comes forth!
To bed the children must depart;
A moment's heaviness they feel,
A sadness at the heart:

'Tis gone—and in a merry fit
They run up stairs in gamesome race;
I, too, infected by their mood,
I could have joined the wanton chase.

Five minutes past—and, oh, the change!
Asleep upon their beds they lie;
Their busy limbs in perfect rest,
And closed the sparkling eye.

LUCY GRAY; OR, SOLITUDE.

Oft I had heard of Lucy Gray:
And, when I crossed the wild,
I chanced to see at break of day
The solitary child.

No mate, no comrade Lucy knew;
She dwelt on a wide moor—
The sweetest thing that ever grew
Beside a human door!

You yet may spy the fawn at play,
The hare upon the green;
But the sweet face of Lucy Gray
Will never more be seen.

"To-night will be a stormy night—
You to the town must go;
And take a lantern, child, to light
Your mother through the snow."

"That, father, will I gladly do:
'Tis scarcely afternoon—
The minster-clock has just struck two,
And yonder is the moon."

At this the father raised his hook,
And snapped a faggot band;
He plied his work,—and Lucy took
The lantern in her hand.

Not blither is the mountain roe:
With many a wanton stroke
Her feet disperse the powdery snow,
That rises up like smoke.

The storm came on before its time:
She wandered up and down;
And many a hill did Lucy climb;
But never reached the town.

The wretched parents all that night
Went shouting far and wide;
But there was neither sound nor sight
To serve them for a guide.

At day-break on a hill they stood
That overlooked the moor,
And thence they saw the bridge of wood,
A furlong from their door.

They wept, and turning homeward, cried,
"In heaven we all shall meet."
When in the snow the mother spied
The print of Lucy's feet.

Then downward from the steep hill's edge
They track the footmarks small;
And through the broken hawthorn hedge,
And by the long stone-wall;

And then an open field they crossed
The marks were still the same,
They tracked them on, nor ever lost,
And to the bridge they came.

They followed from the snowy bank
Those footmarks, one by one,
Into the middle of the plank,
And further there were none!

Yet some maintain that to this day
She is a living child;
That you may see sweet Lucy Gray
Upon the lonesome wild.

O'er rough and smooth she trips along,
And never looks behind,
And sings a solitary song
That whistles in the wind.

ALICE FELL; OR, POVERTY.

THE post-boy drove with fierce career,
For threatening clouds the moon had drowned;
When suddenly I seemed to hear
A moan, a lamentable sound.

As if the wind blew many ways,
I heard the sound—and more and more;
It seemed to follow with the chaise,
And still I heard it as before.

At length I to the boy called out;
He stopped his horses at the word;
But neither cry, nor voice, nor shout,
Nor aught else like it, could be heard.

The boy then smacked his whip, and fast
The horses scampered through the rain;
And soon I heard upon the blast
The voice, and bade him halt again.

Said I, alighting on the ground,
"What can it be, this piteous moan?"
And there a little girl I found,
Sitting behind the chaise, alone

"My cloak!" the word was last and first,
And loud and bitterly she wept,
As if her very heart would burst;
And down from off her seat she leapt.

"What ails you, child?" She sobbed, "Look here!"
I saw it in the wheel entangled,
A weather-beaten rag as e'er
From any garden scarecrow dangled.

'Twas twisted between nave and spoke,
Her help she lent, and with good heed
Together we released the cloak;
A wretched, wretched rag indeed!

"And whither are you going, child,
To-night along these lonesome ways?"
"To Durham," answered she, half wild—
"Then come with me into the chaise."

She sate like one past all relief,
Sob after sob she forth did send
In wretchedness, as if her grief
Could never, never have an end.

"My child, in Durham do you dwell?"
She checked herself in her distress,
And said, "My name is Alice Fell,
I'm fatherless and motherless.

And I to Durham, sir, belong."
And then, as if the thought would choke
Her very heart, her grief grew strong;
And all was for her tattered cloak.

The chaise drove on, our journey's end
Was nigh, and sitting by my side,
As if she had lost her only friend,
She wept, nor would be pacified.

Up to the tavern door we post;
Of Alice and her grief I told;
And I gave money to the host,
To buy a new cloak for the old.

"And let it be of duffil gray,
As warm a cloak as man can sell!"
Proud creature was she the next day,
The little orphan, Alice Fell!

WE ARE SEVEN.

——— A SIMPLE child,
That lightly draws its breath,
And feels its life in every limb,
What should it know of death?

I met a little cottage girl:
She was eight years old, she said;
Her hair was thick with many a curl
That clustered round her head.

She had a rustic, woodland air,
And she was wildly clad:
Her eyes were fair, and very fair;
Her beauty made me glad.

"Sisters and brothers, little maid,
How many may you be?"
"How many? Seven in all," she said,
And wondering looked at me.

"And where are they? I pray you tell."
She answered, "Seven are we;
And two of us at Conway dwell,
And two are gone to sea.

"Two of us in the churchyard lie,
My sister and my brother;
And, in the churchyard cottage, I
Dwell near them with my mother."

"You say that two at Conway dwell,
And two are gone to sea,
Yet ye are seven!—I pray you tell,
Sweet maid, how this may be."

Then did the little maid reply,
"Seven boys and girls are we;
Two of us in the churchyard lie,
Beneath the churchyard tree."

"You run about, my little maid,
Your limbs they are alive;
If two are in the churchyard laid,
Then ye are only five."

"Their graves are green, they may be seen,"
The little maid replied,
"Twelve steps or more from my mother's door,
And they are side by side.

"My stockings there I often knit,
My kerchief there I hem;
And there upon the ground I sit—
I sit and sing to them.

"And often after sunset, sir,
When it is light and fair,
I take my little porringer,
And eat my supper there.

"The first that died was little Jane;
In bed she moaning lay,
Till God released her of her pain;
And then she went away.

"So in the churchyard she was laid;
And when the grass was dry,
Together round her grave we played,
My brother John and I.

"And when the ground was white with snow,
And I could run and slide,
My brother John was forced to go,
And he lies by her side."

"How many are you then," said I,
"If they two are in heaven?"
The little maiden did reply,
"O master! we are seven."

"But they are dead; those two are dead!
Their spirits are in heaven!"
'Twas throwing words away: for still
The little maid would have her will,
And said, "Nay, we are seven!"

ANECDOTE FOR FATHERS.

SHOWING HOW THE PRACTICE OF LYING MAY BE TAUGHT.

I HAVE a boy of five years old;
His face is fair and fresh to see;
His limbs are cast in beauty's mould,
And dearly he loves me.

One morn we strolled on our dry walk,
Our quiet home all full in view,
And held such intermitted talk
As we are wont to do.

My thoughts on former pleasures ran;
I thought of Kilve's delightful shore,
Our pleasant home when spring began,
A long, long year before.

A day it was when I could bear
Some fond regrets to entertain;
With so much happiness to spare,
I could not feel a pain.

The green earth echoed to the feet
Of lambs that bounded through the glade,
From shade to sunshine, and as fleet
From sunshine back to shade.

Birds warbled round me—every trace
Of inward sadness had its charm;
"Kilve," said I, "was a favourite place,
And so is Liswyn farm."

My boy was by my side, so slim
And graceful in his rustic dress!
And, as we talked, I questioned him,
In very idleness.

"Now tell me, had you rather be,"
I said, and took him by the arm,
"On Kilve's smooth shore, by the green
Or here at Liswyn farm?" [sea,

In careless mood he looked at me,
While still I held him by the arm,
And said, "At Kilve I'd rather be
Than here at Liswyn farm."

"Now, little Edward, say why so;
My little Edward, tell me why."
"I cannot tell, I do not know."
"Why, this is strange," said I.

"For here are woods and green-hills
warm:
There surely must some reason be
Why you would change sweet Liswyn
For Kilve by the green sea." [farm

At this my boy hung down his head,
He blushed with shame, nor made reply;
And five times to the child I said,
"Why, Edward, tell me why?"

His head he raised—there was in sight,
It caught his eye, he saw it plain—
Upon the housetop, glittering bright,
A broad and gilded vane.

Then did the boy his tongue unlock;
And thus to me he made reply,
"At Kilve there was no weathercock,
And that's the reason why."

O dearest, dearest boy! my heart
For better lore would seldom yearn,
Could I but teach the hundredth part
Of what from thee I learn.

RURAL ARCHITECTURE.

THERE's George Fisher, Charles Fleming,
and Reginald Shore,
Three rosy-cheeked school-boys, the high-
est not more
Than the height of a counsellor's bag,
To the top of Great How* were once
tempted to climb;
And there they built up, without mortar
or lime,
A man on the peak of the crag.

They built him of stones gathered up as
they lay;
They built him and christened him all in
one day,
An urchin both vigorous and hale;
And so without scruple they called him
Ralph Jones. [his bones:
Now Ralph is renowned for the length of
The Magog of Legberthwaite dale.

Just half a week after, the wind sallied
forth, [north
And, in anger or merriment, out of the
Coming on with a terrible pother,
From the peak of the crag blew the giant
away. [next day
And what did these school-boys?—The very
They went and they built up another.

Some little I've seen of blind boisterous
works [Turks,
By Christian disturbers more savage than
Spirits busy to do and undo:
At remembrance whereof my blood some-
times will flag; [crag,
Then, light-hearted boys, to the top of the
And I'll build up a giant with you.

THE PET-LAMB: A PASTORAL.

THE dew was falling fast, the stars began
to blink; [ture, drink!"
I heard a voice; it said, "Drink, pretty crea-
And, looking o'er the hedge, before me I
espied [at its side.
A snow-white mountain lamb with a maiden

No other sheep was near, the lamb was all
alone, [stone;
And by a slender cord was tethered to a
With one knee on the grass did the little
maiden kneel, [evening meal.
While to that mountain lamb she gave its

The lamb, while from her hand he thus his
supper took,
Seemed to feast with head and ears; and
his tail with pleasure shook.

* Great How is a single and conspicuous hill, which rises towards the foot of Thirlmere, on the western side of the beautiful dale of Legberthwaite, along the high road between Keswick and Ambleside.

"Drink, pretty creature, drink," she said
in such a tone [own.
That I almost received her heart into my

'Twas little Barbara Lewthwaite, a child of
beauty rare! [lovely pair.
I watched them with delight, they were a
Now with her empty can the maiden turned
away; [did she stay.
But ere ten yards were gone her footsteps

Towards the lamb she looked; and from
that shady place [her face:
I unobserved could see the workings of
If nature to her tongue could measured
numbers bring,
Thus, thought I, to her lamb that little
maid might sing:

"What ails thee, young one? what? Why
pull so at thy cord? [and board?
Is it not well with thee? well both for bed
Thy plot of grass is soft, and green as grass
can be; [aileth thee?
Rest, little young one, rest; what is't that

"What is it thou would'st seek? What is
wanting to thy heart?
Thy limbs, are they not strong? And beau-
tiful thou art:
This grass is tender grass; these flowers
they have no peers; [thy ears!
And that green corn all day is rustling in

"If the sun be shining hot, do but stretch
thy woollen chain, [canst gain;
This beech is standing by, its covert thou
For rain and mountain storms? the like
thou need'st not fear—
The rain and storm are things that scarcely
can come here.

"Rest, little young one, rest; thou hast
forgot the day [far away,
When my father found thee first in places
Man flocks were on the hills, but thou
wert owned by none,
And thy mother from thy side for evermore
was gone.

"He took thee in his arms, and in pity
brought thee home.
A blessed day for thee! then whither
wouldst thou roam?
A faithful nurse thou hast; the dam that
did thee yean [have been.
Upon the mountain tops no kinder could

"Thou know'st that twice a day I have
brought thee in this can
Fresh water from the brook, as clear as
ever ran, [wet with dew,
And twice in the day, when the ground is
I bring thee draughts of milk, warm milk
it is and new.

"Thy limbs will shortly be twice as stout
as they are now, [in the plough;
Then I'll yoke thee to my cart like a pony
My playmate thou shalt be; and when the
wind is cold [be thy fold.
Our hearth shall be thy bed, our house shall

"It will not, will not rest!—poor creature,
can it be [ing so in thee?
That 'tis thy mother's heart which is work-
Things that I know not of belike to thee
are dear, [neither see nor hear.
And dreams of things which thou canst

"Alas, the mountain tops that look so
green and fair!
I've heard of fearful winds and darkness
that come there; [and all play,
The little brooks that seem all pastime
When they are angry, roar like lions for
their prey.

"Here thou need'st not dread the raven in
the sky; [is hard by.
Night and day thou art safe,—our cottage
Why bleat so after me? Why pull so at
thy chain? [thee again!"
Sleep—and at break of day I will come to

As homeward through the lane I went
with lazy feet,
This song to myself did I oftentimes repeat;
And it seemed, as I retraced the ballad
line by line, [of it was *mine*.
That but half of it was hers, and one half

Again, and once again, did I repeat the
song; [damsel must belong,
"Nay," said I, "more than half to the
For she looked with such a look, and she
spake with such a tone, [my own."
That I almost received her heart into

THE IDLE SHEPHERD-BOYS; OR, DUNGEON-GHYLL-FORCE.*

A PASTORAL.

THE valley rings with mirth and joy;
Among the hills the echoes play

* *Ghyll*, in the dialect of Cumberland and

A never, never-ending song,
To welcome in the May.
The magpie chatters with delight,
The mountain raven's youngling brood
Have left the mother and the nest,
And they go rambling east and west
In search of their own food;
Or through the glittering vapours dart
In very wantonness of heart.

Beneath a rock upon the grass,
Two boys are sitting in the sun;
Boys that have had no work to do,
Or work that now is done.
On pipes of sycamore they play
The fragments of a Christmas hymn,
Or with that plant which in our dale
We call stag-horn, or fox's tail,
Their rusty hats they trim,
And thus, as happy as the day,
Those shepherds wear the time away.

Along the river's stony marge
The sand-lark chants a joyous song;
The thrush is busy in the wood,
And carols loud and strong.
A thousand lambs are on the rocks,
All newly born! both earth and sky
Keep jubilee; and more than all,
Those boys with their green coronal;
They never hear the cry,
That plaintive cry! which up the hill
Comes from the depth of Dungeon-Ghyll.

Said Walter, leaping from the ground,
"Down to the stump of yon old yew
We'll for our whistles run a race."
——Away the shepherds flew.
They leapt—they ran—and when they came
Right opposite to Dungeon-Ghyll,
Seeing that he should lose the prize,
"Stop!" to his comrade Walter cries—
James stopped with no good will:
Said Walter then, "Your task is here,
'Twill baffle you for half a year.

"Cross, if you dare, where I shall cross—
Come on, and in my footsteps tread!"
The other took him at his word,
And followed as he led.
It was a spot which you may see
If ever you to Langdale go;

Into a chasm a mighty block
Hath fallen, and made a bridge of rock:
The gulf is deep below;
And in a basin black and small
Receives a lofty waterfall.

With staff in hand across the cleft
The challenger pursued his march;
And now, all eyes and feet, hath gained
The middle of the arch.
When list! he hears a piteous moan—
Again!—his heart within him dies—
His pulse is stopped, his breath is lost,
He totters, pallid as a ghost,
And, looking down, espies
A lamb, that in the pool is pent
Within that black and frightful rent.

The lamb had slipped into the stream,
And safe without a bruise or wound
The cataract had borne him down
Into the gulf profound.
His dam had seen him when he fell,
She saw him down the torrent borne:
And, while with all a mother's love
She from the lofty rocks above
Sent forth a cry forlorn,
The lamb, still swimming round and round,
Made answer to that plaintive sound.

When he had learnt what thing it was,
That sent this rueful cry; I ween,
The boy recovered heart, and told
The sight which he had seen.
Both gladly now deferred their task;
Nor was there wanting other aid—
A poet, one who loves the brooks
Far better than the sages' books,
By chance had thither strayed,
And there the helpless lamb he found
By those huge rocks encompassed round.

He drew it gently from the pool,
And brought it forth into the light:
The shepherds met him with his charge,
An unexpected sight!
Into their arms the lamb they took,
Said they, "He's neither maimed nor scarred."
Then up the steep ascent they hied,
And placed him at his mother's side;
And gently did the bard
Those idle shepherd-boys upbraid,
And bade them better mind their trade

Westmoreland, is a short, and, for the most part, a steep narrow valley, with a stream running through it. *Force* is the word universally employed in these dialects for waterfall.

TO H. C. SIX YEARS OLD.

O THOU! whose fancies from afar are brought;
Who of thy words dost make a mock apparel,
And fittest to unutterable thought
The breeze-like motion and the self-born carol;
Thou faery voyager! that dost float,
In such clear water, that thy boat
May rather seem
To brood on air than on an earthly stream;
Suspended in a stream as clear as sky
Where earth and heaven do make one imagery!
O blessed vision! happy child!
That art so exquisitely wild,
I think of thee with many fears
For what may be thy lot in future years.

I thought of times when pain might be thy guest,
Lord of thy house and hospitality!
And grief, uneasy lover! never rest
But when she sate within the touch of thee.
Oh! too industrious folly!
Oh! vain and causeless melancholy!
Nature will either end thee quite;
Or, lengthening out thy season of delight,
Preserve for thee, by individual right,
A young lamb's heart among the full-grown flocks.
What hast thou to do with sorrow,
Or the injuries of to-morrow?
Thou art a dewdrop, which the morn brings forth,
Ill fitted to sustain unkindly shocks;
Or to be trailed along the soiling earth!
A gem that glitters while it lives,
And no forewarning gives;
But, at the touch of wrong, without a strife
Slips in a moment out of life.

INFLUENCE OF NATURAL OBJECTS

IN CALLING FORTH AND STRENGTHENING THE IMAGINATION IN BOYHOOD AND EARLY YOUTH.

[This extract is reprinted from "The Friend."]

WISDOM and Spirit of the universe!
Thou soul, that art the eternity of thought!
And giv'st to forms and images a breath
And everlasting motion! not in vain,
By day or star light, thus from my first dawn
Of childhood did'st thou intertwine for me
The passions that build up our human soul;
Not with the mean and vulgar works of man,—
But with high objects, with enduring things,
With life and nature; purifying thus
The elements of feeling and of thought,
And sanctifying by such discipline
Both pain and fear,—until we recognise
A grandeur in the beatings of the heart.

Nor was this fellowship vouchsafed to me
With stinted kindness. In November days,
When vapours rolling down the valleys made
A lonely scene more lonesome; among woods
At noon; and 'mid the calm of summer nights,
When, by the margin of the trembling lake,
Beneath the gloomy hills, I homeward went
In solitude, such intercourse was mine:
'Twas mine among the fields both day and night,
And by the waters, all the summer long;
And in the frosty season, when the sun
Was set, and visible for many a mile,
The cottage windows through the twilight blazed,
I heeded not the summons:—happy time
It was indeed for all of us; for me
It was a time of rapture!—Clear and loud
The village clock tolled six—I wheeled about,
Proud and exulting like an untired horse
That cares not for his home.—All shod with steel
We hissed along the polished ice, in games
Confederate, imitative of the chase
And woodland pleasures,—the resounding horn,
The pack loud-bellowing, and the hunted hare.
So through the darkness and the cold we flew,
And not a voice was idle: with the din
Meanwhile the precipices rang aloud;
The leafless trees and every icy crag
Tinkled like iron; while the distant hills
Into the tumult sent an alien sound
Of melancholy, not unnoticed, while the stars,
Eastward, were sparkling clear, and in the west
The orange sky of evening died away.

Not seldom from the uproar I retired
Into a silent bay,—or sportively
Glanced sideway, leaving the tumultuous throng,
To cut across the reflex of a star,
Image, that, flying still before me, gleamed

Upon the glassy plain: and oftentimes,
When we had given our bodies to the wind,
And all the shadowy banks on either side
Came sweeping through the darkness, spinning still
The rapid line of motion, then at once
Have I, reclining back upon my heels,
Stopped short; yet still the solitary cliffs
Wheeled by me—even as if the earth had rolled
With visible motion her diurnal round!
Behind me did they stretch in solemn train,
Feebler and feebler, and I stood and watched
Till all was tranquil as a summer sea.

THE LONGEST DAY.

ADDRESSED TO ——

LET us quit the leafy arbour,
And the torrent murmuring by:
Sol has dropped into his harbour,
Weary of the open sky.

Evening now unbinds the fetters
Fashioned by the glowing light;
All that breathe are thankful debtors
To the harbinger of night.

Yet by some grave thoughts attended
Eve renews her calm career;
For the day that now is ended
Is the longest of the year.

Laura! sport, as now thou sportest,
On this platform, light and free;
Take thy bliss, while longest, shortest,
Are indifferent to thee!

Who would check the happy feeling
That inspires the linnet's song?
Who would stop the swallow, wheeling
On her pinions swift and strong?

Yet at this impressive season,
Words which tenderness can speak
From the truths of homely reason,
Might exalt the loveliest cheek;

And, while shades to shades succeeding
Steal the landscape from the sight,
I would urge this moral pleading,
Last forerunner of "Good night!"

Summer ebbs;—each day that follows
Is a reflux from on high,
Tending to the darksome hollows
Where the frosts of winter lie.

He who governs the creation,
In his providence, assigned
Such a gradual declination
To the life of human kind.

Yet we mark it not;—fruits redden,
Fresh flowers blow, as flowers have blown,
And the heart is loth to deaden
Hopes that she so long hath known.

Be thou wiser, youthful maiden!
And when thy decline shall come,
Let not flowers, or boughs fruit-laden,
Hide the knowledge of thy doom.

Now, even now, ere wrapped in slumber
Fix thine eyes upon the sea
That absorbs time, space, and number;
Look towards eternity!

Follow thou the flowing river
On whose breast are thither borne
All deceived, and each deceiver,
Through the gates of night and morn

Through the year's successive portals;
Through the bounds which many a star
Marks, not mindless of frail mortals,
When his light returns from far.

Thus when thou with Time hast travelled
Towards the mighty gulf of things,
And the mazy stream unravelled
With thy best imaginings;

Think, if thou on beauty leanest,
Think how pitiful that stay,
Did not virtue give the meanest
Charms superior to decay.

Duty, like a strict preceptor,
Sometimes frowns, or seems to frown;
Choose her thistle for thy sceptre,
While thy brow youth's roses crown.

Grasp it,—if thou shrink and tremble,
Fairest damsel of the green,
Thou wilt lack the only symbol
That proclaims a genuine queen;

And insures those palms of honour
Which selected spirits wear,
Bending low before the donor,
Lord of heaven's unchanging year!

Poems Founded on the Affections.

THE BROTHERS.

"THESE tourists, Heaven preserve us! needs must live
A profitable life· some glance along,
Rapid and gay, as if the earth were air,
And they were butterflies to wheel about
Long as the summer lasted: some, as wise,
Perched on the forehead of a jutting crag,
Pencil in hand and book upon the knee,
Will look and scribble, scribble on and look,
Until a man might travel twelve stout miles,
Or reap an acre of his neighbour's corn.
But, for that moping son of idleness,
Why can he tarry *yonder*?—In our church-yard
Is neither epitaph nor monument,
Tombstone nor name—only the turf we tread
And a few natural graves."
To Jane, his wife,
Thus spake the homely Priest of Ennerdale.
It was a July evening; and he sate
Upon the long stone-seat beneath the eaves
Of his old cottage,—as it chanced, that day,
Employed in winter's work. Upon the stone
His wife sate near him, teasing matted wool,
While, from the twin cards toothed with glittering wire,
He fed the spindle of his youngest child,
Who turned her large round wheel in the open air
With back and forward steps. Towards the field
In which the parish chapel stood alone,
Girt round with a bare ring of mossy wall,
While half an hour went by, the priest had sent
Many a long look of wonder: and at last,
Risen from his seat, beside the snow-white ridge
Of carded wool which the old man had piled
He laid his implements with gentle care,
Each in the other locked; and, down the path
That from his cottage to the church-yard led,
He took his way, impatient to accost
The stranger, whom he saw still lingering there.

'Twas one well known to him in former days,
A shepherd-lad;—who ere his sixteenth year
Had left that calling, tempted to intrust
His expectations to the fickle winds
And perilous waters,—with the mariners
A fellow-mariner,—and so had fared
Through twenty seasons; but he had been reared
Among the mountains, and he in his heart
Was half a shepherd on the stormy seas.
Oft in the piping shrouds had Leonard heard
The tones of waterfalls, and inland sounds
Of caves and trees:—and when the regular wind
Between the tropics filled the steady sail,
And blew with the same breath through days and weeks,
Lengthening invisibly its weary line
Along the cloudless main, he, in those hours
Of tiresome indolence, would often hang
Over the vessel's side, and gaze and gaze;
And, while the broad green wave and sparkling foam
Flashed round him images and hues that wrought
In union with the employment of his heart,
He, thus by feverish passion overcome,
Even with the organs of his bodily eye,
Below him, in the bosom of the deep,
Saw mountains,—saw the forms of sheep that grazed
On verdant hills—with dwellings among trees,
And shepherds clad in the same country gray
Which he himself had worn.*
And now, at last,
From perils manifold, with some small wealth
Acquired by traffic 'mid the Indian Isles,
To his paternal home he is returned,
With a determined purpose to resume
The life he had lived there; both for the sake
Of many darling pleasures, and the love
Which to an only brother he has borne
In all his hardships, since that happy time

* This description of the Calenture is sketched from an imperfect recollection of an admirable one in prose, by Mr Gilbert, author of "The Hurricane."

When, whether it blew foul or fair, they two
Were brothershepherdson their native hills.
They were the last of all their race and now, [his heart
When Leonard had approached his home,
Failed in him; and, not venturing to inquire
Tidings of one whom he so dearly loved,
Towards the church-yard he had turned aside;
That, as he knew in what particular spot
His family were laid, he thence might learn
If still his brother lived, or to the file
Another grave was added.—He had found
Another grave,—near which a full half-hour
He had remained; but, as he gazed, there grew
Such a confusion in his memory,
That he began to doubt; and he had hopes
That he had seen this heap of turf before—
That it was not another grave; but one
He had forgotten. He had lost his path,
As up the vale, that afternoon, he walked
Through fields which once had been well known to him:
And, oh, what joy the recollection now
Sent to his heart! He lifted up his eyes,
And, looking round, imagined that he saw
Strange alteration wrought on every side
Among the woods and fields, and that the rocks, [changed.
And everlasting hills themselves were
By this the priest, who down the field had come
Unseen by Leonard, at the church-yard gate
Stopped short,—and thence, at leisure, limb by limb
Perused him with a gay complacency.
Ay, thought the vicar, smiling to himself,
'Tis one of those who needs must leave the path
Of the world's business to go wild alone:
His arms have a perpetual holiday;
The happy man will creep about the fields,
Following his fancies by the hour, to bring
Tears down his cheek, or solitary smiles,
Into his face, until the setting sun
Write fool upon his forehead. Planted thus
Beneath a shed that over-arched the gate
Of this rude church-yard, till the stars appeared, [with himself,
The good man might have communed
But that the stranger, who had left the grave, [once,
Approached: he recognised the priest at
And, after greetings interchanged, and given
By Leonard to the vicar as to one
Unknown to him, this dialogue ensued:—

Leonard. You live, sir, in these dales, a quiet life:
Your years make up one peaceful family;
And who would grieve and fret, if, welcome come [other,
And welcome gone, they are so like each
They cannot be remembered? Scarce a funeral [months;
Comes to this churchyard once in eighteen
And yet, some changes must take place among you; [rocks,
And you, who dwell here, even among these
Can trace the finger of mortality,
And see, that with our threescore years and ten
We are not all that perish.——I remember,
(For many years ago I passed this road)
There was a foot-way all along the fields
By the brook-side—'tis gone—and that dark cleft!
To me it does not seem to wear the face
Which then it had!

Priest Nay, sir, for aught I know,
That chasm is much the same—

Leonard. But, surely, yonder—

Priest. Ay, there, indeed, your memory is a friend [tall pike
That does not play you false.—On that
(It is the loneliest place of all these hills)
There were two springs which bubbled side by side,
As if they had been made that they might be
Companions for each other: the huge crag
Was rent with lightning—one hath disappeared;
The other, left behind, is flowing still
For accidents and changes such as these,
We want not store of them —a water-spout
Will bring down half a mountain; what a feast
For folks that wander up and down like you,
To see an acre's breadth of that wide cliff
One roaring cataract!—a sharp May-storm
Will come with loads of January snow,
And in one night send twenty score of sheep
To feed the ravens, or a shepherd dies
By some untoward death among the rocks:
The ice breaks up and sweeps away a bridge— [homes!
A wood is felled —and then for our own
A child is born or christened, a field ploughed,
A daughter sent to service, a web spun,

The old house-clock is decked with a new
face; [dates
And hence, so far from wanting facts or
To chronicle the time, we all have here
A pair of diaries,—one serving, sir,
For the whole dale, and one for each fire-
side— [historians,
Yours was a stranger's judgment: for
Commend me to these valleys!
Leonard. Yet your church-yard
Seems, if such freedom may be used with
you,
To say that you are heedless of the past:
An orphan could not find his mother's
grave: [of brass,
Here's neither head nor footstone, plate
Cross-bones nor skull,—type of our earthly
state [home
Nor emblem of our hopes: the dead man's
Is but a fellow to that pasture-field.
Priest. Why, there, sir, is a thought
that's new to me! [their bread
The stone-cutters, 'tis true, might beg
If every English church-yard were like
ours; [truth:
Yet your conclusion wanders from the
We have no need of names and epitaphs;
We talk about the dead by our fire-sides.
And then, for our immortal part! *we* want
No symbols, sir, to tell us that plain tale:
The thought of death sits easy on the man
Who has been born and dies among the
mountains.
Leonard. Your dalesmen, then, do in
each other's thoughts
Possess a kind of second life: no doubt
You, sir, could help me to the history
Of half these graves?
Priest. For eight-score winters past,
With what I've witnessed, and with what
I've heard,
Perhaps I might; and, on a winter-evening,
If you were seated at my chimney's nook,
By turning o'er these hillocks one by one,
We two could travel, sir, through a strange
round;
Yet all in the broad highway of the world.
Now there's a grave—your foot is half upon
it,—
It looks just like the rest; and yet that man
Died broken-hearted.
Leonard. 'Tis a common case.
We'll take another: who is he that lies
Beneath yon ridge, the last of those three
graves?
It touches on that piece of native rock
Left in the church-yard wall.
Priest That's Walter Ewbank.
He had as white a head and fresh a cheek
As ever were produced by youth and age
Engendering in the blood of hale fourscore.
Through five long generations had the heart
Of Walter's forefathers o'erflowed the
bounds
Of their inheritance, that single cottage—
You see it yonder!—and those few green
fields. [to son,
They toiled and wrought, and still, from sire
Each struggled, and each yielded as before
A little—yet a little—and old Walter,
They left to him the family heart, and land
With other burthens than the crop it bore.
Year after year the old man still kept up
A cheerful mind,—and buffeted with bond,
Interest, and mortgages; at last he sank,
And went into his grave before his time.
Poor Walter! whether it was care that
spurred him
God only knows, but to the very last
He had the lightest foot in Ennerdale:
His pace was never that of an old man:
I almost see him tripping down the path
With his two grandsons after him:—but you,
Unless our landlord be your host to-night,
Have far to travel,—and on these rough
paths
Even in the longest day of midsummer—
Leonard. But those two orphans!
Priest. Orphans!—Such they were—
Yet not while Walter lived:—for, though
their parents
Lay buried side by side as now they lie,
The old man was a father to the boys,
Two fathers in one father: and if tears,
Shed when he talked of them where they
were not,
And hauntings from the infirmity of love,
Are aught of what makes up a mother's
heart,
This old man, in the day of his old age,
Was half a mother to them.—If you weep,
sir,
To hear a stranger talking about strangers,
Heaven bless you when you are among
your kindred!
Ay—you may turn that way—it is a grave
Which will bear looking at.
Leonard. These boys—I hope
They loved this good old man?
Priest. They did—and truly:
But that was what we almost overlooked,
They were such darlings of each other. For,
Though from their cradles they had lived
with Walter,
The only kinsman near them, and though he
Inclined to them by reason of his age,

With a more fond, familiar tenderness ;
They, notwithstanding, had much love to spare,
And it all went into each other's hearts.
Leonard, the elder by just eighteen months,
Was two years taller : 'twas a joy to see,
To hear, to meet them !—From their house the school
Is distant three short miles—and in the time
Of storm and thaw, when every water-course
And unbridged stream, such as you may have noticed
Crossing our roads at every hundred steps,
Was swoln into a noisy rivulet,
Would Leonard then, when elder boys perhaps
Remained at home, go staggering through the fords
Bearing his brother on his back. I've seen him,
On windy days, in one of those stray brooks,
Ay, more than once I've seen him mid-leg deep,
Their two books lying both on a dry stone
Upon the hither side : and once I said,
As I remember, looking round these rocks
And hills on which we all of us were born,
That God who made the great book of the world
Would bless such piety—
Leonard. It may be then—
Priest. Never did worthier lads break English bread ;
The finest Sunday that the autumn saw,
With all its mealy clusters of ripe nuts,
Could never keep these boys away from church,
Or tempt them to an hour of Sabbath breach.
Leonard and James! I warrant every corner
Among these rocks, and every hollow place
Where foot could come, to one or both of them
Was known as well as to the flowers that grow there.
Like roebucks they went bounding o'er the hills ;
They played like two young ravens on the crags :
Then they could write, ay, and speak too, as well
As many of their betters—and for Leonard!
The very night before he went away,
In my own house I put into his hand
A Bible, and I'd wager house and field
That if he is alive, he has it yet.
Leonard. It seems these brothers have not lived to be
A comfort to each other—
Priest. That they might
Live to such end is what both old and young
In this our valley all of us have wished,
And what, for my part I have often prayed:
But Leonard—
Leonard. Then James still is left among you?
Priest. 'Tis of the elder brother I am speaking :
They had an uncle ;—he was at that time
A thriving man, and trafficked on the seas:
And, but for that same uncle, to this hour
Leonard had never handled rope or shroud,
For the boy loved the life which we lead here ;
And though of unripe years, a stripling only,
His soul was knit to this his native soil.
But, as I said, old Walter was too weak
To strive with such a torrent; when he died,
The estate and house were sold ; and all their sheep,
A pretty flock, and which, for aught I know,
Had clothed the Ewbanks for a thousand years :—
Well—all was gone, and they were destitute,
And Leonard, chiefly for his brother's sake,
Resolved to try his fortune on the seas.
Twelve years are passed since we had tidings from him.
If there were one among us who had heard
That Leonard Ewbank was come home again,
From the great Gavel,* down by Leeza's banks,
And down the Enna, far as Egremont,
The day would be a very festival ;
And those two bells of ours, which there you see—
Hanging in the open air—but, O good sir!
This is sad talk—they'll never sound for him—
Living or dead.—When last we heard of him
He was in slavery among the Moors
Upon the Barbary coast.—'Twas not a little
That would bring down his spirit ; and no doubt,
Before it ended in his death, the youth
Was sadly crossed—Poor Leonard ! when we parted,
He took me by the hand, and said to me,
If ever the day came when he was rich,
He would return, and on his father's land
He would grow old among us.

* The Great Gavel, so called, I imagine, from its resemblance to the gable end of a house, is one of the highest of the Cumberland mountains.
The Leeza is a river which flows into the Lake of Ennerdale : on issuing from the Lake, it changes its name, and is called the End, Eyne, or Enna. It falls into the sea a little below Egremont.

Leonard. If that day
Should come, 'twould needs be a glad day
for him;
He would himself, no doubt, be happy then
As any that should meet him—
Priest. Happy! Sir—
Leonard You said his kindred all were
in their graves,
And that he had one brother—
Priest. That is but
A fellow tale of sorrow. From his youth
James, though not sickly, yet was delicate;
And Leonard being always by his side
Had done so many offices about him,
That, though he was not of a timid nature,
Yet still the spirit of a mountain-boy
In him was somewhat checked; and when
his brother
Was gone to sea, and he was left alone,
The little colour that he had was soon
Stolen from his cheek; he drooped, and
pined, and pined—
Leonard. But these are all the graves of
full-grown men!
Priest. Ay, sir, that passed away: we
took him to us;
He was the child of all the dale—he lived
Three months with one and six months
with another, [love:
And wanted neither food, nor clothes, nor
And many, many happy days were his.
But whether blithe or sad, 'tis my belief
His absent brother still was at his heart
And, when he dwelt beneath our roof, we
found
(A practice till this time unknown to him)
That often, rising from his bed at night,
He in his sleep would walk about, and
sleeping [moved!
He sought his brother Leonard —You are
Forgive me, sir: before I spoke to you,
I judged you most unkindly.
Leonard. But this youth,
How did he die at last?
Priest. One sweet May morning,
(It will be twelve years since when spring
returns) [lambs,
He had gone forth among the new-dropped
With two or three companions, whom
their course
Of occupation led from height to height
Under a cloudless sun, till he, at length,
Through weariness, or, haply, to indulge
The humour of the moment, lagged behind.
You see yon precipice;—it wears the shape
Of a vast building made of many crags;
And in the midst is one particular rock
That rises like a column from the vale,
Whence by our shepherds it is called THE
PILLAR.
Upon its aery summit crowned with heath,
The loiterer, not unnoticed by his comrades,
Lay stretched at ease; but, passing by the
place
On their return, they found that he was gone.
No ill was feared; but one of them by
chance
Entering, when evening was far spent, the
house [learned
Which at that time was James's home, there
That nobody had seen him all that day:
The morning came, and still he was un-
heard of: [brook
The neighbours were alarmed, and to the
Some hastened, some towards the lake:
ere noon [rock—
They found him at the foot of that same
Dead, and with mangled limbs. The third
day after
I buried him, poor youth, and there he lies!
Leonard. And that then *is* his grave!—
Before his death
You say that he saw many happy years?
Priest. Ay, that he did—
Leonard. And all went well with him?—
Priest. If he had one, the youth had
twenty homes.
Leonard. And you believe, then, that
his mind was easy?—
Priest. Yes, long before he died, he
found that time
Is a true friend to sorrow; and unless
His thoughts were turned on Leonard's
luckless fortune,
He talked about him with a cheerful love.
Leonard. He could not come to an un-
hallowed end!
Priest. Nay, God forbid!—You recollect
I mentioned
A habit which disquietude and grief
Had brought upon him; and we all con-
jectured [down
That, as the day was warm, he had lain
Upon the grass,—and waiting for his com-
rades, [sleep
He there had fallen asleep; that in his
He to the margin of the precipice
Had walked, and from the summit had
fallen headlong.
And so, no doubt, he perished at the time,
We guess, that in his hands he must have
held
His shepherd's staff, for midway in the cliff
It had been caught; and there, for many
years
It hung, and mouldered there—

The priest here ended—
The stranger would have thanked him, but he felt
A gushing from his heart, that took away
The power of speech. Both left the spot in silence;
And Leonard, when they reached the church-yard gate,
As the priest lifted up the latch, turned round,—
And looking at the grave, he said, "My Brother!"
The vicar did not hear the words and now,
Pointing towards the cottage, he entreated
That Leonard would partake his homely fare:
The other thanked him with a fervent voice;
But added, that, the evening being calm,
He would pursue his journey. So they parted.
It was not long ere Leonard reached a grove
That overhung the road: he there stopped short,
And, sitting down beneath the trees, reviewed
All that the priest had said: his early years
Were with him in his heart: his cherished hopes,
And thoughts which had been his an hour before,
All pressed on him with such a weight, that now,
This vale, where he had been so happy, seemed
A place in which he could not bear to live:
So he relinquished all his purposes.
He travelled on to Egremont: and thence,
That night, he wrote a letter to the priest,
Reminding him of what had passed between them,
And adding, with a hope to be forgiven,
That it was from the weakness of his heart
He had not dared to tell him who he was.

This done, he went on shipboard, and is now
A seaman, a gray-headed mariner.

ARTEGAL AND ELIDURE.

(SEE THE CHRONICLE OF GEOFFREY OF MONMOUTH, AND MILTON'S HISTORY OF ENGLAND.)

WHERE be the temples which, in Britain's Isle,
For his paternal gods, the Trojan raised?
Gone like a morning dream, or like a pile
Of clouds that in cerulean ether blazed!
Ere Julius landed on her white-cliffed shore,
They sank, delivered o'er
To fatal dissolution; and, I ween,
No vestige then was left that such had ever been.

Nathless, a British record (long concealed
In old Armorica, whose secret springs
No Gothic conqueror ever drank) revealed
The wondrous current of forgotten things;
How Brutus came, by oracles impelled,
And Albion's giants quelled,—
A brood whom no civility could melt,
"Who never tasted grace, and goodness ne'er had felt."

By brave Corineus aided, he subdued,
And rooted out the intolerable kind,
And this too-long-polluted land imbued
With goodly arts and usages refined;
Whence golden harvests, cities, warlike towers,
And pleasure's sumptuous bowers,
Whence all the fixed delights of house and home,
Friendships that will not break, and love that cannot roam.

O happy Britain! region all too fair
For self-delighting fancy to endure
That silence only should inhabit there,
Wild beasts, or uncouth savages impure!
But, intermingled with the generous seed,
Grew many a poisonous weed;
Thus fares it still with all that takes its birth
From human care, or grows upon the breast of earth.

Hence, and how soon! that war of vengeance waged
By Guendolen against her faithless lord;
Till she, in jealous fury unassuaged,
Had slain his paramour with ruthless sword:
Then, into Severn hideously defiled,
She flung her blameless child,
Sabrina,—vowing that the stream should bear
That name through every age, her hatred to declare.

So speaks the Chronicle, and tells of Lear
By his ungrateful daughters turned adrift.
Ye lightnings hear his voice!—they cannot hear,
Nor can the winds restore his simple gift.
But one there is, a child of nature meek,
Who comes her sire to seek;
And he, recovering sense, upon her breast
Leans smilingly, and sinks into a perfect rest.

There too we read of Spenser's fairy themes,
And those that Milton loved in youthful
years;
The sage enchanter Merlin's subtle schemes;
The feats of Arthur and his knightly peers;
Of Arthur,—who, to upper light restored
With that terrific sword
Which yet he wields in subterranean war,
Shall lift his country's fame above the polar
star!

What wonder, then, if in such ample field
Of old tradition, one particular flower
Doth seemingly in vain its fragrance yield,
And bloom unnoticed even to this late
hour?
Now, gentle Muses, your assistance grant,
While I this flower transplant
Into a garden stored with poesy;
Where flowers and herbs unite, and haply
some weeds be, [mischief free!
That, wanting not wild grace, are from all

A King more worthy of respect and love
Than wise Gorbonian, ruled not in his day;
And grateful Britain prospered far above
All neighbouring countries through his
righteous sway; [good;
He poured rewards and honours on the
The oppressor he withstood;
And while he served the gods with reve-
rence due, [and cities grew.
Field smiled, and temples rose, and towns

He died, whom Artegal succeeds—his son;
But how unworthy of such sire was he!
A hopeful reign, auspiciously begun,
Was darkened soon by foul iniquity.
From crime to crime he mounted, till at
length
The nobles leagued their strength
With a vexed people, and the tyrant chased;
And, on the vacant throne, his worthier
brother placed.

From realm to realm the humbled exile
went,
Suppliant for aid his kingdom to regain;
In many a court, and many a warrior's tent,
He urged his persevering suit in vain.
Him, in whose wretched heart ambition
failed,
Dire poverty assailed;
And, tired with slights which he no more
could brook, [look.
Towards his native soil he cast a longing

Fair blew the wished-for wind—the voyage
sped;
He landed; and, by many dangers scared,
"Poorly provided, poorly followèd,"
To Calaterium's forest he repaired.
How changed from him who, born to
highest place,
Had swayed the royal mace,
Flattered and feared, despised yet deified,
In Troynovant, his seat by silver Thames's
side!

From that wild region where the crownless
king
Lay in concealment with his scanty train,
Supporting life by water from the spring,
And such chance food as outlaws can ob-
tain,
Unto the few whom he esteems his friends
A messenger he sends;
And from their secret loyalty requires
Shelter and daily bread,—the amount of
his desires.

While he the issue waits, at early morn
Wandering by stealth abroad, he chanced
to hear [horn,
A startling outcry made by hound and
From which the tusky boar hath fled in
fear; [plain,
And, scouring towards him o'er the grassy
Behold the hunter train!
He bids his little company advance
With seeming unconcern and steady coun-
tenance.

The royal Elidure, who leads the chase,
Hath checked his foaming courser—Can it
be? [face,
Methinks that I should recognise that
Though much disguised by long adversity!
He gazed, rejoicing, and again he gazed,
Confounded and amazed—
"It is the king, my brother!" and, by
sound [the ground.
Of his own voice confirmed, he leaps upon

Long, strict, and tender was the embrace
he gave,
Feebly returned by daunted Artegal;
Whose natural affection doubts enslave,
And apprehensions dark and criminal.
Loth to restrain the moving interview,
The attendant lords withdrew;
And, while they stood upon the plain apart,
Thus Elidure, by words, relieved his strug-
gling heart:

"By heavenly Powers conducted, we have
met;
O brother! to my knowledge lost so long,
But neither lost to love, nor to regret,
Nor to my wishes lost;—forgive the wrong,
(Such it may seem) if I thy crown have
Thy royal mantle worn · [borne,
I was their natural guardian; and 'tis just
That now I should restore what hath been
held in trust."

A while the astonished Artegal stood mute,
Then thus exclaimed—"To me, of titles
shorn, [tute,
And stripped of power!—me, feeble, desti-
To me a kingdom!—spare the bitter
scorn!
If justice ruled the breast of foreign kings,
Then, on the wide-spread wings
Of war, had I returned to claim my right,
This will I here avow, not dreading thy
despite"

"I do not blame thee," Elidure replied,
"But, if my looks did with my words agree,
I should at once be trusted, not defied,
And thou from all disquietude be free
May the unsullied goddess of the chase,
Who to this blessed place
At this blest moment led me, if I speak
With insincere intent, on me her vengeance
wreak!

"Were this same spear, which in my hand
I grasp,
The British sceptre, here would I to thee
The symbol yield; and would undo this
clasp,
If it confined the robe of sovereignty.
Odious to me the pomp of regal court,
And joyless sylvan sport, [lorn,
While thou art roving, wretched and for-
Thy couch the dewy earth, thy roof the
forest thorn!"

Then Artegal thus spake—"I only sought,
Within this realm a place of safe retreat;
Beware of rousing an ambitious thought;
Beware of kindling hopes, for me unmeet!
Thou art reputed wise, but in my mind
Art pitiably blind, [rue,
Full soon this generous purpose thou mayst
When that which has been done no wishes
can undo.

"Who, when a crown is fixed upon his
head, [right with right?
Would balance claim with claim, and
But thou—I know not how inspired, how
led— [men s sight!
Wouldst change the course of things in all
And this for one who cannot imitate
Thy virtue—who may hate.
For, if, by such strange sacrifice restored,
He reign, thou still must be his king, and
sovereign lord

"Lifted in magnanimity above
Aught that my feeble nature could perform,
Or even conceive, surpassing me in love
Far as in power the eagle doth the worm;
I, brother! only should be king in name,
And govern to my shame;
A shadow in a hated land, while all
Of glad or willing service to thy share
would fall."

"Believe it not," said Elidure, "respect
Awaits on virtuous life, and ever most
Attends on goodness with dominion decked,
Which stands the universal empire's boast,
This can thy own experience testify·
Nor shall thy foes deny
That, in the gracious opening of thy reign,
Our father's spirit seemed in thee to
breathe again.

"And what if o'er that bright unbosoming
Clouds of disgrace and envious fortune
past!
Have we not seen the glories of the spring
By veil of noontide darkness overcast?
The frith that glittered like a warrior's
shield,
The sky, the gay green field,
Are vanished;—gladness ceases in the
groves, [mountain coves.
And trepidation strikes the blackened

"But is that gloom dissolved? how pass-
ing clear [before!
Seems the wide world—far brighter than
Even so thy latent worth will re-appear,
Gladdening the people's heart from shore
to shore, [atone;
For youthful faults ripe virtues shall
Re-seated on thy throne,
Proof shalt thou furnish that misfortune,
pain, [right to reign
And sorrow, have confirmed thy native

"But, not to overlook what thou mayst
know,
Thy enemies are neither weak nor few;
And circumspect must be our course, and
slow,

Or from my purpose ruin may ensue.
Dismiss thy followers;—let them calmly
Such change in thy estate [wait
As I already have in thought devised;
And which, with caution due, may soon be realised."

The story tells what courses were pursued,
Until King Elidure, with full consent
Of all his peers, before the multitude,
Rose,—and, to consummate this just intent,
Did place upon his brother's head the crown,
Relinquished by his own;
Then to his people cried, "Receive your lord,
[king restored!"
Gorbonian's first-born son, your rightful

The people answered with a loud acclaim:
Yet more;—heart-smitten by the heroic deed,
The reinstated Artegal became
Earth's noblest penitent; from bondage freed
Of vice,—thenceforth unable to subvert
Or shake his high desert.
Long did he reign; and, when he died, the tear [bier.
Of universal grief bedewed his honoured

Thus was a brother by a brother saved;
With whom a crown (temptation that hath set [braved
Discords in hearts of men till they have
Their nearest kin with deadly purpose met)
'Gainst duty weighed, and faithful love, did seem
A thing of no esteem,
And, from this triumph of affection pure,
He bore the lasting name of "pious Elidure!"

THE SPARROW'S NEST.

BEHOLD, within the leafy shade,
Those bright blue eggs together laid!
On me the chance-discovered sight
Gleamed like a vision of delight.
I started—seeming to espy
The home and sheltered bed,—
The sparrow's dwelling, which, hard by,
My father's house, in wet or dry,
My sister Emmeline and I
Together visited.
She looked at it as if she feared it;
Still wishing, dreading to be near it:
Such heart was in her, being then
A little prattler among men.
The blessing of my later years
Was with me when a boy:
She gave me eyes, she gave me ears;
And humble cares, and delicate fears;
A heart, the fountain of sweet tears;
And love, and thought, and joy.

TO A BUTTERFLY.

I'VE watched you now a full half-hour,
Self-poised upon that yellow flower;
And, little butterfly! indeed
I know not if you sleep or feed.
How motionless!—not frozen seas
More motionless! and then
What joy awaits you, when the breeze
Hath found you out among the trees,
And calls you forth again!

This plot of orchard-ground is ours;
My trees they are, my sister's flowers;
Here rest your wings when they are weary;
Here lodge as in a sanctuary!
Come often to us, fear no wrong;
Sit near us, on the bough!
We'll talk of sunshine and of song;
And summer days when we were young;
Sweet childish days, that were as long
As twenty days are now.

A FAREWELL.

FAREWELL, thou little nook of mountain ground,
Thou rocky corner in the lowest stair
Of that magnificent temple which doth bound [rare;
One side of our whole vale with grandeur
Sweet garden-orchard, eminently fair,
The loveliest spot that man hath ever found, [peaceful care,
Farewell!—we leave thee to Heaven's
Thee, and the cottage which thou dost surround.

Our boat is safely anchored by the shore,
And safely she will ride when we are gone;
The flowering shrubs that decorate our door
Will prosper, though untended and alone.
Fields, goods, and far-off chattels we have none: [store
These narrow bounds contain our rivate

Of things earth makes and sun doth shine upon ; [more.
Here they are in our sight—we have no

Sunshine and shower be with you, bud and bell ! [sought ;
For two months now in vain we shall be
We leave you here in solitude to dwell
With these our latest gifts of tender thought ;
Thou, like the morning, in thy saffron coat, [well !
Bright gowan, and marsh-marigold, fare-
Whom from the borders of the lake we brought,
And placed together near our rocky well.

We go for one to whom ye will be dear ;
And she will prize this bower, this Indian shed,
Our own contrivance, building without peer!
A gentle maid, whose heart is lowly bred,
Whose pleasures are in wild fields gathered,
With joyousness, and with a thoughtful cheer,
Will come to you ; to you herself will wed—
And love the blessed life that we lead here.

Dear spot ! which we have watched with tender heed, [blown
Bringing thee chosen plants and blossoms
Among the distant mountains, flower and weed,
Which thou hast taken to thee as thy own,
Making all kindness registered and known ;
Thou for our sakes, though nature's child indeed,
Fair in thyself and beautiful alone,
Hast taken gifts which thou dost little need.

And oh, most constant, yet most fickle place, [dost show
That hast thy wayward moods, as thou
To them who look not daily on thy face ;
Who, being loved, in love no bounds dost know, [them go !"
And say'st when we forsake thee, " Let
Thou easy-hearted thing, with thy wild race
Of weeds and flowers, till we return be slow,
And travel with the year at a soft pace.

Help us to tell her tales of years gone by,
And this sweet spring the best beloved and best.
Joy will be flown in its mortality ;
Something must stay to tell us of the rest.
Here, thronged with primroses, the steep rock's breast
Glittered at evening like a starry sky;
And in this bush our sparrow built her nest,
Of which I sung one song that will not die.

Oh, happy garden ! whose seclusion deep
Hath been so friendly to industrious hours;
And to soft slumbers, that did gently steep
Our spirits, carrying with them dreams of flowers, [bowers;
And wild notes warbled among leafy
Two burning months let summer overleap,
And, coming back with her who will be ours,
Into thy bosom we again shall creep.

STANZAS

WRITTEN IN MY POCKET-COPY OF THOMSON'S "CASTLE OF INDOLENCE."

WITHIN our happy castle there dwelt one
Whom without blame I may not overlook;
For never sun on living creature shone
Who more devout enjoyment with us took:
Here on his hours he hung as on a book;
On his own time here would he float away,
As doth a fly upon a summer brook;
But go to-morrow—or belike to-day—
Seek for him,—he is fled; and whither none can say.

Thus often would he leave our peaceful home,
And find elsewhere his business or delight;
Out of our valley's limits did he roam:
Full many a time, upon a stormy night,
His voice came to us from the neighbouring height:
Oft did we see him driving full in view
At mid-day when the sun was shining bright;
What ill was on him, what he had to do,
A mighty wonder bred among our quiet crew.

Ah! piteous sight it was to see this man
When he came back to us, a withered flower,—
Or like a sinful creature, pale and wan.
Down would he sit; and without strength or power [hour:
Look at the common grass from hour to
And oftentimes, how long I fear to say,

Where apple-trees in blossom made a bower,
Retired in that sunshiny shade he lay:
And, like a naked Indian, slept himself away.

Great wonder to our gentle tribe it was
Whenever from our valley he withdrew;
For happier soul no living creature has
Than he had, being here the long day through.
Some thought he was a lover, and did woo:
Some thought far worse of him, and judged him wrong:
But verse was what he had been wedded to;
And his own mind did like a tempest strong
Come to him thus, and drove the weary wight along.

With him there often walked in friendly guise,
Or lay upon the moss by brook or tree,
A noticeable man with large gray eyes,
And a pale face that seemed undoubtedly
As if a blooming face it ought to be;
Heavy his low-hung lip did oft appear
Deprest by weight of musing phantasy;
Profound his forehead was, though not severe;
Yet some did think that he had little business here.

Sweet heaven forefend! his was a lawful right;
Noisy he was, and gamesome as a boy;
His limbs would toss about him with delight
Like branches when strong winds the trees annoy.
Nor lacked his calmer hours device or toy
To banish listlessness and irksome care;
He would have taught you how you might employ
Yourself; and many did to him repair,—
And, certes, not in vain; he had inventions rare.

Expedients, too, of simplest sort he tried:
Long blades of grass, plucked round him as he lay,
Made—to his ear attentively applied—
A pipe on which the wind would deftly play;
Glasses he had, that little things display,
The beetle panoplied in gems and gold,
A mailèd angel on a battle day;
The mysteries that cups of flowers infold,
And all the gorgeous sights which fairies do behold.

He would entice that other man to hear
His music, and to view his imagery:
And, sooth, these two did love each other dear,
As far as love in such a place could be;
There did they dwell—from earthly labour free,
As happy spirits as were ever seen;
If but a bird, to keep them company,
Or butterfly sate down, they were, I ween,
As pleased as if the same had been a maiden queen.

LOUISA.

I MET Louisa in the shade;
And having seen that lovely maid,
Why should I fear to say
That she is ruddy, fleet, and strong;
And down the rocks can leap along,
Like rivulets in May?

And she hath smiles to earth unknown;
Smiles, that with motion of their own
Do spread, and sink, and rise;
That come and go with endless play,
And ever, as they pass away,
Are hidden in her eyes.

She loves her fire, her cottage-home;
Yet o'er the moorland will she roam
In weather rough and bleak;
And, when against the wind she strains,
Oh, might I kiss the mountain rains,
That sparkle on her cheek!

Take all that's mine "beneath the moon,"
If I with her but half a noon
May sit beneath the walls
Of some old cave, or mossy nook,
When up she winds along the brook
To hunt the waterfalls.

STRANGE fits of passion I have known:
And I will dare to tell,
But in the lover's ear alone,
What once to me befel.

When she I loved was strong and gay
And like a rose in June,
I to her cottage bent my way,
Beneath the evening moon.

Upon the moon I fixed my eye,
All over the wide lea;

My horse trudged on—and we drew nigh
Those paths so dear to me.

And now we reached the orchard plot;
And as we climbed the hill,
Towards the roof of Lucy's cot
The moon descended still.

In one of those sweet dreams I slept,
Kind nature's gentlest boon!
And all the while my eyes I kept
On the descending moon.

My horse moved on; hoof after hoof
He raised, and never stopped:
When down behind the cottage roof,
At once, the bright moon dropped.

What fond and wayward thoughts will slide
Into a lover's head!—
"Oh, mercy!" to myself I cried,
"If Lucy should be dead!"

SHE dwelt among the untrodden ways
Beside the springs of Dove,
A maid whom there were none to praise,
And very few to love.

A violet by a mossy stone
Half-hidden from the eye!
Fair as a star, when only one
Is shining in the sky.

She lived unknown, and few could know
When Lucy ceased to be;
But she is in her grave, and, oh,
The difference to me!

I TRAVELLED among unknown men,
In lands beyond the sea;
Nor, England! did I know till then
What love I bore to thee.

'Tis past, that melancholy dream!
Nor will I quit thy shore
A second time; for still I seem
To love thee more and more.

Among thy mountains did I feel
The joy of my desire;
And she I cherished turned her wheel
Beside an English fire.

Thy mornings showed, thy nights concealed
The bowers where Lucy played;
And thine is too the last green field
That Lucy's eyes surveyed.

ERE with cold beads of midnight dew
Had mingled tears of thine,
I grieved, fond youth! that thou shouldst sue
To haughty Geraldine.

Immoveable by generous sighs,
She glories in a train
Who drag, beneath our native skies,
An oriental chain.

Pine not like them with arms across,
Forgetting in thy care
How the fast-rooted trees can toss
Their branches in mid air.

The humblest rivulet will take
Its own wild liberties;
And, every day, the imprisoned lake
Is flowing in the breeze.

Then, crouch no more on suppliant knee,
But scorn with scorn outbrave;
A Briton, even in love, should be
A subject, not a slave!

TO ——.

LOOK at the fate of summer flowers,
Which blow at daybreak, droop ere even-song;
And, grieved for their brief date, confess that ours,
Measured by what we are and ought to be,
Measured by all that trembling we foresee,
Is not so long!

If human life do pass away,
Perishing yet more swiftly than the flower
Whose frail existence is but of a day;
What space hath virgin's beauty to disclose
Her sweets, and triumph o'er the breathing rose!
Not even an hour!

The deepest grove whose foliage hid
The happiest lovers Arcady might boast,
Could not the entrance of this thought forbid:
Oh, be thou wise as they, soul-gifted maid!
Nor rate too high what must so quickly fade,
So soon be lost.

Then shall love teach some virtuous youth
"To draw out of the object of his eyes,"
The whilst on thee they gaze in simple truth,
Hues more exalted, "a refinèd form,"
That dreads not age, nor suffers from the worm,
And never dies

'TIS said that some have died for love
And here and there a church-yard grave is found
In the cold North's unhallowed ground,—
Because the wretched man himself had slain,
His love was such a grievous pain.
And there is one whom I five years have known;
He dwells alone
Upon Helvellyn's side ·
He loved——the pretty Barbara died,
And thus he makes his moan :
Three years had Barbara in her grave been laid
When thus his moan he made—

"Oh, move, thou cottage, from behind that oak !
Or let the aged tree uprooted lie,
That in some other way yon smoke
May mount into the sky !
The clouds pass on ; they from the heavens depart :
I look—the sky is empty space ,
I know not what I trace ;
But when I cease to look, my hand is on my heart.

"Oh ! what a weight is in these shades ? Ye leaves,
When will that dying murmur be supprest !
Your sound my heart of peace bereaves,
It robs my heart of rest
Thou thrush, that singest loud—and loud and free,
Into yon row of willows flit,
Upon that alder sit ;
Or sing another song, or choose another tree

"Roll back, sweet rill ! back to thy mountain bounds,
And there for ever be thy waters chained !
For thou dost haunt the air with sounds
That cannot be sustained ;
If still beneath that pine-tree's ragged bough
Headlong yon waterfall must come,
Oh, let it then be dumb !—
Be any thing, sweet rill, but that which thou art now.

"Thou eglantine, whose arch so proudly towers,
Even like a rainbow spanning half the vale
Thou one fair shrub, oh ! shed thy flowers,
And stir not in the gale.
For thus to see thee nodding in the air,—
To see thy arch thus stretch and bend,
Thus rise and thus descend,—
Disturbs me till the sight is more than I can bear."

The man who makes this feverish complaint
Is one of giant stature, who could dance
Equipped from head to foot in iron mail.
Ah gentle love ! if ever thought was thine
To store up kindred hours for me, thy face
Turn from me, gentle love ! nor let me walk
Within the sound of Emma's voice, or know
Such happiness as I have known to-day.

A COMPLAINT.

THERE is a change—and I am poor ;
Your love hath been, nor long ago,
A fountain at my fond heart's door,
Whose only business was to flow ;
And flow it did ; not taking heed
Of its own bounty, or my need

What happy moments did I count !
Blest was I then all bliss above !
Now, for this consecrated fount
Of murmuring, sparkling, living love,
What have I ? shall I dare to tell ?
A comfortless and hidden well

A well of love—it may be deep—
I trust it is,—and never dry :
What matter ? if the waters sleep
In silence and obscurity
Such change, and at the very door
Of my fond heart, hath made me poor.

TO ——.

LET other bards of angels sing,
Bright suns without a spot ;
But thou art no such perfect thing ;
Rejoice that thou art not !

Such if thou wert in all men's view,
A universal show,
What would my fancy have to do
My feelings to bestow ?

The world denies that thou art fair,
So, Mary, let it be
If nought in loveliness compare
With what thou art to me.

True beauty dwells in deep retreats,
  Whose veil is unremoved
Till heart with heart in concord beats,
  And the lover is beloved.

How rich that forehead's calm expanse!
How bright that heaven-directed glance!
Waft her to glory, wingèd powers,
Ere sorrow be renewed,
And intercourse with mortal hours
Bring back a humbler mood!
So looked Cecilia when she drew
An angel from his station;
So looked—not ceasing to pursue
Her tuneful adoration!

But hand and voice alike are still;
No sound *here* sweeps away the will
That gave it birth;—in service meek
One upright arm sustains the cheek,
And one across the bosom lies—
That rose, and now forgets to rise,
Subdued by breathless harmonies
Of meditative feeling;
Mute strains from worlds beyond the skies,
Through the pure light of female eyes
Their sanctity revealing!

TO ——.

Oh, dearer far than light and life are
  dear,
Full oft our human foresight I deplore;
Trembling, through my unworthiness, with
  fear [no more!
That friends, by death disjoined, may meet

Misgivings, hard to vanquish or control,
Mix with the day, and cross the hour of rest;
While all the future, for thy purer soul,
With "sober certainties" of love is blest.

If a faint sigh, not meant for human ear,
Tell that these words thy humbleness offend,
Cherish me still—else faltering in the rear
Of a steep march; uphold me to the end.

Peace settles where the intellect is meek,
And love is dutiful in thought and deed;
Through thee communion with that love I
  seek;
The faith Heaven strengthens where *He*
  moulds the creed.

LAMENT OF MARY QUEEN OF SCOTS

ON THE EVE OF A NEW YEAR.

Smile of the moon!—for so I name
That silent greeting from above;
A gentle flash of light that came
From her whom drooping captives love;
Or art thou of still higher birth?
Thou that didst part the clouds of earth,
My torpor to reprove!

Bright boon of pitying Heaven—alas!
I may not trust thy placid cheer!
Pondering that time to-night will pass
The threshold of another year;
For years to me are sad and dull;
My very moments are too full
Of hopelessness and fear.

And yet, the soul-awakening gleam,
That struck perchance the farthest cone
Of Scotland's rocky wilds, did seem
To visit me, and me alone;
Me, unapproached by any friend,
Save those who to my sorrows lend
Tears due unto their own.

To-night, the church-tower bells will ring
Through these wide realms a festive peal;
To the new year a welcoming;
A tuneful offering for the weal
Of happy millions lulled in sleep;
While I am forced to watch and weep,
By wounds that may not heal.

Born all too high, by wedlock raised
Still higher—to be cast thus low!
Would that mine eyes had never gazed
On aught of more ambitious show
Than the sweet flowerets of the fields!
It is my royal state that yields
This bitterness of woe.

Yet how?—for I, if there be truth
In the world's voice, was passing fair,
And beauty, for confiding youth,
Those shocks of passion can prepare
That kill the bloom before its time,
And blanch, without the owner's crime,
The most resplendent hair.

Unblest distinction! showered on me
To bind a lingering life in chains:—
All that could quit my grasp, or flee,
Is gone;—but not the subtle stains
Fixed in the spirit; for even here
Can I be proud that jealous fear
Of what I was remains.

A woman rules my prison's key;
A sister queen, against the bent
Of law and holiest sympathy,
Detains me, doubtful of the event;
Great God, who feel'st for my distress,
My thoughts are all that I possess,
Oh, keep them innocent!

Farewell desire of human aid,
Which abject mortals vainly court,
By friends deceived, by foes betrayed,
Of fears the prey, of hopes the sport;
Nought but the world-redeeming cross
Is able to supply my loss,
My burthen to support.

Hark! the death-note of the year
Sounded by the castle clock!
From her sunk eyes a stagnant tear
Stole forth, unsettled by the shock;
But oft the woods renewed their green,
Ere the tired head of Scotland's queen
Reposed upon the block!

THE COMPLAINT

OF A FORSAKEN INDIAN WOMAN.

[When a Northern Indian, from sickness, is unable to continue his journey with his companions, he is left behind, covered over with deer-skins, and is supplied with water, food, and fuel, if the situation of the place will afford it. He is informed of the track which his companions intend to pursue, and if he is unable to follow or overtake them, he perishes alone in the desert, unless he should have the good fortune to fall in with some other tribes of Indians. The females are equally, or still more, exposed to the same fate. See that very interesting work, Hearne's "Journey from Hudson's Bay to the Northern Ocean." In the high northern latitudes, as the same writer informs us, when the northern lights vary their position in the air, they make a rustling and a crackling noise, as alluded to in the following poem.]

BEFORE I see another day,
Oh, let my body die away!
In sleep I heard the northern gleams;
The stars were mingled with my dreams;
In rustling conflict through the skies,
I heard, I saw the flashes drive,
And yet they are upon my eyes,
And yet I am alive;
Before I see another day,
Oh, let my body die away!

My fire is dead: it knew no pain;
Yet is it dead, and I remain.
All stiff with ice the ashes lie;
And they are dead, and I will die.
When I was well, I wished to live,
For clothes, for warmth, for food, and fire;
But they to me no joy can give,
No pleasure now, and no desire.
Then here contented will I lie!
Alone I cannot fear to die.

Alas! ye might have dragged me on
Another day, a single one!
Too soon I yielded to despair;
Why did ye listen to my prayer?
When ye were gone my limbs were stronger,
And, oh, how grievously I rue,
That, afterwards, a little longer,
My friends, I did not follow you?
For strong and without pain I lay,
My friends, when ye were gone away.

My child! they gave thee to another,
A woman who was not thy mother.
When from my arms my babe they took,
On me how strangely did he look!
Through his whole body something ran,
A most strange working did I see;
As if he strove to be a man,
That he might pull the sledge for me.
And then he stretched his arms, how wild?
Oh, mercy! like a helpless child.

My little joy! my little pride!
In two days more I must have died.
Then do not weep and grieve for me;
I feel I must have died with thee.
O wind, that o'er my head art flying
The way my friends their course did bend,
I should not feel the pain of dying,
Could I with thee a message send;
Too soon, my friends, ye went away;
For I had many things to say.

I'll follow you across the snow;
Ye travel heavily and slow;
In spite of all my weary pain
I'll look upon your tents again.
My fire is dead, and snowy white
The water which beside it stood;
The wolf has come to me to-night,
And he has stolen away my food.
For ever left alone am I,
Then wherefore should I fear to die."

THE LAST OF THE FLOCK.

In distant countries have I been,
And yet I have not often seen
A healthy man, a man full grown,
Weep in the public roads alone
But such a one, on English ground,
And in the broad highway, I met,
Along the broad highway he came,
His cheeks with tears were wet.
Sturdy he seemed, though he was sad,
And in his arms a lamb he had.

He saw me, and he turned aside,
As if he wished himself to hide
Then with his coat he made essay
To wipe those briny tears away.
I followed him, and said, "My friend,
What ails you? wherefore weep you so?"
"Shame on me, sir! this lusty lamb,
He makes my tears to flow.
To-day I fetched him from the rock;
He is the last of all my flock.

"When I was young, a single man,
And after youthful follies ran,
Though little given to care and thought,
Yet, so it was, a ewe I bought;
And other sheep from her I raised,
As healthy sheep as you might see,
And then I married, and was rich
As I could wish to be;
Of sheep I numbered a full score,
And every year increased my store.

"Year after year my stock it grew;
And from this one, this single ewe,
Full fifty comely sheep I raised,
As sweet a flock as ever grazed!
Upon the mountain did they feed,
They throve, and we at home did thrive
This lusty lamb of all my store
Is all that is alive;
And now I care not if we die,
And perish all of poverty.

"Six children, sir! had I to feed;
Hard labour in a time of need!
My pride was tamed, and in our grief
I of the parish asked relief.
They said, I was a wealthy man;
My sheep upon the mountain fed,
And it was fit that thence I took
Whereof to buy us bread.
'Do this: how can we give to you,'
They cried, 'what to the poor is due?'

"I sold a sheep, as they had said,
And bought my little children bread,
And they were healthy with their food;
For me—it never did me good.
A woeful time it was for me,
To see the end of all my gains,
The pretty flock which I had reared
With all my care and pains,
To see it melt like snow away!
For me it was a woeful day.

"Another still! and still another!
A little lamb, and then its mother!
It was a vein that never stopped—
Like blood-drops from my heart they dropped
Till thirty were not left alive.
They dwindled, dwindled, one by one·
And I may say, that many a time
I wished they all were gone—
Reckless of what might come at last
Were but the bitter struggle past

"To wicked deeds I was inclined,
And wicked fancies crossed my mind;
And every man I chanced to see,
I thought he knew some ill of me.
No peace, no comfort could I find,
No ease, within doors or without,
And crazily and wearily
I went my work about,
Bent oftentimes to flee from home,
And hide my head where wild beasts roam

"Sir, 'twas a precious flock to me,
As dear as my own children be,
For daily with my growing store
I loved my children more and more.
Alas! it was an evil time;
God cursed me in my sore distress;
I prayed, yet every day I thought
I loved my children less;
And every week, and every day,
My flock it seemed to melt away.

"They dwindled, sir, sad sight to see!
From ten to five, from five to three,
A lamb, a wether, and a ewe;
And then at last from three to two;
And, of my fifty, yesterday
I had but only one:
And here it lies upon my arm,
Alas! and I have none;—
To-day I fetched it from the rock;
It is the last of all my flock."

REPENTANCE.

A PASTORAL BALLAD.

THE fields which with covetous spirit we sold,
Those beautiful fields, the delight of the day,
Would have brought us more good than a burthen of gold,
Could we but have been as contented as they.

When the troublesome tempter beset us, said I,
"Let him come with his purse proudly grasped in his hand;
But, Allan, be true to me, Allan,—we'll die
Before he shall go with an inch of the land!"

There dwelt we, as happy as birds in their bowers;
Unfettered as bees that in gardens abide;
We could do what we chose with the land, it was ours;
And for us the brook murmured that ran by its side.

But now we are strangers, go early or late;
And often, like one overburdened with sin,
With my hand on the latch of the half-opened gate,
I look at the fields—but I cannot go in!

When I walk by the hedge on a bright summer's day,
Or sit in the shade of my grandfather's tree,
A stern face it puts on, as if ready to say,
"What ails you, that you must come creeping to me?"

With our pastures about us, we could not be sad;
Our comfort was near if we ever were crost,
But the comfort, the blessings, and wealth that we had,
We slighted them all,—and our birthright was lost.

Oh, ill-judging sire of an innocent son,
Who must now be a wanderer!—but peace to that strain!
Think of evening's repose when our labour was done,
The Sabbath's return—and its leisure's soft chain!

And in sickness, if night had been sparing of sleep,
How cheerful, at sunrise, the hill where I stood,
Looking down on the kine, and our treasure of sheep
That besprinkled the field—'twas like youth in my blood!

Now I cleave to the house, and am dull as a snail;
And, oftentimes, hear the church-bell with a sigh,
That follows the thought—We've no land in the vale,
Save six feet of earth where our forefathers lie!

THE AFFLICTION OF MARGARET.

WHERE art thou, my beloved son,
Where art thou, worse to me than dead?
Oh, find me, prosperous or undone!
Or, if the grave be now thy bed,
Why am I ignorant of the same,
That I may rest; and neither blame
Nor sorrow may attend thy name?

Seven years, alas! to have received
No tidings of an only child;
To have despaired, and have believed,
And be for evermore beguiled;
Sometimes with thoughts of very bliss!
I catch at them and then I miss;
Was ever darkness like to this?

He was among the prime in worth,
An object beauteous to behold;
Well born, well bred; I sent him forth
Ingenuous, innocent, and bold:
If things ensued that wanted grace,
As hath been said, they were not base;
And never blush was on my face.

Ah! little doth the young one dream,
When full of play and childish cares,
What power hath even his wildest scream,
Heard by his mother unawares!
He knows it not, he cannot guess:
Years to a mother bring distress;
But do not make her love the less.

Neglect me! no, I suffered long
From that ill thought; and, being blind,
Said, "Pride shall help me in my wrong:
Kind mother have I been, as kind
As ever breathed:" and that is true;
I've wet my path with tears like dew,
Weeping for him when no one knew.

My son, if thou be humbled, poor,
Hopeless of honour and of gain,
Oh! do not dread thy mother's door;
Think not of me with grief and pain:
I now can see with better eyes,
And worldly grandeur I despise,
And fortune with her gifts and lies.

Alas! the fowls of heaven have wings,
And blasts of heaven will aid their flight;
They mount, how short a voyage brings
The wanderers back to their delight!
Chains tie us down by land and sea;
And wishes, vain as mine, may be
All that is left to comfort thee.

Perhaps some dungeon hears thee groan,
Maimed, mangled by inhuman men;
Or thou upon a desert thrown
Inheritest the lion's den;
Or hast been summoned to the deep,
Thou, thou, and all thy mates, to keep
An incommunicable sleep.

I look for ghosts; but none will force
Their way to me:—'tis falsely said
That there was ever intercourse
Betwixt the living and the dead;
For, surely, then I should have sight
Of him I wait for day and night,
With love and longings infinite.

My apprehensions come in crowds;
I dread the rustling of the grass;
The very shadows of the clouds
Have power to shake me as they pass:
I question things and do not find
One that will answer to my mind;
And all the world appears unkind.

Beyond participation lie
My troubles, and beyond relief:
If any chance to heave a sigh,
They pity me and not my grief.
Then come to me, my son, or send
Some tidings that my woes may end;
I have no other earthly friend.

THE COTTAGER TO HER INFANT.

BY A FEMALE FRIEND.

THE days are cold, the nights are long,
The north wind sings a doleful song;
Then hush again upon my breast;
All merry things are now at rest,
Save thee, my pretty love!

The kitten sleeps upon the hearth,
The crickets long have ceased their mirth;
There's nothing stirring in the house
Save one *wee*, hungry, nibbling mouse,
Then why so busy thou?

Nay! start not at that sparkling light,
'Tis but the moon that shines so bright
On the window-pane bedropped with rain
Then, little darling! sleep again!
And wake when it is day.

THE SAILOR'S MOTHER.

ONE morning (raw it was and wet,
A foggy day in winter time)
A woman on the road I met,
Not old, though something past her prime:
Majestic in her person, tall and straight;
And like a Roman matron's was her mien and gait.

The ancient spirit is not dead;
Old times, thought I, are breathing there;
Proud was I that my country bred
Such strength, a dignity so fair:
She begged an alms, like one in poor estate;
I looked at her again, nor did my pride abate.

When from those lofty thoughts I woke,
"What treasure," said I, "do you bear
Beneath the covert of your cloak,
Protected from the cold damp air?"
She answered, soon as she the question heard,
"A simple burden, sir, a little singing-bird.

"I had a son,—the waves might roar,
He feared them not, a sailor gay!
But he will cross the deep no more:
In Denmark he was cast away:
And I have travelled weary miles to see
If aught which he had owned might still remain for me.

"The bird and cage they both were his:
'Twas my son's bird; and neat and trim
He kept it: many voyages
This singing-bird had gone with him:
When last he sailed, he left the bird behind:
From bodings, as might be, that hung upon his mind.

"He to a fellow-lodger's care
Had left it, to be watched and fed,
And pipe its song in safety;—there
I found it when my son was dead;
And now, God help me for my little wit!
I bear it with me, sir! he took so much delight in it.'

THE CHILDLESS FATHER.

"Up, Timothy, up with your staff and away!
Not a soul in the village this morning will stay;
The hare has just started from Hamilton's grounds,
And Skiddaw is glad with the cry of the hounds."

Of coats and of jackets gray, scarlet, and green,
On the slopes of the pastures all colours were seen;
With their comely blue aprons, and caps white as snow,
The girls on the hills made a holiday show.

Fresh sprigs of green box-wood, not six months before,
Filled the funeral basin* at Timothy's door;
A coffin through Timothy's threshold had past;
One child did it bear, and that child was his last.

Now fast up the dell came the noise and the fray,
The horse and the horn, and the hark! hark away!
Old Timothy took up his staff, and he shut
With a leisurely motion the door of his hut.

Perhaps to himself at that moment he said,
"The key I must take, for my Ellen is dead."
But of this in my ears not a word did he speak,
And he went to the chase with a tear on his cheek.

THE EMIGRANT MOTHER.

Once in a lonely hamlet I sojourned,
In which a lady driven from France did dwell;
The big and lesser griefs, with which she mourned,
In friendship, she to me would often tell.

This lady, dwelling upon English ground,
Where she was childless, daily would repair
To a poor neighbouring cottage; as I found,
For sake of a young child whose home was there.

Once, having seen her take with fond embrace
This infant to herself, I framed a lay,
Endeavouring, in my native tongue, to trace
Such things as she unto the child might say:
And thus, from what I knew, had heard, and guessed,
My song the workings of her heart expressed.

"Dear babe, thou daughter of another,
One moment let me be thy mother!
An infant's face and looks are thine,
And sure a mother's heart is mine:
Thy own dear mother's far away,
At labour in the harvest-field:
Thy little sister is at play;
What warmth, what comfort would it yield
To my poor heart, if thou wouldst be
One little hour a child to me!

"Across the waters I am come,
And I have left a babe at home:
A long, long way of land and sea!
Come to me—I'm no enemy:
I am the same who at thy side
Sate yesterday, and made a nest
For thee, sweet baby!—thou hast tried,
Thou know'st the pillow of my breast;
Good, good art thou;—alas to me
Far more than I can be to thee.

"Here, little darling, dost thou lie;
An infant thou, a mother I!
Mine wilt thou be, thou hast no fears;
Mine art thou—spite of these my tears.
Alas! before I left the spot,
My baby and its dwelling-place;
The nurse said to me, 'Tears should not
Be shed upon an infant's face,
It was unlucky'—no, no, no;
No truth is in them who say so!

"My own dear little one will sigh,
Sweet babe! and they will let him die.
'He pines,' they'll say, 'it is his doom.
And you may see his hour is come.'
Oh! had he but thy cheerful smiles,
Limbs stout as thine, and lips as gay,
Thy looks, thy cunning, and thy wiles,
And countenance like a summer's day,
They would have hopes of him—and then
I should behold his face again!

"'Tis gone—like dreams that we forget;
There was a smile or two—yet—yet
I can remember them, I see
The smile worth all the world to me.

* In several parts of the north of England when a funeral takes place, a basin full of sprigs of boxwood is placed at the door of the house from which the coffin is taken up, and each person who attends the funeral ordinarily takes a sprig of this boxwood, and throws it into the grave of the deceased.

Dear baby! I must lay thee down;
Thou troublest me with strange alarms;
Smiles hast thou, bright ones of thy own;
I cannot keep thee in my arms,
By those bewildering glances crost
In which the light of his is lost.

"Oh! how I love thee!—we still stay
Together here this one half day.
My sister's child, who bears my name,
From France to sheltering England came;
She with her mother crossed the sea;
The babe and mother near me dwell:
My darling, she is not to me
What thou art! though I love her well
Rest, little stranger, rest thee here!
Never was any child more dear!

"—I cannot help it—ill intent
I've none, my pretty innocent!
I weep—I know they do thee wrong,
These tears—and my poor idle tongue
Oh, what a kiss was that! my cheek
How cold it is! but thou art good,
Thine eyes are on me—they would speak,
I think, to help me if they could.
Blessings upon that soft, warm face,
My heart again is in its place!

"While thou art mine, my little love,
This cannot be a sorrowful grove;
Contentment, hope, and mother's glee,
I seem to find them all in thee:
Here's grass to play with, here are flowers;
I'll call thee by my darling's name,
Thou hast, I think, a look of ours,
Thy features seem to me the same,
His little sister thou shalt be:
And, when once more my home I see,
I'll tell him many tales of thee."

VAUDRACOUR AND JULIA.

The following tale was written as an episode in a work from which its length may perhaps exclude it The facts are true; no invention as to these has been exercised, as none was needed.

Oh, happy time of youthful lovers, (thus
My story may begin,) oh, balmy time,
In which a love-knot on a lady's brow
Is fairer than the fairest star in heaven!
To such inheritance of blessed fancy
(Fancy that sports more desperately with minds
Than ever fortune hath been known to do)
The high-born Vaudracour was brought, by years
Whose progress had a little overstepped
His stripling prime. A town of small repute,
Among the vine-clad mountains of Auvergne,
Was the youth's birthplace There he wooed a maid
Who heard the heart-felt music of his suit
With answering vows. Plebeian was the stock,
Plebeian, though ingenuous, the stock,
From which her graces and her honours sprung·
And hence the father of the enamoured youth,
With haughty indignation, spurned the thought
Of such alliance.—From their cradles up,
With but a step between their several homes,
Twins had they been in pleasure; after strife
And petty quarrels, had grown fond again,
Each other's advocate, each other's stay;
And strangers to content if long apart,
Or more divided than a sportive pair
Of sea-fowl, conscious both that they are hovering
Within the eddy of a common blast,
Or hidden only by the concave depth
Of neighbouring billows from each other's sight.

Thus, not without concurrence of an age
Unknown to memory, was an earnest given,
By ready nature, for a life of love,
For endless constancy, and placid truth,
But whatsoe'er of such rare treasure lay
Reserved, had fate permitted, for support
Of their maturer years, his present mind
Was under fascination;—he beheld
A vision, and adored the thing he saw.
Arabian fiction never filled the world
With half the wonders that were wrought for him
Earth breathed in one great presence of the spring,
Life turned the meanest of her implements,
Before his eyes, to price above all gold,
The house she dwelt in was a sainted shrine
Her chamber window did surpass in glory
The portals of the dawn, all paradise
Could, by the simple opening of a door,
Let itself in upon him. pathways, walks,
Swarmed with enchantment, till his spirit sank,
Surcharged, within him, —overblest to move
Beneath a sun that wakes a weary world

To its dull round of ordinary cares;
A man too happy for mortality!

So passed the time, till, whether through effect
Of some unguarded moment that dissolved
Virtuous restraint—ah, speak it, think it not!
Deem rather that the fervent youth, who saw
So many bars between his present state
And the dear haven where he wished to be
In honourable wedlock with his love,
Was in his judgment tempted to decline
To perilous weakness, and intrust his cause
To nature for a happy end of all;
Deem that by such fond hope the youth was swayed,
And bear with their transgression, when I add
That Julia, wanting yet the name of wife,
Carried about her for a secret grief
The promise of a mother.
To conceal
The threatened shame, the parents of the maid
Found means to hurry her away by night
And unforewarned, that in some distant spot
She might remain shrouded in privacy,
Until the babe was born. When morning came,
The lover, thus bereft, stung with his loss,
And all uncertain whither he should turn,
Chafed like a wild beast in the toils; but soon
Discovering traces of the fugitives,
Their steps he followed to the maid's retreat.
The sequel may be easily divined,—
Walks to and fro—watchings at every hour;
And the fair captive, who, whene'er she may,
Is busy at her casement as the swallow
Fluttering its pinions, almost within reach,
About the pendent nest, did thus espy
Her lover !—thence a stolen interview,
Accomplished under friendly shade of night.

I pass the raptures of the pair;—such theme
Is, by innumerable poets, touched
In more delightful verse than skill of mine
Could fashion, chiefly by that darling bard
Who told of Juliet and her Romeo,
And of the lark's note heard before its time,
And of the streaks that laced the severing clouds
In the unrelenting east.—Through all her courts
The vacant city slept; the busy winds,
That keep no certain intervals of rest,
Moved not; meanwhile the galaxy displayed
Her fires, that like mysterious pulses beat
Aloft ;—momentous but uneasy bliss!
To their full hearts the universe seemed hung
On that brief meeting's slender filament!

They parted; and the generous Vaudracour
Reached speedily the native threshold, bent
On making (so the lovers had agreed)
A sacrifice of birthright to attain
A final portion from his father's hand;
Which granted, bride and bridegroom then would flee
To some remote and solitary place,
Shady as night, and beautiful as heaven,
Where they may live, with no one to behold
Their happiness, or to disturb their love.
But *now* of this no whisper; not the less,
If ever an obtrusive word were dropped
Touching the matter of his passion, still,
In his stern father's hearing, Vaudracour
Persisted openly that death alone
Should abrogate his human privilege
Divine, of swearing everlasting truth,
Upon the altar, to the maid he loved.

"You shall be baffled in your mad intent
If there be justice in the court of France,"
Muttered the father.—From these words the youth
Conceived a terror,—and, by night or day,
Stirred nowhere without weapons—that full soon
Found dreadful provocation: for at night
When to his chamber he retired, attempt
Was made to seize him by three armèd men,
Acting, in furtherance of the father's will,
Under a private signet of the state.
One, did the youth's ungovernable hand
Assault and slay, and to a second gave
A perilous wound,—he shuddered to behold
The breathless corse; then peacefully resigned
His person to the law, was lodged in prison
And wore the fetters of a criminal.

Have you beheld a tuft of wingèd seed
That, from the dandèlion's naked stalk,
Mounted aloft, is suffered not to use
Its natural gifts for purposes of rest,

Driven by the autumnal whirlwind to and
fro [marked
Through the wide element? or have you
The heavier substance of a leaf-clad bough,
Within the vortex of a foaming flood,
Tormented? by such aid you may conceive
The perturbation of each mind;—ah, no!
Desperate the maid—the youth is stained
with blood!
But as the troubled seed and tortured bough
Is man, subjected to despotic sway.

For him, by private influence with the
court,
Was pardon gained, and liberty procured;
But not without exaction of a pledge
Which liberty and love dispersed in air.
He flew to her from whom they would
divide him— [peace—
He clove to her who could not give him
Yea, his first word of greeting was,—"All
right
Is gone from me; my lately-towering hopes,
To the least fibre of their lowest root,
Are withered;—thou no longer canst be
mine, [woo
I thine—the conscience-stricken must not
The unruffled innocent,—I see thy face,
Behold thee, and my misery is complete!"

"One, are we not?" exclaimed the
maiden—"One, [woe?"
For innocence and youth, for weal and
Then with the father's name she coupled
words
Of vehement indignation; but the youth
Checked her with filial meekness; for no
thought
Uncharitable, no presumptuous rising
Of hasty censure, modelled in the eclipse
Of true domestic loyalty, did e'er
Find place within his bosom.—Once again
The persevering wedge of tyranny
Achieved their separation;—and once
more
Were they united,—to be yet again
Disparted—pitiable lot! But here
A portion of the tale may well be left
In silence, though my memory could add
Much how the youth, in scanty space of
time, [of thoughts
Was traversed from without; much, too,
That occupied his days in solitude
Under privation and restraint; and what,
Through dark and shapeless fear of
things to come.
And what, through strong compunction
for the past,
He suffered—breaking down in heart and
mind!

Doomed to a third and last captivity,
His freedom he recovered on the eve
Of Julia's travail. When the babe was born,
Its presence tempted him to cherish schemes
Of future happiness. "You shall return,
Julia," said he, "and to your father's house
Go with the child.—You have been
wretched; yet [then weighs
The silver shower, whose reckless bur-
Too heavily upon the lily's head,
Oft leaves a saving moisture at its root.
Malice, beholding you, will melt away.
Go!—'tis a town where both of us were
born; [known;
None will reproach you, for our truth is
And if, amidst those once-bright bowers,
our fate
Remain unpitied, pity is not in man.
With ornaments—the prettiest nature yields
Or art can fashion, shall you deck your
boy, [sweet looks
And feed his countenance with your own
Till no one can resist him.—Now, even now,
I see him sporting on the sunny lawn;
My father from the window sees him too;
Startled, as if some new-created thing
Enriched the earth, or faery of the woods
Bounded before him;—but the unweeting
child [heart
Shall by his beauty win his grandsire's
So that it shall be softened, and our loves
End happily—as they began!"
These gleams
Appeared but seldom: oftener was he seen
Propping a pale and melancholy face
Upon the mother's bosom; resting thus
His head upon one breast, while from the
other
The babe was drawing in its quiet food.
That pillow is no longer to be thine,
Fond youth! that mournful solace now
must pass
Into the list of things that cannot be!
Unwedded Julia, terror-smitten, hears
The sentence, by her mother's lip pro-
nounced, [shall tell,
That dooms her to a convent.—Who
Who dares report the tidings to the
lord
Of her affections? So they blindly asked
Who knew not to what quiet depths a
weight
Of agony had pressed the sufferer down:—

The word, by others dreaded, he can hear
Composed and silent, without visible sign
Of even the least emotion. Noting this
When the impatient object of his love
Upbraided him with slackness, he returned
No answer, only took the mother's hand
And kissed it—seemingly devoid of pain,
Or care, that what so tenderly he pressed,
Was a dependant on the obdurate heart
Of one who came to disunite their lives
For ever—sad alternative ! preferred,
By the unbending parents of the maid,
To secret 'spousals meanly disavowed
So be it !
In the city he remained
A season after Julia had withdrawn
To those religious walls. He, too, departs—
Who with him ?—even the senseless little one !
With that sole charge he passed the city-gates,
For the last time, attendant by the side
Of a close chair, a litter, or sedan,
In which the babe was carried. To a hill,
That rose a brief league distant from the town,
The dwellers in that house where he had lodged
Accompanied his steps, by anxious love
Impelled ;—they parted from him there, and stood
Watching below, till he had disappeared
On the hill top. His eyes he scarcely took,
Throughout that journey, from the vehicle
(Slow-moving ark of all his hopes !) that veiled
The tender infant : and at every inn,
And under every hospitable tree
At which the bearers halted or reposed,
Laid him with timid care upon his knees,
And looked, as mothers ne'er were known to look,
Upon the nursling which his arms embraced.

This was the manner in which Vaudracour
Departed with his infant; and thus reached
His father's house, where to the innocent child
Admittance was denied. The young man spake
No words of indignation or reproof,
But of his father begged, a last request,
That a retreat might be assigned to him
Where in forgotten quiet he might dwell,
With such allowance as his wants required;
For wishes he had none. To a lodge that stood
Deep in a forest, with leave given, at the age
Of four-and-twenty summers he withdrew,
And thither took with him his infant babe,
And one domestic, for their common needs,
An aged woman. It consoled him here
To attend upon the orphan, and perform
Obsequious service to the precious child,
Which, after a short time, by some mistake
Or indiscretion of the father, died.
The tale I follow to its last recess
Of suffering or of peace, I know not which;
Theirs be the blame who caused the woe, not mine !

From this time forth he never shared a smile
With mortal creature. An inhabitant
Of that same town, in which the pair had left
So lively a remembrance of their griefs,
By chance of business, coming within reach
Of his retirement, to the forest lodge
Repaired, but only found the matron there,
Who told him that his pains were thrown away,
For that her master never uttered word
To living thing—not even to her.—Behold !
While they were speaking, Vaudracour approached ,
But, seeing some one near, even as his hand
Was stretched towards the garden gate, he shrunk—
And, like a shadow, glided out of view.
Shocked at his savage aspect, from the place
The visitor retired.
Thus lived the youth
Cut off from all intelligence with man,
And shunning even the light of common day ;
Nor could the voice of freedom, which through France
Full speedily resounded, public hope,
Or personal memory of his own deep wrongs,
Rouse him . but in those solitary shades
His days he wasted, an imbecile mind !

THE IDIOT BOY.

'Tis eight o'clock,—a clear March night,
The moon is up—the sky is blue,
The owlet, in the moonlight air,
Shouts, from nobody knows where ;
He lengthens out his lonely shout,
Halloo ! halloo ! a long halloo !

Why bustle thus about your door,
What means this bustle, Betty Foy?
Why are you in this mighty fret?
And why on horseback have you set
Him whom you love, your Idiot Boy?

There's scarce a soul that's out of bed;
Good Betty, put him down again;
His lips with joy they burr at you;
But, Betty! what has he to do
With stirrup, saddle, or with rein?

But Betty's bent on her intent;
For her good neighbour, Susan Gale,
Old Susan, she who dwells alone,
Is sick, and makes a piteous moan,
As if her very life would fail.

There's not a house within a mile,
No hand to help them in distress;
Old Susan lies a-bed in pain,
And sorely puzzled are the twain,
For what she ails they cannot guess.

And Betty's husband's at the wood,
Where by the week he doth abide,
A woodman in the distant vale;
There's none to help poor Susan Gale;
What must be done? what will betide?

And Betty from the lane has fetched
Her pony, that is mild and good,
Whether he be in joy or pain,
Feeding at will along the lane,
Or bringing faggots from the wood.

And he is all in travelling trim,—
And, by the moonlight, Betty Foy
Has up upon the saddle set
(The like was never heard of yet)
Him whom she loves, her Idiot Boy.

And he must post without delay
Across the bridge and through the dale,
And by the church, and o'er the down,
To bring a doctor from the town,
Or she will die, old Susan Gale.

There is no need of boot or spur,
There is no need of whip or wand;
For Johnny has his holly-bough,
And with a *hurly-burly* now
He shakes the green bough in his hand.

And Betty o'er and o'er has told
The boy, who is her best delight,
Both what to follow, what to shun,
What do, and what to leave undone,
How turn to left, and how to right.

And Betty's most especial charge,
Was, "Johnny! Johnny! mind that you
Come home again, nor stop at all,—
Come home again, whate'er befal,
My Johnny, do, I pray you do."

To this did Johnny answer make,
Both with his head, and with his hand,
And proudly shook the bridle too;
And then! his words were not a few,
Which Betty well could understand.

And now that Johnny is just going,
Though Betty's in a mighty flurry,
She gently pats the pony's side,
On which her Idiot Boy must ride.
And seems no longer in a hurry.

But when the pony moved his legs,
Oh! then for the poor Idiot Boy!
For joy he cannot hold the bridle,
For joy his head and heels are idle,
He's idle all for very joy.

And while the pony moves his legs,
In Johnny's left hand you may see
The green bough motionless and dead.
The moon that shines above his head
Is not more still and mute than he.

His heart it was so full of glee,
That till full fifty yards were gone,
He quite forgot his holly whip,
And all his skill in horsemanship,
Oh! happy, happy, happy, John.

And while the mother, at the door,
Stands fixed, her face with joy o'erflows,
Proud of herself, and proud of him,
She sees him in his travelling trim,
How quietly her Johnny goes.

The silence of her Idiot Boy,
What hopes it sends to Betty's heart!
He's at the guide-post—he turns right,
She watches till he's out of sight,
And Betty will not then depart.

Burr, burr—now Johnny's lips they burr,
As loud as any mill, or near it;
Meek as a lamb the pony moves,
And Johnny makes the noise he loves,
And Betty listens, glad to hear it.

Away she hies to Susan Gale:
Her messenger's in merry tune;
The owlets hoot, the owlets curr,
And Johnny's lips they burr, burr, burr,
As on he goes beneath the moon.

His steed and he right well agree;
For of this pony there's a rumour,
That, should he lose his eyes and ears,
And should he live a thousand years,
He never will be out of humour.

But then he is a horse that thinks!
And when he thinks his pace is slack;
Now, though he knows poor Johnny well,
Yet, for his life, he cannot tell
What he has got upon his back.

So through the moonlight lanes they go,
And far into the moonlight dale,
And by the church, and o'er the down,
To bring a doctor from the town
To comfort poor old Susan Gale.

And Betty, now at Susan's side,
Is in the middle of her story,
What comfort soon her boy will bring,
With many a most diverting thing,
Of Johnny's wit, and Johnny's glory.

And Betty, still at Susan's side,
By this time is not quite so flurried:
Demure with porringer and plate
She sits, as if in Susan's fate
Her life and soul were buried.

But Betty, poor good woman! she,
You plainly in her face may read it,
Could lend out of that moment's store,
Five years of happiness or more
To any that might need it.

But yet I guess that now and then
With Betty all was not so well;
And to the road she turns her ears,
And thence full many a sound she hears,
Which she to Susan will not tell.

Poor Susan moans, poor Susan groans;
"As sure as there's a moon in heaven,"
Cries Betty, "he'll be back again;
They'll both be here—'tis almost ten—
Both will be here before eleven."

Poor Susan moans, poor Susan groans;
The clock gives warning for eleven;
'Tis on the stroke—"He must be near,"
Quoth Betty, "and will soon be here,
As sure as there's a moon in heaven."

The clock is on the stroke of twelve,
And Johnny is not yet in sight,
The moon's in heaven, as Betty sees,
But Betty is not quite at ease,
And Susan has a dreadful night.

And Betty, half an hour ago,
On Johnny vile reflections cast:
"A little idle sauntering thing!"
With other names, an endless string;
But now that time is gone and past.

And Betty's drooping at the heart,
That happy time all past and gone,
"How can it be he is so late?
The doctor he has made him wait;
Susan! they'll both be here anon."

And Susan's growing worse and worse,
And Betty's in a sad *quandary*;
And then there's nobody to say
If she must go or she must stay!
She's in a sad *quandary*.

The clock is on the stroke of one;
But neither doctor nor his guide
Appears along the moonlight road;
There's neither horse nor man abroad,
And Betty's still at Susan's side.

And Susan now begins to fear
Of sad mischances not a few,
That Johnny may perhaps be drowned,
Or lost, perhaps, and never found;
Which they must both for ever rue.

She prefaced half a hint of this
With "God forbid it should be true!"
At the first word that Susan said
Cried Betty, rising from the bed,
"Susan, I'd gladly stay with you.

"I must be gone, I must away,
Consider, Johnny's but half wise·
Susan, we must take care of him,
If he is hurt in life or limb"—
"Oh, God forbid!" poor Susan cries.

"What can I do?" says Betty, going,
"What can I do to ease your pain?
Good Susan tell me, and I'll stay;
I fear you're in a dreadful way,
But I shall soon be back again."

"Nay, Betty, go; good Betty, go!
There's nothing that can ease my pain."
Then off she hies; but with a prayer
That God poor Susan's life would spare,
Till she comes back again.

So, through the moonlight lane she goes,
And far into the moonlight dale;
And how she ran, and how she walked,
And all that to herself she talked,
Would surely be a tedious tale.

In high and low, above, below,
In great and small, in round and square,
In tree and tower was Johnny seen,
In bush and brake, in black and green,
'Twas Johnny, Johnny, every where.

The bridge is past—far in the dale;
And now the thought torments her sore,
Johnny perhaps his horse forsook,
To hunt the moon within the brook
And never will be heard of more.

Now is she high upon the down,
Alone amid a prospect wide;
There's neither Johnny nor his horse
Among the fern or in the gorse;
There's neither doctor nor his guide.

"O saints! what is become of him?
Perhaps he's climbed into an oak,
Where he will stay till he is dead;
Or, sadly he has been misled,
And joined the wandering gipsy-folk.

"Or him that wicked pony's carried
To the dark cave, the goblin's hall;
Or in the castle he's pursuing
Among the ghosts his own undoing;
Or playing with the waterfall."

At poor old Susan then she railed,
While to the town she posts away;
"If Susan had not been so ill,
Alas! I should have had him still,
My Johnny, till my dying day."

Poor Betty, in this sad distemper,
The doctor's self could hardly spare;
Unworthy things she talked, and wild;
Even he, of cattle the most mild,
The pony had his share.

And now she's got into the town,
And to the doctor's door she hies;
'Tis silence all on every side;
The town so long, the town so wide,
Is silent as the skies.

And now she's at the doctor's door,
She lifts the knocker, rap, rap, rap;
The doctor at the casement shows
His glimmering eyes that peep and doze!
And one hand rubs his old night-cap.

"Oh, doctor! doctor! where's my Johnny!"
"I'm here, what is't you want with me?"
"Oh, sir! you know I'm Betty Foy
And I have lost my poor dear boy,
You know him—him you often see;

"He's not so wise as some folks be."
"The devil take his wisdom!" said
The doctor, looking somewhat grim,
"What, woman! should I know of him?"
And, grumbling, he went back to bed.

"Oh, woe is me! Oh, woe is me!
Here will I die; here will I die,
I thought to find my lost one here,
But he is neither far nor near,
Oh! what a wretched mother I!"

She stops, she stands, she looks about;
Which way to turn she cannot tell.
Poor Betty! it would ease her pain
If she had heart to knock again;
The clock strikes three—a dismal knell!

Then up along the town she hies,
No wonder if her senses fail,
This piteous news so much it shocked her,
She quite forgot to send the doctor,
To comfort poor old Susan Gale.

And now she's high upon the down,
And she can see a mile of road;
"Oh, cruel! I'm almost threescore;
Such night as this was ne'er before,
There's not a single soul abroad."

She listens, but she cannot hear
The foot of horse, the voice of man;
The streams with softest sound are flowing,
The grass you almost hear it growing,
You hear it now if e'er you can.

The owlets through the long blue night
Are shouting to each other still:
Fond lovers! yet not quite hob nob
They lengthen out the tremulous sob,
That echoes far from hill to hill.

Poor Betty now has lost all hope,
Her thoughts are bent on deadly sin:
A green-grown pond she just has past,
And from the brink she hurries fast,
Lest she should drown herself therein.

And now she sits her down and weeps;
Such tears she never shed before;
"Oh, dear, dear pony! my sweet joy!
Oh, carry back my Idiot Boy!
And we will ne'er o'erload thee more."

A thought is come into her head;
"The pony he is mild and good,
And we have always used him well;
Perhaps he's gone along the dell,
And carried Johnny to the wood."

Then up she springs as if on wings;
She thinks no more of deadly sin;
If Betty fifty ponds should see,
The last of all her thoughts would be
To drown herself therein.

O reader! now that I might tell
What Johnny and his horse are doing!
What they've been doing all this time,
Oh, could I put it into rhyme,
A most delightful tale pursuing!

Perhaps, and no unlikely thought!
He with his pony now doth roam
The cliffs and peaks so high that are,
To lay his hands upon a star,
And in his pocket bring it home.

Perhaps he's turned himself about,
His face unto his horse's tail,
And, still and mute, in wonder lost,
All like a silent horseman-ghost,
He travels on along the vale.

And now, perhaps, is hunting sheep,
A fierce and dreadful hunter he;
Yon valley, now so trim and green,
In five months' time, should he be seen,
A desert wilderness will be!

Perhaps, with head and heels on fire,
And like the very soul of evil,
He's galloping away, away,
And so will gallop on for aye,
The bane of all that dread the devil!

I to the Muses have been bound
These fourteen years, by strong indentures:
O gentle Muses! let me tell
But half of what to him befel,
He surely met with strange adventures.

O gentle Muses! is this kind?
Why will ye thus my suit repel?
Why of your further aid bereave me?
And can ye thus unfriended leave me;
Ye Muses! whom I love so well?

Who's yon, that, near the waterfall,
Which thunders down with headlong force,
Beneath the moon, yet shining fair,
As careless as if nothing were,
Sits upright on a feeding horse?

Unto his horse, there feeding free,
He seems, I think, the rein to give;
Of moon or stars he takes no heed;
Of such we in romances read:
'Tis Johnny! Johnny! as I live.

And that's the very pony too!
Where is she, where is Betty Foy
She hardly can sustain her fears;
The roaring waterfall she hears,
And cannot find her Idiot Boy.

Your pony's worth his weight in gold·
Then calm your terrors, Betty Foy!
She's coming from among the trees,
And now all full in view she sees
Him whom she loves, her Idiot Boy.

And Betty sees the pony too:
Why stand you thus, good Betty Foy?
It is no goblin, 'tis no ghost,
'Tis he whom you so long have lost,
He whom you love, your Idiot Boy.

She looks again—her arms are up—
She screams—she cannot move for joy;
She darts, as with a torrent's force,
She almost has o'erturned the horse
And fast she holds her Idiot Boy.

And Johnny burrs, and laughs aloud,
Whether in cunning or in joy
I cannot tell; but while he laughs,
Betty a drunken pleasure quaffs
To hea. again her Idiot Boy.

And now she's at the pony's tail,
And now is at the pony's head,—
On that side now, and now on this;
And, almost stifled with her bliss,
A few sad tears does Betty shed.

She kisses o'er and o'er again
Him whom she loves, her Idiot Boy;
She's happy here, is happy there,
She is uneasy every where;
Her limbs are all alive with joy.

She pats the pony, where or when
She knows not, happy Betty Foy!
The little pony glad may be,
But he is milder far than she,
You hardly can perceive his joy.

"Oh! Johnny, never mind the doctor;
You've done your best, and that is all."
She took the reins, when this was said,
And gently turned the pony's head
From the loud waterfall.

By this the stars were almost gone,
The moon was setting on the hill,
So pale you scarcely looked at her:
The little birds began to stir,
Though yet their tongues were still.

The pony, Betty, and her boy,
Wind slowly through the woody dale;
And who is she, betimes abroad,
That hobbles up the steep rough road?
Who is it, but old Susan Gale?

Long time lay Susan lost in thought,
And many dreadful fears beset her,
Both for her messenger and nurse;
And as her mind grew worse and worse,
Her body it grew better.

She turned, she tossed herself in bed,
On all sides doubts and terrors met her;
Point after point did she discuss;
And while her mind was fighting thus,
Her body still grew better.

"Alas! what is become of them?
These fears can never be endured,
I'll to the wood."—The word scarce said,
Did Susan rise up from her bed,
As if by magic cured.

Away she posts uphill and down,
And to the wood at length is come;
She spies her friends, she shouts a greeting;
Oh me! it is a merry meeting
As ever was in Christendom.

The owls have hardly sung their last,
While our four travellers homeward wend;
The owls have hooted all night long,
And with the owls began my song,
And with the owls must end.

For while they all were travelling home,
Cried Betty, "Tell us, Johnny, do,
Where all this long night you have been,
What you have heard, what you have seen,
And, Johnny, mind you tell us true."

Now Johnny all night long had heard
The owls in tuneful concert strive;
No doubt too he the moon had seen;
For in the moonlight he had been
From eight o'clock till five.

And thus, to Betty's question, he
Made answer, like a traveller bold,
(His very words I give to you,)
"The cocks did crow to-whoo, to-whoo,
And the sun did shine so cold."
Thus answered Johnny in his glory,
And that was all his travel's story.

MICHAEL.

A PASTORAL POEM.

If from the public way you turn your steps;
Up the tumultuous brook of Green-head Ghyll,
You will suppose that with an upright path
Your feet must struggle; in such bold ascent
The pastoral mountains front you, face to face.
But, courage! for around that boisterous brook
The mountains have all opened out themselves,
And made a hidden valley of their own.
No habitation can be seen· but they
Who journey thither find themselves alone
With a few sheep, with rocks and stones, and kites
That overhead are sailing in the sky.
It is in truth an utter solitude;
Nor should I have made mention of this dell
But for one object which you might pass by,
Might see and notice not. Beside the brook
Appears a straggling heap of unhewn stones!
And to that place a story appertains,
Which, though it be ungarnished with events,
Is not unfit, I deem, for the fireside,
Or for the summer shade. It was the first
Of those domestic tales that spake to me
Of shepherds, dwellers in the valleys, men
Whom I already loved;—not verily
For their own sakes, but for the fields and hills
Where was their occupation and abode.
And hence this tale, while I was yet a boy
Careless of books, yet having felt the power
Of nature, by the gentle agency
Of natural objects led me on to feel
For passions that were not my own, and think
(At random and imperfectly indeed)
On man, the heart of man, and human life.
Therefore, although it be a history
Homely and rude, I will relate the same
For the delight of a few natural hearts;
And, with yet fonder feeling, for the sake
Of youthful poets, who among these hills
Will be my second self when I am gone.

Upon the forest-side in Grasmere Vale
There dwelt a shepherd, Michael was his name;
An old man, stout of heart, and strong of limb.
His bodily frame had been from youth to age
Of an unusual strength: his mind was keen,
Intense, and frugal, apt for all affairs,
And in his shepherd's calling he was prompt

And watchful more than ordinary men.
Hence had he learned the meaning of all winds,
Of blasts of every tone; and, oftentimes,
When others heeded not, he heard the south
Make subterraneous music, like the noise
Of bagpipers on distant Highland hills.
The shepherd, at such warning, of his flock
Bethought him, and he to himself would say,
"The winds are now devising work for me!"
And, truly, at all times, the storm—that drives
The traveller to a shelter—summoned him
Up to the mountains: he had been alone
Amid the heart of many thousand mists,
That came to him and left him on the heights.
So lived he till his eightieth year was past.
And grossly that man errs, who should suppose
That the green valleys, and the streams and rocks,
Were things indifferent to the shepherd's thoughts.
Fields, where with cheerful spirits he had breathed
The common air; the hills, which he so oft
Had climbed with vigorous steps; which had impressed
So many incidents upon his mind
Of hardship, skill or courage, joy or fear;
Which like a book preserved the memory
Of the dumb animals, whom he had saved,
Had fed or sheltered, linking to such acts,
So grateful in themselves, the certainty
Of honourable gain; these fields, these hills,
Which were his living being, even more
Than his own blood—what could they less? had laid
Strong hold on his affections, were to him
A pleasurable feeling of blind love,
The pleasure which there is in life itself.

His days had not been passed in singleness.
His helpmate was a comely matron, old—
Though younger than himself full twenty years.
She was a woman of a stirring life,
Whose heart was in her house: two wheels she had
Of antique form, this large for spinning wool,
That small for flax; and if one wheel had rest,
It was because the other was at work.
The pair had but one inmate in their house,
An only child, who had been born to them
When Michael, telling o'er his years, began
To deem that he was old,—in shepherd's phrase,
With one foot in the grave. This only son,
With two brave sheep-dogs tried in many a storm,
The one of an inestimable worth,
Made all their household. I may truly say,
That they were as a proverb in the vale
For endless industry. When day was gone,
And from their occupations out of doors
The son and father were come home, even then,
Their labour did not cease; unless when all
Turned to their cleanly supper-board, and there,
Each with a mess of pottage and skimmed milk,
Sat round their basket piled with oaten cakes,
And their plain home-made cheese. Yet when their meal
Was ended, Luke (for so the son was named)
And his old father both betook themselves
To such convenient work as might employ
Their hands by the fire-side; perhaps to card
Wool for the housewife's spindle, or repair
Some injury done to sickle, flail, or scythe,
Or other implement of house or field.

Down from the ceiling by the chimney's edge
That in our ancient uncouth country style
Did with a huge projection overbrow
Large space beneath, as duly as the light
Of day grew dim the housewife hung a lamp;
An aged utensil, which had performed
Service beyond all others of its kind.
Early at evening did it burn and late,
Surviving comrade of uncounted hours,
Which going by from year to year had found
And left the couple neither gay perhaps
Nor cheerful, yet with objects and with hopes,
Living a life of eager industry.
And now, when Luke had reached his eighteenth year
There by the light of this old lamp they sat,
Father and son, while late into the night
The housewife plied her own peculiar work,
Making the cottage through the silent hours
Murmur as with the sound of summer flies.
This light was famous in its neighbourhood,
And was a public symbol of the life
The thrifty pair had lived. For, as it chanced,
Their cottage on a plot of rising ground
Stood single, with large prospect, north and south,
High into Easedale, up to Dunmail-Raise,
And westward to the village near the lake;
And from this constant light, so regular
And so far seen, the house itself, by all
Who dwelt within the limits of the vale,
Both old and young, was named THE EVENING STAR.

Thus living on through such a length of
years, [needs
The shepherd, if he loved himself, must
Have loved his helpmate; but to Michael's
heart
This son of his old age was yet more dear—
Less from instinctive tenderness, the same
Blind spirit, which is in the blood of all—
Than that a child, more than all other gifts,
Brings hope with it, and forward looking
thoughts,
And stirrings of inquietude, when they
By tendency of nature needs must fail.
Exceeding was the love he bare to him,
His heart and his heart's joy! For often-
times
Old Michael, while he was a babe in arms,
Had done him female service, not alone
For pastime and delight, as is the use
Of fathers, but with patient mind enforced
To acts of tenderness; and he had rocked
His cradle with a woman's gentle hand.

And, in a later time, ere yet the boy
Had put on boy's attire, did Michael love,
Albeit of a stern unbending mind,
To have the young one in his sight, when
he
Had work by his own door, or when he sat
With sheep before him on his shepherd's
stool, [door
Beneath that large old oak, which near their
Stood,—and, from its enormous breadth of
shade,
Chosen for the shearer's covert from the sun,
Thence in our rustic dialect was called
The CLIPPING TREE,* a name which yet it
bears. [shade,
There, while they two were sitting in the
With others round them, earnest all and
blithe,
Would Michael exercise his heart with looks
Of fond correction and reproof bestowed
Upon the child, if he disturbed the sheep
By catching at their legs, or with his shouts
Scared them, while they lay still beneath
the shears.

And when by Heaven's good grace the
boy grew up
A healthy lad, and carried in his cheek
Two steady roses that were five years old,
Then Michael from a winter coppice cut
With his own hand a sapling, which he
hooped
With iron, making it throughout in all
Due requisites a perfect shepherd's staff,
And gave it to the boy; wherewith equipt
He as a watchman oftentimes was placed
At gate or gap, to stem or turn the flock;
And, to his office prematurely called,
There stood the urchin, as you will divine,
Something between a hindrance and a
help;
And for this course not always, I believe,
Receiving from his father hire of praise;
Though nought was left undone which
staff or voice, [perform.
Or looks, or threatening gestures could

But soon as Luke, full ten years old, could
stand [heights,
Against the mountain blasts; and to the
Not fearing toil, nor length of weary ways,
He with his father daily went, and they
Were as companions, why should I relate
That objects which the shepherd loved
before [came
Were dearer now? that from the boy there
Feelings and emanations—things which
were
Light to the sun and music to the wind;
And that the old man's heart seemed born
again.
Thus in his father's sight the boy grew up;
And now when he had reached his eigh-
teenth year,
He was his comfort and his daily hope.

While in this sort the simple household
lived [came
From day to day, to Michael's ear there
Distressful tidings. Long before the time
Of which I speak, the shepherd had been
bound
In surety for his brother's son, a man
Of an industrious life, and ample means—
But unforeseen misfortunes suddenly
Had prest upon him,—and old Michael
now [ture,
Was summoned to discharge the forfei-
A grievous penalty, but little less
Than half his substance. This unlooked-
for claim
At the first hearing, for a moment took
More hope out of his life than he supposed
That any old man ever could have lost.
As soon as he had gathered so much
strength
That he could look his trouble in the face
It seemed that his sole refuge was to sell
A portion of his patrimonial fields.
Such was his first resolve; he thought again,

* Clipping is the word used in the North of England for shearing.

And his heart failed him. "Isabel," said he,
Two evenings after he had heard the news,
"I have been toiling more than seventy
years,
And in the open sunshine of God's love
Have we all lived; yet if these fields of ours
Should pass into a stranger's hand, I think
That I could not lie quiet in my grave.
Our lot is a hard lot; the sun himself
Has scarcely been more diligent than I;
And I have lived to be a fool at last
To my own family. An evil man
That was, and made an evil choice, if he
Were false to us; and if he were not false,
There are ten thousand to whom loss like this
Had been no sorrow. I forgive him—but
'Twere better to be dumb than to talk thus.
When I began, my purpose was to speak
Of remedies and of a cheerful hope.
Our Luke shall leave us, Isabel; the land
Shall not go from us, and it shall be free;
He shall possess it free as is the wind
That passes over it. We have, thou knowest,
Another kinsman—he will be our friend
In this distress. He is a prosperous man,
Thriving in trade—and Luke to him shall
go, [thrift
And with his kinsman's help and his own
He quickly will repair this loss, and then
May come again to us. If here he stay,
What can be done? Where every one is
poor, [paused,
What can be gained?" At this the old man
And Isabel sat silent, for her mind
Was busy, looking back into past times.
There's Richard Bateman, thought she to
herself,
He was a parish-boy—at the church-door
They made a gathering for him, shillings,
pence, [bought
And halfpennies, wherewith the neighbours
A basket, which they filled with pedlar's
wares;
And with this basket on his arm, the lad,
Went up to London, found a master there,
Who out of many chose the trusty boy
To go and overlook his merchandise
Beyond the seas: where he grew wondrous
rich,
And left estates and moneys to the poor,
And at his birthplace built a chapel floored
With marble, which he sent from foreign
lands. [sort,
These thoughts, and many others of like
Passed quickly through the mind of Isabel
And her face brightened. The old man
was glad,
And thus resumed:—"Well, Isabel! this
scheme
These two days has been meat and drink
to me.
Far more than we have lost is left us yet.
We have enough—I wish indeed that I
Were younger,—but this hope is a good
hope. [best
Make ready Luke's best garments, of the
Buy for him more, and let us send him
forth
To-morrow, or the next day, or to-night:
If he *could* go, the boy should go to-
night." [forth
Here Michael ceased, and to the fields went
With a light heart. The housewife for five
days [long
Was restless morn and night, and all day
Wrought on with her best fingers to pre-
pare
Things needful for the journey of her son.
But Isabel was glad when Sunday came
To stop her in her work: for, when she lay
By Michael's side, she through the two last
nights [sleep:
Heard him, how he was troubled in his
And when they rose at morning she could
see [noon
That all his hopes were gone. That day at
She said to Luke, while they two by them-
selves [go:
Were sitting at the door, "Thou must not
We have no other child but thee to lose,
None to remember—do not go away,
For if thou leave thy father he will die."
The youth made answer with a jocund
voice;
And Isabel, when she had told her fears,
Recovered heart. That evening her best
fare
Did she bring forth, and all together sat
Like happy people round a Christmas fire.

With daylight Isabel resumed her work;
And all the ensuing week the house ap-
peared
As cheerful as a grove in spring: at length
The expected letter from their kinsman
came,
With kind assurances that he would do
His utmost for the welfare of the boy;
To which, requests were added, that forth-
with [more
He might be sent to him. Ten times or
The letter was read over; Isabel
Went forth to show it to the neighbours
round;
Nor was there at that time on English land

A prouder heart than Luke's. When Isabel
Had to her house returned, the old man
said, [word
"He shall depart to-morrow." To this
The housewife answered, talking much of
things
Which, if at such short notice he should go,
Would surely be forgotten. But at length
She gave consent, and Michael was at
ease.

Near the tumultuous brook of Green-
head Ghyll,
In that deep valley, Michael had designed
To build a sheep-fold; and, before he
heard
The tidings of his melancholy loss,
For this same purpose he had gathered up
A heap of stones, which by the streamlet's
edge
Lay thrown together, ready for the work.
With Luke that evening thitherward he
walked; [stopped,
And soon as they had reached the place he
And thus the old man spake to him.—"My
son, [heart
To-morrow thou wilt leave me: with full
I look upon thee, for thou art the same
That wert a promise to me ere thy birth,
And all thy life hast been my daily joy.
I will relate to thee some little part
Of our two histories; 'twill do thee good
When thou art from me, even if I should
speak [After thou
Of things thou canst not know of.——
First cam'st into the world—as oft befalls
To new-born infants—thou didst sleep
away [tongue
Two days, and blessings from thy father's
Then fell upon thee. Day by day passed
on,
And still I loved thee with increasing love.
Never to living ear came sweeter sounds
Than when I heard thee by our own fire-
side [tune;
First uttering, without words, a natural
When thou, a feeding babe, didst in thy
joy [lowed month,
Sing at thy mother's breast. Month fol-
And in the open fields my life was passed
And on the mountains, else I think that
thou [knees.
Hadst been brought up upon thy father's
But we were playmates, Luke: among
these hills, [young
As well thou know'st, in us the old and
Have played together, nor with me didst
thou
Lack any pleasure which a boy can know."
Luke had a manly heart; but at these
words [his hand,
He sobbed aloud. The old man grasped
And said, "Nay, do not take it so—I see
That these are things of which I need not
speak.
Even to the utmost I have been to thee
A kind and a good father: and herein
I but repay a gift which I myself
Received at others' hands; for, though now
old
Beyond the common life of man, I still
Remember them who loved me in my
youth.
Both of them sleep together: here they lived
As all their forefathers had done; and when
At length their time was come, they were
not loath
To give their bodies to the family mould.
I wished that thou shouldst live the life
they lived.
But 'tis a long time to look back, my son,
And see so little gain from threescore years.
These fields were burthened when they
came to me;
Till I was forty years of age, not more
Than half of my inheritance was mine.
I toiled and toiled; God blessed me in my
work, [was free.
And till these three weeks past the land
It looks as if it never could endure
Another master. Heaven forgive me, Luke,
If I judge ill for thee, but it seems good
That thou shouldst go." At this the old
man paused; [they stood,
Then, pointing to the stones near which
Thus, after a short silence, he resumed:
"This was a work for us; and now, my
son,
It is a work for me. But, lay one stone—
Here, lay it for me, Luke, with thine own
hands. [live
Nay, boy, be of good hope;—we both may
To see a better day. At eighty-four
I still am strong and hale;—do thou thy
part,
I will do mine.—I will begin again
With many tasks that were resigned to thee;
Up to the heights, and in among the
storms,
Will I without thee go again, and do
All works which I was wont to do alone,
Before I knew thy face.—Heaven bless
thee, boy! [ing fast
Thy heart these two weeks has been beat-
With many hopes—It should be so—Yes—
yes—

I knew that thou couldst never have a wish
To leave me, Luke: thou hast been bound
to me
Only by links of love: when thou art gone,
What will be left to us!—But, I forget
My purposes. Lay now the corner-stone,
As I requested; and hereafter, Luke,
When thou art gone away, should evil men
Be thy companions, think of me, my son,
And of this moment; hither turn thy
thoughts, [fear
And God will strengthen thee: amid all
And all temptation, Luke, I pray that thou
Mayst bear in mind the life thy fathers
lived,
Who, being innocent, did for that cause
Bestir them in good deeds. Now, fare
thee well— [wilt see
When thou return'st, thou in this place
A work which is not here: a covenant
'Twill be between us——But, whatever fate
Befall thee, I shall love thee to the last,
And bear thy memory with me to the grave."

The shepherd ended here; and Luke
stooped down,
And, as his father had requested, laid
The first stone of the sheep-fold. At the
sight [his heart
The old man's grief broke from him; to
He pressed his son, he kissèd him and
wept;
And to the house together they returned.
Hushed was that house in peace, or
seeming peace, [the boy
Ere the night fell;—with morrow's dawn
Began his journey, and when he had
reached
The public way, he put on a bold face;
And all the neighbours as he passed their
doors [prayers,
Came forth with wishes and with farewell
That followed him till he was out of sight.

A good report did from their kinsman
come,
Of Luke and his well-doing: and the boy
Wrote loving letters, full of wondrous news,
Which, as the housewife phrased it, were
throughout
"The prettiest letters that were ever seen."
Both parents read them with rejoicing
hearts. [again
So, many months passed on: and once
The shepherd went about his daily work
With confident and cheerful thoughts; and
now [hour
Sometimes when he could find a leisure
He to that valley took his way, and there
Wrought at the sheep-fold. Meantime
Luke began
To slacken in his duty; and at length
He in the dissolute city gave himself
To evil courses: ignominy and shame
Fell on him, so that he was driven at last
To seek a hiding-place beyond the seas.

There is a comfort in the strength of love;
'Twill make a thing endurable, which else
Would overset the brain, or break the
heart: [well
I have conversed with more than one who
Remember the old man, and what he was
Years after he had heard this heavy news.
His bodily frame had been from youth to
age [rocks
Of an unusual strength. Among the
He went, and still looked up upon the sun,
And listened to the wind; and as before
Performed all kinds of labour for his sheep,
And for the land his small inheritance.
And to that hollow dell from time to
time
Did he repair, to build the fold of which
His flock had need. 'Tis not forgotten yet
The pity which was then in every heart
For the old man—and 'tis believed by all
That many and many a day he thither
went,
And never lifted up a single stone.

There, by the sheep-fold, sometimes was
he seen
Sitting alone, with that his faithful dog,
Then old, beside him, lying at his feet.
The length of full seven years from time to
time [wrought,
He at the building of this sheep-fold
And left the work unfinished when he died.
Three years, or little more, did Isabel
Survive her husband: at her death the
estate
Was sold, and went into a stranger's hand.
The cottage which was named the EVENING
STAR [the ground
Is gone—the ploughshare has been through
On which it stood; great changes have
been wrought [is left
In all the neighbourhood:—yet the oak
That grew beside their door; and the re-
mains
Of the unfinished sheep-fold may be seen
Beside the boisterous brook of Green-head
Ghyll.

THE WAGGONER.

To Charles Lamb, Esq.

My Dear Friend,—When I sent you, a few weeks ago, the Tale of Peter Bell, you asked "why The Waggoner was not added?" To say the truth,—from the higher tone of imagination, and the deeper touches of passion aimed at in the former, I apprehended, this little piece could not accompany it without disadvantage. In the year 1806, if I am not mistaken, The Waggoner was read to you in manuscript: and, as you have remembered it for so long a time, I am the more encouraged to hope, that, since the localities on which it partly depends did not prevent its being interesting to you, it may prove acceptable to others. Being therefore in some measure the cause of its present appearance, you must allow me the gratification of inscribing it to you; in acknowledgment of the pleasure I have derived from your writings, and of the high esteem with which I am, very truly yours,

William Wordsworth.

Rydal Mount, *May* 20, 1819.

CANTO I.

'Tis spent—this burning day of June!
Soft darkness o'er its latest gleams is stealing;
The dor-hawk, solitary bird,
Round the dim crags on heavy pinions wheeling,
Buzzes incessantly, a tiresome tune;
That constant voice is all that can be heard
In silence deeper far than that of deepest noon!

Confiding glow-worms! 'tis a night
Propitious to your earth-born light;
But, where the scattered stars are seen
In hazy straits the clouds between,
Each, in his station twinkling not,
Seems changed into a pallid spot.
The air, as in a lion's den,
Is close and hot;—and now and then
Comes a tired and sultry breeze
With a haunting and a panting,
Like the stifling of disease;
The mountains rise to wondrous height,
And in the heavens there hangs a weight;
But the dews allay the heat,
And the silence makes it sweet.

Hush, there is some one on the stir!
'Tis Benjamin the waggoner;—
Who long hath trod this toilsome way,
Companion of the night and day.
That far-off tinkling's drowsy cheer,
Mixed with a faint yet grating sound
In a moment lost and found,
The wain announces—by whose side,
Along the banks of Rydal Mere,
He paces on, a trusty guide,—
Listen! you can scarcely hear!
Hither he his course is bending;—
Now he leaves the lower ground,
And up the craggy hill ascending
Many a stop and stay he makes,
Many a breathing-fit he takes;—
Steep the way and wearisome,
Yet all the while his whip is dumb!

The horses have worked with right good will,
And now have gained the top of the hill;
He was patient—they were strong—
And now they smoothly glide along,
Gathering breath, and pleased to win
The praises of mild Benjamin.
Heaven shield him from mishap and snare!
But why so early with this prayer?
Is it for threatenings in the sky?
Or for some other danger nigh?
No, none is near him yet, though he
Be one of much infirmity;
For, at the bottom of the brow,
Where once the Dove and Olive-bough
Offered a greeting of good ale
To all who entered Grasmere Vale;
And called on him who must depart
To leave it with a jovial heart;—
There, where the Dove and Olive-bough
Once hung, a poet harbours now,—
A simple water-drinking bard;
Why need our hero, then, (though frail
His best resolves) be on his guard?
He marches by, secure and bold,—
Yet, while he thinks on times of old,
It seems that all looks wondrous cold;
He shrugs his shoulders—shakes his head—
And, for the honest folk within,
It is a doubt with Benjamin
Whether they be alive or dead!

Here is no danger,—none at all!
Beyond his wish is he secure;
But pass a mile—and *then* for trial,—
Then for the pride of self-denial;
If he resist that tempting door,
Which with such friendly voice will call,
If he resist those casement panes,

And that bright gleam which thence will [fall
Upon his leaders' bells and manes,
Inviting him with cheerful lure;
For still, though all be dark elsewhere,
Some shining notice will be *there*,
Of open house and ready fare.

The place to Benjamin full well
Is known, and by as strong a spell
As used to be that sign of love
And hope—the OLIVE-BOUGH and DOVE
He knows it to his cost, good man!
Who does not know the famous SWAN?
Uncouth although the object be,
An image of perplexity;
Yet not the less it is our boast,
For it was painted by the host;
His own conceit the figure planned,
'Twas coloured all by his own hand;
And that frail child of thirsty clay,
Of whom I sing this rustic lay,
Could tell with self-dissatisfaction
Quaint stories of the bird's attraction!*

Well! that is past—and in despite
Of open door and shining light.
And now the conqueror essays
The long ascent of Dunmail-raise;
And with his team is gentle here
As when he clomb from Rydal Mere;
His whip they do not dread—his voice
They only hear it to rejoice.
To stand or go is at *their* pleasure;
Their efforts and their time they measure
By generous pride within the breast
And, while they strain, and while they rest,
He thus pursues his thoughts at leisure.

Now am I fairly safe to-night—
And never was my heart more light.
I trespassed lately worse than ever—
But Heaven will bless a good endeavour;
And, to my soul's delight, I find
The evil one is left behind.
Yes, let my master fume and fret,
Here am I—with my horses yet!
My jolly team, he finds that ye
Will work for nobody but me!
Good proof of this the country gained,
One day, when ye were vexed and strained—
Intrusted to another's care,
And forced unworthy stripes to bear.
Here was it—on this rugged spot
Which now, contented with our lot,
We climb—that, piteously abused,
Ye plunged in anger and confused:
As chance would have it, passing by
I saw you in your jeopardy:
A word from me was like a charm—
The ranks were taken with one mind;
And your huge burthen, safe from harm,
Moved like a vessel in the wind!
Yes, without me, up hills so high
'Tis vain to strive for mastery.
Then grieve not, jolly team! though tough
The road we travel, steep and rough.
Though Rydal-heights and Dunmail-raise,
And all their fellow banks and braes,
Full often make you stretch and strain,
And halt for breath and halt again,
Yet to their sturdiness 'tis owing
That side by side we still are going!

While Benjamin in earnest mood
His meditations thus pursued,
A storm, which had been smothered long.
Was growing inwardly more strong;
And, in its struggles to get free.
Was busily employed as he.
The thunder had begun to growl—
He heard not, too intent of soul;
The air was now without a breath—
He marked not that 'twas still as death.
But soon large drops upon his head
Fell with the weight of drops of lead;—
He starts—and, at the admonition,
Takes a survey of his condition.
The road is black before his eyes,
Glimmering faintly where it lies;
Black is the sky—and every hill,
Up to the sky, is blacker still;
A huge and melancholy room,
Hung round and overhung with gloom!
Save that above a single height
Is to be seen a lurid light,
Above Helm-crag†—a streak half dead,
A burning of portentous red;
And, near that lurid light, full well
The ASTROLOGER, sage Sidrophel,
Where at his desk and book he sits,
Puzzling on high his curious wits;
He whose domain is held in common
With no one but the ANCIENT WOMAN,
Cowering beside her rifted cell;
As if intent on magic spell;—
Dread pair, that spite of wind and weather,
Still sit upon Helm-crag together!

* This rude piece of self-taught art such is the progress of refinement has been supplanted by a professional production.

† A mountain of Grasmere, the broken summit of which presents two figures, full as distinctly shaped as that of the famous Cobbler, near Arroquhar, in Scotland.

The ASTROLOGER was not unseen
By solitary Benjamin:
But total darkness came anon,
And he and everything was gone.
And suddenly a ruffling breeze,
(That would have sounded through the trees
Had aught of sylvan growth been there)
Was felt throughout the region bare:
The rain rushed down—the road was battered,
As with the force of billows shattered;
The horses are dismayed, nor know
Whether they should stand or go;
And Benjamin is groping near them,
Sees nothing, and can scarcely hear them.
He is astounded,—wonder not,—
With such a charge in such a spot;
Astounded in the mountain gap
By peals of thunder, clap on clap!
And many a terror-striking flash;—
And somewhere, as it seems, a crash,
Among the rocks; with weight of rain,
And sullen motions long and slow,
That to a dreary distance go—
Till, breaking in upon the dying strain,
A rending o'er his head begins the fray again.

Meanwhile, uncertain what to do,
And oftentimes compelled to halt,
The horses cautiously pursue
Their way, without mishap or fault;
And now have reached that pile of stones,
Heaped over brave King Dunmail's bones;
He who had once supreme command,
Last king of rocky Cumberland;
His bones, and those of all his power,
Slain here in a disastrous hour!

When, passing through this narrow strait,
Stony, and dark, and desolate,
Benjamin can faintly hear
A voice that comes from some one near,
A female voice:—"Whoe'er you be,
Stop," it exclaimed, "and pity me!"
And less in pity than in wonder,
Amid the darkness and the thunder,
The waggoner, with prompt command,
Summons his horses to a stand.

The voice, to move commiseration,
Prolonged its earnest supplication—
"This storm that beats so furiously—
This dreadful place! oh, pity me!"

While this was said, with sobs between,
And many tears, but all unseen,
There came a flash—a startling glare,
And all Seat-Sandal was laid bare!

'Tis not a time for nice suggestion,
And Benjamin, without further question,
Taking her for some way-worn rover,
Said, "Mount, and get you under cover!"

Another voice, in tone as hoarse
As a swoln brook with rugged course,
Cried out, "Good brother, why so fast?
I've had a glimpse of you—*avast!*
Or, since it suits you to be civil,
Take her at once—for good and evil!"

"It is my husband," softly said
The woman, as if half afraid:
By this time she was snug within,
Through help of honest Benjamin;
She and her babe, which to her breast
With thankfulness the mother pressed;
And now the same strong voice more near
Said cordially, "My friend, what cheer?
Rough doings these! as God's my judge,
The sky owes somebody a grudge!
We've had in half an hour or less
A twelvemonth's terror and distress!"

Then Benjamin entreats the man
Would mount, too, quickly as he can:
The sailor, sailor now no more,
But such he had been heretofore,
To courteous Benjamin replied,
"Go you your way, and mind not me;
For I must have, whate'er betide,
My ass and fifty things beside,—
Go, and I'll follow speedily!"

The waggon moves—and with its load
Descends along the sloping road;
And to a little tent hard by
Turns the sailor instantly;
For when, at closing-in of day,
The family had come that way,
Green pasture and the soft warm air
Had tempted them to settle there.
Green is the grass for beast to graze,
Around the stones of Dunmail-raise!

The sailor gathers up his bed,
Takes down the canvas overhead;
And, after farewell to the place,
A parting word—though not of grace,
Pursues, with ass and all his store,
The way the waggon went before.

CANTO II.

IF Wytheburn's modest house of prayer,
As lowly as the lowliest dwelling,
Had, with its belfry's humble stock,
A little pair that hang in air,

Been mistress also of a clock,
(And one, too, not in crazy plight)
Twelve strokes that clock would have been telling
Under the brow of old Helvellyn—
Its bead-roll of midnight,
Then, when the hero of my tale
Was passing by, and down the vale
(The vale now silent, hushed I ween,
As if a storm had never been)
Proceeding with an easy mind;
While he, who had been left behind,
Intent to use his utmost haste,
Gained ground upon the waggon fast,
And gives another lusty cheer;
For spite of rumbling of the wheels,
A welcome greeting he can hear;—
It is a fiddle in its glee
Dinning from the CHERRY TREE!

Thence the sound—the light is there—
As Benjamin is now aware,
Who, to his inward thoughts confined,
Had almost reached the festive door,
When, startled by the sailor's roar,
He hears a sound and sees the light,
And in a moment calls to mind
That 'tis the village MERRY-NIGHT!*

Although before in no dejection,
At this insidious recollection
His heart with sudden joy is filled,—
His ears are by the music thrilled,
His eyes take pleasure in the road
Glittering before him bright and broad;
And Benjamin is wet and cold,
And there are reasons manifold
That make the good, towards which he's yearning
Look fairly like a lawful earning.

Nor has thought time to come and go,
To vibrate between yes and no;
"For," cries the sailor, "glorious chance
That blew us hither! Let him dance
Who can or will;—my honest soul
Our treat shall be a friendly bowl!"
He draws him to the door—"Come in,
Come, come," cries he to Benjamin;
And Benjamin—ah, woe is me!
Gave the word,—the horses heard
And halted, though reluctantly.

"Blithe souls and lightsome hearts have we
Feasting at the CHERRY TREE!"

This was the outside proclamation,
This was the inside salutation;
What bustling—jostling—high and low!
A universal overflow;
What tankards foaming from the tap!
What store of cakes in every lap!
What thumping—stumping—over-head!
The thunder had not been more busy:
With such a stir, you would have said,
This little place may well be dizzy!
'Tis who can dance with greatest vigour—
'Tis what can be most prompt and eager;
As if it heard the fiddle's call,
The pewter clatters on the wall;
The very bacon shows its feeling,
Swinging from the smoky ceiling!

A steaming bowl—a blazing fire—
What greater good can heart desire?
'Twere worth a wise man's while to try
The utmost anger of the sky;
To *seek* for thoughts of painful cast,
If such be the amends at last.
Now, should you think I judge amiss,
The CHERRY TREE shows proof of this
For soon, of all the happy there,
Our travellers are the happiest pair.
All care with Benjamin is gone—
A Cæsar past the Rubicon!
He thinks not of his long, long strife;—
The sailor man, by nature gay,
Hath no resolves to throw away;
And he hath now forgot his wife,
Hath quite forgotten her—or may be
Deems that she is happier, laid
Within that warm and peaceful bed;
Under cover, terror over,
Sleeping by her sleeping baby.

With bowl in hand, (it may not stand,)
Gladdest of the gladsome band,
Amid their own delight and fun,
They hear—when every dance is done—
They hear—when every fit is o'er—
The fiddle's *squeak*†—that call to bliss,
Ever followed by a kiss;
They envy not the happy lot,
But enjoy their own the more!

While thus our jocund travellers fare,
Up springs the sailor from his chair—

* A term well known in the north of England, and applied to rural festivals where young persons meet in the evening for the purpose of dancing.

† At the close of each strathspey, or jig, a particular note from the fiddle summons the rustic to the agreeable duty of saluting his partner.

Limps (for I might have told before
That he was lame) across the floor—
Is gone—returns—and with a prize!
With what? a ship of lusty size,
A gallant stately man of war,
Fixed on a smoothly-sliding car
Surprise to all, but most surprise
To Benjamin, who rubs his eyes,
Not knowing that he had befriended
A man so gloriously attended!

"This," cries the sailor, "a third-rate is,
Stand back, and you shall see her gratis!
This was the flag-ship at the Nile,
The Vanguard—you may smirk and smile,
But, pretty maid, if you look near,
You'll find you've much in little here!
A nobler ship did never swim,
And you shall see her in full trim.
I'll set, my friends, to do you honour,
Set every inch of sail upon her."
So said, so done, and masts, sails, yards,
He names them all, and interlards
His speech with uncouth terms of art,
Accomplished in the showman's part,
And then, as from a sudden check,
Cries out—"'Tis there, the quarter-deck
On which brave Admiral Nelson stood—
A sight that would have roused your blood!
One eye he had, which, bright as ten,
Burnt like a fire among his men,
Let this be land, and that be sea,
Here lay the French—and *thus* came we!"

Hushed was by this the fiddle's sound,
The dancers all were gathered round,
And, such the stillness of the house,
You might have heard a nibbling mouse;
While, borrowing helps where'er he may,
The sailor through the story runs
Of ships to ships and guns to guns;
And does his utmost to display
The dismal conflict, and the might
And terror of that wondrous night!
"A bowl, a bowl of double measure,"
Cries Benjamin, "a draught of length,
To Nelson, England's pride and treasure,
Her bulwark and her tower of strength!"
When Benjamin had seized the bowl,
The mastiff from beneath the waggon,
Where he lay, watchful as a dragon,
Rattled his chain—'twas all in vain,
For Benjamin, triumphant soul!
He heard the monitory growl;
Heard—and in opposition quaffed
A deep, determined, desperate draught!
Nor did the battered tar forget,
Or flinch from what he deemed his debt.
Then, like a hero crowned with laurel,
Back to her place the ship he led;
Wheeled her back in full apparel;
And so, flag flying at mast-head,
Re-yoked her to the ass—anon,
Cries Benjamin, "We must be gone."
Thus, after two hours' hearty stay,
Again behold them on their way!

CANTO III.

Right gladly had the horses stirred,
When they the wished-for greeting heard,
The whip's loud notice from the door,
That they were free to move once more
You think these doings must have bred
In them disheartening doubts and dread,
No, not a horse of all the eight,
Although it be a moonless night,
Fears either for himself or freight,
For this they know, (and let it hide,
In part, the offences of their guide,)
That Benjamin, with clouded brains,
Is worth the best with all their pains;
And, if they had a prayer to make,
The prayer would be that they may take
With him whatever comes in course,
The better fortune or the worse, [them
That no one else may have business near
And, drunk or sober, he may steer them.

So, forth in dauntless mood they fare,
And with them goes the guardian pair

Now, heroes, for the true commotion,
The triumph of your late devotion!
Can aught on earth impede delight,
Still mounting to a higher height;
And higher still—a greedy flight!
Can any low-born care pursue her,
Can any mortal clog come to her?
No notion have they—not a thought,
That is from joyless regions brought!
And, while they coast the silent lake,
Their inspiration I partake;
Share their empyreal spirits—yea,
With their enraptured vision, see—
O fancy—what a jubilee!
What shifting pictures—clad in gleam
Of colour bright as feverish dreams!
Earth, spangled sky, and lake serene,
Involved and restless all—a scene
Pregnant with mutual exaltation,
Rich change, and multiplied creation!
This sight to me the muse imparts;—
And then, what kindness in their hearts!
What tears of rapture, what vow-making,
Profound entreaties, and hand-shaking!

What solemn, vacant interlacing,
As if they'd fall asleep embracing!
Then, in the turbulence of glee,
And in the excess of amity,
Says Benjamin, "That ass of thine,
He spoils thy sport, and hinders mine;
If he were tethered to the waggon,
He'd drag as well what he is dragging;
And we, as brother should with brother,
Might trudge it alongside each other?"

Forthwith, obedient to command,
The horses made a quiet stand;
And to the waggon's skirts was tied
The creature, by the mastiff's side
(The mastiff not well pleased to be
So very near such company).
This new arrangement made, the wain
Through the still night proceeds again:
No moon had risen her light to lend;
But indistinctly may be kenned
The VANGUARD, following close behind,
Sails spread, as if to catch the wind!

"Thy wife and child are snug and warm,
Thy ship will travel without harm;
I like," said Benjamin, "her shape and stature;
And this of mine—this bulky creature
Of which I have the steering—this,
Seen fairly, is not much amiss!
We want your streamers, friend, you know;
But altogether, as we go,
We make a kind of handsome show!
Among these hills from first to last,
We've weathered many a furious blast;
Hard passage forcing on, with head
Against the storm, and canvas spread.
I hate a boaster—but to thee
Will say't, who know'st both land and sea,
The unluckiest hulk that sails the brine
Is hardly worse beset than mine,
When cross winds on her quarter beat;
And, fairly lifted from my feet,
I stagger onward—Heaven knows how—
But not so pleasantly as now—
Poor pilot I, by snows confounded,
And many a foundrous pit surrounded!
Yet here we are, by night and day
Grinding through rough and smooth our way,
Through foul and fair our task fulfilling;
And long shall be so yet—God willing!"

"Ay," said the tar, "through fair and foul—
But save us from yon screeching owl!"
That instant was begun a fray
Which called their thoughts another way:
The mastiff, ill-conditioned carl!
What must he do but growl and snarl,
Still more and more dissatisfied
With the meek comrade at his side?
Till, not incensed, though put to proof,
The ass, uplifting a hind hoof,
Salutes the mastiff on the head;
And so were better manners bred,
And all was calmed and quieted.

"Yon screech-owl," says the sailor turning
Back to his former cause of mourning,
"Yon owl!—pray God that all be well!
'Tis worse than any funeral bell;
As sure as I've the gift of sight,
We shall be meeting ghosts to-night!"
Said Benjamin, "This whip shall lay
A thousand if they cross our way.
I know that wanton's noisy station,
I know him and his occupation;
The jolly bird hath learned his cheer
On the banks of Windermere;
Where a tribe of them make merry,
Mocking the man that keeps the ferry,
Halloing from an open throat,
Like travellers shouting for a boat.
The tricks he learned at Windermere
This vagrant owl is playing here—
That is the worst of his employment;
He's in the height of his enjoyment!"

This explanation stilled the alarm,
Cured the foreboder like a charm;
This, and the manner, and the voice,
Summoned the sailor to rejoice;
His heart is up—he fears no evil
From life or death, from man or devil;
He wheeled—and, making many stops,
Brandished his crutch against the mountain tops;
And, while he talked of blows and scars,
Benjamin, among the stars,
Beheld a dancing—and a glancing;
Such retreating and advancing
As, I ween, was never seen
In bloodiest battle since the days of Mars

CANTO IV.

THUS they, with freaks of proud delight,
Beguile the remnant of the night;
And many a snatch of jovial song
Regales them as they wind along;
While to the music from on high,
The echoes make a glad reply.
But the sage muse the revel heeds
No farther than her story needs;

Nor will she servilely attend
The loitering journey to its end
Blithe spirits of her own impel
The muse who scents the morning air,
To take of this transported pair
A brief and unreproved farewell;
To quit the slow-paced waggon's side,
And wander down yon hawthorn dell,
With murmuring Greta for her guide.
There doth she ken the awful form
Of Raven-crag—black as a storm—
Glimmering through the twilight pale,
And Gimmer-crag,* his tall twin-brother,
Each peering forth to meet the other,—
And, while she roves through St. John's Vale,
Along the smooth unpathwayed plain,
By sheep-track, or through cottage lane,
Where no disturbance comes to intrude
Upon the pensive solitude,
Her unsuspecting eye, perchance,
With the rude shepherd's favoured glance,
Beholds the faeries in array,
Whose party-coloured garments gay
The silent company betray;
Red, green, and blue; a moment's sight!
For Skiddaw-top with rosy light
Is touched—and all the band take flight
Fly also, muse! and from the dell
Mount to the ridge of Nathdale Fell;
Thence look thou forth o'er wood and lawn,
Hoar with the frost-like dews of dawn,
Across yon meadowy bottom look,
Where close fogs hide their parent brook;
And see, beyond that hamlet small,
The ruined towers of Threlkeld Hall,
Lurking in a double shade,
By trees and lingering twilight made!
There, at Blencathara's rugged feet,
Sir Lancelot gave a safe retreat
To noble Clifford; from annoy
Concealed the persecuted boy,
Well pleased in rustic garb to feed
His flock, and pipe on shepherd's reed;
Among this multitude of hills,
Crags, woodlands, waterfalls, and rills;
Which soon the morning shall infold,
From east to west, in ample vest
Of massy gloom and radiance bold.

The mists, that o'er the streamlet's bed
Hung low, begin to rise and spread;
Even while I speak, their skirts of gray
Are smitten by a silver ray;

* The crag of the ewe-lamb.

And lo!—up Castrigg's naked steep
(Where, smoothly urged, the vapours sweep
Along—and scatter and divide
Like fleecy clouds self-multiplied)
The stately waggon is ascending
With faithful Benjamin attending,
Apparent now beside his team—
Now lost amid a glittering steam.
And with him goes his sailor friend,
By this time near their journey's end,
And, after their high-minded riot,
Sickening into thoughtful quiet;
As if the morning's pleasant hour
Had for their joys a killing power.

They are drooping, weak, and dull;
But the horses stretch and pull;
With increasing vigour climb,
Eager to repair lost time;
Whether by their own desert,
Knowing there is cause for shame,
They are labouring to avert
At least a portion of the blame,
Which full surely will alight
Upon *his* head, whom, in despite
Of all his faults they love the best,
Whether for him they are distressed;
Or, by length of fasting roused,
Are impatient to be housed;
Up against the hill they strain—
Tugging at the iron chain—
Tugging all with might and main—
Last and foremost, every horse
To the utmost of his force!
And the smoke and respiration
Rising like an exhalation,
Blends with the mist,—a moving shroud
To form—an undissolving cloud;
Which, with slant ray, the merry sun
Takes delight to play upon.
Never surely old Apollo
He, or other god as old,
Of whom in story we are told,
Who had a favourite to follow
Through a battle or elsewhere,
Round the object of his care,
In a time of peril, threw,
Veil of such celestial hue;
Interposed so bright a screen
Him and his enemies between!

Alas, what boots it?—who can hide
When the malicious fates are bent
On working out an ill intent?
Can destiny be turned aside?
No—sad progress of my story!
Benjamin, this outward glory

Cannot shield thee from thy master,
Who from Keswick has pricked forth,
Sour and surly as the north;
And, in fear of some disaster,
Comes to give what help he may,
Or to hear what thou canst say;
If, as needs he must forebode,
Thou hast loitered on the road! [flight—
His doubts—his fears may now take
The wished-for object is in sight;
Yet, trust the muse, it rather hath
Stirred him up to livelier wrath;
Which he stifles, moody man!
With all the patience that he can!
To the end that at your meeting
He may give thee decent greeting.

There he is—resolved to stop,
Till the waggon gains the top;
But stop he cannot—must advance:
Him Benjamin, with lucky glance,
Espies, and instantly is ready,
Self-collected, poised, and steady;
And, to be the better seen,
Issues from his radiant shroud,
From his close attending cloud,
With careless air and open mien.
Erect his port, and firm his going;
So struts yon cock that now is crowing;
And the morning light in grace
Strikes upon his lifted face,
Hurrying the pallid hue away
That might his trespasses betray.
But what can all avail to clear him,
Or what need of explanation,
Parley, or interrogation?
For the master sees, alas!
That unhappy figure near him,
Limping o'er the dewy grass,
Where the road it fringes, sweet,
Soft and cool to way-worn feet;
And, oh, indignity! an ass,
By his noble mastiff's side,
Tethered to the waggon's tail:
And the ship, in all her pride,
Following after in full sail!
Not to speak of babe and mother;
Who, contented with each other,
And, snug as birds in leafy arbour,
Find, within, a blessed harbour!

With eager eyes the master pries:
Looks in and out—and through and
through;
Says nothing—till at last he spies
A wound upon the mastiff's head,
A wound—where plainly might be read
What feats an ass's hoof can do!

But drop the rest:—this aggravation,
This complicated provocation,
A hoard of grievances unsealed;
All past forgiveness it repealed;—
And thus, and through distempered blood
On both sides, Benjamin the good,
The patient, and the tender-hearted,
Was from his team and waggon parted;
When duty of that day was o'er,
Laid down his whip—and served no more.
Nor could the waggon long survive
Which Benjamin had ceased to drive:
It lingered on;—guide after guide
Ambitiously the office tried;
But each unmanageable hill
Called for *his* patience and *his* skill;—
And sure it is, that through this night,
And what the morning brought to light,
Two losses had we to sustain,
We lost both WAGGONER and WAIN!

Accept, O friend, for praise or blame,
The gift of this adventurous song;
A record which I dared to frame,
Though timid scruples checked me long;
They checked me—and I left the theme
Untouched—in spite of many a gleam
Of fancy which thereon was shed,
Like pleasant sunbeams shifting still
Upon the side of a distant hill:
But nature might not be gainsaid;
For what I have and what I miss
I sing of these—it makes my bliss!
Nor is it I who play the part,
But a shy spirit in my heart,
That comes and goes—will sometimes leap
From hiding-places ten years deep;
Or haunts me with familiar face—
Returning, like a ghost unlaid,
Until the debt I owe be paid.
Forgive me, then; for I had been
On friendly terms with this machine:
In him, while he was wont to trace
Our roads, through many a long year's
A living almanack had we: [space,
We had a speaking diary,
That, in this uneventful place,
Gave to the days a mark and name
By which we knew them when they came.
Yes, I, and all about me here,
Through all the changes of the year,
Had seen him through the mountains go,
In pomp of mist or pomp of snow,
Majestically huge and slow:
Or, with a milder grace adorning
The landscape of a summer's morning;

While Grasmere smoothed her liquid plain
The moving image to detain;
And mighty Fairfield, with a chime
Of echoes, to his march kept time;
When little other business stirred,
And little other sound was heard;
In that delicious hour of balm,
Stillness, solitude, and calm,
While yet the valley is arrayed,
On this side with a sober shade;
On that is prodigally bright—
Crag, lawn, and wood—with rosy light.
But most of all, thou lordly wain!
I wish to have thee here again,
When windows flap and chimney roars,
And all is dismal out of doors;
And sitting by my fire, I see
Eight sorry carts, no less a train!
Unworthy successors of thee,
Come straggling through the wind and rain
And oft, as they pass slowly on,
Beneath my window—one by one—
See, perched upon the naked height
The summit of a cumbrous freight,
A single traveller—and there
Another—then perhaps a pair—
The lame, the sickly, and the old;
Men, women, heartless with the cold;
And babes in wet and starveling plight;
Which once, be weather as it might,
Had still a nest within a nest,
Thy shelter—and their mother's breast!
Then most of all, then far the most,
Do I regret what we have lost;
Am grieved for that unhappy sin
Which robbed us of good Benjamin;—
And of his stately charge, which none
Could keep alive when he was gone!

Poems of the Fancy.

A MORNING EXERCISE.

FANCY, who leads the pastimes of the glad,
Full oft is pleased a wayward dart to throw;
Sending sad shadows after things not sad,
Peopling the harmless fields with signs of woe;
Beneath her sway, a simple forest cry
Becomes an echo of man's misery.

Blithe ravens croak of death; and when the owl
Tries his two voices for a favourite strain—
Tu-whit—Tu-whoo! the unsuspecting fowl
Forebodes mishap, or seems but to complain;
Fancy, intent to harass and annoy,
Can thus pervert the evidence of joy.

Through border wilds where naked Indians stray,
Myriads of notes attest her subtle skill;
A feathered task-master cries "WORK AWAY!"
And, in thy iteration, "WHIP-POOR-WILL!"*
Is heard the spirit of a toil-worn slave,
Lashed out of life, not quiet in the grave!

What wonder? at her bidding, ancient lays
Steeped in dire griefs the voice of Philomel;
And that fleet messenger of summer days,
The swallow, twittered subject to like spell;
But ne'er could fancy bend the buoyant lark
To melancholy service—hark! oh, hark!

The daisy sleeps upon the dewy lawn,
Not lifting yet the head that evening bowed;
But *he* is risen, a later star of dawn,
Glittering and twinkling near yon rosy cloud;
Bright gem instinct with music, vocal spark;
The happiest bird that sprang out of the ark!

Hail, blest above all kinds—Supremely skilled
Restless with fixed to balance, high with low,
Thou leav'st the halcyon free her hopes to build
On such forbearance as the deep may show;
Perpetual flight, unchecked by earthly ties,
Leav'st to the wandering bird of paradise

* See Waterton's "Wanderings in South America."

Faithful, though swift as lightning, the meek dove;
Yet more hath nature reconciled in thee;
So constant with thy downward eye of love,
Yet, in aerial singleness, so free;
So humble, yet so ready to rejoice
In power of wing and never-wearied voice!

How would it please old ocean to partake,
With sailors longing for a breeze in vain,
The harmony that thou best lov'st to make
Where earth resembles most his blank domain!
Urania's self might welcome with pleased ear
These matins mounting towards her native sphere.

Chanter by heaven attracted, whom no bars
To day-light known deter from that pursuit,
'Tis well that some sage instinct, when the stars
Come forth at evening, keeps thee still and mute:
For not an eyelid could to sleep incline
Wert thou among them, singing as they shine!

TO THE DAISY.

"Her* divine skill taught me this,
That from every thing I saw
I could some instruction draw,
And raise pleasure to the height
Through the meanest object's sight.
By the murmur of a spring,
Or the least bough's rustelling;
By a daisy whose leaves spread
Shut when Titan goes to bed;
Or a shady bush or tree;
She could more infuse in me
Than all Nature's beauties can
In some other wiser man."—G. WITHER.

In youth from rock to rock I went,
From hill to hill in discontent
Of pleasure high and turbulent,
Most pleased when most uneasy;
But now my own delights I make,—
My thirst at every rill can slake,
And gladly nature's love partake
Of thee, sweet daisy!

When winter decks his few gray hairs,
Thee in the scanty wreath he wears:
Spring parts the clouds with softest airs,
That she may sun thee;
Whole summer fields are thine by right;
And autumn, melancholy wight!
Doth in thy crimson head delight
When rains are on thee.

In shoals and bands, a morrice train,
Thou greet'st the traveller in the lane;
If welcome once thou count'st it gain;
Thou art not daunted,
Nor car'st if thou be set at nought
And oft alone in nooks remote
We meet thee, like a pleasant thought,
When such are wanted.

Be violets in their secret mews
The flowers the wanton zephyrs choose;
Proud be the rose, with rains and dews
Her head impearling;
Thou liv'st with less ambitious aim,
Yet hast not gone without thy fame·
Thou art indeed by many a claim
The poet's darling.

If to a rock from rains he fly,
Or, some bright day of April sky,
Imprisoned by hot sunshine lie
Near the green holly,
And wearily at length should fare;
He needs but look about, and there
Thou art!—a friend at hand, to scare
His melancholy.

A hundred times, by rock or bower,
Ere thus I have lain couched an hour,
Have I derived from thy sweet power
Some apprehension;
Some steady love; some brief delight;
Some memory that had taken flight;
Some chime of fancy wrong or right;
Or stray invention.

If stately passions in me burn,
And one chance look to thee should turn,
I drink out of an humbler urn
A lowlier pleasure;
The homely sympathy that heeds
The common life, our nature breeds;
A wisdom fitted to the needs
Of hearts at leisure.

When, smitten by the morning ray,
I see thee rise, alert and gay,
Then, cheerful flower! my spirits play
With kindred gladness:
And when, at dusk, by dews opprest
Thou sink'st, the image of thy rest
Hath often eased my pensive breast
Of careful sadness.

* His muse.

And all day long I number yet,
All seasons through, another debt,
Which I, wherever thou art met,
To thee am owing;
An instinct call it, a blind sense;
A happy, genial influence,
Coming one knows not how, nor whence,
Nor whither going.

Child of the year! that round dost run
Thy course, bold lover of the sun,
And cheerful when the day's begun
As morning leveret,
Thy long-lost praise* thou shalt regain;
Dear shalt thou be to future men
As in old time;—thou not in vain,
Art nature's favourite.

A WHIRL-BLAST from behind the hill
Rushed o'er the wood with startling sound;
Then—all at once the air was still,
And showers of hailstones pattered round.
Where leafless oaks towered high above,
I sat within an undergrove
Of tallest hollies, tall and green;
A fairer bower was never seen.
From year to year the spacious floor
With withered leaves is covered o'er,
And all the year the bower is green.
But see! where'er the hailstones drop,
The withered leaves all skip and hop,
There's not a breeze—no breath of air—
Yet here, and there, and every where
Along the floor, beneath the shade
By those embowering hollies made,
The leaves in myriads jump and spring,
As if with pipes and music rare
Some Robin Good-fellow were there,
And all those leaves, in festive glee,
Were dancing to the minstrelsy.

THE GREEN LINNET.

BENEATH these fruit-tree boughs that shed
Their snow-white blossoms on thy head,
With brightest sunshine round me spread
Of spring's unclouded weather,
In this sequestered nook how sweet
To sit upon my orchard-seat!
And birds and flowers once more to greet,
My last year's friends together.

One have I marked, the happiest guest
In all this covert of the blest;
Hail to thee, far above the rest
In joy of voice and pinion,
Thou, linnet! in thy green array,
Presiding spirit here to-day,
Dost lead the revels of the May,
And this is thy dominion.

While birds, and butterflies, and flowers
Make all one band of paramours,
Thou, ranging up and down the bowers,
Art sole in thy employment;
A life, a presence like the air,
Scattering thy gladness without care,
Too blest with any one to pair,
Thyself thy own enjoyment.

Upon yon tuft of hazel trees,
That twinkle to the gusty breeze,
Behold him perched in ecstasies,
Yet seeming still to hover;
There! where the flutter of his wings
Upon his back and body flings
Shadows and sunny glimmerings,
That cover him all over.

My sight he dazzles, half deceives,
A bird so like the dancing leaves;
Then flits, and from the cottage eaves
Pours forth his song in gushes;
As if by that exulting strain
He mocked and treated with disdain
The voiceless form he chose to feign,
While fluttering in the bushes.

THE CONTRAST.

WITHIN her gilded cage confined,
I saw a dazzling belle,
A parrot of that famous kind
Whose name is NONPAREIL.

Like beads of glossy jet her eyes;
And, smoothed by nature's skill,
With pearl or gleaming agate vies
Her finely-curvèd bill.

Her plumy mantle's living hues
In mass opposed to mass,
Outshine the splendour that imbues
The robes of pictured glass.

And, sooth to say, an apter mate
Did never tempt the choice
Of feathered thing most delicate
In figure and in voice.

* See, in Chaucer and the elder poets, the honours formerly paid to this flower.

But, exiled from Australian bowers,
And singleness her lot,
She trills her song with tutored powers,
Or mocks each casual note.

No more of pity for regrets
With which she may have striven!
Now but in wantonness she frets,
Or spite, if cause be given;

Arch, volatile, a sportive bird
By social glee inspired,
Ambitious to be seen or heard,
And pleased to be admired!

This moss-lined shed, green, soft, and dry,
Harbours a self-contented wren,
Not shunning man's abode, though shy,
Almost as thought itself, of human ken.

Strange places, coverts unendeared
She never tried, the very nest
In which this child of spring was reared,
Is warmed, through winter, by her feathery breast.

To the bleak winds she sometimes gives
A slender unexpected strain;
That tells the hermitess still lives,
Though she appear not, and be sought in vain.

Say, Dora! tell me by yon placid moon,
If called to choose between the favoured pair
Which would you be,—the bird of the saloon,
By lady fingers tended with nice care,
Caressed, applauded, upon dainties fed,
Or nature's DARKLING of this mossy shed?

TO THE SMALL CELANDINE.*

PANSIES, lilies, kingcups, daisies.
Let them live upon their praises;
Long as there's a sun that sets
Primroses will have their glory;
Long as there are violets,
They will have a place in story:
There's a flower that shall be mine,
'Tis the little celandine.

Eyes of some men travel far
For the finding of a star;
Up and down the heavens they go,
Men that keep a mighty rout!
I'm as great as they, I trow,
Since the day I found thee out,
Little flower!—I'll make a stir
Like a great astronomer.

Modest, yet withal an elf
Bold, and lavish of thyself;
Since we needs must first have met
I have seen thee, high and low,
Thirty years or more, and yet
'Twas a face I did not know;
Thou hast now, go where I may,
Fifty greetings in a day.

Ere a leaf is on a bush,
In the time before the thrush
Has a thought about its nest,
Thou wilt come with half a call,
Spreading out thy glossy breast
Like a careless prodigal;
Telling tales about the sun,
When we've little warmth, or none.

Poets, vain men in their mood!
Travel with the multitude;
Never heed them; I aver
That they all are wanton wooers;
But the thrifty cottager,
Who stirs little out of doors,
Joys to spy thee near her home;
Spring is coming, thou art come!

Comfort have thou of thy merit,
Kindly unassuming spirit;
Careless of thy neighbourhood,
Thou dost show thy pleasant face
On the moor, and in the wood,
In the lane—there's not a place,
Howsoever mean it be,
But 'tis good enough for thee.

Ill befall the yellow flowers,
Children of the flaring hours!
Buttercups, that will be seen
Whether we will see or no;
Others, too, of lofty mien;
They have done as worldlings do,
Taken praise that should be thine,
Little, humble celandine!

Prophet of delight and mirth,
Scorned and slighted upon earth!
Herald of a mighty band,
Of a joyous train ensuing,

* Common Pilewort.

Singing at my heart's command,
In the lanes my thoughts pursuing,
I will sing, as doth behove,
Hymns in praise of what I love!

TO THE SAME FLOWER.

PLEASURES newly found are sweet
When they lie about our feet:
February last, my heart
First at sight of thee was glad;
All unheard of as thou art,
Thou must needs, I think, have had,
Celandine! and long ago,
Praise of which I nothing know.

I have not a doubt but he,
Whosoe'er the man might be,
Who the first with pointed rays
(Workman worthy to be sainted)
Set the sign-board in a blaze,
When the risen sun he painted,
Took the fancy from a glance
At thy glittering countenance.

Soon as gentle breezes bring
News of winter's vanishing,
And the children build their bowers,
Sticking 'kerchief-plots of mould
All about with full-blown flowers,
Thick as sheep in shepherd's fold!
With the proudest thou art there,
Mantling in the tiny square.

Often have I sighed to measure
By myself a lonely pleasure,
Sighed to think, I read a book
Only read, perhaps, by me,
Yet I long could overlook
Thy bright coronet and thee,
And thy arch and wily ways,
And thy store of other praise.

Blithe of heart, from week to week
Thou dost play at hide-and-seek;
While the patient primrose sits
Like a beggar in the cold,
Thou, a flower of wiser wits,
Slipp'st into thy sheltered hold;
Bright as any of the train
When ye all are out again

Thou art not beyond the moon,
But a thing "beneath our shoon:"
Let the bold adventurer thrid
In his bark the polar sea;
Rear who will a pyramid;
Praise it is enough for me,
If there be but three or four
Who will love my little flower.

THE WATERFALL AND THE EGLANTINE

"BEGONE, thou fond presumptuous elf,"
Exclaimed a thundering voice,
"Nor dare to thrust thy foolish self
Between me and my choice!"
A small cascade fresh swoln with snows
Thus threatened a poor briar-rose,
That, all bespattered with his foam,
And dancing high and dancing low,
Was living, as a child might know,
In an unhappy home.

"Dost thou presume my course to block?
Off, off! or, puny thing!
I'll hurl thee headlong with the rock
To which thy fibres cling."
The flood was tyrannous and strong;
The patient briar suffered long,
Nor did he utter groan or sigh,
Hoping the danger would be past:
But, seeing no relief, at last
He ventured to reply.

"Ah!" said the briar, "blame me not;
Why should we dwell in strife?
We who in this sequestered spot
Once lived a happy life!
You stirred me on my rocky bed—
What pleasure through my veins you spread!
The summer long, from day to day,
My leaves you freshened and bedewed;
Nor was it common gratitude
That did your cares repay.

"When spring came on with bud and bell,
Among these rocks did I
Before you hang my wreaths, to tell
The gentle days were nigh!
And in the sultry summer hours,
I sheltered you with leaves and flowers;
And in my leaves—now shed and gone,
The linnet lodged, and for us two
Chanted his pretty songs, when you
Had little voice or none.

"But now proud thoughts are in your breast—
What grief is mine you see.
Ah! would you think, even yet how blest
Together we might be!

Though of both leaf and flower bereft,
Some ornaments to me are left—
Rich store of scarlet hips is mine,
With which I in my humble way,
Would deck you many a winter's day,
A happy eglantine!"

What more he said I cannot tell,
The torrent thundered down the dell
With aggravated haste;
I listened, nor aught else could hear;
The briar quaked, and much I fear
Those accents were his last.

THE OAK AND THE BROOM.

A PASTORAL.

HIS simple truths did Andrew glean
Beside the babbling rills;
A careful student he had been
Among the woods and hills.
One winter's night, when through the trees
The wind was roaring, on his knees
His youngest born did Andrew hold:
And while the rest, a ruddy quire,
Were seated round their blazing fire,
This tale the shepherd told:—

"I saw a crag, a lofty stone
As ever tempest beat!
Out of its head an Oak had grown,
A Broom out of its feet.
The time was March, a cheerful noon—
The thaw-wind, with the breath of June,
Breathed gently from the warm south-west:
When, in a voice sedate with age,
This Oak, a giant and a sage,
His neighbour thus addressed:

"'Eight weary weeks, through rock and clay,
Along this mountain's edge,
The frost hath wrought both night and day,
Wedge driving after wedge.
Look up! and think above your head
What trouble, surely, will be bred;
Last night I heard a crash—'tis true,
The splinters took another road—
I see them yonder—what a load
For such a thing as you!

"'You are preparing as before,
To deck your slender shape;
And yet, just three years back—no more—
You had a strange escape.
Down from yon cliff a fragment broke;
In thunder down, with fire and smoke,
And hitherward pursued its way:
This ponderous block was caught by me,
And o'er your head, as you may see,
'Tis hanging to this day!

"'The thing had better been asleep
Whatever thing it were,
Or breeze, or bird, or dog, or sheep,
That first did plant you there.
For you and your green twigs decoy
The little witless shepherd-boy
To come and slumber in your bower;
And, trust me, on some sultry noon,
Both you and he, Heaven knows how soon
Will perish in one hour.

"'From me this friendly warning take'—
The Broom began to doze,
And thus to keep herself awake
Did gently interpose:
'My thanks for your discourse are due;
That more than what you say is true
I know, and I have known it long;
Frail is the bond by which we hold
Our being whether young or old,
Wise, foolish, weak, or strong.

"'Disasters, do the best we can,
Will reach both great and small;
And he is oft the wisest man
Who is not wise at all.
For me, why should I wish to roam!
This spot is my paternal home,
It is my pleasant heritage;
My father many a happy year
Here spent his careless blossoms, here
Attained a good old age.

"'Even such as his may be my lot.
What cause have I to haunt
My heart with terrors? Am I not
In truth a favoured plant!
On me such bounty summer pours,
That I am covered o'er with flowers;
And, when the frost is in the sky,
My branches are so fresh and gay
That you might look at me and say,
This plant can never die.

"'The butterfly, all green and gold,
To me hath often flown,
Here in my blossoms to behold
Wings lovely as his own.
When grass is chill with rain or dew,
Beneath my shade, the mother ewe
Lies with her infant lamb; I see
The love they to each other make,
And the sweet joy, which they partake,
It is a joy to me.'

"Her voice was blithe, her heart was light;
The Broom might have pursued
Her speech, until the stars of night
Their journey had renewed:
But in the branches of the Oak
Two ravens now began to croak
Their nuptial song, a gladsome air;
And to her own green bower the breeze
That instant brought two stripling bees
To rest, or murmur there.

"One night, my children! from the north
There came a furious blast;
At break of day I ventured forth,
And near the cliff I passed.
The storm had fallen upon the Oak,
And struck him with a mighty stroke,
And whirled, and whirled him far away;
And, in one hospitable cleft,
The little careless Broom was left
To live for many a day."

SONG FOR THE SPINNING WHEEL.

FOUNDED UPON A BELIEF PREVALENT AMONG THE PASTORAL VALES OF WESTMORELAND.

SWIFTLY turn the murmuring wheel!
Night has brought the welcome hour,
When the weary fingers feel
Help, as if from faery power,
Dewy night o'ershades the ground;
Turn the swift wheel round and round!

Now, beneath the starry sky,
Crouch the widely-scattered sheep;—
Ply the pleasant labour, ply!
For the spindle, while they sleep,
Runs with motion smooth and fine,
Gathering up a trustier line.

Short-lived likings may be bred
By a glance from fickle eyes,
But true love is like the thread
Which the kindly wool supplies,
When the flocks are all at rest
Sleeping on the mountain's breast.

THE REDBREAST AND BUTTERFLY.

ART thou the bird whom man loves best,
The pious bird with the scarlet breast,
Our little English robin,
The bird that comes about our doors
When autumn winds are sobbing?
Art thou the Peter of Norway boors?
Their Thomas in Finland,
And Russia far inland?
The bird, who by some name or other
All men who know thee call their brother
The darling of children and men?
Could father Adam open his eyes,*
And see this sight beneath the skies,
He'd wish to close them again.

If the butterfly knew but his friend,
Hither his flight he would bend,
And find his way to me
Under the branches of the tree:
In and out, he darts about,
Can this be the bird, to man so good,
That, after their bewildering,
Did cover with leaves the little children,
So painfully in the wood?

What ailed thee, Robin, that thou couldst pursue
A beautiful creature,
That is gentle by nature?
Beneath the summer sky
From flower to flower let him fly;
'Tis all that he wishes to do
The cheerer thou of our indoor sadness,
He is the friend of our summer gladness:
What hinders, then, that ye should be
Playmates in the sunny weather,
And fly about in the air together!
His beautiful wings in crimson are drest,
A crimson as bright as thine own:
If thou wouldst be happy in thy nest,
O pious bird! whom man loves best,
Love him, or leave him alone!

THE KITTEN AND THE FALLING LEAVES.

THAT way look, my infant, lo!
What a pretty baby show!
See the kitten on the wall,
Sporting with the leaves that fall,
Withered leaves—one—two—and three—
From the lofty elder-tree!
Through the calm and frosty air
Of this morning bright and fair,

* See "Paradise Lost," book xi, where Adam points out to Eve the ominous sign of the eagle chasing "two birds of gayest plume," and the gentle hart and hind pursued by their enemy.

Eddying round and round they sink
Softly, slowly: one might think,
From the motions that are made,
Every little leaf conveyed
Sylph or faery hither tending,—
To this lower world descending,
Each invisible and mute,
In his wavering parachute.
——But the kitten, how she starts,
Crouches, stretches, paws, and darts!
First at one, and then its fellow
Just as light and just as yellow;
There are many now—now one—
Now they stop; and there are none—
What intenseness of desire
In her upward eye of fire!
With a tiger-leap half way
Now she meets the coming prey,
Lets it go as fast, and then
Has it in her power again:
Now she works with three or four
Like an Indian conjuror;
Quick as he in feats of art,
Far beyond in joy of heart.
Were her antics played in the eye
Of a thousand standers-by,
Clapping hands with shout and stare,
What would little tabby care
For the plaudits of the crowd?
Over happy to be proud,
Over wealthy in the treasure
Of her own exceeding pleasure!

'Tis a pretty baby-treat,
Nor, I deem, for me unmeet;
Here, for neither babe nor me,
Other playmate can I see.
Of the countless living things,
That with stir of feet and wings,
(In the sun or under shade
Upon bough or grassy blade)
And with busy revellings,
Chirp and song, and murmurings,
Made this orchard's narrow space,
And this vale so blithe a place;
Multitudes are swept away
Never more to breathe the day:
Some are sleeping; some in bands
Travelled into distant lands;
Others slunk to moor and wood,
Far from human neighbourhood;
And, among the kinds that keep
With us closer fellowship,
With us openly abide,
All have laid their mirth aside.
Where is he that giddy sprite,
Blue-cap, with his colours bright,
Who was blest as bird could be,
Feeding in the apple-tree;
Made such wanton spoil and rout,
Turning blossoms inside out;
Hung with head towards the ground,
Fluttered, perched, into a round
Bound himself, and then unbound?
Lithest, gaudiest harlequin!
Prettiest tumbler ever seen!
Light of heart, and light of limb,
What is now become of him!
Lambs that through the mountains went
Frisking, bleating merriment,
When the year was in its prime,
They are sobered by this time.
If you look to vale or hill,
If you listen, all is still,
Save a little neighbouring rill,
That from out the rocky ground
Strikes a solitary sound.
Vainly glitters hill and plain,
And the air is calm in vain;
Vainly morning spreads the lure
Of a sky serene and pure;
Creature none can she decoy
Into open sign of joy:
Is it that they have a fear
Of the dreary season near?
Or that other pleasures be
Sweeter even than gaiety?

Yet, whate'er enjoyments dwell
In the impenetrable cell
Of the silent heart which nature
Furnishes to every creature;
Whatsoe'er we feel and know
Too sedate for outward show,
Such a light of gladness breaks,
Pretty kitten! from thy freaks,—
Spreads with such a living grace
O'er my little Laura's face;
Yes, the sight so stirs and charms
Thee, baby, laughing in my arms,
That almost I could repine
That your transports are not mine,
That I do not wholly fare
Even as ye do, thoughtless pair!
And I will have my careless season
Spite of melancholy reason;
Will walk through life in such a way
That, when time brings on decay,
Now and then I may possess
Hours of perfect gladsomeness.
—Pleased by any random toy;
By a kitten's busy joy,
Or an infant's laughing eye
Sharing in the ecstasy;

I would fare like that or this,
Find my wisdom in my bliss;
Keep the sprightly soul awake.
And have faculties to take,
Even from things by sorrow wrought,
Matter for a jocund thought,
Spite of care, and spite of grief,
To gambol with life's falling leaf.

A FLOWER GARDEN

TELL me, ye zephyrs! that unfold,
While fluttering o'er this gay recess,
Pinions that fanned the teeming mould
Of Eden's blissful wilderness,
Did only softly-stealing hours,
There close the peaceful lives of flowers?

Say, when the *moving* creatures saw
All kinds commingled without fear,
Prevailed alike indulgent law
For the still growths that prosper here?
Did wanton fawn and kid forbear
The half-blown rose, the lily spare?

Or peeped they often from their beds
And prematurely disappeared,
Devoured like pleasure ere it spreads
A bosom to the sun endeared?
If such their harsh untimely doom,
It falls not *here* on bud or bloom.

All summer long the happy Eve
Of this fair spot her flowers may bind,
Nor e'er, with ruffled fancy, grieve,
From the next glance she casts, to find
That love for little things by fate
Is rendered vain as love for great.

Yet, where the guardian fence is wound,
So subtly is the eye beguiled
It sees not nor suspects a bound,
No more than in some forest wild;
Free as the light in semblance—crost
Only by art in nature lost.

And, though the jealous turf refuse
By random footsteps to be prest,
And feeds on never-sullied dews,
Ye, gentle breezes from the west,
With all the ministers of hope,
Are tempted to this sunny slope!

And hither throngs of birds resort:
Some, inmates lodged in shady nests,
Some, perched on stems of stately port
That nod to welcome transient guests,
While hare and leveret, seen at play,
Appear not more shut out than they

Apt emblem (for reproof of pride)
This delicate enclosure shows
Of modest kindness, that would hide
The firm protection she bestows;
Of manners, like its viewless fence,
Ensuring peace to innocence.

Thus spake the moral muse—her wing
Abruptly spreading to depart,
She left that farewell offering,
Memento for some docile heart,
That may respect the good old age
When fancy was truth's willing page,
And truth would skim the flowery glade,
Though entering but as fancy's shade

TO THE DAISY

WITH little here to do or see
Of things that in the great world be,
Sweet daisy! oft I talk to thee,
        For thou art worthy,
Thou unassuming common-place
Of nature, with that homely face,
And yet with something of a grace,
        Which love makes for thee!

Oft on the dappled turf at ease
I sit, and play with similes,
Loose types of things through all degrees
        Thoughts of thy raising·
And many a fond and idle name
I give to thee, for praise or blame,
As is the humour of the game,
        While I am gazing

A nun demure, of lowly port;
Or sprightly maiden, of love's court,
In thy simplicity the sport
        Of all temptations;
A queen in crown of rubies drest;
A starveling in a scanty vest,
Are all, as seems to suit thee best,
        Thy appellations

A little Cyclops, with one eye
Staring to threaten and defy,
That thought comes next—and instantly
        The freak is over,
The shape will vanish, and behold
A silver shield with boss of gold,
That spreads itself, some faery bold
        In fight to cover!

I see thee glittering from afar;—
And then thou art a pretty star;
Not quite so fair as many are
In heaven above thee!
Yet like a star, with glittering crest,
Self-poised in air thou seem'st to rest;—
May peace come never to his nest,
Who shall reprove thee!

Sweet flower! for by that name at last,
When all my reveries are past,
I call thee, and to that cleave fast,
Sweet silent creature!
That breath'st with me in sun and air,
Do thou, as thou art wont, repair
My heart with gladness, and a share
Of thy meek nature!

TO THE SAME FLOWER.

BRIGHT flower, whose home is everywhere!
A pilgrim bold in nature's care,
And all the long year through the heir
Of joy or sorrow,
Methinks that there abides in thee
Some conc rd with humanity,
Given to no other flower I see
The forest thorough!

Is it that man is soon deprest?
A thoughtless thing! who, once unblest,
Does little on his memory rest,
Or on his reason;
But thou wouldst teach him how to find
A shelter under every wind,
A hope for times that are unkind
And every season.

Thou wander'st the wide world about,
Unchecked by pride or scrupulous doubt,
With friends to greet thee, or without,
Yet pleased and willing;
Meek, yielding to the occasion's call,
And all things suffering from all,
Thy function apostolical
In peace fulfilling.

TO A SKY-LARK.

UP with me! up with me into the clouds!
For thy song, lark, is strong;
Up with me, up with me into the clouds!
Singing, singing,
With clouds and sky about thee ringing,
Lift me, guide me till I find
That spot which seems so to thy mind

I have walked through wildernesses dreary,
And to-day my heart is weary;
Had I now the wings of a faery
Up to thee would I fly.
There is madness about thee, and joy divine
In that song of thine;
Up with me, up with me, high and high
To thy banqueting-place in the sky!

Joyous as morning,
Thou art laughing and scorning;
Thou hast a nest for thy love and thy rest,
And, though little troubled with sloth,
Drunken lark! thou wouldst be loth
To be such a traveller as I.
Happy, happy liver,
With a soul as strong as a mountain river
Pouring out praise to the almighty Giver,
Joy and jollity be with us both!

Alas! my journey, rugged and uneven,
Through prickly moors or dusty ways must wind;
But hearing thee, or others of thy kind,
As full of gladness and as free of heaven,
I, with my fate contented, will plod on,
And hope for higher raptures, when life's day is done.

TO A SEXTON.

LET thy wheelbarrow alone—
Wherefore, sexton, piling still
In thy bone-house bone on bone?
'Tis already like a hill
In a field of battle made,
Where three thousand skulls are laid;
These died in peace each with the other,
Father, sister, friend, and brother.

Mark the spot to which I point!
From this platform, eight feet square,
Take not even a finger joint:
Andrew's whole fire-side is there.
Here, alone, before thine eyes,
Simon's sickly daughter lies,
From weakness now, and pain defended
Whom he twenty winters tended.

Look but at the gardener's pride—
How he glories, when he sees
Roses, lilies, side by side,
Violets in families!
By the heart of man, his tears,
By his hopes and by his fears,
Thou, old grey-beard! art the warden
Of a far superior garden.

Thus then, each to other dear,
Let them all in quiet lie,
Andrew there, and Susan here,
Neighbours in mortality
And, should I live through sun and rain
Seven widowed years without my Jane,
O sexton, do not then remove her,
Let one grave hold the loved and lover!

THE CORONET OF SNOWDROPS.

WHO fancied what a pretty sight
This rock would be if edged around
With living snowdrops? circlet bright!
How glorious to this orchard-ground!
Who loved the little rock, and set
Upon its head this coronet?

Was it the humour of a child?
Or rather of some love-sick maid,
Whose brows, the day that she was styled
The shepherd queen, were thus arrayed?
Of man mature, or matron sage?
Or old-man toying with his age?

I asked—'twas whispered—The device
To each and all might well belong:
It is the spirit of Paradise
That prompts such work, a spirit strong,
That gives to all the self-same bent
Where life is wise and innocent.

SONG

FOR THE WANDERING JEW

THOUGH the torrents from their fountains
Roar down many a craggy steep,
Yet they find among the mountains
Resting-places calm and deep.

Clouds that love through air to hasten,
Ere the storm its fury stills,
Helmet-like themselves will fasten
On the heads of towering hills.

What, if through the frozen centre
Of the Alps the chamois bound,
Yet he has a home to enter
In some nook of chosen ground.

If on windy days the raven
Gambol like a dancing skiff,
Not the less she loves her haven
In the bosom of the cliff

Though the sea-horse in the ocean
Own no dear domestic cave,
Yet he slumbers—by the motion
Rocked of many a gentle wave.

The fleet ostrich, till day closes
Vagrant over desert sands,
Brooding on her eggs reposes
When chill night that care demands.

Day and night my toils redouble,
Never nearer to the goal,
Night and day, I feel the trouble
Of the wanderer in my soul.

THE SEVEN SISTERS;

OR, THE SOLITUDE OF BINNORIE

SEVEN daughters had Lord Archibald,
All children of one mother:
I could not say in one short day
What love they bore each other
A garland of seven lilies wrought!
Seven sisters that together dwell,
But he, bold knight as ever fought,
Their father, took of them no thought,
He loved the wars so well.
Sing, mournfully, oh! mournfully,
The solitude of Binnorie!

Fresh blows the wind, a western wind
And from the shores of Erin,
Across the wave, a rover brave
To Binnorie is steering:
Right onward to the Scottish strand
The gallant ship is borne;
The warriors leap upon the land,
And hark! the leader of the band
Hath blown his bugle horn
Sing, mournfully, oh! mournfully,
The solitude of Binnorie.

Beside a grotto of their own,
With boughs above them closing,
The seven are laid, and in the shade
They lie like fawns reposing.
But now, upstarting with affright
At noise of man and steed,
Away they fly to left, to right—
Of your fair household, father knight,
Methinks you take small heed!
Sing, mournfully, oh! mournfully,
The solitude of Binnorie.

Away the seven fair Campbells fly,
And, over hill and hollow,
With menace proud, and insult loud,
The youthful rovers follow

Cried they, "Your father loves to roam:
Enough for him to find
The empty house when he comes home;
For us your yellow ringlets comb,
For us be fair and kind!"
Sing, mournfully, oh! mournfully,
The solitude of Binnorie.

Some close behind, some side by side,
Like clouds in stormy weather,
They run, and cry, "Nay let us die,
And let us die together."
A lake was near; the shore was steep;
There never foot had been;
They ran, and with a desperate leap
Together plunged into the deep,
Nor ever more were seen.
Sing, mournfully, oh! mournfully,
The solitude of Binnorie.

The stream that flows out of the lake,
As through the glen it rambles,
Repeats a moan o'er moss and stone,
For those seven lovely Campbells.
Seven little islands, green and bare,
Have risen from out the deep:
The fishers say, those sisters fair
By fairies are all buried there,
And there together sleep.
Sing, mournfully, oh! mournfully,
The solitude of Binnorie.

THE DANISH BOY.

BETWEEN two sister moorland rills
There is a spot that seems to lie
Sacred to flowerets of the hills,
And sacred to the sky.
And in this smooth and open dell
There is a tempest-stricken tree;
A corner-stone by lightning cut,
The last stone of a cottage hut;
And in this dell you see
A thing no storm can e'er destroy,
The shadow of a Danish boy.*

In clouds above, the lark is heard,
But drops not here to earth for rest:
Within this nook the lonesome bird
Did never build her nest.
No beast, no bird hath here his home:
Bees, wafted on the breezy air,
Pass high above those fragrant bells
To other flowers; to other dells
Their burthens do they bear;
The Danish boy walks here alone:
The lovely dell is all his own.

A spirit of noon-day is he;
He seems a form of flesh and blood;
Nor piping shepherd shall he be,
Nor herd-boy of the wood.
A regal vest of fur he wears,
In colour like a raven's wing;
It fears not rain, nor wind, nor dew;
But in the storm 'tis fresh and blue
As budding pines in spring;
His helmet was a vernal grace,
Fresh as the bloom upon his face

A harp is from his shoulder slung;
He rests the harp upon his knee;
And there, in a forgotten tongue,
He warbles melody.
Of flocks upon the neighbouring hill
He is the darling and the joy;
And often, when no cause appears,
The mountain ponies prick their ears,
They hear the Danish boy,
While in the dell he sits alone
Beside the tree and corner-stone.

There sits he: in his face you spy
No trace of a ferocious air,
Nor ever was a cloudless sky
So steady or so fair.
The lovely Danish boy is blest
And happy in his flowery cove:
From bloody deeds his thoughts are far
And yet he warbles songs of war,
That seem like songs of love,
For calm and gentle is his mien;
Like a dead boy he is serene.

THE PILGRIM'S DREAM;

OR, THE STAR AND THE GLOW-WORM.

A PILGRIM, when the summer day
Had closed upon his weary way,
A lodging begged beneath a castle's roof;
But him the haughty warder spurned;
And from the gate the pilgrim turned,
To seek such covert as the field
Or heath-besprinkled copse might yield,
Or lofty wood, shower-proof.

* These stanzas were designed to introduce a ballad upon the story of a Danish prince who had fled from battle, and for the sake of the valuables about him, was murdered by the inhabitant of a cottage in which he had taken refuge. The house fell under a curse, and the spirit of the youth, it was believed, haunted the valley where the crime had been committed.

He paced along; and, pensively,
Halting beneath a shady tree,
Whose moss-grown root might serve for
couch or seat,
Fixed on a star his upward eye,
Then, from the tenant of the sky
He turned, and watched with kindred look,
A glow-worm, in a dusky nook,
Apparent at his feet.

The murmur of a neighbouring stream
Induced a soft and slumbrous dream,
A pregnant dream, within whose shadowy
bounds
He recognised the earth-born star,
And *that* which glittered from afar;
And (strange to witness!) from the frame
Of the ethereal orb, there came
Intelligible sounds.

Much did it taunt the humbler light
That now, when day was fled, and night
Hushed the dark earth—fast closing weary
eyes,
A very reptile could presume
To show her taper in the gloom,
As if in rivalship with one
Who sate a ruler on his throne
Erected in the skies.

"Exalted star!" the worm replied.
"Abate this unbecoming pride,
Or with a less uneasy lustre shine,
Thou shrink'st as momently thy rays
Are mastered by the breathing haze;
While neither mist, nor thickest cloud
That shapes in heaven its murky shroud,
Hath power to injure mine.

"But not for this do I aspire
To match the spark of local fire,
That at my will burns on the dewy lawn,
With thy acknowledged glories,—No!
Yet, thus upbraided, I may show
What favours do attend me here,
Till, like thyself, I disappear
Before the purple dawn."

When this in modest guise was said,
Across the welkin seemed to spread
A boding sound—for aught but sleep unfit!
Hills quaked—the rivers backward ran—
That star, so proud of late, looked wan;
And reeled with visionary stir
In the blue depth, like Lucifer
Cast headlong to the pit!

Fire raged,—and when the spangled floor
Of ancient ether was no more,
New heavens succeeded, by the dream
brought forth.
And all the happy souls that rode
Transfigured through that fresh abode,
Had heretofore, in humble trust,
Shone meekly 'mid their native dust,
The glow-worms of the earth!

This knowledge, from an angel's voice
Proceeding, made the heart rejoice
Of him who slept upon the open lea
Waking at morn he murmured not,
And, till life's journey closed, the spot
Was to the pilgrim's soul endeared,
Where by that dream he had been cheered
Beneath the shady tree.

HINT FROM THE MOUNTAINS

FOR CERTAIN POLITICAL PRETENDERS.

"WHO but hails the sight with pleasure
When the wings of genius rise,
Their ability to measure
With great enterprise;
But in man was ne'er such daring
As yon hawk exhibits, pairing
His brave spirit with the war in
The stormy skies!

"Mark him, how his power he uses,
Lays it by, at will resumes!
Mark, ere for his haunt he chooses
Clouds and utter glooms!
There he wheels in downward mazes;
Sunward now his flight he raises,
Catches fire, as seems, and blazes
With uninjured plumes!"

ANSWER.

"Stranger, 'tis no act of courage
Which aloft thou dost discern;
No bold *bird* gone forth to forage
'Mid the tempest stern;
But such mockery as the nations
See, when public perturbations
Lift men from their native stations,
Like yon TUFT OF FERN,

"Such it is,—the aspiring creature
Soaring on undaunted wing
(So you fancied) is by nature
A dull helpless thing,

Dry and withered, light and yellow;—
That to be the tempest's fellow!
Wait and you shall see how hollow
Its endeavouring!"

STRAY PLEASURES.

"*Pleasure is spread through the earth*
In stray gifts, to be claimed by whoever shall find."

By their floating mill,
That lies dead and still,
Behold yon prisoners three,
The miller with two dames, on the breast of the Thames!
The platform is small, but gives room for them all;
And they're dancing merrily.

From the shore come the notes
To their mill where it floats,
To their house and their mill tethered fast;
To the small wooden isle where, their work to beguile,
They from morning to even take whatever is given;—
And many a blithe day they have past.

In sight of the spires,
All alive with the fires
Of the sun going down to his rest,
In the broad open eye of the solitary sky,
They dance,—there are three, as jocund as free,
While they dance on the calm river's breast.

Men and maidens wheel,
They themselves make the reel,
And their music's a prey which they seize;
It plays not for them,—what matter? 'tis theirs;
And if they had care, it has scattered their cares,
While they dance, crying, "Long as ye please!"

They dance not for me,
Yet mine is their glee!
Thus pleasure is spread through the earth
In stray gifts, to be claimed by whoever shall find;
Thus a rich loving-kindness, redundantly kind,
Moves all nature to gladness and mirth.

The showers of the spring
Rouse the birds, and they sing;
If the wind do but stir for his proper delight,
Each leaf, that and this, his neighbour will kiss;
Each wave, one and t'other, speeds after his brother;
They are happy, for that is their right!

ON SEEING A NEEDLECASE IN THE FORM OF A HARP,

THE WORK OF E. M. S.

Frowns are on every muse's face,
Reproaches from their lips are sent,
That mimickry should thus disgrace
The noble instrument.

A very harp in all but size!
Needles for strings in apt gradation!
Minerva's self would stigmatize
The unclassic profanation.

Even her *own* needle that subdued
Arachne's rival spirit,
Though wrought in Vulcan's happiest mood,
Like station could not merit.

And this, too, from the laureate's child,
A living lord of melody!
How will her sire be reconciled
To the refined indignity?

I spake, when whispered a low voice,
"Bard! moderate your ire;
Spirits of all degrees rejoice
In presence of the lyre.

"The minstrels of pygmean bands,
Dwarf genii, moonlight-loving fays,
Have shells to fit their tiny hands
And suit their slender lays.

"Some, still more delicate of ear,
Have lutes (believe my words)
Whose framework is of gossamer,
While sunbeams are the chords.

"Gay sylphs this miniature will court,
Made vocal by their brushing wings,
And sullen gnomes will learn to sport
Around its polished strings;

"Whence strains to love-sick maiden dear,
While in her lonely bower she tries
To cheat the thought she cannot cheer,
By fanciful embroideries.

"Trust, angry bard! a knowing sprite,
Nor think the harp her lot deplores;
Though 'mid the stars the lyre shines bright,
Love *stoops* as fondly as he soars."

ADDRESS TO MY INFANT DAUGHTER,

ON BEING REMINDED, THAT SHE WAS A MONTH OLD ON THAT DAY

HAST thou then survived,
Mild offspring of infirm humanity,
Meek infant! among all forlornest things
The most forlorn, one life of that bright star,
The second glory of the heavens?—Thou hast:
Already hast survived that great decay,
That transformation through the wide earth felt,
And by all nations. In that Being's sight
From whom the race of human kind proceed,
A thousand years are but as yesterday,
And one day's narrow circuit is to Him
Not less capacious than a thousand years
But what is time? What outward glory? Neither
A measure is of Thee, whose claims extend
Through "heaven's eternal year"—Yet hail to thee,
Frail, feeble monthling!—by that name, [methinks,
Thy scanty breathing-time is portioned out
Not idly.—Hadst thou been of Indian birth,
Couched on a casual bed of moss and leaves,
And rudely canopied by leafy boughs,
Or to the churlish elements exposed
On the blank plains,—the coldness of the night,
Or the night's darkness, or its cheerful face
Of beauty, by the changing moon adorned,
Would, with imperious admonition, then
Have scored thine age, and punctually timed
Thine infant history, on the minds of those
Who might have wandered with thee.—Mother's love,
Nor less than mother's love in other breasts,
Will, among us warm clad and warmly housed,
Do for thee what the finger of the heavens
Doth all too often harshly execute
For thy unblest coevals, amid wilds
Where fancy hath small liberty to grace
The affections, to exalt them or refine;
And the maternal sympathy itself,
Though strong, is, in the main, a joyless tie
Of naked instinct, wound about the heart.
Happier, far happier is thy lot and ours!
Even now—To solemnize thy helpless state.
And to enliven in the mind's regard
Thy passive beauty—parallels have risen,
Resemblances, or contrasts, that connect,
Within the region of a father's thoughts,
Thee and thy mate and sister of the sky.
And first,—thy sinless progress, through a world
By sorrow darkened and by care disturbed,
Apt likeness bears to hers, through gathered clouds,
Moving untouched in silver purity,
And cheering oft-times their reluctant gloom
Fair are ye both, and both are free from [stain.
But thou, how leisurely thou fill'st thy horn
With brightness!—leaving her to post along,
And range about—disquieted in change,
And still impatient of the shape she wears
Once up, once down the hill, one journey, babe,
That will suffice thee; and it seems that now
Thou hast fore-knowledge that such task is thine,
Thou travell'st so contentedly, and sleep'st
In such a heedless peace Alas! full soon
Hath this conception, grateful to behold,
Changed countenance, like an object sullied o'er
By breathing mist! and thine appears to be
A mournful labour, while to her is given
Hope—and a renovation without end.
That smile forbids the thought;—for on thy face
Smiles are beginning, like the beams of [dawn,
To shoot and circulate;—smiles have there been seen,—
Tranquil assurances that Heaven supports
The feeble motions of thy life, and cheers
Thy loneliness;—or shall those smiles be called
Feelers of love,—put forth as if to explore
This untried world, and to prepare thy way
Through a strait passage intricate and dim?
Such are they,—and the same are tokens, signs,
Which, when the appointed season hath [arrived,
Joy, as her holiest language, shall adopt;
And reason's godlike power be proud to own.

Poems of the Imagination.

THERE was a boy; ye knew him well, ye cliffs
And islands of Winander! many a time,
At evening, when the earliest stars began
To move along the edges of the hills,
Rising or setting, would he stand alone,
Beneath the trees, or by the glimmering lake;
And there, with fingers interwoven, both hands
Pressed closely palm to palm and to his mouth
Uplifted, he, as through an instrument,
Blew mimic hootings to the silent owls,
That they might answer him.—And they would shout
Across the watery vale, and shout again,
Responsive to his call,—with quivering peals,
And long halloos, and screams, and echoes loud
Redoubled and redoubled; concourse wild
Of mirth and jocund din! And, when it chanced
That pauses of deep silence mocked his skill,
Then, sometimes, in that silence, while he hung
Listening, a gentle shock of mild surprise
Has carried far into his heart the voice
Of mountain torrents; or the visible scene
Would enter unawares into his mind
With all its solemn imagery, its rocks,
Its woods, and that uncertain heaven, received
Into the bosom of the steady lake.

This boy was taken from his mates, and died
In childhood, ere he was full twelve years old.
Fair is the spot, most beautiful the vale
Where he was born: the grassy church-yard hangs
Upon a slope above the village school;
And through that church-yard when my way has led
At evening, I believe, that oftentimes
A long half-hour together I have stood
Mute—looking at the grave in which he lies!

TO ——,

ON HER FIRST ASCENT TO THE SUMMIT OF HELVELLYN.

INMATE of a mountain-dwelling,
Thou hast clomb aloft, and gazed,
From the watch-towers of Helvellyn;
Awed, delighted, and amazed!

Potent was the spell that bound thee,
Not unwilling to obey;
For blue ether's arms, flung round thee,
Stilled the pantings of dismay.

Lo! the dwindled woods and meadows!
What a vast abyss is there!
Lo! the clouds, the solemn shadows,
And the glistenings—heavenly fair!

And a record of commotion
Which a thousant ridges yield;
Ridge, and gulf, and distant ocean
Gleaming like a silver shield!

Take thy flight;—possess, inherit
Alps or Andes—they are thine!
With the morning's roseate spirit,
Sweep their length of snowy line;

Or survey the bright dominions
In the gorgeous colours drest,
Flung from off the purple pinions,
Evening spreads throughout the west!

Thine are all the choral fountains
Warbling in each sparry vault
Of the untrodden lunar mountains;
Listen to their songs!—or halt,

To Niphate's top invited,
Whither spiteful Satan steered;
Or descend where the ark alighted,
When the green earth re-appeared;

For the power of hills is on thee,
As was witnessed through thine eye
Then, when old Helvellyn won thee
To confess their majesty!

TO THE CUCKOO.

O BLITHE new-comer! I have heard,
I hear thee and rejoice.
O Cuckoo! shall I call thee bird,
Or but a wandering voice?

While I am lying on the grass
Thy twofold shout I hear,
From hill to hill it seems to pass,
At once far off and near.

Though babbling only, to the vale,
Of sunshine and of flowers,
Thou bringest unto me a tale
Of visionary hours.

Thrice welcome, darling of the spring!
Even yet thou art to me
No bird: but an invisible thing,
A voice, a mystery.

The same whom in my school-boy days
I listened to; that cry
Which made me look a thousand ways
In bush, and tree, and sky.

To seek thee did I often rove
Through woods and on the green;
And thou wert still a hope, a love;
Still longed for, never seen.

And I can listen to thee yet;
Can lie upon the plain
And listen, till I do beget
That golden time again.

O blessed bird! the earth we pace
Again appears to be
An unsubstantial faery place;
That is fit home for thee!

A NIGHT-PIECE.

THE sky is overcast
With a continuous cloud of texture close,
Heavy and wan, all whitened by the moon,
Which through that veil is indistinctly seen,
A dull, contracted circle, yielding light
So feebly spread, that not a shadow falls,
Chequering the ground—from rock, plant, tree, or tower.
At length a pleasant instantaneous gleam
Startles the pensive traveller while he treads
His lonesome path, with unobserving eye
Bent earthwards: he looks up—the clouds are split
Asunder,—and above his head he sees
The clear moon, and the glory of the heavens.
There, in a black blue vault she sails along,
Followed by multitudes of stars, that, small
And sharp, and bright, along the dark abyss
Drive as she drives;—how fast they wheel away,
Yet vanish not!—the wind is in the tree,
But they are silent;—still they roll along
Immeasurably distant;—and the vault,
Built round by those white clouds, enormous clouds,
Still deepens its unfathomable depth.
At length the vision closes; and the mind,
Not undisturbed by the delight it feels,
Which slowly settles into peaceful calm,
Is left to muse upon the solemn scene.

WATER-FOWL.

"Let me be allowed the aid of verse to describe the evolutions which these visitants sometimes perform, on a fine day towards the close of winter."—*Extract from the Author's Book on the Lakes.*

MARK how the feathered tenants of the flood,
With grace of motion that might scarcely seem
Inferior to angelical, prolong
Their curious pastime! shaping in mid air
(And sometimes with ambitious wing that soars
High as the level of the mountain tops)
A circuit ampler than the lake beneath,
Their own domain;—but ever, while intent
On tracing and retracing that large round,
Their jubilant activity evolves
Hundreds of curves and circles, to and fro,
Upward and downward, progress intricate
Yet unperplexed, as if one spirit swayed
Their indefatigable flight.—'Tis done—
Ten times, or more, I fancied it had ceased;
But lo! the vanished company again
Ascending;—they approach—I hear their wings
Faint, faint at first; and then an eager sound
Past in a moment—and as faint again!
They tempt the sun to sport amid their plumes;
They tempt the water, or the gleaming ice,
To show them a fair image;—'tis themselves,
Their own fair forms, upon the glimmering plain,
Painted more soft and fair as they descend
Almost to touch;—then up again aloft,
Up with a sally and a flash of speed,
As if they scorned both resting-place and rest!

YEW-TREES.

THERE is a yew-tree, pride of Lorton Vale,
Which to this day stands single, in the midst
Of its own darkness, as it stood of yore,
Not loth to furnish weapons for the bands
Of Umfraville or Percy ere they marched
To Scotland's heaths; or those that crossed the sea

And drew their sounding bows at Azincour,
Perhaps at earlier Crecy, or Poictiers
Of vast circumference and gloom profound
This solitary tree!—a living thing
Produced too slowly ever to decay;
Of form and aspect too magnificent
To be destroyed. But worthier still of note
Are those fraternal four of Borrowdale,
Joined in one solemn and capacious grove.
Huge trunks!—and each particular trunk a growth
Of intertwisted fibres serpentine
Up-coiling, and inveterately convolved,—
Nor uninformed with phantasy, and looks
That threaten the profane;—a pillared shade, [hue,
Upon whose grassless floor of red-brown
By sheddings from the pining umbrage tinged
Perennially—beneath whose sable roof
Of boughs, as if for festal purpose decked
With unrejoicing berries, ghostly shapes
May meet at noontide—Fear and trembling Hope,
Silence and Foresight—Death the Skeleton,
And Time the Shadow,—there to celebrate,
As in a natural temple scattered o'er
With altars undisturbed of mossy stone,
United worship; or in mute repose
To lie, and listen to the mountain flood
Murmuring from Glaramara's inmost caves.

VIEW FROM THE TOP OF BLACK COMB.*

This height a ministering angel might select. [name
For from the summit of Black Comb (dread
Derived from clouds and storms!) the amplest range
Of unobstructed prospect may be seen
That British ground commands:—low dusky tracts, [Cambrian hills
Where Trent is nursed, far southward!
To the south-west, a multitudinous show;
And, in a line of eye-sight linked with these,
The hoary peaks of Scotland that give birth
To Teviot's stream, to Annan, Tweed, and Clyde;—
Crowding the quarter whence the sun comes forth
Gigantic mountains rough with crags, beneath, [base,
Right at the imperial station's western
Main Ocean, breaking audibly and stretched
Far into silent regions blue and pale;—
And visibly engirding Mona's Isle,
That, as we left the plain, before our sight
Stood like a lofty mount, uplifting slowly,
(Above the convex of the watery globe)
Into clear view the cultured fields that streak
Her habitable shores; but now appears
A dwindled object, and submits to lie
At the spectator's feet.—Yon azure ridge,
Is it a perishable cloud? Or there
Do we behold the frame of Erin's coast?
Land sometimes by the roving shepherd swain
(Like the bright confines of another world)
Not doubtfully perceived.—Look homeward now!
In depth, in height, in circuit, how serene
The spectacle, how pure! Of nature's works,
In earth, and air, and earth-embracing sea,
A revelation infinite it seems;
Display august of man's inheritance,
Of Britain's calm felicity and power.

* Black Comb stands at the southern extremity of Cumberland; its base covers a much greater extent of ground than any other mountain in these parts; and, from its situation, the summit commands a more extensive view than any other point in Britain.

NUTTING

It seems a day
(I speak of one from many singled out)
One of those heavenly days which cannot die;
When, in the eagerness of boyish hope,
I left our cottage-threshold, sallying forth
With a huge wallet o'er my shoulder slung,
A nutting-crook in hand, and turned my steps
Towards the distant woods, a figure quaint,
Tricked out in proud disguise of cast-off weeds
Which for that service had been husbanded
By exhortation of my frugal dame.
Motley accoutrement, of power to smile
At thorns, and brakes, and brambles,—and in truth, [woods,
More ragged than need was! Among the
And o'er the pathless rocks, I forced my way,
Until, at length, I came to one dear nook
Unvisited, where not a broken bough

Drooped with its withered leaves, ungracious sign
Of devastation, but the hazels rose
Tall and erect, with milk-white clusters hung,
A virgin scene!—A little while I stood,
Breathing with such suppression of the heart
As joy delights in; and with wise restraint
Voluptuous, fearless of a rival, eyed
The banquet,—or beneath the trees I sate
Among the flowers, and with the flowers I played;
A temper known to those, who, after long
And weary expectation, have been blest
With sudden happiness beyond all hope.—
Perhaps it was a bower beneath whose leaves
The violets of five seasons re-appear
And fade, unseen by any human eye;
Where fairy water-breaks do murmur on
For ever,—and I saw the sparkling foam,
And with my cheek on one of those green stones
That, fleeced with moss, beneath the shady trees,
Lay round me, scattered like a flock of sheep,
I heard the murmur and the murmuring sound,
In that sweet mood when pleasure loves to pay
Tribute to ease; and, of its joy secure,
The heart luxuriates with indifferent things,
Wasting its kindliness on stocks and stones,
And on the vacant air. Then up I rose,
And dragged to earth both branch and bough, with crash
And merciless ravage; and the shady nook
Of hazels, and the green and mossy bower,
Deformed and sullied, patiently gave up
Their quiet being: and, unless I now
Confound my present feelings with the past,
Even then, when from the bower I turned away
Exulting, rich beyond the wealth of kings,
I felt a sense of pain when I beheld
The silent trees and the intruding sky.—
Then, dearest maiden! move along these shades
In gentleness of heart: with gentle hand
Touch—for there is a spirit in the woods.

SHE was a phantom of delight
When first she gleamed upon my sight;
A lovely apparition, sent
To be a moment's ornament;
Her eyes as stars of twilight fair;
Like twilight's too, her dusky hair;
But all things else about her drawn
From May-time and the cheerful dawn;
A dancing shape, an image gay,
To haunt, to startle, and waylay.

I saw her upon nearer view,
A spirit, yet a woman too!
Her household motions light and free,
And steps of virgin liberty;
A countenance in which did meet
Sweet records, promises as sweet;
A creature not too bright or good
For human nature's daily food;
For transient sorrows, simple wiles,
Praise, blame, love, kisses, tears, and smiles.

And now I see with eye serene
The very pulse of the machine;
A being breathing thoughtful breath,
A traveller betwixt life and death;
The reason firm, the temperate will,
Endurance, foresight, strength, and skill;
A perfect woman, nobly planned,
To warn, to comfort, and command;
And yet a spirit still, and bright
With something of an angel light.

O NIGHTINGALE! thou surely art
A creature of a fiery heart:—
These notes of thine—they pierce and pierce;
Tumultuous harmony and fierce!
Thou sing'st as if the god of wine
Had helped thee to a valentine;
A song in mockery and despite
Of shades, and dews, and silent night;
And steady bliss, and all the loves
Now sleeping in these peaceful groves.

I heard a stock-dove sing or say
His homely tale this very day;
His voice was buried among trees,
Yet to be come at by the breeze;
He did not cease; but cooed—and cooed
And somewhat pensively he wooed.
He sang of love with quiet blending,
Slow to begin, and never ending;
Of serious faith and inward glee;
That was the song—the song for me!

THREE years she grew in sun and shower.
Then nature said, "A lovelier flower
On earth was never sown;
This child I to myself will take;
She shall be mine, and I will make
A lady of my own.

"Myself will to my darling be
Both law and impulse: and with me
The girl, in rock and plain,
In earth and heaven, in glade and bower,
Shall feel an overseeing power
To kindle or restrain.

"She shall be sportive as the fawn
That wild with glee across the lawn
Or up the mountain springs;
And hers shall be the breathing balm,
And hers the silence and the calm
Of mute insensate things.

"The floating clouds their state shall lend
To her; for her the willow bend:
Nor shall she fail to see
Even in the motions of the storm
Grace that shall mould the maiden's form
By silent sympathy.

"The stars of midnight shall be dear
To her; and she shall lean her ear
In many a secret place
Where rivulets dance their wayward round,
And beauty born of murmuring sound
Shall pass into her face.

"And vital feelings of delight
Shall rear her form to stately height,
Her virgin bosom swell;
Such thoughts to Lucy I will give
While she and I together live
Here in this happy dell."

Thus nature spake—the work was done—
How soon my Lucy's race was run!
She died, and left to me
This heath, this calm and quiet scene;
The memory of what has been,
And never more will be.

A SLUMBER did my spirit seal;
  I had no human fears:
She seemed a thing that could not feel
  The touch of earthly years.

No motion has she now, no force;
  She neither hears nor sees,
Rolled round in earth's diurnal course
  With rocks and stones and trees!

THE HORN OF EGREMONT CASTLE.*

WHEN the brothers reached the gateway,
Eustace pointed with his lance
To the horn which there was hanging;
Horn of the inheritance.
Horn it was which none could sound,
No one upon living ground,
Save he who came as rightful heir
To Egremont's domains and castle fair.

Heirs from ages without record
Had the house of Lucie born,
Who of right had claimed the lordship
By the proof upon the horn:
Each at the appointed hour
Tried the horn,—it owned his power;
He was acknowledged: and the blast,
Which good Sir Eustace sounded was the last.

With his lance Sir Eustace pointed,
And to Hubert thus said he—
"What I speak this horn shall witness
For thy better memory.
Hear, then, and neglect me not!
At this time, and on this spot,
The words are uttered from my heart,
As my last earnest prayer ere we depart.

"On good service we are going
Life to risk by sea and land,
In which course if Christ our Saviour
Do my sinful soul demand,
Hither come thou back straightway,
Hubert, if alive that day;
Return, and sound the horn, that we
May have a living house still left in thee!"

"Fear not!" quickly answered Hubert;
"As I am thy father's son,
What thou askest, noble brother,
With God's favour shall be done."
So were both right well content:
From the castle forth they went,
And at the head of their array
To Palestine the brothers took their way

Side by side they fought, (the Lucies
Were a line for valour famed,)
And where'er their strokes alighted,
There the Saracens were tamed.

* This story is a Cumberland tradition; I have heard it also related of the Hall of Hutton John, an ancient residence of the Huddlestones, in a sequestered valley upon the river Dacor.

Whence, then, could it come—the thought—
By what evil spirit brought?
Oh! can a brave man wish to take [sake?
His brother's life, for land's and castle's

"Sir!" the ruffians said to Hubert,
"Deep he lies in Jordan's flood,"
Stricken by this ill assurance,
Pale and trembling Hubert stood.
"Take your earnings."—Oh! that I
Could have *seen* my brother die!
It was a pang that vexed him then;
And oft returned, again, and yet again.

Months passed on, and no Sir Eustace!
Nor of him were tidings heard.
Wherefore, bold as day, the murderer
Back again to England steered.
To his castle Hubert sped;
He has nothing now to dread.
But silent and by stealth he came,
And at an hour which nobody could name.

None could tell if it were night-time,
Night or day, at even or morn;
For the sound was heard by no one
Of the proclamation-horn.
But bold Hubert lives in glee:
Months and years went smilingly;
With plenty was his table spread;
And bright the lady is who shares his bed.

Likewise he had sons and daughters;
And, as good men do, he sate
At his board by these surrounded,
Flourishing in fair estate.
And while thus in open day
Once he sate, as old books say,
A blast was uttered from the horn,
Where by the castle-gate it hung forlorn.

'Tis the breath of good Sir Eustace!
He is come to claim his right:
Ancient castle, woods, and mountains
Hear the challenge with delight.
Hubert! though the blast be blown
He is helpless and alone:
Thou hast a dungeon, speak the word!
And there he may be lodged, and thou be lord.

Speak!—astounded Hubert cannot;
And if power to speak he had,
All are daunted, all the household
Smitten to the heart, and sad.
'Tis Sir Eustace; if it be
Living man, it must be he!
Thus Hubert thought in his dismay,
And by a postern-gate he slunk away.

Long, and long was he unheard of:
To his brother then he came,
Made confession, asked forgiveness,
Asked it by a brother's name,
And by all the saints in heaven;
And of Eustace was forgiven:
Then in a convent went to hide
His melancholy head, and there he died.

But Sir Eustace, whom good angels
Had preserved from murderers' hands,
And from pagan chains had rescued,
Lived with honour on his lands.
Sons he had, saw sons of theirs:
And through ages, heirs of heirs,
A long posterity renowned, [sound,
Sounded the horn which they alone could

GOODY BLAKE AND HARRY GILL.

A TRUE STORY.

Oh! what's the matter? what's the matter?
What is't that ails young Harry Gill?
That evermore his teeth they chatter,
Chatter, chatter, chatter still!
Of waistcoats Harry has no lack,
Good duffle grey, and flannel fine,
He has a blanket on his back,
And coats enough to smother nine.

In March, December, and in July,
'Tis all the same with Harry Gill;
The neighbours tell, and tell you truly,
His teeth they chatter, chatter still!
At night, at morning, and at noon,
'Tis all the same with Harry Gill;
Beneath the sun, beneath the moon,
His teeth they chatter, chatter still!

Young Harry was a lusty drover,
And who so stout of limb as he?
His cheeks were red as ruddy clover;
His voice was like the voice of three.
Old Goody Blake was old and poor;
Ill fed she was, and thinly clad;
And any man who passed her door
Might see how poor a hut she had.

All day she spun in her poor dwelling:
And then her three hours' work at night,
Alas! 'twas hardly worth the telling,
It would not pay for candle-light.
Remote from sheltered village green,
On a hill's northern side she dwelt,
Where from sea-blasts the hawthorns lean,
And hoary dews are slow to melt.

By the same fire to boil their pottage,
Two poor old dames, as I have known,
Will often live in one small cottage;
But she, poor woman! housed alone.
'Twas well enough when summer came,
The long, warm, lightsome summer-day,
Then at her door the *canty* Dame
Would sit, as any linnet gay.

But when the ice our streams did fetter,
Oh! then how her old bones would shake,
You would have said, if you had met her,
'Twas a hard time for Goody Blake
Her evenings then were dull and dead!
Sad case it was, as you may think,
For very cold to go to bed;
And then for cold not sleep a wink.

Oh, joy for her! whene'er in winter
The winds at night had made a rout,
And scattered many a lusty splinter
And many a rotten bough about.
Yet never had she, well or sick,
As every man who knew her says,
A pile beforehand, turf or stick,
Enough to warm her for three days.

Now, when the frost was past enduring,
And made her poor old bones to ache,
Could anything be more alluring
Than an old hedge to Goody Blake?
And, now and then, it must be said,
When her old bones were cold and chill,
She left her fire, or left her bed,
To seek the hedge of Harry Gill.

Now Harry he had long suspected
This trespass of old Goody Blake;
And vowed that she should be detected,
And he on her would vengeance take.
And oft from his warm fire he'd go,
And to the fields his road would take.
And there, at night, in frost and snow,
He watched to seize old Goody Blake.

And once, behind a rick of barley,
Thus looking out did Harry stand:
The moon was full and shining clearly,
And crisp with frost the stubble land.
He hears a noise— he's all awake—
Again!—on tip-toe down the hill
He softly creeps—'Tis Goody Blake,
She's at the hedge of Harry Gill.

Right glad was he when he beheld her:
Stick after stick did Goody pull:
He stood behind a bush of elder,
Till she had filled her apron full.

When with her load she turned about,
The by-way back again to take;
He started forward with a shout,
And sprang upon poor Goody Blake.

And fiercely by the arm he took her,
And by the arm he held her fast,
And fiercely by the arm he shook her,
And cried, "I've caught you, then, at last!"
Then Goody, who had nothing said,
Her bundle from her lap let fall,
And, kneeling on the sticks, she prayed
To God that is the judge of all.

She prayed, her withered hand uprearing,
While Harry held her by the arm—
"God! who art never out of hearing,
Oh, may he never more be warm!"
The cold, cold moon above her head,
Thus on her knees did Goody pray,
Young Harry heard what she had said:
And icy cold he turned away

He went complaining all the morrow
That he was cold and very chill:
His face was gloom, his heart was sorrow;
Alas! that day for Harry Gill!
That day he wore a riding-coat,
But not a whit the warmer he
Another was on Thursday brought,
And ere the Sabbath he had three.

'Twas all in vain, a useless matter—
And blankets were about him pinned;
Yet still his jaws and teeth they clatter,
Like a loose casement in the wind.
And Harry's flesh it fell away;
And all who see him say, 'tis plain,
That, live as long as live he may,
He never will be warm again.

No word to any man he utters,
A-bed or up, to young or old,
But ever to himself he mutters,
"Poor Harry Gill is very cold."
A-bed or up, by night or day;
His teeth they chatter, chatter still,
Now think, ye farmers all, I pray,
Of Goody Blake and Harry Gill.

I WANDERED lonely as a cloud
That floats on high o'er vales and hills,
When all at once I saw a crowd,
A host of golden daffodils;

Beside the lake, beneath the trees,
Fluttering and dancing in the breeze.

Continuous as the stars that shine
And twinkle on the milky way,
They stretched in never-ending line
Along the margin of a bay:
Ten thousand saw I at a glance,
Tossing their heads in sprightly dance.

The waves beside them danced, but they
Outdid the sparkling waves in glee:—
A poet could not but be gay,
In such a jocund company:
I gazed—and gazed—but little thought
What wealth the show to me had
brought ·

For oft when on my couch I lie
In vacant or in pensive mood,
They flash upon that inward eye
Which is the bliss of solitude,
And then my heart with pleasure fills,
And dances with the daffodils.

THE REVERIE OF POOR SUSAN.

AT the corner of Wood Street, when day-
light appears, [for three years:
Hangs a thrush that sings loud, it has sung
Poor Susan has passed by the spot, and has
heard [bird.
In the silence of morning the song of the

'Tis a note of enchantment; what ails her?
She sees
A mountain ascending, a vision of trees;
Bright volumes of vapour through Loth-
bury glide, [Cheapside.
And a river flows on through the vale of

Green pastures she views in the midst of
the dale, [her pail;
Down which she so often has tripped with
And a single small cottage, a nest like a
dove's [loves.
The one only dwelling on earth that she

She looks, and her heart is in heaven: but
they fade, [shade:
The mist and the river, the hill and the
The stream will not flow, and the hill will
not rise, [her eyes.
And the colours have all passed away from

POWER OF MUSIC.

AN Orpheus! an Orpheus!—yes, faith may
grow bold, [old;—
And take to herself all the wonders of
Near the stately Pantheon you'll meet with
the same [its name.
In the street that from Oxford hath borrowed

His station is there;—and he works on the
crowd, [loud;
He sways them with harmony merry and
He fills with his power all their hearts to
the brim— [him?
Was aught ever heard like his fiddle and

What an eager assembly! what an empire
is this! [bliss;
The weary have life and the hungry have
The mourner is cheered, and the anxious
have rest; [oppress.
And the guilt-burthened soul is no longer

As the moon brightens round her the clouds
of the night,
So he, where he stands, is a centre of light;
It gleams on the face, there, of dusky-
browed Jack, [on back
And the pale-visaged baker's, with basket

That errand-bound 'prentice was passing
in haste— [runs to waste—
What matter! he's caught—and his time
The newsman is stopped, though he stops
on the fret, [in the net!
And the half-breathless lamplighter—he's

The porter sits down on the weight which
he bore; [her store;—
The lass with her barrow wheels hither
If a thief could be here he might pilfer at
ease;
She sees the musician, 'tis all that she sees!

He stands, backed by the wall;—he abates
not his din; [ping in,
His hat gives him vigour, with boons drop
From the old and the young, from the
poorest; and there! [spare.
The one-pennied boy has his penny to

Oh, blest are the hearers, and proud be
the hand [thankful a band;
Of the pleasure it spreads through so
I am glad for him, blind as he is!—all the
while [with a smile.
If they speak 'tis to praise, and they praise

That tall man, a giant in bulk and in height,
Not an inch of his body is free from delight;
Can he keep himself still, if he would? oh, not he!
The music stirs in him like wind through a tree.

Mark that cripple who leans on his crutch; like a tower
That long has leaned forward, leans hour after hour!—
That mother, whose spirit in fetters is bound,
While she dandles the babe in her arms to the sound.

Now, coaches and chariots! roar on like a stream;
Here are twenty souls happy as souls in a dream:
They are deaf to your murmurs—they care not for you,
Nor what ye are flying, nor what ye pursue!

STAR-GAZERS.

WHAT crowd is this? what have we here! we must not pass it by;
A telescope upon its frame, and pointed to the sky:
Long is it as a barber's pole, or mast of little boat,
Some little pleasure-skiff, that doth on Thames's waters float.

The showman chooses well his place, 'tis Leicester's busy Square,
And is as happy in his night, for the heavens are blue and fair;
Calm, though impatient, is the crowd; each stands ready with the fee,
And envies him that's looking—what an insight must it be!

Yet, showman, where can lie the cause? Shall thy implement have blame,
A boaster, that when he is tried, fails, and is put to shame?
Or is it good as others are, and be their eyes in fault?
Their eyes, or minds? or, finally, is this resplendent vault?

Is nothing of that radiant pomp so good as we have here?
Or gives a thing but small delight that never can be dear?
The silver moon with all her vales, and hills of mightiest fame,
Doth she betray us when they're seen! or are they but a name?

Or is it rather that conceit rapacious is and strong,
And bounty never yields so much but it seems to do her wrong?
Or is it that when human souls a journey long have had,
And are returned into themselves they cannot but be sad?

Or must we be constrained to think that these spectators rude,
Poor in estate, of manners base, men of the multitude,
Have souls which never yet have risen, and therefore prostrate lie?
No, no, this cannot be—men thirst for power and majesty!

Does, then, a deep and earnest thought the blissful mind employ
Of him who gazes, or has gazed? a grave and steady joy.
That doth reject all show of pride, admits no outward sign,
Because not of this noisy world, but silent and divine!

Whatever be the cause, 'tis sure that they who pry and pore
Seem to meet with little gain, seem less happy than before;
One after one they take their turn, nor have I one espied
That doth not slackly go away, as if dissatisfied.

THE HAUNTED TREE.

TO ——

THOSE silver clouds collected round the sun
His mid-day warmth abate not, seeming less
To overshade than multiply his beams
By soft reflection—grateful to the sky,
To rocks, fields, woods. Nor doth our human sense
Ask, for its pleasure, screen or canopy
More ample than the time-dismantled oak
Spreads o'er this tuft of heath, which now, attired
In the whole fulness of its bloom, affords
Couch beautiful as e'er for earthly use
Was fashioned; whether by the hand of art,
That eastern sultan, amid flowers enwrought
On silken tissue, might diffuse his limbs

In languor; or, by nature, for repose
Of panting wood-nymph wearied by the chase.
O lady! fairer in thy poet's sight
Than fairest spiritual creature of the groves,
Approach—and thus invited crown with rest
The noon-tide hour;—though truly some there are
Whose footsteps superstitiously avoid
This venerable tree; for, when the wind
Blows keenly, it sends forth a creaking sound
(Above the general roar of woods and crags)
Distinctly heard from far—a doleful note!
As if (so Grecian shepherds would have deemed)
The Hamadryad, pent within, bewailed
Some bitter wrong. Nor is it unbelieved,
By ruder fancy, that a troubled ghost
Haunts this old trunk; lamenting deeds of which
The flowery ground is conscious. But no wind
Sweeps now along this elevated ridge;
Not even a zephyr stirs;—the obnoxious tree
Is mute,—and, in his silence, would look down,
O lovely wanderer of the trackless hills,
On thy reclining form with more delight
Than his coevals, in the sheltered vale
Seem to participate, the whilst they view
Their own far str[illegible]ing arms and leafy heads
Vividly pictured in some glassy pool,
That, for a brief space, checks the hurrying stream!

WRITTEN IN MARCH,

WHILE RESTING ON THE BRIDGE AT THE FOOT OF BROTHER'S WATER.

THE cock is crowing,
The stream is flowing,
The small birds twitter,
The lake doth glitter,
The green field sleeps in the sun;
The oldest and youngest
Are at work with the strongest;
The cattle are grazing,
Their heads never raising;
There are forty feeding like one!

Like an army defeated
The snow hath retreated,
And now doth fare ill
On the top of the bare hill;
The plough-boy is whooping—anon—anon:
There's joy in the mountains;
There's life in the fountains;
Small clouds are sailing,
Blue sky prevailing;
The rain is over and gone!

GIPSIES.

YET are they here the same unbroken knot
Of human beings, in the self-same spot!
Men, women, children, yea, the frame
Of the whole spectacle the same!
Only their fire seems bolder, yielding light,
Now deep and red, the colouring of night;
That on their gipsy-faces falls,
Their bed of straw and blanket-walls.
Twelve hours, twelve bounteous hours, are gone, while I
Have been a traveller under open sky,
Much witnessing of change and cheer,
Yet as I left I find them here!
The weary sun betook himself to rest,
Then issued vesper from the fulgent west,
Outshining like a visible god
The glorious path in which he trod.
And now, ascending, after one dark hour
And one night's diminution of her power,
Behold the mighty moon! this way
She looks as if at them—but they
Regard not her:—oh better wrong and strife,
(By nature transient) than such torpid life;
Life which the very stars reprove
As on their silent tasks they move!
Yet witness all that stirs in heaven or earth!
In scorn I speak not; they are what their birth
And breeding suffer them to be;
Wild outcasts of society!

BEGGARS.

SHE had a tall man's height, or more;
No bonnet screened her from the heat;
Nor claimed she service from the hood
Of a blue mantle, to her feet
Depending with a graceful flow;
Only she wore a cap pure as unsullied snow.

Her skin was of Egyptian brown;
Haughty as if her eye had seen
Its own light to a distance thrown,
She towered—fit person for a queen,
To head those ancient Amazonian files;
Or ruling bandit's wife among the Grecian isles.

Her suit no faltering scruples checked;
Forth did she pour, in current free,
Tales that could challenge no respect
But from a blind credulity;
And yet a boon I gave her; for the creature
Was beautiful to see—a weed of glorious feature:

I left her and pursued my way;
And soon before me did espy
A pair of little boys at play,
Chasing a crimson butterfly:
The taller followed with his hat in hand,
Wreathed round with yellow flowers the gayest of the land.

The other wore a rimless crown
With leaves of laurel stuck about;
And, while both followed up and down,
Each whooping with a merry shout,
In their fraternal features I could trace
Unquestionable lines of that wild suppliant's face.

Yet *they*, so blithe of heart, seemed fit
For finest tasks of earth or air:
Wings let them have, and they might flit
Precursors of Aurora's car,
Scattering fresh flowers; though happier far, I ween,
To hunt their fluttering game o'er rock and level green.

They dart across my path—but lo,
Each ready with a plaintive whine!
Said I, "Not half an hour ago
Your mother has had alms of mine."
"That cannot be," one answered—"she is dead"—
I looked reproof—they saw—but neither hung his head.

"She has been dead, sir, many a day."
"Sweet boys; Heaven hears that rash reply;
It was your mother, as I say!"
And, in the twinkling of an eye,
"Come! come!" cried one, and without more ado,
Off to some other play the joyous vagrants flew!

SEQUEL TO THE FOREGOING,

COMPOSED MANY YEARS AFTER.

WHERE are they now, those wanton boys?
For whose free range the dædal earth
Was filled with animated toys,
And implements of frolic mirth;
With tools for ready wit to guide;
And ornaments of seemlier pride,
More fresh, more bright, than princes wear
For what one moment flung aside,
Another could repair;
What good or evil have they seen
Since I their pastime witnessed here,
Their daring wiles, their sportive cheer?
I ask—but all is dark between!

Spirits of beauty and of grace!
Associates in that eager chase,
Ye, by a course to nature true,
The sterner judgment can subdue;
And waken a relenting smile
When she encounters fraud or guile;
And sometimes ye can charm away
The inward mischief, or allay,
Ye, who within the blameless mind
Your favourite seat of empire find!

They met me in a genial hour,
When universal nature breathed
As with the breath of one sweet flower,—
A time to overrule the power
Of discontent, and check the birth
Of thoughts with better thoughts at strife.
The most familiar bane of life
Since parting innocence bequeathed
Mortality to earth!
Soft clouds, the whitest of the year,
Sailed through the sky—the brooks ran clear;
The lambs from rock to rock were bounding;
With songs the budded groves resounding;
And to my heart is still endeared
The faith with which it then was cheered;
The faith which saw that gladsome pair
Walk through the fire with unsinged hair.
Or, if such thoughts must needs deceive,
Kind spirits! may we not believe
That they so happy and so fair,
Through your sweet influence, and the care
Of pitying Heaven, at least were free
From touch of *deadly* injury?
Destined, whate'er their earthly doom,
For mercy and immortal bloom!

RUTH.

WHEN Ruth was left half desolate,
Her father took another mate;
And Ruth, not seven years old,
A slighted child, at her own will
Went wandering over dale and hill,
In thoughtless freedom bold.

And she had made a pipe of straw,
And from that oaten pipe could draw
All sounds of winds and floods ;
Had built a bower upon the green,
As if she from her birth had been
An infant of the woods.

Beneath her father's roof, alone
She seemed to live, her thoughts her own ;
Herself her own delight,
Pleased with herself, nor sad nor gay ;
And passing thus the live-long day,
She grew to woman's height.

There came a youth from Georgia's shore—
A military casque he wore,
With splendid feathers drest ;
He brought them from the Cherokees ;
The feathers nodded in the breeze,
And made a gallant crest.

From Indian blood you deem him sprung
Ah no ! he spake the English tongue,
And bore a soldier's name,
And, when America was free
From battle and from jeopardy,
He 'cross the ocean came.

With hues of genius on his cheek
In finest tones the youth could speak.
While he was yet a boy,
The moon, the glory of the sun,
And streams that murmur as they run,
Had been his dearest joy.

He was a lovely youth ! I guess
The panther in the wilderness
Was not so fair as he ;
And when he chose to sport and play,
No dolphin ever was so gay
Upon the tropic sea.

Among the Indians he had fought ;
And with him many tales he brought
Of pleasure and of fear ;
Such tales as told to any maid
By such a youth, in the green shade,
Were perilous to hear.

He told of girls—a happy rout !
Who quit their fold with dance and shout,
Their pleasant Indian town,
To gather strawberries all day long ;
Returning with a choral song
When daylight is gone down.

He spake of plants divine and strange
That every hour their blossoms change,
Ten thousand lovely hues !
With budding, fading, faded flowers
They stand the wonder of the bowers
From morn to evening dews.

He told of the magnolia spread
High as a cloud, high over head !
The cypress and her spire ;
Of flowers that with one scarlet gleam
Cover a hundred leagues, and seem
To set the hills on fire.

The youth of green savannas spake,
And many an endless, endless lake,
With all its fairy crowds
Of islands, that together lie
As quietly as spots of sky
Among the evening clouds.

And then he said, "How sweet it were
A fisher or a hunter there,
A gardener in the shade,
Still wandering with an easy mind
To build a household fire, and find
A home in every glade !

"What days and what sweet years ! Ah me !
Our life were life indeed, with thee
So passed in quiet bliss,
And all the while," said he, "to know
That we were in a world of woe,
On such an earth as this !"

And then he sometimes interwove
Dear thoughts about a father's love :
"For there," said he, "are spun
Around the heart such tender ties,
That our own children to our eyes
Are dearer than the sun.

"Sweet Ruth ! and could you go with me
My helpmate in the woods to be,
Our shed at night to rear,
Or run my own adopted bride,
A sylvan huntress at my side,
And drive the flying deer !

"Beloved Ruth !"—No more he said.
The wakeful Ruth at midnight shed
A solitary tear :
She thought again—and did agree
With him to sail across the sea,
And drive the flying deer.

"And now, as fitting is and right,
We in the church our faith will plight,
A husband and a wife."

Even so they did; and I may say
That to sweet Ruth that happy day
Was more than human life.

Through dream and vision did she sink,
Delighted all the while to think
That on those lonesome floods,
And green savannas, she should share
His board with lawful joy, and bear
His name in the wild woods.

But, as you have before been told,
This stripling, sportive, gay, and bold,
And with his dancing crest
So beautiful, through savage lands
Had roamed about, with vagrant bands
Of Indians in the west.

The wind, the tempest roaring high,
The tumult of a tropic sky,
Might well be dangerous food
For him, a youth to whom was given
So much of earth—so much of heaven,
And such impetuous blood.

Whatever in those climes he found
Irregular in sight or sound
Did to his mind impart
A kindred impulse, seemed allied
To his own powers, and justified
The workings of his heart.

Nor less, to feed voluptuous thought,
The beauteous forms of nature wrought,
Fair trees and lovely flowers;
The breezes their own languor lent:
The stars had feelings, which they sent
Into those gorgeous bowers.

Yet, in his worst pursuits, I ween
That sometimes there did intervene
Pure hopes of high intent:
For passions linked to forms so fair
And stately, needs must have their share
Of noble sentiment.

But ill he lived, much evil saw
With men to whom no better law
Nor better life was known;
Deliberately, and undeceived,
Those wild men's vices he received,
And gave them back his own.

His genius and his moral frame
Were thus impaired, and he became
The slave of low desires:
A man who without self-control
Would seek what the degraded soul
Unworthily admires.

And yet he with no feignèd delight
Had wooed the maiden, day and night
Had loved her, night and morn:
What could he less than love a maid
Whose heart with so much nature played?
So kind and so forlorn!

Sometimes, most earnestly, he said,
"O Ruth! I have been worse than dead:
False thoughts, thoughts bold and vain,
Encompassed me on every side
When first, in confidence and pride,
I crossed the Atlantic main.

"It was a fresh and glorious world,
A banner bright that was unfurled
Before me suddenly:
I looked upon those hills and plains,
And seemed as if let loose from chains
To live at liberty.

"But wherefore speak of this? For now,
Sweet Ruth! with thee, I know not how,
I feel my spirit burn—
Even as the east when day comes forth;
And, to the west, and south, and north
The morning doth return."

Full soon that purer mind was gone;
No hope, no wish remained, not one,—
They stirred him now no more;
New objects did new pleasure give;
And once again he wished to live
As lawless as before.

Meanwhile, as thus with him it fared,
They for the voyage were prepared,
And went to the sea-shore;
But, when they thither came, the youth
Deserted his poor bride, and Ruth
Could never find him more.

God help thee, Ruth!—Such pains she had,
That she in half a year was mad,
And in a prison housed;
And there she sang tumultuous songs,
By recollection of her wrongs,
To fearful passion roused.

Yet sometimes milder hours she knew,
Nor wanted sun, nor rain, nor dew,
Nor pastimes of the May,
They all were with her in her cell;
And a wild brook with cheerful knell
Did o'er the pebbles play.

When Ruth three seasons thus had lain,
There came a respite to her pain;

She from her prison fled ;
But of the vagrant none took thought ;
And where it liked her best she sought
Her shelter and her bread

Among the fields she breathed again .
The master-current of her brain
Ran permanent and free ;
And, coming to the banks of Tone,*
There did she rest ; and dwell alone
Under the greenwood tree.

The engines of her pain, the tools
That shaped her sorrow, rocks and pools,
And airs that gently stir
The vernal leaves, she loved them still,
Nor ever taxed them with the ill
Which had been done to her.

A barn her *winter* bed supplies ;
But, till the warmth of summer skies
And summer days is gone,
(And all do in this tale agree)
She sleeps beneath the greenwood tree,
And other home hath none.

An innocent life, yet far astray !
And Ruth will, long before her day,
Be broken down and old ·
Sore aches she needs must have ! but less
Of mind than body's wretchedness,
From damp, and rain, and cold.

If she is pressed by want of food,
She from her dwelling in the wood
Repairs to a road-side ;
And there she begs at one steep place,
Where up and down with easy pace
The horsemen-travellers ride.

That oaten pipe of hers is mute,
Or thrown away : but with a flute
Her loneliness she cheers :
This flute, made of a hemlock stalk,
At evening in his homeward walk
The Quantock woodman hears.

I too, have passed her on the hills
Setting her little water-mills
By spouts and fountains wild—
Such small machinery as she turned
Ere she had wept, ere she had mourned,
A young and happy child !

Farewell ! and when thy days are told,
Ill-fated Ruth ! in hallowed mould
Thy corpse shall buried be ,
For thee a funeral bell shall ring,
And all the congregation sing
A Christian psalm for thee.

* A river in Somersetshire, at no great distance from the Quantock Hills.

LAODAMIA.

"WITH sacrifice before the rising morn
Vows have I made by fruitless hope inspired ;
And from the infernal gods, mid shades forlorn,
Of night, my slaughtered lord have I required .
Celestial pity I again implore ;—
Restore him to my sight—great Jove, restore !"

So speaking, and by fervent love endowed
With faith, the suppliant heavenward lifts her hands ;
While, like the sun emerging from a cloud,
Her countenance brightens—and her eye expands ;
Her bosom heaves and spreads, her stature grows ;
And she expects the issue in repose

O terror ! what hath she perceived ?—O joy !
What doth she look on ?—whom doth she behold ?
Her hero slain upon the beach of Troy ?
His vital presence—his corporeal mould ?
It is—if sense deceive her not—'tis he !
And a god leads him—wingèd Mercury !

Mild Hermes spake—and touched her with his wand
That calms all fear · "Such grace hath crowned thy prayer,
Laodamia ! that at Jove's command
Thy husband walks the paths of upper air .
He comes to tarry with thee three hours' space ;
Accept the gift—behold him face to face !"

Forth sprang the impassioned queen her lord to clasp !
Again that consummation she essayed ;
But unsubstantial form eludes her grasp
As often as that eager grasp was made.
The phantom parts—but parts to re-unite,
And re-assume his place before her sight

"Protesilàus, lo ! thy guide is gone !
Confirm, I pray, the vision with thy voice:
This is our palace.—yonder is thy throne :

Speak, and the floor thou tread'st on will rejoice.
Not to appal me have the gods bestowed
This precious boon,—and blest a sad abode."

"Great Jove, Laodamia! doth not leave
His gifts imperfect :—spectre though I be,
I am not sent to scare thee or deceive ;
But in reward of thy fidelity.
And something also did my worth obtain ;
For fearless virtue bringeth boundless gain.

"Thou know'st, the Delphic oracle foretold
That the first Greek who touched the Trojan strand
Should die ; but me the threat could not withhold :
A generous cause a victim did demand ;
And forth I leapt upon the sandy plain ,
A self-devoted chief—by Hector slain."

"Supreme of heroes—bravest, noblest, best !
Thy matchless courage I bewail no more,
Which then, when tens of thousands were deprest
By doubt, propelled thee to the fatal shore ;
Thou found'st—and I forgive thee—here thou art—
A nobler counsellor than my poor heart.

"But thou, though capable of sternest deed,
Wert kind as resolute, and good as brave ;
And he, whose power restores thee, hath decreed
That thou shouldst cheat the malice of the grave ;
Redundant are thy locks, thy lips as fair
As when their breath enriched Thessalian air.

"No spectre greets me,—no vain shadow this :
Come, blooming hero, place thee by my side !
Give, on this well-known couch, one nuptial kiss
To me, this day, a second time thy bride !"
Jove frowned in heaven ; the conscious Parcæ threw
Upon those roseate lips a Stygian hue.

"This visage tells thee that my doom is past :
Know, virtue were not virtue if the joys
Of sense were able to return as fast
And surely as they vanish.—Earth destroys
Those raptures duly—Erebus disdains :
Calm pleasures there abide—majestic pains.

"Be taught, O faithful consort, to control
Rebellious passion : for the gods approve
The depth, and not the tumult, of the soul ;
A fervent, not ungovernable love.
Thy transports moderate , and meekly mourn
When I depart, for brief is my sojourn—"

"Ah, wherefore ?—Did not Hercules by force
Wrest from the guardian monster of the tomb
Alcestis, a reanimated corse
Given back to dwell on earth in vernal bloom ?
Medea's spells dispersed the weight of years,
And Æson stood a youth 'mid youthful peers.

"The gods to us are merciful—and they
Yet further may relent : for mightier far
Than strength of nerve and sinew, or the sway
Of magic potent over sun and star,
Is love, though oft to agony distrest,
And though his favourite seat be feeble woman's breast.

"But if thou goest I follow—" "Peace !" he said—
She looked upon him and was calmed and cheered ;
The ghastly colour from his lips had fled ;
In his deportment, shape, and mien, appeared
Elysian beauty, melancholy grace,
Brought from a pensive, though a happy place.

He spake of love, such love as spirits feel
In worlds whose course is equable and pure ;
No fears to beat away—no strife to heal—
The past unsighed for, and the future sure ;
Spake of heroic arts in graver mood
Revived, with finer harmony pursued.

Of all that is most beauteous—imaged there
In happier beauty ; more pellucid streams,
An ampler ether, a diviner air,
And fields invested with purpureal gleams,

Climes which the sun, who sheds the brightest day
Earth knows, is all unworthy to survey.

Yet there the soul shall enter which hath earned
That privilege by virtue.—"Ill," said he,
"The end of man's existence I discerned,
Who from ignoble games and revelry
Could draw, when we had parted, vain delight
While tears were thy best pastime,—day and night :

"And while my youthful peers, before my eyes,
(Each hero following his peculiar bent)
Prepared themselves for glorious enterprise
By martial sports,—or, seated in the tent,
Chieftains and kings in council were detained ;
What time the fleet at Aulis lay enchained.

"The wished-for wind was given :—I then revolved
The oracle, upon the silent sea ;
And, if no worthier led the way, resolved
That, of a thousand vessels, mine should be
The foremost prow in pressing to the strand,—
Mine the first blood that tinged the Trojan sand.

"Yet bitter, oft-times bitter, was the pang
When of thy loss I thought, belovèd wife!
On thee too fondly did my memory hang,
And on the joys we shared in mortal life,—
The paths which we had trod—these fountains—flowers ;
My new-planned cities, and unfinished towers.

"But should suspense permit the foe to cry,
'Behold, they tremble!—haughty their array,
Yet of their number no one dares to die!'—
In soul I swept the indignity away :
Old frailties then recurred :—but lofty thought,
In act embodied, my deliverance wrought.

"And thou, though strong in love, art all too weak
In reason, in self-government too slow ;
I counsel thee by fortitude to seek
Our blest re-union in the shades below.
The invisible world with thee hath sympathized ;
Be thy affections raised and solemnized.

"Learn by a mortal yearning to ascend
Towards a higher object.—Love was given,
Encouraged, sanctioned, chiefly for that end :
For this the passion to excess was driven—
That self might be annulled : her bondage prove
The fetters of a dream, opposed to love."

Aloud she shrieked! for Hermes reappears!
Round the dear shade she would have clung—'tis vain.
The hours are past—too brief had they been years ;
And him no mortal effort can detain :
Swift, toward the realms that know not earthly day,
He through the portal takes his silent way,
And on the palace floor a lifeless corse she lay.

By no weak pity might the gods be moved ;
She who thus perished not without the crime
Of lovers that in reason's spite have loved,
Was doomed to wander in a grosser clime,
Apart from happy ghosts—that gather flowers
Of blissful quiet 'mid unfading bowers.

Yet tears to human suffering are due ;
And mortal hopes defeated and o'erthrown
Are mourned by man, and not by man alone,
As fondly he believes.—Upon the side
Of Hellespont (such faith was entertained)
A knot of spiry trees for ages grew
From out the tomb of him for whom she died ;
And ever, when such stature they had gained
That Ilium's walls were subject to their view,
The trees' tall summits withered at the sight ;
A constant interchange of growth and blight! *

HER eyes are wild, her head is bare,
The sun has burnt her coal-black hair ;
Her eyebrows have a rusty stain,
And she came far from over the main.

---

* For the account of these long-lived trees, see Pliny's Natural History, lib. 16, cap. 44 ; and for the features in the character of Protesilaus see the "Iphigenia in Aulis" of Euripides.—Virgil places the shade of Laodamia in a mournful region among unhappy lovers.

She has a baby on her arm,
Or else she were alone;
And underneath the hay-stack warm,
And on the green-wood stone,
She talked and sung the woods among,
And it was in the English tongue.

"Sweet babe! they say that I am mad,
But nay, my heart is far too glad;
And I am happy when I sing
Full many a sad and doleful thing:
Then, lovely baby, do not fear!
I pray thee have no fear of me,
But, safe as in a cradle, here,
My lovely baby! thou shalt be:
To thee I know too much I owe;
I cannot work thee any woe.

A fire was once within my brain,
And in my head a dull, dull pain;
And fiendish faces, one, two, three,
Hung at my breast, and pulled at me.
But then there came a sight of joy:
It came at once to do me good;
I waked, and saw my little boy,
My little boy of flesh and blood;
Oh, joy for me that sight to see!
For he was here, and only he.

"Suck, little babe, oh, suck again!
It cools my blood; it cools my brain.
Thy lips I feel them, baby! they
Draw from my heart the pain away.
Oh! press me with thy little hand;
It loosens something at my chest,
About that tight and deadly band
I feel thy little fingers prest.
The breeze I see is in the tree:
It comes to cool my babe and me.

"Oh! love me, love me, little boy!
Thou art thy mother's only joy;
And do not dread the waves below,
When o'er the sea-rock's edge we go;
The high crag cannot work me harm,
Nor leaping torrents when they howl,
The babe I carry on my arm,
He saves for me my precious soul:
Then happy lie, for blest am I;
Without me my sweet babe would die.

"Then do not fear, my boy! for thee
Bold as a lion I will be;
And I will always be thy guide,
Through hollow snows and rivers wide.
I'll build an Indian bower; I know
The leaves that make the softest bed:
And, if from me thou wilt not go,
But still be true till I am dead,
My pretty thing! then thou shalt sing
As merry as the birds in spring.

"Thy father cares not for my breast,
'Tis thine, sweet baby, there to rest;
'Tis all thine own!—and, if its hue
Be changed, that was so fair to view,
'Tis fair enough for thee, my dove!
My beauty, little child, is flown;
But thou wilt live with me in love,
And what if my poor cheek be brown?
'Tis well for me, thou canst not see
How pale and wan it else would be.

"Dread not their taunts, my little life;
I am thy father's wedded wife;
And underneath the spreading tree
We two will live in honesty
If his sweet boy he could forsake,
With me he never would have stayed.
From him no harm my babe can take,
But he, poor man! is wretched made
And every day we two will pray
For him that's gone and far away

"I'll teach my boy the sweetest things
I'll teach him how the owlet sings.
My little babe! thy lips are still,
And thou hast almost sucked thy fill.
Where art thou gone, my own dear child
What wicked looks are those I see?
Alas! alas! that look so wild,
It never, never came from me:
If thou art mad, my pretty lad,
Then I must be for ever sad.

"Oh, smile on me, my little lamb!
For I thy own dear mother am.
My love for thee has well been tried:
I've sought thy father far and wide.
I know the poisons of the shade,
I know the earth-nuts fit for food;
Then, pretty dear, be not afraid;
We'll find thy father in the wood.
Now laugh and be gay, to the woods away!
And there, my babe, we'll live for aye."

RESOLUTION AND INDEPENDENCE.

THERE was a roaring in the wind all night;
The rain came heavily and fell in floods;
But now the sun is rising calm and bright;
The birds are singing in the distant woods:

Over his own sweet voice the stock-dove broods ; [ters ;
The jay makes answer as the magpie chat-
And all the air is filled with pleasant noise of waters.

All things that love the sun are out of doors
The sky rejoices in the morning's birth ;
The grass is bright with rain-drops ;—on the moors
The hare is running races in her mirth ;
And with her feet she from the plashy earth
Raises a mist , that, glittering in the sun,
Runs with her all the way, wherever she doth run

I was a traveller then upon the moor ;
I saw the hare that raced about with joy ;
I heard the woods, the distant waters, roar,
Or heard them not, as happy as a boy :
The pleasant season did my heart employ
My old remembrances went from me wholly ; [melancholy !
And all the ways of men so vain and

But, as it sometimes chanceth, from the might
Of joy in minds that can no further go,
As high as we have mounted in delight
In our dejection do we sink as low,
To me that morning did it happen so ;
And fears, and fancies, thick upon me came ;
Dim sadness—and blind thoughts, I knew not, nor could name.

I heard the sky-lark warbling in the sky ;
And I bethought me of the playful hare :
Even such a happy child of earth am I ;
Even as these blissful creatures do I fare ;
Far from the world I walk, and from all care ;
But there may come another day to me—
Solitude, pain of heart, distress, and poverty.

My whole life I have lived in pleasant thought,
As if life's business were a summer mood ;
As if all needful things would come unsought
To genial faith, still rich in genial good ;
But how can he expect that others should
Build for him, sow for him, and at his call
Love him, who for himself will take no heed at all?

I thought of Chatterton, the marvellous boy,
The sleepless soul that perished in his pride ;
Of him who walked in glory and in joy
Following his plough, along the mountain-side :
By our own spirits are we deified :
We poets in our youth begin in gladness ;
But thereof comes in the end despondency and madness

Now, whether it were by peculiar grace,
A leading from above, a something given,
Yet it befel, that, in this lonely place,
When I with these untoward thoughts had striven,
Beside a pool bare to the eye of heaven
I saw a man before me unawares :
The oldest man he seemed that ever wore gray hairs.

As a huge stone is sometimes seen to lie
Couched on the bald top of an eminence;
Wonder to all who do the same espy,
By what means it could thither come, and whence ,
So that it seems a thing endued with sense :
Like a sea-beast crawled forth, that on a shelf
Of rock or sand reposeth, there to sun itself ,

Such seemed this man, not all alive nor dead,
Nor all asleep—in his extreme old age :
His body was bent double, feet and head
Coming together in life's pilgrimage ;
As if some dire constraint of pain, or rage
Of sickness felt by him in times long past,
A more than human weight upon his frame had cast.

Himself he propped, his body, limbs, and face,
Upon a long gray staff of shaven wood .
And, still as I drew near with gentle pace,
Upon the margin of that moorish flood
Motionless as a cloud the old man stood ;
That heareth not the loud winds when they call ;
And moveth altogether, if it move at all.

At length, himself unsettling, he the pond
Stirred with his staff, and fixedly did look
Upon the muddy water, which he conned,
As if he had been reading in a book :
And now a stranger's privilege I took ;
And, drawing to his side, to him did say,
"This morning gives us promise of a glorious day."

A gentle answer did the old man make,
In courteous speech which forth he slowly drew :

And him with further words I thus bespake,
"What occupation do you there pursue?
This is a lonesome place for one like you."
He answered, while a flash of mild surprise
Broke from the sable orbs of his yet vivid eyes.

His words came feebly, from a feeble chest,
But each in solemn order followed each,
With something of a lofty utterance drest;
Choice word, and measured phrase, above the reach
Of ordinary men; a stately speech;
Such as grave livers do in Scotland use,
Religious men, who give to God and man their dues.

He told, that to these waters he had come
To gather leeches, being old and poor:
Employment hazardous and wearisome!
And he had many hardships to endure:
From pond to pond he roamed, from moor to moor;
Housing, with God's good help, by choice or chance;
And in this way he gained an honest maintenance.

The old man still stood talking by my side;
But now his voice to me was like a stream
Scarce heard; nor word from word could I divide;
And the whole body of the man did seem
Like one whom I had met with in a dream;
Or like a man from some far region sent,
To give me human strength, by apt admonishment.

My former thoughts returned: the fear that kills;
And hope that is unwilling to be fed;
Cold, pain, and labour, and all fleshly ills;
And mighty poets in their misery dead.
Perplexed, and longing to be comforted
My question eagerly did I renew,
"How is it that you live, and what is it you do?"

He with a smile did then his words repeat;
And said, that, gathering leeches, far and wide
He travelled; stirring thus about his feet
The waters of the pools where they abide.
"Once I could meet with them on every side;
But they have dwindled long by slow decay,
Yet still I persevere, and find them where I may."

While he was talking thus, the lonely place,
The old man's shape, and speech, all troubled me:
In my mind's eye I seemed to see him pace
About the weary moors continually,
Wandering about alone and silently.
While I these thoughts within myself pursued,
He, having made a pause, the same discourse renewed.

And soon with this he other matter blended,
Cheerfully uttered, with demeanour kind,
But stately in the main; and when he ended,
I could have laughed myself to scorn to find
In that decrepit man so firm a mind.
"God," said I, "be my help and stay secure;
I'll think of the leech-gatherer on the lonely moor!"

THE THORN.

"THERE is a thorn—it looks so old,
In truth, you'd find it hard to say
How it could ever have been young,
It looks so old and gray.
Not higher than a two years' child
It stands erect, this aged thorn;
No leaves it has, no thorny points;
It is a mass of knotted joints,
A wretched thing forlorn.
It stands erect, and like a stone
With lichens it is overgrown.

"Like rock or stone, it is o'ergrown,
With lichens to the very top,
And hung with heavy tufts of moss,
A melancholy crop:
Up from the earth these mosses creep,
And this poor thorn they clasp it round
So close, you'd say, that they were bent
With plain and manifest intent
To drag it to the ground;
And all had joined in one endeavour
To bury this poor thorn for ever.

"High on a mountain's highest ridge,
Where oft the stormy winter gale
Cuts like a scythe, while through the clouds
It sweeps from vale to vale;
Not five yards from the mountain path,
This thorn you on your left espy;
And to the left, three yards beyond,
You see a little muddy pond
Of water—never dry;
Though but of compass small, and bare
To thirsty suns and parching air.

"And, close beside this aged thorn,
There is a fresh and lovely sight,
A beauteous heap, a hill of moss,
Just half a foot in height.
All lovely colours there you see,
All colours that were ever seen;
And mossy net-work too is there
As if by hand of lady fair
The work had woven been;
And cups, the darlings of the eye,
So deep is their vermilion dye.

"Ah me! what lovely tints are there!
Of olive green and scarlet bright,
In spikes, in branches, and in stars,
Green, red, and pearly white.
This heap of earth o'ergrown with moss,
Which close beside the thorn you see,
So fresh in all its beauteous dyes,
Is like an infant's grave in size,
As like as like can be:
But never, never any where,
An infant's grave was half so fair.

"Now would you see this aged thorn,
This pond, and beauteous hill of moss,
You must take care and choose your time
The mountain when to cross.
For oft there sits between the heap
So like an infant's grave in size,
And that same pond of which I spoke,
A woman in a scarlet cloak,
And to herself she cries,
'Oh, misery! oh, misery!
Oh, woe is me! oh, misery!'

"At all times of the day and night
This wretched woman thither goes;
And she is known to every star,
And every wind that blows;
And there, beside the thorn, she sits
When the blue daylight's in the skies,
And when the whirlwind's on the hill,
Or frosty air is keen and still,
And to herself she cries,
'Oh, misery! oh, misery!
Oh, woe is me! oh, misery!"

"Now wherefore, thus, by day and night,
In rain, in tempest, and in snow,
Thus to the dreary mountain-top
Does this poor woman go?
And why sits she beside the thorn
When the blue daylight's in the sky,
Or when the whirlwind's on the hill,
Or frosty air is keen and still,
And wherefore does she cry?—
Oh, wherefore? wherefore? tell me why
Does she repeat that doleful cry?"

"I cannot tell; I wish I could;
For the true reason no one knows:
But would you gladly view the spot,
The spot to which she goes;
The hillock like an infant's grave,
The pond—and thorn so old and gray;
Pass by her door—'tis seldom shut—
And, if you see her in her hut,
Then to the spot away!—
I never heard of such as dare
Approach the spot when she is there."

"But wherefore to the mountain-top
Can this unhappy woman go,
Whatever stay is in the skies,
Whatever wind may blow?"
"'Tis known, that twenty years are passed
Since she (her name is Martha Ray)
Gave with a maiden's true good will
Her company to Stephen Hill,
And she was blithe and gay,
While friends and kindred all approved
Of him whom tenderly she loved.

"And they had fixed the wedding day,
The morning that must wed them both;
But Stephen to another maid
Had sworn another oath;
And with this other maid to church
Unthinking Stephen went—
Poor Martha! on that woeful day
A pang of pitiless dismay
Into her soul was sent;
A fire was kindled in her breast,
Which might not burn itself to rest.

"They say, full six months after this,
While yet the summer leaves were green,
She to the mountain-top would go,
And there was often seen.
Alas! her lamentable state
Even to a careless eye was plain;
She was with child, and she was mad;
Yet often she was sober sad
From her exceeding pain
O guilty father,—would that death
Had saved him from that breach of faith!

"Sad case for such a brain to hold
Communion with a stirring child!
Sad case, as you may think, for one
Who had a brain so wild!
Last Christmas-eve we talked of this,
And gray-haired Wilfred of the glen
Held that the unborn infant wrought
About its mother's heart, and brought
Her senses back again:
And when at last her time drew near,
Her looks were calm, her senses clear.

"More know I not, I wish I did,
And it should all be told to you;
For what became of this poor child
No mortal ever knew;
Nay—if a child to her was born
No earthly tongue could ever tell;
And if 'twas born alive or dead,
Far less could this with proof be said;
But some remember well,
That Martha Ray about this time
Would up the mountain often climb.

"And all that winter, when at night
The wind blew from the mountain-peak,
'Twas worth your while, though in the dark,
The church-yard path to seek:
For many a time and oft were heard
Cries coming from the mountain-head:
Some plainly living voices were;
And others, I've heard many swear,
Were voices of the dead:
I cannot think, whate'er they say,
They had to do with Martha Ray.

"But that she goes to this old thorn,
The thorn which I described to you,
And there sits in a scarlet cloak,
I will be sworn is true.
For one day with my telescope,
To view the ocean wide and bright,
When to this country first I came,
Ere I had heard of Martha's name,
I climbed the mountain's height:
A storm came on, and I could see
No object higher than my knee.

"'Twas mist and rain, and storm and rain;
No screen, no fence could I discover;
And then the wind! in faith it was
A wind full ten times over.
I looked around, I thought I saw
A jutting crag,—and off I ran,
Head-foremost, through the driving rain,
The shelter of the crag to gain;
And as I am a man,
Instead of jutting crag, I found
A woman seated on the ground.

"I did not speak—I saw her face;
Her face!—it was enough for me;
I turned about and heard her cry,
'Oh, misery! oh, misery!'
And there she sits, until the moon
Through half the clear blue sky will go;
And, when the little breezes make
The waters of the pond to shake,
As all the country know,
She shudders, and you hear her cry,
'Oh, misery! oh, misery!'

"But what's the thorn? and what the pond?
And what the hill of moss to her?
And what the creeping breeze that comes
The little pond to stir?"
"I cannot tell; but some will say
She hanged her baby on the tree;
Some say she drowned it in the pond,
Which is a little step beyond:
But all and each agree,
The little babe was buried there,
Beneath that hill of moss so fair.

"I've heard the moss is spotted red
With drops of that poor infant's blood·
But kill a new-born infant thus,
I do not think she could!
Some say, if to the pond you go,
And fix on it a steady view,
The shadow of a babe you trace,
A baby and a baby's face,
And that it looks at you;
Whene'er you look on it, 'tis plain
The baby looks at you again.

"And some had sworn an oath that she
Should be to public justice brought;
And for the little infant's bones
With spades they would have sought.
It might not be—the hill of moss
Before their eyes began to stir!
And for full fifty yards around,
The grass—it shook upon the ground!
Yet all do still aver
The little babe is buried there,
Beneath that hill of moss so fair.

"I cannot tell how this may be;
But plain it is, the thorn is bound
With heavy tufts of moss, that strive
To drag it to the ground;
And this I know, full many a time,
When she was on the mountain high,
By day and in the silent night,
When all the stars shone clear and bright,
That I have heard her cry,
'Oh, misery! oh, misery!
Oh, woe is me! oh, misery!'"

HART-LEAP WELL.

Hart-Leap Well is a small spring of water, about five miles from Richmond in Yorkshire, and near the side of the road that leads from Rich-

mond to Askrigg Its name is derived from a remarkable chase, the memory of which is preserved by the monuments spoken of in the second part of the following poem, which monuments do now exist as I have there described them.

THE knight had ridden down from Wensley
 moor
With the slow motion of a summer's cloud,
He turned aside towards a vassal's door,
And "Bring another horse!" he cried
 aloud.

"Another horse!"—That shout the vassal
 heard,
And saddled his best steed, a comely gray,
Sir Walter mounted him; he was the third
Which he had mounted on that glorious
 day.

Joy sparkled in the prancing courser's eyes;
The horse and horseman are a happy pair;
But though Sir Walter like a falcon flies,
There is a doleful silence in the air.

A rout this morning left Sir Walter's hall,
That as they galloped made the echoes roar,
But horse and man are vanished one and
 all;
Such race, I think, was never seen before

Sir Walter, restless as a veering wind,
Calls to the few tired dogs that yet remain:
Blanch, Swift, and Music, noblest of their
 kind,
Follow, and up the weary mountain strain.

The knight hallooed, he cheered, and chid
 them on [stern,
With suppliant gestures and upbraidings
But breath and eyesight fail: and, one by
 one, [fern.
The dogs are stretched among the mountain

Where is the throng, the tumult of the
 race?
The bugles that so joyfully were blown?
This chase it looks not like an earthly
 chase;
Sir Walter and the hart are left alone

The poor hart toils along the mountain
 side;
I will not stop to tell how far he fled;
Nor will I mention by what death he died;
But now the knight beholds him lying
 dead.

Dismounting then, he leaned against a
 thorn;
He had no follower, dog, nor man, nor boy:
He neither cracked his whip, nor blew his
 horn,
But gazed upon the spoil with silent joy.

Close to the thorn on which Sir Walter
 leaned, [feat:
Stood his dumb partner in this glorious
Weak as a lamb the hour that it is yeaned;
And white with foam as if with cleaving
 sleet.

Upon his side the hart was lying stretched;
His nostril touched a spring beneath a hill,
And with the last deep groan his breath had
 fetched [still.
The waters of the spring were trembling

And now, too happy for repose or rest,
(Never had living man such joyful lot!)
Sir Walter walked all round, north, south,
 and west, [spot.
And gazed and gazed upon that darling

And climbing up the hill—(it was at least
Nine roods of sheer ascent) Sir Walter
 found [hunted beast
Three several hoof-marks which the
Had left imprinted on the grassy ground.

Sir Walter wiped his face, and cried, "Till
 now
Such sight was never seen by living eyes:
Three leaps have borne him from this lofty
 brow
Down to the very fountain where he lies.

"I'll build a pleasure-house upon this spot,
And a small arbour, made for rural joy;
'Twill be the traveller's shed, the pilgrim's
 cot,
A place of love for damsels that are coy.

"A cunning artist will I have to frame
A basin for that fountain in the dell!
And they who do make mention of the same,
From this day forth shall call it HART-
 LEAP WELL.

"And, gallant stag! to make thy praises
 known,
Another monument shall here be raised;
Three several pillars, each a rough-hewn
 stone, [grazed.
And planted where thy hoofs the turf have

"And, in the summer-time when days are long,
I will come hither with my paramour;
And with the dancers and the minstrel's song
We will make merry in that pleasant bower

"Till the foundations of the mountains fail
My mansion with its arbour shall endure;—
The joy of them who till the fields of Swale,
And them who dwell among the woods of Ure!"

Then home he went, and left the hart, stone-dead,
With breathless nostrils stretched above the spring.
Soon did the knight perform what he had said,
And far and wide the fame thereof did ring.

Ere thrice the moon into her port had steered,
A cup of stone received the living well;
Three pillars of rude stone Sir Walter reared,
And built a house of pleasure in the dell.

And near the fountain, flowers of stature tall
With trailing plants and trees were intertwined,—
Which soon composed a little sylvan hall,
A leafy shelter from the sun and wind.

And thither, when the summer days were long,
Sir Walter led his wondering paramour;
And with the dancers and the minstrel's song
Made merriment within that pleasant bower

The knight, Sir Walter, died in course of time,
And his bones lie in his paternal vale.—
But there is matter for a second rhyme,
And I to this would add another tale.

PART II.

THE moving accident is not my trade,
To freeze the blood I have no ready arts:
'Tis my delight, alone in summer shade,
To pipe a simple song for thinking hearts.

As I from Hawes to Richmond did repair,
It chanced that I saw standing in a dell
Three aspens at three corners of a square:
And one not four yards distant. near a well.

What this imported I could ill divine:
And pulling now the rein my horse to stop,
I saw three pillars standing in a line,
The last stone pillar on a dark hill-top.

The trees were gray, with neither arms nor head:
Half-wasted the square mound of tawny green;
So that you just might say, as then I said,
"Here in old time the hand of man hath been."

I looked upon the hill both far and near,
More doleful place did never eye survey;
It seemed as if the spring-time came not here,
And nature here were willing to decay.

I stood in various thoughts and fancies lost,
When one, who was in shepherd's garb attired,
Came up the hollow:—him did I accost,
And what this place might be I then inquired.

The shepherd stopped, and that same story told
Which in my former rhyme I have rehearsed.
"A jolly place," said he, "in times of old!
But something ails it now, the spot is cursed.

"You see these lifeless stumps of aspen wood—
Some say that they are beeches, others elms—
These were the bower: and here a mansion stood,
The finest palace of a hundred realms!

"The arbour does its own condition tell;
You see the stones, the fountain, and the stream;
But as to the great lodge! you might as well
Hunt half a day for a forgotten dream.

"There's neither dog nor heifer, horse nor sheep,
Will wet his lips within that cup of stone;
And oftentimes, when all are fast asleep,
This water doth send forth a dolorous groan.

"Some say that here a murder has been done
And blood cries out for blood: but, for my part,
I've guessed, when I've been sitting in the sun,
That it was all for that unhappy hart,

"What thoughts must through the creature's brain have past!
Even from the topmost stone, upon the steep,
Are but three bounds—and look, sir, at this last—
O master! it has been a cruel leap.

"For thirteen hours he ran a desperate race;
And in my simple mind we cannot tell
What cause the hart might have to love this place,
And come and make his death-bed near the well.

"Here on the grass perhaps asleep he sank,
Lulled by this fountain in the summer-tide;
This water was perhaps the first he drank
When he had wandered from his mother's side.

"In April here beneath the scented thorn
He heard the birds their morning carols sing;
And he, perhaps, for aught we know, was born
Not half a furlong from that self-same spring.

"Now, here is neither grass nor pleasant shade;
The sun on drearier hollow never shone;
So will it be, as I have often said,
Till trees, and stones, and fountain, all are gone."

"Gray-headed shepherd, thou hast spoken well;
Small difference lies between thy creed and mine:
This beast not unobserved by nature fell;
His death was mourned by sympathy divine.

"The being that is in the clouds and air,
That is in the green leaves among the groves,
Maintains a deep and reverential care
For the unoffending creatures whom He loves.

"The pleasure-house is dust:—behind, before,
This is no common waste, no common gloom;
But nature, in due course of time, once more
Shall here put on her beauty and her bloom.

"She leaves these objects to a slow decay,
That what we are, and have been, may be known;
But, at the coming of the milder day,
These monuments shall all be overgrown.

"One lesson, shepherd, let us two divide,
Taught both by what she shows, and what conceals,
Never to blend our pleasure or our pride
With sorrow of the meanest thing that feels."

SONG AT THE FEAST OF BROUGHAM CASTLE,

UPON THE RESTORATION OF LORD CLIFFORD, THE SHEPHERD, TO THE ESTATES AND HONOURS OF HIS ANCESTORS.*

HIGH in the breathless hall the minstrel sate,
And Emont's murmur mingled with the song.—
The words of ancient time I thus translate,
A festal strain that hath been silent long:—

* Henry Lord Clifford, etc., etc., who is the subject of this poem, was the son of John Lord Clifford, who was slain at Towton Field, which John Lord Clifford, as is known to the reader of English history, was the person who after the battle of Wakefield slew, in the pursuit, the young Earl of Rutland, son of the Duke of York, who had fallen in the battle, "in part of revenge" (say the authors of the History of Cumberland and Westmoreland); "for the earl's father had slain his." A deed which worthily blemished the author (says Speed); but who, as he adds, "dare promise anything temperate of himself in the heat of martial fury? chiefly when it was resolved not to leave any branch of the York line standing; for so one maketh this lord to speak." This, no doubt, I would observe by the by, was an action sufficiently in the vindictive spirit of the times, and yet not altogether so bad as represented; "for the earl was no child, as some writers would have him, but able to bear arms, being sixteen or seventeen years of age, as is evident from this (say the Memoirs of the Countess of Pembroke, who was laudably anxious to wipe away, as far as could be, this stigma from the illustrious name to which she was born), that he was the next child to King Edward the Fourth, which his mother had by Richard Duke of York, and that king was then eighteen years of age; and for the small distance betwixt her children, see Austin Vincent in his book of Nobility, page 622, where he writes of them all. It may further be observed, that Lord Clifford, who was then himself only twenty-h e years of age, had been a leading man and commander, two or three years together in the army of Lancaster, before this time; and, therefore, would

"From town to town, from tower to tower,
The red rose is a gladsome flower.
Her thirty years of winter past,
The red rose is revived at last;
She lifts her head for endless spring,
For everlasting blossoming:
Both roses flourish, red and white.
In love and sisterly delight
The two that were at strife are blended,
And all old troubles now are ended —
Joy! joy to both! but most to her
Who is the flower of Lancaster!
Behold her how she smiles to-day
On this great throng, this bright array!
Fair greeting doth she send to all
From every corner of the hall;
But chiefly from above the board
Where sits in state our rightful lord,
A Clifford to his own restored!

"They came with banner, spear, and shield;
And it was proved in Bosworth-field.
Not long the avenger was withstood—
Earth helped him with the cry of blood:*
St. George was for us, and the might
Of blessed angels crowned the right.
Loud voice the land has uttered forth,
We loudest in the faithful north:
Our fields rejoice, our mountains ring,
Our streams proclaim a welcoming;
Our strong abodes and castles see
The glory of their loyalty.

"How glad is Skipton at this hour—
Though she is but a lonely tower!
To vacancy and silence left;
Of all her guardian sons bereft—
Knight, squire, or yeoman, page or groom,
We have them at the feast of Brough'm.
How glad Pendragon—though the sleep
Of years be on her!—She shall reap
A taste of this great pleasure, viewing
As in a dream her own renewing.
Rejoiced is Brough, right glad I deem
Beside her little humble stream;
And she that keepeth watch and ward
Her statelier Eden's course to guard;
They both are happy at this hour,
Though each is but a lonely tower:—
But here is perfect joy and pride
For one fair house by Emont's side,
This day distinguished without peer
To see her master and to cheer
Him, and his lady mother dear!

be less likely to think that the Earl of Rutland might be entitled to mercy from his youth.—But independent of this act, at the best a cruel and savage one, the family of Clifford had done enough to draw upon them the vehement hatred of the House of York; so that after the battle of Towton there was no hope for them but in flight and concealment. Henry, the subject of the poem, was deprived of his estate and honours during the space of twenty-four years, all which time he lived as a shepherd in Yorkshire, or in Cumberland, where the estate of his father-in-law (Sir Lancelot Threlkeld) lay. He was restored to his estate and honours in the first year of Henry the Seventh It is recorded that, when called to parliament, he behaved nobly and wisely; but otherwise came seldom to London or the court; and rather delighted to live in the country, where he repaired several of his castles, which had gone to decay during the late troubles." Thus far is chiefly collected from Nicholson and Burn; and I can add, from my own knowledge, that there is a tradition current in the village of Threlkeld and its neighbourhoop, his principal retreat, that, in the course of his shepherd-life he had acquired great astronomical knowledge. I cannot conclude this note without adding a word upon the subject of those numerous and noble feudal edifices, spoken of in the poem, the ruins of some of which are, at this day, so great an ornament to that interesting country. The Cliffords had always been distinguished for an honourable pride in these castles; and we have seen that after the wars of York and Lancaster they were rebuilt; in the civil wars of Charles the First they were again laid waste, and again restored almost to their former magnificence by the celebrated Lady Anne Clifford, Countess of Pembroke, etc., etc. Not more than twenty-five years after this was done, when the estates of Clifford had passed into the Family of Tufton, three of these castles, namely, Brough, Brougham, and Pendragon, were demolished, and the timber and other materials sold by Thomas Earl of Thanet We will hope that when this order was issued, the Earl had not consulted the text of Isaiah, 58th Chapter, 12th Verse, to which the inscription placed over the gate of Pendragon Castle, by the Countess of Pembroke (I believe his grandmother) at the time she repaired that structure, refers the reader "*And they that shall be of thee shall build the old waste places; thou shalt raise up the foundations of many generations; and thou shalt be called the repairer of the breach, the restorer of paths to dwell in*" The Earl of Thanet, the present possessor of the estates, with a due respect for the memory of his ancestors, and a proper sense of the value and beauty of these remains of antiquity, has (I am told) given orders that they shall be preserved from all depredations.

* This line is from the Battle of Bosworth Field, by Sir John Beaumont (brother to the dramatist, whose poems are written with much spirit, elegance, and harmony.

"Oh! it was a time forlorn
When the fatherless was born—
Give her wings that she may fly,
Or she sees her infant die!
Swords that are with slaughter wild
Hunt the mother and the child
Who will take them from the light?
Yonder is a man in sight—
Yonder is a house—but where?
No, they must not enter there.
To the caves, and to the brooks,
To the clouds of heaven she looks;
She is speechless, but her eyes
Pray in ghostly agonies
Blissful Mary, mother mild,
Maid and mother undefiled,
Save a mother and her child!

"Now who is he that bounds with joy
On Carrock's side, a shepherd boy?
No thoughts hath he but thoughts that pass
Light as the wind along the grass.
Can this be he who hither came
In secret, like a smothered flame?
O'er whom such thankful tears were shed
For shelter, and a poor man's bread!
God loves the child; and God hath willed
That those dear words should be fulfilled,
The lady's words, when forced away,
The last she to her babe did say,
'My own, my own, thy fellow-guest
I may not be; but rest thee, rest,
For lowly shepherd's life is best!'

"Alas! when evil men are strong
No life is good, no pleasure long.
The boy must part from Mosedale's groves,
And leave Blencathara's rugged coves,
And quit the flowers that summer brings
To Glenderamakin's lofty springs;
Must vanish, and his careless cheer
Be turned to heaviness and fear.
Give Sir Lancelot Threlkeld praise!
Hear it, good man, old in days!
Thou tree of covert and of rest
For this young bird that is distrest;
Among thy branches safe he lay,
And he was free to sport and play,
When falcons were abroad for prey.

"A recreant harp, that sings of fear
And heaviness in Clifford's ear!
I said, when evil men are strong,
No life is good, no pleasure long,
A weak and cowardly untruth!
Our Clifford was a happy youth,
And thankful through a weary time,
That brought him up to manhood's prime.
Again he wanders forth at will,
And tends a flock from hill to hill:
His garb is humble; ne'er was seen
Such garb with such a noble mien,
Among the shepherd grooms no mate
Hath he, a child of strength and state!
Yet lacks not friends for solemn glee,
And a cheerful company,
That learned of him submissive ways;
And comforted his private days.
To his side the fallow-deer
Came, and rested without fear,
The eagle, lord of land and sea,
Stooped down to pay him fealty;
And both the undying fish that swim
Through Bowscale-Tarn* did wait on him
The pair were servants of his eye
In their immortality;
They moved about in open sight,
To and fro, for his delight.
He knew the rocks which angels haunt
On the mountains visitant;
He hath kenned them taking wing;
And the caves where faeries sing
He hath entered; and been told
By voices how men lived of old.
Among the heavens his eye can see
Face of thing that is to be;
And, if men report him right,
He could whisper words of might.
Now another day is come,
Fitter hope, and nobler doom:
He hath thrown aside his crook,
And hath buried deep his book,
Armour rusting in his halls
On the blood of Clifford calls;†—
'Quell the Scot,' exclaims the lance—
Bear me to the heart of France,
Is the longing of the shield—
Tell thy name, thou trembling field;
Field of death, where'er thou be,
Groan thou with our victory!
Happy day, and mighty hour,
When our shepherd, in his power,

* It is imagined by the people of the country that there are two immortal fish, inhabitants of this Tarn, which lies in the mountains not far from Threlkeld.—Blencathara, mentioned before is the old and proper name of the mountain vulgarly called Saddle-back

† The martial character of the Cliffords is well known to the readers of English history, but it may not be improper here to say, by way of comment on these lines, and what follows, that, besides several others who perished in the same manner, the four immediate progenitors of the person in whose hearing this is supposed to be spoken, all died in the field.

Mailed and horsed, with lance and sword,
To his ancestors restored,
Like a re-appearing star,
Like a glory from afar,
First shall head the flock of war!"

Alas! the fervent harper did not know
That for a tranquil soul the lay was framed,
Who, long compelled in humble walks to go,
Was softened into feeling, soothed, and tamed.

Love had he found in huts where poor men lie;
His daily teachers had been woods and rills,
The silence that is in the starry sky,
The sleep that is among the lonely hills.

In him the savage virtue of the race,
Revenge, and all ferocious thoughts were dead:
Nor did he change; but kept in lofty place
The wisdom which adversity had bred.

Glad were the vales, and every cottage hearth;
The shepherd lord was honoured more and more:
And, ages after he was laid in earth,
"The good Lord Clifford" was the name he bore.

THE ECHO.

Yes, it was the mountain echo,
Solitary, clear, profound,
Answering to the shouting cuckoo,
Giving to her sound for sound!

Unsolicited reply
To a babbling wanderer sent;
Like her ordinary cry,
Like—but oh, how different!

Hears not also mortal life?
Hear not we, unthinking creatures!
Slaves of folly, love, and strife,
Voices of two different natures?

Have not we too;—yes, we have
Answers, and we know not whence;
Echoes from beyond the grave,
Recognised intelligence?

Such rebounds our inward ear
Often catches from afar;—
Giddy mortals! hold them dear;
For of God,—of God they are.

TO A SKYLARK.

Ethereal minstrel! pilgrim of the sky!
Dost thou despise the earth where cares abound?
Or, while the wings aspire, are heart and eye
Both with thy nest upon the dewy ground?
Thy nest which thou canst drop into at will,
Those quivering wings composed, that music still!

To the last point of vision, and beyond,
Mount, daring warbler! that love-prompted strain,
('Twixt thee and thine a never-failing bond)
Thrills not the less the bosom of the plain:
Yet mightst thou seem, proud privilege! to sing
All independent of the leafy spring.

Leave to the nightingale her shady wood;
A privacy of glorious light is thine;
Whence thou dost pour upon the world a flood
Of harmony, with rapture more divine,
Type of the wise who soar, but never roam;
True to the kindred points of heaven and home!

It is no spirit who from heaven hath flown,
And is descending on his embassy;
Nor traveller gone from earth the heavens to espy!
'Tis Hesperus—there he stands with glittering crown,
First admonition that the sun is down!
For yet it is broad daylight! clouds pass by.
A few are near him still—and now the sky,
He hath it to himself—'tis all his own.
O most ambitious star! thy presence brought
A startling recollection to my mind
Of the distinguished few among mankind,
Who dare to step beyond their natural race,
As thou seem'st now to do: nor was a thought
Denied—that even I might one day trace
Some ground not mine; and, strong her strength above,
My soul, an apparition in the place,
Tread there, with steps that no one shall reprove!

FRENCH REVOLUTION,

AS IT APPEARED TO ENTHUSIASTS AT ITS COMMENCEMENT.* REPRINTED FROM "THE FRIEND.'

OH ! pleasant exercise of hope and joy !
For mighty were the auxiliars, which then stood
Upon our side, we who were strong in love!
Bliss was it in that dawn to be alive,
But to be young was very heaven !—Oh ! times,
In which the meagre, stale, forbidding ways
Of custom, law, and statute, took at once
The attraction of a country in romance !
When reason seemed the most to assert her rights,
When most intent on making of herself
A prime enchantress—to assist the work,
Which then was going forward in her name!
Not favoured spots alone, but the whole earth,
The beauty wore of promise—that which sets
(To take an image which was felt no doubt
Among the bowers of paradise itself)
The budding rose above the rose full blown.
What temper at the prospect did not wake
To happiness unthought of? The inert
Were roused, and lively natures rapt away !
They who had fed their childhood upon dreams,
The playfellows of fancy, who had made
All powers of swiftness, subtilty, and strength
Their ministers,—who in lordly wise had stirred
Among the grandest objects of the sense,
And dealt with whatsoever they found there
As if they had within some lurking right
To wield it;—they, too, who of gentle mood
Had watched all gentle motions, and to these
Had fitted their own thoughts, schemers more mild,
And in the region of their peaceful selves;—
Now was it that *both* found, the meek and lofty
Did both find helpers to their heart's desire,
And stuff at hand, plastic as they could wish,—
Were called upon to exercise their skill,
Not in Utopia,—subterraneous fields,—
Or some secreted island, Heaven knows where !
But in the very world, which is the world
Of all of us,—the place where in the end
We find our happiness, or not at all !

* This, and the extract ("The Influence of Natural Objects"), page 28, and the first piece of this class, are from the unpublished poem of which some account is given in the preface to "The Excursion."

THE PASS OF KIRKSTONE.

WITHIN the mind strong fancies work,
A deep delight the bosom thrills,
Oft as I pass along the fork
Of these fraternal hills :
Where, save the rugged road, we find
No appanage of human kind ;
Nor hint of man ; if stone or rock
Seem not his handy-work to mock
By something cognizably shaped ;
Mockery—or model roughly hewn,
And left as if by earthquake strewn,
Or from the flood escaped :—
Altars for Druid service fit ;
(But where no fire was ever lit,
Unless the glow-worm to the skies
Thence offer nightly sacrifice ;
Wrinkled Egyptian monument ;
Green moss-grown tower ; or hoary tent ;
Tents of a camp that never shall be raised ;
On which four thousand years have gazed !

Ye plough-shares sparkling on the slopes !
Ye snow-white lambs that trip
Imprisoned 'mid the formal props
Of restless ownership !
Ye trees, that may to-morrow fall
To feed the insatiate prodigal !
Lawns, houses, chattels, groves, and fields,
All that the fertile valley shields ;
Wages of folly—baits of crime,—
Of life's uneasy game the stake,
Playthings that keep the eyes awake
Of drowsy, dotard time ;—
O care ! O guilt !—O vales and plains,
Here, 'mid his own unvexed domains,
A genius dwells, that can subdue
At once all memory of you,—
Most potent when mists veil the sky,
Mists that distort and magnify ;
While the coarse rushes, to the sweeping breeze,
Sigh forth their ancient melodies !

List to those shriller notes ! *that* march
Perchance was on the blast,
When, through this height's inverted arch,
Rome's earliest legion passed !
They saw, adventurously impelled,
And older eyes than theirs beheld,

This block—and yon, whose church-like frame
Gives to the savage pass its name.
Aspiring road! that lov'st to hide
Thy daring in a vapoury bourn,
Not seldom may the hour return
When thou shalt be my guide;
And I (as often we find cause,
When life is at a weary pause,
And we have panted up the hill
Of duty with reluctant will)
Be thankful, even though tired and faint,
For the rich bounties of constraint;
Whence oft invigorating transports flow
That choice lacked courage to bestow.

My soul was grateful for delight
That wore a threatening brow;
A veil is lifted—can she slight
The scene that opens now!
Though habitation none appear,
The greenness tells, man must be there;
The shelter—that the pérspective
Is of the clime in which we live;
Where toil pursues his daily round;
Where pity sheds sweet tears, and love,
In woodbine bower or birchen grove,
Inflicts his tender wound.
Who comes not hither ne'er shall know
How beautiful the world below;
Nor can he guess how lightly leaps
The brook adown the rocky steeps.
Farewell, thou desolate domain!
Hope, pointing to the cultured plain,
Carols like a shepherd-boy;
And who is she?—Can that be joy!
Who, with a sunbeam for her guide,
Smoothly skims the meadows wide;
While faith, from yonder opening cloud
To hill and vale proclaims aloud,
"Whate'er the weak may dread, the wicked dare,
Thy lot, O man, is good, thy portion fair!"

EVENING ODE,

COMPOSED UPON AN EVENING OF EXTRAORDINARY SPLENDOUR AND BEAUTY.

HAD this effulgence disappeared
With flying haste, I might have sent,
Among the speechless clouds, a look
Of blank astonishment,
But 'tis endued with power to stay,
And sanctify one closing day,
That frail mortality may see—
What is?—ah no, but what *can* be!
Time was when field and watery cove
With modulated echoes rang,
While choirs of fervent angels sang
Their vespers in the grove;
Or, ranged like stars along some sovereign height,
Warbled, for heaven above and earth below,
Strains suitable to both—Such holy rite,
Methinks, if audibly repeated now
From hill or valley, could not move
Sublimer transport, purer love,
Than doth this silent spectacle—the gleam—
The shadow—and the peace supreme!

No sound is uttered,—but a deep
And solemn harmony pervades
The hollow vale from steep to steep,
And penetrates the glades
Far-distant images draw nigh,
Called forth by wondrous potency
Of beamy radiance, that imbues
Whate'er it strikes, with gem-like hues
In vision exquisitely clear,
Herds range along the mountain side;
And glistening antlers are descried;
And gilded flocks appear
Thine is the tranquil hour, purpureal eve!
But long as god-like wish, or hope divine,
Informs my spirit, ne'er can I believe
That this magnificence is wholly thine!
From worlds not quickened by the sun
A portion of the gift is won;
An intermingling of heaven's pomp is spread
On ground which British shepherds tread!

And, if there be whom broken ties
Afflict, or injuries assail,
Yon hazy ridges to their eyes
Present a glorious scale,
Climbing suffused with sunny air,
To stop—no record hath told where!
And tempting fancy to ascend,
And with immortal spirits blend!
Wings at my shoulder seem to play;
But, rooted here, I stand and gaze
On those bright steps that heavenward raise
Their practicable way.
Come forth, ye drooping old men, look abroad,
And see to what fair countries ye are bound!
And if some traveller, weary of his road,
Hath slept since noon-tide on the grassy ground,
Ye genii! to his covert speed;
And wake him with such gentle heed
As may attune his soul to meet the dower
Bestowed on this transcendent hour!

Such hues from their celestial urn
Were wont to stream before my eye.

Where'er it wandered in the morn
Of blissful infancy.
This glimpse of glory, why renewed?
Nay, rather speak with gratitude;
For, if a vestige of those gleams
Survived, 'twas only in my dreams.
Dread Power! whom peace and calmness serve
No less than nature's threatening voice,
If aught unworthy be my choice,
From THEE if I would swerve,
Oh, let thy grace remind me of the light
Full early lost, and fruitlessly deplored;
Which, at this moment, on my waking sight
Appears to shine, by miracle restored!
My soul, though yet confined to earth,
Rejoices in a second birth;
'Tis past, the visionary splendour fades;
And night approaches with her shades.

Note.—The multiplication of mountain ridges, described at the commencement of the third stanza of this ode, as a kind of Jacob's ladder, leading to Heaven, is produced either by watery vapours, or sunny haze;—in the present instance, by the latter cause. Allusions to the ode entitled "Intimations of Immortality," pervade the last stanza of the foregoing poem.

LINES,

COMPOSED A FEW MILES ABOVE TINTERN ABBEY, ON REVISITING THE BANKS OF THE WYE DURING A TOUR.

JULY 13, 1798.

FIVE years have past; five summers, with the length
Of five long winters! and again I hear
These waters, rolling from their mountain-springs
With a sweet inland murmur.*—Once again
Do I behold these steep and lofty cliffs,
That on a wild secluded scene impress
Thoughts of more deep seclusion; and connect
The landscape with the quiet of the sky.
The day is come when I again repose
Here, under this dark sycamore, and view
These plots of cottage-ground, these orchard-tufts,
Which at this season, with their unripe fruits,
Are clad in one green hue, and lose themselves
Among the woods and copses, nor disturb
The wild green landscape. Once again I see
These hedgerows, hardly hedgerows, little lines
Of sportive wood run wild; these pastoral farms,
Green to the very door; and wreaths of smoke
Sent up in silence, from among the trees!
With some uncertain notice, as might seem,
Of vagrant dwellers in the houseless woods,
Or of some hermit's cave, where by his fire
The hermit sits alone.
These beauteous forms,
Through a long absence, have not been to me
As is a landscape to a blind man's eye:
But oft, in lonely rooms, and 'mid the din
Of towns and cities, I have owed to them,
In hours of weariness, sensations sweet,
Felt in the blood, and felt along the heart;
And passing even into my purer mind,
With tranquil restoration:—feelings, too,
Of unremembered pleasure: such, perhaps,
As have no slight or trivial influence
On that best portion of a good man's life,
His little, nameless, unremembered acts
Of kindness and of love. Nor less, I trust,
To them I may have owed another gift,
Of aspect more sublime; that blessed mood,
In which the burthen of the mystery,
In which the heavy and the weary weight
Of all this unintelligible world,
Is lightened:—that serene and blessed mood,
In which the affections gently lead us on,—
Until, the breath of this corporeal frame,
And even the motion of our human blood
Almost suspended, we are laid asleep
In body, and become a living soul:
While with an eye made quiet by the power
Of harmony, and the deep power of joy,
We see into the life of things.
If this
Be but a vain belief, yet, oh! how oft—
In darkness, and amid the many shapes
Of joyless daylight; when the fretful stir
Unprofitable, and the fever of the world,
Have hung upon the beatings of my heart.
How oft, in spirit, have I turned to thee,
O sylvan Wye! Thou wanderer through the woods,
How often has my spirit turned to thee!

And now, with gleams of half-extinguished thought,
With many recognitions dim and faint,
And somewhat of a sad perplexity,
The picture of the mind revives again:
While here I stand, not only with the sense

* The river is not affected by the tides a few miles above Tintern.

Of present pleasure, but with pleasing thoughts
That in this moment there is life and food
For future years. And so I dare to hope,
Though changed, no doubt, from what I was when first
I came among these hills; when like a roe
I bounded o'er the mountains, by the sides
Of the deep rivers, and the lonely streams,
Wherever nature led: more like a man
Flying from something that he dreads, than one
Who sought the thing he loved. For nature then
(The coarser pleasures of my boyish days,
And their glad animal movements all gone by)
To me was all in all.—I cannot paint
What then I was. The sounding cataract
Haunted me like a passion: the tall rock,
The mountain, and the deep and gloomy wood,
Their colours and their forms, were then to me
An appetite; a feeling and a love,
That had no need of a remoter charm,
By thought supplied, or any interest
Unborrowed from the eye.—That time is past,
And all its aching joys are now no more,
And all its dizzy raptures. Not for this
Faint I, nor mourn nor murmur; other gifts
Have followed, for such loss, I would believe,
Abundant recompense. For I have learned
To look on nature, not as in the hour
Of thoughtless youth; but hearing oftentimes
The still, sad music of humanity,
Nor harsh nor grating, though of ample power
To chasten and subdue. And I have felt
A presence that disturbs me with the joy
Of elevated thoughts; a sense sublime
Of something far more deeply interfused,
Whose dwelling is the light of setting suns,
And the round ocean, and the living air,
And the blue sky, and in the mind of man:
A motion and a spirit, that impels
All thinking things, all objects of all thought,
And rolls through all things. Therefore am I still
A lover of the meadows and the woods,
And mountains; and of all that we behold
From this green earth; of all the mighty world
Of eye and ear, both what they half create,*
And what perceive, well pleased to recognise
In nature and the language of the sense,
The anchor of my purest thoughts, the nurse,
The guide, the guardian of my heart, and soul
Of all my moral being.
Nor perchance,
If I were not thus taught, should I the more
Suffer my genial spirits to decay:
For thou art with me, here upon the banks
Of this fair river; thou, my dearest friend,
My dear, dear friend, and in thy voice I catch
The language of my former heart, and read
My former pleasures in the shooting lights
Of thy wild eyes. Oh! yet a little while
May I behold in thee what I was once,
My dear, dear sister! and this prayer I make,
Knowing that nature never did betray
The heart that loved her; 'tis her privilege,
Through all the years of this our life, to lead
From joy to joy: for she can so inform
The mind that is within us, so impress
With quietness and beauty, and so feed
With lofty thoughts, that neither evil tongues,
Rash judgments, nor the sneers of selfish men,
Nor greetings where no kindness is, nor all
The dreary intercourse of daily life,
Shall e'er prevail against us, or disturb
Our cheerful faith, that all which we behold
Is full of blessings. Therefore let the moon
Shine on thee in thy solitary walk;
And let the misty mountain winds be free
To blow against thee: and, in after years,
When these wild ecstasies shall be matured
Into a sober pleasure, when thy mind
Shall be a mansion for all lovely forms,
Thy memory be as a dwelling-place
For all sweet sounds and harmonies; oh! then,
If solitude, or fear, or pain, or grief,
Should be thy portion, with what healing thoughts
Of tender joy wilt thou remember me,
And these my exhortations! Nor, perchance—
If I should be where I no more can hear
Thy voice, nor catch from thy wild eyes these gleams
Of past existence—wilt thou then forget
That on the banks of this delightful stream
We stood together; and that I, so long
A worshipper of nature, hither came,

* This line has a close resemblance to an admirable line of Young, the exact expression of which I cannot recollect.

Unwearied in that service : rather say
With warmer love—oh! with far deeper zeal
Of holier love. Nor wilt thou then forget,
That after many wanderings, many years
Of absence, these steep woods and lofty cliffs,
And this green pastoral landscape, were to me
More dear, both for themselves and for thy sake!

PETER BELL, A TALE.

"What's in a *name*?" . . .

"Brutus will start a spirit as soon as Cæsar!"

TO ROBERT SOUTHEY, ESQ., P. L. ETC. ETC.

MY DEAR FRIEND,—The tale of Peter Bell, which I now introduce to your notice, and to that of the public, has, in its manuscript state, nearly survived its *minority*;—for it first saw the light in the summer of 1798. During this long interval, pains have been taken at different times to make the production less unworthy of a favourable reception; or, rather, to fit it for filling *permanently* a station, however humble, in the literature of my country. This has, indeed, been the aim of all my endeavours in poetry, which, you know, have been sufficiently laborious to prove that I deem the art not lightly to be approached; and that the attainment of excellence in it may laudably be made the principal object of intellectual pursuit by any man, who, with reasonable consideration of circumstances, has faith in his own impulses

The poem of Peter Bell, as the prologue will show, was composed under a belief that the imagination not only does not require for its exercise the intervention of supernatural agency, but that, though such agency be excluded, the faculty may be called forth as imperiously, and for kindred results of pleasure, by incidents, within the compass of poetic probability, in the humblest departments of daily life. Since that prologue was written, *you* have exhibited most splendid effects of judicious daring, in the opposite and usual course. Let this acknowledgment make my peace with the lovers of the supernatural; and I am persuaded it will be admitted, that to you, as a master in that province of the art, the following tale, whether from contrast or congruity, is not an unappropriate offering. Accept it, then, as a public testimony of affectionate admiration from one with whose name yours has been often coupled (to use your own words) for evil and for good; and believe me to be, with earnest wishes that life and health may be granted you to complete the many important works in which you are engaged, and with high respect, most faithfully yours,

WILLIAM WORDSWORTH.

Rydal Mount, April 7, 1819.

PROLOGUE.

THERE'S something in a flying horse,
There's something in a huge balloon;
But through the clouds I'll never float
Until I have a little boat,
Whose shape is like the crescent-moon.

And now I *have* a little boat,
In shape a very crescent-moon:—
Fast through the clouds my boat can sail,
But if perchance your faith should fail,
Look up—and you shall see me soon!

The woods, my friends, are round you roaring,
Rocking and roaring like a sea;
The noise of danger fills your ears,
And ye have all a thousand fears
Both for my little boat and me!

Meanwhile untroubled I admire
The pointed horns of my canoe
And, did not pity touch my breast,
To see how ye are all distrest,
Till my ribs ached, I'd laugh at you!

Away we go, my boat and I—
Frail man ne'er sate in such another;
Whether among the winds we strive,
Or deep into the clouds we dive,
Each is contented with the other.

Away we go—and what care we
For treasons, tumults, and for wars?
We are as calm in our delight
As is the crescent-moon so bright
Among the scattered stars.

Up goes my boat among the stars
Through many a breathless field of light,
Through many a long blue field of ether.

Leaving ten thousand stars beneath her.
Up goes my little boat so bright!

The Crab—the Scorpion—and the Bull—
We pry among them all—have shot
High o'er the red-haired race of Mars,
Covered from top to toe with scars,
Such company I like it not!

The towns in Saturn are decayed,
And melancholy spectres throng them;
The Pleiads, that appear to kiss
Each other in the vast abyss,
With joy I sail among them!

Swift Mercury resounds with mirth,
Great Jove is full of stately bowers;
But these, and all that they contain,
What are they to that tiny grain,
That little earth of ours?

Then back to earth, the dear green earth;
Whole ages if I here should roam,
The world for my remarks and me
Would not a whit the better be;
I've left my heart at home.

And there it is, the matchless earth!
There spreads the famed Pacific Ocean!
Old Andes thrusts yon craggy spear
Through the gray clouds—the Alps are here,
Like waters in commotion!

Yon tawny slip is Libya's sands—
That silver thread the river Dnieper—
And look, where clothed in brightest green
Is a sweet isle, of isles the queen;
Ye fairies, from all evil keep her!

And see the town where I was born!
Around those happy fields we span
In boyish gambols—I was lost
Where I have been, but on this coast
I feel I am a man.

Never did fifty things at once
Appear so lovely, never, never,—
How tunefully the forests ring?
To hear the earth's soft murmuring
Thus could I hang for ever!

"Shame on you!" cried my little boat,
"Was ever such a homesick loon,
Within a living boat to sit,
And make no better use of it,—
A boat twin-sister of the crescent moon!

"Ne'er in the breast of full-grown poet
Fluttered so faint a heart before;—
Was it the music of the spheres
That overpowered your mortal ears!
Such din shall trouble them no more.

"These nether precincts do not lack
Charms of their own;—then come with me—
I want a comrade, and for you
There's nothing that I would not do;
Nought is there that you shall not see.

"Haste! and above Siberian snows
We'll sport amid the boreal morning,
Will mingle with her lustres, gliding
Among the stars, the stars now hiding,
And now the stars adorning.

"I know the secrets of a land
Where human foot did never stray;
Fair is that land as evening skies,
And cool,—though in the depth it lies
Of burning Africa.

"Or we'll into the realms of faery,
Among the lovely shades of things,
The shadowy forms of mountains bare,
And streams, and bowers, and ladies fair,
The shades of palaces and kings!

"Or, if you thirst with hardy zeal
Less quiet regions to explore,
Prompt voyage shall to you reveal
How heaven and earth are taught to feel
The might of magic lore!"

"My little vagrant form of light,
My gay and beautiful canoe,
Well have you played your friendly part;
As kindly take what from my heart
Experience forces—then adieu!

"Temptation lurks among your words;
But, while these pleasures you're pursuing
Without impediment or let,
My radiant pinnace, you forget
What on the earth is doing.

"There was a time when all mankind
Did listen with a faith sincere
To tuneful tongues in mystery versed;
Then poets fearlessly rehearsed
The wonders of a wild career.

"Go—(but the world's a sleepy world,
And 'tis, I fear, an age too late;)
Take with you some ambitious youth;
For, restless wanderer! I, in truth,
Am all unfit to be your mate.

"Long have I loved what I behold,
The night that calms, the day that cheers ;
The common growth of mother earth
Suffices me—her tears, her mirth,
Her humblest mirth and tears.

"The dragon's wing, the magic ring,
I shall not covet for my dower,
If I along that lowly way
With sympathetic heart may stray,
And with a soul of power.

"These given, what more need I desire
To stir—to soothe—or elevate ?
What nobler marvels than the mind
May in life's daily prospect find,
May find or there create ?

"A potent wand doth sorrow wield ;
What spell so strong as guilty fear !
Repentance is a tender sprite ,
If aught on earth have heavenly might,
'Tis lodged within her silent tear.

"But grant my wishes,—let us now
Descend from this ethereal height ,
Then take thy way, adventurous skiff,
More daring far than Hippogriff,
And be thy own delight !

"To the stone-table in my garden,
Loved haunt of many a summer hour,
The squire is come ,—his daughter Bess
Beside him in the cool recess
Sits blooming like a flower.

"With these are many more convened ;
They know not I have been so far—
I see them there, in number nine,
Beneath the spreading Weymouth pine—
I see them—there they are !

"There sits the vicar and his dame ;
And there my good friend, Stephen Otter ,
And, ere the light of evening fail,
To them I must relate the tale
Of Peter Bell the potter."

Off flew my sparkling boat in scorn,
Spurning her freight with indignation ?
And I, as well as I was able,
On two poor legs, toward my stone-table
Limped on with some vexation.

"Oh, here he is ! " cried little Bess—
She saw me at the garden door ;
"We've waited anxiously and long,"
They cried, and all around me throng,
Full nine of them or more!

"Reproach me not—your fears be still—
Be thankful we again have met ,—
Resume, my friends ! within the shade
Your seats, and quickly shall be paid
The well-remembered debt."

I spake with faltering voice, like one
Not wholly rescued from the pale
Of a wild dream, or worse illusion ;
But, straight to cover my confusion,
Began the promised tale.

PART I.

ALL by the moonlight river side
Groaned the poor beast—alas ! in vain ;
The staff was raised to loftier height,
And the blows fell with heavier weight
As Peter struck—and struck again.

Like winds that lash the waves, or smite
The woods, autumnal foliage thinning—
"Hold !" said the squire, "I pray you, hold !
Who Peter was let that be told,
And start from the beginning."

——"A potter,* sir, he was by trade,"
Said I, becoming quite collected ,
"And wheresoever he appeared,
Full twenty times was Peter feared
For once that Peter was respected.

He, two-and-thirty years or more,
Had been a wild and woodland rover ;
Had heard the Atlantic surges roar
On farthest Cornwall's rocky shore,
And trod the cliffs of Dover.

And he had seen Caernarvon's towers,
And well he knew the spire of Sarum ;
And he had been where Lincoln bell
Flings o'er the fen its ponderous knell,
Its far renowned alarum !

At Doncaster, at York, and Leeds
And merry Carlisle had he been ,
And all along the Lowlands fair,
All through the bonny shire of Ayr—
And far as Aberdeen.

And he had been at Inverness ;
And Peter, by the mountain rills,
Had danced his round with Highland lasses
And he had lain beside his asses
On lofty Cheviot Hills :

* In the dialect of the north, a hawker of earthenware is thus designated.

And he had trudged through Yorkshire dales,
Among the rocks and winding *scars;*
Where deep and low the hamlets lie
Beneath their little patch of sky
And little lot of stars:

And all along the indented coast,
Bespattered with the salt-sea foam;
Where'er a knot of houses lay
On headland, or in hollow bay;--
Sure never man like him did roam!

As well might Peter, in the Fleet,
Have been fast bound, a begging debtor;—
He travelled here, he travelled there;—
But not the value of a hair
Was heart or head the better.

He roved among the vales and streams,
In the green wood and hollow dell;
They were his dwellings night and day,—
But nature ne'er could find the way
Into the heart of Peter Bell.

In vain, through every changeful year,
Did nature lead him as before;
A primrose by a river's brim
A yellow primrose was to him,
And it was nothing more.

Small change it made in Peter's heart
To see his gentle panniered train
With more than vernal pleasure feeding,
Where'er the tender grass was leading
Its earliest green along the lane.

In vain, through water, earth, and air
The soul of happy sound was spread,
When Peter, on some April morn,
Beneath the broom or budding thorn,
Made the warm earth his lazy bed.

At noon, when by the forest's edge,
He lay beneath the branches high,
The soft blue sky did never melt
Into his heart,—he never felt
The witchery of the soft blue sky!

On a fair prospect some have looked
And felt, as I have heard them say,
As if the moving time had been
A thing as steadfast as the scene
On which they gazed themselves away.

Within the breast of Peter Bell
These silent raptures found no place:
He was a carl as wild and rude
As ever hue-and-cry pursued,
As ever ran a felon's race.

Of all that lead a lawless life,
Of all that love their lawless lives,
In city or in village small,
He was the wildest far of all;
He had a dozen wedded wives.

Nay, start not! — wedded wives — and twelve!
But how one wife could e'er come near him,
In simple truth I cannot tell;
For be it said of Peter Bell,
To see him was to fear him.

Though nature could not teach his heart
By lovely forms and silent weather,
And tender sounds, yet you might see
At once, that Peter Bell and she
Had often been together.

A savage wildness round him hung
As of a dweller out of doors;
In his whole figure and his mien
A savage character was seen,
Of mountains and of dreary moors.

To all the unshaped half-human thoughts
Which solitary nature feeds
'Mid summer storms or winter's ice,
Had Peter joined whatever vice
The cruel city breeds.

His face was keen as is the wind
That cuts along the hawthorn fence;
Of courage you saw little there,
But, in its stead, a medley air
Of cunning and of impudence.

He had a dark and sidelong walk,
And long and slouching was his gait;
Beneath his looks so bare and bold,
You might perceive, his spirit cold
Was playing with some inward bait.

His forehead wrinkled was and furred;
A work, one half of which was done
By thinking of his *whens* and *hows;*
And half, by knitting of his brows
Beneath the glaring sun.

There was a hardness in his cheek,
There was a hardness in his eye,
As if the man had fixed his face,
In many a solitary place,
Against the wind and open sky!

ONE NIGHT, (and now, my little Bess!
We've reached at last the promised tale,)
One beautiful November night,
When the full moon was shining bright
Upon the rapid river Swale,

Along the river's winding banks
Peter was travelling all alone,—
Whether to buy or sell, or led
By pleasure running in his head,
To me was never known.

He trudged along through copse and brake,
He trudged along o'er hill and dale;
Nor for the moon cared he a tittle,
And for the stars he cared as little,
And for the murmuring river Swale.

But, chancing to espy a path
That promised to cut short the way,
As many a wiser man hath done,
He left a trusty guide for one
That might his steps betray.

To a thick wood he soon is brought
Where cheerfully his course he weaves,
And whistling loud may yet be heard,
Though often buried, like a bird
Darkling among the boughs and leaves.

But quickly Peter's mood is changed,
And on he drives with cheeks that burn
In downright fury and in wrath—
There's little sign the treacherous path
Will to the road return!

The path grows dim, and dimmer still,
Now up—now down—the rover wends
With all the sail that he can carry,
Till brought to a deserted quarry;
And there the pathway ends.

He paused—for shadows of strange shape,
Massy and black, before him lay;
But through the dark, and through the cold,
And through the yawning fissures old,
Did Peter boldly press his way

Right through the quarry;—and behold
A scene of soft and lovely hue!
Where blue and gray, and tender green,
Together make as sweet a scene
As ever human eye did view.

Beneath the clear blue sky he saw
A little field of meadow ground;
But field or meadow name it not,
Call it of earth a small green plot,
With rocks encompassed round.

The Swale flowed under the gray rocks,
But he flowed quiet and unseen,
You need a strong and stormy gale
To bring the noises of the Swale
To that green spot, so calm and green!

And is there no one dwelling here,
No hermit with his beads and glass?
And does no little cottage look
Upon this soft and fertile nook?
Does no one live near this green grass?

Across the deep and quiet spot
Is Peter driving through the grass—
And now he is among the trees;
When, turning round his head, he sees
A solitary ass.

"A prize!" cried Peter, stepping back
To spy about him far and near;
There's not a single house in sight,
No woodman's hut, no cottage light,
Peter, you need not fear!

There's nothing to be seen but woods,
And rocks that spread a hoary gleam,
And this one beast, that from the bed
Of the green meadow hangs his head
Over the silent stream.

His head is with a halter bound;
The halter seizing, Peter leapt
Upon the creature's back, and plied
With ready heel his shaggy side;
But still the ass his station kept.

"What's this!" cried Peter, brandishing
A new-peeled sapling,—though I deem,
This threat was understood full well,
Firm, as before, the sentinel
Stood by the silent stream.

Then Peter gave a sudden jerk,
A jerk that from a dungeon floor
Would have pulled up an iron ring,
But still the heavy-headed thing
Stood just as he had stood before!

Quoth Peter, leaping from his seat,
"There is some plot against me laid,"
Once more the little meadow ground
And all the hoary cliffs around
He cautiously surveyed

All, all is silent—rocks and woods,
All still and silent—far and near!
Only the ass, with motion dull,
Upon the pivot of his skull
Turns round his long left ear.

Thought Peter, What can mean all this?
Some ugly witchcraft must be here!
Once more the ass, with motion dull,
Upon the pivot of his skull
Turned round his long left ear.

Suspicion ripened into dread;
Yet with deliberate action slow,
His staff high-raising, in the pride
Of skill, upon the sounding hide,
He dealt a sturdy blow.

What followed?—yielding to the shock,
The ass, as if to take his ease,
In quiet uncomplaining mood,
Upon the spot where he had stood,
Dropped gently down upon his knees,

And then upon his side he fell,
And by the river's brink did lie;
And, as he lay like one that mourned,
The beast on his tormentor turned
A shining hazel eye.

'Twas but one mild, reproachful look,
A look more tender than severe,
And straight in sorrow, not in dread,
He turned the eye-ball in his head
Towards the river deep and clear.

Upon the beast the sapling rings,—
Heaved his lank sides, his limbs they stirred;
He gave a groan, and then another,
Of that which went before the brother,
And then he gave a third.

And Peter halts to gather breath,
And, while he halts, was clearly shown
(What he before in part had seen)
How gaunt the creature was, and lean,
Yea, wasted to a skeleton!

With legs stretched out and stiff he lay:—
No word of kind commiseration
Fell at the sight from Peter's tongue;
With hard contempt his heart was wrung,
With hatred and vexation.

The meagre beast lay still as death—
And Peter's lips with fury quiver—
Quoth he, "You little mulish dog,
I'll fling your carcase like a log
Head-foremost down the river!"

An impious oath confirmed the threat—
That instant, while outstretched he lay,
To all the echoes, south and north,
And east and west, the ass sent forth
A loud and piteous bray!

This outcry, on the heart of Peter,
Seems like a note of joy to strike,—
Joy at the heart of Peter knocks;—
But in the echo of the rocks
Was something Peter did not like.

Whether to cheer his coward breast,
Or that he could not break the chain,
In this serene and solemn hour,
Twined round him by demoniac power,
To the blind work he turned again.—

Among the rocks and winding crags—
Among the mountains far away—
Once more the ass did lengthen out
More ruefully an endless shout,
The long dry see-saw of his horrible bray!

What is there now in Peter's heart?
Or whence the might of this strange sound?
The moon uneasy looked and dimmer,
The broad blue heavens appeared to glimmer,
And the rocks staggered all around.

From Peter's hand the sapling dropped!
Threat has he none to execute—
"If any one should come and see
That I am here, they'll think," quoth he,
"I'm helping this poor dying brute."

He scans the ass from limb to limb;
And Peter now uplifts his eyes;—
Steady the moon doth look and clear,
And like themselves the rocks appear,
And quiet are the skies.

Whereat, in resolute mood, once more
He stoops the ass's neck to seize—
Foul purpose, quickly put to flight!
For in the pool a startling sight
Meets him, beneath the shadowy trees.

Is it the moon's distorted face?
The ghost-like image of a cloud?
Is it a gallows there portrayed?
Is Peter of himself afraid?
Is it a coffin,—or a shroud?

A grisly idol hewn in stone?
Or imp from witch's lap let fall?
Or a gay ring of shining fairies,
Such as pursue their brisk vagaries
In sylvan bower, or haunted hall?

Is it a fiend that to a stake
Of fire his desperate self is tethering?
Or stubborn spirit doomed to yell
In solitary ward or cell,
Ten thousand miles from all his brethren?

Never did pulse so quickly throb,
And never heart so loudly panted;
He looks, he cannot choose but look;
Like one intent upon a book—
A book that is enchanted.

Ah, well-a-day for Peter Bell!—
He will be turned to iron soon,
Meet statue for the court of fear!
His hat is up—and every hair
Bristles—and whitens in the moon!

He looks—he ponders—looks again
He sees a motion—hears a groan;—
His eyes will burst—his heart will break—
He gives a loud and frightful shriek,
And drops, a senseless weight, as if his life were flown!

PART II.

WE left our hero in a trance,
Beneath the alders, near the river;
The ass is by the river side,
And where the feeble breezes glide,
Upon the stream the moonbeams quiver.

A happy respite!—but at length
He feels the glimmering of the moon;
Wakes with glazed eye, and feebly sighing—
To sink perhaps, where he is lying,
Into a second swoon!

He lifts his head—he sees his staff,
He touches—'tis to him a treasure!
Faint recollection seems to tell
That he is yet where mortals dwell—
A thought received with languid pleasure!

His head upon his elbow propped,
Becoming less and less perplexed,
Skyward he looks—to rock and wood—
And then—upon the glassy flood
His wandering eye is fixed.

Thought he, that is the face of one
In his last sleep securely bound!
So toward the stream his head he bent,
And downward thrust his staff, intent
The river's depth to sound.

Now—like a tempest-shattered bark
That overwhelmed and prostrate lies,
And in a moment to the verge
Is lifted of a foaming surge—
Full suddenly the ass doth rise!

His staring bones all shake with joy—
And close by Peter's side he stands:
While Peter o'er the river bends,
The little ass his neck extends,
And fondly licks his hands.

Such life is in the ass's eyes—
Such life is in his limbs and ears—
That Peter Bell, if he had been
The veriest coward ever seen,
Must now have thrown aside his fears.

The ass looks on—and to his work
Is Peter quietly resigned;
He touches here—he touches there—
And now among the dead man's hair
His sapling Peter has entwined.

He pulls—and looks—and pulls again;
And he whom the poor ass has lost,
The man who had been four days dead,
Head foremost from the river's bed
Uprises—like a ghost!

And Peter draws him to dry land;
And through the brain of Peter pass
Some poignant twitches, fast and faster,
"No doubt," quoth he, "he is the master
Of this poor miserable ass!"

The meagre shadow all this while—
What aim is his? what is he doing?
His sudden fit of joy is flown,—
He on his knees hath laid him down,
As if he were his grief renewing.

But no—his purpose and his wish
The suppliant shows, well as he can;
Thought Peter, whatsoe'er betide,
I'll go, and he my way will guide
To the cottage of the drowned man.

Encouraged by this hope, he mount
Upon the pleased and thankful ass;
And then, without a moment's stay,
That earnest creature turned away,
Leaving the body on the grass.

Intent upon his faithful watch,
The beast four days and nights had passed
A sweeter meadow ne'er was seen,
And there the ass four days had been,
Nor ever once did break his fast!

Yet firm his step, and stout his heart!
The mead is crossed—the quarry's mouth
Is reached—but there the trusty guide
Into a thicket turns aside,
And takes his way towards the south.

When hark a burst of doleful sound!
And Peter honestly might say,
The like came never to his ears,
Though he has been, full thirty years,
A rover—night and day.

'Tis not a plover of the moors,
'Tis not a bittern of the fen;
Nor can it be a barking fox—
Nor night-bird chambered in the rocks—
Nor wild-cat in a woody glen!

The ass is startled—and stops short
Right in the middle of the thicket;
And Peter, wont to whistle loud
Whether alone or in a crowd,
Is silent as a silent cricket.

What ails you now, my little Bess?
Well may you tremble and look grave!
This cry—that rings along the wood,
This cry—that floats adown the flood,
Comes from the entrance of a cave;

I see a blooming wood-boy there,
And, if I had the power to say
How sorrowful the wanderer is,
Your heart would be as sad as his
Till you had kissed his tears away!

Holding a hawthorn branch in hand,
All bright with berries ripe and red,
Into the cavern's mouth he peeps—
Thence back into the moonlight creeps
What seeks the boy?—the silent dead—

His father!—Him doth he require,
Whom he hath sought with fruitless pains,
Among the rocks, behind the trees,
Now creeping on his hands and knees,
Now running o'er the open plains.

And hither is he come at last,
When he through such a day has gone,
By this dark cave to be distrest
Like a poor bird—her plundered nest
Hovering around with dolorous moan!

Of that intense and piercing cry
The listening ass conjectures well;
Wild as it is, he there can read
Some intermingled notes that plead
With touches irresistible;

But Peter, when he saw the ass
Not only stop but turn, and change
The cherished tenor of his pace
That lamentable noise to chase,
It wrought in him conviction strange;

A faith that, for the dead man's sake
And this poor slave who loved him well
Vengeance upon his head will fall,
Some visitation worse than all
Which ever till this night befel

Meanwhile the ass to reach his home,
Is striving stoutly as he may,
But, while he climbs the woody hill,
The cry grows weak—and weaker still
And now at last it dies away!

So with his freight the creature turns
Into a gloomy grove of beech,
Along the shade with footsteps true
Descending slowly, till the two
The open moonlight reach.

And there, along a narrow dell,
A fair smooth pathway you discern,
A length of green and open road—
As if it from a fountain flowed—
Winding away between the fern.

The rocks that tower on either side
Build up a wild fantastic scene;
Temples like those among the Hindoos,
And mosques, and spires, and abbey windows,
And castles all with ivy green!

And, while the ass pursues his way,
Along this solitary dell,
As pensively his steps advance,
The mosques and spires change countenance,
And look at Peter Bell!

That unintelligible cry
Hath left him high in preparation,—
Convinced that he, or soon or late,
This very night, will meet his fate—
And so he sits in expectation!

The strenuous animal hath clomb
With the green path,—and now he wends
Where, shining like the smoothest sea,
In undisturbed immensity
A level plain extends.

But whence that faintly-rustling sound
Which, all too long, the pair hath chased!
—A dancing leaf is close behind,
Light plaything for the sportive wind
Upon that solitary waste.

When Peter spies the withered leaf,
It yields no cure to his distress;

"Where there is not a bush or tree,
The very leaves they follow me—
So huge hath been my wickedness!"

To a close lane they now are come,
Where, as before, the enduring ass
Moves on without a moment's stop,
Nor once turns round his head to crop
A bramble leaf or blade of grass.

Between the hedges as they go,
The white dust sleeps upon the lane,
And Peter, ever and anon
Back-looking, sees, upon a stone
Or in the dust, a crimson stain

A stain—as of a drop of blood
By moonlight made more faint and wan—
Ha! why this comfortless despair?
He knows not how the blood comes there,
And Peter is a wicked man.

At length he spies a bleeding wound,
Where he had struck the creature's head,
He sees the blood, knows what it is,—
A glimpse of sudden joy was his,
But then it quickly fled;

Of him whom sudden death had seized
He thought,—of thee, O faithful ass!
And once again those darting pains,
As meteors shoot through heaven's wide plains,
Pass through his bosom—and repass!

PART III.

I'VE heard of one, a gentle soul,
Though given to sadness and to gloom,
And for the fact will vouch,—one night
It chanced that by a taper's light
This man was reading in his room;

Bending, as you or I might bend
At night o'er any pious book,
When sudden blackness overspread
The snow-white page on which he read,
And made the good man round him look.

The chamber walls were dark all round,—
And to his book he turned again,
The light had left the good man's taper,
And formed itself upon the paper
Into large letters—bright and plain!

The godly book was in his hand—
And, on the page more black than coal,
Appeared, set forth in strange array,
A *word*—which to his dying day
Perplexed the good man's gentle soul

The ghostly word, full plainly seen,
Did never from his lips depart,
But he hath said, poor gentle wight!
It brought full many a sin to light
Out of the bottom of his heart

Dread spirits! to torment the good
Why wander from your course so far,
Disordering colour, form, and stature!
Let good men feel the soul of nature,
And see things as they are.

I know you, potent spirits! well,
How, with the feeling and the sense
Playing, ye govern foes or friends,
Yoked to your will, for fearful ends—
And this I speak in reverence!

But might I give advice to you,
Whom in my fear I love so well,
From men of pensive virtue go,
Dread beings! and your empire show
On hearts like that of Peter Bell.

Your presence I have often felt
In darkness and the stormy night;
And well I know, if need there be,
Ye can put forth your agency
When earth is calm, and heaven is bright.

Then, coming from the wayward world,
That powerful world in which ye dwell,
Come, spirits of the mind! and try
To-night, beneath the moonlight sky,
What may be done with Peter Bell!

Oh, would that some more skilful voice
My further labour might prevent!
Kind listeners, that around me sit,
I feel that I am all unfit
For such high argument.

I've played and danced with my narration—
I loitered long ere I began.
Ye waited then on my good pleasure,—
Pour out indulgence still, in measure
As liberal as ye can!

Our travellers, ye remember well,
Are thridding a sequestered lane;
And Peter many tricks is trying,
And many anodynes applying,
To ease his conscience of its pain.

By this his heart is lighter far;
And, finding that he can account
So clearly for that crimson stain,
His evil spirit up again
Does like an empty bucket mount.

And Peter is a deep logician
Who hath no lack of wit mercurial;
"Blood drops—leaves rustle—yet," quoth he,
"This poor man never, but for me,
Could have had Christian burial.

"And, say the best you can, 'tis plain,
That here hath been some wicked dealing;
No doubt the devil in me wrought;
I'm not the man who could have thought
An ass like this was worth the stealing!"

So from his pocket Peter takes
His shining horn tobacco-box;
And, in a light and careless way,
As men who with their purpose play,
Upon the lid he knocks

Let them whose voice can stop the clouds—
Whose cunning eye can see the wind—
Tell to a curious world the cause
Why, making here a sudden pause,
The ass turned round his head—and *grinned.*

Appalling process! I have marked
The like on heath—in lonely wood,
And, verily, have seldom met
A spectacle more hideous—yet
It suited Peter's present mood.

And, grinning in his turn, his teeth
He in jocose defiance showed—
When, to confound his spiteful mirth,
A murmur, pent within the earth,
In the dead earth beneath the road,

Rolled audibly!—it swept along—
A muffled noise—a rumbling sound!
'Twas by a troop of miners made,
Plying with gunpowder their trade,
Some twenty fathoms under ground.

Small cause of dire effect!—for, surely,
If ever mortal, king or cotter,
Believed that earth was charged to quake
And yawn for his unworthy sake,
'Twas Peter Bell the potter!

But, as an oak in breathless air
Will stand though to the centre hewn;
Or as the weakest things, if frost
Have stiffened them, maintain their post;
So he, beneath the gazing moon!

Meanwhile the pair have reached a spot
Where, sheltered by a rocky cove,
A little chapel stands alone,
With greenest ivy overgrown,
And tufted with an ivy grove

Dying insensibly away
From human thoughts and purposes,
The building seems, wall, roof, and tower
To bow to some transforming power,
And blend with the surrounding trees.

Deep-sighing as he passed along,
Quoth Peter, "In the shire of Fife,
'Mid such a ruin, following still
From land to land a lawless will,
I married my sixth wife!"

The unheeding ass moves slowly on,
And now is passing by an inn
Brimful of a carousing crew,
That make, with curses not a few,
An uproar and a drunken din.

I cannot well express the thoughts
Which Peter in those noises found;—
A stifling power compressed his frame,
As if confusing darkness came
Over that dull and dreary sound.

For well did Peter know the sound;
The language of those drunken joys
To him, a jovial soul, I ween,
But a few hours ago, had been
A gladsome and a welcome noise.

Now, turned adrift into the past,
He finds no solace in his course,
Like planet-stricken men of yore,
He trembles, smitten to the core
By strong compunction and remorse.

But, more than all, his heart is stung,
To think of one, almost a child;
A sweet and playful Highland girl,
As light and beauteous as a squirrel,
As beauteous and as wild!

A lonely house her dwelling was,
A cottage in a heathy dell;
And she put on her gown of green,
And left her mother at sixteen,
And followed Peter Bell

But many good and pious thoughts
Had she; and, in the kirk to pray,
Two long Scotch miles, through rain or snow,
To kirk she had been used to go,
Twice every Sabbath-day.

And, when she followed Peter Bell
It was to lead an honest life;
For he, with tongue not used to falter,
Had pledged his troth before the altar
To love her as his wedded wife.

A mother's hope is hers;—but soon
She drooped and pined like one forlorn;—
From Scripture she a name did borrow;
Benoni, or the child of sorrow,
She called her babe unborn.

For she had learned how Peter lived,
And took it in most grievous part;
She to the very bone was worn,
And, ere that little child was born,
Died of a broken heart

And now the spirits of the mind
Are busy with poor Peter Bell;
Upon the rights of visual sense
Usurping, with a prevalence
More terrible than magic spell.

Close by a brake of flowering furze
(Above it shivering aspens play)
He sees an unsubstantial creature,
His very self in form and feature,
Not four yards from the broad highway:

And stretched beneath the furze he sees
The Highland girl—it is no other;
And hears her crying, as she cried,
The very moment that she died,
"My mother! oh, my mother!"

The sweat pours down from Peter's face,
So grievous is his heart's contrition;
With agony his eye-balls ache
While he beholds by the furze-brake
This miserable vision!

Calm is the well-deserving brute,
His peace, hath no offence betrayed;—
But now, while down that slope he wends,
A voice to Peter's ear ascends,
Resounding from the woody glade:

Though clamorous as a hunter's horn
Re-echoed from a naked rock,
'Tis from the tabernacle—List!
Within, a fervent Methodist
Is preaching to no heedless flock!

"Repent! repent!" he cries aloud,
"While yet ye may find mercy;—strive
To love the Lord with all your might,
Turn to Him, seek Him day and night!
And save your souls alive.

"Repent! repent! though ye have gone
Through paths of wickedness and woe,
After the Babylonian harlot,
And, though your sins be red as scarlet,
They shall be white as snow!"

Even as he passed the door, these words
Did plainly come to Peter's ears:
And they such joyful tidings were,
The joy was more than he could bear!—
He melted into tears.

Sweet tears of hope and tenderness!
And fast they fell, a plenteous shower!
His nerves, his sinews seemed to melt;
Through all his iron frame was felt
A gentle, a relaxing power!

Each fibre of his frame was weak;
Weak all the animal within;
But, in its helplessness, grew mild
And gentle as an infant child,
An infant that has known no sin.

Meanwhile the persevering ass,
Towards a gate in open view,
Turns up a narrow lane; his chest
Against the yielding gate he pressed,
And quietly passed through.

And up the stony lane he goes;
No ghost more softly ever trod;
Among the stones and pebbles, he
Sets down his hoofs inaudibly,
As if with felt his hoofs were shod

Along the lane the trusty ass
Had gone two hundred yards, not more;
When to a lonely house he came,
He turned aside towards the same,
And stopped before the door.

Thought Peter, 'tis the poor man's home!
He listens—not a sound is heard
Save from the trickling household rill,
But, stepping o'er the cottage-sill,
Forthwith a little girl appeared.

She to the meeting-house was bound
In hope some tidings there to gather;
No glimpse it is—no doubtful gleam—
She saw—and uttered with a scream,
"My father! here's my father!"

The very word was plainly heard,
Heard plainly by the wretched mother—
Her joy was like a deep affright;
And forth she rushed into the light,
And saw it was another!

And instantly, upon the earth,
Beneath the full moon shining bright,
Close to the ass's feet she fell;
At the same moment Peter Bell
Dismounts in most unhappy plight.

What could he do?—The woman lay
Breathless and motionless; the mind
Of Peter sadly was confused;
But, though to such demands unused,
And helpless almost as the blind,

He raised her up, and while he held
Her body propped against his knee,
The woman waked—and when she spied
The poor ass standing by her side
She moaned most bitterly.

"Oh! God be praised—my heart's at ease—
For he is dead—I know it well!"
At this she wept a bitter flood;
And, in the best way that he could,
His tale did Peter tell.

He trembles—he is pale as death—
His voice is weak with perturbation—
He turns aside his head—he pauses;
Poor Peter from a thousand causes
Is crippled sore in his narration.

At length she learned how he espied
The ass in that small meadow ground;
And that her husband now lay dead,
Beside that luckless river's bed
In which he had been drowned.

A piercing look the sufferer cast
Upon the beast that near her stands;
She sees 'tis he, that 'tis the same;
She calls the poor ass by his name,
And wrings, and wrings her hands.

"Oh, wretched loss—untimely stroke!
If he had died upon his bed!
He knew not one forewarning pain—
He never will come home again—
Is dead—for ever dead!"

Beside the woman Peter stands:
His heart is opening more and more;
A holy sense pervades his mind:
He feels what he for human kind
Had never felt before.

At length, by Peter's arm sustained,
The woman rises from the ground—
"Oh, mercy! something must be done,—
My little Rachel, you must run,—
Some willing neighbour must be found.

"Make haste—my little Rachel—do,
The first you meet with—bid him come,—
Ask him to lend his horse to-night—
And this good man, whom Heaven requite,
Will help to bring the body home."

Away goes Rachel, weeping loud;—
An infant, waked by her distress,
Makes in the house a piteous cry,
And Peter hears the mother sigh,
"Seven are they, and all fatherless!"

And now is Peter taught to feel
That man's heart is a holy thing;
And Nature, through a world of death,
Breathes into him a second breath,
More searching than the breath of spring.

Upon a stone the woman sits
In agony of silent grief—
From his own thoughts did Peter start;
He longs to press her to his heart,
From love that cannot find relief.

But roused, as if through every limb
Had past a sudden shock of dread,
The mother o'er the threshold flies,
And up the cottage stairs she hies,
And to the pillow gives her burning head.

And Peter turns his steps aside
Into a shade of darksome trees,
Where he sits down, he knows not how,
With his hands pressed against his brow,
His elbows on his tremulous knees.

There, self-involved, does Peter sit
Until no sign of life he makes,
As if his mind were sinking deep
Through years that have been long asleep!
The trance is past away—he wakes,—

He lifts his head—and sees the ass
Yet standing in the clear moonshine.
"When shall I be as good as thou?
Oh! would, poor beast, that I had now
A heart but half as good as thine!"

But *he*—who deviously hath sought
His father through the lonesome woods,
Hath sought, proclaiming to the ear
Of night his inward grief and fear—
He comes—escaped from fields and floods;—

With weary pace is drawing nigh—
He sees the ass—and nothing living
Had ever such a fit of joy
As hath this little orphan boy,
For he has no misgiving!

Towards the gentle ass he springs,
And up about his neck he climbs;
In loving words he talks to him,
He kisses, kisses face and limb,—
He kisses him a thousand times!

This Peter sees, while in the shade
He stood beside the cottage door:
And Peter Bell, the ruffian wild,
Sobs loud, he sobs even like a child,
"Oh! God, I can endure no more!"

Here ends my tale:—for in a trice
Arrived a neighbour with his horse;
Peter went forth with him straightway;
And, with due care, ere break of day
Together they brought back the corse.

And many years did this poor ass,
Whom once it was my luck to see
Cropping the shrubs of Leming Lane,
Help by his labour to maintain
The widow and her family.

And Peter Bell, who, till that night,
Had been the wildest of his clan,
Forsook his crimes, repressed his folly,
And after ten months' melancholy,
Became a good and honest man.

Miscellaneous Sonnets.

TO ——.

HAPPY the feeling from the bosom thrown
In perfect shape (whose beauty time shall spare
Though a breath made it) like a bubble blown
For summer pastime into wanton air;
Happy the thought best likened to a stone
Of the sea-beach, when, polished with nice care,
Veins it discovers exquisite and rare,
Which for the loss of that moist gleam atone
That tempted first to gather it. O chief
Of friends! such feelings if I here present,
Such thoughts, with others mixed less fortunate;
Then smile into my heart a fond belief
That thou, if not with partial joy elate,
Receiv'st the gift for more than mild content!

NUNS fret not at their convent's narrow room;
And hermits are contented with their cells;
And students with their pensive citadels:
Maids at the wheel, the weaver at his loom,
Sit blithe and happy; bees that soar for bloom,
High as the highest peak of Furness Fells,
Will murmur by the hour in foxglove bells:
In truth, the prison, unto which we doom
Ourselves, no prison is: and hence to me,
In sundry moods, 'twas pastime to be bound
Within the sonnet's scanty plot of ground·
Pleased if some souls (for such there needs must be)
Who have felt the weight of too much liberty,
Should find brief solace there, as I have found.

WRITTEN IN VERY EARLY YOUTH.

CALM is all nature as a resting wheel.
The kine are couched upon the dewy grass;
The horse alone, seen dimly as I pass,
Is cropping audibly his later meal:
Dark is the ground; a slumber seems to steal
O'er vale, and mountain, and the starless sky.
Now, in this blank of things, a harmony,
Home-felt, and home-created, seems to heal

That grief for which the senses still supply
Fresh food; for only then, when memory
Is hushed, am I at rest. My friends! restrain
Those busy cares that would allay my pain:
Oh! leave me to myself, nor let me feel
The officious touch that makes me droop again.

ADMONITION.

Intended more particularly for the perusal of those who may have happened to be enamoured of some beautiful place of retreat, in the country of the lakes

Well mayst thou halt, and gaze with brightened eye!
The lovely cottage in the guardian nook
Hath stirred thee deeply; with its own dear brook,
Its own small pasture, almost its own sky!
But covet not the abode,—forbear to sigh,
As many do, repining while they look;
Intruders who would tear from nature's book
This precious leaf, with harsh impiety.
Think what the home must be if it were thine,
Even thine, though few thy wants!—Roof, window, door,
The very flowers are sacred to the poor,
The roses to the porch which they entwine:
Yea, all, that now enchants thee, from the day
On which it should be touched would melt away.

"Beloved vale!" I said, "when I shall con
Those many records of my childish years,
Remembrance of myself and of my peers
Will press me down: to think of what is gone
Will be an awful thought, if life have one."
But, when into the vale I came, no fears
Distressed me, from mine eyes escaped no tears;
Deep thought, or awful vision, had I none.
By doubts and thousand petty fancies crost,
I stood of simple shame the blushing thrall,
So narrow seemed the brooks, the fields so small.
A juggler's balls old time about him tossed;
I looked, I stared, I smiled, I laughed; and all
The weight of sadness was in wonder lost.

Pelion and Ossa flourish side by side,
Together in immortal books enrolled:
His ancient dower Olympus hath not sold;
And that inspiring hill which "did divide
Into two ample horns his forehead wide,"
Shines with poetic radiance as of old;
While not an English mountain we behold
By the celestial muses glorified.
Yet round our sea-girt shore they rise in crowds:
What was the great Parnassus' self to thee,
Mount Skiddaw? In his natural sovereignty
Our British hill is fairer far: he shrouds
His double front among Atlantic clouds,
And pours forth streams more sweet than Castaly.

There is a little unpretending rill
Of limpid water, humbler far than aught
That ever among men or naiads sought
Notice or name!—It quivers down the hill,
Furrowing its shallow way with dubious will;
Yet to my mind this scanty stream is brought
Oftener than Ganges or the Nile, a thought
Of private recollection sweet and still!
Months perish with their moons; year treads on year;
But, faithful Emma, thou with me canst say
That, while ten thousand pleasures disappear,
And flies their memory fast almost as they,
The immortal spirit of one happy day
Lingers beside that rill, in vision clear.

Her only pilot the soft breeze the boat,
Lingers, but fancy is well satisfied, side,
With keen-eyed hope, with memory, at her
And the glad muse at liberty to note
All that to each is precious, as we float
Gently along; regardless who shall chide
If the heavens smile, and leave us free to glide,
Happy associates breathing air remote
From trivial cares. But, fancy and the muse,
Why have I crowded this small bark with you
And others of your kind, ideal crew!
While here sits one whose brightness owes its hues
To flesh and blood; no goddess from above,
No fleeting spirit, but my own true love?

The fairest, brightest hues of ether fade;
The sweetest notes must terminate and die,
O friend! thy flute has breathed a harmony
Softly resounded through this rocky glade;
Such strains of rapture as the genius played
In his still haunt on Bagdad's summit high;*
He who stood visible to Mirza's eye,

* See the Vision of Mirza, in the Spectator.

Never before to human sight betrayed.
Lo, in the vale, the mists of evening spread!
The visionary arches are not there,
Nor the green islands, nor the shining seas;
Yet sacred is to me this mountain's head,
From which I have been lifted on the breeze
Of harmony, above all earthly care.

UPON THE SIGHT OF A BEAUTIFUL PICTURE

(Painted by Sir G. H. Beaumont, Bart.)

PRAISED be the art whose subtle power could stay
Yon cloud, and fix it in that glorious shape;
Nor would permit the thin smoke to escape,
Nor those bright sunbeams to forsake the day;
Which stopped that band of travellers on their way,
Ere they were lost within the shady wood;
And showed the bark upon the glassy flood
For ever anchored in her sheltering bay.
Soul-soothing art! which morning, noon-tide, even
Do serve with all their changeful pageantry;
Thou, with ambition modest yet sublime,
Here, for the sight of mortal man, hast given
To one brief moment caught from fleeting time
The appropriate calm of blest eternity.

'WHY, minstrel, these untuneful murmurings—
Dull, flagging notes that with each other jar?"
"Think, gentle lady, of a harp so far
From its own country, and forgive the strings."
A simple answer! but even so forth springs,
From the Castalian fountain of the heart,
The poetry of life, and all that art
Divine of words quickening insensate things.
From the submissive necks of guiltless men
Stretched on the block, the glittering axe recoils;
Sun, moon, and stars, all struggle in the toils
Of mortal sympathy; what wonder then
If the poor harp distempered music yields
To its sad lord, far from his native fields?

AERIAL rock—whose solitary brow
From this low threshold daily meets my sight,
When I step forth to hail the morning light;
Or quit the stars with lingering farewell—how
Shall fancy pay to thee a grateful vow?
How, with the muse's aid, her love attest?
By planting on thy naked head the crest
Of an imperial castle, which the plough
Of ruin shall not touch. Innocent scheme!
That doth presume no more than to supply
A grace the sinuous vale and roaring stream
Want, through neglect of hoar antiquity.
Rise, then, ye votive towers, and catch a gleam
Of golden sunset, ere it fade and die!

TO SLEEP.

O GENTLE sleep; do they belong to thee,
These twinklings of oblivion! Thou dost love
To sit in meekness, like the brooding dove,
A captive never wishing to be free.
This tiresome night, O sleep! thou art to me
A fly, that up and down himself doth shove
Upon a fretful rivulet, now above
Now on the water vexed with mockery.
I have no pain that calls for patience, no;
Hence am I cross and peevish as a child;
Am pleased by fits to have thee for my foe,
Yet ever willing to be reconciled:
O gentle creature! do not use me so,
But once and deeply let me be beguiled.

TO SLEEP.

A FLOCK of sheep that leisurely pass by,
One after one; the sound of rain, and bees
Murmuring; the fall of rivers, winds and seas,
Smooth fields, white sheets of water, and pure sky;
By turns have all been thought of; yet I lie
Sleepless, and soon the small birds' melodies
Must hear, first uttered from my orchard trees;
And the first cuckoo's melancholy cry.
Even thus last night, and two nights more, I lay,
And could not win thee, sleep! by any stealth,
So do not let me wear to-night away:
Without thee what is all the morning's wealth?
Come, blessed barrier betwixt day and day,
Dear mother of fresh thoughts and joyous health!

TO SLEEP.

FOND words have oft been spoken to thee, sleep!
And thou hast had thy store of tenderest names;
The very sweetest words that fancy frames

When thankfulness of heart is strong and deep!
Dear bosom child we call thee, that dost steep
In rich reward all suffering; balm that tames
All anguish; saint that evil thoughts and aims
Takest away, and into souls dost creep,
Like to a breeze from heaven. Shall I alone,
I surely not a man ungently made,
Call thee worst tyrant by which flesh is crost?
Perverse, self-willed to own and to disown,
Mere slave of them who never for thee prayed,
Still last to come where thou art wanted most!

THE WILD DUCK'S NEST.

THE imperial consort of the fairy king
Owns not a sylvan bower; or gorgeous cell
With emerald floored, and with purpureal shell
Ceilinged and roofed, that is so fair a thing
As this low structure—for the tasks of spring
Prepared by one who loves the buoyant swell
Of the brisk waves, yet here consents to dwell;
And spreads in steadfast peace her brooding-wing.
Words cannot paint the o'ershadowing yew-tree-bough,
And dimly-gleaming nest,—a hollow crown
Of golden leaves inlaid with silver down,
Fine as the mother's softest plumes allow:
I gaze—and almost wish to lay aside
Humanity, weak slave of cumbrous pride!

WRITTEN UPON A BLANK LEAF IN "THE COMPLETE ANGLER."

WHILE flowing rivers yield a blameless sport,
Shall live the name of Walton;—sage benign!
Whose pen, the mysteries of the rod and line
Unfolding, did not fruitlessly exhort
To reverend watching of each still report
That nature utters from her rural shrine.
Meek, nobly versed in simple discipline,
He found the longest summer day too short,
To his loved pastime given by sedgy Lee,
Or down the tempting maze of Shawford brook!
Fairer than life itself, in this sweet book,
The cowslip bank and shady willow tree,
And the fresh meads; where flowed from every nook
Of his full bosom, gladsome piety!

TO THE POET, JOHN DYER.

BARD of the Fleece, whose skilful genius made
That work a living landscape fair and bright;
Nor hallowed less with musical delight
Than those soft scenes through which thy childhood strayed,
Those southern tracts of Cambria, "deep embayed,
With green hills fenced, with ocean's murmur lulled,"
Though hasty fame hath many a chaplet culled
For worthless crowns, while in the pensive shade
Of cold neglect she leaves thy head ungraced,
Yet pure and powerful minds, hearts meek and still,
A grateful few, shall love thy modest lay,
Long as the shepherd's bleating flock shall stray
O'er naked Snowdon's wide aërial waste;
Long as the thrush shall pipe on Grongar Hill!

ON THE DETRACTION WHICH FOLLOWED THE PUBLICATION OF A CERTAIN POEM.

See Milton's sonnet, beginning "A book was writ of late called 'Tetrachordon.'"

A BOOK came forth of late, called "Peter Bell;"
Not negligent the style;—the matter?—good
As aught that song records of Robin Hood;
Or Roy, renowned through many a Scottish dell;
But some (who brook these hackneyed themes full well,
Nor heat at Tam o'Shanter's name their blood)
Waxed wroth, and with foul claws, a harpy brood,
On bard and hero clamorously fell.
Heed not, wild rover once through heath and glen,
Who mad'st at length the better life thy choice,
Heed not such onset! nay, if praise of men
To thee appear not an unmeaning voice,
Lift up that gray-haired forehead, and rejoice
In the just tribute of thy poet's pen!

TO THE RIVER DERWENT.

AMONG the mountains were we nursed, loved stream!
Thou, near the eagle's nest—within brief sail,
I, of his bold wing floating on the gale,

Where thy deep voice could lull me!—Faint the beam
Of human life when first allowed to gleam
On mortal notice.—Glory of the vale,
Such thy meek outset, with a crown though frail
Kept in perpetual verdure by the steam
Of thy soft breath!—Less vivid wreath entwined
Nemæan victor's brow; less bright was worn,
Meed of some Roman chief—in triumph borne
With captives chained; and shedding from his car
The sunset splendours of a finished war
Upon the proud enslavers of mankind!

COMPOSED IN ONE OF THE VALLEYS OF WESTMORELAND ON EASTER SUNDAY.

WITH each recurrence of this glorious morn
That saw the Saviour in His human frame
Rise from the dead, erewhile the cottage-dame
Put on fresh raiment—till that hour unworn;
Domestic hands the home-bred wool had shorn,
And she who span it culled the daintiest fleece,
In thoughtful reverence to the Prince of Peace,
Whose temples bled beneath the platted thorn.
A blest estate when piety sublime
These humble props disdained not! O green dales!
Sad may I be who heard your Sabbath chime
When art's abused inventions were unknown;
Kind nature's various wealth was all your own;
And benefits were weighed in reason's scales!

GRIEF, thou hast lost an ever-ready friend
Now that the cottage spinning-wheel is mute;
And care—a comforter that best could suit
Her froward mood, and softliest reprehend;
And love—a charmer's voice, that used to lend,
More efficaciously than aught that flows
From harp or lute, kind influence to compose
The throbbing pulse,—else troubled without end;
Even joy could tell, joy craving truce and rest
From her own overflow, what power sedate
On those revolving motions did await
Assiduously, to soothe her aching breast—
And—to a point of just relief—abate
The mantling triumphs of a day too blest.

TO S. H.

EXCUSE is needless when with love sincere
Of occupation, not by fashion led,
Thou turn'st the wheel that slept with dust o'erspread;
My nerves from no such murmur shrink—though near,
Soft as the dorhawk's to a distant ear,
When twilight shades bedim the mountain's head.
She who was feigned to spin our vital thread
Might smile, O lady! on a task once dear
To household virtues. Venerable art,
Torn from the poor! yet will kind Heaven protect
Its own, not left without a guiding chart,
If rulers, trusting with undue respect
To proud discoveries of the intellect,
Sanction the pillage of man's ancient heart.

DECAY OF PIETY.

OFT have I seen, ere time had ploughed my cheek,
Matrons and sires—who, punctual to the call
Of their loved church, on fast or festival
Through the long year the house of prayer would seek:
By Christmas snows, by visitation bleak
Of Easter winds, unscared, from hut or hall
They came to lowly bench or sculptured stall,
But with one fervour of devotion meek.
I see the places where they once were known,
And ask, surrounded even by kneeling crowds,
Is ancient piety for ever flown?
Alas! even then they seemed like fleecy clouds
That, struggling through the western sky, have won
Their pensive light from a departed sun!

COMPOSED ON THE EVE OF THE MARRIAGE OF A FRIEND, IN THE VALE OF GRASMERE.

WHAT need of clamorous bells, or ribands gay,
These humble nuptials to proclaim or grace?
Angels of love, look down upon the place,
Shed on the chosen vale a sun-bright day!
Yet no proud gladness would the bride display
Even for such promise;—serious is her face,
Modest her mien; and she, whose thoughts keep pace
With gentleness, in that becoming way

Will thank you. Faultless doth the maid appear,
No disproportion in her soul, no strife:
But, when the closer view of wedded life
Hath shown that nothing human can be clear
From frailty, for that insight may the wife
To her indulgent lord become more dear.

FROM THE ITALIAN OF MICHAEL ANGELO.

Yes! hope may with my strong desire keep pace,
And I be undeluded, unbetrayed;
For if of our affections none find grace
In sight of Heaven, then, wherefore hath God made
The world which we inhabit! Better plea
Love cannot have, than that in loving thee
Glory to that eternal peace is paid,
Who such divinity to thee imparts
As hallows and makes pure all gentle hearts.
His hope is treacherous only whose love dies
With beauty, which is varying every hour;
But, in chaste hearts uninfluenced by the power
Of outward change, there blooms a deathless flower,
That breathes on earth the air of paradise.

FROM THE SAME.

No mortal object did these eyes behold
When first they met the placid light of thine,
And my soul felt her destiny divine,
And hope of endless peace in me grew bold:
Heaven-born, the soul a heaven-ward course must hold;
Beyond the visible world she soars to seek
(For what delights the sense is false and weak)
Ideal form, the universal mould.
The wise man, I affirm, can find no rest
In that which perishes: nor will he lend
His heart to aught which doth on time depend.
'Tis sense, unbridled will, and not true love,
That kills the soul: love betters what is best,
Even here below, but more in heaven above.

FROM THE SAME.
TO THE SUPREME BEING.

The prayers I make will then be sweet indeed
If Thou the spirit give by which I pray:
My unassisted heart is barren clay
That of its native self can nothing feed:
Of good and pious works Thou art the seed,
That quickens only where Thou say'st it may:
Unless Thou show to us Thine own true way
No man can find it. Father! Thou must lead.
Do Thou, then, breathe those thoughts into my mind
By which such virtue may in me be bred
That in Thy holy footsteps I may tread;
The fetters of my tongue do Thou unbind,
That I may have the power to sing of Thee,
And sound Thy praises everlastingly.

Surprised by joy—impatient as the wind
I turned to share the transport—Oh! with whom
But thee deep buried in the silent tomb,
That spot which no vicissitude can find,
Love, faithful love, recalled thee to my mind—
But how could I forget thee?—Through what power,
Even for the least division of an hour,
Have I been so beguiled as to be blind
To my most grievous loss?—That thought's return
Was the worst pang that sorrow ever bore,
Save one, one only, when I stood forlorn,
Knowing my heart's best treasure was no more:
That neither present time, nor years unborn
Could to my sight that heavenly face restore.

Methought I saw the footsteps of a throne
Which mists and vapours from mine eyes did shroud—
Nor view of who might sit thereon allowed;
But all the steps and ground about were strown
With sights the ruefullest that flesh and bone
Ever put on; a miserable crowd,
Sick, hale, old, young, who cried before that cloud,
"Thou art our king, O Death! to thee we groan!"
I seem to mount those steps; the vapours gave
Smooth way; and I beheld the face of one
Sleeping alone within a mossy cave,
With her face up to heaven; that seemed to have
Pleasing remembrance of a thought foregone;
A lovely beauty in a summer grave!

"Weak is the will of man, his judgment blind;
Remembrance persecutes, and hope betrays;

Heavy is woe ,—and joy, for human-kind,
A mournful thing, so transient is the blaze!"
Thus might *he* paint our lot of mortal days
Who wants the glorious faculty assigned
To elevate the more-than-reasoning mind,
And colour life's dark cloud with orient rays
Imagination is that sacred power,
Imagination lofty and refined ,
'Tis hers to pluck the amaranthine flower
Of Faith, and round the sufferer s temples bind [shower,
Wreaths that endure affliction s heaviest
And do not shrink from sorrow's keenest wind.

It is a beauteous evening, calm and free ;
The holy time is quiet as a nun
Breathless with adoration , the broad sun
Is sinking down in its tranquillity ,
The gentleness of heaven is on the sea
Listen ! the mighty Being is awake,
And doth with His eternal motion make
A sound like thunder—everlastingly
Dear child! dear girl ! that walkest with me here, [thought,
If thou appear'st untouched by solemn
Thy nature is not therefore less divine
Thou liest in Abraham's bosom all the year ,
And worshipp'st at the temple's inner shrine,
God being with thee when we know it not.

Where lies the land to which yon ship must go?
Festively she puts forth in trim array ,
As vigorous as a lark at break of day :
Is she for tropic suns, or polar snow?
What boots the inquiry?—Neither friend nor foe
She cares for, let her travel where she may,
She finds familiar names, a beaten way
Ever before her, and a wind to blow
Yet still I ask, what haven is her mark?
And, almost as it was when ships were rare, [and there
(From time to time, like pilgrims, here
Crossing the waters) doubt, and something dark,
Of the old sea some reverential fear,
Is with me at thy farewell, joyous bark !

With ships the sea was sprinkled far and nigh,
Like stars in heaven, and joyously it showed;
Some lying fast at anchor in the road,
Some veering up and down, one knew not why.
A goodly vessel did I then espy
Come like a giant from a haven broad ,
And lustily along the bay she strode,
"Her tackling rich, and of apparel high,
This ship was nought to me, nor I to her
Yet I pursued her with a lover's look ,
This ship to all the rest did I prefer .
When will she turn, and whither? She will brook [must stir
No tarrying , where she comes the winds
On went she,—and due north her journey took

The world is too much with us late and soon, [powers:
Getting and spending, we lay waste our
Little we see in nature that is ours,
We have given our hearts away a sordid boon !
This sea that bares her bosom to the moon
The winds that will be howling at all hours,
And are up-gathered now like sleeping flowers ,
For this, for every thing, we are out of tune ,
It moves us not —Great God ! I'd rather be
A pagan suckled in a creed outworn ;
So might I, standing on this pleasant lea,
Have glimpses that would make me less forlorn ,
Have sight of Proteus rising from the sea ,
Or hear old Triton blow his wreathed horn.

A volant tribe of bards on earth are found,
Who, while the flattering zephyrs round them play, [of clay ;
On "coignes of vantage" hang their nests
How quickly from that aery hold unbound,
Dust for oblivion ! To the solid ground
Of nature trusts the mind that builds for aye ,
Convinced that there, there only, she can lay
Secure foundations. As the year runs round,
Apart she toils within the chosen ring ,
While the stars shine, or while day's purple eye
Is gently closing with the flowers of spring;
Where even the motion of an angel's wing
Would interrupt the intense tranquillity
Of silent hills, and more than silent sky.

How sweet it is, when mother fancy rocks
The wayward brain, to saunter through a wood !
An old place, full of many a lovely brood,
Tall trees, green arbours, and ground-flowers in flocks , [stocks,
And wild rose tip-toe upon hawthorn
Like a bold girl, who plays her agile pranks

At wakes and fairs with wandering mounte-
banks,— [and mocks
When she stands cresting the clown's head,
The crowd beneath her. Verily I think,
Such place to me is sometimes like a dream
Or map of the whole world : thoughts, link
by link, [gleam
Enter through ears and eyesight, with such
Of all things, that at last in fear I shrink,
And leap at once from the delicious stream.

PERSONAL TALK.

I.

I AM not one who much or oft delight
To season my fireside with personal talk,—
Of friends, who live within an easy walk,
Or neighbours, daily, weekly, in my sight :
And, for my chance-acquaintance, ladies
bright, [stalk,
Sons, mothers, maidens withering on the
These all wear out of me, like forms, with
chalk [night,
Painted on rich men's floors for one feast
Better than such discourse doth silence long,
Long, barren silence, square with my desire;
To sit without emotion, hope, or aim,
In the loved presence of my cottage-fire,
And listen to the flapping of the flame,
Or kettle whispering its faint undersong.

II.

"YET life," you say, "is life ; we have seen
and see,
And with a living pleasure we describe ;
And fits of sprightly malice do but bribe
The languid mind into activity.
Sound sense, and love itself, and mirth
and glee
Are fostered by the comment and the gibe."
Even be it so : yet still among your tribe,
Our daily world's true worldlings, rank not
me ! [lies
Children are blest, and powerful; their world
More justly balanced ; partly at their feet,
And part far from them:—sweetest melodies
Are those that are by distance made more
sweet ; [eyes,
Whose mind is but the mind of his own
He is a slave ; the meanest we can meet !

III.

WINGS have we,—and as far as we can go
We may find pleasure : wilderness and
wood, [mood
Blank ocean and mere sky, support that
Which with the lofty sanctifies the low,
Dreams, books, are each a world ; and
books, we know,
Are a substantial world, both pure and good:
Round these, with tendrils strong as flesh
and blood,
Our pastime and our happiness will grow.
There find I personal themes, a plenteous
store ;
Matter wherein right voluble I am :
To which I listen with a ready ear ;
Two shall be named, pre-eminently dear—
The gentle lady married to the Moor ;
And heavenly Una with her milk-white
lamb.

IV.

NOR can I not believe but that hereby
Great gains are mine ; for thus I live remote
From evil-speaking ; rancour, never sought,
Comes to me not : malignant truth, or lie.
Hence have I genial seasons, hence have I
Smooth passions, smooth discourse, and
joyous thought :
And thus from day to day my little boat
Rocks in its harbour, lodging peaceably.
Blessings be with them—and eternal praise,
Who gave us nobler loves and nobler cares—
The poets, who on earth have made us heirs
Of truth and pure delight by heavenly lays !
Oh ! might my name be numbered among
theirs,
Then gladly would I end my mortal days.

TO R. B. HAYDON, ESQ.

HIGH is our calling, friend !—Creative art
(Whether the instrument of words she use,
Or pencil pregnant with ethereal hues,)
Demands the service of a mind and heart,
Though sensitive, yet, in their weakest part,
Heroically fashioned—to infuse
Faith in the whispers of the lonely muse,
While the whole world seems adverse to
desert.
And oh ! when nature sinks, as oft she may,
Through long-lived pressure of obscure
distress,
Still to be strenuous for the bright reward,
And in the soul admit of no decay,
Brook no continuance of weak-mindedness ;
Great is the glory, for the strife is hard !

FROM the dark chambers of dejection freed,
Spurning the unprofitable yoke of care,
Rise, Gillies, rise : the gales of youth shall
bear
Thy genius forward like a winged steed.
Though bold Bellerophon (so Jove decreed

In wrath) fell headlong from the fields of air,
Yet a rich guerdon waits on minds that dare,
If aught be in them of immortal seed,
And reason govern that audacious flight
Which heaven-ward they direct.—Then droop not thou,
Erroneously renewing a sad vow
In the low dell 'mid Roslin's faded grove:
A cheerful life is what the muses love,
A soaring spirit is their prime delight.

FAIR prime of life! were it enough to gild
With ready sunbeams every straggling shower;
And, if an unexpected cloud should lower,
Swiftly thereon a rainbow arch to build
For fancy's errands,—then, from fields half-tilled
Gathering green weeds to mix with poppy flower,
Thee might thy minions crown, and chant thy power,
Unpitied by the wise, all censure stilled.
Ah! show that worthier honours are thy due;
Fair prime of life! arouse the deeper heart;
Confirm the spirit glorying to pursue
Some path of steep ascent and lofty aim;
And, if there be a joy that slights the claim
Of grateful memory, bid that joy depart.

I HEARD (alas! 'twas only in a dream)
Strains—which, as sage antiquity believed,
By waking ears have sometimes been received
Wafted adown the wind from lake or stream;
A most melodious requiem,—a supreme
And perfect harmony of notes, achieved
By a fair swan on drowsy billows heaved,
O'er which her pinions shed a silver gleam.
For is she not the votary of Apollo?
And knows she not, singing as he inspires,
That bliss awaits her which the ungenial hollow *
Of the dull earth partakes not, nor desires?
Mount, tuneful bird, and join the immortal quires!
She soared—and I awoke,—struggling in vain to follow.

RETIREMENT.

IF the whole weight of what we think and feel
Save only far as thought and feeling blend
With action, were as nothing, patriot friend!
From thy remonstrance would be no appeal!
But to promote and fortify the weal
Of our own being, is her paramount end;
A truth which they alone shall comprehend
Who shun the mischief which they cannot heal.
Peace in these feverish times is sovereign bliss;
Here, with no thirst but what the stream can slake,
And startled only by the rustling brake,
Cool air I breathe; while the unincumbered mind,
By some weak aims at services assigned
To gentle natures, thanks not heaven amiss.

TO THE MEMORY OF RAISLEY CALVERT.

CALVERT! it must not be unheard by them
Who may respect my name, that I to thee
Owed many years of early liberty.
This care was thine when sickness did condemn
Thy youth to hopeless wasting, root and stem:
That I, if frugal and severe, might stray
Where'er I liked; and finally array
My temples with the muse's diadem.
Hence, if in freedom I have loved the truth
If there be aught of pure, or good, or great,
In my past verse; or shall be, in the lays
Of higher mood, which now I meditate,—
It gladdens me, O worthy, short-lived youth!
To think how much of this will be thy praise.

SCORN not the sonnet; critic, you have frowned,
Mindless of its just honours;—with this key
Shakspeare unlocked his heart; the melody
Of this small lute gave ease to Petrarch's wound;
A thousand times this pipe did Tasso sound
Camöens soothed with it an exile's grief;
The sonnet glittered a gay myrtle leaf
Amid the cypress with which Dante crowned
His visionary brow: a glow-worm lamp,
It cheered mild Spenser, called from faery-land
To struggle through dark ways; and when a damp
Fell round the path of Milton, in his hand
The thing became a trumpet, whence he blew
Soul-animating strains—alas, too few!

NOT love, nor war, nor the tumultuous swell
Of civil conflict, nor the wrecks of change,
Nor duty struggling with afflictions strange,

* See the "Phædo" of Plato, by which this sonnet was suggested.

Not these alone inspire the tuneful shell;
But where untroubled peace and concord dwell,
There also is the muse not loth to range,
Watching the blue smoke of the elmy grange,
Skyward ascending from the twilight dell.
Meek aspirations please her, lone endeavour,
And sage content, and placid melancholy;
She loves to gaze upon a crystal river,
Diaphanous, because it travels slowly;
Soft is the music that would charm for ever;
The flower of sweetest smell is shy and lowly.

SEPTEMBER, 1815.

While not a leaf seems faded,—while the fields,
With ripening harvest prodigally fair,
In brightest sunshine bask,—this nipping air,
Sent from some distant clime where winter wields
His icy scimitar, a foretaste yields
Of bitter change—and bids the flowers beware;
And whispers to the silent birds, "Prepare
Against the threatening foe your trustiest shields."
For me, who under kindlier laws belong
To nature's tuneful quire, this rustling dry
Through leaves yet green, and yon crystalline sky,
Announce a season potent to renew,
'Mid frost and snow, the instinctive joys of song,
And nobler cares than listless summer knew.

NOVEMBER 1.

How clear, how keen, how marvellously bright
The effluence from yon distant mountain's head,
Which, strewn with snow as smooth as heaven can shed,
Shines like another sun—on mortal sight
Uprisen, as if to check approaching night,
And all her twinkling stars. Who now would tread,
If so he might, yon mountain's glittering head—
Terrestrial—but a surface, by the flight
Of sad mortality's earth-sullying wing,
Unswept, unstained! Nor shall the aërial powers
Dissolve that beauty—destined to endure,
White, radiant, spotless, exquisitely pure,
Through all vicissitudes—till genial spring
Have filled the laughing vales with welcome flowers.

COMPOSED DURING A STORM.

One who was suffering tumult in his soul
Yet failed to seek the sure relief of prayer,
Went forth—his course surrendering to the care
Of the fierce wind, while mid-day lightnings prowl
Insidiously, untimely thunders growl;
While trees, dim-seen, in frenzied numbers tear
The lingering remnant of their yellow hair,
And shivering wolves, surprised with darkness, howl
As if the sun were not. He raised his eye
Soul-smitten—for, that instant, did appear
Large space, 'mid dreadful clouds, of purest sky,
An azure orb—shield of tranquillity,
Invisible, unlooked-for minister
Of providential goodness ever nigh!

TO A SNOWDROP.

Lone flower, hemmed in with snows, and white as they,
But hardier far, once more I see thee bend
Thy forehead, as if fearful to offend,
Like an unbidden guest. Though day by day,
Storms, sallying from the mountain-tops, waylay
The rising sun, and on the plains descend;
Yet art thou welcome, welcome as a friend
Whose zeal outruns his promise! Blue-eyed May
Shall soon behold this border thickly set
With bright jonquils, their odours lavishing
On the soft west-wind and his frolic peers;
Nor will I then thy modest grace forget,
Chaste snowdrop, venturous harbinger of spring,
And pensive monitor of fleeting years!

COMPOSED A FEW DAYS AFTER THE FOREGOING.

When haughty expectations prostrate lie,
And grandeur crouches like a guilty thing,
Oft shall the lowly weak, till nature bring
Mature release, in fair society
Survive, and fortune's utmost anger try;
Like these frail snowdrops that together cling,
And nod their helmets smitten by the wing
Of many a furious whirl-blast sweeping by.
Observe the faithful flowers! if small to great
May lead the thoughts, thus struggling used to stand
The Emathian phalanx, nobly obstinate;

And so the bright immortal Theban band,
Whom onset, fiercely urged at Jove's command,
Might overwhelm—but could not separate!

THE stars are mansions built by nature's hand;
The sun is peopled; and with spirits blest,
Say, can the gentle moon be unpossest?
Huge ocean shows, within his yellow strand,
A habitation marvellously planned,
For life to occupy in love and rest;
All that we see—is dome, or vault, or nest,
Or fort, erected at her sage command.
Is this a vernal thought? Even so, the spring
Gave it while cares were weighing on my heart,
'Mid song of birds, and insects murmuring;
And while the youthful year's prolific art—
Of bud, leaf, blade, and flower—was fashioning
Abodes, where self-disturbance hath no part.

TO LADY BEAUMONT.

LADY! the songs of spring were in the grove
While I was shaping beds for winter flowers;
While I was planting green unfading bowers,
And shrubs to hang upon the warm alcove,
And sheltering wall; and still, as fancy wove
The dream, to time and nature's blended powers
I gave this paradise for winter hours,
A labyrinth, lady! which your feet shall rove.
Yes! when the sun of life more feebly shines,
Becoming thoughts, I trust, of solemn gloom
Or of high gladness you shall hither bring;
And these perennial bowers and murmuring pines
Be gracious as the music and the bloom
And all the mighty ravishment of spring.

TO THE LADY MARY LOWTHER,

With a selection from the poems of Anne, Countess of Winchelsea; and extracts of similar character from other writers; transcribed by a female friend.

LADY! I rifled a Parnassian cave
(But seldom trod) of mildly-gleaming ore;
And culled, from sundry beds, a lucid store
Of genuine crystals, pure as those that pave
The azure brooks where Dian joys to lave
Her spotless limbs; and ventured to explore
Dim shades—for reliques, upon Lethe's shore,
Cast up at random by the sullen wave.
To female hands the treasures were resigned;
And lo this work!—a grotto bright and clear
From stain or taint; in which thy blameless mind
May feed on thoughts though pensive not austere;
Or, if thy deeper spirit be inclined
To holy musing, it may enter here.

There is a pleasure in poetic pains
Which only poets know;—'twas rightly said,
Whom could the muses else allure to tread
Their smoothest paths, to wear their lightest chains?
When happiest fancy has inspired the strains,
How oft the malice of one luckless word
Pursues the enthusiast to the social board,
Haunts him belated on the silent plains!
Yet he repines not, if his thought stand clear
At last of hindrance and obscurity,
Fresh as the star that crowns the brow of morn;
Bright, speckless as a softly-moulded tear
The moment it has left the virgin's eye,
Or rain-drop lingering on the pointed thorn.

THE shepherd, looking eastward, softly said,
"Bright is thy veil, O moon, as thou art bright!"
Forthwith, that little cloud, in ether spread,
And penetrated all with tender light,
She cast away, and showed her fulgent head
Uncovered; dazzling the beholder's sight
As if to vindicate her beauty's right,
Her beauty thoughtlessly disparagèd.
Meanwhile that veil, removed or thrown aside,
Went floating from her, darkening as it went;
And a huge mass, to bury or to hide,
Approached the glory of this firmament;
Who meekly yields, and is obscured;—content
With one calm triumph of a modest pride.

HAIL, Twilight, sovereign of one peaceful hour!
Not dull art thou as undiscerning night:
But studious only to remove from sight
Day's mutable distinctions. Ancient power!
Thus did the waters gleam, the mountains lower,
To the rude Briton, when, in wolf-skin vest
Here roving wild, he laid him down to rest

On the bare rock, or through a leafy bower
Looked ere his eyes were closed. By him was seen
The self-same vision which we now behold,
At thy meek bidding, shadowy power! brought forth; [tween;
These mighty barriers, and the gulf be-
The floods,—the stars,—a spectacle as old
As the beginning of the heavens and earth!

WITH how sad steps, O moon, thou climb'st the sky,
"How silently, and with how wan a face!"
Where art thou? Thou whom I have seen on high [race!
Running among the clouds a wood-nymph's
Unhappy nuns, whose common breath's a sigh [pace!
Which they would stifle, move at such a
The northern wind, to call thee to the chase,
Must blow to-night his bugle horn. Had I
The power of Merlin, goddess! this should be: [riven,
And the keen stars, fast as the clouds were
Should sally forth, an emulous company,
Sparkling, and hurrying through the clear blue heaven; [given,
But, Cynthia! should to thee the palm be
Queen both for beauty and for majesty.

EVEN as the dragon's eye that feels the stress
Of a bedimming sleep, or as a lamp
Suddenly glaring through sepulchral damp,
So burns yon taper 'mid a black recess
Of mountains, silent, dreary, motionless:
The lake below reflects it not; the sky
Muffled in clouds affords no company
To mitigate and cheer its loneliness.
Yet round the body of that joyless thing,
Which sends so far its melancholy light,
Perhaps are seated in domestic ring
A gay society with faces bright, [sing,
Conversing, reading, laughing;—or they
While hearts and voices in the song unite.

MARK the concentred hazels that inclose
Yon old gray stone, protected from the ray
Of noontide suns: and even the beams that play [blows,
And glance, while wantonly the rough wind
Are seldom free to touch the moss that grows
Upon that roof—amid embowering gloom
The very image framing of a tomb,
In which some ancient chieftain finds repose
Among the lonely mountains.—Live, ye trees! [keep
And thou, gray stone, the pensive likeness
Of a dark chamber where the mighty sleep.
Far more than fancy to the influence bends
When solitary nature condescends
To mimic time's forlorn humanities.

CAPTIVITY.

"As the cold aspect of a sunless way
Strikes through the traveller's frame with deadlier chill,
Oft as appears a grove, or obvious hill,
Glistening with unparticipated ray,
Or shining slope where he must never stray;
So joys, remembered without wish or will,
Sharpen the keenest edge of present ill,—
On the crushed heart a heavier burthen lay.
Just Heaven, contract the compass of my mind
To fit proportion with my altered state!
Quench those felicities whose light I find
Reflected in my bosom all too late!
Oh, be my spirit, like my thraldom, strait;
And, like mine eyes that stream with sorrow, blind."

BROOK! whose society the poet seeks
Intent his wasted spirits to renew;
And whom the curious painter doth pursue
Through rocky passes, among flowery creeks, [breaks;
And tracks thee dancing down thy water-
If wish were mine some type of thee to view,
Thee, and not thee thyself, I would not do
Like Grecian artists, give thee human cheeks,
Channels for tears; no naiad shouldst thou be, [hairs;
Have neither limbs, feet, feathers, joints nor
It seems the eternal soul is clothed in thee
With purer robes than those of flesh and blood,
And hath bestowed on thee a better good;
Unwearied joy, and life without its cares.

COMPOSED ON THE BANKS OF A ROCKY STREAM.

DOGMATIC teachers of the snow-white fur!
Ye wrangling schoolmen of the scarlet hood!
Who, with a keenness not to be withstood,
Press the point home,—or falter and demur,
Checked in your course by many a teasing burr;
These natural council-seats your acrid blood
Might cool;—and, as the genius of the flood
Stoops willingly to animate and spur
Each lighter function slumbering in the brain,

Yon eddying balls of foam—these arrowy gleams,
That o'er the pavement of the surging streams
Welter and flash—a synod might detain
With subtle speculations, haply vain,
But surely less so than your far-fetched themes!

THIS, AND THE TWO FOLLOWING, WERE SUGGESTED BY MR. W. WESTALL'S VIEWS OF THE CAVES, ETC., IN YORKSHIRE

PURE element of waters! wheresoe'er
Thou dost forsake thy subterranean haunts,
Green herbs, bright flowers, and berry-bearing plants,
Rise into life and in thy train appear:
And, through the sunny portion of the year,
Swift insects shine, thy hovering pursuivants:
And, if thy bounty fail, the forest pants;
And hart and hind and hunter with his spear,
Languish and droop together. Nor unfelt
In man's perturbèd soul thy sway benign;
And, haply, far within the marble belt
Of central earth, where tortured spirits pine
For grace and goodness lost, thy murmurs melt
Their anguish,—and they blend sweet songs with thine.*

MALHAM COVE.

WAS the aim frustrated by force or guile,
When giants scooped from out the rocky ground
Tier under tier—this semicirque profound?
(Giants—the same who built in Erin's isle
That causeway with incomparable toil!)
Oh, had this vast theatric structure wound
With finished sweep into a perfect round,
No mightier work had gained the plausive smile
Of all-beholding Phœbus! But, alas,
Vain earth!—false world!—Foundations must be laid
In heaven; for, 'mid the wreck of IS and WAS,
Things incomplete, and purposes betrayed
Make sadder transits o'er truth's mystic glass
Than noblest objects utterly decayed.

* Waters (as Mr. Westall informs us in the letter-press prefixed to his admirable views) are invariably found to flow through these caverns.

GORDALE.

AT early dawn, or rather when the air
Glimmers with fading light, and shadowy eve
Is busiest to confer and to bereave,
Then, pensive votary! let thy feet repair
To Gordale-chasm, terrific as the lair
Where the young lions couch;—for so, by leave
Of the propitious hour, thou mayst perceive
The local deity, with oozy hair
And mineral crown, beside his jagged urn
Recumbent. Him thou mayst behold, who hides
His lineaments by day, yet there presides,
Teaching the docile waters how to turn;
Or, if need be, impediment to spurn,
And force their passage to the salt-sea tides!

THE MONUMENT COMMONLY CALLED LONG MEG AND HER DAUGHTERS, NEAR THE RIVER EDEN.

A WEIGHT of awe not easy to be borne*
Fell suddenly upon my spirit—cast
From the dread bosom of the unknown past,
When first I saw that sisterhood forlorn;
And her, whose massy strength and stature scorn
The power of years—pre-eminent, and placed
Apart—to overlook the circle vast.
Speak, giant-mother! tell it to the morn
While she dispels the cumbrous shades of night;
Let the moon hear, emerging from a cloud,
At whose behest uprose on British ground
Thy progeny; in hieroglyphic round
Forth-shadowing, some have deemed, the infinite,
The inviolable God, that tames the proud!

COMPOSED AFTER A JOURNEY ACROSS THE HAMILTON HILLS, YORKSHIRE.

DARK and more dark the shades of evening fell;
The wished-for point was reached, but late the hour;

* The daughters of Long Meg, placed in a perfect circle, eighty yards in diameter, are seventy-two in number, and from more than three yards above ground, to less than so many feet: a little way out of the circle stands *Long Meg* herself, a single stone, eighteen feet high. When the author first saw this monument, as he came upon it by surprise, he might overrate its importance as an object; but, though it will not bear a comparison with Stonehenge, he must

And little could be gained from all that
dower
Of prospect, whereof many thousands tell.
Yet did the glowing west in all its power
Salute us :—there stood Indian citadel,
Temple of Greece, and minster with its
tower
Substantially expressed—a place for bell
Or clock to toll from. Many a tempting isle,
With groves that never were imagined, lay
'Mid seas how steadfast ! objects all for the
eye
Of silent rapture; but we felt the while
We should forget them ; they are of the sky,
And from our earthly memory fade away !

"They are of the sky,
And from our earthly memory fade away."

THESE words were uttered as in pensive
mood [sight:
We turned, departing from that solemn
A contrast and reproach to gross delight,
And life's unspiritual pleasures daily wooed!
But now upon this thought I cannot brood ;
It is unstable as a dream of night ;
Nor will I praise a cloud, however bright,
Disparaging man's gifts, and proper food.
Grove, isle, with every shape of sky-built
dome,
Though clad in colours beautiful and pure,
Find in the heart of man no natural home ;
The immortal mind craves objects that
endure : [roam,
These cleave to it ; from these it cannot
Nor they from it : their fellowship is secure.

COMPOSED UPON WESTMINSTER BRIDGE,
SEPT. 3, 1803.

EARTH has not anything to show more
fair : [by
Dull would he be of soul who could pass
A sight so touching in its majesty:
This city now doth like a garment wear
The beauty of the morning; silent, bare,
Ships, towers, domes, theatres, and temples
lie
Open unto the fields, and to the sky;
All bright and glittering in the smokeless
air.
Never did sun more beautifully steep
In his first splendour valley, rock, or hill ;

say, he has not seen any other relique of those dark ages which can pretend to rival it in singularity and dignity of appearance.

Ne'er saw I, never felt, a calm so deep!
The river glideth at his own sweet will :
Dear God ! the very houses seem asleep ;
And all that mighty heart is lying still !

OXFORD, MAY 30, 1820.

YE sacred nurseries of blooming youth !
In whose collegiate shelter England's
flowers [hours
Expand—enjoying through their vernal
The air of liberty, the light of truth ;
Much have ye suffered from time's gnawing
tooth,
Yet, O ye spires of Oxford ! domes and
towers ! [powers
Gardens and groves ! your presence over-
The soberness of reason ; till, in sooth,
Transformed, and rushing on a bold ex-
change,
I slight my own beloved Cam, to range
Where silver Isis leads my stripling feet ;
Pace the long avenue, or glide adown
The stream-like windings of that glorious
street,
An eager novice robed in fluttering gown !

OXFORD, MAY 30, 1820.

SHAME on this faithless heart ! that could
allow [space ;
Such transport—though but for a moment's
Not while—to aid the spirit of the place—
The crescent moon clove with its glittering
prow [bough,
The clouds, or night-bird sang from shady
But in plain daylight :—She too, at my side,
Who, with her heart's experience satisfied,
Maintains inviolate its slightest vow !
Sweet fancy ! other gifts must I receive ;
Proofs of a higher sovereignty I claim ;
Take from *her* brow the withering flowers
of eve, [restore :
And to that brow life's morning wreath
Let *her* be comprehended in the frame
Of these illusions, or they please no more.

RECOLLECTION OF THE PORTRAIT OF
KING HENRY VIII. TRINITY LODGE,
CAMBRIDGE.

THE imperial stature, the colossal stride,
Are yet before me ; yet do I behold
The broad full visage, chest of amplest
mould, [pride :
The vestments broidered with barbaric
And lo ! a poniard, at the monarch's side,
Hangs ready to be grasped in sympathy

With the keen threatenings of that fulgent
eye, [scried.
Below the white-rimmed bonnet, far de-
Who trembles now at thy capricious mood?
'Mid those surrounding worthies, haughty
king!
We rather think, with grateful mind sedate,
How Providence educeth, from the spring
Of lawless will, unlooked-for streams of
good, [abate.
Which neither force shall check nor time

ON THE DEATH OF HIS MAJESTY GEORGE III.

WARD of the law!—dread shadow of a
king! [room;
Whose realm had dwindled to one stately
Whose universe was gloom immersed in
gloom, [fling,
Darkness as thick as life o'er life could
Save haply for some feeble glimmering
Of faith and hope; if thou, by nature's
doom,
Gently hast sunk into the quiet tomb,
Why should we bend in grief, to sorrow
cling, [flowing tears,
When thankfulness were best!—Fresh-
Or, where tears flow not, sigh succeeding
sigh,
Yield to such after-thought the sole reply
Which justly it can claim. The nation
hears [years,
In this deep knell—silent for threescore
An unexampled voice of awful memory.

JUNE, 1820.

FAME tells of groves—from England far
away*—
Groves that inspire the nightingale to trill
And modulate, with subtle reach of skill
Elsewhere unmatched, her ever-varying lay;
Such bold report I venture to gainsay:
For I have heard the choir of Richmond
Hill
Chanting, with indefatigable bill,
Strains, that recalled to mind a distant
day; [wood,
When, haply under shade of that same
And scarcely conscious of the dashing oars
Plied steadily between those willowy shores,
The sweet-souled poet of "The Seasons"
stood— [mood,
Listening, and listening long, in rapturous
Ye heavenly birds! to your progenitors.

* Wallachia is the country alluded to.

A PARSONAGE IN OXFORDSHIRE.

WHERE holy ground begins, unhallowed
ends,
Is marked by no distinguishable line;
The turf unites, the pathways intertwine;
And, wheresoe'er the stealing footstep
tends, [friends,
Garden, and that domain where kindred,
And neighbours rest together, here con-
found [sound
Their several features, mingled like the
Of many waters, or as evening blends
With shady night. Soft airs, from shrub
and flower, [grave;
Waft fragrant greetings to each silent
And while those lofty poplars gently wave
Their tops, between them comes and goes
a sky
Bright as the glimpses of eternity,
To saints accorded in their mortal hour.

COMPOSED AMONG THE RUINS OF A CASTLE IN NORTH WALES.

THROUGH shattered galleries, 'mid roofless
halls, [trayed,
Wandering with timid footstep oft be-
The stranger sighs, nor scruples to upbraid
Old Time, though he, gentlest among the
thralls
Of destiny, upon these wounds hath laid
His lenient touches, soft as light that falls,
From the wan moon, upon the towers and
walls, [shade.
Light deepening the profoundest sleep of
Relic of kings! wreck of forgotten wars,
To winds abandoned and the prying stars,
Time *loves* thee! at his call the seasons
twine [hoar;
Luxuriant wreaths around thy forehead
And, though past pomp no changes can
restore,
A soothing recompense, his gift, is thine!

TO THE LADY E. B. AND THE HON. MISS P.

Composed in the grounds of Plass Newidd, near
Llangollyn, 1824.

A STREAM, to mingle with your favourite
Dee,
Along the Vale of Meditation flows;*
So styled by those fierce Britons, pleased
to see
In nature's face the expression of repose;

* Glyn Myrvr.

Or haply there some pious hermit chose
To live and die, the peace of heaven his aim;
To whom the wild sequestered region owes,
At this late day, its sanctifying name.
Glyn Cafaillgaroch, in the Cambrian tongue,
In ours the Vale of Friendship, let *this* spot
Be named; where, faithful to a low-roofed cot,
On Deva's banks, ye have abode so long;
Sisters in love—a love allowed to climb,
Even on this earth, above the reach of time!

TO THE TORRENT AT THE DEVIL'S BRIDGE, NORTH WALES.

How art thou named? In search of what strange land
From what huge height, descending? Can such force
Of waters issue from a British source,
Or hath not Pindus fed thee, where the band
Of patriots scoop their freedom out, with hand
Desperate as thine? Or, come the incessant shocks
From that young stream, that smites the throbbing rocks
Of Viamala? There I seem to stand,
As in life's morn; permitted to behold,
From the dread chasm, woods climbing above woods
In pomp that fades not, everlasting snows,
And skies that ne'er relinquish their repose:
Such power possess the family of floods
Over the minds of poets, young or old!

"Gives to airy nothing
A local habitation and a name."

Though narrow be that old man's cares, and near,
The poor old man is greater than he seems:
For he hath waking empire, wide as dreams:
An ample sovereignty of eye and ear.
Rich are his walks with supernatural cheer;
The region of his inner spirit teems
With vital sounds and monitory gleams
Of high astonishment and pleasing fear.
He the seven birds hath seen, that never part,
Seen the Seven Whistlers in their nightly rounds,
And counted them: and oftentimes will start—
For overhead are sweeping Gabriel's hounds,
Doomed, with their impious lord, the flying hart
To chase for ever, on aërial grounds!

Wild Redbreast! hadst thou at *Jemima's* lip
Pecked, as at mine, thus boldly, Love might say,
A half-blown rose had tempted thee to sip
Its glistening dews: but hallowed is the clay
Which the muse warms; and I, whose head is gray,
Am not unworthy of thy fellowship;
Nor could I let one thought—one motion—slip
That might thy sylvan confidence betray.
For are we not all His, without whose care
Vouchsafed, no sparrow falleth to the ground?
Who gives His angels wings to speed through air,
And rolls the planets through the blue profound;
Then peck or perch, fond flutterer! nor forbear
To trust a poet in still musings bound.

When Philoctetes in the Lemnian isle
Lay couched;—upon that breathless monument,
On him, or on his fearful bow unbent,
Some wild bird oft might settle, and beguile
The rigid features of a transient smile,
Disperse the tear, or to the sigh give vent,
Slackening the pains of ruthless banishment
From home affections, and heroic toil.
Nor doubt that spiritual creatures round us move,
Griefs to allay that reason cannot heal;
And very reptiles have sufficed to prove
To fettered wretchedness, that no Bastille
Is deep enough to exclude the light of love,
Though man for brother man has ceased to feel.

While Anna's peers and early playmates tread
In freedom mountain turf and river's marge;
Or float with music in the festal barge;
Rein the proud steed, or through the dance are led;
Her doom it is to press a weary bed—
Till oft her guardian angel, to some charge
More urgent called, will stretch his wings at large,
And friends too rarely prop the languid head.
Yet helped by genius—untired comforter!
The presence even of a stuffed owl for her
Can cheat the time; sending her fancy out
To ivied castles and to moonlight skies,

Though he can neither stir a plume, nor
 shout, [eyes.
Nor veil, with restless film, his staring

TO THE CUCKOO.

NOT the whole warbling grove in concert
 heard [can thrill
When sunshine follows shower, the breast
Like the first summons, cuckoo! of thy
 bill,
With its twin notes inseparably paired.
The captive, 'mid damp vaults unsunned,
 unaired,
Measuring the periods of his lonely doom,
That cry can reach; and to the sick man's
 room
Sends gladness, by no languid smile de-
 clared, [search
The lordly eagle-race through hostile
May perish; time may come when never
 more
The wilderness shall hear the lion roar;
But long as cock shall crow from household
 perch [thy wing,
To rouse the dawn, soft gales shall speed
And thy erratic voice be faithful to the
 spring!

THE INFANT M—— M——.

UNQUIET childhood here by special grace
Forgets her nature, opening like a flower
That neither feeds nor wastes its vital power
In painful struggles. Months each other
 chase, [trace
And nought untunes that infant's voice; a
Of fretful temper sullies not her cheek;
Prompt, lively, self-sufficing, yet so meek
That one enrapt with gazing on her face,
(Which even the placid innocence of death
Could scarcely make more placid, heaven
 more bright,)
Might learn to picture, for the eye of faith,
The virgin, as she shone with kindred light;
A nursling couched upon her mother's
 knee,
Beneath some shady palm of Galilee.

TO ROTHA Q——.

ROTHA, my spiritual child! this head was
 gray
When at the sacred font for thee I stood;
Pledged till thou reach the verge of woman-
 hood,
And shalt become thy own sufficient stay:
Too late, I feel, sweet orphan! was the day
For steadfast hope the contract to fulfil;
Yet shall my blessing hover o'er thee still,
Embodied in the music of this lay,
Breathed forth beside the peaceful moun-
 tain stream* [mother's ear
Whose murmur soothed thy languid
After her throes, this stream of name more
 dear
Since thou dost hear it,—a memorial theme
For others; for thy future self a spell
To summon fancies out of time's dark cell.

TO ——.

SUCH age how beautiful! O lady bright,
Whose mortal lineaments seem all refined
By favouring nature and a saintly mind
To something purer and more exquisite
Than flesh and blood; whene'er thou
 meet'st my sight, [cheek,
When I behold thy blanched unwithered
Thy temples fringed with locks of gleaming
 white, [meek,
And head that droops because the soul is
Thee with the welcome snowdrop I com-
 pare, [that climb
That child of winter, prompting thoughts
From desolation towards the genial prime;
Or with the moon conquering earth's
 misty air, [light
And filling more and more with crystal
As pensive evening deepens into night.

IN my mind's eye a temple, like a cloud
Slowly surmounting some invidious hill,
Rose out of darkness: the bright work
 stood still, [proud,
And might of its own beauty have been
But it was fashioned and to God was
 vowed
By virtues that diffused, in every part,
Spirit divine through forms of human art:
Faith had her arch—her arch when winds
 blow loud,
Into the consciousness of safety thrilled;
And Love her towers of dread foundation
 laid [spire
Under the grave of things; Hope had her
Star-high, and pointing still to something
 higher; [said,
Trembling I gazed, but heard a voice—it
Hell gates are powerless phantoms when
 we build.

* The river Rotha, that flows into Windermere from the lakes of Grasmere and Rydal.

CONCLUSION.

TO ——.

If these brief records, by the Muses' art
Produced as lonely nature or the strife
That animates the scenes of public life
Inspired, may in thy leisure claim a part,
And if these transcripts of the private heart
Have gained a sanction from thy falling tears,
Then I repent not: but my soul hath fears
Breathed from eternity; for as a dart
Cleaves the blank air, life flies: now every day
Is but a glimmering spoke in the swift wheel
Of the revolving week. Away, away,
All fitful cares, all transitory zeal;
So timely grace the immortal wing may heal,
And honour rest upon the senseless clay.

Memorials of a Tour in Scotland,

1803.

DEPARTURE FROM THE VALE OF GRASMERE.

AUGUST 1803.

The gentlest shade that walked Elysian plains
Might sometimes covet dissoluble chains,
Even for the tenants of the zone that lies
Beyond the stars, celestial paradise,
Methinks 'twould heighten joy, to overleap
At will the crystal battlements, and peep
Into some other region, though less fair,
To see how things are made and managed there;
Change for the worse might please, incursion bold
Into the tracts of darkness and of cold,
O'er Limbo lake with aëry flight to steer,
And on the verge of Chaos hang in fear.
Such animation often do I find,
Power in my breast, wings growing in my mind,
Then, when some rock or hill is overpast,
Perchance without one look behind me cast,
Some barrier with which nature, from the birth
Of things, has fenced this fairest spot on earth.
Oh, pleasant transit, Grasmere! to resign
Such happy fields, abodes so calm as thine;
Not like an outcast with himself at strife;
The slave of business, time, or care for life
But moved by choice; or, if constrained in part,
Yet still with nature's freedom at the heart,
To cull contentment upon wildest shores,
And luxuries extract from bleakest moors,
With prompt embrace all beauty to infold,
And having rights in all that we behold
Then why these lingering steps? A bright adieu,
For a brief absence, proves that love is true;
Ne'er can the way be irksome or forlorn,
That winds into itself, for sweet return.

TO THE SONS OF BURNS,

AFTER VISITING THE GRAVE OF THEIR FATHER.

"The poet's grave is in a corner of the churchyard We looked at it with melancholy and painful reflections, repeating to each other his own verses, 'Is there a man whose judgment clear,' etc.'—*Extract from the Journal of my Fellow-Traveller*

'Mid crowded obelisks and urns,
I sought the untimely grave of Burns;
Sons of the bard, my heart still mourns
With sorrow true;
And more would grieve, but that it turns
Trembling to you!

Through twilight shades of good and ill
Ye now are panting up life's hill,
And more than common strength and skill
Must ye display,
If ye would give the better will
Its lawful sway.

Hath nature strung your nerves to bear
Intemperance with less harm, beware!
But if the poet's wit ye share,
Like him can speed
The social hour—for tenfold care
There will be need.

Even honest men delight will take
To spare your failings for his sake,
Will flatter you,—and fool and rake
Your steps pursue;
And of your father's name will make
A snare for you.

Far from their noisy haunts retire,
And add your voices to the quire
That sanctify the cottage fire
With service meet;
There seek the genius of your sire,
His spirit greet;

Or where, 'mid "lonely heights and hows,"
He paid to nature tuneful vows;
Or wiped his honourable brows
Bedewed with toil,
While reapers strove, or busy ploughs
Upturned the soil;

His judgment with benignant ray
Shall guide, his fancy cheer, your way;
But ne'er to a seductive lay
Let faith be given;
Nor deem that "light which leads astray,
Is light from heaven."

Let no mean hope your souls enslave:
Be independent, generous, brave;
Your father such example gave,
And such revere:
But be admonished by his grave,
And think, and fear!

ELLEN IRWIN, OR THE BRAES OF KIRTLE.

FAIR Ellen Irwin, when she sate
Upon the braes of Kirtle,*
Was lovely as a Grecian maid
Adorned with wreaths of myrtle.
Young Adam Bruce beside her lay;
And there did they beguile the day
With love and gentle speeches,
Beneath the budding beeches.

From many knights and many squires
The Bruce had been selected;
And Gordon, fairest of them all,
By Ellen was rejected.
Sad tidings to that noble youth!
For it may be proclaimed with truth,
If Bruce hath loved sincerely,
That Gordon loves as dearly.

But what is Gordon's beauteous face,
And what are Gordon's crosses,
To them who sit by Kirtle's braes
Upon the verdant mosses?
Alas that ever he was born!
The Gordon, couched behind a thorn,
Sees them and their caressing;
Beholds them blest and blessing.

Proud Gordon cannot bear the thoughts
That through his brain are travelling,—
And, starting up, to Bruce's heart
He launched a deadly javelin!
Fair Ellen saw it when it came,
And, stepping forth to meet the same,
Did with her body cover
The youth, her chosen lover.

And, falling into Bruce's arms,
Thus died the beauteous Ellen,
Thus, from the heart of her true-love,
The mortal spear repelling.
And Bruce, as soon as he had slain
The Gordon, sailed away to Spain;
And fought with rage incessant
Against the Moorish crescent.

But many days, and many months,
And many years ensuing,
This wretched knight did vainly seek
The death that he was wooing:
So coming his last help to crave,
Heart-broken, upon Ellen's grave
His body he extended,
And there his sorrow ended.

Now ye, who willingly have heard
The tale I have been telling,
May in Kirkonnel churchyard view
The grave of lovely Ellen:
By Ellen's side the Bruce is laid;
And, for the stone upon its head,
May no rude hand deface it,
And its forlorn HIC JACET!

* The Kirtle is a river in the southern part of Scotland, on whose banks the events here related took place.

TO A HIGHLAND GIRL.

(AT INVERSNAID, UPON LOCH LOMOND.)

SWEET Highland girl, a very shower
Of beauty is thy earthly dower!
Twice seven consenting years have shed
Their utmost bounty on thy head:

And these gray rocks; this household lawn;
These trees, a veil just half withdrawn;
This fall of water, that doth make
A murmur near the silent lake;
This little bay, a quiet road
That holds in shelter thy abode;
In truth together do ye seem
Like something fashioned in a dream;
Such forms as from their covert peep
When earthly cares are laid asleep!
Yet, dream and vision as thou art,
I bless thee with a human heart:
God shield thee to thy latest years!
I neither know thee nor thy peers;
And yet my eyes are filled with tears.

With earnest feeling I shall pray
For thee when I am far away·
For never saw I mien, or face,
In which more plainly I could trace
Benignity and home-bred sense
Ripening in perfect innocence.
Here scattered like a random seed,
Remote from men, thou dost not need
The embarrassed look of shy distress,
And maidenly shamefacedness:
Thou wear'st upon thy forehead clear
The freedom of a mountaineer.
A face with gladness overspread!
Soft smiles, by human kindness bred!
And seemliness complete, that sways
Thy courtesies, about thee plays;
With no restraint, but such as springs
From quick and eager visitings
Of thoughts, that lie beyond the reach
Of thy few words of English speech:
A bondage sweetly brooked, a strife
That gives thy gestures grace and life!
So have I, not unmoved in mind,
Seen birds of tempest-loving kind,
Thus beating up against the wind.

What hand but would a garland cull
For thee, who art so beautiful?
Oh, happy pleasure! here to dwell
Beside thee in some heathy dell;
Adopt your homely ways and dress,
A shepherd, thou a shepherdess!
But I could frame a wish for thee
More like a grave reality:
Thou art to me but as a wave
Of the wild sea: and I would have
Some claim upon thee, if I could,
Though but of common neighbourhood.
What joy to hear thee, and to see!
Thy elder brother I would be,
Thy father anything to thee!

Now thanks to Heaven! that of its grace
Hath led me to this lonely place.
Joy have I had; and going hence
I bear away my recompense.
In spots like these it is we prize
Our memory, feel that she hath eyes:
Then, why should I be loth to stir?
I feel this place was made for her;
To give new pleasure like the past,
Continued long as life shall last.
Nor am I loth, though pleased at heart,
Sweet Highland girl! from thee to part,
For I, methinks, till I grow old,
As fair before me shall behold,
As I do now, the cabin small,
The lake, the bay, the waterfall;
And thee, the spirit of them all!

GLEN-ALMAIN, OR THE NARROW GLEN.

In this still place, remote from men,
Sleeps Ossian, in the Narrow glen;
In this still place, where murmurs on
But one meek streamlet, only one:
He sang of battles, and the breath
Of stormy war, and violent death;
And should, methinks, when all was past,
Have rightfully been laid at last
Where rocks were rudely heaped, and rent
As by a spirit turbulent; [wild
Where sights were rough, and sounds were
And every thing unreconciled;
In some complaining, dim retreat,
For fear and melancholy meet;
But this is calm; there cannot be
A more entire tranquillity.

Does then the bard sleep here indeed?
Or is it but a groundless creed!
What matters it?—I blame them not
Whose fancy in this lonely spot
Was moved; and in such way expressed
Their notion of its perfect rest.
A convent, even a hermit's cell
Would break the silence of this dell:
It is not quiet; is not ease;
But something deeper far than these:
The separation that is here
Is of the grave; and of austere
Yet happy feelings of the dead:
And, therefore, was it rightly said
That Ossian, last of all his race!
Lies buried in this lonely place.

STEPPING WESTWARD.

[While my fellow-traveller and I were walking by the side of Loch Katrine, one fine evening after sunset, in our road to a hut where, in the course of our tour, we had been hospitably entertained some weeks before, we met, in one of the loneliest parts of that solitary region, two well-dressed women, one of whom said to us, by way of greeting, "What! you are stepping westward?"]

"*What! you are stepping westward?*"—["*Yea.*"
'Twould be a *wildish* destiny,
If we, who thus together roam
In a strange land, and far from home,
Were in this place the guests of chance:
Yet who would stop, or fear to advance,
Though home or shelter he had none,
With such a sky to lead him on?

The dewy ground was dark and cold;
Behind, all gloomy to behold;
And stepping westward seemed to be
A kind of *heavenly* destiny;
I liked the greeting; 'twas a sound
Of something without place or bound;
And seemed to give me spiritual right
To travel through that region bright.

The voice was soft, and she who spake
Was walking by her native lake:
The salutation had to me
The very sound of courtesy:
Its power was felt; and while my eye
Was fixed upon the glowing sky,
The echo of the voice inwrought
A human sweetness with the thought
Of travelling through the world that lay
Before me in my endless way.

THE SOLITARY REAPER.

BEHOLD her, single in the field,
Yon solitary Highland lass!
Reaping and singing by herself;
Stop here, or gently pass!
Alone she cuts, and binds the grain,
And sings a melancholy strain;
Oh, listen! for the vale profound
Is overflowing with the sound.

No nightingale did ever chant
More welcome notes to weary bands
Of travellers in some shady haunt,
Among Arabian sands:
Such thrilling voice was never heard
In spring-time from the cuckoo-bird,
Breaking the silence of the seas
Among the farthest Hebrides.

Will no one tell me what she sings?
Perhaps the plaintive numbers flow
For old, unhappy, far-off things,
And battles long ago:
Or is it some more humble lay,
Familiar matter of to-day?
Some natural sorrow, loss, or pain,
That has been, and may be again!

Whate'er the theme, the maiden sang
As if her song could have no ending;
I saw her singing at her work,
And o'er the sickle bending;—
I listened—motionless and still;
And as I mounted up the hill,
The music in my heart I bore,
Long after it was heard no more.

ADDRESS TO KILCHURN CASTLE UPON LOCH AWE.

"From the top of the hill a most impressive scene opened upon our view,—a ruined castle on an island at some distance from the shore, backed by a cove of the mountain Cruachan, down which came a foaming stream. The castle occupied every foot of the island that was visible to us, appearing to rise out of the water,—mists rested upon the mountain side, with spots of sunshine; there was a mild desolation in the low-grounds, a solemn grandeur in the mountains, and the castle was wild, yet stately—not dismantled of turrets—nor the walls broken down, though obviously a ruin."—*Extract from the Journal of my Companion.*

CHILD of loud-throated war! the mountain stream
Roars in thy hearing; but thy hour of rest
Is come, and thou art silent in thy age;
Save when the winds sweep by and sounds are caught
Ambiguous, neither wholly thine nor theirs.
Oh! there is life that breathes not: powers there are
That touch each other to the quick in modes
Which the gross world no sense hath to perceive,
No soul to dream of. What art thou, from care
Cast off—abandoned by thy rugged sire,
Nor by soft peace adopted; though, in place
And in dimension, such that thou mightst seem

N

But a mere footstool to yon sovereign lord,
Hugh Cruachan, (a thing that meaner hills
Might crush, nor know that it had suffered harm ;)
Yet he, not loth, in favour of thy claims
To reverence suspends his own ; submitting
All that the God of nature hath conferred,
All that he has in common with the stars,
To the memorial majesty of time
Impersonated in thy calm decay!

Take, then, thy seat, vicegerent unreproved!
Now, while a farewell gleam of evening light
Is fondly lingering on thy shattered front,
Do thou, in turn, be paramount; and rule
Over the pomp and beauty of a scene
Whose mountains, torrents, lake, and woods, unite
To pay thee homage; and with these are joined,
In willing admiration and respect,
Two hearts, which in thy presence might be called
Youthful as spring. Shade of departed power,
Skeleton of unfleshed humanity,
The chronicle were welcome that should call
Into the compass of distinct regard
The toils and struggles of thy infancy!
Yon foaming flood seems motionless as ice;
Its dizzy turbulence eludes the eye,
Frozen by distance · so, majestic pile,
To the perception of this age, appear
Thy fierce beginnings, softened and subdued
And quieted in character; the strife,
The pride, the fury uncontrollable,
Lost on the aërial heights of the Crusades!*

ROB ROY'S GRAVE.

The history of Rob Roy is sufficiently known; his grave is near the head of Loch Katrine, in one of those small pinfold-like burial-grounds of neglected and desolate appearance, which the traveller meets with in the Highlands of Scotland.

A FAMOUS man is Robin Hood,
The English ballad-singer's joy!
And Scotland has a thief as good,
An outlaw of as daring mood;
She has her brave Rob Roy!
Then clear the weeds from off his grave,
And let us chant a passing stave
In honour of that hero brave!

Heaven gave Rob Roy a dauntless heart
And wondrous length and strength of arm:
Nor craved he more to quell his foes,
Or keep his friends from harm.

Yet was Rob Roy as *wise* as brave;
Forgive me if the phrase be strong;—
A poet worthy of Rob Roy
Must scorn a timid song.

Say, then, that he was wise as brave;
As wise in thought as bold in deed:
For in the principles of things
He sought his moral creed.

Said generous Rob, "What need of books?
Burn all the statutes and their shelves:
They stir us up against our kind;
And worse, against ourselves.

"We have a passion, make a law,
Too false to guide us or control!
And for the law itself we fight
In bitterness of soul.

"And, puzzled, blinded thus, we lose
Distinctions that are plain and few:
These find I graven on my heart:
That tells me what to do.

"The creatures see of flood and field,
And those that travel on the wind!
With them no strife can last; they live
In peace, and peace of mind.

"For why?—because the good old rule
Sufficeth them, the simple plan,
That they should take who have the power
And they should keep who can.

"A lesson that is quickly learned,
A signal this which all can see!
Thus nothing here provokes the strong
To wanton cruelty.

"All freakishness of mind is checked;
He tamed, who foolishly aspires;
While to the measure of his might
Each fashions his desires.

"All kinds, and creatures, stand and fall
By strength of prowess or of wit:
'Tis God's appointment who must sway
And who is to submit.

"Since, then, the rule of right is plain,
And longest life is but a day;
To have my ends, maintain my rights,
I'll take the shortest way."

* The tradition is that the castle was built by a lady during the absence of her lord in Palestine.

And thus among these rocks he lived,
Through summer heat and winter snow :
The eagle, he was lord above,
And Rob was lord below.

So was it—*would*, at least, have been
But through untowardness of fate :
For polity was then too strong ;
He came an age too late.

Or shall we say an age too soon ?
For, were the bold man living *now*,
How might he flourish in his pride,
With buds on every bough !

Then rents and factors, rights of chase,
Sheriffs, and lairds and their domains,
Would all have seemed but paltry things,
Not worth a moment's pains.

Rob Roy had never lingered here,
To these few meagre vales confined ;
But thought how wide the world, the times
How fairly to his mind !

And to his sword he would have said,
"Do thou my sovereign will enact
From land to land through half the earth !
Judge thou of law and fact !

"'Tis fit that we should do our part ;
Becoming, that mankind should learn
That we are not to be surpassed
In fatherly concern.

"Of old things all are over old,
Of good things none are good enough :—
We'll show that we can help to frame
A world of other stuff.

"I, too, will have my kings that take
From me the sign of life and death :
Kingdoms shall shift about, like clouds,
Obedient to my breath."

And, if the word had been fulfilled,
As *might* have been, then, thought of joy !
France would have had her present boast ;
And we our own Rob Roy !

Oh ! say not so ; compare them not ;
I would not wrong thee, champion brave !
Would wrong thee nowhere ; least of all
Here standing by thy grave.

For thou, although with some wild thoughts,
Wild chieftain of a savage clan !
Hadst this to boast of ; thou didst love
The *liberty* of man.

And, had it been thy lot to live
With us who now behold the light,
Thou wouldst have nobly stirred thyself,
And battled for the right.

For thou wert still the poor man's stay,
The poor man's heart, the poor man's hand ;
And all the oppressed, who wanted strength,
Had thine at their command.

Bear witness many a pensive sigh
Of thoughtful herdsman when he strays
Alone upon Loch Veol's heights,
And by Loch Lomond's braes !

And, far and near, through vale and hill,
Are faces that attest the same ;
The proud heart flashing through the eyes,
At sound of Rob Roy's name.

COMPOSED AT —— CASTLE.

DEGENERATE Douglas ! oh, the unworthy lord !
Whom mere despite of heart could so far please,
And love of havoc (for with such disease
Fame taxes him) that he could send forth word,
To level with the dust a noble horde,
A brotherhood of venerable trees,
Leaving an ancient dome, and towers like these,
Beggared and outraged !—Many hearts deplored
The fate of those old trees ; and oft with pain
The traveller, at this day, will stop and gaze
On wrongs, which nature scarcely seems to heed :
For sheltered places, bosoms, nooks, and bays,
And the pure mountains, and the gentle Tweed,
And the green silent pastures, yet remain.

YARROW UNVISITED.

[See the various poems the scene of which is laid upon the banks of the Yarrow ; in particular, the exquisite ballad of Hamilton, beginning

"Busk ye, busk ye, my bonny bonny bride,
Busk ye, busk ye, my winsome marrow !"]

FROM Stirling Castle we had seen
The mazy Forth unravelled ;

Had trod the banks of Clyde, and Tay,
And with the Tweed had travelled;
And when we came to Clovenford,
Then said my "*winsome marrow*,"
"Whate'er betide, we'll turn aside,
And see the Braes of Yarrow."

"Let Yarrow folk, *frae* Selkirk town,
Who have been buying, selling,
Go back to Yarrow, 'tis their own;
Each maiden to her dwelling!
On Yarrow's banks let herons feed,
Hares couch, and rabbits burrow!
But we will downwards with the Tweed,
Nor turn aside to Yarrow.

"There's Gala Water, Leader Haughs,
Both lying right before us;
And Dryburgh, where with chiming Tweed
The lintwhites sing in chorus;
There's pleasant Teviotdale, a land
Made blithe with plough and harrow:
Why throw away a needful day
To go in search of Yarrow?

"What's Yarrow but a river bare,
That glides the dark hills under?
There are a thousand such elsewhere
As worthy of your wonder."
Strange words they seemed of slight and [scorn:
My true love sighed for sorrow:
And looked me in the face, to think
I thus could speak of Yarrow!

"Oh! green," said I, "are Yarrow's [holms,
And sweet is Yarrow flowing!
Fair hangs the apple frae the rock,*
But we will leave it growing.
O'er hilly path, and open strath,
We'll wander Scotland thorough;
But, though so near, we will not turn
Into the dale of Yarrow.

"Let beeves and home-bred kine partake
The sweets of Burn-mill meadow;
The swan on still St. Mary's Lake
Float double, swan and shadow!
We will not see them; will not go,
To-day, nor yet to-morrow;
Enough if in our hearts we know
There's such a place as Yarrow.

"Be Yarrow stream unseen, unknown!
It must, or we shall rue it:
We have a vision of our own;
Ah! why should we undo it?
The treasured dreams of times long past,
We'll keep them, winsome marrow!
For when we're there, although tis 'fair,
'Twill be another Yarrow!

"If care, with freezing years should come,
And wandering seem but folly,—
Should we be loth to stir from home,
And yet be melancholy;
Should life be dull, and spirits low,
'Twill soothe us in our sorrow,
That earth has something yet to show,
The bonny holms of Yarrow!"

* See Hamilton's ballad, as above.

IN THE PASS OF KILLICRANKIE,

AN INVASION BEING EXPECTED, OCTOBER 1803.

Six thousand veterans practised in war's game,
Tried men at Killicrankie were arrayed
Against an equal host that wore the plaid,
Shepherds and herdsmen.—Like a whirlwind came [flame;
The Highlanders, the slaughter spread like
And Garry, thundering down his mountain road,
Was stopped, and could not breathe beneath the load
Of the dead bodies.—'Twas a day of shame
For them whom precept and the pedantry
Of cold mechanic battle do enslave.
Oh, for a single hour of that Dundee,
Who on that day the word of onset gave!
Like conquest would the men of England see;
And her foes find a like inglorious grave.

THE MATRON OF JEDBURGH AND HER HUSBAND.

[At Jedburgh, my companion and I went into private lodgings for a few days: and the following verses were called forth by the character and domestic situation of our hostess.]

Age! twine thy brows with fresh spring flowers,
And call a train of laughing hours;
And bid them dance and bid them sing;
And thou, too, mingle in the ring!
Take to thy heart a new delight;
If not, make merry in despite
That there is one who scorns thy power:—
But dance! for under Jedburgh tower.

A matron dwells, who though she bears
Our mortal complement of years,
Lives in the light of youthful glee,
And she will dance and sing with thee.

Nay! start not at that figure—there!
Him who is rooted to his chair!
Look at him—look again! for he
Hath long been of thy family.
With legs that move not, if they can,
And useless arms, a trunk of man,
He sits, and with a vacant eye;
A sight to make a stranger sigh!
Deaf, drooping, that is now his doom:
His world is in this single room;
Is this a place for mirthful cheer?
Can merrymaking enter here?

The joyous woman is the mate
Of him in that forlorn estate!
He breathes a subterraneous damp;
But bright as vesper shines her lamp;
He is as mute as Jedburgh tower;
She jocund as it was of yore,
With all its bravery on; in times
When all alive with merry chimes,
Upon a sun-bright morn of May,
It roused the vale to holiday.

I praise thee, matron! and thy due
Is praise; heroic praise, and true;
With admiration I behold
Thy gladness unsubdued and bold:
Thy looks, thy gestures, all present
The picture of a life well spent:
This do I see; and something more;
A strength unthought of heretofore!
Delighted am I for thy sake;
And yet a higher joy partake.
Our human nature throws away
Its second twilight, and looks gay;
A land of promise and of pride
Unfolding, wide as life is wide.

Ah! see her helpless charge! inclosed
Within himself as seems, composed;
To fear of loss, and hope of gain,
The strife of happiness and pain,
Utterly dead! yet in the guise
Of little infants, when their eyes
Begin to follow to and fro
The persons that before them go,
He tracks her motions, quick or slow.
Her buoyant spirit can prevail
Where common cheerfulness would fail;
She strikes upon him with the heat
Of July suns: he feels it sweet;
An animal delight, though dim!
'Tis all that now remains for him!

The more I looked, I wondered more—
And, while I scanned them o'er and o'er,
A moment gave me to espy
A trouble in her strong black eye;
A remnant of uneasy light,
A flash of something over bright!
Nor long this mystery did detain
My thoughts; she told in pensive strain
That she had borne a heavy yoke,
Been stricken by a twofold stroke;
Ill health of body; and had pined
Beneath worse ailments of the mind.

So be it!—but let praise ascend
To Him who is our Lord and friend!
Who from disease and suffering
Hath called for thee a second spring;
Repaid thee for that sore distress
By no untimely joyousness;
Which makes of thine a blissful state:
And cheers thy melancholy mate!

FLY, some kind spirit, fly to Grasmere-dale,
Say that we come, and come by this day's light;
Glad tidings!—spread them over field and height;
But chiefly let one cottage hear the tale;
There let a mystery of joy prevail,
The happy kitten bound with frolic might,
And Rover whine, as at a second sight
Of near-approaching good that shall not fail;
And from that infant's face let joy appear;
Yea, let our Mary's one companion child,
That hath her six weeks' solitude beguiled
With intimations manifold and dear,
While we have wandered over wood and wild,
Smile on his mother now with bolder cheer.

THE BLIND HIGHLAND BOY.

A TALE TOLD BY THE FIRESIDE, AFTER RETURNING TO THE VALE OF GRASMERE.

Now we are tired of boisterous joy,
Have romped enough, my little boy!
Jane hangs her head upon my breast,
And you shall bring your stool and rest;
This corner is your own.

There! take your seat, and let me see
That you can listen quietly;
And, as I promised, I will tell
That strange adventure which befel
A poor blind Highland boy.

A *Highland* boy!—why call him so?
Because, my darlings, ye must know,
In land where many a mountain towers,
Far higher hills than these of ours!
He from his birth had lived.

He ne'er had seen one earthly sight:
The sun, the day; the stars, the night;
Or tree, or butterfly, or flower,
Or fish in stream, or bird in bower,
Or woman, man, or child.

And yet he neither drooped nor pined,
Nor had a melancholy mind;
For God took pity on the boy,
And was his friend; and gave him joy
Of which we nothing know.

His mother, too, no doubt above
Her other children him did love:
For, was she here, or was she there,
She thought of him with constant care,
And more than mother's love.

And proud she was of heart, when clad
In crimson stockings, tartan plaid,
And bonnet with a feather gay,
To kirk he on the Sabbath-day
Went hand in hand with her.

A dog, too, had he; not for need,
But one to play with and to feed;
Which would have led him, if bereft
Of company or friends, and left
Without a better guide.

And then the bagpipes he could blow;
And thus from house to house would go,
And all were pleased to hear and see;
For none made sweeter melody
Than did the poor blind boy.

Yet he had many a restless dream;
Both when he heard the eagles scream,
And when he heard the torrents roar,
And heard the water beat the shore
Near which their cottage stood.

Beside a lake their cottage stood,
Not small like ours, a peaceful flood;
But one of mighty size, and strange;
That, rough or smooth, is full of change,
And stirring in its bed.

For to this lake by night and day,
The great sea-water finds its way
Through long, long windings of the hills;
And drinks up all the pretty rills,
And rivers large and strong:

Then hurries back the road it came—
Returns, on errand still the same;
This did it when the earth was new;
And this for evermore will do,
As long as earth shall last.

And with the coming of the tide,
Come boats and ships that safely ride,
Between the woods and lofty rocks;
And to the shepherds with their flocks
Bring tales of distant lands.

And of those tales, whate'er they were,
The blind boy always had his share;
Whether of mighty towns, or vales
With warmer suns and softer gales,
Or wonders of the deep.

Yet more it pleased him, more it stirred,
When from the water-side he heard
The shouting, and the jolly cheers,
The bustle of the mariners
In stillness or in storm.

But what do his desires avail?
For he must never handle sail;
Nor mount the mast, nor row, nor float
In sailor's ship, or fisher's boat
Upon the rocking waves.

His mother often thought, and said,
What sin would be upon her head
If she should suffer this. "My son,
Whate'er you do, leave this undone;
The danger is so great."

Thus lived he by Loch Leven's side,
Still sounding with the sounding tide,
And heard the billows leap and dance,
Without a shadow of mischance,
Till he was ten years old.

When one day (and now mark me well,
Ye soon shall know how this befel)
He in a vessel of his own,
On the swift flood is hurrying down
Towards the mighty sea.

In such a vessel never more
May human creature leave the shore!
If this or that way he should stir,
Woe to the poor blind mariner!
For death will be his doom.

But say what bears him?—Ye have seen
The Indian's bow, his arrows keen,
Rare beasts, and birds with plumage bright
Gifts which, for wonder or delight,
Are brought in ships from far.

Such gifts had those seafaring men
Spread round that haven in the glen;
Each hut, perchance, might have its own,
And to the boy they all were known;
He knew and prized them all.

The rarest was a turtle shell
Which he, poor child, had studied well;
A shell of ample size, and light
As the pearly car of Amphitrite,
That sportive dolphins drew.

And, as a coracle that braves
On Vaga's breast the fretful waves,
This shell upon the deep would swim,
And gaily lift its fearless brim
Above the tossing surge.

And this the little blind boy knew:
And he a story strange, yet true,
Had heard, how in a shell like this
An English boy, oh, thought of bliss!
Had stoutly launched from shore;

Launched from the margin of a bay
Among the Indian isles, where lay
His father's ship, and had sailed far,
To join that gallant ship of war,
In his delightful shell.

Our Highland boy oft visited
The house which held this prize; and, led
By choice or chance, did thither come
One day when no one was at home,
And found the door unbarred.

While there he sate, alone and blind,
That story flashed upon his mind;—
A bold thought roused him, and he took
The shell from out its secret nook,
And bore it on his head.

He launched his vessel—and in pride
Of spirit, from Loch Leven's side,
Stepped into it—his thoughts all free
As the light breezes that with glee
Sang through the adventurer's hair.

A while he stood upon his feet;
He felt the motion—took his seat;
Still better pleased as more and more
The tide retreated from the shore,
And sucked and sucked him in.

And there he is in face of heaven!
How rapidly the child is driven!
The fourth part of a mile I ween
He thus had gone, ere he was seen
By any human eye.

But when he was first seen, oh, me,
What shrieking and what misery!
For many saw; among the rest
His mother, she who loved him best,
She saw her poor blind boy.

But for the child, the sightless boy,
It is the triumph of his joy!
The bravest traveller in balloon,
Mounting as if to reach the moon,
Was never half so blessed.

And let him, let him go his way,
Alone, and innocent, and gay!
For, if good angels love to wait
On the forlorn unfortunate,
This child will take no harm.

But now the passionate lament,
Which from the crowd on shore was sent,
The cries which broke from old and young
In Gaelic, or the English tongue,
Are stifled—all is still.

And quickly with a silent crew
A boat is ready to pursue;
And from the shore their course they take,
And swiftly down the running lake
They follow the blind boy.

But soon they move with softer pace;
So have ye seen the fowler chase
On Grasmere's clear unruffled breast
A youngling of the wild-duck's nest
With deftly-lifted oar.

Or as the wily sailors crept
To seize (while on the deep it slept)
The hapless creature which did dwell
Erewhile within the dancing shell,
They steal upon their prey.

With sound the least that can be made
They follow, more and more afraid,
More cautious as they draw more near,
But in his darkness he can hear,
And guesses their intent.

"*Lei-gha—Lei-gha*"—then did he cry,
"*Lei-gha—Lei-gha*"—most eagerly;
Thus did he cry, and thus did pray,
And what he meant was, "Keep away,
And leave me to myself!"

Alas! and when he felt their hands—
You've often heard of magic wands,
That with a motion overthrow
A palace of the proudest show,
Or melt it into air.

So all his dreams, that inward light
With which his soul had shone so bright,
All vanished ;—'twas a heartfelt cross
To him, a heavy, bitter loss,
As he had ever known.

But hark ! a gratulating voice
With which the very hills rejoice :
'Tis from the crowd, who tremblingly
Had watched the event, and now can see
That he is safe at last.

And then, when he was brought to land,
Full sure they were a happy band,
Which gathering round did on the banks
Of that great water give God thanks,
And welcomed the poor child.

And in the general joy of heart
The blind boy's little dog took part ;
He leapt about, and oft did kiss
His master's hands in sign of bliss,
With sound like lamentation.

But most of all, his mother dear,
She who had fainted with her fear,
Rejoiced when waking she espies
The child ; when she can trust her eyes ;
And touches the blind boy.

She led him home, and wept amain,
When he was in the house again :
Tears flowed in torrents from her eyes ;
She could not blame him, or chastise :
She was too happy far.

Thus, after he had fondly braved
The perilous deep, the boy was saved ;
And, though his fancies had been wild,
Yet he was pleased and reconciled
To live in peace on shore.

And in the lonely Highland dell
Still do they keep the turtle shell ;
And long the story will repeat
Of the blind boy's adventurous feat,
And how he was preserved.*

Memorials of a Tour in Scotland.

1814.

THE BROWNIE'S CELL.

[Suggested by a beautiful ruin upon one of the islands of Loch Lomond, a place chosen for the retreat of a solitary individual from whom this habitation acquired its name.]

To barren heath and quaking fen,
Or depth of labyrinthine glen ;
Or into trackless forest set
With trees, whose lofty umbrage met ;
World-wearied men withdrew of yore,—
(Penance their trust, and prayer their store;)
And in the wilderness were bound
To such apartments as they found ;
Or with a new ambition raised ;
That God might suitably be praised.

High lodged the *warrior*, like a bird of prey ;
Or where broad waters round him lay ;
But this wild ruin is no ghost
Of his devices—buried, lost !
Within this little lonely isle
There stood a consecrated pile ;
Where tapers burned, and mass was sung,
For them whose timid spirits clung
To mortal succour, though the tomb
Had fixed, for ever fixed, their doom !

Upon those servants of another world
When maddening power her bolts had hurled,
Their habitation shook ;—it fell,
And perished—save one narrow cell ;
Whither, at length, a wretch retired ;
Who neither grovelled nor aspired ;
He, struggling in the net of pride,
The future scorned, the past defied ;

* It is recorded in Dampier's Voyages, that a boy, the son of a captain of a man-of-war, seated himself in a turtle shell, and floated in it from the shore to his father's ship, which lay at anchor at the distance of half a mile. In deference to the opinion of a friend, I have substituted such a shell for the less elegant vessel in which my blind voyager did actually intrust himself to the dangerous current of Loch Leven, as was related to me by an eye-witness.

Still tempering from the unguilty forge
Of vain conceit, an iron scourge!

Proud remnant was he of a fearless race,
Who stood and flourished face to face
With their perennial hills;—but crime
Hastening the stern decrees of time,
Brought low a power, which from its home
Burst when repose grew wearisome;
And taking impulse from the sword,
And mocking its own plighted word,
Had found, in ravage widely dealt
Its warfare's bourne, its travel's belt!

All, all were dispossessed, save him whose smile
Shot lightning through this lonely isle!
No right had he but what he made
To this small spot, his leafy shade;
But the ground lay within that ring
To which he only dared to cling;
Renouncing here, as worse than dead,
The craven few who bowed the head
Beneath the change, who heard a claim
How loud! yet lived in peace with shame.

From year to year this shaggy mortal went
(So seemed it) down a strange descent;
Till they, who saw his outward frame,
Fixed on him an unhallowed name;
Him—free from all malicious taint,
And guiding, like the Patmos saint,
A pen unwearied—to indite,
In his lone isle, the dreams of night;
Impassioned dreams, that strove to span
The faded glories of his clan!

Suns that through blood their western harbour sought,
And stars that in their courses fought,—
Towers rent, winds combating with woods—
Lands deluged by unbridled floods,—
And beast and bird that from the spell
Of sleep took import terrible,
These types mysterious (if the show
Of battle and the routed foe
Had failed) would furnish an array
Of matter for the dawning day!

How disappeared he?—ask the newt and toad,
Inheritors of his abode;
The otter crouching undisturbed,
In her dank cleft;—but be thou curbed,
O froward fancy! 'mid a scene
Of aspect winning and serene;
For those offensive creatures shun
The inquisition of the sun!
And in this region flowers delight,
And all is lovely to the sight.

Spring finds not here a melancholy breast,
When she applies her annual test
To dead and living; when her breath
Quickens, as now, the withered heath;—
Nor flaunting summer—when he throws
His soul into the briar-rose;
Or calls the lily from her sleep;
Prolonged beneath the bordering deep:
Nor autumn, when the viewless wren
Is warbling near the Brownie's den.

Wild relique! beauteous as the chosen spot
In Nysa's isle, the embellished grot;
Whither by care of Libyan Jove
(High servant of paternal love),
Young Bacchus was conveyed—to lie
Safe from his step-dame Rhea's eye;
Where bud, and bloom, and fruitage, glowed,
Close crowding round the infant god,
All colours, and the liveliest streak
A foil to his celestial cheek!

COMPOSED AT CORRA LINN.

IN SIGHT OF WALLACE'S TOWER.

"How Wallace fought for Scotland, left the name
Of Wallace to be found, like a wild flower,
All over his dear country; left the deeds
Of Wallace, like a family of ghosts,
To people the steep rocks and river banks,
Her natural sanctuaries, with a local soul
Of independence and stern liberty."—*MS.*

LORD of the vale! astounding flood!
The dullest leaf in this thick wood
Quakes—conscious of thy power;
The caves reply with hollow moan;
And vibrates to its central stone,
Yon time-cemented tower!

And yet how fair the rural scene!
For thou, O Clyde, hast ever been
Beneficent as strong;
Pleased in refreshing dews to steep
The little trembling flowers that peep
Thy shelving rocks among.

Hence all who love their country, love
To look on thee—delight to rove
Where they thy voice can hear;
And, to the patriot warrior's shade,
Lord of the vale! to heroes laid
In dust, that voice is dear!

Along thy banks, at dead of night
Sweeps visibly the Wallace wight;

Or stands in warlike vest,
Aloft, beneath the moon's pale beam,
A champion worthy of the stream,
Yon gray tower's living crest !

But clouds and envious darkness hide
A form not doubtfully descried :—
Their transient mission o'er,
Oh, say to what blind region flee
These shapes of awful phantasy?
To what untrodden shore?

Less than divine command they spurn ;
But this we from the mountains learn,
And this the valleys show,
That never will they deign to hold
Communion where the heart is cold
To human weal and woe.

The man of abject soul in vain
Shall walk the Marathonian plain ;
Or thrid the shadowy gloom,
That still invests the guardian pass
Where stood, sublime, Leonidas,
Devoted to the tomb.

Nor deem that it can aught avail
For such to glide with oar or sail
Beneath the piny wood,
Where Tell once drew, by Uri's lake,
His vengeful shafts—prepared to slake
Their thirst in tyrant's blood.

EFFUSION,

IN THE PLEASURE-GROUND ON THE BANKS OF THE BRAN, NEAR DUNKELD.

"The waterfall, by a loud roaring, warned us when we must expect it. We were first, however, conducted into a small apartment, where the gardener desired us to look at the picture of Ossian, which, while he was telling the history of the young artist who executed the work, disappeared, parting in the middle—flying asunder as by the touch of magic—and lo! we are at the entrance of a splendid apartment, which was almost dizzy and alive with waterfalls, that tumbled in all directions; the great cascade, opposite the window, which faced us, being reflected in innumerable mirrors upon the ceiling and against the walls."—*Extract from the Journal of my Fellow-Traveller.*

WHAT he—who 'mid the kindred throng
Of heroes that inspired his song,
Doth yet frequent the hill of storms,
The stars dim-twinkling through their
forms !
What ! Ossian here—a painted thrall,
Mute fixture on a stuccoed wall ;
To serve, an unsuspected screen
For show that must not yet be seen :
And, when the moment comes, to part
And vanish by mysterious art ;
Head, harp, and body, split asunder,
For ingress to a world of wonder ;
A gay saloon, with waters dancing
Upon the sight wherever glancing ;
One loud cascade in front, and lo !
A thousand like it, white as snow—
Streams on the walls, and torrents foam
As active round the hollow dome,
Illusive cataracts ! of their terrors
Not stript, nor voiceless in the mirrors,
That catch the pageant from the flood
Thundering adown a rocky wood !
Strange scene, fantastic and uneasy
As ever made a maniac dizzy,
When disenchanted from the mood
That loves on sullen thoughts to brood !

O nature, in thy changeful visions,
Through all thy most abrupt transitions,
Smooth, graceful, tender, or sublime,
Ever averse to pantomime,
Thee neither do they know nor us
Thy servants, who can trifle thus ;
Else surely had the sober powers
Of rock that frowns, and stream that roars
Exalted by congenial sway
Of spirits, and the undying lay,
And names that moulder not away,
Awakened some redeeming thought
More worthy of this favoured spot ;
Recalled some feeling—to set free
The bard from such indignity !

The effigies of a valiant wight*
I once beheld, a Templar knight ;
Not prostrate, not like those that rest
On tombs, with palms together pressed,
But sculptured out of living stone,
And standing upright and alone,
Both hands with rival energy
Employed in setting his sword free
From its dull sheath—stern sentinel
Intent to guard St. Robert's cell ;
As if with memory of the affray
Far distant, when, as legends say,
The monks of Fountains thronged to
force
From its dear home the hermit's corse,

* On the banks of the river Nid, near Knaresborough.

That in their keeping it might lie,
To crown their abbey's sanctity.
So had they rushed into the grot
Of sense despised, a world forgot,
And torn him from his loved retreat,
Where altar-stone and rock-hewn seat
Still hint that quiet best is found,
Even by the *living*, under ground;
But a bold knight, the selfish aim
Defeating, put the monks to shame,
There where you see his image stand
Bare to the sky, with threatening brand
Which lingering Nid is proud to show
Reflected in the pool below.

Thus, like the men of earliest days,
Our sires set forth their grateful praise;
Uncouth the workmanship, and rude!
But, nursed in mountain solitude,
Might some aspiring artist dare
To seize whate'er, through misty air,
A ghost, by glimpses, may present
Of imitable lineament,
And give the phantom such array
As less should scorn the abandoned clay;
Then let him hew, with patient stroke,
An Ossian out of mural rock,
And leave the figurative man
Upon thy margin, roaring Bran!
Fixed, liked the Templar of the steep,
An everlasting watch to keep;
With local sanctities in trust;
More precious than a hermit's dust;
And virtues through the mass infused,
Which old idolatry abused.

What though the granite would deny
All fervour to the sightless eye;
And touch from rising suns in vain
Solicit a Memnonian strain;
Yet, in some fit of anger sharp,
The wind might force the deep-grooved harp
To utter melancholy moans
Not unconnected with the tones
Of soul-sick flesh and weary bones;
While grove and river notes would lend,
Less deeply sad, with these to blend!

Vain pleasures of luxurious life,
For ever with yourselves at strife;
Through town and country both deranged
By affectations interchanged,
And all the perishable gauds
That heaven-deserted man applauds;
When will your hapless patrons learn
To watch and ponder—to discern
The freshness, the eternal youth,
Of admiration sprung from truth;
From beauty infinitely growing
Upon a mind with love o'erflowing;
To sound the depths of every art
That seeks its wisdom through the heart?

Thus (where the intrusive pile, ill-graced
With baubles of theatric taste,
O'erlooks the torrent breathing showers
On motley bands of alien flowers,
In stiff confusion set or sown,
Till nature cannot find her own,
Or keep a remnant of the sod
Which Caledonian heroes trod)
I mused; and, thirsting for redress,
Recoiled into the wilderness.

YARROW VISITED.

SEPTEMBER, 1814.

AND is this—Yarrow?—*This* the stream
Of which my fancy cherished,
So faithfully, a waking dream?
An image that hath perished!
Oh, that some minstrel's harp were near,
To utter notes of gladness,
And chase this silence from the air,
That fills my heart with sadness!

Yet why?—A silvery current flows
With uncontrolled meanderings;
Nor have these eyes by greener hills
Been soothed, in all my wanderings.
And, through her depths, Saint Mary's Lake
Is visibly delighted;
For not a feature of those hills
Is in the mirror slighted.

A blue sky bends o'er Yarrow vale,
Save where that pearly whiteness
Is round the rising sun diffused,
A tender hazy brightness;
Mild dawn of promise! that excludes
All profitless dejection;
Though not unwilling here to admit
A pensive recollection.

Where was it that the famous flower
Of Yarrow vale lay bleeding?
His bed perchance was yon smooth mound
On which the herd is feeding:
And haply from this crystal pool,
Now peaceful as the morning,
The water-wraith ascended thrice—
And gave his doleful warning.

Delicious is the lay that sings
The haunts of happy lovers.

The path that leads them to the grove,
The leafy grove that covers:
And pity sanctifies the verse
That paints, by strength of sorrow,
The unconquerable strength of love;
Bear witness, rueful Yarrow!

But thou, that didst appear so fair
To fond imagination,
Dost rival in the light of day
Her delicate creation:
Meek loveliness is round thee spread,
A softness still and ho y;
The grace of forest charms decayed,
And pastoral melancholy.

That region left, the vale unfolds
Rich groves of lofty stature,
With Yarrow winding through the pomp
Of cultivated nature;
And, rising from those lofty groves,
Behold a ruin hoary!
The shattered front of Newark's towers,
Renowned in Border story.

Fair scenes for chi dhood's opening bloom,
For sportive youth to stray in;
For manhood to enjoy his strength;
And age to wear away in!

Yon cottage seems a bower of bliss,
A covert for protection
Of tender thoughts that nestle there,
The brood of chaste affection.

How sweet, on this autumnal day,
The wild-wood fruits to gather,
And on my true love's forehead plant
A crest of blooming heather!
And what if I enwreathed my own!
'Twere no offence to reason;
The sober hills thus deck their brows
To meet the wintry season.

I see—but not by sight alone,
Loved Yarrow, have I won thee!
A ray of fancy still survives—
Her sunshine plays upon thee!
Thy ever youthful waters keep
A course of lively pleasure
And gladsome notes my lips can breathe
According to the measure.

The vapours linger round the heights,
They melt—and soon must vanish;
One hour is theirs, no more is mine—
Sad thought, which I would banish,
But that I know where'er I go,
Thy genuine image, Yarrow!
Will dwell with me to heightened joy,
And cheer my mind in sorrow.

Poems on the Naming of Places.

ADVERTISEMENT.

By persons resident in the country and attached to rural objects, many places will be found unnamed or of unknown names, where little incidents must have occurred, or feelings been experienced, which will have given to such places a private and peculiar interest. From a wish to give some sort of record to such incidents, or renew the gratification of such feelings, names have been given to places by the author and some of his friends, and the following poems written in consequence.

It was an April morning: fresh and clear
The rivulet, delighting in its strength,
Ran with a young man's speed; and yet the voice
Of waters which the winter had supplied
Was softened down into a vernal tone.
The spirit of enjoyment and desire,
And hopes and wishes, from all living things
Went circling, like a multitude of sounds.
The budding groves appeared as if in haste
To spur the steps of June; as if their shades
Of *various* green were hindrances that stood

Between them and their object: yet, meanwhile,
There was such deep contentment in the air,
That every naked ash and tardy tree
Yet leafless, seemed as though the countenance
With which it looked on this delightful day
Were native to the summer.—Up the brook
I roamed in the confusion of my heart,
Alive to all things and forgetting all.
At length I to a sudden turning came
In this continuous glen, where down a rock
The stream, so ardent in its course before,
Sent forth such sallies of glad sound, that all
Which I till then had heard, appeared the voice
Of common pleasure: beast and bird, the lamb,
The shepherd's dog, the linnet and the thrush
Vied with this waterfall, and made a song
Which, while I listened, seemed like the wild growth
Or like some natural produce of the air,
That could not cease to be. Green leaves were here;
But 'twas the foliage of the rocks, the birch,
The yew, the holly, and the bright green thorn,
With hanging islands of resplendent furze:
And on a summit, distant a short space,
By any who should look beyond the dell,
A single mountain cottage might be seen.
I gazed and gazed, and to myself I said,
"Our thoughts at least are ours; and this wild nook,
My Emma, I will dedicate to thee."
Soon did the spot become my other home,
My dwelling, and my out-of-doors abode.
And, of the shepherds who have seen me there,
To whom I sometimes in our idle talk
Have told this fancy, two or three, perhaps,
Years after we are gone and in our graves,
When they have cause to speak of this wild place,
May call it by the name of Emma's Dell.

TO JOANNA.

AMID the smoke of cities did you pass
The time of early youth; and there you learned,
From years of quiet industry, to love
The living beings by your own fire-side,
With such a strong devotion, that your heart
Is slow towards the sympathies of them
Who look upon the hills with tenderness,
And make dear friendships with the streams and groves.
Yet we, who are transgressors in this kind,
Dwelling retired in our simplicity
Among the woods and fields, we love you well,
Joanna! and I guess, since you have been
So distant from us now for two long years,
That you will gladly listen to discourse
However trivial, if you thence are taught
That they, with whom you once were happy, talk
Familiarly of you and of old times.

While I was seated, now some ten days past,
Beneath those lofty firs, that overtop
Their ancient neighbour, the old steeple tower,
The vicar from his gloomy house hard by
Came forth to greet me; and when he had asked,
"How fares Joanna; that wild-hearted maid!
And when will she return to us?" he paused;
And, after short exchange of village news,
He with grave looks demanded, for what cause,
Reviving obsolete idolatry,
I, like a Runic priest, in characters
Of formidable size had chiselled out
Some uncouth name upon the native rock,
Above the Rotha, by the forest side.
Now by those dear immunities of heart
Engendered betwixt malice and true love,
I was not loth to be so catechised,
And this was my reply:—"As it befel,
One summer morning we had walked abroad
At break of day, Joanna and myself.
'Twas that delightful season when the broom,
Full-flowered, and visible on every steep,
Along the copses runs in veins of gold.
Our pathway led us on to Rotha's banks;
And when we came in front of that tall rock
Which looks toward the east, I there stopped short,
And traced the lofty barrier with my eye
From base to summit; such delight I found
To note in shrub and tree, in stone and flower,
That intermixture of delicious hues,
Along so vast a surface, all at once,
In one impression, by connecting force
Of their own beauty, imaged in the heart.

When I had gazed perhaps two minutes space,
Joanna, looking in my eyes, beheld
That ravishment of mine, and laughed aloud.
The rock, like something starting from a sleep,
Took up the lady's voice, and laughed again:
That ancient woman seated on Helm-Crag
Was ready with her cavern: Hammer-Scar,
And the tall steep of Silver-how, sent forth
A noise of laughter; southern Loughrigg heard,
And Fairfield answered with a mountain tone:
Helvellyn far into the clear blue sky
Carried the lady's voice, — old Skiddaw blew
His speaking trumpet;—back out of the clouds
Of Glaramara southward came the voice:
And Kirkstone tossed it from his misty head.
Now whether (said I to our cordial friend,
Who in the hey-day of astonishment
Smiled in my face) this were in simple truth
A work accomplished by the brotherhood
Of ancient mountains, or my ear was touched
With dreams and visionary impulses
To me alone imparted, sure I am
That there was a loud uproar in the hills:
And, while we both were listening, to my side
The fair Joanna drew, as if she wished
To shelter from some object of her fear.
And hence, long afterwards, when eighteen moons
Were wasted, as I chanced to walk alone
Beneath this rock, at sunrise, on a calm
And silent morning, I sat down, and there,
In memory of affections, old and true,
I chiselled out in those rude characters
Joanna's name upon the living stone.
And I, and all who dwell by my fire-side,
Have called the lovely rock, Joanna's Rock." *

THERE is an eminence,—of these our hills
The last that parleys with the setting sun.
We can behold it from our orchard-seat;
And when at evening we pursue our walk
Along the public way, this cliff, so high
Above us, and so distant in its height,
Is visible; and often seems to send
Its own deep quiet to restore our hearts.
The meteors make of it a favourite haunt:
The star of Jove, so beautiful and large
In the mid heavens, is never half so fair
As when he shines above it. 'Tis in truth
The loneliest place we have among the clouds.
And she who dwells with me, whom I have loved
With such communion, that no place on earth
Can ever be a solitude to me,
Hath to this lonely summit given my name.

A NARROW girdle of rough stones and crags,
A rude and natural causeway, interposed
Between the water and a winding slope
Of copse and thicket, leaves the eastern shore
Of Grasmere safe in its own privacy.
And there, myself and two beloved friends,
One calm September morning, ere the mist
Had altogether yielded to the sun,
Sauntered on this retired and difficult way.
Ill suits the road with one in haste, but we
Played with our time; and, as we strolled along,
It was our occupation to observe
Such objects as the waves had tossed ashore,
Feather, or leaf, or weed, or withered bough,
Each on the other heaped, along the line
Of the dry wreck. And, in our vacant mood,
Not seldom did we stop to watch some tuft
Of dandelion seed or thistle's beard,
That skimmed the surface of the dead calm lake,
Suddenly halting now—a lifeless stand!
And starting off again with freak as sudden;
In all its sportive wanderings, all the while,
Making report of an invisible breeze
That was its wings, its chariot, and its horse,

* In Cumberland and Westmoreland are several inscriptions, upon the native rock, which, from the wasting of time, and the rudeness of the workmanship, have been mistaken for Runic. They are, without doubt, Roman.

The Rotha, mentioned in this poem, is the river which, flowing through the lakes of Grasmere and Rydal, falls into Wynander.—On Helm-Crag, that impressive single mountain at the head of the vale of Grasmere, is a rock which from most points of view bears a striking resemblance to an old woman cowering. Close by this rock is one of those fissures or caverns, which in the language of the country are called dungeons. Most of the mountains here mentioned immediately surround the vale of Grasmere; of the others, some are at a considerable distance, but they belong to the same cluster.

Its playmate, rather say its moving soul.
And often, trifling with a privilege
Alike indulged to all, we paused, one now,
And now the other, to point out, perchance
To pluck, some flower or water-weed, too fair
Either to be divided from the place
On which it grew, or to be left alone
To its own beauty. Many such there are,
Fair ferns and flowers, and chiefly that tall fern,
So stately, of the Queen Osmunda named;
Plant lovelier in its own retired abode
On Grasmere's beach, than naiad by the side
Of Grecian brook, or lady of the mere,
Sole-sitting by the shores of old romance,
So fared we that bright morning: from the fields,
Meanwhile, a noise was heard, the busy mirth
Of reapers, men and women, boys and girls.
Delighted much to listen to those sounds,
And feeding thus our fancies, we advanced
Along the indented shore; when suddenly,
Through a thin veil of glittering haze was seen
Before us, on a point of jutting land,
The tall and upright figure of a man
Attired in peasant's garb, who stood alone,
Angling beside the margin of the lake.
Improvident and reckless, we exclaimed,
The man must be, who thus can lose a day
Of the mid-harvest, when the labourer's hire
Is ample, and some little might be stored
Wherewith to cheer him in the winter time.
Thus talking of that peasant, we approached
Close to the spot where with his rod and line
He stood alone; whereat he turned his head
To greet us—and we saw a man worn down
By sickness, gaunt and lean, with sunken cheeks
And wasted limbs, his legs so long and lean
That for my single self I looked at them,
Forgetful of the body they sustained.—
Too weak to labour in the harvest field,
The man was using his best skill to gain
A pittance from the dead unfeeling lake
That knew not of his wants. I will not say
What thoughts immediately were ours, nor how
The happy idleness of that sweet morn,
With all its lovely images, was changed
To serious musing and to self-reproach.
Nor did we fail to see within ourselves
What need there is to be reserved in speech,
And temper all our thoughts with charity.
Therefore, unwilling to forget that day,
My friend, myself, and she who then received
The same admonishment, have called the place
By a memorial name, uncouth indeed
As e'er by mariner was given to bay
Or foreland, on a new-discovered coast;
And Point Rash Judgment is the name it bears.

TO M. H.

Our walk was far among the ancient trees;
There was no road, nor any woodman's path;
But the thick umbrage, checking the wild growth
Of weed and sapling, along soft green turf
Beneath the branches, of itself had made
A track, that brought us to a slip of lawn,
And a small bed of water in the woods.
All round this pool both flocks and herds might drink
On its firm margin, even as from a well,
Or some stone-basin which the herdsman's hand
Had shaped for their refreshment; nor did sun,
Or wind from any quarter, ever come,
But as a blessing, to this calm recess,
This glade of water and this one green field.
The spot was made by nature for herself,
The travellers know it not, and 'twill remain
Unknown to them: but it is beautiful;
And if a man should plant his cottage near,
Should sleep beneath the shelter of its trees,
And blend its waters with his daily meal,
He would so love it, that in his death hour
Its image would survive among his thoughts;
And therefore, my sweet Mary, this still nook,
With all its beeches, we have named from you.

When, to the attractions of the busy world,
Preferring studious leisure, I had chosen
A habitation in this peaceful vale,
Sharp season followed of continual storm
In deepest winter; and, from week to week,

Pathway, and lane, and public road, were
clogged [hill
With frequent showers of snow. Upon a
At a short distance from my cottage stands
A stately fir-grove, whither I was wont
To hasten, for I found beneath the roof
Of that perennial shade, a cloistral place
Of refuge, with an unincumbered floor.
Here, in safe covert, on the shallow snow,
And, sometimes, on a speck of visible
earth, [loth
The redbreast near me hopped ; nor was I
To sympathise with vulgar coppice birds
That, for protection from the nipping
blast,
Hither repaired.—A single beech-tree grew
Within this grove of firs ; and, on the fork
Of that one beech, appeared a thrush's
nest ;
A last year's nest, conspicuously built
At such small elevation from the ground
As gave sure sign that they, who in that
house
Of nature and of love had made their home
Amid the fir-trees, all the summer long
Dwelt in a tranquil spot. And oftentimes,
A few sheep, stragglers from some moun-
tain-flock,
Would watch my motions with suspicious
stare,
From the remotest outskirts of the grove,—
Some nook where they had made their
final stand,
Huddling together from two fears—the fear
Of me and of the storm. Full many
an hour
Here did I lose. But in this grove the
trees [thriven
Had been so thickly planted, and had
In such perplexed and intricate array,
That vainly did I seek, between their stems,
A length of open space, where to and fro
My feet might move without concern or
care.
And, baffled thus, before the storm relaxed,
I ceased the shelter to frequent,—and
prized,
Less than I wished to prize, that calm
recess.

The snows dissolved, and genial spring
returned [haunts
To clothe the fields with verdure. Other
Meanwhile were mine ; till, one bright
April day,
By chance retiring from the glare of noon
To this forsaken covert, there I found
A hoary pathway traced between the trees,
And winding on with such an easy line
Along a natural opening, that I stood
Much wondering how I could have sought
in vain
For what was now so obvious. To abide,
For an allotted interval of ease,
Beneath my cottage roof, had newly come
From the wild sea a cherished visitant ;
And with the sight of this same path—
begun,
Begun and ended, in the shady grove,
Pleasant conviction flashed upon my mind
That, to this opportune recess allured,
He had surveyed it with a finer eye,
A heart more wakeful ; and had worn the
track
By pacing here, unwearied and alone,
In that habitual restlessness of foot [o'er
With which the sailor measures o'er and
His short domain upon the vessel's deck,
While she is travelling through the dreary
sea.

When thou hadst quitted Esthwaite's
pleasant shore,
And taken thy first leave of those green
hills [youth.
And rocks that were the play-ground of thy
Year followed year, my brother! and we two,
Conversing not, knew little in what mould
Each other's minds were fashioned ; and at
length,
When once again we met in Grasmere vale,
Between us there was little other bond
Than common feelings of fraternal love.
But thou, a school-boy, to the sea hadst
carried
Undying recollections ; nature there
Was with thee ; she, who loved us both,
she still [become
Was with thee ; and even so didst thou
A *silent* poet ; from the solitude [heart
Of the vast sea didst bring a watchful
Still couchant, an inevitable ear,
And an eye practised like a blind man's
touch.
Back to the joyless ocean thou art gone ;
Nor from this vestige of thy musing hours
Could I withhold thy honoured name, and
now
I love the fir-grove with a perfect love.
Thither do I withdraw when cloudless suns
Shine hot, or wind blows troublesome and
strong :
And there I sit at evening, when the steep
Of Silver-how, and Grasmere's peaceful
lake, [stems
And one green island, gleam between the

Of the dark firs, a visionary scene!
And, while I gaze upon the spectacle
Of clouded splendour, on this dream-like sight
Of solemn loveliness, I think on thee,
My brother, and on all which thou hast lost.
Nor seldom, if I rightly guess, while thou,
Muttering the verses which I muttered first
Among the mountains, through the midnight watch
Art pacing thoughtfully the vessel's deck
In some far region, here, while o'er my head,
At every impulse of the moving breeze,
The fir-grove murmurs with a sea-like sound,
Alone I tread this path;—for aught I know,
Timing my steps to thine and, with a store
Of undistinguishable sympathies,
Mingling most earnest wishes for the day
When we, and others whom we love, shall meet
A second time, in Grasmere's happy vale

Note—This wish was not granted, the lamented person, not long after, perished by shipwreck, in discharge of his duty as commander of the Honourable East India Company's vessel, the *Earl of Abergavenny*

Inscriptions.

IN THE GROUNDS OF COLEORTON, THE SEAT OF SIR GEORGE BEAUMONT, BART., LEICESTERSHIRE.

THE embowering rose, the acacia, and the pine,
Will not unwillingly their place resign;
If but the cedar thrive that near them stands,
Planted by Beaumont's and by Wordsworth's hands.
One wooed the silent art with studious pains,—
These groves have heard the other's pensive strains;
Devoted thus, their spirits did unite
By interchange of knowledge and delight
May nature's kindliest powers sustain the tree,
And love protect it from all injury!
And when its potent branches, wide outthrown,
Darken the brow of this memorial stone,
Here may some painter sit in future days,
Some future poet meditate his lays,
Not mindless of that distant age renowned
When inspiration hovered o'er this ground,
The haunt of him who sang how spear and shield
In civil conflict met on Bosworth field;
And of that famous youth, full soon removed
From earth, perhaps by Shakspeare's self approved,
Fletcher's associate, Jonson's friend beloved

IN A GARDEN OF THE SAME

OFT is the medal faithful to its trust
When temples, columns, towers are laid in dust,
And 'tis a common ordinance of fate
That things obscure and small outlive the great:
Hence, when yon mansion and the flowery trim
Of this fair garden, and its alleys dim,
And all its stately trees are passed away
This little niche, unconscious of decay,
Perchance may still survive.—And be it known
That it was scooped within the living stone,—
Not by the sluggish and ungrateful pains
Of labourer plodding for his daily gains,
But by an industry that wrought in love,
With help from female hands, that proudly strove
To aid the work, what time these walks and bowers
Were shaped to cheer dark winter's lonely hours

WRITTEN AT THE REQUEST OF SIR GEORGE BEAUMONT BART, AND IN HIS NAME, FOR AN URN, PLACED BY HIM AT THE TERMINATION OF A NEWLY-PLANTED AVENUE, IN THE SAME GROUNDS.

YE lime-trees, ranged before this hallowed urn
Shoot forth with lively power at spring's return;

And be not slow a stately growth to rear
Of pillars, branching off from year to year,
Till they have learned to frame a darksome aisle;—
That may recall to mind that awful pile
Where Reynolds, 'mid our country's noblest dead,
In the last sanctity of fame is laid.
There, though by right the excelling painter sleep
Where death and glory a joint Sabbath keep,
Yet not the less his spirit would hold dear
Self-hidden praise, and friendship's private tear:
Hence, on my patrimonial grounds, have I
Raised this frail tribute to his memory,
From youth a zealous follower of the art
That he professed, attached to him in heart:
Admiring, loving, and with grief and pride
Feeling what England lost when Reynolds died.

FOR A SEAT IN THE GROVES OF COLEORTON.

BENEATH yon eastern ridge, the craggy bound,
Rugged and high, of Charnwood's forest ground,
Stand yet, but, stranger! hidden from thy view,
The ivied ruins of forlorn Grace Dieu;
Erst a religious house, which day and night
With hymns resounded, and the chanted rite:
And when those rites had ceased, the spot gave birth
To honourable men of various worth:
There, on the margin of a streamlet wild,
Did Francis Beaumont sport, an eager child;
There, under shadow of the neighbouring rocks,
Sang youthful tales of shepherds and their flocks;
Unconscious prelude to heroic themes,
Heart-breaking tears, and melancholy dreams
Of slighted love, and scorn, and jealous rage,
With which his genius shook the buskined stage.
Communities are lost, and empires die,
And things of holy use unhallowed lie;
They perish;—but the intellect can raise,
From airy words alone, a pile that ne'er decays.

WRITTEN WITH A PENCIL UPON A STONE IN THE WALL OF THE HOUSE (AN OUT-HOUSE) ON THE ISLAND AT GRASMERE.

RUDE is this edifice, and thou hast seen
Buildings, albeit rude, that have maintained
Proportions more harmonious, and approached
To somewhat of a closer fellowship
With the ideal grace. Yet, as it is,
Do take it in good part:—alas! the poor
Vitruvius of our village had no help
From the great city; never, on the leaves
Of red morocco folio saw displayed
The skeletons and pre-existing ghosts
Of beauties yet unborn, the rustic box,
Snug cot, with coach-house, shed, and hermitage.
Thou see'st a homely pile, yet to these walls
The heifer comes in the snow-storm, and here
The new-dropped lamb finds shelter from the wind.
And hither does one poet sometimes row
His pinnace, a small vagrant barge, up-piled
With plenteous store of heath and withered fern,
(A lading which he with his sickle cuts
Among the mountains) and beneath this roof
He makes his summer couch, and here at noon
Spreads out his limbs, while, yet unshorn, the sheep,
Panting beneath the burthen of their wool,
Lie round him, even as if they were a part
Of his own household; nor, while from his bed
He through that door-place looks toward the lake
And to the stirring breezes, does he want
Creations lovely as the work of sleep—
Fair sights and visions of romantic joy!

WRITTEN WITH A SLATE-PENCIL ON A STONE, ON THE SIDE OF THE MOUNTAIN OF BLACK COMB.

STAY, bold adventurer; rest a while thy limbs
On this commodious seat! for much remains
Of hard ascent before thou reach the top
Of this huge eminence,—from blackness named,
And, to far-travelled storms of sea and land,
A favourite spot of tournament and war!
But thee may no such boisterous visitants
Molest; may gentle breezes fan thy brow;
And neither cloud conceal, nor misty air
Bedim, the grand terraqueous spectacle,
From centre to circumference, unveiled!

Know, if thou grudge not to prolong thy rest,
That on the summit whither thou art bound,
A geographic labourer pitched his tent,
With books supplied and instruments of art,
To measure height and distance, lonely task,
Week after week pursued!—To him was given
Full many a glimpse (but sparingly bestowed
On timid man) of nature's processes
Upon the exalted hills. He made report
That once, while there he plied his studious work
Within that canvas dwelling, suddenly
The many-coloured map before his eyes
Became invisible: for all around
Had darkness fallen—unthreatened, unproclaimed—
As if the golden day itself had been
Extinguished in a moment; total gloom,
In which he sat alone, with unclosed eyes,
Upon the blinded mountain's silent top!

WRITTEN WITH A SLATE-PENCIL UPON A STONE, THE LARGEST OF A HEAP LYING NEAR A DESERTED QUARRY, UPON ONE OF THE ISLANDS AT RYDAL.

STRANGER! this hillock of mis-shapen stones
Is not a ruin of the ancient time,
Nor, as perchance thou rashly deem'st, the cairn
Of some old British chief: 'tis nothing more
Than the rude embryo of a little dome
Or pleasure-house, once destined to be built
Among the birch-trees of this rocky isle.
But, as it chanced, Sir William having learned
That from the shore a full-grown man might wade,
And make himself a freeman of this spot
At any hour he chose, the knight forthwith
Desisted, and the quarry and the mound
Are monuments of his unfinished task.
The block on which these lines are traced, perhaps,
Was once selected as the corner-stone
Of the intended pile, which would have been
Some quaint odd plaything of elaborate skill,
So that, I guess, the linnet and the thrush,
And other little builders who dwell here,
Had wondered at the work. But blame him not,
For old Sir William was a gentle knight
Bred in this vale, to which he appertained
With all his ancestry. Then peace to him,
And for the outrage which he had devised
Entire forgiveness!—But if thou art one
On fire with thy impatience to become
An inmate of these mountains,—if, disturbed
By beautiful conceptions, thou hast hewn
Out of the quiet rock the elements
Of thy trim mansion destined soon to blaze
In snow-white splendour,—think again, and, taught
By old Sir William and his quarry, leave
Thy fragments to the bramble and the rose;
There let the vernal slow-worm sun himself,
And let the redbreast hop from stone to stone.

INSCRIPTIONS SUPPOSED TO BE FOUND IN AND NEAR A HERMIT'S CELL.

HOPES what are they?—Beads of morning
Strung on slender blades of grass;
Or a spider's web adorning
In a strait and treacherous pass.

What are fears but voices airy?
Whispering harm where harm is not;
And deluding the unwary
Till the fatal bolt is shot!

What is glory?—in the socket
See how dying tapers fare!
What is pride?—a whizzing rocket
That would emulate a star.

What is friendship?—do not trust her,
Nor the vows which she has made;
Diamonds dart their brightest lustre
From a palsy-shaken head.

What is truth?—a staff rejected;
Duty?—an unwelcome clog;
Joy?—a moon by fits reflected
In a swamp or watery bog;

Bright, as if through ether steering,
To the traveller's eye it shone:
He hath hailed it re-appearing—
And as quickly it is gone;

Gone, as if for ever hidden;
Or mis-shapen to the sight,
And by sullen weeds forbidden
To resume its native light.

What is youth?—a dancing billow,
(Winds behind, and rocks before!)
Age?—a drooping, tottering willow
On a flat and lazy shore.

What is peace?—when pain is over,
And love ceases to rebel,
Let the last faint sigh discover
That precedes the passing knell!

INSCRIBED UPON A ROCK.

PAUSE, traveller! whosoe'er thou be
Whom chance may lead to this retreat
Where silence yields reluctantly
Even to the fleecy straggler's bleat;

Give voice to what my hand shall trace,
And fear not lest an idle sound
Of words unsuited to the place
Disturb its solitude profound.

I saw this rock, while vernal air
Blew softly o'er the russet heath,
Uphold a monument as fair
As church or abbey furnisheth.

Unsullied did it meet the day,
Like marble white, like ether pure;
As if beneath some hero lay,
Honoured with costliest sepulture.

My fancy kindled as I gazed;
And, ever as the sun shone forth,
The flattered structure glistened, blazed,
And seemed the proudest thing on earth.

But frost had reared the gorgeous pile
Unsound as those which fortune builds;
To undermine with secret guile,
Sapped by the very beam that gilds.

And, while I gazed, with sudden shock
Fell the whole fabric to the ground;
And naked left this dripping rock,
With shapeless ruin spread around!

HAST thou seen, with flash incessant,
Bubbles gliding under ice,
Bodied forth and evanescent,
No one knows by what device?

Such are thoughts!—A wind-swept meadow
Mimicking a troubled sea,
Such is life; and death a shadow
From the rock eternity!

NEAR THE SPRING OF THE HERMITAGE.

TROUBLED long with warring notions,
Long impatient of thy rod,
I resign my soul's emotions
Unto thee, mysterious God!

What avails the kindly shelter
Yielded by this craggy rent,
If my spirit toss and welter
On the waves of discontent?

Parching summer hath no warrant
To consume this crystal well;
Rains that make each rill a torrent,
Neither sully it nor swell.

Thus, dishonouring not her station,
Would my life present to thee,
Gracious God, the pure oblation,
Of divine tranquillity!

NOT seldom, clad in radiant vest,
Deceitfully goes forth the morn;
Not seldom evening in the west
Sinks smilingly forsworn.

The smoothest seas will sometimes prove,
To the confiding bark, untrue;
And, if she trust the stars above,
They can be treacherous too.

The umbrageous oak, in pomp outspread,
Full oft, when storms the welkin rend,
Draws lightning down upon the head
It promised to defend.

But thou art true, incarnate Lord,
Who didst vouchsafe for man to die;
Thy smile is sure, thy plighted word
No change can falsify!

I bent before thy gracious throne,
And asked for peace on suppliant knee;
And peace was given,—nor peace alone,
But faith sublimed to ecstasy!

FOR THE SPOT WHERE THE HERMITAGE STOOD ON ST. HERBERT'S ISLAND, DERWENT WATER.

STRANGER! this shapeless heap of stones and earth
Is the last relic of St. Herbert's cell.
Here stood his threshold; here was spread the roof
That sheltered him, a self-secluded man,
After long exercise in social cares
And offices humane, intent to adore
The Deity, with undistracted mind,
And meditate on everlasting things,
In utter solitude.—But he had left
A fellow-labourer, whom the good man loved
As his own soul. And, when with eye [upraised

To heaven he knelt before the crucifix,
While o'er the lake the cataract of Lodore
Pealed to his orisons, and when he paced
Along the beach of this small isle and thought
Of his companion, he would pray that both
(Now that their earthly duties were fulfilled)
Might die in the same moment. Nor in vain
So prayed he:—as our chronicles report,
Though here the hermit numbered his last day,
Far from St. Cuthbert his beloved friend,
Those holy men both died in the same hour.

Sonnets Dedicated to Liberty.

COMPOSED BY THE SEA-SIDE, NEAR CALAIS, AUGUST, 1802.

FAIR star of evening, splendour of the west,
Star of my country!—on the horizon's brink
Thou hangest, stooping, as might seem, to sink
On England's bosom: yet well pleased to rest,
Meanwhile, and be to her a glorious crest
Conspicuous to the nations. Thou, I think,
Shouldst be my country's emblem; and shouldst wink,
Bright star! with laughter on her banners, drest
In thy fresh beauty. There! that dusky spot
Beneath thee, it is England; there it lies.
Blessings be on you both! one hope, one lot,
One life, one glory! I with many a fear
For my dear country, many heartfelt sighs,
Among men who do not love her, linger here.

CALAIS, AUGUST, 1802.

Is it a reed that's shaken by the wind,
Or what is it that ye go forth to see?
Lords, lawyers, statesmen, squires of low degree,
Men known, and men unknown, sick, lame, and blind,
Post forward all, like creatures of one kind,
With first-fruit offerings crowd to bend the knee
In France, before the new-born majesty.
'Tis even thus. Ye men of prostrate mind!
A seemly reverence may be paid to power;
But that's a loyal virtue, never sown
In haste, nor springing with a transient shower:
When truth, when sense, when liberty were flown,
What hardship had it been to wait an hour?
Shame on you, feeble heads, to slavery prone!

TO A FRIEND. COMPOSED NEAR CALAIS, ON THE ROAD LEADING TO ARDRES, AUGUST 7, 1802.

JONES! while from Calais southward you and I
Urged our accordant steps, this public way
Streamed with the pomp of a too-credulous day,*
When faith was pledged to new-born liberty:
A homeless sound of joy was in the sky;
The antiquated earth, as one might say,
Beat like the heart of man: songs, garlands, play,
Banners, and happy faces, far and nigh!
And now, sole register that these things were,
Two solitary greetings have I heard,
"*Good morrow, citizen!*" a hollow word,
As if a dead man spake it! Yet despair
Touches me not, though pensive as a bird
Whose vernal coverts winter hath laid bare.

1801.

I GRIEVED for Bonaparté, with a vain
And an unthinking grief! for, who aspires
To genuine greatness but from just desires,
And knowledge such as *he* could never gain?
'Tis not in battles that from youth we train
The governor who must be wise and good,
And temper with the sternness of the brain
Thoughts motherly, and meek as womanhood.
Wisdom doth live with children round her knees:

* 14th July, 1790.—[The day on which the unfortunate Louis XVI. took the oath of fidelity to the new constitution.]

Books, leisure, perfect freedom, and the talk [walk
Man holds with week-day man in the hourly
Of the mind's business: these are the degrees [the stalk
By which true sway doth mount; this is
True power doth grow on; and her rights are these.

CALAIS, AUGUST 15, 1802.

FESTIVALS have I seen that were not names:
This is young Bonaparté's natal day,
And his is henceforth an established sway,
Consul for life. With worship France proclaims [games.
Her approbation, and with pomps and
Heaven grant that other cities may be gay!
Calais is not: and I have bent my way
To the sea-coast, noting that each man frames
His business as he likes. Far other show
My youth here witnessed, in a prouder time;
The senselessness of joy was then sublime!
Happy is he, who, caring not for pope,
Consul, or king, can sound himself to know
The destiny of man, and live in hope.

ON THE EXTINCTION OF THE VENETIAN REPUBLIC.

ONCE did she hold the gorgeous East in fee; [worth
And was the safeguard of the West: the
Of Venice did not fall below her birth,
Venice, the eldest child of liberty.
She was a maiden city, bright and free;
No guile seduced, no force could violate;
And when she took unto herself a mate,
She must espouse the everlasting sea!
And what if she had seen those glories fade,
Those titles vanish, and that strength decay;
Yet shall some tribute of regret be paid
When her long life hath reached its final day: [the shade
Men are we, and must grieve when even
Of that which once was great, is passed away.

THE KING OF SWEDEN.

THE voice of song from distant lands shall call [youth
To that great king; shall hail the crowned
Who, taking counsel of unbending truth,
By one example hath set forth to all
How they with dignity may stand; or fall:
If fall they must. Now, whither doth it tend?
And what to him and his shall be the end?
That thought is one which neither can appal
Nor cheer him: for the illustrious Swede hath done [*above*
The thing which ought to be: he stands
All consequences; work he hath begun
Of fortitude, and piety, and love,
Which all his glorious ancestors approve·
The heroes bless him, him their rightful son.

TO TOUSSAINT L'OUVERTURE.

TOUSSAINT, the most unhappy man of men!
Whether the whistling rustic tend his plough
Within thy hearing, or thy head be now
Pillowed in some deep dungeon's earless den;
O miserable chieftain! where and when
Wilt thou find patience? Yet die not! do thou
Wear rather in thy bonds a cheerful brow:
Though fallen thyself, never to rise again,
Live, and take comfort. Thou hast left behind [and skies:
Powers that will work for thee, air, earth,
There's not a breathing of the common wind
That will forget thee; thou hast great allies;
Thy friends are exultations, agonies,
And love, and man's unconquerable mind.

SEPTEMBER 1, 1802.

Among the capricious acts of tyranny that disgraced these times, was the chasing of all negroes from France by decree of the government: we had a fellow-passenger who was one of the expelled.

DRIVEN from the soil of France, a female came
From Calais with us, brilliant in array,
A negro woman like a lady gay,
Yet downcast as a woman fearing blame;
Meek, destitute, as seemed, of hope or aim
She sate, from notice turning not away,
But on all proffered intercourse did lay
A weight of languid speech,—or at the same
Was silent, motionless in eyes and face.
Meanwhile those eyes retained their tropic fire,
Which, burning independent of the mind,
Joined with the lustre of her rich attire
To mock the outcast—O ye heavens be kind!
And feel, thou earth, for this afflicted race!

COMPOSED IN THE VALLEY, NEAR DOVER, ON THE DAY OF LANDING.

HERE, on our native soil we breathe once more. [that sound
The cock that crows, the smoke that curls,
Of bells,—those boys who in yon meadow-ground [the roar
In white-sleeved shirts are playing,—and
Of the waves breaking on the chalky shore,
All, all are English. Oft have I looked round [found
With joy in Kent's green vales; but never
Myself so satisfied in heart before.
Europe is yet in bonds; but let that pass,
Thought for another moment. Thou art free,
My country! and 'tis joy enough and pride
For one hour's perfect bliss, to tread the grass
Of England once again, and hear and see,
With such a dear companion at my side.

SEPTEMBER, 1802.

INLAND, within a hollow vale, I stood;
And saw, while sea was calm and air was clear, [how near!
The coast of France, the coast of France
Drawn almost into frightful neighbourhood.
I shrunk, for verily the barrier flood
Was like a lake, or river bright and fair,
A span of waters; yet what power is there!
What mightiness for evil and for good!
Even so doth God protect us if we be
Virtuous and wise. Winds blow, and waters roll,
Strength to the brave, and power, and deity,
Yet in themselves are nothing! One decree
Spake laws to *them*, and said that by the soul
Only the nations shall be great and free!

THOUGHT OF A BRITON ON THE SUBJUGATION OF SWITZERLAND.

TWO voices are there; one is of the sea,
One of the mountains; each a mighty voice
In both from age to age thou didst rejoice,
They were thy chosen music, liberty!
There came a tyrant, and with holy glee
Thou fought'st against him; but hast vainly striven. [driven,
Thou from thy Alpine holds at length art
Where not a torrent murmurs heard by thee.
Of one deep bliss thine ear hath been bereft;
Then cleave, oh, cleave to that which still is left; [it be
For, high-souled maid, what sorrow would
That mountain floods should thunder as before,
And ocean bellow from his rocky shore,
And neither awful voice be heard by thee!

WRITTEN IN LONDON, SEPTEMBER, 1802.

O FRIEND! I know not which way I must look
For comfort, being, as I am, oppressed,
To think that now our life is only drest
For show; mean handy-work of craftsman, cook, [brook
Or groom!—We must run glittering like a
In the open sunshine, or we are unblest:
The wealthiest man among us is the best;
No grandeur now in nature or in book
Delights us. Rapine, avarice, expense,
This is idolatry; and these we adore;
Plain living and high thinking are no more,
The homely beauty of the good old cause
Is gone; our peace, our fearful innocence
And pure religion breathing household laws

LONDON, 1802.

MILTON! thou shouldst be living at this hour:
England hath need of thee; she is a fen
Of stagnant waters; altar, sword, and pen,
Fireside, the heroic wealth of hall and bower,
Have forfeited their ancient English dower
Of inward happiness. We are selfish men;
Oh! raise us up, return to us again;
And give us manners, virtue, freedom, power.
Thy soul was like a star, and dwelt apart;
Thou hadst a voice whose sound was like the sea;
Pure as the naked heavens, majestic, free,
So didst thou travel on life's common way,
In cheerful godliness; and yet thy heart
The lowliest duties on herself did lay.

GREAT men have been among us; hands that penned [none:
And tongues that uttered wisdom, better
The later Sidney, Marvel, Harrington,
Young Vane, and others who called Milton friend.
These moralists could act and comprehend:
They knew how genuine glory was put on;
Taught us how rightfully a nation shone

In splendour: what strength was, that
would not bend ['tis strange,
But in magnanimous meekness. France,
Hath brought forth no such souls as we
had then.
Perpetual emptiness! unceasing change!
No single volume paramount, no code,
No master spirit, no determined road;
But equally a want of books and men!

IT is not to be thought of that the flood
Of British freedom, which, to the open sea
Of the world's praise, from dark antiquity
Hath flowed, "with pomp of waters un-
withstood,"
Roused though it be full often to a mood
Which spurns the check of salutary bands,
That this most famous stream in bogs and
sands
Should perish; and to evil and to good
Be lost for ever. In our halls is hung
Armoury of the invincible knights of old:
We must be free or die, who speak the
tongue [morals hold
That Shakspeare spake: the faith and
Which Milton held. In everything we
are sprung
Of earth's first blood, have titles manifold.

WHEN I have borne in memory what has
tamed [depart
Great nations, how ennobling thoughts
When men change swords for ledgers, and
desert [unnamed
The student's bower for gold, some fears
I had, my country!—am I to be blamed?
But when I think of thee, and what thou
art,
Verily, in the bottom of my heart,
Of those unfilial fears I am ashamed.
But dearly must we prize thee; we who
find
In thee a bulwark for the cause of men;
And I by my affection was beguiled.
What wonder if a poet now and then,
Among the many movements of his mind,
Felt for thee as a lover or a child?

OCTOBER, 1803.

ONE might believe that natural miseries
Had blasted France, and made of it a land
Unfit for men, and that in one great band
Her sons were bursting forth, to dwell at
ease.
But 'tis a chosen soil, where sun and breeze
Shed gentle favours; rural works are there
And ordinary business without care;
Spot rich in all things that can soothe and
please! [dearth
How piteous then that there should be such
Of knowledge; that whole myriads should
unite [despite:
To work against themselves such fell
Should come in frensy and in drunken
mirth,
Impatient to put out the only light
Of liberty that yet remains on earth!

THERE is a bondage worse, far worse, to
bear [and wall,
Than his who breathes, by roof, and floor,
Pent in, a tyrant's solitary thrall;
'Tis his who walks about in the open air
One of a nation who, henceforth, must wear
Their fetters in their souls. For who could
be,
Who, even the best, in such condition, free
From self-reproach, reproach which he
must share
With human nature? Never be it ours
To see the sun how brightly it will shine,
And know that noble feelings, manly
powers, [and pine,
Instead of gathering strength, must droop
And earth with all her pleasant fruits and
flowers
Fade, and participate in man's decline.

OCTOBER, 1803.

THESE times touch moneyed worldlings
with dismay: [air
Even rich men, brave by nature, taint the
With words of apprehension and despair:
While tens of thousands, thinking on the
affray,
Men unto whom sufficient for the day
And minds not stinted or untilled are given,
Sound, healthy children of the God of
heaven,
Are cheerful as the rising sun in May.
What do we gather hence but firmer faith
That every gift of noble origin [breath?
Is breathed upon by hope's perpetual
That virtue and the faculties within
Are vital,—and that riches are akin
To fear, to change, to cowardice and
death!

ENGLAND! the time is come when thou
shouldst wean
Thy heart from its emasculating food;

The truth should now be better understood;
Old things have been unsettled; we have seen [been
Fair seedtime, better harvest might have
But for thy trespasses; and at this day,
If for Greece, Egypt, India, Africa,
Aught good were destined, thou wouldst step between.
England! all nations in this charge agree.
But worse, more ignorant in love and hate,
Far, far more abject is thine enemy:
Therefore the wise pray for thee, though the freight
Of thy offences be a heavy weight:
Oh, grief! that earth's best hopes rest all with thee!

OCTOBER, 1803.

WHEN, looking on the present face of things,
I see one man, of men the meanest too!
Raised up to sway the world, to do, undo,
With mighty nations for his underlings,
The great events with which old story rings
Seem vain and hollow. I find nothing great;
Nothing is left which I can venerate;
So that almost a doubt within me springs
Of Providence, such emptiness at length
Seems at the heart of all things. But, great God!
I measure back the steps which I have trod;
And tremble, seeing whence proceeds the strength [sublime
Of such poor instruments, with thoughts
I tremble at the sorrow of the time.

TO THE MEN OF KENT. OCTOBER, 1803.

VANGUARD of liberty, ye men of Kent,
Ye children of a soil that doth advance
Her haughty brow against the coast of France,
Now is the time to prove your hardiment!
To France be words of invitation sent!
They from their fields can see the countenance [lance,
Of your fierce war, may ken the glittering
And hear you shouting forth your brave intent.
Left single, in bold parley, ye of yore,
Did from the Norman win a gallant wreath;
Confirmed the charters that were yours before;— [breath;
No parleying now! In Britain is one
We all are with you now from shore to shore:
Ye men of Kent, 'tis victory or death!

ANTICIPATION. OCTOBER, 1803.

SHOUT, for a mighty victory is won!
On British ground the invaders are laid low;
The breath of Heaven has drifted them like snow,
And left them lying in the silent sun,
Never to rise again! the work is done.
Come forth, ye old men, now in peaceful show,
And greet your sons! drums beat and trumpets blow!
Make merry, wives! ye little children, stun
Your grandames' ears with pleasure of your noise! [must be
Clap, infants, clap your hands! Divine
That triumph, when the very worst, the pain, [slain,
And even the prospect of our brethren
Had something in it which the heart enjoys:—
In glory will they sleep and endless sanctity

NOVEMBER, 1806.

ANOTHER year!—another deadly blow!
Another mighty empire overthrown!
And we are left, or shall be left, alone;
The last that dare to struggle with the foe.
'Tis well! from this day forward we shall know
That in ourselves our safety must be sought;
That by our own right hands it must be wrought, [low.
That we must stand unpropped, or be laid
O dastard whom such foretaste doth not cheer!
We shall exult, if they who rule the land
Be men who hold its many blessings dear,
Wise, upright, valiant; not a servile band,
Who are to judge of danger which they fear,
And honour which they do not understand.

ODE.

WHO rises on the banks of Seine,
And binds her temples with the civic wreath?
What joy to read the promise of her mien!
How sweet to rest her wide-spread wings beneath!
But they are ever playing,
And twinkling in the light,
And if a breeze be straying,
That breeze she will invite;
And stands on tiptoe, conscious she is fair,
And calls a look of love into her face,

And spreads her arms—as if the general air
Alone could satisfy her wide embrace.
Melt, principalities, before her melt!
Her love ye hailed—her wrath have felt;
But she through many a change of form hath gone, [creature,
And stands amidst you now, an armèd
Whose panoply is not a thing put on,
But the live scales of a portentous nature;
That, having wrought its way from birth to birth, [to the earth!
Stalks round—abhorred by Heaven, a terror

I marked the breathings of her dragon crest;
My soul, a sorrowful interpreter,
In many a midnight vision bowed
Before the ominous aspect of her spear;
Whether the mighty beam, in scorn upheld,
Threatened her foes,—or, pompously at rest,
Seemed to bisect her orbèd shield,
As stretches a blue bar of solid cloud
Across the setting sun, and through the fiery west.

So did she daunt the earth, and God defy!
And, wheresoe'er she spread her sovereignty,
Pollution tainted all that was most pure.
Have we not known—and live we not to tell—
That Justice seemed to hear her final knell?
Faith buried deeper in her own deep breast
Her stores, and sighed to find them insecure!
And Hope was maddened by the drops that fell [lived rest:
From shades, her chosen place of short-
Shame followed shame—and woe supplanted woe—
Is this the only change that time can show?
How long shall vengeance sleep? Ye patient heavens, how long?
Infirm ejaculation! from the tongue
Of nations wanting virtue to be strong
Up to the measure of accorded might,
And daring not to feel the majesty of right.

Weak spirits are there—who would ask,
Upon the pressure of a painful thing,
The lion's sinews, or the eagle's wing;
Or let their wishes loose, in forest glade,
Among the lurking powers
Of herbs and lowly flowers,
Or seek, from saints above, miraculous aid;
That man may be accomplished for a task
Which his own nature hath enjoined—and why?
If, when that interference hath relieved him,
He must sink down to languish
In worse than former helplessness—and lie
Till the caves roar,—and, imbecility
Again engendering anguish,
The same weak wish returns, that had before deceived him.

But Thou, Supreme Disposer! mayst not speed
The course of things, and change the creed,
Which hath been held aloft before men's sight
Since the first framing of societies,
Whether, as bards have told in ancient song,
Built up by soft seducing harmonies;
Or prest together by the appetite,
And by the power, of wrong!

ON A CELEBRATED EVENT IN ANCIENT HISTORY.

A ROMAN master stands on Grecian ground, [games
And to the concourse of the Isthmian
He, by his herald's voice, aloud proclaims
The liberty of Greece!—the words rebound
Until all voices in one voice are drowned;
Glad acclamation by which air was rent!
And birds, high flying in the element,
Dropped to the earth, astonished at the sound!
A melancholy echo of that noise
Doth sometimes hang on musing fancy's ear: [dear;
Ah! that a *conqueror's* word should be so
Ah! that a *boon* could shed such rapturous joys!
A gift of that which is not to be given
By all the blended powers of earth and heaven.

UPON THE SAME EVENT.

WHEN, far and wide, swift as the beams of morn
The tidings passed of servitude repealed,
And of that joy which shook the Isthmian field,
The rough Ætolians smiled with bitter scorn.
"'Tis known," cried they, "that he, who would adorn
His envied temples with the Isthmian crown,
Must either win, through effort of his own,
The prize, or be content to see it worn

By more deserving brows.—Yet so ye prop,
Sons of the brave who fought at Marathon!
Your feeble spirits. Greece her head hath bowed,
As if the wreath of liberty thereon
Would fix itself as smoothly as a cloud,
Which, at Jove's will, descends on Pelion's top."

TO THOMAS CLARKSON, ON THE FINAL PASSING OF THE BILL FOR THE ABOLITION OF THE SLAVE TRADE, MARCH, 1807.

CLARKSON! it was an obstinate hill to climb:
How toilsome, nay, how dire it was, by thee
Is known,—by none, perhaps, so feelingly;
But thou, who, starting in thy fervent prime,
Didst first lead forth this pilgrimage sublime,
Hast heard the constant voice its charge repeat,
Which, out of thy young heart's oracular seat,
First roused thee.—Oh, true yoke-fellow of Time
With unabating effort, see, the palm
Is won, and by all nations shall be worn!
The bloody writing is for ever torn,
And thou henceforth shalt have a good man's calm,
A great man's happiness; thy zeal shall find
Repose at length, firm friend of human kind!

A PROPHECY. FEBRUARY, 1807.

HIGH deeds, O Germans, are to come from you!
Thus in your books the record shall be found,
"A watchword was pronounced, a potent sound,
ARMINIUS!—all the people quaked like dew
Stirred by the breeze—they rose a nation, true,
True to herself—the mighty Germany,
She of the Danube and the Northern sea,
She rose, and off at once the yoke she threw.
All power was given her in the dreadful trance;
Those new-born kings she withered like a flame."
Woe to them all! but heaviest woe and shame
To that Bavarian who did first advance
His banner in accursed league with France,
First open traitor to a sacred name!

CLOUDS, lingering yet, extend in solid bars
Through the gray west; and lo! these waters, steeled
By breezeless air to smoothest polish, yield
A vivid repetition of the stars;
Jove—Venus—and the ruddy crest of Mars,
Amid his fellows beauteously revealed
At happy distance from earth's groaning field,
Where ruthless mortals wage incessant wars.
Is it a mirror?—or the nether sphere
Opening to view the abyss in which it feeds
Its own calm fires?—But list! a voice is near;
Great Pan himself low-whispering through the reeds,
"Be thankful, thou; for if unholy deeds
Ravage the world, tranquillity is here!"

Go back to antique ages, if thine eyes
The genuine mien and character would trace
Of the rash spirit that still holds her place,
Prompting the world's audacious vanities!
See, at her call, the Tower of Babel rise;
The Pyramid extend its monstrous base,
For some aspirant of our short-lived race,
Anxious an airy name to immortalize.
There, too, ere wiles and politic dispute
Gave specious colouring to aim and act,
See the first mighty hunter leave the brute
To chase mankind, with men in armies packed
For his field-pastime, high and absolute,
While, to dislodge his game, cities are sacked!

COMPOSED WHILE THE AUTHOR WAS ENGAGED IN WRITING A TRACT OCCASIONED BY THE CONVENTION OF CINTRA, 1808.

NOT 'mid the world's vain objects! that enslave
The free-born soul,—that world whose vaunted skill
In selfish interest perverts the will,
Whose factions lead astray the wise and brave;
Not there! but in dark wood and rocky cave,
And hollow vale which foaming torrents fill
With omnipresent murmur as they rave
Down their steep beds, that never shall be still:
Here, mighty nature! in this school sublime
I weigh the hopes and fears of suffering Spain:
For her consult the auguries of time,

And through the human heart explore my way,
And look and listen—gathering, whence I may,
Triumph, and thoughts no bondage can restrain.

COMPOSED AT THE SAME TIME AND ON THE SAME OCCASION.

I DROPPED my pen :—and listened to the wind
That sang of trees up-torn and vessels tost;
A midnight harmony, and wholly lost
To the general sense of men by chains confined
Of business, care, or pleasure,—or resigned
To timely sleep. Thought I, the impassioned strain,
Which, without aid of numbers, I sustain,
Like acceptation from the world will find.
Yet some with apprehensive ear shall drink
A dirge devoutly breathed o'er sorrows past,
And to the attendant promise will give heed—
The prophecy,—like that of this wild blast,
Which, while it makes the heart with sadness shrink,
Tells also of bright calms that shall succeed.

HOFFER.

OF mortal parents is the hero born
By whom the undaunted Tyrolese are led?
Or is it Tell's great spirit, from the dead
Returned to animate an age forlorn?
He comes like Phœbus through the gates of morn
When dreary darkness is discomfited :
Yet mark his modest state! upon his head,
That simple crest, a heron's plume is worn.
O liberty! they stagger at the shock ;
The murderers are aghast; they strive to flee,
And half their host is buried :—rock on rock
Descends :—beneath this godlike warrior, see!
Hills, torrents, woods, embodied to bemock
The tyrant, and confound his cruelty.

ADVANCE—come forth from thy Tyrolean ground,
Dear liberty! stern nymph of soul untamed,
Sweet nymph, oh, rightly of the mountains named
Through the long chain of Alps from mound to mound
And o'er the eternal snows, like echo, bound,—
Like echo, when the hunter-train at dawn
Have roused her from her sleep: and forest-lawn,
Cliffs, woods, and caves her viewless steps resound
And babble of her pastime!—On, dread power!
With such invisible motion speed thy flight,
Through hanging clouds, from craggy height to height,
Through the green vales and through the herdsman's bower,
That all the Alps may gladden in thy might,
Here, there, and in all places at one hour.

FEELINGS OF THE TYROLESE.

THE land we from our fathers had in trust,
And to our children will transmit, or die :
This is our maxim, this our piety ;
And God and nature say that it is just.
That which we *would* perform in arms—we must!
We read the dictate in the infant's eye ;
In the wife's smile ; and in the placid sky ;
And, at our feet, amid the silent dust
Of them that were before us.—Sing aloud
Old songs, the precious music of the heart!
Give, herds and flocks, your voices to the wind!
While we go forth, a self-devoted crowd,
With weapons in the fearless hand, to assert
Our virtue and to vindicate mankind.

ALAS! what boots the long, laborious quest
Of moral prudence, sought through good and ill;
Or pains abstruse—to elevate the will,
And lead us on to that transcendent rest
Where every passion shall the sway attest
Of reason, seated on her sovereign hill;
What is it, but a vain and curious skill,
If sapient Germany must lie deprest,
Beneath the brutal sword? Her haughty schools
Shall blush; and may not we with sorrow say,
A few strong instincts and a few plain rules,
Among the herdsmen of the Alps, have wrought
More for mankind at this unhappy day
Than all the pride of intellect and thought?

AND is it among rude untutored dales,
There, and there only, that the heart is true?
And, rising to repel or to subdue,
Is it by rocks and woods that man prevails?

Ah, no! though nature's dread protection fails,
There is a bulwark in the *soul*. This knew
Iberian burghers when the sword they drew
In Zaragoza, naked to the gales
Of fiercely-breathing war. The truth was felt
By Palafox, and many a brave compeer,
Like him of noble birth and noble mind;
By ladies, meek-eyed women without fear;
And wanderers of the street, to whom is dealt
The bread which without industry they find.

O'ER the wide earth, on mountain and on plain,
Dwells in the affections and the soul of man
A godhead, like the universal Pan,
But more exalted, with a brighter train.
And shall his bounty be dispensed in vain,
Showered equally on city and on field,
And neither hope nor steadfast promise yield
In these usurping times of fear and pain?
Such doom awaits us. Nay, forbid it Heaven!
We know the arduous strife, the eternal laws
To which the triumph of all good is given,
High sacrifice, and labour without pause,
Even to the death:—else wherefore should the eye
Of man converse with immortality?

ON THE FINAL SUBMISSION OF THE TYROLESE.

IT was a *moral* end for which they fought;
Else how, when mighty thrones were put to shame,
Could they, poor shepherds, have preserved an aim,
A resolution, or enlivening thought?
Nor hath that moral good been *vainly* sought;
For in their magnanimity and fame
Powers have they left, an impulse and a claim
Which neither can be overturned nor bought.
Sleep, warriors, sleep! among your hills repose!
We know that ye, beneath the stern control
Of awful prudence, keep the unvanquished soul.
And, when, impatient of her guilt and woes,
Europe breaks forth; then, shepherds! shall ye rise
For perfect triumph o'er your enemies.

HAIL, Zaragoza! If with unwet eye
We can approach, thy sorrow to behold,
Yet is the heart not pitiless nor cold;
Such spectacle demands not tear or sigh.
These desolate remains are trophies high
Of more than martial courage in the breast
Of peaceful civic virtue: they attest
Thy matchless worth to all posterity.
Blood flowed before thy sight without remorse;
Disease consumed thy vitals; war upheaved
The ground beneath thee with volcanic force;
Dread trials! yet encountered and sustained
Till not a wreck of help or hope remained,
And law was from *necessity* received.

SAY, what is honour?—'Tis the finest sense
Of *justice* which the human mind can frame,
Intent each lurking frailty to disclaim,
And guard the way of life from all offence
Suffered or done. When lawless violence
A kingdom doth assault, and in the scale
Of perilous war her weightiest armies fail,
Honour is hopeful elevation—whence
Glory, and triumph. Yet with politic skill
Endangered states may yield to terms unjust,
Stoop their proud heads, but not unto the dust,—
A foe's most favourite purpose to fulfil:
Happy occasions oft by self-mistrust
Are forfeited; but infamy doth kill.

THE martial courage of a day is vain,
An empty noise of death the battle's roar,
If vital hope be wanting to restore,
Or fortitude be wanting to sustain,
Armies or kingdoms. We have heard a strain
Of triumph, how the labouring Danube bore
A weight of hostile corses: drenched with gore
Were the wide fields, the hamlets heaped with slain.
Yet see, the mighty tumult overpast,
Austria a daughter of her throne hath sold!
And her Tyrolean champion we behold
Murdered like one ashore by shipwreck cast,
Murdered without relief. Oh! blind as bold,
To think that such assurance can stand fast!

BRAVE Schill! by death delivered, take thy flight
From Prussia's timid region. Go, and rest
With heroes 'mid the islands of the blest,
Or in the fields of empyrean light.
A meteor wert thou in a darksome night;
Yet shall thy name conspicuous and sublime,
Stand in the spacious firmament of time,
Fixed as a star: such glory is thy right.
Alas! it may not be: for earthly fame
Is fortune's frail dependent; yet there lives
A judge, who, as man claims by merit, gives;
To whose all-pondering mind a noble aim,
Faithfully kept, is as a noble deed:
In whose pure sight all virtue doth succeed.

CALL not the royal Swede unfortunate,
Who never did to fortune bend the knee;
Who slighted fear, rejected steadfastly
Temptation; and whose kingly name and state
Have "perished by his choice, and not his fate!"
Hence lives he, to his inner self endeared;
And hence, wherever virtue is revered,
He sits a more exalted potentate,
Throned in the hearts of men. Should Heaven ordain
That this great servant of a righteous cause
Must still have sad or vexing thoughts to endure,
Yet may a sympathising spirit pause,
Admonished by these truths, and quench all pain
In thankful joy and gratulation pure.

LOOK now on that adventurer who hath paid
His vows to fortune; who, in cruel slight
Of virtuous hope, of liberty, and right,
Hath followed wheresoe'er a way was made
By the blind goddess;—ruthless, undismayed;
And so hath gained at length a prosperous height
Round which the elements of worldly might
Beneath his haughty feet, like clouds, are laid!
Oh, joyless power that stands by lawless force!
Curses are *his* dire portion, scorn and hate,
Internal darkness and unquiet breath;
And, if old judgments keep their sacred course,
Him from that height shall Heaven precipitate
By violent and ignominious death.

Is there a power that can sustain and cheer
The captive chieftain, by a tyrant's doom,
Forced to descend alive into his tomb,
A dungeon dark! where he must waste the year,
And lie cut off from all his heart holds dear;
What time his injured country is a stage
Whereon deliberate valour and the rage
Of righteous vengeance side by side appear,
Filling from morn to night the heroic scene
With deeds of hope and everlasting praise:
Say can he think of this with mind serene
And silent fetters? Yes, if visions bright
Shine on his soul, reflected from the days
When he himself was tried in open light.

1810.

AH! where is Palafox? Nor tongue nor pen
Reports of him, his dwelling or his grave!
Does yet the unheard-of vessel ride the wave?
Or is she swallowed up, remote from ken
Of pitying human nature? Once again
Methinks that we shall hail thee, champion brave,
Redeemed to baffle that imperial slave,
And through all Europe cheer desponding men
With new-born hope. Unbounded is the might
Of martyrdom, and fortitude, and right.
Hark, how thy country triumphs!—Smilingly
The Eternal looks upon her sword that gleams,
Like his own lightning, over mountains high,
On rampart, and the banks of all her streams.

IN due observance of an ancient rite,
The rude Biscayans, when their children lie
Dead in the sinless time of infancy,
Attire the peaceful corse in vestments white;
And, in like sign of cloudless triumph bright,

They bind the unoffending creature's brows
With happy garlands of the pure white rose ;
This done, a festal company unite
In choral song ; and, while the uplifted cross
Of Jesus goes before, the child is borne
Uncovered to his grave. Her piteous loss
The lonesome mother cannot choose but mourn ;
Yet soon by Christian faith is grief subdued,
And joy attends upon her fortitude.

FEELINGS OF A NOBLE BISCAYAN AT ONE OF THESE FUNERALS. 1810.

YET, yet, Biscayans ! we must meet our foes
With firmer soul, yet labour to regain
Our ancient freedom ; else 'twere worse than vain
To gather round the bier these festal shows.
A garland fashioned of the pure white rose
Becomes not one whose father is a slave :
Oh ! bear the infant covered to his grave !
These venerable mountains now inclose
A people sunk in apathy and fear.
If this endure, farewell, for us, all good !
The awful light of heavenly innocence
Will fail to illuminate the infant's bier ;
And guilt and shame, from which is no defence,
Descend on all that issues from our blood.

THE OAK OF GUERNICA.

The ancient oak of Guernica, says Laborde in his account of Biscay, is the most venerable natural monument. Ferdinand and Isabella, in the year 1476, after hearing mass in the Church of Santa Maria de la Antigua, repaired to this tree, under which they swore to the Biscayans to maintain their *fueros* (privileges). What other interest belongs to it in the minds of this people will appear from the following

SUPPOSED ADDRESS TO THE SAME. 1810.

OAK of Guernica ! Tree of holier power
Than that which in Dodona did enshrine
(So faith too fondly deemed) a voice divine,
Heard from the depths of its aërial bower,
How canst thou flourish at this blighting hour?
What hope, what joy can sunshine bring to thee,
Or the soft breezes from the Atlantic sea,
The dews of morn, or April's tender shower?
Stroke merciful and welcome would that be
Which should extend thy branches on the ground,
If never more within their shady round
Those lofty-minded law-givers shall meet,
Peasant and lord, in their appointed seat,
Guardians of Biscay's ancient liberty.

INDIGNATION OF A HIGH-MINDED SPANIARD. 1810.

WE can endure that he should waste our lands,
Despoil our temples, and by sword and flame
Return us to the dust from which we came ;
Such food a tyrant's appetite demands :
And we can brook the thought that by his hands
Spain may be overpowered, and he possess,
For his delight, a solemn wilderness,
Where all the brave lie dead. But when of bands,
Which he will break for us, he dares to speak,
Of benefits, and of a future day
When our enlightened minds shall bless his sway,
Then, the strained heart of fortitude proves weak ;
Our groans, our blushes, our pale cheeks declare
That he has power to inflict what we lack strength to bear.

AVAUNT all specious pliancy of mind
In men of low degree, all smooth pretence !
I better like a blunt indifference
And self-respecting slowness, disinclined
To win me at first sight : and be there joined
Patience and temperance with this high reserve,
Honour that knows the path and will not swerve ;
Affections, which, if put to proof, are kind ;
And piety towards God. Such men of old
Were England's native growth ; and, throughout Spain,
Forests of such do at this day remain ;
Then for that country let our hopes be bold ;
For matched with these shall policy prove vain,
Her arts, her strength, her iron, and her gold.

1810.

O'ERWEENING statesmen have full long relied
On fleets and armies, and external wealth :

But from *within* proceeds a nation's health ,
Which shall not fail, though poor men cleave with pride
To the paternal floor ; or turn aside,
In the thronged city, from the walks of gain,
As being all unworthy to detain
A soul by contemplation sanctified
There are who cannot languish in this strife,
Spaniards of every rank, by whom the good
Of such high course was felt and understood ,
Who to their country's cause have bound a life,
Erewhile by solemn consecration given
To labour, and to prayer, to nature, and to heaven *

THE FRENCH AND THE SPANISH GUERILLAS.

HUNGER, and sultry heat, and nipping blast
From bleak hill-top, and length of march by night
Through heavy swamp, or over snow-clad height,
These hardships ill sustained, these dangers past,
The roving Spanish bands are reached at last,
Charged, and dispersed like foam ; but as a flight
Of scattered quails by signs to reunite,
So these,—and, heard of once again, are chased
With combinations of long-practised art
And newly-kindled hope ; but they are fled,
Gone are they, viewless as the buried dead ;
Where now ?—Their sword is at the foeman's heart !
And thus from year to year his walk they thwart,
And hang like dreams around his guilty bed

SPANISH GUERILLAS. 1811.

THEY seek, are sought ; to daily battle led,
Shrink not, though far outnumbered by their foes
For they have learnt to open and to close
The ridges of grim war ; and at their head
Are captains such as erst their country bred
Or fostered, self-supported chiefs,—like those
Whom hardy Rome was fearful to oppose,
Whose desperate shock the Carthaginian fled.

* See Laborde's character of the Spanish people : from him the sentiment of these last two lines is taken

In one who lived unknown a shepherd's life
Redoubted Viriatus breathes again ,
And Mina, nourished in the studious shade,
With that great leader* vies, who, sick of strife
And bloodshed, longed in quiet to be laid
In some green island of the western main.

1811.

THE power of armies is a visible thing,
Formal, and circumscribed in time and space ;
But who the limits of that power shall trace
Which a brave people into light can bring
Or hide, at will,—for freedom combating,
By just revenge inflamed? No foot may chase,
No eye can follow to a *fatal* place
That power, that spirit, whether on the wing
Like the strong wind, or sleeping like the wind
Within its awful caves.—From year to year
Springs this indigenous produce far and near ,
No craft this subtle element can bind,
Rising like water from the soil, to find
In every nook a lip that it may cheer.

1811.

HERE pause : the poet claims at least this praise,
That virtuous liberty hath been the scope
Of his pure song which did not shrink from hope
In the worst moment of these evil days ;
From hope, the paramount *duty* that Heaven lays,
For its own honour, on man's suffering heart.
Never may from our souls one truth depart,
That an *accursed* thing it is to gaze
On prosperous tyrants with a dazzled eye ;
Nor, touched with due abhorrence of *their* guilt
For whose dire ends tears flow, and blood is spilt,
And justice labours in extremity,
Forget thy weakness, upon which is built,
O wretched man, the throne of tyranny !

THE FRENCH ARMY IN RUSSIA 1812-13.

HUMANITY, delighting to behold
A fond reflection of her own decay,

* Sertorius.

Hath painted winter like a traveller—old,
Propped on a staff—and, through the sullen day,
In hooded mantle, limping o'er the plain,
As though his weakness were disturbed by pain:
Or, if a juster fancy should allow
An undisputed symbol of command,
The chosen sceptre is a withered bough,
Infirmly grasped within a palsied hand
These emblems suit the helpless and forlorn,
But mighty winter the device shall scorn

For he it was—dread winter! who beset,
Flinging round van and rear his ghastly net,
That host,—when from the regions of the pole
They shrunk, insane ambition's barren goal,
That host, as huge and strong as e'er defied
Their God, and placed their trust in human pride!
As fathers persecute rebellious sons,
He smote the blossoms of their warrior youth,
He called on frost's inexorable tooth
Life to consume in manhood's firmest hold;
Nor spared the reverend blood that feebly runs;
For why, unless for liberty enrolled
And sacred home, ah! why should hoary age be bold?

Fleet the Tartar's reinless steed,
But fleeter far the pinions of the wind,
Which from Siberian caves the monarch freed, [kind
And sent him forth, with squadrons of his
And bade the snow their ample backs bestride,
And to the battle ride
No pitying voice commands a halt,
No courage can repel the dire assault,
Distracted, spiritless, benumbed, and blind,
Whole legions sink—and, in one instant, find [descry,
Burial and death look for them—and
When morn returns, beneath the clear blue sky,
A soundless waste, a trackless vacancy!

ON THE SAME OCCASION.

Ye storms, resound the praises of your king!
And ye mild seasons—in a sunny clime,
Midway on some high hill, while father Time
Looks on delighted—meet in festal ring,
And loud and long of winter's triumph sing!
Sing ye, with blossoms crowned, and fruits, and flowers, [showers,
Of winter's breath surcharged with sleety
And the dire flapping of his hoary wing!
Knit the blithe dance upon the soft green grass, [your gain,
With feet, hands, eyes, looks, lips, report
Whisper it to the billows of the main,
And to the aerial zephyrs as they pass,
That old decrepit winter—*He* hath slain,
That host, which rendered all your bounties vain!

By Moscow self-devoted to a blaze
Of dreadful sacrifice, by Russian blood
Lavished in fight with desperate hardihood,
The unfeeling elements no claim shall raise
To rob our human nature of just praise
For what she did and suffered Pledges
Of a deliverance absolute and pure [sure
She gave, if faith might tread the beaten ways [High
Of Providence. But now did the Most
Exalt His still small voice,—to quell that host
Gathered His Power, a manifest Ally;
He whose heaped waves confounded the proud boast [Frost,
Of Pharaoh, said to Famine, Snow, and
Finish the strife by deadliest victory!

THE GERMANS ON THE HEIGHTS OF HOCKHEIM.

Abruptly paused the strife,—the field throughout
Resting upon his arms each warrior stood,
Checked in the very act and deed of blood,
With breath suspended, like a listening scout.
O silence! thou wert mother of a shout,
That through the texture of yon azure dome
Cleaves its glad way, a cry of harvest-home
Uttered to Heaven in ecstasy devout!
The barrier Rhine hath flashed, through battle-smoke, [view,
On men who gaze heart-smitten by the
As if all Germany had felt the shock!
Fly, wretched Gauls! ere they the charge renew [the yoke)
Who have seen (themselves delivered from
The unconquerable stream his course pursue.*

* The event is thus recorded in the journals of

NOVEMBER, 1813.

Now that all hearts are glad, all faces
bright, [flow
Our aged sovereign sits; to the ebb and
Of states and kingdoms, to their joy or woe,
Insensible he sits deprived of sight,
And lamentably wrapt in twofold night,
Whom no weak hopes deceived, whose
mind ensued,
Through perilous war, with regal fortitude,
Peace that should claim respect from law-
less might. [divine
Dread King of kings, vouchsafe a ray
To his forlorn condition! let thy grace
Upon his inner soul in mercy shine;
Permit his heart to kindle, and embrace
(Though were it only for a moment's
space)
The triumphs of this hour; for they are
THINE!

ON THE DISINTERMENT OF THE REMAINS OF THE DUKE D'ENGHIEN.

DEAR reliques! from a pit of vilest mould
Uprisen—to lodge among ancestral kings;
And to inflict shame's salutary stings
On the remorseless hearts of men grown
old
In a blind worship; men perversely bold
Even to this hour, yet at this hour they
quake; [sake,
And some their monstrous idol shall for-
If, to the living, truth was ever told
By aught surrendered from the hollow
grave: [brave!
O murdered prince! meek, loyal, pious,
The power of retribution once was given;
But 'tis a rueful thought that willow-
bands
So often tie the thunder-wielding hands
Of justice, sent to earth from highest
heaven!

---

the day: "When the Austrians took Hockheim, in one part of the engagement they got to the brow of the hill, whence they had their first view of the Rhine They instantly halted—not a gun was fired—not a voice heard they stood gazing on the river, with those feelings which the events of the last fifteen years at once called up Prince Schwartzenberg rode up to know the cause of this sudden stop: they then gave three cheers, rushed after the enemy, and drove them into the water."

OCCASIONED BY THE BATTLE OF WATERLOO.

(*The last six lines are intended for an Inscription.*)

FEBRUARY, 1816

INTREPID sons of Albion! not by you
Is life despised; ah, no, the spacious earth
Ne'er saw a race who held, by right of birth,
So many objects to which love is due.
Ye slight not life—to God and nature true;
But death, becoming death, is dearer far,
When duty bids you bleed in open war
Hence hath your prowess quelled that
impious crew
Heroes! for instant sacrifice prepared,
Yet filled with ardour, and on triumph bent,
'Mid direst shocks of mortal accident,
To you who fell, and you whom slaughter
spared, [event,
To guard the fallen, and consummate the
Your country rears this sacred monument!

FEBRUARY, 1816

OH! for a kindling touch of that pure
flame
Which taught the offering of song to rise
From thy lone bower, beneath Italian skies,
Great Filicaia! With celestial aim
It rose—thy saintly rapture to proclaim,
Then, when the imperial city stood re-
leased [East,
From bondage threatened by the embattled
And Christendom respired, from guilt
and shame
Redeemed, from miserable fear set free
By one day's feat, one mighty victory.
—Chant the deliverer's praise in every
tongue! [waxed dim,
The cross shall spread, the crescent hath
He conquering, as in earth and heaven
was sung, [GOD BY HIM.
HE CONQUERING THROUGH GOD, AND

OCCASIONED BY THE SAME BATTLE. FEBRUARY, 1816.

THE bard, whose soul is meek as dawning
day, [severe;
Yet trained to judgments righteously
Fervid, yet conversant with holy fear,
As recognizing one Almighty sway.
He whose experienced eye can pierce the
array

Of past events,—to whom, in vision clear,
The aspiring heads of future things appear,
Like mountain-tops whose mists have rolled away:
Assoiled from all incumbrance of our time,*
He only, if such breathe, in strains devout
Shall comprehend this victory sublime,
And worthily rehearse the hideous rout,
Which the blest angels, from their peaceful clime
Beholding, welcomed with a choral shout

EMPERORS and kings, how oft have temples rung
With impious thanksgiving, the Almighty's scorn!
How oft above their altars have been hung
Trophies that led the good and wise to mourn
Triumphant wrong, battle of battle born,
And sorrow that to fruitless sorrow clung!
Now, from Heaven-sanctioned victory, peace is sprung,
In this firm hour salvation lifts her horn.
Glory to arms! but conscious that the nerve
Of popular reason, long mistrusted, freed
Your thrones, from duty, princes! fear to swerve,
Be just, be grateful, nor, the oppressor's creed
Reviving, heavier chastisement deserve
Than ever forced unpitied hearts to bleed

ODE.

COMPOSED IN JANUARY, 1816.

"Carmina possumus
Donare, et pretium dicere muneri
Non incisa notis marmora publicis,
Per quæ spiritus et vita redit bonis
Post mortem ducibus
—————— clarius indicant
Laudes, quam ——— Pierides: neque
Si chartæ sileant quod bene feceris,
Mercedem tuleris"—HOR Car. 8, Lib 4

WHEN the soft hand of sleep had closed the latch
On the tired household of corporeal sense,
And Fancy, keeping unreluctant watch,
Was free her choicest favours to dispense;
I saw, in wondrous pérspective displayed,
A landscape more august than happiest skill
Of pencil ever clothed with light and shade,
An intermingled pomp of vale and hill,
City, and naval stream, suburban grove,
And stately forest where the wild deer rove;
Nor wanted lurking hamlet, dusky towns,
And scattered rural farms of aspect bright,
And, here and there, between the pastoral downs,
The azure sea upswelled upon the sight
Fair prospect, such as Britain only shows!
But not a living creature could be seen
Through its wide circuit, hushed in deep repose,
Yea, even to sadness, quiet and serene!
Amid this solitude of earth and sky,
Through portal clear as loop-hole in a storm
Opening before the sun's triumphant eye,
Issued, to sudden view, a radiant form!
Earthward it glided with a swift descent
Saint George himself this visitant may be,
And ere a thought could ask on what intent
He sought the regions of humanity,
A thrilling voice was heard, that vivified
City and field and flood,—aloud it cried,

"Though from my celestial home,
Like a champion armed I come,
On my helm the dragon crest,
And the red cross on my breast,
I, the guardian of this land,
Speak not now of toilsome duty—
Well obeyed was that command,
Hence bright days of festive beauty;
Haste, virgins, haste!—the flowers which summer gave
Have perished in the field;
But the green thickets plenteously shall yield
Fit garlands for the brave,
That will be welcome, if by you entwined!
Haste, virgins, haste,—and you, ye matrons grave,
Go forth with rival youthfulness of mind,
And gather what ye find
Of hardy laurel and wild holly boughs,
To deck your stern defenders' modest brows!
Such simple gifts prepare,
Though they have gained a worthier meed,
And in due time shall share
Those palms and amaranthine wreaths
Unto their martyred countrymen decreed,
In realms where everlasting freshness breathes!"

And lo! with crimson banners proudly streaming,
And upright weapons innocently gleaming,
Along the surface of a spacious plain
Advance in order the redoubted bands,
And there receive green chaplets from the hands
Of a fair female train,

* "From all this world's encumbrance did himself assoil."—SPENSER

Maids and matrons—dight
In robes of dazzling white,—
While from the crowd bursts forth a
rapturous noise
By the cloud-capt hills retorted,—
And a throng of rosy boys
In loose fashion tell their joys,—
And gray-haired sires, on staffs supported,
Look round—and by their smiling seem
to say,
Thus strives a grateful country to display
The mighty debt which nothing can repay!

Anon before my sight a palace rose,
Built of all precious substances,—so pure
And exquisite, that sleep alone bestows
Ability like splendour to endure;
Entered, with streaming thousands, through
the gate, [of state,
I saw the banquet spread beneath a dome
A lofty dome, that dared to emulate
The heaven of sable night
With starry lustre; and had power to throw
Solemn effulgence, clear as solar light,
Upon a princely company below,
While the vault rang with choral harmony,
Like some nymph-haunted grot beneath
the roaring sea
No sooner ceased that peal, than on the
Of exultation hung a dirge, [verge
Breathed from a soft and lonely instrument,
That kindled recollections
Of agonized affections;
And, though some tears the strain attended,
The mournful passion ended
In peace of spirit, and sublime content!

But garlands wither,—festal shows depart,
Like dreams themselves; and sweetest
Albeit of effect profound, [sound,
It was—and it is gone!
Victorious England! bid the silent art
Reflect, in glowing hues that shall not fade,
These high achievements, even as she arrayed
With second life the deed of Marathon,
Upon Athenian walls
So may she labour for thy civic halls;
And be the guardian spaces
Of consecrated places,
As nobly graced by sculpture's patient toil;
And let imperishable structures grow
Fixed in the depths of this courageous soil,
Expressive signals of a glorious strife,
And competent to shed a spark divine
Into the torpid breast of daily life; [shine,
Records on which the morning sun may
As changeful ages flow,
With gratulation thoroug[illegible]gn!

And ye, Pierian sisters, sprung from Jove
And sage Mnemosyne,—full long debarred
From your first mansions,—exiled all too
long
From many a hallowed stream and grove,
Dear native regions where ye wont to rove,
Chanting for patriot heroes the reward
Of never-dying song!
Now, (for, though truth descending from
above
The Olympian summit hath destroyed for
aye
Your kindred deities, *ye* live and move
And exercise unblamed a generous sway)
Now, on the margin of some spotless foun-
tain,
Or top serene of unmolested mountain,
Strike audibly the noblest of your lyres,
And for a moment meet my soul's desires!
That I, or some more favoured bard, may
hear
What ye, celestial maids! have often sung
Of Britain's acts,—may catch it with rapt
ear,
And give the treasure to our British tongue!
So shall the characters of that proud page
Support their mighty theme from age to age;
And, in the desert places of the earth,
When they to future empires have given
birth,
So shall the people gather and believe
The bold report, transferred to every clime,
And the whole world, not envious but ad-
And to the like aspiring, [miring,
Own that the progeny of this fair isle
Had power as lofty actions to achieve
As were performed in man's heroic prime,
Nor wanted, when their fortitude had held
Its even tenor, and the foe was quelled,
A corresponding virtue to beguile
The hostile purpose of wide-wasting time;
That not in vain they laboured to secure,
For their great deeds, perpetual memory,
And fame as largely spread as land and sea,
By works of spirit high and passion pure.

THANKSGIVING ODE.

JANUARY 18, 1816.

ADVERTISEMENT.

WHOLLY unworthy of touching upon the momentous subject here treated would that poet be, before whose eyes the present distresses under which this kingdom labours could interpose a veil sufficiently thick to hide, or even to obscure, the splendour of this great moral triumph If the author has given way to exultation, unchecked by these distresses, it might be sufficient to protect him from a charge of insensibility, should he state his own belief that the sufferings will be transitory On the wisdom of a very large majority of the British nation rested that generosity which poured out the treasures of this country for the deliverance of Europe and in the same national wisdom, presiding in time of peace over an energy not inferior to that which has been displayed in war, *they* confide, who encourage a firm hope, that the cup of our wealth will be gradually replenished There will, doubtless, be no few ready to indulge in regrets and repinings, and to feed a morbid satisfaction, by aggravating these burthens in imagination, in order that calamity so confidently prophesied, as it has not taken the shape which their sagacity allotted to it, may appear as grievous as possible under another But the body of the nation will not quarrel with the gain, because it might have been purchased at a less price: and, acknowledging in these sufferings, which they feel to have been in a great degree unavoidable, a consecration of their noble efforts, they will vigorously apply themselves to remedy the evil.

Nor is it at the expense of rational patriotism or in disregard of sound philosophy, that the author hath given vent to feelings tending to encourage a martial spirit in the bosoms of his countrymen, at a time when there is a general outcry against the prevalence of these dispositions The British army, both by its skill and valour in the field, and by the discipline which has rendered it much less formidable than the armies of other powers to the inhabitants of the several countries where its operations were carried on, has performed services that will not allow the language of gratitude and admiration to be suppressed or restrained (whatever be the temper of the public mind) through a scrupulous dread lest the tribute due to the past should prove an injurious incentive for the future Every man deserving the name of Briton adds his voice to the chorus which extols the exploits of his countrymen, with a consciousness, at times overpowering the effort, that they transcend all praise —But this particular sentiment, thus irresistibly excited, is not sufficient The nation would err grievously, if she suffered the abuse which other states have made of military power, to prevent her from perceiving that no people ever was, or can be, independent, free, or secure, much less great, in any sane application of the word, without martial propensities and an assiduous cultivation of military virtues Nor let it be overlooked, that the benefits derivable from these sources are placed within the reach of Great Britain, under conditions peculiarly favourable The same insular position which, by rendering territorial incorporation impossible, utterly precludes the desire of conquest under the most seductive shape it can assume, enables her to rely, for her defence against foreign foes, chiefly upon a species of armed force from which her own liberties have nothing to fear Such are the privileges of her situation; and, by permitting, they invite her to give way to the courageous instincts of human nature, and to strengthen and to refine them by culture But some have more than insinuated that a design exists to subvert the civil character of the English people by unconstitutional applications and unnecessary increase of military power The advisers and abettors of such a design, were it possible that it should exist, would be guilty of the most heinous crime, which, upon this planet, can be committed The author, trusting that this apprehension arises from the delusive influences of an honourable jealousy, hopes that the martial qualities he venerates will be fostered by adhering to those good old usages which experience has sanctioned and by availing ourselves of new means of indisputable promise particularly by applying, in its utmost possible extent, that system of tuition whose master-spring is a habit of gradually enlightened subordination,—by imparting knowledge, civil, moral, and religious, in such measure that the mind, among all classes of the community, may love, admire, and be prepared and accomplished to defend that country under whose protection its faculties have been unfolded, and its riches acquired,—by just dealing towards all orders of the state, so that no members of it being trampled upon, courage may everywhere continue to rest immovably upon its ancient English foundation, personal self-respect,—by adequate rewards, and permanent honours, conferred upon the deserving, by encouraging athletic exercises and manly sports among the peasantry of the country —and by especial care to provide and support institutions, in which, during a time of peace, a reasonable proportion of the youth of the country may be instructed in military science

The author has only to add, that he should feel little satisfaction in giving to the world these limited attempts to celebrate the virtues of his country, if he did not encourage a hope that a subject, which it has fallen within his province to treat only in the mass, will by other poets be illustrated in that detail which its importance calls for, and which will allow opportunities to give the merited applause to PERSONS as well as to THINGS

This Ode was published along with other pieces, now interspersed through this Volume.

ODE.

THE MORNING OF THE DAY APPOINTED FOR A GENERAL THANKSGIVING.

JANUARY 18, 1816.

HAIL, orient conqueror of gloomy night!
Thou that canst shed the bliss of gratitude
On hearts howe'er insensible or rude;
Whether thy orient visitations smite
The haughty towers where monarchs dwell,
Or thou, impartial sun, with presence bright

Cheer'st the low threshold of the peasant's cell!
Not unrejoiced I see thee climb the sky
In naked splendour, clear from mist or haze,
Or cloud approaching to divert the rays,
Which even in deepest winter testify
Thy power and majesty,
Dazzling the vision that presumes to gaze.
Well does thine aspect usher in this day;
As aptly suits therewith that modest pace
Submitted to the chains
That bind thee to the path which God ordains
That thou shalt trace,
Till, with the heavens and earth, thou pass away!
Nor less, the stillness of these frosty plains,
Their utter stillness, and the silent grace
Of yon ethereal summits white with snow,
(Whose tranquil pomp, and spotless purity,
Report of storms gone by
To us who tread below)
Do with the service of this day accord.
Divinest object, which the uplifted eye
Of mortal man is suffered to behold;
Thou, who upon yon snow-clad heights hast poured
Meek splendour, nor forget'st the humble vale,
Thou who dost warm earth's universal mould,
And for thy bounty wert not unadored
By pious men of old;
Once more, heart-cheering sun, I bid thee hail!
Bright be thy course to-day, let not this promise fail!

'Mid the deep quiet of this morning hour,
All nature seems to hear me while I speak,
By feelings urged, that do not vainly seek
Apt language, ready as the tuneful notes
That stream in blithe succession from the throats
Of birds in leafy bower,
Warbling a farewell to a vernal shower.
There is a radiant but a short-lived flame,
That burns for poets in the dawning east;
And oft my soul hath kindled at the same,
When the captivity of sleep had ceased;
But he who fixed immovably the frame
Of the round world, and built, by laws as strong,
A solid refuge for distress,
The towers of righteousness;
He knows that from a holier altar came
The quickening spark of this day's sacrifice;
Knows that the source is nobler whence doth rise
The current of this matin song;
That deeper far it lies
Than aught dependent on the fickle skies.

Have we not conquered?—By the vengeful sword?
Ah, no, by dint of magnanimity;
That curbed the baser passions, and left free
A loyal band to follow their liege lord,
Clear-sighted honour—and his staid compeers,
Along a track of most unnatural years,
In execution of heroic deeds;
Whose memory, spotless as the crystal beads
Of morning dew upon the untrodden meads,
Shall live enrolled above the starry spheres
Who to the murmurs of an earthly string,
Of Britain's acts would sing,
He with enraptured voice will tell
Of one whose spirit no reverse could quell;
Of one that 'mid the failing never failed:
Who paints how Britain struggled and prevailed
Shall represent her labouring with an eye
Of circumspect humanity;
Shall show her clothed with strength and skill,
All martial duties to fulfil;
Firm as a rock in stationary fight:
In motion rapid as the lightning's gleam;
Fierce as a flood-gate bursting in the night
To rouse the wicked from their giddy dream—
Woe, woe to all that face her in the field!
Appalled she may not be, and cannot yield.

And thus is missed the sole true glory
That can belong to human story!
At which *they* only shall arrive
Who through the abyss of weakness dive.
The very humblest are too proud of heart:
And one brief day is rightly set apart
To Him who lifteth up and layeth low;
For that Almighty God to whom we owe,
Say not that we have vanquished—but that we survive.

How dreadful the dominion of the impure!
Why should the song be tardy to proclaim
That less than power unbounded could not tame
That soul of evil—which, from hell let loose,
Had filled the astonished world with such abuse,
As boundless patience only could endure?
Wide-wasted regions—cities wrapt in flame—
Who sees, and feels, may lift a streaming eye
To heaven,—who never saw may heave a sigh;
But the foundation of our nature shakes,
And with an infinite pain the spirit aches,

When desolated countries, towns on fire,
Are but the avowed attire
Of warfare waged with desperate mind
Against the life of virtue in mankind;
Assaulting without ruth
The citadels of truth;
While the whole forest of civility
Is doomed to perish, to the last fair tree!

A crouching purpose—a distracted will—
Opposed to hopes that battened upon scorn,
And to desires whose ever-waxing horn
Not all the light of earthly power could fill;
Opposed to dark, deep plots of patient
And to celerities of lawless force [skill,
Which, spurning God, had flung away
remorse— [redress?
What could they gain but shadows of
So bad proceeded propagating worse;
And discipline was passion's dire excess.
Widens the fatal web, its lines extend,*
And deadlier poisons in the chalice blend—
When will your trials teach you to be
wise?
Oh, prostrate lands, consult your agonies!

No more—the guilt is banished,
And, with the guilt, the shame is fled;
And, with the guilt and shame, the woe
hath vanished,
Shaking the dust and ashes from her head!
No more—these lingerings of distress
Sully the limpid stream of thankfulness.
What robe can gratitude employ
So seemly as the radiant vest of joy?
What steps so suitable as those that move
In prompt obedience to spontaneous mea-
Of glory—and felicity—and love, [sures
Surrendering the whole heart to sacred
pleasures?

Land of our fathers! precious unto me
Since the first joys of thinking infancy;
When of thy gallant chivalry I read,
And hugged the volume on my sleepless
bed!
O England!—dearer far than life is dear,
If I forget thy prowess, never more
Be thy ungrateful son allowed to hear
Thy green leaves rustle, or thy torrents roar!
But how can *he* be faithless to the past,
Whose soul, intolerant of base decline,
Saw in thy virtue a celestial sign,

* "A discipline the rule whereof is passion."—LORD BROOK.

That bade him hope, and to his hope
cleave fast! [length
The nations strove with puissance;—at
Wide Europe heaved, impatient to be cast,
With *all* her living strength,
With *all* her armèd powers,
Upon the offensive shores.
The trumpet blew a universal blast!
But thou art foremost in the field;—there
stand:
Receive the triumph destined to thy hand!
All states have glorified themselves; their
claims
Are weighed by Providence, in balance
even; [names,
And now, in preference to the mightiest
To thee the exterminating sword is given.
Dread mark of approbation, justly gained!
Exalted office, worthily sustained!

Imagination, ne'er before content,
But aye ascending, restless in her pride,
From all that man's performance could
present,
Stoops to that closing deed magnificent,
And with the embrace is satisfied.
Fly, ministers of fame,
Whate'er your means, whatever help ye
claim, [delight!
Bear through the world these tidings of
Hours, days, and months, have borne them,
in the sight [shower,
Of mortals, travelling faster than the
That landward stretches from the sea,
The morning's splendours to devour;
But *this* appearance scattered ecstasy,
And heart-sick Europe blessed the healing
power.
*The shock is given—the adversaries
bleed—*
Lo, justice triumphs! Earth is freed!
Such glad assurance suddenly went forth—
It pierced the caverns of the sluggish
north—
It found no barrier on the ridge
Of Andes—frozen gulfs became its bridge—
The vast Pacific gladdens with the freight—
Upon the lakes of Asia 'tis bestowed—
The Arabian desert shapes a willing road,
Across her burning breast,
For this refreshing incense from the west!
Where snakes and lions breed,
Where towns and cities thick as stars
appear,
Wherever fruits are gathered, and where'er
The upturned soil receives the hopeful
seed—

While the sun rules, and cross the shades
of night—
The unwearied arrow hath pursued its
flight! [heed,
The eyes of good men thankfully give
And in its sparkling progress read
How virtue triumphs, from her bondage
freed!
Tyrants exult to hear of kingdoms won,
And slaves are pleased to learn that mighty
feats are done; [tracted borders
Even the proud realm, from whose dis-
This messenger of good was launched in
air, [disorders,
France, conquered France, amid her wild
Feels, and hereafter shall the truth declare,
That she too lacks not reason to rejoice,
And utter England's name with sadly-
plausive voice.

Preserve, O Lord! within our hearts
The memory of thy favour,
That else insensibly departs,
And loses its sweet savour!
Lodge it within us!—as the power of light
Lives inexhaustibly in precious gems,
Fixed on the front of eastern diadems,
So shine our thankfulness for ever bright!
What offering, what transcendent monu-
Shall our sincerity to thee present? [ment
Not work of hands; but trophies that may
reach
To highest heaven—the labour of the soul,
That builds, as thy unerring precepts teach,
Upon the inward victories of each,
Her hope of lasting glory for the whole.
Yet might it well become that city now,
Into whose breast the tides of grandeur
flow,
To whom all persecuted men retreat;
If a new temple lift her votive brow
Upon the shore of silver Thames—to greet
The peaceful guest advancing from afar.
Bright be the distant fabric, as a star
Fresh risen—and beautiful within!—there
meet
Dependence infinite, proportion just;
A pile that grace approves, that time can
trust
With his most sacred wealth, heroic dust!

But if the valiant of this land
In reverential modesty demand,
That all observance, due to them, be paid
Where their serene progenitors are laid;
Kings, warriors, high-souled poets, saint-
like sages, [ages;
England's illustrious sons of long, long
Be it not unordained that solemn rites,
Within the circuit of those Gothic walls,
Shall be performed at pregnant intervals;
Commemoration holy, that unites
The living generations with the dead;
By the deep soul-moving sense
Of religious eloquence,—
By visual pomp, and by the tie
Of sweet and threatening harmony;
Soft notes, awful as the omen
Of destructive tempests coming,
And escaping from that sadness
Into elevated gladness;
While the white-robed choir at-
tendant,
Under mouldering banners pen-
dant,
Provoke all potent symphonies to raise
Songs of victory and praise,
For them who bravely stood unhurt, or
bled [graves
With medicable wounds, or found their
Upon the battle-field, or under ocean's
waves;
Or were conducted home in single state,
And long procession—there to lie,
Where their sons' sons, and all posterity,
Unheard by them, their deeds shall cele
brate!
Nor will the God of peace and love
Such martial service disapprove.
He guides the pestilence—the
cloud
Of locusts travels on his breath;
The region that in hope was
ploughed
His drought consumes, his mildew taints
with death;
He springs the hushed volcano's mine;
He puts the earthquake on her still design,
Darkens the sun, hath bade the forest sink,
And, drinking towns and cities, still can
drink [Thine!
Cities and towns—'tis Thou—the work is
The fierce tornado sleeps within thy
courts—
He hears the word—he flies—
And navies perish in their ports;
For thou art angry with thine enemies!
For these, and for our errors
And sins, that point their terrors,
We bow our heads before Thee, and we
laud
And magnify thy name, Almighty God!
But thy most dreaded instrument
In working out a pure intent,
Is man—arrayed for mutual
slaughter,—

Yea, Carnage is thy daughter!
Thou cloth'st the wicked in their dazzling mail,
And by thy just permission they prevail;
Thine arm from peril guards the coasts
Of them who in thy laws delight:
Thy presence turns the scale of doubtful fight,
Tremendous God of battles Lord of Hosts!
To Thee—to Thee—
On this appointed day shall thanks ascend,
That Thou hast brought our warfare to an end,
And that we need no second victory!
Ha! what a ghastly sight for man to see,
And to the heavenly saints in peace who dwell,
For a brief moment, terrible;
But to thy sovereign penetration, fair,
Before whom all things are, that were,
All judgments that have been, or e'er shall be;
Links in the chain of thy tranquillity!
Along the bosom of this favoured nation,
Breathe thou, this day, a vital undulation!
Let all who do this land inherit
Be conscious of thy moving spirit!
Oh, 'tis a goodly ordinance,—the sight,
Though sprung from bleeding war, is one of pure delight;
Bless thou the hour, or ere the hour arrive,
When a whole people shall kneel down in prayer,
And, at one moment, in one rapture, strive
With lip and heart to tell their gratitude
For thy protecting care, [Lord
Their solemn joy—praising the Eternal
For tyranny subdued,
And for the sway of equity renewed,
For liberty confirmed, and peace restored!

But hark—the summons!—down the placid lake
Floats the soft cadence of the church-tower bells; [wake
Bright shines the sun, as if his beams might
The tender insects sleeping in their cells
Bright shines the sun—and not a breeze to shake
The drops that tip the melting icicles.
Oh, enter now His temple gate!
Inviting words—perchance already flung.
(As the crowd press devoutly down the aisle
Of some old minster's venerable pile)
From voices into zealous passion stung,
While the tubed engine feels the inspiring blast, [cast
And has begun—its clouds of sound to
Towards the empyreal heaven,
As if the fretted roof were riven.
Us, humbler ceremonies now await,
But in the bosom, with devout respect,
The banner of our joy we will erect,
And strength of love our souls shall elevate
For to a few collected in his name,
Their heavenly Father will incline an ear
Gracious to service hallowed by its aim,—
Awake! the majesty of God revere!
Go—and with foreheads meekly bowed
Present your prayers—go—and rejoice aloud—

The Holy One will hear!
And what 'mid silence deep, with faith sincere,
Ye, in your low and undisturbed estate,
Shall simply feel and purely meditate
Of warnings—from the unprecedented might, [closed;
Which, in our time, the impious have dis-
And of more arduous duties thence imposed
Upon the future advocates of right;
Of mysteries revealed,
And judgments unrepealed,—
Of earthly revolution,
And final retribution,—
To his omniscience will appear
An offering not unworthy to find place,
On this high Day of Thanks, before the Throne of Grace!

Memorials of a Tour on the Continent.

1820.

DEDICATION.

Dear fellow-travellers! think not that the muse
Presents to notice these memorial lays,
Hoping the general eye thereon will gaze,
As on a mirror that gives back the hues
Of living nature: no—though free to choose
The greenest bowers, the most inviting ways,
The fairest landscapes and the brightest days,
Her skill she tried with less ambitious views.
For you she wrought;—ye only can supply
The life, the truth, the beauty: she confides
In that enjoyment which with you abides,
Trusts to your love and vivid memory;
Thus far contented, that for you her verse
Shall lack not power the "melting soul to pierce."

W. Wordsworth

Rydal Mount, *January*, 1822

FISH-WOMEN ON LANDING AT CALAIS.

'Tis said, fantastic ocean doth enfold
The likeness of whate'er on land is seen;
But, if the Nereid sisters and their queen,
Above whose heads the tide so long hath rolled,
The dames resemble whom we here behold,
How terrible beneath the opening waves
To sink, and meet them in their fretted caves,
Withered, grotesque—immeasurably old,
And shrill and fierce in accent!—Fear it not;
For they earth's fairest daughters do excel;
Pure undecaying beauty is their lot;
Their voices into liquid music swell,
Thrilling each pearly cleft and sparry grot—
The undisturbed abodes where sea-nymphs dwell!

BRUGES.*

Bruges I saw attired with golden light
(Streamed from the west) as with a robe of power:
'Tis passed away;—and now the sunless hour,
That slowly introducing peaceful night
Best suits with fallen grandeur, to my sight
Offers the beauty, the magnificence,
And sober graces, left her for defence
Against the injuries of time, the spite
Of fortune, and the desolating storms
Of future war. Advance not—spare to hide,
O gentle power of darkness!—these mild hues;
Obscure not yet these silent avenues
Of stateliest architecture, where the forms
Of nun-like females, with soft motion glide!

---

* This is not the first poetical tribute which in our times has been paid to this beautiful city. Mr. Southey, in the "Poet's Pilgrimage," speaks of it in lines which I cannot deny myself the pleasure of connecting with my own:—

"Time hath not wronged her, nor hath ruin sought
Rudely her splendid structures to destroy,
Save in those recent days, with evil fraught,
When mutability, in drunken joy
Triumphant, and from all restraint released
Let loose her fierce and many-headed beast.

"But for the scars in that unhappy rage
Inflicted, firm she stands and undecayed;
Like our first sires, a beautiful old age
Is hers in venerable years arrayed;
And yet, to her, benignant stars may bring,
What fate denies to man,—a second spring.

"When I may read of tilts in days of old,
And tourneys graced by chieftains of renown,
Fair dames, grave citizens, and warriors bold,
If fancy would portray some stately town,
Which for such pomp fit theatre should be,
Fair Bruges, I shall then remember thee."

In this city are many vestiges of the splendour of the Burgundian dukedom; and the long black mantle universally worn by the females is probably a remnant of the old Spanish connexion, which, if I do not much deceive myself, is trace-

BRUGES.

THE spirit of antiquity—enshrined
In sumptuous buildings, vocal in sweet song,
In picture, speaking with heroic tongue,
And with devout solemnities entwined—
Strikes to the seat of grace within the mind:
Hence forms that glide with swan-like ease along;
Hence motions, even amid the vulgar throng,
To an harmonious decency confined;
As if the streets were consecrated ground,
The city one vast temple—dedicate
To mutual respect in thought and deed;
To leisure, to forbearances sedate;
To social cares from jarring passions freed;
A nobler peace than that in deserts found!

AFTER VISITING THE FIELD OF WATERLOO.

A WINGED goddess, clothed in vesture wrought
Of rainbow colours; one whose port was bold
Whose overburthened hand could scarcely hold
The glittering crowns and garlands which it brought,
Hovered in air above the far-famed spot.
She vanished—leaving prospect blank and cold
Of wind-swept corn that wide around us rolled
In dreary billows, wood, and meagre cot,
And monuments that soon must disappear:
Yet a dread local recompense we found;
While glory seemed betrayed, while patriot zeal
Sank in our hearts, we felt as men *should* feel
With such vast hoards of hidden carnage near,
And horror breathing from the silent ground!

SCENERY BETWEEN NAMUR AND LIEGE.

WHAT lovelier home could gentle fancy choose?
Is this the stream, whose cities, heights, and plains,
War's favourite playground, are with crimson stains
Familiar, as the morn with pearly dews?
The morn, that now, along the silver Meuse,
Spreading her peaceful ensigns, calls the swains
To tend their silent boats and ringing wains,
Or strip the bough whose mellow fruit bestrews
The ripening corn beneath it. As mine eyes
Turn from the fortified and threatening hill,
How sweet the prospect of yon watery glade,
With its gray rocks clustering in pensive shade,
That, shaped like old monastic turrets, rise
From the smooth meadow ground, serene and still!

AIX-LA-CHAPELLE.

WAS it to disenchant, and to undo,
That we approached the seat of Charlemaine?
To sweep from many an old romantic strain
That faith which no devotion may renew!
Why does this puny church present to view
Its feeble columns? and that scanty chair!
This sword that one of our weak times might wear;
Objects of false pretence, or meanly true!
If from a traveller's fortune I might claim
A palpable memorial of that day,
Then would I seek the Pyrenean breach
Which Roland clove with huge two-handed sway,
And to the enormous labour left his name,
Where unremitting frosts the rocky crescent bleach.*

ible in the grave deportment of its inhabitants. Bruges is comparatively little disturbed by that curious contest, or rather conflict, of Flemish with French propensities in matters of taste, so conspicuous through other parts of Flanders. The hotel to which we drove at Ghent furnished an odd instance. In the passages were paintings and statues, after the antique, of Hebe and Apollo; and in the garden a little pond, about a yard and a half in diameter, with a weeping willow bending over it, and under the shade of that tree, in the centre of the pond, a wooden painted statue of a Dutch or Flemish boor, looking ineffably tender upon his mistress, and embracing her. A living duck, tethered at the feet of the statues, alternately tormented a miserable eel and itself with endeavours to escape from its bonds and prison. Had we chanced to espy the hostess of the hotel in this quaint rural retreat, the exhibition would have been complete. She was a true Flemish figure, in the dress of the days of Holbein,—her symbol of office a weighty bunch of keys, pendent from her portly waist. In Brussels, the modern taste in costume, architecture, etc., has got the mastery; in Ghent there is a struggle; but in Bruges old images are still paramount, and an air of monastic life among the quiet goings-on of a thinly-peopled city is inexpressibly soothing; a pensive grace seems to be cast over all, even the very children. —*Extract from Journal.*

* Let a wall of rocks be imagined from three to six hundred feet in height, and rising be

IN THE CATHEDRAL AT COLOGNE.

OH, for the help of angels to complete
This temple—angels governed by a plan
Thus gloriously pursued by daring man,
Studious that *He* might not disdain the seat
Who dwells in heaven! But that inspiring heat
Hath failed, and now, ye powers! whose gorgeous wings
And splendid aspect yon emblazonings
But faintly picture, 'twere an office meet
For you, on these unfinished shafts to try
The midnight virtues of your harmony:—
This vast design might tempt you to repeat
Strains that call forth upon empyreal ground
Immortal fabrics—rising to the sound
Of penetrating harps and voices sweet!

IN A CARRIAGE, UPON THE BANKS OF THE RHINE.

AMID this dance of objects sadness steals
O'er the defrauded heart—while sweeping by,
As in a fit of Thespian jollity,
Beneath her vine-leaf crown the green earth reels.
Backward, in rapid evanescence, wheels
The venerable pageantry of time,
Each beetling rampart—and each tower sublime,
And what the dell unwillingly reveals
Of lurking cloistral arch, through trees espied
Near the bright river's edge. Yet why repine?
Pedestrian liberty shall yet be mine
To muse, to creep, to halt at will, to gaze
Freedom which youth with copious hand supplied,
May in fit measure bless my later days.

HYMN, FOR THE BOATMEN AS THEY APPROACH THE RAPIDS, UNDER THE CASTLE OF HEIDELBERG.

JESU! bless our slender boat,
By the current swept along;
Loud its threatenings—let them not
Drown the music of a song,
Breathed thy mercy to implore,
Where these troubled waters roar!

Saviour, in Thy image, seen
Bleeding on that precious rood;
If, while through the meadows green
Gently wound the peaceful flood,
We forgot Thee, do not Thou
Disregard Thy suppliants now!

Hither, like yon ancient tower
Watching o'er the river's bed,
Fling the shadow of Thy power,
Else we sleep among the dead;
Thou who trod'st the billowy sea,
Shield us in our jeopardy!

Guide our bark among the waves;
Through the rocks our passage smooth;
Where the whirlpool frets and raves
Let Thy love its anger soothe:
All our hope is placed in Thee;
Miserere Domine! *

THE SOURCE OF THE DANUBE.

NOT, like his great compeers, indignantly†
Doth Danube spring to life! The wandering stream
(Who loves the cross, yet to the crescent's gleam
Unfolds a willing breast) with infant glee
Slips from his prison walls and fancy, free
To follow in his track of silver light,
Reaches, with one brief moment's rapid flight,
The vast encincture of that gloomy sea.

tween France and Spain, so as physically to separate the two kingdoms—let us fancy this wall curved like a crescent, with its convexity towards France. Lastly, let us suppose, that in the very middle of the wall a breach of three hundred feet wide has been beaten down by the famous *Roland*, and we may have a good idea of what the mountaineers call the 'Breche de Roland.'—Raymond's Pyrenees.

* See the beautiful song in Mr. Coleridge's tragedy of "Remorse."

† Before this quarter of the Black Forest was inhabited, the source of the Danube might have suggested some of those sublime images which Armstrong has so finely described; at present, the contrast is most striking. The spring appears in a capacious stone basin upon the front of a ducal palace, with a pleasure-ground opposite; then, passing under the pavement, takes the form of a little, clear, bright, black, vigorous rill, barely wide enough to tempt the agility of a child five years old to leap over it,—and entering the garden, it joins, after a course of a few hundred yards, a stream much more considerable than itself. The *copiousness* of the spring at *Donischingen* must have procured for it the honour of being named the source of the Danube.

Whose waves the Orphean lyre forbad to meet
In conflict; whose rough winds forgot their jars—
To waft the heroic progeny of Greece,
When the first ship sailed for the golden fleece,
Argo, exalted for that daring feat
To bear in heaven a shape distinct with stars

MEMORIAL NEAR THE OUTLET OF THE LAKE OF THUN.

DEM
ANDENKEN
MEINES FREUNDES
ALOYS REDING
MDCCCXVIII.

Aloys Reding, it will be remembered, was captain-general of the Swiss forces, which, with a courage and perseverance worthy of the cause, opposed the flagitious and too successful attempt of Bonaparte to subjugate their country

---

AROUND a wild and woody hill
A gravelled pathway treading,
We reached a votive stone that bears
The name of Aloys Reding.

Well judged the friend who placed it there
For silence and protection,
And haply with a finer care
Of dutiful affection.

The sun regards it from the west,
Sinking in summer glory;
And, while he sinks, affords a type
Of that pathetic story.

And oft he tempts the patriot Swiss
Amid the grove to linger;
Till all is dim, save this bright stone
Touched by his golden finger.

COMPOSED IN ONE OF THE CATHOLIC CANTONS OF SWITZERLAND

DOOMED as we are our native dust
To wet with many a bitter shower,
It ill befits us to disdain
The altar, to deride the fane,
Where patient sufferers bend, in trust
To win a happier hour.

I love, where spreads the village lawn,
Upon some knee-worn cell to gaze,
Hail to the firm unmoving cross,
Aloft, where pines their branches toss
And to the chapel far withdrawn,
That lurks by lonely ways!

Where'er we roam—along the brink
Of Rhine—or by the sweeping Po,
Through Alpine vale, or champain wide
Whate'er we look on, at our side
Be Charity,—to bid us think,
And feel, if we would know

ON APPROACHING THE STAUB-BACH LAUTERBRUNNEN.*

TRACKS let me follow far from human kind
Which these illusive greetings may not reach,
Where only nature tunes her voice to teach
Careless pursuits, and raptures unconfined.
No mermaid warbles (to allay the wind
That drives some vessel toward a dangerous beach)
More thrilling melodies! no cavernèd witch,
Chanting a love-spell, ever intertwined
Notes shrill and wild with art more musical!
Alas! that from the lips of abject want
And idleness in tatters mendicant
The strain should flow—enjoyment to enthral,
And with regret and useless pity haunt
This bold this pure, this sky-born *waterfall!*

---

* "The Staub-bach" is a narrow stream, which, after a long course on the heights, comes to the sharp edge of a somewhat overhanging precipice, overleaps it with a bound, and, after a fall of 930 feet, forms again a rivulet The vocal powers of these musical beggars may seem to be exaggerated; but this wild and savage air was utterly unlike any sounds I had ever heard; the notes reached me from a distance, and on what occasion they were sung I could not guess, only they seemed to belong, in some way or other, to the waterfall, and reminded me of religious services chanted to streams and fountains in pagan times Mr Southey has thus accurately characterized the peculiarity of this music: "While we were at the waterfall, some half score peasants, chiefly women and girls, assembled just out of reach of the spring, and set up,—surely, the wildest chorus that ever was heard by human ears,—a song not of articulate sounds, but in which the voice was used as a mere instrument of music, more flexible than any which art could produce,—sweet, powerful, and thrilling beyond description."—See notes to "A Tale of Paraguay"

THE FALL OF THE AAR.—HANDEC.

FROM the fierce aspect of this river throwing
His giant body o'er the steep rock's brink,
Back in astonishment and fear we shrink:
But gradually a calmer look bestowing,
Flowers we espy beside the torrent growing;
Flowers that peep forth from many a cleft and chink,
And, from the whirlwind of his anger drink
Hues ever fresh, in rocky fortress blowing;
They suck, from breath that threatening to destroy
Is more benignant than the dewy eve,
Beauty, and life, and motions as of joy:
Nor doubt but He to whom yon pine-trees nod
Their heads in sign of worship, nature's God,
These humbler adorations will receive.

SCENE ON THE LAKE OF BRIENTZ.

"WHAT know we of the blest above
But that they sing and that they love?"
Yet, if they ever did inspire
A mortal hymn, or shaped the choir,
Now, where those harvest damsels float
Homeward in their rugged boat,
(While all the ruffling winds are fled,
Each slumbering on some mountain's head),
Now, surely, hath that gracious aid
Been felt, that influence is displayed.
Pupils of Heaven, in order stand
The rustic maidens, every hand
Upon a sister's shoulder laid,—
To chant, as glides the boat along,
A simple, but a touching, song;
To chant, as angels do above,
The melodies of peace in love!

ENGELBERG, THE HILL OF ANGELS.

FOR gentlest uses, oft-times nature takes
The work of fancy from her willing hands;
And such a beautiful creation makes
As renders needless spells and magic wands,
And for the boldest tale belief commands.
When first mine eyes beheld that famous hill
The sacred Engelberg;* celestial bands,
With intermingling motions soft and still,
Hung round its top, on wings that changed their hues at will.
Clouds do not name those visitants; they were
The very angels whose authentic lays,
Sung from that heavenly ground in middle air,
Made known the spot where piety should raise
A holy structure to the Almighty's praise.
Resplendent apparition! if in vain
My ears did listen, 'twas enough to gaze;
And watch the slow departure of the train,
Whose skirts the glowing mountain thirsted to detain!

* The convent whose site was pointed out, according to tradition, in this manner, is seated at its base. The architecture of the building is unimpressive, but the situation is worthy of the honour which the imagination of the mountaineers has conferred upon it.

OUR LADY OF THE SNOW.

MEEK Virgin mother, more benign
Than fairest star upon the height
Of thy own mountain† set to keep
Lone vigils through the hours of sleep,
What eye can look upon thy shrine
Untroubled at the sight?

These crowded offerings as they hang
In sign of misery relieved,
Even these, without intent of theirs,
Report of comfortless despairs,
Of many a deep and cureless pang
And confidence deceived.

To thee, in this aërial cleft,
As to a common centre, tend
All sufferings that no longer rest
On mortal succour, all distrest
That pine of human hope bereft,
Nor wish for earthly friend.

And hence, O Virgin mother mild!
Though plenteous flowers around thee blow,
Not only from the dreary strife
Of winter, but the storms of life,
Thee have thy votaries aptly styled
Our Lady of the Snow.

Even for the man who stops not here,
But down the irriguous valley hies,
Thy very name, O lady! flings,
O'er blooming fields and gushing springs,
A holy shadow soft and dear
Of chastening sympathies!

Nor falls that intermingling shade
To summer gladsomeness unkind;
It chastens only to requite
With gleams of fresher, purer light;
While, o'er the flower-enamelled glade,
More sweetly breathes the wind.

† Mount Righi

But on !—a tempting downward way,
A verdant path before us lies ;
Clear shines the glorious sun above ;
Then give free course to joy and love,
Deeming the evil of the day
Sufficient for the wise.

EFFUSION IN PRESENCE OF THE PAINTED TOWER OF TELL, AT ALTORE.

This tower is said to stand upon the spot where grew the linden-tree against which his sou was placed, when the father's archery was put to proof under circumstances so famous in Swiss history.

WHAT though the Italian pencil wrought not here,
Nor such fine skill as did the meed bestow
On Marathonian valour, yet the tear
Springs forth in presence of this gaudy show,
While narrow cares their limits overflow.
Thrice happy, burghers, peasants, warriors old,
Infants in arms, and ye, that as ye go
Home-ward or school-ward, ape what ye behold ;
Heroes before your time, in frolic fancy bold !

But when that calm spectatress from on high
Looks down—the bright and solitary moon,
Who never gazes but to beautify ;
And snow-fed torrents, which the blaze of noon
Roused into fury, murmur a soft tune
That fosters peace, and gentleness recalls ;
Then might the passing monk receive a boon
Of saintly pleasure from these pictured walls,
While, on the warlike groups, the mellowing lustre falls.

How blest the souls who when their trials come
Yield not to terror or despondency,
But face like that sweet boy their mortal doom,
Whose head the ruddy apple tops, while he
Expectant stands beneath the linden tree,
Not quaking like the timid forest game ;
He smiles—the hesitating shaft to free,
Assured that Heaven its justice will proclaim,
And to his father give its own unerring aim.

THE TOWN OF SCHWYTZ.

BY antique fancy trimmed—though lowly, bred
To dignity—in thee, O Schwytz ! are seen
The genuine features of the golden mean ;
Equality by prudence governed,
Or jealous nature ruling in her stead ;
And, therefore, art thou blest with peace, serene
As that of the sweet fields and meadows green
In unambitious compass round thee spread,
Majestic Berne, high on her guardian steep,
Holding a central station of command,
Might well be styled this noble body's head ;
Thou, lodged 'mid mountainous entrenchments deep,
Its heart ; and ever may the heroic land
Thy name, O Schwytz, in happy freedom keep !*

ON HEARING THE "RANZ DES VACHES" ON THE TOP OF THE PASS OF ST. GOTHARD.

I LISTEN—but no faculty of mine
Avails those modulations to detect,
Which, heard in foreign lands, the Swiss affect
With tenderest passion, leaving him to pine
(So fame reports) and die ; his sweet-breathed kine
Remembering, and green Alpine pastures decked
With vernal flowers. Yet may we not reject
The tale as fabulous.—Here while I recline
Mindful how others love this simple strain,
Even here, upon this glorious mountain named
Of God himself from dread pre-eminence—
Aspiring thoughts, by memory reclaimed,
Yield to the music's touching influence,
And joys of distant home my heart enchain.

THE CHURCH OF SAN SALVADOR, SEEN FROM THE LAKE OF LUGANO.

This church was almost destroyed by lightning a few years ago, but the altar and the image of the patron saint were untouched The mount, upon the summit of which the church is built, stands amid the intricacies of the

* Nearly 500 years (says Ebel, speaking of the French invasion) had elapsed, when, for the first time, foreign soldiers were seen upon the frontiers of this small canton, to impose upon it the laws of their governors.

Lake of Lugano: and is, from a hundred points of view, its principal ornament, rising to the height of 2000 feet, and, on one side, nearly perpendicular. The ascent is toilsome, but the traveller who performs it will be amply rewarded. Splendid fertility, rich woods, and dazzling waters, seclusion and confinement of view contrasted with sea-like extent of plain fading into the sky; and this again, in an opposite quarter, with an horizon of the loftiest and boldest Alps—unite in composing a prospect more diversified by magnificence, beauty, and sublimity, than perhaps any other point in Europe of so inconsiderable an elevation commands.

THOU sacred pile! whose turrets rise
From yon steep mountain's loftiest stage,
Guarded by lone San Salvador;
Sink (if thou must) as heretofore,
To sulphurous bolts a sacrifice,
But ne'er to human rage!

On Horeb's top, on Sinai, deigned
To rest the universal lord:
Why leap the fountains from their cells
Where everlasting bounty dwells?
That, while the creature is sustained,
His God may be adored.

Cliffs, fountains, rivers, seasons, times,
Let all remind the soul of heaven;
Our slack devotion needs them all
And faith, so oft of sense the thrall,
While she, by aid of nature, climbs,
May hope to be forgiven.

Glory, and patriotic love,
And all the pomps of this frail "spot
Which men call earth," have yearned to [seek,
Associate with the simply meek,
Religion in the sainted grove,
And in the hallowed grot.

Thither, in times of adverse shocks,
Of fainting hopes and backward wills,
Did mighty Tell repair of old—
A hero cast in nature's mould,
Deliverer of the steadfast rocks
And of the ancient hills!

He, too, of battle-martyrs chief!
Who, to recall his daunted peers,
For victory shaped an open space,
By gathering with a wide embrace,
Into his single heart, a sheaf
Of fatal Austrian spears.*

* Arnold Winkelreid, at the battle of Sempach, broke an Austrian phalanx in this manner.

FORT FUENTES

"The ruins of Fort Fuentes form the crest of a rocky eminence that rises from the plain at the head of the Lake of Como, commanding views up the Valteline, and toward the town of Chiavenna. The prospect in the latter direction is characterized by melancholy sublimity. We rejoiced at being favoured with a distinct view of those Alpine heights; not, as we had expected from the breaking up of the storm, steeped in celestial glory, yet in communion with clouds floating or stationary—scatterings from heaven. The ruin is interesting, both in mass and detail. An inscription upon elaborately-sculptured marble lying on the ground, records that the fort had been erected by Count Fuentes in the year 1600, during the reign of Philip the Third; and the chapel, about twenty years after, by one of his descendants. Marble pillars of gateways are yet standing, and a considerable part of the chapel walls: a smooth green turf has taken the place of the pavement, and we could see no trace of altar or image; but everywhere something to remind one of former splendour, and of devastation and tumult. In our ascent we had passed abundance of wild vines intermingled with bushes: near the ruins were some, ill tended, but growing willingly; and rock, turf, and fragments of the pile, are alike covered or adorned with a variety of flowers, among which the rose-coloured pink was growing in great beauty. While descending, we discovered on the ground, apart from the path, and at a considerable distance from the ruined chapel, a statue of a child in pure white marble, uninjured by the explosion that had driven it so far down the hill. 'How little,' we exclaimed, 'are these things valued here! Could we but transport this pretty image to our own garden!' Yet it seemed it would have been a pity any one should remove it from its couch in the wilderness, which may be its own for hundreds of years."
—*Extract from Journal.*

DREAD hour! when upheaved by war's sulphurous blast, [stone
This sweet-visaged cherub of Parian
So far from the holy inclosure was cast,
To couch in this thicket of brambles alone,

To rest where the lizard may bask in the palm [or speck,
Of his half-open hand pure from blemish
And the green, gilded snake, without troubling the calm [his neck
Of the beautiful countenance, twine round

The event is one of the most famous in the annals of Swiss heroism; and pictures and prints of it are frequent throughout the country.

Where haply (kind service to piety due !)
When winter the grove of its mantle bereaves,
Some bird (like our own honoured redbreast) may strew
The desolate slumberer with moss and with leaves

Fuentes once harboured the good and the brave,
Nor to her was the dance of soft pleasure unknown,
Her banners for festal enjoyment did wave
While the thrill of her fifes through the mountains was blown :

Now gads the wild vine o'er the pathless ascent—
Oh, silence of nature, how deep is thy sway,
When the whirlwind of human destruction is spent,
Our tumults appeased, and our strifes passed away !

THE ITALIAN ITINERANT, AND THE SWISS GOATHERD.

PART I.

Now that the farewell tear is dried,
Heaven prosper thee, be hope thy guide !
Hope be thy guide, adventurous boy ;
The wages of thy travel, joy !
Whether for London bound—to trill
Thy mountain notes with simple skill ;
Or on thy head to poise a show
Of images in seemly row ;
The graceful form of milk-white steed,
Or bird that soared with Ganymede ;
Or through our hamlets thou wilt bear
The sightless Milton, with his hair
Around his placid temples curled ;
And Shakspeare at his side—a freight,
If clay could think and mind were weight,
For him who bore the world !
Hope be thy guide, adventurous boy ;
The wages of thy travel, joy !

But thou, perhaps, (alert and free
Though serving sage philosophy)
Wilt ramble over hill and dale,
A vendor of the well-wrought scale
Whose sentient tube instructs to time
A purpose to a fickle clime ;
Whether thou choose this useful part,
Or minister to finer art,
Though robbed of many a cherished dream,
And crossed by many a shattered scheme,
What stirring wonders wilt thou see
In the proud isle of liberty !
Yet will the wanderer sometimes pine
With thoughts which no delights can chase,
Recal a sister's last embrace,
His mother's neck entwine ;
Nor shall forget the maiden coy
That *would* have loved the bright-haired boy !

My song, encouraged by the grace
That beams from his ingenuous face,
For this adventurer scruples not
To prophesy a golden lot ,
Due recompence, and safe return
To Como's steeps—his happy bourne !
Where he, aloft in garden glade,
Shall tend, with his own dark-eyed maid,
The towering maize, and prop the twig
That ill supports the luscious fig ,
Or feed his eye in paths sun-proof
With purple of the trellis-roof
That through the jealous leaves escapes
From Cadenabbia's pendant grapes.
Oh, might he tempt that goatherd-child
To share his wanderings ! him whose look
Even yet my heart can scarcely brook,
So touchingly he smiled,
As with a rapture caught from heaven,
For unasked alms in pity given.

PART II.

With nodding plumes, and lightly drest
Like foresters in leaf-green vest,
The Helvetian mountaineers, on ground
For Tell's dread archery renowned,
Before the target stood—to claim
The guerdon of the steadiest aim.
Loud was the rifle-gun's report,
A startling thunder quick and short !
But, flying through the heights around,
Echo prolonged a tell-tale sound
Of hearts and hands alike "prepared
The treasures they enjoy to guard ?"
And, if there be a favoured hour
When heroes are allowed to quit
The tomb, and on the clouds to sit
With tutelary power,
On their descendants shedding grace,
This was the hour, and that the place.

But truth inspired the bards of old
When of an iron age they told,
Which to unequal laws gave birth,
That drove Astræa from the earth.
A gentle boy (perchance with blood
As noble as the best endued,
But seemingly a thing despised,
Even by the sun and air unprized,
For not a tinge or flowery streak
Appeared upon his tender cheek

Heart-deaf to those rebounding notes,
Of pleasure, by his silent goats,
Sate far apart in forest shed,
Pale, ragged, bare his feet and head,
Mute as the snow upon the hill,
And, as the saint he prays to, still.
Ah, what avails heroic deed?
What liberty? if no defence
Be won for feeble innocence—
Father of all! though wilful manhood read
His punishment in soul-distress,
Grant to the morn of life its natural blessedness!

THE LAST SUPPER, BY LEONARDO DA VINCI, IN THE REFECTORY OF THE CONVENT OF MARIA DELLA GRAZIA, MILAN.

THOUGH searching damps and many an envious flaw
Have marred this work,* the calm ethereal grace,
The love deep-seated in the Saviour's face,
The mercy, goodness, have not failed to awe
The elements; as they do melt and thaw
The heart of the beholder—and erase
(At least for one rapt moment) every trace
Of disobedience to the primal law.
The annunciation of the dreadful truth
Made to the twelve, survives. lip, forehead, cheek,
And hand reposing on the board in ruth
Of what it utters † while the unguilty seek
Unquestionable meanings, still bespeak
A labour worthy of eternal youth!

THE ECLIPSE OF THE SUN, 1820.

HIGH on her speculative tower
Stood science waiting for the hour
When sol was destined to endure
That darkening of his radiant face
Which superstition strove to chase,
Erewhile, with rites impure.

Afloat beneath Italian skies,
Through regions fair as Paradise
We gaily passed,—till nature wrought
A silent and unlooked-for change,
That checked the desultory range
Of joy and sprightly thought.

Where'er was dipped the toiling oar,
The waves danced round us as before,
As lightly, though of altered hue;
Mid recent coolness, such as falls
At noon-tide from umbrageous walls
That screen the morning dew.

No vapour stretched its wings; no cloud
Cast far or near a murky shroud,
The sky an azure field displayed,
'Twas sunlight sheathed and gently charmed,
Of all its sparkling rays disarmed,
And as in slumber laid —

Or something night and day between,
Like moonshine, but the hue was green,
Still moonshine, without shadow, spread
On jutting rock, and curvèd shore
Where gazed the peasant from his door
And on the mountain's head.

It tinged the Julian steeps—it lay,
Lugano! on thy ample bay,
The solemnizing veil was drawn
O'er villas, terraces, and towers,
To Albogasio's olive bowers
Porlezza's verdant lawn.

But fancy, with the speed of fire,
Hath fled to Milan's loftiest spire,
And there alights 'mid that aerial host
Of figures human and divine,‡
White as the snows of Apennine
Indurated by frost.

* This picture of the Last Supper has not only been grievously injured by time, but parts are said to have been painted over again These niceties may be left to connoisseurs.—I speak of it as I felt The copy exhibited in London some years ago, and the engraving by Morghen, are both admirable: but in the original is a power which neither of those works has attained, or even approached

† "The hand
Sang with the voice, and this the argument."
—MILTON.

‡ The statues ranged round the spire and along the roof of the cathedral of Milan, have been found fault with by persons whose exclusive taste is unfortunate for themselves. It is true that the same expense and labour, judiciously directed to purposes more strictly architectural, might have much heightened the general effect of the building· for, seen from the ground, the statues appear diminutive. But the *coup d'œil*, from the best point of view, which is half way up the spire, must strike an unprejudiced person with admiration and surely the selection and arrangement of the figures is exquisitely fitted to support the religion of the country in the imaginations and feelings of the spectator. It was with great pleasure that I saw, during the two ascents which we made, several children, of different ages, tripping up

Awe-stricken she beholds the array
That guards the temple night and day;
Angels she sees that might from heaven
have flown,
And virgin saints—who not in vain
Have striven by purity to gain
The beatific crown;

Sees long-drawn files, concentric rings
Each narrowing above each;—the
wings—
The uplifted palms, the silent marble lips,
The starry zone of sovereign height,*
All steeped in this portentous light!
All suffering dim eclipse!

Thus after man had fallen, (if aught
These perishable spheres have wrought
May with that issue be compared)
Throngs of celestial visages,
Darkening like water in the breeze,
A holy sadness shared.

Lo! while I speak, the labouring sun
His glad deliverance has begun:
The cypress waves its sombre plume
More cheerily; and town and tower,
The vineyard and the olive bower,
Their lustre re-assume!

O ye, who guard and grace my home
While in far-distant lands we roam,
Was such a vision given to you?
Or, while we looked with favoured eyes,
Did sullen mist hide lake and skies
And mountains from your view?

I ask in vain—and know far less
If sickness, sorrow, or distress
Have spared my dwelling to this hour:
Sad blindness, but ordained to prove
Our faith in Heaven's unfailing love
And all-controlling power.

THE THREE COTTAGE GIRLS.

How blest the maid whose heart—yet free
From love's uneasy sovereignty,
Beats with a fancy running high
Her simple cares to magnify.
Whom labour, never urged to toil,
Hath cherished on a healthful soil,
Who knows not pomp, who heeds not pelf,
Whose heaviest sin it is to look
Askance upon her pretty self
Reflected in some crystal brook;
Whom grief hath spared—who sheds no tear
But in sweet pity; and can hear
Another's praise from envy clear.

Such, (but, O lavish nature! why
That dark unfathomable eye,
Where lurks a spirit that replies
To stillest mood of softest skies,
Yet hints at peace to be o'erthrown,
Another's first, and then her own?)
Such, haply, yon Italian maid,
Our lady's laggard votaress,
Halting beneath the chestnut shade
To accomplish there her loveliness:
Nice aid maternal fingers lend;
A sister serves with slacker hand;
Then, glittering like a star, she joins the
festal band.

How blest (if truth may entertain
Coy fancy with a bolder strain)
The Helvetian girl—who daily braves,
In her light skiff, the tossing waves,
And quits the bosom of the deep
Only to climb the rugged steep?
Say whence that modulated shout?
From wood-nymph of Diana's throng?
Or does the greeting to a rout
Of giddy bacchanals belong?
Jubilant outcry!—rock and glade
Resounded—but the voice obeyed
The breath of an Helvetian maid.

Her beauty dazzles the thick wood;
Her courage animates the flood;
Her step the elastic green-sward meets
Returning unreluctant sweets;
The mountains (as ye heard) rejoice
Aloud, saluted by her voice!
Blithe paragon of Alpine grace,
Be as thou art—for through thy veins
The blood of heroes runs its race!
And nobly wilt thou brook the chains
That, for the virtuous, life prepares;
The fetters which the matron wears;
The patriot mother's weight of anxious
cares!

"Sweet Highland girl! a very shower†
Of beauty was thy earthly dower,"

---

and down the slender spire, and pausing to look around them, with feelings much more animated than could have been derived from these, or the finest works of art if placed within easy reach. Remember also that you have the Alps on one side, and on the other the Apennines, with the Plain of Lombardy between!

* Above the highest circle of figures is a zone of metallic stars.

† See Address to a Highland Girl, p. 147.

When thou didst pass before my eyes,
Gay vision under sullen skies,
While hope and love around thee played,
Near the rough Falls of Inversnaid!
Time cannot thin thy flowing hair,
Nor take one ray of light from thee;
For in my fancy thou dost share
The gift of immortality;
And there shall bloom, with thee allied,
The votaress by Lugano's side;
And that intrepid nymph, on Uri's steep, descried!

THE COLUMN, INTENDED BY BONAPARTE FOR A TRIUMPHAL EDIFICE IN MILAN, NOW LYING BY THE WAY-SIDE IN THE SIMPLON PASS.

AMBITION, following down this far-famed slope
Her pioneer, the snow-dissolving sun,
While clarions prate of kingdoms to be won,
Perchance in future ages here may stop;
Taught to mistrust her flattering horoscope
By admonition from this prostrate stone;
Memento uninscribed of pride o'erthrown,
Vanity's hieroglyphic; a choice trope
In fortune's rhetoric. Daughter of the rock,
Rest where thy course was stayed by power divine!
The soul transported sees, from hint of thine,
Crimes which the great Avenger's hand provoke,
Hears combats whistling o'er the ensanguined heath;
What groans! what shrieks! what quietness in death!

STANZAS COMPOSED IN THE SIMPLON PASS.

VALLOMBROSA! I longed in thy shadiest wood
To slumber, reclined on the moss-covered floor,
To listen to Anio's precipitous flood,
When the stillness of evening hath deepened its roar;
To range through the temples of Pæstum, to muse
In Pompeii, preserved by her burial in earth:
On pictures to gaze, where they drank in their hues;
And murmur sweet songs on the ground of their birth!

The beauty of Florence, the grandeur of Rome,
Could I leave them unseen, and not yield to regret?
With a hope (and no more) for a season to come,
Which ne'er may discharge the magnificent debt?
Thou fortunate region! whose greatness inurned,
Awoke to new life from its ashes and dust;
Twice-glorified-fields! if in sadness I turned
From your infinite marvels, the sadness was just.

Now, risen ere the light-footed chamois retires
From dew-sprinkled grass to heights guarded with snow,
Toward the mists that hang over the land of my sires,
From the climate of myrtles contented I go.
My thoughts become bright like yon edging of pines,
How black was its hue in the region of air!
But, touched from behind by the sun, it now shines
With threads that seem part of his own silver hair.

Though the burthen of toil with dear friends we divide,
Though by the same zephyr our temples are fanned
As we rest in the cool orange-bower side by side,
A yearning survives which few hearts shall withstand:
Each step hath its value while homeward we move;—
Oh, joy, when the girdle of England appears!
What moment in life is so conscious of love,
So rich in the tenderest sweetness of tears?

ECHO UPON THE GEMMI.

WHAT beast of chase hath broken from the cover?
Stern Gemmi listens to as full a cry,
As multitudinous a harmony,
As e'er did ring the heights of Latmos over,
When, from the soft couch of her sleeping lover,
Up-starting, Cynthia skimmed the mountain-dew
In keen pursuit—and gave, where'er she flew,
Impetuous motion to the stars above her.
A solitary wolf-dog, ranging on
Through the bleak concave, wakes this wondrous chime
Of aëry voices locked in unison,—
Faint—far off—near—deep—solemn and sublime!
So, from the body of one guilty deed,
A thousand ghostly fears, and haunting thoughts, proceed!

PROCESSIONS. SUGGESTED ON A SABBATH MORNING IN THE VALE OF CHAMOUNY.

To appease the gods, or public thanks to yield;
Or to solicit knowledge of events,
Which in her breast futurity concealed,
And that the past might have its true intents
Feelingly told by living monuments,
Mankind of yore were prompted to devise
Rites such as yet Persepolis presents
Graven on her cankered walls,—solemnities
That moved in long array before admiring eyes.

The Hebrews thus, carrying in joyful state
Thick boughs of palm, and willows from the brook,
Marched round the altar—to commemorate
How, when their course they through the desert took,
Guided by signs which ne'er the sky forsook,
They lodged in leafy tents and cabins low;
Green boughs were borne, while for the blast that shook
Down to the earth the walls of Jericho,
These shout hosannas,—these the startling trumpets blow!

And thus, in order, 'mid the sacred grove
Fed in the Libyan waste by gushing wells,
The priests and damsels of Ammonian Jove
Provoked responses with shrill canticles;
While, in a ship begirt with silver bells,
They round the altar bore the horned god,
Old Cham, the solar deity, who dwells
Aloft, yet in a tilting vessel rode,
When universal sea the mountains overflowed.

Why speak of Roman pomps? the haughty claims
Of chiefs triumphant after ruthless wars;
The feast of Neptune—and the cereal games,
With images, and crowns, and empty cars;
The dancing Salii—on the shields of Mars
Smiting with fury; and the deeper dread
Scattered on all sides by the hideous jars
Of Corybantian cymbals, while the head
Of Cybelè was seen, sublimely turreted!

At length a spirit more subdued and soft
Appeared to govern Christian pageantries
The cross, in calm processions, borne aloft
Moved to the chant of sober litanies
Even such, this day, came wafted on the breeze [fair
From a long train—in hooded vestments
Enwrapt—and winding, between Alpine trees [prayer
Spiry and dark, around their house of
Below the icy bed of bright Argentiere.

Still, in the vivid freshness of a dream,
The pageant haunts me as it met our eyes!
Still, with those white-robed shapes—a living stream,
The glacier pillars join in solemn guise.*
For the same service by mysterious ties;
Numbers exceeding credible account
Of number, pure and silent votaries
Issuing or issued from a wintry fount;
The impenetrable heart of that exalted mount!

They too, who send so far a holy gleam
While they the church engird with motion slow,
A product of that awful mountain seem,
Poured from its vaults of everlasting snow;
Not virgin-lilies marshalled in bright row,
Not swans descending with the stealthy tide,
A livelier sisterly resemblance show
Than the fair forms that in long order glide,
Bear to the glacier band—those shapes aloft descried!

Trembling, I look upon the secret springs
Of that licentious craving in the mind
To act the God among external things,
To bind, on apt suggestion, or unbind;
And marvel not that antique faith inclined
To crowd the world with metamorphosis,
Vouchsafed in pity or in wrath assigned·
Such insolent temptations wouldst thou miss, [dark abyss!
Avoid these sights; nor brood o'er fable's

---

* This procession is a part of the sacramental service performed once a month In the valley of Engelberg we had the good fortune to be present at the *grand festival* of the virgin—but the procession on that day, though consisting of upwards of 1000 persons, assembled from all the branches of the sequestered valley, was much less striking (notwithstanding the sublimity of the surrounding scenery) it wanted both the simplicity of the other, and the accompaniment of the glacier columns, whose sisterly resemblance to the *moving* figures gave it a most beautiful and solemn peculiarity.

ELEGIAC STANZAS.

The lamented youth whose untimely death gave occasion to these elegiac verses, was Frederick William Goddard, from Boston in North America. He was in his twentieth year, and had resided for some time with a clergyman in the neighbourhood of Geneva for the completion of his education. Accompanied by a fellow-pupil, a native of Scotland, he had just set out on a Swiss tour when it was his misfortune to fall in with a friend of mine who was hastening to join our party. The travellers, after spending a day together on the road from Berne and at Soleure, took leave of each other at night, the young man having intended to proceed directly to Zurich. But early in the morning my friend found his new acquaintances, who were informed of the object of his journey, and the friends he was in pursuit of, equipped to accompany him. We met at Lucerne the succeeding evening, and Mr G and his fellow-student became in consequence our travelling companions for a couple of days We ascended the Righi together; and, after contemplating the sunrise from that noble mountain, we separated at an hour and on a spot well suited to the parting of those who were to meet no more Our party descended through the valley of our Lady of the Snow, and our late companions, to Art We had hoped to meet in a few weeks at Geneva. but on the third succeeding day (on the 21st of August) Mr Goddard perished, being overset in a boat while crossing the lake of Zurich His companion saved himself by swimming. and was hospitably received in the mansion of a Swiss gentleman (Mr Keller) situated on the eastern coast of the lake. The corpse of poor G was cast ashore on the estate of the said gentleman, who generously performed all the rites of hospitality which could be rendered to the dead as well as to the living He caused the handsome mural monument to be erected in the church at Küsnacht, which records the premature fate of the young American, and on the shores too of the lake the traveller may read an inscription pointing out the spot where the body was deposited by the waves.

LULLED by the sound of pastoral bells,
Rude nature's pilgrims did we go,
From the dread summit of the Queen*
Of mountains through a deep ravine,
Where, in her holy chapel, dwells
'Our Lady of the Snow.'

The sky was blue, the air was mild;
Free were the streams and green the bowers:
As if, to rough assaults unknown,
The genial spot had *ever* shown
A countenance that sweetly smiled—
The face of summer-hours.

And we were gay, our hearts at ease;
With pleasure dancing through the frame
We journeyed. all we knew of care—
Our path that straggled here and there,
Of trouble—but the fluttering breeze,
Of winter—but a name.

If foresight could have rent the veil
Of three short days—but hush—no more
Calm is the grave, and calmer none
Than that to which thy cares are gone,
Thou victim of the stormy gale,
Asleep on Zurich's shore!

O Goddard! what art thou?—a name—
A sunbeam followed by a shade!
No more, for aught that time supplies,
The great, the experienced, and the wise
Too much from this frail earth we claim,
And therefore are betrayed.

We met, while festive mirth ran wild,
Where, from a deep lake's mighty urn,
Forth slips, like an enfranchised slave,
A sea-green river, proud to lave,
With current swift and undefiled,
The towers of old Lucerne.

We parted upon solemn ground
Far lifted towards the unfading sky;
But all our thoughts were *then* of earth
That gives to common pleasures birth;
And nothing in our hearts we found
That prompted even a sigh.

Fetch, sympathising powers of air,
Fetch, ye that post o'er seas and lands,
Herbs moistened by Virginian dew,
A most untimely sod to strew,
That lacks the ornamental care
Of kindred human hands!

Beloved by every gentle muse
He left his Transatlantic home:
Europe, a realized romance,
Had opened on his eager glance;
What present bliss!—what golden views!
What stores for years to come!

Though lodged within no vigorous frame,
His soul her daily task renewed,
Blithe as the lark on sun-gilt wings
High poised—or as the wren that sings
In shady places to proclaim
Her modest gratitude.

Not vain is sadly-uttered praise;
The words of truth's memorial vow

* Mount Righi—Regina Montium.

Are sweet as morning fragrance shed
From flowers 'mid Goldau's* ruins bred,
As evening's fondly-lingering rays,
On Righi's silent brow

Lamented youth! to thy cold clay
Fit obsequies the stranger paid,
And piety shall guard that stone
Which hath not left the spot unknown
Where the wild waves resigned their prey,
And *that* which marks thy bed.

And, when thy mother weeps for thee,
Lost youth! a solitary mother,
This tribute from a casual friend
A not unwelcome aid may lend,
To feed the tender luxury,
The rising pang to smother.

SKY-PROSPECT. FROM THE PLAIN OF FRANCE.

Lo! in the burning west, the craggy nape
Of a proud Ararat! and, thereupon,
The ark, her melancholy voyage done!
Yon rampant cloud mimics a lion's shape,
There—combats a huge crocodile—agape
A golden spear to swallow! and that brown
And massy grove, so near yon blazing town,
Stirs—and recedes—destruction to escape!
Yet all is harmless as the Elysian shades
Where spirits dwell in undisturbed repose,
Silently disappears, or quickly fades,—
Meek nature's evening comment on the
shows
That for oblivion take their daily birth,
From all the fuming vanities of earth!

ON BEING STRANDED NEAR THE HARBOUR OF BOULOGNE.†

Why cast ye back upon the Gallic shore,
Ye furious waves! a patriotic son
Of England—who in hope her coast had
won, [o'er?
His project crowned, his pleasant travel
Well—let him pace this noted beach once
more,
That gave the Roman his triumphal shells;
That saw the Corsican his cap and bells
Haughtily shake, a dreaming conqueror!
Enough, my country's cliffs I can behold,
And proudly think, beside the murmuring
sea,
Of checked ambition, tyranny controlled,
And folly cursed with endless memory
These local recollections ne'er can cloy,
Such ground I from my very heart enjoy!

AFTER LANDING. THE VALLEY OF DOVER —NOV 1820.

Where be the noisy followers of the game
Which faction breeds? the turmoil where?
that past [man's blast,
Through Europe, echoing from the news
And filled our hearts with grief for England's
shame. [aim
Peace greets us;—rambling on without an
We mark majestic herds of cattle free
To ruminate‡ couched on the grassy lea,
And hear far-off the mellow horn proclaim
The season's harmless pastime Ruder
sound
Stirs not; enrapt I gaze with strange delight,
While consciousnesses, not to be disowned,
Here only serve a feeling to invite
That lifts the spirit to a calmer height,
And makes the rural stillness more profound.

DESULTORY STANZAS,
UPON RECEIVING THE PRECEDING SHEETS FROM THE PRESS.

Is then the final page before me spread,
Nor further outlet left to mind or heart?
Presumptuous book! too forward to be
read—
How can I give thee licence to depart?
One tribute more,—unbidden feelings start
Forth from their coverts—slighted objects
rise—
My spirit is the scene of such wild art

---

* One of the villages desolated by the fall of part of the mountain Rossberg.

† Near the town of Boulogne, and overhanging the beach, are the remains of a tower which bears the name of Caligula, who here terminated his western expedition, of which these sea-shells were the boasted spoils And at no great distance from these ruins, Bonaparte, standing upon a mound of earth, harangued his "army of England," reminded them of the exploits of Cæsar, and pointed towards the white cliffs upon which their standards *were to float* He recommended also a subscription to be raised among the soldiery to erect on that ground, in memory of the foundation of the "Legion of Honour," a column—which was not completed at the time we were there

‡ This is a most grateful sight for an Englishman returning to his native land Everywhere one misses, in the cultivated grounds abroad, the animating and soothing accompaniment of animals ranging and selecting their own food at will

As on Parnassus rules, when lightning flies,
Visibly leading on the thunder's harmonies.

All that I saw returns upon my view,
All that I heard comes back upon my ear,
All that I felt this moment doth renew;
And where the foot with no unmanly fear
Recoiled—and wings alone could travel—there
I move at ease, and meet contending themes
That press upon me, crossing the career
Of recollections vivid as the dreams
Of midnight,—cities—plains—forests—and mighty streams

Where mortal never breathed I dare to sit
Among the interior Alps, gigantic crew,
Who triumphed o'er diluvian power!—and yet
What are they but a wreck and residue,
Whose only business is to perish?—true
To which sad course, these wrinkled sons of time
Labour their proper greatness to subdue;
Speaking of death alone, beneath a clime
Where life and rapture flow in plenitude sublime

Fancy hath flung for me an airy bridge
Across thy long deep valley, furious Rhone!
Arch that *here* rests upon the granite ridge
Of Monte Rosa—*there* on frailer stone
Of secondary birth—the Jungfrau's cone;
And, from that arch, down-looking on the vale
The aspect I behold of every zone;
A sea of foliage tossing with the gale,
Blithe autumn's purple crown, and winter's icy mail!

Far as St. Maurice, from yon eastern forks,*
Down the main avenue my sight can range.
And all its branchy vales, and all that lurks
Within them, church, and town, and huts and grange,
For my enjoyment meet in vision strange;
Snows—torrents;—to the region's utmost bound,
Life, death, in amicable interchange—
But list! the avalanche—the hush profound
That follows, yet more awful than that awful sound!

* Les Fourches, the point at which the two chains of mountains part, that inclose the Valais, which terminates at St Maurice.

Is not the chamois suited to his place?
The eagle worthy of her ancestry?
Let empires fall; but ne'er shall ye disgrace
Your noble birthright, ye that occupy
Your council-seats beneath the open sky,
On Sarnen's Mount,† there judge if fit and right,
In simple democratic majesty:
Soft breezes fanning your rough brows—the might
And purity of nature spread before your sight!

From this appropriate court, renowned Lucerne
Calls me to pace her honoured bridge‡ that cheers
The patriot's heart with pictures rude and stern,
An uncouth chronicle of glorious years.
Like portraiture, from loftier source, endears
That work of kindred frame, which spans the lake
Just at the point of issue, where it fears
The form and motion of a stream to take;
Where it begins to stir, *yet* voiceless as a snake.

Volumes of sound, from the cathedral rolled,
This long-roofed vista penetrate—but see,

† Sarnen, one of the two capitals of the Canton of Underwalden; the spot here alluded to is close to the town, and is called the Landenberg, from the tyrant of that name, whose chateau formerly stood there. On the 1st of January, 1308, the great day which the confederated heroes had chosen for the deliverance of their country, all the castles of the governors were taken by force or stratagem; and the tyrants themselves conducted, with their creatures, to the frontiers, after having witnessed the destruction of their strongholds. From that time the Landenberg has been the place where the legislators of this division of the Canton assemble. The site, which is well described by Ebel, is one of the most beautiful in Switzerland.

‡ The bridges of Lucerne are roofed, and open at the sides, so that the passenger has, at the same time the benefit of shade, and a view of the magnificent country. The pictures are attached to the rafters; those from Scripture history on the cathedral-bridge, amount, according to my notes to 240. Subjects from the Old Testament face the passenger as he goes towards the cathedral, and those from the New as he returns. The pictures on these bridges, as well as those in most other parts of Switzerland, are not to be spoken of as works of art; but they are instruments admirably answering the purpose for which they were designed.

One after one, its tablets, that unfold
The whole design of Scripture history,
From the first tasting of the fatal tree,
Till the bright star appeared in eastern skies,
Announcing ONE was born mankind to free;
His acts, his wrongs, his final sacrifice;
Lessons for every heart, a Bible for all eyes

Our pride misleads, our timid likings kill
Long may these homely works devised of old,
These simple efforts of Helvetian skill,
Aid, with congenial influence, to uphold
The state,—the country's destiny to mould;
Turning, for them who pass, the common dust
Of servile opportunity to gold,
Filling the soul with sentiments august—
The beautiful, the brave, the holy, and the just!

No more,—time halts not in his noiseless march— [flood,
Nor turns, nor winds, as doth the liquid
Life slips from underneath us, like that arch
Of airy workmanship whereon we stood,
Earth stretched below, heaven in our neighbourhood.
Go forth, my little book! pursue thy way,
Go forth, and please the gentle and the good;
Nor be a whisper stifled, if it say
That treasures, yet untouched, may grace some future lay.

TO ENTERPRISE *

KEEP for the young the impassioned smile
Shed from thy countenance, as I see thee stand
High on a chalky cliff of Britain's Isle,
A slender volume grasping in thy hand—
(Perchance the pages that relate
The various turns of Crusoe's fate).
Ah! spare the exulting smile,
And drop thy pointing finger bright
As the first flash of beacon-light,
But neither veil thy head in shadows dim,
Nor turn thy face away
From one who, in the evening of his day,
To thee would offer no presumptuous hymn!

Bold spirit! who art free to rove
Among the starry courts of Jove,
And oft in splendour dost appear
Embodied to poetic eyes,
While traversing this nether sphere,
Where mortals call thee Enterprise
Daughter of Hope! her favourite child
Whom she to young Ambition bore,
When hunter's arrow first defiled
The grove, and stained the turf with gore
Thee winged Fancy took, and nursed
On broad Euphrates' palmy shore,
Or where the mightier waters burst
From caves of Indian mountains hoar!
She wrapped thee in a panther's skin,
And thou, whose earliest thoughts held dear
Allurements that were edged with fear,
(The food that pleased thee best, to win)
From rocky fortress in mid air
The flame-eyed eagle oft wouldst scare
With infant shout,—as often sweep,
Paired with the ostrich, o'er the plain;
And, tired with sport, wouldst sink asleep
Upon the couchant lion's mane!
With rolling years thy strength increased!
And, far beyond thy native East,
To thee, by varying titles known,
As variously thy power was shown,
Did incense-bearing altars rise,
Which caught the blaze of sacrifice,
From suppliants panting for the skies!

What though this ancient earth be trod
No more by step of demi-god,
Mounting from glorious deed to deed
As thou from clime to clime didst lead,
Yet still, the bosom beating high,
And the hushed farewell of an eye
Where no procrastinating gaze
A last infirmity betrays,
Prove that thy heaven-descended sway
Shall ne'er submit to cold decay.
By thy divinity impelled,
The stripling seeks the tented field;
The aspiring virgin kneels, and, pale
With awe, receives the hallowed veil,
A soft and tender heroine
Vowed to severer discipline;
Inflamed by thee, the blooming boy
Makes of the whistling shrouds a toy,
And of the ocean's dismal breast
A playground and a couch of rest;
Thou to his dangers dost enchain,
'Mid the blank world of snow and ice,
The chamois-chaser, awed in vain
By chasm or dizzy precipice;
And hast thou not with triumph seen
How soaring mortals glide serene

* This poem having risen out of the "Italian Itinerant," etc., (page 197), it is here annexed

From cloud to cloud, and brave the light
With bolder than Icarian flight?
Or, in their bells of crystal dive
Where winds and waters cease to strive,
For no unholy visitings,
Among the monsters of the deep,
And all the sad and precious things
Which there in ghastly silence sleep;
Within our fearless reach are placed
The secrets of the burning waste,—
Egyptian tombs unlock their dead,
Nile trembles at his fountain head;
Thou speak'st—and lo! the polar seas
Unbosom their last mysteries.
But oh! what transports, what sublime reward,
Won from the world of mind, dost thou prepare
For philosophic sage—or high-souled bard
Who, for thy service trained in lonely woods,
Hath fed on pageants floating through the air,
Or calentured in depth of limpid floods;
Nor grieves—though doomed, through silent night, to bear
The domination of his glorious themes,
Or struggle in the net-work of thy dreams!

If there be movements in the patriot's soul,
From source still deeper, and of higher worth,
'Tis thine the quickening impulse to control,
And in due season send the mandate forth;
Thy call an abject nation can restore,
When but a single mind resolves to crouch no more.

Dread minister of wrath!
Who to their destined punishment dost urge
The Pharaohs of the earth, the men of hardened heart!
Not unassisted by the flattering stars,
Thou strew'st temptation o'er the path
When they in pomp depart,
With trampling horses and refulgent cars—
Soon to be swallowed by the briny surge;
Or cast, for lingering death, on unknown strands:
Or stifled under weight of desert sands—
An army now, and now a living hill
Heaving with convulsive throes.—
It quivers—and is still;
Or to forget their madness and their woes,
Wrapt in a winding-sheet of spotless snows!

Back flows the willing current of my song:
If to provoke such doom the impious dare.
Why should it daunt a blameless prayer?
Bold goddess! range our youth among;
Nor let thy genuine impulse fail to beat
In hearts no longer young;
Still may a veteran few have pride
In thoughts whose sternness makes them sweet;
In fixed resolves by reason justified;
That to their object cleave like sleet
Whitening a pine-tree's northern side,
While fields are naked far and wide.

But, if such homage thou disdain
As doth with mellowing years agree,
One rarely absent from thy train
More humble favours may obtain
For thy contented votary
She, who incites the frolic lambs
In presence of their heedless dams,
And to the solitary fawn
Vouchsafes her lessons—bounteous nymph
That wakes the breeze—the sparkling lymph
Doth hurry to the lawn;
She, who inspires that strain of joyance holy
Which the sweet bird, misnamed the melancholy
Pours forth in shady groves, shall plead for me,
And vernal mornings opening bright
With views of undefined delight,
And cheerful songs, and suns that shine
On busy days, with thankful nights, be mine.

But thou, O goddess! in thy favourite isle
(Freedom's impregnable redoubt,
The wide earth's store-house fenced about
With breakers roaring to the gales
That stretch a thousand thousand sails)
Quicken the slothful, and exalt the vile!
Thy impulse is thy life of fame;
Glad hope would almost cease to be
If torn from thy society;
And love, when worthiest of the name,
Is proud to walk the earth with thee!

Ecclesiastical Sketches.*

"A verse may catch a wandering soul, that flies
Profounder tracts, and by a blest surprise
Convert delight into a sacrifice"

ADVERTISEMENT

During the month of December, 1820, I accompanied a much loved and honoured friend in a walk through different parts of his estate, with a view to fix upon the site of a new church which he intended to erect It was one of the most beautiful mornings of a mild season,—our feelings were in harmony with the cherishing influences of the scene, and, such being our purpose, we were naturally led to look back upon past events with wonder and gratitude, and on the future with hope Not long afterwards some of the sonnets which will be found towards the close of this series were produced as a private memorial of that morning's occupation

The Catholic question, which was agitated in Parliament about that time, kept my thoughts in the same course, and it struck me that certain points in the ecclesiastical history of the country might advantageously be presented to view in verse Accordingly I took up the subject, and what I now offer to the reader was the result

When the work was far advanced, I was agreeably surprised to find that my friend, Mr Southey, was engaged, with similar views, in writing a concise history of the Church *in* England If our productions, thus unintentionally coinciding, shall be found to illustrate each other, it will prove a high gratification to me, which I am sure my friend will participate

W. WORDSWORTH.

Rydal Mount, *January* 24, 1822.

PART I.

FROM THE INTRODUCTION OF CHRISTIANITY INTO BRITAIN, TO THE CONSUMMATION OF THE PAPAL DOMINION.

INTRODUCTION.

I who accompanied with faithful pace
Cerulean Duddon from his cloud-fed spring,
And loved with spirit ruled by his to sing
Of mountain-quiet and boon nature's grace;
I, who essayed the nobler stream to trace
Of liberty, and smote the plausive string
Till the checked torrent, proudly triumphing,
Won for herself a lasting resting-place:
Now seek upon the heights of time the source
Of a Holy River, on whose banks are found
Sweet pastoral flowers, and laurels that have crowned
Full oft the unworthy brow of lawless force;
Where, for the delight of him who tracks its course,
Immortal amaranth and palms abound.

CONJECTURES.

If there be prophets on whose spirits rest
Past things, revealed like future, they can tell
What powers, presiding o'er the sacred well
Of Christian faith, this savage island blessed
With its first bounty. Wandering through the west,
Did holy Paul† a while in Britain dwell,

* For the convenience of passing from one point of the subject to another without shocks of abruptness, this work has taken the shape of a series of sonnets; but the reader, it is hoped, will find that the pictures are often so closely connected as to have the effect of a poem in a form of stanza, to which there is no objection but one that bears on the poet only—its difficulty.

† Stillingfleet adduces many arguments in support of this opinion, but they are unconvin-

And call the fountain forth by miracle,
And with dread signs the nascent stream invest? [prison doors
Or he, whose bonds dropped off, whose
Flew open, by an angel's voice unbarred?
Or some of humbler name, to these wild shores [woe
Storm-driven, who, having seen the cup of
Pass from their master, sojourned here to guard [flow?
The precious current they had taught to

TREPIDATION OF THE DRUIDS.

SCREAMS round the arch-druid's brow the seamew*—white [ring
As Menai's foam; and towards the mystic
Where augurs stand, the future questioning,
Slowly the cormorant aims her heavy flight,
Portending ruin to each baleful rite,
That, in the lapse of ages hath crept o'er
Diluvian truths, and patriarchal lore.
Haughty the bard;—can these meek doctrines blight
His transports? wither his heroic strains?
But all shall be fulfilled;—the Julian spear
A way first opened: and, with Roman chains,
The tidings come of Jesus crucified;
They come—they spread—the weak, the suffering, hear;
Receive the faith, and in the hope abide.

DRUIDICAL EXCOMMUNICATION.

MERCY and love have met thee on thy road,
Thou wretched outcast, from the gift of fire
And food cut off by sacerdotal ire,
From every sympathy that man bestowed!
Yet shall it claim our reverence, that to God,
Ancient of days! that to the eternal Sire
These jealous ministers of law aspire,
As to the one sole fount whence wisdom flowed,
Justice and order. Tremblingly escaped,
As if with prescience of the coming storm,
That intimation when the stars were shaped, [truth
And still, 'mid yon thick woods, the primal
Glimmers through many a superstitious form
That fills the soul with unavailing ruth.

UNCERTAINTY.

DARKNESS surrounds us; seeking, we are lost [coves,
On Snowdon's wilds, amid Brigantian
Or where the solitary shepherd roves
Along the plain of Sarum, by the ghost
Of time and shadows of tradition, crost;
And where the boatman of the Western isles [piles
Slackens his course—to mark those holy
Which yet survive on bleak Iona's coast.
Nor these, nor monuments of eldest fame
Nor Taliesin's unforgotten lays,
Nor characters of Greek or Roman fame,
To an unquestionable source have led;
Enough—if eyes that sought the fountain-head,
In vain, upon the growing rill may gaze.

PERSECUTION.

LAMENT! for Diocletian's fiery sword
Works busy as the lightning; but instinct
With malice ne'er to deadliest weapon linked,
Which God's ethereal storehouses afford:
Against the followers of the incarnate Lord
It rages;—some are smitten in the field—
Some pierced beneath the ineffectual shield
Of sacred home;—with pomp are others gored
And dreadful respite. Thus was Alban tried,
England's first martyr, whom no threats could shake;
Self-offered victim, for his friend he died,
And for the faith—nor shall his name forsake [rise†
That hill, whose flowery platform seems to
By nature decked for holiest sacrifice.

cing. The latter part of this sonnet refers to a favourite notion of Catholic writers, that Joseph of Arimathea and his companions brought Christianity into Britain, and built a rude church at Glastonbury; alluded to hereafter, in a passage upon the dissolution of monasteries.

* This water-fowl was, among the Druids, an emblem of those traditions connected with the deluge that made an important part of their mysteries. The cormorant was a bird of bad omen.

† This hill at St. Alban's must have been an object of great interest to the imagination of the venerable Bede, who thus describes it with a delicate feeling delightful to meet with in that rude age, traces of which are frequent in his works:—"Variis herbarum floribus depictus imò usquequaque vestitus, in quo nihil repentè arduum, nihil præceps, nihil abruptum, quem

RECOVERY.

As, when a storm hath ceased, the birds regain
Their cheerfulness, and busily retrim
Their nests, or chant a gratulating hymn
To the blue ether and bespangled plain,
Even so, in many a reconstructed fane,
Have the survivors of this storm renewed
Their holy rites with vocal gratitude.
And solemn ceremonial they ordain
To celebrate their great deliverance;
Most feelingly instructed 'mid their fear,
That persecution, blind with rage extreme,
May not the less, through Heaven's mild countenance,
Even in her own despite, both feed and cheer,
For all things are less dreadful than they seem.

TEMPTATIONS FROM ROMAN REFINEMENTS

WATCH, and be firm! for soul-subduing vice,
Heart-killing luxury, on your steps await.
Fair houses, baths, and banquets delicate
And temples flashing, bright as polar ice,
Their radiance through the woods, may yet suffice
To sap your hardy virtue, and abate
Your love of Him upon whose forehead sate
The crown of thorns; whose life-blood flowed, the price
Of your redemption. Shun the insidious arts
That Rome provides, less dreading from her frown
Than from her wily praise, her peaceful gown,
Language and letters;—these, though fondly viewed
As humanizing graces, are but parts
And instruments of deadliest servitude!

DISSENSIONS.

THAT heresies should strike (if truth be scanned
Presumptuously) their roots both wide and deep
Is natural as dreams to feverish sleep.
Lo! Discord at the altar dares to stand
Uplifting toward high heaven her fiery brand,
A cherished priestess of the new-baptized!
But chastisement shall follow peace despised.
The Pictish cloud darkens the enervate land
By Rome abandoned, vain are suppliant cries,
And prayers that would undo her forced farewell,
For she returns not.—Awed by her own knell,
She casts the Britons upon strange allies,
Soon to become more dreaded enemies
Than heartless misery called them to repel.

STRUGGLE OF THE BRITONS AGAINST THE BARBARIANS.

RISE!—they *have* risen: of brave Aneurin ask
How they have scourged old foes, perfidious friends:
The spirit of Caractacus defends
The patriots, animates their glorious task,—
Amazement runs before the towering casque
Of Arthur, bearing through the stormy field
The Virgin sculptured on his Christian shield —
Stretched in the sunny light of victory bask
The hosts that followed Urien as he strode
O'er heaps of slain;—from Cambrian wood and moss
Druids descend, auxiliars of the Cross;
Bards, nursed on blue Plinlimmon's still abode,
Rush on the fight, to harps preferring swords,
And everlasting deeds to burning words!

SAXON CONQUEST.

NOR wants the cause the panic-striking aid
Of hallelujahs* tost from hill to hill—
For instant victory. But Heaven's high will
Permits a second and a darker shade
Of pagan light. Afflicted and dismayed,
The relics of the sword flee to the mountains:
O wretched land! whose tears have flowed like fountains;
Whose arts and honours in the dust are laid,
By men yet scarcely conscious of a care
For other monuments than those of earth,†
Who, as the fields and woods have given them birth,

laterıbus longè latèque deductum in modum æquoris natura complanat, dignum videlicet cum pro insita sibi specie venustatis jam olim reddens, qui beati martyris cruore dicaretur "

* Alluding to the victory gained under Germanus.—See Bede.

† The last six lines of this sonnet are chiefly from the prose of Daniel; and here I will state (though to the readers whom this poem will chiefly interest it is unnecessary), that my obli-

Will build their savage fortunes only there,
Content, if foss, and barrow, and the girth
Of long-drawn rampart, witness what they were.

MONASTERY OF OLD BANGOR.*

THE *oppression of the tumult—wrath and scorn—*
The tribulation—and the gleaming blades—
Such is the impetuous spirit that pervades
The song of Taliesin,†—Ours shall mourn
The *unarmed* host who by their prayers would turn
The sword from Bangor's walls, and guard the store
Of aboriginal and Roman lore,
And Christian monuments that now must burn
To senseless ashes. Mark! how all things swerve
From their known course, or vanish like a dream;
Another language spreads from coast to coast;
Only perchance some melancholy stream
And some indignant hills old names preserve,
When laws, and creeds, and people all are lost!

CASUAL INCITEMENT.

A BRIGHT-HAIRED company of youthful slaves,
Beautiful strangers, stand within the pale
Of a sad market, ranged for public sale,
Where Tiber's stream the immortal city laves;
Angli by name, and not an angel waves
His wing who seemeth lovelier in Heaven's eye
Than they appear to holy Gregory,
Who, having learnt that name, salvation craves
For them, and for their land. The earnest sire,
His questions urging, feels in slender ties
Of chiming sound commanding sympathies;
DE-IRIANS—he would save them from God's IRE,
Subjects of Saxon ÆLLA—they shall sing
Glad HALLElujahs to the eternal King!

GLAD TIDINGS.

FOR ever hallowed be this morning fair,
Blest be the unconscious shore on which ye tread,
And blest the silver cross, which ye, instead
Of martial banner, in procession bear;
The cross preceding Him who floats in air,
The pictured Saviour!—By Augustin led,
They come—and onward travel without dread,
Chanting in barbarous ears a tuneful prayer,
Sung for themselves, and those whom they would free!
Rich conquest waits them:—the tempestuous sea
Of ignorance, that ran so rough and high,
And heeded not the voice of clashing swords,
These good men humble by a few bare words,
And calm with fear of God's divinity.

PAULINUS ‡

BUT, to remote Northumbria's royal hall,
Where thoughtful Edwin, tutored in the school
Of sorrow still maintains a heathen rule,
Who comes with functions apostolical?

gations to other prose writers are frequent—obligations which, even if I had not a pleasure in courting, it would have been presumptuous to shun, in treating an historical subject. I must, however, particularise Fuller, to whom I am indebted in the sonnet upon Wicliffe, and in other instances And upon the Acquittal of the Seven Bishops I have done little more than versify a lively description of that event in the memoirs of the first Lord Lonsdale

* "Ethelforth reached the convent of Bangor; he perceived the monks, twelve hundred in number, offering prayers for the success of their countrymen. 'If they are praying against us,' he exclaimed, 'they are fighting against us;' and he ordered them to be first attacked: they were destroyed; and, appalled by their fate, the courage of Brocmail wavered, and he fled from the field in dismay. Thus abandoned by their leader, his army soon gave way, and Ethelforth obtained a decisive conquest. Ancient Bangor itself soon fell into his hands, and was demolished; the noble monastery was levelled to the ground; its library, which is mentioned as a large one, the collection of ages, the repository of the most precious monuments of the ancient Britons, was consumed, half-ruined walls, gates, and rubbish, were all that remained of the magnificent edifice"—See Turner's valuable history of the Anglo-Saxons.

The account Bede gives of this remarkable event, suggests a most striking warning against national and religious prejudices

† Taliesin was present at the battle which preceded this desolation.

‡ The person of Paulinus is thus described by Bede, from the memory of an eye-witness:—"Longæ staturæ, paululum incurvus, nigro capillo, facie macilento, naso adunco, pertenui venerabilis simul et terribilis aspectu"

Mark him, of shoulders curved, and stature tall,
Black hair, and vivid eye, and meagre cheek,
His prominent features like an eagle's beak,
A man whose aspect doth at once appal,
And strike with reverence. The monarch leans
Towards the truth this delegate propounds,
Repeatedly his own deep mind he sounds
With careful hesitation,—then convenes
A synod of his counsellors;—give ear,
And what a pensive sage doth utter, hear!

PERSUASION.

"MAN's life is like a sparrow,* mighty king!
That, stealing in while by the fire you sit
Housed with rejoicing friends, is seen to flit
Safe from the storm, in comfort tarrying.
Here did it enter—there, on hasty wing
Flies out, and passes on from cold to cold;
But whence it came we know not, nor behold
Whither it goes. Even such that transient thing,
The human soul; not utterly unknown
While in the body lodged, her warm abode,
But from what world she came, what woe or weal
On her departure waits, no tongue hath [shown;
This mystery if the stranger can reveal,
His be a welcome cordially bestowed!"

CONVERSION.

PROMPT transformation works the novel lore;
The council closed, the priest in full career
Rides forth, an armèd man, and hurls a spear
To desecrate the fane which heretofore
He served in folly.—Woden falls—and Thor
Is overturned; the mace, in battle heaved
(So might they dream) till victory was achieved,
Drops, and the god himself is seen no more.
Temple and altar sink, to hide their shame
Amid oblivious weeds "*Oh, come to me,*
Ye heavy laden!" such the inviting voice
Heard near fresh streams,†—and thousands, who rejoice
In the new rite—the pledge of sanctity,
Shall, by regenerate life, the promise claim

APOLOGY.

NOR scorn the aid which fancy oft doth lend
The soul's eternal interests to promote;
Death, darkness, danger, are our natural lot,
And evil spirits *may* our walk attend
For aught the wisest know or comprehend.
Then be *good* spirits free to breathe a note
Of elevation; let their odours float
Around these converts; and their glories blend,
Outshining nightly tapers, or the blaze
Of the noon-day. Nor doubt that golden cords [raise
Of good works, mingling with the visions
The soul to purer worlds: and *who* the line
Shall draw, the limits of the power define,
That even imperfect faith to man affords?

PRIMITIVE SAXON CLERGY ‡

How beautiful your presence, how benign,
Servants of God! who not a thought will share

---

* See the original of this speech in Bede — The conversion of Edwin, as related by him is highly interesting—and the breaking up of this council accompanied with an event so striking and characteristic, that I am tempted to give it at length, in a translation "Who, exclaimed the king, when the council was ended, shall first desecrate the altars and the temples? I, answered the chief priest, for who more fit than myself, through the wisdom which the true God hath given me to destroy, for the good example of others, what in foolishness I worshipped? Immediately, casting away vain superstition, he besought the king to grant him, what the laws did not allow to a priest, arms and a courser; which mounting, and furnished with a sword and lance, he proceeded to destroy the idols. The crowd, seeing this, thought him mad—he, however, halted not, but approaching he profaned the temple, casting against it the lance which he had held in his hand, and, exulting in acknowledgment of the true God, he ordered his companions to pull down the temple, with all its inclosures The place is shown where those idols formerly stood, not far from York, at the source of the river Derwent, and is at this day called Gormund Gaham."

† The early propagators of Christianity were accustomed to preach near rivers for the convenience of baptism

‡ Having spoken of the zeal, disinterestedness, and temperance of the clergy of those times, Bede thus proceeds:—"Unde et in magna erat veneratione tempore illo religionis habitus, ita ut ubicunque clericus aliquis, aut monachus adveniret, gaudenter ab omnibus tanquam Dei famulus exciperetur Etiam si in itinere pergens inveniretur, accurrebant, et flexâ cervice

With the vain world, who, outwardly as bare
As winter trees, yield no fallacious sign
That the firm soul is clothed with fruit divine!
Such priest, when service worthy of his care
Has called him forth to breathe the common air
Might seem a saintly image from its shrine
Descended.—happy are the eyes that meet
The apparition; evil thoughts are stayed
At his approach, and low-bowed necks entreat
A benediction from his voice or hand;
Whence grace, through which the heart can understand;
And vows, that bind the will, in silence made.

OTHER INFLUENCES.

AH, when the frame, round which in love we clung,
Is chilled by death, does mutual service fail?
Is tender pity then of no avail?
Are intercessions of the fervent tongue
A waste of hope?—From this sad source have sprung
Rites that console the spirit, under grief
Which ill can brook more rational relief:
Hence prayers are shaped amiss, and dirges sung
For those whose doom is fixed! The way is smooth
For power that travels with the human heart:
Confession ministers, the pang to soothe
In him who at the ghost of guilt doth start.
Ye holy men, so earnest in your care,
Of your own mighty instruments beware!

SECLUSION.

LANCE, shield, and sword relinquished—at his side
A bead-roll, in his hand a claspèd book,
Or staff more harmless than a shepherd's crook,
The war-worn chieftain quits the world—to hide
His thin autumnal locks where monks abide
In cloistered privacy. But not to dwell
In soft repose he comes. Within his cell
Round the decaying trunk of human pride,
At morn, and eve, and midnight's silent hour,
Do penitential cogitations cling:

vel manu signari, vel ore illius se benedici, gaudebant. Verbis quoque horum exhortatoriis diligenter auditum præbebant."—Lib. iii, cap 26.

Like ivy, round some ancient elm, they twine
In grisly folds and strictures serpentine;
Yet, while they strangle without mercy, bring
For recompense their own perennial bower

CONTINUED.

METHINKS that to some vacant hermitage
My feet would rather turn—to some dry nook
Scooped out of living rock, and near a brook
Hurled down a mountain-cove from stage to stage,
Yet tempering, for my sight, its bustling rage
In the soft heaven of a translucent pool;
Thence creeping under forest arches cool,
Fit haunt of shapes whose glorious equipage
Would elevate my dreams. A beechen bowl,
A maple dish, my furniture should be;
Crisp, yellow leaves my bed; the hooting owl
My night-watch: nor should e'er the crested fowl
From thorp or vill his matins sound for me,
Tired of the world and all its industry.

REPROOF

BUT what if one, through grove or flowery mead,
Indulging thus at will the creeping feet
Of a voluptuous indolence, should meet
Thy hovering shade, O venerable Bede!
The saint, the scholar, from a circle freed
Of toil stupendous, in a hallowed seat
Of learning, where thou heard'st the billows beat
On a wild coast, rough monitors to feed
Perpetual industry. Sublime recluse!
The recreant soul, that dares to shun the debt
Imposed on human kind, must first forget
Thy diligence, thy unrelaxing use
Of a long life; and, in the hour of death,
The last dear service of thy passing breath?*

SAXON MONASTERIES, AND LIGHTS AND SHADES OF THE RELIGION

BY such examples moved to unbought pains
The people work like congregated bees;†

* He expired dictating the last words of a translation of St. John's Gospel.

† See in Turner's History, vol iii, p 528, the account of the erection of Ramsey monastery. Penances were removable by the performances of acts of charity and benevolence

Eager to build the quiet fortresses
Where piety, as they believe, obtains
From heaven a *general* blessing, timely rains
Or needful sunshine; prosperous enterprise,
And peace, and equity.—Bold faith! yet rise
The sacred structures for less doubtful gains.
The sensual think with reverence of the palms [grave,
Which the chaste votaries seek, beyond the
If penance be redeemable, thence alms
Flow to the poor, and freedom to the slave,
And, if full oft the sanctuary save
Lives black with guilt, ferocity it calms.

MISSIONS AND TRAVELS.

NOT sedentary all: there are who roam
To scatter seeds of life on barbarous shores;
Or quit with zealous step their knee-worn floors
To seek the general mart of Christendom;
Whence they, like richly-laden merchants, come
To their beloved cells:—or shall we say
That, like the red-cross knight, they urge their way,
To lead in memorable triumph home
Truth—their immortal Una? Babylon,
Learned and wise, hath perished utterly,
Nor leaves her speech one word to aid the sigh [are gone
That would lament her;—Memphis, Tyre,
With all their arts,—but classic lore glides on
By these religious saved for all posterity.

ALFRED

BEHOLD a pupil of the monkish gown,
The pious Alfred, king to justice dear;
Lord of the harp and liberating spear;
Mirror of princes! Indigent renown
Might range the starry ether for a crown
Equal to *his* deserts, who, like the year,
Pours forth his bounty, like the day doth cheer, [frown.
And awes like night with mercy-tempered
Ease from this noble miser of his time
No moment steals, pain narrows not his cares.* [gem,
Though small his kingdom as a spark or
Of Alfred boasts remote Jerusalem,
And Christian India, through her wide-spread clime,
In sacred converse gifts with Alfred shares

HIS DESCENDANTS

CAN aught survive to linger in the veins
Of kindred bodies—an essential power
That may not vanish in one fatal hour,
And wholly cast away terrestrial chains?
The race of Alfred covets glorious pains
When dangers threaten, dangers ever new!
Black tempests bursting, blacker still in view!
But manly sovereignty its hold retains;
The root sincere, the branches bold to strive
With the fierce tempest, while, within the round
Of their protection, gentle virtues thrive;
As oft, 'mid some green plot of open ground
Wide as the oak extends its dewy gloom,
The fostered hyacinths spread their purple bloom.

INFLUENCE ABUSED.

URGED by ambition, who with subtlest skill
Changes her means, the enthusiast as a dupe
Shall soar, and as a hypocrite can stoop,
And turn the instruments of good to ill,
Moulding the credulous people to his will
Such Dunstan:—from its Benedictine coop
Issues the master mind, at whose fell swoop
The chaste affections tremble to fulfil
Their purposes Behold, pre-signified,
The night of spiritual sway! his thoughts, his dreams,
Do in the supernatural world abide:
So vaunt a throng of followers, filled with pride
In shows of virtue pushed to its extremes,
And sorceries of talent misapplied

DANISH CONQUESTS.

WOE to the crown that doth the cowl obey!†
Dissension checks the arms that would restrain
The incessant rovers of the Northern main
And widely spreads once more a pagan sway
But gospel-truth is potent to allay

* Through the whole of his life Alfred was subject to grievous maladies.

† The violent measures carried on under the influence of *Dunstan* for strengthening the Benedictine order, were a leading cause of the second series of Danish invasions —See *Turner.*

Fierceness and rage; and soon the cruel
Dane [reign,
Feels, through the influence of her gentle
His native superstitions melt away.
Thus, often, when thick gloom the east o'er-
shrouds, [appear
The full-orbed moon, slow-climbing, doth
Silently to consume the heavy clouds;
How no one can resolve; but every eye
Around her sees, while air is hushed, a clear
And widening circuit of ethereal sky

CANUTE.

A PLEASANT music floats along the mere,
From monks in Ely chanting service high,
Whileas Canùte the king is rowing by:
"My oarsmen," quoth the mighty king,
"draw near, [hear!"
That we the sweet song of the monks may
He listens, (all past conquests and all
schemes
Of future vanishing like empty dreams,)
Heart-touched, and haply not without a tear.
The royal minstrel, ere the choir is still,
While his free barge skims the smooth flood
along,
Gives to that rapture an accordant rhyme.*
O suffering earth! be thankful; sternest
clime
And rudest age are subject to the thrill
Of heaven-descended piety and song.

THE NORMAN CONQUEST.

THE woman-hearted confessor prepares
The evanescence of the Saxon line.
Hark! 'tis the tolling curfew! the stars
shine, [cares
But of the lights that cherish household
And festive gladness, burns not one that
dares
To twinkle after that dull stroke of thine,
Emblem and instrument, from Thames to
Tyne, [snares!
Of force that daunts, and cunning that en-
Yet as the terrors of the lordly bell,
That quench, from hut to palace, lamps
and fires,
Touch not the tapers of the sacred quires,
Even so a thraldom studious to expel
Old laws and ancient customs to derange,
Brings to religion no injurious change.

* Which is still extant.

THE COUNCIL OF CLERMONT.

"AND shall," the Pontiff asks, "profane-
ness flow
From Nazareth—source of Christian piety,
From Bethlehem, from the mounts of agony
And glorified ascension? Warriors go,
With prayers and blessings we your path
will sow;
Like Moses hold our hands erect, till ye
Have chased far off by righteous victory
These sons of Amalek, or laid them low!"
"God willeth it," the whole assembly cry;
Shout which the enraptured multitude as-
tounds! [reply:—
The Council-roof and Clermont's towers
"God willeth it," from hill to hill rebounds,
And in awe-stricken countries far and nigh
Through "nature's hollow arch," the voice
resounds.†

CRUSADES.

THE turbaned race are poured in thicken-
ing swarms [taine,
Along the west; though driven from Aqui-
The crescent glitters on the towers of
Spain;
And soft Italia feels renewed alarms;
The scimitar, that yields not to the charms
Of ease, the narrow Bosporus will disdain;
Nor long (that crossed) would Grecian hills
detain [arms.
Their tents, and check the current of their
Then blame not those who, by the mightiest
lever
Known to the moral world, imagination,
Upheave (so seems it) from her natural
station [(was never
All Christendom:—they sweep along—
So huge a host!)—to tear from the un-
believer [vation.
The precious tomb, their haven of sal-

RICHARD I.

REDOUBTED king, of courage leonine,
I mark thee, Richard! urgent to equip
Thy warlike person with the staff and scrip;
I watch thee sailing o'er the midland brine;
In conquered Cyprus see thy bride decline

† The decision of this council was believed to be instantly known in remote parts of Europe.

Her blushing cheek, love-vows upon her
lip, [ship,
And see love-emblems streaming from thy
As thence she holds her way to Palestine
My song (a fearless homager) would attend
Thy thundering battle-axe as it cleaves the
press
Of war, but duty summons her away
To tell, how finding in the rash distress
Of those enthusiast powers a constant friend,
Through giddier heights hath clomb the
papal sway

AN INTERDICT.

REALMS quake by turns proud arbitress
of grace, [the power
The Church, by mandate shadowing forth
She arrogates o'er heaven's eternal door,
Closes the gates of every sacred place,
Straight from the sun and tainted air s em-
brace [morn
All sacred things are covered · cheerful
Grows sad as night—no seemly garb is
worn,
Nor is a face allowed to meet a face
With natural smile of greeting Bells are
dumb:
Ditches are graves—funereal rites denied,
And in the church-yard he must take his
bride [come
Who dares be wedded ! Fancies thickly
Into the pensive heart ill-fortified,
And comfortless despairs the soul benumb.

PAPAL ABUSES.

As with the stream our voyage we pursue,
The gross materials of this world present
A marvellous study of wild accident;
Uncouth proximities of old and new;
And bold transfigurations, more untrue
(As might be deemed) to disciplined intent
Than aught the sky's fantastic element,
When most fantastic, offers to the view.
Saw we not Henry scourged at Becket's
shrine? [crown,
Lo! John self-stripped of his insignia;—
Sceptre and mantle, sword and ring, laid
down [line
At a proud legate's feet! The spears that
Baronial halls, the opprobrious insult feel;
And angry ocean roars a vain appeal.

SCENE IN VENICE

BLACK demons hovering o'er his mitred
head,
To Cæsar's successor the pontiff spake:
"Ere I absolve thee, stoop! that on thy
neck [tread."
Levelled with earth this foot of mine may
Then, he who to the altar had been led,
He, whose strong arm the orient could not
check,
He, who had held the soldan at his beck,
Stooped, of all glory disinherited,
And even the common dignity of man!
Amazement strikes the crowd,—while many
turn
Their eyes away in sorrow, others burn
With scorn, invoking a vindictive ban
From outraged nature, but the sense of most
In abject sympathy with power is lost

PAPAL DOMINION.

UNLESS to Peter's chair the viewless wind
Must come and ask permission when to
blow, [now
What further empire would it have? for
A ghostly domination, unconfined
As that by dreaming bards to love assigned,
Sits there in sober truth—to raise the low,
Perplex the wise, the strong to overthrow—
Through earth and heaven to bind and to
unbind! [—rebuff
Resist—the thunder quails thee!—crouch
Shall be thy recompense! from land to land
The ancient thrones of Christendom are
For occupation of a magic wand, [stuff
And 'tis the pope that wields it,—whether
rough [hand!
Or smooth his front, our world is in his

PART II.

TO THE CLOSE OF THE TROUBLES IN THE REIGN OF CHARLES I.

CISTERTIAN MONASTERY.

"*Here man more purely lives,* less oft doth
fall,
More promptly rises, walks with nicer heed*

* "Bonum est nos hic esse, quia homo vivit

More safely rests, dies happier, is freed
Earlier from cleansing fires, and gains withal
A brighter crown. '—On yon Cistertian wall
That confident assurance may be read;
And, to like shelter, from the world have fled
Increasing multitudes. The potent call
Doubtless shall cheat full oft the heart's desires;
Yet, while the rugged age on pliant knee
Vows to rapt fancy humble fealty,
A gentler life spreads round the holy spires;
Where'er they rise, the sylvan waste retires,
And aëry harvests crown the fertile lea

MONKS AND SCHOOLMEN.

RECORD we too, with just and faithful pen,
That many hooded Cenobites there are,
Who in their private cells have yet a care
Of public quiet, unambitious men,
Counsellors for the world, of piercing ken;
Whose fervent exhortations from afar
Move princes to their duty, peace or war;
And oft-times in the most forbidding den
Of solitude, with love of science strong,
How patiently the yoke of thought they bear!
How subtly glide its finest threads along!
Spirits that crowd the intellectual sphere
With mazy boundaries, as the astronomer
With orb and cycle girds the starry throng.

OTHER BENEFITS.

AND not in vain embodied to the sight
Religion finds even in the stern retreat
Of feudal sway her own appropriate seat;
From the collegiate pomps on Windsor's height,
Down to the humble altar, which the knight
And his retainers of the embattled hall
Seek in domestic oratory small,
For prayer in stillness, or the chanted rite;
Then chiefly dear, whose foes are planted round,
Who teach the intrepid guardians of the place,
Hourly exposed to death, with famine worn,
And suffering under many a perilous wound,
How sad would be their durance, if forlorn
Of offices dispensing heavenly grace!

CONTINUED.

AND what melodious sounds at times prevail!
And, ever and anon, how bright a gleam
Pours on the surface of the turbid stream!
What heartfelt fragrance mingles with the gale
That swells the bosom of our passing sail!
For where, but on *this* river's margin, blow
Those flowers of chivalry, to bind the brow
Of hardihood with wreaths that shall not fail?
Fair court of Edward! wonder of the world
I see a matchless blazonry unfurled
Of wisdom, magnanimity, and love,
And meekness tempering honourable pride;
The lamb is couching by the lion's side,
And near the flame-eyed eagle sits the dove.

CRUSADERS.

NOR can imagination quit the shores
Of these bright scenes without a farewell glance
Given to those dream-like issues—that romance
Of many-coloured life which fortune pours
Round the crusaders, till on distant shores
Their labours end; or they return to lie,
The vow performed, in cross-legged effigy,
Devoutly stretched upon their chancel floors
Am I deceived? Or is their requiem chanted
By voices never mute when heaven unties
Her inmost, softest, tenderest harmonies,
Requiem which earth takes up with voice undaunted
When she would tell how good, and brave, and wise,
For their high guerdon not in vain have panted!

TRANSUBSTANTIATION.

ENOUGH! for see, with dim association
The tapers burn, the odorous incense feeds
A greedy flame; the pompous mass proceeds:
The priest bestows the appointed consecration;
And, while the Host is raised, its elevation
An awe and supernatural horror breeds,
And all the people bow their heads like reeds

purius, cadit rarius, surgit velocius, incedit cautius, quiescit securius, moritur felicius, purgatur citius, præmiatur copiosius."—Bernard. "This sentence," says Dr. Whitaker, "is usually inscribed on some conspicuous part of the Cistertian houses"

To a soft breeze, in lowly adoration
This Valdo brooked not. On the banks of Rhone [thence,
He taught, till persecution chased him
To adore the Invisible, and Him alone
Nor were his followers loth to seek defence,
'Mid woods and wilds, on Nature's craggy throne, [sense
From rites that trample upon soul and

WALDENSES.

THESE who gave earliest notice, as the lark [gratulate,
Springs from the ground the morn to
Who rather rose the day to antedate,
By striking out a solitary spark,
When all the world with midnight gloom was dark—
The harbingers of good whom bitter hate
In vain endeavoured to exterminate,
Fell obloquy pursues with hideous bark,*
But they desist not; and the sacred fire,
Rekindled thus, from dens and savage woods
Moves, handed on with never-ceasing care,
Through courts, through camps, o'er limitary floods;
Nor lacks this sea-girt isle a timely share
Of the new flame, not suffered to expire.

ARCHBISHOP CHICHLEY TO HENRY V.

"WHAT beast in wilderness or cultured field
The lively beauty of the leopard shows?
What flower in meadow-ground or garden grows
That to the towering lily doth not yield?
Let both meet only on thy royal shield!

* The list of foul names bestowed upon those poor creatures is long and curious; and, as is, alas! too natural, most of the opprobrious appellations are drawn from circumstances into which they were forced by their persecutors, who even consolidated their miseries into one reproachful term, calling them Patarenians or Paturins, from *pati*, to suffer.

" Dwellers with wolves she names them, for the pine
And green oak are their covert; as the gloom
Of night oft foils their enemy's design,
She calls them riders on the flying broom
Sorcerers, whose frame and aspect have become
One and the same through practices malign."

Go forth, great king, ! claim what thy birth bestows;
Conquer the Gallic lily which thy foes
Dare to usurp;—thou hast a sword to wield, [mitred sire
And Heaven will crown the right."—The
Thus spake—and lo! a fleet, for Gaul addrest, [ing seas,
Ploughs her bold course across the wonder-
For, sooth to say, ambition, in the breast
Of youthful heroes, is no sullen fire,
But one that leaps to meet the fanning breeze

WARS OF YORK AND LANCASTER.

THUS is the storm abated by the craft
Of a shrewd counsellor, eager to protect
The Church, whose power hath recently been checked, [the shaft
Whose monstrous riches threatened So
Of victory mounts high, and blood is quaffed
In fields that rival Cressy and Poictiers—
Pride to be washed away by bitter tears,
For deep as hell itself, the avenging draught
Of civil slaughter! Yet, while temporal power [truth
Is by these shocks exhausted, spiritual
Maintains the else endangered gift of life;
Proceeds from infancy to lusty youth;
And, under cover of this woeful strife,
Gathers unblighted strength from hour to hour.

WICLIFFE.

ONCE more the Church is seized with sudden fear,
And at her call is Wicliffe disinhumed;
Yea, his dry bones to ashes are consumed,
And flung into the brook that travels near;
Forthwith that ancient voice which streams can hear, [the wind,
Thus speaks, (that voice which walks upon
Though seldom heard by busy human kind,)
"As thou these ashes, little brook! wilt bear
Into the Avon, Avon to the tide
Of Severn, Severn to the narrow seas,
Into main ocean they, this deed accurst
An emblem yields to friends and enemies
How the bold teacher's doctrine, sanctified
By truth shall spread throughout the world dispersed."

CORRUPTIONS OF THE HIGHER CLERGY.

"WOE to you, prelates! rioting in ease
And cumbrous wealth the shame of your estate;
You on whose progress dazzling trains await
Of pompous horses; whom vain titles please,
Who will be served by others on their knees,
Yet will yourselves to God no service pay;
Pastors who neither take nor point the way
To Heaven; for either lost in vanities
Ye have no skill to teach, or if ye know
And speak the word——" Alas! of fearful things
'Tis the most fearful when the people's eye
Abuse hath cleared from vain imaginings;
And taught the general voice to prophesy
Of justice armed, and pride to be laid low.

ABUSE OF MONASTIC POWER.

AND what is penance with her knotted thong,
Mortification with the shirt of hair,
Wan cheek, and knees indurated with prayer,
Vigils and fastings rigorous as long,
If cloistered avarice scruple not to wrong
The pious, humble, useful secular,
And rob the people of his daily care,
Scorning that world whose blindness makes her strong?
Inversion strange! that unto one who lives
For self, and struggles with himself alone,
The amplest share of heavenly favour gives;
That to a monk allots, in the esteem
Of God and man, place higher than to him
Who on the good of others builds his own!

MONASTIC VOLUPTUOUSNESS.

YET more, — round many a convent's blazing fire
Unhallowed threads of revelry are spun;
There Venus sits disguisèd like a nun,—
While Bacchus, clothed in semblance of a friar,
Pours out his choicest beverage high and higher
Sparkling, until it cannot choose but run
Over the bowl, whose silver lip hath won
An instant kiss of masterful desire—
To stay the precious waste. In every brain
Spreads the dominion of the sprightly juice,
Through the wide world, to madding fancy dear,
Till the arched roof, with resolute abuse
Of its grave echoes, swells a choral strain,
Whose votive burthen is—"Our kingdom's here!"

DISSOLUTION OF THE MONASTERIES.

THREATS come which no submission may assuage;
No sacrifice avert, no power dispute;
The tapers shall be quenched, the belfries mute,
And, 'mid their choirs unroofed by selfish rage,
The warbling wren shall find a leafy cage;
The gadding bramble hang her purple fruit;
And the green lizard and the gilded newt
Lead unmolested lives, and die of age.*
The owl of evening and the woodland fox
For their abode the shrines of Waltham choose:
Proud Glastonbury can no more refuse
To stoop her head before these desperate shocks—
She whose high pomp displaced, as story tells,
Arimathean Joseph's wattled cells.

THE SAME SUBJECT.

THE lovely nun (submissive but more meek
Through saintly habit, than from effort due
To unrelenting mandates that pursue
With equal wrath the steps of strong and weak)
Goes forth—unveiling timidly her cheek
Suffused with blushes of celestial hue,
While through the convent gate to open view
Softly she glides, another home to seek.
Not Iris, issuing from her cloudy shrine,
An apparition more divinely bright!
Not more attractive to the dazzled sight
Those watery glories, on the stormy brine
Poured forth, while summer suns at distance shine,
And the green vales lie hushed in sober light!

* These two lines are adopted from a MS. written about the year 1770, which accidentally fell into my possession. The close of the preceding sonnet on monastic voluptuousness is taken from the same source, as is the verse, "There Venus sits," &c.

CONTINUED

YET some noviciates of the cloistral shade,
Or chained by vows, with undissembled glee
The warrant hail—exulting to be free ,
Like ships before whose keels, full long embayed
In polar ice, propitious winds have made
Unlooked-for outlet to an open sea,
Their liquid world, for bold discovery,
In all her quarters temptingly displayed !
Hope guides the young ; but when the old must pass
The threshold, whither shall they turn to [find
The hospitality—the alms (alas !
Alms may be needed) which that house bestowed ?
Can they, in faith and worship, train the [mind
To keep this new and questionable road ?

SAINTS.

YE, too, must fly before a chasing hand,
Angels and saints, in every hamlet mourned !
Ah ! if the old idolatry be spurned,
Let not your radiant shapes desert the land :
Her adoration was not your demand,
The fond heart proffered it--the servile heart ;
And therefore are ye summoned to depart,
Michael, and thou, St. George, whose flaming brand
The dragon quelled ; and valiant Margaret
Whose rival sword a like opponent slew .
And rapt Cecilia, seraph-haunted queen
Of harmony ; and weeping Magdalene,
Who in the penitential desert met
Gales sweet as those that over Eden blew !

THE VIRGIN.

MOTHER ! whose virgin bosom was uncrost
With the least shade of thought to sin allied;
Woman ! above all women glorified,
Our tainted nature's solitary boast ;
Purer than foam on central ocean tost ;
Brighter than eastern skies at daybreak strewn
With fancied roses, than the unblemished [moon
Before her wane begins on heaven's blue coast ;
Thy image falls to earth Yet some, I ween,
Not unforgiven the suppliant knee might bend,
As to a visible power, in which did blend
All that was mixed and reconciled in thee
Of mother's love with maiden purity,
Of high with low, celestial with terrene !

APOLOGY

NOT utterly unworthy to endure
Was the supremacy of crafty Rome ,
Age after age to the arch of Christendom
Aerial keystone haughtily secure ;
Supremacy from Heaven transmitted pure
As many hold , and, therefore, to the tomb
Pass, some through fire — and by the scaffold some—
Like saintly Fisher, and unbending More.
"Lightly for both the bosom's lord did sit
Upon his throne ," unsoftened, undismayed
By aught that mingled with the tragic scene
Of pity or fear , and More's gay genius played
With the inoffensive sword of native wit,
Than the bare axe more luminous and keen.

IMAGINATIVE REGRETS

DEEP is the lamentation ! Not alone
From sages justly honoured by mankind,
But from the ghostly tenants of the wind
Demons and spirits, many a dolorous groan
Issues for that dominion overthrown :
Proud Tiber grieves, and far-off Ganges, blind
As his own worshippers , and Nile, reclined
Upon his monstrous urn, the farewell moan
Renews.—Through every forest, cave, and den,
Where frauds were hatched of old, hath [sorrow past—
Hangs o'er the Arabian prophet's native waste
Where once his airy helpers schemed and planned
'Mid phantom lakes bemocking thirsty men,
And stalking pillars built of fiery sand.

REFLECTIONS.

GRANT, that by this unsparing hurricane
Green leaves with yellow mixed are torn away,
And goodly fruitage with the mother spray,
'Twere madness—wished we, therefore, to detain,
With hands stretched forth in mollified [disdain,

The "trumpery" that ascends in bare display,—
Bulls, pardons, relics, cowls, black, white, and gray,
Unwhirled—and flying o'er the ethereal plain
Fast bound for Limbo Lake.—And yet not choice
But habit rules the unreflecting herd,
And airy bonds are hardest to disown;
Hence, with the spiritual sovereignty transferred
Unto itself, the crown assumes a voice
Of reckless mastery, hitherto unknown.

TRANSLATION OF THE BIBLE.

But to outweigh all harm, the sacred Book,
In dusty sequestration wrapt too long,
Assumes the accents of our native tongue;
And he who guides the plough, or wields the crook,
With understanding spirit now may look
Upon her records, listen to her song,
And sift her laws—much wondering that the wrong,
Which faith has suffered, Heaven could calmly brook.
Transcendent boon! noblest that earthly king
Ever bestowed to equalise and bless
Under the weight of mortal wretchedness!
But passions spread like plagues, and thousands wild
With bigotry shall tread the offering
Beneath their feet—detested and defiled.

THE POINT AT ISSUE.

For what contend the wise? for nothing less
Than that pure faith dissolve the bonds of sense;
The soul restored to God by evidence
Of things not seen—drawn forth from their recess,
Root there, and not in forms, her holiness;
That faith which to the patriarchs did dispense
Sure guidance, ere a ceremonial fence
Was needful round men thirsting to transgress;
That faith, more perfect still, with which the Lord
Of all, himself a Spirit, in the youth
Of Christian aspiration, deigned to fill
The temples of their hearts—who, with His word
Informed, were resolute to do His will,
And worship Him in spirit and in truth.

EDWARD VI.

"Sweet is the holiness of youth"—so felt
Time-honoured Chaucer when he framed the lay
By which the prioress beguiled the way,
And many a pilgrim's rugged heart did melt.
Hadst thou, loved bard! whose spirit often dwelt
In the clear land of vision, but foreseen
King, child, and seraph, blended in the mien
Of pious Edward kneeling as he knelt
In meek and simple infancy, what joy
For universal Christendom had thrilled
Thy heart! what hopes inspired thy genius, skilled
(O great precursor, genuine morning star)
The lucid shafts of reason to employ,
Piercing the papal darkness from afar!

EDWARD SIGNING THE WARRANT FOR THE EXECUTION OF JOAN OF KENT.

The tears of man in various measure gush
From various sources; gently overflow
From blissful transport some—from clefts of woe
Some with ungovernable impulse rush;
And some, coëval with the earliest blush
Of infant passion, scarcely dare to show
Their pearly lustre—coming but to go;
And some break forth when others' sorrows crush
The sympathising heart. Nor these, nor yet
The noblest drops to admiration known,
To gratitude, to injuries forgiven,
Claim Heaven's regard like waters that have wet
The innocent eyes of youthful monarchs, driven
To pen the mandates nature doth disown.

REVIVAL OF POPERY.

Melts into silent shades the youth, discrowned
By unrelenting death. O people keen
For change, to whom the new looks always green!
They cast, they cast with joy upon the ground
Their gods of wood and stone; and, at the sound
Of counter-proclamation, now are seen,
(Proud triumph is it for a sullen queen!)
Lifting them up, the worship to confound

Of the Most High. Again do they invoke
The creature, to the creature glory give;
Again with frankincense the altars smoke
Like those the heathen served; and mass is sung;
And prayer, man's rational prerogative,
Runs through blind channels of an unknown tongue.

LATIMER AND RIDLEY.

HOW fast the Marian death-list is unrolled!
See Latimer and Ridley* in the might
Of faith stand coupled for a common flight!
One (like those prophets whom God sent of old)
Transfigured, from this kindling hath foretold
A torch of inextinguishable light;
The other gains a confidence as bold;
And thus they foil their enemy's despite.
The penal instruments, the shows of crime,
Are glorified while this once-mitred pair
Of saintly friends, the "murtherer's chain partake,
Corded, and burning at the social stake:"
Earth never witnessed object more sublime
In constancy, in fellowship more fair!

CRANMER.

OUTSTRETCHING flame-ward his upbraided hand
(O God of mercy, may no earthly seat
Of judgment such presumptuous doom repeat!)
Amid the shuddering throng doth Cranmer stand;
Firm as the stake to which with iron band
His frame is tied; firm from the naked feet
To the bare head, the victory complete;
The shrouded body, to the soul's command,
Answering with more than Indian fortitude,
Through all her nerves with finer sense endued,
Till breath departs in blissful aspiration:
Then, 'mid the ghastly ruins of the fire,
Behold the unalterable heart entire,
Emblem of faith untouched, miraculous attestation!†

GENERAL VIEW OF THE TROUBLES OF THE REFORMATION.

AID, glorious martyrs, from your fields of light
Our mortal ken! Inspire a perfect trust
(While we look round) that Heaven's decrees are just:
Which few can hold committed to a fight
That shows, even on its better side, the might
Of proud self-will, rapacity, and lust,
'Mid clouds enveloped of polemic dust,
Which showers of blood seem rather to incite
Than to allay.—Anathemas are hurled
From both sides; veteran thunders (the brute test
Of truth) are met by fulminations new—
Tartarian flags are caught at, and unfurled—
Friends strike at friends—the flying shall pursue—
And victory sickens, ignorant where to rest!

ENGLISH REFORMERS IN EXILE.

SCATTERING, like birds escaped the fowler's net,
Some seek with timely flight a foreign strand;
Most happy, re-assembled in a land
By dauntless Luther freed, could they forget
Their country's woes. But scarcely have they met,
Partners in faith, and brothers in distress,
Free to pour forth their common thankfulness,
Ere hope declines; their union is beset

* "M. Latimer very quietly suffered his keeper to pull off his hose, and his other aray, which to looke unto was very simple; and being stripped into his shrowd, he seemed as comely a person to them that were present, as one should lightly see: and whereas in his clothes hee appeared a withered and crooked sillie (weak) olde man, he now stood bolt upright, as comely a father as one might lightly behold. . . . Then they brought a faggotte, kindled with fire, and laid the same downe at doctor Ridley's feete. To whom M. Latimer spake in this manner, 'Bee of good comfort, master Ridley, and play the man: wee shall this day light such a candle by God's grace in England, as I trust shall never bee put out.'"—Fox's *Acts, etc.*

Similar alterations in the outward figure and deportment of persons brought to like trial were not uncommon. See note to the above passage in Dr. Wordsworth's Ecclesiastical Biography, for an example in a humble Welsh fisherman.

† For the belief in this fact see the contemporary historians.

With speculative notions rashly sown,
Whence thickly-sprouting growth of poisonous weeds;
Their forms are broken staves; their passions steeds
That master them. How enviably blest
Is he who can, by help of grace, enthrone
The peace of God within his single breast!

ELIZABETH.

Hail, virgin queen! o'er many an envious bar
Triumphant—snatched from many a treacherous wile!
All hail, sage lady, whom a grateful isle
Hath blest, respiring from that dismal war
Stilled by thy voice! But quickly from afar
Defiance breathes with more malignant aim;
And alien storms with home-bred ferments claim
Portentous fellowship. Her silver car
By sleepless prudence ruled, glides slowly on;
Unhurt by violence, from menaced taint
Emerging pure, and seemingly more bright!
For, wheresoe'er she moves, the clouds anon
Disperse; or, under a divine constraint,
Reflect some portion of her glorious light!

EMINENT REFORMERS.

Methinks that I could trip o'er heaviest soil,
Light as a buoyant bark from wave to wave,
Were mine the trusty staff that Jewel gave
To youthful Hooker, in familiar style
The gift exalting, and with playful smile:*
For thus equipped, and bearing on his head
The donor's farewell blessing, can he dread
Tempest, or length of way, or weight of toil?
More sweet than odours caught by him who sails
Near spicy shores of Araby the blest,
A thousand times more exquisitely sweet,
The freight of holy feeling which we meet,
In thoughtful moments, wafted by the gales
From fields where good men walk, or bowers wherein they rest.

THE SAME.

Holy and heavenly spirits as they are,
Spotless in life, and eloquent as wise,
With what entire affection do they prize
Their new-born Church! labouring with earnest care
To baffle all that may her strength impair;
That Church — the unperverted gospel's seat;
In their afflictions a divine retreat;
Source of their liveliest hope, and tenderest prayer!
The truth exploring with an equal mind,
In doctrine and communion they have sought
Firmly between the two extremities to steer;
But theirs the wise man's ordinary lot,
To trace right courses for the stubborn blind,
And prophesy to ears that will not hear.

DISTRACTIONS.

Men, who have ceased to reverence, soon defy
Their forefathers; lo! sects are formed—and split
With morbid restlessness,—the ecstatic fit
Spreads wide; though special mysteries multiply,
The saints must govern, is their common cry;
And so they labour; deeming Holy Writ
Disgraced by aught that seems content to sit

---

* "On foot they went, and took Salisbury in their way, purposely to see the good bishop, who made Mr. Hooker sit at his own table,—which Mr. Hooker boasted of with much joy and gratitude when he saw his mother and friends; and at the bishop's parting with him, the bishop gave him good counsel, and his benediction, but forgot to give him money; which when the bishop had considered, he sent a servant in all haste to call Richard back to him, and at Richard's return, the bishop said to him, 'Richard, I sent for you back to lend you a horse which hath carried me many a mile, and, I thank God, with much ease,' and presently delivered into his hand a walking-staff, with which he professed he had travelled through many parts of Germany; and he said, 'Richard, I do not give, but lend you my horse; be sure you be honest, and bring my horse back to me at your return this way to Oxford. And I do now give you ten groats to bear your charges to Exeter; and here is ten groats more, which I charge you to deliver to your mother, and tell her I send her a bishop's benediction with it, and beg the continuance of her prayers for me. And if you bring my horse back to me, I will give you ten groats more to carry you on foot to the college; and so God bless you, good Richard.'"—See Walton's *Life of Richard Hooker.*

Beneath the roof of settled modesty
The Romanist exults, fresh hope he draws
From the confusion—craftily incites
The overweening—personates the mad *—
To heap disgust upon the worthier cause.
Totters the throne, the new-born Church is sad,
For every wave against her peace unites

GUNPOWDER PLOT.

FEAR hath a hundred eyes that all agree
To plague her beating heart, and there is one
(Nor idlest that!) which holds communion
With things that were not, yet were *meant* to be.
Aghast within its gloomy cavity
That eye (which sees as if fulfilled and done
Crimes that might stop the motion of the sun)
Beholds the horrible catastrophe
Of an assembled senate unredeemed
From subterraneous treason's darkling power;
Merciless act of sorrow infinite!
Worse than the product of that dismal night,
When gushing, copious as a thunder-shower,
The blood of Huguenots through Paris streamed.

ILLUSTRATION.

THE Virgin Mountain,† wearing like a queen
A brilliant crown of everlasting snow,
Sheds ruin from her sides; and men below
Wonder that aught of aspect so serene
Can link with desolation. Smooth and green,
And seeming, at a little distance, slow,
The waters of the Rhine; but on they go
Fretting and whitening, keener and more keen,
Till madness seizes on the whole wide flood,
Turned to a fearful thing whose nostrils breathe
Blasts of tempestuous smoke—wherewith he tries
To hide himself, but only magnifies;
And doth in more conspicuous torment writhe,
Deafening the region in his ireful mood.

TROUBLES OF CHARLES THE FIRST.

SUCH is the contrast, which where'er we move,
To the mind's eye religion doth present;
Now with her own deep quietness content;
Then, like the mountain, thundering from above
Against the ancient pine-trees of the grove
And the land's humblest comforts. Now her mood
Recals the transformation of the flood,
Whose rage the gentle skies in vain reprove,
Earth cannot check. Oh, terrible excess
Of headstrong will! Can this be piety?
No—some fierce maniac hath usurped her name,
And scourges England struggling to be free.
Her peace destroyed! her hopes a wilderness!
Her blessings cursed—her glory turned to shame!

LAUD.‡

PREJUDGED by foes determined not to spare,
An old weak man for vengeance thrown aside,
Laud, "in the painful art of dying" tried,
(Like a poor bird entangled in a snare
Whose heart still flutters, though his wings forbear
To stir in useless struggle) hath relied
On hope that conscious innocence supplied,
And in his prison breathes celestial air.
Why tarries, then, thy chariot? Wherefore stay,
O death! the ensanguined yet triumphant wheels,

* A common device in religious and political conflicts.—See STRYPE *in support of this instance.*

† The Jungfrau.

‡ In this age a word cannot be said in praise of Laud, or even in compassion for his fate, without incurring a charge of bigotry, but fearless of such imputation, I concur with Hume, "that it is sufficient for his vindication to observe, that his errors were the most excusable of all those which prevailed during that zealous period" A key to the right understanding of those parts of his conduct that brought the most odium upon him in his own time, may be found in the following passage of his speech before the bar of the House of Peers:—"Ever since I came in place, I have laboured nothing more, than that the external public worship of God, so much slighted in divers parts of this kingdom, might be preserved, and that with as much decency and uniformity as might be For I evidently saw, that the publick neglect of God's service in the outward face of it, and the nasty lying of many places dedicated to that service, *had almost cast a damp upon the true and inward worship of God, which, while we live in the body needs external helps, and all little enough to keep it in any vigour.*"

Which thou prepar'st, full often to convey,
(What time a state with madding faction reels)
The saint or patriot to the world that heals
All wounds, all perturbations doth allay?

AFFLICTIONS OF ENGLAND.

HARP! couldst thou venture, on thy boldest string,
The faintest note to echo which the blast
Caught from the hand of Moses as it past
O'er Sinai's top, or from the shepherd king,
Early awake, by Siloa's brook, to sing
Of dread Jehovah; then, should wood and waste
Hear also of that name, and mercy cast
Off to the mountains, like a covering
Of which the Lord was weary. Weep, oh! weep,
Weep with the good, beholding king and priest
Despised by that stern God to whom they raise
Their suppliant hands; but holy is the feast
He keepeth; like the firmament his ways;
His statutes like the chambers of the deep.

PART III.

FROM THE RESTORATION TO THE PRESENT TIMES.

I SAW the figure of a lovely maid
Seated alone beneath a darksome tree,
Whose fondly overhanging canopy
Set off her brightness with a pleasing shade,
Substance she seemed (and *that* my heart betrayed,
For she was one I loved exceedingly),
But while I gazed in tender reverie
(Or was it sleep that with my fancy played?)
The bright corporeal presence, form, and face,
Remaining still distinct, grew thin and rare,
Like sunny mist; at length the golden hair,
Shape, limbs, and heavenly features, keeping pace
Each, with the other, in a lingering race
Of dissolution, melted into air.

PATRIOTIC SYMPATHIES.

LAST night, without a voice, this vision spake
Fear to my spirit—passion that might seem
Wholly dissevered from our present theme:
Yet do I love my country—and partake
Of kindred agitations for her sake;
She visits oftentimes my midnight dream;
Her glory meets me with the earliest beam
Of light, which tells that morning is awake.
If aught impair her beauty or destroy,
Or but forebode destruction, I deplore
With filial love the sad vicissitude;
If she hath fallen and righteous Heaven restore
The prostrate, then my spring-time is renewed,
And sorrow bartered for exceeding joy.

CHARLES THE SECOND.

WHO comes with rapture greeted, and caressed
With frantic love—his kingdom to regain?
Him virtue's nurse, adversity, in vain
Received, and fostered in her iron breast
For all she taught of hardiest and of best,
Or would have taught, by discipline of pain
And long privation, now dissolves amain,
Or is remembered only to give zest
To wantonness.—Away, Circean revels!
Already stands our country on the brink
Of bigot rage, that all distinction levels
Of truth and falsehood, swallowing the good name,
And, with that draught, the life-blood: misery, shame,
By poets loathed; from which historians shrink!

LATITUDINARIANISM

YET truth is keenly sought for, and the wind
Charged with rich words poured out in thought's defence;
Whether the Church inspire that eloquence,
Or a Platonic piety confined
To the sole temple of the inward mind;
And one there is who builds immortal lays,
Though doomed to tread in solitary ways,
Darkness before, and danger's voice behind!
Yet not alone, nor helpless to repel
Sad thoughts; for from above the starry sphere
Come secrets, whispered nightly to his ear;
And the pure spirit of celestial light
Shines through his soul—"that he may see and tell
Of things invisible to mortal sight."

CLERICAL INTEGRITY.

NOR shall the eternal roll of praise reject
Those unconforming; whom one rigorous day
Drives from their cures, a voluntary prey
To poverty and grief, and disrespect,
And some to want — as if by tempests wrecked
On a wild coast; how destitute! did they
Feel not that conscience never can betray,
That peace of mind is virtue's sure effect.
Their altars they forego, their homes they quit,
Fields which they love, and paths they daily trod,
And cast the future upon Providence;
As men the dictate of whose inward sense
Outweighs the world; whom self-deceiving wit
Lures not from what they deem the cause of God

PERSECUTION OF THE SCOTTISH COVENANTERS.

WHEN Alpine vales threw forth a suppliant cry,
The majesty of England interposed
And the sword stopped, the bleeding wounds were closed;
And faith preserved her ancient purity.
How little boots that precedent of good,
Scorned or forgotten, thou canst testify,
For England's shame, O sister realm! from wood,
Mountain, and moor, and crowded street, where lie
The headless martyrs of the Covenant,
Slain by compatriot-protestants that draw
From councils senseless as intolerant
Their warrant. Bodies fall by wild sword-law;
But who would force the soul, tilts with a straw
Against a champion cased in adamant.

ACQUITTAL OF THE BISHOPS.

A VOICE, from long-expecting thousands sent,
Shatters the air, and troubles tower and spire—
For justice hath absolved the innocent,
And tyranny is balked of her desire:
Up, down, the busy Thames—rapid as fire
Coursing a train of gunpowder—it went,
And transport finds in every street a vent,
Till the whole city rings like one vast quire.
The fathers urge the people to be still
With outstretched hands and earnest speech—in vain!
Yea, many, haply wont to entertain
Small reverence for the mitre's offices,
And to religion's self no friendly will,
A prelate's blessing ask on bended knees.

WILLIAM THE THIRD.

CALM as an under-current—strong to draw
Millions of waves into itself, and run,
From sea to sea, impervious to the sun
And ploughing storm—the spirit of Nassau
(By constant impulse of religious awe
Swayed, and thereby enabled to contend
With the wide world's commotions) from its end
Swerves not—diverted by a casual law.
Had mortal action e'er a nobler scope?
The hero comes to liberate, not defy:
And, while he marches on with righteous hope,
Conqueror beloved! expected anxiously!
The vacillating bondman of the pope,
Shrinks from the verdict of his steadfast eye.

OBLIGATIONS OF CIVIL TO RELIGIOUS LIBERTY.

UNGRATEFUL country, if thou e'er forget
The sons who for thy civil rights have bled!
How, like a Roman, Sidney bowed his head,
And Russel's milder blood the scaffold wet,
But these had fallen for profitless regret
Had not thy holy Church her champions bred;
And claims from other worlds inspirited
The star of liberty to rise. Nor yet
(Grave this within thy heart!) if spiritual things
Be lost, through apathy, or scorn, or fear,
Shalt thou thy humbler franchises support,
However hardly won or justly dear;
What came from Heaven to Heaven by nature clings,
And, if dissevered thence, its course is short.

DOWN a swift stream, thus far, a bold design
Have we pursued, with livelier stir of heart
Than his who sees, borne forward by the Rhine,

The living landscapes greet him, and depart,
Sees spires fast sinking—up again to start!
And strives the towers to number, that recline
O'er the dark steeps, or on the horizon line
Striding with shattered crests the eye athwart;—
So have we hurried on with troubled pleasure:
Henceforth, as on the bosom of a stream
That slackens, and spreads wide a watery gleam,
We, nothing loth a lingering course to measure,
May gather up our thoughts, and mark at leisure
Features that else had vanished like a dream.

WALTON'S BOOK OF LIVES.

THERE are no colours in the fairest sky
So fair as these The feather whence the pen
Was shaped that traced the lives of these good men
Dropped from an angel's wing. With moistened eye
We read of faith and purest charity
In statesman, priest, and humble citizen.
Oh, could we copy their mild virtues, then
What joy to live, what blessedness to die!
Methinks their very names shine still and bright;
Apart, like glow-worms on a summer night;
Or lonely tapers when from far they fling
A guiding ray, or seen, like stars on high,
Satellites burning in a lucid ring
Around meek Walton's heavenly memory.

SACHEVERELL.

A SUDDEN conflict rises from the swell
Of a proud slavery met by tenets strained
In liberty's behalf. Fears, true or feigned,
Spread through all ranks; and lo! the sentinel
Who loudest rang his pulpit 'larum bell,
Stands at the bar—absolved by female eyes,
Mingling their light with graver flatteries,
Lavished on *him* that England may rebel
Against her ancient virtue. High and Low,
Watchwords of party, on all tongues are rife,
As if a Church, though sprung from Heaven, must owe
To opposites and fierce extremes her life—
Not to the golden mean, and quiet flow
Of truths that soften hatred, temper strife.

PLACES OF WORSHIP.

As star that shines dependent upon star
Is to the sky while we look up in love;
As to the deep fair ships which though they move
Seem fixed, to eyes that watch them from afar;
As to the sandy desert fountains are,
With palm-groves shaded at wide intervals,
Whose fruit around the sun-burnt native falls
Of roving tired or desultory war;
Such to this British isle her Christian fanes,
Each linked to each for kindred services;
Her spires, her steeple-towers with glittering vanes
Far-kenned, her chapels lurking among trees,
Where a few villagers on bended knees
Find solace which a busy world disdains

PASTORAL CHARACTER.

A GENIAL hearth, a hospitable board,
And a refined rusticity, belong
To the neat mansion,* where, his flock among,
The learned pastor dwells, their watchful lord.

* Among the benefits arising, as Mr Coleridge has well observed, from a Church establishment of endowments corresponding with the wealth of the country to which it belongs, may be reckoned as eminently important, the examples of civility and refinement which the clergy, stationed at intervals, afford to the whole people. The established clergy in many parts of England have long been, as they continue to be, the principal bulwark against barbarism, and the link which unites the sequestered peasantry with the intellectual advancement of the age. Nor is it below the dignity of the subject to observe that their taste, as acting upon rural residences and scenery, often furnishes models which country gentlemen, who are more at liberty to follow the caprices of fashion, might profit by. The precincts of an old residence must be treated by ecclesiastics with respect, both from prudence and necessity. I remember being much pleased some years ago, at Rose Castle, the rural seat of the see of Carlisle, with a style of garden and architecture, which, if the place had belonged to a wealthy layman, would no doubt have been swept away. A parsonage-house generally stands not far from the church; this proximity imposes favourable restraints, and sometimes suggests an affecting union of the accommodations and elegances of life with the outward signs of piety and mortality With pleasure I recall to mind a happy instance of this in the residence of an old and much-valued friend in Oxfordshire. The house and church

Though meek and patient as a sheathèd sword,
Though pride's least lurking thought appear [a wrong
To human kind; though peace be on his tongue,
Gentleness in his heart; can earth afford
Such genuine state, pre-eminence so free,
As when, arrayed in Christ's authority,
He from the pulpit lifts his awful hand;
Conjures, implores, and labours all he can
For re-subjecting to divine command
The stubborn spirit of rebellious man?

THE LITURGY.

YES, if the intensities of hope and fear
Attract us still, and passionate exercise
Of lofty thoughts, the way before us lies
Distinct with signs—through which, in fixed career,
As through a zodiac, moves the ritual year
Of England's Church—stupendous mysteries!
Which whoso travels in her bosom, eyes
As he approaches them, with solemn cheer.
Enough for us to cast a transient glance
The circle through, relinquishing its story
For those whom Heaven hath fitted to advance, [Glory—
And, harp in hand, rehearse the King of
From His mild advent till His countenance
Shall dissipate the seas and mountains hoary.

BAPTISM.

BLEST be the Church, that, watching o'er the needs
Of infancy, provides a timely shower,
Whose virtue changes to a Christian flower
The sinful product of a bed of weeds!
Fitliest beneath the sacred roof proceeds
The ministration, while parental love
Looks on, and grace descendeth from above [pleads.
As the high service pledges now, now
There, should vain thoughts outspread their wings and fly
To meet the coming hours of festal mirth,
The tombs which hear and answer that brief cry,
The infant's notice of his second birth,
Recal the wandering soul to sympathy
With what man hopes from Heaven, yet fears from earth

CATECHISING.

FROM little down to least—in due degree,
Around the pastor, each in new-wrought vest,
Each with a vernal posy at his breast,
We stood, a trembling, earnest company!
With low soft murmur, like a distant bee,
Some spake, by thought-perplexing fears betrayed,
And some a bold unerring answer made;
How fluttered then thy anxious heart for me,
Beloved mother! Thou whose happy hand
Had bound the flowers I wore, with faithful tie: [mand
Sweet flowers! at whose inaudible com-
Her countenance, phantom-like, doth re-appear:
Oh, lost too early for the frequent tear,
And ill requited by this heart-felt sigh!

CONFIRMATION.

THE young-ones gathered in from hill and dale,
With holiday delight on every brow
'Tis passed away; far other thoughts prevail,
For they are taking the baptismal vow
Upon their conscious selves, their own lips speak
The solemn promise. Strongest sinews fail,
And many a blooming, many a lovely cheek
Under the holy fear of God turns pale,
While on each head His lawn-robed servant lays
An apostolic hand, and with prayer seals
The covenant. The Omnipotent will raise
Their feeble souls, and bear with *his* regrets, [feels
Who, looking round the fair assemblage,
That ere the sun goes down their childhood sets.

stand parallel to each other, at a small distance; a circular lawn, or rather grass-plot, spreads between them; shrubs and trees curve from each side of the dwelling, veiling, but not hiding the church From the front of this dwelling, no part of the burial-ground is seen, but, as you wind by the side of the shrubs towards the steeple end of the church, the eye catches a single, small, low, monumental head-stone, moss-grown, sinking into, and gently inclining towards, the earth Advance, and the church-yard, populous and gay with glittering tomb-stones, opens upon the view This humble and beautiful parsonage called forth a tribute, for which see "A Parsonage in Oxfordshire," in Miscellaneous Sonnets

CONFIRMATION CONTINUED.

I SAW a mother's eye intensely bent
Upon a maiden trembling as she knelt;
In and for whom the pious mother felt
Things that we judge of by a light too faint,
Tell, if ye may, some star-crowned muse, or saint! [relieved—
Tell what rushed in, from what she was
Then, when her child the hallowing touch received,
And such vibration to the mother went
That tears burst forth amain. Did gleams appear?
Opened a vision of that blissful place
Where dwells a sister-child? And was power given
Part of her lost one's glory back to trace
Even to this rite? For thus *she* knelt, and, ere [heaven.
The summer-leaf had faded, passed to

SACRAMENT.

By chain yet stronger must the soul be tied·
One duty more, last stage of this ascent,
Brings to thy food, memorial Sacrament!
The offspring, haply at the parents' side.
But not till they, with all that do abide
In heaven, have lifted up their hearts to laud
And magnify the glorious name of God,
Fountain of Grace, whose Son for sinners died.
Here must my song in timid reverence pause:
But shrink not ye whom to the saving rite
The altar calls, come early under laws
That can secure for you a path of light
Through gloomiest shade; put on (nor dread its weight)
Armour divine, and conquer in your cause!

RURAL CEREMONY.*

CONTENT with calmer scenes around us spread
And humbler objects, give we to a day
Of annual joy one tributary lay;
This day when, forth by rustic music led,
The village children, while the sky is red
With evening lights, advance in long array
Through the still church-yard, each with garland gay,

* This is still continued in many churches in Westmorland. It takes place in the month of July, when the floor of the stalls is strewn with fresh rushes; and hence it is called the "rush-bearing"

That, carried sceptre-like, o'ertops the head
Of the proud bearer. To the wide church door, [fathers bore
Charged with these offerings which their
For decoration in the papal time,
The innocent procession softly moves,—
The spirit of Laud is pleased in heaven's pure clime,
And Hooker's voice the spectacle approves!

REGRETS.

WOULD that our scrupulous sires had dared to leave
Less scanty measure of those graceful rites
And usages, whose due return invites
A stir of mind too natural to deceive;
Giving the memory help when she would weave [lights
A crown for hope! I dread the boasted
That all too often are but fiery blights,
Killing the bud o'er which in vain we grieve
Go, seek when Christmas snows discomfort bring [church
The counter spirit, found in some gay
Green with fresh holly, every pew a perch
In which the linnet or the thrush might sing,
Merry and loud, and safe from prying search,
Strains offered only to the genial spring.

MUTABILITY.

FROM low to high doth dissolution climb,
And sinks from high to low, along a scale
Of awful notes, whose concord shall not
A musical but melancholy chime, [fail;
Which they can hear who meddle not with crime,
Nor avarice, nor over-anxious care.
Truth fails not; but her outward forms that bear
The longest date do melt like frosty rime,
That in the morning whitened hill and plain
And is no more, drop like the tower sublime
Of yesterday, which royally did wear
Its crown of weeds, but could not even sustain
Some casual shout that broke the silent air,
Or the unimaginable touch of time.

OLD ABBEYS

MONASTIC domes! following my downward way, [fall!
Untouched by due regret I marked your

Now, ruin, beauty, ancient stillness, all
Dispose to judgments temperate as we lay
On our past selves in life's declining day
For as, by discipline of time made wise,
We learn to tolerate the infirmities
And faults of others, gently as he may
Towards our own the mild instructor deals,
Teaching us to forget them or forgive.*
Perversely curious, then for hidden ill
Why should we break time's charitable seals?
Once ye were holy, ye are holy still;
Your spirit let me freely drink and live!

EMIGRANT FRENCH CLERGY

EVEN while I speak, the sacred roofs of France
Are shattered into dust; and self-exiled
From altars threatened, levelled, or defiled,
Wander the ministers of God, as chance
Opens a way for life, or consonance
Of faith invites. More welcome to no land
The fugitives than to the British strand,
Where priest and layman with the vigilance
Of true compassion greet them Creed and test
Vanish before the unreserved embrace
Of Catholic humanity:—distrest
They came,—and, while the moral tempest roars
Throughout the country they have left, our shores
Give to their faith a dreadless resting-place.

CONGRATULATION.

THUS all things lead to charity—secured
By them who blessed the soft and happy gale
That landward urged the great deliverer's sail,
Till in the sunny bay his fleet was moored!
Propitious hour! had we, like them, endured
Sore stress of apprehension,† with a mind
Sickened by injuries, dreading worse designed,
From month to month trembling and unassured,
How had we then rejoiced! But we have felt,
As a loved substance, their futurity,
Good, which they dared not hope for, we have seen,
A state whose generous will through earth is dealt;
A state—which, balancing herself between
Licence and slavish order, dares be free.

NEW CHURCHES

BUT liberty, and triumphs on the main,
And laurelled armies—not to be withstood,
What serve they? if, on transitory good
Intent, and sedulous of abject gain,
The state (ah, surely not preserved in vain!)
Forbear to shape due channels which the flood
Of sacred truth may enter—till it brood
O'er the wide realm, as o'er the Egyptian plain
The all-sustaining Nile No more—the time
Is conscious of her want, through England's bounds,
In rival haste, the wished-for temples rise!
I hear their Sabbath bells' harmonious chime
Float on the breeze—the heavenliest of all sounds
That hill or vale prolongs or multiplies!

CHURCH TO BE ERECTED.

BE this the chosen site;—the virgin sod,
Moistened from age to age by dewy eve,
Shall disappear—and grateful earth receive
The corner-stone from hands that build to God
Yon reverend hawthorns, hardened to the rod
Of winter storms, yet budding cheerfully,
Those forest oaks of Druid memory,
Shall long survive, to shelter the abode
Of genuine faith Where, haply, 'mid this band
Of daisies, shepherds sate of yore and wove
May-garlands, let the holy altar stand
For kneeling adoration; while—above,
Broods, visibly portrayed, the mystic Dove
That shall protect from blasphemy the land.

CONTINUED

MINE ear has rung, my spirit sunk subdued,
Sharing the strong emotion of the crowd,
When each pale brow to dread hosannas bowed
While clouds of incense mounting veiled the rood,

* This is borrowed from an affecting passage in Mr George Dyer's history of Cambridge

† See Burnet, who is unusually animated on this subject. the east wind, so anxiously expected and prayed for, was called the "Protestant wind"

That glimmered like a pine-tree dimly viewed
Through Alpine vapours. Such appalling rite [might
Our Church prepares not, trusting to the
Of simple truth with grace divine imbued;
Yet will we not conceal the precious cross,
Like men ashamed:* the sun with his first smile [pile;
Shall greet that symbol crowning the low
And the fresh air of "incense-breathing morn"
Shall wooingly embrace it; and green moss
Creep round its arms through centuries unborn.

NEW CHURCH-YARD.

THE encircling ground, in native turf arrayed,
Is now by solemn consecration given
To social interests, and to favouring heaven;
And where the rugged colts their gambols played, [glade,
And wild deer bounded through the forest
Unchecked as when by merry outlaw driven,
Shall hymns of praise resound at morn and even;
And so, full soon, the lonely sexton's spade
Shall wound the tender sod. Encincture small,
But infinite its grasp of joy and woe!
Hopes, fears, in never-ending ebb and flow— [dust"—
The spousal trembling—and the "dust to
The prayers, the contrite struggle, and the trust [all!
That to the Almighty Father looks through

CATHEDRALS, ETC.

OPEN your gates, ye everlasting piles!
Types of the spiritual Church which God hath reared;
Not loth we quit the newly-hallowed sward
And humble altar, 'mid your sumptuous aisles
To kneel—or thrid your intricate defiles—
Or down the nave to pace in motion slow;
Watching, with upward eye, the tall tower grow
And mount, at every step, with living wiles
Instinct—to rouse the heart and lead the will
By a bright ladder to the world above.
Open your gates, ye monuments of love
Divine! thou, Lincoln, on thy sovereign hill!
Thou, stately York! and ye, whose splendours cheer
Isis and Cam, to patient science dear!

INSIDE OF KING'S COLLEGE CHAPEL, CAMBRIDGE.

TAX not the royal saint with vain expense,
With ill-matched aims the architect who planned,
Albeit labouring for a scanty band
Of white-robed scholars only, this immense
And glorious work of fine intelligence!
Give all thou canst; high Heaven rejects the lore
Of nicely-calculated less or more;
So deemed the man who fashioned for the sense [roof
These lofty pillars, spread that branching
Self-poised, and scooped into ten thousand cells, [dwells
Where light and shade repose, where music
Lingering—and wandering on as loth to die;
Like thoughts whose very sweetness yieldeth proof
That they were born for immortality.

THE SAME.

WHAT awful pérspective! while from our sight [hide
With gradual stealth the lateral windows
Their portraitures, their stone-work glimmers, dyed
In the soft chequerings of a sleepy light.
Martyr, or king, or sainted eremite,
Whoe'er ye be, that thus—yourselves unseen—
Imbue your prison-bars with solemn sheen,
Shine on! until ye fade with coming night!
But, from the arms of silence—list! oh, list!
The music bursteth into second life;—
The notes luxuriate—every stone is kissed
By sound, or ghost of sound, in mazy strife;
Heart-thrilling strains, that cast before the
Of the devout a veil of ecstasy! [eye

CONTINUED.

THEY dreamt not of a perishable home
Who thus could build. Be mine, in hours of fear
Or grovelling thought, to seek a refuge here;

* The Lutherans have retained the cross within their churches; it is to be regretted that we have not done the same.

Or through the aisles of Westminster to
roam; [foam
Where bubbles burst, and folly's dancing
Melts, if it cross the threshold; where the
wreath [path
Of awe-struck wisdom droops: or let my
Lead to that younger pile, whose sky-like
dome
Hath typified by reach of daring art
Infinity's embrace; whose guardian crest,
The silent cross, among the stars shall
spread
As now, when she hath *also* seen her breast
Filled with mementos, satiate with its part
Of grateful England's overflowing dead.

EJACULATION.

GLORY to God! and to the Power who
came
In filial duty, clothed with love divine;
That made His human tabernacle shine
Like ocean burning with purpureal flame;
Or like the Alpine mount, that takes its
name [and even,
From roseate hues,* far kenned at morn
In hours of peace, or when the storm is
driven
Along the nether region's rugged frame!
Earth prompts—Heaven urges; let us seek
the light
Studious of that pure intercourse begun
When first our infant brows their lustre
won; [bright
So, like the mountain, may we grow more
From unimpeded commerce with the sun,
At the approach of all-involving night.

* Some say that Monte Rosa takes its name from a belt of rock at its summit—a very unpoetical, and scarcely a probable supposition.

CONCLUSION.

WHY sleeps the future, as a snake enrolled
Coil within coil, at noon-tide? For the
Word [plored,
Yields, if with unpresumptuous faith ex-
Power at whose touch the sluggard shall
unfold, [behold,
His drowsy rings. Look forth! that stream
That stream upon whose bosom we have
passed
Floating at ease while nations have effaced
Nations, and death has gathered to his fold
Long lines of mighty kings—look forth,
my soul!
(Nor in this vision be thou slow to trust)
The living waters, less and less by guilt
Stained and polluted, brighten as they roll,
Till they have reached the eternal city—
built
For the perfected spirits of the just!

The White Doe of Rylstone;[1]

OR,

THE FATE OF THE NORTONS.

ADVERTISEMENT.

During the Summer of 1807, the author visited, for the first time, the beautiful scenery that surrounds Bolton Priory, in Yorkshire; and the poem of the White Doe, founded upon a tradition connected with the place, was composed at the close of the same year

In trellised shed with clustering roses gay,
And, Mary! oft beside our blazing fire,
When years of wedded life were as a day
Whose current answers to the heart's desire,
Did we together read in Spenser's lay,
How Una, sad of soul—in sad attire,
The gentle Una, born of heavenly birth,
To seek her knight went wandering o'er the earth.

Ah, then, beloved! pleasing was the smart,
And the tear precious in compassion shed
For her, who, pierced by sorrow's thrilling dart,
Did meekly bear the pang unmerited;
Meek as that emblem of her lowly heart
The milk-white lamb which in a line she led,—
And faithful, loyal in her innocence,
Like the brave lion slain in her defence.

Notes could we hear as of a faery shell
Attuned to words with sacred wisdom fraught,
Free fancy prized each specious miracle,
And all its finer inspiration caught,
Till, in the bosom of our rustic cell,
We by a lamentable change were taught
That "bliss with mortal man may not abide:"—
How nearly joy and sorrow are allied!

For us the stream of fiction ceased to flow,
For us the voice of melody was mute.
But, as soft gales dissolve the dreary snow,
And give the timid herbage leave to shoot,
Heaven's breathing influence failed not to bestow
A timely promise of unlooked-for fruit,
Fair fruit of pleasure and serene content
From blossoms wild of fancies innocent.

It soothed us—it beguiled us—then, to hear
Once more of troubles wrought by magic spell;
And griefs whose aery motion comes not near
The pangs that tempt the spirit to rebel;
Then, with mild Una in her sober cheer,
High over hill and low adown the dell
Again we wandered, willing to partake
All that she suffered for her dear lord's sake.

Then, too, this song of mine once more could please,
Where anguish, strange as dreams of restless sleep,
Is tempered and allayed by sympathies
Aloft ascending, and descending deep,
Even to the inferior kinds; whom forest trees
Protect from beating sunbeams, and the sweep
Of the sharp winds;—fair creatures!—to whom Heaven
A calm and sinless life, with love, hath given.

This tragic story cheered us; for it speaks
Of female patience winning firm repose;
And of the recompense which conscience seeks
A bright, encouraging example shows;
Needful when o'er wide realms the tempest breaks,
Needful amid life's ordinary woes;
Hence, not for them unfitted who would bless
A happy hour with holier happiness.

[1] See Notes at end of poem, page 251.

He serves the muses erringly and ill,
Whose aim is pleasure light and fugitive
Oh, that my mind were equal to fulfil
The comprehensive mandate which they give—
Vain aspiration of an earnest will!
Yet in this moral strain a power may live,
Beloved wife! such solace to impart
As it hath yielded to thy tender heart.

Rydal Mount, Westmoreland,
April 20, 1815

CANTO 1

"They that deny a God, destroy man's nobility, for certainly man is of kinn to the beasts by his body: and if he be not of kinn to God by his spirit, he is a base ignoble creature. It destroys likewise magnanimity, and the raising of humane nature. for take an example of a dogg, and mark what a generosity and courage he will put on, when he finds himself maintained by a man, who to him is instead of a God, or *melior natura* Which courage is manifestly such, as that creature without that confidence of a better nature than his own could never attain. So man, when he resteth and assureth himself upon Divine protection and favour, gathereth a force and faith which human nature in itself could not obtain"—
LORD BACON

FROM Bolton's old monastic tower(2)
The bells ring loud with gladsome power,
The sun is bright, the fields are gay
With people in their best array
Of stole and doublet, hood and scarf,
Along the banks of crystal Wharf,
Through the vale retired and lowly,
Trooping to that summons holy
And, up among the moorlands, see
What sprinklings of blithe company!
Of lasses and of shepherd grooms,
That down the steep hills force their way,
Like cattle through the budded brooms;
Path, or no path, what care they?
And thus in joyous mood they hie
To Bolton's mouldering Priory

What would they there?—Full fifty years
That sumptuous pile, with all its peers,
Too harshly hath been doomed to taste
The bitterness of wrong and waste:
Its courts are ravaged; but the tower
Is standing with a voice of power,
That ancient voice which wont to call
To mass or some high festival;
And in the shattered fabric's heart
Remaineth one protected part;
A rural chapel, neatly drest,(3)
In covert like a little nest;
And thither old and young repair,
This Sabbath day, for praise and prayer

Fast the church-yard fills,—anon
Look again, and they all are gone,
The cluster round the porch, and the folk
Who sate in the shade of the Prior's Oak.(4)
And scarcely have they disappeared
Ere the prelusive hymn is heard —
With one consent the people rejoice,
Filling the church with a lofty voice!
They sing a service which they feel.
For 'tis the sun-rise now of zeal,
And faith and hope are in their prime,
In great Eliza's golden time

A moment ends the fervent din,
And all is hushed, without and within;
For though the priest, more tranquilly,
Recites the holy liturgy,
The only voice which you can hear
Is the river murmuring near.
When soft!—the dusky trees between,
And down the path through the open green,
Where is no living thing to be seen;
And through yon gateway, where is found,
Beneath the arch with ivy bound,
Free entrance to the church-yard ground,
And right across the verdant sod
Towards the very house of God,—
Comes gliding in with lovely gleam,
Comes gliding in serene and slow,
Soft and silent as a dream,
A solitary doe!
White she is as lily of June,
And beauteous as the silver moon
When out of sight the clouds are driven,
And she is left alone in heaven;
Or like a ship some gentle day
In sunshine sailing far away,
A glittering ship, that hath the plain
Of ocean for her own domain

Lie silent in your graves, ye dead!
Lie quiet in your church-yard bed!
Ye living, tend your holy cares;
Ye multitude, pursue your prayers,
And blame not me if my heart and sight
Are occupied with one delight!
'Tis a work for Sabbath hours
If I with this bright creature go,
Whether she be of forest bowers,
From the bowers of earth below;
Or a spirit, for one day given,
A gift of grace from purest heaven.

What harmonious pensive changes
Wait upon her as she ranges
Round and through this pile of state,
Overthrown and desolate !
Now a step or two her way
Is through space of open day,
Where the enamoured sunny light
Brightens her that was so bright ;
Now doth a delicate shadow fall,
Falls upon her like a breath,
From some lofty arch or wall,
As she passes underneath :
Now some gloomy nook partakes
Of the glory that she makes,—
High-ribbed vault of stone, or cell
With perfect cunning framed as well
Of stone, and ivy, and the spread
Of the elder's bushy head ;
Some jealous and forbidding cell,
That doth the living stars repel,
And where no flower hath leave to dwell.

The presence of this wandering doe
Fills many a damp obscure recess
With lustre of a saintly show ;
And, re-appearing, she no less
To the open day gives blessedness.
But say, among these holy places,
Which thus assiduously she paces,
Comes she with a votary's task,
Rite to perform, or boon to ask ?
Fair pilgrim ! harbours she a sense
Of sorrow, or of reverence ?
Can she be grieved for quire or shrine,
Crushed as if by wrath divine ?
For what survives of house where God
Was worshipped, or where man abode ;
For old magnificence undone ;
Or for the gentler work begun
By nature, softening and concealing,
And busy with a hand of healing,—
For altar, whence the cross was rent,
Now rich with mossy ornament,
Or dormitory's length laid bare,
Where the wild rose blossoms fair ;
And sapling ash, whose place of birth
Is that lordly chamber's hearth?
She sees a warrior carved in stone,
Among the thick weeds, stretched alone ;
A warrior, with his shield of pride
Cleaving humbly to his side,
And hands in resignation prest,
Palm to palm, on his tranquil breast :
Methinks she passeth by the sight,
As a common creature might :
If she be doomed to inward car
Or service, it must lie elsewhere.
But hers are eyes serenely bright,
And on she moves—with pace how light ?
Nor spares to stoop her head, and taste
The dewy turf with flowers bestrown ;
And thus she fares, until at last
Beside the ridge of a grassy grave
In quietness she lays her down ;
Gently as a weary wave
Sinks, when the summer breeze hath died,
Against an anchored vessel's side ;
Even so, without distress, doth she
Lie down in peace, and lovingly.

The day is placid in its going,
To a lingering motion bound,
Like the river in its flowing—
Can there be a softer sound ?
So the balmy minutes pass,
While this radiant creature lies
Couched upon the dewy grass,
Pensively with downcast eyes.
When now again the people rear
A voice of praise, with awful cheer !
It is the last, the parting song ;
And from the temple forth they throng—
And quickly spread themselves abroad—
While each pursues his several road.
But some, a variegated band,
Of middle-aged, and old, and young,
And little children by the hand
Upon their leading mothers hung,
Turn, with obeisance gladly paid,
Towards the spot, where, full in view,
The lovely doe of whitest hue,
Her Sabbath couch has made.

It was a solitary mound ;
Which two spears' length of level ground
Did from all other graves divide :
As if in some respect of pride ;
Or melancholy's sickly mood,
Still shy of human neighbourhood ;
Or guilt, that humbly would express
A penitential loneliness.

"Look, there she is, my child ! draw near;
She fears not, wherefore should we fear ?
She means no harm ;"—but still the boy,
To whom the words were softly said,
Hung back, and smiled and blushed for joy
A shame-faced blush of glowing red !
Again the mother whispered low,
"Now you have seen the famous doe ;
From Rylstone she hath found her way
Over the hills this Sabbath-day ;
Her work, whate'er it be, is done,
And she will depart when we are gone ;

Thus doth she keep from year to year,
Her Sabbath morning, foul or fair "

This whisper soft repeats what he
Had known from early infancy.
Bright is the creature—as in dreams
The boy had seen her—yea, more bright,
But is she truly what she seems?
He asks with insecure delight,
Asks of himself—and doubts—and still
The doubt returns against his will:
Though he, and all the standers by,
Could tell a tragic history
Of facts divulged, wherein appear
Substantial motive, reason clear,
Why thus the milk-white doe is found
Couchant beside that lonely mound,
And why she duly loves to pace
The circuit of this hallowed place.
Nor to the child's inquiring mind
Is such perplexity confined:
For, spite of sober truth, that sees
A world of fixed remembrances
Which to this mystery belong,
If, undeceived, my skill can trace
The characters of every face,
There lack not strange delusion here,
Conjecture vague, and idle fear,
And superstitious fancies strong,
Which do the gentle creature wrong.

That bearded, staff-supported sire,
(Who in his youth hath often fed
Full cheerily on convent-bread,
And heard old tales by the convent-fire,
And lately hath brought home the scars
Gathered in long and distant wars)
That old man—studious to expound
The spectacle—hath mounted high
To days of dim antiquity;
When Lady Aaliza mourned(5)
Her son, and felt in her despair,
The pang of unavailing prayer,
Her son in Wharf's abysses drowned,
The noble boy of Egremound
From which affliction, when God's grace
At length had in her heart found place,
A pious structure, fair to see,
Rose up—this stately priory!
The lady's work,—but now laid low, [go
To the grief of her soul that doth come and
In the beautiful form of this innocent doe:
Which, though seemingly doomed in its
breast to sustain
A softened remembrance of sorrow and pain,
Is spotless, and holy, and gentle, and bright;
And glides o'er the earth like an angel of
light.

Pass, pass who will, yon chantry door,(6)
And, through the chink in the fractured floor
Look down, and see a griesly sight;
A vault where the bodies are buried upright!
There, face by face and hand by hand,
The Claphams and Mauleverers stand,
And, in his place, among son and sire,
Is John de Clapham, that fierce esquire,
A valiant man, and a name of dread,
In the ruthless wars of the White and Red,
Who dragged Earl Pembroke from Banbury
church, [the porch!
And smote off his head on the stones of
Look down among them, if you dare,
Oft does the White Doe loiter there,
Prying into the darksome rent,
Nor can it be with good intent,—
So thinks that dame of haughty air,
Who hath a page her book to hold,
And wears a frontlet edged with gold.
Well may her thoughts be harsh. for she
Numbers among her ancestry
Earl Pembroke, slain so impiously!

That slender youth, a scholar pale,
From Oxford come to his native vale,
He also hath his own conceit
It is, thinks he, the gracious fairy,
Who loved the Shepherd Lord to meet(7)
In his wanderings solitary
Wild notes she in his hearing sang,
A song of nature's hidden powers;
That whistled like the wind, and rang
Among the rocks and holly bowers.
'Twas said that she all shapes could wear;
And oftentimes before him stood,
Amid the trees of some thick wood,
In semblance of a lady fair,
And taught him signs, and showed him
sights,
In Craven's dens, on Cumbrian heights;
When under cloud of fear he lay,
A shepherd clad in homely gray,
Nor left him at his later day.
And hence, when he, with spear and shield
Rode full of years to Flodden field,
His eye could see the hidden spring,
And how the current was to flow,
The fatal end of Scotland's king,
And all that hopeless overthrow.
But not in wars did he delight,
This Clifford wished for worthier might:
Nor in broad pomp, or courtly state:
Him his own thoughts did elevate,—
Most happy in the shy recess
Of Barden's humble quietness.
And choice of studious friends had he
Of Bolton's dear fraternity;

Who, standing on this old church tower,
In many a calm propitious hour,
Perused, with him, the starry sky;
Or, in their cells, with him did pry
For other lore,—through strong desire
Searching the earth with chemic fire:
But they and their good works are fled—
And all is now disquieted—
And peace is none, for living or dead!

Ah, pensive scholar, think not so,
But look again at the radiant doe!
What quiet watch she seems to keep,
Alone, beside that grassy heap!

Why mention other thoughts unmeet
For vision so composed and sweet?
While stand the people in a ring,
Gazing, doubting, questioning,
Yea, many overcome in spite
Of recollections clear and bright;
Which yet do unto some impart
An undisturbed repose of heart,
And all the assembly own a law
Of orderly respect and awe;
But see—they vanish, one by one.
And last, the doe herself is gone.

Harp! we have been full long beguiled
By busy dreams, and fancies wild;
To which, with no reluctant strings,
Thou hast attuned thy murmurings;
And now before this pile we stand
In solitude, and utter peace;
But, harp! thy murmurs may not cease—
Thou hast breeze-like visitings,
For a spirit with angel's wings
Hath touched thee, and a spirit's hand:
A voice is with us—a command
To chant, in strains of heavenly glory,
A tale of tears, a mortal story.

CANTO II.

THE harp in lowliness obeyed;
And first we sang of the green-wood shade,
And a solitary maid;
Beginning, where the song must end,
With her, and with her sylvan friend;
Her friend who stood before her sight,
Her only unextinguished light;
The last companion in a dearth
Of love, upon a hopeless earth.

For she it was—this maid, who wrought
Meekly, with foreboding thought,
In vermeil colours and in gold
An unblest work; which, standing by,
Her father did with joy behold,—
Exulting in the imagery;
A banner, one that did fulfil
Too perfectly his headstrong will·
For on this banner had her hand
Embroidered (such was the command)
The sacred cross; and figured there
The five dear wounds our Lord did bear;
Full soon to be uplifted high,
And float in rueful company!

It was the time when England's queen
Twelve years had reigned, a sovereign dread;
Nor yet the restless crown had been
Disturbed upon her virgin head;
But now the inly-working north
Was ripe to send its thousands forth,
A potent vassalage, to fight
In Percy's and in Neville's right,
Two earls fast leagued in discontent,
Who gave their wishes open vent;
And boldly urged a general plea,
The rites of ancient piety
To be triumphantly restored,
By the dread justice of the sword!
And that same banner, on whose breast
The blameless lady had exprest
Memorials chosen to give life
And sunshine to a dangerous strife;
That banner, waiting for the call,
Stood quietly in Rylstone Hall.

It came,—and Francis Norton said,
"O father! rise not in this fray—
The hairs are white upon your head;
Dear father, hear me when I say
It is for you too late a day!
Bethink you of your own good name:
A just and gracious queen have we,
A pure religion, and the claim
Of peace on our humanity.
'Tis meet that I endure your scorn,—
I am your son, your eldest born,
But not for lordship or for land,
My father, do I clasp your knees—
The banner touch not, stay your hand,—
This multitude of men disband,
And live at home in blameless ease;
For these my brethren's sake, for me;
And, most of all, for Emily!"

Loud noise was in the crowded hall,
And scarcely could the father hear
That name—which had a dying fall,
The name of his only daughter dear,—

And on the banner which stood near
He glanced a look of holy pride,
And his moist eyes were glorified ;
Then seized the staff, and thus did say—
"Thou, Richard, bear'st thy father's name,
Keep thou this ensign till the day
When I of thee require the same
Thy place be on my better hand ;—
And seven as true as thou, I see,
Will cleave to this good cause and me."
He spake, and eight brave sons straightway
All followed him, a gallant band!

Forth when sire and sons appeared
A gratulating shout was reared,
With din of arms and minstrelsy,
From all his warlike tenantry,
All horsed and harnessed with him to ride,
A shout to which the hills replied!

But Francis, in the vacant hall,
Stood silent under dreary weight,—
A phantasm, in which roof and wall
Shook—tottered—swam before his sight ;
A phantasm like a dream of night!
Thus overwhelmed, and desolate,
He found his way to a postern-gate ;
And, when he walked at length, his eye
Was on the calm and silent sky,
With air about him breathing sweet,
And earth's green grass beneath his feet ;
Nor did he fail ere long to hear
A sound of military cheer,
Faint—but it reached that sheltered spot ;
He heard, and it disturbed him not.

There stood he, leaning on a lance
Which he had grasped unknowingly,—
Had blindly grasped in that strong trance,
That dimness of heart agony ;
There stood he, cleansed from the despair
And sorrow of his fruitless prayer.
The past he calmly hath reviewed :
But where will be the fortitude
Of this brave man, when he shall see
That form beneath the spreading tree,
And know that it is Emily?
Oh! hide them from each other, hide,
Kind Heaven, this pair severely tried!

He saw her where in open view
She sate beneath the spreading yew,—
Her head upon her lap, concealing
In solitude her bitter feeling ;
How could he choose but shrink or sigh?
He shrunk, and muttered inwardly,
"Might ever son *command* a sire,
The act were justified to-day."

This to himself—and to the maid,
Whom now he had approached, he said,
"Gone are they,—they have their desire,
And I with thee one hour will stay,
To give thee comfort if I may."

He paused, her silence to partake,
And long it was before he spake [round,
Then, all at once, his thoughts turned
And fervent words a passage found.

"Gone are they, bravely, though misled;
With a dear father at their head!
The sons obey a natural lord ;
The father had given solemn word
To noble Percy,—and a force,
Still stronger, bends him to his course
This said, our tears to-day may fall
As at an innocent funeral
In deep and awful channel runs
This sympathy of sire and sons,
Untried our brothers were beloved,
And now their faithfulness is proved,
For faithful we must call them, bearing
That soul of conscientious daring.
There were they all in circle—there
Stood Richard, Ambrose, Christopher,
John with a sword that will not fail,
And Marmaduke in fearless mail,
And those bright twins were side by side ;
And there by fresh hopes beautified,
Stood he, whose arm yet lacks the power
Of man, our youngest, fairest flower!
I, by the right of eldest born,
And in a second father's place,
Presumed to grapple with their scorn,
And meet their pity face to face,
Yea, trusting in God's holy aid,
I to my father knelt and prayed,
And one, the pensive Marmaduke,
Methought, was yielding inwardly,
And would have laid his purpose by,
But for a glance of his father's eye,
Which I myself could scarcely brook

"Then, be we, each, and all, forgiven.
Thee, chiefly thee, my sister dear,
Whose pangs are registered in heaven.
The stifled sigh, the hidden tear,
And smiles, that dared to take their place,
Meek filial smiles, upon thy face,
As that unhallowed banner grew
Beneath a loving old man's view
Thy part is done—thy painful part ;
Be thou then satisfied in heart!
A further, though far easier, task
Than thine hath been, my duties ask ;

With theirs my efforts cannot blend,
I cannot for such cause contend;
Their aims I utterly forswear;
But I in body will be there.
Unarmed and naked will I go,
Be at their side, come weal or woe:
On kind occasions I may wait,
See, hear, obstruct, or mitigate.
Bare breast I take and an empty hand."*
Therewith he threw away the lance,
Which he had grasped in that strong trance,
Spurned it—like something that would [stand
Between him and the pure intent
Of love on which his soul was bent.

"For thee, for thee, is left the sense
Of trial past without offence
To God or man;—such innocence,
Such consolation, and the excess
Of an unmerited distress;
In that thy very strength must lie.
O sister, I could prophesy!
The time is come that rings the knell
Of all we loved, and loved so well;
Hope nothing, if I thus may speak
To thee a woman, and thence weak;
Hope nothing, I repeat; for we
Are doomed to perish utterly:
'Tis meet that thou with me divide
The thought while I am by thy side,
Acknowledging a grace in this,
A comfort in the dark abyss:
But look not for me when I am gone,
And be no farther wrought upon.
Farewell all wishes, all debate,
All prayers for this cause, or for that!
Weep, if that aid thee; but depend
Upon no help of outward friend;
Espouse thy doom at once, and cleave
To fortitude without reprieve.
For we must fall, both we and ours,—
This mansion and these pleasant bowers,
Walks, pools, and arbours, homestead, hall,
Our fate is theirs, will reach them all;
The young horse must forsake his manger,
And learn to glory in a stranger;
The hawk forget his perch—the hound
Be parted from his ancient ground:
The blast will sweep us all away,
One desolation, one decay! [saying
And even this creature!" which words
He pointed to a lovely doe,
A few steps distant, feeding, straying,
Fair creature, and more white than snow!

* See the old ballad,—"The Rising of the North."

"Even she will to her peaceful woods
Return, and to her murmuring floods,
And be in heart and soul the same
She was before she hither came,—
Ere she had learned to love us all,
Herself beloved in Rylstone Hall.
But thou, my sister, doomed to be
The last leaf which by Heaven's decree
Must hang upon a blasted tree;
If not in vain we breathed the breath
Together of a purer faith—
If hand in hand we have been led,
And thou, (oh, happy thought this day!)
Not seldom foremost in the way—
If on one thought our minds have fed,
And we have in one meaning read—
If, when at home our private weal
Hath suffered from the shock of zeal,
Together we have learned to prize
Forbearance and self-sacrifice—
If we like combatants have fared,
And for this issue been prepared—
If thou art beautiful, and youth
And thought endue thee with all truth—
Be strong;—be worthy of the grace
Of God, and fill thy destined place:
A soul, by force of sorrows high,
Uplifted to the purest sky
Of undisturbed humanity!"

He ended,—or she heard no more:
He led her from the yew-tree shade,
And at the mansion's silent door,
He kissed the consecrated maid;
And down the valley he pursued,
Alone, the armèd multitude.

CANTO III.

Now joy for you and sudden cheer,
Ye watchmen upon Brancepeth towers; (8)
Looking forth in doubt and fear,
Telling melancholy hours!
Proclaim it, let your masters hear
That Norton with his band is near!
The watchmen from their station high
Pronounced the word,—and the earls descry
Forthwith the armèd company
Marching down the banks of Were.

Said fearless Norton to the pair
Gone forth to hail him on the plain—
"This meeting, noble lords! looks fair,
I bring with me a goodly train;
Their hearts are with you:—hill and dale
Have helped us:—Ure we crossed, and Swale.

And horse and harness followed—see
The best part of their yeomanry!
Stand forth, my sons!—these eight are mine,
Whom to this service I commend;
Which way soe'er our fate incline,
These will be faithful to the end,
They are my all"—voice failed him here,
"My all save one, a daughter dear!
Whom I have left, the mildest birth,
The meekest child on this blessed earth,
I had—but these are by my side,
These eight, and this is a day of pride!
The time is ripe—with festive din
Lo! how the people are flocking in,—
Like hungry fowls to the feeder's hand
When snow lies heavy upon the land."

He spake bare truth; for far and near
From every side came noisy swarms
Of peasants in their homely gear;
And, mixed with these to Brancepeth came
Grave gentry of estate and name,
And captains known for worth in arms·
And prayed the earls in self-defence
To rise, and prove their innocence —
"Rise, noble earls, put forth your might
For holy Church, and the people's right!"

The Norton fixed, at this demand,
His eye upon Northumberland,
And said, "The minds of men will own
No loyal rest while England's crown
Remains without an heir, the bait
Of strife and factions desperate;
Who, paying deadly hate in kind
Through all things else, in this can find
A mutual hope, a common mind;
And plot, and pant to overwhelm
All ancient honour in the realm
Brave earls! to whose heroic veins
Our noblest blood is given in trust,
To you a suffering state complains,
And ye must raise her from the dust
With wishes of still bolder scope
On you we look, with dearest hope,
Even for our altars,—for the prize
In heaven, of life that never dies;
For the old and holy Church we mourn,
And must in joy to her return.
Behold!"—and from his son whose stand
Was on his right, from that guardian hand
He took the banner, and unfurled
The precious folds—"behold," said he,
"The ransom of a sinful world;
Let this your preservation be,—
The wounds of hands and feet and side,
And the sacred cross on which Jesus died!
This bring I from an ancient hearth,
These records wrought in pledge of love
By hands of no ignoble birth,
A maid o'er whom the blessed Dove
Vouchsafed in gentleness to brood
While she the holy work pursued."
"Uplift the standard!" was the cry
From all the listeners that stood round;
"Plant it,—by this we live or die"—
The Norton ceased not for that sound,
But said, "The prayer which ye have heard
Much injured earls! by these preferred,
Is offered to the saints, the sigh
Of tens of thousands, secretly."—
"Uplift it!" cried once more the band,
And then a thoughtful pause ensued.
"Uplift it, !" said Northumberland—
Whereat, from all the multitude,
Who saw the banner reared on high
In all its dread emblazonry,
With tumult and indignant rout
A voice of uttermost joy brake out.
The transport was rolled down the river of Were,
And Durham, the time-honoured Durham, did hear,
And the towers of Saint Cuthbert were stirred by the shout!

Now was the North in arms.—they shine
In warlike trim from Tweed to Tyne,
At Percy's voice; and Neville sees
His followers gathering in from Tees
From Were, and all the little rills—
Concealed among the forked hills—
Seven hundred knights, retainers all
Of Neville, at their master's call
Had sate together in Raby hall!
Such strength that earldom held of yore;
Nor wanted at this time rich store
Of well-appointed chivalry.
Not loth the sleepy lance to wield,
And greet the old paternal shield,
They heard the summons,—and, furthermore,
Horsemen and foot of each degree,
Unbound by pledge of fealty,
Appeared, with free and open hate
Of novelties in Church and State,
Knight, burgher, yeoman, and esquire;
And Romish priest, in priest's attire
And thus, in arms, a zealous band
Proceeding under joint command,
To Durham first their course they bear.
And in Saint Cuthbert's ancient seat
Sang mass, and tore the Book of Prayer,—
And trod the Bible beneath their feet.

Thence marching southward smooth and free,
"They mustered their host at Wetherby,
Full sixteen thousand, fair to see;"*
The choicest warriors of the North!
But none for beauty and for worth
Like those eight sons—embosoming
Determined thoughts—who, in a ring
Each with a lance, erect and tall,
A falchion, and a buckler small,
Stood by their sire, on Clifford-moor,
To guard the standard which he bore.
With feet that firmly pressed the ground
They stood, and girt their father round;
Such was his choice,—no steed will he
Henceforth bestride;—triumphantly
He stood upon the grassy sod,
Trusting himself to the earth, and God.
Rare sight to embolden and inspire!
Proud was the field of sons and sire,
Of him the most; and sooth to say,
No shape of man in all the array
So graced the sunshine of that day.
The monumental pomp of age
Was with this goodly personage;
A stature undepressed in size,
Unbent, which rather seemed to rise,
In open victory o'er the weight
Of seventy years, to higher height;
Magnific limbs of withered state,—
A face to fear and venerate,—
Eyes dark and strong, and on his head
Bright locks of silver hair, thick-spread.
Which a brown morion half-concealed,
Light as a hunter's of the field;
And thus, with girdle round his waist,
Whereon the banner-staff might rest
At need, he stood, advancing high
The glittering, floating pageantry.

Who sees him?—many see, and one
With unparticipated gaze;
Who 'mong these thousand friends hath none,
And treads in solitary ways.
He, following wheresoe'er he might,
Hath watched the banner from afar,
As shepherds watch a lonely star,
Or mariners the distant light
That guides them on a stormy night.
And now upon a chosen plot
Of rising ground, yon heathy spot!
He takes this day his far-off stand,
With breast unmailed, unweaponed hand.
Bold is his aspect; but his eye
Is pregnant with anxiety,
While, like a tutelary power,
He there stands fixed, from hour to hour;
Yet sometimes in more humble guise,
Stretched out upon the ground he lies;
As if it were his only task
Like herdsmen in the sun to bask,
Or by his mantle's help to find
A shelter from the nipping wind:
And thus, with short oblivion blest,
His weary spirits gather rest.
Again he lifts his eyes; and lo!
The pageant glancing to and fro;
And hope is wakened by the sight,
He thence may learn, ere fall of night,
Which way the tide is doomed to flow.

To London were the chieftains bent;
But what avails the bold intent?
A royal army is gone forth
To quell the rising of the North;
They march with Dudley at their head,
And, in seven days' space, will to York be led!
Can such a mighty host be raised
Thus suddenly, and brought so near?
The earls upon each other gazed;
And Neville was opprest with fear;
For, though he bore a valiant name,
His heart was of a timid frame,
And bold if both had been, yet they
"Against so many may not stay."†
And therefore will retreat to seize
A stronghold on the banks of Tees;
There wait a favourable hour,
Until Lord Dacre with his power
From Naworth comes; and Howard's aid
Be with them; openly displayed.

While through the host, from man to man,
A rumour of this purpose ran,
The standard giving to the care
Of him who heretofore did bear
That charge, impatient Norton sought
The chieftains to unfold his thought,
And thus abruptly spake,—"We yield
(And can it be?) an unfought field!
How often hath the strength of Heaven
To few triumphantly been given!
Still do our very children boast
Of mitred Thurston, what a host
He conquered!(9)—Saw we not the plain,
(And flying shall behold again)
Where faith was proved?—while to battle moved
The standard on the sacred wain

* From the old ballad.

† From the old ballad.

On which the gray-haired barons stood,
And the infant heir of Mowbray's blood,
Beneath the saintly ensigns three,
Stood confident of victory!
Shall Percy blush, then, for his name?
Must Westmoreland be asked with shame,
Whose were the numbers, where the loss,
In that other day of Neville's Cross?(10)
When, as the vision gave command,
The Prior of Durham with holy hand
Saint Cuthbert's relic did uprear
Upon the point of a lofty spear,
And God descended in His power,
While the monks prayed in maiden's bower
Less would not at our need be due
To us, who war against the untrue,—
The delegates of heaven we rise,
Convoked the impious to chastise;
We, we the sanctities of old
Would re-establish and uphold."
The Chiefs were by his zeal confounded,
But word was given—and the trumpet sounded;
Back through the melancholy host
Went Norton, and resumed his post.
Alas! thought he, and have I borne
This banner, raised so joyfully,
This hope of all posterity,
Thus to become at once the scorn
Of babbling winds as they go by,
A spot of shame to the sun's bright eye,
To the frail clouds a mockery!
"Even these poor eight of mine would stem;"
Half to himself, and half to them
He spake, "would stem, or quell a force
Ten times their number, man and horse,
This by their own unaided might,
Without their father in their sight,
Without the cause for which they fight;
A cause, which on a needful day
Would breed us thousands brave as they."
So speaking he his reverend head
Raised towards that imagery once more·
But the familiar prospect shed
Despondency unfelt before:
A shock of intimations vain,
Dismay, and superstitious pain,
Fell on him, with the sudden thought
Of her by whom the work was wrought:
Oh, wherefore was her countenance bright
With love divine and gentle light?
She did in passiveness obey,
But her faith leaned another way
Ill tears she wept.—I saw them fall,
I overheard her as she spake
Sad words to that mute animal,
The White Doe in the hawthorn brake;
She steeped, but not for Jesu's sake,
This cross in tears:—by her, and one
Unworthier far, we are undone—
Her brother was it who assailed
Her tender spirit and prevailed.
Her other parent, too, whose head
In the cold grave hath long been laid,
From reason's earliest dawn beguiled
The docile, unsuspecting child.
Far back—far back my mind must go
To reach the well-spring of this woe!
While thus he brooded, music sweet
Was played to cheer them in retreat;
But Norton lingering in the rear
Thought followed thought—and ere the last
Of that unhappy train was past,
Before him Francis did appear.

"Now when 'tis not your aim to oppose,"
Said he, "in open field your foes,
Now that from this decisive day
Your multitude must melt away,
An unarmed man may come unblamed;
To ask a grace, that was not claimed
Long as your hopes were high, he now
May hither bring a fearless brow,
When his discountenance can do
No injury—may come to you.
Though in your cause no part I bear,
Your indignation I can share;
Am grieved this backward march to see,
How careless and disorderly!
I scorn your chieftains, men who lead,
And yet want courage at their need,
Then look at them with open eyes!
Deserve they further sacrifice?
My father! I would help to find
A place of shelter till the rage
Of cruel men do like the wind
Exhaust itself and sink to rest;
Be brother now to brother joined!
Admit me in the equipage
Of your misfortunes, that at least,
Whatever fate remains behind,
I may bear witness in my breast
To your nobility of mind!"

"Thou enemy, my bane and blight!
Oh! bold to fight the coward's fight
Against all good!"—but why declare,
At length, the issue of this prayer?
Or how, from his depression raised,
The father on the son had gazed,
Suffice it that the son gave way,
Nor strove that passion to allay,
Nor did he turn aside to prove
His brothers' wisdom or their love—
But calmly from the spot withdrew;

The like endeavours to renew,
Should e'er a kindlier time ensue.

CANTO IV.

FROM cloudless ether looking down,
The moon, this tranquil evening, sees
A camp and a beleaguered town,
And castle like a stately crown
On the steep rocks of winding Tees;
And southward far, with moors between,
Hill-tops, and floods, and forest green,
The bright moon sees that valley small
Where Rylstone's old sequestered hall
A venerable image yields
Of quiet to the neighbouring fields;
While from one pillared chimney breathes
The smoke, and mounts in silver wreaths.
The courts are hushed;—for timely sleep
The greyhounds to their kennel creep;
The peacock in a broad ash-tree
Aloft is roosted for the night,
He who in proud prosperity
Of colours manifold and bright
Walked round, affronting the daylight;
And higher still above the bower
Where he is perched, from yon lone tower
The hall-clock in the clear moonshine
With glittering finger points at nine.
Ah! who could think that sadness here
Hath any sway? or pain, or fear?
A soft and lulling sound is heard
Of streams inaudible by day;
The garden pool's dark surface, stirred
By the night insects in their play,
Breaks into dimples small and bright;
A thousand, thousand rings of light,
That shape themselves and disappear
Almost as soon as seen:—and, lo!
Not distant far, the milk-white doe:
The same fair creature who was nigh
Feeding in tranquillity,
When Francis uttered to the maid
His last words in the yew-tree shade;—
The same fair creature, who hath found
Her way into forbidden ground;
Where now, within this spacious plot
For pleasure made, a goodly spot,
With lawns and beds of flowers and shades
Of trellis-work in long arcades,
And cirque and crescent framed by wall
Of close-clipt foliage green and tall,
Converging walks, and fountains gay,
And terraces in trim array,—
Beneath yon cypress spiring high,
With pine and cedar spreading wide
Their darksome boughs on either side,
In open moonlight doth she lie;
Happy as others of her kind,
That, far from human neighbourhood,
Range unrestricted as the wind,
Through park, or chase, or savage wood.

But where at this still hour is she,
The consecrated Emily?
Even while I speak behold the maid
Emerging from the cedar shade
To open moonshine, where the doe
Beneath the cypress-spire is laid;
Like a patch of April snow,
Upon a bed of herbage green,
Lingering in a woody glade,
Or behind a rocky screen,
Lonely relic! which, if seen
By the shepherd, is passed by
With an inattentive eye.
Nor more regard doth she bestow
Upon the uncomplaining doe!

Yet the meek creature was not free,
Erewhile, from some perplexity:
For thrice hath she approached, this day
The thought-bewildered Emily;
Endeavouring, in her gentle way,
Some smile or look of love to gain,—
Encouragement to sport or play;
Attempts which by the unhappy maid
Have all been slighted or gainsaid.
Yet is she soothed: the viewless breeze
Comes fraught with kindlier sympathies
Ere she hath reached yon rustic shed
Hung with late-flowering woodbine, spread
Along the walls and overhead;
The fragrance of the breathing flowers
Revives a memory of those hours
When here, in this remote alcove,
(While from the pendant woodbine came
Like odours, sweet as if the same)
A fondly-anxious mother strove
To teach her salutary fears
And mysteries above her years.
Yes, she is soothed:—an image faint—
And yet not faint—a presence bright
Returns to her;—'tis that blest saint
Who with mild looks and language mild
Instructed here her darling child,
While yet a prattler on the knee,
To worship in simplicity
The invisible God, and take for guide
The faith reformed and purified.
'Tis flown—the vision, and the sense
Of that beguiling influence!
"But oh! thou angel from above,
Thou spirit of mat rnal love,

That stood'st before my eyes more clear
Than ghosts are fabled to appear
Sent on embassies of fear;
As thou thy presence hast to me
Vouchsafed, in radiant ministry,
Descend on Francis—through the air
Of this sad earth to him repair,
Speak to him with a voice and say,
That he must cast despair away!"

Then from within the embowered retreat
Where she had found a grateful seat
Perturbed she issues.—She will go,
Herself will follow to the war,
And clasp her father's knees,—ah, no
She meets the insuperable bar,
The injunctions by her brother laid,
His parting charge—but ill obeyed!
That interdicted all debate,
All prayer for this cause or for that,
All efforts that would turn aside
The headlong current of their fate·
Her duty is to stand and wait;
In resignation to abide
The shock, AND FINALLY SECURE
O'ER PAIN AND GRIEF A TRIUMPH PURE.
She knows, she feels it, and is cheered,
At least her present pangs are checked.
But now an ancient man appeared,
Approaching her with grave respect.
Down the smooth walk which then she trod
He paced along the silent sod,
And greeting her thus gently spake
"An old man's privilege I take,
Dark is the time—a woeful day!
Dear daughter of affliction, say
How can I serve you? point the way."

"Rights have you, and may well be bold
You with my father have grown old
In friendship;—go—from him—from me—
Strive to avert this misery.
This would I beg; but on my mind
A passive stillness is enjoined.
If prudence offer help or aid,
On *you* is no restriction laid;
You not forbidden to recline
With hope upon the Will divine."

"Hope," said the sufferer's zealous friend,
"Must not forsake us till the end.—
In Craven's wilds is many a den,
To shelter persecuted men:
Far under ground is many a cave,
Where they might lie as in the grave,
Until this storm hath ceased to rave;
Or let them cross the river Tweed,
And be at once from peril freed!"

"Ah tempt me not!" she faintly sighed;
"I will not counsel nor exhort,—
With my condition satisfied,
But you, at least, may make report
Of what befalls;—be this your task—
This may be done,—'tis all I ask!"

She spake—and from the lady's sight
The sire, unconscious of his age,
Departed promptly as a page
Bound on some errand of delight.
The noble Francis—wise as brave,
Thought he, may have the skill to save.
With hopes in tenderness concealed,
Unarmed he followed to the field.
Him will I seek! the insurgent powers
Are now besieging Barnard's towers,—
"Grant that the moon which shines this night
May guide them in a prudent flight!"

But quick the turns of chance and change,
And knowledge has a narrow range,
Whence idle fears, and needless pain,
And wishes blind, and efforts vain.—
Their flight the fair moon may not see,
For, from mid-heaven, already she
Hath witnessed their captivity
She saw the desperate assault
Upon that hostile castle made;—
But dark and dismal is the vault
Where Norton and his sons are laid!
Disastrous issue! He had said
"This night yon haughty towers must yield
Or we for ever quit the field
Neville is utterly dismayed,
For promise fails of Howard's aid;
And Dacre to our call replies
That he is unprepared to rise
My heart is sick; this weary pause
Must needs be fatal to the cause.
The breach is open—on the wall,
This night, the banner shall be planted!
'Twas done.—his sons were with him—all;—
They belt him round with hearts undaunted;
And others follow,—sire and son
Leap down into the court—'Tis won"—
They shout aloud—but Heaven decreed
Another close
To that brave deed,
Which struck with terror friends and foes!
The friend shrinks back—the foe recoils
From Norton and his filial band;
But they, now caught within the toils,
Against a thousand cannot stand —
The foe from numbers courage drew,
And overpowered that gallant few.

"A rescue for the standard!" cried
The father from within the walls;
But, see, the sacred standard falls!—
Confusion through the camp spread wide:
Some fled—and some their fears detained:
But ere the moon had sunk to rest
In her pale chambers of the west,
Of that rash levy nought remained.

CANTO V.

High on a point of rugged ground,
Among the wastes of Rylstone Fell,
Above the loftiest ridge or mound
Where foresters or shepherds dwell,
An edifice of warlike frame(11)
Stands single (Norton Tower its name);
It fronts all quarters, and looks round
O'er path and road, and plain and dell,
Dark moor, and gleam of pool and stream,
Upon a prospect without bound.

The summit of this bold ascent,
Though bleak and bare, and seldom free
As Pendle-hill or Pennygent
From wind, or frost, or vapours wet;
Had often heard the sound of glee
When there the youthful Nortons met,
To practise games and archery:
How proud and happy they! the crowd
Of lookers-on how pleased and proud!
And from the scorching noon-tide sun,
From showers, or when the prize was won,
They to the watch-tower did repair.
Commodious pleasure-house! and there
Would mirth run round, with generous fare;
And the stern old lord of Rylstone-hall,
He was the proudest of them all!

But now, his child, with anguish pale,
Upon the height walks to and fro;
'Tis well that she hath heard the tale,
Received the bitterness of woe:
For she *had* hoped, had hoped and feared,
Such rights did feeble nature claim;
And oft her steps had hither steered,
Though not unconscious of self-blame;
For she her brother's charge revered,
His farewell words; and by the same,
Yea, by her brother's very name,
Had, in her solitude, been cheered.

She turned to him, who with his eye
Was watching her while on the height
She sate, or wandered restlessly,
O'erburthened by her sorrow's weight;
To him who this dire news had told,
And now beside the mourner stood
(That gray-haired man of gentle blood,
Who with her father had grown old
In friendship, rival hunters they,
And fellow-warriors in their day);
To Rylstone he the tidings brought;
Then on this place the maid had sought:
And told, as gently as could be,
The end of that sad tragedy,
Which it had been his lot to see.

To him the lady turned: "You said
That Francis lives, *he* is not dead?"

"Your noble brother hath been spared,
To take his life they have not dared.
On him and on his high endeavour
The light of praise shall shine for ever!
Nor did he (such Heaven's will) in vain
His solitary course maintain;
Not vainly struggled in the might
Of duty, seeing with clear sight;
He was their comfort to the last,
Their joy till every pang was past.

"I witnessed when to York they came—
What, lady, if their feet were tied!
They might deserve a good man's blame;
But, marks of infamy and shame,
These were their triumph, these their pride,
Nor wanted 'mid the pressing crowd
Deep feeling, that found utterance loud,
'Lo, Francis comes,' there were who cried,
'A prisoner once, but now set free!
'Tis well, for he the worst defied
For the sake of natural piety;
He rose not in this quarrel, he
His father and his brothers wooed,
Both for their own and country's good,
To rest in peace—he did divide,
He parted from them; but at their side
Now walks in unanimity—
Then peace to cruelty and scorn,
While to the prison they are borne,
Peace, peace to all indignity!'

"And so in prison were they laid—
Oh, hear me, hear me, gentle maid,
For I am come with power to bless,
By scattering gleams, through your distress,
Of a redeeming happiness.
Me did a reverent pity move
And privilege of ancient love;
And, in your service, I made bold—
And entrance gained to that stronghold.

"Your father gave me cordial greeting;
But to his purposes, that burned

Within him, instantly returned—
He was commanding and entreating,
And said, 'We need not stop, my son!
But I will end what is begun;
'Tis matter which I do not fear
To intrust to any living ear.'
And so to Francis he renewed
His words more calmly thus pursued

"'Might this our enterprise have sped,
Change wide and deep the land had seen,
A renovation from the dead,
A spring-tide of immortal green.
The darksome altars would have blazed
Like stars when clouds are rolled away;
Salvation to all eyes that gazed,
Once more the rood had been upraised
To spread its arms, and stand for aye
Then, then, had I survived to see
New life in Bolton Priory;
The voice restored, the eye of truth
Re-opened that inspired my youth,
To see her in her pomp arrayed,
This banner (for such vow I made)
Should on the consecrated breast
Of that same temple, have found rest.
I would myself have hung it high,
Glad offering of glad victory!

"'A shadow of such thought remains
To cheer this sad and pensive time;
A solemn fancy yet sustains
One feeble being—bids me climb
Even to the last—one effort more
To attest my faith, if not restore.

"'Hear then,' said he, 'while I impart,
My son, the last wish of my heart
The banner strive thou to regain;
And, if the endeavour be not vain,
Bear it—to whom if not to thee
Shall I this lonely thought consign?—
Bear it to Bolton Priory,
And lay it on Saint Mary's shrine,—
To wither in the sun and breeze
'Mid those decaying sanctities.
There let at least the gift be laid,
The testimony there displayed;
Bold proof that with no selfish aim,
But for lost faith and Christ's dear name,
I helmeted a brow though white,
And took a place in all men's sight;
Yea, offered up this beauteous brood,
This fair unrivalled brotherhood,
And turned away from thee, my son!
And left—but be the rest unsaid,
The name untouched, the tear unshed.—
My wish is known, and I have done:
Now promise, grant this one request,
This dying prayer, and be thou blest!'

"Then Francis answered fervently,
'If God so will, the same shall be'

"Immediately, this solemn word
Thus scarcely given, a noise was heard,
And officers appeared in state
To lead the prisoners to their fate.
They rose, oh! wherefore should I fear
To tell, or, lady, you to hear?
They rose—embraces none were given—
They stood like trees when earth and heaven
Are calm; they knew each other's worth,
And reverently the band went forth:
They met, when they had reached the door,
The banner which a soldier bore,
One marshalled thus with base intent
That he in scorn might go before,
And, holding up this monument,
Conduct them to their punishment;
So cruel Sussex, unrestrained
By human feeling, had ordained.
The unhappy banner Francis saw,
And, with a look of calm command
Inspiring universal awe,
He took it from the soldier's hand;
And all the people that were round
Confirmed the deed in peace profound.
High transport did the father shed
Upon his son—and they were led,
Led on, and yielded up their breath,
Together died, a happy death!
But Francis, soon as he had braved
This insult, and the banner saved,
That moment, from among the tide
Of the spectators occupied
In admiration or dismay,
Bore unobserved his charge away."

These things, which thus had in the sight
And hearing passed of him who stood
With Emily, on the watch-tower height,
In Rylstone's woeful neighbourhood,
He told, and oftentimes with voice
Of power to comfort or rejoice,
For deepest sorrows that aspire,
Go high, no transport ever higher.
"Yet, yet in this affliction," said
The old man to the silent maid,
"Yet, lady! Heaven is good—the night
Shows yet a star which is most bright;
Your brother lives—he lives—is come
Perhaps already to his home;
Then let us leave this dreary place."
She yielded, and with gentle pace,

Though without one uplifted look,
To Rylstone Hall her way she took.

CANTO VI.

Why comes not Francis?—Joyful cheer
In that parental gratulation,
And glow of righteous indignation,
Went with him from the doleful city:—
He fled—yet in his flight could hear
The death-sound of the minster-bell;
That sullen stroke pronounced farewell
To Marmaduke, cut off from pity!
To Ambrose that! and then a knell
For him, the sweet half-opened flower!
For all—all dying in one hour!
Why comes not Francis? Thoughts of love
Should bear him to his sister dear
With motion fleet as winged dove,
Yea, like a heavenly messenger,
An angel-guest, should he appear.
Why comes he not?—for westward fast
Along the plain of York he past;
The banner-staff was in his hand,
The imagery concealed from sight,
And 'cross the expanse, in open flight,
Reckless of what impels or leads,
Unchecked he hurries on,—nor heeds
The sorrow of the villages;
Spread by triumphant cruelties
Of vengeful military force,
And punishment without remorse
He marked not, heard not as he fled;
All but the suffering heart was dead
For him, abandoned to blank awe,
To vacancy, and horror strong;
And the first object which he saw,
With conscious sight, as he swept along,—
It was the banner in his hand!
He felt, and made a sudden stand.

He looked about like one betrayed:
What hath he done? what promise made?
Oh, weak, weak moment! to what end
Can such a vain oblation tend,
And he the bearer?—Can he go
Carrying this instrument of woe,
And find, find anywhere, a right
To excuse him in his country's sight?
No, will not all men deem the change
A downward course, perverse and strange?
Here is it,—but how, when? must she,
The unoffending Emily,
Again this piteous object see?

Such conflict long did he maintain
Within himself, and found no rest:
Calm liberty he could not gain;
And yet the service was unblest
His own life into danger brought
By this sad burden, even that thought,
Exciting self-suspicion strong,
Swayed the brave man to his wrong.
And how, unless it were the sense
Of all-disposing Providence,
Its will intelligibly shown,
Finds he the banner in his hand,
Without a thought to such intent,
Or conscious effort of his own;
And no obstruction to prevent
His father's wish, and last command!
And, thus beset, he heaved a sigh;
Remembering his own prophecy
Of utter desolation, made
To Emily in the yew-tree shade:
He sighed, submitting to the power,
The might of that prophetic hour.
"No choice is left, the deed is mine—
Dead are they, dead!—and I will go,
And, for their sakes, come weal or woe,
Will lay the relic on the shrine."

So forward with a steady will
He went, and traversed plain and hill;
And up the vale of Wharf his way
Pursued;—and, on the second day,
He reached a summit whence his eyes
Could see the tower of Bolton rise
There Francis for a moment's space
Made halt—but hark! a noise behind
Of horsemen at an eager pace!
He heard, and with misgiving mind.
'Tis Sir George Bowes who leads the band
They come, by cruel Sussex sent,
Who, when the Nortons from the hand
Of death had drunk their punishment,
Bethought him, angry and ashamed,
How Francis had the banner claimed,
And with that charge had disappeared;
By all the standers-by revered.
His whole bold carriage (which had quelled
Thus far the opposer, and repelled
All censure, enterprise so bright
That even bad men had vainly striven
Against that overcoming light)
Was then reviewed, and prompt word given,
That to what place soever fled
He should be seized, alive or dead.

The troop of horse had gained the height
Where Francis stood in open sight.
They hem him round—"Behold the proof,
Behold the ensign in his hand!
He did not arm, he walked aloof!
For why?—to save his father's land:—

Worst traitor of them all is he,
A traitor dark and cowardly !"

"I am no traitor," Francis said,
"Though this unhappy freight I bear ;
It weakens me, my heart hath bled
Till it is weak—but you, beware,
Nor do a suffering spirit wrong,
Whose self-reproaches are too strong !"
At this he from the beaten road
Retreated towards a brake of thorn,
Which like a place of 'vantage showed ;
And there stood bravely, though forlorn.
In self-defence with warlike brow
He stood,—nor weaponless was now ;
He from a soldier's hand had snatched
A spear,—and with his eyes he watched
Their motions, turning round and round :
His weaker hand the banner held ;
And straight, by savage zeal impelled,
Forth rushed a pikeman, as if he,
Not without harsh indignity,
Would seize the same :—instinctively–
To smite the offender—with his lance
Did Francis from the brake advance ;
But, from behind, a treacherous wound
Unfeeling, brought him to the ground,
A mortal stroke :—oh, grief to tell !
Thus, thus, the noble Francis fell :
There did he lie of breath forsaken ;
The banner from his grasp was taken,
And borne exultingly away ;
And the body was left on the ground where [it lay.

Two days, as many nights he slept
Alone, unnoticed, and unwept ;
For at that time distress and fear
Possessed the country far and near ;
The third day, one, who chanced to pass,
Beheld him stretched upon the grass.
A gentle forester was he,
And of the Norton tenantry ;
And he had heard that by a train
Of horsemen Francis had been slain.
Much was he troubled—for the man
Hath recognized his pallid face ;
And to the nearest huts he ran,
And called the people to the place.
How desolate is Rylstone Hall !
Such was the instant thought of all ;
And if the lonely lady there
Should be, this sight she cannot bear !
Such thought the forester expressed ;
And all were swayed, and deemed it best
That, if the priest should yield assent
And join himself to their intent,
Then, they, for Christian pity's sake,
In holy ground a grave would make ;
That straightway buried he should be
In the church-yard of the priory.

Apart, some little space, was made
The grave where Francis must be laid.
In no confusion or neglect
This did they,—but in pure respect
That he was born of gentle blood ;
And that there was no neighbourhood
Of kindred for him in that ground ;
So to the church-yard they are bound,
Bearing the body on a bier
In decency and humble cheer ;
And psalms are sung with holy sound.

But Emily hath raised her head,
And is again disquieted ;
She must behold !—so many gone,
Where is the solitary one ?
And forth from Rylstone Hall stepped she,
To seek her brother forth she went,
And tremblingly her course she bent
Toward Bolton's ruined priory.
She comes, and in the vale hath heard
The funeral dirge ;—she sees the knot
Of people, sees them in one spot—
And darting like a wounded bird
She reached the grave, and with her breast
Upon the ground received the rest,—
The consummation, the whole ruth
And sorrow of this final truth !

CANTO VII.

THOU spirit, whose angelic hand
Was to the harp a strong command,
Called the submissive strings to wake
In glory for this maiden's sake,
Say, spirit ! whither hath she fled
To hide her poor afflicted head ?
What mighty forest in its gloom
Enfolds her ?—is a rifted tomb
Within the wilderness her seat ?
Some island which the wild waves beat,
Is that the sufferer's last retreat ?
Or some aspiring rock that shrouds
Its perilous front in mists and clouds ?
High-climbing rock—low sunless dale—
Sea—desert—what do these avail ?
Oh, take her anguish and her fears
Into a deep recess of years !

'Tis done ;—despoil and desolation(12)
O'er Rylstone's fair domain have blown ;
The walks and pools neglect hath sown
With weeds, the bowers are overthrown,
Or have given way to slow mutation,
While, in their ancient habitation

The Norton name hath been unknown.
The lordly mansion of its pride
Is stripped; the ravage hath spread wide
Through park and field, a perishing
That mocks the gladness of the spring!
And with this silent gloom agreeing
There is a joyless human being,
Of aspect such as if the waste
Were under her dominion placed:
Upon a primrose bank, her throne
Of quietness, she sits alone;
There seated, may this maid be seen,
Among the ruins of a wood,
Erewhile a covert bright and green,
And where full many a brave tree stood;
That used to spread its boughs, and ring
With the sweet birds' carolling.
Behold her, like a virgin queen,
Neglecting in imperial state
These outward images of fate,
And carrying inward a serene
And perfect sway, through many a thought
Of chance and change, that hath been brought
To the subjection of a holy,
Though stern and rigorous, melancholy!
The like authority, with grace
Of awfulness, is in her face,—
There hath she fixed it; yet it seems
To o'ershadow by no native right
That face, which cannot lose the gleams,
Lose utterly the tender gleams
Of gentleness and meek delight,
And loving-kindness ever bright:
Such is her sovereign mien;—her dress
(A vest, with woollen cincture tied,
A hood of mountain-wool undyed)
Is homely,—fashioned to express
A wandering pilgrim's humbleness.

And she *hath* wandered, long and far,
Beneath the light of sun and star;
Hath roamed in trouble and in grief,
Driven forward like a withered leaf,
Yea, like a ship at random blown
To distant places and unknown.
But now she dares to seek a haven
Among her native wilds of Craven;
Hath seen again her father's roof,
And put her fortitude to proof;
The mighty sorrow hath been borne,
And she is thoroughly forlorn:
Her soul doth in itself stand fast,
Sustained by memory of the past
And strength of reason; held above
The infirmities of mortal love;
Undaunted, lofty, calm, and stable,
And awfully impenetrable.

And so, beneath a mouldered tree,
A self-surviving leafless oak,
By unregarded age from stroke
Of ravage saved—sate Emily.
There did she rest, with head reclined,
Herself most like a stately flower,
(Such have I seen) whom chance of birth
Hath separated from its kind,
To live and die in a shady bower,
Single on the gladsome earth.

When, with a noise like distant thunder,
A troop of deer came sweeping by;
And, suddenly, behold a wonder!
For, of that band of rushing deer,
A single one in mid career
Hath stopped, and fixed its large full eye
Upon the Lady Emily,
A doe most beautiful, clear-white,
A radiant creature, silver-bright!

Thus checked, a little while it stayed;
A little thoughtful pause it made;
And then advanced with stealth-like pace,
Drew softly near her—and more near,
Stopped once again;—but, as no trace
Was found of anything to fear,
Even to her feet the creature came,
And laid its head upon her knee,
And looked into the lady's face,
A look of pure benignity,
And fond unclouded memory;
It is, thought Emily, the same,
The very doe of other years!
The pleading look the lady viewed,
And, by her gushing thoughts subdued,
She melted into tears—
A flood of tears, that flowed apace
Upon the happy creature's face.

Oh, moment ever blest! O pair!
Beloved of Heaven, Heaven's choicest care,
This was for you a precious greeting,—
For both a bounteous fruitful meeting.
Joined are they, and the sylvan doe
Can she depart? can she forego
The lady, once her playful peer,
And now her sainted mistress dear?
And will not Emily receive
This lovely chronicler of things
Long past, delights and sorrowings?
Lone sufferer! will not she believe
The promise in that speaking face,
And take this gift of Heaven with grace?

That day, the first of a reunion
Which was to teem with high communion,

That day of balmy April weather,
They tarried in the wood together
And when, ere fall of evening-dew,
She from this sylvan haunt withdrew,
The white doe tracked with faithful pace
The lady to her dwelling-place.
That nook where, on paternal ground,
A habitation she had found,
The master of whose humble board
Once owned her father for his lord,
A hut, by tufted trees defended,
Where Rylstone brook with Wharf is blended

When Emily by morning light
Went forth, the doe was there in sight.
She shrunk.—with one frail shock of pain
Received and followed by a prayer,
She saw the creature once again;
Shun will she not, she feels, will bear;—
But, wheresoever she looked round,
All now was trouble-haunted ground.
So doth the sufferer deem it good
Even once again this neighbourhood
To leave.—Unwooed, yet unforbidden,
The white doe followed up the vale,
Up to another cottage—hidden
In the deep fork of Amerdale;(13)
And there may Emily restore
Herself, in spots unseen before.
Why tell of mossy rock, or tree,
By lurking Denbrook's pathless side,
Haunts of a strengthening amity
That calmed her, cheered, and fortified?
For she hath ventured now to read
Of time, and place, and thought, and deed,
Endless history that lies
In her silent follower's eyes!
Who with a power like human reason
Discerns the favourable season,
Skilled to approach or to retire,—
From looks conceiving her desire,
From look, deportment, voice, or mien,
That vary to the heart within.
If she too passionately wreathed
Her arms, or over-deeply breathed,
Walked quick or slowly, every mood
In its degree was understood,
Then well may their accord be true,
And kindly intercourse ensue.
Oh! surely 'twas a gentle rousing
When she by sudden glimpse espied
The white doe on the mountain browsing,
Or in the meadow wandered wide!
How pleased, when down the straggler sank
Beside her, on some sunny bank!
How soothed, when in thick bower inclosed,
They like a nested pair reposed!

Fair vision! when it crossed the maid
Within some rocky cavern laid,
The dark cave's portal gliding by,
White as whitest cloud on high,
Floating through an azure sky.
What now is left for pain or fear?
That presence, dearer and more dear,
Did now a very gladness yield
At morning to the dewy field,
While they, side by side, were straying,
And the shepherd's pipe was playing,
And with a deeper peace endued
The hour of moonlight solitude

With her companion, in such frame
Of mind, to Rylstone back she came;
And, wandering through the wasted groves,
Received the memory of old loves,
Undisturbed and undistrest,
Into a soul which now was blest
With a soft spring-day of holy,
Mild, delicious, melancholy:
Not sunless gloom or unenlightened,
But by tender fancies brightened.

When the bells of Rylstone played(14)
Their Sabbath music—"God us ayde!"
That was the sound they seemed to speak;
Inscriptive legend, which I ween
May on those holy bells be seen,
That legend, and her grandsire's name;
And oftentimes the lady meek
Had in her childhood read the same,
Words which she slighted at that day
But now, when such sad change was wrought,
And of that lonely name she thought,
The bells of Rylstone seemed to say,
While she sat listening in the shade,
With vocal music, "God us ayde;"
And all the hills were glad to bear
Their part in this effectual prayer.

Nor lacked she reason's firmest power;
But with the white doe at her side
Up doth she climb to Norton tower,
And thence looks round her far and wide;
Her fate there measures—all is stilled,—
The weak one hath subdued her heart,
Behold the prophecy fulfilled,
Fulfilled, and she sustains her part!
But here her brother's words have failed;
Here hath a milder doom prevailed;
That she, of him and all bereft,
Hath yet this faithful partner left;
This single creature that disproves
His words, remains for her, and loves.

If tears are shed, they do not fall
For loss of him, for one or all;
Yet, sometimes, sometimes doth she weep,
Moved gently in her soul's soft sleep;
A few tears down her cheek descend
For this her last and living friend.

Bless, tender hearts, their mutual lot,
And bless for both this savage spot!
Which Emily doth sacred hold
For reasons dear and manifold—
Here hath she, here before her sight,
Close to the summit of this height,
The grassy rock-encircled pound(15)
In which the creature first was found
So beautiful the spotless thrall,
(A lovely youngling white as foam,)
That it was brought to Rylstone Hall;
Her youngest brother led it home,
The youngest, then a lusty boy,
Brought home the prize—and with what joy!

But most to Bolton's sacred pile,
On favouring nights, she loved to go:
There ranged through cloister, court, and aisle,
Attended by the soft-paced doe;
Nor feared she in the still moonshine
To look upon Saint Mary's shrine;
Nor on the lonely turf that showed
Where Francis slept in his last abode.
For that she came; there oft and long
She sate in meditation strong:
And, when she from the abyss returned
Of thought, she neither shrunk nor mourned;
Was happy that she lived to greet
Her mute companion as it lay
In love and pity at her feet;
How happy in its turn to meet
That recognition! the mild glance
Beamed from that gracious countenance;
Communication, like the ray
Of a new morning, to the nature
And prospects of the inferior creature!

A mortal song we frame, by dower
Encouraged of celestial power;
Power which the viewless spirit shed
By whom we were first visited;
Whose voice we heard, whose hand and wings
Swept like a breeze the conscious strings,
When, left in solitude, erewhile
We stood before this ruined pile,
And, quitting unsubstantial dreams,
Sang in this presence kindred themes;
Distress and desolation spread
Through human heart, and pleasure dead,—
Dead—but to live again on earth,
A second and yet nobler birth;
Dire overthrow, and yet how high
The re-ascent in sanctity!
From fair to fairer; day by day
A more divine and loftier way!
Even such this blessed pilgrim trod,
By sorrow lifted towards her God;
Uplifted to the purest sky
Of undisturbed mortality.
Her own thoughts loved she; and could bend
A dear look to her lowly friend,—
There stopped;—her thirst was satisfied
With what this innocent spring supplied—
Her sanction inwardly she bore,
And stood apart from human cares:
But to the world returned no more,
Although with no unwilling mind
Help did she give at need, and joined
The Wharfdale peasants in their prayers.
At length, thus faintly, faintly tied
To earth, she was set free, and died.
Thy soul, exalted Emily,
Maid of the blasted family,
Rose to the God from whom it came!
In Rylstone church her mortal frame
Was buried by her mother's side.

Most glorious sunset!—and a ray
Survives—the twilight of this day;
In that fair creature whom the fields
Support, and whom the forest shields;
Who, having filled a holy place,
Partakes, in her degree, Heaven's grace;
And bears a memory and a mind
Raised far above the law of kind;
Haunting the spots with lonely cheer
Which her dear mistress once held dear:
Loves most what Emily loved most—
The inclosure of this church-yard ground;
Here wanders like a gliding ghost,
And every Sabbath here is found;
Comes with the people when the bells
Are heard among the moorland dells,
Finds entrance through yon arch, where way
Lies open on the Sabbath-day;
Here walks amid the mournful waste
Of prostrate altars, shrines defaced,
And floors encumbered with rich show
Of fret-work imagery laid low;
Paces softly, or makes halt,
By fractured cell, or tomb, or vault,
By plate of monumental brass
Dim-gleaming among weeds and grass,
And sculptured forms of warriors brave,
But chiefly by that single grave,
That one sequestered hillock green,
The pensive visitant is seen.

Where doth the gentle creature lie
With those adversities unmoved,
Calm spectacle, by earth and sky
In their benignity approved!
And aye, methinks, this hoary pile,
Subdued by outrage and decay,
Looks down upon her with a smile,
A gracious smile, that seems to say,
"Thou, thou art not a child of time,
But daughter of the eternal prime!"

NOTES

Note 1 page 232

THE poem of "The White Doe of Rylstone" is founded on a local tradition, and on the ballad in Percy's Collection, entitled, "The Rising of the North" The tradition is as follows — "About this time," not long after the dissolution, "a white doe, say the aged people of the neighbourhood, long continued to make a weekly pilgrimage from Rylstone over the fells of Bolton, and was constantly found in the abbey church-yard during divine service, after the close of which she returned home as regularly as the rest of the congregation"—Dr Whitaker's "History of the Deanery of Craven" Rylstone was the property and residence of the Nortons, distinguished in that ill-advised and unfortunate insurrection, which led me to connect with this tradition the principal circumstances of their fate, as recorded in the ballad

"Bolton Priory," says Dr Whitaker in his excellent book, "The History and Antiquities of the Deanery of Craven," "stands upon a beautiful curvature of the Wharf, on a level sufficiently elevated to protect it from inundations, and low enough for every purpose of picturesque effect.

"Opposite to the east window of the priory church, the river washes the foot of a rock nearly perpendicular, and of the richest purple, where several of the mineral beds, which break out, instead of maintaining their usual inclination to the horizon, are twisted by some inconceivable process into undulating and spiral lines To the south all is soft and delicious, the eye reposes upon a few rich pastures, a moderate reach of the river, sufficiently tranquil to form a mirror to the sun, and the bounding hills beyond, neither too near nor too lofty to exclude, even in winter, any portion of his rays

"But, after all, the glories of Bolton are on the North Whatever the most fastidious taste could require to constitute a perfect landscape is not only found here, but in its proper place In front, and immediately under the eye, is a smooth expanse of park-like inclosure, spotted with native elm, ash, etc., of the finest growth: on the right a skirting oak wood, with jutting points of gray rock; on the left a rising copse. Still forward, are seen the aged groves of Bolton Park, the growth of centuries, and farther yet, the barren and rocky distances of Simon seat and Barden Fell contrasted with the warmth, fertility, and luxuriant foliage of the valley below

"About half a mile above Bolton the valley closes, and either side of the Wharf is overhung by solemn woods, from which huge perpendicular masses of gray rock jut out at intervals

"This sequestered scene was almost inaccessible till of late, that ridings have been cut on both sides of the river, and the most interesting points laid open by judicious thinnings in the woods Here a tributary stream rushes from a waterfall, and bursts through a woody glen to mingle its waters with the Wharf; there the Wharf itself is nearly lost in a deep cleft in the rock, and next becomes a horned flood inclosing a woody island—sometimes it reposes for a moment, and then resumes its native character lively, irregular, and impetuous

"The cleft mentioned above is the tremendous Strid This chasm, being incapable of receiving the winter floods, has formed on either side, a broad strand of naked gritstone full of rock-basins, or 'pots of the Linn,' which bear witness to the restless impetuosity of so many northern torrents. But if here Wharf is lost to the eye, it amply repays another sense by its deep and solemn roar, like 'the voice of the angry spirit of the waters,' heard far above and beneath, amidst the silence of the surrounding woods

"The terminating object of the landscape is the remains of Barden tower, interesting from their form and situation, and still more so from the recollections which they excite"

Note 2 Page 233 col 1

"*From Bolton's old monastic tower*"

It is to be regretted that at the present day Bolton Abbey wants this ornament: but the poem, according to the imagination of the poet, is composed in Queen Elizabeth's time "Formerly," says Dr Whitaker, "over the transept was a tower. This is proved not only from the mention of bells at the dissolution, when they could have had no other place, but from the pointed roof of the choir, which must have terminated westward, in some building of superior height to the ridge."

Note 3 Page 233, col. 2.

"*A rural chapel, neatly drest*"

"The nave of the church having been reserved at the dissolution, for the use of the Saxon cure, is still a parochial chapel; and, at this day, is as well kept as the neatest English cathedral"

Note 4 Page 233, col. 2.

"*Who sate in the shade of the prior's oak*"

"At a small distance from the great gateway stood the prior's oak, which was felled about the year 1720, and sold for 70*l* According to the price of wood at that time, it could scarcely have contained less than 1400 feet of timber.

Note 5. Page 235, col. 1.

"When Lady Aaliza mourned."

The detail of this tradition may be found in Dr. Whitaker's book, and in a poem of this collection, entitled, "The Force of Prayer," &c.

Note 6. Page 235, col. 2.

"Pass, pass who will, yon chantry door."

"At the east end of the north aisle of Bolton Priory church is a chantry belonging to Bethmesly Hall, and a vault, where, according to tradition, the Claphams" (who inherited this estate, by the female line from the Mauleverers) "were interred upright." John de Clapham, of whom this ferocious act is recorded, was a name of great note in his time: "he was a vehement partisan of the House of Lancaster, in whom the spirit of his chieftains, the Cliffords, seemed to survive."

Note 7. Page 235, col. 2.

"Who loved the Shepherd Lord to meet."

At page 109 of this volume will be found a poem entitled, "Song at the Feast of Brougham Castle, upon the Restoration of Lord Clifford the Shepherd to the Estates and Honours of his Ancestors." To that poem is annexed an account of this personage, chiefly extracted from Burn's and Nicholson's History of Cumberland and Westmoreland. It gives me pleasure to add these further particulars concerning him from Dr. Whitaker, who says, "He retired to the solitude of Barden, where he seems to have enlarged the tower out of a common keeper's lodge, and where he found a retreat equally favourable to taste, to instruction, and to devotion. The narrow limits of his residence show that he had learned to despise the pomp of greatness, and that a small train of servants could suffice him who had lived to the age of thirty a servant himself. I think this nobleman resided here almost entirely when in Yorkshire, for all his charters which I have seen are dated at Barden.

"His early habits, and the want of those artificial measures of time which even shepherds now possess, had given him a turn for observing the motions of the heavenly bodies, and, having purchased such an apparatus as could then be procured, he amused and informed himself by those pursuits, with the aid of the canons of Bolton, some of whom are said to have been well versed in what was then known of the science.

"I suspect this nobleman to have been sometimes occupied in a more visionary pursuit, and probably in the same company. For, from the family evidences, I have met with two MSS. on the subject of alchemy, which, from the character, spelling, etc., may almost certainly be referred to the reign of Henry the Seventh. If these were originally deposited with the MSS. of the Cliffords, it might have been for the use of this nobleman. If they were brought from Bolton at the dissolution, they must have been the work of those canons whom he almost exclusively conversed with.

"In these peaceful employments Lord Clifford spent the whole reign of Henry the Seventh and the first years of his son. But in the year 1513, when almost sixty years old, he was appointed to a principal command over the army which fought at Flodden, and showed that the military genius of the family had neither been chilled in him by age, nor extinguished by habits of peace.

"He survived the battle of Flodden ten years, and died April 23rd, 1523, aged about 70. I shall endeavour to appropriate to him a tomb, vault, and chantry, in the choir of the church at Bolton, as I should be sorry to believe that he was deposited, when dead, at a distance from the place which in his lifetime he loved so well.

"By his last will he appointed his body to be interred at Shap, if he died in Westmoreland; or at Bolton, if he died in Yorkshire."

With respect to the canons of Bolton, Dr. Whitaker shows from MSS. that not only alchemy but astronomy was a favourite pursuit with them.

Note 8. Page 238, col. 2.

"Ye watchmen upon Brancepeth towers."

Brancepeth Castle stands near the river Were, a few miles from the city of Durham. It formerly belonged to the Nevilles, Earls of Westmoreland. See Dr. Percy's account.

Note 9. Page 240, col. 2.

"Of mitred Thurston, when a host
He conquered!"

See the historians for the account of this memorable battle, usually denominated the Battle of the Standard.

Note 10. Page 241, col. 1.

"In that other day of Neville's Cross."

"In the night before the battle of Durham was strucken and begun, the 17th day of October, anno 1346, there did appear to John Fosser, then prior of the abbey of Durham, commanding him to take the holy corporax-cloth, wherewith St. Cuthbert did cover the chalice when he used to say mass, and to put the same holy relique like to a banner-cloth upon the point of a spear, and the next morning to go and repair to a place on the west side of the city of Durham, called the Red Hills, where the maid's bower wont to be, and there to remain and abide till the end of the battle. To which vision, the prior obeying, and taking the same for a revelation of God's grace and mercy by the mediation of holy St. Cuthbert, did accordingly the next morning, with the monks of the said Abbey, repair to the said Red Hills, and there most devoutly humbling and prostrating themselves in prayer for the victory in the said battle: (a great multitude of the Scots running and pressing by them, with intention to have spoiled them, yet had no power to commit any violence under such holy persons, so occupied in prayer, being protected and defended by the mighty providence of Almighty God, and by the mediation of holy St Cuthbert, and by the presence of the holy relique› And, after many conflicts and warlike exploits there had and done between the English men and the King of Scots and his company, the said battle ended, and the victory was obtained, to the great overthrow and confusion of the Scots, their enemies And then the said prior and monks, accompanied with Ralph Lord Nevil, and John Nevil his son, and the Lord Percy, and many other nobles of England, returned home and went to the abbey church, there joining in hearty prayer and thanksgiving to God and holy St Cuthbert for the victory atchieved that day "

This battle was afterwards called the Battle of Nevilles Cross, from the following circumstance:—

"On the west side of the city of Durham, where two roads pass each other, a most notable, famous, and goodly cross of stone-work was erected and set up to the honour of God for the victory there obtained in the field of battle, and known by the name of Nevil s Cross, and built at the sole cost of the Lord Ralph Nevil, one of the most excellent and chief persons in the said battle." The relique of St Cuthbert afterwards became of great importance in military events For soon after this battle, says the same author, "The prior caused a goodly and sumptuous banner to be made, (which is then described at great length,) and in the midst of the same banner-cloth was the said holy relique and corporax-cloth enclosed, etc , etc , and so sumptuously finished, and absolutely perfected, this banner was dedicated to holy St Cuthbert, of intent and purpose, that for the future it should be carried to any battle, as occasion should serve; and was never carried and showed at any battle but by the especial grace of God Almighty, and the mediation of holy St. Cuthbert, it brought home victory: which banner-cloth, after the dissolution of the abbey, fell into the possession of Dean Whittingham, whose wife was called Katharine, being a Frenchwoman, (as is most credibly reported by eyewitnesses,) did most injuriously burn the same in her fire, to the open contempt and disgrace of all ancient and goodly reliques "—Extracted from a book entitled, "Durham Cathedral, as it stood before the Dissolution of the Monastery " It appears, from the old metrical history, that the abovementioned banner was carried by the Earl of Surrey to Flodden field.

Note 11. Page 244, col. 1

" *An edifice of warlike frame*
Stands single (*Norton Tower its name*)."

It is so called to this day, and is thus described by Dr. Whitaker:—" Rylstone Fell yet exhibits a monument of the old warfare between the Nortons and the Cliffords. On a point of very high ground, commanding an immense prospect, and protected by two deep ravines, are the remains of a square tower, expressly said by Dodsworth to have been built by Richard Norton The walls are of strong grout work, about four feet thick It seems to have been three stories high Breaches have been industriously made in all the sides, almost to the ground, to render it untenable

" But Norton Tower was probably a sort of pleasure-house in summer, as there are, adjoining to it, several large mounds (two of them are pretty entire), of which no other account can be given than that they were butts for large companies of archers

" The place is savagely wild, and admirably adapted to the uses of a watch-tower "

Note 12 Page 247, col 2

——" *despoil and desolation*
O'er Rylstone's fair domain have blown "

" After the attainder of Richard Norton, his estates were forfeited to the crown, where they remained till the 2nd or 3rd of James; they were then granted to Francis Earl of Cumberland " From an accurate survey made at that time, several particulars have been extracted by Dr W. It appears that the mansion-house was then in decay Immediately adjoining is a close, called the Vivery, so called undoubtedly from the French *Vivier*, or modern Latin *Vivarium*, for there are near the house large remains of a pleasure-ground, such as were introduced in the earlier part of Elizabeth's time, with topiary works, fish-ponds, an island, etc The whole township was ranged by an hundred and thirty red deer, the property of the lord, which, together with the wood, had, after the attainder of Mr. Norton, been committed to Sir Stephen Tempest. The wood, it seems, had been abandoned to depredations, before which time it appears, that the neighbourhood must have exhibited a forest-like and sylvan scene In this survey, among the old tenants, is mentioned one Richard Kitchen, butler to Mr Norton, who rose in rebellion with his master, and was executed at Ripon "

Note 13 Page 249, col 1

" *In the deep fork of Amerdale.*"

"At the extremity of the parish of Burnsal, the valley of Wharf forks off into two great branches, one of which retains the name of Wharfdale to the source of the river; the other is usually called Littondale, but more anciently and properly Amerdale Dern-brook, which runs along an obscure valley from the N.W is derived from a Teutonic word, signifying concealment."—Dr. WHITAKER

Note 14 Page 249, col 2

" *When the bells of Rylstone played*
Their Sabbath music—' God us ayde.' "

On one of the bells of Rylstone church, which seems coeval with the building of the tower, is this cipher, J N. for John Norton, and the motto, " God us ayde."

Note 15. Page 250, col. 1.

"The grassy rock-encircled pound"

Which is thus described by Dr. Whitaker:—"On the plain summit of the hill are the foundations of a strong wall stretching from the S.W. to the N.E. corner of the tower, and to the edge of a very deep glen. From this glen, a ditch, several hundred yards long, runs south to another deep and rugged ravine. On the N. and W., where the banks are very steep, no wall or mound is discoverable, paling being the only fence that could stand on such ground.

"From the 'Minstrelsy of the Scottish Border,' it appears that such pounds for deer, sheep, etc., were far from being uncommon in the south of Scotland. The principle of them was something like that of a wire mouse-trap. On the declivity of a steep hill, the bottom and sides of which were fenced so as to be impassable, a wall was constructed nearly level with the surface on the outside, yet so high within that without wings it was impossible to escape in the opposite direction. Care was probably taken that these inclosures should contain better feed than the neighbouring parks or forests: and whoever is acquainted with the habits of these sequacious animals, will easily conceive, that if the leader was once tempted to descend into the snare, an herd would follow."

I cannot conclude without recommending to the notice of all lovers of beautiful scenery—Bolton Abbey and its neighbourhood. This enchanting spot belongs to the Duke of Devonshire: and the superintendence of it has for some years been intrusted to the Rev. William Carr, who has most skilfully opened out its features; and, in whatever he has added, has done justice to the place by working with an invisible hand of art in the very spirit of nature.

The Prioress's Tale.

(FROM CHAUCER.)

"Call up him who left half told
The story of Cambuscan bold."

In the following poem I have allowed myself no further deviation from the original than was necessary for the fluent reading and instant understanding of the author: so much, however, is the language altered since Chaucer's time, especially in pronunciation, that much was to be removed, and its place supplied with as little incongruity as possible. The ancient accent has been retained in a few conjunctions as *also* and *alway*, from a conviction that such sprinklings of antiquity would be admitted, by persons of taste, to have a graceful accordance with the subject. The fierce bigotry of the prioress forms a fine background for her tender-hearted sympathies with the mother and child; and the mode in which the story is told amply atones for the extravagance of the miracle.

"O LORD, our Lord! how wondrously," (quoth she)
"Thy name in this large world is spread abroad!
For not alone by men of dignity
Thy worship is performed and precious laud;
But by the mouths of children, gracious God!
Thy goodness is set forth; they when they lie
Upon the breast thy name do glorify.

"Wherefore in praise, the worthiest that I may,
Jesu! of thee, and the white lily-flower
Which did thee bear, and is a maid for aye,
To tell a story I will use my power;
Not that I may increase her honour's dower,
For she herself is honour, and the root
Of goodness, next her Son our soul's best boot.

"O mother maid! O maid and mother free!
O bush unburnt! burning in Moses' sight!
That down didst ravish from the Deity,
Through humbleness, the Spirit that did alight
Upon thy heart, whence, through that glory's might,
Conceivèd was the Father's sapience,
Help me to tell it in thy reverence!

"Lady, thy goodness, thy magnificence,
Thy virtue, and thy great humility,
Surpass all science and all utterance;
For sometimes, lady! ere men pray to thee
Thou go'st before in thy benignity,
The light to us vouchsafing of thy prayer,
To be our guide unto thy Son so dear.

"My knowledge is so weak, O blissful queen!
To tell abroad thy mighty worthiness,
That I the weight of it may not sustain;
But as a child of twelve months old or less,
That laboureth his language to express,
Even so fare I, and therefore, I thee pray,
Guide thou my song which I of thee shall say.

"There was in Asia, in a mighty town,
'Mong Christian folk, a street where Jews might be;
Assigned to them and given them for their own
By a great lord, for gain and usury,
Hateful to Christ and to his company;
And through this street who list might ride and wend;
Free was it, and unbarred at either end.

"A little school of Christian people stood
Down at the farther end, in which there were
A nest of children come of Christian blood,
That learnèd in that school from year to year
Such sort of doctrine as men usèd there,
That is to say, to sing and read alsò
As little children in their childhood do.

"Among these children was a widow's son,
A little scholar, scarcely seven years old,
Who day by day unto his school hath gone,
And eke, when he the image did behold
Of Jesu's mother, as he had been told,
This child was wont to kneel adown and say
Ave Marie, as he goeth by the way.

"This widow thus her little son hath taught
Our blissful lady, Jesu's mother dear,
To worship aye, and he forgat it not,
For simple infant hath a ready ear.
Sweet is his holiness of youth: and hence,
Calling to mind this matter when I may,
Saint Nicholas in my presence standeth aye,
For he so young to Christ did reverence.

"This little child, while in the school he sate
His primer conning with an earnest cheer,
The whilst the rest their anthem book repeat
The *Alma Redemptoris* did he hear,
And as he durst he drew him near and near,
And hearkened to the words and to the note,
Till the first verse he learned it all by rote.

"This Latin knew he nothing what it said,
For he too tender was of age to know;
But to his comrade he repaired, and prayed
That he the meaning of this song would show,
And unto him declare why men sing so;
This oftentimes, that he might be at ease,
This child did him beseech on his bare knees.

"His schoolfellow, who elder was than he,
Answered him thus:—'This song, I have heard say,
Was fashioned for our blissful lady free;
Her to salute, and also her to pray
To be our help upon our dying day
If there is more in this, I know it not,
Song do I learn,—small grammar I have got.'

"'And is this song fashioned in reverence
Of Jesu's mother?' said this Innocent,
'Now, certès, I will use my diligence
To con it all ere Christmas-tide be spent;
Although I for my primer shall be shent,
And shall be beaten three times in an hour,
Our lady I will praise with all my power'

"His schoolfellow, whom he had so besought,
As they went homeward taught him privily;
And then he sang it well and fearlessly,
From word to word according to the note:
Twice in a day it passèd through his throat,
Homeward and schoolward whensoe'er he went,
On Jesu's mother fixed was his intent

"Through all the Jewry (this before said I,)
This little child, as he came to and fro,
Full merrily then would he sing and cry,
O Alma Redemptoris! high and low
The sweetness of Christ's mother piercèd so
His heart, that her to praise, to her to pray,
He cannot stop his singing by the way.

"The serpent, Satan, our first foe, that hath
His wasp's nest in Jew's heart, upswelled—'O woe,
O Hebrew people!' said he in his wrath,
'Is it an honest thing? Shall this be so?
That such a boy where'er he lists shall go
In your despite, and sing his hymns and saws,
Which is against the reverence of our laws!'

"From that day forward have the Jews conspired
Out of the world this innocent to chase,
And to this end a homicide they hired,
That in an alley had a privy place,
And, as the child 'gan to the school to pace,
This cruel Jew him seized, and held him fast
And cut his throat, and in a pit him cast.

"I say that him into a pit they threw,
A loathsome pit, whence noisome scents exhale;
O cursed folk! away, ye Herods new!
What may your ill intentions you avail?
Murder will out; certès it will not fail;
Know, that the honour of high God may spread,
The blood cries out on your accursèd deed.

"O martyr 'stablished in virginity!
Now mayest thou sing for aye before the throne,
Following the Lamb celestial," quoth she,
"Of which the great Evangelist Saint John,
In Patmos wrote, who saith of them that go
Before the Lamb singing continually,
That never fleshly woman they did know

'Now this poor widow waiteth all that night
After her little child, and he came not;
For which, by earliest glimpse of morning light [thought
With face all pale with dread and busy
She at the school and elsewhere him hath sought,
Until thus far she learned, that he had been
In the Jews' street, and there he last was seen.

"With mother's pity in her breast inclosed
She goeth as she were half out of her mind,
To every place wherein she hath supposed
By likelihood her little son to find;
And ever on Christ's mother meek and kind
She cried, till to the Jewry she was brought,
And him among the accursèd Jews she sought.

"She asketh, and she piteously doth pray
To every Jew that dwelleth in that place
To tell her if her child had passed that way;
They all said nay; but Jesu of his grace
Gave to her thought, that in a little space
She for her son in that same spot did cry
Where he was cast into a pit hard by.

"O thou great God that dost perform thy laud
By mouths of innocents, lo! here thy might,
This gem of chastity, this emerald,
And eke of martyrdom this ruby bright,
There, where with mangled throat he lay upright,
The *Alma Redemptoris* 'gan to sing
So loud, that with his voice the place did ring.

"The Christian folk that through the Jewry went
Come to the spot in wonder at the thing;
And hastily they for the provost sent;
Immediately he came not tarrying,
And praiseth Christ that is our heavenly king,
And eke his mother, honour of mankind:
Which done, he bade that they the Jews should bind.

"This child with piteous lamentation then
Was taken up, singing his song alway,
And with procession great and pomp of men
To the next abbey him they bare away,
His mother swooning by the bier lay.
And scarcely could the people that were near
Remove the second Rachel from the bier.

"Torment and shameful death to every one
This provost doth for those bad Jews prepare
That of this murder wist, and that anon:
Such wickedness his judgments cannot spare;
Who will do evil, evil shall he bear;
Them therefore with wild horses did he draw,
And after that he hung them by the law.

"Upon his bier this innocent doth lie
Before the altar while the mass doth last:
The abbot with his convent's company
Then sped themselves to bury him full fast,
And, when they holy water on him cast,
Yet spake this child when sprinkled was the water,
And sang, *O Alma Redemptoris Mater!*

"This abbot, for he was a holy man,
As all monks are, or surely ought to be,
In supplication to the child began;
Thus saying, 'O dear child! I summon thee
In virtue of the holy Trinity,
Tell me the cause why thou dost sing this hymn,
Since that thy throat is cut, as it doth seem.'

"'My throat is cut unto the bone, I trow,'
Said this young child, 'and by the law of kind
I should have died, yea, many hours ago;
But Jesus Christ, as in the books ye find,
Will that his glory last, and be in mind;
And, for the worship of his mother dear,
Yet may I sing, *O Alma!* loud and clear.

"'This well of mercy Jesu's mother sweet
After my knowledge I have loved alway,
And in the hour when I my death did meet

To me she came, and thus to me did say,
'Thou in thy dying sing this holy lay,'
As ye have heard ; and soon as I had sung
Methought she laid a grain upon my tongue.

"'Wherefore I sing, nor can from song refrain,
In honour of that blissful maiden free,
Till from my tongue off taken is the grain;
And after that thus said she unto me,
'My little child, then will I come for thee
Soon as the grain from off thy tongue they take,
Be not dismayed, I will not thee forsake!'

"This holy monk, this abbot—him mean I,
Touched then his tongue, and took away the grain ;
And he gave up the ghost full peacefully ,
And, when the abbot had this wonder seen,
His salt tears trickled down like showers of rain,
And on his face he dropped upon the ground
And still he lay as if he had been bound.

"Eke the whole convent on the pavement lay,
Weeping and praising Jesu's mother dear ;
And after that they rose, and took their way
And lifted up this martyr from the bier
And in a tomb of precious marble clear
Inclosed his uncorrupted body sweet.—
Where'er he be, God grant us him to meet!

"Young Hugh of Lincoln! in like sort laid low
By cursed Jews—thing well and widely known,
For not long since was dealt the cruel blow
Pray also thou for us, while here we tarry,
Weak sinful folk, that God with pitying eye,
In mercy would his mercy multiply
On us, for reverence of his mother Mary!

The River Duddon.

A SERIES OF SONNETS.

ADVERTISEMENT.

The River Duddon rises upon Wrynose Fell, on the confines of Westmoreland, Cumberland, and Lancashire ; and, serving as a boundary to the two last counties, for the space of about twenty-five miles, enters the Irish Sea, between the Isle of Walney and the Lordship of Milium

TO THE REV. DR. WORDSWORTH.

(WITH THE SONNETS TO THE RIVER DUDDON, AND OTHER POEMS IN THIS COLLECTION.)

The minstrels played their Christmas tune
To-night beneath my cottage eaves ;
While, smitten by a lofty moon,
The encircling laurels, thick with leaves,
Gave back a rich and dazzling sheen,
That overpowered their natural green.

Through hill and valley every breeze
Had sunk to rest with folded wings :
Keen was the air, but could not freeze
Nor check the music of the strings ;
So stout and hardy were the band
That scraped the chords with strenuous hand.

And who but listened ?—till was paid
Respect to every inmate's claim :
The greeting given, the music played,
In honour of each household name,
Duly pronounced with lusty call,
And "Merry Christmas" wished to all !

O brother ! I revere the choice
That took thee from thy native hills ;
And it is given thee to rejoice :
Though public care full often tills
(Heaven only witness of the toil)
A barren and ungrateful soil.

Yet, would that thou, with me and mine,
Hadst heard this never-failing rite ;
And seen on other faces shine
A true revival of the light,
Which nature, and these rustic powers,
In simple childhood, spread through ours !

For pleasure hath not ceased to wait
On these expected annual rounds,
Whether the rich man's sumptuous gate
Call forth the unelaborate sounds,
Or they are offered at the door
That guards the lowliest of the poor.

How touching, when, at midnight, sweep
Snow-muffled winds, and all is dark,
To hear—and sink again to sleep !
Or, at an earlier call, to mark,
By blazing fire, the still suspense
Of self-complacent innocence ;

The mutual nod,—the grave disguise
Of hearts with gladness brimming o'er :
And some unbidden tears that rise
For names once heard, and heard no more ;
Tears brightened by the serenade
For infant in the cradle laid !

Ah ! not for emerald fields alone,
With ambient streams more pure and bright
Than fabled Cytherea's zone
Glittering before the Thunderer's sight,
Is to my heart of hearts endeared,
The ground where we were born and reared !

Hail, ancient manners ! sure defence,
Where they survive, of wholesome laws ;
Remnants of love whose modest sense
Thus into narrow room withdraws ;
Hail, usages of pristine mould,
And ye, that guard them, mountains old !

Bear with me, brother ! quench the thought
That slights this passion, or condemns ;
If thee fond fancy ever brought
From the proud margin of the Thames,
And Lambeth's venerable towers,
To humbler streams, and greener bowers.

Yes, they can make, who fail to find,
Short leisure even in busiest days,
Moments, to cast a look behind,
And profit by those kindly rays
That through the clouds do sometimes steal,
And all the far-off past reveal

Hence, while the imperial city's din
Beats frequent on thy satiate ear,
A pleased attention I may win
To agitations less severe,
That neither overwhelm nor cloy,
But fill the hollow vale with joy!

I.

NOT envying shades which haply yet may throw
A grateful coolness round that rocky spring,
Blandusia, once responsive to the string
Of the Horatian lyre with babbling flow,
Careless of flowers that in perennial blow
Round the moist marge of Persian fountains cling;
Heedless of Alpine torrents thundering
Through icy portals radiant as heaven's bow;
I seek the birthplace of a native stream
All hail, ye mountains! hail, thou morning light!
Better to breathe upon this aery height
Than pass in needless sleep from dream to dream:
Pure flow the verse, pure, vigorous, free, and bright,
For Duddon, long-loved Duddon is my theme!

II.

CHILD of the clouds! remote from every taint
Of sordid industry thy lot is cast,
Thine are the honours of the lofty waste;
Not seldom, when with heat the valleys faint,
Thy hand-maid frost with spangled tissue quaint
Thy cradle decks, to chant thy birth thou hast
No meaner poet than the whistling blast,
And desolation is thy patron-saint!
She guards thee, ruthless power! who would not spare
Those mighty forests, once the bison's screen,
Where stalked the huge deer to his shaggy lair*
Through paths and alleys roofed with sombre green,
Thousands of years before the silent air
Was pierced by whizzing shaft of hunter keen!

III.

How shall I paint thee?—Be this naked stone
My seat while I give way to such intent,
Pleased could my verse, a speaking monument,
Make to the eyes of men thy features known
But as of all those tripping lambs not one
Outruns his fellows, so hath nature lent
To thy beginning naught that doth present
Peculiar grounds for hope to build upon.
To dignify the spot that gives thee birth,
No sign of hoar antiquity's esteem
Appears, and none of modern fortune's care;
Yet thou thyself hast round thee shed a gleam
Of brilliant moss, instinct with freshness rare;
Prompt offering to thy foster-mother, earth!

IV.

TAKE, cradled nursling of the mountain, take
This parting glance, no negligent adieu!
A Protean change seems wrought while I pursue
The curves, a loosely-scattered chain doth make,
Or rather thou appear'st a glistening snake,
Silent, and to the gazer's eye untrue,
Thridding with sinuous lapse the rushes, through
Dwarf willows gliding, and by ferny brake.
Starts from a dizzy steep the undaunted rill
Robed instantly in garb of snow-white foam;
And laughing dares the adventurer, who hath clomb
So high, a rival purpose to fulfil;
Else let the dastard backward wend, and roam,
Seeking less bold achievement, where he will!

V.

SOLE listener, Duddon! to the breeze that played
With thy clear voice, I caught the fitful sound
Wafted o'er sullen moss and craggy mound,
Unfruitful solitudes, that seemed to upbraid

* The deer alluded to is the Leigh, a gigantic species long since extinct.

The sun in heaven !—but now, to form a
shade
For thee, green alders have together wound
Their foliage; ashes flung their arms
around
And birch-trees risen in silver colonnade
And thou hast also tempted here to rise,
'Mid sheltering pines, this cottage rude and
grey,
Whose ruddy children, by the mother's eyes
Carelessly watched, sport through the summer day,
Thy pleased associates·—light as endless May
On infant bosoms lonely nature lies.

VI

FLOWERS.

ERE yet our course was graced with social
trees
It lacked not old remains of hawthorn bowers,
Where small birds warbled to their paramours,
And, earlier still, was heard the hum of bees;
I saw them ply their harmless robberies,
And caught the fragrance which the sundry
flowers,
Fed by the stream with soft perpetual showers,
Plenteously yielded to the vagrant breeze.
There bloomed the strawberry of the
wilderness;
The trembling eyebright showed her sapphire blue, (1)
The thyme her purple, like the blush of
even;
And, if the breath of some to no caress
Invited, forth they peeped so fair to view,
All kinds alike seemed favourites of Heaven.

VII.

"CHANGE me, some god, into that
breathing rose!"
The love-sick stripling fancifully sighs,
The envied flower, beholding, as it lies
On Laura's breast, in exquisite repose;
Or he would pass into her bird, that throws
The darts of song from out its wiry cage;
Enraptured,—could he for himself engage
The thousandth part of what the nymph
bestows,
And what the little careless innocent
Ungraciously receives Too daring choice!
There are whose calmer mind it would
content
To be an unculled floweret of the glen,
Fearless of plough and scythe; or darkling
wren,
That tunes on Duddon's banks her slender voice.

VIII.

WHAT aspect bore the man who roved or
fled,
First of his tribe, to this dark dell—who first
In this pellucid current slaked his thirst?
What hopes came with him? what designs
were spread
Along his path? His unprotected bed
What dreams encompassed? Was the
intruder nursed
In hideous usages, and rites accursed,
That thinned the living and disturbed the
dead?
No voice replies;—the earth, the air is mute,
And thou, blue streamlet, murmuring
yield'st no more
Than a soft record that whatever fruit
Of ignorance thou mightst witness heretofore,
Thy function was to heal and to restore,
To soothe and cleanse, not madden and
pollute!

IX.

THE STEPPING-STONES.

THE struggling rill insensibly is grown
Into a brook of loud and stately march,
Crossed ever and anon by plank and arch,
And, for like use, lo! what might seem a
zone
Chosen for ornament· stone matched with stone
In studied symmetry, with interspace
For the clear waters to pursue their race
Without restraint.—How swiftly have they
flown,
Succeeding — still succeeding! Here the child
Puts, when the high-swoln flood runs fierce
and wild,
His budding courage to the proof,—and here
Declining manhood learns to note the sly
And sure encroachments of infirmity,
Thinking how fast time runs, life's end how
near!

X

THE SAME SUBJECT.

NOT so that pair whose youthful spirits
dance
With prompt emotion, urging them to pass;
A sweet confusion checks the shepherd-lass,
Blushing she eyes the dizzy flood askance,—
To stop ashamed—too timid to advance;
She ventures once again—another pause!
His outstretched hand he tauntingly withdraws—
She sues for help with piteous utterance!

Chidden she chides again, the thrilling touch [aid
Both feel when he renews the wished-for
Ah! if their fluttering hearts should stir too much
Should beat too strongly, both may be betrayed.
The frolic loves who, from yon high rock, see
The struggle, clap their wings for victory!

XI.

THE FAERY CHASM.

No fiction was it of the antique age;
A sky-blue stone, within this sunless cleft,
Is of the very footmarks unbereft
Which tiny elves impressed, on that smooth stage
Dancing with all their brilliant equipage
In secret revels—haply after theft
Of some sweet babe, flower stolen, and coarse weed left
For the distracted mother to assuage
Her grief with, as she might!—But, where, oh! where
Is traceable a vestige of the notes
That ruled those dances, wild in character?
Deep underground?—Or in the upper air,
On the shrill wind of midnight? or where floats
O'er twilight fields the autumnal gossamer?

XII.

HINTS FOR THE FANCY.

On, loitering muse—the swift stream chides us—on!
Albeit his deep-worn channel doth immure
Objects immense portrayed in miniature,
Wild shapes for many a strange comparison!
Niagaras, Alpine passes, and anon
Abodes of Naiads, calm abysses pure,
Bright liquid mansions, fashioned to endure
When the broad oak drops, a leafless skeleton
And the solidities of mortal pride,
Palace and tower, are crumbled into dust!
The bard who walks with Duddon for his guide,
Shall find such toys of fancy thickly set;—
Turn from the sight, enamoured muse—we must;
And, if thou canst, leave them without regret!

XIII

OPEN PROSPECT

Hail to the fields—with dwellings sprinkled o'er,
And one small hamlet, under a green hill,
Clustered with barn and byre, and spouting mill! [more,
A glance suffices;—should we wish for
Gay June would scorn us but when bleak winds roar [ash,
Through the stiff lance-like shoots of pollard
Dread swell of sound! loud as the gusts that lash
The matted forests of Ontario's shore
By wasteful steel unsmitten, then would I
Turn into port,—and, reckless of the gale
Reckless of angry Duddon sweeping by
While the warm hearth exalts the mantling ale,
Laugh with the generous household heartily
At all the merry pranks of Donnerdale!

XIV

O mountain stream! the shepherd and his cot
Are privileged inmates of deep solitude;
Nor would the nicest anchorite exclude
A field or two of brighter green, or plot
Of tillage-ground, that seemeth like a spot
Of stationary sunshine—thou hast viewed
These only, Duddon! with their paths renewed [not.
By fits and starts, yet this contents thee
Thee hath some awful spirit impelled to leave,
Utterly to desert, the haunts of men,
Though simple thy companions were and few, [cleave
And through this wilderness a passage
Attended but by thy own voice, save when
The clouds and fowls of the air thy way pursue!

XV.

From this deep chasm—where quivering sunbeams play
Upon its loftiest crags—mine eyes behold
A gloomy niche, capacious, blank, and cold, [gray;
A concave free from shrubs and mosses
In semblance fresh, as if, with dire affray,
Some statue, placed amid these regions old
For tutelary service, thence had rolled,
Startling the flight of timid yesterday!
Was it by mortals sculptured?—weary slaves

Of slow endeavour! or abruptly cast
Into rude shape by fire, with roaring blast
Tempestuously let loose from central caves?
Or fashioned by the turbulence of waves,
Then, when o'er highest hills the deluge past?

XVI.

AMERICAN TRADITION.

SUCH fruitless questions may not long beguile
Or plague the fancy, 'mid the sculptured shows
Conspicuous yet where Oroonoko flows;
There would the Indian answer with a smile
Aimed at the white man's ignorance, the while
Of the Great Waters telling how they rose,
Covered the plains, and, wandering where they chose,
Mounted through every intricate defile,
Triumphant.—Inundation wide and deep,
O'er which his fathers urged, to ridge and steep
Else unapproachable, their buoyant way;
And carved, on mural cliff's undreaded side,
Sun, moon, and stars, and beast of chase or prey;
Whate'er they sought, shunned, loved, or deified!*

XVII.

RETURN.

A DARK plume fetch me from yon blasted yew,
Perched on whose top the Danish raven croaks;
Aloft, the imperial bird of Rome invokes
Departed ages, shedding where he flew
Loose fragments of wild wailing, that bestrew
The clouds, and thrill the chambers of the rocks,
And into silence hush the timorous flocks,
That, calmly couching while the nightly dew
Moistened each fleece, beneath the twinkling stars
Slept amid that lone camp on Hardknot's height,
Whose guardians bent the knee to Jove and Mars:
Or, near that mystic round of Druid frame
Tardily sinking by its proper weight
Deep into patient earth, from whose smooth breast it came!(2)

XVIII.

SEATHWAITE CHAPEL.

SACRED religion, "mother of form and fear,"
Dread arbitress of mutable respect.
New rites ordaining, when the old are wrecked,
Or cease to please the fickle worshipper;
If one strong wish may be embosomed here,
Mother of love! for this deep vale, protect
Truth's holy lamp, pure source of bright effect,
Gifted to purge the vapoury atmosphere
That seeks to stifle it;—as in those days
When this low pile a gospel teacher knew,
Whose good works formed an endless retinue:†
Such priest as Chaucer sang in fervent lays;
Such as the Heaven-taught skill of Herbert drew;
And tender Goldsmith crowned with deathless praise!

XIX.

TRIBUTARY STREAM.

MY frame hath often trembled with delight
When hope presented some far-distant good,
That seemed from Heaven descending, like the flood
Of yon pure waters, from their aëry height
Hurrying with lordly Duddon to unite;
Who, 'mid a world of images imprest
On the calm depth of his transparent breast,
Appears to cherish most that torrent white,
The fairest, softest, liveliest of them all!
And seldom hath ear listened to a tune
More lulling than the busy hum of noon,
Swoln by that voice—whose murmur musical
Announces to the thirsty fields a boon
Dewy and fresh, till showers again shall fall.

XX.

THE PLAIN OF DONNERDALE.

THE old inventive poets, had they seen,
Or rather felt, the entrancement that detains
Thy waters, Duddon! 'mid these flowery plains,
The still repose, the liquid lapse serene,
Transferred to bowers imperishably green,
Had beautified Elysium! But these chains

* See Humboldt's Personal Narrative.

† See Note to Sonnet xvi.

Will soon be broken,—a rough course remains,
Rough as the past, where thou, of placid mien,
Innocuous as a firstling of the flock,
And countenanced like a soft cerulean sky,
Shalt change thy temper, and, with many a shock
Given and received in mutual jeopardy,
Dance like a Bacchanal, from rock to rock,
Tossing her frantic thyrsus wide and high!

XXI

WHENCE that low voice?—A whisper from the heart,
That told of days long past, when here I roved
With friends and kindred tenderly beloved,
Some who had early mandates to depart,
Yet are allowed to steal my path athwart
By Duddon's side; once more do we unite,
Once more beneath the kind earth's tranquil light;
And smothered joys into new being start.
From her unworthy seat, the cloudy stall
Of time, breaks forth triumphant Memory;
Her glistening tresses bound, yet light and free
As golden locks of birch, that rise and fall
On gales that breathe too gently to recal
Aught of the fading year's inclemency!

XXII.

TRADITION.

A LOVE-LORN maid, at some far-distant time,
Came to this hidden pool, whose depths surpass
In crystal clearness Dian's looking-glass,
And, gazing, saw that rose, which from the prime
Derives its name, reflected as the chime
Of echo doth reverberate some sweet sound:
The starry treasure from the blue profound
She longed to ravish;—shall she plunge, or climb
The humid precipice, and seize the guest
Of April, smiling high in upper air?
Desperate alternative! what fiend could dare
To prompt the thought?—Upon the steep rock's breast
The lonely primrose yet renews its bloom,
Untouched memento of her hapless doom!

XXIII.

SHEEP-WASHING.

SAD thoughts, avaunt!—the favour of the year,
Poured on the fleece-encumbered flock, invites
To laving currents, for prelusive rites
Duly performed before the dalesmen shear
Their panting charge. The distant mountains hear,
Hear and repeat, the turmoil that unites
Clamour of boys with innocent despites
Of barking dogs, and bleatings from strange fear
Meanwhile, if Duddon's spotless breast receive
Unwelcome mixtures as the uncouth noise
Thickens, the pastoral river will forgive
Such wrong; nor need *we* blame the licensed joys,
Though false to nature's quiet equipoise.
Frank are the sports, the stains are fugitive.

XXIV.

THE RESTING-PLACE.

MID-NOON is past;—upon the sultry mead
No zephyr breathes, no cloud its shadow throws:
If we advance unstrengthened by repose,
Farewell the solace of the fragrant reed!
This nook, with woodbine hung and straggling weed,
Tempting recess as ever pilgrim chose,
Half grot, half arbour, proffers to inclose
Body and mind from molestation freed,
In narrow compass—narrow as itself:
Or if the fancy, too industrious elf,
Be loth that we should breathe a while exempt
From new incitements friendly to our task,
There wants not stealthy prospect, that may tempt
Loose idless to forego our wily mask.

XXV.

METHINKS 'twere no unprecedented feat
Should some benignant minister of air
Lift, and incircle with a cloudy chair,
The one for whom my heart shall ever beat
With tenderest love;—or, if a safer seat
Atween his downy wings be furnished, there
Would lodge her, and the cherished burden bear
O'er hill and valley to this dim retreat!

Rough ways my steps have trod ; too rough and long [ease :
For her companionship ; here dwells soft
With sweets which she partakes not some distaste [wrong ;
Mingles, and lurking consciousness of
Languish the flowers , the waters seem to waste
Their vocal charm ; their sparklings cease to please.

XXVI.

RETURN, content ! for fondly I pursued,
Even when a child, the streams—unheard, unseen ; [between ;
Through tangled woods, impending rocks
Or, free as air, with flying inquest viewed
The sullen reservoirs whence their bold brood, [keen,
Pure as the morning, fretful, boisterous,
Green as the salt-sea billows, white and green,
Poured down the hills, a choral multitude !
Nor have I tracked their course for scanty gains , [joys,
They taught me random cares and truant
That shield from mischief and preserve from stains [of boys ;
Vague minds, while men are growing out
Maturer fancy owes to their rough noise
Impetuous thoughts that brook not servile reins

XXVII.

FALLEN, and diffused into a shapeless heap,
Or quietly self-buried in earth's mould,
Is that embattled house, whose massy keep
Flung from yon cliff a shadow large and cold.—
There dwelt the gay, the bountiful, the bold,
Till nightly lamentations, like the sweep
Of winds—though winds were silent, struck a deep
And lasting terror through that ancient hold.
Its line of warriors fled ;—they shrunk when tried
By ghostly power :—but Time's unsparing hand
Hath plucked such foes, like weeds, from out the land ;
And now, if men with men in peace abide,
All other strength the weakest may withstand,
All worse assaults may safely be defied.

XXVIII.

JOURNEY RENEWED.

I ROSE while yet the cattle, heat-opprest,
Crowded together under rustling trees,
Brushed by the current of the water-breeze,
And for *their* sakes, and love of all that rest,
On Duddon's margin, in the sheltering nest;
For all the startled scaly tribes that slink
Into his coverts, and each fearless link
Of dancing insects forged upon his breast ;
For these, and hopes and recollections worn
Close to the vital seat of human clay ;
Glad meetings,—tender partings—that upstay [sworn
The drooping mind of absence, by vows
In his pure presence near the trysting thorn ,
I thanked the leader of my onward way.

XXIX.

No record tells of lance opposed to lance,
Horse charging horse, 'mid these retired domains ; [veins
Tells that their turf drank purple from the
Of heroes fallen, or struggling to advance,
Till doubtful combat issued in a trance
Of victory, that struck through heart and reins,
Even to the inmost seat of mortal pains,
And lightened o'er the pallid countenance.
Yet, to the loyal and the brave, who lie
In the black earth, neglected and forlorn,
The passing winds memorial tribute pay ;
The torrents chant their praise, inspiring scorn
Of power usurped with proclamation high,
And glad acknowledgment of lawful sway.

XXX

WHO swerves from innocence, who makes divorce
Of that serene companion—a good name,
Recovers not his loss, but walks with shame,
With doubt, with fear, and haply with remorse.
And oft-times he, who, yielding to the force
Of chance temptation, ere his journey end,
From chosen comrade turns, or faithful friend,
In vain shall rue the broken intercourse.
Not so with such as loosely wear the chain

That binds them, pleasant river! to thy side — [hasty stride,
Through the rough copse wheel thou with
I choose to saunter o'er the grassy plain,
Sure, when the separation has been tried,
That we, who part in love, shall meet again.

XXXI.

THE Kirk of Ulpha to the pilgrim's eye
Is welcome as a star, that doth present
Its shining forehead through the peaceful rent
Of a black cloud diffused o'er half the sky
Or as a fruitful palm-tree towering high
O'er the parched waste beside an Arab's tent; [ward bent,
Or the Indian tree whose branches, down-
Take root again, a boundless canopy
How sweet were leisure! could it yield no more [to recline,
Than 'mid that wave-washed churchyard
From pastoral graves extracting thoughts divine,
Or there to pace, and mark the summits hoar
Of distant moon-lit mountains faintly shine,
Soothed by the unseen river's gentle roar.

XXXII.

NOT hurled precipitous from steep to steep;
Lingering no more 'mid flower-enamelled lands
And blooming thickets; nor by rocky bands
Held,—but in radiant progress toward the deep
Where mightiest rivers into powerless sleep
Sink, and forget their nature,—*now* expands
Majestic Duddon, over smooth flat sands
Gliding in silence with unfettered sweep!
Beneath an ampler sky a region wide
Is opened round him:—hamlets, towers, and towns, [afar;
And blue-topped hills, behold him from
In stately mien to sovereign Thames allied
Spreading his bosom under Kentish downs,
With commerce freighted, or triumphant war

XXXIII.

CONCLUSION.

BUT here no cannon thunders to the gale;
Upon the wave no haughty pendants cast
A crimson splendour; lowly is the mast
That rises here, and humbly spread the sail;
While, less disturbed than in the narrow vale
Through which with strange vicissitudes he passed,
The wanderer seeks that receptacle vast
Where all his unambitious functions fail
And may thy poet, cloud-born stream! be free,
The sweets of earth contentedly resigned,
And each tumultuous working left behind
At seemly distance, to advance like thee,
Prepared, in peace of heart, in calm of mind
And soul, to mingle with eternity!

XXXIV.

AFTER-THOUGHT.

I THOUGHT of thee, my partner and my guide,
As being past away. Vain sympathies!
For, backward, Duddon! as I cast my eyes,
I see what was, and is, and will abide,
Still glides the stream, and shall not cease to glide;
The form remains, the function never dies;
While we, the brave, the mighty, and the wise,
We men, who in our morn of youth defied
The elements, must vanish,—be it so!
Enough, if something from our hands have power
To live, and act, and serve the future hour,
And if, as toward the silent tomb we go,
Through love, through hope, and faith's transcendant dower,
We feel that we are greater than we know. (3)

POSTSCRIPT.

A POET, whose works are not yet known as they deserve to be, thus enters upon his description of the "Ruins of Rome:"

> "The rising sun
> Flames on the ruins in the purer air
> Towering aloft."

and ends thus—

> "The setting sun displays
> His visible great round, between yon towers,
> As through two shady cliffs"

Mr. Crowe, in his excellent loco-descriptive poem, "Lewesdon Hill," is still more expeditious, finishing the whole on a May-morning, before breakfast

> "To-morrow for severer thought, but now
> To breakfast, and keep festival to-day"

Sonnets dedicated to Liberty and Order.

I.

UPON THE LATE GENERAL FAST.

March, 1832.

RELUCTANT call it was; the rite delayed;
And in the Senate some there were who doffed
The last of their humanity, and scoffed
At providential judgments, undismayed
By their own daring. But the people prayed
As with one voice; their flinty heart grew soft
With penitential sorrow, and aloft
Their spirit mounted, crying, "God us aid!"
Oh that with aspirations more intense,
Chastised by self-abasement more profound,
This People, once so happy, so renowned
For liberty, would seek from God defence
Against far heavier ill, the pestilence
Of revolution, impiously unbound!

II.

SAID Secrecy to Cowardice and Fraud,
Falsehood and Treachery, in close council met,
Deep under ground, in Pluto's cabinet,
"The frost of England's pride will soon be thawed;
Hooded the open brow that overawed
Our schemes; the faith and honour, never yet
By us with hope encountered, be upset;—
For once I burst my bands, and cry, applaud!"
Then whispered she, "The Bill is carrying out!"
They heard, and, starting up, the Brood of Night
Clapped hands, and shook with glee their matted locks;
All Powers and Places that abhor the light
Joined in the transport, echoed back their shout,
Hurrah for ——, hugging his Ballot-Box!

III.

BLEST Statesman he, whose Mind's unselfish will
Leaves him at ease among grand thoughts: whose eye
Sees that, apart from magnanimity,
Wisdom exists not; nor the humbler skill
Of Prudence, disentangling good and ill
With patient care. What though assaults run high,
They daunt not him who holds his ministry,
Resolute, at all hazards, to fulfil
Its duties;—prompt to move, but firm to wait,—
Knowing, things rashly sought are rarely found:
That, for the functions of an ancient State—
Strong by her charters, free because unbound,
Servant of Providence, not slave of Fate—
Perilous is sweeping change, all chance unsound.

IV.

IN ALLUSION TO VARIOUS RECENT HISTORIES AND NOTICES OF THE FRENCH REVOLUTION.

PORTENTOUS change when History can appear
As the cool Advocate of foul device;
Reckless audacity extol, and jeer
At consciences perplexed with scruples nice!
They who bewail not must abhor the sneer
Born of Conceit, Power's blind Idolater;
Or haply sprung from vaunting Cowardice
Betrayed by mockery of holy fear.
Hath it not long been said the wrath of Man
Works not the righteousness of God? Oh bend,
Bend, ye Perverse! to judgments from on High,
Laws that lay under Heaven's perpetual ban
All principles of action that transcend
The sacred limits of humanity.

V.

WHO ponders national events shall find
An awful balancing of loss and gain,
Joy based on sorrow, good with ill combined,
And proud deliverance issuing out of pain
And direful throes; as if the All-ruling Mind,

With whose perfection it consists to ordain
Volcanic burst, earthquake, and hurricane,
Dealt in like sort with feeble human kind
By laws immutable. But woe for him
Who thus deceived shall lend an eager hand
To social havoc. Is not Conscience ours,
And Truth, whose eye guilt only can make dim;
And Will, whose office, by divine command,
Is to control and check disordered Powers!

VI.

CONCLUDED.

LONG-FAVOURED England! be not thou misled
By monstrous theories of alien growth,
Lest alien frenzy seize thee, waxing wroth,
Self-smitten till thy garments reek dyed red
With thy own blood, which tears in torrents shed
Fail to wash out, tears flowing ere thy troth
Be plighted, not to ease but sullen sloth,
Or wan despair—the ghost of false hope fled
Into a shameful grave. Among thy youth,
My Country! if such warning be held dear,
Then shall a Veteran's heart be thrilled with joy,
One who would gather from eternal truth,
For time and season, rules that work to cheer—
Not scourge, to save the People—not destroy.

VII.

MEN of the Western World! in Fate's dark book
Whence these opprobrious leaves of dire portent?
Think ye your British Ancestors forsook
Their native Land, for outrage provident;
From unsubmissive necks the bridle shook
To give, in their Descendants, freer vent
And wider range to passions turbulent,
To mutual tyranny, a deadlier look?
Nay, said a voice, soft as the south wind's breath,
Dive through the stormy surface of the flood
To the great current flowing underneath;
Explore the countless springs of silent good;
So shall the truth be better understood,
And thy grieved Spirit brighten strong in faith.

VIII.

TO THE PENNSYLVANIANS.

DAYS undefiled by luxury or sloth,
Firm self-denial, manners grave and staid,
Rights equal, laws with cheerfulness obeyed,
Words that require no sanction from an oath,
And simple honesty a common growth—
This high repute, with bounteous Nature's aid,
Won confidence, now ruthlessly betrayed
At will, your power the measure of your troth!—
All who revere the memory of Penn
Grieve for the land on whose wild woods his name
Was fondly grafted with a virtuous aim,
Renounced, abandoned by degenerate Men
For state-dishonour black as ever came
To upper air from Mammon's loathsome den.

IX.

AT BOLOGNA, IN REMEMBRANCE OF THE LATE INSURRECTIONS, 1837.

I.

AH, why deceive ourselves! by no mere fit
Of sudden passion roused shall men attain
True freedom where for ages they have lain
Bound in a dark abominable pit,
With life's best sinews more and more unknit,
Here, there, a banded few who loathe the Chain
May rise to break it: effort worse than vain
For thee, O great Italian nation, split
Into those jarring fractions.—Let thy scope
Be one fixed mind for all, thy rights approve
To thy own conscience gradually renewed;
Learn to make Time the father of wise Hope,
Then trust thy cause to the arm of Fortitude,
The light of Knowledge, and the warmth of Love.

X.

CONTINUED.

2

HARD task! exclaim the undisciplined, to lean
On Patience coupled with such slow endeavour
That long-lived servitude must last for ever.
Perish the grovelling few, who, prest between

Wrongs and the terror of redress, would wean
Millions from glorious aims. Our chains to sever
Let us break forth in tempest now or never!—
What, is there then no space for golden mean
And gradual progress?—Twilight leads to day,
And, even within the burning zones of earth,
The hastiest sunrise yields a temperate ray;
The softest breeze to fairest flowers gives birth:
Think not that Prudence dwells in dark abodes,
She scans the future with the eye of gods.

XI.

CONCLUDED

3.

As leaves are to the tree whereon they grow
And wither, every human generation
Is to the Being of a mighty nation,
Locked in our world's embrace through weal and woe;
Thought that should teach the zealot to forego
Rash schemes, to abjure all selfish agitation,
And seek through noiseless pains and moderation
The unblemished good they only can bestow.
Alas! with most who weigh futurity
Against time present, passion holds the scales:
Hence equal ignorance of both prevails,
And nations sink, or, struggling to be free,
Are doomed to flounder on, like wounded whales
Tossed on the bosom of a stormy sea.

XII.

YOUNG ENGLAND—what is then become of Old,
Of dear Old England? Think they she is dead,
Dead to the very name? Presumption fed
On empty air! That name will keep its hold
In the true filial bosom's inmost fold
For ever.—The Spirit of Alfred at the head
Of all who for her rights watch'd, toil'd and bled,
Knows that this prophecy is not too bold.
What—how! shall she submit in will and deed
To Beardless Boys—an imitative race,
The *servum pecus* of a Gallic breed?
Dear Mother! if thou *must* thy steps retrace,
Go where at least meek Innocency dwells;
Let Babes and Sucklings be thy oracles.

XIII.

FEEL for the wrongs to universal ken
Daily exposed, woe that unshrouded lies;
And seek the Sufferer in his darkest den,
Whether conducted to the spot by sighs
And moanings, or he dwells (as if the wren
Taught him concealment) hidden from all eyes
In silence and the awful modesties
Of sorrow;—feel for all, as brother Men.
Rest not in hope Want's icy chain to thaw
By casual boons and formal charities;
Learn to be just, just through impartial law:
Far as ye may, erect and equalise;
And, what ye cannot reach by statute, draw
Each from his fountain of self-sacrifice!

Sonnets upon the Punishment of Death.

IN SERIES.

I.

SUGGESTED BY THE VIEW OF LANCASTER CASTLE (ON THE ROAD FROM THE SOUTH).

THIS Spot—at once unfolding sight so fair
Of sea and land, with yon grey towers that still
Rise up as if to lord it over air—
Might soothe in human breasts the sense of ill,
Or charm it out of memory; yea, might fill
The heart with joy and gratitude to God
For all His bounties upon man bestowed
Why bears it then the name of "Weeping Hill"?
Thousands, as toward yon old Lancastrian Towers,
A prison's crown, along this way they past
For lingering durance or quick death with shame,

From this bare eminence thereon have cast
Their first look—blinded as tears fell in showers
Shed on their chains, and hence that doleful name.

II.

TENDERLY do we feel by Nature's law
For worst offenders: though the heart will heave
With indignation, deeply moved we grieve,
In after thought, for Him who stood in awe
Neither of God nor man, and only saw,
Lost wretch, a horrible device enthroned
On proud temptations, till the victim groaned
Under the steel his hand had dared to draw.
But O, restrain compassion, if its course,
As oft befalls, prevent or turn aside
Judgments and aims and acts whose higher source
Is sympathy with the unforewarned, who died
Blameless—with them that shuddered o'er his grave,
And all who from the law firm safety crave

III.

THE Roman Consul doomed his sons to die
Who had betrayed their country. The stern word
Afforded (may it through all time afford)
A theme for praise and admiration high.
Upon the surface of humanity
He rested not, its depths his mind explored;
He felt; but his parental bosom's lord
Was Duty,—Duty calmed his agony.
And some, we know, when they by wilful act
A single human life have wrongly taken,
Pass sentence on themselves, confess the fact,
And, to atone for it, with soul unshaken
Kneel at the feet of Justice, and, for faith
Broken with all mankind, solicit death

IV.

Is *Death*, when evil against good has fought
With such fell mastery that a man may dare
By deeds the blackest purpose to lay bare—
Is Death, for one to that condition brought,
For him, or any one, the thing that ought
To be *most* dreaded? Lawgivers, beware,
Lest, capital pains remitting till ye spare
The murderer, ye, by sanction to that thought
Seemingly given, debase the general mind;
Tempt the vague will tried standards to disown,
Nor only palpable restraints unbind,
But upon Honour's head disturb the crown,
Whose absolute rule permits not to withstand
In the weak love of life his least command.

V.

NOT to the object specially designed,
Howe'er momentous in itself it be,
Good to promote or curb depravity,
Is the wise Legislator's view confined
His Spirit, when most severe, is oft most kind;
As all Authority in earth depends
On Love and Fear, their several powers he blends,
Copying with awe the one Paternal mind.
Uncaught by processes in show humane,
He feels how far the act would derogate
From even the humblest functions of the State;
If she, self-shorn of Majesty, ordain
That never more shall hang upon her breath
The last alternative of Life or Death.

VI.

YE brood of conscience—Spectres! that frequent
The bad Man's restless walk, and haunt his bed—
Fiends in your aspect, yet beneficent
In act, as hovering Angels when they spread
Their wings to guard the unconscious Innocent—
Slow be the Statutes of the land to share
A laxity that could not but impair
Your power to punish crime, and so prevent.
And ye, Beliefs! coiled serpent-like about
The adage on all tongues, "Murder will out,"
How shall your ancient warnings work for good
In the full might they hitherto have shown,
If for deliberate shedder of man's blood
Survive not Judgment that requires his own?

VII.

BEFORE the world had past her time of youth,
While polity and discipline were weak,
The precept eye for eye, and tooth for tooth,
Came forth—a light, though but as of daybreak,

Strong as could then be borne. A Master meek
Proscribed the spirit fostered by that rule,
Patience *his* law, long-suffering *his* school,
And love the end, which all through peace must seek.
But lamentably do they err who strain
His mandates, given rash impulse to controul
And keep vindictive thirstings from the soul,
So far that, if consistent in their scheme,
They must forbid the State to inflict a pain,
Making of social order a mere dream.

VIII.

Fit retribution, by the moral code
Determined, lies beyond the State's embrace,
Yet, as she may, for each peculiar case
She plants well-measured terrors in the road
Of wrongful acts. Downward it is and broad,
And, the main fear once doomed to banishment,
Far oftener then, bad ushering worse event,
Blood would be spilt that in his dark abode
Crime might lie better hid. And, should the change
Take from the horror due to a foul deed,
Pursuit and evidence so far must fail,
And, guilt escaping, passion then might plead
In angry spirits for her old free range,
And the "wild justice of revenge" prevail.

IX.

Though to give timely warning and deter
Is one great aim of penalty, extend
Thy mental vision further and ascend
Far higher, else full surely shalt thou err.
What is a State? The wise behold in her
A creature born of time, that keeps one eye
Fixed on the statutes of Eternity,
To which her judgments reverently defer.
Speaking through Law's dispassionate voice, the State
Endues her conscience with external life
And being, to preclude or swell the strife
Of individual will, to elevate
The grovelling mind, the erring to recal,
And fortify the moral sense of all.

X.

Our bodily life, some plead, that life the shrine
Of an immortal spirit, is a gift
So sacred, so informed with light divine,
That no tribunal, though most wise to sift
Deed and intent, should turn the Being adrift
Into that world where penitential tear
May not avail, nor prayer have for God's ear
A voice—that world whose veil no hand can lift
For earthly sight. "Eternity and Time,"
They urge, "have interwoven claims and rights
Not to be jeopardised through foulest crime:
The sentence rule by mercy's heaven-born lights."
Even so: but measuring not by finite sense
Infinite Power, perfect Intelligence.

XI.

Ah, think how one compelled for life to abide
Locked in a dungeon needs must eat the heart
Out of his own humanity, and part
With every hope that mutual cares provide;
And, should a less unnatural doom confide
In life-long exile on a savage coast,
Soon the relapsing penitent may boast
Of yet more heinous guilt, with fiercer pride.
Hence thoughtful Mercy, Mercy sage and pure,
Sanctions the forfeiture that Law demands,
Leaving the final issue in *His* hands
Whose goodness knows no change, whose love is sure,
Who sees, foresees; who cannot judge amiss,
And wafts at will the contrite soul to bliss.

XII.

See the Condemned alone within his cell,
And prostrate at some moment when remorse
Stings to the quick, and, with resistless force,
Assaults the pride she strove in vain to quell.
Then mark him, him who could so long rebel,
The crime confessed, a kneeling Penitent
Before the Altar, where the Sacrament
Softens his heart, till from his eyes outwell
Tears of salvation. Welcome death! while Heaven

Does in this change exceedingly rejoice;
While yet the solemn heed the State hath given
Helps him to meet the last Tribunal's voice
In faith, which fresh offences, were he cast
On old temptations, might for ever blast.

XIII.

CONCLUSION.

YES, though He well may tremble at the sound
Of his own voice, who from the judgment-seat
Sends the pale convict to his last retreat
In death; though Listeners shudder all around,
They know the dread requital's source profound;
Nor is, they feel, its wisdom obsolete—
(Would that it were!) the sacrifice unmeet
For Christian Faith. But hopeful signs abound.
The social rights of man breathe purer air;
Religion deepens her preventive care;
Then, moved by needless fear of past abuse,
Strike not from Law's firm hand that awful rod,
But leave it thence to drop for lack of use:
Oh, speed the blessed hour, Almighty God!

XIV.

APOLOGY.

THE formal World relaxes her cold chain
For One who speaks in numbers; ampler scope
His utterance finds, and, conscious of the gain,
Imagination works with bolder hope
The cause of grateful reason to sustain;
And, serving Truth, the heart more strongly beats
Against all barriers which his labour meets
In lofty place, or humble Life's domain.
Enough;—before us lay a painful road,
And guidance have I sought in duteous love
From Wisdom's heavenly Father. Hence hath flowed
Patience, with trust that, whatsoe'er the way
Each takes in this high matter, all may move
Cheered with the prospect of a brighter day.

1840.

Sonnets and Stanzas.

THOUGH the bold wings of Poesy affect
The clouds, and wheel around the mountain tops
Rejoicing, from her loftiest height she drops
Well pleased to skim the plain with wild flowers deckt,
Or muse in solemn grove whose shades protect
The lingering dew—there steals along, or stops,
Watching the least small bird that round her hops,
Or creeping worm, with sensitive respect.
Her functions are they therefore less divine,
Her thoughts less deep, or void of grave intent
Her simplest fancies? Should that fear be thine,
Aspiring Votary, ere thy hand present
One offering, kneel before her modest shrine,
With brow in penitential sorrow bent!

A POET!—He hath put his heart to school,
Nor dares to move unpropped upon the staff
Which Art hath lodged within his hand—must laugh
By precept only, and shed tears by rule.
Thy Art be Nature; the live current quaff,
And let the groveller sip his stagnant pool,
In fear that else, when Critics grave and cool
Have killed him, Scorn should write his epitaph.
How does the Meadow-flower its bloom unfold?
Because the lovely little flower is free
Down to its root, and, in that freedom bold;
And so the grandeur of the Forest-tree
Comes not by casting in a formal mould,
But from its *own* divine vitality.

THE most alluring clouds that mount the sky
Owe to a troubled element their forms,
Their hues to sunset. If with raptured eye

We watch their splendour, shall we covet storms,
And wish the Lord of day his slow decline
Would hasten, that such pomp may float on high?
Behold, already they forget to shine,
Dissolve—and leave to him who gazed a sigh,
Not loth to thank each moment for its boon
Of pure delight, come whencesoe'er it may,
Peace let us seek,—to steadfast things attune
Calm expectations: leaving to the gay
And volatile their love of transient bowers,
The house that cannot pass away be ours.

ON A PORTRAIT OF THE DUKE OF WELLINGTON UPON THE FIELD OF WATERLOO, BY HAYDON.

BY Art's bold privilege Warrior and War-horse stand
On ground yet strewn with their last battle's wreck;
Let the Steed glory while his Master's hand
Lies fixed for ages on his conscious neck;
But by the Chieftain's look, though at his side
Hangs that day's treasured sword, how firm a check
Is given to triumph and all human pride!
Yon trophied Mound shrinks to a shadowy speck
In his calm presence! Him the mighty deed
Elates not, brought far nearer the grave's rest,
As shows that time-worn face, for he such seed
Has sown as yields, we trust, the fruit of fame
In Heaven; hence no one blushes for thy name,
Conqueror,'mid some sad thoughts, divinely blest!

HARK! 'tis the Thrush, undaunted, undeprest,
By twilight premature of cloud and rain;
Nor does that roaring wind deaden his strain
Who carols thinking of his Love and nest,
And seems, as more incited, still more blest.
Thanks; thou hast snapped a fireside Prisoner's chain,
Exulting Warbler! eased a fretted brain,
And in a moment charmed my cares to rest.
Yes, I will forth, bold Bird! and front the blast
That we may sing together, if thou wilt,
So loud, so clear, my Partner through life's day,
Mute in her nest love-chosen, if not love-built
Like thine, shall gladden, as in seasons past
Thrilled by loose snatches of the social Lay.

Rydal Mount, 1838.

'TIS he whose yester-evening's high disdain
Beat back the roaring storm—but how subdued
His day-break note, a sad vicissitude!
Does the hour's drowsy weight his glee restrain?
Or, like the nightingale, her joyous vein
Pleased to renounce, does this dear Thrush attune
His voice to suit the temper of yon Moon?
Doubly depressed, setting, and in her wane?
Rise, tardy Sun! and let the Songster prove
(The balance trembling between night and morn
No longer) with what ecstasy upborne
He can pour forth his spirit. In heaven above,
And earth below, they best can serve true gladness
Who meet most feelingly the calls of sadness.

A PLEA FOR AUTHORS, MAY 1838.

FAILING imperial measure to dispense
To every suitor, Equity is lame;
And social justice, stript of reverence
For natural rights, a mockery and a shame;
Law but a servile dupe of false pretence,
If, guarding grossest things from common claim,
Now and for ever, She, to works that came
From mind and spirit, grudge a short-lived fence.
"What! lengthened privilege, a lineal tie
For *Books!*" Yes, heartless Ones, or be it proved
That 'tis a fault in us to have lived and loved
Like others, with like temporal hopes to die;
No public harm that Genius from her course
Be turned; and streams of truth dried up even at their source.

AT DOVER.

FROM the Pier's head, musing, and with increase
Of wonder, I have watched this sea-side Town,
Under the white cliff's battlemented crown,
Hushed to a depth of more than Sabbath peace:
The streets and quays are thronged, but why disown
Their natural utterance: whence this strange release
From social noise—silence elsewhere unknown?—
A spirit whispered, "Let all wonder cease;
Ocean's overpowering murmurs have set free
Thy sense from pressure of life's common din;
As the dread Voice that speaks from out the sea
Of God's eternal Word, the Voice of Time
Doth deaden, shocks of tumult, shrieks of crime,
The shouts of folly, and the groans of sin."

INTENT on gathering wool from hedge and brake,
Yon busy Little-ones rejoice that soon
A poor old Dame would bless them for the boon:
Great is their glee while flake they add to flake
With rival earnestness; far other strife
Than will hereafter move them, if they make
Pastime their idol, give their day of life
To pleasure snatched for reckless pleasure's sake.
Can pomp and show allay one heart-born grief?
Pains which the World inflicts can she requite?
Not for an interval however brief;
The silent thoughts that search for steadfast light,
Love from her depths, and Duty in her might,
And Faith—these only yield secure relief.

ON THE PLANET VENUS AS AN EVENING STAR.

WHAT strong allurement draws, what spirit guides
Thee, Vesper! brightening still, as if the nearer
Thou com'st to man's abode the spot grew dearer
Night after night? True is it Nature hides
Her treasures less and less. Man now presides
In power where once he trembled at his weakness;
Science advances with gigantic strides;
But are we aught enriched in love and meekness?
Aught dost thou see, bright Star! of pure and wise,
More than in humbler times graced human story;
That makes our hearts more apt to sympathise
With heaven, our souls more fit for future glory,
When earth shall vanish from our closing eyes,
Ere we lie down in our last dormitory?

So fair, so sweet, withal so sensitive,
Would that the little Flowers were born to live,
Conscious of half the pleasure which they give;

That to this mountain-daisy's self were known
The beauty of its star-shaped shadow, thrown
On the smooth surface of this naked stone!

And what if hence a bold desire should mount
High as the Sun, that he could take account
Of all that issues from his glorious fount!

So might he ken how by his sovereign aid
These delicate companionships are made;
And how he rules the pomp of light and shade;

And were the Sister-power that shines by night
So privileged, what a countenance of delight
Would through the clouds break forth on human sight!

Fond fancies! wheresoe'er shall turn thine eye
On earth, air, ocean, or the starry sky,
Converse with Nature in pure sympathy.

All vain desires, all lawless wishes quelled,
Be Thou to love and praise alike impelled,
Whatever boon is granted or withheld.

Poems of Sentiment and Reflection.

EXPOSTULATION AND REPLY.

"WHY, William, on that old gray stone,
Thus for the length of half a day,
Why, William, sit you thus alone,
And dream your time away?

"Where are your books?—that light bequeathed
To beings else forlorn and blind!
Up! up! and drink the spirit breathed
From dead men to their kind.

"You look round on your mother earth,
As if she for no purpose bore you;
As if you were her first-born birth,
And none had lived before you!"

One morning thus, by Esthwaite lake,
When life was sweet, I knew not why,
To me my good friend Matthew spake,
And thus I made reply—

"The eye—it cannot choose but see;
We cannot bid the ear be still;
Our bodies feel, where'er they be,
Against, or with our will.

"Nor less I deem that there are powers
Which of themselves our minds impress;
That we can feed this mind of ours
In a wise passiveness.

"Think you, 'mid all this mighty sum
Of things for ever speaking,
That nothing of itself will come,
But we must still be seeking?

"Then ask not wherefore, here, alone,
Conversing as I may,
I sit upon this old gray stone,
And dream my time away."

THE TABLES TURNED.

AN EVENING SCENE, ON THE SAME SUBJECT.

UP! up! my friend, and quit your books;
Or surely you'll grow double:
Up! up! my friend, and clear your looks
Why all this toil and trouble?

The sun, above the mountain's head,
A freshening lustre mellow
Through all the long green fields has spread
His first sweet evening yellow.

Books! 'tis a dull and endless strife:
Come, hear the woodland linnet,
How sweet his music! on my life,
There's more of wisdom in it.

And hark! how blithe the throstle sings!
He, too, is no mean preacher:
Come forth into the light of things,
Let nature be your teacher.

She has a world of ready wealth,
Our minds and hearts to bless—
Spontaneous wisdom breathed by health,
Truth breathed by cheerfulness.

One impulse from a vernal wood
May teach you more of man,
Of moral evil and of good,
Than all the sages can.

Sweet is the lore which nature brings,
Our meddling intellect
Mis-shapes the beauteous forms of things
We murder to dissect.

Enough of science and of art;
Close up these barren leaves;
Come forth, and bring with you a heart
That watches and receives.

WRITTEN IN GERMANY.

ON ONE OF THE COLDEST DAYS OF THE CENTURY.

The reader must be apprised, that the stoves in North Germany generally have the impression of a galloping horse upon them, this being part of the Brunswick Arms

A PLAGUE on your languages, German and Norse !
Let me have the song of the kettle ,
And the tongs and the poker, instead of that horse
That gallops away with such fury and force
On his dreary dull plate of black metal

See that fly,—a disconsolate creature ! per-
A child of the field or the grove ; [haps
And, sorrow for him ! the dull treacherous heat [retreat,
Has seduced the poor fool from his winter
And he creeps to the edge of my stove.

Alas ! how he fumbles about the domains
Which this comfortless oven environ !
He cannot find out in what track he must crawl, [wall,
Now back to the tiles, and now back to the
And now on the brink of the iron.

Stock-still there he stands like a traveller bemazed ;
The best of his skill he has tried ; [forth
His feelers, methinks, I can see him put
To the east and the west, to the south and the north ;
But he finds neither guide-post nor guide.

How his spindles sink under him, foot, leg, and thigh ;
His eyesight and hearing are lost ;
Between life and death his blood freezes and thaws ;
And his two pretty pinions of blue dusky
Are glued to his sides by the frost. [gauze

No brother, no mate has he near him—while I [love ,
Can draw warmth from the cheek of my
As blest and as glad in this desolate gloom,
As if green summer grass were the floor of my room,
And woodbines were hanging above.

Yet, God is my witness, thou small helpless
Thy life I would gladly sustain [thing !
Till summer comes up from the south, and with crowds
Of thy brethren a march thou shouldst sound through the clouds,
And back to the forests again !

CHARACTER OF THE HAPPY WARRIOR.

WHO is the happy warrior? Who is he
That every man in arms should wish to be?
It is the generous spirit, who, when brought
Among the tasks of real life, hath wrought
Upon the plan that pleased his childish thought [light
Whose high endeavours are an inward
That makes the path before him always bright .
Who, with a natural instinct to discern
What knowledge can perform, is diligent to learn ;
Abides by this resolve, and stops not there,
But makes his moral being his prime care ;
Who, doomed to go in company with pain,
And fear, and bloodshed, miserable train !
Turns his necessity to glorious gain ;
In face of these doth exercise a power
Which is our human nature's highest dower ;
Controls them and subdues, transmutes, bereaves, [receives ;
Of their bad influence, and their good
By objects, which might force the soul to abate
Her feeling, rendered more compassionate ;
Is placable—because occasions rise
So often that demand such sacrifice ;
More skilful in self-knowledge, even more pure,
As tempted more ; more able to endure,
As more exposed to suffering and distress ;
Thence, also, more alive to tenderness.
'Tis he whose law is reason ; who depends
Upon that law as on the best of friends ;
Whence, in a state where men are tempted still
To evil for a guard against worse ill,
And what in quality or act is best
Doth seldom on a right foundation rest,
He fixes good on good alone, and owes
To virtue every triumph that he knows ;
Who, if he rise to station of command,
Rises by open means , and there will stand
On honourable terms, or else retire,
And in himself possess his own desire ;
Who comprehends his trust, and to the same

Keeps faithful with a singleness of aim ;
And therefore does not stoop, nor lie in wait
For wealth, or honours, or for worldly state ;
Whom they must follow ; on whose head must fall,
Like showers of manna, if they come at all .
Whose powers shed round him in the common strife,
Or mild concerns of ordinary life,
A constant influence, a peculiar grace ;
But who, if he be called upon to face
Some awful moment to which Heaven has joined
Great issues, good or bad for human kind,
Is happy as a lover ; and attired
With sudden brightness, like a man inspired ;
And, through the heat of conflict, keeps the law
In calmness made, and sees what he foresaw ,
Or if an unexpected call succeed,
Come when it will, is equal to the need .
He who though thus endued as with a sense
And faculty for storm and turbulence,
Is yet a soul whose master-bias leans
To homefelt pleasures and to gentle scenes ;
Sweet images ! which, wheresoe'er he be,
Are at his heart ; and such fidelity
It is his darling passion to approve ;
More brave for this, that he hath much to love :—
'Tis, finally, the man, who, lifted high
Conspicuous object in a nation's eye,
Or left unthought-of in obscurity,—
Who, with a toward or untoward lot,
Prosperous or adverse, to his wish or not,
Plays, in the many games of life, that one
Where what he most doth value must be won ·
Whom neither shape of danger can dismay,
Nor thought of tender happiness betray ;
Who, not content that former worth stand fast,
Looks forward, persevering to the last,
From well to better, daily self-surpast :
Who, whether praise of him must walk the earth
For ever, and to noble deeds give birth,
Or he must go to dust without his fame,
And leave a dead unprofitable name,
Finds comfort in himself and in his cause ;
And, while the mortal mist is gathering, draws
His breath in confidence of Heaven's applause :
This is the happy warrior ; this is he
Whom every man in arms should wish to be.

A POET'S EPITAPH.

ART thou a statesman, in the van
Of public business trained and bred ?
First learn to love one living man ;
Then mayst thou think upon the dead.

A lawyer art thou ?—draw not nigh ;
Go, carry to some fitter place
The keenness of that practised eye,
The hardness of that sallow face.

Art thou a man of purple cheer ?
A rosy man, right plump to see ?
Approach , yet, doctor, not too near ·
This grave no cushion is for thee.

Or art thou one of gallant pride,
A soldier, and no man of chaff ?
Welcome !—but lay thy sword aside,
And lean upon a peasant's staff.

Physician art thou ? One, all eyes,
Philosopher ! a fingering slave,
One that would peep and botanise
Upon his mother's grave ?

Wrapt closely in thy sensual fleece,
O turn aside,—and take, I pray,
That he below may rest in peace,
That abject thing, thy soul, away !

A moralist perchance appears ;
Led, Heaven knows how ! to this poor sod:
And he has neither eyes nor ears ;
Himself his world, and his own God:

One to whose smooth-rubbed soul can cling
Nor form, nor feeling, great nor small ;
A reasoning self-sufficient thing,
An intellectual all in all !

Shut close the door , press down the latch;
Sleep in thy intellectual crust ;
Nor lose ten tickings of thy watch
Near this unprofitable dust.

But who is he, with modest looks,
And clad in homely russet brown ?
He murmurs near the running brooks
A music sweeter than their own.

He is retired as noontide dew,
Or fountain in a noon-day grove ;
And you must love him, ere to you
He will seem worthy of your love.

The outward shows of sky and earth,
Of hill and valley he has viewed ,
And impulses of deeper birth
Have come to him in solitude

In common things that round us lie
Some random truths he can impart,
The harvest of a quiet eye
That broods and sleeps on his own heart.

But he is weak, both man and boy,
Hath been an idler in the land ,
Contented if he might enjoy
The things which others understand.

Come hither in thy hour of strength ;
Come, weak as is a breaking wave !
Here stretch thy body at full length ;
Or build thy house upon this grave.

TO THE SPADE OF A FRIEND,

(AN AGRICULTURIST)

COMPOSED WHILE WE WERE LABOURING TOGETHER IN HIS PLEASURE-GROUND

SPADE ! with which Wilkinson hath tilled his lands,
And shaped these pleasant walks by Emont's side,
Thou art a tool of honour in my hands ,
I press thee, through the yielding soil, with pride.

Rare master has it been thy lot to know ,
Long hast thou served a man to reason true ;
Whose life combines the best of high and low,
The toiling many and the resting few ,

Health, meekness, ardour, quietness secure,
And industry of body and of mind ,
And elegant enjoyments, that are pure
As nature is ;—too pure to be refined.

Here often hast thou heard the poet sing
In concord with his river murmuring by;
Or in some silent field, while timid spring
Is yet uncheered by other minstrelsy.

Who shall inherit thee when death has laid
Low in the darksome cell thine own dear lord ?
That man will have a trophy, humble spade!
A trophy nobler than a conqueror's sword !

If he be one that feels, with skill to part
False praise from true, or greater from the less,
Thee will he welcome to his hand and heart,
Thou monument of peaceful happiness !

With thee he will not dread a toilsome day,
His powerful servant, his inspiring mate !
And, when thou art past service, worn away,
Thee a surviving soul shall consecrate.

His thrift thy uselessness will never scorn ;
An *heirloom* in his cottage wilt thou be —
High will he hang thee up, and will adorn
His rustic chimney with the last of thee !

TO MY SISTER.

WRITTEN AT A SMALL DISTANCE FROM MY HOUSE, AND SENT BY MY LITTLE BOY.

IT is the first mild day of March :
Each minute sweeter than before,
The redbreast sings from the tall larch
That stands beside our door.

There is a blessing in the air,
Which seems a sense of joy to yield
To the bare trees and mountains bare,
And grass in the green field.

My sister ! ('tis a wish of mine)
Now that our morning meal is done,
Make haste, your morning task resign ;
Come forth and feel the sun.

Edward will come with you ; and pray
Put on with speed your woodland dress ;
And bring no book : for this one day
We'll give to idleness.

No joyless forms shall regulate
Our living calendar :
We from to-day, my friend, will date
The opening of the year.

Love, now a universal birth,
From heart to heart is stealing,
From earth to man, from man to earth
It is the hour of feeling.

One moment now may give us more
Than fifty years of reason .
Our minds shall drink at every pore
The spirit of the season.

Some silent laws our hearts will make,
Which they shall long obey :
We for the year to come may take
Our temper from to-day.

And from the blessed power that rolls
About, below, above,
We'll frame the measure of our souls :
They shall be turned to love.

Then come, my sister ! come, I pray,
With speed put on your woodland dress;
And bring no book : for this one day
We'll give to idleness.

TO A YOUNG LADY,

WHO HAD BEEN REPROACHED FOR TAKING LONG WALKS IN THE COUNTRY.

DEAR child of nature, let them rail !
There is a nest in a green dale,
A harbour and a hold,
Where thou, a wife and friend, shalt see
Thy own delightful days, and be
A light to young and old.

There, healthy as a shepherd-boy,
And treading among flowers of joy,
That at no season fade,
Thou, while thy babes around thee cling,
Shalt show us how divine a thing
A woman may be made.

Thy thoughts and feelings shall not die,
Nor leave thee when gray-hairs are nigh,
A melancholy slave ;
But an old age serene and bright,
And lovely as a Lapland night,
Shall lead thee to thy grave.

LINES

WRITTEN IN EARLY SPRING.

I HEARD a thousand blended notes,
While in a grove I sat reclined,
In that sweet mood when pleasant thoughts
Bring sad thoughts to the mind.

To her fair works did nature link
The human soul that through me ran ;
And much it grieved my heart to think
What man has made of man.

Through primrose tufts in that sweet bower
The periwinkle trailed its wreaths ;
And 'tis my faith that every flower
Enjoys the air it breathes.

The birds around me hopped and played ;
Their thoughts I cannot measure :—
But the least motion which they made,
It seemed a thrill of pleasure.

The budding twigs spread out their fan,
To catch the breezy air ;
And I must think, do all I can,
That there was pleasure there.

From Heaven if this belief be sent,
If such be nature's holy plan,
Have I not reason to lament
What man has made of man?

SIMON LEE, THE OLD HUNTSMAN,

WITH AN INCIDENT IN WHICH HE WAS CONCERNED.

IN the sweet shire of Cardigan,
Not far from pleasant Ivor-hall,
An old man dwells, a little man,
'Tis said he once was tall.
Full five-and-thirty years he lived
A running huntsman merry ;
And still the centre of his cheek
Is blooming as a cherry.

Worn out by hunting feats—bereft
By time of friends and kindred, see !
Old Simon to the world is left
In liveried poverty.
His master's dead,—and no one now
Dwells in the Hall of Ivor ;
Men, dogs, and horses, all are dead ;
He is the sole survivor.

No man like him the horn could sound,
And hill and valley rang with glee
When echo bandied, round and round,
The halloo of Simon Lee.
In those proud days, he little cared
For husbandry or tillage ;
To blither tasks did Simon rouse
The sleepers of the village.

He all the country could outrun,
Could leave both man and horse behind;
And often, ere the chase was done,
He reeled and was stone-blind.

And still there's something in the world
At which his heart rejoices ,
For when the chiming hounds are out,
He dearly loves their voices !

But he is lean and he is sick,
His body, dwindled and awry,
Rests upon ankles swoln and thick ,
His legs are thin and dry.
One prop he has, an only one,
His wife, an aged woman,
Lives with him, near the waterfall,
Upon the village common.

Beside their moss-grown hut of clay,
Not twenty paces from the door,
A scrap of land they have, but they
Are poorest of the poor.
This scrap of land he from the heath
Inclosed when he was stronger ;
" But what," saith he, " avails the land
Which I can till no longer?"

Oft, working by her husband's side,
Ruth does what Simon cannot do ;
For she, with scanty cause for pride,
Is stouter of the two.
And, though you with your utmost skill
From labour could not wean them,
Alas ! 'tis very little—all
Which they can do between them.

Few months of life has he in store,
As he to you will tell,
For still, the more he works, the more
Do his weak ankles swell
My gentle reader, I perceive
How patiently you've waited,
And now I fear that you expect
Some tale will be related.

O reader ! had you in your mind
Such stores as silent thought can bring,
O gentle reader ! you would find
A tale in everything.
What more I have to say is short,
And you must kindly take it :
It is no tale ; but, should you think,
Perhaps a tale you'll make it.

One summer-day I chanced to see
This old man doing all he could
To unearth the root of an old tree,
A stump of rotten wood.
The mattock tottered in his hand ,
So vain was his endeavour,
That at the root of the old tree
He might have worked for ever

" You're overtasked, good Simon Lee,
Give me your tool," to him I said ;
And at the word right gladly he
Received my proffered aid
I struck, and with a single blow
The tangled root I severed,
At which the poor old man so long
And vainly had endeavoured.

The tears into his eyes were brought,
And thanks and praises seemed to run
So fast out of his heart, I thought
They never would have done.
I've heard of hearts unkind, kind deeds
With coldness still returning,
Alas ! the gratitude of men
Hath oftener left me mourning.

INCIDENT

CHARACTERISTIC OF A FAVOURITE DOG.

ON his morning rounds the master
Goes to learn how all things fare ;
Searches pasture after pasture,
Sheep and cattle eyes with care ,
And for silence or for talk,
He hath comrades in his walk ,
Four dogs, each pair of different breed,
Distinguished two for scent, and two for speed.

See a hare before him started !
Off they fly in earnest chase ,
Every dog is eager-hearted,
All the four are in the race .
And the hare whom they pursue,
Hath an instinct what to do ;
Her hope is near : no turn she makes ;
But, like an arrow, to the river takes.

Deep the river was, and crusted
Thinly by a one night's frost ;
But the nimble hare hath trusted
To the ice, and safely crost ;
She hath crost, and without heed
All are following at full speed,
When, lo ! the ice, so thinly spread,
Breaks—and the greyhound, Dart, is over head !

Better fate have Prince and Swallow—
See them cleaving to the sport !
Music has no heart to follow,
Little Music, she stops short.
She hath neither wish nor heart,
Hers is now another part :

A loving creature she, and brave!
And fondly strives her struggling friend to save.

From the brink her paws she stretches,
Very hands as you would say!
And afflicting moans she fetches,
As he breaks the ice away.
For herself she hath no fears,—
Him alone she sees and hears,—
Makes efforts and complainings; nor gives o'er
Until her fellow sank, and re-appeared no more.

TRIBUTE

TO THE MEMORY OF THE SAME DOG.

Lie here, without a record of thy worth,
Beneath a covering of the common earth!
It is not from unwillingness to praise,
Or want of love, that here no stone we raise;
More thou deserv'st; but *this* man gives to man,
Brother, to brother, *this* is all we can.
Yet they to whom thy virtues made thee dear
Shall find thee through all changes of the year:
This oak points out thy grave; the silent tree
Will gladly stand a monument of thee.

I grieved for thee, and wished thy end were past;
And willingly have laid thee here at last:
For thou hadst lived, till everything that cheers
In thee had yielded to the weight of years;
Extreme old age had wasted thee away;
And left thee but a glimmering of the day;
Thy ears were deaf; and feeble were thy knees,
I saw thee stagger in the summer breeze,
Too weak to stand against its sportive breath,
And ready for the gentlest stroke of death.
It came, and we were glad; yet tears were shed;
Both man and woman wept when thou wert dead;
Not only for a thousand thoughts that were,
Old household thoughts, in which thou hadst thy share;
But for some precious boons vouchsafed to thee,
Found scarcely any where in like degree!
For love, that comes to all—the holy sense,
Best gift of God—in thee was most intense;
A chain of heart, a feeling of the mind,
A tender sympathy, which did thee bind
Not only to us men, but to thy kind:
Yea, for thy fellow-brutes in thee we saw
The soul of love, love's intellectual law:—
Hence, if we wept, it was not done in shame;
Our tears from passion and from reason came,
And, therefore, shalt thou be an honoured name!

MATTHEW.

In the school of —— is a tablet, on which are inscribed, in gilt letters, the names of the several persons who have been schoolmasters there since the foundation of the school, with the time at which they entered upon and quitted their office. Opposite one of those names the author wrote the following lines:—

If nature, for a favourite child
In thee hath tempered so her clay
That every hour thy heart runs wild
Yet never once doth go astray,

Read o'er these lines; and then review
This tablet, that thus humbly rears
In such diversity of hue
Its history of two hundred years.

When through this little wreck of fame,
Cipher and syllable! thine eye
Has travelled down to Matthew's name,
Pause with no common sympathy.

And, if a sleeping tear should wake,
Then be it neither checked nor stayed:
For Matthew a request I make
Which for himself he had not made.

Poor Matthew, all his frolics o'er,
Is silent as a standing pool:
Far from the chimney's merry roar,
And murmur of the village school.

The sighs which Matthew heaved were sighs
Of one tired out with fun and madness;
The tears which came to Matthew's eyes
Were tears of light, the dew of gladness.

Yet, sometimes, when the secret cup
Of still and serious thought went round,
It seemed as if he drank it up—
He felt with spirit so profound.

Thou soul of God's best earthly mould!
Thou happy soul! and can it be
That these two words of glittering gold
Are all that must remain of thee?

THE TWO APRIL MORNINGS.

We walked along, while bright and red
Uprose the morning sun
And Matthew stopped, he looked, and said,
"The will of God be done!"

A village schoolmaster was he,
With hair of glittering gray;
As blithe a man as you could see
On a spring holiday.

And on that morning, through the grass,
And by the steaming rills,
We travelled merrily, to pass
A day among the hills.

"Our work," said I, "was well begun;
Then, from thy breast what thought,
Beneath so beautiful a sun,
So sad a sigh has brought?"

A second time did Matthew stop;
And fixing still his eye
Upon the eastern mountain-top,
To me he made reply:

"Yon cloud with that long purple cleft
Brings fresh into my mind
A day like this which I have left
Full thirty years behind.

"And just above yon slope of corn
Such colours, and no other,
Were in the sky, that April morn,
Of this the very brother.

"With rod and line I sued the sport
Which that sweet season gave,
And, coming to the church, stopped short
Beside my daughter's grave.

"Nine summers had she scarcely seen,
The pride of all the vale,
And then she sang;—she would have been
A very nightingale.

"Six feet in earth my Emma lay;
And yet I loved her more,
For so it seemed, than till that day
I e'er had loved before.

"And turning from her grave, I met,
Beside the churchyard yew,
A blooming girl, whose hair was wet
With points of morning dew.

"A basket on her head she bare,
Her brow was smooth and white·
To see a child so very fair,
It was a pure delight!

"No fountain from its rocky cave
E'er tripped with foot so free;
She seemed as happy as a wave
That dances on the sea.

"There came from me a sigh of pain
Which I could ill confine,
I looked at her, and looked again·
And did not wish her mine."

Matthew is in his grave, yet now,
Methinks, I see him stand,
As at that moment, with a bough
Of wilding in his hand

THE FOUNTAIN.

A CONVERSATION.

We talked with open heart, and tongue
Affectionate and true,
A pair of friends, though I was young,
And Matthew seventy-two.

We lay beneath a spreading oak,
Beside a mossy seat;
And from the turf a fountain broke,
And gurgled at our feet.

"Now Matthew!" said I, "let us match
This water's pleasant tune
With some old Border song, or catch,
That suits a summer's noon,

"Or of the church clock and the chimes
Sing here beneath the shade,
That half-mad thing of witty rhymes
Which you last April made!"

In silence Matthew lay, and eyed,
The spring beneath the tree;
And thus the dear old man replied,
The gray-haired man of glee·

"Down to the vale this water steers,
How merrily it goes!
'Twill murmur on a thousand years,
And flow as now it flows.

"And here, on this delightful day,
I cannot choose but think
How oft, a vigorous man, I lay
Beside this fountain's brink.

"My eyes are dim with childish tears,
My heart is idly stirred,
For the same sound is in my ears
Which in those days I heard.

"Thus fares it still in our decay:
And yet the wiser mind
Mourns less for what age takes away
Than what it leaves behind.

"The blackbird in the summer trees,
The lark upon the hill,
Let loose their carols when they please,
Are quiet when they will.

"With nature never do *they* wage
A foolish strife: they see
A happy youth, and their old age
Is beautiful and free:

"But we are pressed by heavy laws;
And often glad no more,
We wear a face of joy, because
We have been glad of yore.

"If there is one who need bemoan
His kindred laid in earth,
The household hearts that were his own,
It is the man of mirth.

"My days, my friend, are almost gone,
My life has been approved,
And many love me; but by none
Am I enough beloved."

"Now both himself and me he wrongs,
The man who thus complains!
I live and sing my idle songs
Upon these happy plains,

"And, Matthew, for thy children dead
I'll be a son to thee!"
At this he grasped my hand, and said,
"Alas! that cannot be."

We rose up from the fountain-side;
And down the smooth descent
Of the green sheep-track did we glide;
And through the wood we went;

And, ere we came to Leonard's rock,
He sang those witty rhymes
About the crazy old church clock,
And the bewildered chimes.

If thou indeed derive thy light from Heaven,
Shine, poet, in thy place, and be content!
The star that from the zenith darts its beams,
Visible though it be to half the earth,
Though half a sphere be conscious of its brightness,
Is yet of no diviner origin,
No purer essence, than the one that burns,
Like an untended watch-fire, on the ridge
Of some dark mountain; or than those which seem
Humbly to hang, like twinkling winter lamps,
Among the branches of the leafless trees.

WRITTEN IN A BLANK LEAF OF MACPHERSON'S "OSSIAN."

Oft have I caught from fitful breeze
Fragments of far-off melodies,
With ear not coveting the whole,
A part so charmed the pensive soul ·
While a dark storm before my sight
Was yielding, on a mountain height
Loose vapours have I watched, that won
Prismatic colours from the sun;
Nor felt a wish that heaven would show
The image of its perfect bow.
What need, then, of these finished strains?
Away with counterfeit remains!
An abbey in its lone recess,
A temple of the wilderness,
Wrecks though they be, announce with feeling
The majesty of honest dealing.
Spirit of Ossian! if imbound
In language thou mayst yet be found,
If aught (intrusted to the pen,
Or floating on the tongues of men,
Albeit shattered and impaired)
Subsist thy dignity to guard,
In concert with memorial claim
Of old gray stone, and high-born name,
That cleaves to rock or pillared cave,
Where moans the blast or beats the wave,
Let truth, stern arbitress of all
Interpret that original,
And for presumptuous wrongs atone;
Authentic words be given, or none!

Time is not blind;—yet he, who spares
Pyramid pointing to the stars,
Hath preyed with ruthless appetite
On all that marked the primal flight
Of the poetic ecstasy
Into the land of mystery

No tongue is able to rehearse
One measure, Orpheus! of thy verse,
Musæus, stationed with his lyre
Supreme among the Elysian quire,
Is, for the dwellers upon earth,
Mute as a lark ere morning's birth.
Why grieve for these, though passed away
The music, and extinct the lay?
When thousands, by severer doom,
Full early to the silent tomb
Have sunk, at nature's call, or strayed
From hope and promise, self-betrayed;
The garland withering on their brows,
Stand with remorse for broken vows,
Frantic—else how might they rejoice?
And friendless, by their own sad choice.

Hail, bards of mightier grasp! on you
I chiefly call, the chosen few,
Who cast not off the acknowledged guide,
Who faltered not, nor turned aside;
Whose lofty genius could survive
Privation, under sorrow thrive;
In whom the fiery muse revered
The symbol of a snow-white beard,
Bedewed with meditative tears
Dropped from the lenient cloud of years.

Brothers in soul! though distant times
Produced you, nursed in various climes,
Ye, when the orb of life had waned,
A plenitude of love retained,
Hence, while in you each sad regret
By corresponding hope was met,
Ye lingered among human kind,
Sweet voices for the passing wind,
Departing sunbeams, loth to stop,
Though smiling on the last hill top!

Such to the tender-hearted maid
Even ere her joys begin to fade;
Such, haply, to the rugged chief
By fortune crushed, or tamed by grief,
Appears, on Morven's lonely shore,
Dim-gleaming through imperfect lore,
The Son of Fingal; such was blind
Mæonides of ampler mind;
Such Milton, to the fountain head
Of glory by Urania led!

VERNAL ODE.

"Rerum natura tota est nusquam magis quam in minimis."—PLIN. *Nat. Hist.*

BENEATH the concave of an April sky,
When all the fields with freshest green were dight,
Appeared, in presence of that spiritual eye
That aids or supersedes our grosser sight,
The form and rich habiliments of one
Whose countenance bore resemblance to the sun,
When it reveals, in evening majesty,
Features half lost amid their own pure light
Poised, like a weary cloud, in middle air
He hung,—then floated with angelic ease
(Softening that bright effulgence by degrees)
Till he had reached a summit sharp and bare,
Where oft the venturous heifer drinks the noontide breeze
Upon the apex of that lofty cone
Alighted, there the stranger stood alone,
Fair as a gorgeous fabric of the East
Suddenly raised by some enchanter's power,
Where nothing was; and firm as some old tower
Of Britain's realm, whose leafy crest
Waves high, embellished by a gleaming shower!

Beneath the shadow of his purple wings
Rested a golden harp,—he touched the strings;
And, after prelude of unearthly sound
Poured through the echoing hills around,
He sang—
"No wintry desolations,
Scorching blight, or noxious dew,
Affect my native habitations,
Buried in glory, far beyond the scope
Of man's inquiring gaze, but imaged to his hope
(Alas, how faintly!) in the hue
Profound of night's ethereal blue;
And in the aspect of each radiant orb;—
Some fixed, some wandering with no timid curb;
But wandering star and fixed, to mortal eye,
Blended in absolute serenity,
And free from semblance of decline;
Fresh as if evening brought their natal hour;
Her darkness splendour gave her silence power,
To testify of love and grace divine.

"And though to every draught of vital breath
Renewed throughout the bounds of earth or ocean,
The melancholy gates of death
Respond with sympathetic motion;
Though all that feeds on nether air,
Howe'er magnificent or fair,
Grows but to perish, and intrust
Its ruins to their kindred dust;

Yet, by the Almighty's ever-during care,
Her procreant vigils nature keeps
Amid the unfathomable deeps;
And saves the peopled fields of earth
From dread of emptiness or dearth. [sky
Thus, in their stations, lifting toward the
The foliaged head in cloud-like majesty,
The shadow-casting race of trees survive:
Thus, in the train of spring, arrive
Sweet flowers;—what living eye hath viewed
Their myriads?—endlessly renewed,
Wherever strikes the sun's glad ray;
Where'er the subtle waters stray;
Wherever sportive zephyrs bend
Their course or genial showers descend!
Mortals, rejoice! the very angels quit
Their mansions unsusceptible of change,
Amid your pleasant bowers to sit,
And through your sweet vicissitudes to range!"
Oh, nursed at happy distance from the cares
Of a too-anxious world, mild pastoral muse!
That, to the sparkling crown Urania wears,
And to her sister Clio's laurel wreath,
Prefer'st a garland culled from purple heath, [dews;
Or blooming thicket moist with morning
Was such bright spectacle vouchsafed to me?
And was it granted to the simple ear
Of thy contented votary
Such melody to hear!
Him rather suits it, side by side with thee,
Wrapped in a fit of pleasing indolence,
While thy tired lute hangs on the hawthorn tree,
To lie and listen, till o'er-drowsed sense
Sinks, hardly conscious of the influence,
To the soft murmur of the vagrant bee.
A slender sound! yet hoary time
Doth to the *soul* exalt it with the chime
Of all his years;—a company
Of ages coming, ages gone;
(Nations from before them sweeping,
Regions in destruction steeping,)
But every awful note in unison
With that faint utterance, which tells
Of treasure sucked from buds and bells,
For the pure keeping of those waxen cells;
Where she, a statist prudent to confer
Upon the public weal; a warrior bold,—
Radiant all over with unburnished gold,
And armed with living spear for mortal fight;
A cunning forager
That spreads no waste;—a social builder;
In whom all busy offices unite [one
With all fine functions that afford delight,
Safe through the winter storm in quiet dwells!

And is she brought within the power
Of vision?—o'er this tempting flower
Hovering until the petals stay
Her flight, and take its voice away!—
Observe each wing—a tiny van!—
The structure of her laden thigh,
How fragile!—yet of ancestry
Mysteriously remote and high,
High as the imperial front of man,
The roseate bloom on woman's cheek;
The soaring eagle's curvèd beak;
The white plumes of the floating swan;
Old as the tiger's paw, the lion's mane
Ere shaken by that mood of stern disdain
At which the desert trembles.—Humming bee! [unknown;
Thy sting was needless then, perchance
The seeds of malice were not sown;
All creatures met in peace, from fierceness free,
And no pride blended with their dignity.
Tears had not broken from their source;
Nor anguish strayed from her Tartarian den;
The golden years maintained a course
Not undiversified, though smooth and even; [shadow, then
We were not mocked with glimpse and
Bright seraphs mixed familiarly with men;
And earth and stars composed a universal heaven!

ODE TO LYCORIS.

MAY, 1817.

AN age hath been when earth was proud
Of lustre too intense
To be sustained; and mortals bowed
The front in self-defence.
Who *then*, if Dian's crescent gleamed,
Or Cupid's sparkling arrow streamed
While on the wing the urchin played,
Could fearlessly approach the shade?
Enough for one soft vernal day,
If I, a bard of ebbing time,
And nurtured in a fickle clime,
May haunt this horned bay;
Whose amorous water multiplies
The flitting halcyon's vivid dyes;
And smooths her liquid breast—to show
These swan-like specks of mountain snow,

White as the pair that slid along the plains
Of heaven, when Venus held the reins!

In youth we love the darksome lawn
Brushed by the owlet's wing;
Then twilight is preferred to dawn,
And autumn to the spring.
Sad fancies do we then affect,
In luxury of disrespect
To our own prodigal excess
Of too familiar happiness.
Lycoris (if such name befit
Thee, thee my life's celestial sign!)
When nature marks the year's decline,
Be ours to welcome it;
Pleased with the harvest hope that runs
Before the path of milder suns,
Pleased while the sylvan world displays
Its ripeness to the feeding gaze;
Pleased when the sullen winds resound the [knell
Of the resplendent miracle.

But something whispers to my heart
That, as we downward tend,
Lycoris! life requires an *art*
To which our souls must bend;
A skill—to balance and supply;
And, ere the flowing fount be dry,
As soon it must, a sense to sip,
Or drink, with no fastidious lip.
Frank greeting, then, to that blithe guest
Diffusing smiles o'er land and sea
To aid the vernal Deity
Whose home is in the breast!
May pensive autumn ne'er present
A claim to her disparagement!
While blossoms and the budding spray
Inspire us in our own decay;
Still, as we nearer draw to life's dark goal,
Be hopeful spring the favourite of the soul!

TO THE SAME.

ENOUGH of climbing toil!—Ambition treads [and rough,
Here, as 'mid busier scenes, ground steep
Or slippery even to peril! and each step,
As we for most uncertain recompense
Mount toward the empire of the fickle clouds,
Each weary step, dwarfing the world below,
Induces, for its old familiar sights,
Unacceptable feelings of contempt,
With wonder mixed—that man could e'er be tied,
In anxious bondage to such nice array
And formal fellowship of petty things!
Oh! 'tis the *heart* that magnifies this life,
Making a truth and beauty of her own;
And moss-grown alleys, circumscribing shades,
And gurgling rills, assist her in the work
More efficaciously than realms outspread,
As in a map, before the adventurer's gaze—
Ocean and earth contending for regard.

The umbrageous woods are left—how far beneath!
But lo! where darkness seems to guard the mouth
Of yon wild cave, whose jagged brows are fringed
With flaccid threads of ivy, in the still
And sultry air, depending motionless.
Yet cool the space within, and not uncheered
(As whoso enters shall ere long perceive)
By stealthy influx of the timid day
Mingling with night, such twilight to compose
As Numa loved; when, in the Egerian grot,
From the sage nymph appearing at his wish,
He gained whate'er a regal mind might ask,
Or need, of council breathed through lips divine.

Long as the heat shall rage, let that dim cave
Protect us, there deciphering as we may
Diluvian records; or the sighs of earth
Interpreting; or counting for old time
His minutes, by reiterated drops,
Audible tears, from some invisible source
That deepens upon fancy—more and more
Drawn toward the centre whence those sighs creep forth
To awe the lightness of humanity.
Or, shutting up thyself within thyself,
There let me see thee sink into a mood
Of gentler thought, protracted till thine eye
Be calm as water when the winds are gone,
And no one can tell whither. Dearest friend!
We two have known such happy hours together,

That, were power granted to replace them (fetched
From out the pensive shadows where they lie)
In the first warmth of their original sunshine,
Loth should I be to use it: passing sweet
Are the domains of tender memory!

FIDELITY.

A BARKING sound the shepherd hears,
A cry as of a dog or fox;
He halts and searches with his eyes
Among the scattered rocks:
And now at distance can discern
A stirring in a brake of fern;
And instantly a dog is seen,
Glancing through that covert green.

The dog is not of mountain breed;
Its motions, too, are wild and shy;
With something, as the shepherd thinks,
Unusual in its cry:
Nor is there any one in sight
All round, in hollow or on height;
Nor shout, nor whistle strikes his ear;
What is the creature doing here?

It was a cove, a huge recess,
That keeps, till June, December's snow;
A lofty precipice in front,
A silent tarn* below!
Far in the bosom of Helvellyn,
Remote from public road or dwelling,
Pathway, or cultivated land;
From trace of human foot or hand.

There sometimes doth a leaping fish
Send through the tarn a lonely cheer;
The crags repeat the raven's croak,
In symphony austere;
Thither the rainbow comes—the cloud—
And mists that spread the flying shroud;
And sunbeams; and the sounding blast,
That, if it could, would hurry past;
But that enormous barrier binds it fast.

Not free from boding thoughts, a while
The shepherd stood: then makes his way
Towards the dog, o'er rocks and stones,
As quickly as he may;
Not far had gone before he found
A human skeleton on the ground;
The appalled discoverer with a sigh
Looks round, to learn the history.

From those abrupt and perilous rocks
The man had fallen, that place of fear!
At length upon the shepherd's mind
It breaks, and all is clear:
He instantly recalled the name,
And who he was, and whence he came;
Remembered, too, the very day
On which the traveller passed this way.

But hear a wonder, for whose sake
This lamentable tale I tell!
A lasting monument of words
This wonder merits well.
The dog, which still was hovering nigh,
Repeating the same timid cry,
This dog had been through three months' space
A dweller in that savage place.

Yes, proof was plain that since the day
When this ill-fated traveller died,
The dog had watched about the spot,
Or by his master's side:
How nourished here through such long time
He knows who gave that love sublime;
And gave that strength of feeling great
Above all human estimate.

* A tarn is a *small* mere or lake, mostly high up in the mountains.

TO THE LADY FLEMING.

ON SEEING THE FOUNDATION PREPARING FOR THE ERECTION OF —— CHAPEL, WESTMORELAND.

BLEST is this isle—our native land;
Where battlement and moated gate
Are objects only for the hand
Of hoary time to decorate:
Where shady hamlet, town that breathes
Its busy smoke in social wreaths,
No rampart's stern defence require,
Nought but the heaven-directed spire,
And steeple tower (with pealing bells
Far heard)—our only citadels.

O lady! from a noble line
Of chieftains sprung, who stoutly bore
The spear, yet gave to works divine
A bounteous help in days of yore,

[As records mouldering in the dell
Of nightshade* haply yet may tell)
Thee kindred aspirations moved
To build, within a vale beloved,
For him upon whose high behests
All peace depends, all safety rests

Well may the villagers rejoice!
Nor heat, nor cold, nor weary ways,
Will be a hindrance to the voice
That would unite in prayer and praise,
More duly shall wild-wandering youth
Receive the curb of sacred truth,
Shall tottering age, bent earthward, hear
The promise, with uplifted ear!
And all shall welcome the new ray
Imparted to their Sabbath-day

Even strangers, slackening here their pace,
Shall hail this work of pious care,
Lifting its front with modest grace
To make a fair recess more fair;
And to exalt the passing hour;
Or soothe it, with a healing power
Drawn from the sacrifice fulfilled,
Before this rugged soil was tilled,
Or human habitation rose
To interrupt the deep repose!

Not yet the corner stone is laid
With solemn rite; but fancy sees
The tower time-stricken, and in shade
Embosomed of coeval trees;
Hears, o'er the lake, the warning clock
As it shall sound with gentle shock
At evening, when the ground beneath
Is ruffled o'er with cells of death;
Where happy generations lie,
Here tutored for eternity.

Lives there a man whose sole delights
Are trivial pomp and city noise,
Hardening a heart that loathes or slights
What every natural heart enjoys?
Who never caught a noon-tide dream
From murmur of a running stream;
Could strip, for aught the prospect yields
To him, their verdure from the fields;
And take the radiance from the clouds
In which the sun his setting shrouds.

A soul so pitiably forlorn,
If such do on this earth abide,
May season apathy with scorn,
May turn indifference to pride,
And still be not unblest—compared
With him who grovels, self-debarred
From all that lies within the scope
Of holy faith and Christian hope;
Or, shipwrecked, kindles on the coast
False fires, that others may be lost.

Alas! that such perverted zeal
Should spread on Britain's favoured ground?
That public order, private weal,
Should e'er have felt or feared a wound
From champions of the desperate law
Which from their own blind hearts they draw;
Who tempt their reason to deny
God, whom their passions dare defy,
And boast that *they alone* are free
Who reach this dire extremity!

But turn we from these "bold bad" men;
The way, mild lady! that hath led
Down to their "dark opprobrious den,"
Is all too rough for thee to tread
Softly as morning vapours glide
Through Mosedale-cove from Carrock's side,
Should move the tenor of *his* song
Who means to charity no wrong,
Whose offering gladly would accord
With this day's work in thought and word

Heaven prosper it! may peace and love,
And hope, and consolation fall,
Through its meek influence from above,
And penetrate the hearts of all;
All who, around the hallowed fane,
Shall sojourn in this fair domain;
Grateful to thee, while service pure,
And ancient ordinance, shall endure,
For opportunity bestowed
To kneel together, and adore their God!

* Bekangs Ghyll—or the Vale of Nightshade—in which stands St. Mary's Abbey, in Low Furness.

ON THE SAME OCCASION.

"Oh! gather whencesoe'er ye safely may
The help which slackening piety requires,
Nor deem that he perforce must go astray
Who treads upon the footmarks of his sires.

Our churches, invariably perhaps, stand east and west, but *why* is by few persons *exactly* known; nor, that the degree of deviation from due east, often noticeable in the ancient ones, was determined, in each particular case, by the point in the horizon, at which the sun rose upon the day of the saint to whom the church was dedicated. These observances of our ancestors, and the causes of them, are the subject of the following stanzas.

WHEN in the antique age of bow and spear
And feudal rapine clothed with iron mail,
Came ministers of peace, intent to rear
The mother church in yon sequestered vale;

Then, to her patron saint a previous rite
Resounded with deep swell and solemn close,
Through unremitting vigils of the night,
Till from his couch the wished-for sun uprose.

He rose, and straight — as by divine command,
They who had waited for that sign to trace
Their work's foundation, gave with careful hand,
To the high altar its determined place;

Mindful of Him who in the Orient born
There lived, and on the cross his life resigned,
And who, from out the regions of the morn,
Issuing in pomp, shall come to judge mankind.

So taught *their* creed; — nor failed the eastern sky,
'Mid these more awful feelings, to infuse
The sweet and natural hopes that shall not die
Long as the sun his gladsome course renews.

For us hath such prelusive vigil ceased;
Yet still we plant, like men of elder days,
Our Christian altar faithful to the east,
Whence the tall window drinks the morning rays;

That obvious emblem giving to the eye
Of meek devotion, which erewhile it gave,
That symbol of the dayspring from on high,
Triumphant o'er the darkness of the grave.

THE FORCE OF PRAYER;*

OR, THE FOUNDING OF BOLTON PRIORY.

(A TRADITION.)

"What is good for a bootless bene?"
With these dark words begins my tale;
And their meaning is, Whence can comfort spring
When prayer is of no avail?

"What is good for a bootless bene?"
The falconer to the lady said;
And she made answer, "Endless sorrow!"
For she knew that her son was dead.

She knew it by the falconer's words,
And from the look of the falconer's eye;
And from the love which was in her soul
For her youthful Romilly.

Young Romilly through Barden woods
Is ranging high and low;
And holds a greyhound in a leash,
To let slip upon buck or doe.

The pair have reached that fearful chasm,
How tempting to bestride!
For lordly Wharf is there pent in,
With rocks on either side.

This striding-place is called The Strid,
A name which it took of yore:
A thousand years hath it borne that name
And shall a thousand more.

And hither is young Romilly come,
And what may now forbid
That he, perhaps for the hundredth time,
Shall bound across The Strid?

He sprang in glee, — for what cared he
That the river was strong, and the rocks were steep?
But the greyhound in the leash hung back
And checked him in his leap.

The boy is in the arms of Wharf,
And strangled by a merciless force;
For never more was young Romilly seen
Till he rose a lifeless corse.

Now there is stillness in the vale,
And deep unspeaking sorrow:
Wharf shall be to pitying hearts
A name more sad than Yarrow.

If for a lover the lady wept,
A solace she might borrow
From death, and from the passion of death; —
Old Wharf might heal her sorrow.

* See "The White Doe of Rylstone," page 232.

She weeps not for the wedding-day
Which was to be to-morrow:
Her hope was a farther-looking hope,
And hers is a mother's sorrow.

He was a tree that stood alone,
And proudly did its branches wave,
And the root of this delightful tree
Was in her husband's grave!

Long, long in darkness did she sit,
And her first words were, "Let there be
In Bolton, on the field of Wharf,
A stately priory!"

The stately priory was reared,
And Wharf, as he moved along,
To matins joined a mournful voice,
Nor failed at even-song

And the lady prayed in heaviness
That looked not for relief!
But slowly did her succour come,
And a patience to her grief.

Oh! there is never sorrow of heart
That shall lack a timely end,
If but to God we turn, and ask
Of Him to be our Friend!

A FACT, AND AN IMAGINATION;

OR, CANUTE AND ALFRED.

THE Danish conqueror, on his royal chair,
Mustering a face of haughty sovereignty,
To aid a covert purpose, cried—"Oh, ye
Approaching waters of the deep, that share
With this green isle my fortunes, come not where
Your master's throne is set!"—Absurd decree!
A mandate uttered to the foaming sea
Is to its motion less than wanton air.
Then Canute, rising from the invaded throne,
Said to his servile courtiers, "Poor the reach,
The undisguised extent, of mortal sway!
He only is a king, and he alone
Deserves the name (this truth the billows preach)
Whose everlasting law, sea, earth, and heaven obey."
This just reproof the prosperous Dane
Drew, from the influx of the main,
For some whose rugged northern mouths would strain
At oriental flattery;
And Canute (truth more worthy to be known)
From that time forth did for his brows disown
The ostentatious symbol of a crown;
Esteeming earthly royalty
Contemptible and vain

Now hear what one of elder days,
Rich theme of England's fondest praise,
Her darling Alfred, *might* have spoken;
To cheer the remnant of his host
When he was driven from coast to coast,
Distressed and harassed, but with mind unbroken
"My faithful followers, lo! the tide is spent,
That rose, and steadily advanced to fill
The shores and channels, working nature's will
Among the mazy streams that backward went,
And in the sluggish pools where ships are pent,
And now, its task performed, the flood stands still
At the green base of many an inland hill,
In placid beauty and sublime content!
Such the repose that sage and hero find,
Such measured rest the sedulous and good
Of humbler name, whose souls do, like the flood
Of ocean, press right on; or gently wind,
Neither to be diverted nor withstood,
Until they reach the bounds by Heaven assigned."

"*A little onward lend thy guiding hand
To these dark steps, a little further on!*"
What trick of memory to *my* voice hath brought
This mournful iteration? For though Time,
The conqueror, crowns the conquered, on this brow
Planting his favourite silver diadem,
Nor he, nor minister of his—intent
To run before him, hath enrolled me yet,
Though not unmenaced, among those who lean
Upon a living staff, with borrowed sight.
O my Antigone, beloved child!
Should that day come—but hark! the birds salute
The cheerful dawn, brightening for me the east;
For me, thy natural leader, once again
Impatient to conduct thee, not as erst
A tottering infant, with compliant stoop
From flower to flower supported, but to curb

Thy nymph-like step swift-bounding o'er the lawn,
Along the loose rocks, or the slippery verge
Of foaming torrent.—From thy orisons
Come forth; and, while the morning air is yet
Transparent as the soul of innocent youth,
Let me, thy happy guide, now point thy way,
And now precede thee, winding to and fro,
Till we by perseverance gain the top
Of some smooth ridge, whose brink precipitous
Kindles intense desire for powers withheld
From this corporeal frame; whereon who stands,
Is seized with strong incitement to push forth
His arms, as swimmers use, and plunge—dread thought!
For pastime plunge—into the "abrupt abyss,"
Where ravens spread their plumy vans, at ease!

And yet more gladly thee would I conduct
Through woods and spacious forests,—to behold
There, how the original of human art,
Heaven-prompted nature, measures and erects
Her temples, fearless for the stately work,
Though waves in every breeze its high-arched roof,
And storms the pillars rock. But we such schools
Of reverential awe will chiefly seek
In the still summer noon, while beams of light,
Reposing here, and in the aisles beyond
Traceably gliding through the dusk, recall
To mind the living presences of nuns;
A gentle, pensive, white-robed sisterhood,
Whose saintly radiance mitigates the gloom
Of those terrestrial fabrics, where they serve,
To Christ, the Sun of Righteousness, espoused.

Now also shall the page of classic lore,
To these glad eyes from bondage freed, again
Lie open; and the book of Holy Writ,
Again unfolded, passage clear shall yield
To heights more glorious still, and into shades
More awful, where advancing hand in hand
We may be taught, O darling of my care!
To calm the affections, elevate the soul,
And consecrate our lives to truth and love.

SEPTEMBER, 1819.

THE sylvan slopes with corn-clad fields
Are hung, as if with golden shields,
Bright trophies of the sun!
Like a fair sister of the sky,
Unruffled doth the blue lake lie,
The mountains looking on.

And, sooth to say, yon vocal grove,
Albeit uninspired by love,
By love untaught to ring,
May well afford to mortal ear
An impulse more profoundly dear
Than music of the spring.

For *that* from turbulence and heat
Proceeds, from some uneasy seat
In nature's struggling frame,
Some region of impatient life;
And jealousy, and quivering strife,
Therein a portion claim.

This, this is holy;—while I hear
These vespers of another year,
This hymn of thanks and praise,
My spirit seems to mount above
The anxieties of human love,
And earth's precarious days.

But list!—though winter storms be nigh
Unchecked is that soft harmony:
There lives who can provide
For all his creatures; and in Him,
Even like the radiant seraphim,
These choristers confide.

UPON THE SAME OCCASION.

DEPARTING summer hath assumed
An aspect tenderly illumed,
The gentlest look of spring;
That calls from yonder leafy shade
Unfaded, yet prepared to fade,
A timely caroling.

No faint and hesitating trill,
Such tribute as to winter chill

The lonely redbreast pays!
Clear, loud, and lively is the din,
From social warblers gathering in
Their harvest of sweet lays.

Nor doth the example fail to cheer
Me, conscious that my leaf is sere,
And yellow on the bough:—
Fall, rosy garlands, from my head!
Ye myrtle wreaths, your fragrance shed
Around a younger brow!

Yet will I temperately rejoice:
Wide is the range, and free the choice
Of undiscordant themes,
Which, haply, kindred souls may prize
Not less than vernal ecstasies,
And passion's feverish dreams.

For deathless powers to verse belong,
And they like demi-gods are strong
On whom the muses smile;
But some their function have disclaimed,
Best pleased with what is aptliest framed
To enervate and defile.

Not such the initiatory strains
Committed to the silent plains
In Britain's earliest dawn:
Trembled the groves, the stars grew pale,
While all too-daringly the veil
Of nature was withdrawn!

Nor such the spirit-stirring note
When the live chords Alcæus smote,
Inflamed by sense of wrong;
Woe! woe to tyrants! from the lyre
Broke threateningly, in sparkles dire
Of fierce vindictive song.

And not unhallowed was the page
By winged love inscribed, to assuage
The pangs of vain pursuit;
Love listening while the Lesbian maid
With finest touch of passion swayed
Her own Æolian lute.

O ye who patiently explore
The wreck of Herculanean lore,
What rapture! could ye seize
Some Theban fragment, or unrol
One precious, tender-hearted scroll
Of pure Simonides.

That were, indeed, a genuine birth
Of poesy; a bursting forth
Of genius from the dust.
What Horace gloried to behold,
What Maro loved, shall we enfold?
Can haughty time be just!

THE PILLAR OF TRAJAN.

WHERE towers are crushed, and unforbidden weeds
O'er mutilated arches shed their seeds,
And temples, doomed to milder change, unfold
A new magnificence that vies with old;
Firm in its pristine majesty hath stood
A votive column, spared by fire and flood,—
And, though the passions of man's fretful race
Have never ceased to eddy round its base,
Not injured more by touch of meddling hands
Than a lone obelisk, 'mid Nubian sands,
Or aught in Syrian deserts left to save
From death the memory of the good and brave.
Historic figures round the shaft embost
Ascend, with lineaments in air not lost:
Still as he turns, the charmed spectator sees
Group winding after group with dream-like ease;
Triumphs in sunbright gratitude displayed,
Or softly stealing into modest shade.
So, pleased with purple clusters to entwine
Some lofty elm-tree, mounts the daring vine;
The woodbine so, with spiral grace, and breathes
Wide-spreading odours from her flowery wreaths.

Borne by the muse from rills in shepherds' ears
Murmuring but one smooth story for all years,
I gladly commune with the mind and heart
Of him who thus survives by classic art,
His actions witness, venerate his mien,
And study Trajan as by Pliny seen;
Behold how fought the chief whose conquering sword
Stretched far as earth might own a single lord:

In the delight of moral prudence schooled,
How feelingly at home the sovereign ruled;
Best of the good—in pagan faith allied
To more than man by virtue deified.

Memorial pillar! 'mid the wrecks of time
Preserve thy charge with confidence sublime—
The exultations, pomps, and cares of Rome,
Whence half the breathing world received its doom;
Things that recoil from language; that, if shown
By apter pencil, from the light had flown.
A pontiff, Trajan *here* the gods implores,
There greets an embassy from Indian shores;
Lo! he harangues his cohorts—*there* the storm
Of battle meets him in authentic form!
Unharnessed, naked, troops of Moorish horse
Sweep to the charge; more high, the Dacian force,
To hoof and finger mailed;—yet, high or low,
None bleed, and none lie prostrate but the foe;
In every Roman, through all turns of fate,
Is Roman dignity inviolate;
Spirit in him pre-eminent; who guides,
Supports, adorns, and over all presides;
Distinguished only by inherent state
From honoured instruments that round him wait;
Rise as he may, his grandeur scorns the test
Of outward symbol, nor will deign to rest
On aught by which another is depressed.*
Alas! that one thus disciplined could toil
To enslave whole nations on their native soil;
So emulous of Macedonian fame,
That, when his age was measured with his aim,
He drooped, 'mid else unclouded victories,
And turned his eagles back with deep-drawn sighs;
Oh, weakness of the great! Oh, folly of the wise!

* See Forsyth.

Where now the haughty empire that was spread
With such fond hope? her very speech is dead;
Yet glorious art the sweep of time defies,
And Trajan still, through various enterprise,
Mounts, in this fine illusion, toward the skies:
Still are we present with the imperial chief,
Nor cease to gaze upon the bold relief
Till Rome, to silent marble unconfined,
Becomes with all her years a vision of the mind.

DION.

(SEE PLUTARCH.)

FAIR is the swan, whose majesty, prevailing
O'er breezeless water, on Locarno's lake,
Bears him on while proudly sailing
He leaves behind a moon-illumined wake:
Behold! the mantling spirit of reserve
Fashions his neck into a goodly curve;
An arch thrown back between luxuriant wings
Of whitest garniture, like fir-tree boughs
To which on some unruffled morning clings
A flaky weight of winter's purest snows!
Behold!—as with a gushing impulse heaves
That downy prow, and softly cleaves
The mirror of the crystal flood,
Vanish inverted hill, and shadowy wood,
And pendant rocks, where'er, in gliding state,
Winds the mute creature without visible mate
Or rival, save the queen of night
Showering down a silver light,
From heaven, upon her chosen favourite!

So pure, so bright, so fitted to embrace,
Where'er he turned, a natural grace
Of haughtiness without pretence,
And to unfold a still magnificence,
Was princely Dion in the power
And beauty of his happier hour.
Nor less the homage that was seen to wait
On Dion's virtues, when the lunar beam
Of Plato's genius, from its lofty sphere,
Fell round him in the grove of Academe
Softening their inbred dignity austere;—

That he, not too elate
With self-sufficing solitude,
But with majestic lowliness endued,
Might in the universal bosom reign,
And from affectionate observance gain
Help, under every change of adverse fate

Five thousand warriors—Oh, the rapturous day!
Each crowned with flowers and armed with spear and shield,
Or ruder weapon which their course might yield,
To Syracuse advance in bright array.
Who leads them on?—The anxious people see
Long-exiled Dion marching at their head,
He also crowned with flowers of Sicily,
And in a white, far-beaming, corselet clad!
Pure transport undisturbed by doubt or fear
The gazers feel; and rushing to the plain,
Salute those strangers as a holy train
Or blest procession (to the immortals dear)
That brought their precious liberty again.
Lo! when the gates are entered, on each hand,
Down the long street, rich goblets filled with wine
In seemly order stand,
On tables set, as if for rites divine;—
And, as the great deliverer marches by,
He looks on festal ground with fruits bestrown;
And flowers are on his person thrown
In boundless prodigality;
Nor doth the general voice abstain from prayer,
Invoking Dion's tutelary care,
As if a very Deity he were!

Mourn, hills and groves of Attica! and mourn
Ilissus, bending o'er thy classic urn!
Mourn, and lament for him whose spirit dreads
Your once-sweet memory, studious walks and shades!
For him who to divinity aspired,
Not on the breath of popular applause,
But through dependence on the sacred laws
Framed in the schools where wisdom dwelt retired,
Intent to trace the ideal path of right
(More fair than heaven's broad causeway paved with stars)
Which Dion learned to measure with delight;
But he hath overleaped the eternal bars;
And, following guides whose craft holds no consent
With aught that breathes the ethereal element,
Hath stained the robes of civil power with blood,
Unjustly shed, though for the public good.
Whence doubts that came too late, and wishes vain,
Hollow excuses, and triumphant pain;
And oft his cogitations sink as low
As, through the abysses of a joyless heart,
The heaviest plummet of despair can go,
But whence that sudden check? that fearful start!
He hears an uncouth sound—
Anon his lifted eyes
Saw at a long-drawn gallery's dusky bound,
A shape of more than mortal size
And hideous aspect, stalking round and round;
A woman's garb that phantom wore,
And fiercely swept the marble floor,—
Like Auster whirling to and fro,
His force on Caspian foam to try;
Or Boreas when he scours the snow
That skins the plains of Thessaly,
Or when aloft on Mænalus he stops
His flight, 'mid eddying pine-tree tops

So, but from toil less sign of profit reaping
The sullen spectre to her purpose bowed,
Sweeping—vehemently sweeping—
No pause admitted, no design avowed?
"Avaunt, inexplicable guest!—avaunt!"
Exclaimed the chieftain—"Let me rather see
The coronal that coiling vipers make;
The torch that flames with many a lurid flake,
And the long train of doleful pageantry
Which they behold, whom vengeful furies haunt:
Who, while they struggle from the scourge to flee,
Move where the blasted soil is not unworn,
And, in their anguish, bear what other minds have borne!"

But shapes that come not at an earthly call,
Will not depart when mortal voices bid;
Lords of the visionary eye whose lid
Once raised, remains aghast and will not fall!
Ye gods, thought he, that servile implement
Obeys a mystical intent!

Your minister would brush away
The spots that to my soul adhere;
But should she labour night and day,
They will not, cannot disappear; [look
Whence angry perturbations,—and that
Which no philosophy can brook!

Ill-fated chief; there are whose hopes are built
Upon the ruins of thy glorious name;
Who, through the portal of one moment's guilt,
Pursue thee with their deadly aim!
O matchless perfidy! portentous lust
Of monstrous crime!—that horror-striking blade,
Drawn in defiance of the gods, hath laid
The noble Syracusan low in dust!
Shudder the walls—the marble city wept—
And sylvan places heaved a pensive sigh;
But in calm peace the appointed victim slept,
As he had fallen in magnanimity;
Of spirit too capacious to require
That destiny her course should change; too just
To his own native greatness to desire
That wretched boon, days lengthened by mistrust.
So were the hopeless troubles, that involved
The soul of Dion, instantly dissolved
Released from life and cares of princely state,
He left this moral grafted on his fate—
"Him only pleasure leads, and peace attends,
Him, only him, the shield of Jove defends,
Whose means are fair and spotless as his ends."

MEMORY.

A PEN—to register; a key—
That winds through secret wards;
Are well assigned to memory
By allegoric bards.

As aptly, also, might be given
A pencil to her hand;
That, softening objects, sometimes even
Outstrips the heart's demand;

That smooths foregone distress, the lines
Of lingering care subdues,
Long-vanished happiness refines,
And clothes in brighter hues:

Yet, like a tool of fancy, works
Those spectres to dilate
That startle conscience, as she lurks
Within her lonely seat.

Oh, that our lives, which flee so fast,
In purity were such,
That not an image of the past
Should fear that pencil's touch!

Retirement then might hourly look
Upon a soothing scene,
Age steal to his allotted nook,
Contented and serene;

With heart as calm as lakes that sleep,
In frosty moonlight glistening;
Or mountain rivers, where they creep
Along a channel smooth and deep,
To their own far-off murmurs listening.

ODE TO DUTY.

STERN daughter of the voice of God!
O Duty! if that name thou love,
Who art a light to guide, a rod
To check the erring, and reprove;
Thou who art victory and law
When empty terrors overawe;
From vain temptations dost set free;
And calm'st the weary strife of frail humanity!

There are who ask not if thine eye
Be on them; who, in love and truth,
Where no misgiving is, rely
Upon the genial sense of youth;
Glad hearts! without reproach or blot;
Who do thy work, and know it not:
Long may the kindly impulse last!
But thou, if they should totter, teach them to stand fast!

Serene will be our days and bright,
And happy will our nature be,
When love is an unerring light,
And joy its own security.
And they a blissful course may hold
Even now, who, not unwisely bold,
Live in the spirit of this creed;
Yet find that other strength, according to their need.

I, loving freedom, and untried ;
No sport of every random gust,
Yet being to myself a guide,
Too blindly have reposed my trust ·
And oft, when in my heart was heard
Thy timely mandate, I deferred
The task, in smoother walks to stray ;
But thee I now would serve more strictly, if I may.

Through no disturbance of my soul,
Or strong compunction in me wrought,
I supplicate for thy control ;
But in the quietness of thought .
Me this unchartered freedom tires ;
I feel the weight of chance-desires ·
My hopes no more must change their name,
I long for a repose that ever is the same.

Stern lawgiver ! yet thou dost wear
The Godhead's most benignant grace ;
Nor know we anything so fair
As is the smile upon thy face
Flowers laugh before thee on their beds ;
And fragrance in thy footing treads ,
Thou dost preserve the stars from wrong ,
And the most ancient heavens, through thee, are fresh and strong.

To humbler functions, awful power !
I call thee I myself commend
Unto thy guidance from this hour ;
Oh, let my weakness have an end !
Give unto me, made lowly wise,
The spirit of self-sacrifice ;
The confidence of reason give ;
And in the light of truth thy bondman let me live !

Poems Referring to the Period of Old Age.

THE OLD CUMBERLAND BEGGAR.

The class of beggars, to which the old man here described belongs, will probably soon be extinct. It consisted of poor, and, mostly, old and infirm persons, who confined themselves to a stated round in their neighbourhood, and had certain fixed days, on which, at different houses, they regularly received alms, sometimes in money, but mostly in provisions.

I SAW an aged beggar in my walk ;
And he was seated, by the highway side,
On a low structure of rude masonry
Built at the foot of a huge hill, that they
Who lead their horses down the steep rough road
May thence remount at ease. The aged man
Had placed his staff across the broad smooth stone
That overlays the pile ; and, from a bag
All white with flour, the dole of village dames,
He drew his scraps and fragments, one by one ;
And scanned them with a fixed and serious look
Of idle computation. In the sun,
Upon the second step of that small pile,
Surrounded by those wild unpeopled hills,
He sat, and ate his food in solitude :
And ever, scattered from his palsied hand,
That, still attempting to prevent the waste,
Was baffled still, the crumbs in little showers
Fell on the ground ; and the small mountain birds,
Not venturing yet to peck their destined meal,
Approached within the length of half his staff.

Him from my childhood have I known ; and then
He was so old, he seems not older now ;
He travels on, a solitary man,
So helpless in appearance, that for him
The sauntering horseman-traveller does not throw
With careless hand his alms upon the ground,
But stops,—that he may safely lodge the coin
Within the old man's hat ; nor quits him so,
But still, when he has given his horse the rein,
Watches the aged beggar with a look
Sidelong—and half-reverted. She who tends
The toll-gate, when in summer at her door
She turns her wheel, if on the road she sees
The aged beggar coming, quits her work,
And lifts the latch for him that he may pass.
The post boy, when his rattling wheels o'ertake
The aged beggar in the woody lane,
Shouts to him from behind ; and, if thus warned
The old man does not chang his course, the boy

Turns with less noisy wheels to the road-side,
And passes gently by—without a curse
Upon his lips, or anger at his heart
He travels on, a solitary man,
His age has no companion. On the ground
His eyes are turned, and, as he moves along
They move along the ground, and, evermore,
Instead of common and habitual sight
Of fields with rural works, of hill and dale,
And the blue sky, one little span of earth
Is all his prospect. Thus, from day to day,
Bow-bent, his eyes for ever on the ground,
He plies his weary journey, seeing still,
And seldom knowing that he sees, some straw,
Some scattered leaf, or marks which, in one track,
The nails of cart or chariot-wheel have left
Impressed on the white road,—in the same line,
At distance still the same. Poor traveller!
His staff trails with him; scarcely do his feet
Disturb the summer dust, he is so still
In look and motion, that the cottage curs,
Ere he have passed the door, will turn away,
Weary of barking at him. Boys and girls,
The vacant and the busy, maids and youths,
And urchins newly breeched—all pass him by:
Him even the slow-paced waggon leaves behind

But deem not this man useless.—Statesmen! ye
Who are so restless in your wisdom, ye
Who have a broom still ready in your hands
To rid the world of nuisances; ye proud,
Heart-swoln, while in your pride ye contemplate
Your talents, power, and wisdom, deem him not
A burthen of the earth! 'Tis nature's law
That none, the meanest of created things,
Of forms created the most vile and brute,
The dullest or most noxious, should exist
Divorced from good—a spirit and pulse of good,
A life and soul, to every mode of being
Inseparably linked. While thus he creeps
From door to door, the villagers in him
Behold a record which together binds
Past deeds and offices of charity,
Else unremembered, and so keeps alive
The kindly mood in hearts which lapse of years,
And that half-wisdom half-experience gives,
Make slow to feel, and by sure steps resign
To selfishness and cold oblivious cares
Among the farms and solitary huts,
Hamlets and thinly-scattered villages,
Where'er the aged beggar takes his rounds,
The mild necessity of use compels
To acts of love; and habit does the work
Of reason; yet prepares that after-joy
Which reason cherishes. And thus the soul,
By that sweet taste of pleasure unpursued,
Doth find itself insensibly disposed
To virtue and true goodness. Some there are

By their good works exalted, lofty minds
And meditative, authors of delight
And happiness, which to the end of time
Will live, and spread, and kindle : even such minds
In childhood, from this solitary being,
Or from like wanderer, haply have received
(A thing more precious far than all that books
Or the solicitudes of love can do !)
That first mild touch of sympathy and thought,
In which they found their kindred with a world
Where want and sorrow were. The easy man
Who sits at his own door,—and, like the pear
That overhangs his head from the green wall,
Feeds in the sunshine ; the robust and young,
The prosperous and unthinking, they who live
Sheltered, and flourish in a little grove
Of their own kindred ;—all behold in him
A silent monitor, which on their minds
Must needs impress a transitory thought
Of self-congratulation, to the heart
Of each recalling his peculiar boons,
His charters and exemptions ; and, perchance,
Though he to no one give the fortitude
And circumspection needful to preserve
His present blessings, and to husband up
The respite of the seasons, he, at least,
And 'tis no vulgar service, makes them felt.

Yet further.—Many, I believe, there are
Who live a life of virtuous decency,
Men who can hear the decalogue and feel
No self-reproach ; who of the moral law
Established in the land where they abide
Are strict observers ; and not negligent,
In acts of love to those with whom they dwell,
Their kindred, and the children of their blood.
Praise be to such, and to their slumbers peace !
But of the poor man ask, the abject poor ;
Go, and demand of him, if there be here
In this cold abstinence from evil deeds,
And these inevitable charities,
Wherewith to satisfy the human soul?
No—man is dear to man ; the poorest poor
Long for some moments in a weary life
When they can know and feel that they have been,
Themselves, the fathers and the dealers out
Of some small blessings ; have been kind to such
As needed kindness, for this single cause,
That we have all of us one human heart.
Such pleasure is to one kind being known,
My neighbour, when with punctual care, each week,
Duly as Friday comes, though pressed herself
By her own wants, she from her store of meal
Takes one unsparing handful for the scrip
Of this old mendicant, and, from her door
Returning with exhilarated heart,
Sits by her fire, and builds her hope in heaven

Then let him pass, a blessing on his head!
And while in that vast solitude to which
The tide of things has borne him, he appears
To breathe and live but for himself alone,
Unblamed, uninjured, let him bear about
The good which the benignant law of Heaven
Has hung around him: and, while life is his,
Still let him prompt the unlettered villagers
To tender offices and pensive thoughts.
Then let him pass, a blessing o. his head!
And, long as he can wander, let him breathe
The freshness of the valleys; let his blood
Struggle with frosty air and winter snows;
And let the chartered wind that sweeps the heath
Beat his gray locks against his withered face.
Reverence the hope whose vital anxiousness
Gives the last human interest to his heart.
May never House, misnamed of Industry,
Make him a captive! for that pent-up din,
Those life-consuming sounds that clog the air,
Be his the natural silence of old age!
Let him be free of mountain solitudes;
And have around him, whether heard or not,
The pleasant melody of woodland birds.
Few are his pleasures: if his eyes have now
Been doomed so long to settle on the earth
That not without some effort they behold
The countenance of the horizontal sun,
Rising or setting, let the light at least
Find a free entrance to their languid orbs.
And let him, *where* and *when* he will, sit down
Beneath the trees, or by the grassy bank
Of highway side, and with the little birds
Share his chance-gathered meal; and, finally,
As in the eye of nature he has lived,
So in the eye of nature let him die!

THE FARMER OF TILSBURY VALE.

'Tis not for the unfeeling, the falsely refined,
The squeamish in taste, and narrow of mind,
And the small critic wielding his delicate pen,
That I sing of old Adam, the pride of old men.

He dwells in the centre of London's wide town;
His staff is a sceptre—his gray hairs a crown;
Erect as a sunflower he stands, and the streak
Of the unfaded rose still enlivens his cheek.

'Mid the dews, in the sunshine of morn,—'mid the joy
Of the fields, he collected that bloom, when a boy;
There fashioned that countenance, which, in spite of a stain
That his life hath received, to the last will remain.

A farmer he was; and his house far and near
Was the boast of the country for excellent cheer:
How oft have I heard in sweet Tilsbury vale
Of the silver-rimmed horn whence he dealt his mild ale!

Yet Adam was far as the farthest from ruin,
His fields seemed to know what their master was doing;
And turnips, and corn-land, and meadow, and lea,
All caught the infection—as generous as he.

Yet Adam prized little the feast and the bowl,—
The fields better suited the ease of his soul:
He strayed through the fields like an indolent wight,
The quiet of nature was Adam's delight.

For Adam was simple in thought, and the poor,
Familiar with him, made an inn of his door:
He gave them the best that he had; or, to say
What less may mislead you, they took it away.

Thus thirty smooth years did he thrive on his farm;
The genius of plenty preserved him from harm:
At length, what to most is a season of sorrow,
His means are run out, he must beg, or must borrow.

To the neighbours he went,—all were free with their money;
For his hive had so long been replenished with honey,
That they dreamt not of dearth;—he continued his rounds,
Knocked here—and knocked there, pounds still adding to pounds.

He paid what he could with this ill-gotten pelf,
And something, it might be, reserved for himself:
Then, (what is too true,) without hinting a word,
Turned his back on the country; and off like a bird.

You lift up your eyes!—but I guess that you frame
A judgment too harsh of the sin and the shame;
In him it was scarcely a business of art,
For this he did all in the *ease* of his heart.

To London—a sad emigration I ween—
With his gray hairs he went from the brook and the green;
And there with small wealth but his legs and his hands,
As lonely he stood as a crow on the sands.

All trades, as need was, did old Adam assume,—
Served as stable-boy, errand-boy, porter, and groom;
But nature is gracious, necessity kind,
And, in spite of the shame that may lurk in his mind,

He seems ten birthdays younger, is green and is stout;
Twice as fast as before does his blood run about;
You would say that each hair of his beard was alive,
And his fingers are busy as bees in a hive.

For he's not like an old man that leisurely goes
About work that he knows, in a track that he knows;
But often his mind is compelled to demur,
And you guess that the more then his body must stir

In the throng of the town like a stranger is he,
Like one whose own country's far over the sea;
And nature, while through the great city he hies,
Full ten times a day takes his heart by surprise

This gives him the fancy of one that is young,
More of soul in his face than of words on his tongue,
Like a maiden of twenty he trembles and sighs,
And tears of fifteen will come into his eyes

What's a tempest to him, or the dry parching heats?
Yet he watches the clouds that pass over the streets,
With a look of such earnestness often will stand,
You might think he'd twelve reapers at work in the Strand.

Where proud Covent Garden, in desolate hours
Of snow and hoar-frost, spreads her fruit and her flowers,
Old Adam will smile at the pains that have made
Poor winter look fine in such strange masquerade.

'Mid coaches and chariots, a waggon of straw,
Like a magnet, the heart of old Adam can draw,
With a thousand soft pictures his memory will teem,
And his hearing is touched with the sounds of a dream.

Up the Haymarket hill he oft whistles his way,
Thrusts his hands in the waggon, and smells at the hay,
He thinks of the fields he so often hath mown,
And is happy as if the rich freight were his own

But chiefly to Smithfield he loves to repair,—
If you pass by at morning, you'll meet with him there
The breath of the cows you may see him inhale,
And his heart all the while is in Tilsbury Vale

Now farewell, old Adam! when low thou art laid,
May one blade of grass spring up over thy head,
And I hope that thy grave, wheresoever it be,
Will hear the wind sigh through the leaves of a tree

THE SMALL CELANDINE.

THERE is a flower, the lesser Celandine,
That shrinks, like many more, from cold and rain;
And, the first moment that the sun may shine,
Bright as the sun itself, 'tis out again!

When hailstones have been falling, swarm on swarm,
Or blasts the green field and the trees distressed,
Oft have I seen it muffled up from harm,
In close self-shelter, like a thing at rest.

But lately, one rough day, this flower I passed
And recognized it, though an altered form,
Now standing forth an offering to the blast,
And buffeted at will by rain and storm

I stopped, and said with inly-muttered voice,
"It doth not love the shower, nor seek the cold:
This neither is its courage nor its choice,
But its necessity in being old.

"The sunshine may not cheer it, nor the dew;
It cannot help itself in its decay;
Stiff in its members, withered, changed of hue."
And, in my spleen, I smiled that it was gray.

To be a prodigal's favourite—then, worse truth,
A miser's pensioner—behold our lot!
O man, that from thy fair and shining youth
Age might but take the things youth needed not!

THE TWO THIEVES;

OR, THE LAST STAGE OF AVARICE.

OH, now that the genius of Bewick were mine,
And the skill which he learned on the banks of the Tyne!
Then the muses might deal with me just as they chose,
For I'd take my last leave both of verse and of prose.

What feats would I work with my magical hand!
Book-learning and books should be banished the land:
And, for hunger and thirst, and such troublesome calls,
Every alehouse should then have a feast on its walls.

The traveller would hang his wet clothes on a chair;
Let them smoke, let them burn, not a straw would he care
For the Prodigal Son, Joseph's dream and his sheaves,
Oh, what would they be to my tale of two thieves?

The one, yet unbreeched, is not three birthdays old,
His grandsire that age more than thirty times told;
There are ninety good seasons of fair and foul weather
Between them, and both go a-stealing together.

With chips is the carpenter strewing his floor?
Is a cart-load of turf at an old woman's door?
Old Daniel his hand to the treasure will slide!
And his grandson's as busy at work by his side.

Old Daniel begins, he stops short—and his eye,
Through the lost look of dotage, is cunning and sly.
'Tis a look which at this time is hardly his own,
But tells a plain tale of the days that are flown.

He once had a heart which was moved by the wires
Of manifold pleasures and many desires:
And what if he cherished his purse! 'Twas no more
Than treading a path trod by thousands before.

'Twas a path trod by thousands; but Daniel is one
Who went something further than others have gone,
And now with old Daniel you see how it fares,
You see to what end he has brought his gray hairs.

The pair sally forth hand in hand ere the sun
Has peered o'er the beeches, their work is begun
And yet, into whatever sin they may fall,
This child but half knows it, and that not at all

They hunt through the streets with deliberate tread,
And each, in his turn, is both leader and led,
And, wherever they carry their plots and their wiles,
Every face in the village is dimpled with smiles.

Neither checked by the rich nor the needy they roam;
The gray-headed sire has a daughter at home,
Who will gladly repair all the damage that's done,
And three, were it asked, would be rendered for one.

Old man! whom so oft I with pity have eyed,
I love thee, and love the sweet boy at thy side:
Long yet mayst thou live! for a teacher we see
That lifts up the veil of our nature in thee.

ANIMAL TRANQUILLITY AND DECAY.

A SKETCH

THE little hedgerow birds,
That peck along the road, regard him not.
He travels on, and in his face, his step,
His gait, is one expression; every limb,
His look and bending figure, all bespeak
A man who does not move with pain, but moves
With thought.—He is insensibly subdued
To settled quiet: he is one by whom
All effort seems forgotten; one to whom
Long patience hath such mild composure given
That patience now doth seem a thing of which
He hath no need He is by nature led
To peace so perfect, that the young behold
With envy, what the old man hardly feels.

Epitaphs and Elegiac Poems.

EPITAPHS.

TRANSLATED FROM CHIABRERA.

PERHAPS some needful service of the state
Drew Titus from the depth of studious bowers,
And doomed him to contend in faithless courts,
Where gold determines between right and wrong.
Yet did at length his loyalty of heart,
And his pure native genius, lead him back
To wait upon the bright and gracious Muses,
Whom he had early loved. And not in vain
Such course he held! Bologna's learned schools
Were gladdened by the sage's voice, and hung
With fondness on those sweet Nestorian strains.
There pleasure crowned his days; and all his thoughts
A roseate fragrance breathed.*—O human life,
That never art secure from dolorous change!
Behold a high injunction suddenly
To Arno's side conducts him, and he charmed
A Tuscan audience: but full soon was called
To the perpetual silence of the grave.
Mourn, Italy, the loss of him who stood
A champion steadfast and invincible,
To quell the rage of literary war!

O THOU who movest onward with a mind
Intent upon thy way, pause, though in haste!
'Twill be no fruitless moment. I was born
Within Savona's walls, of gentle blood.
On Tiber's banks my youth was dedicate
To sacred studies; and the Roman shepherd
Gave to my charge Urbino's numerous flock.
Much did I watch, much laboured, nor had power
To escape from many and strange indignities;
Was smitten by the great ones of the world,
But did not fall; for virtue braves all shocks,
Upon herself resting immoveably.
Me did a kindlier fortune then invite
To serve the glorious Henry, King of France,

* "Ivi vivea giocondo e i suoi pensieri
Erano tutti rose."
The translator had not skill to come nearer to his original.

And in his hands I saw a high reward
Stretched out for my acceptance—but death came.
Now, reader, learn from this my fate—how false,
How treacherous to her promise is the world,
And trust in God—to whose eternal doom
Must bend the sceptred potentates of earth.

THERE never breathed a man who when his life
Was closing might not of that life relate
Toils long and hard.—The warrior will report
Of wounds, and bright swords flashing in the field,
And blast of trumpets He who hath been doomed
To bow his forehead in the courts of kings,
Will tell of fraud and never-ceasing hate,
Envy and heart-inquietude, derived
From intricate cabals of treacherous friends.
I, who on shipboard lived from earliest youth,
Could represent the countenance horrible
Of the vexed waters, and the indignant rage
Of Auster and Bootes. Forty years
Over the well-steered galleys did I rule:—
From huge Pelorus to the Atlantic pillars
Rises no mountain to mine eyes unknown;
And the broad gulfs I traversed oft—and—oft:
Of every cloud which in the heavens might stir
I knew the force, and hence the rough sea's pride
Availed not to my vessel's overthrow.
What noble pomp and frequent have not I
On regal decks beheld! yet in the end
I learn that one poor moment can suffice
To equalize the lofty and the low.
We sail the sea of life—a *calm* one finds,
And one a *tempest*—and, the voyage o'er,
Death is the quiet haven of us all
If more of my condition ye would know,
Savona was my birthplace, and I sprang
Of noble parents. sixty years and three
Lived I——then yielded to a slow disease.

DESTINED to war from very infancy
Was I, Roberto Dati, and I took
In Malta the white symbol of the cross.
Nor in life's vigorous season did I shun
Hazard or toil, among the sands was seen
Of Libya, and not seldom, on the banks
Of wide Hungarian Danube, 'twas my lot
To hear the sanguinary trumpet sounded.
So lived I, and repined not at such fate;
This only grieves me, for it seems a wrong,
That stripped of arms I to my end am brought
On the soft down of my paternal home.
Yet haply Arno shall be spared all cause
To blush for me. Thou, loiter not nor halt
In thy appointed way, and bear in mind
How fleeting and how frail is human life.

NOT without heavy grief of heart did he,
On whom the duty fell (for at that time
The father sojourned i a distant land),
Deposit in the hollow of this tomb
A brother's child, most tenderly beloved!
Francesco was the name the youth had borne,
Pozzobonnelli his illustrious house;
And, when beneath this stone the corse was laid
The eyes of all Savona streamed with tears.
Alas! the twentieth April of his life
Had scarcely flowered: and at this early time,
By genuine virtue he inspired a hope
That greatly cheered his country: to his kin
He promised comfort; and the flattering thoughts
His friends had in their fondness entertained,*
He suffered not to languish or decay.
Now is there not good reason to break forth
Into a passionate lament?—O Soul!
Short while a pilgrim in our nether world,
Do thou enjoy the calm empyreal air;
And r und this earthly tomb let roses rise,
An everlasting spring! in memory
Of that delightful fragrance which was once
From thy mild manners, quietly exhaled.

PAUSE, courteous spirit!—Balbi supplicates
That thou, with no reluctant voice, for him
Here laid in mortal darkness, wouldst prefer
A prayer to the Redeemer of the world.
This to the dead by sacred right belongs;
All else is nothing.—Did occasion suit
To tell his worth, the marble of this tomb
Would ill suffice: for Plato's lore sublime,
And all the wisdom of the Stagyrite,
Enriched and beautified his studious mind:
With Archimedes also he conversed
As with a chosen friend, nor did he leave
Those laureat wreaths ungathered which the nymphs
Twine on the top of Pindus.—Finally,
Himself above each lower thought uplifting,
His ears he closed to listen to the song
Which Sion's kings did consecrate of old;
And fixed his Pindus upon Lebanon.
A blessed man! who of protracted days
Made not, as thousands do, a vulgar sleep;
But truly did *he* live his life.—Urbino,
Take pride in him!—O passenger, farewell!

* In justice to the author, I subjoin the original—

"e degli amici
Non lasciava languire i bei pensieri."

LINES

Composed at Grasmere, during a walk, one evening, after a stormy day, the author having just read in a newspaper that the dissolution of Mr Fox was hourly expected

LOUD is the vale ! the voice is up
With which she speaks when storms are gone,
A mighty unison of streams !
Of all her voices, one !

Loud is the vale ;—this inland depth
In peace is roaring like the sea ;
Yon star upon the mountain-top
Is listening quietly.

Sad was I, even to pain deprest,
Importunate and heavy load ! *
The Comforter hath found me here,
Upon this lonely road ;

And many thousands now are sad—
Wait the fulfilment of their fear ;
For he must die who is their stay,
Their glory disappear.

A power is passing from the earth
To breathless nature's dark abyss ;
But when the mighty pass away
What is it more than this—

That man, who is from God sent forth,
Doth yet again to God return ?
Such ebb and flow must ever be ,
Then wherefore should we mourn ?

LINES

Written, November 13, 1814, on a blank leaf in a copy of the author's poem, "The Excursion upon hearing of the death of the late vicar of Kendal.

To public notice, with reluctance strong,
Did I deliver this unfinished song ;
Yet for one happy issue ,—and I look
With self-congratulation on the book
Which pious, learned Murfitt saw and read ;—
Upon my thoughts his saintly spirit fed ;
He conned the new-born lay with grateful heart—
Foreboding not how soon he must depart ;
Unweeting that to him the joy was given
Which good men take with them from earth to heaven.

* " Importuna e grave salma."—MICHAEL ANGELO

ELEGIAC STANZAS,

SUGGESTED BY A PICTURE OF PEELE CASTLE, IN A STORM, PAINTED BY SIR GEORGE BEAUMONT.

I WAS thy neighbour once, thou rugged pile!
Four summer weeks I dwelt in sight of thee:
I saw thee every day; and all the while
Thy form was sleeping on a glassy sea.

So pure the sky, so quiet was the air;
So like, so very like, was day to day!
Whene'er I looked, thy image still was there;
It trembled, but it never passed away.

How perfect was the calm! it seemed no sleep,
No mood which season takes away or brings:
I could have fancied that the mighty deep
Was even the gentlest of all gentle things.

Ah! THEN, if mine had been the painter's hand,
To express what then I saw; and add the gleam,
The light that never was on sea or land,
The consecration and the poet's dream;

I would have planted thee, thou hoary pile!
Amid a world how different from this!
Beside a sea that could not cease to smile;
On tranquil land, beneath a sky of bliss.

A picture had it been of lasting ease,
Elysian quiet, without toil or strife;
No motion but the moving tide, a breeze,
Or merely silent nature's breathing life.

Such, in the fond illusion of my heart,
Such picture would I at that time have made:
And seen the soul of truth in every part;
A steadfast peace that might not be betrayed.

So once it would have been,—'tis so no more;
I have submitted to a new control:
A power is gone, which nothing can restore;
A deep distress hath humanized my soul.

Not for a moment could I now behold
A smiling sea, and be what I have been:
The feeling of my loss will ne'er be old;
This, which I know, I speak with mind serene.

Then, Beaumont, friend! who would have been the friend,
If he had lived, of him whom I deplore,
This work of thine I blame not, but commend;
This sea in anger, and that dismal shore.

Oh, 'tis a passionate work!—yet wise and well:
Well chosen is the spirit that is here;
That hulk which labours in the deadly swell,
This rueful sky, this pageantry of fear;

And this huge castle, standing here sublime,
I love to see the look with which it braves,
Cased in the unfeeling armour of old time,
The lightning, the fierce wind, and trampling waves.

Farewell, farewell, the heart that lives alone,
Housed in a dream, at distance from the kind!
Such happiness, wherever it be known,
Is to be pitied; for 'tis surely blind

But welcome fortitude, and patient cheer,
And frequent sights of what is to be borne!
Such sights, or worse, as are before me here.—
Not without hope we suffer and we mourn.

TO THE DAISY.

Sweet flower! belike one day to have
A place upon thy poet's grave,
I welcome thee once more:
But he, who was on land, at sea,
My brother, too, in loving thee,
Although he loved more silently,
Sleeps by his native shore.

Ah! hopeful, hopeful was the day
When to that ship he bent his way,
To govern and to guide:
His wish was gained: a little time
Would bring him back in manhood's prime,
And free for life, these hills to climb,
With all his wants supplied.

And full of hope day followed day
While that stout ship at anchor lay
Beside the shores of Wight;
The May had then made all things green:
And floating there in pomp serene,
That ship was goodly to be seen,
His pride and his delight!

Yet then, when called ashore, he sought
The tender peace of rural thought;
In more than happy mood
To your abodes, bright daisy flowers!
He then would steal at leisure hours,
And loved you glittering in your bowers,
A starry multitude.

But hark the word!—the ship is gone;—
From her long course returns!—anon
Sets sail!—in season due,
Once more on English earth they stand:
But, when a third time from the land
They parted, sorrow was at hand
For him and for his crew

Ill-f ted vessel!—ghastly shock!
At length delivered from the rock,
The deep she hath regained;
And through the stormy night they steer,
Labouring for life, in hope and fear,
Towards a safer shore—how near,
Yet not to be attained!

"Silence!" the brave commander cried;
To that calm word a shriek replied,
It was the last death-shriek.
—A few (my soul oft sees that sight)
Survive upon the tall mast's height:
But one dear remnant of the night—
For him in vain I seek.

Six weeks beneath the moving sea
He lay in slumber quietly;
Unforced by wind or wave
To quit the ship for which he died,
(All claims of duty satisfied;)
And there they found him at her side
And bore him to the grave.

Vain service! yet not vainly done
For this, if other end were none,
That he, who had been cast
Upon a way of life unmeet
For such a gentle soul and sweet,
Should find an undisturbed retreat
Near what he loved at last;

That neighbourhood of grove and field
To him a resting-place should yield.
A meek man and a brave!
The birds shall sing and ocean make
A mournful murmur for *his* sake;
And thou, sweet flower, shalt sleep and wake
Upon his senseless grave.*

"Late, late yestreen, I saw the new moone
Wi' the auld moon in hir arme."
—*Ballad of Sir Patrick Spence, Percy's Reliques.*

ONCE I could hail (howe'er serene the sky)
The moon re-entering her monthly round,
No faculty yet given me to espy
The dusky shape within her arms imbound,
That thin memento of effulgence lost
Which some have named her predecessor's ghost.

* See, in Poems on the Naming of Places, the one beginning "When, to the attractions of the busy world," page 163

Young, like the crescent that above me shone,
Nought I perceived within it dull or dim;
All that appeared was suitable to one
Whose fancy had a thousand fields to skim;
To expectations spreading with wild growth,
And hope that kept with me her plighted troth.

I saw (ambition quickening at the view)
A silver boat launched on a boundless flood;
A pearly crest, like Dian's when it threw
Its brightest splendour round a leafy wood;
But not a hint from under-ground, no sign
Fit for the glimmering brow of Proserpine.

Or was it Dian's self that seemed to move
Before me? nothing blemished the fair sight;
On her I looked whom jocund fairies love,
Cynthia, who puts the *little* stars to flight,
And by that thinning magnifies the great
For exaltation of her sovereign state.

And when I learned to mark the spectral shape,
As each new moon obeyed the call of time,
If gloom fell on me, swift was my escape.
Such happy privilege hath life's gay prime,
To see or not to see, as best may please
A buoyant spirit, and a heart at ease.

Now, dazzling stranger! when thou meet'st my glancc,
Thy dark associate ever I discern,
Emblem of thoughts too eager to advance
While I salute my joys, thoughts sad or stern,
Shades of past bliss, or phantoms that to gain
Their fill of promised lustre wait in vain.

So changes mortal life with fleeting years,
A mournful change, should reason fail to bring
The timely insight that ca n temper fears,
And from vicissitude remove its sting;
While faith aspires to seats in that domain
Where joys are perfect, neither wax nor wane.

ELEGIAC STANZAS.

1824.

OH, for a dirge! But why complain?
Ask rather a triumphal strain
When Fermor's race is run;
A garland of immortal boughs
To bind around the Christian's brows,
Whose glorious work is done.

We pay a high and holy debt;
No tears of passionate regret

Shall stain this votive lay;
Ill-worthy, Beaumont! were the grief
That flings itself on wild relief
When saints have passed away.

Sad doom, at sorrow's shrine to kneel,
For ever covetous to feel
And impotent to bear:
Such once was hers—to think and think
On severed love, and only sink
From anguish to despair!

But nature to its inmost part
Had faith refined, and to her heart
A peaceful cradle given;
Calm as the dew-drops, free to rest
Within a breeze-fanned rose's breast
Till it exhales to heaven.

Was ever spirit that could bend
So graciously?—that could descend
Another's need to suit,
So promptly from her lofty throne!—
In works of love, in these alone,
How restless, how minute!

Pale was her hue; yet mortal cheek
Ne'er kindled with a livelier streak
When aught had suffered wrong,—
When aught that breathes had felt a wound
Such look the oppressor might confound,
However proud and strong.

But hushed be every thought that springs
From out the bitterness of things;
Her quiet is secure;
No thorns can pierce her tender feet,
Whose life was, like the violet sweet,
As climbing jasmine pure;—

As snowdrop on an infant's grave,
Or lily heaving with the wave
That feeds it and defends;
As vesper, ere the star hath kissed
The mountain top, or breathed the mist
That from the vale ascends.

Thou takest not away, O death!
Thou strik'st—and absence perisheth
Indifference is no more;
The future brightens on our sight;
For on the past hath fallen a light
That tempts us to adore.

INVOCATION TO THE EARTH.

FEBRUARY, 1816.

REST, rest, perturbèd earth !
Oh, rest, thou doleful mother of mankind !"
A spirit sang in tones more plaintive than the wind :
"From regions where no evil thing has birth
I come—thy stains to wash away,
Thy cherished fetters to unbind,
To open thy sad eyes upon a milder day.
The heavens are thronged with martyrs that have risen
From out thy noisome prison ;
The penal caverns groan
With tens of thousands rent from off the tree
Of hopeful life,—by battle's whirlwind blown
Into the deserts of eternity.

"Unpitied havoc ! Victims unlamented !
But not on high, where madness is resented,
And murder causes some sad tears to flow,
Though, from the widely-sweeping blow,
The choirs of angels spread, triumphantly augmented.

"False parent of mankind !
Obdurate, proud, and blind,
I sprinkle thee with soft celestial dews,
Thy lost maternal heart to re-infuse !
Scattering this far-fetched moisture from my wings,
Upon the act a blessing I implore,
Of which the rivers in their secret springs,
The rivers stained so oft with human gore,
Are conscious ;—may the like return no more !
May Discord—for a seraph's care
Shall be attended with a bolder prayer—
May she, who once disturbed the seats of bliss
These mortal spheres above,
Be chained for ever to the black abyss !
And thou, O rescued earth, by peace and love,
And merciful desires, thy sanctity approve !"

The spirit ended his mysterious rite,
And the pure vision closed in darkness infinite.

ODE.

INTIMATIONS OF IMMORTALITY FROM RECOLLECTIONS OF EARLY CHILDHOOD.

"The child is father of the man ;
And I could wish my days to be
Bound each to each by natural piety."

See page 20.

THERE was a time when meadow, grove, and stream,
The earth, and every common sight,
To me did seem
Apparelled in celestial light,

The glory and the freshness of a dream.
It is not now as it hath been of yore ,—
Turn wheresoe'er I may,
By night or day,
The things which I have seen I now can see no more.

The rainbow comes and goes
And lovely is the rose ;
The moon doth with delight
Look round her when the heavens are bare ;
Waters on a starry night
Are beautiful and fair ;
The sunshine is a glorious birth ;
But yet I know, where'er I go,
That there hath passed away a glory from the earth

Now, while the birds thus sing a joyous song,
And while the young lambs bound
As to the tabor's sound,
To me alone there came a thought of grief :
A timely utterance gave that thought relief,
And I again am strong :
The cataracts blow their trumpets from the steep,
No more shall grief of mine the season wrong ;
I hear the echoes through the mountains throng,
The winds come to me from the fields of sleep,
And all the earth is gay ;
Land and sea
Give themselves up to jollity,
And with the heart of May
Doth every beast keep holiday ;—
Thou child of joy,
Shout round me, let me hear thy shouts, thou happy
shepherd boy !

Ye blessed creatures, I have heard the call
Ye to each other make ; I see
The heavens laugh with you in your jubilee ;
My heart is at your festival,
My head hath its coronal,
The fulness of your bliss, I feel—I feel it all.
Oh evil day ! if I were sullen
While the earth itself is adorning,
This sweet May-morning,
And the children are pulling,
On every side,
In a thousand valleys far and wide,
Fresh flowers ; while the sun shines warm,
And the babe leaps up on his mother's arm :—
I hear, I hear, with joy I hear !
But there's a tree, of many, one,
A single field which I have looked upon,
Both of them speak of something that is gone :
The pansy at my feet
Doth the same tale repeat ;
Whither is fled the visionary gleam ?
Where is it now, the glory and the dream ?

Our birth is but a sleep and a forgetting:
The soul that rises with us, our life's star,
Hath had elsewhere its setting,
And cometh from afar:
Not in entire forgetfulness,
And not in utter nakedness,
But trailing clouds of glory do we come
From God, who is our home:
Heaven lies about us in our infancy!
Shades of the prison-house begin to close
Upon the growing boy,
But he beholds the light, and whence it flows,
He sees it in his joy;
The youth, who daily farther from the east
Must travel, still is nature's priest,
And by the vision splendid
Is on his way attended;
At length the man perceives it die away,
And fade into the light of common day.

Earth fills her lap with pleasures of her own;
Yearnings she hath in her own natural kind,
And, even with something of a mother's mind,
And no unworthy aim,
The homely nurse doth all she can
To make her foster-child, her inmate man,
Forget the glories he hath known,
And that imperial palace whence he came.

Behold the child among his new-born blisses,
A six-years' darling of a pigmy size!
See where 'mid work of his own hand he lies,
Fretted by sallies of his mother's kisses,
With light upon him from his father's eyes!
See, at his feet, some little plan or chart,
Some fragment from his dream of human life,
Shaped by himself with newly-learned art;
A wedding or a festival,
A mourning or a funeral,
And this hath now his heart,
And unto this he frames his song.
Then will he fit his tongue
To dialogues of business, love, or strife;
But it will not be long
Ere this be thrown aside,
And with new joy and pride
The little actor cons another part,
Filling from time to time his "humorous stage"
With all the persons, down to palsied age,
That life brings with her in her equipage;
As if his whole vocation
Were endless imitation.

Thou, whose exterior semblance doth belie
Thy soul's immensity;
Thou best philosopher, who yet dost keep
Thy heritage, thou eye among the blind,

That, deaf and silent, read'st the eternal deep,
Haunted for ever by the eternal mind,—
Mighty prophet! seer blest!
On whom those truths do rest,
Which we are toiling all our lives to find,
In darkness lost, the darkness of the grave;
Thou, over whom thy immortality
Broods like the day, a master o'er a slave,
A presence which is not to be put by;
Thou little child, yet glorious in the might
Of heaven-born freedom on thy being's height,
Why with such earnest pains dost thou provoke
The years to bring the inevitable yoke,
Thus blindly with thy blessedness at strife?
Full soon thy soul shall have her earthly freight,
And custom lie upon thee with a weight,
Heavy as frost, and deep almost as life!

O joy! that in our embers
Is something that doth live,
That nature yet remembers
What was so fugitive!
The thought of our past years in me doth breed
Perpetual benediction: not indeed
For that which is most worthy to be blest;
Delight and liberty, the simple creed
Of childhood, whether busy or at rest,
With new-fledged hope still fluttering in his breast:
Not for these I raise
The song of thanks and praise;
But for those obstinate questionings
Of sense and outward things,
Fallings from us, vanishings;
Blank misgivings of a creature
Moving about in worlds not realised,
High instincts before which our mortal nature
Did tremble like a guilty thing surprised:
But for those first affections,
Those shadowy recollections,
Which, be they what they may,
Are yet the fountain light of all our day,
Are yet a master light of all our seeing;
Uphold us, cherish, and have power to make
Our noisy years seem moments in the being
Of the eternal silence: truths that wake
To perish never;
Which neither listlessness, nor mad endeavour,
Nor man nor boy,
Nor all that is at enmity with joy,
Can utterly abolish or destroy!
Hence, in a season of calm weather,
Though inland far we be,
Our souls have sight of that immortal sea
Which brought us hither,
Can in a moment travel thither,
And see the children sport upon the shore,
And hear the mighty waters rolling evermore.

Then sing, ye birds, sing, sing a joyous song!
And let the young lambs bound
As to the tabor's sound!
We in thought will join your throng,
Ye that pipe and ye that play,
Ye that through your hearts to-day
Feel the gladness of the May!
What though the radiance which was once so bright
Be now for ever taken from my sight,
Though nothing can bring back the hour
Of splendour in the grass, of glory in the flower;
We will grieve not, rather find
Strength in what remains behind;
In the primal sympathy
Which having been must ever be,
In the soothing thoughts that spring
Out of human suffering,
In the faith that looks through death,
In years that bring the philosophic mind.

And O ye fountains, meadows, hills, and groves,
Think not of any severing of our loves!
Yet in my heart of hearts I feel your might:
I only have relinquished one delight
To live beneath your more habitual sway.
I love the brooks which down their channels fret,
Even more than when I tripped lightly as they;
The innocent brightness of a new-born day
Is lovely yet;
The clouds that gather round the setting sun
Do take a sober colouring from an eye
That hath kept watch o'er man's mortality;
Another race hath been, and other palms are won.
Thanks to the human heart by which we live,
Thanks to its tenderness, its joys, and fears,
To me the meanest flower that blows can give
Thoughts that do often lie too deep for tears.

OBSERVATIONS

PREFIXED TO THE SECOND EDITION OF SEVERAL OF THE FOREGOING POEMS, PUBLISHED UNDER THE TITLE OF "LYRICAL BALLADS."

SEVERAL of these poems have already been submitted to general perusal. They were published, as an experiment, which, I hoped, might be of some use to ascertain, how far, by fitting to metrical arrangement a selection of the real language of men in a state of vivid sensation, that sort of pleasure and that quantity of pleasure may be imparted, which a poet may rationally endeavour to impart.

I had formed no very inaccurate estimate of the probable effect of those poems: I flattered myself that they who should be pleased with them would read them with more than common pleasure; and, on the other hand, I was well aware, that by those who should dislike them, they would be read with more than common dislike. The result has differed from my expectation in this only, that I have pleased a greater number than I ventured to hope I should please.

* * * * * * * * * *

Several of my friends are anxious for the success of these poems from a belief, that, if the views with which they were composed were indeed realised, a class of poetry would be produced well adapted to interest mankind permanently, and not unimportant in the multiplicity, and in the quality of its moral relations: and on this account they have advised me to add a systematic defence of the theory upon which the poems were written. But I was unwilling to undertake the task, because I knew that on this occasion the reader would look coldly upon my arguments, since I might be suspected of having been principally influenced by the selfish and foolish hope of *reasoning* him into an approbation of these particular poems: and I was still more unwilling to undertake the task, because, adequately to display my opinions, and fully to enforce my arguments, would require a space wholly disproportionate to the extent of the work. For to treat the subject with the clearness and coherence of which I believe it susceptible, it would be necessary to give a full account of the present state of the public taste in this country, and to determine how far this taste is healthy or depraved; which, again, could not be determined, without pointing out, in what manner language and the human mind act and react on each other, and without retracing the revolutions, not of literature alone, but likewise of society itself. I have therefore altogether declined to enter regularly upon this defence; yet I am sensible, that there would be some impropriety in abruptly obtruding upon the public, without a few words of introduction, poems so materially different from those upon which general approbation is at present bestowed.

It is supposed, that by the act of writing in verse an author makes a formal engagement that he will gratify certain known habits of association; that he not only thus apprises the reader that certain classes of ideas and expressions will be found in his book, but that others will be carefully excluded. This exponent or symbol held forth by metrical language must in different eras of literature have excited very different expectations, for example, in the age of Catullus, Terence, and Lucretius, and that of Statius or Claudian; and in our own country, in the age of Shakspeare and Beaumont and Fletcher, and that of Donne and Cowley, or Dryden, or Pope. I will not take upon me to determine the exact import of the promise which by the act of writing in verse an author, in the present day, makes to his reader; but I am certain it will appear to many persons that I have not fulfilled the terms of an engagement thus voluntarily contracted. They who have been accustomed to the gaudiness and inane phraseology of many modern writers, if they persist in reading this book to its conclusion, will, no doubt, frequently have to struggle with feelings of strangeness and awkwardness: they will look round for poetry, and will be induced to inquire by what species of courtesy these attempts can be permitted to assume that title. I hope therefore the reader will not censure me, if I attempt to state what I have proposed to myself to perform ; and also (as far as the limits of this notice will permit) to explain some of the chief reasons which have determined me in the choice of my purpose that at least he may be spared any unpleasant feeling of disappointment, and that I myself may be protected from the most dishonourable accusation which can be brought against an author, namely, that of an indolence which prevents him from endeavouring to ascertain what is his duty, or, when his duty is ascertained, prevents him from performing it.

The principal object, then, which I proposed to myself in these poems was to choose incidents and situations from common life, and to relate or describe them, throughout, as far as was possible, in a selection of language really used by men, and, at the same time, to throw over them a certain colouring of imagination, whereby ordinary things should be presented to the mind in an unusual way , and, further, and above all, to make these incidents and situations interesting by tracing in them, truly though not ostentatiously, the primary laws f our nature . chiefly, as far as regards the manner in which we associate ideas in a state of excitement. Low and rustic life was generally chosen, because, in that condition, the essential passions of the heart find a better soil in which they can attain their maturity, are less under restraint, and speak a plainer and more emphatic language ; because in that condition of life our elementary feelings co-exist in a state of greater simplicity, and, consequently, may be more accurately contemplated, and more forcibly communicated ; because the manners of rural life germinate from those elementary feelings , and from the necessary character of rural occupations, are more easily comprehended, and are more durable ; and lastly, because in that condition the passions of men are incorporated with the beautiful and permanent forms of nature. The language, too, of these men is adopted (purified indeed from what appears to be its real defects, from all lasting and rational causes of dislike or disgust) because such men hourly communicate with the best objects from which the best part of language is originally derived ; and because, from their rank in society and the sameness and narrow circle of their intercourse, being less under the influence of social vanity, they convey their feelings and notions in simple and unelaborated expressions. Accordingly, such a language, arising out of repeated experience and regular feelings, is a more permanent and a far more philosophical language than that which is frequently substituted for it by poets, who think that they are conferring honour upon themselves and their art, in proportion as they separate themselves from the sympathies of men, and indulge in arbitrary and capricious habits of expression, in order to furnish food for fickle tastes, and fickle appetites, of their own creation.*

I cannot, however, be insensible to the present outcry against the triviality and meanness, both of thought and language, which some of my contemporaries have occasionally introduced into their metrical compositions ; and I acknowledge that this defect, where it exists, is more dishonourable to the writer's own character than false refinement or arbitrary innovation, though I should contend at the same time, that it is far less pernicious in the sum of its consequences. From such verses the poems in these volumes will be found distinguished at least by one mark of difference, that each of them has a worthy *purpose.* Not that I mean to say, I always began to write with a distinct purpose formally conceived ; but my habits of meditation have so formed my feelings, as that my descriptions of such objects as strongly excite those feelings, will be found to carry along with them a *purpose* If in this opinion I am mistaken, I can have little right to the name of a poet. For all good poetry is the spontaneous overflow of powerful feelings and though this be true, poems to which any value can be attached were never produced on any variety of subjects but by a man, who, being possessed of more than usual organic sensibility, had also thought long and deeply. For our continued influxes of feeling are modified and directed by our thoughts, which are indeed the representatives of all our past feelings ; and, as by contemplating the relation of these general representatives to each other, we discover what is really important to men, so,

* It is worth while here to observe, that the affecting parts of Chaucer are almost always expressed in language pure and universally intelligible even to this day

by the repetition and continuance of this act, our feelings will be connected with important subjects, till at length, if we be originally possessed of much sensibility, such habits of mind will be produced, that, by obeying blindly and mechanically the impulses of those habits, we shall describe objects, and utter sentiments, of such a nature, and in such connection with each other, that the understanding of the being to whom we address ourselves, if he be in a healthful state of association, must necessarily be in some degree enlightened, and his affections ameliorated.

I have said that each of these poems has a purpose. I have also informed my reader what this purpose will be found principally to be: namely, to illustrate the manner in which our feelings and ideas are associated in a state of excitement. But, speaking in language somewhat more appropriate, it is to follow the fluxes and refluxes of the mind when agitated by the great and simple affections of our nature. This object I have endeavoured in these short essays to attain by various means; by tracing the maternal passion through many of its more subtle windings, as in the poems of the Idiot Boy and the Mad Mother; by accompanying the last struggles of a human being, at the approach of death, cleaving in solitude to life and society, as in the poem of the Forsaken Indian; by showing, as in the stanzas entitled "We are Seven," the perplexity and obscurity which in childhood attend our notion of death, or rather our utter inability to admit that notion; or by displaying the strength of fraternal, or, to speak more philosophically, of moral attachment when early associated with the great and beautiful objects of nature, as in "The Brothers;" or, as in the incident of Simon Lee, by placing my reader in the way of receiving from ordinary moral sensations another and more salutary impression than we are accustomed to receive from them. It has also been part of my general purpose to attempt to sketch characters under the influence of less impassioned feelings, as in the Two April Mornings, The Fountain, The Old Man Travelling, The Two Thieves, etc., characters of which the elements are simple, belonging rather to nature than to manners, such as exist now, and will probably always exist, and which from their constitution may be distinctly and profitably contemplated. I will not abuse the indulgence of my reader by dwelling longer upon this subject; but it is proper that I should mention one other circumstance which distinguishes these poems from the popular poetry of the day; it is this, that the feeling therein developed gives importance to the action and situation, and not the action and situation to the feeling. My meaning will be rendered perfectly intelligible by referring my reader to the poems entitled Poor Susan and the Childless Father, particularly to the last stanza of the latter poem.

I will not suffer a sense of false modesty to prevent me from asserting, that I point my reader's attention to this mark of distinction, far less for the sake of these particular poems than from the general importance of the subject. The subject is indeed important! For the human mind is capable of being excited without the application of gross and violent stimulants; and he must have a very faint perception of its beauty and dignity who does not know this, and who does not further know, that one being is elevated above another, in proportion as he possesses this capability. It has therefore appeared to me, that to endeavour to produce or enlarge this capability is one of the best services in which, at any period, a writer can be engaged; but this service, excellent at all times, is especially so at the present day. For a multitude of causes, unknown to former times, are now acting with a combined force to blunt the discriminating powers of the mind, and unfitting it for all voluntary exertion, to reduce it to a state of almost savage torpor. The most effective of these causes are the great national events which are daily taking place, and the increasing accumulation of men in cities, where the uniformity of their occupation produces a craving for extraordinary incident, which the rapid communication of intelligence hourly gratifies. To this tendency of life and manners the literature and theatrical exhibitions of the country have conformed themselves. The invaluable works of our elder writers, I had almost said the works of Shakspeare and Milton, are driven into neglect by frantic novels, sickly and stupid German tragedies, and deluges of idle and extravagant stories in verse.—When I think upon this degrading thirst after outrageous stimulation, I am almost ashamed to have spoken of the feeble effort with which I have endeavoured to counteract it; and, reflecting upon the magnitude of the general evil, I shall be oppressed with no dishonourable melancholy, had

I not a deep impression of certain inherent and indestructible qualities of the human mind, and likewise of certain powers in the great and permanent objects that act upon it, which are equally inherent and indestructible ; and did I not further add to this impression a belief, that the time is approaching when the evil will be systematically opposed, by men of greater powers, and with far more distinguished success.

Having dwelt thus long on the subjects and aim of these poems, I shall request the reader's permission to apprise him of a few circumstances relating to their *style*, in order, among other reasons, that I may not be censured for not having performed what I never attempted. The reader will find that personifications of abstract ideas rarely occur in these volumes ; and, I hope, are utterly rejected, as an ordinary device to elevate the style, and raise it above prose. I have proposed to myself to intimate, and, as far as is possible, to adopt the very language of men ; and assuredly such personifications do not make any natural or regular part of that language. They are, indeed, a figure of speech occasionally prompted by passion, and I have made use of them as such ; but I have endeavoured utterly to reject them as a mechanical device of style, or as a family language which writers in metre seem to lay claim to by prescription. I have wished to keep my reader in the company of flesh and blood, persuaded that by so doing I shall interest him. I am, however, well aware that others who pursue a different track may interest him likewise ; I do not interfere with their claim, I only wish to prefer a different claim of my own. There will also be found in these pieces little of what is usually called poetic diction ; I have taken as much pains to avoid it as others ordinarily take to produce it ; this I have done for the reason already alleged, to bring my language near to the language of men, and further, because the pleasure which I have proposed to myself to impart, is of a kind very different from that which is supposed by many persons to be the proper object of poetry. I do not know how, without being culpably particular, I can give my reader a more exact notion of the style in which I wished these poems to be written, than by informing him that I have at all times endeavoured to look steadily at my subject, consequently, I hope that there is in these poems little falsehood of description, and that my ideas are expressed in language fitted to their respective importance. Something I must have gained by this practice, as it is friendly to one property of all good poetry, namely, good sense ; but it has necessarily cut me off from a large portion of phrases and figures of speech which from father to son have long been regarded as the common inheritance of poets. I have also thought it expedient to restrict myself still further, having abstained from the use of many expressions, in themselves proper and beautiful, but which have been foolishly repeated by bad poets, till such feelings of disgust are connected with them as it is scarcely possible by any art of association to overpower.

If in a poem there should be found a series of lines, or even a single line, in which the language, though naturally arranged, and according to the strict laws of metre, does not differ from that of prose, there is a numerous class of critics, who, when they stumble upon these prosaisms, as they call them, imagine that they have made a notable discovery, and exult over the poet as over a man ignorant of his own profession. Now, these men would establish a canon of criticism which the reader will conclude he must utterly reject, if he wishes to be pleased with these pieces. And it would be a most easy task to prove to him, that not only the language of a large portion of every good poem, even of the most elevated character, must necessarily, except with reference to the metre, in no respect differ from that of good prose, but likewise that some of the most interesting parts of the best poems will be found to be strictly the language of prose, when prose is well written. The truth of this assertion might be demonstrated by innumerable passages from almost all the poetical writings, even of Milton himself. I have not space for much quotation ; but, to illustrate the subject in a general manner, I will here adduce a short composition of Gray, who was at the head of those who, by their reasonings, have attempted to widen the space of separation betwixt prose and metrical composition, and was more than any other man curiously elaborate in the structure of his own poetic diction :—

"In vain to me the smiling mornings shine,
And reddening Phœbus lifts his golden fire :

The birds, in vain their amorous descant join,
Or cheerful fields resume their green attire.
These ears, alas! for other notes repine;
A different object do these eyes require;
My lonely anguish melts no heart but mine;
And in my breast the imperfect joys expire:
Yet morning smiles the busy race to cheer,
And new-born pleasure brings to happier men;
The fields to all their wonted tribute bear;
To warm their little loves the birds complain,
I fruitless mourn to him that cannot hear,
And weep the more because I weep in vain."

It will easily be perceived, that the only part of this sonnet which is of any value is the lines printed in italics: it is equally obvious, that, except in the rhyme, and in the use of the single word "fruitless" for fruitlessly, which is so far a defect, the language of these lines does in no respect differ from that of prose.

By the foregoing quotation I have shown that the language of prose may yet be well adapted to poetry; and I have previously asserted, that a large portion of the language of every good poem can in no respect differ from that of good prose. I will go further. I do not doubt that it may be safely affirmed, that there neither is, nor can be, any essential difference between the language of prose and metrical composition. We are fond of tracing the resemblance between poetry and painting, and, accordingly, we call them sisters: but where shall we find bonds of connexion sufficiently strict to typify the affinity betwixt metrical and prose composition? They both speak by and to the same organs; the bodies in which both of them are clothed may be said to be of the same substance, their affections are kindred, and almost identical, not necessarily differing even in degree; poetry* sheds no tears "such as angels weep," but natural and human tears; she can boast of no celestial ichor that distinguishes her vital juices from those of prose; the same human blood circulates through the veins of them both.

If it be affirmed that rhyme and metrical arrangement of themselves constitute a distinction which overturns what I have been saying on the strict affinity of metrical language with that of prose, and paves the way for other artificial distinctions which the mind voluntarily admits, I answer that the language of such poetry as I am recommending is, as far as is possible, a selection of the language really spoken by men; that this selection, wherever it is made with true taste and feeling, will of itself form a distinction far greater than would at first be imagined, and will entirely separate the composition from the vulgarity and meanness of ordinary life; and, if metre be superadded thereto, I believe that a dissimilitude will be produced altogether sufficient for the gratification of a rational mind. What other distinction would we have? Whence is it to come? And where is it to exist? Not surely, where the poet speaks through the mouths of his characters: it cannot be necessary here, either for elevation of style, or any of its supposed ornaments: for if the poet's subject be judiciously chosen, it will naturally, and upon fit occasion, lead him to passions the language of which, if selected truly and judiciously, must necessarily be dignified and variegated, and alive with metaphors and figures. I forbear to speak of an incongruity which would shock the intelligent reader, should the poet interweave any foreign splendour of his own with that which the passion naturally suggests: it is sufficient to say that such addition is unnecessary. And, surely, it is more probable that those passages, which with propriety abound with metaphors and figures, will have their due effect, if, upon other occasions where the passions are of a milder character, the style also be subdued and temperate.

But, as the pleasure which I hope to give by the poems I now present to the reader must depend entirely on just notions upon this subject, and, as it is in itself of the

---

* I here use the word "poetry" (though against my own judgment) as opposed to the word prose, and synonymous with metrical composition. But much confusion has been introduced into criticism by this contradistinction of poetry and prose, instead of the more philosophical one of poetry and matter of fact, or science. The only strict antithesis to prose is metre: nor is this, in truth, a *strict* antithesis; because lines and passages of metre so naturally occur in writing prose, that it would be scarcely possible to avoid them, even were it desirable.

highest importance to our taste and moral feelings, I cannot content myself with these detached remarks. And if, in what I am about to say, it shall appear to some that my labour is unnecessary, and that I am like a m .n fighting a battle without enemies, I would remind such persons, that, whatever may be the language outwardly holden by men, a practical faith in the opinions which I am wishing to establish is almost unknown. If my conclusions are admitted, and carried as far as they must be carried if admitted at all, our judgments concerning the works of the greatest poets both ancient and modern will be far different from what they are at present, both when we praise, and when we censure: and our moral feelings influencing and influenced by these judgments will, I believe, be corrected and purified.

Taking up the subject, then, upon general grounds, I ask what is meant by the word poet? What is a poet? To whom does he address himself? And what language is to be expected from him? He is a man speaking to men: a man, it is true, endued with more lively sensibility, more enthusiasm and tenderness, who has a greater knowledge of human nature, and a more comprehensive soul, than are supposed to be common among mankind; a man pleased with his own passions and volitions, and who rejoices more than other men in the spirit of life that is in him; delighting to ntemplate similar volitions and passions as manifested in the goings-on of the universe, and habitually impelled to create them where he does not find them. To these qualities he has added, a disposition to be affected more than other men by absent things as if they were present; and ability f conjuring up in himself passions, which are indeed far from being the same as thos produced by real events, yet (especially in those parts of the general sympathy which are pleasing and delightful) do more nearly resemble the passions produced by real events, than anything which, from the motions of their own minds merely, other men are accustomed to feel in themselves; whence, and from practice, he has acquired a greater readiness and power in expressing what he thinks and feels, and especially those thoughts and feelings which, by his own choice, or from the structure of his own mind, arise in him without immediate external excitement.

But, whatever portion of this faculty we may suppose even the greatest poet to possess, there cannot be a doubt but that the language which it wi" suggest to him, must, in liveliness and truth, fall far short of that which is uttered by men in real life, under the actual pressure of those passions, certain shadows of which the poet thus produces, or feels to be produced, in himself.

However exalted a notion we would wish to cherish of the character of a poet, it is obvious, that, while he describ s and imitates passions, his situation is altogether slavish and mechanical, compared with the freedom and power of real and substantial action and suffering. So that it will be the wish of the poet to bring his feelings near to those of the persons whose feelings he describes, nay, for short spaces of time, perhaps to let himself slip into an entire delusion, and even confound and identify his own feelings with theirs; modifying only the language which is thus suggested to him by a considera- tion that he describes for a particular purpose, that of giving pleasure. Here then, he will apply the principle on which I have so much insisted, namely, that of selection; on this he will depend for removing what would otherwise be painful or disgusting in the passion; he will feel that there is no necessity to trick out or to elevate nature · and the more industriously he applies this principle, the deeper will be his faith that no words, which *his* fanc r imagination can suggest, will be to be compared with those which are the emanat s of reality and truth.

But it may be said by those who do not object to the general spirit of these remarks, that, as it is impossible for the poet to produce upon all occasions language as exqui- sitely fitted for the passion as that which the real passion itself suggests, it is proper that, he should consider himself as in the situation of a translat r, who deems himself justified when he substitutes excellences of another kind for those which are unattainable by him; and endeavours occasionally to surpass his original, in order to make some amends for the general inferiority to which he feels that he must submit. But this would be to encourage idleness and unmanly despair. Further, it is the language of men who speak of what they do not understand; who talk of poetry as of a matter of amusement and idle pleasure; who will converse with us as gravely about a *taste* for poetry, as they express it, as if it were a thing as indifferent as a taste for rope-dancing, or Frontinac, or sherry. Aristotle, I have been told, hath said, that poetry is the most philosophic of all writing: it is so: its object is truth, not individual and local, but general, and operative; not standing upon external testimony, but carried alive into the heart by passion; truth which is its own testimony, which gives strength and divinity to the tribunal to which it appeals, and receives them from the same tribunal. Poetry is the image of man and nature. The obstacles which stand in the way of the fidelity of the biographer and historian, and of their consequent utility, are incalculably greater than those which are to be encountered by the poet who has an adequate notion of the dignity of his art. The poet writes under one restriction only, namely, that of the necessity of giving immediate pleasure to a human being possessed of that information which may be expected from him, not as a lawyer, a physician, a mariner, an astronomer, or a natural philosopher, but as a man. Except this one restriction, there is no object standing between the poet and the image of things; between this, and the biographer and historian there are a thousand.

Nor let this necessity of producing immediate pleasure be considered as a degradation of the poet's art. It is far otherwise. It is an acknowledgment of the beauty of the universe, an acknowledgment the more sincere, because it is not formal, but indirect; it is a task light and easy to him who looks at the world in the spirit of love: further, it is an homage paid to the native and naked dignity of man, to the grand elementary principle of pleasure, by which he knows, and feels, and lives, and moves. We have no sympathy but what is propagated by pleasure: I would not be misunderstood: but wherever we sympathise with pain, it will be found that the sympathy is produced and carried on by subtle combinations with pleasure. We have no knowledge, that is, no general principles drawn from the contemplation of particular facts, but what has been built up by pleasure, and exists in us by pleasure alone. The man of science, the chemist and mathematician, whatever difficulties and disgusts they may have had to struggle with, know and feel this. However painful may be the objects with which the anatomist's knowledge is connected he feels that his knowledge is pleasure; and where he has no pleasure he has no knowledge. What then does the poet? He considers man and the objects that surround him as acting and re-acting upon each other, so as to produce an infinite complexity of pain and pleasure; he considers man in his own nature and in his ordinary life as contemplating this with a certain quantity of immediate knowledge, with certain convictions, intuitions, and deductions, which by habit become of the nature of intuitions; he considers him as looking upon this complex scene of ideas and sensations, and finding everywhere objects that immediately excite in him sympathies which, from the necessities of his nature, are accompanied by an overbalance of enjoyment.

To this knowledge which all men carry about with them, and to these sympathies in which, without any other discipline than that of our daily life, we are fitted to take delight, the poet principally directs his attention. He considers man and nature as essentially adapted to each other, and the mind of man as naturally the mirror of the fairest and most interesting qualities of nature. And thus the poet, prompted by this feeling of pleasure which accompanies him through the whole course of his studies, converses with general nature with affections akin to those, which, through labour and length of time, the man of science has raised up in himself, by conversing with those particular parts of nature which are the objects of his studies. The knowledge both of the poet and the man of science is pleasure; but the knowledge of the one cleaves to us as a necessary part of our existence, our natural and inalienable inheritance; the other is a personal and individual acquisition, slow to come to us, and by no habitual and direct sympathy connecting us with our fellow-beings. The man of science seeks truth as a remote and unknown benefactor; he cherishes and loves it in his solitude: the poet, singing a song in which all human beings join with him, rejoices in the presence of truth as our visible friend and hourly companion. Poetry is the breath and finer spirit of all knowledge; it is the impassioned expression which is in the countenance of all science. Emphatically may it be said of the poet, as Shakspeare hath said of man, "that he looks before and after." He is the rock of defence of human nature; an upholder and preserver, carrying everywhere with him relationship and love. In spite of difference of soil and climate, of language and manners, of laws and customs, in spite of things silently gone out of mind, and things violently destroyed, the poet binds together by passion and knowledge the vast empire of human society, as it is spread over the whole earth, and over all time The objects of the poet s thoughts are everywhere ; though the eyes and senses of man are, it is true, his favourite guides, yet he will follow wheresoever he can find n atmosphere of sensation in which to move his wings. Poetry is the first and last of all knowledge—it is as immortal as the heart of man. If the labours of men of science should ever create any material revolution, direct or indirect, in our condition, and in the impressions which we habitually receive, the poet will sleep then no more than at present, but he will be ready to follow the steps of the man of science, not only in those general indirect effects, but he will be at his side, carrying sensation into the midst of the objects of the science itself. The remotest discoveries of the chemist, the botanist, or mineralogist, will be as proper objects of the poet's art as any upon which it can be employed, if the time should ever come when these things shall be familiar to us, and the relations under which they are contemplated by the followers of these respective sciences shall be manifestly and palpably material to us as enjoying and suffering beings. If the time should ever come when what is now called science, thus familiarised to men, shall be ready to put on, as it were, a form of flesh and blood, the poet will lend his divine spirit to aid the transfiguration, and will welcome the being thus produced, as a dear and genuine inmate of the household of man.—It is not, then, to be supposed that any one, who holds that sublime notion of poetry which I have attempted to convey, will break in upon the sanctity and truth of his pictures by transitory and accidental ornaments, and endeavour to excite admiration of himself by arts, the necessity of which must manifestly depend upon the assumed meanness of his subject.

What I have thus far said applies to poetry in general ; but especially to those parts of composition where the poet speaks through the mouths of his characters , and upon this point it appears to have such weight, that I will conclude, there are few persons of good sense, who would not allow that the dramatic parts of composition are defective, in proportion as they deviate from the real language of nature, and are coloured by a diction of the poet's own, either peculiar to him as an individual poet or belonging simply to poets in general, to a body of men who, from the circumstance of their compositions being in metre, it is expected will employ a particular language

It is not, then, in the dramatic parts of composition that we look for this distinction of language ; but still it may be proper and necessary where the poet speaks to us in his own person and character. To this I answer by referring my reader to the description which I have before given of a poet. Among the qualities which I have enumerated as principally conducing to form a poet, is implied nothing differing in kind from other men, but only in degree. The sum of what I have there said is, that the poet is chiefly distinguished from other men by a greater promptness to think and feel without immediate external excitement, and a greater power in expressing such thoughts and feelings as are produced in him in that manner. But these passions and thoughts and feelings are the general passions and thoughts and feelings of men. And with what are they connected? Undoubtedly with our moral sentiments and animal sensations, and with the causes which excite these ; with the operations of the elements, and the appearances of the visible universe with storm and sunshine, with the revolutions of the seasons, with cold and heat, with loss of friends and kindred, with injuries and resentments, gratitude and hope, with fear and sorrow. These, and the like, are the sensations and objects which the poet describes, as they are the sensations of other men, and the objects which interest them. The poet thinks and feels in the spirit of the passions of men. How, then, can his language differ in any material degree from that of all other men who feel vividly and see clearly? It might be *proved* that it is impossible. But supposing that this were not the case, the poet might then be allowed to use a peculiar language when expressing his feelings for his own gratification, or that of men like himself. But poets do not write for poets alone, but for men. Unless therefore we are advocates for that admiration which depends upon ignorance, and that pleasure which arises from hearing what we do not understand, the poet must descend from this supposed height, and, in order to excite rational sympathy, he must express himself as other men express themselves. To this it may be added, that while he is only selecting from the real language of men, or, which amounts to the same thing, composing accurately in the spirit of such selection, he is treading upon safe ground, and we know what we are to expect from him. Our feelings are the same with respect to metre; for, as it may be proper to remind the reader, the distinction of metre is regular and uniform, and not like that which is produced by what is usually called poetic diction,* arbitrary, and subject to infinite caprices upon which no calculation whatever can be made. In the one case, the reader is utterly at the mercy of the poet respecting what imagery or diction he may choose to connect with the passion, whereas, in the other, the metre obeys certain laws, to which the poet and reader both willingly submit because they are certain, and because no interference is made by them with the passion but such as the concurring testimony of ages has shown to heighten and improve the pleasure which coexists with it

It will now be proper to answer an obvious question, namely, Why, professing these opinions, have I written in verse? To this, in addition to such answer as is included in what I have already said, I reply, in the first place, Because, however I may have restricted myself, there is still left open to me what confessedly constitutes the most valuable object of all writing, whether in prose or verse, the great and universal passions of men, the most general and interesting of their occupations, and the entire world of nature, from which I am at liberty to supply myself with endless combinations of forms and imagery. Now, supposing for a moment that whatever is interesting in these objects may be as vividly described in prose, why am I to be condemned, if to such description I have endeavoured to superadd he charm which, by the consent of all nations, is acknowledged to exist in metrical language? To this, by such as are unconvinced by what I have already said, it may be answered that a very small part of the pleasure given by poetry depends upon the metre, and that it is injudicious to write in metre, unless it be accompanied with the other artificial distinctions of style with which metre is usually accompanied, and that, by such deviation, more will be lost from the shock which will thereby be given to the reader's associations than will be counterbalanced by any pleasure which he can derive from the general power of numbers In answer to those who still contend for the necessity of accompanying metre with certain appropriate colours of style in order to the accomplishment of its appropriate end, and who also, in my opinion, greatly underrate the power of metre in itself, it might, perhaps, as far as relates to these poems, have been almost sufficient to observe, that poems are extant, written upon more humble subjects, and in a more naked and simple style than I have aimed at, which poems have continued to give pleasure from generation to generation. Now, if nakedness and simplicity be a defect, the fact here mentioned affords a strong presumption that poems somewhat less naked and simple are capable of affording pleasure at the present day; and, what I wished *chiefly* to attempt, at present, was to justify myself for having written under the impression of this belief

But I might point out various causes why, when the style is manly, and the subject of some importance, words metrically arranged will long continue to impart such a pleasure to mankind as he who is sensible of the extent of that pleasure will be desirous to impart. The end of poetry is to produce excitement in co-existence with an overbalance of pleasure Now, by the supposition, excitement is an unusual and irregular state of the mind; ideas and feelings do not, in that state, succeed each other in accustomed order. But, if the words by which this excitement is produced are in themselves powerful, or the images and feelings have an undue proportion of pain connected with them, there is some danger that the excitement may be carried beyond its proper bounds. Now the co-presence of something regular, something to which the mind has been accustomed in various moods and in a less excited state, cannot but have great efficacy in tempering and restraining the passion by an intertexture of ordinary feeling, and of feeling not strictly and necessarily connected with the passion. This is unquestionably true, and hence, though the opinion will at first appear paradoxical, from the tendency of metre to divest language, in a certain degree, of its reality, and thus to

* See Appendix, page 331

throw a sort of half consciousness of unsubstantial existence over the whole composition, there can be little doubt, but that more pathetic situations and sentiments, that is, those which have a greater proportion of pain connected with them, may be endured in metrical composition, especially in rhyme, than in prose The metre of the old ballads is very artless; yet they contain many passages which would illustrate this opinion, and, I hope, if the poems referred to be attentively perused, similar instances will be found in them. This opinion may be further illustrated by appealing to the reader's own experience of the reluctance with which he comes to the re-perusal of the distressful parts of "Clarissa Harlowe," or the "Gamester" While Shakspeare's writings, in the most pathetic scenes, never acted upon us, as pathetic, beyond the bounds of pleasure—an effect which, in a much greater degree than might at first be imagined, is to be ascribed to small, but continual and regular impulses of pleasurable surprise from the metrical arrangement —On the other hand, (what it must be allowed will much more frequently happen), if th poet's words should be incommensurate with the passion, and inadequate to raise the reader to a height of desirable excitement, then, (unless th poet's choice of his metre has been grossly injudicious,) in the feelings of pleasure which the reader has been accustomed to connect with metre in general, and in the feeling, whether cheerful or melancholy, which he has been accustomed to connect with that particular movement of metre, there will be found something which will greatly contribute to impart passion to the words, and to effect the complex end which the poet proposes to himself.

If I had undertaken a systematic defence of the theory upon which these poems are written, it would have been my duty to develop the various causes upon which the pleasure received from metrical language depends. Among the chief of these causes is to be reckoned a principle which must be well known to those who have made any of the arts the object of accurate reflection; I mean the pleasure which the mind derives from the perception of similitude in dissimilitude. This principle is the great spring of the activity of our minds, and their chief feeder. From this principle the direction of the sexual appetite, and all the passions connected with it, take their origin; it is the life of our ordinary conversation; and upon the accuracy with which similitude in dissimilitude, and dissimilitude in similitude are perceived, depend our taste and our moral feelings. It would not have been a useless employment to have applied this principle to the consideration of metre, and to have shown that metre is hence enabled to afford much pleasure, and to have pointed out in what manner that pleasure is produced. But my limits will not permit me to enter upon this subject, and I must content myself with a general summary

I have said that poetry is the spontaneous overflow of powerful feelings it takes its origin from emotion recollected in tranquillity the emotion is contemplated till, by a species of re-action, the tranquillity gradually disappears, and an emotion, kindred to that which was before the subject of contemplation, is gradually produced, and does itself actually exist in the mind. In this mood successful composition generally begins, and in a mood similar to this it is carried on; but the emotion of whatever kind, and in whatever degree, from various causes, is qualified by various pleasures, so that in describing any passions whatsoever, which are voluntarily described, the mind will, upon the whole, be in a state of enjoyment. Now, if nature be thus cautious in preserving in a state of enjoyment a being thus employed, the poet ought to profit by the lesson thus held forth to him, and ought especially to take care, that, whatever passions he communicates to his reader, those passions, if his reader's mind be sound and vigorous, should always be accompanied with an over-balance of pleasure. Now the music of harmonious metrical language, the sense of difficulty overcome, and the blind association of pleasure which has been previously received from works of rhyme or metre of the same or similar construction, an indistinct perception perpetually renewed of language closely resembling that of real life, and yet, in the circumstance of metre, differing from it so widely—all these imperceptibly make up a complex feeling of delight, which is of the most important use in tempering the painful feeling which will always be found intermingled with powerful descriptions of the deeper passions. This effect is always produced in pathetic and impassioned poetry; while, in lighter compositions, the ease and gracefulness with which the poet manages his numbers are themselves confessedly a principal source of the gratification of the reader. I might, perhaps, include all which it is *necessary* to say upon this subject, by affirming what few persons will deny, that, of two descriptions either of passions, manners, or characters, each of them equally well executed, the one in prose and the other in verse, the verse will be read a hundred times where the prose is read once. We see that Pope, by the power of verse alone, has contrived to render the plainest common sense interesting, and even frequently to invest it with the appearance of passion. In consequence of these convictions I related in metre the tale of Goody Blake and Harry Gill, which is one of the rudest of this collection. I wished to draw attention to the truth, that the power of the human imagination is sufficient to produce such changes even in our physical nature as might almost appear miraculous. The truth is an important one; the fact (for it is a *fact*) is a valuable illustration of it: and I have the satisfaction of knowing that it has been communicated to many hundreds of people who would never have heard of it, had it not been narrated as a ballad, and in a more impressive metre than is usual in ballads.

Having thus explained a few of the reasons why I have written in verse, and why I have chosen subjects from common life, and endeavoured to bring my language near to the real language of men, if I have been too minute in pleading my own cause, I have at the same time been treating a subject of general interest; and it is for this reason that I request the reader's permission to add a few words with reference solely to these particular poems, and to some defects which will probably be found in them. I am sensible that my associations must have sometimes been particular instead of general, and that, consequently, giving to things a false importance, sometimes from diseased impulses, I may have written upon unworthy subjects; but I am less apprehensive on this account, than that my language may frequently have suffered from those arbitrary connexions of feelings and ideas with particular words and phrases, from which no man can altogether protect himself. Hence I have no doubt, that, in some instances, feelings, even of the ludicrous, may be given to my readers by expressions which appeared to me tender and pathetic. Such faulty expressions, were I convinced they were faulty at present, and that they must necessarily continue to be so, I would willingly take all reasonable pains to correct. But it is dangerous to make these alterations on the simple authority of a few individuals, or even of certain classes of men; for where the understanding of an author is not convinced, or his feelings altered, this cannot be done without great injury to himself: for his own feelings are his stay and support; and, if he sets them aside in one instance, he may be induced to repeat this act till his mind loses all confidence in itself, and becomes utterly debilitated. To this it may be added, that the reader ought never to forget that he is himself exposed to the same errors as the poet, and, perhaps, in a much greater degree: for there can be no presumption in saying, that it is not probable he will be so well acquainted with the various stages of meaning through which words have passed, or with the fickleness or stability or the relations of particular ideas to each other; and, above all, since he is so much less interested in the subject, he may decide lightly and carelessly.

Long as I have detained my reader, I hope he will permit me to caution him against a mode of false criticism which has been applied to poetry, in which the language closely resembles that of life and nature. Such verses have been triumphed over in parodies of which Dr. Johnson's stanza is a fair specimen.

> "I put my hat upon my head
> And walked into the Strand,
> And there I met another man
> Whose hat was in his hand."

Immediately under these lines I will place one of the most justly-admired stanzas of the "Babes in the Wood."

> "These pretty babes with hand in hand
> Went wandering up and down;
> But never more they saw the man
> Approaching from the town."

In both these stanzas the words, and the order of the words, in no respect differ from the most unimpassioned conversation. There are words in both, for example, "the Strand," and "the town," connected with none but the most familiar ideas; yet the one stanza we admit as admirable, and the other as a fair example of the superlatively contemptible. Whence arises this difference? Not from the metre, not from the language, not from the order of the words; but the *matter* expressed in Dr. Johnson's stanza is contemptible The proper method of treating trivial and simple verses, to which Dr. Johnson's stanza would be a fair parallelism, is not to say, This is a bad kind of poetry, or, This is not poetry, but this wants sense, it is neither interesting in itself, nor can it *lead* to anything interesting; the images neither originate in that sane state of feeling which arises out of thought, nor can they excite thought or feeling in the reader. This is the only sensible manner of dealing with such verses. Why trouble yourself about the species till you have previously decided upon the genus? Why take pains to prove that an ape is not a Newton, when it is self-evident that he is not a man?

I have one request to make of my reader, which is, that in judging these poems he would decide by his own feelings genuinely, and not by reflection upon what will probably be the judgment of others. How common is it to hear a person say, "I myself do not object to this style of composition, or this or that expression, but, to such and such classes of people, it will appear mean or ludicrous!" This mode of criticism, so destructive o. all sound unadulterated judgment, is almost universal · I have therefore to request, that the reader will abide independently, by his own feelings, and that, if he finds himself affected, he would not suffer such conjectures to interfere with his pleasure.

If an author, by any single composition, has impressed us with respect for his talents, it is useful to consider this as affording a presumption, that on other occasions where we have been displeased, he, nevertheless, may not have written ill or absurdly; and, further, to give him so much credit for this one composition as may induce us to review what has displeased us, with more care than we should otherwise have bestowed upon it. This is not only an act of justice, but, in our decisions upon poetry especially, may conduce, in a high degree, to the improvement of our own taste. for an *accurate* taste in poetry, and in all the other arts, as Sir Joshua Reynolds has observed, is an *acquired* talent, which can only be produced by thought and a long-continued intercourse with the best models of composition. This is mentioned, not with so ridiculous a purpose as to prevent the most inexperienced reader from judging for himself (I have already said that I wish him to judge for himself), but merely to temper the rashness of decision, and to suggest, that, if poetry be a subject on which much time has not been bestowed, the judgment may be erroneous; and that, in many cases, it necessarily will be so

I know that nothing would have so effectually contributed to further the end which I have in view, as to have shown of what kind the pleasure is, and how that pleasure is produced, which is confessedly produced by metrical composition essentially different from that which I have here endeavoured to recommend: for the reader will say that he has been pleased by such composition; and what can I do more for him? The power of any art is limited, and he will suspect, that, if I propose to furnish him with new friends, it is only upon condition of his abandoning his old friends. Besides, as I have said, the reader is himself conscious of the pleasure which he has received from such composition, composition to which he has peculiarly attached the endearing name of poetry; and all men feel an habitual gratitude, and something of an honourable bigotry for the objects which have long continued to please them; we not only wish to be pleased, but to be pleased in that particular way in which we have been accustomed to be pleased. There is a host of arguments in these feelings, and I should be the less able to combat them successfully, as I am willing to allow, that, in order entirely to enjoy the poetry which I am recommending, it would be necessary to give up much of what is ordinarily enjoyed. But, would my limits have permitted me to point out how this pleasure is produced, I might have removed many obstacles, and assisted my reader in perceiving that the powers of language are not so limited as he may suppose; and that it is possible for poetry to give other enjoyments, of a purer, more lasting, and more exquisite nature. This part of my subject I have not altogether neglected; but it has been less my present aim to prove, that the interest excited by some other kind of poetry is less vivid, and less worthy of the nobler powers of the mind, than to offer reasons for presuming, that, if the object which I have proposed to myself were adequately attained, a species of poetry would be produced, which is genuine poetry; in its nature well adapted to interest mankind permanently, and likewise important in the multiplicity and quality of its moral relations.

From what has been said, and from a perusal of the poems, the reader will be able clearly to perceive the object which I have proposed to myself. he will determine how far I have attained this object, and, what is a much more important question, whether it be worth attaining: and upon the decision of these two questions will rest my claim to the approbation of the public.

APPENDIX.

ON POETIC DICTION.

As, perhaps, I have no right to expect from a reader of observations on a volume of poems that attentive perusal without which it is impossible, imperfectly as I have been compelled to express my meaning, that what is there said should, throughout, be fully understood, I am the more anxious to give an exact notion of the sense in which I use the phrase *poetic diction;* and for this purpose I will here add a few words concerning the origin of the phraseology which I have condemned under that name.

The earliest poets of all nations generally wrote from passion excited by real events; they wrote naturally, and as men · feeling powerfully as they did, their language was daring, and figurative. In succeeding times, poets, and men ambitious of the fame of poets, perceiving the influence of such language, and desirous of producing the same effect without having the same animating passion, set themselves to a mechanical adoption of these figures of speech, and made use of them, sometimes with propriety, but much more frequently applied them to feelings and ideas with which they had no natural connexion whatsoever. A language was thus insensibly produced, differing materially from the real language of men in *any situation.* The reader or hearer of this distorted language found himself in a perturbed and unusual state of mind; when affected by the genuine language of passion he had been in a perturbed and unusual state of mind also: in both cases he was willing that his common judgment and understanding should be laid asleep, and he had no instinctive and infallible perception of the true to make him reject the false; the one served as a passport for the other. The agitation and confusion of mind were in both cases delightful, and no wonder if he confounded the one with the other, and believed them both to be produced by the same, or similar causes. Besides, the poet spake to him in the character of a man to be looked up to, a man of genius and authority. Thus, and from a variety of other causes, this distorted language was received with admiration: and poets, it is probable, who had before contented themselves for the most part with misapplying only expressions which at first had been dictated by real passion, carried the abuse still further, and introduced phrases composed apparently in the spirit of the original figurative language of passion, yet altogether of their own invention, and distinguished by various degrees of wanton deviation from good sense and nature.

It is indeed true that the language of the earliest poets was felt to differ materially from ordinary language, because it was the language of extraordinary occasions, but it was really spoken by men—language which the poet himself had uttered when he had been affected by the events which he described, or which he had heard uttered by those around him. To this language it is probable that metre of some sort or other was early superadded. This separated the genuine language of poetry still further from common life, so that whoever read or heard poems of these earliest poets felt himself moved in a way in which he had not been accustomed to be moved in real life, and by causes manifestly different from those which acted upon him in real life. This was the great temptation to all the corruptions which have followed: under the protection of this feeling succeeding poets constructed a phraseology which had one thing, it is true, in common with the genuine language of poetry, namely, that it was not heard in ordinary conversation; that it was unusual. But the first poets, as I have said, spake a language which, though unusual, was still the language of men. This circumstance, however, was disregarded by their successors, they found that they could please by easier means: they became proud of a language which they themselves had invented, and which was uttered only by themselves; and, with the spirit of a fraternity, they arrogated it to themselves as their own. In process of time metre became a symbol or promise of this unusual language, and whoever took upon him to write in metre, according as he possessed more or less of true poetic genius, introduced less or more of this adulterated phraseology into his compositions, and the true and the false became so inseparably interwoven that the taste of men was gradually perverted; and this language was received as a natural language: and at length, by the influence of books upon men, did to a certain degree really become so. Abuses of this kind were imported from one nation to another, and with the progress of refinement this diction became daily more and more corrupt, thrusting out of sight the plain humanities of nature by a motley masquerade of tricks, quaintness, hieroglyphics, and enigmas.

It would be highly interesting to point out the causes of the pleasure given by this extravagant and absurd language; but this is not the place; it depends upon a great variety of causes, but upon none perhaps more than its influence in impressing a notion of the peculiarity and exaltation of the poet's character, and in flattering the reader's self-love by bringing him nearer to a sympathy with that character; an effect which is accomplished by unsettling ordinary habits of thinking, and thus assisting the reader to approach to that perturbed and dizzy state of mind in which if he does not find himself, he imagines that he is *balked* of a peculiar enjoyment which poetry can and ought to bestow.

The sonnet which I have quoted from Gray, in the preface, except the lines printed in Italics, consists of little else but this diction, though not of the worst kind; and, indeed, if I may be permitted to say so, it is far too common in the best writers, both ancient and modern. Perhaps I can in no way, by positive example, more easily give my reader a notion of what I mean by the phrase *poetic diction*, than by referring him to a comparison between the metrical paraphrase which we have of passages in the Old and New Testament, and those passages as they exist in our common translation. See Pope's "Messiah" throughout; Prior's "Did sweeter sounds adorn my flowing tongue," etc. etc. "Though I speak with the tongues of men and of angels," etc. etc. See 1st Corinthians, chapter xiii. By way of immediate example, take the following of Dr Johnson:—

"Turn on the prudent ant thy heedless eyes,
Observe her labours, sluggard, and be wise;
No stern command, no monitory voice,
Prescribes her duties, or directs her choice;
Yet, timely provident, she hastes away
To snatch the blessings of a plenteous day;
When fruitful summer loads the teeming plain,
She crops the harvest and she stores the grain.
How long shall sloth usurp thy useless hours,
Unnerve thy vigour, and enchain thy powers?
While artful shades thy downy couch inclose,
And soft solicitation courts repose,
Amidst the drowsy charms of dull delight,
Year chases year with unremitted flight,
Till want now following, fraudulent and slow,
Shall spring to seize thee, like an ambushed foe."

From this hubbub of words pass to the original. "Go to the ant, thou sluggard, consider her ways, and be wise: which having no guide, overseer, or ruler, provideth her meat in the summer, and gathereth her food in the harvest. How long wilt thou sleep, O sluggard? Wilt thou arise out of thy sleep? Yet a little sleep, a little slumber, a little folding of the hands to sleep. So shall thy poverty come as one that travaileth, and thy want as an armed man."—Proverbs vi. 6—11.

One more quotation, and I have done. It is from Cowper's verses, supposed to be written by Alexander Selkirk:—

"Religion! what treasure untold
Resides in that heavenly word?
More precious than silver and gold,
Or all that this earth can afford.

"But the sound of the church-going bell
These valleys and rocks never heard,
Ne'er sighed at the sound of a knell,
Or smiled when a sabbath appeared

"Ye winds, that have made me your sport
Convey to this desolate shore
Some cordial endearing report
Of a land I must visit no more.

"My friends, do they now and then send
A wish or a thought after me?
Oh, tell me I yet have a friend,
Though a friend I am never to see."

I have quoted this passage as an instance of three different styles of composition. The first four lines are poorly expressed; some critics would call the language prosaic; the fact is, it would be bad prose, so bad, that it is scarcely worse in metre. The epithet "church-going" applied to a bell, and that by so chaste a writer as Cowper, is an instance of the strange abuses which poets have introduced into their language till they and their readers take them as matters of course, if they do not single them out expressly as objects of admiration. The two lines, "Ne'er sighed at the sound," etc., are, in my opinion, an instance of the language of passion wrested from its proper use, and, from the mere circumstance of the composition being in metre, applied upon an occasion that does not justify such violent expressions; and I should condemn the passage, though perhaps few readers will agree with me, as vicious poetic diction. The last stanza is throughout admirably expressed: it would be equally good whether in prose or verse, except that the reader has an exquisite pleasure in seeing such natural language so naturally connected with metre. The beauty of this stanza tempts me to conclude with a principle which ought never to be lost sight of,—namely, that in works of imagination and sentiment, in proportion as ideas and feelings are valuable, whether the composition be in prose or in verse, they require and exact one and the same language. Metre is but adventitious to composition, and the phraseology for which that passport is necessary, even where it is graceful at all, will be little valued by the judicious.

The Excursion.

TO THE RIGHT HONOURABLE

WILLIAM, EARL OF LONSDALE, K.G., etc. etc.

OFT, through thy fair domains, illustrious peer!
In youth I roamed, on youthful pleasures bent;
And mused in rocky cell or sylvan tent,
Beside swift-flowing Lowther's current clear.
Now, by thy care befriended, I appear
Before thee, Lonsdale, and this work present,
A token (may it prove a monument!)
Of high respect and gratitude sincere.
Gladly would I have waited till my task
Had reached its close; but life is insecure,
And hope full oft fallacious as a dream:
Therefore, for what is here produced I ask
Thy favour; trusting that thou wilt not deem
The offering, though imperfect, premature.

WILLIAM WORDSWORTH.

Rydal Mount, Westmoreland, *July* 29, 1814.

PREFACE TO THE EDITION OF 1814.

THE title announces that this is only a portion of a poem; and the reader must be here apprised that it belongs to the second part of a long and laborious work, which is to consist of three parts.—The author will candidly acknowledge that, if the first of these had been completed, and in such a manner as to satisfy his own mind, he should have preferred the natural order of publication, and have given that to the world first; but, as the second division of the work was designed to refer more to passing events, and to an existing state of things, than the others were meant to, more continuous exertion was naturally bestowed upon it, and greater progress made here than in the rest of the poem; and as this part does not depend upon the preceding, to a degree which will materially injure its own peculiar interest, the author, complying with the earnest entreaties of some valued friends, presents the following pages to the public.

It may be proper to state whence the poem, of which "The Excursion" is a part, derives its title of "The Recluse."—Several years ago, when the author retired to his native mountains, with the hope of being enabled to construct a literary work that might live, it was a reasonable thing that he should take a review of his own mind, and examine how far nature and education had qualified him for such employment. As subsidiary to this preparation, he undertook to record, in verse, the origin and progress of his own powers, as far as he was acquainted with them. That work, addressed to a dear friend, most distinguished for his knowledge and genius, and to whom the author's intellect is deeply indebted, has been long finished; and the result of the investigation which gave rise to it was a determination to compose a philosophical poem, containing views of man, nature, and society · and to be entitled, "The Recluse;" as having for its principal subject the sensations and opinions of a poet living in retirement. The preparatory poem is biographical, and conducts the history of the author's mind to the point when he was emboldened to hope that his faculties were sufficiently matured for entering upon the arduous labour which he had proposed to himself; and the two works have the same kind of relation to each other, if he may so express himself, as the ante-chapel has to the body of a Gothic church. Continuing this allusion, he may be permitted to add, that his minor pieces, which have been long before the public, being now properly arranged, will be found by the attentive reader to have such connexion with the main work as may give them claim to be likened to the little cells, oratories, and sepulchral recesses, ordinarily included in those edifices.

The author would not have deemed himself justified in saying, upon this occasion, so much of performances either unfinished, or unpublished, if he had not thought that the labour bestowed by him upon what he has heretofore and now laid before the public, entitled him to candid attention for such a statement as he thinks necessary to throw light upon his endeavours to please, and he would hope, to benefit his countrymen.—Nothing further need be added, than that the first and third parts of "The Recluse" will consist chiefly of meditations in the author's own person; and that in the intermediate part ("The Excursion") the intervention of the characters speaking is employed, and something of a dramatic form is adopted.

It is not the author's intention formally to announce a system: it was more animating to him to proceed in a different course; and if he shall succeed in conveying to the mind clear thoughts, lively images, and strong feelings, the reader will have no difficulty in extracting the system for himself. And in the meantime the following passage taken from the conclusion of the first book of "The Recluse," may be acceptable as a kind of prospectus of the design and scope of the whole poem:—

"On man, on nature, and on human life
Musing in solitude, I oft perceive
Fair trains of imagery before me rise,
Accompanied by feelings of delight
Pure, or with no unpleasing sadness mixed;
And I am conscious of affecting thoughts
And dear remembrances whose presence soothes
Or elevates the mind, intent to weigh
The good and evil of our mortal state.
To these emotions, whencesoe'er they come,
Whether from breath of outward circumstance,
Or from the soul—an impulse to herself,
I would give utterance in numerous verse.
Of truth, of grandeur, beauty, love, and hope—
And melancholy fear subdued by faith;
Of blessed consolations in distress;
Of moral strength, and intellectual power;
Of joy in widest commonalty spread;
Of the individual mind that keeps her own
Inviolate retirement, subject there
To conscience only, the law supreme
Of that Intelligence which governs all;
I sing—'fit audience let me find though few!'

"So prayed, more gaining than he asked, the bard.
Holiest of men.—Urania, I shall need
Thy guidance, or a greater muse, if such
Descend to earth or dwell in highest heaven,

For I must tread on shadowy ground, must sink
Deep—and, aloft ascending, breathe in worlds
To which the heaven of heavens is but a veil.
All strength—all terror, single, or in bands,
That ever was put forth in personal form;
Jehovah—with his thunder, and the choir
Of shouting angels, and the empyreal thrones—
I pass them unalarmed. Not Chaos, not
The darkest pit of lowest Erebus,
Nor aught of blinder vacancy—scooped out
By help of dreams, can breed such fear and awe
As fall upon us often when we look
Into our minds, into the mind of man,
My haunt, and the main region of my song.
Beauty—a living presence of the earth,
Surpassing the most fair ideal forms
Which craft of delicate spirits hath composed
From earth's materials—waits upon my steps;
Pitches her tents before me as I move,
An hourly neighbour, Paradise, and groves
Elysian, fortunate fields—like those of old
Sought in the Atlantic main, why should they be
A history only of departed things,
Or a mere fiction of what never was?
For the discerning intellect of man,
When wedded to his goodly universe
In love and holy passion, shall find these
A simple produce of the common day.
I, long before the blissful hour arrives,
Would chant in lowly peace, the spousal verse
Of this great consummation: and by words
Which speak of nothing more than what we are,
Would I arouse the sensual from their sleep
Of death, and win the vacant and the vain
To noble raptures; while my voice proclaims
How exquisitely the individual mind
(And the progressive powers perhaps no less
Of the whole species) to the external world
Is fitted:—and how exquisitely, too,
Theme this but little heard of among men,
The external world is fitted to the mind;
And the creation (by no lower name
Can it be called) which they with blended might
Accomplish!—this is our high argument.
Such grateful haunts foregoing, if I oft
Must turn elsewhere—to travel near the tribes
And fellowships of man, and see ill sights
Of madding passions mutually inflamed;
Must hear humanity in fields and groves
Pipe solitary anguish; or must hang
Brooding above the fierce confederate storm
Of sorrow, barricadoed evermore
Within the walls of cities; may these sounds
Have their authentic comment,—that even these
Hearing, I be not downcast or forlorn!
Descend, prophetic spirit! that inspir'st
The human soul of universal earth,
Dreaming on things to come; and dost possess

A metropolitan temple in the hearts
Of mighty poets; upon me bestow
A gift of genuine insight; that my song
With star-like virtue in its place may shine;
Shedding benignant influence,—and secure,
Itself, from all malevolent effect
Of those mutations that extend their sway
Throughout the nether sphere!—And if with this
I mix more lowly matter; with the thing
Contemplated, describe the mind of man
Contemplating, and who, and what he was,
The transitory being that beheld
This vision,—when and where, and how he lived;
Be not this labour useless. If such theme
May sort with highest objects, then, dread Power!
Whose gracious favour is the primal source
Of all illumination, may my life
Express the image of a better time,
More wise desires, and simpler manners;—nurse
My heart in genuine freedom:—all pure thoughts
Be with me;—so shall thy unfailing love
Guide, and support, and cheer me to the end!"

BOOK I.

ARGUMENT.

A summer forenoon—The author reaches a ruined cottage upon a common, and there meets with a revered friend, the Wanderer, of whom he gives an account—The Wanderer, while resting under the shade of the trees that surround the cottage, relates the history of its last inhabitant.

THE WANDERER.

'TWAS summer, and the sun had mounted high:
Southward the landscape indistinctly glared
Through a pale steam; but all the northern downs,
In clearest air ascending, showed far off
A surface dappled o'er with shadows flung
From brooding clouds; shadows that lay in spots
Determined and unmoved, with steady beams
Of bright and pleasant sunshine interposed;
Pleasant to him who on the soft cool moss
Extends his careless limbs along the front
Of some huge cave, whose rocky ceiling casts
A twilight of its own, an ample shade,
Where the wren warbles; while the dreaming man,
Half conscious of the soothing melody,
With side-long eye looks out upon the scene,
By power of that impending covert thrown,
To finer distance. Other lot was mine;
Yet with good heart that soon I should obtain
As grateful resting-place, and livelier joy.
Across a bare wide common I was toiling
With languid steps that by the slippery ground
Were baffled; nor could my weak arm disperse
The host of insects gathering round my face,
And ever with me as I paced along.

Upon that open level stood a grove,
The wished-for port to which my course was bound.
Thither I came, and there, amid the gloom
Spread by a brotherhood of lofty elms,
Appeared a roofless hut; four naked walls
That stared upon each other! I looked round,
And to my wish and to my hope espied
Him whom I sought; a man of reverend age,
But stout and hale, for travel unimpaired.
There was he seen upon the cottage bench,
Recumbent in the shade, as if asleep;
An iron-pointed staff lay at his side.

Him had I marked the day before—alone
And stationed in the public way, with face
Turned toward the sun then setting, while that staff
Afforded to the figure of the man
Detained for contemplation or repose,
Graceful support; his countenance meanwhile
Was hidden from my view, and he remained
Unrecognised; but, stricken by the sight,
With slackened footsteps I advanced, and soon
A glad congratulation we exchanged
At such unthought-of meeting.—For the night
We parted, nothing willingly; and now
He by appointment waited for me here,
Beneath the shelter of these clustering elms.

We were tried friends: amid a pleasant vale,
In the antique market village where were passed
My school-days, an apartment he had owned,
To which at intervals the Wanderer drew,
And found a kind of home or harbour there.
He loved me; from a swarm of rosy boys
Singled out me, as he in sport would say,
For my grave looks—too thoughtful for my years.
As I grew up, it was my best delight
To be his chosen comrade. Many a time,
On holidays, we rambled through the woods:
We sate—we walked; he pleased me with report
Of things which he had seen; and often touched
Abstrusest matter, reasonings of the mind
Turned inward; or at my request would sing
Old songs—the product of his native hills;
A skilful distribution of sweet sounds,
Feeding the soul, and eagerly imbibed
As cool refreshing water, by the care
Of the industrious husbandman, diffused
Through a parched meadow-ground, in time of drought.
Still deeper welcome found his pure discourse:
How precious when in riper days I learned
To weigh with care his words, and to rejoice
In the plain presence of his dignity!

Oh! many are the poets that are sown
By nature; men endowed with highest gifts,
The vision and the faculty divine,
Yet wanting the accomplishment of verse

(Which, in the docile season of their youth,
It was denied them to acquire, through lack
Of culture and the inspiring aid of books,
Or haply by a temper too severe,
Or a nice backwardness afraid of shame);
Nor having e'er, as life advanced, been led
By circumstance to take unto the height
The measure of themselves, these favoured beings,
All but a scattered few, live out their time,
Husbanding that which they possess within,
And go to the grave, unthought of. Strongest minds
Are often those of whom the noisy world
Hears least; else surely this man had not left
His graces unrevealed and unproclaimed.
But, as the mind was filled with inward light
So not without distinction had he lived,
Beloved and honoured—far as he was known.
And some small portion of his eloquent speech,
And something that may serve to set in view
The feeling-pleasures of his loneliness,
His observations, and the thoughts his mind
Had dealt with—I will here record in verse;
Which, if with truth it correspond, and sink
Or rise, as venerable nature leads,
The high and tender muses shall accept
With gracious smile, deliberately pleased,
And listening Time reward with sacred praise.

Among the hills of Athol he was born:
Where, on a small hereditary farm,
An unproductive slip of rugged ground,
His parents, with their numerous offspring, dwelt;
A virtuous household, though exceeding poor!
Pure livers were they all, austere and grave,
And fearing God; the very children taught
Stern self-respect, a reverence for God's Word,
And an habitual piety, maintained
With strictness scarcely known on English ground.

From his sixth year, the boy of whom I speak,
In summer, tended cattle on the hills;
But, through the inclement and the perilous days
Of long-continuing winter, he repaired,
Equipped with satchel, to a school, that stood
Sole building on a mountain's dreary edge,
Remote from view of city's spire, or sound
Of minster clock! From that bleak tenement
He, many an evening, to his distant home
In solitude returning, saw the hills
Grow larger in the darkness, all alone
Beheld the stars come out above his head,
And travelled through the wood with no one near
To whom he might confess the things he saw.
So the foundations of his mind were laid.
In such communion, not from terror free,
While yet a child, and long before his time,
He had perceived the presence and the power
Of greatness; and deep feelings had impressed

Great objects on his mind, with portraiture
And colour so distinct, that on his mind
They lay like substances, and almost seemed
To haunt the bodily sense. He had received
A precious gift; for, as he grew in years,
With these impressions would he still compare
All his remembrances, thoughts, shapes, and forms;
And, being still unsatisfied with aught
Of dimmer character, he thence attained
An active power to fasten images
Upon his brain; and on their pictured lines
Intensely brooded, even till they acquired
The liveliness of dreams. Nor did he fail,
While yet a child, with a child's eagerness
Incessantly to turn his ear and eye
On all things which the moving seasons brought
To feed such appetite: nor this alone
Appeased his yearning:—in the after day
Of boyhood, many an hour in caves forlorn,
And 'mid the hollow depths of naked crags
He sate, and even in their fixed lineaments,
Or from the power of a peculiar eye,
Or by creative feeling overborne,
Or by predominance of thought oppressed,
Even in their fixed and steady lineaments
He traced an ebbing and a flowing mind,
Expressions ever varying!
Thus informed,
He had small need of books; for many a tale
Traditionary round the mountains hung,
And many a legend, peopling the dark woods,
Nourished imagination in her growth,
And gave the mind that apprehensive power
By which she is made quick to recognise
The moral properties and scope of things.
But eagerly he read, and read again,
Whate'er the minister's old shelf supplied;
The life and death of martyrs, who sustained,
With will inflexible, those fearful pangs
Triumphantly displayed in records left
Of persecution, and the Covenant—times
Whose echo rings through Scotland to this hour!
And there, by lucky hap, had been preserved
A straggling volume, torn and incomplete,
That left half told the preternatural tale,
Romance of giants, chronicle of fiends,
Profuse in garniture of wooden cuts
Strange and uncouth; dire faces, figures dire,
Sharp-kneed, sharp-elbowed, and lean-ankled too,
With long and ghostly shanks—forms which once seen
Could never be forgotten!
In his heart,
Where fear sate thus, a cherished visitant,
Was wanting yet the pure delight of love
By sound diffused, or by the breathing air,
Or by the silent looks of happy things,
Or flowing from the universal face
Of earth and sky. But he had felt the power

Of nature, and already was prepared,
By his intense conceptions, to receive
Deeply the lesson deep of love which he,
Whom nature, by whatever means, has taught
To feel intensely, cannot but receive.

Such was the boy—but for the growing youth
What soul was his, when, from the naked top
Of some bold headland, he beheld the sun
Rise up, and bathe the world in light! He looked—
Ocean and earth, the solid frame of earth
And ocean's liquid mass, beneath him lay
In gladness and deep joy. The clouds were touched,
And in their silent faces did he read
Unutterable love. Sound needed none,
Nor any voice of joy, his spirit drank
The spectacle: sensation, soul, and form
All melted into him, they swallowed up
His animal being; in them did he live,
And by them did he live; they were his life.
In such access of mind, in such high hour
Of visitation from the living God,
Thought was not, in enjoyment it expired.
No thanks he breathed, he proffered no request;
Rapt into still communion that transcends
The imperfect offices of prayer and praise,
His mind was a thanksgiving to the power
That made him; it was blessedness and love!

A herdsman on the lonely mountain tops,
Such intercourse was his, and in this sort
Was his existence oftentimes *possessed.*
Oh, then how beautiful, how bright appeared
The written promise! Early had he learned
To reverence the volume that displays
The mystery, the life which cannot die;
But in the mountains did he *feel* his faith.
Responsive to the writing, all things there
Breathed immortality, revolving life,
And greatness still revolving, infinite;
There littleness was not, the least of things
Seemed infinite; and there his spirit shaped
Her prospects, now did he believe,—he *saw.*
What wonder if his being thus became
Sublime and comprehensive! Low desires,
Low thoughts had there no place; yet was his heart
Lowly; for he was meek in gratitude,
Oft as he called these ecstasies to mind
And whence they flowed; and from them he acquired
Wisdom, which works through patience; thence he learned
In oft-recurring hours of sober thought
To look on nature with a humble heart,
Self-questioned where it did not understand,
And with a superstitious eye of love.

So passed the time; yet to the nearest town
He duly went with what small overplus
His earnings might supply, and brought away
And book that most had tempted his desires

While at the stall he read. Among the hills
He gazed upon that mighty orb of song,
The divine Milton. Lore of different kind,
The annual savings of a toilsome life,
His schoolmaster supplied; books that explain
The purer elements of truth involved
In lines and numbers, and, by charm severe,
(Especially perceived where nature droops
And feeling is suppressed) preserve the mind
Busy in solitude and poverty.
These occupations oftentimes deceived
The listless hours, while in the hollow vale,
Hollow and green, he lay on the green turf
In pensive idleness. What could he do,
Thus daily thirsting, in that lonesome life,
With blind endeavours? Yet, still uppermost,
Nature was at his heart as if he felt,
Though yet he knew not how, a wasting power
In all things that from her sweet influence
Might tend to wean him. Therefore with her hues,
Her forms, and with the spirit of her forms,
He clothed the nakedness of austere truth.
While yet he lingered in the rudiments
Of science, and among her simplest laws,
His triangles—they were the stars of heaven,
The silent stars! Oft did he take delight
To measure the altitude of some tall crag
That is the eagle's birthplace, or some peak
Familiar with forgotten years, that shows
Inscribed, as with the silence of the thought,
Upon its bleak and visionary sides,
The history of many a winter storm,
Or obscure records of the path of fire.

And thus, before his eighteenth year was told,
Accumulated feelings pressed his heart
With still increasing weight; he was o'erpowered
By nature, by the turbulence subdued
Of his own mind; by mystery and hope,
And the first virgin passion of a soul
Communing with the glorious universe.
Full often wished he that the winds might rage
When they were silent; far more fondly now
Than in his earlier season did he love
Tempestuous nights—the conflict and the sounds
That live in darkness:—from his intellect
And from the stillness of abstracted thought
He asked repose; and, failing oft to win
The peace required, he scanned the laws of light
Amid the roar of torrents, where they send
From hollow clefts up to the clearer air
A cloud of mist that, smitten by the sun,
Varies its rainbow hues. But vainly thus
And vainly by all other means, he strove
To mitigate the fever of his heart.

In dreams, in study, and in ardent thought,
Thus was he reared; much wanting to assist

The growth of intellect, yet gaining more,
And every moral feeling of his soul
Strengthened and braced, by breathing in content
The keen, the wholesome air of poverty,
And drinking from the well of homely life
But, from past liberty, and tried restraints,
He now was summoned to select the course
Of humble industry that promised best
To yield him no unworthy maintenance.
Urged by his mother, he essayed to teach
A village school—but wandering thoughts were then
A misery to him ; and the youth resigned
A task he was unable to perform.

That stern yet kindly spirit, who constrains
The Savoyard to quit his native rocks,
The free-born Swiss to leave his narrow vales,
(Spirit attached to regions mountainous
Like their own steadfast clouds) did now impel
His restless mind to look abroad with hope.
An irksome drudgery seems it to plod on,
Through hot and dusty ways, or pelting storm,
A vagrant merchant bent beneath his load !
Yet do such travellers find their own delight ;
And their hard service, deemed debasing now,
Gained merited respect in simpler times ;
When squire and priest, and they who round them dwelt
In rustic sequestration—all dependent
Upon the pedlar's toil—supplied their wants,
Or pleased their fancies with the wares he brought.
Not ignorant was the youth that still no few
Of his adventurous countrymen were led
By perseverance in this track of life
To competence and ease ;—for him it bore
Attractions manifold ;—and this he chose.
His parents on the enterprise bestowed
Their farewell benediction, ' ut with hearts
Foreboding evil. From his native hills
He wandered far ; much did he see of men,
Their manners, their enjoyments, and pursuits,
Their passions, and their feelings ; chiefly those
Essential and eternal in the heart,
That, 'mid the simpler forms of rural life,
Exist more simple in their elements,
And speak a plainer language. In the woods,
A lone enthusiast, and among the fields,
Itinerant in this labour, he had passed
The better portion of his time ; and there
Spontaneously had his affections thriven
Amid the bounties of the year, the peace,
And liberty of nature ; there he kept
In solitude and solitary thought
His mind in a just equipoise of love.
Serene it was, unclouded by the cares
Of ordinary life ; unvexed, unwarped,
By partial bondage. In his steady course,
No piteous revolutions had he felt,
No wild varieties of joy and grief.

Unoccupied by sorrow of its own,
His heart lay open; and by nature tuned
And constant disposition of his thoughts
To sympathy with man, he was alive
To all that was enjoyed where'er he went;
And all that was endured; for in himself
Happy, and quiet in his cheerfulness,
He had no painful pressure from without
That made him turn aside from wretchedness
With coward fears. He could *afford* to suffer
With those whom he saw suffer. Hence it came
That in our best experience he was rich,
And in the wisdom of our daily life.
For hence, minutely, in his various rounds,
He had observed the progress and decay
Of many minds, of minds and bodies too;
The history of many families;
How they had prospered; how they were o'erthrown
By passion or mischance; or such misrule
Among the unthinking masters of the earth
As makes the nations groan.—This active course
He followed till provision for his wants
Had been obtained;—the Wanderer then resolved
To pass the remnant of his days—untasked
With needless services—from hardship free.
His calling laid aside, he lived at ease:
But still he loved to pace the public roads
And the wild paths; and, by the summer's warmth
Invited, often would he leave his home
And journey far, revisiting the scenes
That to his memory were most endeared.
Vigorous in health, of hopeful spirits, undamped
By worldly-mindedness, or anxious care;
Observant, studious, thoughtful, and refreshed
By knowledge gathered up from day to day;—
Thus had he lived a long and innocent life.

The Scottish Church, both on himself and those
With whom from childhood he grew up, had held
The strong hand of her purity; and still
Had watched him with an unrelenting eye.
This he remembered in his riper age
With gratitude, and reverential thoughts.
But by the native vigour of his mind,
By his habitual wanderings out of doors,
By loneliness, and goodness, and kind works,
Whate'er, in docile childhood or in youth,
He had imbibed of fear or darker thought,
Was melted all away: so true was this,
That sometimes his religion seemed to me
Self-taught, as of a dreamer in the woods;
Who to the model of his own pure heart
Shaped his belief as grace divine inspired,
Or human reason dictated with awe.
And surely never did there live on earth
A man of kindlier nature. The rough sports
And teasing ways of children vexed not him;
'ndulgent listener was he to the tongue

Of garrulous age; nor did the sick man's tale,
To his fraternal sympathy addressed,
Obtain reluctant hearing.
Plain his garb;
Such as might suit a rustic sire, prepared
For Sabbath duties; yet he was a man
Whom no one could have passed without remark
Active and nervous was his gait; his limbs
And his whole figure breathed intelligence.
Time had compressed the freshness of his cheek
Into a narrower circle of deep red,
But had not tamed his eye; that, under brows
Shaggy and gray, had meanings which it brought
From years of youth; which, like a being made
Of many beings, he had wondrous skill
To blend with knowledge of the years to come,
Human, or such as lie beyond the grave.

So was he framed; and such his course of life
Who now, with no appendage but a staff,
The prized memorial of relinquished toils,
Upon that cottage bench reposed his limbs,
Screened from the sun. Supine the Wanderer lay
His eyes as if in drowsiness half shut,
The shadows of the breezy elms above
Dappling his face. He had not heard the sound
Of my approaching steps, and in the shade
Unnoticed did I stand, some minutes' space.
At length I hailed him, seeing that his hat
Was moist with water-drops, as if the brim
Had newly scooped a running stream. He rose,
And ere our lively greeting into peace
Had settled, "'Tis," said I, "a burning day;
My lips are parched with thirst, but you, it seems,
Have somewhere found relief." He, at the word,
Pointing towards a sweet-briar, bade me climb
The fence where that aspiring shrub looked out
Upon the public way. It was a plot
Of garden-ground run wild, its matted weeds
Marked with the steps of those, whom, as they passed.
The gooseberry trees that shot in long lank slips,
Or currants, hanging from their leafless stems
In scanty strings, had tempted to o'erleap
The broken wall. I looked around, and there,
Where two tall hedgerows of thick alder boughs
Joined in a cold damp nook, espied a well
Shrouded with willow-flowers and plumy fern.
My thirst I slaked, and from the cheerless spot
Withdrawing, straightway to the shade returned
Where sate the old man on the cottage bench;
And while, beside him, with uncovered head,
I yet was standing, freely to respire,
And cool my temples in the fanning air,
Thus did he speak—"I see around me here
Things which you cannot see: we die, my friend
Nor we alone, but that which each man loved

And prized in his peculiar nook of earth
Dies with him, or is changed; and very soon
Even of the good is no memorial left.
The poets, in their elegies and songs
Lamenting the departed, call the groves,
They call upon the hills and streams to mourn,
And senseless rocks, nor idly; for they speak,
In these their invocations, with a voice
Obedient to the strong creative power
Of human passion. Sympathies there are
More tranquil, yet perhaps of kindred birth,
That steal upon the meditative mind,
And grow with thought. Beside yon spring I stood,
And eyed its waters till we seemed to feel
One sadness, they and I. For them a bond
Of brotherhood is broken: time has been
When, every day, the touch of human hand
Dislodged the natural sleep that binds them up
In mortal stillness; and they ministered
To human comfort. Stooping down to drink,
Upon the slimy foot-stone I espied
The useless fragment of a wooden bowl,
Green with the moss of years, and subject only
To the soft handling of the elements:
There let the relic lie—fond thought—vain words!
Forgive them—never did my steps approach
This humble door but she who dwelt therein
A daughter's welcome gave me, and I loved her
As my own child. Oh, sir! the good die first,
And they whose hearts are dry as summer dust
Burn to the socket. Many a passenger
Hath blessed poor Margaret for her gentle looks,
When she upheld the cool refreshment drawn
From that forsaken spring; and no one came
But he was welcome; no one went away
But that it seemed she loved him. She is dead,
The light extinguished of her lonely hut,
The hut itself abandoned to decay,
And she forgotten in the quiet grave!

"I speak," continued he, "of one whose stock
Of virtues bloomed beneath this lowly roof
She was a woman of a steady mind,
Tender and deep in her excess of love,
Not speaking much, pleased rather with the joy
Of her own thoughts by some especial care
Her temper had been framed, as if to make
A being—who by adding love to peace
Might live on earth a life of happiness.
Her wedded partner lacked not on his side
The humble worth that satisfied her heart:
Frugal, affectionate, sober, and withal
Keenly industrious. She with pride would tell
That he was often seated at his loom,
In summer, ere the mower was abroad
Among the dewy grass,—in early spring,
Ere the last star had vanished.- They who passed
At evening, from behind the garden fence

Might hear his busy spade, which he would ply,
After his daily work, until the light
Had failed, and every leaf and flower were lost
In the dark hedges. So their days were spent
In peace and comfort; and a pretty boy
Was their best hope,—next to the God in heaven.

"Not twenty years ago, but you I think
Can scarcely bear it now in mind, there came
Two blighting seasons, when the fields were left
With half a harvest. It pleased Heaven to add
A worse affliction in the plague of war;
This happy land was stricken to the heart!
A wanderer then among the cottages
I, with my freight of winter raiment, saw
The hardships of that season; many rich
Sank down, as in a dream, among the poor;
And of the poor did many cease to be,
And their place knew them not. Meanwhile, abridged
Of daily comforts, gladly reconciled
To numerous self-denials, Margaret
Went struggling on through those calamitous years
With cheerful hope, until the second autumn,
When her life's helpmate on a sick-bed lay,
Smitten with perilous fever. In disease
He lingered long; and when his strength returned,
He found the little he had stored, to meet
The hour of accident or crippling age,
Was all consumed. A second infant now
Was added to the troubles of a time
Laden, for them and all of their degree,
With care and sorrow; shoals of artisans
From ill-requited labour turned adrift
Sought daily bread from public charity,
They, and their wives and children—happier far
Could they have lived as do the little birds
That peck along the hedgerows, or the kite
That makes her dwelling on the mountain rocks!

"A sad reverse it was for him who long
Had filled with plenty, and possessed in peace,
This lonely cottage. At his door he stood,
And whistled many a snatch of merry tunes
That had no mirth in them; or with his knife
Carved uncouth figures on the heads of sticks—
Then, not less idly, sought, through every nook
In house or garden, any casual work
Of use or ornament; and with a strange,
Amusing, yet uneasy novelty,
He blended, where he might, the various tasks
Of summer, autumn, winter, and of spring.
But this endured not; his good humour soon
Became a weight in which no pleasure was;
And poverty brought on a petted mood
And a sore temper: day by day he drooped,
And he would leave his work—and to the town,
Without an errand, would direct his steps,
Or wander here and there among the fields.

One while he would speak lightly of his babes,
And with a cruel tongue: at other times
He tossed them with a false unnatural joy
And 'twas a rueful thing to see the looks
Of the poor innocent children. 'Every smile,'
Said Margaret to me, here beneath these trees,
'Made my heart bleed.'"
At this the Wanderer paused
And, looking up to those enormous elms,
He said, "'Tis now the hour of deepest noon.
At this still season of repose and peace,
This hour, when all things which are not at rest
Are cheerful; while this multitude of flies
Is filling all the air with melody;
Why should a tear be in an old man's eye?
Why should we thus, with an untoward mind,
And in the weakness of humanity,
From natural wisdom turn our hearts away,
To natural comfort shut our eyes and ears,
And, feeding on disquiet, thus disturb
The calm of nature with our restless thoughts?"

He spake with somewhat of a solemn tone:
But, when he ended, there was in his face
Such easy cheerfulness, a look so mild,
That for a little time it stole away
All recollection, and that simple tale
Passed from my mind like a forgotten sound.
A while on trivial things we held discourse,
To me soon tasteless. In my own despite,
I thought of that poor woman as of one
Whom I had known and loved. He had rehearsed
Her homely tale with such familiar power,
With such an active countenance, an eye
So busy, that the things of which he spake
Seemed present; and, attention now relaxed,
A heart-felt chillness crept along my veins.
I rose; and, having left the breezy shade,
Stood drinking comfort from the warmer sun,
That had not cheered me long—ere, looking round
Upon that tranquil ruin, I returned,
And begged of the old man that, for my sake,
He would resume his story.
He replied,
"It were a wantonness, and would demand
Severe reproof, if we were men whose hearts
Could hold vain dalliance with the misery
Even of the dead; contented thence to draw
A momentary pleasure, never marked
By reason, barren of all future good.
But we have known that there is often found
In mournful thoughts, and always might be found,
A power to virtue friendly; were't not so,
I am a dreamer among men, indeed
An idle dreamer! 'Tis a common tale,
An ordinary sorrow of man's life,

A tale of silent suffering, hardly clothed
In bodily form.—But, without further bidding,
I will proceed.
While thus it fared with them,
To whom this cottage, till those hapless years,
Had been a blessed home, it was my chance
To travel in a country far remote;
And when these lofty elms once more appeared,
What pleasant expectations lured me on
O'er the flat common!—With quick step I reached
The threshold, lifted with light hand the latch;
But, when I entered, Margaret looked at me
A little while; then turned her head away
Speechless,—and sitting down upon a chair
Wept bitterly. I wist not what to do,
Or how to speak to her. Poor wretch! at last
She rose from off her seat, and then,—O sir!
I cannot *tell* how she pronounced my name.—
With fervent love, and with a face of grief
Unutterably helpless, and a look
That seemed to cling upon me, she inquired
If I had seen her husband. As she spake
A strange surprise and fear came to my heart,
Nor had I power to answer ere she told
That he had disappeared—not two months gone.
He left his house: two wretched days had passed
And on the third, as wistfully she raised
Her head from off her pillow, to look forth,
Like one in trouble, for returning light,
Within her chamber-casement she espied
A folded paper, lying as if placed
To meet her waking eyes. This tremblingly
She opened—found no writing, but beheld
Pieces of money carefully inclosed,
Silver and gold—'I shuddered at the sight,'
Said Margaret, 'for I knew it was his hand
Which placed it there: and ere that day was ended
That long and anxious day! I learned from one
Sent hither by my husband to impart
The heavy news,—that he had joined a troop
Of soldiers going to a distant land.
He left me thus—he could not gather heart
To take a farewell of me; for he feared
That I should follow with my babes, and sink
Beneath the misery of that wandering life.'

"This tale did Margaret tell with many tears:
And, when she ended, I had little power
To give her comfort, and was glad to take
Such words of hope from her own mouth as served
To cheer us both:—but long we had not talked
Ere we built up a pile of better thoughts,
And with a brighter eye she looked around
As if she had been shedding tears of joy.
We parted.—'Twas the time of early spring;
I left her busy with her garden tools;
And well remember, o'er that fence she looked
And, while I paced along the footway path,

Called out, and sent a blessing after me,
With tender cheerfulness; and with a voice
That seemed the very sound of happy thoughts.

"I roved o'er many a hill and many a dale,
With my accustomed load; in heat and cold,
Through many a wood, and many an open ground,
In sunshine and in shade, in wet and fair,
Drooping or blithe of heart, as might befal;
My best companions now the driving winds,
And now the "trotting brooks" and whispering trees,
And now the music of my own sad steps,
With many a short-lived thought that passed between,
And disappeared.—I journeyed back this way,
When, in the warmth of midsummer, the wheat
Was yellow; and the soft and bladed grass
Springing afresh had o'er the hay-field spread
Its tender verdure. At the door arrived,
I found that she was absent. In the shade
Where now we sit, I waited her return.
Her cottage, then a cheerful object, wore
Its customary look,—only, it seemed,
The honeysuckle, crowding round the porch,
Hung down in heavier tufts: and that bright weed,
The yellow stonecrop, suffered to take root
Along the window's edge, profusely grew,
Blinding the lower panes. I turned aside,
And strolled into her garden. It appeared
To lag behind the season, and had lost
Its pride of neatness. Daisy-flowers and thrift
Had broken their trim lines, and straggled o'er
The paths they used to deck:—carnations, once
Prized for surpassing beauty, and no less
For the peculiar pains they had required,
Declined their languid heads, without support.
The cumbrous bind-weed, with its wreaths and bells
Had twined about her two small rows of pease,
And dragged them to the earth.—Ere this an hour
Had wasted.—Back I turned my restless steps;
A stranger passed; and, guessing whom I sought,
He said that she was used to ramble far.
The sun was sinking in the west; and now
I sate with sad impatience. From within
Her solitary infant cried aloud;
Then, like a blast that dies away self-stilled,
The voice was silent. From the bench I rose;
But neither could divert nor soothe my thoughts.
The spot, though fair, was very desolate—
The longer I remained more desolate:
And, looking round me, now I first observed
The corner stones, on either side the porch,
With dull red stains discoloured, and stuck o'er
With tufts and hairs of wool, as if the sheep,
That fed upon the common, thither came
Familiarly; and found a couching-place
Even at her threshold. Deeper shadows fell
From these tall elms;—the cottage-clock struck eight;—
I turned, and saw her distant a few steps.

Her face was pale and thin, her figure too
Was changed. As she unlocked the door, she said,
'It grieves me you have waited here so long,
But, in good truth, I've wandered much of late,
And, sometimes—to my shame I speak—have need
Of my best prayers to bring me back again.'
While on the board she spread our evening meal,
She told me—interrupting not the work
Which gave employment to her listless hands—
That she had parted with her elder child;
To a kind master on a distant farm
Now happily apprenticed.—'I perceive
You look at me, and you have cause; to-day
I have been travelling far; and many days
About the fields I wander, knowing this
Only, that what I seek I cannot find,
And so I waste my time for I am changed;
And to myself,' said she, 'have done much wrong
And to his helpless infant. I have slept
Weeping, and weeping have I waked; my tears
Have flowed as if my body were not such
As others are; and I could never die.
But I am now in mind and in my heart
More easy; and I hope,' said she, 'that Heaven
Will give me patience to endure the things
Which I behold at home.' It would have grieved
Your very soul to see her; sir, I feel
The story linger in my heart; I fear
'Tis long and tedious; but my spirit clings
To that poor woman:—so familiarly
Do I perceive her manner, and her look,
And presence, and so deeply do I feel
Her goodness, that, not seldom, in my walks
A momentary trance comes over me;
And to myself I seem to muse on one
By sorrow laid asleep,—or borne away,
A human being destined to awake
To human life, or something very near
To human life, when he shall come again
For whom she suffered. Yes, it would have grieved
Your very soul to see her: evermore
Her eyelids drooped, her eyes were downward cast;
And, when she at her table gave me food,
She did not look at me. Her voice was low,
Her body was subdued. In every act
Pertaining to her house affairs, appeared
The careless stillness of a thinking mind
Self-occupied: to which all outward things
Are like an idle matter. Still she sighed,
But yet no motion of the breast was seen,
No heaving of the heart. While by the fire
We sate together, sighs came on my ear,
I knew not how, and hardly whence they came.

"Ere my departure, to her care I gave,
For her son's use, some tokens of regard,
Which with a look of welcome she received,
And I exhorted her to place her trust

In God's good love, and seek his help by prayer.
I took my staff, and when I kissed her babe
The tears stood in her eyes. I left her then
With the best hope and comfort I could give;
She thanked me for my wish;—but for my hope
Methought she did not thank me.
I returned,
And took my rounds along this road again
Ere on its sunny bank the primrose flower
Peeped forth, to give an earnest of the spring.
I found her sad and drooping; she had learned
No tidings of her husband; if he lived,
She knew not that he lived; if he were dead,
She knew not he was dead. She seemed the same
In person and appearance; but her house
Bespake a sleepy hand of negligence;
The floor was neither dry nor neat, the hearth
Was comfortless, and her small lot of books,
Which, in the cottage window, heretofore
Had been piled up against the corner panes
In seemly order, now, with straggling leaves
Lay scattered here and there, open or shut,
As they had chanced to fall. Her infant babe
Had from its mother caught the trick of grief,
And sighed among its playthings. Once again
I turned towards the garden gate, and saw,
More plainly still, that poverty and grief
Were now come nearer to her: weeds defaced
The hardened soil, and knots of withered grass:
No ridges there appeared of clear black mould,
No winter greenness; of her herbs and flowers,
It seemed the better part were gnawed away
Or trampled into earth; a chain of straw,
Which had been twined about the slender stem
Of a young apple-tree, lay at its root,
The bark was nibbled round by truant sheep.
Margaret stood near, her infant in her arms,
And, noting that my eye was on the tree,
She said, 'I fear it will be dead and gone
Ere Robert come again.' Towards the house
Together we returned; and she inquired
If I had any hope:—but for her babe
And for her little orphan boy, she said,
She had no wish to live, that she must die
Of sorrow. Yet I saw the idle loom
Still in its place; his Sunday garments hung
Upon the self-same nail; his very staff
Stood undisturbed behind the door. And when,
In bleak December, I retraced this way,
She told me that her little babe was dead,
And she was left alone. She now, released
From her maternal cares, had taken up
The employment common through these wilds, and gained
By spinning hemp a pittance for herself;
And for this end had hired a neighbour's boy
To give her needful help. That very time
Most willingly she put her work aside,
And walked with me along the miry road

Heedless how far; and in such piteous sort
That any heart had ached to hear her, begged
That, wheresoe'er I went, I still would ask
For him whom she had lost. We parted then—
Our final parting; for from that time forth
Did many seasons pass ere I returned
Into this tract again.
                                        Nine tedious years;
From their first separation, nine long years,
She lingered in unquiet widowhood;
A wife and widow. Needs must it have been
A sore heart-wasting. I have heard, my friend,
That in yon arbour oftentimes she sate
Alone, through half the vacant Sabbath-day;
And, if a dog passed by, she still would quit
The shade, and look abroad. On this old bench
For hours she sate; and evermore her eye
Was busy in the distance, shaping things
That made her heart beat quick. You see that path,
Now faint,—the grass has crept o'er its gray line;
There, to and fro, she paced through many a day
Of the warm summer, from a belt of hemp
That girt her waist, spinning the long-drawn thread
With backward steps. Yet ever as there passed
A man whose garments showed the soldier's red,
Or crippled mendicant in sailor's garb,
The little child who sate to turn the wheel
Ceased from his task; and she with faltering voice
Made many a fond inquiry; and when they,
Whose presence gave no comfort, were gone by,
Her heart was still more sad. And by yon gate,
That bars the traveller's road, she often stood,
And when a stranger horseman came, the latch
Would lift, and in his face look wistfully:
Most happy, if, from aught discovered there
Of tender feeling, she might dare repeat
The same sad question. Meanwhile her poor hut
Sank to decay: for he was gone whose hand,
At the first nipping of October frost,
Closed up each chink, and with fresh bands of straw
Chequered the green-grown thatch. And so she lived
Through the long winter, reckless and alone;
Until her house by frost, and thaw, and rain,
Was sapped; and while she slept the nightly damps
Did chill her breast; and in the stormy day
Her tattered clothes were ruffled by the wind;
Even at the side of her own fire. Yet still
She loved this wretched spot, nor would for worlds
Have parted hence; and still that length of road,
And this rude bench, one torturing hope endeared,
Fast rooted at her heart: and here, my friend,
In sickness she remained; and here she died,
Last human tenant of these ruined walls."

The old man ceased: he saw that I was moved;
From that low bench, rising instinctively
I turned aside in weakness, nor had power
To thank him for the tale which he had told.

I stood, and leaning o'er the garden wall,
Reviewed that woman's sufferings; and it seemed
To comfort me while with a brother's love
I blessed her—in the impotence of grief.
At length towards the cottage I returned
Fondly,—and traced, with interest more mild,
That secret spirit of humanity
Which, 'mid the calm oblivious tendencies
Of nature, 'mid her plants, and weeds, and flowers,
And silent overgrowings, still survived.
The old man, noting this, resumed, and said,
"My friend! enough to sorrow you have given,
The purposes of wisdom ask no more;
Be wise and cheerful; and no longer read
The forms of things with an unworthy eye.
She sleeps in the calm earth, and peace is here.
I well remember that those very plumes,
Those weeds, and the high spear-grass on that wall,
By mist and silent rain-drops silvered o'er,
As once I passed, did to my heart convey
So still an image of tranquillity,
So calm and still, and looked so beautiful
Amid the uneasy thoughts which filled my mind,
That what we feel of sorrow and despair
From ruin and from change, and all the grief
The passing shows of being leave behind,
Appeared an idle dream that could not live
Where meditation was. I turned away,
And walked along my road in happiness."

He ceased. Ere long the sun declining shot
A slant and mellow radiance, which began
To fall upon us, while beneath the trees,
We sate on that low bench: and now we felt,
Admonished thus, the sweet hour coming on.
A linnet warbled from those lofty elms,
A thrush sang loud, and other melodies,
At distance heard, peopled the milder air.
The old man rose, and, with a sprightly mien
Of hopeful preparation, grasped his staff:
Together casting then a farewell look
Upon those silent walls, we left the shade;
And, ere the stars were visible, had reached
A village inn,—our evening resting-place.

BOOK II.

ARGUMENT.

The author describes his travels with the Wanderer, whose character is further illustrated—Morning scene, and view of a village wake—Wanderer's account of a friend whom he purposes to visit—View from an eminence of the valley which his friend had chosen for his retreat—Feelings of the author at the sight of it—Sound of singing from below—A funeral procession—Descent into the valley—Observations drawn from the Wanderer at sight of a book accidentally discovered in a recess in the valley—Meeting with the Wanderer's friend, the Solitary—Wanderer's description of the mode of burial in this mountainous district—Solitary contrasts with this, that of the individual carried a few minutes before from the cottage—Brief conversation—The cottage

entered—description of the Solitary's apartment—Repast there—View from the window of two mountain summits—and the Solitary's description of the companionship they afford him—Account of the departed inmate of the cottage—Description of a grand spectacle upon the mountains, with its effect upon the Solitary's mind—Quit the house.

THE SOLITARY.

IN days of yore how fortunately fared
The minstrel! wandering on from hall to hall,
Baronial court or royal; cheered with gifts
Munificent, and love, and ladies' praise;
Now meeting on his road an armèd knight,
Now resting with a pilgrim by the side
Of a clear brook,—beneath an abbey's roof
One evening sumptuously lodged; the next
Humbly in a religious hospital;
Or, with some merry outlaws of the wood;
Or haply shrouded in a hermit's cell.
Him, sleeping or awake, the robber spared;
He walked—protected from the sword of war
By virtue of that sacred instrument
His harp, suspended at the traveller's side;
His dear companion wheresoe'er he went
Opening from land to land an easy way
By melody, and by the charm of verse.
Yet not the noblest of that honoured race
Drew happier, loftier, more impassioned thoughts
From his long journeyings and eventful life,
Than this obscure itinerant had skill
To gather, ranging through the tamer ground
Of these our unimaginative days;
Both while he trod the earth in humblest guise
Accoutred with his burthen and his staff;
And now, when free to move with lighter pace.

What wonder, then, if I, whose favourite school
Hath been the fields, the roads, and rural lanes,
Looked on this guide with reverential love?
Each with the other pleased, we now pursued
Our journey—beneath favourable skies.
Turn wheresoe'er we would, he was a light
Unfailing: not a hamlet could we pass,
Rarely a house, that did not yield to him
Remembrances; or from his tongue call forth
Some way-beguiling tale. Nor less regard
Accompanied those strains of apt discourse,
Which nature's various objects might inspire,
And in the silence of his face I read
His overflowing spirit. Birds and beasts,
And the mute fish that glances in the stream
And harmless reptile crawling in the sun,
And gorgeous insect hovering in the air,
The fowl domestic, and the household dog,
In his capacious mind—he loved them all.
Their rights acknowledging, he felt for all.
Oft was occasion given me to perceive
How the calm pleasures of the pasturing herd
To happy contemplation soothed his walk;

How the poor brute's condition, forced to run
Its course of suffering in the public road,
Sad contrast! all too often smote his heart
With unavailing pity. Rich in love
And sweet humanity, he was, himself,
To the degree that he desired, beloved.
Greetings and smiles we met with all day long
From faces that he knew; we took our seats
By many a cottage hearth, where he received
The welcome of an inmate come from far.
Nor was he loth to enter ragged huts,
Huts where his charity was blest; his voice
Heard as the voice of an experienced friend.
And, sometimes, where the poor man held dispute
With his own mind, unable to subdue
Impatience through inaptness to perceive
General distress in his particular lot;
Or cherishing resentment, or in vain
Struggling against it, with a soul perplexed,
And finding in herself no steady power
To draw the line of comfort that divides
Calamity, the chastisement of Heaven,
From the injustice of our brother men;
To him appeal was made as to a judge;
Who, with an understanding heart, allayed
The perturbation; listen'd to the plea;
Resolved the dubious point; and sentence gave
So grounded, so applied, that it was heard
With soften'd spirit—even when it condemned.

Such intercourse I witnessed, while we roved,
Now as his choice directed, now as mine;
Or both, with equal readiness of will,
Of course submitting to the changeful breeze
Of accident. But when the rising sun
Had three times called us to renew our walk,
My fellow-traveller claimed with earnest voice,
As if the thought were but a moment old,
An absolute dominion for the day.
We started—and he led towards the hills;
Up through an ample vale, with higher hills
Before us, mountains stern and desolate;
But, in the majesty of distance, now
Set off, and to our ken appearing fair
Of aspect, with aërial softness clad,
And beautified with morning's purple beams.

The wealthy, the luxurious, by the stress
Of business roused, or pleasure, ere their time,
May roll in chariots, or provoke the hoofs
Of the fleet coursers they bestride, to raise
From earth the dust of morning, slow to rise;
And they, if blest with health and hearts at ease,
Shall lack not their enjoyment;—but how faint
Compared with ours! who, pacing side by side,
Could, with an eye of leisure, look on all
That we beheld; and lend the listening sense
To every grateful sound of earth and air;

Pausing at will—our spirits braced, our thoughts
Pleasant as roses in the thickets blown,
And pure as dew bathing their crimson leaves.

Mount slowly, sun! that we may journey long,
By this dark hill protected from thy beams!
Such is the summer pilgrim's frequent wish;
But quickly from among our morning thoughts
'Twas chased away: for, toward the western side
Of the broad vale, casting a casual glance,
We saw a throng of people:—wherefore met?
Blithe notes of music, suddenly let loose
On the thrilled ear, and flags uprising, yield
Prompt answer: they proclaim the annual wake,
Which the bright season favours.—Tabor and pipe
In purpose join to hasten and reprove
The laggard rustic; and repay with boons
Of merriment a party-coloured knot,
Already formed upon the village green.
Beyond the limits of the shadow cast
By the broad hill, glistened upon our sight
That gay assemblage. Round them and above,
Glitter, with dark recesses interposed,
Casement, and cottage-roof, and stems of trees
Half-veiled in vapoury cloud, the silver steam
Of dews fast melting on their leafy boughs
By the strong sunbeams smitten. Like a mast
Of gold, the maypole shines; as if the rays
Of morning, aided by exhaling dew,
With gladsome influence could re-animate
The faded garlands hanging from its sides.

Said I, "The music and the sprightly scene
Invite us; shall we quit our road, and join
These festive matins?"—He replied, "Not loth
Here would I linger, and with you partake,
Not one hour merely, but till evening's close,
The simple pastimes of the day and place.
By the fleet racers, ere the sun be set,
The turf of yon large pasture will be skimmed;
There, too, the lusty wrestlers shall contend:
But know we not that he who intermits
The appointed task and duties of the day,
Untunes full oft the pleasures of the day;
Checking the finer spirits that refuse
To flow when purposes are lightly changed?
We must proceed—a length of journey yet
Remains untraced." Then, pointing with his staff
Towards those craggy summits, his intent
He thus imparted:

"In a spot that lies
Among yon mountain fastnesses concealed,
You will receive, before the hour of noon,
Good recompense, I hope, for this day's toil—
From sight of one who lives secluded there,
Lonesome and lost: of whom, and whose past life,
(Not to forestal such knowledge as may be

More faithfully collected from himself,)
This brief communication shall suffice.

"Though now sojourning there, he, like myself
Sprang from a stock of lowly parentage
Among the wilds of Scotland, in a tract
Where many a sheltered and well-tended plant,
Bears, on the humblest ground of social life,
Blossoms of piety and innocence.
Such grateful promises his youth displayed ·
And, having shown in study forward zeal,
He to the ministry was duly called;
And straight incited by a curious mind
Filled with vague hopes, he undertook the charge
Of chaplain to a military troop
Cheered by the Highland bagpipe, as they marched
In plaided vest,—his fellow-countrymen,
The office filling, yet by native power
And force of native inclination, made
An intellectual ruler in the haunts
Of social vanity—he walked the world,
Gay, and affecting graceful gaiety;
Lax, buoyant—less a pastor with his flock
Than a soldier among soldiers—lived and roamed
Where fortune led:—and fortune, who oft proves
The careless wanderer's friend, to him made known
A blooming lady—a conspicuous flower,
Admired for beauty, for her sweetness praised;
Whom he had sensibility to love,
Ambition to attempt, and skill to win.

"For this fair bride, most rich in gifts of mind,
Nor sparingly endowed with worldly wealth,
His office he relinquished; and retired
From the world's notice to a rural home.
Youth's season yet with him was scarcely past,
And she was in youth's prime. How full their joy
How free their love! nor did that love decay,
Nor joy abate, till, pitiable doom!
In the short course of one undreaded year
Death blasted all.—Death suddenly o'erthrew
Two lovely children—all that they possessed!
The mother followed:—miserably bare
The one survivor stood; he wept, he prayed
For his dismissal, day and night, compelled
By pain to turn his thoughts towards the grave,
And face the regions of eternity.
An uncomplaining apathy displaced
This anguish; and, indifferent to delight,
To aim and purpose, he consumed his days,
To private interest dead, and public care.
So lived he; so he might have died.
But now,
To the wide world's astonishment, appeared
A glorious opening, the unlooked-for dawn,
That promised everlasting joy to France!
Her voice of social transport reached even him!
He broke from his contracted bounds, repaired

To the great city, an emporium then
Of golden expectations, and receiving
Freights every day from a new world of hope.
Thither his popular talents he transferred ;
And, from the pulpit, zealously maintained
The cause of Christ and civil liberty,
As one ; and moving to one glorious end.
Intoxicating service ! I might say
A happy service ; for he was sincere
As vanity and fondness for applause,
And new and shapeless wishes, would allow

"That righteous cause (such power hath freedom bound
For one hostility, in friendly league
Ethereal natures and the worst of slaves ,
Was served by rival advocates that came
From regions opposite as heaven and hell.
One courage seemed to animate them all .
And, from the dazzling conquests daily gained
By their united efforts, there arose
A proud and most presumptuous confidence
In the transcendent wisdom of the age,
And her discernment , not alone in rights,
And in the origin and bounds of power,
Social and temporal ; but in laws divine,
Deduced by reason, or to faith revealed.
And overweening trust was raised , and fear
Cast out,—alike of person and of thing.
Plague from this union spread, whose subtle bane
The strongest did not easily escape ;
And he, what wonder ! took a mortal taint.
How shall I trace the change, how bear to tell
That he broke faith with them whom he had laid
In earth's dark chambers with a Christian's hope !
An infidel contempt of Holy Writ
Stole by degrees upon his mind ; and hence
Life, like that Roman Janus, double-faced ;
Vilest hypocrisy, the laughing, gay
Hypocrisy, not leagued with fear, but pride
Smooth words he had to wheedle simple souls ;
But, for disciples of the inner school,
Old freedom was old servitude, and they
The wisest whose opinions stooped the least
To know restraints : and who most boldly drew
Hopeful prognostications from a creed,
That, in the light of false philosophy,
Spread like a halo round a misty moon,
Widening its circle as the storms advance.

"His sacred function was at length renounced
And every day and every place enjoyed
The unshackled layman's natural liberty ;
Speech, manners, morals, all without disguise.
I do not wish to wrong him ;—though the course
Of private life licentiously displayed
Unhallowed actions—planted like a crown
Upon the insolent aspiring brow
Of spurious notions—worn as open signs

Of prejudice subdued—he still retained,
'Mid such abasement, what he had received
From nature—an intense and glowing mind.
Wherefore, when humbled Liberty grew weak,
And mortal sickness on her face appeared,
He coloured objects to his own desire
As with a lover's passion. Yet his moods
Of pain were keen as those of better men,
Nay, keener—as his fortitude was less.
And he continued, when worse days were come,
To deal about his sparkling eloquence,
Struggling against the strange reverse with zeal
That showed like happiness; but, in despite
Of all this outside bravery, within,
He neither felt encouragement nor hope.
For moral dignity, and strength of mind,
Were wanting; and simplicity of life;
And reverence for himself; and, last and best,
Confiding thoughts, through love and fear of Him
Before whose sight the troubles of this world
Are vain as billows in a tossing sea.

"The glory of the times fading away,
The splendour, which had given a festal air
To self-importance, hallowed it, and veiled
From his own sight,—this gone, he forfeited
All joy in human nature; was consumed,
And vexed, and chafed, by levity and scorn,
And fruitless indignation; galled by pride;
Made desperate by contempt of men who throve
Before his sight in power or fame, and won,
Without desert, what he desired; weak men,
Too weak even for his envy or his hate!
Tormented thus, after a wandering course
Of discontent, and inwardly opprest
With malady—in part, I fear, provoked
By weariness of life, he fixed his home,
Or, rather say, sate down by very chance,
Among these rugged hills; where now he dwells,
And wastes the sad remainder of his hours
In self-indulging spleen, that doth not want
Its own voluptuousness; on this resolved,
With this content, that he will live and die
Forgotten,—at safe distance from a 'world
Not moving to his mind.'"

These serious words
Closed the preparatory notices
That served my fellow-traveller to beguile
The way, while we advanced up that wide vale.
Diverging now (as if his quest had been
Some secret of the mountains, cavern, fall
Of water—or some boastful eminence,
Renowned for splendid prospect far and wide)
We scaled, without a track to ease our steps,
A steep ascent; and reached a dreary plain,
With a tumultuous waste of huge hill tops
Before us; savage region! which I paced
Dispirited: when, all at once, behold!

Beneath our feet, a little lowly vale,
A lowly vale, and yet uplifted high
Among the mountains, even as if the spot
Had been, from eldest time by wish of theirs,
So placed,—to be shut out from all the world!
Urn-like it was in shape, deep as an urn,
With rocks encompassed, save that to the south
Was one small opening, where a heath-clad ridge
Supplied a boundary less abrupt and close;
A quiet treeless nook, with two green fields,
A liquid pool that glittered in the sun,
And one bare dwelling, one abode, no more!
It seemed the home of poverty and toil,
Though not of want. the little fields, made green
By husbandry of many thrifty years,
Paid cheerful tribute to the moorland house
There crows the cock, single in his domain;
The small birds find in spring no thicket there
To shroud them; only from the neighbouring vales
The cuckoo, straggling up to the hill tops,
Shouteth faint tidings of some gladder place.

Ah! what a sweet recess, thought I, is here!
Instantly throwing down my limbs at ease
Upon a bed of heath;—full many a spot
Of hidden beauty have I chanced to espy
Among the mountains; never one like this,
So lonesome, and so perfectly secure,
Not melancholy—no, for it is green,
And bright, and fertile, furnished in itself
With the few needful things that life requires.
In rugged arms how soft it seems to lie,
How tenderly protected! Far and near
We have an image of the pristine earth,
The planet in its nakedness; were this
Man's only dwelling, sole appointed seat,
First, last, and single in the breathing world,
It could not be more quiet: peace is here
Or nowhere; days unruffled by the gale
Of public news or private; years that pass
Forgetfully; uncalled upon to pay
The common penalties of mortal life,
Sickness, or accident, or grief, or pain.

On these and kindred thoughts intent I lay,
In silence musing by my comrade's side,
He also silent when from out the heart
Of that profound abyss a solemn voice
Or several voices in one solemn sound,
Was heard—ascending: mournful, deep, and slow
The cadence, as of psalms—a funeral dirge!
We listened, looking down upon the hut,
But seeing no one; meanwhile from below
The strain continued, spiritual as before,
And now distinctly could I recognize
These words:—"*Shall in the grave thy love be known,*
In death thy faithfulness?"—"God rest his soul!"

The wanderer cried, abruptly breaking silence,—
"He is departed, and finds peace at last!"

This scarcely spoken, and those holy strains
Not ceasing, forth appeared in view a band
Of rustic persons, from behind the hut
Bearing a coffin in the midst, with which
They shaped their course along the sloping side
Of that small valley; singing as they moved;
A sober company and few, the men
Bare-headed, and all decently attired!
Some steps when they had thus advanced, the dirge
Ended; and, from the stillness that ensued
Recovering, to my friend I said, "You spake,
Methought, with apprehension that these rites
Are paid to him upon whose shy retreat
This day we purposed to intrude."—"I did so,
But let us hence, that we may learn the truth:
Perhaps it is not he but some one else
For whom this pious service is performed;
Some other tenant of the solitude."

So, to a steep and difficult descent
Trusting ourselves, we wound from crag to crag,
Where passage could be won; and, as the last
Of the mute train, upon the heathy top
Of that off-sloping outlet, disappeared,
I, more impatient in my downward course,
Had landed upon easy ground; and there
Stood waiting for my comrade. When behold
An object that enticed my steps aside!
A narrow, winding entry opened out
Into a platform—that lay, sheepfold-wise,
Inclosed between an upright mass of rock
And one old moss-grown wall;—a cool recess,
And fanciful! For, where the rock and wall
Met in an angle, hung a penthouse, framed
By thrusting two rude staves into the wall
And overlaying them with mountain sods;
To weather-fend a little turf-built seat
Whereon a full-grown man might rest, nor dread
The burning sunshine, or a transient shower;
But the whole plainly wrought by children's hands!
Whose skill had thronged the floor with a proud show
Of baby-houses, curiously arranged;
Nor wanting ornament of walks between,
With mimic trees inserted in the turf,
And gardens interposed. Pleased with the sight,
I could not choose but beckon to my guide,
Who, entering, round him threw a careless glance,
Impatient to pass on, when I exclaimed,
"Lo! what is here?" and stooping down, drew forth
A book, that, in the midst of stones and moss,
A wreck of party-coloured earthenware,
Aptly disposed, had lent its help to raise
One of those petty structures. "Gracious Heaven!"
The Wanderer cried, "it cannot but be his,
And he is gone!" The book, which in my hand

Had opened of itself, (for it was swoln
With searching damp, and seemingly had lain
To the injurious elements exposed
From week to week,) I found to be a work
In the French tongue, a novel of Voltaire,
His famous Optimist "Unhappy man!"
Exclaimed my friend, "here then has been to him
Retreat within retreat, a sheltering-place
Within how deep a shelter! He had fits,
Even to the last, of genuine tenderness,
And loved the haunts of children: here, no doubt,
Pleasing and pleased, he shared their simple sports,
Or sate companionless, and here the book,
Left and forgotten in his careless way,
Must by the cottage children have been found
Heaven bless them, and their inconsiderate work!
To what odd purpose have the darlings turned
This sad memorial of their hapless friend!"

"Me," said I, "most doth it surprise, to find
Such book in such a place!" "A book it is,"
He answered, "to the person suited well,
Though little suited to surrounding things;
'Tis strange, I grant; and stranger still had been
To see the man who owned it, dwelling here,
With one poor shepherd, far from all the world!
Now, if our errand hath been thrown away,
As from these intimations I forebode,
Grieved shall I be—less for my sake than yours,
And least of all for him who is no more."

By this, the book was in the old man's hand;
And he continued, glancing on the leaves
An eye of scorn, "The lover," said he, "doomed
To love when hope hath failed him—whom no depth
Of privacy is deep enough to hide,
Hath yet his bracelet or his lock of hair,
And that is joy to him. When change of times
Hath summoned kings to scaffolds, do but give
The faithful servant, who must hide his head
Henceforth in whatsoever nook he may,
A kerchief sprinkled with his master's blood,
And he too hath his comforter. How poor,
Beyond all poverty how destitute,
Must that man have been left, who, hither driven,
Flying or seeking, could yet bring with him
No dearer relique, and no better stay,
Than this dull product of a scoffer's pen,
Impure conceits discharging from a heart
Hardened by impious pride!—I did not fear
To tax you with this journey;"—mildly said
My venerable friend, as forth we stepped
Into the presence of the cheerful light—
"For I have knowledge that you do not shrink
From moving spectacles,—but let us on."

So speaking, on he went, and at the word
I followed, till he made a sudden stand:

For full in view, approaching through a gate
That opened from the inclosure of green fields
Into the rough uncultivated ground,
Behold the man whom he had fancied dead!
I knew, from his deportment, mien, and dress,
That it could be no other; a pale face,
A tall and meagre person, in a garb
Not rustic, dull and faded like himself!
He saw us not, though distant but few steps;
For he was busy, dealing, from a store
Upon a broad leaf carried, choicest strings
Of red ripe currants; gift by which he strove,
With intermixture of endearing words,
To soothe a child, who walked beside him, weeping
As if disconsolate.—"They to the grave
Are bearing him, my little one," he said;
"To the dark pit; but he will feel no pain;
His body is at rest, his soul in heaven."

More might have followed—but my honoured friend
Broke in upon the speaker with a frank
And cordial greeting.—Vivid was the light
That flashed and sparkled from the other's eyes;
He was all fire: the sickness from his face
Passed like a fancy that is swept away;
Hands joined he with his visitant,—a grasp,
An eager grasp; and, many moments' space,
When the first glow of pleasure was no more,
And much of what had vanished was returned,
An amicable smile retained the life
Which it had unexpectedly received,
Upon his hollow cheek. "How kind!" he said,
"Nor could your coming have been better timed;
For this, you see, is in our narrow world
A day of sorrow. I have here a charge"—
And, speaking thus, he patted tenderly
The sun-burnt forehead of the weeping child—
"A little mourner, whom it is my task
To comfort;—but how came ye?—if yon track
(Which doth at once befriend us and betray)
Conducted hither your most welcome feet,
You could not miss the funeral train—they yet
Have scarcely disappeared." "This blooming child,"
Said the old man, "is of an age to weep
At any grave or solemn spectacle,
Inly distressed, or overpowered with awe,
He knows not why;—but he, perchance, this day,
Is shedding orphan's tears; and you yourself
Must have sustained a loss."—"The hand of death,"
He answered, "has been here; but could not well
Have fallen more lightly, if it had not fallen
Upon myself."—The other left these words
Unnoticed, thus continuing.—
"From yon crag,
Down whose steep sides we dropped into the vale,
We heard the hymn they sang—a solemn sound
Heard any where, but in a place like this
'Tis more than human! Many precious rites

And customs of our rural ancestry
Are gone, or stealing from us, this, I hope.
Will last for ever. Often have I stopped,
So much I felt the awfulness of life,
In that one moment when the corse is lifted
In silence, with a hush of decency,
Then from the threshold moves with song of peace,
And confidential yearnings, to its home,
Its final home in earth What traveller—who—
(How far soe'er a stranger) does not own
The bond of brotherhood, when he sees them go,
A mute procession on the houseless road;
Or passing by some single tenement
Or clustered dwellings, where again they raise
The monitory voice? But most of all
It touches, it confirms, and elevates,
Then, when the body, soon to be consigned
Ashes to ashes, dust bequeathed to dust,
Is raised from the church aisle, and forward borne
Upon the shoulders of the next in love,
The nearest in affection or in blood,
Yea, by the very mourners who had knelt
Beside the coffin, resting on its lid
In silent grief their unuplifted heads,
And heard meanwhile the Psalmist's mournful plaint,
And that most awful scripture which declares
We shall not sleep, but we shall all be changed!
Have I not seen?—Ye likewise may have seen—
Son, husband, brothers—brothers side by side,
And son and father also side by side,
Rise from that posture:—and in concert move,
On the green turf following the vested priest,
Four dear supporters of one senseless weight,
From which they do not shrink, and under which
They faint not, but advance towards the grave
Step after step—together, with their firm
Unhidden faces; he that suffers most
He outwardly, and inwardly perhaps
The most serene, with most undaunted eye!
Oh! blest are they who live and die like these,
Loved with such love, and with such sorrow mourned!"

"That poor man taken hence to-day," replied
The Solitary, with a faint sarcastic smile
Which did not please me, "must be deemed, I fear,
Of the unblest; for he will surely sink
Into his mother earth without such pomp
Of grief, depart without occasion given
By him for such array of fortitude.
Full seventy winters hath he lived, and mark!
This simple child will mourn his one short hour,
And I shall miss him; scanty tribute! yet,
This wanting, he would leave the sight of men,
If love were his sole claim upon their care,
Like a ripe date which in the desert falls
Without a hand to gather it." At this
I interposed, though loth to speak, and said,
"Can it be thus among so small a band

As ye must needs be here? in such a place
I would not willingly, methinks, lose sight
Of a departing cloud."—"'Twas not for love"—
Answered the sick man with a careless voice—
"That I came hither; neither have I found
Among associates who have power of speech,
Nor in such other converse as is here,
Temptation so prevailing as to change
That mood, or undermine my first resolve."—
Then, speaking in like careless sort, he said
To my benign companion,—"Pity 'tis
That fortune did not guide you to this house
A few days earlier; then you would have seen
What stuff the dwellers in a solitude,
That seems by nature hollowed out to be
The seat and bosom of pure innocence,
Are made of; an ungracious matter this!
Which for truth's sake, yet in remembrance too
Of past discussions with this zealous friend
And advocate of humble life, I now
Will force upon his notice; undeterred
By the example of his own pure course,
And that respect and deference which a soul
May fairly claim, by niggard age enriched
In what she values most—the love of God
And his frail creature man;—but ye shall hear.
I talk—and ye are standing in the sun
Without refreshment!"
Saying this, he led
Towards the cottage;—homely was the spot;
And to my feeling, ere we reached the door,
Had almost a forbidding nakedness;
Less fair, I grant, even painfully less fair,
Than it appeared when from the beetling rock
We had looked down upon it. All within,
As left by the departed company,
Was silent; and the solitary clock
Ticked, as I thought, with melancholy sound.—
Following our guide, we clomb the cottage stairs
And reached a small apartment dark and low,
Which was no sooner entered, than our host
Said gaily, "This is my domain, my cell,
My hermitage, my cabin,—what you will—
I love it better than a snail his house.
But now ye shall be feasted with our best."
So, with more ardour than an unripe girl
Left one day mistress of her mother's stores,
He went about his hospitable task.
My eyes were busy, and my thoughts no less,
And pleased I looked upon my gray-haired friend
As if to thank him; he returned that look,
Cheered plainly, and yet serious. What a wreck
Had we around us! scattered was the floor,
And, in like sort, chair, window-seat, and shelf,
With books, maps, fossils, withered plants and flowers.
And tufts of mountain moss; mechanic tools
Lay intermixed with scraps of paper,—some
Scribbled with verse: a broken angling-rod

And shattered telescope, together linked
By cobwebs, stood within a dusty nook;
And instruments of music, some half-made,
Some in disgrace, hung dangling from the walls.
But speedily the promise was fulfilled;
A feast before us, and a courteous host
Inviting us in glee to sit and eat.
A napkin, white as foam of that rough brook
By which it had been bleached, o'erspread the board·
And was itself half-covered with a load
Of dainties,—oaten bread, curd, cheese, and cream,
And cakes of butter curiously embossed,
Butter that had imb bed a golden tinge
From meadow flowers, hue delicate as theirs
Faintly reflected in a lingering stream;
Nor lacked, for more delight on that warm day,
Our table, small parade of garden fruits,
And whortle-berries from the mountain side
The child, who long ere this had stilled his sobs,
Was now a help to his late comforter,
And moved a willing page, as he was bid,
Ministering to our need

In genial mood,
While at our pastoral banquet thus we sate
Fronting the window of that little cell,
I could not, ever and anon, forbear
To glance an upward look on two huge peaks,
That from some other vale peered into this.
"Those lusty twins," exclaimed our host, "if here
It were your lot to dwell, would soon become
Your prized companions.—Many are the notes
Which, in his tuneful course, the wind draws forth
From rocks, woods, caverns, heaths, and dashing shores;
And well those lofty brethren bear their part
In the wild concert—chiefly when the storm
Rides high; then all the upper air they fill
With roaring sound, that ceases not to flow,
Like smoke, along the level of the blast,
In mighty current; theirs, too, is the song
Of stream and headlong flood that seldom fails;
And, in the grim and breathless hour of noon,
Methinks that I have heard them echo back
The thunder's greeting·—nor have nature's laws
Left them ungifted with a power to yield
Music of finer tone; a harmony,
So do I call it; though it be the hand
Of silence, though there be no voice;—the clouds,
The mist, the shadows, light of golden suns,
Motions of moonlight, all come hither—touch,
And have an answer—thither come, and shape
A language not unwelcome to sick hearts
And idle spirits:—there the sun himself,
At the calm close of summer's longest day,
Rests his substantial orb;—between those heights
And on the top of either pinnacle,
More keenly than elsewhere in night's blue vault,
Sparkle the stars, as of their station proud.
Thoughts are not busier in the mind of man

Than the mute agents stirring there :—alone
Here do I sit and watch."
A fall of voice,
Regretted like the nightingale's last note,
Had scarcely closed this high-wrought rhapsody,
Ere with inviting smile the wanderer said,
"Now for the tale with which you threatened us!"
"In truth the threat escaped me unawares;
Should the tale tire you, let this challenge stand
For my excuse. Dissevered from mankind,
As to your eyes and thoughts we must have seemed
When ye looked down upon us from the crag,
Islanders of a stormy mountain sea,
We are not so;—perpetually we touch
Upon the vulgar ordinance of the world,
And, he, whom this our cottage hath to-day
Relinquished, lived dependent for his bread
Upon the laws of public charity.
The housewife, tempted by such slender gains
As might from that occasion be distilled,
Opened, as she before had done for me,
Her doors to admit this homeless pensioner;
The portion gave of coarse but wholesome fare
Which appetite required—a blind dull nook
Such as she had—the *kennel* of his rest!
This, in itself not ill, would yet have been
Ill borne in earlier life, but his was now
The still contentedness of seventy years.
Calm did he sit beneath the wide-spread tree
Of his old age; and yet less calm and meek,
Winningly meek or venerably calm,
Than slow and torpid; paying in this wise
A penalty, if penalty it were,
For spendthrift feats, excesses of his prime.
I loved the old man, for I pitied him!
A task it was, I own, to hold discourse
With one so slow in gathering up his thoughts,
But he was a cheap pleasure to my eyes;
Mild, inoffensive, ready in *his* way,
And helpful to his utmost power: and there
Our housewife knew full well what she possessed!
He was her vassal of all labour, tilled
Her garden, from the pasture fetched her kine;
And, one among the orderly array
Of hay-makers, beneath the burning sun
Maintained his place; or heedfully pursued
His course, on errands bound, to other vales,
Leading sometimes an inexperienced child,
Too young for any profitable task.
So moved he like a shadow that performed
Substantial service. Mark me now, and learn
For what reward! The moon her monthly round
Hath not completed since our dame, the queen
Of this one cottage and this lonely dale,
Into my little sanctuary rushed—
Voice to a rueful treble humanized,
And features in deplorable dismay.
I treat the matter lighty, but alas!

It is most serious: persevering rain
Had fallen in torrents, all the mountain tops
Were hidden, and black vapours coursed their sides;
This had I seen and saw; but, till she spake,
Was wholly ignorant that my ancient friend,
Who at her bidding, early and alone,
Had clomb aloft to delve the moorland turf
For winter fuel, to his noontide meal
Returned not, and now, haply on the heights
Lay at the mercy of this raging storm.
"Inhuman!"—said I, "was an old man's life
Not worth the trouble of a thought?—alas!
This notice comes too late." With joy I saw
Her husband enter—from a distant vale.
We sallied forth together; found the tools
Which the neglected veteran had dropped,
But through all quarters looked for him in vain.
We shouted—but no answer! Darkness fell
Without remission of the blast or shower,
And fears for our own safety drove us home
I, who weep little, did, I will confess,
The moment I was seated here alone,
Honour my little cell with some few tears
Which anger and resentment could not dry.
All night the storm endured; and, soon as help
Had been collected from the neighbouring vale,
With morning we renewed our quest · the wind
Was fallen, the rain abated, but the hills
Lay shrouded in impenetrable mist,
And long and hopelessly we sought in vain.
Till, chancing on that lofty ridge to pass
A heap of ruin, almost without walls,
And wholly without roof (the bleached remains
Of a small chapel, where, in ancient time,
The peasants of these lonely valleys used
To meet for worship on that central height)—
We there espied the object of our search,
Lying full three parts buried among tufts
Of heath-plant, under and above him strewn,
To baffle, as he might, the watery storm:
And there we found him breathing peaceably,
Snug as a child that hides itself in sport
'Mid a green hay-cock in a sunny field.
We spake—he made reply, but would not stir
At our entreaty; less from want of power
Than apprehension and bewildering thoughts.
So was he lifted gently from the ground,
And with their freight the shepherds homeward moved
Through the dull mist, I following—when a step,
A single step that freed me from the skirts
Of the blind vapour, opened to my view
Glory beyond all glory ever seen
By waking sense or by the dreaming soul!
The appearance instantaneously disclosed,
Was of a mighty city—boldly say
A wilderness of building, sinking far
And self-withdrawn into a wondrous depth,
Far sinking into splendour—without end!

Fabric it seemed of diamond and of gold,
With alabaster domes, and silver spires,
And blazing terrace upon terrace, high
Uplifted; here, serene pavilions bright
In avenues disposed; there towers begirt
With battlements that on their restless fronts
Bore stars—illumination of all gems!
By earthly nature had the effect been wrought
Upon the dark materials of the storm
Now pacified; on them, and on the coves
And mountain-steeps and summits, whereunto
The vapours had receded, taking there
Their station under a cerulean sky
Oh, 'twas an unimaginable sight!
Clouds, mists, streams, watery rocks and emerald turf
Clouds of all tincture, rocks and sapphire sky,
Confused, commingled, mutually inflamed,
Molten together, and composing thus,
Each lost in each, that marvellous array
Of temple, palace, citadel, and huge
Fantastic pomp of structure without name,
In fleecy folds voluminous enwrapped.
Right in the midst, where interspace appeared
Of open court, an object like a throne
Beneath a shining canopy of state
Stood fixed; and fixed resemblances were seen
To implements of ordinary use,
But vast in size, in substance glorified;
Such as by Hebrew prophets were beheld
In vision—forms uncouth of mightiest power,
For admiration and mysterious awe.
Below me was the earth; this little vale
Lay low beneath my feet; 'twas visible—
I saw not, but I felt that this was there.
That which I *saw* was the revealed abode
Of spirits in beatitude: my heart
Swelled in my breast.—'I have been dead,' I cried,
'And now I live! Oh! wherefore do I live?'
And with that pang I prayed to be no more!—
But I forget our charge, as utterly
I then forgot him:—there I stood and gazed;
The apparition faded not away,
And I descended.—Having reached the house,
I found its rescued inmate safely lodged,
And in serene possession of himself,
Beside a genial fire, that seemed to spread
A gleam of comfort o'er his pallid face.
Great show of joy the housewife made, and truly
Was glad to find her conscience set at ease;
And not less glad, for sake of her good name,
That the poor sufferer had escaped with life.
But, though he seemed at first to have received
No harm, and uncomplaining as before
Went through his usual tasks, a silent change
Soon showed itself: he lingered three short weeks;
And from the cottage hath been borne to-day.

'So ends my dolorous tale, and glad I am

That it is ended." At these words he turned—
And, with blithe air of open fellowship,
Brought from the cupboard wine and stouter cheer,
Like one who would be merry. Seeing this.
My gray-haired friend said courteously—"Nay, nay,
You have regaled us as a hermit ought,
Now let us forth into the sun!"—Our host
Rose, though reluctantly, and forth we went.

BOOK III.

ARGUMENT.

Images in the valley—Another recess in it entered and described—Wanderer's sensations—Solitary's excited by the same objects—Contrast between these—Despondency of the Solitary gently reproved—Conversation exhibiting the Solitary's past and present opinions and feelings, till he enters upon his own history at length—His domestic felicity—Afflictions—Dejection—Roused by the French Revolution—Disappointment and disgust—Voyage to America—Disappointment and disgust pursue him—His return—His languor and depression of mind, from want of faith in the great truths of religion, and want of confidence in the virtue of mankind.

DESPONDENCY.

A HUMMING bee—a little tinkling rill—
A pair of falcons wheeling on the wing,
In clamorous agitation, round the crest
Of a tall rock, their airy citadel—
By each and all of these the pensive ear
Was greeted in the silence that ensued,
When through the cottage threshold we had passed
And, deep within that lonesome valley, stood
Once more, beneath the concave of a blue
And cloudless sky.—Anon! exclaimed our host,
Triumphantly dispersing with the taunt
The shade of discontent which on his brow
Had gathered,—"Ye have left my cell,—but see
How nature hems you in with friendly arms!
And by her help ye are my prisoners still.
But which way shall I lead you?—how contrive,
In spot so parsimoniously endowed,
That the brief hours, which yet remain, may reap
Some recompense of knowledge or delight?"
So saying, round he looked as if perplexed;
And, to remove those doubts, my gray-haired friend
Said—"Shall we take this pathway for our guide?—
Upward it winds, as if, in summer heats,
Its line had first been fashioned by the flock
A place of refuge seeking at the root
Of yon black yew-tree; whose protruded boughs
Darken the silver bosom of the crag,
From which she draws her meagre sustenance.
There in commodious shelter may we rest,
Or let us trace this streamlet to its source;
Feebly it tinkles with an earthy sound,
And a few steps may bring us to the spot
Where, haply, crowned with flowerets and green herbs,

The mountain infant to the sun comes forth,
Like human life from darkness."—A quick turn
Through a strait passage of encumbered ground
Proved that such hope was vain :—for now we stood
Shut out from prospect of the open vale,
And saw the water that composed this rill,
Descending, disembodied and diffused
O'er the smooth surface of an ample crag,
Lofty and steep, and naked as a tower,
All further progress here was barred ;—And who,
Thought I, if master of a vacant hour,
Here would not linger, willingly detained?
Whether to such wild objects he were led
When copious rains have magnified the stream
Into a loud and white-robed waterfall,
Or introduced at this more quiet time.

Upon a semicirque of turf-clad ground,
The hidden nook discovered to our view
A mass of rock resembling, as it lay
Right at the foot of that moist precipice,
A stranded ship, with keel upturned,—that rests
Fearless of winds and waves. Three several stones
Stood near, of smaller size, and not unlike
To monumental pillars : and from these
Some little space disjoined, a pair were seen,
That with united shoulders bore aloft
A fragment, like an altar, flat and smooth :
Barren the table, yet thereon appeared
A tall and shining holly, that had found
A hospitable chink, and stood upright,
As if inserted by some human hand
In mockery, to wither in the sun,
Or lay its beauty flat before a breeze,
The first that entered. But no breeze did now
Find entrance ; high, or low, appeared no trace
Of motion, save the water that descended,
Diffused adown that barrier of steep rock,
And softly creeping, like a breath of air,
Such as is sometimes seen, and hardly seen,
To brush the still breast of a crystal lake.

"Behold a cabinet for sages built,
Which kings might envy !"—Praise to this effect
Broke from the happy old man's reverend lip ;
Who to the Solitary turned, and said,
"In sooth, with love's familiar privilege,
You have decried the wealth which is your own.
Among these rocks and stones, methinks, I see
More than the heedless impress that belongs
To lonely nature's casual work : they bear
A semblance strange of power intelligent,
And of design not wholly worn away.
Boldest of plants that ever faced the wind,
How gracefully that slender shrub looks forth
From its fantastic birthplace ! And I own,
Some shadowy intimations haunt me here,
That in these shows a chronicle survives

Of purposes akin to those of man,
But wrought with mightier arm than now prevails.
Voiceless the stream descends into the gulf
With timid lapse ;—and lo! while in this strait
I stand—the chasm of sky above my head
Is heaven's profoundest azure, no domain
For fickle, short-lived clouds to occupy,
Or to pass through, but rather an abyss
In which the everlasting stars abide;
And whose soft gloom, and boundless depth, might tempt
The curious eye to look for them by day.
Hail contemplation! from the stately towers,
Reared by the industrious hand of human art
To lift thee high above the misty air,
And turbulence of murmuring cities vast,
From academic groves, that have for thee
Been planted, hither come and find a lodge
To which thou mayst resort for holier peace,—
From whose calm centre thou, through height or depth
Mayst penetrate, wherever truth shall lead;
Measuring through all degrees, until the scale
Of time and conscious nature disappear,
Lost in unsearchable eternity!"

A pause ensued; and with minuter care
We scanned the various features of the scene:
And soon the tenant of that lonely vale
With courteous voice thus spake—
"I should have grieved
Hereafter, not escaping self-reproach,
If from my poor retirement ye had gone
Leaving this nook unvisited: but, in sooth,
Your unexpected presence has so roused
My spirits, that they were bent on enterprise;
And, like an ardent hunter, I forgot,
Or, shall I say?—disdained, the game that lurks
At my own door. The shapes before our eyes,
And their arrangement, doubtless must be deemed
The sport of nature, aided by blind chance,
Rudely to mock the works of toiling man.
And hence, this upright shaft of unhewn stone,
From fancy, willing to set off her stores
By sounding titles, hath acquired the name
Of Pompey's pillar; *that* I gravely style
My Theban obelisk, and, there, behold
A Druid cromlech!—thus I entertain
The antiquarian humour, and am pleased
To skim along the surfaces of things,
Beguiling harmlessly the listless hours.
But, if the spirit be oppressed by sense
Of instability, revolt, decay,
And change, and emptiness, these freaks of nature
And her blind helper chance, do *then* suffice
To quicken, and to aggravate—to feed
Pity and scorn, and melancholy pride,
Not less than that huge pile (from some abyss
Of mortal power unquestionably sprung)
Whose hoary diadem of pendant rocks

Confines the shrill-voiced whirlwind, round and round
Eddying within its vast circumference,
On Sarum's naked plain;—than pyramid
Of Egypt, unsubverted, undissolved;
Or Syria's marble ruins towering high
Above the sandy desert, in the light
Of sun or moon—Forgive me, if I say
That an appearance, which hath raised your minds
To an exalted pitch, (the self-same cause
Different effect producing) is for me
Fraught rather with depression than delight,
Though shame it were, could I not look around,
By the reflection of your pleasure, pleased.
Yet happier, in my judgment, even than you
With your bright transports fairly may be deemed,
The wandering herbalist,—who, clear alike
From vain, and, that worse evil, vexing thoughts,
Casts, if he ever chance to enter here,
Upon these uncouth forms a slight regard
Of transitory interest, and peeps round
For some rare floweret of the hills, or plant
Of craggy fountain; what he hopes for wins,
Or learns, at least, that 'tis not to be won:
Then, keen and eager, as a fine-nosed hound
By soul-engrossing instinct driven along
Through wood or open field, the harmless man
Departs, intent upon his onward quest!
Nor is that fellow-wanderer, so deem I,
Less to be envied, (you may trace him oft
By scars which his activity has left
Beside our roads and pathways, though, thank Heaven
This covert nook reports not of his hand,)
He, who with pocket hammer smites the edge
Of luckless rock or prominent stone, disguised
In weather-stains, or crusted o'er by nature
With her first growths—detaching by the stroke
A chip, or splinter—to resolve his doubts;
And, with that ready answer satisfied,
The substance classes by some barbarous name,
And hurries on; or from the fragments picks
His specimen, if but haply interveined
With sparkling mineral, or should crystal cube
Lurk in its cells—and thinks himself enriched,
Wealthier, and doubtless wiser, than before!
Intrusted safely—each to his pursuit
Earnest alike, let both from hill to hill
Range; if it please them, speed from clime to clime;
The mind is full—no pain is in their sport."

"Then," said I, interposing; "one is near,
Who cannot but possess in your esteem
Place worthier still of envy. May I name,
Without offence, that fair-faced cottage-boy?
Dame nature's pupil of the lowest form,
Youngest apprentice in the school of art!
Him, as we entered from the open glen,
You might have noticed, busily engaged,
Heart, soul, and hands,—in mending the defects

Left in the fabric of the leaky dam,
Raised for enabling this penurious stream
To turn a slender mill (that new-made plaything)
For his delight—the happiest he of all!"

"Far happiest,' answered the desponding man,
"If such as now he is, he might remain!
Ah! what avails imagination high
Or question deep? what profits all that earth,
Or heaven's blue vault, is suffered to put forth
Of impulse or allurement, for the soul
To quit the beaten track of life, and soar
Far as she finds a yielding element
In past or future; far as she can go
Through time or space; if neither in the one,
Nor in the other region, nor in aught
That fancy, dreaming o'er the map of things,
Hath placed beyond these penetrable bounds,
Words of assurance can be heard; if nowhere
A habitation for consummate good,
Nor for progressive virtue, by the search
Can be attained, a better sanctuary
From doubt and sorrow, than the senseless grave?"

"Is this," the gray-haired wanderer mildly said,
"The voice, which we so lately overheard,
To that same child, addressing tenderly
The consolations of a hopeful mind?
'*His body is at rest, his soul in heaven.*'
These were your words; and, verily, methinks
Wisdom is oft-times nearer when we stoop
Than when we soar."

The other, not displeased,
Promptly replied,—"My notion is the same.
And I, without reluctance, could decline
All act of inquisition whence we rise,
And what, when breath had ceased, we may become.
Here are we, in a bright and breathing world—
Our origin, what matters it? In lack
Of worthier explanation, say at once
With the American (a thought which suits
The place where now we stand) that certain men
Leap out together from a rocky cave;
And these were the first parents of mankind:
Or, if a different image be recalled
By the warm sunshine, and the jocund voice
Of insects—chirping out their careless lives
On these soft beds of thyme-besprinkled turf,
Choose, with the gay Athenian, a conceit
As sound—blithe race! whose mantles were bedecked
With golden grasshoppers, in sign that they
Had sprung, like those bright creatures, from the soil
Whereon their endless generations dwelt.
But stop!—these theoretic fancies jar
On serious minds; then, as the Hindoos draw
Their holy Ganges from a skyey fount,
Even so deduce the stream of human life
From seats of power divine; and hope, or trust,

That our existence winds her stately course
Beneath the sun, like Ganges, to make part
Of a living ocean ; or, to sink ingulfed
Like Niger, in impenetrable sands
And utter darkness : thought which may be faced,
Though comfortless !—Not of myself I speak ;
Such acquiescence neither doth imply,
In me, a meekly-bending spirit soothed
By natural piety ; nor a lofty mind,
By philosophic discipline prepared
For calm subjection to acknowledged law ;
Pleased to have been, contented not to be.
Such palms I boast not ;—no ! to me, who find,
Reviewing my past way, much to condemn,
Little to praise, and nothing to regret,
(Save some remembrances of dream-like joys
That scarcely seem to have belonged to me,)
If I must take my choice between the pair
That rule alternately the weary hours,
Night is than day more acceptable ;—sleep
Doth, in my estimate of good, appear
A better state than waking ; death than sleep :
Feelingly sweet is stillness after storm,
Though under covert of the wormy ground !

"Yet be it said, in justice to myself,
That in more genial times, when I was free
To explore the destiny of human kind,
(Not as an intellectual game pursued
With curious subtilty, from wish to cheat
Irksome sensations ; but by love of truth
Urged on, or haply by intense delight
In feeding thought, wherever thought could feed,)
I did not rank with those (too dull or nice,
For to my judgment such they then appeared,
Or too aspiring, thankless at the best)
Who, in this frame of human life perceive
An object whereunto their souls are tied
In discontented wedlock ; nor did e'er,
From me, those dark impervious shades, that hang
Upon the region whither we are bound,
Exclude a power to enjoy the vital beams
Of present sunshine.—Deities that float
On wings, angelic spirits, I could muse
O'er what from eldest time we have been told
Of your bright forms and glorious faculties,
And with the imagination be content,
Not wishing more ; repining not to tread
The little sinuous path of earthly care,
By flowers embellished, and by springs refreshed.
'Blow winds of autumn !—let your chilling breath
Take the live herbage from the mead, and strip
The shady forest of its green attire,—
And let the bursting clouds to fury rouse
The gentle brooks !—Your desolating sway,'
Thus I exclaimed, 'no sadness sheds on me.
And no disorder in your rage I find.
What dignity, what beauty in this change

From mild to angry, and from sad to gay,
Alternate and revolving! How benign,
How rich in animation and delight,
How bountiful these elements—compared
With aught, as more desirable and fair,
Devised by fancy for the golden age,
Or the perpetual warbling that prevails
In Arcady, beneath unaltered skies,
Through the long year in constant quiet bound,
Night hushed as night, and day serene as day!'
But why this tedious record?—Age, we know,
Is garrulous, and solitude is apt
To anticipate the privilege of age.
From far ye come; and surely with a hope
Of better entertainment—let us hence!"

Loth to forsake the spot, and still more loth
To be diverted from our present theme,
I said, "My thoughts agreeing, sir, with yours,
Would push this censure farther,—for, if smiles
Of scornful pity be the just reward
Of poesy, thus courteously employed
In framing models to improve the scheme
Of man's existence, and recast the world,
Why should not grave philosophy be styled,
Herself, a dreamer of a kindred stock,
A dreamer yet more spiritless and dull?
Yes, shall the fine immunities she boasts
Establish sounder titles of esteem
For her, who (all too timid and reserved
For onset, for resistance too inert,
Too weak for suffering, and for hope too tame)
Placed among flowery gardens, curtained round
With world-excluding groves, the brotherhood
Of soft Epicureans, taught—if they
The ends of being would secure, and win
The crown of wisdom—to yield up their souls
To a voluptuous unconcern, preferring
Tranquillity to all things. Or is she,"
I cried, "more worthy of regard, the power,
Who, for the sake of sterner quiet, closed
The Stoic's heart against the vain approach
Of admiration, and all sense of joy?"

His countenance gave notice that my zeal
Accorded little with his present mind;
I ceased, and he resumed,—"Ah! gentle sir,
Slight, if you will, the *means*; but spare to slight
The *end* of those, who did, by system, rank,
As the prime object of a wise man's aim,
Security from shock of accident,
Release from fear; and cherished peaceful days
For their own sakes, as mortal life's chief good,
And only reasonable felicity.
What motive drew, what impulse, I would ask,
Through a long course of later ages, drove
The hermit to his cell in forest wide;
Or what detained him, till his closing eyes

Took their last farewell of the sun and stars,
Fast anchored in the desert?—Not alone
Dread of the persecuting sword—remorse,
Wrongs unredressed, or insults unavenged
And unavengeable, defeated pride,
Prosperity subverted, maddening want,
Friendship betrayed, affection unreturned,
Love with despair, or grief in agony:—
Not always from intolerable pangs
He fled; but, compassed round by pleasure, sighed
For independent happiness; craving peace,
The central feeling of all happiness,
Not as a refuge from distress or pain,
A breathing-time, vacation, or a truce,
But for its absolute self; a life of peace,
Stability without regret or fear;
That hath been, is, and shall be evermore!
Such the reward he sought; and wore out life,
There, where on few external things his heart
Was set, and those his own; or, if not his,
Subsisting under nature's steadfast law.

"What other yearning was the master tie
Of the monastic brotherhood; upon rock
Aërial, or in green secluded vale,
One after one, collected from afar,
An undissolving fellowship!—What but this,
The universal instinct of repose,
The longing for confirmed tranquillity,
Inward and outward; humble, yet sublime:—
The life where hope and memory are as one;
Earth quiet and unchanged; the human soul
Consistent in self-rule; and heaven revealed
To meditation, in that quietness!
Such was their scheme:—thrice happy he who gained
The end proposed! And,—though the same were missed
By multitudes, perhaps obtained by none,—
They, for the attempt, and for the pains employed,
Do, in my present censure, stand redeemed
From the unqualified disdain, that once
Would have been cast upon them, by my voice
Delivering its decisions from the seat
Of forward youth:—that scruples not to solve
Doubts, and determine questions, by the rules
Of inexperienced judgment, ever prone
To overweening faith; and is inflamed,
By courage, to demand from real life
The test of act and suffering—to provoke
Hostility, how dreadful when it comes,
Whether affliction be the foe, or guilt!

"A child of earth, I rested, in that stage
Of my past course to which these thoughts advert,
Upon earth's native energies; forgetting
That mine was a condition which required
Nor energy, nor fortitude—a calm
Without vicissitude; which, if the like
Had been presented to my view elsewhere,

I might have even been tempted to despise.
But that which was serene was also bright,
Enlivened happiness, with joy o'erflowing,
With joy, and—oh! that memory should survive
To speak the word—with rapture! Nature's boon,
Life's genuine inspiration, happiness
Above what rules can teach, or fancy feign;
Abused, as all possessions are abused
That are not prized according to their worth.
And yet, what worth? what good is given to men,
More solid than the gilded clouds of heaven?
What joy more lasting than a vernal flower?
None! 'tis the general plaint of human kind
In solitude, and mutually addressed
From each to all, for wisdom's sake:—This truth
The priest announces from his holy seat;
And, crowned with garlands in the summer grove,
The poet fits it to his pensive lyre.
Yet, ere that final resting-place be gained
Sharp contradictions may arise by doom
Of this same life, compelling us to grieve
That the prosperities of love and joy
Should be permitted, oft-times, to endure
So long, and be at once cast down for ever.
Oh! tremble ye to whom hath been assigned
A course of days composing happy months,
And they as happy years; the present still
So like the past, and both so firm a pledge
Of a congenial future, that the wheels
Of pleasure move without the aid of hope:
For mutability is nature's bane;
And slighted hope will be avenged, and, when
Ye need her favours, ye shall find her not;
But, in her stead—fear—doubt—and agony!"

This was the bitter language of the heart;
But, while he spake, look, gesture, tone of voice,
Though discomposed and vehement, were such
As skill and graceful nature might suggest
To a proficient of the tragic scene
Standing before the multitude, beset
With dark events Desirous to divert
Or stem the current of the speaker's thoughts,
We signified a wish to leave that place
Of stillness and close privacy, a nook
That seemed for self-examination made,
Or, for confession, in the sinner's need,
Hidden from all men's view. To our attempt
He yielded not; but, pointing to a slope
Of mossy turf defended from the sun,
And, on that couch inviting us to rest,
Full on that tender-hearted man he turned
A serious eye, and thus his speech renewed.

"You never saw, your eyes did never look
On the bright form of her whom once I loved:—
Her silver voice was heard upon the earth,
A sound unknown to you; else, honoured friend

Your heart had borne a pitiable share
Of what I suffered, when I wept that loss,
And suffer now, not seldom, from the thought
That I remember, and can weep no more.—
Stripped as I am of all the golden fruit
Of self-esteem ; and by the cutting blasts
Of self-reproach familiarly assailed ;
I would not yet be of such wintry bareness,
But that some leaf of your regard should hang
Upon my naked branches :—lively thoughts
Give birth, full often, to unguarded words ;
I grieve that, in your presence, from my tongue
Too much of frailty hath already dropped ;
But that too much demands still more.
You know,
Revered compatriot ;—and to you, kind sir,
(Not to be deemed a stranger, as you come
Following the guidance of these welcome feet
To our secluded vale) it may be told,
That my demerits did not sue in vain
To one on whose mild radiance many gazed
With hope, and all with pleasure. This fair bride,
In the devotedness of youthful love,
Preferring me to parents, and the choir
Of gay companions, to the natal roof,
And all known places and familiar sights,
(Resigned with sadness gently weighing down
Her trembling expectations, but no more
Than did to her due honour, and to me
Yielded, that day, a confidence sublime
In what I had to build upon)—this bride,
Young, modest, meek, and beautiful, I led
To a low cottage in a sunny bay,
Where the salt sea innocuously breaks,
And the sea breeze as innocently breathes,
On Devon's leafy shores ;—a sheltered hold,
In a soft clime encouraging the soil
To a luxuriant bounty !—As our steps
Approach the embowered abode—our chosen seat—
See, rooted in the earth, her kindly bed,
The unendangered myrtle, decked with flowers,
Before the threshold stands to welcome us !
While, in the flowering myrtle's neighbourhood,
Not overlooked, but courting no regard,
Those native plants, the holly and the yew,
Gave modest intimation to the mind
How willingly their aid they would unite
With the green myrtle, to endear the hours
Of winter, and protect that pleasant place.
Wild were the walks upon those lonely downs,
Track leading into track, how marked, how worn
Into bright verdure, between fern and gorse
Winding away its never-ending line
On their smooth surface, evidence was none ;
But, there, lay open to our daily haunt,
A range of unappropriated earth,
Where youth's ambitious feet might move at large ;
Whence, unmolested wanderers, we beheld

The shining giver of the day diffuse
His brightness, o'er a tract of sea and land
Gay as our spirits, free as our desires,
As our enjoyments boundless.—From those heights
We dropped, at pleasure, into sylvan combs;
Where arbours of impenetrable shade,
And mossy seats, detained us side by side,
With hearts at ease, and knowledge in our hearts
'That all the grove and all the day was ours.'

"But nature called my partner to resign
Her share in the pure freedom of that life,
Enjoyed by us in common —To my hope,
To my heart's wish, my tender mate became
The thankful captive of maternal bonds;
And those wild paths were left to me alone
There could I meditate on follies past,
And, like a weary voyager escaped
From risk and hardship, inwardly retrace
A course of vain delights and thoughtless guilt,
And self-indulgence—without shame pursued.
There, undisturbed, could think of, and could thank
Her—whose submissive spirit was to me
Rule and restraint—my guardian—shall I say
That earthly Providence, whose guiding love
Within a port of rest had lodged me safe;
Safe from temptation, and from danger far?
Strains followed of acknowledgment addressed
To an Authority enthroned above
The reach of sight; from whom, as from their source,
Proceed all visible ministers of good
That walk the earth—Father of heaven and earth,
Father, and King, and Judge, adored and feared!
These acts of mind, and memory, and heart,
And spirit,—interrupted and relieved
By observations transient as the glance
Of flying sunbeams, or to the outward form
Cleaving with power inherent and intense,
As the mute insect fixed upon the plant
On whose soft leaves it hangs, and from whose cup
Draws imperceptibly its nourishment,—
Endeared my wanderings; and the mother's kiss
And infant's smile, awaited my return.

"In privacy we dwelt—a wedded pair—
Companions daily, often all day long;
Not placed by fortune within easy reach
Of various intercourse, nor wishing aught
Beyond the allowance of our own fire-side,
The twain within our happy cottage born,
Inmates, and heirs of our united love;
Graced mutually by difference of sex,
By the endearing names of nature bound,
And with no wider interval of time
Between their several births than served for one
To establish something of a leader's sway,
Yet left them joined by sympathy in age;
Equals in pleasure, fellows in pursuit.

On these two pillars rested as in air
Our solitude.
It soothes me to perceive,
Your courtesy withholds not from my words
Attentive audience. But oh! gentle friends,
As times of quiet and unbroken peace
Though, for a nation, times of blessedness,
Give back faint echoes from the historian's page;
So, in the imperfect sounds of this discourse,
Depressed I hear, how faithless is the voice
Which those most blissful days reverberate.
What special record can, or need, be given
To rules and habits, whereby much was done,
But all within the sphere of little things,
Of humble, though, to us, important cares,
And precious interests? Smoothly did our life
Advance, not swerving from the path prescribed;
Her annual, her diurnal round alike
Maintained with faithful care. And you divine
The worst effects that our condition saw
If you imagine changes slowly wrought,
And in their progress imperceptible;
Not wished for, sometimes noticed with a sigh
(Whate'er of good or lovely they might bring),
Sighs of regret, for the familiar good,
And loveliness endeared—which they removed.

"Seven years of occupation undisturbed
Established seemingly a right to hold
That happiness: and use and habit gave
To what an alien spirit had acquired
A patrimonial sanctity. And thus,
With thoughts and wishes bounded to this world,
I lived and breathed; most grateful, if to enjoy
Without repining or desire for more,
For different lot, or change to higher sphere,
(Only except some impulses of pride
With no determined object, though upheld
By theories with suitable support)
Most grateful, if in such wise to enjoy
Be proof of gratitude for what we have;
Else, I allow, most thankless.—But, at once,
From some dark seat of fatal power was urged
A claim that shattered all.—Our blooming girl,
Caught in the gripe of death, with such brief time
To struggle in as scarcely would allow
Her cheek to change its colour, was conveyed
From us, to regions inaccessible;
Where height, or depth, admits not the approach
Of living man, though longing to pursue.
With even as brief a warning—and how soon,
With what short interval of time between,
I tremble yet to think of—our last prop,
Our happy life's only remaining stay—
The brother followed; and was seen no more!

"Calm as a frozen lake when ruthless winds
Blow fiercely, agitating earth and sky,

The mother now remained, as if in her,
Who, to the lowest region of the soul,
Had been erewhile unsettled and disturbed,
This second visitation had no power
To shake; but only to bind up and seal
And to establish thankfulness of heart
In Heaven's determinations, ever just;
The eminence on which her spirit stood
Mine was unable to attain Immense
The space that severed us! But, as the sight
Communicates with heaven's ethereal orbs
Incalculably distant; so, I felt
That consolation may descend from far;
(And, that is intercourse, and union, too)
While, overcome with speechless gratitude,
And, with a holier love inspired, I looked
On her—at once superior to my woes
And partner of my loss.—Oh, heavy change!
Dimness o'er this clear luminary crept
Insensibly;—the immortal and divine
Yielded to mortal reflux; her pure glory,
As from the pinnacle of worldly state
Wretched ambition drops astounded, fell
Into a gulf obscure of silent grief,
And keen heart-anguish—of itself ashamed,
Yet obstinately cherishing itself:
And, so consumed, she melted from my arms;
And left me, on this earth, disconsolate.

"What followed cannot be reviewed in thought;
Much less retraced in words If she, of life
Blameless; so intimate with love and joy,
And all the tender motions of the soul,
Had been supplanted, could I hope to stand—
Infirm, dependent, and now destitute?
I called on dreams and visions, to disclose
That which is veiled from waking thought; conjured
Eternity, as men constrain a ghost
To appear and answer; to the grave I spake
Imploringly;—looked up, and asked the heavens
If angels traversed their cerulean floors,
If fixed or wandering star could tidings yield
Of the departed spirit—what abode
It occupies—what consciousness retains
Of former loves and interests. Then my soul
Turned inward,—to examine of what stuff
Time's fetters are composed, and life was put
To inquisition, long and profitless!
By pain of heart—now checked—and now impelled-
The intellectual power, through words and things,
Went sounding on, a dim and perilous way,
And from those transports, and these toils abstruse,
Some trace am I enabled to retain
Of time, else lost; existing unto me
Only by records in myself not found.

"From that abstraction I was roused,—and how?
Even as a thoughtful shepherd by a flash

Of lightning startled in a gloomy cave
Of these wild hills. For lo! the dread Bastile,
With all the chambers in its horrid towers,
Fell to the ground:—by violence o'erthrown
Of indignation; and with shouts that drowned
The crash it made in falling! From the wreck
A golden palace rose, or seemed to rise,
The appointed seat of equitable law
And mild paternal sway. The potent shock
I felt; the transformation I perceived,
As marvellously seized as in that moment
When, from the blind mist issuing, I beheld
Glory—beyond all glory ever seen,
Confusion infinite of heaven and earth,
Dazzling the soul! Meanwhile prophetic harps
In every grove were ringing, 'War shall cease;
Did ye not hear that conquest is abjured?
Bring garlands, bring forth choicest flowers, to deck
The tree of liberty.'—My heart rebounded;
My melancholy voice the chorus joined:
'Be joyful all ye nations! in all lands,
Ye that are capable of joy be glad!
Henceforth whate'er is wanting to yourselves
In others ye shall promptly find;—and all
Be rich by mutual and reflected wealth.'

"Thus was I reconverted to the world;
Society became my glittering bride,
And airy hopes my children. From the depths
Of natural passion, seemingly escaped,
My soul diffused herself in wide embrace
Of institutions, and the forms of things;
As they exist, in mutable array,
Upon life's surface. What, though in my veins
There flowed no Gallic blood, nor had I breathed
The air of France, not less than Gallic zeal
Kindled and burnt among the sapless twigs
Of my exhausted heart. If busy men
In sober conclave met, to weave a web
Of amity, whose living threads should stretch
Beyond the seas, and to the farthest pole,
There did I sit, assisting. If, with noise
And acclamation, crowds in open air
Expressed the tumult of their minds, my voice
There mingled, heard or not. The powers of song
I left not uninvoked; and, in still groves,
Where mild enthusiasts tuned a pensive lay
Of thanks and expectation, in accord
With their belief, I sang Saturnian rule
Returned,—a progeny of golden years
Permitted to descend, and bless mankind.
With promises the Hebrew Scriptures teem:
I felt the invitation; and resumed
A long-suspended office in the house
Of public worship, where, the glowing phrase
Of ancient inspiration serving me,
I promised also,—with undaunted trust
Foretold, and added prayer to prophecy;

The admiration winning of the crowd ;
The help desiring of the pure devout.

"Scorn and contempt forbid me to proceed!
But history, time's slavish scribe, will tell
How rapidly the zealots of the cause
Disbanded—or in hostile ranks appeared ;
Some tired of honest service ; these, outdone,
Disgusted, therefore, or appalled, by aims
Of fiercer zealots—so confusion reigned,
And the more faithful were compelled to exclaim,
As Brutus did to virtue, 'Liberty,
I worshipped thee, and find thee but a shade!'

"Such recantation had for me no charm,
Nor would I bend to it ; who should have grieved
At aught, however fair, that bore the mien
Of a conclusion, or catastrophe.
Why then conceal, that, when the simply good
In timid selfishness withdrew, I sought
Other support, not scrupulous whence it came,
And, by what compromise it stood not nice?
Enough if notions seem to be high pitched,
And qualities determined. Among men
So charactered did I maintain a strife
Hopeless, and still more hopeless every hour ;
But, in the process, I began to feel
That, if the emancipation of the world
Were missed, I should at least secure my own,
And be in part compensated. For rights,
Widely—inveterately usurped upon,
I spake with vehemence ; and promptly seized
Whate'er abstraction furnished for my needs
Or purposes ; nor scrupled to proclaim,
And propagate, by liberty of life,
Those new persuasions. Not that I rejoiced,
Or even found pleasure, in such vagrant course
For its own sake ; but farthest from the walk
Which I had trod in happiness and peace,
Was most inviting to a troubled mind ;
That, in a struggling and distempered world,
Saw a seductive image of herself.
Yet, mark the contradictions of which man
Is still the sport! Here nature was my guide,
The nature of the dissolute ; but thee,
O fostering nature! I rejected—smiled
At others' tears in pity ; and in scorn
At those which thy soft influence sometimes drew
From my unguarded heart.—The tranquil shores
Of Britain circumscribed me ; else, perhaps,
I might have been entangled among deeds
Which, now, as infamous, I should abhor—
Despise, as senseless : for my spirit relished
Strangely the exasperation of that land,
Which turned an angry beak against the down
Of her own breast ; confounded into hope
Of disencumbering thus her fretful wings.

But all was quieted by iron bonds
Of military sway. The shifting aims,
The moral interests, the creative might,
The varied functions and high attributes
Of civil action, yielded to a power
Formal, and odious, and contemptible.
In Britain, ruled a panic dread of change;
The weak were praised, rewarded, and advanced;
And, from the impulse of a just disdain
Once more did I retire into myself.
There feeling no contentment, I resolved
To fly, for safeguard, to some foreign shore,
Remote from Europe; from her blasted hopes;
Her fields of carnage, and polluted air.

"Fresh blew the wind, when o'er the Atlantic main
The ship went gliding with her thoughtless crew:
And who among them but an exile, freed
From discontent, indifferent, pleased to sit
Among the busily employed, not more
With obligation charged, with service taxed,
Than the loose pendant—to the idle wind
Upon the tall mast, streaming:—but, ye powers
Of soul and sense—mysteriously allied,
Oh, never let the wretched, if a choice
Be left him, trust the freight of his distress
To a long voyage on the silent deep!
For, like a plague, will memory break out;
And, in the blank and solitude of things,
Upon his spirit, with a fever's strength,
Will conscience prey.—Feebly must they have felt
Who, in old time, attired with snakes and whips
The vengeful Furies. *Beautiful* regards
Were turned on me—the face of her I loved;
The wife and mother, pitifully fixing
Tender reproaches, insupportable!
Where now that boasted liberty? No welcome
From unknown objects I received; and those,
Known and familiar, which the vaulted sky
Did, in the placid clearness of the night,
Disclose, had accusations to prefer
Against my peace. Within the cabin stood
That volume—as the compass for the soul—
Revered among the nations. I implored
Its guidance; but the infallible support
Of faith was wanting. Tell me, why refused
To one by storms annoyed and adverse winds;
Perplexed with currents; of his weakness sick;
Of vain endeavours tired; and by his own,
And by his nature's, ignorance, dismayed?

"Long-wished-for sight, the western world appeared;
And, when the ship was moored, I leaped ashore
Indignantly—resolved to be a man,
Who, having o'er the past no power, would live
No longer in subjection to the past,
With abject mind—from a tyrannic lord
Inviting penance, fruitlessly endured.

So, like a fugitive, whose feet have cleared
Some boundary, which his followers may not cross
In prosecution of their deadly chase,
Respiring I looked round.—How bright the sun,
How promising the breeze!—Can aught produced
In the old world compare, thought I, for power
And majesty with this gigantic stream,
Sprung from the desert? And behold a city
Fresh, youthful, and aspiring! What are these
To me, or I to them? as much at least
As he desires that they should be, whom winds
And waves have wafted to this distant shore,
In the condition of a damaged seed,
Whose fibres cannot, if they would, take root
Here may I roam at large, my business is,
Roaming at large, to observe, and not to feel;
And, therefore, not to act—convinced that all
Which bears the name of action, howsoe'er
Beginning, ends in servitude—still painful,
And mostly profitless And, sooth to say,
On nearer view, a motley spectacle
Appeared, of high pretensions—unreproved
But by the obstreperous voice of higher still;
Big passions strutting on a petty stage;
Which a detached spectator may regard
Not unamused.—But ridicule demands
Quick change of objects, and, to laugh alone.
At a composing distance from the haunts
Of strife and folly—though it be a treat
As choice as musing leisure can bestow,
Yet in the very centre of the crowd,
To keep the secret of a poignant scorn,
Howe'er to airy demons suitable,
Of all unsocial courses, is least fit
For the gross spirit of mankind,—the one
That soonest fails to please, and quickliest turns
Into vexation.—Let us, then, I said,
Leave this unknit republic to the scourge
Of her own passions; and to regions haste,
Whose shades have never felt the encroaching axe,
Or soil endured a transfer in the mart
Of dire rapacity. There man abides,
Primeval nature's child A creature weak
In combination (wherefore else driven back
So far, and of his old inheritance
So easily deprived?) but, for that cause,
More dignified, and stronger in himself,
Whether to act, judge, suffer, or enjoy.
True, the intelligence of social art
Hath overpowered his forefathers, and soon
Will sweep the remnant of his line away;
But contemplations, worthier, nobler far
Than her destructive energies attend
His independence, when along the side
Of Mississippi, or that northern stream
That spreads into successive seas, he walks:
Pleased to perceive his own unshackled life,
And his innate capacities of soul,

There imaged : or, when having gained the top
Of some commanding eminence, which yet
Intruder ne'er beheld, he thence surveys
Regions of wood and wide savanna, vast
Expanse of unappropriated earth,
With mind that sheds a light on what he sees ;
Free as the sun, and lonely as the sun,
Pouring above his head its radiance down
Upon a living and rejoicing world !

"So, westward, tow'rd the unviolated woods
I bent my way ; and, roaming far and wide,
Failed not to greet the merry mocking-bird ;
And, while the melancholy muccawiss
(The sportive bird's companion in the grove)
Repeated, o'er and o'er, his plaintive cry,
I sympathised at leisure with the sound,
But that pure archetype of human greatness,
I found him not. There, in his stead, appeared
A creature, squalid, vengeful, and impure ;
Remorseless, and submissive to no law
But superstitious fear, and abject sloth.
Enough is told ! Here am I—Ye have heard
What evidence I seek, and vainly seek ;
What from my fellow-beings I require,
And cannot find ; what I myself have lost,
Nor can regain ; how languidly I look
Upon this visible fabric of the world,
May be divined—perhaps it hath been said :—
But spare your pity, if there be in me
Aught that deserves respect : for I exist—
Within myself—not comfortless.—The tenor
Which my life holds, he readily may conceive
Whoe'er hath stood to watch a mountain brook
In some still passage of its course, and seen,
Within the depths of its capacious breast,
Inverted trees, and rocks, and azure sky ;
And, on its glassy surface, specks of foam,
And conglobated bubbles undissolved,
Numerous as stars ; that, by their onward lapse,
Betray to sight the motion of the stream,
Else imperceptible ; meanwhile, is heard
A softened roar, a murmur ; and the sound
Though soothing, and the little floating isles
Though beautiful, are both by nature charged
With the same pensive office ; and make known
Through what perplexing labyrinths, abrupt
Precipitations, and untoward straits,
The earth-born wanderer hath passed ; and quickly,
That respite o'er, like traverses and toils
Must be again encountered.—Such a stream
Is human life ; and so the spirit fares
In the best quiet to its course allowed ;
And such is mine,—save only for a hope
That my particular current soon will reach
The unfathomable gulf, where all is still !"

BOOK IV.

ARGUMENT.

State of feeling produced by the foregoing narrative—A belief in a superintending Providence the only adequate support under affliction—Wanderer's ejaculation—Account of his own devotional feelings in youth involved—Acknowledges the difficulty of a lively faith—Hence immoderate sorrow—Doubt or despondence not therefore to be inferred—Consolation to the Solitary—Exhortations—How received—Wanderer applies his discourse to that other cause of dejection in the Solitary's mind—Disappointment from the French Revolution—States grounds of hope—Insists on the necessity of patience and fortitude with respect to the course of great revolutions—Knowledge the source of tranquillity—Rural solitude favourable to knowledge of the inferior creatures—Study of their habits and ways recommended—Exhortation to bodily exertion and communion with nature—Morbid solitude pitiable—Superstition better than apathy—Apathy and destitution unknown in the infancy of society—The various modes of religion prevented it —Illustrated in the Jewish, Persian, Babylonian, Chaldean, and Grecian modes of belief—Solitary interposes—Wanderer points out the influence of religious and imaginative feeling in the humble ranks of society—Illustrated from present and past times—These principles tend to recall exploded superstitions and popery—Wanderer rebuts this charge, and contrasts the dignities of the Imagination with the presumptive littleness of certain modern philosophers—Recommends other lights and guides—Asserts the power of the soul to regenerate herself—Solitary asks how—Reply—Personal appeal—Happy that the imagination and the affections mitigate the evils of that intellectual slavery which the calculating understanding is apt to produce—Exhortation to activity of body renewed—How to commune with nature—Wanderer concludes with a legitimate union of the imagination, affections, understanding, and reason—Effect of his discourse—Evening—Return to the cottage

DESPONDENCY CORRECTED.

HERE closed the tenant of that lonely vale
His mournful narrative—commenced in pain,
In pain commenced, and ended without peace:
Yet tempered, not unfrequently with strains
Of native feeling, grateful to our minds;
And doubtless yielding some relief to his,
While we sate listening with compassion due.
Such pity yet surviving, with firm voice,
That did not falter, though the heart was moved,
The Wanderer said—
"One adequate support
For the calamities of mortal life
Exists, one only;—an assured belief
That the procession of our fate, howe'er
Sad or disturbed, is ordered by a Being
Of infinite benevolence and power,
Whose everlasting purposes embrace
All accidents, converting them to good.
The darts of anguish fix not where the seat
Of suffering hath been thoroughly fortified
By acquiescence in the Will Supreme
For time and for eternity; by faith,
Faith, absolute in God, including hope,
And the defence that lies in boundless love
Of His perfections; with habitual dread
Of aught unworthily conceived, endured
Impatiently; ill-done, or left undone,
To the dishonour of His holy name.
Soul of our souls, and safeguard of the world,
Sustain, Thou only canst, the sick of heart:

Restore their languid spirits, and recall
Their lost affections unto Thee and Thine!"

Then, as we issued from that covert nook,
He thus continued—lifting up his eyes
To heaven.—"How beautiful this dome of sky.
And the vast hills, in fluctuation fixed
At Thy command, how awful! Shall the soul,
Human and rational, report of Thee
Even less than these?—Be mute who will, who can,
Yet will I praise Thee with impassioned voice:
My lips, that may forget Thee in the crowd,
Cannot forget Thee here; where Thou hast built,
For Thy own glory, in the wilderness!
Me didst Thou constitute a priest of thine,
In such a temple as we now behold
Reared for Thy presence: therefore am I bound
To worship here and everywhere—as one
Not doomed to ignorance, though forced to tread,
From childhood up, the ways of poverty,
From unreflecting ignorance preserved,
And from debasement rescued.—By Thy grace
The particle divine remained unquenched;
And, 'mid the wild weeds of a rugged soil,
Thy bounty caused to flourish deathless flowers,
From Paradise transplanted; wintry age
Impends, the frost will gather round my heart;
And, if they wither, I am worse than dead!
Come, labour, when the worn-out frame requires
Perpetual Sabbath; come, disease and want;
And sad exclusion through decay of sense;
But leave me unabated trust in Thee—
And let Thy favour, to the end of life,
Inspire me with ability to seek
Repose and hope among eternal things—
Father of heaven and earth! and I am rich,
And will possess my portion in content!

"And what are things eternal?—Powers depart,"
The grey-haired Wanderer steadfastly replied,
Answering the question which himself had asked,
"Possessions vanish, and opinions change,
And passions hold a fluctuating seat
But, by the storms of circumstance unshaken,
And subject neither to eclipse nor wane,
Duty exists; immutably survive,
For our support, the measures and the forms,
Which an abstract intelligence supplies;
Whose kingdom is where time and space are not:
Of other converse, which mind, soul, and heart,
Do, with united urgency, require,
What more, that may not perish? Thou, dread Source,
Prime, self-existing Cause and End of all,
That, in the scale of being fill their place,
Above our human region, or below,
Set and sustained;—Thou—who didst wrap the cloud
Of infancy around us, that Thyself,
Therein, with our simplicity a while

Mightst hold, on earth, communion undisturbed—
Who from the anarchy of dreaming sleep,
Or from its death-like void, with punctual care,
And touch as gentle as the morning light,
Restorest us daily to powers of sense,
And reason's steadfast rule—Thou, Thou alone
Art everlasting, and the blessed spirits,
Which Thou includest, as the sea her waves:
For adoration Thou endurest, endure
For consciousness the motions of Thy will;
For apprehension those transcendant truths
Of pure intellect that stand as laws,
(Submission constituting strength and power)
Even to Thy Being's infinite majesty!
This Universe shall pass away—a work
Glorious! because the shadow of thy might,
A step, or link, for intercourse with Thee
Ah! if the time must come, in which my feet
No more shall stray where meditation leads,
By flowing stream, through wood, or craggy wild,
Loved haunts like these, the unprisoned mind
May yet have scope to range among her own,
Her thoughts, her images, her high desires.
If the dear faculty of sight should fail,
Still, it may be allowed me to remember
What visionary powers of eye and soul
In youth were mine, when stationed on the top
Of some huge hill—expectant, I beheld
The sun rise up, from distant climes returned
Darkness to chase, and sleep, and bring the day
His bounteous gift! or saw him towards the deep
Sink with a retinue of flaming clouds
Attended; then my spirit was entranced
With joy exalted to beatitude;
The measure of my soul was filled with bliss,
And holiest love, as earth, sea, air, with light,
With pomp, with glory, with magnificence!

"Those fervent raptures are for ever flown·
And, since their date, my soul hath undergone
Change manifold, for better or for worse;
Yet cease I not to struggle, and aspire
Heavenward: and chide the part of me that flags,
Through sinful choice; or dread necessity,
On human nature, from above, imposed.
'Tis, by comparison, an easy task
Earth to despise; but, to converse with Heaven—
This is not easy:—to relinquish all
We have, or hope, of happiness and joy,
And stand in freedom loosened from this world,
I deem not arduous.—but must needs confess
That 'tis a thing impossible to frame
Conceptions equal to the soul's desires;
And the most difficult of tasks to *keep*
Heights which the soul is competent to gain
Man is of dust: ethereal hopes are his,
Which, when they should sustain themselves aloft,
Want due consistence· like a pillar of smoke,

That with majestic energy from earth
Rises, but, having reached the thinner air,
Melts, and dissolves, and is no longer seen.
From this infirmity of mortal kind
Sorrow proceeds, which else were not,—at least
If grief be something hallowed and ordained,
If in proportion, it be just and meet,
Through this, 'tis able to maintain its hold,
In that excess which conscience disapproves.
For who could sink and settle to that point
Of selfishness; so senseless who could be
As long and perseveringly to mourn
For any object of his love, removed
From this unstable world, if he could fix
A satisfying view upon that state
Of pure, imperishable blessedness,
Which reason promises, and Holy Writ
Insures to all believers?—Yet mistrust
Is of such incapacity, methinks,
No natural branch; despondency far less.
And, if there be whose tender frames have drooped
Even to the dust; apparently, through weight
Of anguish unrelieved, and lack of power
An agonizing sorrow to transmute,
Infer not hence a hope from those withheld
When wanted most; a confidence impaired
So pitiably, that, having ceased to see
With bodily eyes, they are borne down by love
Of what is lost, and perish through regret.
Oh! no, full oft the innocent sufferer sees
Too clearly; feels too vividly; and longs
To realize the vision, with intense
And overconstant yearning—there—there lies
The excess, by which the balance is destroyed.
Too, too contracted are these walls of flesh,
This vital warmth too cold, these visual orbs,
Though inconceivably endowed, too dim
For any passion of the soul that leads
To ecstasy, and, all the crooked paths
Of time and change disdaining, takes its course
Along the line of limitless desires.
I, speaking now from such disorder free,
Nor rapt, nor craving, but in settled peace,
I cannot doubt that they whom you deplore
Are glorified; or, if they sleep, shall wake
From sleep, and dwell with God in endless love.
Hope, below this, consists not with belief
In mercy, carried infinite degrees
Beyond the tenderness of human hearts
Hope, below this, consists not with belief
In perfect wisdom, guiding mightiest power,
That finds no limits but her own pure will.

"Here then we rest; not fearing for our creed
The worst that human reasoning can achieve,
To unsettle or perplex it: yet with pain
Acknowledging, and grievous self-reproach,
That, though immovably convinced, we want

Zeal, and the virtue to exist by faith
As soldiers live by courage; as, by strength
Of heart, the sailor fights with roaring seas.
Alas! the endowment of immortal power
Is matched unequally with custom, time,
And domineering faculties of sense
In *all;* in most with superadded foes,
Idle temptations—open vanities,
Ephemeral offspring of the unblushing world;
And in the private regions of the mind,
Ill-governed passions, ranklings of despite,
Immoderate wishes, pining discontent,
Distress and care. What then remains?—To seek
Those helps, for his occasions ever near,
Who lacks not will to use them; vows, renewed
On the first motion of a holy thought;
Vigils of contemplation; praise; and prayer,
A stream, which, from the fountain of the heart,
Issuing, however feebly, nowhere flows
Without access of unexpected strength.
But, above all, the victory is most sure
For him, who, seeking faith by virtue, strives
To yield entire submission to the law
Of conscience; conscience reverenced and obeyed,
As God's most intimate presence in the soul,
And his most perfect image in the world.
Endeavour thus to live; these rules regard;
These helps solicit; and a steadfast seat
Shall then be yours among the happy few
Who dwell on earth, yet breathe empyreal air,
Sons of the morning. For your nobler part,
Ere disencumbered of her mortal chains,
Doubt shall be quelled and trouble chased away;
With only such degree of sadness left
As may support longings of pure desire;
And strengthen love, rejoicing secretly
In the sublime attractions of the grave."

While in this strain, the venerable sage
Poured forth his aspirations, and announced
His judgments, near that lonely house we paced
A plot of greensward, seemingly preserved
By nature's care from wreck of scattered stones,
And from encroachment of encircling heath:
Small space! but, for reiterated steps,
Smooth and commodious; as a stately deck
Which to and fro the mariner is used
To tread for pastime, talking with his mates,
Or haply thinking of far-distant friends,
While the ship glides before a steady breeze.
Stillness prevailed around us: and the voice
That spake was capable to lift the soul
Toward regions yet more tranquil. But, methought,
That he whose fixed despondency had given
Impulse and motive to that strong discourse,
Was less upraised in spirit than abashed;
Shrinking from admonition, like a man
Who feels that to exhort is to reproach.

Yet not to be diverted from his aim,
The sage continued.—"For that other loss,
The loss of confidence in social man,
By the unexpected transports of our age
Carried so high, that every thought—which looked
Beyond the temporal destiny of the kind—
To many seemed superfluous; as no cause
For such exalted confidence could e'er
Exist; so, none is now for fixed despair;
The two extremes are equally disowned
By reason; if, with sharp recoil, from one
You have been driven far as its opposite,
Between them seek the point whereon to build
Sound expectations. So doth he advise
Who shared at first the illusion; but was soon
Cast from the pedestal of pride by shocks
Which nature gently gave, in woods and fields;
Nor unreproved by Providence, thus speaking
To the inattentive children of the world:
'Vain-glorious generation! What new powers
On you have been conferred? what gifts withheld
From your progenitors, have ye received,
Fit recompense of new desert? what claim
Are ye prepared to urge, that my decrees
For you should undergo a sudden change;
And the weak functions of one busy day,
Reclaiming and extirpating, perform
What all the slowly-moving years of time,
With their united force, have left undone?
By nature's gradual processes be taught;
By story be confounded! Ye aspire
Rashly, to fall once more; and that false fruit,
Which to your over-weening spirits, yields
Hope of a flight celestial, will produce
Misery and shame. But wisdom of her sons
Shall not the less, though late, be justified.'
Such timely warning, said the Wanderer, gave
That visionary voice; and, at this day,
When a Tartarian darkness overspreads
The groaning nations; when the impious rule,
By will or by established ordinance,
Their own dire agents, and constrain the good
To acts which they abhor; though I bewail
This triumph, yet the pity of my heart
Prevents me from not owning that the law
By which mankind now suffers, is most just.
For by superior energies; more strict
Affiance in each other; faith more firm
In their unhallowed principles; the bad
Have fairly earned a victory o'er the weak,
The vacillating, inconsistent good.
Therefore, not unconsoled, I wait—in hope
To see the moment when the righteous cause
Shall gain defenders zealous and devout
As they who have opposed her; in which virtue
Will, to her efforts, tolerate no bounds
That are not lofty as her rights; aspiring
By impulse of her own ethereal zeal.

That spirit only can redeem mankind
And when that sacred spirit shall appear,
Then shall our triumph be complete as theirs.
Yet, should this confidence prove vain, the wise
Have still the keeping of their proper peace:
Are guardians of their own tranquillity,
They act, or they recede, observe, and feel;
'Knowing the heart of man is set to be
The centre of this world, about the which
Those revolutions of disturbances
Still roll, where all the aspects of misery
Predominate; whose strong effects are such
As he must bear, being powerless to redress;
And that unless above himself he can
*Erect himself, how poor a thing is man!'**

"Happy is he who lives to understand—
Not human nature only, but explores
All natures,—to the end that he may find
The law that governs each, and where begins
The union, the partition where, that makes
Kind and degree, among all visible beings,
The constitutions, powers, and faculties,
Which they inherit, cannot step beyond,—
And cannot fall beneath; that do assign
To every class its station and its office,
Through all the mighty commonwealth of things;
Up from the creeping plant to sovereign man.
Such converse, if directed by a meek,
Sincere, and humble spirit, teaches love;
For knowledge is delight; and such delight
Breeds love; yet, suited as it rather is
To thought and to the climbing intellect,
It teaches less to love, than to adore;
If that be not indeed the highest love!"

"Yet," said I, tempted here to interpose,
"The dignity of life is not impaired
By aught that innocently satisfies
The humbler cravings of the heart; and he
Is a still happier man, who, for those heights
Of speculation not unfit, descends;
And such benign affections cultivates
Among the inferior kinds; not merely those
That he may call his own, and which depend,
As individual objects of regard,
Upon his care,—from whom he also looks
For signs and tokens of a mutual bond,—
But others, far beyond this narrow sphere,
Whom, for the very sake of love, he loves.
Nor is it a mean praise of rural life
And solitude, that they do favour most,
Most frequently call forth, and best sustain
These pure sensations; that can penetrate
The obstreperous city; on the barren seas
Are not unfelt,—and much might recommend,

* Daniel.

How much they might inspirit and endear,
The loneliness of this sublime retreat!"

"Yes," said the sage, resuming the discourse
Again directed to his downcast friend,
"If, with the froward will and grovelling soul
Of man offended, liberty is here,
And invitation every hour renewed,
To mark *their* placid state, who never heard
Of a command which they have power to break,
Or rule which they are tempted to transgress;
These, with a soothed or elevated heart,
May we behold; their knowledge register;
Observe their ways; and, free from envy, find
Complacence there;—but wherefore this to you?
I guess that, welcome to your lonely hearth,
The redbreast feeds in winter from your hand;
A box, perchance, is from your casement hung
For the small wren to build in;—not in vain,
The barriers disregarding that surround
This deep abiding-place, before your sight
Mounts on the breeze the butterfly—and soars,
Small creature as she is, from earth's bright flowers
Into the dewy clouds. Ambition reigns
In the waste wilderness the soul ascends
Towards her native firmament of heaven,
When the fresh eagle, in the month of May,
Upborne, at evening, on replenished wing,
This shaded valley leaves,—and leaves the dark
Empurpled hills,—conspicuously renewing
A proud communication with the sun
Low sunk beneath the horizon!—List!—I heard,
From yon huge breast of rock, a solemn bleat,
Sent forth as if it were the mountain's voice,
As if the visible mountain made the cry.
Again!"—The effect upon the soul was such
As he expressed, from out the mountain's heart
The solemn bleat appeared to issue, startling
The blank air—for the region all around
Stood silent, empty of all shape of life:
It was a lamb—left somewhere to itself,
The plaintive spirit of the solitude!—
He paused, as if unwilling to proceed,
Through consciousness that silence in such place
Was best,—the most affecting eloquence.
But soon his thoughts returned upon themselves,
And, in soft tone of speech, he thus resumed:

"Ah! if the heart, too confidently raised,
Perchance too lightly occupied, or lulled
Too easily, despise or overlook
The vassalage that binds her to the earth,
Her sad dependence upon time, and all
The trepidations of mortality,
What place so destitute and void—but there
The little flower her vanity shall check;
The trailing worm reprove her thoughtless pride?

"These craggy regions, these chaotic wilds
Does that benignity pervade, that warms
The mole contented with her darksome walk
In the cold ground: and to the emmet gives
Her foresight, and intelligence that makes
The tiny creatures strong by social league,
Supports the generations, multiplies
Their tribes, till we behold a spacious plain
Or grassy bottom, all, with little hills—
Their labour—covered, as a lake with waves;
Thousands of cities, in the desert place
Built up of life, and food, and means of life!
Nor wanting here, to entertain the thought,
Creatures, that in communities exist,
Less, as might seem, for general guardianship
Or through dependence upon mutual aid,
Than by participation of delight
And a strict love of fellowship, combined.
What other spirit can it be that prompts
The gilded summer flies to mix and weave
Their sports together in the solar beam,
Or in the gloom of twilight hum their joy?
More obviously, the self-same influence rules
The feathered kinds; the fieldfare's pensive flock,
The cawing rooks, and sea-mews from afar,
Hovering above these inland solitudes,
By the rough wind unscattered, at whose call
Their voyage was begun! nor is its power
Unfelt among the sedentary fowl
That seek yon pool, and there prolong their stay
In silent congress; or together roused
Take flight; while with their clang the air resounds,
And, over all, in that ethereal arch,
Is the mute company of changeful clouds;
Bright apparition suddenly put forth,
The rainbow smiling on the faded storm,
The mild assemblage of the starry heavens;
And the great sun, earth's universal lord!

"How bountiful is nature! he shall find
Who seeks not; and to him who hath not asked,
Large measure shall be dealt. Three Sabbath-days
Are scarcely told, since, on a service bent
Of mere humanity, you clomb those heights;
And what a marvellous and heavenly show
Was to your sight revealed! the swains moved on,
And heeded not; you lingered, and perceived.
There is a luxury in self-dispraise;
And inward self-disparagement affords
To meditative spleen a grateful feast.
Trust me, pronouncing on your own desert,
You judge unthankfully; distempered nerves
Infect the thoughts: the languor of the frame
Depresses the soul's vigour. Quit your couch—
Cleave not so fondly to your moody cell
Nor let the hallowed powers, that shed from heaven
Stillness and rest, with disapproving eye
Look down upon your taper, through a watch

Of midnight hours, unseasonably twinkling
In this deep hollow; like a sullen star
Dimly reflected in a lonely pool.
Take courage, and withdraw yourself from ways
That run not parallel to nature's course.
Rise with the lark! your matins shall obtain
Grace, be their composition what it may,
If but with hers performed; climb once again,
Climb every day those ramparts, meet the breeze
Upon their tops,—adventurous as a bee
That from your garden thither soars, to feed
On new-blown heath, let yon commanding rock
Be your frequented watch-tower, roll the stone
In thunder down the mountains; with all your might
Chase the wild goat; and, if the bold red deer
Fly to these harbours, driven by hound and horn
Loud echoing, add your speed to the pursuit.
So, wearied to your hut shall you return,
And sink at evening into sound repose."

The Solitary lifted tow'rd the hills
A kindling eye,—poetic feelings rushed
Into my bosom, whence these words broke forth:
"Oh! what a joy it were, in vigorous health,
To have a body (this our vital frame
With shrinking sensibility endued,
And all the nice regards of flesh and blood)
And to the elements surrender it
As if it were a spirit!—How divine,
The liberty, for frail, for mortal man
To roam at large among unpeopled glens
And mountainous retirements, only trod
By devious footsteps: regions consecrate
To oldest time! and, reckless of the storm
That keeps the raven quiet in her nest,
Be as a presence or a motion—one
Among the many there; and, while the mists
Flying, and rainy vapours, call out shapes
And phantoms from the crags and solid earth,
As fast as a musician scatters sounds
Out of an instrument; and, while the streams
(As at a first creation, and in haste
To exercise their untried faculties,)
Descending from the region of the clouds,
And starting from the hollows of the earth,
More multitudinous every moment, rend
Their way before them—what a joy to roam
An equal among mightiest energies;
And haply sometimes with articulate voice,
Amid the deafening tumult, scarcely heard
By him that utters it, exclaim aloud,
'Be this continued so from day to day,
Nor let the fierce commotion have an end,
Ruinous though it be, from month to month!'"

"Yes," said the Wanderer, taking from my lips
The strain of transport, "whatsoe'er in youth
Has, through ambition of his soul, given way

To such desires, and grasped at such delight,
Shall feel congenial stirrings late and long ;
In spite of all the weakness that life brings,
Its cares and sorrows ; he though taught to own
The tranquillizing power of time, shall wake,
Wake sometimes to a noble restlessness—
Loving the sports which once he gloried in.

"Compatriot, friend, remote are Garry's Hills,
The streams far distant of your native glen ;
Yet is their form and image here expressed
With brotherly resemblance. Turn your steps
Wherever fancy leads, by day, by night,
Are various engines working, not the same
As those by which your soul in youth was moved,
But by the great Artificer endued
With no inferior power. You dwell alone ;
You walk, you live, you speculate alone ;
Yet doth remembrance, like a sovereign prince,
For you a stately gallery maintain
Of gay or tragic pictures. You have seen,
Have acted, suffered, travelled far, observed
With no incurious eye ; and books are yours,
Within whose silent chambers treasure lies
Preserved from age to age ; more precious far
Than that accumulated store of gold
And orient gems, which, for a day of need,
The Sultan hides within ancestral tombs.
These hoards of truth you can unlock at will :
And music waits upon your skilful touch,—
Sounds which the wandering shepherd from these heights
Hears, and forgets his purpose ;—furnished thus
How can you droop, if willing to be raised?

A piteous lot it were to flee from man—
Yet not rejoice in nature. He—whose hours
Are by domestic pleasures uncaressed
And unenlivened ; who exists whole years
Apart from benefits received or done
'Mid the transactions of the bustling crowd ;
Who neither hears, nor feels a wish to hear,
Of the world's interests—such a one hath need
Of a quick fancy, and an active heart,
That, for the day's consumption, books may yield
A not unwholesome food, and earth and air
Supply his morbid humour with delight.
Truth has her pleasure-grounds, her haunts of ease
And easy contemplation,—gay parterres,
And labyrinthine walks, her sunny glades
And shady groves for recreation framed:
These may he range, if willing to partake
Their soft indulgences, and in due time
May issue thence, recruited for the tasks
And course of service truth requires from those
Who tend her altars, wait upon her throne,
And guard her fortresses. Who thinks and feels,
And recognizes ever and anon
The breeze of nature stirring in his soul,

Why need such man go desperately astray,
And nurse 'the dreadful appetite of death?'
If tired with systems—each in its degree
Substantial—and all crumbling in their turn,
Let him build systems of his own, and smile
At the fond work—demolished with a touch:
If unreligious, let him be at once,
Among ten thousand innocents, enrolled
A pupil in the many-chambered school
Where superstition weaves her airy dreams.

"Life's autumn past, I stand on winter's verge,
And daily lose what I desire to keep!
Yet rather would I instantly decline
To the traditionary sympathies
Of a most rustic ignorance, and take
A fearful apprehension from the owl
Or death-watch,—and as readily rejoice,
If two auspicious magpies crossed my way;
To this would rather bend than see and hear
The repetitions wearisome of sense,
Where soul is dead, and feeling hath no place;
Where knowledge, ill begun in cold remark
On outward things, with formal inference ends:
Or, if the mind turn inward, 'tis perplexed,
Lost in a gloom of uninspired research;
Meanwhile, the heart within the heart, the seat
Where peace and happy consciousness should dwell;
On its own axis restlessly revolves,
Yet nowhere finds the cheering light of truth.

"Upon the breast of new-created earth
Man walked; and when and wheresoe'er he moved,
Alone or mated, solitude was not.
He heard, upon the wind, the articulate voice
Of God; and angels to his sight appeared,
Crowning the glorious hills of Paradise;
Or through the groves gliding like morning mist
Enkindled by the sun. He sate—and talked
With wingèd messengers: who daily brought
To his small island in the ethereal deep
Tidings of joy and love.—From these pure heights
(Whether of actual vision, sensible
To sight and feeling, or that in this sort
Have condescendingly been shadowed forth
Communications spiritually maintained,
And intuitions moral and divine)
Fell human-kind—to banishment condemned
That flowing years repealed not: and distress
And grief spread wide; but man escaped the doom
Of destitution;—solitude was not.
Jehovah—shapeless Power above all powers,
Single and one, the omnipresent God,
By vocal utterance, or blaze of light,
Or cloud of darkness, localized in heaven;
On earth, enshrined within the wandering ark,
Or, out of Sion, thundering from His throne
Between the cherubim—on the chosen race

Showered miracles, and ceased not to dispense
Judgments, that filled the land from age to age
With hope, and love, and gratitude, and fear;
And with amazement smote;—thereby to assert
His scorned, or unacknowledged sovereignty.
And when the One, ineffable of name,
Of nature indivisible, withdrew
From mortal adoration or regard,
Not then was Deity ingulfed, nor man,
The rational creature, left, to feel the weight
Of his own reason, without sense or thought
Of higher reason and a purer will,
To benefit and bless, through mightier power.
Whether the Persian—zealous to reject
Altar and image, and the inclusive walls
And roofs of temples built by human hands—
To loftiest heights ascending, from their tops,
With myrtle-wreathed tiara on his brow,
Presented sacrifice to moon and stars,
And to the winds and mother elements,
And the whole circle of the heavens, for him
A sensitive existence, and a God,
With lifted hands invoked, and songs of praise:
Or, less reluctantly to bonds of sense
Yielding his soul, the Babylonian framed
For influence undefined a personal shape;
And, from the plain, with toil immense, upreared
Tower eight times planted on the top of tower;
That Belus, nightly to his splendid couch
Descending, there might rest; upon that height
Pure and serene, diffused—to overlook
Winding Euphrates, and the city vast
Of his devoted worshippers, far-stretched,
With grove, and field, and garden, interspersed,
Their town, and foodful region for support
Against the pressure of beleaguering war.

"Chaldean shepherds, ranging trackless fields,
Beneath the concave of unclouded skies
Spread like a sea, in boundless solitude,
Looked on the polar star, as on a guide
And guardian of their course, that never closed
His steadfast eye. The planetary five
With a submissive reverence they beheld;
Watched, from the centre of their sleeping flocks
Those radiant Mercuries, that seemed to move
Carrying through ether, in perpetual round,
Decrees and resolutions of the gods;
And, by their aspects, signifying works
Of dim futurity, to man revealed.
The imaginative faculty was lord
Of observations natural; and, thus
Led on, those shepherds made report of stars
In set rotation passing to and fro,
Between the orbs of our apparent sphere
And its invisible counterpart, adorned
With answering constellations, under earth,
Removed from all approach of living sight,

But present to the dead, who, so they deemed,
Like those celestial messengers beheld
All accidents, and judges were of all.

"The lively Grecian, in a land of hills,
Rivers, and fertile plains, and sounding shores,
Under a cope of variegated sky,
Could find commodious place for every god,
Promptly received, as prodigally brought,
From the surrounding countries, at the choice
Of all adventurers. With unrivalled skill,
As nicest observation furnished hints
For studious fancy, did his hand bestow
On fluent operations a fixed shape;
Metal or stone, idolatrously served.
And yet—triumphant o'er this pompous show
Of art, this palpable array of sense,
On every side encountered; in despite
Of the gross fictions, chanted in the streets
By wandering rhapsodists; and in contempt
Of doubt and bold denials hourly urged
Amid the wrangling schools—a spirit hung,
Beautiful region! o'er thy towns and farms,
Statues and temples, and memorial tombs;
And emanations were perceived, and acts
Of immortality, in nature's course,
Exemplified by mysteries, that were felt
As bonds, on grave philosopher imposed
And armed warrior; and in every grove
A gay or pensive tenderness prevailed,
When piety more awful had relaxed.
'Take, running river, take these locks of mine'—
Thus would the votary say—'this severed hair,
My vow fulfilling, do I here present,
Thankful for my beloved child's return.
Thy banks, Cephisus, he again hath trod,
Thy murmurs heard; and drunk the crystal lymph
With which thou dost refresh the thirsty lip,
And moisten all day long these flowery fields!'
And doubtless, sometimes, when the hair was shed
Upon the flowing stream, a thought arose
Of life continuous—being unimpaired!
That hath been, is, and where it was and is
There shall endure,—existence unexposed
To the blind walk of mortal accident;
From diminution safe and weakening age;
While man grows old, and dwindles, and decays;
And countless generations of mankind
Depart; and leave no vestige where they trod.

"We live by admiration, hope, and love;
And even as these are well and wisely fixed,
In dignity of being we ascend.
But what is error?" "Answer he who can!"
The sceptic somewhat haughtily exclaimed,
"Love, hope, and admiration—are they not
Mad fancy's favourite vassals? Does not Life
Use them, full oft, as pioneers to ruin,

Guides to destruction? Is it well to trust
Imagination's light when reason's fails,
The unguarded taper where the guarded faints?
Stoop from those heights, and soberly declare
What error is; and, of our errors, which
Doth most debase the mind; the genuine seats
Of power, where are they? Who shall regulate
With truth the scale of intellectual rank?"

"Methinks," persuasively the sage replied,
"That for this arduous office you possess
Some rare advantages. Your early days
A grateful recollection must supply
Of much exalted good by Heaven vouchsafed
To dignify the humblest state.—Your voice
Hath, in my hearing, often testified
That poor men's children, they, and they alone,
By their condition taught, can understand
The wisdom of the prayer that daily asks
For daily bread. A consciousness is yours
How feelingly religion may be learned
In smoky cabins, from a mother's tongue—
Heard while the dwelling vibrates to the din
Of the contiguous torrent, gathering strength
At every moment—and, with strength, increase
Of fury; or, while snow is at the door,
Assaulting and defending, and the wind,
A sightless labourer, whistles at his work—
Fearful, but resignation tempers fear,
And piety is sweet to infant minds.
The shepherd lad, who in the sunshine carves,
On the green turf, a dial—to divide
The silent hours; and who to that report
Can portion out his pleasures, and adapt
His round of pastoral duties, is not left
With less intelligence for *moral* things
Of gravest import. Early he erceives,
Within himself, a measure and a rule,
Which to the sun of truth he can apply,
That shines for him, and shines for all mankind.
Experience daily fixing his regards
On nature's wants, he knows how few they are,
And where they lie, how answered and appeased.
This knowledge ample recompense affords
For manifold privations; he refers
His notions to this standard; on this rock
Rests his desires; and hence, in after life,
Soul-strengthening patience, and sublime content.
Imagination—not permitted here
To waste her powers, as in the worldling's mind,
On fickle pleasures, and superfluous cares,
And trivial ostentation—is left free
And puissant to range the solemn walks
Of time and nature, girded by a zone
That, while it binds, invigorates and supports.
Acknowledge, then, that whether by the side
Of his poor hut, or on the mountain top,
Or in the cultured field, a man so bred

(Take from him what you will upon the score
Of ignorance or illusion) lives and breathes
For noble purposes of mind: his heart
Beats to the heroic song of ancient days;
His eye distinguishes, his soul creates.
And those illusions, which excite the scorn
Or move the pity of unthinking minds,
Are they not mainly outward ministers
Of inward conscience? with whose service charged
They come and go, appear and disappear,
Diverting evil purposes, remorse
Awakening, chastening an intemperate grief,
Or pride of heart abating: and, whene'er
For less important ends those phantoms move,
Who would forbid them, if their presence serve,
Among wild mountains and unpeopled heaths,
Filling a space, else vacant, to exalt
The forms of nature, and enlarge her powers?

"Once more to distant ages of the world
Let us revert, and place before our thoughts
The face which rural solitude might wear
To the unenlightened swains of pagan Greece.
In that fair clime, the lonely herdsman, stretched
On the soft grass through half a summer's day,
With music lulled his indolent repose:
And, in some fit of weariness, if he,
When his own breath was silent, chanced to hear
A distant strain, far sweeter than the sounds
Which his poor skill could make, his fancy fetched,
Even from the blazing chariot of the sun,
A beardless youth, who touched a golden lute,
And filled the illumined groves with ravishment.
The nightly hunter, lifting up his eyes
Towards the crescent moon, with grateful heart
Called on the lovely wanderer who bestowed
That timely light, to share his joyous sport:
And hence, a beaming goddess with her nymphs,
Across the lawn and through the darksome grove
(Not unaccompanied with tuneful notes
By echo multiplied from rock or cave)
Swept in the storm of chase, as moon and stars
Glance rapidly along the clouded heaven,
When winds are blowing strong. The traveller slaked
His thirst from rill or gushing fount, and thanked
The Naiad.—Sunbeams, upon distant hills
Gliding apace, with shadows in their train,
Might, with small help from fancy, be transformed
Into fleet Oreads sporting visibly.
The Zephyrs, fanning as they passed, their wings,
Lacked not, for love, fair objects, whom they wooed
With gentle whisper. Withered boughs grotesque,
Stripped of their leaves and twigs by hoary age,
From depth of shaggy covert peeping forth
In the low vale, or on steep mountain side;
And, sometimes, intermixed with stirring horns
Of the live deer, or goat's depending beard,—
These were the lurking satyrs, a wild brood

Of gamesome deities; or Pan himself,
The simple shepherd's awe-inspiring god!"

As this apt strain proceeded, I could mark
Its kindly influence, o'er the yielding brow
Of our companion, gradually diffused;
While, listening, he had paced the noiseless turf,
Like one whose untried ear a murmuring stream
Detains, but tempted now to interpose,
He with a smile exclaimed—
"'Tis well you speak
At a safe distance from our native land,
And from the mansions where our youth was taught.
The true descendants of those godly men
Who swept from Scotland, in a flame of zeal,
Shrine, altar, image, and the massy piles
That harboured them,—the souls retaining yet
The churlish features of that after race
Who fled to caves, and woods, and naked rocks,
In deadly scorn of superstitious rites,
Or what their scruples construed to be such—
How, think you, would they tolerate this scheme
Of fine propensities, that tends, if urged
Far as it might be urged, to sow afresh
The weeds of Romish phantasy, in vain
Uprooted; would re-consecrate our wells
To good Saint Fillan and to fair Saint Anne,
And from long banishment recall Saint Giles,
To watch again with tutelary love
O'er stately Edinburgh throned on crags?
A blessed restoration, to behold
The patron, on the shoulders of his priests,
Once more parading through her crowded streets;
Now simply guarded by the sober powers
Of science, and philosophy, and sense!"

This answer followed—"You have turned my thoughts
Upon our brave progenitors, who rose
Against idolatry with warlike mind,
And shrunk from vain observances, to lurk
In caves, and woods, and under dismal rocks,
Deprived of shelter, covering, fire, and food
Why?—for this very reason that they felt,
And did acknowledge, wheresoe'er they moved,
A spiritual presence, oft-times misconceived;
But still a high dependence, a divine
Bounty and government, that filled their hearts
With joy, and gratitude, and fear, and love;
And from their fervent lips drew hymns of praise,
That through the desert rang Though avoured less,
Far less, than these, yet such, in their degree,
Were those bewildered pagans of old time.
Beyond their own poor natures and above
They looked; were humbly thankful for the good
Which the warm sun solicited—and earth
Bestowed, were gladsome,—and their moral sense
They fortified with reverence for the gods,
And they had hopes that overstepped the grave.

"Now, shall our great discoverers," he exclaimed,
Raising his voice triumphantly, "obtain
From sense and reason less than these obtained,
Though far misled? Shall men for whom our age
Unbaffled powers of vision hath prepared,
To explore the world without and world within,
Be joyless as the blind? Ambitious souls—
Whom earth, at this late season, hath produced
To regulate the moving spheres, and weigh
The planets in the hollow of their hand;
And they who rather dive than soar, whose pains
Have solved the elements, or analysed
The thinking principle—shall they in fact
Prove a degraded race? and what avails
Renown, if their presumption make them such?
Oh! there is laughter at their work in heaven!
Inquire of ancient wisdom; go, demand
Of mighty nature, if 'twas ever meant
That we should pry far off, yet be unraised;
That we should pore, and dwindle as we pore,
Viewing all objects unremittingly
In disconnexion dead and spiritless;
And still dividing, and dividing still,
Break down all grandeur, still unsatisfied
With the perverse attempt, while littleness
May yet become more little; waging thus
An impious warfare with the very life
Of our own souls!—And if indeed there be
An all-pervading spirit, upon whom
Our dark foundations rest, could He design
That this magnificent effect of power,
The earth we tread, the sky that we behold
By day, and all the pomp which night reveals,
That these—and that superior mystery
Our vital frame, so fearfully devised,
And the dread soul within it—should exist
Only to be examined, pondered, searched,
Probed, vexed, and criticised?—Accuse me not
Of arrogance, unknown wanderer as I am,
If, having walked with nature threescore years,
And offered, far as frailty would allow,
My heart a daily sacrifice to truth,
I now affirm of nature and of truth,
Whom I have served, that their Divinity
Revolts, offended at the ways of men
Swayed by such motives, to such end employed;
Philosophers, who, though the human soul
Be of a thousand faculties composed,
And twice ten thousand interests, do yet prize
This soul, and the transcendent universe,
No more than as a mirror that reflects
To proud self-love her own intelligence;
That one, poor, finite object, in the abyss
Of infinite being, twinkling restlessly!

"Nor higher place can be assigned to him
And his compeers—the laughing sage of France.
Crowned was he, if my memory do not err,

With laurel planted upon hoary hairs,
In sign of conquest by his wit achieved,
And benefits his wisdom had conferred.
His tottering body was with wreaths of flowers
Opprest, far less becoming ornaments
Than spring oft twines about a mouldering tree;
Yet so it pleased a fond, a vain old man,
And a most frivolous people. Him I mean
Who penned, to ridicule confiding faith,
This sorry legend; which by chance we found
Piled in a nook, through malice, as might seem,
Among more innocent rubbish."—Speaking thus,
With a brief notice when, and how, and where,
We had espied the book, he drew it forth;
And courteously, as if the act removed,
At once, all traces from the good man's heart
Of unbenign aversion or contempt,
Restored it to its owner. "Gentle friend,"
Herewith he grasped the Solitary's hand,
"You have known better lights and guides than these—
Ah! let not aught amiss within dispose
A noble mind to practise on herself,
And tempt opinion to support the wrongs
Of passion: whatsoe'er be felt or feared,
From higher judgment-seats make no appeal
To lower: can you question that the soul
Inherits an allegiance, not by choice
To be cast off, upon an oath proposed
By each new upstart notion? In the ports
Of levity no refuge can be found,
No shelter, for a spirit in distress.
He, who by wilful disesteem of life,
And proud insensibility to hope
Affronts the eye of solitude, shall learn
That her mild nature can be terrible;
That neither she nor silence lack the power
To avenge their own insulted majesty.
O blest seclusion! when the mind admits
The law of duty; and can therefore move
Through each vicissitude of loss and gain,
Linked in entire complacence with her choice;
When youth's presumptuousness is mellowed down,
And manhood's vain anxiety dismissed;
When wisdom shows her seasonable fruit,
Upon the boughs of sheltering leisure hung
In sober plenty; when the spirit stoops
To drink with gratitude the crystal stream
Of unreproved enjoyment; and is pleased
To muse,—and be saluted by the air
Of meek repentance, wafting wall-flower scents
From out the crumbling ruins of fallen pride
And chambers of transgression, now forlorn.
Oh, calm contented days, and peaceful nights!
Who, when such good can be obtained, would strive
To reconcile his manhood to a couch
Soft, as may seem, but, under that disguise,
Stuffed with the thorny substance of the past,
For fixed annoyance; and full oft beset

With floating dreams, disconsolate and black,
The vapoury phantoms of futurity?

"Within the soul a faculty abides,
That with interpositions, which would hide
And darken, so can deal, that they become
Contingencies of pomp; and serve to exalt
Her native brightness. As the ample moon,
In the deep stillness of a summer even
Rising behind a thick and lofty grove,
Burns like an unconsuming fire of light,
In the green trees; and, kindling on all sides
Their leafy umbrage, turns the dusky veil
Into a substance glorious as her own,
Yea, with her own incorporated, by power
Capacious and serene; like power abides
In man's celestial spirit; virtue thus
Sets forth and magnifies herself; thus feeds
A calm, a beautiful, and silent fire,
From the incumbrances of mortal life,
From error, disappointment,—nay, from guilt;
And sometimes, so relenting justice wills,
From palpable oppressions of despair."

The Solitary by these words was touched
With manifest emotion, and exclaimed,
"But how begin? and whence?—The mind is free;
Resolve'—the haughty moralist would say,
'This single act is all that we demand.'
Alas! such wisdom bids a creature fly
Whose very sorrow is, that time hath shorn
His natural wings!—To friendship let him turn
For succour; but perhaps he sits alone
On stormy waters, in a little boat
That holds but him, and can contain no more!
Religion tells of amity sublime
Which no condition can preclude; of One
Who sees all suffering, comprehends all wants,
All weakness fathoms, can supply all needs;
But is that bounty absolute?—His gifts,
Are they not still, in some degree, rewards
For acts of service? Can His love extend
To hearts that own not Him? Will showers of grace,
When in the sky no promise may be seen,
Fall to refresh a parched and withered land?
Or shall the groaning spirit cast her load
At the Redeemer's feet?"
In rueful tone,
With some impatience in his mien, he spake;
Back to my mind rushed all that had been urged
To calm the sufferer when his story closed;
I looked for counsel as unbending now;
But a discriminating sympathy
Stooped to this apt reply.—
"As men from men
Do, in the constitution of their souls,
Differ, by mystery not to be explained;
And as we fall by various ways, and sink

One deeper than another, self-condemned,
Through manifold degrees of guilt and shame,
So manifold and various are the ways
Of restoration, fashioned to the steps
Of all infirmity, and tending all
To the same point,—attainable by all;
Peace in ourselves, and union with our God.
For you, assuredly, a hopeful road
Lies open: we have heard from you a voice
At every moment softened in its course
By tenderness of heart; have seen your eye,
Even like an altar lit by fire from heaven,
Kindle before us.—Your discourse this day,
That, like the fabled Lethe, wished to flow
In creeping sadness, through oblivious shades
Of death and night, has caught at every turn
The colours of the sun. Access for you
Is yet preserved to principles of truth,
Which the imaginative will upholds
In seats of wisdom, not to be approached
By the inferior faculty that moulds,
With her minute and speculative pains,
Opinion, ever changing!—I have seen
A curious child, who dwelt upon a tract
Of inland ground, applying to his ear
The convolutions of a smooth-lipped shell;
To which, in silence hushed, his very soul
Listened intensely; and his countenance soon
Brightened with joy; for murmurings from within
Were heard, sonorous cadences! whereby
To his belief, the monitor expressed
Mysterious union with its native sea.
Even such a shell the universe itself
Is to the ear of faith; and there are times,
I doubt not, when to you it doth impart
Authentic tidings of invisible things;
Of ebb and flow, and ever-during power;
And central peace, subsisting at the heart
Of endless agitation. Here you stand,
Adore, and worship, when you know it not;
Pious beyond the intention of your thought;
Devout above the meaning of your will.
Yes, you have felt, and may not cease to feel.
The estate of man would be indeed forlorn
If false conclusions of the reasoning power
Made the eye blind, and closed the passages
Through which the ear converses with the heart.
Has not the soul, the being of your life,
Received a shock of awful consciousness,
In some calm season, when these lofty rocks
At night's approach bring down the unclouded sky,
To rest upon their circumambient walls;
A temple framing of dimensions vast,
And yet not too enormous for the sound
Of human anthems,—choral song, or burst
Sublime of instrumental harmony,
To glorify the Eternal! What if these
Did never break the stillness that prevails

Here, if the solemn nightingale be mute,
And the soft woodlark here did never chant
Her vespers, nature fails not to provide
Impulse and utterance. The whispering air
Sends inspiration from the shadowy heights,
And blind recesses of the caverned rocks;
The little rills, and waters numberless,
Inaudible by daylight, blend their notes
With the loud streams: and often, at the hour
When issue forth the first pale stars, is heard,
Within the circuit of this fabric huge,
One voice—the solitary raven, flying
Athwart the concave of the dark-blue dome,
Unseen, perchance above all power of sight—
An iron knell! with echoes from afar
Faint—and still fainter—as the cry, with which
The wanderer accompanies her flight
Through the calm region, fades upon the ear,
Diminishing by distance till it seemed
To expire, yet from the abyss is caught again
And yet again recovered!
But descending
From these imaginative heights, that yield
Far-stretching views into eternity,
Acknowledge that to nature's humbler power
Your cherished sullenness is forced to bend
Even here, where her amenities are sown
With sparing hand. Then trust yourself abroad
To range her blooming bowers, and spacious fields,
Where on the labours of the happy throng
She smiles, including in her wide embrace
City, and town, and tower,—and sea with ships
Sprinkled;—be our companion while we track
Her rivers populous with gliding life;
While, free as air, o'er printless sands we march,
Or pierce the gloom of her majestic woods;
Roaming, or resting under grateful shade
In peace and meditative cheerfulness;
Where living things, and things inanimate,
Do speak, at Heaven's command, to eye and ear,
And speak to social reason's inner sense,
With inarticulate language.
For the man
Who, in this spirit, communes with the forms
Of nature, who with understanding heart
Doth know and love such objects as excite
No morbid passions, no disquietude,
No vengeance, and no hatred, needs must feel
The joy of that pure principle of love
So deeply, that, unsatisfied with aught
Less pure and exquisite, he cannot choose
But seek for objects of a kindred love
In fellow-natures, and a kindred joy.
Accordingly he by degrees perceives
His feelings of aversion softened down;
A holy tenderness pervade his frame.
His sanity of reason not impaired,
Say rather, all his thoughts now flowing clear.

From a clear fountain flowing, he looks round
And seeks for good, and finds the good he seeks;
Until abhorrence and contempt are things
He only knows by name; and if he hear,
From other mouths, the language which they speak,
He is compassionate; and has no thought,
No feeling, which can overcome his love.

"And further; by contemplating these forms
In the relations which they bear to man,
He shall discern, how, through the various
Which silently they yield, are multiplied
The spiritual presences of absent things.
Trust me, that for the instructed, time will come
When they shall meet no object but may teach
Some acceptable lesson to their minds
Of human suffering, or of human joy.
So shall they learn, while all things speak of man,
Their duties from all forms, and general laws,
And local accidents, shall tend alike
To rouse, to urge; and, with the will, confer
The ability to spread the blessings wide
Of true philanthropy The light of love
Not failing, perseverance from their steps
Departing not, for them shall be confirmed
The glorious habit by which sense is made
Subservient still to moral purposes,
Auxiliar to divine. That change shall clothe
The naked spirit, ceasing to deplore
The burthen of existence Science then
Shall be a precious visitant; and then,
And only then, be worthy of her name.
For then her heart shall kindle; her dull eye,
Dull and inanimate, no more shall hang
Chained to its object in brute slavery;
But taught with patient interest to watch
The processes of things, and serve the cause
Of order and distinctness, not for this
Shall it forget that its most noble use,
Its most illustrious province, must be found
In furnishing clear guidance, a support
Not treacherous, to the mind's *excursive* power.
So build we up the being that we are;
Thus deeply drinking-in the soul of things
We shall be wise perforce, and while inspired
By choice, and conscious that the will is free,
Unswerving shall we move, as if impelled
By strict necessity, along the path
Of order and of good. Whate'er we see,
Whate'er we feel, by agency direct
Or indirect shall tend to feed and nurse
Our faculties, shall fix in calmer seats
Of moral strength, and raise to loftier heights
Of love divine, our intellectual soul."

Here closed the sage that eloquent hárangue,
Poured forth with fervour in continuous stream;
Such as, remote 'mid savage wilderness,

An Indian chief discharges from his breast
Into the hearing of assembled tribes,
In open circle seated round, and hushed
As the unbreathing air, when not a leaf
Stirs in the mighty woods.—So did he speak :
The words he uttered shall not pass away ;
For they sank into me—the bounteous gift
Of one whom time and nature had made wise,
Gracing his language with authority
Which hostile spirits silently allow ;
Of one accustomed to desires that feed
On fruitage gathered from the tree of life ;
To hopes on knowledge and experience built ;
Of one in whom persuasion and belief
Had ripened into faith, and faith become
A passionate intuition ; whence the soul,
Though bound to earth by ties of pity and love,
From all injurious servitude was free.

The sun, before his place of rest were reached,
Had yet to travel far, but unto us,
To us who stood low in that hollow dell,
He had become invisible,—a pomp
Leaving behind of yellow radiance spread
Upon the mountain side in contrast bold
With ample shadows, seemingly no less
Than those resplendent lights, his rich bequest,
A dispensation of his evening power.
Adown the path that from the glen had led
The funeral train, the shepherd and his mate
Were seen descending ; forth to greet them ran
Our little page ; the rustic pair approach ;
And in the matron's aspect may be read
A plain assurance that the words which told
How that neglected pensioner was sent
Before his time into a quiet grave,
Had done to her humanity no wrong :
But we are kindly welcomed—promptly served
With ostentatious zeal.—Along the floor
Of the small cottage in the lonely dell
A grateful couch was spread for our repose ;
Where, in the guise of mountaineers, we slept,
Stretched upon fragrant heath, and lulled by sound
Of far-off torrents charming the still night,
And to tired limbs and over-busy thoughts
Inviting sleep and soft forgetfulness.

BOOK V.

ARGUMENT.

Farewell to the valley—Reflections—Sight of a large and populous vale—Solitary consents to go forward—Vale described—The pastor's dwelling, and some account of him—The churchyard—Church and monuments—The Solitary musing, and where—Roused—In the churchyard the Solitary communicates the thoughts which had recently passed through his mind—Lofty tone of the Wanderer's discourse of yesterday adverted to—Rite of baptism, and the professions accompanying it, contrasted with the real state of human life—Inconsistency of the best men—Acknowledgment that practice falls far below the injunctions of duty as existing in the mind—General complaint of a falling-off in the value of life after the time of youth—Outward appearances of content and happiness in degree illusive—Pastor approaches—Appeal made to him—His answer—Wanderer in sympathy with him—Suggestion that the least ambitious inquirers may be most free from error—The pastor is desired to give some portraits of the living or dead from his own observation of life among these mountains—and for what purpose—Pastor consents—Mountain cottage—Excellent qualities of its inhabitants—Solitary expresses his pleasure, but denies the praise of virtue to worth of this kind—Feelings of the priest before he enters upon his account of persons interred in the churchyard—Graves of unbaptized infants—What sensations they excite—Funeral and sepulchral observances, whence—Ecclesiastical establishments, whence derived—Profession of belief in the doctrine of immortality.

THE PASTOR.

FAREWELL, deep valley, with thy one rude house,
And its small lot of life-supporting fields,
And guardian rocks!—Farewell, attractive seat!
To the still influx of the morning light
Open, and day's pure cheerfulness, but veiled
From human observation, as if yet
Primeval forests wrapped thee round with dark
Impenetrable shade; once more farewell,
Majestic circuit, beautiful abyss,
By nature destined from the birth of things,
For quietness profound!
Upon the side
Of that brown slope, the outlet of the vale,
Lingering behind my comrades, thus I breathed
A parting tribute to a spot that seemed
Like the fixed centre of a troubled world.
And now, pursuing leisurely my way,
How vain, thought I, it is by change of place
To seek that comfort which the mind denies;
Yet trial and temptation oft are shunned
Wisely; and by such tenure do we hold
Frail life's possessions, that even they whose fate
Yields no peculiar reason of complaint
Might, by the promise that is here, be won
To steal from active duties, and embrace
Obscurity, and calm forgetfulness.
Knowledge, methinks, in these disordered times,
Should be allowed a privilege to have
Her anchorites, like piety of old;
Men, who, from faction sacred, and unstained
By war, might, if so minded, turn aside
Uncensured, and subsist, a scattered few
Living to God and nature, and content
With that communion. Consecrated be
The spots where such abide! But happier still
The man, whom, furthermore, a hope attends
That meditation and research may guide
His privacy to principles and powers
Discovered or invented, or set forth,
Through his acquaintance with the ways of truth,
In lucid order; so that, when his course
Is run, some faithful eulogist may say,
He sought not praise, and praise did overlook
His unobtrusive merit; but his life,

Sweet to himself, was exercised in good
That shall survive his name and memory.

Acknowledgments of gratitude sincere
Accompanied these musings ; fervent thanks
For my own peaceful lot and happy choice ;
A choice that from the passions of the world
Withdrew, and fixed me in a still retreat,
Sheltered, but not to social duties lost ;
Secluded, but not buried ; and with song
Cheering my days, and with industrious thought,
With ever-welcome company of books,
By virtuous friendship's soul-sustaining aid,
And with the blessings of domestic love.

Thus occupied in mind I paced along,
Following the rugged road, by sledge or wheel,
Worn in the moorland, till I overtook
My two associates, in the morning sunshine
Halting together on a rocky knoll,
From which the road descended rapidly
To the green meadows of another vale.

Here did our pensive host put forth his hand
In sign of farewell "Nay," the old man said,
"The fragrant air its coolness still retains ,
The herds and flocks are yet abroad to crop
The dewy grass ; you cannot leave us now,
We must not part at this inviting hour."
He yielded, though reluctant , for his mind
Instinctively disposed him to retire
To his own covert ; as a billow, heaved
Upon the beach, rolls back into the sea.
So we descend ; and winding round a rock
Attain a point that showed the valley—stretched
In length before us ; and, not distant far,
Upon a rising ground a gray church-tower,
Whose battlements were screened by tufted trees.
And, towards a crystal mere, that lay beyond
Among steep hills and woods embosomed, flowed
A copious stream with boldly-winding course ;
Here traceable, there hidden—there again
To sight restored, and glittering in the sun
On the stream's bank, and everywhere, appeared
Fair dwellings, single, or in social knots ;
Some scattered o'er the level, others perched
On the hill sides, a cheerful quiet scene,
Now in its morning purity arrayed.

"As, 'mid some happy valley of the Alps,"
Said I, "once happy, ere tyrannic power,
Wantonly breaking in upon the Swiss,
Destroyed their unoffending commonwealth,
A popular equality reigns here,
Save for one house of state beneath whose roof
A rural lord might dwell." "No feudal pomp,"
Replied our friend, a chronicler who stood
Where'er he moved upon familiar ground,
"Nor feudal power is there ; but there abides,

In his allotted home, a genuine priest,
The shepherd of his flock, or, as a king
Is styled, when most affectionately praised,
The father of his people. Such is he;
And rich and poor, and young and old, rejoice
Under his spiritual sway. He hath vouchsafed
To me some portions of a kind regard;
And something also of his inner mind
Hath he imparted—but I speak of him
As he is known to all. The calm delights
Of unambitious piety he chose,
And learning's solid dignity; though born
Of knightly race, nor wanting powerful friends,
Hither, in prime of manhood, he withdrew
From academic bowers He loved the spot,
Who does not love his native soil? He prized
The ancient rural character, composed
Of simple manners, feelings unsuppressed
And undisguised, and strong and serious thought;
A character reflected in himself,
With such embellishment as well beseems
His rank and sacred function. This deep vale
Winds far in reaches hidden from our eyes,
And one a turreted manorial hall
Adorns, in which the good man's ancestors
Have dwelt through ages—patrons of this cure.
To them, and to his own judicious pains,
The vicar's dwelling, and the whole domain,
Owes that presiding aspect which might well
Attract your notice; statelier than could else
Have been bestowed, through course of common chance,
On an unwealthy mountain benefice."

This said, oft halting we pursued our way;
Nor reached the village churchyard till the sun,
Travelling at steadier pace than ours, had risen,
Above the summits of the highest hills,
And round our path darted oppressive beams.

As chanced, the portals of the sacred pile
Stood open, and we entered. On my frame,
At such transition from the fervid air,
A grateful coolness fell, that seemed to strike
The heart, in concert with that temperate awe
And natural reverence, which the place inspired.
Not raised in nice proportions was the pile,
But large and massy, for duration built;
With pillars crowded, and the roof upheld
By naked rafters intricately crossed,
Like leafless underboughs, 'mid some thick grove,
All withered by the depth of shade above.
Admonitory texts inscribed the walls,
Each, in its ornamental scroll inclosed,
Each also crowned with winged heads—a pair
Of rudely-painted cherubim. The floor
Of nave and aisle, in unpretending guise,
Was occupied by oaken benches, ranged
In seemly rows; the chancel only showed

Some inoffensive marks of earthly state
And vain distinction. A capacious pew
Of sculptured oak stood here, with drapery lined;
And marble monuments were here displayed
Thronging the walls; and on the floor beneath
Sepulchral stones appeared, with emblems graven
And foot-worn epitaphs, and some with small
And shining effigies of brass inlaid.
The tribute by these various records claimed
Without reluctance did we pay; and read
The ordinary chronicle of birth,
Office, alliance, and promotion—all
Ending in dust; of upright magistrates,
Grave doctors strenuous for the mother Church,
And uncorrupted senators, alike
To king and people true. A brazen plate,
Not easily deciphered, told of one
Whose course of earthly honour was begun
In quality of page among the train
Of the eighth Henry, when he crossed the seas
His royal state to show, and prove his strength
In tournament, upon the fields of France.
Another tablet registered the death,
And praised the gallant bearing, of a knight
Tried in the sea-fights of the second Charles.
Near this brave knight his father lay entombed;
And, to the silent language giving voice,
I read,—how in his manhood's earlier day
He, 'mid the afflictions of intestine war
And rightful government subverted, found
One only solace—that he had espoused
A virtuous lady tenderly beloved
For her benign perfections; and yet more
Endeared to him, for this, that in her state
Of wedlock richly crowned with Heaven's regard,
She with a numerous issue filled his house,
Who throve, like plants, uninjured by the storm
That laid their country waste. No need to speak
Of less particular notices assigned
To youth or maiden gone before their time,
And matrons and unwedded sisters old;
Whose charity and goodness were rehearsed
In modest panegyric. "These dim lines,
What would they tell?" said I,—but, from the task
Of puzzling out that faded narrative,
With whisper soft my venerable friend
Called me; and looking down the darksome aisle,
I saw the tenant of the lonely vale
Standing apart; with curved arm reclined
On the baptismal font; his pallid face
Upturned, as if his mind were rapt, or lost
In some abstraction;—gracefully he stood,
The semblance bearing of a sculptured form
That leans upon a monumental urn
In peace, from morn to night, from year to year.

Him from that posture did the sexton rouse;
Who entered, humming carelessly a tune,

Continuation haply of the notes
That had beguiled the work from which he came,
With spade and mattock o'er his shoulder hung,
To be deposited, for future need,
In their appointed place. The pale recluse
Withdrew; and straight we followed,—to a spot
Where sun and shade were intermixed, for there
A broad oak stretching forth its leafy arms
From an adjoining pasture, overhung
Small space of that green churchyard with a light
And pleasant awning. On the moss-grown wall
My ancient friend and I together took
Our seats; and thus the Solitary spake,
Standing before us:—"Did you note the mien
Of that self-solaced, easy-hearted churl,
Death's hireling, who scoops out his neighbour's grave,
Or wraps an old acquaintance up in clay,
As unconcerned as when he plants a tree?
I was abruptly summoned by his voice
From some affecting images and thoughts,
And from the company of serious words.
Much, yesterday, was said in glowing phrase
Of our sublime dependencies and hopes
For future states of being; and the wings
Of speculation, joyfully outspread,
Hovered above our destiny on earth:—
But stoop, and place the prospect of the soul
In sober contrast with reality,
And man's substantial life If this mute earth
Of what it holds could speak, and every grave
Were as a volume, shut, yet capable
Of yielding its contents to eye and ear,
We should recoil, stricken with sorrow and shame,
To see disclosed, by such dread proof, how ill
That which is done accords with what is known
To reason, and by conscience is enjoined;
How idly, how perversely, life's whole course,
To this conclusion, deviates from the line,
Or of the end stops short, proposed to all
At her aspiring outset. Mark the babe
Not long accustomed to this breathing world;
One that hath barely learned to shape a smile;
Though yet irrational of soul to grasp
With tiny fingers—to let fall a tear;
And, as the heavy cloud of sleep dissolves,
To stretch his limbs, bemocking, as might seem
The outward functions of intelligent man;
A grave proficient in amusive feats
Of puppetry, that from the lap declare
His expectations, and announce his claims
To that inheritance which millions rue
That they were ever born to! In due time
A day of solemn ceremonial comes;
When they, who for this minor hold in trust
Rights that transcend the humblest heritage
Of mere humanity, present their charge,
For this occasion daintily adorned,
At the baptismal font. And when the pure

And consecrating element hath cleansed
The original stain, the child is there received
Into the second ark, Christ's Church, with trust
That he, from wrath redeemed, therein shall float
Over the billows of this troublesome world
To the fair land of everlasting life.
Corrupt affections, covetous desires,
Are all renounced; high as the thought of man
Can carry virtue, virtue is professed;
A dedication made, a promise given
For due provision to control and guide,
And unremitting progress to insure
In holiness and truth."

"You cannot blame,"
Here interposing fervently I said,
"Rites which attest that man by nature lies
Bedded for good and evil in a gulf
Fearfully low; nor will your judgment scorn
Those services, whereby attempt is made
To lift the creature toward that eminence
On which, now fallen, erewhile in majesty
He stood; or if not so, whose top serene
At least he feels 'tis given him to descry;
Not without aspirations, evermore
Returning, and injunctions from within
Doubt to cast off and weariness, in trust
That what the soul perceives, if glory lost,
May be, through pains and persevering hope,
Recovered; or, if hitherto unknown,
Lies within reach, and one day shall be gained."

"I blame them not," he calmly answered—"no;
The outward ritual and established forms
With which communities of men invest
These inward feelings, and the aspiring vows
To which the lips give public utterance
Are both a natural process; and by me
Shall pass uncensured; though the issue prove,
Bringing from age to age its own reproach,
Incongruous, impotent, and blank.—But, oh!
If to be weak is to be wretched—miserable,
As the lost angel by a human voice
Hath mournfully pronounced, then, in my mind,
Far better not to move at all than move
By impulse sent from such illusive power,
That finds and cannot fasten down; that grasps
And is rejoiced, and loses while it grasps;
That tempts, emboldens—doth a while sustain,
And then betrays; accuses and inflicts
Remorseless punishment; and so retreads
The inevitable circle: better far
Than this, to graze the herb in thoughtless peace,
By foresight or remembrance, undisturbed!

"Philosophy! and thou, more vaunted name,
Religion! with thy statelier retinue.

Faith, hope, and charity—from the visible world
Choose for your emblems whatsoe'er ye find
Of safest guidance and of firmest trust,—
The torch, the star, the anchor, nor except
The cross itself, at whose unconscious feet
The generations of mankind have knelt
Ruefully seized, and shedding bitter tears,
And through that conflict seeking rest—of you,
High-titled powers, am I constrained to ask,
Here standing, with the unvoyageable sky
In faint reflection of infinitude
Stretched overhead, and at my pensive feet
A subterraneous magazine of bones,
In whose dark vaults my own shall soon be laid,
Where are your triumphs? your dominion where?
And in what age admitted and confirmed?
Not for a happy land do I inquire,
Island or grove, that hides a blessed few
Who, with obedience willing and sincere,
To your serene authorities conform;
But whom, I ask, of individual souls,
Have ye withdrawn from passion's crooked ways,
Inspired, and thoroughly fortified!—If the heart
Could be inspected to its inmost folds
By sight undazzled with the glare of praise,
Who shall be named—in the resplendent line
Of sages, martyrs, confessors—the man
Whom the best might of conscience, truth, and hope,
For one day's little compass, has preserved
From painful and discreditable shocks
Of contradiction, from some vague desire
Culpably cherished, or corrupt relapse
To some unsanctioned fear?"

"If this be so,
And man," said I, "be in his noblest shape
Thus pitiably infirm, then, He who made,
And who shall judge the creature, will forgive
Yet, in its general tenor, your complaint
Is all too true; and surely not misplaced:
For from this pregnant spot of ground such thoughts
Rise to the notice of a serious mind
By natural exhalation. With the dead
In their repose, the living in their mirth,
Who can reflect, unmoved, upon the round
Of smooth and solemnized complacencies,
By which, in Christian lands, from age to age
Profession mocks performance Earth is sick,
And Heaven is weary, of the hollow words
Which states and kingdoms utter when they talk
Of truth and justice. Turn to private life
And social neighbourhood, look we to ourselves;
A light of duty shines on every day
For all; and yet how few are warmed or cheered!
How few who mingle with their fellow-men
And still remain self-governed, and apart,
Like this our honoured friend; and thence acquire
Right to expect his vigorous decline,
That promises to the end a blest old age!"

"Yet," with a smile of triumph thus exclaimed
The Solitary, "in the life of man,
If to the poetry of common speech
Faith may be given, we see as in a glass
A true reflection of the circling year,
With all its seasons. Grant that spring is there,
In spite of many a rough untoward blast,
Hopeful and promising with buds and flowers;
Yet where is glowing summer's long rich day,
That *ought* to follow faithfully expressed?
And mellow autumn, charged with bounteous fruit,
Where is she imaged? in what favoured clime
Her lavish pomp, and ripe magnificence?
Yet, while the better part is missed, the worse
In man's autumnal season is set forth
With a resemblance not to be denied,
And that contents him; bowers that hear no more
The voice of gladness, less and less supply
Of outward sunshine and internal warmth;
And, with this change, sharp air and falling leaves,
Foretelling total winter, blank and cold.

"How gay the habitations that bedeck
This fertile valley! Not a house but seems
To give assurance of content within;
Embosomed happiness, and placid love;
As if the sunshine of the day were met
With answering brightness in the hearts of all
Who walk this favoured ground. But chance-regards,
And notice forced upon incurious ears;
These, if these only, acting in despite
Of the encomiums by my friend pronounced
On humble life, forbid the judging mind
To trust the smiling aspect of this fair
And noiseless commonwealth. The simple race
Of mountaineers (by nature's self removed
From foul temptations, and by constant care
Of a good shepherd tended as themselves
Do tend their flocks) partake man's general lot
With little mitigation. They escape,
Perchance, guilt's heavier woes; and do not feel
The tedium of fantastic idleness;
Yet life, as with the multitude, with them,
Is fashioned like an ill-constructed tale;
That on the outset wastes its gay desires,
Its fair adventures, its enlivening hopes,
And pleasant interests—for the sequel leaving
Old things repeated with diminished grace,
And all the laboured novelties at best
Imperfect substitutes, whose use and power
Evince the want and weakness whence they spring."

While in this serious mood we held discourse,
The reverend pastor toward the churchyard gate
Approached; and, with a mild respectful air
Of native cordiality, our friend
Advanced to greet him. With a gracious mien
Was he received, and mutual joy prevailed.

A while they stood in conference, and I guess
That he, who now upon the mossy wall
Sate by my side, had vanished, if a wish
Could have transferred him to his lonely house
Within the circuit of those guardian rocks.
For me, I looked upon the pair, well pleased:
Nature had framed them both, and both were marked
By circumstance, with intermixture fine
Of contrast and resemblance. To an oak
Hardy and grand, a weather-beaten oak,
Fresh in the strength and majesty of age,
One might be likened: flourishing appeared,
Though somewhat past the fulness of his prime,
The other—like a stately sycamore,
That spreads, in gentler pomp, its honeyed shade.

A general greeting was exchanged; and soon
The pastor learned that his approach had given
A welcome interruption to discourse
Grave, and in truth too often sad.—"Is man
A child of hope? Do generations press
On generations, without progress made?
Halts the individual, ere his hairs be gray,
Perforce? Are we a creature in whom good
Preponderates, or evil? Doth the will
Acknowledge reason's law? A living power
Is virtue, or no better than a name,
Fleeting as health or beauty, and unsound?
So that the only substance which remains,
(For thus the tenor of complaint hath run)
Among so many shadows, are the pains
And penalties of miserable life,
Doomed to decay, and then expire in dust!
Our cogitations this way have been drawn,
These are the points," the Wanderer said, "on which
Our inquest turns.—Accord, good sir! the light
Of your experience, to dispel this gloom:
By your persuasive wisdom shall the heart
That frets, or languishes, be stilled and cheered."

"Our nature," said the priest, in mild reply,
"Angels may weigh and fathom: they perceive,
With undistempered and unclouded spirit,
The object as it is; but, for ourselves,
That speculative height we may not reach.
The good and evil are our own; and we
Are that which we would contemplate from far.
Knowledge, for us, is difficult to gain—
Is difficult to gain and hard to keep—
As virtue's self; like virtue is beset
With snares, tried, tempted, subject to decay.
Love, admiration, fear, desire, and hate,
Blind were we without these: through these alone
Are capable to notice or discern
Or to record, we judge, but cannot be
Indifferent judges. 'Spite of proudest boast,
Reason, best reason, is to imperfect man
An effort only, and a noble aim;

A crown, an attribute of sovereign power,
Still to be courted—never to be won!
Look forth, or each man dive into himself,
What sees he but a creature too perturbed,
That is transported to excess; that yearns,
Regrets, or trembles wrongly, or too much;
Hopes rashly, in disgust as rash recoils;
Battens on spleen, or moulders in despair?
Thus truth is missed, and comprehension fails;
And darkness and delusion round our path
Spread from disease, whose subtile injury lurks
Within the very faculty of sight.

"Yet for the general purposes of faith
In Providence, for solace and support,
We may not doubt that who can best subject
The will to reason's law, and strictliest live
And act in that obedience, he shall gain
The clearest apprehension of those truths,
Which unassisted reason's utmost power
Is too infirm to reach. But—waiving this,
And our regards confining within bounds
Of less exalted consciousness—through which
The very multitude are free to range—
We safely may affirm that human life
Is either fair and tempting, a soft scene
Grateful to sight, refreshing to the soul,
Or a forbidding tract of cheerless view:
Even as the same is looked at, or approached.
Thus, when in changeful April snow has fallen,
And fields are white, if from the sullen north
Your walk conduct you hither, ere the sun
Hath gained his noontide height, this churchyard, filled
With mounds transversely lying side by side
From east to west, before you will appear
An unillumined, blank, and dreary plain,
With more than wintery cheerlessness and gloom
Saddening the heart. Go forward, and look back.
Look, from the quarter whence the lord of light,
Of life, of love, and gladness doth dispense
His beams; which, unexcluded in their fall,
Upon the southern side of every grave
Have gently exercised a melting power,
Then will a vernal prospect greet your eye,
All fresh and beautiful, and green and bright,
Hopeful and cheerful:—vanished is the snow,
Vanished or hidden; and the whole domain,
To some, too lightly minded, might appear
A meadow carpet for the dancing hours.
This contrast, not unsuitable to life,
Is to that other state more opposite,
Death, and its two-fold aspect; wintery—one,
Cold, sullen, blank, from hope and joy shut out;
The other, which the ray divine hath touched,
Replete with vivid promise, bright as spring."

"We see, then, as we feel," the Wanderer thus
With a complacent animation spake,

"And, in your judgment, sir! the mind's repose
On evidence is not to be insured
By act of naked reason. Moral truth
Is no mechanic structure, built by rule,
And which, once built, retains a steadfast shape
And undisturbed proportions; but a thing
Subject, you deem, to vital accidents;
And, like the water-lily, lives and thrives,
Whose root is fixed in stable earth, whose head
Floats on the tossing waves. With joy sincere
I re-salute these sentiments, confirmed
By your authority. But how acquire
The inward principle that gives effect
To outward argument; the passive will
Meek to admit; the active energy,
Strong and unbounded to embrace, and firm
To keep and cherish? How shall man unite
With self-forgetting tenderness of heart
An earth-despising dignity of soul?
Wise in that union, and without it blind!"

"The way," said I, "to court, if not obtain
The ingenuous mind, apt to be set aright;
This, in the lonely dell discoursing, you
Declared at large; and by what exercise
From visible nature or the inner self
Power may be trained, and renovation brought
To those who need the gift. But, after all,
Is aught so certain as that man is doomed
To breathe beneath a vault of ignorance?
The natural roof of that dark house in which
His soul is pent! How little can be known—
This is the wise man's sigh; how far we err—
This is the good man's not unfrequent pang!
And they perhaps err least, the lowly class
Whom a benign necessity compels
To follow reason's least ambitious course;
Such do I mean who, unperplexed by doubt,
And unincited by a wish to look
Into high objects farther than they may,
Pace to and fro, from morn till eventide,
The narrow avenue of daily toil
For daily bread."
"Yes," buoyantly exclaimed
The pale recluse—"praise to the sturdy plough,
And patient spade, and shepherd's simple crook,
And ponderous loom—resounding while it holds
Body and mind in one captivity;
And let the light mechanic tool be hailed
With honour; which, encasing by the power
Of long companionship, the artist's hand,
Cuts off that hand, with all its world of nerves,
From a too busy commerce with the heart!
Inglorious implements of craft and toil,
Both ye that shape and build, and ye that force,
By slow solicitation, earth to yield
Her annual bounty, sparingly dealt forth
With wise reluctance, you would I extol

Not for gross good alone which ye produce,
But for the impertinent and ceaseless strife
Of proofs and reasons ye preclude—in those
Who to your dull society are born,
And with their humble birthright rest content.
Would I had ne'er renounced it!"

A slight flush
Of moral anger previously had tinged
The old man's cheek; but, at this closing turn
Of self-reproach, it passed away. Said he,
"That which we feel we utter; as we think
So have we argued; reaping for our pains
No visible recompense. For our relief
You," to the pastor turning thus he spake,
"Have kindly interposed. May I entreat
Your further help? The mine of real life
Dig for us; and present us, in the shape
Of virgin ore, that gold which we, by pains,
Fruitless as those of aëry alchemists,
Seek from the torturing crucible. There lies
Around us a domain where you have long
Watched both the outward course and inner heart;
Give us, for our abstractions, solid facts;
For our disputes, plain pictures. Say what man
He is who cultivates yon hanging field;
What qualities of mind she bears, who comes,
For morn and evening service with her pail,
To that green pasture; place before our sight
The family who dwell within yon house
Fenced round with glittering laurel; or in that
Below, from which the curling smoke ascends.
Or rather, as we stand on holy earth,
And have the dead around us, take from them
Your instances; for they are both best known,
And by frail man most equitably judged.
Epitomise the life; pronounce, you can,
Authentic epitaphs on some of these
Who, from their lowly mansions hither brought,
Beneath this turf lie mouldering at our feet.
So, by your records, may our doubts be solved;
And so, not searching higher, we may learn
To prize the breath we share with human kind
And look upon the dust of man with awe."

The priest replied.—"An office you impose
For which peculiar requisites are mine:
Yet much, I feel, is wanting—else the task
Would be most grateful. True indeed it is
That they whom death has hidden from our sight
Are worthiest of the mind's regard; with these
The future cannot contradict the past:
Mortality's last exercise and proof
Is undergone; the transit made that shows
The very soul, revealed as she departs.
Yet, on your first suggestion, will I give,
Ere we descend into these silent vaults,
One picture from the living.—

You behold,
High on the breast of yon dark mountain—dark
With stony barrenness, a shining speck
Bright as a sunbeam sleeping till a shower
Brush it away, or cloud pass over it;
And such it might be deemed—a sleeping sunbeam;
But 'tis a plot of cultivated ground,
Cut off, an island in the dusky waste;
And that attractive brightness is its own.
The lofty site, by nature framed to tempt
Amid a wilderness of rocks and stones
The tiller's hand, a hermit might have chosen,
For opportunity presented, thence
Far forth to send his wandering eye o'er land
And ocean, and look down upon the works,
The habitations, and the ways of men,
Himself unseen! But no tradition tells
That ever hermit dipped his maple dish
In the sweet spring that lurks 'mid yon green fields;
And no such visionary views belong
To those who occupy and till the ground,
And on the bosom of the mountain dwell,
A wedded pair in childless solitude.
A house of stones collected on the spot,
By rude hands built, with rocky knolls in front,
Backed also by a ledge of rock, whose crest
Of birch-trees waves above the chimney top:
A rough abode—in colour, shape, and size,
Such as in unsafe times of Border war
Might have been wished for and contrived, to elude
The eye of roving plunderer—for their need
Suffices; and unshaken bears the assault
Of their most dreaded foe, the strong south-west
In anger blowing from the distant sea.
Alone within her solitary hut;
There, or within the compass of her fields,
At any moment may the dame be found,
True as the stock-dove to her shallow nest
And to the grove that holds it. She beguiles
By intermingled work of house and field
The summer's day, and winter's; with success
Not equal, but sufficient to maintain,
Even at the worst, a smooth stream of content,
Until the expected hour at which her mate
From the far-distant quarry's vault returns;
And by his converse crowns a silent day
With evening cheerfulness. In powers of mind,
In scale of culture, few among my flock
Hold lower rank than this sequestered pair;
But humbleness of heart descends from heaven;
And that best gift of Heaven hath fallen on them;
Abundant recompense for every want.
Stoop from your height, ye proud, and copy these!
Who, in their noiseless dwelling-place, can hear
The voice of wisdom whispering Scripture texts
For the mind's government, or temper's peace;
And recommending, for their mutual need,
Forgiveness, patience, hope, and charity!"

"Much was I pleased," the gray-haired Wanderer said,
"When to those shining fields our notice first
You turned; and yet more pleased have from your lips
Gathered this fair report of them who dwell
In that retirement, whither by such course
Of evil hap and good as oft awaits
A lone wayfaring man, I once was brought.
Dark on my road the autumnal evening fell
While I was traversing yon mountain-pass,
And night succeeded with unusual gloom;
So that my feet and hands at length became
Guides better than mine eyes—until a light
High in the gloom appeared, too high, methought,
For human habitation, but I longed
To reach it, destitute of other hope.
I looked with steadiness as sailors look
On the north star, or watch-tower's distant lamp,
And saw the light—now fixed—and shifting now—
Not like a dancing meteor, but in line
Of never-varying motion, to and fro.
It is no night-fire of the naked hills,
Thought I, some friendly covert must be near.
With this persuasion thitherward my steps
I turn, and reach at last the guiding light;
Joy to myself! but to the heart of her
Who there was standing on the open hill
(The same kind matron whom your tongue hath praised)
Alarm and disappointment! The alarm
Ceased when she learned through what mishap I came,
And by what help had gained those distant fields.
Drawn from her cottage, on that open height,
Bearing a lanthorn in her hand she stood,
Or paced the ground—to guide her husband home,
By that unwearied signal kenned afar;
An anxious duty! which the lofty site,
Traversed but by a few irregular paths,
Imposes, whensoever untoward chance
Detains him after his accustomed hour
When night lies black upon the hills. 'But come,
Come,' said the matron, 'to our poor abode,
Those dark rocks hide it!' Entering, I beheld
A blazing fire—beside a cleanly hearth
Sate down! and to her office, with leave asked,
The dame returned.—Or ere that glowing pile
Of mountain turf required the builder's hand
Its wasted splendour to repair, the door
Opened, and she re-entered with glad looks,
Her helpmate following. Hospitable fare,
Frank conversation, made the evening's treat:
Need a bewildered traveller wish for more?
But more was given; I studied as we sate
By the bright fire, the good man's face—composed
Of features elegant; an open brow
Of undisturbed humanity; a cheek
Suffused with something of a feminine hue:
Eyes beaming courtesy and mild regard;
But, in the quicker turns of the discourse,
Expression slowly varying, that evinced

A tardy apprehension. From a fount
Lost, thought I, in the obscurities of time,
But honoured once, these features and that mien
May have descended, though I see them here.
In such a man, so gentle and subdued,
Withal so graceful in his gentleness,
A race illustrious for heroic deeds,
Humbled, but not degraded, may expire.
This pleasing fancy (cherished and upheld
By sundry recollections of such fall
From high to low, ascent from low to high,
As books record, and even the careless mind
Cannot but notice among men and things)
Went with me to the place of my repose.

"Roused by the crowing cock at dawn of day,
I yet had risen too late to interchange
A morning salutation with my host,
Gone forth already to the far-off seat
Of his day's work 'Three dark mid-winter months
Pass, said the matron, 'and I never see,
Save when the Sabbath brings its kind release,
My helpmate s face by light of day. He quits
His door in darkness, nor till dusk returns.
And, through Heaven's blessing, thus we gain the bread
For which we pray, and for the wants provide
Of sickness, accident, and helpless age.
Companions have I many; many friends,
Dependents, comforters—my wheel, my fire,
All day the house-clock ticking in mine ear,
The cackling hen, the tender chicken brood,
And the wild birds that gather round my porch.
This honest sheep-dog's countenance I read;
With him can talk, nor blush to waste a word
On creatures less intelligent and shrewd.
And if the blustering wind that drives the clouds
Care not for me, he lingers round my door,
And makes me pastime when our tempers suit;
But, above all, my thoughts are my support.'
The matron ended—nor could I forbear
To exclaim—'Oh, happy I yielding to the law
Of these privations, richer in the main!
While thankless thousands are oppressed and clogged
By ease and leisure—by the very wealth
And pride of opportunity made poor;
While tens of thousands falter in their path,
And sink through utter want of cheering light;
For you the hours of labour do not flag;
For you each evening hath its shining star,
And every Sabbath-day its golden sun!'"

"Yes!" said the Solitary with a smile
That seemed to break from an expanding heart,
"The untutored bird may found, and so construct,
And with such soft materials line her nest,
Fixed in the centre of a prickly brake,
That the thorns wound her not; they only guard.
Powers not unjustly likened to those gifts

Of happy instinct which the woodland bird
Shares with her species, nature's grace sometimes
Upon the individual doth confer
Among her higher creatures born and trained
To use of reason And, I own, that tired
Of the ostentatious world—a swelling stage
With empty actions and vain passions stuffed,
And from the private struggles of mankind
Hoping for less than I could wish to hope,
Far less than once I trusted and believed—
I love to hear of those, who, not contending
Nor summoned to contend for virtue's prize,
Miss not the humbler good at which they aim;
Blest with a kindly faculty to blunt
The edge of adverse circumstance, and turn
Into their contraries the petty plagues
And hindrances with which they stand beset.
In early youth, among my native hills,
I knew a Scottish peasant, who possessed
A few small crofts of stone-encumbered ground;
Masses of every shape and size, that lay
Scattered about beneath the mouldering walls
Of a rough precipice; and some, apart,
In quarters unobnoxious to such chance,
As if the moon had showered them down in spite;
But he repined not. Though the plough was scared
By these obstructions, 'round the shady stones
A fertilising moisture,' said the swain,
'Gathers and is preserved, and feeding dews
And damps, through all the droughty summer day,
From out their substance issuing, maintain
Herbage that never fails; no grass springs up
So green, so fresh, so plentiful, as mine!'
But thinly sown these natures; rare, at least,
The mutual aptitude of seed and soil
That yields such kindly product He—whose bed
Perhaps yon loose sods cover, the poor pensioner
Brought yesterday from our sequestered dell
Here to lie down in lasting quiet—he,
If living now,—could otherwise report
Of rustic loneliness: that gray-haired orphan—
So call him, for humanity to him
No parent was—could feelingly have told,
In life, in death, what solitude can breed
Of selfishness, and cruelty and vice;
Or, if it breed not, hath not power to cure.
But your compliance, sir! with our request
My words too long have hindered."

Undeterred,
Perhaps incited rather, by these shocks,
In no ungracious opposition, given
To the confiding spirit of his own
Experienced faith, the reverend pastor said,
Around him looking, "Where shall I begin?
Who shall be first selected from my flock
Gathered together in their peaceful fold?"
He paused—and having lifted up his eyes
To the pure heaven, he cast them down again

Upon the earth beneath his feet, and spake.
"To a mysteriously-consorted pair
This place is consecrate; to death and life,
And to the best affections that proceed
From their conjunction. Consecrate to faith
In Him who bled for man upon the cross,
Hallowed to revelation, and no less
To reason's mandates; and the hopes divine
Of pure imagination;—above all,
To charity, and love, that have provided,
Within these precincts a capacious bed
And receptacle, open to the good
And evil, to the just and the unjust,
In which they find an equal resting-place:
Even as the multitude of kindred brooks
And streams whose murmur fills this hollow vale,
Whether their course be turbulent or smooth,
Their waters clear or sullied, all are lost
Within the bosom of yon crystal lake,
And end their journey in the same repose!

"And blest are they who sleep, and we that know
While in a spot like this we breathe and walk,
That all beneath us by the wings are covered
Of motherly humanity, outspread
And gathering all within their tender shade,
Though loth and slow to come! A battle-field,
In stillness left when slaughter is no more,
With this compared, is a strange spectacle!
A rueful sight the wild shore strewn with wrecks,
And trod by people in afflicted quest
Of friends and kindred whom the angry sea
Restores not to their prayer! Ah! who would think
That all the scattered subjects which compose
Earth's melancholy vision through the space
Of all her climes; these wretched, these depraved,
To virtue lost, insensible of peace,
From the delights of charity cut off,
To pity dead, the oppressor and the opprest;
Tyrants who utter the destroying word,
And slaves who will consent to be destroyed—
Were of one species with the sheltered few,
Who, with a dutiful and tender hand,
Did lodge in an appropriated spot,
This file of infants; some that never breathed
The vital air; and others, who, allowed
That privilege, did yet expire too soon,
Or with too brief a warning, to admit
Administration of the holy rite
That lovingly consigns the babe to the arms
Of Jesus, and his everlasting care.
These that in trembling hope are laid apart;
And the besprinkled nursling, unrequired
Till he begins to smile upon the breast
That feeds him; and the tottering little one
Taken from air and sunshine when the rose
Of infancy first blooms upon his cheek;
The thinking, thoughtless schoolboy; the bold youth

Of soul impetuous, and the bashful maid
Smitten while all the promises of life
Are opening round her; those of middle age,
Cast down while confident in strength they stand,
Like pillars fixed more firmly, as might seem,
And more secure, by very weight of all
That, for support, rests on them: the decayed
And burthensome; and, lastly, that poor few
Whose light of reason is with age extinct;
The hopeful and the hopeless, first and last,
The earliest summoned and the longest spared—
Are here deposited, with tribute paid
Various, but unto each some tribute paid;
As if, amid these peaceful hills and groves,
Society were touched with kind concern;
And gentle 'nature grieved, that one should die;'
Or, if the change demanded no regret,
Observed the liberating stroke—and blessed.
And whence that tribute? wherefore these regards?
Not from the naked *heart* alone of man
(Though claiming high distinction upon earth
As the sole spring and fountain-head of tears,
His own peculiar utterance for distress
Or gladness), no," the philosophic priest
Continued, "'tis not in the vital seat
Of feeling to produce them, without aid
From the pure soul, the soul sublime and pure;
With her two faculties of eye and ear,
The one by which a creature, whom his sins
Have rendered prone, can upward look to heaven;
The other that empowers him to perceive
The voice of Deity, on height and plain
Whispering those truths in stillness, which the Word,
To the four quarters of the winds, proclaims.
Not without such assistance could the use
Of these benign observances prevail.
Thus are they born, thus fostered, and maintained;
And by the care prospective of our wise
Forefathers who, to guard against the shocks,
The fluctuation and decay of things
Embodied and established these high truths
In solemn institutions:—men convinced
That life is love and immortality,
The being one, and one the element.
There lies the channel, and original bed,
From the beginning, hollowed out and scooped
For man's affections—else betrayed and lost,
And swallowed up 'mid deserts infinite!
This is the genuine course, the aim, and end
Of prescient reason, all conclusions else
Are abject, vain, presumptuous, and perverse.
The faith partaking of those holy times,
Life, I repeat, is energy of love,
Divine or human; exercised in pain,
In strife, and tribulation; and ordained,
If so approved and sanctified, to pass,
Through shades and silent rest, to endless joy."

BOOK VI.

ARGUMENT.

Poet's address to the state and Church of England– The pastor not inferior to the ancient Worthies of the Church—He begins his narratives with an instance of unrequited love—Anguish of mind subdued—and how—The lonely miner, an instance of perseverance, which leads by contrast to an example of abused talents, irresolution, and weakness—Solitary, applying this covertly to his own case, asks for an instance of some stranger, whose dispositions may have led him to end his days here—Pastor, in answer, gives an account of the harmonizing influence of solitude upon two men, of opposite principles, who had encountered agitations in public life—The rule by which peace may be obtained expressed—and where—Solitary hints at an overpowering fatality—Answer of the pastor—What subjects he will exclude from his narratives—Conversation upon this—Instance of an unamiable character, a female—and why given—Contrasted with this, a meek sufferer, from unguarded and betrayed love—Instance of heavier guilt, and its consequences to the offender—With this instance of a marriage contract broken is contrasted one of a widower, evidencing his faithful affection towards his deceased wife by his care of their female children

THE CHURCHYARD AMONG THE MOUNTAINS.

HAIL to the crown by freedom shaped—to gird
An English sovereign's brow ! and to the throne
Whereon he sits ! Whose deep foundations lie
In veneration and the people's love ;
Whose steps are equity, whose seat is law.
Hail to the state of England ! And conjoin
With this a salutation as devout,
Made to the spiritual fabric of her Church ;
Founded in truth ; by blood of martyrdom
Cemented ; by the hands of wisdom reared
In beauty of holiness, with ordered pomp,
Decent, and unreproved The voice, that greets
The majesty of both, shall pray for both ,
That mutually protected and sustained,
They may endure as long as sea surrounds
This favoured land, or sunshine warms her soil.
And oh, ye swelling hills, and spacious plains !
Besprent from shore to shore with steeple-towers,
And spires whose "silent finger points to heaven ;"
Nor wanting, at wide intervals, the bulk
Of ancient minster, lifted above the cloud
Of the dense air, which town or city breeds
To intercept the sun's glad beams—may ne'er
That true succession fail of English hearts,
Who, with ancestral feeling can perceive
What in those holy structures ye possess
Of ornamental interest, and the charm
Of pious sentiment diffused afar,
And human charity, and social love.
Thus never shall the indignities of time
Approach their reverend graces, unopposed ;
Nor shall the elements be free to hurt
Their fair proportions ; nor the blinder rage
Of bigot zeal madly to overturn ;
And, if the desolating hand of war
Spare them, they shall continue to bestow—
Upon the thronged abodes of busy men

(Depraved, and ever prone to fill their minds
Exclusively with transitory things)
An air and mien of dignified pursuit;
Of sweet civility—on rustic wilds.
The poet fostering for his native land
Such hope, entreats that servants may abound
Of those pure altars worthy, ministers
Detached from pleasure, to the love of gain
Superior, insusceptible of pride,
And by ambitious longings undisturbed;
Men, whose delight is where their duty lands
Or fixes them; whose least distinguished day
Shines with some portion of that heavenly lustre
Which makes the Sabbath lovely in the sight
Of blessed angels, pitying human cares.
And, as on earth it is the doom of truth
To be perpetually attacked by foes
Open or covert, be that priesthood still,
For her defence, replenished with a band
Of strenuous champions, in scholastic arts
Thoroughly disciplined, nor (if in course
Of the revolving world's disturbances
Cause should recur, which righteous Heaven avert!
To meet such trial) from their spiritual sires
Degenerate; who, constrained to wield the sword
Of disputation, shrunk not though assailed
With hostile din, and combating in sight
Of angry umpires, partial and unjust;
And did, thereafter, bathe their hands in fire,
So to declare the conscience satisfied:
Nor for their bodies would accept release;
But, blessing God, and praising him, bequeathed,
With their last breath, from out the smouldering flame,
The faith which they by diligence had earned,
Or, through illuminating grace, received,
For their dear countrymen, and all mankind.
Oh, high example, constancy divine!

Even such a man (inheriting the zeal
And from the sanctity of elder times
Not deviating,—a priest, the like of whom,
If multiplied, and in their stations set,
Would o'er the bosom of a joyful land
Spread true religion, and her genuine fruits)
Before me stood that day; on holy ground
Fraught with the relics of mortality,
Exalting tender themes, by just degrees
To lofty raised; and to the highest, last:
The head and mighty paramount of truths;
Immortal life in never-fading worlds,
For mortal creatures, conquered and secured.

That basis laid, those principles of faith
Announced as a preparatory act
Of reverence to the spirit of the place;
The pastor casts his eyes upon the ground,
Not, as before, like one oppressed with awe,

But with a mild and social cheerfulness,
Then to the Solitary turned, and spake—

"At morn or eve, in your retired domain,
Perchance you not unfrequently have marked
A visitor,—in quest of herbs and flowers;
Too delicate employ, as would appear,
For one who, though of drooping mien, had yet
From nature's kindliness received a frame
Robust as ever rural labour bred."

The Solitary answered:—"Such a form
Full well I recollect. We often crossed
Each other's path; but, as the intruder seemed
Fondly to prize the silence which he kept,
And I as willingly did cherish mine,
We met, and passed like shadows. I have heard,
From my good host, that he was crazed in brain
By unrequited love; and scaled the rocks,
Dived into caves, and pierced the matted woods,
In hope to find some virtuous herb, of power
To cure his malady!"
                                        The vicar smiled.
"Alas! before to-morrow's sun goes down
His habitation will be here: for him
That open grave is destined."
                                        "Died he then
Of pain and grief?" the Solitary asked.
"Believe it not—oh! never could that be!"

"He loved," the vicar answered, "deeply loved
Loved fondly, truly, fervently; and dared
At length to tell his love, but sued in vain;
Rejected—yea, repelled—and, if with scorn
Upon the haughty maiden's brow, 'tis but
A high-prized plume which female beauty wears
In wantonness of conquest, or puts on
To cheat the world, or from herself to hide
Humiliation, when no longer free.
That he could brook, and glory in,—but when
The tidings came that she whom he had wooed
Was wedded to another, and his heart
Was forced to rend away its only hope,
Then, pity could have scarcely found on earth
An object worthier of regard than he,
In the transition of that bitter hour!
Lost was she, lost; nor could the sufferer say
That in the act of preference he had been
Unjustly dealt with; but the maid was gone!
Had vanished from his prospects and desires;
Not by translation to the heavenly choir
Who have put off their mortal spoils—ah, no!
She lives another's wishes to complete,—
'Joy be their lot, and happiness,' he cried,
'His lot and hers, as misery is mine!'

Such was that strong concussion; but the man
Who trembled, trunk and limbs, like some huge oak

By a fierce tempest shaken, soon resumed
The steadfast quiet natural to a mind
Of composition gentle and sedate,
And in its movements circumspect and slow.
To books, and to the long-forsaken desk,
O'er which enchained by science he had loved
To bend, he stoutly re-addressed himself,
Resolved to quell his pain, and search for truth
With keener appetite (if that might be)
And closer industry. Of what ensued
Within the heart no outward sign appeared
Till a betraying sickliness was seen
To tinge his cheek ; and through his frame it crept
With slow mutation unconcealable ;
Such universal change as autumn makes
In the fair body of a leafy grove
Discoloured, then divested. 'Tis affirmed
By poets skilled in nature's secret ways
That love will not submit to be controlled
By mastery —and the good man lacked not friends
Who strove to instil this truth into his mind,
A mind in all heart-mysteries unversed.
" Go to the hills," said one, " remit a while
This baneful diligence :—at early morn
Court the fresh air, explore the heaths and woods ;
And, leaving it to others, to foretell,
By calculations sage, the ebb and flow
Of tides, and when the moon will be eclipsed,
Do you, for your own benefit, construct
A calendar of flowers, plucked as they blow
Where health abides, and cheerfulness, and peace "
The attempt was made ;—'tis needless to report
How hopelessly ;—but innocence is strong,
And an entire simplicity of mind,
A thing most sacred in the eye of Heaven,
That opens, for such sufferers, relief
Within their souls, a fount of grace divine ;
And doth commend their weakness and disease
To nature's care, assisted in her office
By all the elements that round her wait
To generate, to preserve, and to restore ;
And by her beautiful array of forms
Shedding sweet influence from above, or pure
Delight exhaling from the ground they tread."

" Impute it not to impatience, if,' exclaimed
The Wanderer, " I infer that he was healed
By perseverance in the course prescribed.'

" You do not err ; the powers that had been lost
By slow degrees, were gradually regained ;
The fluttering nerves composed ; the beating heart
In rest established ; and the jarring thoughts
To harmony restored.—But yon dark mould
Will cover him, in height of strength—to eart'
Hastily smitten, by a fever's force ;
Yet not with strokes so sudden as refused
Time to look back with tenderness on her

Whom he had loved in passion,—and to send
Some farewell words—with one, but one, request,
That from his dying hand she would accept,
Of his possessions, that which most he prized;
A book, upon whose leaves some chosen plants
By his own hand disposed with nicest care,
In undecaying beauty were preserved,
Mute register, to him, of time and place,
And various fluctuations in the breast;
To her, a monument of faithful love
Conquered, and in tranquillity retained!

"Close to his destined habitation lies
One who achieved a humbler victory,
Though marvellous in its kind. A place there is
High in these mountains, that allured a band
Of keen adventurers to unite their pains
In search of precious ore: who tried, were foiled,
And all desisted, all save him alone.
He, taking counsel of his own clear thoughts,
And trusting only to his own weak hands,
Urged unremittingly the stubborn work,
Unseconded, uncountenanced; then, as time
Passed on, while still his lonely efforts found
No recompense, derided; and, at length,
By many pitied, as insane of mind;
By others dreaded as the luckless thrall
Of subterranean spirits feeding hope
By various mockery of sight and sound;
Hope, after hope, encouraged and destroyed.
But when the Lord of seasons had matured
The fruits of earth through space of twice ten years.
The mountain's entrails offered to his view
And trembling grasp the long-deferred reward.
Not with more transport did Columbus greet
A world, his rich discovery! But our swain,
A very hero till his point was gained,
Proved all unable to support the weight
Of prosperous fortune. On the fields he looked
With an unsettled liberty of thought,
Of schemes and wishes; in the daylight walked
Giddy and restless; ever and anon
Quaffed in his gratitude immoderate cups;
And truly might be said to die of joy!
He vanished; but conspicuous to this day
The path remains that linked his cottage-door
To the mine's mouth; a long, and slanting track,
Upon the rugged mountain's stony side,
Worn by his daily visits to and from
The darksome centre of a constant hope.
The vestige, neither force of beating rain
Nor the vicissitudes of frost and thaw
Shall cause to fade, till ages pass away:
And it is named, in memory of the event,
The path of perseverance."

"Thou, from whom
Man has his strength," exclaimed the Wanderer, "oh
Do Thou direct it!—to the virtuous grant

The penetrative eye which can perceive
In this blind world the guiding vein of hope,
That, like this labourer, such may dig their way,
'Unshaken, unseduced, unterrified;'
Grant to the wise *his* firmness of resolve!"

"That prayer were not superfluous," said the priest
"Amid the noblest relics, proudest dust,
That Westminster, for Britain's glory, holds,
Within the bosom of her awful pile,
Ambitiously collected Yet the sigh,
Which wafts that prayer to Heaven, is due to all,
Wherever laid, who living fell below
Their virtue's humbler mark; a sigh of *pain*
If to the opposite extreme they sank.
How would you pity her who yonder rests;
Him, farther off, the pair, who here are laid;
But above all, that mixture of earth's mould
Whom sight of this green hillock to my mind
Recalls!—He lived not till his locks were nipped
By seasonable frost of age; nor died
Before his temples, prematurely forced
To mix the manly brown with silver gray
Gave obvious instance of the sad effect
Produced, when thoughtless folly hath usurped
The natural crown that sage experience wears.
Gay, volatile, ingenious, quick to learn,
And prompt to exhibit all that he possessed
Or could perform; a zealous actor—hired
Into the troop of mirth, a soldier—sworn
Into the lists of giddy enterprise—
Such was he; yet, as if within his frame
Two several souls alternately had lodged,
Two sets of manners could the youth put on;
And, fraught with antics as the Indian bird
That writhes and chatters in her wiry cage,
Was graceful, when it pleased him, smooth and still
As the mute swan that floats adown the stream,
Or, on the waters of the unruffled lake,
Anchors her placid beauty. Not a leaf,
That flutters on the bough, more light than he,
And not a flower, that droops in the green shade,
More winningly reserved! If ye inquire
How such consummate elegance was bred
Amid these wilds, this answer may suffice,
'Twas nature's will; who sometimes undertakes
For the reproof of human vanity,
Art to outstrip in her peculiar walk.
Hence, for this favourite, lavishly endowed
With personal gifts, and bright instinctive wit,
While both, embellishing each other, stood
Yet farther recommended by the charm
Of fine demeanour, and by dance and song,
And skill in letters, every fancy shaped
Fair expectations; nor when to the world's
Capacious field forth went the adventurer, there
Were he and his attainments overlooked,
Or scantily rewarded; but all hopes,

Cherished for him, he suffered to depart,
Like blighted buds; or clouds that mimicked land
Before the sailor's eye! or diamond drops
That sparkling decked the morning grass; or aught
That *was* attractive—and hath ceased to be!
Yet, when this prodigal returned, the rites
Of joyful greeting were on him bestowed,
Who, by humiliation undeterred,
Sought for his weariness a place of rest
Within his father's gates—Whence came he?—clothed
In tattered garb, from hovels where abides
Necessity, the stationary host
Of vagrant poverty; from rifted barns
Where no one dwells but the wide-staring owl
And the owl's prey; from these bare haunts to which
He had descended from the proud saloon,
He came the ghost of beauty and of health,
The wreck of gaiety! But soon revived
In strength, in power refitted, he renewed
His suit to fortune; and she smiled again
Upon a fickle ingrate. Thrice he rose,
Thrice sank as willingly. For he, whose nerves
Were used to thrill with pleasure, while his voice
Softly accompanied the tuneful harp,
By the nice finger of fair ladies, touched
In glittering halls, was able to derive
Not less enjoyment from an abject choice.
Who happier for the moment—who more blithe
Than this fallen spirit? in those dreary holds
His talents lending to exalt the freaks
Of merry-making beggars,—now, provoked
To laughter multiplied in louder peals
By his malicious wit; then, all enchained
With mute astonishment, themselves to see
In their own arts outdone, their fame eclipsed,
As by the very presence of the fiend
Who dictates and inspires illusive feats,
For knavish purposes! The city, too,
(With shame I speak it) to her guilty bowers
Allured him, sunk so low in self-respect
As there to linger, there to eat his bread,
Hired minstrel of voluptuous blandishment;
Charming the air with skill of hand or voice,
Listen who would, be wrought upon who might,
Sincerely wretched hearts, or falsely gay.
Such the too frequent tenor of his boast
In ears that relished the report;—but all
Was from his parents happily concealed;
Who saw enough for blame and pitying love.
They also were permitted to receive
His last, repentant breath; and closed his eyes,
No more to open on that irksome world
Where he had long existed in the state
Of a young fowl beneath one mother hatched,
Though from another sprung—of different kind:
Where he had lived, and could not cease to live,
Distracted in propensity; content
With neither element of good or ill;

And yet in both rejoicing; man unblest;
Of contradictions infinite the slave,
Till his deliverance, when mercy made him
One with himself, and one with them who sleep."

"'Tis strange," observed the Solitary, "strange
It seems, and scarcely less than pitiful,
That in a land where charity provides
For all that can no longer feed themselves,
A man like this should choose to bring his shame
To the parental door; and with his sighs
Infect the air which he had freely breathed
In happy infancy. He could not pine,
Through lack of converse; no, he must have found
Abundant exercise for thought and speech
In his dividual being, self-reviewed,
Self-catechised, self-punished.—Some there are
Who, drawing near their final home, and much
And daily longing that the same were reached,
Would rather shun than seek the fellowship
Of kindred mould.—Such haply here are laid?"

"Yes," said the priest, "the genius of our hills,
Who seems, by these stupendous barriers cast
Round his domain, desirous not alone
To keep his own, but also to exclude
All other progeny, doth sometimes lure,
Even by this studied depth of privacy,
The unhappy alien hoping to obtain
Concealment, or seduced by wish to find
In place from outward molestation free,
Helps to eternal ease. Of many such
Could I discourse; but as their stay was brief,
So their departure only left behind
Fancies, and loose conjectures. Other trace
Survives, for worthy mention, of a pair
Who, from the pressure of their several fates,
Meeting as strangers, in a petty town
Whose blue roofs ornament a distant reach
Of this far-winding vale, remained as friends
True to their choice; and gave their bones in trust
To this loved cemetery, here to lodge
With unescutcheoned privacy interred
Far from the family-vault.—A chieftain one
By right of birth, within whose spotless breast
The fire of ancient Caledonia burned.
He, with the foremost whose impatience hailed
The Stuart, landing to resume, by force
Of arms, the crown which bigotry had lost,
Aroused his clan; and, fighting at their head,
With his brave sword endeavoured to prevent
Culloden's fatal overthrow.—Escaped
From that disastrous rout, to foreign shores
He fled, and when the lenient hand of time
Those troubles had appeased, he sought and gained,
For his obscured condition, an obscure
Retreat, within this nook of English ground.
The other, born in Britain's southern tract,

Had fixed his milder loyalty, and placed
His gentler sentiments of love and hate,
There, where *they* placed them who in conscience prized
The new succession, as a line of kings
Whose oath had virtue to protect the land
Against the dire assaults of Papacy
And arbitrary rule. But launch thy bark
On the distempered flood of public life,
And cause for most rare triumph will be thine
If, spite of keenest eye and steadiest hand,
The stream, that bears thee forward, prove not, soon
Or late, a perilous master. He, who oft,
Under the battlements and stately trees
That round his mansion cast a sober gloom,
Had moralized on this, and other truths
Of kindred import, pleased and satisfied,
Was forced to vent his wisdom with a sigh
Heaved from the heart in fortune's bitterness,
When he had crushed a plentiful estate
By ruinous contest, to obtain a seat
In Britain's senate. Fruitless was the attempt:
And while the uproar of that desperate strife
Continued yet to vibrate on his ear,
The vanquished Whig, beneath a *borrowed* name,
(For the mere sound and echo of his own
Haunted him with sensation of disgust
That he was glad to lose) slunk from the world
To the deep shade of these untravelled wilds:
In which the Scottish laird had long possessed
An undisturbed abode.—Here, then, they met,
Two doughty champions; flaming Jacobite
And sullen Hanoverian! You might think
That losses and vexations, less severe
Than those which they had severally sustained,
Would have inclined each to abate his zeal
For his ungrateful cause; no,—I have heard
My reverend father tell that, 'mid the calm
Of that small town encountering thus, they filled,
Daily, its bowling-green with harmless strife;
Plagued with uncharitable thoughts the church;
And vexed the market-place. But in the breasts
Of these opponents gradually was wrought,
With little change of general sentiment,
Such change towards each other, that their days
By choice were spent in constant fellowship;
And if, at times, they fretted with the yoke,
Those very bickerings made them love it more.

"A favourite boundary to their lengthened walks
This churchyard was. And whether they had come
Treading their path in sympathy and linked
In social converse, or by some short space
Discreetly parted to preserve the peace,
One spirit seldom failed to extend its sway
Over both minds, when they a while had marked
The visible quiet of this holy ground,
And breathed its soothing air;—the spirit of hope
And saintly magnanimity; that, spurning

The field of selfish difference and dispute,
And every care which transitory things,
Earth, and the kingdoms of the earth, create,
Doth, by a rapture of forgetfulness,
Preclude forgiveness, from the praise debarred,
Which else the Christian virtue might have claimed.
There live who yet remember here to have seen
Their courtly figures,—seated on the stump
Of an old yew, their favourite resting-place.
But, as the remnant of the long-lived tree
Was disappearing by a swift decay,
They, with joint care, determined to erect,
Upon its site, a dial, that might stand
For public use preserved, and thus survive
As their own private monument; for this
Was the particular spot, in which they wished,
(And Heaven was pleased to accomplish the desire)
That, undivided, their remains should lie.
So, where the mouldered tree had stood, was raised
Yon structure, framing, with the ascent of steps
That to the decorated pillar lead,
A work of art more sumptuous than might seem
To suit this place; yet built in no proud scorn
Of rustic homeliness; they only aimed
To ensure for it respectful guardianship.
Around the margin of the plate, whereon
The shadow falls to note the stealthy hours,
Winds an inscriptive legend."—At these words
Thither we turned; and, gathered, as we read,
The appropriate sense, in Latin numbers couched,—
"*Time flies; it is his melancholy task*
To bring, and bear away, delusive hopes,
And re-produce the troubles he destroys;
But, while his blindness thus is occupied,
Discerning mortal! do thou serve the will
Of time's eternal Master, and that peace
Which the world wants, shall be for thee confirmed."

"Smooth verse, inspired by no unlettered muse,"
Exclaimed the sceptic, "and the strain of thought
Accords with nature's language;—the soft voice
Of yon white torrent falling down the rocks
Speaks, less distinctly, to the same effect.
If, then, their blended influence be not lost
Upon our hearts, not wholly lost I grant,
Even upon mine, the more are we required
To feel for those, among our fellow-men,
Who, offering no obeisance to the world,
Are yet made desperate by 'too quick a sense
Of constant infelicity'—cut off
From peace like exiles on some barren rock,
Their life's appointed prison; not more free
Than sentinels, between two armies, set,
With nothing better, in the chill night air,
Than their own thoughts to comfort them.—Say why
That ancient story of Prometheus chained?
The vulture—the inexhaustible repast
Drawn from his vitals? Say what meant the woes

By Tantalus entailed upon his race,
And the dark sorrows of the line of Thebes?
Fictions in form, but in their substance truths,
Tremendous truths! familiar to the men
Of long-past times; nor obsolete in ours.
Exchange the shepherd's frock of native gray
For robes with regal purple tinged; convert
The crook into a sceptre; give the pomp
Of circumstance, and here the tragic Muse
Shall find apt subjects for her highest art.
Amid the groves, beneath the shadowy hills,
The generations are prepared; the pangs,
The internal pangs are ready; the dread strife
Of poor humanity's afflicted will
Struggling in vain with ruthless destiny."

"Though," said the priest in answer," these be terms
Which a divine philosophy rejects,
We, whose established and unfailing trust
Is in controlling Providence, admit
That, through all stations, human life abounds
With mysteries,—for, if faith were left untried,
How could the might, that lurks within her, then
Be shown? her glorious excellence—that ranks
Among the first of powers and virtues—proved?
Our system is not fashioned to preclude
That sympathy which you for others ask;
And I could tell, not travelling for my theme
Beyond these humble graves, of grievous crimes
And strange disasters; but I pass them by,
Loth to disturb what Heaven hath hushed in peace.
Still less, far less, am I inclined to treat
Of man degraded in his Maker's sight
By the deformities of brutish vice:
For, in such portraits, though a vulgar face
And a coarse outside of repulsive life
And unaffecting manners might at once
Be recognised by all"— "Ah! do not think,"
The Wanderer somewhat eagerly exclaimed,
"Wish could be ours that you, for such poor gain,
(Gain shall I call it?—gain of what?—for whom?)
Should breathe a word tending to violate
Your own pure spirit. Not a step we look for
In slight of that forbearance and reserve
Which common human-heartedness inspires,
And mortal ignorance and frailty claim,
Upon this sacred ground, if nowhere else."

"True," said the Solitary, "be it far
From us to infringe the laws of charity.
Let judgment here in mercy be pronounced:
This, self-respecting nature prompts, and this
Wisdom enjoins; but, if the thing we seek
Be genuine knowledge, bear we then in mind
How, from his lofty throne, the sun can fling
Colours as bright on exhalations bred
By weedy pool or pestilential swamp,

As by the rivulet sparkling where it runs,
Or the pellucid lake."
"Small risk," said I,
"Of such illusion do we here incur;
Temptation here is none to exceed the truth;
No evidence appears that they who rest
Within this ground, were covetous of praise,
Or of remembrance even, deserved or not.
Green is the churchyard, beautiful and green;
Ridge rising gently by the side of ridge;
A heaving surface—almost wholly free
From interruption of sepulchral stones,
And mantled o'er with aboriginal turf
And everlasting flowers. These dalesmen trust
The lingering gleam of their departed lives
To oral records and the silent heart;
Depository faithful, and more kind
Than fondest epitaphs: for, if that fail,
What boots the sculptured tomb? and who can blame,
Who rather would not envy, men that feel
This mutual confidence; if, from such source,
The practice flow,—if thence, or from a deep
And general humility in death?
Nor should I much condemn it, if it spring
From disregard of time's destructive power,
As only capable to prey on things
Of earth, and human nature's mortal part.
Yet—in less simple districts, where we see
Stone lift its forehead emulous of stone
In courting notice, and the ground all paved
With commendations of departed worth;
Reading, where'er we turn, of innocent lives,
Of each domestic charity fulfilled,
And sufferings meekly borne—I, for my part,
Though with the silence pleased that here prevails,
Among those fair recitals also range,
Soothed by the natural spirit which they breathe.
And, in the centre of a world whose soil
Is rank with all unkindness, compassed round
With such memorials, I have sometimes felt
That 'twas no momentary happiness
To have *one* inclosure where the voice that speaks
In envy or detraction is not heard;
Which malice may not enter; where the traces
Of evil inclinations are unknown;
Where love and pity tenderly unite
With resignation; and no jarring tone
Intrudes, the peaceful concert to disturb
Of amity and gratitude."
"Thus sanctioned,"
The pastor said, "I willingly confine
My narratives to subjects that excite
Feelings with these accordant; love, esteem,
And admiration; lifting up a veil,
A sunbeam introducing among hearts
Retired and covert; so that ye shall have
Clear images before your gladdened eyes
Of nature's unambitious underwood.

And flowers that prosper in the shade. And when
I speak of such among my flock as swerved
Or fell, those only will I single out
Upon whose lapse, or error, something more
Than brotherly forgiveness may attend
To such will we restrict our notice , else
Better my tongue were mute. And yet there are,
I feel, good reasons why we should not leave
Wholly untraced a more forbidding way.
For strength to persevere and to support,
And energy to conquer and repel ;—
These elements of virtue, that declare
The native grandeur of the human soul,
Are oft-times not unprofitably shown
In the perverseness of a selfish course ·
Truth every day exemplified, no less
In the gray cottage by the murmuring stream
Than in fantastic conqueror's roving camp,
Or 'mid the factious senate, unappalled
While merciless proscription ebbs and flows.
There," said the vicar, pointing as he spake,
"A woman rests in peace , surpassed by few
In power of mind, and eloquent discourse
Tall was her stature ; her complexion dark
And saturnine · her head not raised to hold
Converse with Heaven, nor yet deprest towards earth
But in projection carried, as she walked
For ever musing. Sunken were her eyes ;
Wrinkled and furrowed with habitual thought
Was her broad forehead ; like the brow of one
Whose visual nerve shrinks from a painful glare
Of overpowering light.—While yet a child,
She, 'mid the humble flowerets of the vale,
Towered like the imperial thistle, not unfurnished
With its appropriate grace, yet rather seeking
To be admired, than coveted and loved.
Even at that age, she ruled as sovereign queen
'Mid her companions ; else their simple sports,
Wanting all relish for her strenuous mind,
Had crossed her, only to be shunned with scorn.
Oh! pang of sorrowful regret for those
Whom, in their youth, sweet study has enthralled,
That they have lived for harsher servitude,
Whether in soul, in body, or estate!
Such doom was hers ; yet nothing could subdue
Her keen desire of knowledge ; nor efface
Those brighter images—by books impressed
Upon her memory , faithfully as stars
That occupy their places,—and, though oft
Hidden by clouds, and oft bedimmed by haze,
Are not to be extinguished, or impaired

"Two passions, both degenerate, for they both
Began in honour, gradually obtained
Rule over her, and vexed her daily life ;
An unrelenting avaricious thrift ;
And a strange thraldom of maternal love,
That held her spirit, in its own despite,

Bound—by vexation, and regret, and scorn,
Constrained forgiveness, and relenting vows,
And tears, in pride suppressed, in shame concealed—
To a poor dissolute son, her only child.
Her wedded days had opened with mishap,
Whence dire dependence.—What could she perform
To shake the burthen off! Ah! there was felt
Indignantly, the weakness of her sex.
She mused—resolved, adhered to her resolve;
The hand grew slack in almsgiving, the heart
Closed by degrees to charity; Heaven's blessing
Not seeking from that source, she placed her trust
In ceaseless pains and parsimonious care,
Which got, and sternly hoarded each day's gain.

"Thus all was re-established, and a pile
Constructed, that sufficed for every end,
Save the contentment of the builder's mind;
A mind by nature indisposed to aught
So placid, so inactive, as content;
A mind intolerant of lasting peace,
And cherishing the pang which it deplored.
Dread life of conflict! which I oft compared
To the agitation of a brook that runs
Down rocky mountains—buried now and lost
In silent pools, and now in eddies chained,—
But never to be charmed to gentleness;
Its best attainment fits of such repose
As timid eyes might shrink from fathoming.

"A sudden illness seized her in the strength
Of life's autumnal season.—Shall I tell
How on her bed of death the matron lay,
To Providence submissive, so she thought;
But fretted, vexed, and wrought upon—almost
To anger, by the malady, that griped
Her prostrate frame with unrelaxing power,
As the fierce eagle fastens on the lamb?
She prayed, she moaned—her husband's sister watched
Her dreary pillow, waited on her needs;
And yet the very sound of that kind foot
Was anguish to her ears!—'And must she rule,'
This was the dying woman heard to say
In bitterness, 'and must she rule and reign,
Sole mistress of this house, when I am gone?
Sit by my fire—possess what I possessed—
Tend what I tended—calling it her own!'
Enough;—I fear, too much.—One vernal evening,
While she was yet in prime of health and strength,
I well remember, while I passed her door:
Musing with loitering step, and upward eye
Turned towards the planet Jupiter, that hung
Above the centre of the vale, a voice
Roused me, her voice; it said, 'That glorious star
In its untroubled element will shine
As now it shines, when we are laid in earth,
And safe from all our sorrows.'—She is safe,
And her uncharitable acts, I trust,

And harsh unkindnesses, are all forgiven;
Though, in this vale, remembered with deep awe!"

THE vicar paused; and towards a seat advanced.
A long stone-seat, fixed in the churchyard wall;
Part shaded by cool sycamore, and part
Offering a sunny resting-place to them
Who seek the house of worship, while the bells
Yet ring with all their voices, or before
The last hath ceased its solitary knoll.
Under the shade we all sate down, and there
His office, uninvited, he resumed.

"As on a sunny bank, a tender lamb
Lurks in safe shelter from the winds of March,
Screened by its parent, so that little mound
Lies guarded by its neighbour; the small heap
Speaks for itself; an infant there doth rest,
The sheltering hillock is the mother's grave.
If mild discourse, and manners that conferred
A natural dignity on humblest rank;
If gladsome spirits, and benignant looks,
That for a face not beautiful did more
Than beauty for the fairest face can do;
And if religious tenderness of heart,
Grieving for sin, and penitential tears
Shed when the clouds had gathered and distained
The spotless ether of a maiden life;
If these may make a hallowed spot of earth
More holy in the sight of God or man;
Then, o'er that mould, a sanctity shall brood,
Till the stars sicken at the day of doom.

"Ah! what a warning for a thoughtless man,
Could field or grove, or any spot of earth,
Show to his eye an image of the pangs
Which it hath witnessed; render back an echo
Of the sad steps by which it hath been trod!
There, by her innocent baby's precious grave,
Yea, doubtless, on the turf that roofs her own,
The mother oft was seen to stand or kneel
In the broad day, a weeping Magdalene.
Now she is not; the swelling turf reports
Of the fresh shower, but of poor Ellen's tears
Is silent, nor is any vestige left
Of the path worn by mournful tread of her
Who, at her heart's light bidding, once had moved
In virgin fearlessness, with step that seemed
Caught from the pressure of elastic turf
Upon the mountains gemmed with morning dew,
In the prime hour of sweetest scents and airs.
Serious and thoughtful was her mind; and yet,
By reconcilement exquisite and rare,
The form, port, motions of this cottage-girl

Were such as might have quickened and inspired
A Titian's hand, addrest to picture forth
Oread or Dryad glancing through the shade
What time the hunter's earliest horn is heard
Startling the golden hills. A wide-spread elm
Stands in our valley, named the joyful tree;
From dateless usage which our peasants hold
Of giving welcome to the first of May
By dances, round its trunk.—And if the sky
Permit, like honours, dance and song, are paid
To the Twelfth Night; beneath the frosty stars
Or the clear moon. The queen of these gay sports,
If not in beauty, yet in sprightly air,
Was hapless Ellen.—No one touched the ground
So deftly, and the nicest maiden's locks
Less gracefully were braided;—but this praise,
Methinks, would better suit another place.

"She loved, and fondly deemed herself beloved.
The road is dim, the current unperceived,
The weakness painful and most pitiful,
By which a virtuous woman, in pure youth,
May be delivered to distress and shame.
Such fate was hers.—The last time Ellen danced,
Among her equals, round the joyful tree,
She bore a secret burthen; and full soon
Was left to tremble for a breaking vow—
Then, to bewail a sternly-broken vow,
Alone, within her widowed mother's house.
It was the season sweet, of budding leaves,
Of days advancing towards their utmost length,
And small birds singing to their happy mates.
Wild is the music of the autumnal wind
Among the faded woods; but these blithe notes
Strike the deserted to the heart:—I speak
Of what I know, and what we feel within.
Beside the cottage in which Ellen dwelt
Stands a tall ash-tree; to whose topmost twig
A thrush resorts, and annually chants,
At morn and evening, from that naked perch,
While all the undergrove is thick with leaves,
A time-beguiling ditty, for delight
Of his fond partner, silent in the nest.
'Ah why,' said Ellen, sighing to herself,
'Why do not words, and kiss, and solemn pledge,
And nature that is kind in woman's breast,
And reason that in man is wise and good,
And fear of Him who is a righteous Judge,
Why do not these prevail for human life,
To keep two hearts together, that began
Their spring-time with one love, and that have need
Of mutual pity and forgiveness, sweet
To grant, or be received; while that poor bird,
Oh, come and hear him! Thou who hast to me
Been faithless, hear him, though a lowly creature,
One of God's simple children that yet know not
The universal Parent, how he sings,
As if he wished the firmament of heaven

Should listen, and give back to him the voice
Of his triumphant constancy and love;
The proclamation that he makes, how far
His darkness doth transcend our fickle light!'

"Such was the tender passage, not by me
Repeated without loss of simple phrase,
Which I perused, even as the words had been
Committed by forsaken Ellen's hand
To the blank margin of a valentine,
Bedropped with tears. 'Twill please you to be told
That, studiously withdrawing from the eye
Of all companionship, the sufferer yet
In lonely reading found a meek resource.
How thankful for the warmth of summer days,
When she could slip into the cottage-barn,
And find a secret oratory there;
Or, in the garden, under friendly veil
Of their long twilight, pore upon her book
By the last lingering help of open sky,
Till the dark night dismissed her to her bed!
Thus did a waking fancy sometimes lose
The unconquerable pang of despised love.

"A kindlier passion opened on her soul
When that poor child was born. Upon its face
She looked as on a pure and spotless gift
Of unexpected promise, where a grief
Or dread was all that had been thought of—joy
Far livelier than bewildered traveller feels
Amid a perilous waste, that all night long
Hath harassed him—toiling through fearful storm,
When he beholds the first pale speck serene
Of day-spring, in the gloomy east revealed,
And greets it with thanksgiving. 'Till this hour,'
Thus in her mother's hearing Ellen spake,
'There was a stony region in my heart;
But He, at whose command the parchèd rock
Was smitten, and poured forth a quenching stream
Hath softened that obduracy, and made
Unlooked-for gladness in the desert place,
To save the perishing; and, henceforth, I look
Upon the light with cheerfulness, for thee
My infant! and for that good mother dear,
Who bore me,—and hath prayed for me in vain;—
Yet not in vain, it shall not be in vain'
She spake, nor was the assurance unfulfilled;
And if heart-rending thoughts would oft return,
They stayed not long.—The blameless infant grew;
The child whom Ellen and her mother loved
They soon were proud of, tended it and nursed,
A soothing comforter, although forlorn;
Like a poor singing-bird from distant lands;
Or a choice shrub, which he, who passes by
With vacant mind, not seldom may observe
Fair-flowering in a thinly-peopled house,
Whose window, somewhat sadly, it adorns.
Through four months' space the infant drew its food

From the maternal breast ; then scruples rose ;
Thoughts, which the rich are free from, came and crossed
The sweet affection. She no more could bear
By her offence to lay a two-fold weight
On a kind parent willing to forget
Their slender means , so, to that parent's care
Trusting her child, she left their common home,
And with contented spirit undertook
A foster-mother's office.
'Tis perchance,
Unknown to you that in these simple vales
The natural feeling of equality
Is by domestic service unimpaired ;
Yet, though such service be, with us, removed
From sense of degradation, not the less
The ungentle mind can easily find means
To impose severe restraints and laws unjust :
Which hapless Ellen now was doomed to feel.
For (blinded by an over-anxious dread
Of such excitement and divided thought
As with her office would but ill accord)
The pair, whose infant she was bound to nurse,
Forbade her all communion with her own ;
Week after week, the mandate they enforced.
So near !—yet not allowed, upon that sight
To fix her eyes—alas ! 'twas hard to bear !
But worse affliction must be borne—far worse ;
For 'tis Heaven's will—that, after a disease
Begun and ended within three days' space,
Her child should die ; as Ellen now exclaimed,
Her own—deserted child !—Once, only once,
She saw it in that mortal malady :
And, on the burial day, could scarcely gain
Permission to attend its obsequies
She reached the house—last of the funeral train ;
And some one, as she entered, having chanced
To urge unthinkingly their prompt departure,
'Nay,' said she, with commanding look, a spirit
Of anger never seen in her before,
'Nay, ye must wait my time !' and down she sate,
And by the unclosed coffin kept her seat
Weeping and looking, looking on and weeping,
Upon the last sweet slumber of her child,
Until at length her soul was satisfied.

"You see the infant's grave ;—and to this spot,
The mother, oft as she was sent abroad,
And whatsoe'er the errand, urged her steps :
Hither she came , and here she stood, or knelt
In the broad day—a rueful Magdalene !
So call her ; for not only she bewailed
A mother's loss, but mourned in bitterness
Her own transgression ; penitent sincere
As ever raised to Heaven a streaming eye.
At length the parents of the foster-child,
Noting that in despite of their commands
She still renewed and could not but renew
Those visitations, ceased to send her forth ;

Or, to the garden's narrow bounds, confined.
I failed not to remind them that they erred ;
For holy nature might not thus be crossed,
Thus wronged in woman's breast : in vain I pleaded—
But the green stalk of Ellen's life was snapped,
And the flower dropped ; as every eye could see,
It hung its head in mortal languishment
Aided by this appearance, I at length
Prevailed ; and, from those bonds released, she went
Home to her mother's house. The youth was fled ;
The rash betrayer could not face the shame
Or sorrow which his senseless guilt had caused ;
And little would his presence, or proof given
Of a relenting soul, have now availed ,
For, like a shadow, he was passed away
From Ellen's thoughts ; had perished to her mind
For all concerns of fear, or hope, or love,
Save only those which to their common shame,
And to his moral being appertained :
Hope from that quarter would, I know, have brought
A heavenly comfort ; there she recognised
An unrelaxing bond, a mutual need ;
There, and, as seemed, there only.—She had built.
Her fond maternal heart had built, a nest,
In blindness all too near the river's edge ;
That work a summer flood with hasty swell
Had swept away ; and now her spirit longed
For its last flight to heaven's security.
The bodily frame was wasted day by day ;
Meanwhile, relinquishing all other cares,
Her mind she strictly tutored to find peace
And pleasure in endurance. Much she thought,
And much she read ; and brooded feelingly
Upon her own unworthiness.—To me,
As to a spiritual comforter and friend,
Her heart she opened , and no pains were spared
To mitigate, as gently as I could,
The sting of self-reproach, with healing words.
Meek Saint ! through patience glorified on earth !
In whom, as by her lonely hearth she sate,
The ghastly face of cold decay put on
A sun-like beauty, and appeared divine !
May I not mention—that, within those walls,
In due observance of her pious wish,
The congregation joined with me in prayer
For her soul's good ? Nor was that office vain.
Much did she suffer but, if any friend,
Beholding her condition, at the sight
Gave way to words of pity or complaint,
She stilled them with a prompt reproof, and said,
'He who afflicts me knows what I can bear ,
And, when I fail, and can endure no more,
Will mercifully take me to himself.'
So, through the cloud of death, her spirit passed
Into that pure and unknown world of love,
Where injury cannot come :—and here is laid
The mortal body by her infant's side."

The vicar ceased; and downcast looks made known
That each had listened with his inmost heart.
For me, the emotion scarcely was less strong
Or less benign than that which I had felt
When, seated near my venerable friend,
Beneath those shady elms, from him I heard
The story that retraced the slow decline
Of Margaret sinking on the lonely heath,
With the neglected house to which she clung.
I noted that the Solitary's cheek
Confessed the power of nature.—Pleased though sad,
More pleased than sad, the gray-haired Wanderer sate;
Thanks to his pure imaginative soul,
Capacious and serene, his blameless life,
His knowledge, wisdom, love of truth, and love
Of human kind! He it was who first broke
The pensive silence, saying, "Blest are they
Whose sorrow rather is to suffer wrong
Than to do wrong, although themselves have erred.
This tale gives proof that Heaven most gently deals
With such, in their affliction.—Ellen's fate,
Her tender spirit, and her contrite heart,
Call to my mind dark hints which I have heard
Of one who died within this vale, by doom
Heavier, as his offence was heavier far.
Where, sir, I pray you, where are laid the bones
Of Wilfred Armathwaite?"—The vicar answered,
"In that green nook, close by the churchyard wall,
Beneath yon hawthorn, planted by myself
In memory and for warning, and in sign
Of sweetness where dire anguish had been known,
Of reconcilement after deep offence,
There doth he rest.—No theme his fate supplies
For the smooth glozings of the indulgent world;
Nor need the windings of his devious course
Be here retraced;—enough that, by mishap
And venial error, robbed of competence,
And her obsequious shadow, peace of mind,
He craved a substitute in troubled joy;
Against his conscience rose in arms, and, braving
Divine displeasure, broke the marriage-vow.
That which he had been weak enough to do
Was misery in remembrance, he was stung,
Stung by his inward thoughts, and by the smiles
Of wife and children stung to agony.
Wretched at home, he gained no peace abroad;
Ranged through the mountains, slept upon the earth,
Asked comfort of the open air, and found
No quiet in the darkness of the night,
No pleasure in the beauty of the day.
His flock he slighted: his paternal fields
Became a clog to him, whose spirit wished
To fly, but whither? And this gracious church,
That wears a look so full of peace, and hope,
And love, benignant mother of the vale,
How fair amid her brood of cottages!
She was to him a sickness and reproach.
Much to the last remained unknown: but this

Is sure, that through remorse and grief he died;
Though pitied among men, absolved by God,
He could not find forgiveness in himself,
Nor could endure the weight of his own shame.

"Here rests a mother. But from her I turn,
And from her grave.—Behold—upon that bridge,
That, stretching boldly from the mountain side,
Carries into the centre of the vale
Its rocks and woods—the cottage where she dwelt,
And where yet dwells her faithful partner, left
(Full eight years past) the solitary prop
Of many helpless children I begin
With words that might be prelude to a tale
Of sorrow and dejection; but I feel
No sadness, when I think of what mine eyes
See daily in that happy family.
Bright garland form they for the pensive brow
Of their undrooping father's widowhood,
Those six fair daughters, budding yet—not one,
Not one of all the band a full-blown flower!
Depressed, and desolate of soul, as once
That father was, and filled with anxious fear,
Now, by experience taught, he stands assured,
That God, who takes away, yet takes not half
Of what he seems to take; or gives it back,
Not to our prayer, but far beyond our prayer;
He gives it—the boon produce of a soil
Which our endeavours have refused to till,
And hope hath never watered The abode
Whose grateful owner can attest these truths,
Even were the object nearer to our sight,
Would seem in no distinction to surpass
The rudest habitations. Ye might think
That it had sprung self-raised from earth, or grown
Out of the living rock, to be adorned
By nature only, but, if thither led,
Ye would discover, then, a studious work
Of many fancies, prompting many hands.
Brought from the woods the honeysuckle twines
Around the porch, and seems, in that trim place,
A plant no longer wild; the cultured rose
There blossoms, strong in health, and will be soon
Roof-high; the wild pink crowns the garden wall,
And with the flowers are intermingled stones
Sparry and bright, rough scatterings of the hills.
These ornaments, that fade not with the year,
A hardy girl continues to provide;
Who mounting fearlessly the rocky heights,
Her father's prompt attendant, does for him
All that a boy could do; but with delight
More keen and prouder daring; yet hath she,
Within the garden, like the rest, a bed
For her own flowers and favourite herbs—a space,
By sacred charter, holden for her use.
These, and whatever else the garden bears
Of fruit or flower, permission asked or not,
I freely gather; and my leisure draws

A not unfrequent pastime from the sight
Of the bees murmuring round their sheltered hives
In that inclosure; while the mountain rill,
That sparkling thrids the rocks, attunes his voice
To the pure course of human life, which there
Flows on in solitude. But, when the gloom
Of night is falling round my steps, then most
This dwelling charms me; often I stop short;
(Who could refrain?) and feed by stealth my sight
With prospect of the company within,
Laid open through the blazing window.—there
I see the eldest daughter at her wheel
Spinning amain, as if to overtake
The never-halting time; or, in her turn,
Teaching some novice of the sisterhood
That skill in this, or other household work,
Which, from her father's honoured hand, herself,
While she was yet a little-one, had learned.
Mild man! he is not gay, but they are gay;
And the whole house seems filled with gaiety.
Thrice happy, then, the mother may be deemed,
The wife, who rests beneath that turf, from which
I turned, that ye in mind might witness where,
And how, her spirit yet survives on earth."

BOOK VII.

ARGUMENT.

Impression of these narratives upon the author's mind—Pastor invited to give account of certain graves that lie apart—Clergyman and his family—Fortunate influence of change of situation—Activity in extreme old age—Another clergyman, a character of resolute virtue—Lamentations over misdirected applause—Instance of less exalted excellence in a deaf man—Elevated character of a blind man—Reflection upon blindness—Interrupted by a peasant who passes—His animal cheerfulness and careless vivacity—He occasions a digression on the fall of beautiful and interesting trees—A female infant's grave—Joy at her birth—Sorrow at her departure—A youthful peasant—his patriotic enthusiasm—distinguished qualities and untimely death—Exultation of the Wanderer, as a patriot, in this picture—Solitary, how affected—Monument of a knight—Traditions concerning him—Peroration of the Wanderer on the transitoriness of things and the revolutions of society—Hints at his own past calling—Thanks the Pastor.

THE CHURCHYARD AMONG THE MOUNTAINS.

CONTINUED.

WHILE thus from theme to theme the historian passed,
The words he uttered, and the scene that lay
Before our eyes, awakened in my mind
Vivid remembrance of those long-past hours;
When, in the hollow of some shadowy vale,
(What time the splendour of the setting sun
Lay beautiful on Snowdon's sovereign brow,
On Cader Idris, or huge Penmanmaur)
A wandering youth, I listened with delight
To pastoral melody or warlike air,
Drawn from the chords of the ancient British harp
By some accomplished master; while he sate

Amid the quiet of the green recess,
And there did inexhaustibly dispense
An interchange of soft or solemn tunes,
Tender or blithe , now, as the varying mood
Of his own spirit urged,—now, as a voice
From youth or maiden, or some honoured chief
Of his compatriot villagers (that hung
Around him, drinking in the impassioned notes
Of the time-hallowed minstrelsy) required
For their heart's ease or pleasure. Strains of power
Were they, to seize and occupy the sense ;
But to a higher mark than song can reach
Rose this pure eloquence And, when the stream
Which overflowed the soul was passed away,
A consciousness remained that it had left,
Deposited upon the silent shore
Of memory, images and precious thoughts,
That shall not die, and cannot be destroyed.

"These grassy heaps lie amicably close,"
Said I, "like surges heaving in the wind
Upon the surface of a mountain pool ;
Whence comes it, then, that yonder we behold
Five graves, and only five, that rise together
Unsociably sequestered, and encroaching
On the smooth playground of the village school ?"

The vicar answered. "No disdainful pride
In them who rest beneath, nor any course
Of strange or tragic accident, hath helped
To place those hillocks in that lonely guise.
Once more look forth, and follow with your sight
The length of road that from yon mountain's base
Through bare inclosures stretches, till its line
Is lost within a little tuft of trees,—
Then, reappearing in a moment, quits
The cultured fields,—and up the heathy waste,
Mounts, as you see, in mazes serpentine,
Towards an easy outlet of the vale.
That little shady spot, that sylvan tuft,
By which the road is hidden, also hides
A cottage from our view,—though I discern,
(Ye scarcely can) amid its sheltering trees,
The smokeless chimney-top.—All unembowered
And naked stood that lowly parsonage
(For such in truth it is, and appertains
To a small chapel in the vale beyond)
When hither came its last inhabitant.

"Rough and forbidding were the choicest roads
By which our northern wilds could then be crossed ;
And into most of these secluded vales
Was no access for wain, heavy or light.
So, at his dwelling-place the priest arrived
With store of household goods, in panniers slung
On sturdy horses graced with jingling bells,
And on the back of more ignoble beast ;
That, with like burthen of effects most prized

Or easiest carried, closed the motley train.
Young was I then, a schoolboy of eight years:
But still, methinks, I see them as they passed
In order, drawing tow'rds their wished-for home.
Rocked by the motion of a trusty ass
Two ruddy children hung, a well-poised freight,
Each in his basket nodding drowsily;
Their bonnets, I remember, wreathed with flowers
Which told it was the pleasant month of June;
And, close behind, the comely matron rode,
A woman of soft speech and gracious smile,
And with a lady's mien.—From far they came,
Even from Northumbrian hills; yet theirs had been
A merry journey—rich in pastime—cheered
By music, prank, and laughter-stirring jest,
And freak put on, arch word dropped—to swell
The cloud of fancy and uncouth surmise
That gathered round the slowly-moving train.
'Whence do they come? and with what errand charged?
Belong they to the fortune-telling tribe
Who pitch their tents beneath the green-wood tree?
Or are they strollers, furnished to enact
Fair Rosamond, and the Children of the Wood,
And, by that whiskered Tabby's aid, set forth
The lucky venture of sage Whittington,
When the next village hears the show announced
By blast of trumpet?' Plenteous was the growth
Of such conjectures, overheard, or seen
On many a staring countenance portrayed
Of boor or burgher, as they marched along.
And more than once their steadiness of face
Was put to proof, and exercise supplied
To their inventive humour, by stern looks,
And questions in authoritative tone,
From some staid guardian of the public peace,
Checking the sober steed on which he rode,
In his suspicious wisdom; oftener still
By notice indirect, or blunt demand
From traveller halting in his own despite,
A simple curiosity to ease
Of which adventures, that beguiled and cheered
Their grave migration, the good pair would tell,
With undiminished glee, in hoary age

"A priest he was by function; but his course
From his youth up, and high as manhood's noon,
(The hour of life to which he then was brought)
Had been irregular, I might say, wild;
By books unsteadied, by his pastoral care
Too little checked An active, ardent mind;
A fancy pregnant with resource and scheme
To cheat the sadness of a rainy day:
Hands apt for all ingenious arts and games;
A generous spirit, and a body strong
To cope with stoutest champions of the bowl;
Had earned for him sure welcome, and the rights
Of a prized visitant, in the jolly hall
Of country squire, or at the statelier board

Of duke or earl, from scenes of courtly pomp
Withdrawn,—to while away the summer hours
In condescension among rural guests

"With these high comrades he had revelled long,
Frolicked industriously, a simple clerk,
By hopes of coming patronage beguiled
Till the heart sickened. So each loftier aim
Abandoning and all his showy friends,
For a life's stay, though slender, yet assured,
He turned to this secluded chapelry,
That had been offered to his doubtful choice
By an unthought-of patron Bleak and bare
They found the cottage, their allotted home:
Naked without, and rude within, a spot
With which the scantily-provided cure
Not long had been endowed: and far remote
The chapel stood, divided from that house
By an unpeopled tract of mountain waste.
Yet cause was none, whate'er regret might hang
On his own mind, to quarrel with the choice
Or the necessity that fixed him here;
Apart from old temptations, and constrained
To punctual labour in his sacred charge.
See him a constant preacher to the poor!
And visiting, though not with saintly zeal,
Yet when need was, with no reluctant will,
The sick in body, or distrest in mind;
And, by as salutary change, compelled
To rise from timely sleep, and meet the day
With no engagement, in his thoughts, more proud
Or splendid than his garden could afford,
His fields,—or mountains by the heath-cock ranged,
Or the wild brooks, from which he now returned
Contented to partake the quiet meal
Of his own board, where sate his gentle mate
And three fair children, plentifully fed,
Though simply, from their little household farm;
With acceptable treat of fish or fowl
By nature yielded to his practised hand—
To help the small but certain comings-in
Of that spare benefice. Yet not the less
Theirs was a hospitable board, and theirs
A charitable door.—So days and years
Passed on,—the inside of that rugged house
Was trimmed and brightened by the matron's care,
And gradually enriched with things of price,
Which might be lacked for use or ornament.
What, though no soft and costly sofa there
Insidiously stretched out its lazy length,
And no vain mirror glittered on the walls,
Yet were the windows of the low abode
By shutters weather-fended, which at once
Repelled the storm and deadened its loud roar
There snow-white curtains hung in decent folds;
Tough moss, and long-enduring mountain plants,
That creep along the ground with sinuous trail,
Were nicely braided and composed a work

Like Indian mats, that with appropriate grace
Lay at the threshold and the inner doors;
And a fair carpet, woven of home-spun wool,
But tinctured daintily with florid hues,
For seemliness and warmth, on festal days,
Covered the smooth blue slabs of mountain stone
With which the parlour-floor in simplest guise
Of pastoral homesteads, had been long inlaid.
These pleasing works the housewife's skill produced,
Meanwhile the unsedentary master's hand
Was busier with his task—to rid, to plant,
To rear for food, for shelter, and delight;
A thriving covert! And when wishes, formed
In youth, and sanctioned by the riper mind,
Restored me to my native valley, here
To end my days; well pleased was I to see
The once-bare cottage, on the mountain-side,
Screened from assault of every bitter blast,
While the dark shadows of the summer leaves
Danced in the breeze, upon its mossy roof.
Time, which had thus afforded willing help
To beautify with nature's fairest growth
This rustic tenement, had gently shed,
Upon its master's frame, a wintry grace;
The comeliness of unenfeebled age
But how could I say, gently? for he still
Retained a flashing eye, a burning palm,
A stirring foot, a head which beat at nights
Upon its pillow with a thousand schemes.
Few likings had he dropped, few pleasures lost:
Generous and charitable, prompt to serve;
And still his harsher passions kept their hold,
Anger and indignation; still he loved
The sound of titled names, and talked in glee
Of long-past banquetings with high-born friends:
Then, from those lulling fits of vain delight
Uproused by recollected injury, railed
At their false ways disdainfully,—and oft
In bitterness, and with a threatening eye
Of fire, incensed beneath its hoary brow.
These transports, with staid look of pure good-will
And with soft smile, his consort would reprove
She, far behind him in the race of years,
Yet keeping her first mildness, was advanced
Far nearer, in the habit of her soul,
To that still region whither all are bound.
Him might we liken to the setting sun
As seen not seldom on some gusty day,
Struggling and bold, and shining from the west
With an inconstant and unmellowed light;
She was a soft attendant cloud, that hung
As if with wish to veil the restless orb;
From which it did itself imbibe a ray
Of pleasing lustre.—But no more of this;
I better love to sprinkle on the sod
That now divides the pair, or rather say
That still unites them, praises, like heaven's dew,
Without reserve descending upon both.

"Our very first in eminence of years
This old man stood, the patriarch of the vale!
And, to his unmolested mansion, death
Had never come, through space of forty years;
Sparing both old and young in that abode.
Suddenly then they disappeared: not twice
Had summer scorched the fields; not twice had fallen,
On those high peaks, the first autumnal snow,
Before the greedy visiting was closed,
And the long-privileged house left empty—swept
As by a plague: yet no rapacious plague
Had been among them; all was gentle death,
One after one, with intervals of peace.
A happy consummation! an accord
Sweet, perfect,—to be wished for! save that here
Was something to which mortal sense might sound
Like harshness,—that the old gray-headed sire,
The oldest, he was taken last,—survived
When the meek partner of his age, his son,
His daughter, and that late and high-prized gift,
His little smiling grandchild, were no more.

"'All gone, all vanished! he deprived and bare,
How will he face the remnant of his life?
What will become of him?' we said, and mused
In sad conjectures—'Shall we meet him now
Haunting with rod and line the craggy brooks?
Or shall we overhear him, as we pass,
Striving to entertain the lonely hours
With music?' (for he had not ceased to touch
The harp or viol which himself had framed,
For their sweet purposes, with perfect skill.)
'What titles will he keep? will he remain
Musician, gardener, builder, mechanist,
A planter, and a rearer from the seed?
A man of hope and forward-looking mind
Even to the last!'—Such was he, unsubdued.
But Heaven was gracious; yet a little while,
And this survivor, with his cheerful throng
Of open schemes, and all his inward hoard
Of unsunned griefs, too many and too keen,
Was overcome by unexpected sleep,
In one blest moment. Like a shadow thrown
Softly and lightly from a passing cloud,
Death fell upon him, while reclined he lay
For noon-tide solace on the summer grass,
The warm lap of his mother earth: and so,
Their lenient term of separation past,
That family, (whose graves you there behold,)
By yet a higher privilege, once more
Were gathered to each other."

Calm of mind
And silence waited on these closing words;
Until the Wanderer (whether moved by fear
Lest in those passages of life were some
That might have touched the sick heart of his friend
Too nearly, or intent to reinforce
His own firm spirit in degree depressed

By tender sorrow for our mortal state)
Thus silence broke : "Behold a thoughtless man
From vice and premature decay preserved
By useful habits, to a fitter soil
Transplanted ere too late.—The hermit, lodged
In the untrodden desert, tells his beads,
With each repeating its allotted prayer,
And thus divides and thus relieves the time ;
Smooth task, with his compared, whose mind could string,
Not scantily, bright minutes on the thread
Of keen domestic anguish,—and beguile
A solitude, unchosen, unprofessed ;
Till gentlest death released him.—Far from us
Be the desire—too curiously to ask
How much of this is but the blind result
Of cordial spirits and vital temperament,
And what to higher powers is justly due.
But you, sir, know that in a neighbouring vale
A priest abides before whose life such doubts
Fall to the ground ; whose gifts of nature lie
Retired from notice, lost in attributes
Of reason,—honourably effaced by debts
Which her poor treasure-house is content to owe,
And conquests over her dominion gained,
To which her forwardness must needs submit
In this one man is shown a temperance—proof
Against all trials , industry severe
And constant as the motion of the day ;
Stern self-denial round him spread, with shade
That might be deemed forbidding, did not there
All generous feelings flourish and rejoice ;
Forbearance, charity in deed and thought,
And resolution competent to take
Out of the bosom of simplicity
All that her holy customs recommend,
And the best ages of the world prescribe.
Preaching, administering, in every work
Of his sublime vocation, in the walks
Of worldly intercourse 'twixt man and man,
And in his humble dwelling, he appears
A labourer, with moral virtue girt,
With spiritual graces, like a glory, crowned."

"Doubt can be none," the pastor said, "for whom
This portraiture is sketched.—The great, the good,
The well-beloved, the fortunate, the wise,
These titles emperors and chiefs have borne,
Honour assumed or given : and him, the Wonderful,
Our simple shepherds, speaking from the heart,
Deservedly have styled.—From his abode
In a dependent chapelry, that lies
Behind yon hill, a poor and rugged wild,
Which in his soul he lovingly embraced,—
And, having once espoused, would never quit ;
Hither, ere long, that lowly, great, good man
Will be conveyed. An unelaborate stone
May cover him ; and by its help, perchance,
A century shall hear his name pronounced,

With images attendant on the sound;
Then, shall the slowly gathering twilight close
In utter night, and of his course remain
No cognizable vestiges, no more
Than of this breath, which shapes itself in words
To speak of him, and instantly dissolves.
Noise is there not enough in doleful war,
But that the heaven-born poet must stand forth
And lend the echoes of his sacred shell
To multiply and aggravate the din?
Pangs are there not enough in hopeless love—
And, in requited passion, all too much
Of turbulence, anxiety, and fear—
But that the minstrel of the rural shade
Must tune his pipe, insidiously to nurse
The perturbation in the suffering breast,
And propagate its kind, where'er he may?
Ah, who (and with such rapture as befits
The hallowed theme) will rise and celebrate
The good man's deeds and purposes; retrace
His struggles, his discomfiture deplore,
His triumphs hail, and glorify his end?
That virtue, like the fumes and vapoury clouds
Through fancy's heat redounding in the brain,
And like the soft infections of the heart,
By charm of measured words may spread o'er field,
Hamlet, and town; and piety survive
Upon the lips of men in hall or bower;
Not for reproof, but high and warm delight,
And grave encouragement, by song inspired.
Vain thought! but wherefore murmur or repine?
The memory of the just survives in heaven:
And, without sorrow, will this ground receive
That venerable clay. Meanwhile the best
Of what it holds confines us to degrees
In excellence less difficult to reach,
And milder worth: nor need we travel far
From those to whom our last regards were paid,
For such example.
Almost at the root
Of that tall pine, the shadow of whose bare
And slender stem, while here I sit at eve,
Oft stretches towards me, like a long straight path
Traced faintly in the greensward, there, beneath
A plain blue stone, a gentle dalesman lies,
From whom, in early childhood, was withdrawn
The precious gift of hearing. He grew up
From year to year in loneliness of soul;
And this deep mountain valley was to him
Soundless, with all its streams The bird of dawn
Did never rouse this cottager from sleep
With startling summons; not for his delight
The vernal cuckoo shouted; not for him
Murmured the labouring bee. When stormy winds
Were working the broad bosom of the lake
Into a thousand thousand sparkling waves,
Rocking the trees, or driving cloud on cloud
Along the sharp edge of yon lofty crags,

The agitated scene before his eye
Was silent as a picture: evermore
Were all things silent, wheresoe'er he moved.
Yet, by the solace of his own pure thoughts
Upheld, he duteously pursued the round
Of rural labours; the steep mountain-side
Ascended with his staff and faithful dog;
The plough he guided, and the scythe he swayed,
And the ripe corn before his sickle fell
Among the jocund reapers. For himself,
All watchful and industrious as he was,
He wrought not; neither field nor flock he owned:
No wish for wealth had place within his mind;
Nor husband's love, nor father's hope or care.
Though born a younger brother, need was none
That from the floor of his paternal home
He should depart, to plant himself anew.
And when, mature in manhood, he beheld
His parents laid in earth, no loss ensued
Of rights to him; but he remained well pleased,
By the pure bond of independent love,
An inmate of a second family,
The fellow-labourer and friend of him
To whom the small inheritance had fallen.
Nor deem that his mild presence was a weight
That pressed upon his brother's house, for books
Were ready comrades whom he could not tire,—
Of whose society the blameless man
Was never satiate. Their familiar voice,
Even to old age, with unabated charm
Beguiled his leisure hours; refreshed his thoughts:
Beyond its natural elevation raised
His introverted spirit; and bestowed
Upon his life an outward dignity
Which all acknowledged. The dark winter night,
The stormy day, had each its own resource;
Song of the muses, sage historic tale,
Science severe, or word of Holy Writ
Announcing immortality and joy
To the assembled spirits of the just,
From imperfection and decay secure.
Thus soothed at home, thus busy in the field,
To no perverse suspicion he gave way,
No languor, peevishness, nor vain complaint:
And they, who were about him, did not fail
In reverence, or in courtesy; they prized
His gentle manners:—and his peaceful smiles,
The gleams of his slow-varying countenance,
Were met with answering sympathy and love.

"At length, when sixty years and five were told,
A slow disease insensibly consumed
The powers of nature; and a few short steps
Of friends and kindred bore him from his home
(Yon cottage shaded by the woody crags)
To the profounder stillness of the grave.
Nor was his funeral denied the grace
Of many tears, virtuous and thoughtful grief;

Heart-sorrow rendered sweet by gratitude.
And now that monumental stone preserves
His name, and unambitiously relates
How long, and by what kindly outward aids,
And in what pure contentedness of mind,
The sad privation was by him endured
And yon tall pine-tree, whose composing sound
Was wasted on the good man's living ear,
Hath now its own peculiar sanctity;
And, at the touch of every wandering breeze,
Murmurs, not idly, o'er his peaceful grave.

"Soul-cheering light, most bountiful of things!
Guide of our way, mysterious comforter!
Whose sacred influence, spread through earth and heaven
We all too thanklessly participate,
Thy gifts were utterly withheld from him
Whose place of rest is near yon ivied porch.
Yet, of the wild brooks ask if he complained;
Ask of the channelled rivers if they held
A safer, easier, more determined course.
What terror doth it strike into the mind
To think of one, who cannot see, advancing
Towards some precipice's airy brink!
But, timely warned, *he* would have stayed his steps;
Protected, say enlightened, by his ear,
And on the very edge of vacancy
Not more endangered than a man whose eye
Beholds the gulf beneath —No floweret blooms
Throughout the lofty range of these rough hills,
Or in the woods, that could from him conceal
Its birth-place; none whose figure did not live
Upon his touch. The bowels of the earth
Enriched with knowledge his industrious mind;
The ocean paid him tribute from the stores
Lodged in her bosom; and, by science led,
His genius mounted to the plains of heaven.
Methinks I see him—how his eye-balls rolled,
Beneath his ample brow, in darkness paired,—
But each instinct with spirit; and the frame
Of the whole countenance alive with thought,
Fancy, and understanding; while the voice
Discoursed of natural or moral truth
With eloquence, and such authentic power,
That, in his presence, humbler knowledge stood
Abashed, and tender pity overawed."

"A noble—and, to unreflecting minds,
A marvellous spectacle," the wanderer said,
"Beings like these present! But proof abounds
Upon the earth that faculties, which seem
Extinguished, do not, *therefore*, cease to be.
And to the mind among her powers of sense
This transfer is permitted,—not alone
That the bereft their recompense may win;
But for remoter purposes of love
And charity; nor last nor least for this,
That to the imagination may be given

A type and shadow of an awful truth;
How, likewise, under sufferance divine,
Darkness is banished from the realms of death,
By man's imperishable spirit, quelled.
Unto the men who see not as we see
Futurity was thought, in ancient times,
To be laid open, and they prophesied
And know ye not that from the blind have flowed
The highest, holiest, raptures of the lyre;
And wisdom married to immortal verse?"

Among the humble worthies, at our feet
Lying insensible to human praise,
Love, or regret,—*whose* lineaments would next
Have been portrayed, I guess not; but it chanced
That near the quiet churchyard where we sate
A team of horses, with a ponderous freight
Pressing behind, adown a rugged slope,
Whose sharp descent confounded their array,
Came at that moment, ringing noisily.

"Here," said the pastor, "do we muse, and mourn
The waste of death, and lo! the giant oak
Stretched on his bier—that massy timber wain;
Nor fail to note the man who guides the team."

He was a peasant of the lowest class:
Gray locks profusely round his temples hung
In clustering curls, like ivy, which the bite
Of winter cannot thin; the fresh air lodged
Within his cheek, as light within a cloud;
And he returned our greeting with a smile.
When he had passed, the Solitary spake:
"A man he seems of cheerful yesterdays
And confident to-morrows,—with a face
Not worldly-minded; for it bears too much
Of nature's impress,—gaiety and health,
Freedom and hope; but keen, withal, and shrewd.
His gestures note,—and hark! his tones of voice
Are all vivacious as his mien and looks."

The pastor answered. "You have read him well.
Year after year is added to his store
With *silent* increase: summers, winters—past,
Past or to come; yea, boldly might I say,
Ten summers and ten winters of a space
That lies beyond life's ordinary bounds,
Upon his sprightly vigour cannot fix
The obligation of an anxious mind,
A pride in having, or a fear to lose;
Possessed like outskirts of some large domain,
By any one more thought of than by him
Who holds the land in fee, its careless lord!
Yet is the creature rational—endowed
With foresight; hears, too, every Sabbath day,
The Christian promise with attentive ear;
Nor will, I trust, the Majesty of heaven

Reject the incense offered up by him,
Though of the kind which beasts and birds present
In grove or pasture ; cheerfulness of soul,
From trepidation and repining free.
How many scrupulous worshippers fall down
Upon their knees and daily homage pay
Less worthy, less religious even, than his!

"This qualified respect, the old man's due,
Is paid without reluctance ; but in truth,"
(Said the good vicar with a fond half-smile,)
"I feel at times a motion of despite
Towards one, whose bold contrivances and skill,
As you have seen, bear such conspicuous part
In works of havoc ; taking from these vales,
One after one, their proudest ornaments.
Full oft his doings leave me to deplore
Tall ash-tree sown by winds, by vapours nursed,
In the dry crannies of the pendent rocks ,
Light birch, aloft upon the horizon's edge,
A veil of glory for the ascending moon ,
And oak whose roots by noontide dew were damped,
And on whose forehead inaccessible
The raven lodged in safety —Many a ship
Launched into Morecamb Bay, to *him* hath owed
Her strong knee-timbers, and the mast that bears
The loftiest of her pendants. He, from park
Or forest, fetched the enormous axle-tree
That whirls (how slow itself!) ten thousand spindles :
And the vast engine labouring in the mine,
Content with meaner prowess, must have lacked
The trunk and body of its marvellous strength,
If his undaunted enterprise had failed
Among the mountain coves.
Yon household fir,
A guardian planted to fence off the blast,
But towering high the roof above, as if
Its humble destination were forgot ;
That sycamore, which annually holds
Within its shade, as in a stately tent
On all sides opening to the fanning breeze,
A grave assemblage, seated while they shear
The fleece-incumbered flock ;—the joyful elm,
Around whose trunk the maidens dance in May ;—
And the Lord's Oak ;—would plead their several rights
In vain, if he were master of their fate ;
His sentence to the axe would doom them all.
But, green in age and lusty as he is,
And promising to keep his hold on earth
Less, as might seem, in rivalship with men
Than with the forest's more enduring growth,
His own appointed hour will come at last ,
And like the haughty spoilers of the world,
This keen destroyer, in his turn, must fall.

"Now from the living pass we once again :
From age," the priest continued, "turn your thoughts ;
From age, that often unlamented drops,

And mark that daisied hillock, three spans long!
Seven lusty sons sate daily round the board
Of Gold-rill side; and when the hope had ceased
Of other progeny, a daughter then
Was given, the crowning bounty of the whole;
And so acknowledged with a tremulous joy
Felt to the centre of that heavenly calm
With which by nature every mother's soul
Is stricken, in the moment when her throes
Are ended, and her ears have heard the cry
Which tells her that a living child is born,—
And she lies conscious, in a blissful rest,
That the dread storm is weathered by them both.
The father—him at his unlooked-for gift
A bolder transport seizes. From the side
Of his bright hearth, and from his open door;
Day after day the gladness is diffused
To all that come, and almost all that pass;
Invited, summoned, to partake the cheer
Spread on the never-empty board, and drink
Health and good wishes to his new-born girl,
From cups replenished by his joyous hand.
Those seven fair brothers variously were moved
Each by the thoughts best suited to his years:
But most of all and with most thankful mind
The hoary grandsire felt himself enriched;
A happiness that ebbed not, but remained
To fill the total measure of the soul!
From the low tenement, his own abode,
Whither, as to a little private cell,
He had withdrawn from bustle, care, and noise,
To spend the Sabbath of old age in peace,
Once every day he duteously repaired
To rock the cradle of the slumbering babe:
For in that female infant's name he heard
The silent name of his departed wife!
Heart-stirring music! hourly heard that name;
Full blest he was. 'Another Margaret Green,
Oft did he say, 'was come to Gold-rill side.'
Oh! pang unthought of, as the precious boon
Itself had been unlooked for;—oh! dire stroke
Of desolating anguish for them all!
Just as the child could totter on the floor,
And, by some friendly finger's help upstayed,
Range round the garden walk, while she perchance
Was catching at some novelty of spring,
Ground-flower, or glossy insect from its cell
Drawn by the sunshine—at that hopeful season
The winds of March, smiting insidiously,
Raised in the tender passage of the throat
Viewless obstruction; whence—all unforewarned,
The household lost their pride and soul's delight.
But time hath power to soften all regrets,
And prayer and thought can bring to worst distress
Due resignation. Therefore, though some tears
Fail not to spring from either parent's eye
Oft as they hear of sorrow like their own,
Yet this departed little one, too long

The innocent troubler of their quiet, sleeps
In what may now be called a peaceful grave.

"On a bright day, the brightest of the year,
These mountains echoed with an unknown sound,
A volley, thrice repeated o'er the corse
Let down into the hollow of that grave,
Whose shelving sides are red with naked mould.
Ye rains of April, duly wet this earth!
Spare, burning sun of midsummer, these sods,
That they may knit together, and therewith
Our thoughts unite in kindred quietness!
Nor so the valley shall forget her loss.
Dear youth, by young and old alike beloved,
To me as precious as my own!—Green herbs
May creep (I wish that they would softly creep)
Over thy last abode, and we may pass
Reminded less imperiously of thee;—
The ridge itself may sink into the breast
Of earth, the great abyss, and be no more;
Yet shall not thy remembrance leave our hearts,
Thy image disappear!
The mountain ash
No eye can overlook, when 'mid a grove
Of yet unfaded trees she lifts her head
Decked with autumnal berries, that outshine
Spring's richest blossoms; and ye may have marked
By a brook side or solitary tarn,
How she her station doth adorn,—the pool
Glows at her feet, and all the gloomy rocks
Are brightened round her In his native vale
Such and so glorious did this youth appear;
A sight that kindled pleasure in all hearts
By his ingenuous beauty, by the gleam
Of his fair eyes, by his capacious brow,
By all the graces with which nature's hand
Had lavishly arrayed him. As old bards
Tell in their idle songs of wandering gods,
Pan or Apollo, veiled in human form;
Yet, like the sweet-breathed violet of the shade,
Discovered in their own despite to sense
Of mortals, (if such fables without blame
May find chance-mention on this sacred ground,)
So, through a simple rustic garb's disguise,
And through the impediment of rural cares,
In him revealed a scholar's genius shone,
And so, not wholly hidden from men's sight,
In him the spirit of a hero walked
Our unpretending valley.—How the coit
Whizzed from the stripling's arm! If touched by him,
The inglorious foot-ball mounted to the pitch
Of the lark's flight,—or shaped a rainbow curve,
Aloft, in prospect of the shouting field!
The indefatigable fox had learned
To dread his perseverance in the chase.
With admiration would he lift his eyes
To the wide-ruling eagle, and his hand
Was loth to assault the majesty he loved;

Else had the strongest fastnesses proved weak
To guard the royal brood. The sailing glead,
The wheeling swallow, and the darting snipe,
The sportive sea-gull dancing with the waves,
And cautious water-fowl, from distant climes,
Fixed at their seat, the centre of the mere,
Were subject to young Oswald's steady aim.

"From Gallia's coast a tyrant hurled his threats;
Our country marked the preparation vast
Of hostile forces; and she called—with voice
That filled her plains and reached her utmost shores,
And in remotest vales was heard—to arms!
Then, for the first time, here you might have seen
The shepherd's gray to martial scarlet changed,
That flashed uncouthly through the woods and fields.
Ten hardy striplings, all in bright attire,
And graced with shining weapons, weekly marched,
From this lone valley, to a central spot
Where, in assemblage with the flower and choice
Of the surrounding district, they might learn
The rudiments of war; ten—hardy, strong,
And valiant; but young Oswald, like a chief
And yet a modest comrade, led them forth
From their shy solitude, to face the world,
With a gay confidence and seemly pride;
Measuring the soil beneath their happy feet
Like youths released from labour, and yet bound
To most laborious service, though to them
A festival of unencumbered ease;
The inner spirit keeping holiday,
Like vernal ground to Sabbath sunshine left.

"Oft have I marked him, at some leisure hour,
Stretched on the grass or seated in the shade
Among his fellows, while an ample map
Before their eyes lay carefully outspread,
From which the gallant teacher would discourse,
Now pointing this way and now that—'Here flows,'
Thus would he say, 'the Rhine, that famous stream!
Eastward, the Danube toward this inland sea,
A mightier river, winds from realm to realm;—
And, like a serpent, shows his glittering back
Bespotted with innumerable isles.
Here reigns the Russian, there the Turk; observe
His capital city!—Thence—along a tract
Of livelier interest to his hopes and fears
His finger moved, distinguishing the spots
Where wide-spread conflict then most fiercely raged;
Nor left unstigmatized those fatal fields
On which the sons of mighty Germany
Were taught a base submission.—'Here behold
A nobler race, the Switzers, and their land;
Vales deeper far than these of ours, huge woods,
And mountains white with everlasting snow!'
And, surely, he, that spake with kindling brow,
Was a true patriot, hopeful as the best
Of that young peasantry, who, in our days,

Have fought and perished for Helvetia's rights,-
Ah, not in vain! –or those who, in old time,
For work of happier issue, to the side
Of Tell came trooping from a thousand huts,
When he had risen alone! No braver youth
Descended from Judean heights to march
With righteous Joshua; or appeared in arms
When grove was felled, and altar was cast down,
And Gideon blew the trumpet, soul-enflamed,
And strong in hatred of idolatry."

This spoken, from his seat the pastor rose,
And moved towards the grave; instinctively
His steps we followed, and my voice exclaimed,
"Power to the oppressors of the world is given,
A might of which they dream not. Oh! the curse,
To be the awakener of divinest thoughts,
Father and founder of exalted deeds,
And to whole nations bound in servile straits
The liberal donor of capacities
More than heroic! this to be, nor yet
Have sense of one connatural wish, nor yet
Deserve the least return of human thanks;
Winning no recompense but deadly hate
With pity mixed, astonishment with scorn!"

When these involuntary words had ceased,
The Pastor said, "So Providence is served;
The forked weapon of the skies can send
Illumination into deep, dark holds,
Which the mild sunbeam hath not power to pierce.
Why do ye quake, intimidated thrones?
For, not unconscious of the mighty debt
Which to outrageous wrong the sufferer owes,
Europe, through all her habitable seats,
Is thirsting for *their* overthrow, who still
Exist, as pagan temples stood of old,
By very horror of their impious rites
Preserved, are suffered to extend their pride,
Like cedars on the top of Lebanon
Darkening the sun —But less impatient thoughts,
And love 'all hoping and expecting all,'
This hallowed grave demands; where rests in peace
A humble champion of the better cause;
A peasant youth, so call him, for he asked
No higher name; in whom our country showed,
As in a favourite son, most beautiful
In spite of vice, and misery, and disease,
Spread with the spreading of her wealthy arts,
England, the ancient and the free, appeared,
In him to stand, before my swimming eyes,
Unconquerably virtuous and secure.
No more of this, lest I offend his dust:
Short was his life, and a brief tale remains.

"One summer's day—a day of annual pomp
And solemn chase—from morn to sultry noon

His steps had followed, fleetest of the fleet,
The red-deer driven along its native heights
With cry of hound and horn ; and, from that toil
Returned with sinews weakened and relaxed,
This generous youth, too negligent of self,
Plunged—'mid a gay and busy throng convened
To wash the fleeces of his father's flock—
Into the chilling flood.
Convulsions dire
Seized him that self-same night ; and through the space
Of twelve ensuing days his frame was wrenched
Till nature rested from her work in death.
To him, thus snatched away, his comrades paid
A soldier's honours. At his funeral hour
Bright was the sun, the sky was cloudless blue—
A golden lustre slept upon the hills ;
And if by chance a stranger, wandering there,
From some commanding eminence had looked
Down on this spot, well pleased would he have seen
A glittering spectacle ; but every face
Was pallid,—seldom hath that eye been moist
With tears that wept not then ; nor were the few
Who from their dwellings came not forth to join
In this sad service, less disturbed than we.
They started at the tributary peal
Of instantaneous thunder, which announced
Through the still air the closing of the grave ;
And distant mountains echoed with a sound
Of lamentation never heard before !"

The pastor ceased.—My venerable friend
Victoriously upraised his clear bright eye ;
And, when that eulogy was ended, stood
Enrapt,—as if his inward sense perceived
The prolongation of some still response,
Sent by the ancient soul of this wide land,
The spirit of its mountains and its seas,
Its cities, temples, fields, its awful power,
Its rights and virtues—by that Deity
Descending ; and supporting his pure heart
With patriotic confidence and joy.
And, at the last of those memorial words,
The pining Solitary turned aside,
Whether through manly instinct to conceal
Tender emotions spreading from the heart
To his worn cheek ; or with uneasy shame
För those cold humours of habitual spleen,
That fondly seeking in dispraise of man
Solace and self-excuse, had sometimes urged
To self-abuse, a not ineloquent tongue.
Right tow'rd the sacred edifice his steps
Had been directed ; and we saw him now
Intent upon a monumental stone,
Whose uncouth form was grafted on the wall
Or rather seemed to have grown into the side
Of the rude pile · as oft-times trunks of trees,
Where nature works in wild and craggy spots,

Are seen incorporate with the living rock—
To endure for aye. The vicar, taking note
Of his employment, with a courteous smile
Exclaimed, "The sagest antiquarian's eye
That task would foil," then, letting fall his voice
While he advanced, thus spake. "Tradition tells
That, in Eliza's golden days, a knight
Came on a war-horse sumptuously attired,
And fixed his home in this sequestered vale.
'Tis left untold if here he first drew breath,
Or as a stranger reached this deep recess,
Unknowing, and unknown. A pleasing thought
I sometimes entertain, that, haply bound
To Scotland's court in service of his queen,
Or sent on mission to some northern chief
Of England's realm, this vale he might have seen
With transient observation; and thence caught
An image fair, which, brightening in his soul
When joy of war and pride of chivalry
Languished beneath accumulated years,
Had power to draw him from the world—resolved
To make that paradise his chosen home
To which his peaceful fancy oft had turned.
Vague thoughts are these, but, if belief may rest
Upon unwritten story fondly traced
From sire to son, in this obscure retreat
The knight arrived, with pomp of spear and shield,
And borne upon a charger covered o'er
With gilded housings. And the lofty steed—
His sole companion, and his faithful friend,
Whom he, in gratitude, let loose to range
In fertile pastures—was beheld with eyes
Of admiration and delightful awe
By those untravelled dalesmen. With less pride,
Yet free from touch of envious discontent,
They saw a mansion at his bidding rise,
Like a bright star, amid the lowly band
Of their rude homesteads. Here the warrior dwelt,
And, in that mansion, children of his own,
Or kindred, gathered round him. As a tree
That falls and disappears, the house is gone;
And, through improvidence, or want of love
For ancient worth and honourable things,
The spear and shield are vanished, which the knight
Hung in his rustic hall. One ivied arch
Myself have seen, a gateway, last remains
Of that foundation in domestic care
Raised by his hands. And now no trace is left
Of the mild-hearted champion, save this stone,
Faithless memorial! and his family name
Borne by yon clustering cottages, that sprang
From out the ruins of his stately lodge:
These and the name and title at full length,—
Sir Alfred Irthing, with appropriate words
Accompanied, still extant, in a wreath
Or posy—girding round the several fronts
Of three clear-sounding and harmonious bells,
That in the steeple hang, his pious gift."

"So fails, so languishes, grows dim, and dies,"
The gray-haired Wanderer pensively exclaimed,
"All that this world is proud of. From their spheres
The stars of human glory are cast down;
Perish the roses and the flowers of kings,
Princes, and emperors, and the crowns and palms
Of all the mighty, withered and consumed!
Nor is power given to lowliest innocence,
Long to protect her own. The man himself
Departs; and soon is spent the line of those
Who, in the bodily image, in the mind,
In heart or soul, in station or pursuit,
Did most resemble him. Degrees and ranks,
Fraternities and orders—heaping high
New wealth upon the burthen of the old,
And placing trust in privilege confirmed
And re-confirmed—are scoffed at with a smile
Of greedy foretaste, from the secret stand
Of desolation aimed: to slow decline
These yield, and these to sudden overthrow;
Their virtue, service, happiness, and state
Expire; and nature's pleasant robe of green,
Humanity's appointed shroud, enwraps
Their monuments and their memory. The vast frame
Of social nature changes evermore
Her organs and her members with decay
Restless, and restless generation, powers
And functions dying and produced at need,—
And by this law the mighty whole subsists:
With an ascent and progress in the main;
Yet, oh! how disproportioned to the hopes
And expectations of self-flattering minds!
The courteous knight, whose bones are here interred,
Lived in an age conspicuous as our own
For strife and ferment in the minds of men,
Whence alteration, in the forms of things,
Various and vast. A memorable age!
Which did to him assign a pensive lot,
To linger 'mid the last of those bright clouds,
That, on the steady breeze of honour, sailed
In long procession calm and beautiful.
He who had seen his own bright order fade,
And its devotion gradually decline,
(While war, relinquishing the lance and shield,
Her temper changed, and bowed to other laws,)
Had also witnessed in his morn of life,
That violent commotion, which o'erthrew,
In town, and city, and sequestered glen,
Altar, and cross, and church of solemn roof,
And old religious house—pile after pile;
And shook the tenants out into the fields,
Like wild beasts without home! Their hour was come;
But why no softening thought of gratitude,
No just remembrance, scruple, or wise doubt?
Benevolence is mild; nor borrows help,
Save at worst need, from bold impetuous force,
Fitliest allied to anger and revenge.
But human-kind rejoices in the might

Of mutability ; and airy hopes,
Dancing around her, hinder and disturb
Those meditations of the soul, that feed
The retrospective virtues. Festive songs
Break from the maddened nations at the sight
Of sudden overthrow ; and cold neglect
Is the sure consequence of slow decay.
Even," said the Wanderer, "as that courteous knight,
Bound by his vow to labour for redress
Of all who suffer wrong, and to enact
By sword and lance the law of gentleness,
If I may venture of myself to speak,
Trusting that not incongruously I blend
Low things with lofty, I too shall be doomed
To outlive the kindly use and fair esteem
Of the poor calling which my youth embraced
With no unworthy prospect. But enough ;
Thoughts crowd upon me—and 'twere seemlier now
To stop, and yield our gracious teacher thanks
For the pathetic records which his voice
Hath here delivered ; words of heartfelt truth,
Tending to patience when affliction strikes ,
To hope and love ; to confident repose
In God ; and reverence for the dust of man."

BOOK VIII.

ARGUMENT.

Pastor's apprehensions that he might have detained his auditors too long—Invitation to his house—Solitary disinclined to comply—rallies the Wanderer; and somewhat playfully draws a comparison between his itinerant profession and that of the knight-errant—which leads to Wanderer's giving an account of changes in the country from the manufacturing spirit—Favourable effects—The other side of the picture, and chiefly as it has affected the humbler classes—Wandered asserts the hollowness of all national grandeur if unsupported by moral worth—gives instances—Physical science unable to support itself—Lamentations over an excess of manufacturing industry among the humbler classes of society—Picture of a child employed in a cotton-mill—Ignorance and degradation of children among the agricultural population reviewed—Conversation broken off by a renewed invitation by the pastor—Path leading to his house—Its appearance described—His daughter—His wife—His son (a boy) enters with his companion—Their happy appearance—The Wanderer how affected by the sight of them.

THE PARSONAGE.

THE pensive sceptic of the lonely vale
To those acknowledgments subscribed his own,
With a sedate compliance, which the priest
Failed not to notice, inly pleased, and said,
"If ye, by whom invited I commenced
These narratives of calm and humble life,
Be satisfied, 'tis well,—the end is gained .
And, in return for sympathy bestowed
And patient listening, thanks accept from me.
Life, death, eternity ! momentous themes
Are they—and might demand a seraph's tongue,
Were they not equal to their own support ;

And therefore no incompetence of mine
Could do them wrong. The universal forms
Of human nature, in a spot like this,
Present themselves at once to all men's view;
Ye wished for act and circumstance that make
The individual known and understood;
And such as my best judgment could select
From what the place afforded have been given;
Though apprehensions crossed me, in the course
Of this self-pleasing exercise, that ye
My zeal to his would liken, who unlocks
A cabinet with gems or pictures stored,
And draws them forth—soliciting regard
To this, and this, as worthier than the last,
Till the spectator, who a while was pleased
More than the exhibitor himself, becomes
Weary and faint, and longs to be released.
But let us hence! my dwelling is in sight,
And there—"
At this the Solitary shrunk
With backward will; but, wanting not address
That inward motion to disguise, he said
To his compatriot, smiling as he spake:
"The peaceable remains of this good knight
Would be disturbed, I fear, with wrathful scorn,
If consciousness could reach him where he lies
That one, albeit of these degenerate times,
Deploring changes past, or dreading change
Foreseen, had dared to couple, even in thought,
The fine vocation of the sword and lance
With the gross aims and body-bending toil
Of a poor brotherhood who walk the earth
Pitied, and where they are not known, despised.
Yet, by the good knight's leave, the two estates
Are graced with some resemblance Errant those,
Exiles and wanderers—and the like are these,
Who, with their burthen, traverse hill and dale,
Carrying relief for nature's simple wants.
What though no higher recompense they seek
Than honest maintenance, by irksome toil
Full oft procured, yet such may claim respect,
Among the intelligent, for what this course
Enables them to be and to perform.
Their tardy steps give leisure to observe,
While solitude permits the mind to feel;
Instructs and prompts her to supply defects
By the division of her inward self,
For grateful converse · and to these poor men
(As I have heard you boast with honest pride)
Nature is bountiful, where'er they go;
Kind nature's various wealth is all their own.
Versed in the characters of men; and bound,
By tie of daily interest, to maintain
Conciliatory manners and smooth speech:
Such have been, and still are in their degree,
Examples efficacious to refine
Rude intercourse, apt agents to expel,
By importation of unlooked-for arts.

Barbarian torpor, and blind prejudice;
Raising, through just gradation, savage life
To rustic, and the rustic to urbane
Within their moving magazines is lodged
Power that comes forth to quicken and exalt
Affections seated in the mother's breast,
And in the lover's fancy; and to feed
The sober sympathies of long-tried friends.
By these itinerants, as experienced men,
Counsel is given; contention they appease
With gentle language; in remotest wilds,
Tears wipe away, and pleasant tidings bring:
Could the proud quest of chivalry do more?"

"Happy," rejoined the Wanderer, "they who gain
A panegyric from your generous tongue!
But if to these wayfarers once pertained
Aught of romantic interest, 'tis gone;
Their purer service, in this realm at least,
Is past for ever.—An inventive age
Has wrought, if not with speed of magic, yet
To most strange issues. I have lived to mark
A new and unforeseen creation rise
From out the labours of a peaceful land,
Wielding her potent enginery to frame
And to produce, with appetite as keen
As that of war, which rests not night or day,
Industrious to destroy! With fruitless pains
Might one like me *now* visit many a tract
Which, in his youth, he trod and trod again,
A lone pedestrian with a scanty freight,
Wished for, or welcome, wheresoe'er he came,
Among the tenantry of thorpe and vill;
Or straggling burgh, of ancient charter proud,
And dignified by battlements and towers
Of some stern castle, mouldering on the brow
Of a green hill or bank of rugged stream.
The foot-path faintly marked, the horse-track wild,
And formidable length of plashy lane,
(Prized avenues ere others had been shaped
Or easier links connecting place with place)
Have vanished,—swallowed up by stately roads
Easy and bold, that penetrate the gloom
Of Britain's farthest glens. The earth has lent
Her waters, air her breezes, and the sail
Of traffic glides with ceaseless interchange,
Glistening along the low and woody dale,
Or on the naked mountain's lofty side.
Meanwhile, at social industry's command,
How quick, how vast an increase! From the germ
Of some poor hamlet, rapidly produced
Here a huge town, continuous and compact,
Hiding the face of earth for leagues—and there,
Where not a habitation stood before,
Abodes of men irregularly massed
Like trees in forests—spread through spacious tracts.
O'er which the smoke of unremitting fires
Hangs permanent, and plentiful as wreaths

Of vapour glittering in the morning sun.
And, wheresoe'er the traveller turns his steps,
He sees the barren wilderness erased,
Or disappearing; triumph that proclaims
How much the mild directress of the plough
Owes to alliance with these new-born arts!
Hence is the wide sea peopled,—hence the shores
Of Britain are resorted to by ships
Freighted from every climate of the world
With the world's choicest produce. Hence that sum
Of keels that rest within her crowded ports,
Or lie at anchor in her sounds and bays,
That animating spectacle of sails
Which, through her inland regions, to and fro
Pass with the respirations of the tide,
Perpetual, multitudinous! Finally,
Hence a dread arm of floating power, a voice
Of thunder daunting those who would approach
With hostile purposes the blessed isle—
Truth's consecrated residence, the seat
Impregnable of liberty and peace!

"And yet, O happy pastor of a flock
Faithfully watched, and, by that loving care
And Heaven's good providence, preserved from taint!
With you I grieve, when on the darker side
Of this great change I look; and there behold,
Such outrage done to nature as compels
The indignant power to justify herself;
Yea, to avenge her violated rights,
For England's bane.—When soothing darkness spreads
O'er hill and vale," the Wanderer thus expressed
His recollections, "and the punctual stars,
While all things else are gathering to their homes,
Advance, and in the firmament of heaven
Glitter—but undisturbing, undisturbed,
As if their silent company were charged
With peaceful admonitions for the heart
Of all-beholding man, earth's thoughtful lord;
Then, in full many a region, once like this
The assured domain of calm simplicity
And pensive quiet, an unnatural light,
Prepared for never-resting labour's eyes,
Breaks from a many-windowed fabric huge:
And at the appointed hour a bell is heard—
Of harsher import than the curfew-knoll
That spake the Norman conqueror's stern behest—
A local summons to unceasing toil!
Disgorged are now the ministers of day;
And, as they issue from the illumined pile,
A fresh band meets them, at the crowded door—
And in the courts—and where the rumbling stream
That turns the multitude of dizzy wheels,
Glares, like a troubled spirit, in its bed
Among the rocks below. Men, maidens, youths,
Mother and little children, boys and girls,
Enter, and each the wonted task resumes
Within this temple—where is offered up

To gain, the master idol of the realm,
Perpetual sacrifice. Even thus of old
Our ancestors, within the still domain
Of vast cathedral or conventual church,
Their vigils kept; where tapers day and night
On the dim altar burned continually,
In token that the house was evermore
Watching to God. Religious men were they;
Nor would their reason, tutored to aspire
Above this transitory world, allow
That there should pass a moment of the year,
When in their land the Almighty's service ceased.

"Triumph who will in these profaner rites
Which we, a generation self-extolled,
As zealously perform! I cannot share
His proud complacency; yet I exult,
Casting reserve away, exult to see
An intellectual mastery exercised
O'er the blind elements; a purpose given,
A perseverance fed; almost a soul
Imparted—to brute matter. I rejoice,
Measuring the force of those gigantic powers,
That by the thinking mind have been compelled
To serve the will of feeble-bodied man.
For with the sense of admiration blends
The animating hope that time may come
When strengthened, yet not dazzled, by the might
Of this dominion over nature gained,
Men of all lands shall exercise the same
In due proportion to their country's need;
Learning, though late, that all true glory rests,
All praise, all safety, and all happiness,
Upon the moral law. Egyptian Thebes;
Tyre by the margin of the sounding waves;
Palmyra, central in the desert, fell;
And the arts died by which they had been raised.
Call Archimedes from his buried tomb
Upon the plain of vanished Syracuse,
And feelingly the sage shall make report
How insecure, how baseless in itself,
Is the philosophy, whose sway depends
On mere material instruments:—how weak
Those arts, and high inventions, if unpropped
By virtue.—He with sighs of pensive grief,
Amid his calm abstractions, would admit
That not the slender privilege is theirs
To save themselves from blank forgetfulness!"

When from the Wanderer's lips these words had fallen,
I said, "And, did in truth these vaunted arts
Possess such privilege, how could we escape
Regret and painful sadness, who revere,
And would preserve as things above all price,
The old domestic morals of the land,
Her simple manners, and the stable worth
That dignified and cheered a low estate?
Oh! where is now the character of peace,

Sobriety, and order, and chaste love,
And honest dealing, and untainted speech,
And pure good-will, and hospitable cheer,
That made the very thought of country-life
A thought of refuge, for a mind detained
Reluctantly amid the bustling crowd?
Where now the beauty of the Sabbath kept
With conscientious reverence, as a day
By the Almighty law-giver pronounced
Holy and blest? and where the winning grace
Of all the lighter ornaments attached
To time and season, as the year rolled round?"

"Fled!" was the Wanderer's passionate response,
"Fled utterly! or only to be traced
In a few fortunate retreats like this;
Which I behold with trembling, when I think
What lamentable change, a year—a month—
May bring; that brook converting as it runs
Into an instrument of deadly bane
For those, who, yet untempted to forsake
The simple occupations of their sires,
Drink the pure water of its innocent stream
With lip almost as pure.—Domestic bliss,
(Or call it comfort, by a humbler name,)
How art thou blighted for the poor man's heart!
Lo! in such neighbourhood, from morn to eve,
The habitations empty! or perchance
The mother left alone,—no helping hand
To rock the cradle of her peevish babe;
No daughters round her, busy at the wheel,
Or in despatch of each day's little growth
Of household occupation; no nice arts
Of needle-work; no bustle at the fire,
Where once the dinner was prepared with pride;
Nothing to speed the day, or cheer the mind,
Nothing to praise, to teach, or to command!
The father, if perchance he still retain
His old employments, goes to field or wood,
No longer led or followed by the sons;
Idlers perchance they were,—but in *his* sight,
Breathing fresh air, and treading the green earth;
Till their short holiday of childhood ceased,
Ne'er to return! That birthright now is lost.
Economists will tell you that the state
Thrives by the forfeiture——unfeeling thought,
And false as monstrous! Can the mother thrive
By the destruction of her innocent sons?
In whom a premature necessity
Blocks out the forms of nature, preconsumes
The reason, famishes the heart, shuts up
The infant being in itself, and makes
Its very spring a season of decay!
The lot is wretched, the condition sad,
Whether a pining discontent survive,
And thirst for change; or habit hath subdued
The soul depressed, dejected—even to love
Of her dull tasks, and close captivity.

Oh, banish far such wisdom as condemns
A native Briton to these inward chains,
Fixed in his soul, so early and so deep,
Without his own consent, or knowledge, fixed!
He is a slave to whom release comes not,
And cannot come. The boy, where'er he turns,
Is still a prisoner; when the wind is up
Among the clouds and in the ancient woods;
Or when the sun is shining in the east,
Quiet and calm. Behold him—in the school
Of his attainment? no, but with the air
Fanning his temples under heaven's blue arch.
His raiment, whitened o'er with cotton flakes,
Or locks of wool, announces whence he comes.
Creeping his gait and cowering—his lip pale—
His respiration quick and audible;
And scarcely could you fancy that a gleam
From out those languid eyes could break, or blush
Mantle upon his cheek. Is this the form,
Is that the countenance, and such the port,
Of no mean being? One who should be clothed
With dignity befitting his proud hope;
Who, in his very childhood, should appear
Sublime—from present purity and joy!
The limbs increase; but liberty of mind
Is gone for ever; this organic frame
So joyful in her motions, is become
Dull, to the joy of her own motions dead;
And even the touch so exquisitely poured
Through the whole body with a languid will
Performs her functions; rarely competent
To impress a vivid feeling on the mind
Of what there is delightful in the breeze,
The gentle visitations of the sun,
Or lapse of liquid element,—by hand,
Or foot, or lip, in summer's warmth—perceived.
Can hope look forward to a manhood raised
On such foundations?"

"Hope is none for him!"
The pale recluse indignantly exclaimed,
"And tens of thousands suffer wrong as deep.
Yet be it asked, in justice to our age,
If there were not, before those arts appeared,
These structures rose, commingling old and young,
And unripe sex with sex, for mutual taint;
Then, if there were not, in our far-famed isle,
Multitudes, who from infancy had breathed
Air unimprisoned, and had lived at large;
Yet walked beneath the sun, in human shape,
As abject, as degraded? At this day
Who shall enumerate the crazy huts
And tottering hovels, whence do issue forth
A ragged offspring, with their own blanched hair
Crowned like the image of fantastic fear;
Or wearing, we might say, in that white growth
An ill-adjusted turban, for defence
Or fierceness, wreathed around their sun-burnt brows,
By savage nature's unassisted care.

Naked and coloured like the soil, the feet
On which they stand; as if thereby they drew
Some nourishment, as trees do by their roots,
From earth, the common mother of us all.
Figure and mien, complexion and attire,
Are leagued to strike dismay, but outstretched hand
And whining voice denote them supplicants
For the least boon that pity can bestow.
Such on the breast of darksome heaths are found;
And with their parents dwell upon the skirts
Of furze-clad commons, such are born and reared
At the mine's mouth, under impending rocks;
Or in the chambers of some natural cave;
Or where their ancestors erected huts,
For the convenience of unlawful gain,
In forest purlieus; and the like are bred,
All England through, where nooks and slips of ground,
Purloined, in times less jealous than our own,
From the green margin of the public way,
A residence afford them, 'mid the bloom
And gaiety of cultivated fields.
Such (we will hope the lowest in the scale)
Do I remember oft-times to have seen
'Mid Buxton's dreary heights. Upon the watch,
Till the swift vehicle approach, they stand,
Then, following closely with the cloud of dust,
An uncouth feat exhibit, and are gone
Heels over head like tumblers on a stage.
Up from the ground they snatch the copper coin,
And, on the freight of merry passengers
Fixing a steady eye, maintain their speed;
And spin—and pant—and overhead again,
Wild pursuivants! until their breath is lost,
Or bounty tires—and every face, that smiled
Encouragement, hath ceased to look that way.
But, like the vagrants of the Gipsy tribe,
These, bred to little pleasure in themselves,
Are profitless to others. Turn we then
To Britons born and bred within the pale
Of civil policy, and early trained
To earn, by wholesome labour in the field,
The bread they eat. A sample should I give
Of what this stock produces to enrich
The tender age of life, ye would exclaim,
'Is this the whistling plough-boy whose shrill notes
Impart new gladness to the morning air?'
Forgive me if I venture to suspect
That many, sweet to hear of in soft verse,
Are of no finer frame:—his joints are stiff,
Beneath a cumbrous frock, that to the knees
Invests the thriving churl, his legs appear,
Fellows to those that lustily upheld
The wooden stools for everlasting use,
Whereon our fathers sate. And mark his brow!
Under whose shaggy canopy are set
Two eyes, not dim, but of a healthy stare:
Wide, sluggish, blank, and ignorant, and strange·
Proclaiming boldly that they never drew

A look or motion of intelligence
From infant conning of the Christ-cross-row,
Or puzzling through a primer, line by line,
Till perfect mastery crown the pains at last.
What kindly warmth from touch of fostering hand,
What penetrating power of sun or breeze,
Shall e'er dissolve the crust wherein his soul
Sleeps, like a caterpillar sheathed in ice?
This torpor is no pitiable work
Of modern ingenuity, no town
Nor crowded city may be taxed with aught
Of sottish vice or desperate breach of law,
To which in after years he may be roused.
This boy the fields produce: his spade and hoe-
The carter's whip that on his shoulder rests
In air high-towering with a boorish pomp,
The sceptre of his sway; his country's name,
Her equal rights, her churches and her schools-
What have they done for him? And, let me ask,
For tens of thousands uninformed as he?
In brief, what liberty of mind is here?"

This ardent sally pleased the mild good man,
To whom the appeal couched in its closing words
Was pointedly addressed; and to the thoughts
That, in assent or opposition, rose
Within his mind, he seemed prepared to give
Prompt utterance; but, rising from our seat,
The hospitable vicar interposed
With invitation urgently renewed.
We followed, taking as he led, a path
Along a hedge of hollies, dark and tall,
Whose flexile boughs, descending with a weight
Of leafy spray, concealed the stems and roots
That gave them nourishment When frosty winds
Howl from the north, what kindly warmth methought
Is here, how grateful this impervious screen!
Not shaped by simple wearing of the foot
On rural business passing to and fro
Was the commodious walk; a careful hand
Had marked the line, and strewn the surface o'er
With pure cerulean gravel, from the heights
Fetched by the neighbouring brook.—Across the vale
The stately fence accompanied our steps;
And thus the pathway, by perennial green
Guarded and graced, seemed fashioned to unite,
As by a beautiful yet solemn chain,
The pastor's mansion with the house of prayer

Like image of solemnity, conjoined
With feminine allurement soft and fair,
The mansion's self displayed;—a reverend pile
With bold projections and recesses deep;
Shadowy, yet gay and lightsome as it stood
Fronting the noontide sun. We paused to admire
The pillared porch, elaborately embossed;
The low wide windows with their mullions old,
The cornice richly fretted, of grey stone;

And that smooth slope from which the dwelling rose,
By beds and banks Arcadian of gay flowers
And flowering shrubs, protected and adorned;
Profusion bright! and every flower assuming
A more than natural vividness of hue,
From unaffected contrast with the gloom
Of sober cypress, and the darker foil
Of yew, in which survived some traces, here
Not unbecoming, of grotesque device
And uncouth fancy From behind the roof
Rose the slim ash and massy sycamore,
Blending their diverse foliage with the green
Of ivy, flourishing and thick, that clasped
The huge round chimneys, harbour of delight
For wren and redbreast,—where they sit and sing
Their slender ditties when the trees are bare.
Nor must I leave untouched (the picture else
Were incomplete) a relique of old times
Happily spared, a little Gothic niche
Of nicest workmanship; that once had held
The sculptured image of some patron saint,
Or of the blessed Virgin looking down
On all who entered those religious doors.

But lo! where from the rocky garden mount
Crowned by its antique summer-house, descends,
Light as the silver fawn, a radiant girl:
For she hath recognized her honoured friend,
The Wanderer ever welcome! A prompt kiss
The gladsome child bestows at his request;
And, up the flowery lawn as we advance,
Hangs on the old man with a happy look,
And with a pretty restless hand of love.
We enter—by the lady of the place
Cordially greeted. Graceful was her port:
A lofty stature undepressed by time,
Whose visitation had not wholly spared
The finer lineaments of form and face;
To that complexion brought which prudence trusts in
And wisdom loves.—But when a stately ship
Sails in smooth weather by the placid coast
On homeward voyage, what—if wind and wave,
And hardship undergone in various climes,
Have caused her to abate the virgin pride,
And that full trim of inexperienced hope
With which she left her haven—not for this,
Should the sun strike her, and the impartial breeze
Play on her streamers, fails she to assume
Brightness and touching beauty of her own,
That charm all eyes. So bright, so fair, appeared
This goodly matron, shining in the beams
Of unexpected pleasure. Soon the board
Was spread, and we partook a plain repast.

Here, resting in cool shelter, we beguiled
The mid-day hours with desultory talk;
From trivial themes to general argument
Passing, as accident or fancy led,
Or courtesy prescribed. While question rose

And answer flowed, the fetters of reserve
Dropping from every mind, the Solitary
Resumed the manners of his happier days;
And, in the various conversation, bore
A willing, nay, at times, a forward part,
Yet with the grace of one who in the world
Had learned the art of pleasing, and had now
Occasion given him to display his skill,
Upon the steadfast vantage-ground of truth.
He gazed with admiration unsuppressed
Upon the landscape of the sun bright vale,
Seen, from the shady room in which we sate,
In softened perspective; and more than once
Praised the consummate harmony serene
Of gravity and elegance—diffused
Around the mansion and its whole domain;
Not, doubtless, without help of female taste
And female care.—"A blessed lot is yours!"
The words escaped his lip with a tender sigh
Breathed over them, but suddenly the door
Flew open, and a pair of lusty boys
Appeared—confusion checking their delight.
Not brothers they in feature or attire,
But fond companions, so I guessed, in field,
And by the river's margin—whence they come,
Anglers elated with unusual spoil.
One bears a willow-panier on his back,
The boy of plainer garb, whose blush survives
More deeply tinged. Twin might the other be
To that fair girl who from the garden mount
Bounded—triumphant entry this for him.
Between his hands he holds a smooth blue stone
On whose capacious surface see outspread
Large store of gleaming crimson-spotted trouts;
Ranged side by side, and lessening by degrees
Up to the dwarf that tops the pinnacle.
Upon the board he lays the sky-blue stone
With its rich freight;—their number he proclaims
Tells from what pool the noblest had been dragged;
And where the very monarch of the brook,
After long struggle, had escaped at last—
Stealing alternately at them and us
(As doth his comrade too) a look of pride.
And verily the silent creatures made
A splendid sight, together thus exposed;
Dead—but not sullied or deformed by death,
That seemed to pity what he could not spare.

But oh, the animation in the mien
Of those two boys! Yea, in the very words
With which the young narrator was inspired,
When, as our questions led, he told at large
Of that day's prowess! Him might I compare,
His look, tones, gestures, eager eloquence,
To a bold brook that splits for better speed,
And, at the self-same moment, works its way
Through many channels, ever and anon
Parted and reunited: his compeer

To the still lake, whose stillness is to sight
As beautiful, as grateful to the mind.
But to what object shall the lovely girl
Be likened? She whose countenance and air
Unite the graceful qualities of both,
Even as she shares the pride and joy of both.

My gray-haired friend was moved; his vivid eye
Glistened with tenderness; his mind, I knew,
Was full; and had, I doubted not, returned,
Upon this impulse, to the theme—erewhile
Abruptly broken-off. The ruddy boys
Withdrew, on summons to their well-earned meal;
And he—(to whom all tongues resigned their rights
With willingness, to whom the general ear
Listened with readier patience than to strain
Of music, lute, or harp,—a long delight
That ceased not when his voice had ceased) as one
Who from truth's central point serenely views
The compass of his argument,—began
Mildly, and with a clear and steady tone.

BOOK IX.

ARGUMENT.

Wanderer asserts that an active principle pervades the universe—Its noblest seat the human soul—How lively this principle is in childhood—Hence the delight in old age of looking back upon childhood—The dignity, powers, and privileges of age asserted—These not to be looked for generally but under a just government—Right of a human creature to be exempt from being considered as a mere instrument—Vicious inclinations are best kept under by giving good ones an opportunity to show themselves—The condition of multitudes deplored from want of due respect to this truth on the part of their superiors in society—Former conversation recurred to, and the Wanderer's opinions set in a clearer light—Genuine principles of equality—Truth placed within reach of the humblest.—Happy state of the two boys again adverted to—Earnest wish expressed for a system of national education established universally by government—Glorious effects of this foretold—Wanderer breaks off—Walk to the lake—Embark—Description of scenery and amusements—Grand spectacle from the side of a hill—Address of priest to the Supreme Being—in the course of which he contrasts with ancient barbarism the present appearance of the scene before him—The change ascribed to Christianity—Apostrophe to his flock, living and dead—Gratitude to the Almighty—Return over the lake—Parting with the Solitary—Under what circumstances.

DISCOURSE OF THE WANDERER, AND AN EVENING VISIT TO THE LAKE.

"To every form of being is assigned,"
Thus calmly spake the venerable sage,
"An *active* principle: howe'er removed
From sense and observation, it subsists
In all things, in all natures, in the stars
Of azure heaven, the unenduring clouds,
In flower and tree, in every pebbly stone
That paves the brooks, the stationary rocks,
The moving waters, and the invisible air.
Whate'er exists hath properties that spread

Beyond itself, communicating good,
A simple blessing, or with evil mixed;
Spirit that knows no insulated spot,
No chasm, no solitude; from link to link
It circulates, the soul of all the worlds.
This is the freedom of the universe;
Unfolded still the more, more visible,
The more we know; and yet is reverenced least.
And least respected, in the human mind,
Its most apparent home. The food of hope
Is meditated action; robbed of this
Her sole support, she languishes and dies
We perish also; for we live by hope
And by desire; we see by the glad light,
And breathe the sweet air of futurity,
And so we live, or else we have no life.
To-morrow—nay, perchance this very hour,
(For every moment hath its own to-morrow!)
Those blooming boys, whose hearts are almost sick
With present triumph, will be sure to find
A field before them freshened with the dew
Of other expectations;—in which course
Their happy year spins round. The youth obeys
A like glad impulse; and so moves the man
'Mid all his apprehensions, cares, and fears,—
Or so he ought to move. Ah, why in age
Do we revert so fondly to the walks
Of childhood—but that there the soul discerns
The dear memorial footsteps unimpaired
Of her own native vigour—thence can hear
Reverberations; and a choral song,
Commingling with the incense that ascends
Undaunted, toward the imperishable heavens,
From her own lonely altar?—Do not think
That good and wise will ever be allowed,
Though strength decay, to breathe in such estate
As shall divide them wholly from the stir
Of hopeful nature. Rightly is it said
That man descends into the Vale of years;
Yet have I thought that we might also speak,
And not presumptuously, I trust, of age,
As of a final Eminence, though bare
In aspect and forbidding, yet a point
On which 'tis not impossible to sit
In awful sovereignty—a place of power—
A throne, that may be likened unto his,
Who, in some placid day of summer, looks
Down from a mountain-top,—say one of those
High peaks that bound the vale where now we are.
Faint, and diminished to the gazing eye,
Forest and field, and hill and dale appear,
With all the shapes upon their surface spread:
But, while the gross and visible frame of things
Relinquishes its hold upon the sense,
Yea, almost on the mind herself, and seems
All unsubstantialized,—how loud the voice
Of waters, with invigorated peal
From the full river in the vale below

Ascending!—For on that superior height
Who sits, is disencumbered from the press
Of near obstructions, and is privileged
To breathe in solitude above the host
Of ever-humming insects, 'mid thin air
That suits not them. The murmur of the leaves
Many and idle, visits not his ear;
This he is freed from, and from thousand notes
Not less unceasing, not less vain than these,—
By which the finer passages of sense
Are occupied; and the soul, that would incline
To listen, is prevented or deterred.

"And may it not be hoped, that, placed by age
In like removal, tranquil though severe,
We are not so removed for utter loss;
But for some favour, suited to our need?
What more than that the severing should confer
Fresh power to commune with the invisible world,
And hear the mighty stream of tendency
Uttering, for elevation of our thought,
A clear sonorous voice, inaudible
To the vast multitude; whose doom it is
To run the giddy round of vain delight,
Or fret and labour on the plain below.

"But, if to such sublime ascent the hopes
Of man may rise, as to a welcome close
And termination of his mortal course,
Them only can such hope inspire whose minds
Have not been starved by absolute neglect;
Nor bodies crushed by unremitting toil;
To whom kind nature, therefore, may afford
Proof of the sacred love she bears for all;
Whose birth-right reason, therefore may insure.
For me, consulting what I feel within
In times when most existence with herself
Is satisfied, I cannot but believe,
That, far as kindly nature hath free scope,
And reason's sway predominates, even so far,
Country, society, and time itself,
That saps the individual's bodily frame,
And lays the generations low in dust,
Do, by the Almighty Ruler's grace, partake
Of one maternal spirit, bringing forth
And cherishing with ever-constant love,
That tires not, nor betrays. Our life is turned
Out of her course, wherever man is made
An offering, or a sacrifice, a tool
Or implement, a passive thing employed
As a brute mean, without acknowledgment
Of common right or interest in the end;
Used or abused, as selfishness may prompt.
Say, what can follow for a rational soul
Perverted thus, but weakness in all good,
And strength in evil? Hence an after-call
For chastisement, and custody, and bonds,
And oft-times death, avenger of the past,

And the sole guardian in whose hands we dare
Intrust the future.—Not for these sad issues
Was man created ; but to obey the law
Of life, and hope, and action And tis known
That when we stand upon our native soil,
Unelbowed by such objects as oppress
Our active powers, those powers themselves become
Strong to subvert our noxious qualities
They sweep distemper from the busy day,
And make the vessel of the big round year
Run o'er with gladness , whence the being moves
In beauty through the world ; and all who see
Bless him, rejoicing in his neighbourhood."

"Then," said the Solitary, "by what force
Of language shall a feeling heart express
Her sorrow for that multitude in whom
We look for health from seeds that have been sown
In sickness, and for increase in a power
That works but by extinction ? On themselves
They cannot lean, nor turn to their own hearts
To know what they must do ; their wisdom is
To look into the eyes of others, thence
To be instructed what they must avoid .
Or rather let us say, how least observed,
How with most quiet and most silent death,
With the least taint and injury to the air
The oppressor breathes, their human form divine,
And their immortal soul, may waste away."

The sage rejoined, "I thank you—you have spared
My voice the utterance of a keen regret,
A wide compassion which with you I share.
When, heretofore, I placed before your sight
A little-one, subjected to the arts
Of modern ingenuity, and made
The senseless member of a vast machine,
Serving as doth a spindle or a wheel,
Think not, that, pitying him, I could forget
The rustic boy, who walks the fields, untaught ;
The slave of ignorance, and oft of want,
And miserable hunger. Much, too much
Of this unhappy lot, in early youth
We both have witnessed, lot which I myself
Shared, though in mild and merciful degree·
Yet was the mind to hindrances exposed,
Through which I struggled, not without distress
And sometimes injury, like a lamb enthralled
'Mid thorns and brambles , or a bird that breaks
Through a strong net, and mounts upon the wind,
Though with her plumes impaired. If they, whose souls
Should open while they range the richer fields
Of merry England, are obstructed less
By indigence, their ignorance is not less,
Nor less to be deplored For who can doubt
That tens of thousands at this day exist
Such as the boy you painted, lineal heirs
Of those who once were vassals of her soil,

Following its fortunes like the beasts or trees
Which it sustained. But no one takes delight
In this oppression; none are proud of it;
It bears no sounding name, nor ever bore;
A standing grievance, an indigenous vice
Of every country under heaven. My thoughts
Were turned to evils that are new and chosen,
A bondage lurking under shape of good,—
Arts, in themselves beneficent and kind,
But all too fondly followed and too far;
To victims, which the merciful can see
Nor think that they are victims; turned to wrongs
By women who have children of their own,
Beheld without compassion, yea with praise!
I spake of mischief by the wise diffused
With gladness, thinking that the more it spreads
The healthier, the securer, we become;
Delusion which a moment may destroy!
Lastly, I mourned for those whom I had seen
Corrupted and cast down, on favoured ground,
Where circumstances and nature had combined
To shelter innocence, and cherish love;
Who, but for this intrusion, would have lived,
Possessed of health, and strength, and peace of mind;
Thus would have lived, or never have been born.

"Alas! what differs more than man from man!
And whence that difference? whence but from himself?
For see the universal race endowed
With the same upright form!—The sun is fixed,
And the infinite magnificence of heaven,
Fixed within reach of every human eye;
The sleepless ocean murmurs for all ears;
The vernal field infuses fresh delight
Into all hearts. Throughout the world of sense,
Even as an object is sublime or fair,
That object is laid open to the view
Without reserve or veil; and as a power
Is salutary, or an influence sweet,
Are each and all enabled to perceive
That power, that influence, by impartial law.
Gifts nobler are vouchsafed alike to all;
Reason,—and, with that reason, smiles and tears;
Imagination, freedom in the will,
Conscience to guide and check, and death to be
Foretasted, immortality presumed.
Strange, then, nor less than monstrous might be deemed
The failure, if the Almighty, to this point
Liberal and undistinguishing, should hide
The excellence of moral qualities
From common understanding; leaving truth
And virtue, difficult, abstruse, and dark;
Hard to be won, and only by a few;
Strange, should he deal herein with nice respects,
And frustrate all the rest! Believe it not:
The primal duties shine aloft—like stars;
The charities that soothe, and heal, and bless,
Are scattered at the feet of man—like flowers.

The generous inclination, the just rule,
Kind wishes, and good actions, and pure thoughts—
No mystery is here ; no special boon
For high and not for low, for proudly graced
And not for meek of heart The smoke ascends
To heaven as lightly from the cottage hearth
As from the haughty palace. He, whose soul
Ponders this true equality, may walk
The fields of earth with gratitude and hope ;
Yet, in that meditation, will he find
Motive to sadder grief, as we have found,—
Lamenting ancient virtues overthrown,
And for the injustice grieving, that hath made
So wide a difference betwixt man and man.

"But let us rather turn our gladdened thoughts
Upon the brighter scene. How blest that pair
Of blooming boys (whom we beheld even now)
Blest in their several and their common lot !
A few short hours of each returning day
The thriving prisoners of their village school.
And thence let loose, to seek their pleasant homes
Or range the grassy lawn in vacancy,
To breathe and to be happy, run and shout ;
Idle,—but no delay, no harm, no loss ;
For every genial power of heaven and earth,
Through all the seasons of the changeful year,
Obsequiously doth take upon herself
To labour for them ; bringing each in turn
The tribute of enjoyment, knowledge, health,
Beauty, or strength ! Such privilege is theirs,
Granted alike in the outset of their course
To both , and, if that partnership must cease,
I grieve not," to the pastor here he turned,
"Much as I glory in that child of yours,
Repine not, for his cottage-comrade, whom
Belike no higher destiny awaits
Than the old hereditary wish fulfilled,
The wish for liberty to live—content
With what Heaven grants, and die—in peace of mind,
Within the bosom of his native vale.
At least, whatever fate the noon of life
Reserves for either, this is sure, that both
Have been permitted to enjoy the dawn ;
Whether regarded as a jocund time,
That in itself may terminate, or lead
In course of nature to a sober eve.
Both have been fairly dealt with ; looking back
They will allow that justice has in them
Been shown—alike to body and to mind."

He paused, as if revolving in his soul
Some weighty matter, then, with fervent voice
And an impassioned majesty, exclaimed,
"Oh, for the coming of that glorious time
When, prizing knowledge as her noblest wealth
And best protection, this imperial realm,
While she exacts allegiance shall admit

An obligation, on her part, to *teach*
Them who are born to serve her and obey:
Binding herself by statute to secure
For all the children whom her soil maintains
The rudiments of letters, and inform
The mind with moral and religious truth,
Both understood and practised,—so that none
However destitute, be left to droop
By timely culture unsustained; or run
Into a wild disorder; or be forced
To drudge through weary life without the aid
Of intellectual implements and tools;
A savage horde among the civilised,
A servile band among the lordly free!
This sacred right, the lisping babe proclaims
To be inherent in him, by Heaven's will,
For the protection of his innocence;
And the rude boy,—who, having overpast
The sinless age, by conscience is enrolled,
Yet mutinously knits his angry brow,
And lifts his wilful hand on mischief bent,
Or turns the godlike faculty of speech
To impious use—by process indirect
Declares his due, while he makes known his need.
This sacred right is fruitlessly announced,
This universal plea in vain addressed,
To eyes and ears of parents who themselves
Did, in the time of their necessity,
Urge it in vain; and therefore, like a prayer
That from the humblest roof ascends to Heaven
It mounts to reach the state's parental ear;
Who, if indeed she own a mother's heart,
And be not most unfeelingly devoid
Of gratitude to Providence, will grant
The unquestionable good; which, England, safe
From interference of external force,
May grant at leisure; without risk incurred
That what in wisdom for herself she doth,
Others shall e'er be able to undo.

"Look! and behold, from Calpe's sunburnt cliffs
To the flat margin of the Baltic sea,
Long-reverenced titles cast away as weeds;
Laws overturned;—and territory split,
Like fields of ice rent by the polar wind,
And forced to join in less obnoxious shapes,
Which, ere they gain consistency, by a gust
Of the same breath are shattered and destroyed.
Meantime the sovereignty of these fair isles
Remains entire and indivisible;
And, if that ignorance were removed, which breeds
Within the compass of their several shores
Dark discontent, or loud commotion, each
Might still preserve the beautiful repose
Of heavenly bodies shining in their spheres.
The discipline of slavery is unknown
Amongst us,—hence the more do we require
The discipline of virtue; order else

Cannot subsist, nor confidence, nor peace.
Thus, duties rising out of good possessed,
And prudent caution needful to avert
Impending evil, equally require
That the whole people should be taught and trained,
So shall licentiousness and black resolve
Be rooted out, and virtuous habits take
Their place, and genuine piety descend,
Like an inheritance, from age to age.

"With such foundations laid, avaunt the fear
Of numbers crowded on their native soil,
To the prevention of all healthful growth
Through mutual injury! Rather in the law
Of increase and the mandate from above
Rejoice!—and ye have special cause for joy.
For, as the element of air affords
An easy passage to the industrious bees
Fraught with their burthens; and a way as smooth
For those ordained to take their sounding flight
From the thronged hive, and settle where they list
In fresh abodes, their labour to renew;
So the wide waters, open to the power,
The will, the instincts, and appointed needs
Of Britain, do invite her to cast off
Her swarms, and in succession send them forth;
Bound to establish new communities
On every shore whose aspect favours hope
Or bold adventure; promising to skill
And perseverance their deserved reward.
Yes," he continued, kindling as he spake,
"Change wide, and deep, and silently performed,
This land shall witness; and as days roll on,
Earth's universal frame shall feel the effect
Even till the smallest habitable rock,
Beaten by lonely billows, hear the songs
Of humanized society; and bloom
With civil arts, that send their fragrance forth,
A grateful tribute to all-ruling Heaven.
From culture, unexclusively bestowed
On Albion's noble race in freedom born,
Expect these mighty issues; from the pains
And faithful care of unambitious schools
Instructing simple childhood's ready ear:
Thence look for these magnificent results!
Vast the circumference of hope—and ye
Are at its centre, British lawgivers;
Ah! sleep not there in shame! Shall wisdom's voice
From out the bosom of these troubled times
Repeat the dictates of her calmer mind,
And shall the venerable halls ye fill
Refuse to echo the sublime decree?
Trust not to partial care a general good;
Transfer not to futurity a work
Of urgent need.—Your country must complete
Her glorious destiny.—Begin even now,
Now, when oppression, like the Egyptian plague
Of darkness, stretched o'er guilty Europe, makes

The brightness more conspicuous, that invests
The happy island where ye think and act:
Now, when destruction is a prime pursuit,
Show to the wretched nations for what end
The powers of civil polity were given!"

Abruptly here, but with a graceful air,
The sage broke off. No sooner had he ceased
Than, looking forth, the gentle lady said,
"Behold, the shades of afternoon have fallen
Upon this flowery slope; and see—beyond—
The lake, though bright, is of a placid blue;
As if preparing for the peace of evening.
How temptingly the landscape shines!—The air
Breathes invitation; easy is the walk
To the lake's margin, where a boat lies moored
Beneath her sheltering tree."—Upon this hint
We rose together: all were pleased—but most
The beauteous girl, whose cheek was flushed with joy
Light as a sunbeam glides along the hills
She vanished—eager to impart the scheme
To her loved brother and his shy compeer.
Now was there bustle in the vicar's house
And earnest preparation.—Forth we went,
And down the vale along the streamlet's edge
Pursued our way, a broken company,
Mute or conversing, single or in pairs
Thus having reached a bridge, that overarched
The hasty rivulet where it lay becalmed
In a deep pool, by happy chance we saw
A two-fold image; on a grassy bank
A snow-white ram, and in the crystal flood
Another and the same! Most beautiful,
On the green turf, with his imperial front
Shaggy and bold, and wreathed horns superb,
The breathing creature stood; as beautiful,
Beneath him, showed his shadowy counterpart.
Each had his glowing mountains, each his sky,
And each seemed centre of his own fair world;
Antipodes unconscious of each other,
Yet, in partition, with their several spheres,
Blended in perfect stillness, to our sight!

"Ah! what a pity were it to disperse,
Or to disturb so fair a spectacle,
And yet a breath can do it!"
These few words
The lady whispered, while we stood and gazed,
Gathered together, all, in still delight,
Not without awe. Thence passing on, she said,
In like low voice to my particular ear,
"I love to hear that eloquent old man
Pour forth his meditations, and descant
On human life from infancy to age.
How pure his spirit! in what vivid hues
His mind gives back the various forms of things,
Caught in their fairest, happiest attitude!
While he is speaking, I have power to see

Even as he sees ; but when his voice hath ceased
Then, with a sigh, I sometimes feel, as now,
That combinations so serene and bright,
Like those reflected in yon quiet pool,
Cannot be lasting in a world like ours,
To great and small disturbances exposed."
More had she said—but sportive shouts were heard ;
Sent from the jocund hearts of those two boys,
Who, bearing each a basket on his arm,
Down the green field came tripping after us.
When we had cautiously embarked, the pair
Now for a prouder service were addrest ;
But an inexorable law forbade,
And each resigned the oar which he had seized.
Whereat, with willing hand I undertook
The needful labour ; grateful task !—to me
Pregnant with recollections of the time
When, on thy bosom, spacious Windermere !
A youth, I practised this delightful art ;
Tossed on the waves alone, or 'mid a crew
Of joyous comrades.—Now, the reedy marge
Cleared, with a strenuous arm I dipped the oar,
Free from obstruction and the boat advanced
Through crystal water, smoothly as a hawk,
That, disentangled from the shady boughs
Of some thick wood, her place of covert, cleaves
With correspondent wings the abyss of air.
"Observe," the vicar said, "yon rocky isle
With birch-trees fringed ; my hand shall guide the helm.
While thitherward we bend our course ; or while
We seek that other, on the western shore,—
Where the bare columns of those lofty firs,
Supporting gracefully a massy dome
Of sombre foliage, seem to imitate
A Grecian temple rising from the deep."

"Turn where we may," said I, "we cannot err
In this delicious region."- Cultured slopes,
Wild tracts of forest-ground, and scattered groves,
And mountains bare—or clothed with ancient woods,
Surrounded us ; and, as we held our way
Along the level of the glassy flood,
They ceased not to surround us ; change of place,
From kindred features diversely combined,
Producing change of beauty ever new.
Ah ! that such beauty, varying in the light
Of living nature, cannot be portrayed
By words, nor by the pencil's silent skill ;
But is the property of him alone
Who hath beheld it, noted it with care,
And in his mind recorded it with love !
Suffice it, therefore, if the rural muse
Vouchsafe sweet influence, while her poet speaks
Of trivial occupations well devised,
And unsought pleasures springing up by chance ;
As if some friendly genius had ordained
That, as the day thus far had been enriched

By acquisition of sincere delight,
The same should be continued to its close.

One spirit animating old and young,
A gipsy fire we kindled on the shore
Of the fair isle with birch-trees fringed—and there,
Merrily seated in a ring, partook
The beverage drawn from China's fragrant herb.
Launched from our hands, the smooth stone skimmed the lake;
With shouts we roused the echoes;—stiller sounds
The lovely girl supplied—a simple song,
Whose low tones reached not to the distant rocks
To be repeated thence, but gently sank
Into our hearts; and charmed the peaceful flood.
Rapaciously we gathered flowery spoils
From land and water; lilies of each hue—
Golden and white, that float upon the waves
And court the wind; and leaves of that shy plant,
(Her flowers were shed) the lily of the vale,
That loves the ground, and from the sun withholds
Her pensive beauty, from the breeze her sweets.

Such product, and such pastime did the place
And season yield; but as we re-embarked,
Leaving, in quest of other scenes, the shore
Of that wild spot, the Solitary said,
In a low voice, yet careless who might hear,
"The fire, that burned so brightly to our wish,
Where is it now? Deserted on the beach
It seems extinct; nor shall the fanning breeze
Revive its ashes. What care we for this,
Whose ends are gained? Behold an emblem here
Of one day's pleasure, and all mortal joys!
And in this unpremeditated slight
Of that which is no longer needed, see
The common course of human gratitude!"

This plaintive note disturbed not the repose
Of the still evening. Right across the lake
Our pinnace moves: then, coasting creek and bay,
Glades we behold—and into thickets peep—
Where couch the spotted deer; or raised our eyes
To shaggy steeps on which the careless goat
Browsed by the side of dashing waterfalls.
Thus did the bark, meandering with the shore,
Pursue her voyage, till a natural pier
Of jutting rock invited us to land.
Alert to follow as the pastor led,
We clomb a green hill's side; and as we clomb,
The valley, opening out her bosom, gave
Fair prospect, intercepted less and less,
Of the flat meadows and indented coast
Of the smooth lake—in compass seen:—far off,
And yet conspicuous, stood the old church-tower,
In majesty presiding over fields
And habitations, seemingly preserved
From the intrusion of a restless world
By rocks impassable and mountains huge.

Soft heath this elevated spot supplied,
And choice of moss-clad stones, whereon we couched
Or sat reclined—admiring quietly
The general aspect of the scene; but each
Not seldom over anxious to make known
His own discoveries; or to favourite points
Directing notice merely from a wish
To impart a joy, imperfect while unshared.
That rapturous moment ne'er shall I forget
When these particular interests were effaced
From every mind! already had the sun,
Sinking with less than ordinary state,
Attained his western bound; but rays of light
Now suddenly diverging from the orb
Retired behind the mountain tops or veiled
By the dense air—shot upwards to the crown
Of the blue firmament—aloft—and wide
And multitudes of little floating clouds,
Ere we, who saw, of change were conscious, pierced
Through their ethereal texture, had become
Vivid as fire—clouds separately poised,
Innumerable multitude of forms
Scattered through half the circle of the sky;
And giving back, and shedding each on each,
With prodigal communion, the bright hues
Which from the unapparent fount of glory
They had imbibed, and ceased not to receive.
That which the heavens displayed, the liquid deep
Repeated, but with unity sublime!

While from the grassy mountain's open side
We gazed, in silence hushed, with eyes intent
On the refulgent spectacle—diffused
Through earth, sky, water, and all visible space,
The priest in holy transport thus exclaimed—

"Eternal Spirit! universal God!
Power inaccessible to human thought,
Save by degrees and steps which thou hast deigned
To furnish, for this effluence of thyself,
To the infirmity of mortal sense
Vouchsafed, this local, transitory type
Of thy paternal splendours, and the pomp
Of those who fill thy courts in highest heaven,
The radiant cherubim;—accept the thanks
Which we, thy humble creatures, here convened,
Presume to offer; we, who from the breast
Of the frail earth, permitted to behold
The faint reflections only of thy face,
Are yet exalted, and in soul adore!
Such as they are who in thy presence stand
Unsullied, incorruptible, and drink
Imperishable majesty streamed forth
From thy empyreal throne, the elect of earth
Shall be—divested at the appointed hour
Of all dishonour—cleansed from mortal stain.
Accomplish, then, their number; and conclude
Time's weary course! Or, if, by thy decree,
The consummation that will come by stealth

Be yet far distant, let thy Word prevail,
Oh! let thy Word prevail, to take away
The sting of human nature. Spread the law,
As it is written in thy holy Book,
Throughout all lands let every nation hear
The high behest, and every heart obey;
Both for the love of purity, and hope
Which it affords, to such as do thy will
And persevere in good, that they shall rise,
To have a nearer view of thee, in heaven.
Father of Good! this prayer in bounty grant,
In mercy grant it to thy wretched sons.
Then, not till then, shall persecutions cease,
And cruel wars expire. The way is marked,
The guide appointed, and the ransom paid
Alas! the nations, who of yore received
These tidings, and in Christian temples meet
The sacred truth to acknowledge, linger still;
Preferring bonds and darkness to a state
Of holy freedom, by redeeming love
Proffered to all, while yet on earth detained.

"So fare the many, and the thoughtful few,
Who in the anguish of their souls bewail
This dire perverseness, cannot choose but ask,
Shall it endure?—Shall enmity and strife,
Falsehood and guile, be left to sow their seed;
And the kind never perish?—Is the hope
Fallacious, or shall righteousness obtain
A peaceable dominion, wide as earth,
And ne'er to fail? Shall that blest day arrive
When they, whose choice or lot it is to dwell
In crowded cities, without fear shall live
Studious of mutual benefit; and he,
Whom morning wakes, among sweet dews and flowers
Of every clime, to till the lonely field,
Be happy in himself!—The law of faith
Working through love such conquest shall it gain,
Such triumph over sin and guilt achieve?
Almighty Lord, thy further grace impart!
And with that help the wonder shall be seen
Fulfilled, the hope accomplished; and thy praise
Be sung with transport and unceasing joy"

"Once," and with mild demeanour, as he spake,
On us the venerable pastor turned
His beaming eye that had been raised to Heaven,
"Once, while the name Jehovah was a sound,
Within the circuit of this sea-girt isle,
Unheard, the savage nations bowed the head
To gods delighting in remorseless deeds,
Gods which themselves had fashioned, to promote
Ill purposes, and flatter foul desires.
Then in the bosom of yon mountain cove,
To those inventions of corrupted man
Mysterious rites were solemnized; and there,
Amid impending rocks and gloomy woods,
Of those terrific idols, some received
Such dismal service, that the loudest voice

Of the swoln cataracts (which now are heard
Soft murmuring) was too weak to overcome,
Though aided by wild winds, the groans and shrieks
Of human victims, offered up to appease
Or to propitiate. And if living eyes
Had visionary faculties to see
The thing that hath been as the thing that is,
Aghast we might behold this crystal mere
Bedimmed with smoke, in wreaths voluminous,
Flung from the body of devouring fires,
To Taranis erected on the heights
By priestly hands, for sacrifice, performed
Exultingly, in view of open day
And full assemblage of a barbarous host;
Or to Andates, female power! who gave
(For so they fancied) glorious victory.
A few rude monuments of mountain-stone
Survive; all else is swept away.—How bright
The appearances of things! From such, how changed
The existing worship; and, with those compared,
The worshippers how innocent and blest!
So wide the difference, a willing mind,
At this affecting hour, might almost think
That Paradise, the lost abode of man,
Was raised again · and to a happy few,
In its original beauty, here restored.
Whence but from thee, the true and only God,
And from the faith derived through Him who bled
Upon the cross, this marvellous advance
Of good from evil; as if one extreme
We left—the other gained.—O ye, who come
To kneel devoutly in yon reverend pile,
Called to such office by the peaceful sound
Of Sabbath bells; and ye, who sleep in earth,
All cares forgotten, round its hallowed walls!
For you, in presence of this little band
Gathered together on the green hill-side,
Your pastor is emboldened to prefer
Vocal thanksgivings to the eternal King;
Whose love, whose counsel, whose commands have made
Your very poorest rich in peace of thought
And in good works, and him, who is endowed
With scantiest knowledge, master of all truth
Which the salvation of his soul requires.
Conscious of that abundant favour showered
On you, the children of my humble care,
And this dear land, our country while on earth
We sojourn, have I lifted up my soul,
Joy giving voice to fervent gratitude.
These barren rocks, your stern inheritance;
These fertile fields, that recompense your pains;
The shadowy vale, the sunny mountain top,
Woods waving in the wind their lofty heads,
Or hushed; the roaring waters and the still;
They see the offering of my lifted hands—
They hear my lips present their sacrifice—
They know if I be silent morn or even:
For, though in whispers speaking, the full heart

Will find a vent; and thought is praise to Him,
Audible praise, to Thee, Omniscient Mind,
From Whom all gifts descend, all blessings flow!"

This vesper service closed, without delay,
From that exalted station to the plain
Descending, we pursued our homeward course,
In mute composure, o'er the shadowy lake,
Beneath a faded sky. No trace remained
Of those celestial splendours; grey the vault,
Pure, cloudless ether, and the star of eve
Was wanting;—but inferior lights appeared
Faintly, too faint almost for sight; and some
Above the darkened hills stood boldly forth
In twinkling lustre, ere the boat attained
Her mooring-place;—where, to the sheltering tree,
Our youthful voyagers bound fast her prow
With prompt yet careful hands. This done, we paced
The dewy fields, but ere the Vicar's door
Was reached, the Solitary checked his steps;
Then, intermingling thanks, on each bestowed
A farewell salutation,—and, the like
Receiving, took the slender path that leads
To the one cottage in the lonely dell;
But turned not without welcome promise given,
That he would share the pleasures and pursuits
Of yet another summer's day, consumed
In wandering with us through the valleys fair,
And o'er the mountain-wastes. "Another sun,"
Said he, "shall shine upon us, ere we part,—
Another sun, and peradventure more;
If time, with free consent, is yours to give,—
And season favours."

To enfeebled power,
From this communion with uninjured minds,
What renovation had been brought; and what
Degree of healing to a wounded spirit,
Dejected, and habitually disposed
To seek, in degradation of the kind,
Excuse and solace for her own defects;
How far those erring notions were reformed;
And whether aught, of tendency as good
And pure, from further intercourse ensued;
This—(if delightful hopes, as heretofore,
Inspire the serious song, and gentle hearts
Cherish, and lofty minds approve the past)
My future labours may not leave untold.

YARROW REVISITED,

AND

OTHER POEMS,

COMPOSED (TWO EXCEPTED) DURING A TOUR IN SCOTLAND, AND ON THE ENGLISH BORDER, IN THE AUTUMN OF 1831.

YARROW REVISITED.

[The following Stanzas are a memorial of a day passed with Sir Walter Scott, and other Friends visiting the Banks of the Yarrow under his guidance, immediately before his departure from Abbotsford, for Naples.]

THE gallant Youth, who may have gained,
  Or seeks, a "Winsome Marrow,"
Was but an Infant in the lap
  When first I looked on Yarrow;
Once more, by Newark's Castle-gate
  Long left without a Warder,
I stood, looked, listened, and with Thee,
  Great Minstrel of the Border!

Grave thoughts ruled wide on that sweet day,
  Their dignity installing
In gentle bosoms, while sere leaves
  Were on the bough, or falling;
But breezes played, and sunshine gleamed—
  The forest to embolden;
Reddened the fiery hues, and shot
  Transparence through the golden.

For busy thoughts the Stream flowed on
  In foamy agitation;
And slept in many a crystal pool
  For quiet contemplation:
No public and no private care
  The freeborn mind enthralling,
We made a day of happy hours,
  Our happy days recalling.

Brisk Youth appeared, the Morn of youth,
  With freaks of graceful folly,—
Life's temperate Noon, her sober Eve
  Her Night not melancholy,
Past, present, future, all appeared
  In harmony united,
Like guests that meet, and some from far,
  By cordial love invited.

And if, as Yarrow, through the woods
  And down the meadow ranging,
Did meet us with unaltered face,
  Though we were changed and changing
If, *then*, some natural shadows spread
  Our inward prospect over,
The soul's deep valley was not slow
  Its brightness to recover.

Eternal blessings on the Muse,
  And her divine employment!
The blameless Muse, who trains her Sons
  For hope and calm enjoyment;
Albeit sickness lingering yet
  Has o'er their pillow brooded;
And Care waylay their steps—a Sprite
  Not easily eluded.

For thee, O SCOTT! compelled to change
  Green Eildon-hill and Cheviot
For warm Vesuvio's vine-clad slopes;
  And leave thy Tweed and Teviot
For mild Sorento's breezy waves;
  May classic Fancy, linking
With native Fancy her fresh aid,
  Preserve thy heart from sinking!

O! while they minister to thee,
  Each vying with the other,
May Health return to mellow Age,
  With Strength, her venturous brother;
And Tiber, and each brook and rill
  Renowned in song and story,
With unimagined beauty shine,
  Nor lose one ray of glory!

For Thou, upon a hundred streams,
  By tales of love and sorrow,
Of faithful love, undaunted truth,
  Hast shed the power of Yarrow;
And streams unknown, hills yet unseen,
  Where'er thy path invite thee,
At parent Nature's grateful call,
  With gladness must requite Thee.

A gracious welcome shall be thine,
  Such looks of love and honour
As thy own Yarrow gave to me
  When first I gazed upon her;
Beheld what I had feared to see,
  Unwilling to surrender
Dreams treasured up from early days,
  The holy and the tender.

And what, for this frail world, were all
  That mortals do or suffer,
Did no responsive harp, no pen,
  Memorial tribute offer?
Yea, what were mighty Nature's self?
  Her features, could they win us,
Unhelped by the poetic voice
  That hourly speaks within us?

Nor deem that localised Romance
  Plays false with our affections;
Unsanctifies our tears—made sport
  For fanciful dejections:
Ah, no! the visions of the past
  Sustain the heart in feeling
Life as she is—our changeful Life,
  With friends and kindred dealing.

Bear witness, Ye, whose thoughts that day
  In Yarrow's groves were center'd;
Who through the silent portal arch
  Of mouldering Newark enter'd,
And clomb the winding stair that once
  Too timidly was mounted
By the "last Minstrel," (not the last)
  Ere he his Tale recounted!

Flow on for ever, Yarrow Stream!
  Fulfil thy pensive duty,
Well pleased that future Bards should chant
  For simple hearts thy beauty,
To dream-light dear while yet unseen,
  Dear to the common sunshine,
And dearer still, as now I feel,
  To memory's shadowy moonshine!

SONNETS.

I.

ON THE DEPARTURE OF SIR WALTER SCOTT FROM ABBOTSFORD FOR NAPLES.

A TROUBLE, not of clouds, or weeping rain,
Nor of the setting sun's pathetic light
Engendered, hangs o'er Eildon's triple height:
Spirits of Power, assembled there, complain
For kindred Power departing from their sight;
While Tweed, best pleased in chanting a blithe strain,
Saddens his voice again, and yet again.
Lift up your hearts, ye Mourners! for the might
Of the whole world's good wishes with him goes;
Blessings and prayers in nobler retinue
Than sceptred King or laurelled Conqueror knows,
Follow this wondrous Potentate. Be true,
Ye winds of ocean, and the midland sea,
Wafting your Charge to soft Parthenope!

II.

A PLACE OF BURIAL IN THE SOUTH OF SCOTLAND.

PART fenced by man, part by a ragged steep
That curbs a foaming brook, a Grave-yard lies;
The Hare's best couching-place for fearless sleep;
Which moonlit Elves, far seen by credulous eyes,
Enter in dance. Of Church, or Sabbath ties,
No vestige now remains; yet thither creep
Bereft Ones, and in lowly anguish weep
Their prayers out to the wind and naked skies.
Proud tomb is none; but rudely-sculptured knights,
By humble choice of plain old times, are seen
Level with earth, among the hillocks green:
Union not sad, when sunny daybreak smites
The spangled turf, and neighbouring thickets ring
With *jubilate* from the choirs of spring!

III.

ON THE SIGHT OF A MANSE IN THE SOUTH OF SCOTLAND.

SAY, ye far-travelled clouds, far-seeing hills,
Among the happiest-looking Homes of men
Scatter'd all Britain over, through deep glen,
On airy upland, and by forest rills,
And o'er wide plains whereon the sky distils

Her lark's loved warblings; does aught meet your ken
More fit to animate the Poet's pen,
Aught that more surely by its aspect fills
Pure minds with sinless envy, than the Abode
Of the good Priest: who, faithful through all hours
To his high charge, and truly serving God,
Has yet a heart and hand for trees and flowers,
Enjoys the walks his Predecessors trod,
Nor covets lineal rights in lands and towers.

IV.

COMPOSED IN ROSLIN CHAPEL DURING A STORM.

THE wind is now thy organist;—a clank
(We know not whence) ministers for a bell
To mark some change of service. As the swell
Of music reached its height, and even when sank
The notes, in prelude, ROSLIN! to a blank
Of silence, how it thrilled thy sumptuous roof,
Pillars, and arches—not in vain time-proof,
Though Christian rites be wanting! From what bank
Came those live herbs? by what hand were they sown
Where dew falls not, where rain-drops seem unknown?
Yet in the Temple they a friendly niche
Share with their sculptured fellows, that, green-grown,
Copy their beauty more and more, and preach,
Though mute, of all things blending into one

V.

THE TROSSACHS.

THERE'S not a nook within this solemn Pass,
But were an apt confessional for One
Taught by his summer spent, his autumn gone,
That Life is but a tale of morning grass,
Withered at eve. From scenes of art that chase
That thought away, turn, and with watchful eyes
Feed it 'mid Nature's old felicities,
Rocks, rivers, and smooth lakes more clear than glass
Untouched, unbreathed upon. Thrice happy quest,
If from a golden perch of aspen spray
(October's workmanship to rival May)
The pensive warbler of the ruddy breast
This moral sweeten by a heaven-taught lay,
Lulling the year, with all its cares, to rest.

VI

THE Pibroch's note, discountenanced or mute,
The Roman kilt, degraded to a toy
Of quaint apparel for a half-spoilt boy;
The target mouldering like ungathered fruit,
The smoking steam-boat eager in pursuit,
As eagerly pursued; the umbrella spread
To weather-fend the Celtic herdsman's head—
All speak of manners withering to the root,
And some old honours, too, and passions high:
Then may we ask, though pleased that thought should range
Among the conquests of civility,
Survives imagination—to the change
Superior? Help to virtue does it give?
If not, O Mortals, better cease to live!

VII.

COMPOSED IN THE GLEN OF LOCH ETIVE.

THIS Land of Rainbows, spanning glens whose walls,
Rock-built, are hung with rainbow-coloured mists,
Of far-stretched meres, whose salt flood never rests,
Of tuneful caves and playful waterfalls,
Of mountains varying momently their crests—
Proud be this Land! whose poorest huts are halls
Where Fancy entertains becoming guests;
While native song the heroic Past recalls.
Thus, in the net of her own wishes caught,
The Muse exclaimed; but Story now must hide
Her trophies, Fancy crouch;—the course of pride
Has been diverted, other lessons taught,
That make the Patriot-spirit bow her head
Where the all-conquering Roman feared to tread

VIII.

EAGLES.

COMPOSED AT DUNOLLIE CASTLE, IN THE BAY OF OBAN.

DISHONOURED Rock and Ruin! that, by law
Tyrannic, keep the Bird of Jove embarred
Like a lone criminal whose life is spared.
Vexed is he, and screams aloud. The last I saw
Was on the wing; stooping, he struck with awe
Man, bird, and beast; then, with a consort paired,
From a bold headland, their loved aery's guard,
Flew high above Atlantic waves, to draw
Light from the fountain of the setting sun.
Such was this Prisoner once; and, when his plumes
The sea-blast ruffles as the storm comes on,
In spirit, for a moment, he resumes
His rank 'mong freeborn creatures that live free,
His power, his beauty, and his majesty.

IX.

IN THE SOUND OF MULL.

TRADITION, be thou mute! Oblivion, throw
Thy veil, in mercy, o'er the records hung
Round strath and mountain, stamped by the ancient tongue
On rock and ruin darkening as we go,—
Spots where a word, ghost-like, survives to show
What crimes from hate, or desperate love, have sprung;
From honour misconceived, or fancied wrong,
What feuds, not quenched but fed by mutual woe:
Yet, though a wild vindictive Race, untamed
By civil arts and labours of the pen,
Could gentleness be scorned by these fierce Men,
Who, to spread wide the reverence that they claimed
For patriarchal occupations, named
Yon towering Peaks, "Shepherds of Etive Glen?"*

X.

AT TYNDRUM.

ENOUGH of garlands, of the Arcadian crook,
And all that Greece and Italy have sung
Of Swains reposing myrtle groves among!
Ours couch on naked rocks, will cross a brook
Swoln with chill rains, nor ever cast a look
This way or that, or give it even a thought
More than by smoothest pathway may be brought
Into a vacant mind. Can written book
Teach what *they* learn? Up, hardy Mountaineer!
And guide the Bard, ambitious to be one
Of Nature's privy council, as thou art,
On cloud-sequestered heights, that see and hear
To what dread Power He delegates his part
On earth, who works in the heaven of heavens, alone.

XI.

THE EARL OF BREADALBANE'S RUINED MANSION, AND FAMILY BURIAL-PLACE, NEAR KILLIN.

WELL sang the Bard who called the Grave, in strains
Thoughtful and sad, the "Narrow House." No style
Of fond sepulchral flattery can beguile
Grief of her sting; nor cheat, where he detains
The sleeping dust, stern Death: how reconcile
With truth, or with each other, decked Remains
Of a once warm Abode, and that *new* Pile,
For the departed, built with curious pains
And mausolean pomp? Yet here they stand
Together,—'mid trim walks and artful bowers,
To be looked down upon by ancient hills,
That, for the living and the dead, demand
And prompt a harmony of genuine powers
Concord that elevates the mind, and stills.

XII.

REST AND BE THANKFUL, AT THE HEAD OF GLENCROE.

DOUBLING and doubling with laborious walk,
Who, that has gained at length the wished-for Height,
This brief this simple way-side call can slight,
And rest not thankful? Whether cheered by talk
With some loved Friend, or by the unseen Hawk
Whistling to clouds and sky-born streams, that shine
At the sun's outbreak, as with light divine

* In Gaelic, *Buachaill Eite*.

Ere they descend to nourish root and stalk
Of valley flowers Nor, while the limbs repose,
Will we forget that, as the Fowl can keep
Absolute stillness, poised aloft in air,
And Fishes front, unmoved, the torrent's sweep,—
So may the Soul, through powers that Faith bestows,
Win rest, and ease, and peace, with bliss that Angels share.

XIII.

HIGHLAND HUT.

SEE what gay wild flowers deck this earth-built Cot,
Whose smoke, forth-issuing whence and how it may,
Shines in the greeting of the Sun's first ray
Like wreaths of vapour without stain or blot.
The limpid mountain rill avoids it not,
And why shouldst thou? If rightly trained and bred,
Humanity is humble,—finds no spot
Which her Heaven-guided feet refuse to tread.
The walls are cracked, sunk is the flowery roof,
Undressed the pathway leading to the door,
But love, as Nature loves, the lonely Poor;
Search, for their worth, some gentle heart wrong-proof,
Meek, patient, kind, and, were its trials fewer,
Belike less happy.—Stand no more aloof!

XIV.

THE BROWNIE.

[Upon a small island not far from the head of Loch Lomond, are some remains of an ancient building, which was for several years the abode of a solitary Individual, one of the last survivors of the Clan of Macfarlane, once powerful in that neighbourhood Passing along the shore opposite this island in the year 1814, the Author learned these particulars, and that this person then living there had acquired the appellation of "*The Brownie*" The following Sonnet is a sequel to the Brownie's Cell, p. 156]

"How disappeared he?" Ask the newt and toad;
Ask of his fellow men, and they will tell
How he was found, cold as an icicle,
Under an arch of that forlorn abode;
Where he, unpropp'd, and by the gathering flood
Of years hemm'd round, had dwelt, prepared to try
Privation's worst extremities, and die
With no one near save the omnipresent God.
Verily so to live was an awful choice—
A choice that wears the aspect of a doom;
But in the mould of mercy all is cast
For Souls familiar with the eternal Voice;
And this forgotten Taper to the last
Drove from itself, we trust, all frightful gloom.

XV.

TO THE PLANET VENUS, AN EVENING STAR.

COMPOSED AT LOCH LOMOND.

THOUGH joy attend thee orient at the birth
Of dawn, it cheers the lofty spirit most
To watch thy course when Day-light, fled from earth,
In the grey sky hath left his lingering ghost,
Perplexed as if between a splendour lost
And splendour slowly mustering Since the Sun,
The absolute, the world-absorbing One,
Relinquished half his empire to the host
Emboldened by thy guidance, holy Star,
Holy as princely, who that looks on thee
Touching, as now, in thy humility
The mountain borders of this seat of care,
Can question that thy countenance is bright,
Celestial Power, as much with love as light?

XVI.

BOTHWELL CASTLE.

IMMURED in Bothwell's Towers, at times the Brave
(So beautiful is Clyde) forgot to mourn
The liberty they lost at Bannockbourn.
Once on those steeps *I* roamed at large, and have
In mind the landscape, as if still in sight;
The river glides, the woods before me wave;
But, by occasion tempted, now I crave
Needless renewal of an old delight.
Better to thank a dear and long-past day
For joy its sunny hours were free to give
Than blame the present, that our wish hath crost.
Memory, like Sleep, hath powers which dreams obey,
Dreams, vivid dreams, that are not fugitive:
How little that she cherishes is lost!

XVII.

PICTURE OF DANIEL IN THE LION'S DEN AT HAMILTON PALACE.

AMID a fertile region green with wood
And fresh with rivers, well doth it become
The Ducal Owner, in his Palace-home
To naturalise this tawny Lion brood;
Children of Art, that claim strange brotherhood,
Couched in their Den, with those that roam at large
Over the burning wilderness, and charge
The wind with terror while they roar for food.
But *these* are satiate, and a stillness drear
Calls into life a more enduring fear;
Yet is the Prophet calm, nor would the cave
Daunt him—if his Companions, now bedrowsed
Yawning and listless, were by hunger roused:
Man placed him here, and God, he knows, can save.

XVIII.

THE AVON (*a feeder of the Annan*).

AVON—a precious, an immortal name!
Yet is it one that other Rivulets bear
Like this unheard-of, and their channels wear
Like this contented, though unknown to Fame·
For great and sacred is the modest claim
Of streams to Nature's love, where'er they flow;
And ne'er did genius slight them, as they go,
Tree, flower, and green herb, feeding without blame.
But Praise can waste her voice on work of tears,
Anguish, and death: full oft where innocent blood
Has mixed its current with the limpid flood,
Her heaven-offending trophies Glory rears;
Never for like distinction may the good
Shrink from *thy* name, pure Rill, with unpleased ears!

XIX.

SUGGESTED BY A VIEW FROM AN EMINENCE IN INGLEWOOD FOREST.

THE forest huge of ancient Caledon
Is but a name, nor more is Inglewood,
That swept from hill to hill, from flood to flood:
On her last thorn the nightly Moon has shone,
Yet still, though unappropriate Wild be none
Fair parks spread wide where Adam Bell might deign
With Clym o' the Clough, were they alive again,
To kill for merry feast their venison.
Nor wants the holy Abbot's gliding Shade
His Church with monumental wreck bestrown;
The feudal Warrior-chief, a Ghost unlaid,
Hath still his Castle, though a Skeleton,
That he may watch by night, and lessons con
Of Power that perishes, and Rights that fade.

XX.

HART'S-HORN TREE, NEAR PENRITH.

HERE stood an Oak, that long had borne affixed
To his huge trunk, or, with more subtle art,
Among its withering topmost branches mixed,
The palmy antlers of a hunted Hart,
Whom the dog Hercules pursued—his part
Each desperately sustaining, till at last
Both sank and died, the life-veins of the chased
And chaser bursting here with one dire smart.
Mutual the Victory, mutual the Defeat!
High was the trophy hung with pitiless pride;
Say, rather, with that generous sympathy
That wants not, even in rudest breasts, a seat;
And, for this feeling's sake, let no one chide
Verse that would guard thy memory, *Hart's-horn Tree!*

XXI

COUNTESS'S PILLAR.

[On the roadside between Penrith and Appleby, there stands a pillar with the following inscription:—

"This pillar was erected, in the year 1656, by Anne Countess Dowager of Pembroke, &c, for a memorial of her last parting with her pious mother, Margaret Countess Dowager of Cumberland, on the 2nd of April, 1616; in memory whereof she hath left an annuity of 4*l* to be distributed to the poor of the parish of Brougham, every 2nd day of April for ever, upon the stone table placed hard by. Laus Deo!"]

WHILE the Poor gather round, till the end of time
May this bright flower of Charity display
Its bloom, unfolding at the appointed day;

Flower than the loveliest of the vernal prime
Lovelier—transplanted from heaven's purest clime!
"Charity never faileth." on that creed,
More than on written testament or deed,
The pious Lady built with hope sublime.
Alms on this stone to be dealt out, *for ever!*
"*Laus Deo.*" Many a Stranger passing by
Has with that parting mixed a filial sigh,
Blest its humane Memorial's fond endeavour;
And, fastening on those lines an eye tear-glazed,
Has ended, though no Clerk, with "God be praised!"

XXII.

ROMAN ANTIQUITIES.

(FROM THE ROMAN STATION AT OLD PENRITH.)

How profitless the relics that we cull,
Troubling the last holds of ambitious Rome,
Unless they chasten fancies that presume
Too high, or idle agitations lull!
Of the world's flatteries if the brain be full,
To have no seat for thought were better doom,
Like this old helmet, or the eyeless skull
Of him who gloried in its nodding plume
Heaven out of view, our wishes what are they?
Our fond regrets, insatiate in their grasp?
The Sage's theory? the Poet's lay?
Mere Fibulæ without a robe to clasp;
Obsolete lamps, whose light no time recalls;
Urns without ashes, tearless lacrymals!

APOLOGY.

No more: the end is sudden and abrupt,
Abrupt—as without preconceived design
Was the beginning, yet the several Lays
Have moved in order, to each other bound
By a continuous and acknowledged tie
Though unapparent, like those Shapes distinct
That yet survive ensculptured on the walls
Of Palace, or of Temple, 'mid the wreck
Of famed Persepolis; each following each,
As might beseem a stately embassy,
In set array; these bearing in their hands
Ensign of civil power, weapon of war,
Or gift, to be presented at the Throne
Of the Great King; and others, as they go
In priestly vest, with holy offerings charged,
Or leading victims drest for sacrifice,
Nor will the Muse condemn, or treat with scorn
Our ministration, humble but sincere,
That from a threshold loved by every Muse
Its impulse took—that sorrow-stricken door,
Whence, as a current from its fountain head,
Our thoughts have issued, and our feelings flowed,
Receiving, willingly or not, fresh strength
From kindred sources; while around us sighed
(Life's three first seasons having passed away)
Leaf-scattering winds, and hoar-frost sprinklings fell,
Foretaste of winter, on the moorland heights;
And every day brought with it tidings new
Of rash change, ominous for the public weal.
Hence, if dejection have too oft encroached
Upon that sweet and tender melancholy
Which may itself be cherished and caressed
More than enough, a fault so natural,
Even with the young the hopeful or the gay,
For prompt forgiveness will not sue in vain.

THE HIGHLAND BROACH.

If to Tradition faith be due,
And echoes from old verse speak true,
Ere the meek Saint, Columba, bore
Glad tidings to Iona's shore,
No common light of nature blessed
The mountain region of the west,
A land where gentle manners ruled
O'er men in dauntless virtues schooled,
That raised, for centuries, a bar
Impervious to the tide of war;
Yet peaceful Arts did entrance gain
Where haughty Force had striven in vain,
And, 'mid the works of skilful hands,
By wanderers brought from foreign lands
And various climes, was not unknown
The clasp that fixed the Roman Gown;
The Fibula, whose shape, I ween,
Still in the Highland Broach is seen,
The silver Broach of massy frame,
Worn at the breast of some grave Dame
On road or path, or at the door
Of fern-thatched Hut on heathy moor:
But delicate of yore its mould,
And the material finest gold;

As might beseem the fairest Fair,
Whether she graced a royal chair,
Or shed, within a vaulted Hall,
No fancied lustre on the wall
Where shields of mighty Heroes hung,
While Fingal heard what Ossian sung.

The heroic Age expired—it slept
Deep in its tomb:—the bramble crept
O'er Fingal's hearth; the grassy sod
Grew on the floors his Sons had trod:
Malvina! where art thou? Their state
The noblest-born must abdicate,
The fairest, while with fire and sword
Come Spoilers—horde impelling horde,
Must walk the sorrowing mountains, drest
By ruder hands in homelier vest.
Yet still the female bosom lent,
And loved to borrow, ornament;
Still was its inner world a place
Reached by the dews of heavenly grace;
Still pity to this last retreat
Clove fondly; to his favourite seat
Love wound his way by soft approach,
Beneath a massier Highland Broach.

When alternations came of rage
Yet fiercer, in a darker age;
And feuds, where, clan encountering clan,
The weaker perished to a man;
For maid and mother, when despair
Might else have triumphed, baffling prayer,
One small *possession* lacked not power,
Provided in a calmer hour,
To meet such need as might befall—
Roof, raiment, bread, or burial:
For woman, even of tears bereft,
The hidden silver Broach was left.

As generations come and go,
Their arts, their customs, ebb and flow;
Fate, fortune, sweep strong powers away,
And feeble, of themselves, decay;
What poor abodes the heir-loom hide,
In which the castle once took pride!
Tokens, once kept as boasted wealth,
If saved at all, are saved by stealth.
Lo! ships, from seas by nature barred,
Mount along ways by man prepared;
And in far-stretching vales, whose streams
Seek other seas, their canvas gleams.
Lo! busy towns spring up, on coasts
Thronged yesterday by airy ghosts;
Soon, like a lingering star forlorn
Among the novelties of morn,
While young delights on old encroach,
Will vanish the last Highland Broach.

But when, from out their viewless bed,
Like vapours, years have rolled and spread
And this poor verse, and worthier lays,
Shall yield no light of love or praise,
Then, by the spade, or cleaving plough,
Or torrent from the mountain's brow,
Or whirlwind, reckless what his might
Entombs, or forces into light,
Blind Chance, a volunteer ally,
That oft befriends Antiquity,
And clears Oblivion from reproach,
May render back the Highland Broach.

THE EGYPTIAN MAID;

OR,

THE ROMANCE OF THE WATER LILY.

[For the names and persons in the following poem, see the "History of the renowned Prince Arthur and his Knights of the Round Table;" for the rest the Author is answerable; only it may be proper to add, that the Lotus, with the bust of the goddess appearing to rise out of the full-blown flower, was suggested by the beautiful work of ancient art, once included among the Townley Marbles, and now in the British Museum.]

While Merlin paced the Cornish sands,
Forth-looking toward the Rocks of Scilly,
The pleased Enchanter was aware
Of a bright Ship that seemed to hang in air,
Yet was she work of mortal hands,
And took from men her name—The Water Lily.

Such was the wind, that landward blew;
And, as the Moon, o'er some dark hill ascendant,
Grows from a little edge of light
To a full orb, this Pinnace bright
Became, as nearer to the Coast she drew,
More glorious, with spread sail and streaming pendant.

Upon this winged Shape so fair
Sage Merlin gazed with admiration:
Her lineaments, thought he, surpass
Aught that was ever shown in magic glass;
Was ever built with subtle care;
Or, at a touch, set forth with wondrous transformation.

Now, though a Mechanist, whose skill
Shames the degenerate grasp of modern science,
Grave Merlin (and belike the more
For practising occult and perilous lore)
Was subject to a freakish will
That sapped good thoughts, or scared them with defiance.

Provoked to envious spleen, he cast
An altered look upon the advancing Stranger
Whom he had hailed with joy, and cried,
"My Art shall help to tame her pride—"
Anon the breeze became a blast,
And the waves rose, and sky portended danger.

With thrilling word, and potent sign
Traced on the beach, his work the Sorcerer urges;
The clouds in blacker clouds are lost,
Like spiteful Fiends that vanish, crossed
By Fiends of aspect more malign;
And the winds roused the Deep with fiercer scourges.

But worthy of the name she bore
Was this Sea-flower, this buoyant Galley;
Supreme in loveliness and grace
Of motion, whether in the embrace
Of trusty anchorage, or scudding o'er
The main flood roughened into hill and valley.

Behold, how wantonly she laves
Her sides, the Wizard's craft confounding;
Like something out of Ocean sprung
To be for ever fresh and young,
Breasts the sea-flashes, and huge waves
Top-gallant high, rebounding and rebounding!

But Ocean under magic heaves,
And cannot spare the Thing he cherished:
Ah! what avails that She was fair,
Luminous, blithe, and debonair?
The storm has stripped her of her leaves;
The Lily floats no longer!—She hath perished.

Grieve for her,—She deserves no less;
So like, yet so unlike, a living Creature!
No heart had she, no busy brain;
Though loved, she could not love again;
Though pitied, *feel* her own distress;
Nor aught that troubles us, the fools of Nature.

Yet is there cause for gushing tears;
So richly was this Galley laden;
A fairer than Herself she bore,
And, in her struggles, cast ashore;
A lovely One, who nothing hears
Of wind or wave—a meek and guileless Maiden.

Into a cave had Merlin fled
From mischief, caused by spells himself had muttered;
And, while repentant all too late,
In moody posture there he sate,
He heard a voice, and saw, with half-raised head,
A Visitant by whom these words were uttered:

"On Christian service this frail Bark
Sailed" (hear me, Merlin!) "under high protection,
Though on her prow a sign of heathen power
Was carved—a Goddess with a Lily flower
The old Egyptian's emblematic mark
Of joy immortal and of pure affection.

"Her course was for the British strand,
Her freight it was a Damsel peerless;
God reigns above, and Spirits strong
May gather to avenge this wrong
Done to the Princess, and her Land
Which she in duty left, though sad not cheerless.

"And to Caerleon's loftiest tower
Soon will the Knights of Arthur's Table
A cry of lamentation send,
And all will weep who there attend,
To grace that Stranger's bridal hour,
For whom the sea was made unnavigable

"Shame! should a Child of Royal Line
Die through the blindness of thy malice."
Thus to the Necromancer spake
Nina, the Lady of the Lake,
A gentle Sorceress, and benign,
Who ne'er embittered any good man's chalice

"What boots," continued she, "to mourn?
To expiate thy sin endeavour!
From the bleak isle where she is laid,
Fetched by our art, the Egyptian Maid
May yet to Arthur's court be borne
Cold as she is, ere life be fled for ever.

"My pearly Boat, a shining Light,
That brought me down that sunless river,
Will bear me on from wave to wave,
And back with her to this sea-cave;
Then Merlin! for a rapid flight
Through air to thee my charge will I deliver.

"The very swiftest of thy Cars
Must, when my part is done, be ready;
Meanwhile, for further guidance, look
Into thy own prophetic book;
And, if that fail, consult the Stars
To learn thy course, farewell! be prompt and steady."

This scarcely spoken, she again
Was seated in her gleaming Shallop,
That, o'er the yet-distempered Deep,
Pursued its way with bird-like sweep,
Or like a steed, without a rein,
Urged o'er the wilderness in sportive gallop.

Soon did the gentle Nina reach
That Isle without a house or haven;
Landing, she found not what she sought,
Nor saw of wreck or ruin aught
But a carved Lotus cast upon the shore
By the fierce waves, a flower in marble graven.

Sad relique, but how fair the while!
For gently each from each retreating
With backward curve, the leaves revealed
The bosom half, and half concealed,
Of a Divinity, that seemed to smile
On Nina as she passed, with hopeful greeting.

No quest was hers of vague desire,
Of tortured hope and purpose shaken,
Following the margin of a bay,
She spied the lonely Cast-away,
Unmarred, unstripped of her attire,
But with closed eyes,—of breath and bloom forsaken.

Then Nina, stooping down, embraced,
With tenderness and mild emotion,
The Damsel, in that trance embound;
And, while she raised her from the ground,
And in the pearly shallop placed,
Sleep fell upon the air, and stilled the ocean

The turmoil hushed, celestial springs
Of music opened, and there came a blending
Of fragrance, underived from earth,
With gleams that owed not to the Sun their birth.
And that soft rustling of invisible wings
Which Angels make, on works of love descending.

And Nina heard a sweeter voice
Than if the Goddess of the Flower had spoken:
"Thou hast achieved, fair Dame! what none
Less pure in spirit could have done;
Go, in thy enterprise rejoice!
Air, earth, sea, sky, and heaven, success betoken"

So cheered she left that Island bleak,
A bare rock of the Scilly cluster;
And, as they traversed the smooth brine,
The self-illumined Brigantine
Shed, on the Slumberer's cold wan cheek
And pallid brow, a melancholy lustre.

Fleet was their course, and when they came
To the dim cavern, whence the river
Issued into the salt-sea flood,
Merlin, as fixed in thought he stood,
Was thus accosted by the Dame:
"Behold to thee my Charge I now deliver

"But where attends thy chariot—where?"
Quoth Merlin, "Even as I was bidden,
So have I done; as trusty as thy barge
My vehicle shall prove—O precious Charge!
If this be sleep, how soft! if death, how fair!
Much have my books disclosed, but the end is hidden."

He spake, and gliding into view
Forth from the grotto's dimmest chamber
Came two mute Swans, whose plumes of dusky white
Changed, as the pair approached the light,
Drawing an ebon car, their hue
(Like clouds of sunset) into lucid amber

Once more did gentle Nina lift
The Princess, passive to all changes:
The car received her; then up-went
Into the ethereal element
The Birds with progress smooth and swift
As thought, when through bright regions memory ranges.

Sage Merlin, at the Slumberer's side,
Instructs the Swans their way to measure;
And soon Caerleon's towers appeared,
And notes of minstrelsy were heard

From rich pavilions spreading wide,
For some high day of long-expected pleasure.

Awe-stricken stood both Knights and Dames
Ere on firm ground the car alighted:
Eftsoons astonishment was past,
For in that face they saw the last
Last lingering look of clay, that tames
All pride, by which all happiness is blighted.

Said Merlin, "Mighty King, fair Lords,
Away with feast and tilt and tourney!
Ye saw, throughout this Royal House,
Ye heard, a rocking marvellous
Of turrets, and a clash of swords
Self-shaken, as I closed my airy journey.

"Lo! by a destiny well known
To mortals, joy is turned to sorrow;
This is the wished-for Bride, the Maid
Of Egypt, from a rock conveyed
Where she by shipwreck had been thrown;
Ill sight! but grief may vanish ere the morrow."

"Though vast thy power, thy words are weak,"
Exclaimed the King, "a mockery hateful;
Dutiful Child! her lot how hard!
Is this her piety's reward?
Those watery locks, that bloodless cheek!
O winds without remorse! O shore ungrateful!

"Rich robes are fretted by the moth,
Towers, temples, fall by stroke of thunder;
Will that, or deeper thoughts, abate
A Father's sorrow for her fate?
He will repent him of his troth;
His brain will burn, his stout heart split asunder.

"Alas! and I have caused this woe;
For, when my prowess from invading Neighbours
Had freed his Realm, he plighted word
That he would turn to Christ our Lord,
And his dear Daughter on a Knight bestow
Whom I should choose for love and matchless labours

"Her birth was heathen, but a fence
Of holy Angels round her hovered,
A Lady added to my court
So fair, of such divine report
And worship, seemed a recompence
For fifty kingdoms by my sword recovered.

"Ask not for whom, O champions true!
She was reserved by me her life's betrayer,
She who was meant to be a bride
Is now a corse, then put aside
Vain thoughts, and speed ye, with observance due
Of Christian rites, in Christian ground to lay her"

"The tomb,' said Merlin, "may not close
Upon her yet, earth hide her beauty;
Not froward to thy sovereign will
Esteem me, Liege! if I, whose skill
Wafted her hither, interpose
To check this pious haste of erring duty

"My books command me to lay bare
The secret thou art bent on keeping;
Here must a high attest be given,
What Bridegroom was for her ordained by Heaven;
And in my glass significants there are
Of things that may to gladness turn this weeping.

"For this, approaching, One by One,
Thy Knights must touch the cold hand of the Virgin;
So, for the favoured One, the Flower may bloom
Once more; but, if unchangeable her doom,
If life departed be for ever gone,
Some blessed assurance, from this cloud emerging,

"May teach him to bewail his loss,
Not with a grief that, like a vapour, rises
And melts; but grief devout that shall endure
And a perpetual growth secure
Of purposes which no false thought shall cross
A harvest of high hopes and noble enterprises"

"So be it," said the King,—"anon,
Here, where the Princess lies, begin the trial;
Knights each in order as ye stand
Step forth."—To touch the pallid hand
Sir Agravaine advanced; no sign he won
From Heaven or Earth,—Sir Kaye had like denial

Abashed, Sir Dinas turned away;
Even for Sir Percival was no disclosure;
Though he, devoutest of all Champions, ere
He reached the ebon car, the bier

Whereon diffused like snow the Damsel lay,
Full thrice had crossed himself in meek composure.

Imagine (but ye Saints! who can?)
How in still air the balance trembled;
The wishes, peradventure the despites
That overcame some not ungenerous Knights;
And all the thoughts that lengthened out a span
Of time to Lords and Ladies thus assembled.

What patient confidence was here!
And there how many bosoms panted!
While drawing toward the Car Sir Gawaine, mailed
For tournament, his Beaver vailed,
And softly touched, but, to his princely cheer
And high expectancy, no sign was granted.

Next, disencumbered of his harp,
Sir Tristram, dear to thousands as a brother,
Came to the proof, nor grieved that there ensued
No change,—the fair Izonda he had wooed
With love too true, a love with pangs too sharp,
From hope too distant, not to dread another.

Not so Sir Launcelot,—from Heaven's grace
A sign he craved, tired slave of vain contrition,
The royal Guinever looked passing glad
When his touch failed.—Next came Sir Galahad;
He paused, and stood entranced by that still face
Whose features he had seen in noontide vision.

For late, as near a murmuring stream
He rested 'mid an arbour green and shady,
Nina, the good Enchantress, shed
A light around his mossy bed;
And, at her call, a waking dream
Prefigured to his sense the Egyptian Lady.

Now, while his bright-haired front he bowed,
And stood, far-kenned by mantle furred with ermine,
As o'er the insensate Body hung
The enrapt, the beautiful, the young
Belief sank deep into the crowd
That he the solemn issue would determine.

Nor deem it strange, the Youth had worn
That very mantle on a day of glory,
The day when he achieved that matchless feat,
The marvel of the PERILOUS SEAT,
Which whosoe'er approached of strength was shorn,
Though King or Knight the most renowned in story.

He touched with hesitating hand,
And lo! those Birds, far-famed through Love's dominions,
The Swans, in triumph clap their wings;
And their necks play, involved in rings,
Like sinless snakes in Eden's happy land;—
"Mine is she," cried the Knight;—again they clapped their pinions.

"Mine was she—mine she is, though dead,
And to her name my soul shall cleave in sorrow;"
Whereat, a tender twilight streak
Of colour dawned upon the Damsel's cheek;
And her lips, quickening with uncertain red,
Seemed from each other a faint warmth to borrow.

Deep was the awe, the rapture high,
Of love emboldened, hope with dread entwining,
When, to the mouth, relenting Death
Allowed a soft and flower-like breath,
Precursor to a timid sigh,
To lifted eyelids, and a doubtful shining.

In silence did King Arthur gaze
Upon the signs that pass away or tarry;
In silence watched the gentle strife
Of Nature leading back to life,
Then eased his Soul at length by praise
Of God, and Heaven's pure Queen—the blissful Mary.

Then said he, "Take her to thy heart
Sir Galahad! a treasure that God giveth,
Bound by indissoluble ties to thee
Through mortal change and immortality;
Be happy and unenvied, thou who art
A goodly Knight that hath no Peer that liveth!"

Not long the Nuptials were delayed,
And sage tradition still rehearses
The pomp the glory of that hour
When toward the Altar from her bower
King Arthur led the Egyptian Maid,
And Angels carolled these far-echoed verses:—

Who shrinks not from alliance
Of evil with good Powers,
To God proclaims defiance,
And mocks whom he adores

A Ship to Christ devoted
From the Land of Nile did go,
Alas! the bright Ship floated,
An idol at her Prow.

By magic domination,
The Heaven-permitted vent
Of purblind mortal passion,
Was wrought her punishment.

The Flower, the Form within it,
What served they in her need?
Her port she could not win it,
Nor from mishap be freed.

The tempest overcame her,
And she was seen no more;
But gently gently blame her,
She cast a Pearl ashore.

The Maid to Jesu hearkened,
And kept to him her faith,
Till sense in death was darkened,
Or sleep akin to death

But Angels round her pillow
Kept watch, a viewless band;
And, billow favouring billow,
She reached the destined strand.

Blest Pair! whate'er befall you,
Your faith in Him approve
Who from frail earth can call you,
To bowers of endless love!

ODE,

COMPOSED ON MAY MORNING.

While from the purpling east departs
The Star that led the dawn,
Blithe Flora from her couch upstarts,
For May is on the lawn.
A quickening hope, a freshening glee,
Foreran the expected Power,
Whose first-drawn breath, from bush and tree,
Shakes off that pearly shower.

All Nature welcomes Her whose sway
Tempers the year's extremes,
Who scattereth lustres o'er noon-day,
Like morning's dewy gleams;
While mellow warble, sprightly trill,
The tremulous heart excite;
And hums the balmy air to still
The balance of delight.

Time was, blest Power! when Youths and Maids
At peep of dawn would rise,
And wander forth in forest glades
Thy birth to solemnize
Though mute the song—to grace the rite
Untouched the hawthorn bough,
Thy Spirit triumphs o'er the slight,
Man changes, but not Thou!

Thy feathered Lieges bill and wings
In love's disport employ,
Warmed by thy influence, creeping Things
Awake to silent joy:
Queen art thou still for each gay Plant
Where the slim wild Deer roves;
And served in depths where Fishes haunt
Their own mysterious groves.

Cloud-piercing Peak, and trackless Heath
Instinctive homage pay;
Nor wants the dim-lit Cave a wreath
To honour Thee, sweet May!
Where Cities fanned by thy brisk airs
Behold a smokeless sky,
Their puniest Flower-pot-nursling dares
To open a bright eye.

And if, on this thy natal morn,
The Pole, from which thy name
Hath not departed, stands forlorn
Of song and dance and game,
Still from the village-green a vow
Aspires to thee addrest,
Wherever peace is on the brow,
Or love within the breast

Yes! where Love nestles thou canst teach
The soul to love the more,
Hearts also shall thy lessons reach
That never loved before.
Stript is the haughty One of pride,
The bashful freed from fear,
While rising, like the ocean-tide,
In flows the joyous year.

Hush, feeble lyre! weak words, refuse
  The service to prolong!
To yon exulting Thrush the Muse
  Intrusts the imperfect song;
His voice shall chant, in accents clear,
  Throughout the live-long day,
Till the first silver Star appear,
  The sovereignty of May.

TO MAY.

THOUGH many suns have risen and set
  Since thou, blithe May, wert born,
And Bards, who hailed thee, may forget
  Thy gifts, thy beauty scorn;
There are who to a birthday strain
  Confine not harp and voice,
But evermore throughout thy reign
  Are grateful and rejoice!

Delicious odours! music sweet,
  Too sweet to pass away!
Oh for a deathless song to meet
  The soul's desire—a lay
That, when a thousand years are told,
  Should praise thee, genial Power!
Through summer heat, autumnal cold,
  And winter's dreariest hour.

Earth, Sea, thy presence feel—nor less
  If yon ethereal blue
With its soft smile the truth express,
  The Heavens have felt it too.
The inmost heart of man if glad
  Partakes a livelier cheer;
And eyes that cannot but be sad
  Let fall a brightened tear.

Since thy return, through days and weeks
  Of hope that grew by stealth,
How many wan and faded cheeks
  Have kindled into health!
The Old, by thee revived, have said,
  "Another year is ours;"
And wayworn Wanderers, poorly fed,
  Have smiled upon thy flowers.

Who tripping lisps a merry song
  Amid his playful peers?
The tender Infant who was long
  A prisoner of fond fears;
But now, when every sharp-edged blast
  Is quiet in its sheath,
His Mother leaves him free to taste
  Earth's sweetness in thy breath.

Thy help is with the Weed that creeps
  Along the humblest ground,
No Cliff so bare but on its steeps
  Thy favours may be found,
But most on some peculiar nook
  That our own hands have drest,
Thou and thy train are proud to look,
  And seem to love it best.

And yet how pleased we wander forth
  When May is whispering, "Come!
Choose from the bowers of virgin earth
  The happiest for your home;
Heaven's bounteous love throngh me is spread
  From sunshine, clouds, winds, waves,
Drops on the mouldering turret's head,
  And on your turf-clad graves!"

Such greeting heard, away with sighs
  For lilies that must fade,
Or "the rathe primrose as it dies
  Forsaken" in the shade!
Vernal fruitions and desires
  Are linked in endless chase;
While, as one kindly growth retires,
  Another takes its place.

And what if thou, sweet May, hast known
  Mishap by worm and blight,
If expectations newly blown
  Have perished in thy sight;
If loves and joys, while up they sprung,
  Were caught as in a snare;
Such is the lot of all the young,
  However bright and fair.

Lo! Streams that April could not check
  Are patient of thy rule;
Gurgling in foamy water-break,
  Loitering in glassy pool:
By thee, thee only, could be sent
  Such gentle Mists as glide,
Curling with unconfirmed intent,
  On that green mountain's side

How delicate the leafy veil
  Through which yon House of God
Gleams 'mid the peace of this deep dale
  By few but shepherds trod!
And lowly Huts, near beaten ways,
  No sooner stand attired
In thy fresh wreaths, than they for praise
  Peep forth, and are admired.

Season of fancy and of hope,
  Permit not for one hour
A blossom from thy crown to drop,
  Nor add to it a flower!

Keep, lovely May, as if by touch
  Of self-restraining art,
This modest charm of not too much,
  Part seen, imagined part!

INSCRIPTION.

THE massy Ways, carried across these Heights
By Roman Perseverance, are destroyed,
Or hidden under ground, like sleeping worms.
How venture then to hope that Time will spare
This humble Walk? Yet on the mountain's side
A Poet's hand first shaped it; and the steps
Of that same Bard, repeated to and fro
At morn, at noon, and under moonlight skies,
Through the vicissitudes of many a year,
Forbade the weeds to creep o'er its grey line.
No longer, scattering to the heedless winds
The vocal raptures of fresh poesy,
Shall he frequent these precincts; locked no more
In earnest converse with beloved Friends,
Here will he gather stores of ready bliss,
As from the beds and borders of a garden
Choice flowers are gathered! But, if Power may spring
Out of a farewell yearning favoured more
Than kindred wishes mated suitably
With vain regrets, the Exile would consign
This Walk, his loved possession, to the care
Of those pure Minds that reverence the Muse.

ELEGIAC MUSINGS

IN THE GROUNDS OF COLEORTON HALL, THE SEAT OF THE LATE SIR GEORGE BEAUMONT, BART.

[In these grounds stands the Parish Church, wherein is a mural monument, the Inscription upon which, in deference to the earnest request of the deceased, is confined to name, dates, and these words:—"Enter not into judgment with thy servant, O LORD!"]

WITH copious eulogy in prose and rhyme
Graven on the tomb we struggle against Time,
Alas, how feebly! but our feelings rise
And still we struggle when a good man dies:
Such offering BEAUMONT dreaded and forbade,
A spirit meek in self-abasement clad.
Yet *here* at least, though few have numbered days
That shunned so modestly the light of praise,
His graceful manners, and the temperate ray
Of that arch fancy which would round him play,
Brightening a converse never known to swerve
From courtesy and delicate reserve;
That sense—the bland philosophy of life
Which checked discussion ere it warmed to strife;
Those fine accomplishments, and varied powers,
Might have their record among sylvan bowers.
—Oh, fled for ever! vanished like a blast
That shook the leaves in myriads as it passed;
Gone from this world of earth, air, sea, and sky,
From all its spirit-moving imagery,
Intensely studied with a Painter's eye,
A Poet's heart; and, for congenial view,
Portrayed with happiest pencil, not untrue
To common recognitions while the line
Flowed in a course of sympathy divine—
Oh! severed too abruptly from delights
That all the seasons shared with equal rights—
Rapt in the grace of undismantled age,
From soul-felt music, and the treasured page,
Lit by that evening lamp which loved to shed
Its mellow lustre round thy honoured head,
While Friends beheld thee give with eye, voice, mien,
More than theatric force to Shakspeare's scene—
Rebuke us not!—The mandate is obeyed
That said, "Let praise be mute where I am laid;"
The holier deprecation, given in trust
To the cold Marble, waits upon thy dust;
Yet have we found how slowly genuine grief
From *silent* admiration wins relief.
Too long abashed thy Name is like a Rose
That doth "within itself its sweetness close;"
A drooping Daisy changed into a cup
In which her bright-eyed beauty is shut up.
Within these Groves, where still are flitting by
Shades of the Past, oft noticed with a sigh,

Shall stand a votive Tablet, haply free,
When towers and temples fall, to speak of Thee!
If sculptured emblems of our mortal doom
Recall not there the wisdom of the Tomb,
Green ivy, risen from out the cheerful earth,
Shall fringe the lettered stone; and herbs spring forth,
Whose fragrance, by soft dews and rain unbound,
Shall penetrate the heart without a wound;
While truth and love their purposes fulfil,
Commemorating genius, talent, skill,
That could not lie concealed where Thou wert known;
Thy virtues *He* must judge, and *He* alone,
The God upon whose mercy they are thrown.

EPITAPH.

By a blest Husband guided Mary came
From nearest kindred, Vernon her new name;
She came; though meek of soul, in seemly pride
Of happiness and hope, a youthful Bride.
O dread reverse! if aught *be* so, which proves
That God will chasten whom he dearly loves.
Faith bore her up through pains in mercy given,
And troubles that were each a step to Heaven:
Two Babes were laid in earth before she died;
A third now slumbers at the Mother's side;
Its Sister-twin survives, whose smiles afford
A trembling solace to her widowed Lord.

Reader! if to thy bosom cling the pain
Of recent sorrow combated in vain;
Or if thy cherished grief have failed to thwart
Time still intent on his insidious part,
Lulling the Mourner's best good thoughts asleep,
Pilfering regrets we would, but cannot, keep;
Bear with Him—judge *Him* gently who makes known
His bitter loss by this memorial Stone;
And pray that in his faithful breast the grace
Of resignation find a hallowed place.

INSCRIPTION

INTENDED FOR A STONE IN THE GROUNDS OF RYDAL MOUNT.

In these fair Vales hath many a Tree
At Wordsworth's suit been spared;
And from the Builder's hand this Stone,
For some rude beauty of its own,
Was rescued by the Bard:
So let it rest;—and time will come
When here the tender-hearted
May heave a gentle sigh for him,
As one of the departed.

WRITTEN IN AN ALBUM.

Small service is true service while it lasts,
Of Friends, however humble, scorn not one:
The Daisy, by the shadow that it casts,
Protects the lingering dew-drop from the Sun.

INCIDENT AT BRUGÈS.

In Brugès town is many a street
Whence busy life hath fled;
Where, without hurry, noiseless feet,
The grass-grown pavement tread.
There heard we, halting in the shade
Flung from a Convent-tower,
A harp that tuneful prelude made
To a voice of thrilling power.

The measure, simple truth to tell,
Was fit for some gay throng;
Though from the same grim turret fell
The shadow and the song.
When silent were both voice and chords
The strain seemed doubly dear,
Yet sad as sweet, for *English* words
Had fallen upon the ear.

It was a breezy hour of eve;
And pinnacle and spire
Quivered and seemed almost to heave
Clothed with innocuous fire;
But where we stood, the setting sun
Showed little of his state;
And, if the glory reached the Nun,
'Twas through an iron grate.

Not always is the heart unwise,
Nor pity idly born,
If even a passing Stranger sighs
For them who do not mourn.

Sad is thy doom, self-solaced dove,
  Captive, whoe'er thou be!
Oh! what is beauty, what is love,
  And opening life to thee?

Such feeling pressed upon my soul,
  A feeling sanctified
By one soft trickling tear that stole
  From the Maiden at my side;
Less tribute could she pay than this.
  Borne gaily o'er the sea,
Fresh from the beauty and the bliss
  Of English liberty?

A JEWISH FAMILY.

(IN A SMALL VALLEY OPPOSITE ST. GOAR, UPON THE RHINE.)

GENIUS of Raphael! if thy wings
  Might bear thee to this glen,
With faithful memory left of things
  To pencil dear and pen,
Thou wouldst forego the neighbouring Rhine,
  And all his majesty,
A studious forehead to incline
  O'er this poor family.

The Mother—her thou must have seen,
  In spirit, ere she came
To dwell these rifted rocks between,
  Or found on earth a name;
An image, too, of that sweet Boy,
  Thy inspirations give
Of playfulness, and love, and joy,
  Predestined here to live.

Downcast, or shooting glances far,
  How beautiful his eyes,
That blend the nature of the star
  With that of summer skies!
I speak as if of sense beguiled;
  Uncounted months are gone,
Yet am I with the Jewish Child,
  That exquisite St John.

I see the dark brown curls, the brow,
  The smooth transparent skin,
Refined, as with intent to show
  The holiness within,
The grace of parting Infancy
  By blushes yet untamed,
Age faithful to the mother's knee,
  Nor of her arms ashamed.

Two lovely Sisters, still and sweet
  As flowers, stand side by side;
Their soul-subduing looks might cheat
  The Christian of his pride
Such beauty hath the Eternal poured
  Upon them not forlorn,
Though of a lineage once abhorred,
  Nor yet redeemed from scorn.

Mysterious safeguard, that, in spite
  Of poverty and wrong,
Doth here preserve a living light,
  From Hebrew fountains sprung;
That gives this ragged group to cast
  Around the dell a gleam
Of Palestine, of glory past,
  And proud Jerusalem!

DEVOTIONAL INCITEMENTS.

"Not to the earth confined,
Ascend to heaven"

WHERE will they stop, those breathing Powers,
The Spirits of the new-born flowers?
They wander with the breeze, they wind
Where'er the streams a passage find;
Up from their native ground they rise
In mute aërial harmonies;
From humble violet modest thyme
Exhaled, the essential odours climb,
As if no space below the sky
Their subtle flight could satisfy:
Heaven will not tax our thoughts with pride
If like ambition be *their* guide.

  Roused by this kindliest of May-showers,
The spirit-quickener of the flowers,
That with moist virtue softly cleaves
The buds, and freshens the young leaves,
The Birds pour forth their souls in notes
Of rapture from a thousand throats,
Here checked by too impetuous haste,
While there the music runs to waste,
With bounty more and more enlarged,
Till the whole air is overcharged;
Give ear, O Man! to their appeal
And thirst for no inferior zeal,
Thou, who canst *think*, as well as feel.

  Mount from the earth, aspire! aspire!
So pleads the town's cathedral choir,
In strains that from their solemn height
Sink, to attain a loftier flight.

While incense from the altar breathes
Rich fragrance in embodied wreaths;
Or, flung from swinging censer, shrouds
The taper lights, and curls in clouds
Around angelic Forms, the still
Creation of the painter's skill,
That on the service wait concealed
One moment, and the next revealed.
—Cast off your bonds, awake, arise,
And for no transient ecstasies!
What else can mean the visual plea
Of still or moving imagery?
The iterated summons loud,
Not wasted on the attendant crowd,
Nor wholly lost upon the throng
Hurrying the busy streets along?

Alas! the sanctities combined
By art to unsensualise the mind,
Decay and languish; or, as creeds
And humours change, are spurned like weeds:
The solemn rites, the awful forms,
Founder amid fanatic storms;
The priests are from their altars thrust,
The temples levelled with the dust:
Yet evermore, through years renewed
In undisturbed vicissitude
Of seasons balancing their flight
On the swift wings of day and night,
Kind Nature keeps a heavenly door
Wide open for the scattered Poor.
Where flower-breathed incense to the skies
Is wafted in mute harmonies;
And ground fresh cloven by the plough
Is fragrant with a humbler vow,
Where birds and brooks from leafy dells
Chime forth unwearied canticles,
And vapours magnify and spread
The glory of the sun's bright head,
Still constant in her worship, still
Conforming to the almighty Will,
Whether men sow or reap the fields,
Her admonitions Nature yields;
That not by bread alone we live,
Or what a hand of flesh can give;
That every day should leave some part
Free for a sabbath of the heart;
So shall the seventh be truly blest,
From morn to eve, with hallowed rest.

THE ARMENIAN LADY'S LOVE.

[The subject of the following poem is from the Orlandus of the author's friend, Kenelm Henry Digby; and the liberty is taken of inscribing it to him as an acknowledgment, however unworthy, of pleasure and instruction derived from his numerous and valuable writings, illustrative of the piety and chivalry of the olden time.]

1.

You have heard "a Spanish Lady
How she wooed an English Man;"*
Hear now of a fair Armenian,
Daughter of the proud Soldàn;
How she loved a Christian Slave, and told her pain
By word, look, deed, with hope that he might love again.

2.

"Pluck that rose, it moves my liking,"
Said she, lifting up her veil,
"Pluck it for me, gentle Gardener,
Ere it wither and grow pale."
"Princess fair, I till the ground, but may not take
From twig or bed an humbler flower, even for your sake."

3.

"Grieved am I, submissive Christian!
To behold thy captive state;
Women, in your land, may pity
(May they not?) the unfortunate."
"Yes, kind Lady! otherwise Man could not bear
Life, which to every one that breathes is full of care."

4.

"Worse than idle is compassion
If it end in tears and sighs;
Thee from bondage would I rescue
And from vile indignities;
Nurtured, as thy mien bespeaks, in high degree,
Look up—and help a hand that longs to set thee free."

5.

"Lady, dread the wish, nor venture
In such peril to engage;
Think how it would stir against you
Your most loving Father's rage:

* See in Percy's Reliques, that fine old ballad, "The Spanish Lady's Love;" from which Poem the form of stanza, as suitable to dialogue, is adopted

Sad deliverance would it be, and yoked with shame,
Should troubles overflow on her from whom it came."

6.

"Generous Frank! the just in effort
Are of inward peace secure;
Hardships for the brave encountered,
Even the feeblest may endure:
If Almighty Grace through me thy chains unbind,
My Father for slave's work may seek a slave in mind."

7.

"Princess, at this burst of goodness,
My long-frozen heart grows warm!"
"Yet you make all courage fruitless,
Me to save from chance of harm:
Leading such Companion I that gilded Dome,
Yon Minarets, would gladly leave for his worst home."

8.

"Feeling tunes your voice, fair Princess!
And your brow is free from scorn,
Else these words would come like mockery,
Sharper than the pointed thorn."
"Whence the undeserved mistrust? Too wide apart
Our faith hath been,—O would that eyes could see the heart!"

9.

"Tempt me not, I pray; my doom is
These base implements to wield;
Rusty Lance, I ne'er shall grasp thee,
Ne'er assoil my cobwebb'd shield!
Never see my native land, nor castle towers,
Nor Her who thinking of me there counts widowed hours."

10.

"Prisoner! pardon youthful fancies;
Wedded? If you *can*, say no!—
Blessed is and be your Consort;
Hopes I cherished let them go!
Handmaid's privilege would leave my purpose free,
Without another link to my felicity."

11.

"Wedded love with loyal Christians,
Lady, is a mystery rare;
Body, heart, and soul in union,
Make one being of a pair."
"Humble love in me would look for no return,
Soft as a guiding star that cheers, but cannot burn."

12.

"Gracious Allah! by such title
Do I dare to thank the God,
Him who thus exalts thy spirit,
Flower of an unchristian sod!
Or hast thou put off wings which thou in heaven dost wear?
What have I seen, and heard, or dreamt? where am I? where?"

13.

Here broke off the dangerous converse:
Less impassioned words might tell
How the pair escaped together,
Tears not wanting, nor a knell
Of sorrow in her heart while through her Father's door,
And from her narrow world, she passed for evermore.

14.

But affections higher, holier,
Urged her steps; she shrunk from trust
In a sensual creed that trampled
Woman's birthright into dust.
Little be the wonder then, the blame be none,
If she, a timid Maid, hath put such boldness on.

15.

Judge both Fugitives with knowledge:
In those old romantic days
Mighty were the soul's commandments
To support, restrain, or raise.
Foes might hang upon their path, snakes rustle near,
But nothing from their inward selves had they to fear.

16.

Thought infirm ne'er came between them,
Whether printing desert sands
With accordant steps, or gathering
Forest-fruit with social hands;
Or whispering like two reeds that in the cold moonbeam
Bend with the breeze their heads, beside a crystal stream.

17.

On a friendly deck reposing
They at length for Venice steer;
There, when they had closed their voyage
One, who daily on the Pier

Watched for tidings from the East, beheld his Lord,
Fell down and clasped his knees for joy, not uttering word.

18

Mutual was the sudden transport;
Breathless questions followed fast,
Years contracting to a moment,
Each word greedier than the last;
"Hie thee to the Countess, Friend! return with speed,
And of this Stranger speak by whom her Lord was freed.

19.

"Say that I, who might have languished,
Drooped and pined till life was spent,
Now before the gates of Stolberg
My Deliverer would present
For a crowning recompence, the precious grace
Of her who in my heart still holds her ancient place.

20.

"Make it known that my Companion
Is of royal Eastern blood,
Thirsting after all perfection,
Innocent, and meek, and good,
Though with misbelievers bred; but that dark night
Will Holy Church disperse by beams of Gospel Light."

21.

Swiftly went that grey-haired Servant,
Soon returned a trusty Page
Charged with greetings, benedictions,
Thanks and praises, each a gage
For a sunny thought to cheer the Stranger's way,
Her virtuous scruples to remove, her fears allay.

22.

Fancy (while, to banners floating,
High on Stolberg's Castle walls,
Deafening noise of welcome mounted,
Trumpets, Drums, and Atabals,)
The devout embraces still, while such tears fell
As made a meeting seem most like a dear farewell.

23.

Through a haze of human nature,
Glorified by heavenly light,
Looked the beautiful Deliverer
On that overpowering sight,
While across her virgin cheek pure blushes strayed,
For every tender sacrifice her heart had made.

24.

On the ground the weeping Countess
Knelt, and kissed the Stranger's hand;
Act of self-devoted homage,
Pledge of an eternal band:
Nor did aught of future days that kiss belie,
Which, with a generous shout, the crowd did ratify.

25.

Constant to the fair Armenian,
Gentle pleasures round her moved,
Like a tutelary Spirit
Reverenced, like a Sister, loved.
Christian meekness smoothed for all the path of life,
Who, loving most, should wiseliest love, their only strife.

26.

Mute Memento of that union
In a Saxon Church survives,
Where a cross-legged Knight lies sculptured
As between two wedded Wives—
Figures with armorial signs of race and birth,
And the vain rank the Pilgrims bore while yet on earth.

THE PRIMROSE OF THE ROCK

A ROCK there is whose homely front
The passing Traveller slights;
Yet there the Glow-worms hang their lamps,
Like stars, at various heights;
And one coy Primrose to that Rock
The vernal breeze invites.

What hideous warfare hath been waged,
What kingdoms overthrown,
Since first I spied that Primrose-tuft
And marked it for my own;
A lasting link in Nature's chain
From highest Heaven let down!

The Flowers, still faithful to the stems
Their fellowship renew;
The stems are faithful to the root,
That worketh out of view;
And to the rock the root adheres
In every fibre true.

Close clings to earth the living rock,
Though threatening still to fall;
The earth is constant to her sphere;
And God upholds them all:
So blooms this lonely Plant, nor dreads
Her annual funeral.

* * * * *

Here closed the meditative Strain,
But air breathed soft that day,
The hoary mountain-heights were cheered,
The sunny vale looked gay;
And to the Primrose of the Rock
I gave this after-lay.

I sang, Let myriads of bright flowers,
Like Thee, in field and grove
Revive unenvied,—mightier far
Than tremblings that reprove
Our vernal tendencies to hope
Is God's redeeming love

That love which changed, for wan disease,
For sorrow that had bent
O'er hopeless dust, for withered age,
Their moral element,
And turned the thistles of a curse
To types beneficent.

Sin-blighted though we are, we too,
The reasoning Sons of Men,
From one oblivious winter called
Shall rise, and breathe again;
And in eternal summer lose
Our threescore years and ten.

To humbleness of heart descends
This prescience from on high,
The faith that elevates the Just,
Before and when they die,
And makes each soul a separate heaven,
A court for Deity.

PRESENTIMENTS.

PRESENTIMENTS! they judge not right
Who deem that ye from open light
Retire in fear of shame;
All *heaven-born* Instincts shun the touch
Of vulgar sense, and, being such,
Such privilege ye claim.

The tear whose source I could not guess,
The deep sigh that seemed fatherless,
Were mine in early days;
And now, unforced by Time to part
With Fancy, I obey my heart,
And venture on your praise.

What though some busy Foes to good,
Too potent over nerve and blood,
Lurk near you, and combine
To taint the health which ye infuse,
This hides not from the moral Muse
Your origin divine.

How oft from you, derided Powers!
Comes Faith that in auspicious hours
Builds castles, not of air;
Bodings unsanctioned by the will
Flow from your visionary skill,
And teach us to beware.

The bosom-weight, your stubborn gift,
That no philosophy can lift,
Shall vanish, if ye please,
Like morning mist; and, where it lay,
The spirits at your bidding play
In gaiety and ease.

Star-guided Contemplations move
Through space, though calm, not raised above
Prognostics that ye rule;
The naked Indian of the Wild,
And haply, too, the cradled Child,
Are pupils of your school

But who can fathom your intents,
Number their signs or instruments?
A rainbow, a sunbeam,
A subtle smell that Spring unbinds,
Dead pause abrupt of midnight winds,
An echo, or a dream.

The laughter of the Christmas hearth
With sighs of self-exhausted mirth
Ye feelingly reprove;
And daily, in the conscious breast,
Your visitations are a test
And exercise of love.

When some great change gives boundless scope
To an exulting Nation's hope,
Oft, startled and made wise
By your low-breathed interpretings,
The simply-meek foretaste the springs
Of bitter contraries.

Ye daunt the proud array of War,
Pervade the lonely Ocean far
As sail hath been unfurled;
For Dancers in the festive hall
What ghastly Partners hath your call
Fetched from the shadowy world!

'Tis said, that warnings ye dispense
Emboldened by a keener sense;
That men have lived for whom,
With dread precision, ye made clear
The hour that in a distant year
Should knell them to the tomb.

Unwelcome Insight! Yet there are
Blest times when mystery is laid bare,
Truth shows a glorious face,
While on that Isthmus which commands
The councils of both worlds she stands,
Sage Spirits! by your grace.

God, who instructs the Brutes to scent
All changes of the element,
Whose wisdom fixed the scale
Of Natures, for our wants provides
By higher, sometimes humbler, guides,
When lights of Reason fail.

SONNETS.

THE POET AND THE CAGED TURTLE-DOVE.

As often as I murmur here
My half-formed melodies,
Straight from her osier mansion near
The Turtledove replies:
Though silent as a leaf before,
The captive promptly coos;
Is it to teach her own soft lore,
Or second my weak Muse?

I rather think, the gentle Dove
Is murmuring a reproof,
Displeased that I from lays of love
Have dared to keep aloof;
That I, a Bard of hill and dale,
Have carolled, fancy free,
As if nor dove, nor nightingale,
Had heart or voice for me.

If such thy meaning, O forbear,
Sweet Bird! to do me wrong;
Love, blessed Love, is every where
The spirit of my song:
'Mid grove, and by the calm fireside,
Love animates my lyre;
That coo again!—'tis not to chide,
I feel, but to inspire.

CHATSWORTH! thy stately mansion, and the pride
Of thy domain, strange contrast do present
To house and home in many a craggy rent
Of the wild Peak; where new-born waters glide
Through fields whose thrifty Occupants abide
As in a dear and chosen banishment,
With every semblance of entire content;
So kind is simple Nature, fairly tried!
Yet He whose heart in childhood gave her troth
To pastoral dales, thin set with modest farms,
May learn, if judgment strengthen with his growth,
That, not for Fancy only, pomp hath charms;
And, strenuous to protect from lawless harms
The extremes of favoured life, may honour both

DESPONDING Father! mark this altered bough,
So beautiful of late, with sunshine warmed,
Or moist with dews; what more unsightly now,
Its blossoms shrivelled, and its fruit, if formed,
Invisible? yet Spring her genial brow
Knits not o'er that discolouring and decay
As false to expectation. Nor fret thou
At like unlovely process in the May
Of human life: a Stripling's graces blow,
Fade and are shed, that from their timely fall
(Misdeem it not a cankerous change) may grow
Rich mellow bearings, that for thanks shall call;
In *all* men, sinful is it to be slow
To hope—in *Parents*, sinful above all.

ROMAN ANTIQUITIES DISCOVERED AT BISHOPSTONE, HEREFORDSHIRE.

WHILE poring Antiquarians search the ground
Upturned with curious pains, the Bard, a Seer,
Takes fire:—The men that have been reappear;
Romans for travel girt, for business gowned,
And some recline on couches, myrtle-crowned,
In festal glee: why not? For fresh and clear,
As if its hues were of the passing year,
Dawns this time-buried pavement. From that mound
Hoards may come forth of Trajans, Maximins,
Shrunk into coins with all their warlike toil:

Or a fierce impress issues with its foil
Of tenderness—the Wolf, whose suckling Twins [wins
The unlettered Ploughboy pities when he
The casual treasure from the furrowed soil.

ST. CATHERINE OF LEDBURY.

When human touch, as monkish books attest,
Nor was applied nor could be, Ledbury bells
Broke forth in concert flung adown the dells, [crest,
And upward, high as Malvern's cloudy
Sweet tones, and caught by a noble Lady blest
To rapture! Mabel listened at the side
Of her loved Mistress soon the music died,
And Catherine said, "Here I set up my rest." [had sought
Warned in a dream, the Wanderer long
A home that by such miracle of sound
Must be revealed:—she heard it now, or felt
The deep, deep joy of a confiding thought,
And there, a saintly Anchoress she dwelt
Till she exchanged for heaven that happy ground.

THE RUSSIAN FUGITIVE

[Peter Henry Bruce, having given in his entertaining Memoir the substance of the following Tale, affirms, that, besides the concurring reports of others, he had the story from the Lady's own mouth.

The Lady Catherine, mentioned towards the close, was the famous Catherine, then bearing that name as the acknowledged Wife of Peter the Great.]

PART I.

1.

Enough of rose-bud lips, and eyes
Like harebells bathed in dew,
Of cheek that with carnation vies,
And veins of violet hue;
Earth wants not beauty that may scorn
A likening to frail flowers;
Yea, to the stars, if they were born
For seasons and for hours

2.

Through Moscow's gates, with gold unbarred,
Stepped one at dead of night,
Whom such high beauty could not guard
From meditated blight;
By stealth she passed, and fled as fast
As doth the hunted fawn,
Nor stopped, till in the dappling east
Appeared unwelcome dawn.

3.

Seven days she lurked in brake and field,
Seven nights her course renewed,
Sustained by what her scrip might yield,
Or berries of the wood;
At length, in darkness travelling on,
When lowly doors were shut,
The haven of her hope she won,
Her Foster-mother's hut.

4

"To put your love to dangerous proof
I come," said she, "from far;
For I have left my Father's roof,
In terror of the Czar."
No answer did the Matron give,
No second look she cast;
She hung upon the Fugitive,
Embracing and embraced.

5.

She led her Lady to a seat
Beside the glimmering fire,
Bathed duteously her wayworn feet,
Prevented each desire·
The cricket chirped, the house-dog dozed,
And on that simple bed,
Where she in childhood had reposed,
Now rests her weary head.

6.

When she, whose couch had been the sod,
Whose curtain pine or thorn,
Had breathed a sigh of thanks to God,
Who comforts the forlorn,
While over her the Matron bent
Sleep sealed her eyes, and stole
Feeling from limbs with travel spent,
And trouble from the soul.

7

Refreshed, the Wanderer rose at morn,
And soon again was dight
In those unworthy vestments worn
Through long and perilous flight;
And "O beloved Nurse," she said,
"My thanks with silent tears
Have unto Heaven and You been paid
Now listen to my fears!

8.

"Have you forgot"—and here she smiled—
"The babbling flatteries
You lavished on me when a child
Disporting round your knees?
I was your lambkin, and your bird,
Your star, your gem, your flower;
Light words, that were more lightly heard
In many a cloudless hour!

9.

"The blossom you so fondly praised
Is come to bitter fruit;
A mighty One upon me gazed;
I spurned his lawless suit,
And must be hidden from his wrath:
You, Foster-father dear,
Will guide me in my forward path;
I may not tarry here!

10.

"I cannot bring to utter woe
Your proved fidelity."—
"Dear Child, sweet Mistress, say not so!
For you we both would die."
"Nay, nay, I come with semblance feigned
And cheek embrowned by art,
Yet, being inwardly unstained,
With courage will depart."

11.

"But whither would you, could you, flee?
A poor Man's counsel take;
The Holy Virgin gives to me
A thought for your dear sake;
Rest shielded by our Lady's grace;
And soon shall you be led
Forth to a safe abiding-place,
Where never foot doth tread."

PART II.

1.

THE Dwelling of this faithful pair
In a straggling village stood,
For One who breathed unquiet air
A dangerous neighbourhood;
But wide around lay forest ground
With thickets rough and blind;
And pine-trees made a heavy shade
Impervious to the wind.

2.

And there, sequestered from the sight,
Was spread a treacherous swamp,
On which the noonday sun shed light
As from a lonely lamp;
And midway in the unsafe morass,
A single Island rose
Of firm dry ground, with healthful grass
Adorned, and shady boughs.

3.

The Woodman knew, for such the craft
This Russian Vassal plied,
That never fowler's gun, nor shaft
Of archer, there was tried;
A sanctuary seemed the spot
From all intrusion free;
And there he planned an artful Cot
For perfect secrecy.

4.

With earnest pains unchecked by dread
Of Power's far-stretching hand,
The bold good Man his labour sped
At nature's pure command;
Heart-soothed, and busy as a wren,
While, in a hollow nook,
She moulds her sight-eluding den
Above a murmuring brook.

5.

His task accomplished to his mind,
The twain ere break of day
Creep forth, and through the forest wind
Their solitary way;
Few words they speak, nor dare to slack
Their pace from mile to mile,
Till they have crossed the quaking marsh,
And reached the lonely isle.

6.

The sun above the pine-trees showed
A bright and cheerful face;
And Ina looked for her abode,
The promised hiding-place,
She sought in vain, the Woodman smiled,
No threshold could be seen,
Nor roof, nor window, all seemed wild
As it had ever been.

7

Advancing, you might guess an hour,
The front with such nice care
Is masked, "if house it be or bower,"
But in they entered are;
As shaggy as were wall and roof
With branches intertwined,
So smooth was all within, air-proof,
And delicately lined.

8.

And hearth was there, and maple dish,
  And cups in seemly rows,
And couch—all ready to a wish
  For nurture or repose,
And Heaven doth to her virtue grant
  That here she may abide
In solitude, with every want
  By cautious love supplied

9.

No Queen, before a shouting crowd,
  Led on in bridal state,
E'er struggled with a heart so proud,
  Entering her palace gate,
Rejoiced to bid the world farewell,
  No saintly Anchoress
E'er took possession of her cell
  With deeper thankfulness.

10.

"Father of all, upon thy care
  And mercy am I thrown;
Be thou my safeguard!"—such her prayer
  When she was left alone,
Kneeling amid the wilderness
  When joy had passed away,
And smiles, fond efforts of distress
  To hide what they betray!

11.

The prayer is heard, the Saints have seen,
  Diffused through form and face,
Resolves devotedly serene;
  That monumental grace
Of Faith, which doth all passions tame
  That reason *should* control;
And shows in the untrembling frame
  A statue of the soul.

PART III.

1.

'TIS sung in ancient minstrelsy
  That Phœbus wont to wear
"The leaves of any pleasant tree
  Around his golden hair,"*
Till Daphne, desperate with pursuit
  Of his imperious love,
At her own prayer transformed, took root,
  A laurel in the grove.

2.

Then did the Penitent adorn
  His brow with laurel green;
And 'mid his bright locks never shorn
  No meaner leaf was seen;
And Poets sage, through every age,
  About their temples wound
The bay, and Conquerors thanked the Gods,
  With laurel chaplets crowned.

3

Into the mists of fabling Time
  So far runs back the praise
Of Beauty, that disdains to climb
  Along forbidden ways;
That scorns temptation, power defies
  Where mutual love is not,
And to the tomb for rescue flies
  When life would be a blot.

4

To this fair Votaress, a fate
  More mild doth Heaven ordain
Upon her Island desolate;
  And words, not breathed in vain,
Might tell what intercourse she found,
  Her silence to endear,
What birds she tamed, what flowers the ground
  Sent forth her peace to cheer.

5.

To one mute Presence, above all,
  Her soothed affections clung,
A picture on the Cabin wall
  By Russian usage hung—
The Mother-maid, whose countenance bright
  With love abridged the day,
And, communed with by taper light,
  Chased spectral fears away.

6.

And oft, as either guardian came,
  The joy in that retreat
Might any common friendship shame,
  So high their hearts would beat;
And to the lone Recluse, whate'er
  They brought, each visiting
Was like the crowding of the year
  With a new burst of spring.

7.

But, when she of her Parents thought,
  The pang was hard to bear;
And, if with all things not enwrought,
  That trouble still is near.

* From Golding's Translation of Ovid's Metamorphoses. See also his Dedicatory Epistle as fixed to the same work

Before her flight she had not dared
 Their constancy to prove,
Too much the heroic Daughter feared
 The weakness of their love.

8.

Dark is the Past to them, and dark
 The Future still must be,
Till pitying Saints conduct her bark
 Into a safer sea—
Or gentle Nature close her eyes,
 And set her Spirit free
From the altar of this sacrifice,
 In vestal purity.

9.

Yet, when above the forest-glooms
 The white swans southward passed,
High as the pitch of their swift plumes
 Her fancy rode the blast;
And bore her tow'rd the fields of France,
 Her Father's native land,
To mingle in the rustic dance,
 The happiest of the band!

10.

Of those beloved fields she oft
 Had heard her father tell
In phrase that now with echoes soft
 Haunted her lonely cell;
She saw the hereditary bowers,
 She heard the ancestral stream;
The Kremlin and its haughty towers
 Forgotten like a dream!

PART IV.

1.

THE ever-changing Moon had traced
 Twelve times her monthly round,
When through the unfrequented Waste
 Was heard a startling sound;
A shout thrice sent from one who chased
 At speed a wounded Deer,
Bounding through branches interlaced
 And where the wood was clear.

2.

The fainting creature took the marsh,
 And toward the Island fled,
While plovers screamed with tumult harsh
 Above his antlered head;
This, Ina saw; and, pale with fear,
 Shrunk to her citadel;
The desperate Deer rushed on, and near
 The tangled covert fell.

3.

Across the marsh, the game in view,
 The Hunter followed fast,
Nor paused, till o'er the Stag he blew
 A death-proclaiming blast;
Then, resting on her upright mind,
 Came forth the Maid—"In me
Behold," she said, "a stricken Hind
 Pursued by destiny!

4.

"From your deportment, Sir! I deem
 That you have worn a sword,
And will not hold in light esteem
 A suffering woman's word;
There is my covert, there perchance
 I might have lain concealed,
My fortunes hid, my countenance
 Not even to you revealed.

5.

"Tears might be shed, and I might pray
 Crouching and terrified,
That what has been unveiled to-day,
 You would in mystery hide;
But I will not defile with dust
 The knee that bends to adore
The God in heaven;—attend, be just:
 This ask I, and no more!

6.

"I speak not of the winter's cold,
 For summer's heat exchanged,
While I have lodged in this rough hold,
 From social life estranged;
Nor yet of trouble and alarms:
 High Heaven is my defence;
And every season has soft arms
 For injured Innocence.

7.

"From Moscow to the Wilderness
 It was my choice to come,
Lest virtue should be harbourless,
 And honour want a home;
And happy were I, if the Czar
 Retain his lawless will,
To end life here like this poor Deer,
 Or a Lamb on a green hill."

8.

"Are you the Maid," the Stranger cried
 "From Gallic Parents sprung,
Whose vanishing was rumoured wide,
 Sad theme for every tongue;

Who foiled an Emperor's eager quest?
  You, Lady, forced to wear
These rude habiliments, and rest
  Your head in this dark lair!"

9.

But wonder, pity, soon were quelled;
  And in her face and mien
The soul's pure brightness he beheld
  Without a veil between.
He loved, he hoped,—a holy flame
  Kindled 'mid rapturous tears,
The passion of a moment came
  As on the wings of years.

10

"Such bounty is no gift of chance,"
  Exclaimed he; "righteous Heaven,
Preparing your deliverance,
  To me the charge hath given.
The Czar full oft in words and deeds
  Is stormy and self-willed;
But, when the Lady Catherine pleads,
  His violence is stilled.

11.

"Leave open to my wish the course,
  And I to her will go;
From that humane and heavenly source,
  Good, only good, can flow."
Faint sanction given, the Cavalier
  Was eager to depart,
Though question followed question, dear
  To the Maiden's filial heart.

12.

Light was his step,—his hopes, more light,
  Kept pace with his desires;
And the third morning gave him sight
  Of Moscow's glittering spires.
He sued:—heart-smitten by the wrong,
  To the lorn Fugitive
The Emperor sent a pledge as strong
  As sovereign power could give.

13.

O more than mighty change! If e'er
  Amazement rose to pain,
And over-joy produced a fear
  Of something void and vain,
'Twas when the Parents, who had mourned
  So long the lost as dead,
Beheld their only Child returned,
  The household floor to tread.

14

Soon gratitude gave way to love
  Within the Maiden's breast:
Delivered and Deliverer move
  In bridal garments drest,
Meek Catherine had her own reward,
  The Czar bestowed a dower,
And universal Moscow shared
  The triumph of that hour.

15

Flowers strewed the ground; the nuptial feast
  Was held with costly state,
And there, 'mid many a noble Guest,
  The Foster-parents sate,
Encouraged by the imperial eye,
  They shrank not into shade;
Great was their bliss, the honour high
  To them and nature paid!

SONNETS.

Why art thou silent! Is thy love a plant
Of such weak fibre that the treacherous air
Of absence withers what was once so fair?
Is there no debt to pay, no boon to grant?
Yet have my thoughts for thee been vigilant
(As would my deeds have been) with hourly care,
The mind's least generous wish a mendicant
For naught but what thy happiness could spare.
Speak, though this soft warm heart, once free to hold
A thousand tender pleasures, thine and mine,
Be left more desolate, more dreary cold
Than a forsaken bird's-nest filled with snow
'Mid its own bush of leafless eglantine,
Speak, that my torturing doubts their end may know!

Four fiery steeds impatient of the rein
Whirled us o'er sunless ground beneath a sky
As void of sunshine, when, from that wide Plain,
Clear tops of far-off Mountains we descry,
Like a Sierra of cerulean Spain,
All light and lustre. Did no heart reply?
Yes, there was One,—for One, asunder fly
The thousand links of that ethereal chain;

And green vales open out, with grove and field,
And the fair front of many a happy home;
Such tempting spots as into vision come
While soldiers, of the weapons that they wield
Weary, and sick of strifeful Christendom,
Gaze on the moon by parting clouds revealed.

TO THE AUTHOR'S PORTRAIT.

[Painted at Rydal Mount, by W. Pickersgill, Esq., for St. John's College, Cambridge.]

Go, faithful Portrait! and where long hath knelt
Margaret, the saintly Foundress, take thy place;
And, if Time spare the colours for the grace
Which to the work surpassing skill hath dealt,
Thou, on thy rock reclined, though Kingdoms melt
And States be torn up by the roots, wilt seem
To breathe in rural peace, to hear the stream,
To think and feel as once the Poet felt.
Whate'er thy fate, those features have not grown
Unrecognised through many a household tear,
More prompt more glad to fall than drops of dew
By morning shed around a flower half blown;
Tears of delight, that testified how true
To life thou art, and, in thy truth, how dear!

GOLD AND SILVER FISHES,

IN A VASE.

THE soaring Lark is blest as proud
  When at Heaven's gate she sings;
The roving Bee proclaims aloud
  Her flight by vocal wings;
While Ye, in lasting durance pent,
  Your silent lives employ
For something "more than dull content
  Though haply less than joy."

Yet might your glassy prison seem
  A place where joy is known,
Where golden flash and silver gleam
  Have meanings of their own;
While, high and low, and all about,
  Your motions, glittering Elves!
Ye weave—no danger from without,
  And peace among yourselves.

Type of a sunny human breast
  Is your transparent cell;
Where Fear is but a transient guest,
  No sullen humours dwell;
Where, sensitive of every ray
  That smites this tiny sea,
Your scaly panoplies repay
  The loan with usury.

How beautiful! Yet none knows why
  This ever-graceful change,
Renewed—renewed incessantly—
  Within your quiet range.
Is it that ye with conscious skill
  For mutual pleasure glide;
And sometimes, not without your will,
  Are dwarfed, or magnified?

Fays—Genii of gigantic size—
  And now, in twilight dim,
Clustering like constellated Eyes
  In wings of Cherubim,
When they abate their fiery glare:
  Whate'er your forms express,
Whate'er ye seem, whate'er ye are,
  All leads to gentleness.

Cold though your nature be, 'tis pure;
  Your birthright is a fence
From all that haughtier kinds endure
  Through tyranny of sense.
Ah! not alone by colours bright
  Are Ye to Heaven allied,
When, like essential Forms of light,
  Ye mingle, or divide.

For day-dreams soft as e'er beguiled
  Day-thoughts while limbs repose;
For moonlight fascinations mild
  Your gift, ere shutters close;
Accept, mute Captives! thanks and praise:
  And may this tribute prove
That gentle admirations raise
  Delight resembling love.

LIBERTY.

(SEQUEL TO THE ABOVE.)

[Addressed to a Friend; the Gold and Silver Fishes having been removed to a pool in the pleasure-ground of Rydal Mount.]

"The liberty of a people consists in being governed by laws which they have made for themselves, under whatever form it be of government The liberty of a private man, in being master of his own time and actions, as far as may consist with the laws of God and of his country Of this latter we are here to discourse "—COWLEY.

THOSE breathing Tokens of your kind regard,
(Suspect not, Anna, that their fate is hard;
Not soon does aught to which mild fancies cling,
In lonely spots, become a slighted thing,)
Those silent Inmates now no longer share,
Nor do they need, our hospitable care,
Removed in kindness from their glassy Cell
To the fresh waters of a living Well,
That spreads into an elfin pool opaque
Of which close boughs a glimmering mirror make,
On whose smooth breast with dimples light and small
The fly may settle, leaf or blossom fall
—*There* swims, of blazing sun and beating shower
Fearless (but how obscured!) the golden Power,
That from his bauble prison used to cast
Gleams by the richest jewel unsurpast;
And near him, darkling like a sullen Gnome,
The silver Tenant of the crystal dome,
Dissevered both from all the mysteries
Of hue and altering shape that charmed all eyes.
They pined, perhaps, they languished while they shone;
And, if not so, what matters beauty gone
And admiration lost, by change of place
That brings to the inward creature no disgrace?
But if the change restore his birthright, then,
Whate'er the difference, boundless is the gain.
Who can divine what impulses from God
Reach the caged Lark, within a town-abode,
From his poor inch or two of daisied sod?
O yield him back his privilege! No sea
Swells like the bosom of a man set free;
A wilderness is rich with liberty.
Roll on, ye spouting Whales, who die or keep
Your independence in the fathomless Deep!
Spread, tiny Nautilus, the living sail;
Dive, at thy choice, or brave the freshening gale!
If unreproved the ambitious Eagle mount
Sunward to seek the daylight in its fount,
Bays, gulfs, and ocean's Indian width, shall be,
Till the world perishes, a field for thee!

While musing here I sit in shadow cool,
And watch these mute Companions, in the pool,
Among reflected boughs of leafy trees,
By glimpses caught—disporting at their ease—
Enlivened, braced, by hardy luxuries,
I ask what warrant fixed them (like a spell
Of witchcraft fixed them) in the crystal Cell;
To wheel with languid motion round and round,
Beautiful, yet in a mournful durance bound.
Their peace, perhaps, our lightest footfall marred,
On their quick sense our sweetest music jarred,
And whither could they dart, if seized with fear?
No sheltering stone, no tangled root was near.
When fire or taper ceased to cheer the room,
They wore away the night in starless gloom;
And, when the sun first dawned upon the streams,
How faint their portion of his vital beams!
Thus, and unable to complain, they fared,
While not one joy of ours by them was shared.

Is there a cherished Bird (I venture now
To snatch a sprig from Chaucer's reverend brow)—
Is there a brilliant Fondling of the cage,
Though sure of plaudits on his costly stage,
Though fed with dainties from the snow white hand
Of a kind Mistress, fairest of the land,
But gladly would escape, and, if need were,
Scatter the colours from the plumes that bear
The emancipated captive through blithe air
Into strange woods, where he at large may live
On best or worst which they and Nature give?
The Beetle loves his unpretending track,
The Snail the house he carries on his back:
The far-fetched Worm with pleasure would disown
The bed we give him, though of softest down,
A noble instinct; in all kinds the same,
All Ranks! What Sovereign, worthy of the name,
If doomed to breathe against his lawful will
An element that flatters him—to kill,
But would rejoice to barter outward show
For the least boon that freedom can bestow?

But most the Bard is true to inborn right,
Lark of the dawn, and Philomel of night,
Exults in freedom, can with rapture vouch
For the dear blessings of a lowly couch,
A natural meal—days, months, from Nature's hand;
Time, place, and business, all at his command!
Who bends to happier duties, who more wise
Than the industrious Poet, taught to prize,
Above all grandeur, a pure life uncrossed
By cares in which simplicity is lost?
That life—the flowery path which winds by stealth,
Which Horace needed for his spirit's health;
Sighed for, in heart and genius, overcome
By noise, and strife, and questions wearisome,
And the vain splendours of Imperial Rome?
Let easy mirth his social hours inspire,
And fiction animate his sportive lyre,
Attuned to verse that crowning light Distress
With garlands cheats her into happiness,
Give *me* the humblest note of those sad strains
Drawn forth by pressure of his gilded chains,
As a chance sunbeam from his memory fell
Upon the Sabine Farm he loved so well;
Or when the prattle of Bandusia's spring
Haunted his ear—he only listening—
He proud to please, above all rivals, fit
To win the palm of gaiety and wit;
He, doubt not, with involuntary dread,
Shrinking from each new favour to be shed,
By the World's Ruler, on his honoured head!

In a deep vision's intellectual scene,
Such earnest longings and regrets as keen
Depressed the melancholy Cowley, laid
Under a fancied yew-tree's luckless shade;
A doleful bower for penitential song,
Where Man and Muse complained of mutual wrong,
While Cam's ideal current glided by,
And antique Towers nodded their foreheads high,
Citadels dear to studious privacy.
But Fortune, who had long been used to sport
With this tried Servant of a thankless Court,
Relenting met his wishes; and to You
The *remnant* of his days at least was true,
You, whom, though long deserted, he loved best;
You, Muses, Books, Fields, Liberty and Rest!

But happier they who, fixing hope and aim
On the humanities of peaceful fame,
Enter *betimes* with more than martial fire
The generous course, aspire, and still aspire;
Upheld by warnings heeded not too late
Stifle the contradictions of their fate,
And to one purpose cleave, their being's godlike mate!

Thus, gifted Friend, but with the placid brow
That Woman ne'er should forfeit, keep *thy* vow;
With modest scorn reject whate'er would blind
The ethereal eyesight, cramp the winged mind!
Then, with a blessing granted from above
To every act, word, thought, and look of love,
Life's book for Thee may lie unclosed, till age
Shall with a thankful tear bedrop its latest page.*

EVENING VOLUNTARIES

I.

CALM is the fragrant air, and loth to lose
Day's grateful warmth, tho' moist with falling dews.
Look for the stars, you'll say that there are none;
Look up a second time, and, one by one,

* There is now, alas! no possibility of the anticipation, with which the above Epistle concludes, being realised: nor were the verses ever seen by the Individual for whom they were intended. She accompanied her husband, the Rev. Wm. Fletcher, to India, and died of cholera, at the age of thirty-two or thirty-three years, on her way from Shalapore to Bombay, deeply lamented by all who knew her.

Her enthusiasm was ardent, her piety steadfast; and her great talents would have enabled her to be eminently useful in the difficult path of life to which she had been called. The opinion she entertained of her own performances, given to the world under her maiden name, Jewsbury, was modest and humble, and, indeed, far below their merits, as is often the case with those who are making trial of their powers with a hope to discover what they are best fitted for. In one quality—viz, quickness in the motions of her mind, she was in the author's estimation unequalled.

You mark them twinkling out with silvery light,
And wonder how they could elude the sight.
The birds, of late so noisy in their bowers,
Warbled a while with faint and fainter powers,
But now are silent as the dim-seen flowers
Nor does the Village Church-clock's iron tone
The time's and season's influence disown,
Nine beats distinctly to each other bound
In drowsy sequence; how unlike the sound
That, in rough winter, oft inflicts a fear
On fireside Listeners, doubting what they hear!
The Shepherd, bent on rising with the sun,
Had closed his door before the day was done,
And now with thankful heart to bed doth creep,
And join his little Children in their sleep.
The Bat, lured forth where trees the lane o'ershade,
Flits and reflits along the close arcade;
Far-heard the Dor-hawk chases the white Moth
With burring note, which Industry and Sloth
Might both be pleased with, for it suits them both.
Wheels and the tread of hoofs are heard no more;
One Boat there was, but it will touch the shore
With the next dipping of its slackened oar;
Faint sound, that, for the gayest of the gay,
Might give to serious thought a moment's sway,
As a last token of Man's toilsome day!

II.

NOT in the lucid intervals of life
That come but as a curse to Party-strife,
Not in some hour when Pleasure with a sigh
Of languor puts his rosy garland by;
Not in the breathing-times of that poor Slave
Who daily piles up wealth in Mammon's cave,
Is Nature felt, or can be; nor do words,
Which practised Talent readily affords,
Prove that her hand has touched responsive chords;
Nor has her gentle beauty power to move
With genuine rapture and with fervent love
The soul of Genius, if he dares to take
Life's rule from passion craved for passion's sake;
Untaught that meekness is the cherished bent
Of all the truly Great and all the Innocent.
But who is innocent? By grace divine,
Not otherwise, O Nature! we are thine
Through good and evil thine, in just degre
Of rational and manly sympathy
To all that Earth from pensive hearts is stealing,
And Heaven is now to gladdened eyes revealing,
Add every charm the Universe can show
Through every change its aspects undergo
Care may be respited, but not repealed,
No perfect cure grows on that bounded field
Vain is the pleasure, a false calm the peace,
If He, through whom alone our conflicts cease,
Our virtuous hopes without relapse advance,
Come not to speed the Soul's deliverance;
To the distempered Intellect refuse
His gracious help, or give what we abuse.

III.

(BY THE SIDE OF RYDAL MERE.)

THE Linnet's warble, sinking towards a close,
Hints to the Thrush 'tis time for their repose;
The shrill-voiced Thrush is heedless, and again
The Monitor revives his own sweet strain;
But both will soon be mastered, and the copse
Be left as silent as the mountain-tops,
Ere some commanding Star dismiss to rest
The throng of Rooks, that now, from twig or nest,
(After a steady flight on home-bound wings,
And a last ame of mazy hoverings
Around their ancient grove) with cawing noise
Disturb the liquid music's equipoise.
O Nightingale! Who ever heard thy song
Might here be moved, till Fancy grows so strong
That listening sense is pardonably cheated
Where wood or stream by thee was never greeted.

Surely, from fairest spots of favoured lands,
Were not some gifts withheld by jealous hands,
This hour of deepening darkness here would be,
As a fresh morning for new harmony;
And Lays as prompt would hail the dawn of night;
A *dawn* she has both beautiful and bright,
When the East kindles with the full moon's light.

Wanderer by spring with gradual progress led,
For sway profoundly felt as widely spread;
To king, to peasant, to rough sailor, dear,
And to the soldier's trumpet-wearied ear;
How welcome wouldst thou be to this green Vale
Fairer than Tempe! Yet, sweet Nightingale!
From the warm breeze that bears thee on alight
At will, and stay thy migratory flight;
Build, at thy choice, or sing, by pool or fount,
Who shall complain, or call thee to account?
The wisest, happiest, of our kind are they
That ever walk content with Nature's way,
God's goodness measuring bounty as it may;
For whom the gravest thought of what they miss,
Chastening the fulness of a present bliss,
Is with that wholesome office satisfied,
While unrepining sadness is allied
In thankful bosoms to a modest pride.

IV.

SOFT as a cloud is yon blue Ridge—the Mere
Seems firm as solid crystal, breathless, clear,
And motionless; and, to the gazer's eye,
Deeper than Ocean, in the immensity
Of its vague mountains and unreal sky!
But, from the process in that still retreat,
Turn to minuter changes at our feet;
Observe how dewy Twilight has withdrawn
The crowd of daisies from the shaven lawn,
And has restored to view its tender green,
That, while the sun rode high, was lost beneath their dazzling sheen.
—An emblem this of what the sober Hour
Can do for minds disposed to feel its power!
Thus oft, when we in vain have wished away
The petty pleasures of the garish day,
Meek Eve shuts up the whole usurping host
(Unbashful dwarfs each glittering at his post)
And leaves the disencumbered spirit free
To reassume a staid simplicity.
'Tis well—but what are helps of time and place,
When wisdom stands in need of nature's grace;
Why do good thoughts, invoked or not, descend,
Like Angels from their bowers, our virtues to befriend;
If yet To-morrow, unbelied, may say,
"I come to open out, for fresh display,
The elastic vanities of yesterday?"

V.

THE leaves that rustled on this oak-crowned hill,
And sky that danced among those leaves, are still;
Rest smooths the way for sleep; in field and bower
Soft shades and dews have shed their blended power
On drooping eyelid and the closing flower;
Sound is there none at which the faintest heart
Might leap, the weakest nerve of superstition start;
Save when the Owlet's unexpected scream
Pierces the ethereal vault; and 'mid the gleam
Of unsubstantial imagery—the dream,
From the hushed vale's realities, transferred
To the still lake, the imaginative Bird
Seems, 'mid inverted mountains, not unheard.

Grave Creature! whither, while the moon shines bright
On thy wings opened wide for smoothest flight,
Thou art discovered in a roofless tower,
Rising from what may once have been a lady's bower:
Or spied where thou sitt'st moping in thy mew
At the dim centre of a churchyard yew;
Or, from a rifted crag or ivy tod
Deep in a forest, thy secure abode,
Thou giv'st, for pastime's sake, by shriek or shout,
A puzzling notice of thy whereabout;

May the night never come, the day be seen,
When I shall scorn thy voice or mock thy mien!
In classic ages men perceived a soul
Of sapience in thy aspect, headless Owl!
Thee Athens reverenced in the studious grove;
And, near the golden sceptre grasped by Jove,
His Eagle's favourite perch, while round him sate
The Gods revolving the decrees of Fate,
Thou, too, wert present at Minerva's side—
Hark to that second larum! far and wide
The elements have heard, and rock and cave replied.

VI.

THE Sun, that seemed so mildly to retire,
Flung back from distant climes a streaming fire,
Whose blaze is now subdued to tender gleams,
Prelude of night's approach with soothing dreams.
Look round;—of all the clouds not one is moving;
'Tis the still hour of thinking, feeling, loving.
Silent, and steadfast as the vaulted sky,
The boundless plain of waters seems to lie:—
Comes that low sound from breezes rustling o'er
The grass-crowned headland that conceals the shore!
No, 'tis the earth-voice of the mighty sea,
Whispering how meek and gentle he *can* be!

Thou Power supreme! who, arming to rebuke
Offenders, dost put off the gracious look,
And clothe thyself with terrors like the flood
Of ocean roused into his fiercest mood,
Whatever discipline thy Will ordain
For the brief course that must for me remain;
Teach me with quick-eared spirit to rejoice
In admonitions of thy softest voice!
Whate'er the path these mortal feet may trace,
Breathe through my soul the blessing of thy grace,
Glad, through a perfect love, a faith sincere
Drawn from the wisdom that begins with fear;
Glad to expand, and, for a season, free
From finite cares, to rest absorbed in Thee!

VII.

(BY THE SEA-SIDE.)

THE sun is couched, the sea-fowl gone to rest,
And the wild storm hath somewhere found a nest;
Air slumbers—wave with wave no longer strives,
Only a heaving of the deep survives,
A tell-tale motion! soon will it be laid,
And by the tide alone the water swayed.
Stealthy withdrawings, interminglings mild
Of light with shade in beauty reconciled—
Such is the prospect far as sight can range,
The soothing recompence, the welcome change.
Where now the ships that drove before the blast,
Threatened by angry breakers as they passed;
And by a train of flying clouds bemocked;
Or, in the hollow surge, at anchor rocked
As on a bed of death? Some lodge in peace,
Saved by His care who bade the tempest cease;
And some, too heedless of past danger, court
Fresh gales to waft them to the far-off port;
But near, or hanging sea and sky between,
Not one of all those wingèd Powers is seen,
Seen in her course, nor 'mid this quiet heard;
Yet oh! how gladly would the air be stirred
By some ackowledgment of thanks and praise,
Soft in its temper as those vesper lays
Sung to the Virgin while accordant oars
Urge the slow bark along Calabrian shores;
A sea-born service through the mountains felt
Till into one loved vision all things melt:
Or like those hymns that soothe with graver sound
The gulfy coast of Norway iron-bound;
And, from the wide and open Baltic, rise
With punctual care, Lutherian harmonies.
Hush, not a voice is here! but why repine,
Now when the star of eve comes forth to shine
On British waters with that look benign?
Ye mariners, that plough your onward way,
Or in the haven rest, or sheltering bay,
May *silent* thanks to at least God be given
With a full heart, "our thoughts are heard in heaven!"

THE LABOURER'S NOON-DAY HYMN.

Up to the throne of God is borne
The voice of praise at early morn,
And he accepts the punctual hymn
Sung as the light of day grows dim.

Nor will he turn his ear aside
From holy offerings at noontide:
Then here reposing let us raise
A song of gratitude and praise.

What though our burthen be not light
We need not toil from morn to night;
The respite of the mid-day hour
Is in the thankful Creature's power.

Blest are the moments, doubly blest,
That, drawn from this one hour of rest,
Are with a ready heart bestowed
Upon the service of our God!

Why should we crave a hallowed spot?
An Altar is in each man's cot,
A Church in every grove that spreads
Its living roof above our heads.

Look up to Heaven! the industrious Sun
Already half his race hath run;
He cannot halt nor go astray,
But our immortal Spirits may.

Lord! since his rising in the East,
If we have faltered or transgressed,
Guide, from thy love's abundant source,
What yet remains of this day's course:

Help with thy grace, through life's short day
Our upward and our downward way;
And glorify for us the west,
When we shall sink to final rest.

A WREN'S NEST.

Among the dwellings framed by birds
  In field or forest with nice care,
Is none that with the little Wren's
  In snugness may compare.

No door the tenement requires,
  And seldom needs a laboured roof;
So is it to the fiercest sun
  Impervious and storm-proof.

So warm, so beautiful withal,
  In perfect fitness for its aim,
That to the K[illegible]
  Their in[illegible]

And when for their abodes they seek
  An opportune recess,
The Hermit has no finer eye
  For shadowy quietness.

These find, 'mid ivied Abbey walls,
  A canopy in some still nook;
Others are pent-housed by a brae
  That overhangs a brook.

There to the brooding Bird her Mate
  Warbles by fits his low clear song;
And by the busy Streamlet both
  Are sung to all day long.

Or in sequestered lanes they build,
  Where, till the flitting Bird's return,
Her eggs within the nest repose,
  Like relics in an urn.

But still, where general choice is good,
  There is a better and a best;
And, among fairest objects, some
  Are fairer than the rest;

This, one of those small Builders proved
  In a green covert, where, from out
The forehead of a pollard oak,
  The leafy antlers sprout;

For She who planned the mossy Lodge,
  Mistrusting her evasive skill,
Had to a Primrose looked for aid
  Her wishes to fulfil.

High on the trunk's projecting brow,
  And fixed an infant's span above
The budding flowers, peeped forth the nest
  The prettiest of the grove!

The treasure proudly did I show
  To some whose minds without disdain
Can turn to little things, but once
  Looked up for it in vain:

'Tis gone—a ruthless Spoiler's prey,
  Who heeds not beauty, love, or song,
'Tis gone! (so seemed it) and we grieved
  Indignant at the wrong.

Just three days after, passing by
  In clearer light the moss-built cell
I saw, espied its shaded mouth,
  And felt that all was well.

The Primrose for a veil had spread
  The largest of her upright leaves;
And [illegible] berign,
  A [illegible] F[illegible] deceives.

Concealed from friends who might disturb
Thy quiet with no ill intent,
Secure from evil eyes and hands
On barbarous plunder bent,

Rest, mother-bird! and when thy young
Take flight, and thou art free to roam,
When withered is the guardian flower,
And empty thy late home,

Think how ye prospered, thou and thine,
Amid the unviolated grove
Housed near the growing primrose tuft
In foresight, or in love.

SONNETS.

COMPOSED OR SUGGESTED DURING A TOUR IN SCOTLAND IN THE SUMMER OF 1833.

[Having been prevented by the lateness of the season, in 1831, from visiting Staffa and Iona, the author made these the principal objects of a short tour in the summer of 1833, of which the following series of sonnets is a Memorial. The course pursued was down the Cumberland river Derwent, and to Whitehaven; thence (by the Isle of Man, where a few days were passed) up the Frith of Clyde to Greenock, then to Oban, Staffa, Iona; and back towards England, by Loch Awe, Inverary, Loch Goil-head, Greenock, and through parts of Renfrewshire, Ayrshire, and Dumfriesshire to Carlisle, and thence up the river Eden, and homewards by Ullswater.]

I.

Adieu, Rydalian Laurels! that have grown
And spread as if ye knew that days might come
When ye would shelter in a happy home,
On this fair Mount, a Poet of your own,
One who ne'er ventured for a Delphic crown
To sue the God; but, haunting your green shade
All seasons through, is humbly pleased to braid
Ground-flowers, beneath your guardianship, self sown.
Farewell! no Minstrels now with harp new-strung
For summer wandering quit their household bowers;
Yet not for this wants Poesy a tongue
To cheer the Itinerant on whom she pours
Her spirit, wh[illegible]
Or musing sits [illegible]

II.

Why should the Enthusiast, journeying through this Isle,
Repine as if his hour were come too late?
Not unprotected in her mouldering state,
Antiquity salutes him with a smile,
'Mid fruitful fields that ring with jocund toil,
And pleasure-grounds where Taste, refined Co-mate
Of Truth and Beauty, strives to imitate,
Far as she may, primeval Nature's style.
Fair land! by Time's parental love made free,
By social Order's watchful arms embraced,
With unexampled union meet in thee,
For eye and mind, the present and the past;
With golden prospect for futurity,
If what is rightly reverenced may last.

III.

They called Thee merry England, in old time;
A happy people won for thee that name
With envy heard in many a distant clime
And, spite of change, for me thou keep'st the same
Endearing title, a responsive chime
To the heart's fond belief, though some there are
Whose sterner judgments deem that word a snare
For inattentive Fancy, like the lime
Which foolish birds are caught with. Can, I ask,
This face of rural beauty be a mask
For discontent, and poverty, and crime;
These spreading towns a cloak for lawless will;
Forbid it, Heaven!—that "merry England" still
May be thy rightful name, in prose and rhyme!

IV.

TO THE RIVER GRETA, NEAR KESWICK.

Greta, what fearful listening! when huge stones
Rumble along thy bed, block after block:
Or, whirling with reiterated shock,
Combat, while darkness aggravates the [illegible]
[illegible] moans

Heard on his rueful margin) thence wert named
The Mourner, thy true nature was defamed,
And the habitual murmur that atones
For thy worst rage, forgotten. Oft as Spring
Decks, on thy sinuous banks, her thousand thrones,
Seats of glad instinct and love's carolling,
The concert, for the happy, then may vie
With liveliest peals of birth-day harmony:
To a grieved heart, the notes are benisons.

V.

COMPOSED ON A MAY MORNING, 1838.

LIFE with yon Lambs, like day, is just begun,
Yet nature seems to them a heavenly guide.
Does joy approach? they meet the coming tide;
And sullenness avoid, as now they shun
Pale twilight's lingering glooms,—and in the sun
Couch near their dams, with quiet satisfied;
Or gambol—each with his shadow at his side,
Varying its shape wherever he may run.
As they from turf yet hoar with sleepy dew
All turn, and court the shining and the green,
Where herbs look up, and opening flowers are seen;
Why to God's goodness cannot We be true,
And so, His gifts and promises between,
Feed to the last on pleasures ever new?

VI.

IN SIGHT OF THE TOWN OF COCKERMOUTH,

(WHERE THE AUTHOR WAS BORN, AND HIS FATHER'S REMAINS ARE LAID

A POINT of life between my Parents' dust,
And yours, my buried Little-ones! am I;
And to those graves looking habitually
In kindred quiet I repose my trust
Death to the innocent is more than just,
And, to the sinner, mercifully bent;
So may I hope, if truly I repent
And meekly bear the ills which bear I must:
And You, my Offspring! that do still remain,
Yet may outstrip me in the appointed race,
If e'er, through fault of mine, in mutual pain
We breathed together for a moment's space,
The wrong, by love provoked, let love arraign,
And only love keep in your hearts a place

VII.

ADDRESS FROM THE SPIRIT OF COCKERMOUTH CASTLE.

THOU look'st upon me, and dost fondly think,
Poet! that, stricken as both are by years,
We, differing once so much, are now Compeers,
Prepared, when each has stood his time, to sink
Into the dust. Erewhile a sterner link
United us; when thou, in boyish play,
Entering my dungeon, didst become a prey
To soul-appalling darkness. Not a blink
Of light was there;—and thus did I, thy Tutor,
Make thy young thoughts acquainted with the grave;
While thou wert chasing the winged butterfly
Through my green courts, or climbing, a bold suitor,
Up to the flowers whose golden progeny
Still round my shattered brow in beauty wave.

VIII.

NUN'S WELL, BRIGHAM.

THE cattle crowding round this beverage clear
To slake their thirst, with reckless hoofs have trod
The encircling turf into a barren clod,
Through which the waters creep, then disappear,
Born to be lost in Derwent flowing near;
Yet, o'er the brink, and round the lime-stone-cell
Of the pure spring (they call it the "Nun's Well,"
Name that first struck by chance my startled ear)

A tender Spirit broods—the pensive Shade
Of ritual honours to this Fountain paid
By hooded Votaries with saintly cheer;
Albeit oft the Virgin-mother mild
Looked down with pity upon eyes beguiled
Into the shedding of "too soft a tear."

IX.

TO A FRIEND

(ON THE BANKS OF THE DERWENT)

PASTOR and Patriot! at whose bidding rise
These modest Walls, amid a flock that need
For one who comes to watch them and to feed
A fixed abode, keep down presageful sighs.
Threats which the unthinking only can despise,
Perplex the Church, but be thou firm,—be true
To thy first hope, and this good work pursue,
Poor as thou art A welcome sacrifice
Dost Thou prepare, whose sign will be the smoke
Of thy new hearth, and sooner shall its wreaths,
Mounting while earth her morning incense breathes,
From wandering fiends of air receive a yoke,
And straightway cease to aspire, than God disdain
This humble tribute as ill-timed or vain.

X.

MARY QUEEN OF SCOTS,

(LANDING AT THE MOUTH OF THE DERWENT, WORKINGTON)

DEAR to the Loves, and to the Graces vowed,
The Queen drew back the wimple that she wore;
And to the throng how touchingly she bowed
That hailed her landing on the Cumbrian shore;
Bright as a Star (that, from a sombre cloud
Of pine-tree foliage poised in air, forth darts,
When a soft summer gale at evening parts
The gloom that did its loveliness enshroud)
She smiled, but Time, the old Saturnian Seer,
Sighed on the wing as her foot pressed the strand,
With step prelusive to a long array
Of woes and degradations hand in hand,
Weeping captivity, and shuddering fear
Stilled by the ensanguined block of Fotheringay!

XI.

IN THE CHANNEL, BETWEEN THE COAST OF CUMBERLAND AND THE ISLE OF MAN.

RANGING the Heights of Scawfell or Black-coom,
In his lone course the Shepherd oft will pause,
And strive to fathom the mysterious laws
By which the clouds, arrayed in light or gloom,
On Mona settle, and the shapes assume
Of all her peaks and ridges What He draws
From sense, faith, reason, fancy, of the cause
He will take with him to the silent tomb:
Or, by his fire, a Child upon his knee,
Haply the untaught Philosopher may speak
Of the strange sight, nor hide his theory
That satisfies the simple and the meek,
Blest in their pious ignorance, though weak
To cope with Sages undevoutly free.

XII.

AT SEA OFF THE ISLE OF MAN.

BOLD words affirmed, in days when faith was strong,
That no adventurer's bark had power to gain
These shores if he approached them bent on wrong;
For, suddenly up-conjured from the Main,
Mists rose to hide the Land—that search, though long
And eager, might be still pursued in vain
O Fancy, what an age was *that* for song!
That age, when not by *laws* inanimate,
As men believed, the waters were impelled,
The air controlled, the stars their courses held,
But element and orb on *acts* did wait

Of *Powers* endued with visible form, instinct
With will, and to their work by passion linked.

XIII.

DESIRE we past illusions to recall?
To reinstate wild fancy would we hide
Truths whose thick veil Science has drawn aside.
No,—let this Age, high as she may, install
In her esteem the thirst that wrought man's fall,
The universe is infinitely wide,
And conquering Reason, if self-glorified,
Can nowhere move uncrossed by some new wall
Or gulf of mystery, which thou alone,
Imaginative Faith! canst overleap,
In progress toward the fount of Love,—the throne
Of Power, whose ministering Spirits records keep
Of periods fixed, and laws established, less
Flesh to exalt than prove its nothingness.

XIV.

ON ENTERING DOUGLAS BAY, ISLE OF MAN.

"Dignum laude virum Musa vetat mori."

THE feudal Keep, the bastions of Cohorn,
Even when they rose to check or to repel
Tides of aggressive war, oft served as well
Greedy ambition, armed to treat with scorn
Just limits; but yon Tower, whose smiles adorn
This perilous bay, stands clear of all offence;
Blest work it is of love and innocence,
A Tower of refuge to the else forlorn.
Spare it, ye waves, and lift the mariner,
Struggling for life, into its saving arms!
Spare, too, the human helpers! Do they stir
'Mid your fierce shock like men afraid to die?
No, their dread service nerves the heart it warms,
And they are led by noble HILLARY.

XV.

BY THE SEA-SHORE, ISLE OF MAN.

WHY stand we gazing on the sparkling brine
With wonder, smit by its transparency,
And all-enraptured with its purity?
Because the unstained, the clear, the crystalline,
Have ever in them something of benign;
Whether in gem, in water, or in sky,
A sleeping infant's brow, or wakeful eye
Of a young maiden, only not divine.
Scarcely the hand forbears to dip its palm
For beverage drawn as from a mountain well:
Temptation centres in the liquid calm;
Our daily raiment seems no obstacle
To instantaneous plunging in, deep Sea!
And revelling in long embrace with Thee.

XVI.

ISLE OF MAN.

A YOUTH too certain of his power to wade
On the smooth bottom of this clear bright sea,
To sight so shallow, with a bather's glee
Leapt from this rock, and surely, had not aid
Been near, must soon have breathed out life, betrayed
By fondly trusting to an element
Fair, and to others more than innocent;
Then had sea-nymphs sung dirges for him laid
In peaceful earth: for, doubtless, he was frank,
Utterly in himself devoid of guile;
Knew not the double-dealing of a smile;
Nor aught that makes men's promises a blank,
Or deadly snare: and He survives to bless
The Power that saved him in his strange distress.

XVII.

THE RETIRED MARINE OFFICER, ISLE OF MAN.

NOT pangs of grief for lenient time too keen,
Grief that devouring waves had caused, nor guilt
Which they had witnessed, swayed the man who built

This homestead, placed where nothing could be seen,
Naught heard of ocean, troubled or serene.
A tired Ship-soldier on paternal land,
That o'er the channel holds august command,
The dwelling raised,—a veteran Marine;
Who, in disgust, turned from the neighbouring sea
To shun the memory of a listless life
That hung between two callings. May no strife
More hurtful here beset him, doom'd, though free,
Self-doom'd to worse inaction, till his eye
Shrink from the daily sight of earth and sky!

XVIII.

BY A RETIRED MARINER,

(A FRIEND OF THE AUTHOR.)

FROM early youth I ploughed the restless Main,
My mind as restless and as apt to change;
Through every clime and ocean did I range,
In hope at length a competence to gain;
For poor to Sea I went, and poor I still remain.
Year after year I strove, but strove in vain,
And hardships manifold did I endure,
For Fortune on me never deign'd to smile;
Yet I at last a resting-place have found,
With just enough life's comforts to procure,
In a snug Cove on this our favoured Isle,
A peaceful spot where Nature's gifts abound;
Then sure I have no reason to complain,
Though poor to Sea I went, and poor I still remain

XIX.

AT BALA-SALA, ISLE OF MAN.

(SUPPOSED TO BE WRITTEN BY A FRIEND OF THE AUTHOR.

BROKEN in fortune; but in mind entire
And sound in principle, I seek repose
Where ancient trees this convent pile enclose,*
In ruin beautiful. When vain desire
Intrudes on peace, I pray the eternal Sire
To cast a soul-subduing shade on me,
A grey-haired, pensive, thankful Refugee,
A shade but with some sparks of heavenly fire
Once to these cells vouchsafed. And when I note
The old Tower's brow yellowed as with the beams
Of sunset ever there, albeit streams
Of stormy weather-stains that semblance wrought,
I thank the silent Monitor, and say
"Shine so, my aged brow, at all hours of the day!"

* Rusher Abbey.

XX.

TYNWALD HILL.

ONCE on the top of Tynwald's formal mound
(Still marked with green turf circles narrowing
Stage above stage) would sit this Island's King,
The laws to promulgate, enrobed and crowned;
While, compassing the little mount around,
Degrees and Orders stood, each under each;
Now, like to things within fate's easiest reach,
The power is merged, the pomp a grave has found.
Off with yon cloud, old Snafell! that thine eye
Over three Realms may take its widest range;
And let, for them, thy fountains utter strange
Voices, thy winds break forth in prophecy,
If the whole State must suffer mortal change,
Like Mona's miniature of sovereignty.

XXI.

DESPOND who will—*I* heard a voice exclaim,
"Though fierce the assault, and shatter'd the defence,
It cannot be that Britain's social frame,
The glorious work of time and providence,
Before a flying season's rash pretence,
Should fall; that She, whose virtue put to shame,
When Europe prostrate lay, the Conqueror's aim,

Should perish, self-subverted. Black and dense
The cloud is; but brings *that* a day of doom
To Liberty? Her sun is up the while,
That orb whose beams round Saxon Alfred shone,
Then laugh, ye innocent Vales! ye Streams, sweep on,
Nor let one billow of our heaven-blest Isle
Toss in the fanning wind a humbler plume."

XXII.

IN THE FRITH OF CLYDE, AILSA CRAG.

(JULY 17, 1833.)

SINCE risen from ocean, ocean to defy,
Appeared the Crag of Ailsa; ne'er did morn
With gleaming lights more gracefully adorn
His sides, or wreathe with mist his forehead high:
Now, faintly darkening with the sun's eclipse,
Still is he seen, in lone sublimity,
Towering above the sea and little ships;
For dwarfs the tallest seem while sailing by,
Each for her haven; with her freight of Care,
Pleasure, or Grief, and Toil that seldom looks
Into the secret of to-morrow's fare;
Though poor, yet rich, without the wealth of books,
Or aught that watchful Love to Nature owes
For her mute Powers, fix'd Forms, and transient Shows.

XXIII.

ON THE FRITH OF CLYDE.

(IN A STEAM-BOAT.)

ARRAN! a single-crested Teneriffe,
A St. Helena next—in shape and hue;
Varying her crowded peaks and ridges blue;
Who but must covet a cloud-seat or skiff
Built for the air, or winged Hippogriff,
That he might fly, where no one could pursue,
From this dull Monster and her sooty crew,
And, like a God, light on thy topmost cliff.
Impotent wish! which reason would despise
If the mind knew no union of extremes,
No natural bond between the boldest schemes
Ambition frames, and heart-humilities.
Beneath stern mountains many a soft vale lies,
And lofty springs give birth to lowly streams.

XXIV.

ON REVISITING DUNOLLY CASTLE.

THE captive Bird was gone;—to cliff or moor
Perchance had flown, delivered by the storm;
Or he had pined, and sunk to feed the worm:
Him found we not; but, climbing a tall tower,
There saw, impaved with rude fidelity
Of art mosaic, in a roofless floor,
An Eagle with stretched wings, but beamless eye—
An Eagle that could neither wail nor soar.
Effigies of the Vanished, (shall I dare
To call thee so?) or symbol of past times,
That towering courage, and the savage deeds
Those times were proud of, take Thou too a share,
Not undeserved, of the memorial rhymes
That animate my way where'er it leads!

XXV.

THE DUNOLLY EAGLE.

NOT to the clouds, not to the cliff, he flew;
But when a storm, on sea or mountain bred,
Came and delivered him, alone he sped
Into the Castle-dungeon's darkest mew.
Now, near his Master's house in open view
He dwells, and hears indignant tempests howl,
Kennelled and chained. Ye tame domestic Fowl,
Beware of him! Thou, saucy Cockatoo,
Look to thy plumage and thy life! The Roe,
Fleet as the west wind, is for *him* no quarry;
Balanced in ether he will never tarry,
Eyeing the sea's blue depths. Poor Bird! even so
Doth Man of Brother-man a creature make,
That clings to slavery for its own sad sake

XXVI.

CAVE OF STAFFA.

We saw, but surely, in the motley crowd,
Not One of us has *felt*, the far-famed sight;
How *could* we feel it? each the other's blight,
Hurried and hurrying, volatile and loud.
O for those motions only that invite
The Ghost of Fingal to his tuneful Cave!
By the breeze entered, and wave after wave
Softly embosoming the timid light!
And by *one* Votary who at will might stand
Gazing, and take into his mind and heart,
With undistracted reverence, the effect
Of those proportions where the almighty hand
That made the worlds, the sovereign Architect,
Has deigned to work as if with human Art!

XXVII.

CAVE OF STAFFA.

Thanks for the lessons of this Spot—fit school
For the presumptuous thoughts that would assign
Mechanic laws to agency divine;
And, measuring heaven by earth, would overrule
Infinite Power. The pillared vestibule,
Expanding yet precise, the roof embowed,
Might seem designed to humble Man, when proud
Of his best workmanship by plan and tool
Down-bearing with his whole Atlantic weight
Of tide and tempest on the Structure's base,
And flashing upwards to its topmost height,
Ocean has proved its strength, and of its grace
In calms is conscious, finding for its freight
Of softest music some responsive place.

XXVIII.

CAVE OF STAFFA.

Ye shadowy Beings, that have rights and claims
In every cell of Fingal's mystic Grot,
Where are ye? Driven or venturing to the spot,
Our Fathers glimpses caught of your thin Frames,
And, by your mien and bearing, knew your names;
And they could hear *his* ghostly song who trod
Earth, till the flesh lay on him like a load,
While he struck his desolate harp without hopes or aims.
Vanished ye are, but subject to recall;
Why keep *we* else the instincts whose dread law
Ruled here of yore, till what men felt they saw,
Not by black arts but magic natural!
If eyes be still sworn vassals of belief,
Yon light shapes forth a Bard, that shade a Chief.

XXIX.

FLOWERS ON THE TOP OF THE PILLARS AT THE ENTRANCE OF THE CAVE

Hope smiled when your nativity was cast,
Children of Summer! Ye fresh flowers that brave
What Summer here escapes not, the fierce wave,
And whole artillery of the western blast,
Battering the Temple's front, its long-drawn nave
Smiting, as if each moment were the last
But ye, bright flowers, on frieze and architrave
Survive, and once again the Pile stands fast,
Calm as the Universe, from specular Towers
Of heaven contemplated by Spirits pure—
Suns and their systems, diverse yet sustained
In symmetry, and fashioned to endure,
Unhurt, the assault of Time with all his hours,
As the supreme Artificer ordained.

XXX.

On to Iona!—What can she afford
To *us* save matter for a thoughtful sigh,
Heaved over ruin with stability
In urgent contrast? To diffuse the Word
(Thy Paramount, mighty Nature! and Time's Lord)
Her Temples rose, 'mid pagan gloom; but why,
Even for a moment, has our verse deplored
Their wrongs, since they fulfilled their destiny?
And when, subjected to a common doom
Of mutability, those far-famed Piles
Shall disappear from both the sister Isles,

Iona's Saints, forgetting not past days,
Garlands shall wear of amaranthine bloom,
While heaven's vast sea of voices chants
their praise.

XXXI.

IONA.

(UPON LANDING.)

WITH earnest look, to every voyager,
Some ragged child holds up for sale his
store
Of wave-worn pebbles, pleading on the
shore
Where once came monk and nun with
gentle stir,
Blessings to give, news ask, or suit prefer.
But see yon neat trim church, a grateful
speck
Of novelty amid this sacred wreck—
Nay spare thy scorn, haughty Philosopher!
Fallen though she be, this Glory of the west,
Still on her sons the beams of mercy shine;
And "hopes, perhaps more heavenly bright
than thine,
A grace by thee unsought and unpossest,
A faith more fixed, a rapture more divine
Shall gild their passage to eternal rest."

XXXII.

THE BLACK STONES OF IONA.

[See Martin's Voyage among the Western Isles.]

HERE on their knees men swore: the stones
were black,
Black in the People's minds and words, yet
they
Were at that time, as now, in colour grey.
But what is colour, if upon the rack
Of conscience souls are placed by deeds that
lack
Concord with oaths? What differ night and
day
Then, when before the Perjured on his way
Hell opens, and the heavens in vengeance
crack
Above his head uplifted in vain prayer
To Saint, or Fiend, or to the Godhead whom
He had insulted—Peasant, King, or Thane.
Fly where the culprit may, guilt meets a
doom;
And, from invisible worlds at need laid bare,
Come links for social order's awful chain.

XXXIII.

HOMEWARD we turn. Isle of Columba's
Cell,
Where Christian piety's soul-cheering spark
(Kindled from Heaven between the light
and dark
Of time) shone like the morning star, fare-
well!—
Remote St. Kilda, art thou visible?
No—but farewell to thee, beloved sea-mark
For many a voyage made in Fancy's bark,
When, with more hues than in the rainbow
dwell
Thou a mysterious intercourse dost hold;
Extracting from clear skies and air serene,
And out of sun-bright waves, a lucid veil,
That thickens, spreads, and, mingling fold
with fold
Makes known, when thou no longer canst
be seen,
Thy whereabout, to warn the approaching
sail.

XXXIV.

GREENOCK.

"Per me si va nella Città dolente."

We have not passed into a doleful City,
We who were led to-day down a grim Dell,
By some too boldly named "the Jaws of
Hell:"
Where be the wretched Ones, the sights for
pity?
These crowded streets resound no plaintive
ditty:
As from the hive where bees in summer dwell,
Sorrow seems here excluded; and that knell,
It neither damps the gay, nor checks the
witty.
Too busy Mart! thus fared it with old Tyre,
Whose Merchants Princes were, whose
decks were thrones:
Soon may the punctual sea in vain respire
To serve thy need, in union with that Clyde
Whose nursling current brawls o'er mossy
stones,
The poor, the lonely herdsman's joy and
pride.

XXXV.

"THERE!" said a stripling, pointing with
meet pride
Towards a low roof with green trees half
concealed,
"Is Mossgiel farm; and that's the very field

Where Burns ploughed up the Daisy" Far and wide
A plain below stretched sea-ward, while, descried
Above sea-clouds, the Peaks of Arran rose;
And, by that simple notice, the repose
Of earth, sky, sea, and air, was vivified.
Beneath "the random *bield* of clod or stone"
Myriads of Daisies have shone forth in flower
Near the lark's nest, and in their natural hour
Have passed away, less happy than the One
That by the unwilling ploughshare died to prove
The tender charm of Poetry and Love.

XXXVI.

FANCY AND TRADITION.

THE Lovers took within this ancient grove
Their last embrace; beside those crystal springs
The Hermit saw the Angel spread his wings
For instant flight; the Sage in yon alcove
Sate musing; on that hill the Bard would rove,
Not mute, where now the Linnet only sings:
Thus everywhere to truth Tradition clings,
Or Fancy localises Powers we love.
Were only History licensed to take note
Of things gone by, her meagre monuments
Would ill suffice for persons and events·
There is an ampler page for man to quote,
A readier book of manifold contents,
Studied alike in palace and in cot.

XXXVII.

THE RIVER EDEN, CUMBERLAND.

EDEN ! till now thy beauty had I viewed
By glimpses only, and confess with shame
That verse of mine, whate'er its varying mood,
Repeats but once the sound of thy sweet name;
Yet fetched from Paradise that honour came,
Rightfully borne; for Nature gives thee flowers
That have no rivals among British bowers,
And thy bold rocks are worthy of their fame
Measuring thy course, fair Stream ! at length I pay
To my life's neighbour dues of neighbourhood;
But I have traced thee on thy winding way
With pleasure sometimes by the thought restrained
That things far off are toiled for, while a good
Not sought, because too near, is seldom gained.

XXXVIII.

MONUMENT OF MRS HOWARD,

(*by Nollekens,*)

IN WETHERAL CHURCH, NEAR CORBY, ON THE BANKS OF THE EDEN

STRETCHED on the dying Mother's lap, lies dead
Her new-born Babe, dire issue of bright hope!
But Sculpture here, with the divinest scope
Of luminous faith, heavenward hath raised that head
So patiently; and through one hand has spread
A touch so tender for the insensate Child,
Earth's lingering love to parting reconciled
Brief parting—for the spirit is all but fled;
That we, who contemplate the turns of life
Through this still medium, are consoled and cheered;
Feel with the Mother, think the severed Wife
Is less to be lamented than revered;
And own that Art, triumphant over strife
And pain, hath powers to Eternity endeared.

XXXIX.

TRANQUILLITY ! the sovereign aim wert thou
In heathen schools of philosophic lore;
Heart-stricken by stern destiny of yore
The Tragic Muse thee served with thoughtful vow;
And what of hope Elysium could allow
Was fondly seized by Sculpture, to restore
Peace to the Mourner's soul; but He who wore
The crown of thorns around his bleeding brow

Warmed our sad being with his glorious light:
Then Arts, which still had drawn a softening grace
From shadowy fountains of the Infinite,
Communed with that Idea face to face;
And move around it now as planets run,
Each in its orbit, round the central Sun.

XL.

NUNNERY.

THE floods are roused, and will not soon be weary;
Down from the Pennine Alps* how fiercely sweeps
CROGLIN, the stately Eden's tributary!
He raves, or through some moody passage creeps
Plotting new mischief—out again he leaps
Into broad light, and sends, through regions airy,
That voice which soothed the Nuns while on the steeps
They knelt in prayer, or sang to blissful Mary.
That union ceased: then, cleaving easy walks
Through crags, and smoothing paths beset with danger,
Came studious Taste; and many a pensive Stranger
Dreams on the banks, and to the river talks.
What change shall happen next to Nunnery Dell?
Canal, and Viaduct, and Railway, tell!

XLI.

STEAMBOATS, VIADUCTS, AND RAILWAYS.

MOTIONS and Means, on land and sea at war
With old poetic feeling, not for this,
Shall ye, by Poets even, be judged amiss!
Nor shall your presence, howsoe'er it mar
The loveliness of Nature, prove a bar
To the Mind's gaining that prophetic sense
Of future change, that point of vision whence
May be discovered what in soul ye are.

* The Chain of Crossfell, which parts Cumberland and Westmoreland from Northumberland and Durham.

In spite of all that beauty may disown
In your harsh features, Nature doth embrace
Her lawful offspring in Man's art; and Time,
Pleased with your triumphs o'er *his* brother Space,
Accepts from your bold hands the proffered crown
Of hope, and smiles on you with cheer sublime.

XLII.

LOWTHER! in thy majestic Pile are seen
Cathedral pomp and grace, in apt accord
With the baronial castle's sterner mien;
Union significant of God adored,
And charters won and guarded by the sword
Of ancient honour; whence that goodly state
Of Polity which wise men venerate,
And will *maintain*, if God his help afford.
Hourly the democratic torrent swells;
For airy promises and hopes suborned
The strength of backward-looking thoughts is scorned.
Fall if ye must, ye Towers and Pinnacles,
With what ye symbolise, authentic Story
Will say, Ye disappeared with England's Glory!

XLIII.

TO THE EARL OF LONSDALE.

"Magistratus indicat virum."

LONSDALE! it were unworthy of a Guest,
Whose heart with gratitude to thee inclines,
If he should speak, by fancy touched, of signs
On thy Abode harmoniously imprest,
Yet be unmoved with wishes to attest
How in thy mind and moral frame agree
Fortitude and that Christian Charity
Which, filling, consecrates the human breast.
And if the Motto on thy scutcheon teach
With truth, "THE MAGISTRACY SHOWS THE MAN;"
That searching test thy public course has stood;
As will be owned alike by bad and good,
Soon as the measuring of life's little span
Shall place thy virtues out of Envy's reach.

XLIV.

TO CORDELIA M——,

HALLSTEADS, ULLSWATER.

NOT in the mines beyond the western main,
You tell me, Delia! was the metal sought,
Which a fine skill, of Indian growth, has wrought
Into this flexible yet faithful Chain,
Nor is it silver of romantic Spain
You say, but from Helvellyn's depths was brought,
Our own domestic mountain Thing and thought
Mix strangely; trifles light, and partly vain,
Can prop, as you have learnt, our nobler being·
Yes, Lady, while about your neck is wound
(Your casual glance oft meeting) this bright cord,
What witchery, for pure gifts of inward seeing,
Lurks in it, Memory's Helper, Fancy's Lord,
For precious tremblings in your bosom found!

XLV.

CONCLUSION.

MOST sweet it is with unuplifted eye
To pace the ground if path there be or none,
While a fair region round the traveller lies,
Which he forbears again to look upon;
Pleased rather with some soft ideal scene,
The work of Fancy or some happy tone
Of meditation, stepping in between
The beauty coming and the beauty gone.
If Thought and Love desert us, from that day
Let us break off all commerce with the Muse;
With Thought and Love companions of our way,
Whate'er the senses take or may refuse,
The Mind's internal heaven shall shed her dews
Of inspiration on the humblest lay.

LINES

WRITTEN IN THE ALBUM OF THE COUNTESS OF ——.

Nov 5, 1834.

LADY! a Pen, perhaps, with thy regard,
Among the Favoured, favoured not the least,
Left, 'mid the Records of this Book inscribed,
Deliberate traces, registers of thought
And feeling, suited to the place and time
That gave them birth:—months passed, and still this hand,
That had not been too timid to imprint
Words which the virtues of thy Lord inspired,
Was yet not bold enough to write of Thee.
And why that scrupulous reserve? In sooth
The blameless cause lay in the Theme itself.
Flowers are there many that delight to strive
With the sharp wind, and seem to court the shower,
Yet are by nature careless of the sun
Whether he shine on them or not; and some,
Where'er he moves along the unclouded sky,
Turn a broad front full on his flattering beams·
Others do rather from their notice shrink,
Loving the dewy shade,—a humble Band,
Modest and sweet, a Progeny of earth,
Congenial with thy mind and character,
High-born Augusta!

Towers, and stately Groves,
Bear witness for me, thou, too, Mountain-stream!
From thy most secret haunts, and ye Parterres,
Which she is pleased and proud to call her own,
Witness how oft upon my noble Friend
Mute offerings, tribute from an inward sense
Of admiration and respectful love,
Have waited, till the affections could no more
Endure that silence, and broke out in song,
Snatches of music taken up and dropt
Like those self-solacing those under notes
Trilled by the redbreast, when autumnal leaves
Are thin upon the bough. Mine, only mine,
The pleasure was, and no one heard the praise.

Checked, in the moment of its issue checked;
And reprehended by a fancied blush
From the pure qualities that called it forth.

Thus Virtue lives debarred from Virtue's meed;
Thus, Lady, is retiredness a veil
That, while it only spreads a softening charm
O'er features looked at by discerning eyes,
Hides half their beauty from the common gaze;
And thus, even on the exposed and breezy hill
Of lofty station, female goodness walks,
When side by side with lunar gentleness
As in a cloister. Yet the grateful Poor
(Such the immunities of low estate,
Plain Nature's enviable privilege,
Her sacred recompence for many wants)
Open their hearts before Thee, pouring out
All that they think and feel, with tears of joy;
And benedictions not unheard in Heaven:
And friend in the ear of friend, where speech is free
To follow truth, is eloquent as they.

Then let the Book receive in these prompt lines
A just memorial; and thine eyes consent
To read that they, who mark thy course, behold
A life declining with the golden light
Of summer, in the season of sere leaves;
See cheerfulness undamped by stealing Time;
See studied kindness flow with easy stream,
Illustrated with inborn courtesy;
And an habitual disregard of self
Balanced by vigilance for others' weal.

And shall the verse not tell of lighter gifts
With these ennobling attributes conjoined
And blended, in peculiar harmony,
By Youth's surviving spirit? What agile grace!
A nymph-like liberty, in nymph-like form,
Beheld with wonder; whether floor or path
Thou tread, or on the managed steed art borne,
Fleet as the shadows, over down or field,
Driven by strong winds at play among the clouds.

Yet one word more—one farewell word—a wish!
Which came, but it has passed into a prayer,
That, as thy sun in brightness is declining,
So, at an hour yet distant for *their* sakes
Whose tender love, here faltering on the way
Of a diviner love, will be forgiven,—
So may it set in peace, to rise again
For everlasting glory won by faith.

THE SOMNAMBULIST.

I.

List, ye who pass by Lyulph's Tower*
At eve; how softly then
Doth Aira-force, that torrent hoarse,
Speak from the woody glen!
Fit music for a solemn vale!
And holier seems the ground
To him who catches on the gale
The spirit of a mournful tale,
Embodied in the sound.

2.

Not far from that fair site whereon
The Pleasure-house is reared,
As Story says, in antique days,
A stern-brow'd house appeared;
Foil to a jewel rich in light
There set, and guarded well;
Cage for a bird of plumage bright,
Sweet-voiced, nor wishing for a flight
Beyond her native dell.

3.

To win this bright bird from her cage,
To make this gem their own,
Came Barons bold, with store of gold,
And Knights of high renown;
But one she prized, and only One;
Sir Eglamore was he;
Full happy season, when was known,
Ye Dales and Hills! to you alone
Their mutual loyalty—

4.

Known chiefly, Aira! to thy glen,
Thy brook, and bowers of holly;
Where Passion caught what Nature taught
That all but love is folly;

* A pleasure-house built by the late Duke of Norfolk upon the banks of Ullswater. Force is the word used in the Lake District for Waterfall.

Where Fact with Fancy stooped to play,
  Doubt came not, nor regret;
To trouble hours that winged their way,
As if through an immortal day
  Whose sun could never set.

5.

But in old times Love dwelt not long
  Sequester'd with repose;
Best throve the fire of chaste desire,
  Fanned by the breath of foes.
"A conquering lance is beauty's test,
  And proves the lover true;"
So spake Sir Eglamore, and pressed
The drooping Emma to his breast,
  And looked a blind adieu.

6.

They parted.—Well with him it fared
  Through wide-spread regions errant;
A knight of proof in love's behoof,
  The thirst of fame his warrant:
And she her happiness can build
  On woman's quiet hours;
Though faint, compared with spear and shield,
The solace beads and masses yield,
  And needlework and flowers.

7.

Yet blest was Emma when she heard
  Her Champion's praise recounted;
Though brain would swim, and eyes grow dim,
  And high her blushes mounted;
Or when a bold heroic lay
  She warbled from full heart:
Delightful blossoms for the *May*
Of absence! but they will not stay,
  Born only to depart.

8.

Hope wanes with her, while lustre fills
  Whatever path he chooses;
As if his orb, that owns no curb,
  Received the light hers loses.
He comes not back; an ampler space
  Requires for nobler deeds;
He ranges on from place to place,
Till of his doings is no trace
  But what her fancy breeds.

9.

His fame may spread, but in the past
  Her spirit finds its centre;
Clear sight she has of what he was,
  And that would now content her.

"Still is he my devoted knight?"
  The tear in answer flows;
Month falls on month with heavier weight,
Day sickens round her, and the night
  Is empty of repose.

10.

In sleep she sometimes walked abroad,
  Deep sighs with quick words blending
Like that pale Queen whose hands are seen
  With fancied spots contending;
But *she* is innocent of blood,—
  The moon is not more pure
That shines aloft, while through the wood
She thrids her way, the sounding Flood
  Her melancholy lure!

11.

While 'mid the fern-brake sleeps the doe,
  And owls alone are waking,
In white arrayed, glides on the Maid
  The downward pathway taking,
That leads her to the torrent's side
  And to a holly bower;
By whom on this still night descried?
By whom in that lone place espied?
  By thee, Sir Eglamore!

12.

A wandering Ghost, so thinks the Knight,
  His coming step has thwarted,
Beneath the boughs that heard their vows,
  Within whose shade they parted.
Hush, hush, the busy Sleeper see!
  Perplexed her fingers seem,
As if they from the holly tree
Green twigs would pluck, as rapidly
  Flung from her to the stream.

13.

What means the Spectre? Why intent
  To violate the Tree,
Thought Eglamore, by which I swore
  Unfading constancy?
Here am I, and to-morrow's sun,
  To her I left, shall prove
That bliss is ne'er so surely won
As when a circuit has been run
  Of valour, truth, and love.

14.

So from the spot whereon he stood,
  He moved with stealthy pace;
And, drawing nigh, with his living eye,
  He recognised the face;

And whispers caught, and speeches small,
Some to the green-leaved tree,
Some muttered to the torrent-fall,—
"Roar on, and bring him with thy call;
I heard, and so may he!"

15.

Soul-shattered was the Knight, nor knew
If Emma's Ghost it were,
Or boding Shade, or if the Maid
Her very self stood there.
He touched, what followed who shall tell?
The soft touch snapped the thread
Of slumber—shrieking back she fell,
And the Stream whirled her down the dell
Along its foaming bed.

16.

In plunged the Knight! when on firm ground
The rescued Maiden lay,
Her eyes grew bright with blissful light,
Confusion passed away;
She heard, ere to the throne of grace
Her faithful Spirit flew,
His voice; beheld his speaking face,
And, dying, from his own embrace,
She felt that he was true

17.

So was he reconciled to life:
Brief words may speak the rest;
Within the dell he built a cel ,
And there was Sorrow's gı est;
In hermits' weeds repose he ound,
From vain temptations free;
Beside the torrent dwelling—bound
By one deep heart-controlling sound,
And awed to piety.

18.

Wild stream of Aira, hold thy course,
Nor fear memorial lays,
Where clouds that spread in solemn shade,
Are edged with golden rays!
Dear art thou to the light of Heaven,
Though minister of sorrow;
Sweet is thy voice at pensive Even;
And thou, in Lovers' hearts forgiven,
Shall take thy place with Yarrow!

TO ——,

UPON THE BIRTH OF HER FIRST-BORN CHILD, MARCH, 1833.

"Tum porro puer, ut sævis projectus ab undis
Navita; nudus humi jacet," &c.—LUCRETIUS.

LIKE a shipwreck'd Sailor tost
By rough waves on a perilous coast,
Lies the Babe, in helplessness
And in tenderest nakedness,
Flung by labouring nature forth
Upon the mercies of the earth.
Can its eyes beseech? no more
Than the hands are free to implore:
Voice but serves for one brief cry,
Plaint was it? or prophecy
Of sorrow that will surely come?
Omen of man's grievous doom!

But, O Mother! by the close
Duly granted to thy throes;
By the silent thanks now tending
Incense-like to Heaven, descending
Now to mingle and to move
With the gush of earthly love,
As a debt to that frail Creature,
Instrument of struggling Nature
For the blissful calm, the peace
Known but to this *one* release;
Can the pitying spirit doubt
That from human-kind springs out
From the penalty a sense
Of more than mortal recompence?

As a floating summer cloud,
Though of gorgeous drapery proud,
To the sun-burnt traveller,
Or the stooping labourer,
Ofttimes makes its bounty known
By its shadow round him thrown;
So, by chequerings of sad cheer,
H[illegible]venly guardians, brooding near,
Of their presence tell—too bright
Haply for corporeal sight!
Ministers of grace divine
Feelingly their brows incline
O'er this seeming Castaway
Breathing, in the light of day,
Something like the faintest breath
That has power to baffle death—
Beautiful, while very weakness
Captivates like passive meekness!

And, sweet Mother! under warrant
Of the universal Parent,
Who repays in season due
Them who have, like thee, been true
To the filial chain let down
From his everlasting throne,

Angels hovering round thy couch,
With their softest whispers vouch,
That, whatever griefs may fret,
Cares entangle, sins beset
This thy first-born, and with tears
Stain her cheek in future years,
Heavenly succour, not denied
To the Babe, whate'er betide,
Will to the Woman be supplied!

Mother! blest be thy calm ease;
Blest the starry promises,
And the firmament benign
Hallowed be it, where they shine!
Yes, for them whose souls have scope
Ample for a wingèd hope,
And can earthward bend an ear
For needful listening, pledge is here,
That, if thy new-born Charge shall tread
In thy footsteps, and be led
By that other Guide, whose light
Of manly virtues, mildly bright,
Gave him first the wished-for part
In thy gentle virgin heart,
Then, amid the storms of life
Presignified by that dread strife
Whence ye have escaped together,
She may look for serene weather,
In all trials sure to find
Comfort for a faithful mind,
Kindlier issues, holier rest,
Than even now await her prest,
Conscious Nursling, to thy breast!

THE WARNING

A SEQUEL TO THE FOREGOING.

MARCH, 1833

List, the winds of March are blowing;
Her ground-flowers shrink, afraid of showing
Their meek heads to the nipping air,
Which ye feel not, happy pair!
Sunk into a kindly sleep.
We, meanwhile, our hope will keep,
And if Time leagued with adverse Change
(Too busy fear!) shall cross its range,
Whatsoever check they bring,
Anxious duty hindering,
To like hope our prayers will cling.

Thus, while the ruminating spirit feeds
Upon each home-event as life proceeds,
Affections pure and holy in their source
Gain a fresh impulse, run a livelier course;
Hopes that within the Father's heart prevail,
Are in the experienced Grandsire's slow to fail,
And if the Harp pleased his gay youth, it rings
To his grave touch with no unready strings,
While thoughts press on, and feelings overflow,
And quick words round him fall like flakes of snow.

Thanks to the Powers that yet maintain their sway,
And have renewed the tributary Lay
Truths of the heart flock in with eager pace,
And Fancy greets them with a fond embrace;
Swift as the rising sun his beam extends
She shoots the tidings forth to distant friends,
Their gifts she hails (deemed precious as they prove
For the unconscious Babe an unbelated love!)
But from this peaceful centre of delight
Vague sympathies have urged her to take flight.
She rivals the fleet Swallow, making rings
In the smooth lake where'er he dips his wings:
—Rapt into upper regions, like the Bee
That sucks from mountain heath her honey fee,
Or, like the warbling Lark intent to shroud
His head in sunbeams or a bowery cloud,
She soars—and here and there her pinions rest
On proud towers, like this humble cottage, blest
With a new visitant, an infant guest—
Towers where red streamers flout the breezy sky
In pomp foreseen by her creative eye,
When feasts shall crowd the Hall, and steeple bells
Glad proclamation make, and heights and dells
Catch the blithe music as it sinks or swells,
And harboured ships, whose pride is on the sea,
Shall hoist their topmast flags in sign of glee,
Honouring the hope of noble ancestry

But who (though neither reckoning ills assigned
By Nature, nor reviewing in the mind

The track that was, and is, and must be, worn
With weary feet by all of woman born)—
Shall *now* by such a gift with joy be moved,
Nor feel the fulness of that joy reproved?
Not He, whose last faint memory will command
The truth that Britain was his native land;
Whose infant soul was tutored to confide
In the cleansed faith for which her martyrs died;
Whose boyish ear the voice of her renown
With rapture thrilled; whose Youth revered the crown
Of Saxon liberty that Alfred wore,
Alfred, dear Babe, thy great Progenitor!
—Not He, who from her mellowed practice drew
His social sense of just, and fair, and true;
And saw, thereafter, on the soil of France
Rash Polity begin her maniac dance,
Foundations broken up, the deeps run wild,
Nor grieved to see, (himself not unbeguiled)—
Woke from the dream, the dreamer to upbraid,
And learn how sanguine expectations fade
When novel trusts by folly are betrayed,—
To see presumption, turning pale, refrain
From further havoc, but repent in vain,—
Good aims lie down, and perish in the road
Where guilt had urged them on, with ceaseless goad,
Till undiscriminating Ruin swept
The Land, and Wrong perpetual vigils kept;
With proof before her that on public ends
Domestic virtue vitally depends.

Can such a one, dear Babe! though glad and proud
To welcome Thee, repel the fears that crowd
Into his English breast, and spare to quake
Not for his own, but for thy innocent sake?
Too late—or, should the providence of God
Lead, through blind ways by sin and sorrow trod,
Justice and peace to a secure abode,
Too soon—thou com'st into this breathing world;
Ensigns of mimic outrage are unfurled.
Who shall preserve or prop the tottering Realm?
What hand suffice to govern the state-helm?
If, in the aims of men, the surest test
Of good or bad (whate'er be sought for or profest)
Lie in the means required, or ways ordained,
For compassing the end, else never gained;
Yet governors and governed both are blind
To this plain truth, or fling it to the wind;
If to expedience principle must bow;
Past, future, shrinking up beneath the incumbent Now;
If cowardly concession still must feed
The thirst for power in men who ne'er concede;
If generous Loyalty must stand in awe
Of subtle Treason, with his mask of law;
Or with bravado insolent and hard,
Provoking punishment, to win reward;
If office help the factious to conspire,
And they who *should* extinguish, fan the fire—
Then, will the sceptre be a straw, the crown
Sit loosely, like the thistle's crest of down;
To be blown off at will, by Power that spares it
In cunning patience, from the head that wears it.

Lost people, trained to theoretic feud;
Lost above all, ye labouring multitude!
Bewildered whether ye, by slanderous tongues
Deceived, mistake calamities for wrongs;
And over fancied usurpations brood,
Oft snapping at revenge in sullen mood;
Or, from long stress of real injuries fly
To desperation for a remedy;
In bursts of outrage spread your judgments wide,
And to your wrath cry out, "Be thou our guide;"
Or, bound by oaths, come forth to tread earth's floor
In marshalled thousands, darkening street and moor
With the worst shape mock-patience ever wore;
Or, to the giddy top of self-esteem
By Flatterers carried, mount into a dream
Of boundless suffrage, at whose sage behest
Justice shall rule, disorder be supprest,
And every man sit down as Plenty's Guest!
—O for a bridle bitted with remorse
To stop your Leaders in their headstrong course!
Oh may the Almighty scatter with his grace
These mists, and lead you to a safer place,
By paths no human wisdom can foretrace!

May He pour round you, from worlds far above
Man's feverish passions, his pure light of love,
That quietly restores the natural mien
To hope, and makes truth willing to be seen!
Else shall your blood-stained hands in frenzy reap
Fields gaily sown when promises were cheap.
Why is the Past belied with wicked art,
The Future made to play so false a part,
Among a people famed for strength of mind,
Foremost in freedom, noblest of mankind?
We act as if we joyed in the sad tune
Storms make in rising, valued in the moon
Naught but her changes. Thus, ungrateful Nation!
If thou persist, and, scorning moderation,
Spread for thyself the snares of tribulation,
Whom, then, shall meekness guard? What saving skill
Lie in forbearance, strength in standing still?
—Soon shall the Widow (for the speed of Time
Naught equals when the hours are winged with crime)
Widow, or Wife, implore on tremulous knee,
From him who judged her Lord, a like decree;
The skies will weep o'er old men desolate:
Ye little ones! Earth shudders at your fate,
Outcasts and homeless orphans——

But turn, my Soul, and from the sleeping Pair
Learn thou the beauty of omniscient care!
Be strong in faith, bid anxious thoughts lie still;
Seek for the good and cherish it—the ill
Oppose, or bear with a submissive will.

If this great world of joy and pain
Revolve in one sure track,
If Freedom, set, will rise again,
And Virtue, flown, come back;
Woe to the purblind crew who fill
The heart with each day's care;
Nor gain, from past or future, skill
To bear, and to forbear!

SONNET,*

COMPOSED AFTER READING A NEWSPAPER OF THE DAY.

"People! your chains are severing link by link,
Soon shall the Rich be levelled down—the Poor
Meet them half way." Vain boast! for These, the more
They thus would rise, must low and lower sink
Till, by repentance stung, they fear to think,
While all lie prostrate, save the tyrant few
Bent in quick turns each other to undo,
And mix the poison, they themselves must drink.
Mistrust thyself, vain Country! cease to cry
"Knowledge will save me from the threatened woe."
For, if than other rash ones more thou know,
Yet on presumptuous wing as far would fly
Above thy knowledge as they dared to go,
Thou wilt provoke a heavier penalty.

LOVING AND LIKING:

IRREGULAR VERSES ADDRESSED TO A CHILD.

[In the former editions of the author's Miscellaneous Poems are three pieces addressed to Children:—the following, a few lines excepted, is by the same Writer, and, as it belongs to the same unassuming class of compositions, she has been prevailed upon to consent to its publication.]

There's more in words than I can teach:
Yet listen, Child!—I would not preach;
But only give some plain directions
To guide your speech and your affections.
Say not you *love* a roasted Fowl,
But you may love a screaming Owl,
And, if you can, the unwieldy Toad
That crawls from his secure abode
Within the mossy garden wall
When evening dews begin to fall.
Oh mark the beauty of his eye:
What wonders in that circle lie!
So clear, so bright, our fathers said
He wears a jewel in his head!

* This Sonnet ought to have followed No. VII. in the series of 1831, but was omitted by mistake.

And when, upon some showery day,
Into a path or public way
A Frog leaps out from bordering grass,
Startling the timid as they pass,
Do you observe him, and endeavour
To take the intruder into favour;
Learning from him to find a reason
For a light heart in a dull season.
And you may love him in the pool,
That is for him a happy school,
In which he swims, as taught by nature,
A pattern for a human creature,
Glancing amid the water bright,
And sending upward sparkling light
Nor blush if o'er your heart be stealing
A love for things that have no feeling:
The spring's first Rose, by you espied,
May fill your breast with joyful pride,
And you may love the Strawberry Flower,
And love the Strawberry in its bower;
But when the fruit, so often praised
For beauty, to your lip is raised,
Say not you *love* the delicate treat,
But *like* it, enjoy it, and thankfully eat.
Long may you love your pensioner Mouse,
Though one of a tribe that torment the house:
Nor dislike for her cruel sport the Cat,
That deadly foe of both mouse and rat;
Remember she follows the law of her kind,
And Instinct is neither wayward nor blind.
Then think of her beautiful gliding form,
Her tread that would not crush a worm,
And her soothing song by the winter fire,
Soft as the dying throbs of the lyre.

I would not circumscribe your love:
It may soar with the Eagle and brood with the Dove,
May pierce the earth with the patient Mole,
Or track the Hedgehog to his hole.
Loving and liking are the solace of life,
They foster all joy, and extinguish all strife.
You love your father and your mother,
Your grown-up and your baby brother;
You love your sister, and your friends,
And countless blessings which God sends:
And while these right affections play,
You *live* each moment of your day,
They lead you on to full content,
And likings fresh and innocent,
That store the mind, the memory feed,
And prompt to many a gentle deed:
But *likings* come, and pass away;
'Tis *love* that remains till our latest day:
Our heavenward guide is holy love,
And it will be our bliss with saints above.

ST. BEES,

SUGGESTED IN A STEAMBOAT OFF ST. BEES' HEADS, ON THE COAST OF CUMBERLAND.

[St. Bees' Heads, anciently called the Cliff of Baruth, are a conspicuous sea-mark for all vessels sailing in the N E parts of the Irish Sea. In a bay, one side of which is formed by the southern headland, stand the village of St Bees: a place distinguished from very early times, for its religious and scholastic foundations.

"St. Bees," say Nicholson and Burns, "had its name from Bega, an holy woman from Ireland, who is said to have founded here, about the year of our Lord 650, a small monastery, where afterwards a church was built in memory of her

"The aforesaid religious house being destroyed by the Danes, was restored by William de Meschiens, son of Ranulph, and brother of Ranulph de Meschiens, first Earl of Cumberland after the Conquest; and made a cell of a prior and six Benedictine monks to the Abbey of St Mary at York"

Several traditions of miracles, connected with the foundation of the first of these religious houses, survive among the people of the neighbourhood; one of which is alluded to in the following Stanzas and another, of a somewhat bolder and more peculiar character, has furnished the subject of a spirited poem by the Rev. R Parkinson, M.A., late Divinity Lecturer of St. Bees' College, and Fellow of the Collegiate Church of Manchester

After the dissolution of the monasteries, Archbishop Grindal founded a free school at St. Bees, from which the counties of Cumberland and Westmoreland have derived great benefit, and under the patronage of the Earl of Lonsdale, a college has been established there for the education of ministers for the English Church. The old Conventual Church has been repaired under the superintendence of the Rev Dr Ainger, the Head of the College; and is well worthy of being visited by any strangers who might be led to the neighbourhood of this celebrated spot.

The form of stanza in the following Piece, and something in the style of versification, are adopted from the "St Monica," a poem of much beauty upon a monastic subject, by Charlotte Smith; a lady to whom English verse is under greater obligations, than are likely to be either acknowledged or remembered. She wrote little, and that little unambitiously, but with true feeling for nature]

I.

If Life were slumber on a bed of down,
Toil unimposed, vicissitudes unknown,
Sad were our lot: no Hunter of the Hare
Exults like him whose javelin from the lair

Has roused the Lion, no one plucks the
Rose,
Whose proffered beauty in safe shelter
blows
'Mid a trim garden's summer luxuries,
With joy like his who climbs on hands and
knees,
For some rare Plant, yon Headland of St
Bees.

2

This independence upon oar and sail,
This new indifference to breeze or gale,
This straight-lined progress, furrowing a
flat lea,
And regular as if locked in certainty,
Depress the hours Up, Spirit of the Storm!
That Courage may find something to per-
form;
That Fortitude, whose blood disdains to
freeze
At Danger's bidding, may confront the seas,
Firm as the towering Headlands of St.
Bees.

3.

Dread Cliff of Baruth! *that* wild wish may
sleep,
Bold as if Men and Creatures of the Deep
Breathed the same Element: too many
wrecks
Have struck thy sides, too many ghastly
decks
Hast thou looked down upon, that such a
thought
Should here be welcome, and in verse en-
wrought·
With thy stern aspect better far agrees
Utterance of thanks that we have past with
ease,
As Millions thus shall do, the Headlands
of St. Bees.

4.

Yet, while each useful Art augments her
store,
What boots the gain if Nature should lose
more?
And Wisdom, that once held a Christian
place
In Man's intelligence sublimed by grace?
When Bega sought of yore the Cumbrian
coast,
Tempestuous winds her holy errand cross'd,
As high and higher heaved the billows, faith
Grew with them, mightier than the powers
of death.

She knelt in prayer—the waves their wrath
appease;
And, from her vow well weighed in Heaven's
decrees,
Rose, where she touched the strand, the
Chauntry of St. Bees

5.

"Cruel of heart were they, bloody of hand,"
Who in these Wilds then struggled for
command,
The strong were merciless, without hope
the weak;
Till this bright Stranger came, fair as Day
break,
And as a Cresset true that darts its length
Of beamy lustre from a tower of strength;
Guiding the Mariner through troubled seas,
And cheering oft his peaceful reveries,
Like the fixed Light that crowns yon head-
land of St. Bees.

6.

To aid the Votaress, miracles believed
Wrought in men's minds, like miracles
achieved;
So piety took root; and Song might tell
What humanizing Virtues round her Cell
Sprang up, and spread their fragrance wide
around;
How savage bosoms melted at the sound
Of gospel-truth enchained in harmonies
Wafted o'er waves, or creeping through
close trees,
From her religious Mansion of St. Bees

7

When her sweet Voice, that instrument of
love,
Was glorified, and took its place, above
The silent stars, among the angelic Quire,
Her Chauntry blazed with sacrilegious fire!
And perished utterly, but her good deeds
Had sown the spot that witnessed them
with seeds
Which lay in earth expectant, till a breeze
With quickening impulse answered their
mute pleas,
And lo! a *statelier* Pile, the Abbey of St
Bees.

8.

There were the naked clothed, the hungry
fed;
And Charity extended to the Dead
Her intercessions made for the soul's rest
Of tardy Penitents; or for the best

Among the good (when love might else have slept,
Sickened, or died) in pious memory kept.
Thanks to the austere and simple Devotees,
Who, to that service bound by venial fees,
Kept watch before the Altars of St. Bees.

9.

Were not, in sooth, their Requiems sacred ties
Woven out of passion's sharpest agonies,
Subdued, composed, and formalized by art,
To fix a wiser sorrow in the heart?
The prayer for them whose hour was past away
Said to the Living, profit while ye may!
A little part, and that the worst, he sees
Who thinks that priestly cunning holds the keys
That best unlock the secrets of St. Bees.

10.

Conscience, the timid being's inmost light,
Hope of the dawn and solace of the night,
Cheers these Recluses with a steady ray
In many an hour when judgment goes astray.
Ah! scorn not hastily their rule who try
Earth to despise, and flesh to mortify;
Consume with zeal, in wingèd ecstacies
Of prayer and praise forget their rosaries,
Nor hear the loudest surges of St. Bees.

11.

Yet none so prompt to succour and protect
The forlorn Traveller, or Sailor wrecked
On the bare coast; nor do they grudge the boon
Which staff and cockle hat and sandal shoon
Claim for the Pilgrim: and, though chidings sharp
May sometimes greet the strolling Minstrel's harp,
It is not then when, swept with sportive ease,
It charms a feast-day throng of all degrees,
Brightening the archway of reverend St. Bees.

12.

How did the Cliffs and echoing Hills rejoice
What time the Benedictine Brethren's voice,
Imploring, or commanding with meet pride,
Summoned the Chiefs to lay their feuds aside.
And under one blest ensign serve the Lord
In Palestine. Advance, indignant Sword!
Flaming till thou from Paynim hands release
That Tomb, dread centre of all sanctities
Nursed in the quiet Abbey of St. Bees.

13.

On, Champions, on!—But mark! the passing Day
Submits her intercourse to milder sway,
With high and low whose busy thoughts from far
Follow the fortunes which they may not share.
While in Judea Fancy loves to roam,
She helps to make a Holy-land at home:
The Star of Bethlehem from its sphere invites
To sound the crystal depth of maiden rights,
And wedded life, through scriptural mysteries,
Heavenward ascends with all her charities,
Taught by the hooded Celibates of St. Bees

14.

Who with the ploughshare clove the barren moors,
And to green meadows changed the swampy shores?
Thinned the rank woods, and for the cheerful Grange
Made room where Wolf and Boar were used to range?
Who taught, and showed by deeds, that gentler chains
Should bind the Vassal to his Lord's domains?
The thoughtful Monks, intent their God to please,
For Christ's dear sake, by human sympathies
Poured from the bosom of thy Church, St. Bees!

15.

But all availed not; by a mandate given
Through lawless will the Brotherhood was driven
Forth from their cells;—their ancient House laid low
In Reformation's sweeping overthrow.
But now once more the local Heart revives,
The inextinguishable Spirit strives.
Oh may that Power who hushed the stormy seas,
And cleared the way for the first Votaries,
Prosper the new-born College of St. Bees!

16.

Alas! the Genius of our age from Schools
Less humble draws her lessons, aims, and rules
To Prowess guided by her insight keen
Matter and Spirit are as one Machine,
Boastful Idolatress of formal skill
She in her own would merge the eternal will.
Expert to move in paths that Newton trod,
From Newton's Universe would banish God
Better, if Reason's triumphs match with these,
Her flight before the bold credulities
That furthered the first teaching of St. Bees.

[The three following Sonnets are an intended addition to the "Ecclesiastical Sketches," the first to stand second, and the two that succeed, seventh and eighth, in the second part of the Series. They are placed here as having some connection with the foregoing Poem]

DEPLORABLE his lot who tills the ground,
His whole life long tills it, with heartless toil
Of villain-service, passing with the soil
To each new Master, like a steer or hound,
Or like a rooted tree, or stone earth-bound;
But, mark how gladly, through their own domains,
The Monks relax or break these iron chains;
While Mercy, uttering, through their voice, a sound
Echoed in Heaven, cries out, "Ye Chiefs, abate
These legalized oppressions! Man, whose name
And nature God disdained not, Man, whose soul
Christ died for, cannot forfeit his high claim
To live and move exempt from all controul
Which fellow-feeling doth not mitigate!"

THE VAUDOIS.

BUT whence came they who for the Saviour Lord
Have long borne witness as the Scriptures teach?
Ages ere Valdo raised his voice to preach
In Gallic ears the unadulterate Word,
Their fugitive Progenitors explored
Subalpine vales, in quest of safe retreats
Where that pure Church survives, though summer heats
Open a passage to the Romish sword,
Far as it dares to follow. Herbs self-sown,
And fruitage gathered from the chestnut wood,
Nourish the Sufferers then; and mists, that brood
O'er chasms with new-fallen obstacles bestrown,
Protect them; and the eternal snow that daunts
Aliens, is God's good winter for their haunts.

PRAISED be the Rivers, from their mountain-springs
Shouting to Freedom, "Plant thy Banners here!"
To harassed Piety, "Dismiss thy fear,
And in our Caverns smooth thy ruffled wings!"
Nor be unthanked their tardiest lingerings
'Mid reedy fens wide-spread and marshes drear,
Their own creation, till their long career
End in the sea engulphed. Such welcomings
As came from mighty Po when Venice rose,
Greeted those simple Heirs of truth divine
Who near his fountains sought obscure repose,
Yet were prepared as glorious lights to shine,
Should that be needed for their sacred Charge;
Blest Prisoners They, whose spirits are at large!

THE REDBREAST.

(SUGGESTED IN A WESTMORELAND COTTAGE.)

DRIVEN in by Autumn's sharpening air,
From half-stripped woods and pastures bare,
Brisk Robin seeks a kindlier home:
Not like a beggar is he come,
But enters as a looked-for guest,
Confiding in his ruddy breast,

As if it were a natural shield
Charged with a blazon on the field,
Due to that good and pious deed
Of which we in the Ballad read.
But pensive fancies putting by,
And wild-wood sorrows, speedily
He plays the expert ventriloquist;
And, caught by glimpses now—now missed,
Puzzles the listener with a doubt
If the soft voice he throws about
Comes from within doors or without!
Was ever such a sweet confusion,
Sustained by delicate illusion?
He's at your elbow—to your feeling
The notes are from the floor or ceiling;
And there's a riddle to be guessed,
'Till you have marked his heaving breast,
Where tiny sinking and faint swell,
Betray the Elf that loves to dwell
In Robin's bosom, as a chosen cell.

Heart-pleased we smile upon the Bird
If seen, and with like pleasure stirred
Commend him, when he's only heard.
But small and fugitive *our* gain
Compared with *his* who long hath lain,
With languid limbs and patient head,
Reposing on a lone sick-bed;
Where now he daily hears a strain
That cheats him of too busy cares,
Eases his pain, and helps his prayers.
And who but this dear Bird beguiled
The fever of that pale-faced Child?
Now cooling, with his passing wing,
Her forehead, like a breeze of Spring;
Recalling now, with descant soft
Shed round her pillow from aloft,
Sweet thoughts of angels hovering nigh,
And the invisible sympathy
Of "Matthew, Mark, and Luke, and John,
Blessing the bed she lies upon:"*
And sometimes, just as listening ends
In slumber, with the cadence blends
A dream of that low-warbled hymn
Which Old-folk, fondly pleased to trim
Lamps of faith now burning dim,
Say that the Cherubs carved in stone,
When clouds gave way at dead of night,
And the moon filled the church with light,
Used to sing in heavenly tone,
Above and round the sacred places
They guard, with wingèd baby-faces.

* The words—

"Matthew, Mark, and Luke, and John,
Bless the bed that I lie on,"

are part of a child's prayer, still in general use through the northern counties.

Thrice-happy Creature! in all lands
Nurtured by hospitable hands:
Free entrance to this cot has he,
Entrance and exit both *yet* free;
And, when the keen unruffled weather
That thus brings man and bird together,
Shall with its pleasantness be past,
The casement closed and door made fast,
To keep at bay the howling blast,
He needs not fear the season's rage,
For the whole house is Robin's cage.
Whether the bird flit here or there,
O'er table *lilt*, or perch on chair,
Though some may frown, and make a stir
To scare him as a trespasser,
And he belike will flinch or start,
Good friends he has to take his part;
One chiefly, who with voice and look
Pleads for him from the chimney nook,
Where sits the Dame, and wears away
Her long and vacant holiday;
With images about her heart,
Reflected, from the years gone by,
On human nature's second infancy.

TO ——.

[Miss not the occasion; by the forelock take
That subtle Power, the never-halting Time,
Lest a mere moment's putting-off should make
Mischance almost as heavy as a crime.]

"WAIT, prithee, wait!" this answer Lesbia threw
Forth to her Dove, and took no further heed;
Her eye was busy, while her fingers flew
Across the harp, with soul-engrossing speed;
But from that bondage when her thoughts were freed
She rose, and towards the close-shut casement drew,
Whence the poor unregarded Favourite, true
To old affections, had been heard to plead
With flapping wing for entrance. What a shriek
Forced from that voice so lately tuned to a strain
Of harmony!—a shriek of terror, pain,
And self-reproach!—for, from aloft, a Kite
Pounced, and the Dove, which from its ruthless beak
She could not rescue, perished in her sight!

RURAL ILLUSIONS.

I.

SYLPH was it? or a Bird more bright
 Than those of fabulous stock?
A second darted by;—and lo!
 Another of the flock,
Through sunshine flitting from the bough
 To nestle in the rock.
Transient deception! a gay freak
 Of April's mimicries!
Those brilliant Strangers, hailed with joy
 Among the budding trees,
Proved last year's leaves, pushed from the spray
 To frolic on the breeze.

2.

Maternal Flora! show thy face,
 And let thy hand be *seen*
Which sprinkles here these tiny flowers,
 That, as they touch the green,
Take root (so seems it) and look up
 In honour of their Queen.
Yet, sooth, those little starry specks,
 That not in vain aspired
To be confounded with live growths,
 Most dainty, most admired,
Were only blossoms dropped from twigs
 Of their own offspring tired.

3.

Not such the World's illusive shows;
 Her wingless flutterings,
Her blossoms which, though shed, outbrave
 The Floweret as it springs,
For the Undeceived, smile as they may,
 Are melancholy things:
But gentle Nature plays her part
 With ever-varying wiles,
And transient feignings with plain truth
 So well she reconciles,
That those fond Idlers most are pleased
 Whom oftenest she beguiles.

THIS LAWN, &c.

THIS Lawn, a carpet all alive
With shadows flung from leaves—to strive
 In dance, amid a press
Of sunshine—an apt emblem yields
Of Worldlings revelling in the fields
 Of strenuous idleness;
Less quick the stir when tide and breeze
Encounter, and to narrow seas
 Forbid a moment's rest;
The medley less when boreal Lights
Glance to and fro like aery Sprites
 To feats of arms addrest!

Yet, spite of all this eager strife,
This ceaseless play, the genuine life
 That serves the steadfast hours,
Is in the grass beneath, that grows
Unheeded, and the mute repose
 Of sweetly-breathing flowers.

THOUGHT ON THE SEASONS.

FLATTERED with promise of escape
 From every hurtful blast,
Spring takes, O sprightly May! thy shape,
 Her loveliest and her last.

Less fair is summer riding high
 In fierce solstitial power,
Less fair than when a lenient sky
 Brings on her parting hour.

When earth repays with golden sheaves
 The labours of the plough,
And ripening fruits and forest leaves
 All brighten on the bough,

What pensive beauty autumn shows,
 Before she hears the sound
Of winter rushing in, to close
 The emblematic round!

Such be our Spring, our Summer such;
 So may our Autumn blend
With hoary Winter, and Life touch,
 Through heaven-born hope, her end!

HUMANITY.

(WRITTEN IN THE YEAR 1829.)

Not from his fellows only man may learn
Rights to compare and duties to discern:
All creatures and all objects, in degree,
Are friends and patrons of humanity.—MS.

[The Rocking-stones, alluded to in the beginning of the following verses, are supposed to have been used, by our British ancestors, both for judicial and religious purposes. Such stones are not uncommonly found, at this day, both in Great Britain and in Ireland.]

WHAT though the Accused, upon his own appeal
To righteous Gods when Man has ceased to feel,

Or at a doubting Judge's stern command,
Before the STONE OF POWER no longer stand—
To take his sentence from the balanced Block,
As, at his touch, it rocks, or seems to rock;
Though, in the depths of sunless groves, no more
The Druid-priest the hallowed Oak adore;
Yet, for the Initiate, rocks and whispering trees
Do still perform mysterious offices!
And still in beast and bird a function dwells,
That, while we look and listen, sometimes tells
Upon the heart, in more authentic guise
Than Oracles, or wingèd Auguries,
Spake to the Science of the ancient wise.
Not uninspired appear their simplest ways;
Their voices mount symbolical of praise—
To mix with hymns that Spirits make and hear;
And to fallen Man their innocence is dear.
Enraptured Art draws from those sacred springs
Streams that reflect the poetry of things!
Where Christian Martyrs stand in hues portrayed,
That, might a wish avail, would never fade,
Borne in their hands the Lily and the Palm
Shed round the Altar a celestial calm;
There, too, behold the Lamb and guileless Dove
Prest in the tenderness of virgin love
To saintly bosoms!—Glorious is the blending
Of right Affections, climbing or descending
Along a scale of light and life, with cares
Alternate; carrying holy thoughts and prayers
Up to the sovereign seat of the Most High,
Descending to the worm in charity;*
Like those good Angels whom a dream of night
Gave, in the Field of Luz, to Jacob's sight;
All, while *he* slept, treading the pendent stairs
Earthward or heavenward, radiant Messengers,
That, with a perfect will in one accord
Of strict obedience, served the Almighty Lord;
And with untired humility forbore
The ready service of the wings they wore.

What a fair World were ours for Verse to paint,
If Power could live at ease with self-restraint!
Opinion bow before the naked sense
Of the great Vision,—faith in Providence;
Merciful over all existence, just
To the least particle of sentient dust;
And, fixing by immutable decrees,
Seedtime and harvest for his purposes!
Then would be closed the restless oblique eye
That looks for evil like a treacherous spy,
Disputes would then relax, like stormy winds
That into breezes sink; impetuous Minds
By discipline endeavour to grow meek
As Truth herself, whom they profess to seek.
Then Genius, shunning fellowship with Pride,
Would braid his golden locks at Wisdom's side;
Love ebb and flow untroubled by caprice;
And not alone *harsh* tyranny would cease,
But unoffending creatures find release
From *qualified* oppression, whose defence
Rests on a hollow plea of recompence;
Thought-tempered wrongs, for each humane respect
Oft worse to bear, or deadlier in effect
Witness those glances of indignant scorn
From some high-minded Slave, impelled to spurn
The kindness that would make him less forlorn;
Or, if the soul to bondage be subdued,
His look of pitiable gratitude!

Alas for thee, bright Galaxy of Isles,
Where day departs in pomp, returns with smiles—
To greet the flowers and fruitage of a land,
As the sun mounts, by sea-borne breezes fanned;
A land whose azure mountain-tops are seats
For Gods in council, whose green vales, Retreats
Fit for the Shades of Heroes, mingling there
To breathe Elysian peace in upper air.

Though cold as winter, gloomy as the grave,
Stone-walls a Prisoner make, but not a Slave
Shall Man assume a property in Man?
Lay on the moral Will a withering ban?

* The author is indebted, here, to a passage in one of Mr. Digby's valuable works.

Shame that our laws at distance should protect
Enormities, which they at home reject!
"Slaves cannot breathe in England"—a proud boast!
And yet a mockery! if, from coast to coast,
Though *fettered* slave be none, her floors and soil
Groan underneath a weight of slavish toil,
For the poor Many, measured out by rules
Fetched with cupidity from heartless schools,
That to an Idol, falsely called "the Wealth
Of Nations," sacrifice a People's health,
Body and mind and soul, a thirst so keen
Is ever urging on the vast machine
Of sleepless Labour, 'mid whose dizzy wheels
The Power least prized is that which thinks and feels.

Then, for the pastimes of this delicate age,
And all the heavy or light vassalage
Which for their sakes we fasten, as may suit
Our varying moods, on human kind or brute,
'Twere well in little, as in great, to pause,
Lest Fancy trifle with eternal laws.
There are to whom even garden, grove, and field,
Perpetual lessons of forbearance yield;
Who would not lightly violate the grace
The lowliest flower possesses in its place,
Nor shorten the sweet life, too fugitive,
Which nothing less than Infinite Power could give.

LINES

SUGGESTED BY A PORTRAIT FROM THE PENCIL OF F. STONE.

BEGUILED into forgetfulness of care
Due to the day's unfinished task, of pen
Or book regardless, and of that fair scene
In Nature's prodigality displayed
Before my window, oftentimes and long
I gaze upon a Portrait whose mild gleam
Of beauty never ceases to enrich
The common light, whose stillness charms the air,
Or seems to charm it, into like repose;
Whose silence, for the pleasure of the ear,
Surpasses sweetest music. There she sits
With emblematic purity attired
In a white vest, white as her marble neck
Is, and the pillar of the throat *would be*
But for the shadow by the drooping chin
Cast into that recess—the tender shade
The shade and light, both there and everywhere,
And through the very atmosphere she breathes,
Broad, clear, and toned harmoniously, with skill
That might from nature have been learnt in the hour
When the lone Shepherd sees the morning spread
Upon the mountains. Look at her, whoe'er
Thou be, that kindling with a poet's soul
Hast loved the painter's true Promethean craft
Intensely—from Imagination take
The treasure, what mine eyes behold see thou,
Even though the Atlantic Ocean roll between.

A silver line, that runs from brow to crown,
And in the middle parts the braided hair,
Just serves to show how delicate a soil
The golden harvest grows in, and those eyes,
Soft and capacious as a cloudless sky
Whose azure depth their colour emulates,
Must needs be conversant with *upward* looks,
Prayer's voiceless service, but now, seeking naught
And shunning naught, their own peculiar life
Of motion they renounce, and with the head
Partake its inclination towards earth
In humble grace, and quiet pensiveness
Caught at the point where it stops short of sadness.

Offspring of soul-bewitching Art, make me
Thy confidant! say, whence derived that air
Of calm abstraction? Can the ruling thought
Be with some lover far away, or one
Crossed by misfortune, or of doubted faith?
Inapt conjecture! Childhood here, a moon
Crescent in simple loveliness serene,
Has but approached the gates of womanhood,
Not entered them; her heart is yet unpierced
By the blind Archer-god, her fancy free:
The fount of feeling, if unsought elsewhere,
Will not be found.

Her right hand, as it lies
Across the slender wrist of the left arm
Upon her lap reposing, holds—but mark
How slackly, for the absent mind permits
No firmer grasp—a little wild-flower, joined
As in a posy, with a few pale ears
Of yellowing corn, the same that overtopped
And in their common birthplace sheltered it
'Till they were plucked together; a blue flower
Called by the thrifty husbandman *a weed;*
But Ceres, in her garland, might have worn
That ornament, unblamed. The floweret, held
In scarcely conscious fingers, was, she knows,
(Her Father told her so) in Youth's gay dawn
Her Mother's favourite; and the orphan Girl,
In her own dawn—a dawn less gay and bright,
Loves it while there in solitary peace
She sits, for that departed Mother's sake.
—Not from a source less sacred is derived
(Surely I do not err) that pensive air
Of calm abstraction through the face diffused
And the whole person.

Words have something told
More than the pencil can, and verily
More than is needed, but the precious Art
Forgives their interference—Art divine,
That both creates and fixes, in despite
Of Death and Time, the marvels it hath wrought.

Strange contrasts have we in this world of ours!
That posture, and the look of filial love
Thinking of past and gone, with what is left
Dearly united, might be swept away
From this fair Portrait's fleshly Archetype,
Even by an innocent fancy's slightest freak
Banished, nor ever, haply, be restored
To their lost place, or meet in harmony
So exquisite; but *here* do they abide,
Enshrined for ages. Is not then the Art
Godlike, a humble branch of the divine,
In visible quest of immortality,
Stretched forth with trembling hope? In every realm,
From high Gibraltar to Siberian plains,
Thousands, in each variety of tongue
That Europe knows, would echo this appeal;
One above all, a Monk who waits on God
In the magnific Convent built of yore
To sanctify the Escurial palace. He
Guiding, from cell to cell and room to room,
A British Painter (eminent for truth
In character, and depth of feeling, shown
By labours that have touched the hearts of kings,
And are endeared to simple cottagers)
Left not unvisited a glorious work,
Our Lord's Last Supper, beautiful as when first
The appropriate Picture, fresh from Titian's hand,
Graced the Refectory: and there, while both
Stood with eyes fixed upon that Masterpiece,
The hoary Father in the Stranger's ear
Breathed out these words:—"Here daily do we sit,
Thanks given to God for daily bread, and here
Pondering the mischiefs of these restless Times,
And thinking of my Brethren, dead, dispersed,
Or changed and changing, I not seldom gaze
Upon this solemn Company unmoved
By shock of circumstance, or lapse of years,
Until I cannot but believe that they—
They are in truth the Substance, we the Shadows."

So spake the mild Jeronymite, his griefs
Melting away within him like a dream
Ere he had ceased to gaze, perhaps to speak:
And I, grown old, but in a happier land,
Domestic Portrait! have to verse consigned
In thy calm presence those heart-moving words:
Words that can soothe, more than they agitate;
Whose spirit, like the angel that went down
Into Bethesda's pool, with healing virtue
Informs the fountain in the human breast
That by the visitation was disturbed.
——But why this stealing tear? Companion mute,
On thee I look, not sorrowing; fare thee well,
My Song's Inspirer, once again farewell!

The pile of buildings, composing the palace and convent of San Lorenzo, has, in common usage, lost its proper name in that of the *Escurial*, a village at the foot of the hill upon which the splendid edifice, built by Philip the Second, stands. It need scarcely be added, that Wilkie is the painter alluded to.

THE FOREGOING SUBJECT RESUMED.

AMONG a grave fraternity of Monks,
For One, but surely not for One alone,
Triumphs, in that great work, the Painter's skill,
Humbling the body, to exalt the soul;
Yet representing, amid wreck and wrong
And dissolution and decay, the warm
And breathing life of flesh, as if already
Clothed with impassive majesty, and graced
With no mean earnest of a heritage
Assigned to it in future worlds Thou, too,
With thy memorial flower, meek Portraiture!
From whose serene companionship I passed,
Pursued by thoughts that haunt me still, thou also—
Though but a simple object, into light
Called forth by those affections that endear
The private hearth, though keeping thy sole seat
In singleness, and little tried by time,
Creation, as it were, of yesterday—
With a congenial function art endued
For each and all of us, together joined,
In course of nature, under a low roof
By charities and duties that proceed
Out of the bosom of a wiser vow.
To a like salutary sense of awe,
Or sacred wonder, growing with the power
Of meditation that attempts to weigh,
In faithful scales, things and their opposites,
Can thy enduring quiet gently raise
A household small and sensitive,—whose love,
Dependent as in part its blessings are
Upon frailties dissolving or dissolved
On earth, will be revived, we trust, in heaven.

STANZAS ON THE POWER OF SOUND.

ARGUMENT.

The Ear addressed, as occupied by a spiritual functionary, in communion with sounds, individual, or combined in studied harmony — Sources and effects of those sounds (to the close of 6th Stanza).—The power of music, whence proceeding, exemplified in the idiot.—Origin of music, and its effect in early ages—how produced (to the middle of 10th Stanza).—The mind recalled to sounds acting casually and severally —Wish uttered (11th Stanza) that these could be united into a scheme or system for moral interests and intellectual contemplation —(Stanza 12th) The Pythagorean theory of numbers and music, with their supposed power over the motions of the universe—imaginations consonant with such a theory —Wish expressed (in 11th Stanza) realised, in some degree, by the representation of all sounds under the form of thanksgiving to the Creator —(Last Stanza) the destruction of earth and the planetary system—the survival of audible harmony, and its support in the Divine Nature, as revealed in Holy Writ

1.

THY functions are ethereal,
As if within thee dwelt a glancing Mind,
Organ of Vision And a Spirit aerial
Informs the cell of hearing, dark and blind
Intricate labyrinth, more dread for thought
To enter than oracular cave;
Strict passage, through which sighs are brought,
And whispers, for the heart, their slave;
And shrieks, that revel in abuse
Of shivering flesh; and warbled air,
Whose piercing sweetness can unloose
The chains of frenzy, or entice a smile
Into the ambush of despair;
Hosannas pealing down the long-drawn aisle,
And requiems answered by the pulse that beats
Devoutly, in life's last retreats!

2.

The headlong Streams and Fountains
Serve Thee, Invisible Spirit, with untired powers;
Cheering the wakeful Tent on Syrian mountains,
They lull perchance ten thousand thousand flowers.
That roar, the prowling Lion's *Here I am*,
How fearful to the desert wide!
That bleat, how tender! of the Dam
Calling a straggler to her side.
Shout, Cuckoo! let the vernal soul
Go with thee to the frozen zone,
Toll from thy loftiest perch, lone Bell-bird toll!
At the still hour to Mercy dear,
Mercy from her twilight throne
Listening to Nun's faint sob of holy fear,
To Sailor's prayer breathed from a darkening sea,
Or Widow's cottage lullaby.

3.

Ye Voices, and ye Shadows,
And Images of voice—to hound and horn
From rocky steep and rock-bestudded meadows
Flung back, and, in the sky's blue caves, reborn,
On with your pastime! till the church-tower bells
A greeting give of *measured* glee;
And milder echoes from their cells
Repeat the bridal symphony.
Then, or far earlier, let us rove
Where mists are breaking up or gone,
And from aloft look down into a cove
Besprinkled with a careless quire,
Happy Milk-maids, one by one
Scattering a ditty each to her desire,
A liquid concert matchless by nice Art,
A stream as if from one full heart.

4.

Blest be the song that brightens
The blind Man's gloom, exalts the Veteran's mirth;
Unscorned the Peasant's whistling breath, that lightens
His duteous toil of furrowing the green earth.
For the tired Slave, Song lifts the languid oar,
And bids it aptly fall, with chime
That beautifies the fairest shore,
And mitigates the harshest clime.
Yon Pilgrims see—in lagging file
They move; but soon the appointed way
A choral *Ave Marie* shall beguile,
And to their hope the distant shrine
Glisten with a livelier ray:
Nor friendless He, the Prisoner of the Mine,
Who from the well-spring of his own clear breast
Can draw, and sing his griefs to rest.

5.

When civic renovation
Dawns on a kingdom, and for needful haste
Best eloquence avails not, Inspiration
Mounts with a tune, that travels like a blast
Piping through cave and battlemented tower;
Then starts the Sluggard, pleased to meet
That voice of Freedom, in its power
Of promises, shrill, wild, and sweet!
Who, from a martial *pageant*, spreads
Incitements of a battle-day,
Thrilling the unweaponed crowd with plumeless heads;
Even She whose Lydian airs inspire
Peaceful striving, gentle play
Of timid hope and innocent desire
Shot from the dancing Graces, as they move
Fanned by the plausive wings of Love.

6.

How oft along thy mazes,
Regent of Sound, have dangerous Passions trod!
O Thou, through whom the Temple rings with praises,
And blackening clouds in thunder speak of God,
Betray not by the cozenage of sense
Thy Votaries, wooingly resigned
To a voluptuous influence
That taints the purer, better mind;
But lead sick Fancy to a harp
That hath in noble tasks been tried;
And, if the Virtuous feel a pang too sharp,
Soothe it into patience,—stay
The uplifted arm of Suicide;
And let some mood of thine in firm array
Knit every thought the impending issue needs,
Ere Martyr burns, or Patriot bleeds!

7.

As Conscience, to the centre
Of Being, smites with irresistible pain,
So shall a solemn cadence, if it enter
The mouldy vaults of the dull Idiot's brain,
Transmute him to a wretch from quiet hurled—
Convulsed as by a jarring din;
And then aghast, as at the world
Of reason partially let in
By concords winding with a sway
Terrible for sense and soul!
Or, awed he, weeps, struggling to quell dismay.
Point not these mysteries to an Art
Lodged above the starry pole;
Pure modulations flowing from the heart
Of divine Love, where Wisdom, Beauty, Truth
With Order dwell, in endless youth?

8.

Oblivion may not cover
All treasures hoarded by the Miser, Time.
Orphean Insight! Truth's undaunted Lover,
To the first leagues of tutored Passion climb,

When Music deigned within this grosser sphere
Her subtle essence to enfold,
And Voice and Shell drew forth a tear
Softer than Nature's self could mould
Yet *strenuous* was the infant Age
Art, daring because souls could feel,
Stirred nowhere but an urgent equipage
Of rapt imagination sped her march
Through the realms of woe and weal·
Hell to the lyre bowed low; the upper arch
Rejoiced that clamorous spell and magic verse
Her wan disasters could disperse

9.

The GIFT to King Amphion
That walled a city with its melody
Was for belief no dream; thy skill, Arion!
Could humanise the creatures of the sea,
Where men were monsters. A last grace he craves,
Leave for one chant;—the dulcet sound
Steals from the deck o'er willing waves,
And listening Dolphins gather round.
Self-cast, as with a desperate course,
'Mid that strange audience, he bestrides
A proud One docile as a managed horse;
And singing, while the accordant hand
Sweeps his harp, the Master rides;
So shall he touch at length a friendly strand,
And he, with his Preserver, shine star-bright
In memory, through silent night.

10.

The pipe of Pan, to Shepherds
Couched in the shadow of Menalian Pines,
Was passing sweet; the eyeballs of the Leopards,
That in high triumph drew the Lord of vines,
How did they sparkle to the cymbal's clang!
While Fauns and Satyrs beat the ground
In cadence,—and Silenus swang
This way and that, with wild-flowers crowned.
To life, to *life* give back thine Ear:
Ye who are longing to be rid
Of Fable, though to truth subservient, hear
The little sprinkling of cold earth that fell
Echoed from the coffin lid;
The Convict's summons in the steeple knell
"The vain distress-gun," from a leeward shore,
Repeated—heard, and heard no more!

11

For terror, joy, or pity,
Vast is the compass, and the swell of notes:
From the Babe's first cry to voice of regal City,
Rolling a solemn sea-like bass, that floats
Far as the woodlands—with the trill to blend
Of that shy Songstress, whose love-tale
Might tempt an Angel to descend,
While hovering o'er the moonlight vale
O for some soul-affecting scheme
Of *moral* music, to unite
Wanderers whose portion is the faintest dream [bear
Of memory!—O that they might stoop to
Chains, such precious chains of sight
As laboured minstrelsies through ages wear!
O for a balance fit the truth to tell
Of the Unsubstantial, pondered well!

12

By one pervading Spirit
Of tones and numbers all things are controlled, [merit
As Sages taught, where faith was found to
Initiation in that mystery old.
The Heavens, whose aspect makes our minds as still
As they themselves *appear* to be,
Innumerable voices fill
With everlasting harmony,
The towering Headlands, crowned with mist,
Their feet among the billows, know
That Ocean is a mighty harmonist,
Thy pinions, universal Air,
Ever waving to and fro,
Are delegates of harmony, and bear
Strains that support the Seasons in their round;
Stern Winter loves a dirge-like sound.

13.

Break forth into thanksgiving,
Ye banded Instruments of wind and chords;
Unite, to magnify the Ever-living,
Your inarticulate notes with the voice of words!
Nor hushed be service from the lowing mead,
Nor mute the forest hum of noon.
Thou too be heard, lone Eagle! freed
From snowy peak and cloud, attune

Thy hungry barkings to the hymn
Of joy, that from her utmost walls
The six-days' Work by flaming Seraphim,
Transmits to Heaven! As Deep to Deep
Shouting through one valley calls
All worlds, all natures, mood and measure keep
For praise and ceaseless gratulation poured
Into the ear of God, their Lord!

14.

A voice to Light gave Being;
To Time, and Man his earth-born Chronicler;
A Voice shall finish doubt and dim foreseeing,
And sweep away life's visionary stir;
The Trumpet (we, intoxicate with pride,
Arm at its blast for deadly wars)
To archangelic lips applied,
The grave shall open, quench the stars
O Silence! are Man's noisy years
No more than moments of thy life?
Is Harmony, blest Queen of smiles and tears,
With her smooth tones and discords just;
Tempered into rapturous strife,
Thy destined Bond-slave? No! though Earth be dust
And vanish, though the Heavens dissolve, her stay
Is in the WORD, that shall not pass away.

TO THE MOON.

(COMPOSED BY THE SEA-SIDE,—ON THE COAST OF CUMBERLAND.)

WANDERER! that stoop'st so low, and com'st so near
To human life's unsettled atmosphere;
Who lov'st with Night and Silence to partake,
So might it seem, the cares of them that wake;
And, through the cottage lattice softly peeping,
Dost shield from harm the humblest of the sleeping;
What pleasure once encompassed those sweet names
Which yet in thy behalf the Poet claims,
An idolizing dreamer as of yore!—
I slight them all; and, on this sea-beat shore
Sole-sitting, only can to thoughts attend
That bid me hail thee as the SAILOR'S FRIEND;
So call thee for heaven's grace through thee made known
By confidence supplied and mercy shown.
When not a twinkling star or beacon's light
Abates the perils of a stormy night;
And for less obvious benefits, that find
Their way, with thy pure help, to heart and mind;
Both for the adventurer starting in life's prime;
And veteran ranging round from clime to clime,
Long baffled hope's slow fever in his veins,
And wounds and weakness oft his labour's sole remains.

The aspiring Mountains and the winding Streams
Empress of Night! are gladdened by thy beams;
A look of thine the wilderness pervades,
And penetrates the forest's inmost shades;
Thou, chequering peaceably the minster's gloom,
Guid'st the pale Mourner to the lost one's tomb;
Canst reach the Prisoner—to his grated cell
Welcome, though silent and intangible!—
And lives there one, of all that come and go
On the great waters toiling to and fro,
One, who has watched thee at some quiet hour
Enthroned aloft in undisputed power,
Or crossed by vapoury streaks and clouds that move
Catching the lustre they in part reprove—
Nor sometimes felt a fitness in thy sway
To call up thoughts that shun the glare of day,
And make the serious happier than the gay?

Yes, lovely Moon! if thou so mildly bright
Dost rouse, yet surely in thy own despite,
To fiercer mood the phrenzy-stricken brain,
Let me a compensating faith maintain;
That there's a sensitive, a tender part
Which thou canst touch in every human heart,
For healing and composure.—But, as least
And mightiest billows ever have confessed
Thy domination; as the whole vast Sea
Feels through her lowest depths thy sovereignty;
So shines that countenance with especial grace
On them who urge the keel her *plains* to trace
Furrowing its way right onward. The most rude,
Cut off from home and country, may have stood—

Even till long gazing hath bedimmed his eye,
Or the mute rapture ended in a sigh—
Touched by accordance of thy placid cheer,
With some internal lights to memory dear,
Or fancies stealing forth to soothe the breast
Tired with its daily share of earth's unrest,—
Gentle awakenings, visitations meek,
A kindly influence whereof few will speak,
Though it can wet with tears the hardiest cheek.

And when thy beauty in the shadowy cave
Is hidden, buried in its monthly grave;
Then, while the Sailor mid an open sea
Swept by a favouring wind that leaves thought free,
Paces the deck—no star perhaps in sight,
And nothing save the moving ship's own light
To cheer the long dark hours of vacant night—
Oft with his musings does thy image blend,
In his mind's eye thy crescent horns ascend,
And thou art still, O Moon, that SAILOR'S FRIEND!

TO THE MOON.

(RYDAL.)

QUEEN of the Stars!— so gentle so benign,
That ancient Fable did to thee assign,
When darkness creeping o'er thy silver brow
Warned thee these upper regions to forego,
Alternate empire in the shades below—
A Bard, who, lately near the wide-spread sea
Traversed by gleaming ships looked up to thee
With grateful thoughts, doth now thy rising hail
From the close confines of a shadowy vale.
Glory of night, conspicuous yet serene,
Nor less attractive when by glimpses seen
Through cloudy umbrage, well might that fair face,
And all those attributes of modest grace,
In days when Fancy wrought unchecked by fear,
Down to the green earth fetch thee from thy sphere,
To sit in leafy woods by fountains clear!

O still beloved (for thine, meek Power, are charms
That fascinate the very Babe in arms,
While he, uplifted towards thee, laughs outright,
Spreading his little palms in his glad Mother's sight)
O still beloved, once worshipped! Time, that frowns
In his destructive flight on earthly crowns,
Spares thy mild splendour, still those far-shot beams
Tremble on dancing waves and rippling streams
With stainless touch, as chaste as when thy praise
Was sung by Virgin-choirs in festal lays;
And through dark trials still dost thou explore
Thy way for increase punctual as of yore,
When teeming Matrons—yielding to rude faith
In mysteries of birth and life and death
And painful struggle and deliverance—prayed
Of thee to visit them with lenient aid.
What though the rites be swept away, the fanes
Extinct that echoed to the votive strains;
Yet thy mild aspect does not, cannot cease,
Love to promote and purity and peace;
And Fancy, unreproved, even yet may trace
Faint types of suffering in thy beamless face.

Then, silent Monitress! let us—not blind
To worlds unthought of till the searching mind
Of Science laid them open to mankind—
Told, also, how the voiceless heavens declare
God's glory; and acknowledging thy share
In that blest charge; let us—without offence
To ought of highest, holiest, influence—
Receive whatever good 'tis given thee to dispense.
May sage and simple, catching with one eye
The moral intimations of the sky,
Learn from thy course, where'er their own be taken,
"To look on tempests, and be never shaken;"
To keep with faithful step the appointed way
Eclipsing or eclipsed, by night or day,
And from example of thy monthly range
Gently to brook decline and fatal change;
Meek, patient, steadfast, and with loftier scope,
Than thy revival yields, for gladsome hope

IMPROMPTU.

THE sun has long been set,
The stars are out by twos and threes,
The little birds are piping yet
Among the bushes and the trees;
There's a cuckoo, and one or two thrushes,
And a far-off wind that rushes,
And a sound of water that gushes,
And the cuckoo's sovereign cry
Fills all the hollow of the sky
Who would 'go parading'
In London, 'and masquerading,'
On such a night of June
With that beautiful half-moon,
And all these innocent blisses?
On such a night as this is!

SONNET.

I WATCH, and long have watched, with calm regret
Yon slowly-sinking star—immortal Sire
(So might he seem) of all the glittering quire!
Blue ether still surrounds him—yet—and yet;
But now the horizon's rocky parapet
Is reached, where, forfeiting his bright attire,
He burns—transmuted to a dusky fire—
Then pays submissively the appointed debt
To the flying moments, and is seen no more.
Angels and gods! we *struggle* with our fate,
While health, power, glory, from their height decline,
Depressed; and then extinguished: and our state,
In this, how different, lost Star, from thine,
That no to-morrow shall our beams restore!

ELEGIAC PIECES.

TO LAMB.

To a good Man of most dear memory
This Stone is sacred. Here he lies apart
From the great city where he first drew breath,
Was reared and taught; and humbly earned his bread,
To the strict labours of the merchant's desk [tasks
By duty chained. Not seldom did those
Tease, and the thought of time so spent depress,
His spirit, but the recompense was high;
Firm Independence, Bounty's rightful sire;
Affections, warm as sunshine, free as air;
And when the precious hours of leisure came, [converse sweet
Knowledge and Wisdom, gained from
With books, or while he ranged the crowded streets
With a keen eye, and overflowing heart.
So genius triumphed over seeming wrong,
And poured out truth in works by thoughtful love
Inspired—works potent over smiles and tears,
And as round mountain-tops the lightning plays,
Thus innocently sported, breaking forth
As from a cloud of some grave sympathy,
Humour and wild instinctive wit, and all
The vivid flashes of his spoken words.
From the most gentle creature nursed in fields
Had been derived the name he bore—a name,
Wherever Christian altars have been raised,
Hallowed to meekness and to innocence;
And if in him meekness at times gave way,
Provoked out of herself by troubles strange,
Many and strange, that hung about his life;
Still, at the centre of his being, lodged
A soul by resignation sanctified·
And if too often, self-reproached, he felt
That innocence belongs not to our kind,
A power that never ceased to abide in him,
Charity, 'mid the multitude of sins
That she can cover, left not his exposed
To an unforgiving judgment from just Heaven.
O, he was good, if e'er a good Man lived!

* * * * *

From a reflecting mind and sorrowing heart [wish,
Those simple lines flowed with an earnest
Though but a doubting hope, and they might serve
Fitly to guard the precious dust of him
Whose virtues called them forth. That aim is missed; [quired
For much that truth most urgently re-
Had from a faltering pen been asked in vain;
Yet, haply, on the printed page received,

The imperfect record, there may stand
unblamed [air
As long as verse of mine shall breathe the
Of memory, or see the light of love

Thou wert a scorner of the fields, my
Friend ! [the fields,
But more in show than truth ; and from
And from the mountains, to thy rural
grave
Transported, my soothed spirit hovers o'er
Its green untrodden turf, and blowing
flowers ; [still
And taking up a voice shall speak (though
Awed by the theme's peculiar sanctity
Which words less free presumed not even
to touch)
Of that fraternal love, whose heaven-lit
lamp
From infancy, through manhood to the last
Of threescore years, and to thy latest hour,
Burnt on with ever-strengthening light,
enshrined
Within thy bosom.

"Wonderful" hath been
The love established between man and
man,
"Passing the love of women," and between
Man and his help-mate in fast wedlock
joined [of love
Through God, is raised a spirit and soul
Without whose blissful influence Paradise
Had been no Paradise, and earth were
now [form,
A waste where creatures bearing human
Direst of savage beasts, would roam in
fear, [on ;
Joyless and comfortless. Our days glide
And let him grieve who cannot choose but
grieve [Vine,
That he hath been an Elm without his
And her bright dower of clustering
charities, [have clung
That, round his trunk and branches might
Enriching and adorning. Unto thee
Not so enriched, not so adorned, to thee
Was given (say rather thou of later birth
Wert given to her) a Sister—'tis a word
Timidly uttered, for she *lives*, the meek,
The self-restraining, and the ever-kind ;
In whom thy reason and intelligent heart
Found—for all interests, hopes, and tender
cares, [powers,
All softening, humanizing, hallowing,
Whether withheld, or or her sake un-
sought—
More than sufficient recompense !

Her love
(What weakness prompts the voice to tell
it here !) [years,
Was as the love of mothers ; and when
Lifting the boy to man's estate, had called
The long-protected to assume the part
Of a protector, the first filial tie
Was undissolved, and, in or out of sight,
Remained imperishably interwoven
With life itself. Thus, 'mid a shifting
world,
Did they together testify of time
And season's difference—a double tree
With two collateral stems sprung from one
root ; [have been
Such were they—such thro' life they *might*
In union, in partition only such ; [High ;
Otherwise wrought the will of the Most
Yet, through all visitations and all trials,
Still they were faithful ; like two vessels
launched
From the same beach one ocean to explore
With mutual help, and sailing—to their
league
True, as inexorable winds, or bars
Floating or fixed of polar ice, allow.

But turn we rather, let my spirit turn
With thine, O silent and invisible Friend !
To those dear intervals, nor rare nor brief,
When reunited, and by choice withdrawn
From miscellaneous converse, ye were
taught
That the remembrance of foregone distress,
And the worse fear of future ill (which oft
Doth hang around it, as a sickly child
Upon its mother) may be both alike
Disarmed of power to unsettle present good
So prized; and things inward and outward
held
In such an even balance, that the heart
Acknowledges God's grace, his mercy feels,
And in its depth of gratitude is still.

O gift divine of quiet sequestration !
The hermit, exercised in prayer and praise,
And feeding daily on the hope of heaven,
Is happy in his vow, and fondly cleaves
To life-long singleness ; but happier far
Was to your souls, and, to the thoughts of
others,
A thousand times more beautiful appeared
Your *dual* loneliness. The sacred tie
Is broken ; yet why grieve? for time but
holds
His moiety in trust, till Joy shall lead
To the blest world where parting is un-
known.

EXTEMPORE EFFUSION UPON THE DEATH OF JAMES HOGG.

WHEN first descending from the moorlands,
I saw the Stream of Yarrow glide
Along a bare and open valley,
The Ettrick Shepherd was my guide.

When last along its banks I wandered,
Through groves that had begun to shed
Their golden leaves upon the pathways,
My steps the Border Minstrel led.

The mighty Minstrel breathes no longer,
Mid mouldering ruins low he lies;
And death upon the braes of Yarrow,
Has closed the Shepherd-poet's eyes:

Nor has the rolling year twice measured,
From sign to sign, its steadfast course,
Since every mortal power of Coleridge,
Was frozen at its marvellous source;

The 'rapt One, of the godlike forehead,
The heaven-eyed creature sleeps in earth:
And Lamb, the frolic and the gentle,
Has vanished from his lonely hearth.

Like clouds that rake the mountain-summits,
Or waves that own no curbing hand,
How fast has brother followed brother,
From sunshine to the sunless land!

Yet I, whose lids from infant slumbers
Were earlier raised, remain to hear
A timid voice, that asks in whispers,
"Who next will drop and disappear?"

Our haughty life is crowned with darkness,
Like London with its own black wreath,
On which with thee, O Crabbe! forth-looking,
I gazed from Hampstead's breezy heath.

As if but yesterday departed,
Thou too art gone before; but why,
O'er ripe fruit, seasonably gathered,
Should frail survivors heave a sigh?

Mourn rather for that holy Spirit,
Sweet as the spring, as ocean deep;
For Her who, ere her summer faded,
Has sunk into a breathless sleep.

No more of old romantic sorrows,
For slaughtered Youth or love-lorn Maid!
With sharper grief is Yarrow smitten,
And Ettrick mourns with her their poet dead.

TRANSLATIONS OF EPITAPHS.

FROM CHIABRERA.

WEEP not, beloved Friends! nor let the air
For me with sighs be troubled. Not from life
Have I been taken; this is genuine life
And this alone—the life which now I live
In peace eternal; where desire and joy
Together move in fellowship without end.—
Francesco Ceni after death enjoined
That thus his tomb should speak for him
And surely
Small cause there is for that fond wish of ours
Long to continue in this world; a world
That keeps not faith, nor yet can point a hope
To good, whereof itself is destitute.

TRUE is it that Ambrosio Salinero
With an untoward fate was long involved
In odious litigation; and full long,
Fate harder still! had he to endure assaults
Of racking malady. And true it is
That not the less a frank courageous heart
And buoyant spirit triumphed over pain;
And he was strong to follow in the steps
Of the fair Muses. Not a covert path
Leads to the dear Parnassian forest's shade,
That might from him be hidden; not a track
Mounts to pellucid Hippocrene, but he
Had traced its windings.—This Savona knows,
Yet no sepulchral honours to her Son
She paid, for in our age the heart is ruled
Only by gold. And now a simple stone
Inscribed with this memorial here is raised
By his bereft, his lonely, Chiabrera.
Think not, O Passenger! who read'st the lines
That an exceeding love hath dazzled me;
No—he was One whose memory ought to spread
Where'er Permessus bears an honoured name,
And live as long as its pure stream shall flow.

O FLOWER of all that springs from gentle blood,
And all that generous nurture breeds, to make
Youth amiable; O friend so true of soul

To fair Aglaia; by what envy moved,
Lelius! has death cut short thy brilliant day
In its sweet opening? and what dire mishap
Has from Savona torn her best delight?
For thee she mourns, nor e'er will cease to mourn;
And, should the outpourings of her eyes suffice not
For her heart's grief, she will entreat Sebeto
Not to withhold his bounteous aid, Sebeto
Who saw thee, on his margin, yield to death
In the chaste arms of thy belovèd Love!
What profit riches? what does youth avail?
Dust are our hopes,—I, weeping bitterly,
Penned these sad lines, nor can forbear to pray
That every gentle Spirit hither led
May read them not without some bitter tears.

THE NORMAN BOY.

High on a broad unfertile tract of forest-skirted Down,
Nor kept by Nature for herself, nor made by man his own,
From home and company remote and every playful joy,
Served, tending a few sheep and goats, a ragged Norman Boy.

Him never saw I, nor the spot; but from an English Dame,
Stranger to me and yet my friend, a simple notice came,
With suit that I would speak in verse of that sequestered child
Whom, one bleak winter's day, she met upon the dreary Wild.

His flock, along the woodland's edge with relics sprinkled o'er
Of last night's snow, beneath a sky threatening the fall of more,
Where tufts of herbage tempted each, were busy at their feed,
And the poor Boy was busier still, with work of anxious heed.

There *was* he, where of branches rent and withered and decayed,
For covert from the keen north wind, his hands a hut had made.
A tiny tenement, forsooth, and frail, as needs must be
A thing of such materials framed, by a builder such as he

The hut stood finished by his pains, nor seemingly lacked aught
That skill or means of his could add, but the architect had wrought
Some limber twigs into a Cross, well-shaped with fingers nice,
To be engrafted on the top of his small edifice.

That Cross he now was fastening there, as the surest power and best
For supplying all deficiencies, all wants of the rude nest
In which, from burning heat, or tempest driving far and wide,
The innocent Boy, else shelterless, his lonely head must hide

That Cross belike he also raised as a standard for the true
And faithful service of his heart in the worst that might ensue
Of hardship and distressful fear, amid the houseless waste
Where he, in his poor self so weak, by Providence was placed.

——Here, Lady! might I cease, but nay, let *us* before we part
With this dear holy shepherd-boy breathe a prayer of earnest heart,
That unto him, where'er shall lie his life's appointed way,
The Cross, fixed in his soul, may prove an all-sufficing stay.

THE POET'S DREAM.

SEQUEL TO THE NORMAN BOY.

Just as those final words were penned, the sun broke out in power,
And gladdened all things; but, as chanced, within that very hour,
Air blackened, thunder growled, fire flashed from clouds that hid the sky,
And, for the Subject of my Verse, I heaved a pensive sigh.

Nor could my heart by second thoughts from heaviness be cleared,
For bodied forth before my eyes the cross-crowned hut appeared,
And, while around it storm as fierce seemed troubling earth and air,
I saw, within, the Norman Boy kneeling alone in prayer.

The Child, as if the thunder's voice spake with articulate call,
Bowed meekly in submissive fear, before the Lord of All;
His lips were moving; and his eyes, upraised to sue for grace,
With soft illumination cheered the dimness of that place.

How beautiful is holiness!—what wonder if the sight,
Almost as vivid as a dream, produced a dream at night?
It came with sleep and showed the Boy, no cherub, not transformed,
But the poor ragged Thing whose ways my human heart had warmed.

Me had the dream equipped with wings, so I took him in my arms,
And lifted from the grassy floor, stilling his faint alarms,
And bore him high through yielding air my debt of love to pay,
By giving him, for both our sakes, an hour of holiday.

I whispered, "Yet a little while, dear Child! thou art my own,
To show thee some delightful thing, in country or in town.
What shall it be? a mirthful throng? or that holy place and calm
St. Denis, filled with royal tombs, or the Church of Notre Dame?

"St. Ouen's golden Shrine? Or choose what else would please thee most
Of any wonder, Normandy, or all proud France, can boast!"
"My Mother," said the Boy, "was born near to a blessèd Tree,
The Chapel Oak of Allonville; good Angel, show it me!"

On wings, from broad and steadfast poise let loose by this reply,
For Allonville, o'er down and dale, away then did we fly;
O'er town and tower we flew, and fields in May's fresh verdure drest;
The wings they did not flag; the Child, though grave, was not deprest.

But who shall show, to waking sense, the gleam of light that broke
Forth from his eyes, when first the Boy looked down on that huge oak,
For length of days so much revered, so famous where it stands
For twofold hallowing—Nature's care, and work of human hands?

Strong as an Eagle with my charge I glided round and round
The wide-spread boughs, for view of door, window, and stair that wound
Gracefully up the gnarled trunk; nor left we unsurveyed
The pointed steeple peering forth from the centre of the shade.

I lighted—opened with soft touch the chapel's iron door,
Past softly, leading in the Boy; and, while from roof to floor
From floor to roof all round his eyes the Child with wonder cast,
Pleasure on pleasure crowded in, each livelier than the last.

For, deftly framed within the trunk, the sanctuary showed,
By light of lamp and precious stones, that glimmer here, there glowed,
Shrine, Altar, Image, Offerings hung in sign of gratitude;
Sight that inspired accordant thoughts; and speech I thus renewed:

"Hither the Afflicted come, as thou hast heard thy Mother say,
And, kneeling, supplication make to our Lady de la Paix;
What mournful sighs have here been heard, and, when the voice was stopt
By sudden pangs, what bitter tears have on this pavement dropt!

"Poor Shepherd of the naked Down, a favoured lot is thine,
Far happier lot, dear Boy, than brings full many to this shrine;
From body pains and pains of soul thou needest no release,
Thy hours as they flow on are spent, if not in joy, in peace.

"Then offer up thy heart to God in thankfulness and praise,
Give to Him prayers, and many thoughts, in thy most busy days;
And in His sight the fragile Cross, on thy small hut, will be
Holy as that which long hath crowned the Chapel of this Tree;

"Holy as that far seen which crowns the sumptuous Church in Rome
Where thousands meet to worship God under a mighty Dome:
He sees the bending multitude, He hears the choral rites,
Yet not the loss, in children's hymns and lonely prayer, delights.

"God for His service needeth not proud work of human skill;
They please Him best who labour most to do in peace His will:
So let us strive to live, and to our spirits will be given
Such wings as, when our Saviour calls, shall bear us up to heaven."

The Boy no answer made by words, but, so earnest was his look,
Sleep fled, and with it fled the dream—recorded in this book,
Lest all that passed should melt away in silence from my mind,
As visions still more bright have done, and left no trace behind.

But oh! that Country-man of thine, whose eye, loved Child, can see
A pledge of endless bliss in acts of early piety,
In verse, which to thy ear might come, would treat this simple theme,
Nor leave untold our happy flight in that adventurous dream.

Alas the dream, to thee, poor Boy! to thee from whom it flowed,
Was nothing, scarcely can be aught, yet 'twas bounteously bestowed,
If I may dare to cherish hope that gentle eyes will read
Not loth, and listening little-ones, heart-touched, their fancies feed.

THE WESTMORELAND GIRL.

TO MY GRANDCHILDREN.

PART I.

SEEK who will delight in fable,
I shall tell you truth. A Lamb
Leapt from this steep bank to follow
'Cross the brook its thoughtless dam.

Far and wide on hill and valley
Rain had fallen, unceasing rain,
And the bleating mother's Young-one
Struggled with the flood in vain:

But, as chanced, a Cottage-maiden
(Ten years scarcely had she told)
Seeing, plunged into the torrent,
Clasped the Lamb and kept her hold.

Whirled adown the rocky channel,
Sinking, rising, on they go,
Peace and rest, as seems, before them
Only in the lake below.

Oh! it was a frightful current
Whose fierce wrath the Girl had braved;
Clap your hands with joy, my Hearers,
Shout in triumph, both are saved;

Saved by courage that with danger
Grew, by strength the gift of love,
And belike a guardian angel
Came with succour from above.

PART II.

Now, to a maturer Audience,
Let me speak of this brave Child
Left among her native mountains
With wild Nature to run wild.

So, unwatched by love maternal,
Mother's care no more her guide,
Fared this little bright-eyed Orphan
Even while at her father's side.

Spare your blame,—remembrance makes him
Loth to rule by strict command;
Still upon his cheek are living
Touches of her infant hand,

Dear caresses given in pity,
Sympathy that soothed his grief,
As the dying mother witnessed
To her thankful mind's relief.

Time passed on; the Child was happy,
Like a Spirit of air she moved,
Wayward, yet by all who knew her
For her tender heart beloved.

Scarcely less than sacred passions,
Bred in house, in grove, and field,
Link her with the inferior creatures,
Urge her powers their rights to shield.

Anglers, bent on reckless pastime,
Learn how she can feel alike
Both for tiny harmless minnow
And the fierce and sharp-toothed pike.

Merciful protectress, kindling
Into anger or disdain;
Many a captive hath she rescued,
Others saved from lingering pain.

Listen yet awhile;—with patience
Hear the homely truths I tell,
She in Grasmere's old church-steeple
Tolled this day the passing-bell.

Yes, the wild Girl of the mountains
To their echoes gave the sound,
Notice punctual as the minute,
Warning solemn and profound.

She, fulfilling her sire's office,
Rang alone the far-heard knell,
Tribute, by her hand, in sorrow,
Paid to One who loved her well.

When his spirit was departed,
On that service she went forth;
Nor will fail the like to render
When his corse is laid in earth.

What then wants the child to temper,
In her breast, unruly fire,
To control the froward impulse
And restrain the vague desire?

Easily a pious training
And a steadfast outward power
Would supplant the weeds and cherish,
In their stead, each opening flower.

Thus the fearless Lamb-deliv'rer,
Woman-grown, meek-hearted, sage,
May become a blest example
For her sex, of every age.

Watchful as a wheeling eagle,
Constant as a soaring lark,
Should the country need a heroine
She might prove our Maid of Arc

Leave that thought; and here be uttered
Prayer that Grace divine may raise
Her humane courageous spirit
Up to heaven, thro' peaceful ways.

YES, THOU ART FAIR.

Yes! thou art fair, yet be not moved
To scorn the declaration,
That sometimes I in thee have loved
My fancy's own creation

Imagination needs must stir;
Dear Maid, this truth believe,
Minds that have nothing to confer
Find little to perceive.

Be pleased that nature made thee fit
To feed my heart's devotion,
By laws to which all Forms submit
In sky, air, earth, and ocean.

WHAT HEAVENLY SMILES.

What heavenly smiles! O Lady mine
Through my very heart they shine;
And, if my brow gives back their light,
Do thou look gladly on the sight;
As the clear Moon with modest pride
Beholds her own bright beams
Reflected from the mountain's side
And from the headlong streams.

THE WIDOW ON WINDERMERE SIDE.

I.

How beautiful when up a lofty height
Honour ascends among the humblest poor,
And feeling sinks as deep! See there the door
Of One, a Widow, left beneath a weight
Of blameless debt. On evil Fortune's spite
She wasted no complaint, but strove to make
A just repayment, both for conscience-sake
And that herself and hers should stand upright
In the world's eye. Her work when daylight failed
Paused not, and through the depth of night she kept
Such earnest vigils, that belief prevailed
With some, the noble Creature never slept;
But, one by one, the hand of death assailed
Her children from her inmost heart bewept.

II.

The Mother mourned, nor ceased her tears to flow
Till a winter's noon-day placed her buried Son
Before her eyes, last child of many gone—
His raiment of angelic white, and lo!
His very feet bright as the dazzling snow

Which they are touching; yea, far brighter, even
As that which comes, or seems to come, from heaven,
Surpasses aught these elements can show
Much she rejoiced, trusting that from that hour
Whate'er befell she could not grieve or pine,
But the Transfigured, in and out of season,
Appeared, and spiritual presence gained a power
Over material forms that mastered reason
Oh, gracious Heaven, in pity make her thine!

III.

But why that prayer? as if to her could come
No good but by the way that leads to bliss
Through Death,—so judging we should judge amiss
Since reason failed want is her threatened doom,
Yet frequent transports mitigate the gloom:
Nor of those maniacs is she one that kiss
The air or laugh upon a precipice,
No, passing through strange sufferings toward the tomb,
She smiles as if a martyr's crown were won·
Oft, when light breaks through clouds or waving trees,
With outspread arms and fallen upon her knees
The Mother hails in her descending Son
An Angel, and in earthly ecstasies
Her own angelic glory seems begun.

FAREWELL LINES.

"HIGH bliss is only for a higher state,"
But, surely, if severe afflictions borne
With patience merit the reward of peace,
Peace ye deserve; and may the solid good,
Sought by a wise though late exchange, and here
With bounteous hand beneath a cottage-roof
To you accorded, never be withdrawn,
Nor for the world's best promises renounced
Most soothing was it for a welcome Friend,
Fresh from the crowded city, to behold
That lonely union, privacy so deep,
Such calm employments, such entire content.
So when the rain is over, the storm laid,
A pair of herons oft-times have I seen,
Upon a rocky islet, side by side,
Drying their feathers in the sun, at ease;
And so, when night with grateful gloom had fallen,
'Two glow-worms in such nearness that they shared,
As seemed, their soft self-satisfying light,
Each with the other, on the dewy ground,
Where He that made them blesses their repose.—
When wandering among lakes and hills I note,
Once more, those creatures thus by nature paired,
And guarded in their tranquil state of life,
Even as your happy presence to my mind
Their union brought, will they repay the debt,
And send a thankful spirit back to you,
With hope that we, dear Friends! shall meet again.

GLAD sight wherever new with old
Is joined through some dear homeborn tie;
The life of all that we behold
Depends upon that mystery.
Vain is the glory of the sky,
The beauty vain of field and grove,
Unless, while with admiring eye
We gaze, we also learn to love.

LOVE LIES BLEEDING.

YOU call it "Love lies bleeding,"—so you may,
Though the red Flower, not prostrate, only droops,
As we have seen it here from day to day,
From month to month, life passing not away.
A flower how rich in sadness! Even thus stoops,
(Sentient by Grecian sculpture's marvellous power)
Thus leans, with hanging brow and body bent
Earthward in uncomplaining languishment.
The dying Gladiator. So, sad Flower!
('Tis Fancy guides me willing to be led,
Though by a slender thread),
So drooped Adonis bathed in sanguine dew
Of his death wound, when he from innocent air

The gentlest breath of resignation drew;
While Venus in a passion of despair
Rent, weeping over him, her golden hair
Spangled with drops of that celestial shower.
She suffered, as Immortals sometimes do;
But pangs more lasting far *that* Lover knew
Who first, weighed down by scorn, in some lone bower
Did press this semblance of unpitied smart
Into the service of his constant heart,
His own dejection, downcast Flower! could share
With thine, and gave the mournful name which thou wilt ever bear.

COMPANION TO THE FOREGOING.

Never enlivened with the liveliest ray
That fosters growth or checks or cheers decay,
Nor by the heaviest rain-drops more deprest,
This Flower, that first appeared as summer's guest,
Preserves her beauty mid autumnal leaves,
And to her mournful habits fondly cleaves.
When files of stateliest plants have ceased to bloom,
One after one submitting to their doom,
When her coevals each and all are fled,
What keeps her thus reclined upon her lonesome bed?

The old mythologists, more impressed than we
Of this late day by character in tree
Or herb, that claimed peculiar sympathy,
Or by the silent lapse of fountain clear,
Or with the language of the viewless air
By bird or beast made vocal, sought a cause
To solve the mystery, not in Nature's laws
But in man's fortunes. Hence a thousand tales
Sung to the plaintive lyre in Grecian vales
Nor doubt that something of their spirit swayed
The fancy-stricken Youth or heart-sick Maid,
Who, while each stood companionless and eyed
This undeparting Flower in crimson dyed,
Thought of a wound which death is slow to cure,
A fate that has endured and will endure,
And, patience coveting yet passion feeding,
Called the dejected Lingerer, *Love lie bleeding*.

AIREY-FORCE VALLEY.

——Not a breath of air
Ruffles the bosom of this leafy glen.
From the brook's margin, wide around, the trees
Are steadfast as the rocks; the brook itself,
Old as the hills that feed it from afar,
Doth rather deepen than disturb the calm
Where all things else are still and motionless.
And yet, even now, a little breeze, perchance
Escaped from boisterous winds that rage without,
Has entered, by the sturdy oaks unfelt,
But to its gentle touch how sensitive
Is the light ash! that, pendent from the brow
Of yon dim cave, in seeming silence makes
A soft eye-music of slow-waving boughs,
Powerful almost as vocal harmony
To stay the wanderer's steps and soothe his thoughts.

THE SIMPLON PASS.

——Brook and road
Were fellow-travellers in this gloomy Pass,
And with them did we journey several hours
At a slow step. The immeasurable height
Of woods decaying, never to be decayed,
The stationary blasts of waterfalls,
And in the narrow rent, at every turn,
Winds thwarting winds bewildered and forlorn,
The torrents shooting from the clear blue sky,
The rocks that muttered close upon our ears,
Black drizzling crags that spake by the wayside
As if a voice were in them, the sick sight
And giddy prospect of the raving stream,
The unfettered clouds and region of the heavens,
Tumult and peace, the darkness and the light—
Were all like workings of one mind, the features
Of the same face, blossoms upon one tree,
Characters of the great Apocalypse,
The types and symbols of Eternity;
Of first, and last, and midst, and without end.

1799.

THE LYRE.

LYRE! though such power do in thy magic live
As might from India's farthest plain
Recall the not unwilling Maid,
Assist me to detain
The lovely Fugitive:
Check with thy notes the impulse which, betrayed
By her sweet farewell looks, I longed to aid.
Here let me gaze enrapt upon that eye,
The impregnable and awe-inspiring fort
Of contemplation, the calm port
By reason fenced from winds that sigh
Among the restless sails of vanity.
But if no wish be hers that we should part,
A humbler bliss would satisfy my heart.
Where all things are so fair,
Enough by her dear side to breathe the air
Of this Elysian weather;
And, on or in, or near, the brook, espy
Shade upon the sunshine lying
Faint and somewhat pensively,
And downward Image gaily vying
With its upright living tree
Mid silver clouds, and openings of blue sky,
As soft almost and deep as her cerulean eye.

Nor less the joy with many a glance
Cast up the Stream or down at her beseeching,
To mark its eddying foam-balls prettily distrest
By ever-changing shape and want of rest;
Or watch, with mutual teaching,
The current as it plays
In flashing leaps and stealthy creeps
Adown a rocky maze,
Or note (translucent summer's happiest chance!)
In the slope-channel floored with pebbles bright,
Stones of all hues, gem emulous of gem,
So vivid that they take from keenest sight
The liquid veil that seeks not to hide them.

THE TRIAD.

SHOW me the noblest Youth of present time,
Whose trembling fancy would to love give birth;
Some God or Hero, from the Olympian clime
Returned, to seek a Consort upon earth:
Or, in no doubtful prospect let me see
The brightest star of ages yet to be,
And I will mate and match him blissfully.

I will not fetch a Naiad from a flood
Pure as herself—(song lacks not mightier power)
Nor leaf-crowned Dryad from a pathless wood,
Nor sea-nymph glistening from her coral bower,
Mere Mortals, bodied forth in vision still,
Shall with Mount Ida's triple lustre fill
The chaster coverts of a British hill.

"Appear!—obey my lyre's command!
Come, like the Graces, hand in hand!
For ye, though not by birth allied,
Are Sisters in the bond of love;
Nor shall the tongue of envious pride
Presume those interweavings to reprove
In you, which that fair progeny of Jove,
Learned from the tuneful spheres that glide
In endless union, earth and sea above."
—I sing in vain,—the pines have hushed their wavings:
A peerless Youth expectant at my side,
Breathless as they, with unabated craving
Looks to the earth, and to the vacant air:
And, with a wandering eye that seems to chide,
Asks of the clouds what occupants they hide:—
But why solicit more than sight could bear,
By casting on a moment all we dare?
Invoke we those bright beings one by one;
And what was boldly promised, truly shall be done.

"Fear not a constraining measure!
—Yielding to this gentle spell,
Lucida[1] from domes of pleasure,
Or from cottage-sprinkled dell,
Come to regions solitary,
Where the eagle builds her aery,
Above the hermit's long-forsaken cell!"
—She comes!—behold
That Figure, like a ship with snow-white sail!
Nearer she draws; a breeze uplifts her veil,
Upon her coming wait
As pure a sunshine and as soft a gale
As e'er, on herbage covering earthy mold,
Tempted the bird of Juno to unfold
His richest splendour—when his veering gait
And every motion of his starry train
Seem governed by a strain
Of music, audible to him alone,

"O Lady, worthy of earth's proudest throne!
Nor less, by excellence of nature, fit
Beside an unambitious hearth to sit
Domestic queen, where grandeur is unknown;
What living man could fear
The worst of Fortune's malice, wert Thou near,
Humbling that lily-stem, thy sceptre meek,
That its fair flowers may from his cheek
Brush the too happy tear?
—Queen, and handmaid lowly!
Whose skill can speed the day with lively cares,
And banish melancholy
By all that mind invents or hand prepares;
O Thou, against whose lip, without its smile
And in its silence even, no heart is proof;
Whose goodness, sinking deep, would reconcile
The softest Nursling of a gorgeous palace
To the bare life beneath the hawthorn-roof
Of Sherwood's Archer, or in caves of Wallace—
Who that hath seen thy beauty could content
His soul with but a *glimpse* of heavenly day?
Who that hath loved thee, but would lay
His strong hand on the wind, if it were bent
To take thee in thy majesty away?
—Pass onward (even the glancing deer
Till we depart intrude not here;)
That mossy slope, o'er which the woodbine throws
A canopy, is smoothed for thy repose!"

Glad moment is it when the throng
Of warblers in full concert strong
Strive, and not vainly strive, to rout
The lagging shower, and force coy Phœbus out,
Met by the rainbow's form divine,
Issuing from her cloudy shrine;—
So may the thrillings of the lyre
Prevail to further our desire,
While to these shades a sister Nymph I call.

"Come, if the notes thine ear may pierce,
Come, youngest of the lovely Three,
Submissive to the might of verse
And the dear voice of harmony,
By none more deeply felt than Thee!"
—I sang; and lo! from pastimes virginal
She hastens to the tents
Of nature, and the lonely elements.
Air sparkles round her with a dazzling sheen;
But mark her glowing cheek, her vesture green!
And, as if wishful to disarm
Or to repay the potent Charm,
She bears the stringèd lute of old romance,
That cheered the trellised arbour's privacy,
And soothed war-wearied knights in raftered hall.
How vivid, yet how delicate, her glee!
So tripped the Muse, inventress of the dance;
So, truant in waste woods, the blithe Euphrosyne!

But the ringlets of that head
Why are they ungarlanded?
Why bedeck her temples less
Than the simplest shepherdess?
Is it not a brow inviting
Choicest flowers that ever breathed,
Which the myrtle would delight in
With Idalian rose enwreathed?
But her humility is well content
With *one* wild floweret (call it not forlorn)
FLOWER OF THE WINDS, beneath her bosom worn—
Yet more for love than ornament.

Open, ye thickets! let her fly,
Swift as a Thracian Nymph o'er field and height!
For She, to all but those who love her, shy,
Would gladly vanish from a Stranger's sight;
Though where she is beloved and loves,
Light as the wheeling butterfly she moves;
Her happy spirit as a bird is free,
That rifles blossoms on a tree,
Turning them inside out with arch audacity.
Alas! how little can a moment show
Of an eye where feeling plays
In ten thousand dewy rays;
A face o'er which a thousand shadows go;
—She stops—is fastened to that rivulet's side;
And there (while, with sedater mien,
O'er timid waters that have scarcely left
Their birth-place in the rocky cleft
She bends) at leisure may be seen
Features to old ideal grace allied,
Amid their smiles and dimples dignified—
Fit countenance for the soul of primal truth
The bland composure of eternal youth!

What more changeful than the sea?
But over his great tides

Fidelity presides,
And this light-hearted Maiden constant is as he.
High is her aim as heaven above,
And wide as ether her good will,
And, like the lowly reed, her love
Can drink its nurture from the scantiest rill:
Insight as keen as frosty star
Is to *her* charity no bar,
Nor interrupts her frolic graces
When she is, far from these wild places
Encircled by familiar faces.

O the charm that manners draw,
Nature, from thy genuine law!
If from what her hand would do,
Her voice would utter, aught ensue
Untoward or unfit,
She, in benign affections pure,
In self-forgetfulness secure,
Sheds round the transient harm or vague mischance
A light unknown to tutored elegance:
Hers is not a cheek shame-stricken,
But her blushes are joy-flushes;
And the fault (if fault it be)
Only ministers to quicken
Laughter-loving gaiety,
And kindle sportive wit—
Leaving this Daughter of the mountains free
As if she knew that Oberon king of Faery
Had crossed her purpose with some quaint vagary,
And heard his viewless bands
Over their mirthful triumph clapping hands

"Last of the Three, though eldest born,
Reveal thyself, like pensive Morn
Touched by the skylark's earliest note,
Ere humbler gladness be afloat.
But whether in the semblance drest
Of Dawn—or Eve, fair vision of the west,
Come with each anxious hope subdued
By woman's gentle fortitude,
Each grief, through meekness, settling into rest.
—Or I would hail thee when some high-wrought page
Of a closed volume lingering in thy hand
Has raised thy spirit to a peaceful stand
Among the glories of a happier age."

Her brow hath opened on me—see it there
Brightening the umbrage of her hair;
So gleams the crescent moon, that loves
To be descried, through shady groves.
Tenderest bloom is on her cheek;
Wish not for a richer streak;
Nor dread the depth of meditative eye;
But let thy love, upon that azure field
Of thoughtfulness and beauty, yield
Its homage offered up in purity
What would'st thou more? In sunny glade,
Or under leaves of thickest shade,
Was such a stillness e'er diffused
Since earth grew calm while angels mused?
Softly she treads, as if her foot were loth
To crush the mountain dew-drops—soon to melt
On the flower's breast; as if she felt
That flowers themselves, whate'er their hue,
With all their fragrance, all their glistening,
Call to the heart for inward listening—
And though for bridal wreaths and tokens true
Welcomed wisely; though a growth
Which the careless shepherd sleeps on
As fitly spring from turf the mourner weeps on—
And without wrong are cropped the marble tomb to strew
The charm is over, the mute Phantoms gone,
Nor will return—but droop not, favoured Youth;
The apparition that before thee shone
Obeyed a summons covetous of truth.
From these wild rocks thy footsteps I will guide
To bowers in which thy fortune may be tried,
And one of the bright Three become thy happy Bride.

1828

THE WISHING-GATE.

[In the vale of Grasmere, by the side of the old highway leading to Ambleside, is a gate, which, time out of mind, has been called the Wishing-gate, from a belief that wishes formed or indulged there have a favourable issue.]

Hope rules a land for ever green:
All powers that serve the bright-eyed Queen
Are confident and gay;
Clouds at her bidding disappear
Points she to aught?—the bliss draws near,
And Fancy smooths the way.

Not such the land of Wishes—there
Dwells fruitless day-dreams, lawless prayer,
And thoughts with things at strife;

Yet how forlorn should *ye* depart,
Ye superstitions of the *heart*,
How poor, were human life!

When magic lore abjured its might,
Ye did not forfeit one dear right,
One tender claim abate;
Witness this symbol of your sway,
Surviving near the public way,
The rustic Wishing-gate!

Inquire not if the faery race
Shed kindly influence on the place,
Ere northward they retired;
If here a warrior left a spell,
Panting for glory as he fell;
Or here a saint expired.

Enough that all around is fair,
Composed with Nature's finest care,
And in her fondest love—
Peace to embosom and content—
To overawe the turbulent,
The selfish to reprove.

Yea! even the Stranger from afar,
Reclining on this moss-grown bar,
Unknowing and unknown,
The infection of the ground partakes,
Longing for his Beloved—who makes
All happiness her own.

Then why should conscious spirits fear
The mystic stirrings that are here,
The ancient faith disclaim?
The local Genius ne'er befriends
Desires whose course in folly ends,
Whose just reward is shame.

Smile if thou wilt, but not in scorn,
If some, by ceaseless pains outworn
Here crave an easier lot;
If some have thirsted to renew
A broken vow, or bind a true,
With firmer, holier knot.

And not in vain, when thoughts are cast
Upon the irrevocable past,
Some Penitent sincere
May for a worthier future sigh,
While trickles from his downcast eye
No unavailing tear.

The Worldling, pining to be freed
From turmoil, who would turn or speed
The current of his fate,
Might stop before this favoured scene,
At Nature's call, nor blush to lean
Upon the Wishing-gate.

The Sage, who feels how blind, how weak
Is man, though loth such help to *seek*,
Yet, passing, here might pause,
And thirst for insight to allay
Misgiving, while the crimson day
In quietness withdraws;

Or when the church-clock's knell profound
To Time's first step across the bound
Of midnight makes reply:
Time pressing on with starry crest,
To filial sleep upon the breast
Of dread eternity.

1828.

THE WISHING-GATE DESTROYED.

'TIS gone—with old belief and dream
That round it clung, and tempting scheme
Released from fear and doubt;
And the bright landscape too must lie,
By this blank wall, from every eye,
Relentlessly shut out.

Bear witness ye who seldom passed
That opening—but a look ye cast
Upon the lake below,
What spirit-stirring power it gained
From faith which here was entertained
Though reason might say no.

Blest is that ground, where, o'er the springs
Of history, Glory claps her wings,
Fame sheds the exulting tear;
Yet earth is wide, and many a nook
Unheard of is, like this, a book
For modest meanings dear.

It was in sooth a happy thought
That grafted, on so fair a spot,
So confident a token
Of coming good;—the charm is fled;
Indulgent centuries spun a thread,
Which one harsh day has broken.

Alas! for him who gave the word;
Could he no sympathy afford,
Derived from earth or heaven,
To hearts so oft by hope betrayed;
Their very wishes wanted aid
Which here was freely given?

Where, for the love-lorn maiden's wound,
Will now so readily be found
A balm of expectation?
Anxious for far-off children, where
Shall mothers breathe a like sweet air
Of home-felt consolation?

And not unfelt will prove the loss
'Mid trivial care and petty cross
And each day's shallow grief,
Though the most easily beguiled
Were oft among the first that smiled
At their own fond belief.

If still the reckless change we mourn,
A reconciling thought may turn
To harm that might lurk here,
Ere judgment prompted from within
Fit aims, with courage to begin,
And strength to persevere.

Not Fortune's slave is Man: our state
Enjoins, while firm resolves await
On wishes just and wise,
That strenuous action follow both,
And life be one perpetual growth
Of heaven-ward enterprise.

So taught, so trained, we boldly face
All accidents of time and place;
Whatever props may fail,
Trust in that sovereign law can spread
New glory o'er the mountain's head,
Fresh beauty through the vale.

That truth informing mind and heart,
The simplest cottager may part,
Ungrieved, with charm and spell;
And yet, lost Wishing-gate, to thee
The voice of grateful memory
Shall bid a kind farewell!

THE CUCKOO-CLOCK.

Wouldst thou be taught, when sleep has taken flight,
By a sure voice that can most sweetly tell,
How far-off yet a glimpse of morning light,
And if to lure the truant back be well,
Forbear to covet a Repeater's stroke,
That, answering to thy touch, will sound the hour;
Better provide thee with a Cuckoo-clock
For service hung behind thy chamber-door;
And in due time the soft spontaneous shock,
The double note, as if with living power,
Will to composure lead—or make thee blithe as bird in bower.

List, Cuckoo—Cuckoo!—oft tho' tempests howl,
Or nipping frost remind thee trees are bare,
How cattle pine, and droop the shivering fowl,
Thy spirits will seem to feed on balmy air:
I speak with knowledge,—by that Voice beguiled,
Thou wilt salute old memories as they throng
Into thy heart; and fancies, running wild
Through fresh green fields, and budding groves among,
Will make thee happy, happy as a child;
Of sunshine wilt thou think, and flowers, and song,
And breathe as in a world where nothing can go wrong.

And know—that, even for him who shuns the day
And nightly tosses on a bed of pain;
Whose joys, from all but memory swept away,
Must come unhoped for, if they come again:
Know—that, for him whose waking thoughts, severe
As his distress is sharp, would scorn my theme,
The mimic notes, striking upon his ear
In sleep, and intermingling with his dream,
Could from sad regions send him to a dear
Delightful land of verdure, shower and gleam,
To mock the *wandering* Voice beside some haunted stream.

O bounty without measure! while the grace
Of Heaven doth in such wise, from humblest springs,
Pour pleasure forth, and solaces that trace
A mazy course along familiar things,
Well may our hearts have faith that blessings come,
Streaming from founts above the starry sky,
With angels when their own untroubled home
They leave, and speed on nightly embassy
To visit earthly chambers,—and for whom?
Yea, both for souls who God's forbearance try,
And those that seek His help, and for His mercy sigh.

TO THE CLOUDS.

Army of Clouds! ye wingèd Host in troops
Ascending from behind the motionless brow
Of that tall rock, as from a hidden world,
O whither with such eagerness of speed?
What seek ye, or what shun ye? of the gale
Companions, fear ye to be left behind,

Or racing o'er your blue ethereal field
Contend ye with each other? of the sea
Children, thus post ye over vale and height
To sink upon your mother's lap—and rest?
Or were ye rightlier hailed, when first mine eyes
Beheld in your impetuous march the likeness
Of a wide army pressing on to meet
Or overtake some unknown enemy?—
But your smooth motions suit a peaceful aim;
And Fancy, not less aptly pleased, compares
Your squadrons to an endless flight of birds
Aerial, upon due migration bound
To milder climes; or rather do ye urge
In caravan your hasty pilgrimage
To pause at last on more aspiring heights
Than these, and utter your devotion there
With thunderous voice? Or are ye jubilant,
And would ye, tracking your proud lord the Sun,
Be present at his setting; or the pomp
Of Persian mornings would ye fill, and stand
Poising your splendours high above the heads
Of worshippers kneeling to their up-risen God?
Whence, whence, ye Clouds! this eagerness of speed?
Speak, silent creatures.—They are gone, are fled,
Buried together in yon gloomy mass
That loads the middle heaven; and clear and bright
And vacant doth the region which they thronged
Appear; a calm descent of sky conducting
Down to the unapproachable abyss,
Down to that hidden gulf from which they rose
To vanish—fleet as days and months and years,
Fleet as the generations of mankind,
Power, glory, empire, as the world itself,
The lingering world, when time hath ceased to be,
But the winds roar, shaking the rooted trees,
And see! a bright precursor to a train
Perchance as numerous, overpeers the rock
That sullenly refuses to partake
Of the wild impulse. From a fount of life
Invisible, the long procession moves
Luminous or gloomy, welcome to the vale
Which they are entering, welcome to mine eye
That sees them, to my soul that owns in them,
And in the bosom of the firmament
O'er which they move, wherein they are contained,
A type of her capacious self and all
Her restless progeny.
A humble walk
Here is my body doomed to tread, this path,
A little hoary line and faintly traced,
Work, shall we call it, of the shepherd's foot
Or of his flock?—joint vestige of them both.
I pace it unrepining, for my thoughts
Admit no bondage and my words have wings.
Where is the Orphean lyre, or Druid harp
To accompany the verse? The mountain blast
Shall be our *hand* of music; he shall sweep
The rocks, and quivering trees, and billowy lake.
And search the fibres of the caves, and they
Shall answer, for our song is of the Clouds,
And the wind loves them; and the gentle gales—
Which by their aid re-clothe the naked lawn
With annual verdure, and revive the woods,
And moisten the parched lips of thirsty flowers—
Love them; and every idle breeze of air
Bends to the favourite burthen. Moon and stars
Keep their most solemn vigils when the Clouds
Watch also, shifting peaceably their place
Like bands of ministering Spirits, or when they lie,
As if some Protean art the change had wrought,
In listless quiet o'er the ethereal deep
Scattered, a Cyclades of various shapes
And all degrees of beauty. O ye Lightnings!
Ye are their perilous offspring; and the Sun—
Source inexhaustible of life and joy,
And type of man's far-darting reason, therefore
In old time worshipped as the god of verse,
A blazing intellectual deity—
Loves his own glory in their looks, and showers
Upon that unsubstantial brotherhood
Visions with all but beatific light
Enriched—too transient were they not renewed
From age to age, and did not, while we gaze
In silent rapture, credulous desire
Nourish the hope that memory lacks not power

To keep the treasure unimpaired. Vain thought!
Yet why repine, created as we are
For joy and rest, albeit to find them only
Lodged in the bosom of eternal things?

SUGGESTED BY A PICTURE OF THE BIRD OF PARADISE.

THE gentlest poet, with free thoughts endowed,
And a true master of the glowing strain,
Might scan the narrow province with disdain
That to the Painter's skill is here allowed.
This, this the Bird of Paradise! disclaim
The daring thought, forget the name:
This the Sun's Bird, whom Glendoveers might own
As no unworthy Partner in their flight
Through seas of ether, where the ruffling sway
Of nether air's rude billows is unknown;
Whom Sylphs, if e'er for casual pastime they
Through India's spicy regions wing their way,
Might bow to as their Lord. What character,
O sovereign Nature! I appeal to thee,
Of all thy feathered progeny
Is so unearthly, and what shape so fair?
So richly decked in variegated down,
Green, sable, shining yellow, shadowy brown,
Tints softly with each other blended,
Hues doubtfully begun and ended;
Or intershooting, and to sight
Lost and recovered, as the rays of light
Glance on the conscious plumes touched here and there?
Full surely, when with such proud gifts of life
Began the pencil's strife,
O'erweening Art was caught as in a snare.

A sense of seemingly presumptuous wrong
Gave the first impulse to the Poet's song;
But, of his scorn repenting soon, he drew
A juster judgment from a calmer view;
And, with a spirit freed from discontent,
Thankfully took an effort that was meant
Not with God's bounty, Nature's love, to vie,
Or made with hope to please that inward eye
Which ever strives [illegible] itself to satisfy,
But to recal the truth by some faint trace
Of power ethereal and celestial grace,
That in the living Creature find on earth a place.

POOR ROBIN.*

Now when the primrose makes a splendid show,
And lilies face the March-winds in full blow,
And humbler growths as moved with one desire
Put on, to welcome spring, their best attire,
Poor Robin is yet flowerless, but how gay
With his red stalks upon this sunny day!
And, as his tufts of leaves he spreads, content
With a hard bed and scanty nourishment,
Mixed with the green, some shine not lacking power
To rival summer's brightest scarlet flower;
And flowers they well might seem to passers-by
If looked at only with a careless eye;
Flowers—or a richer produce (did it suit
The season) sprinklings of ripe strawberry fruit.

But while a thousand pleasures come unsought,
Why fix upon his wealth or want a thought?
Is the string touched in prelude to a lay
Of pretty fancies that would round him play
When all the world acknowledged elfin sway?
Or does it suit our humour to commend
Poor Robin as a sure and crafty friend,
Whose practice teaches, spite of names to show
Bright colours whether they deceive or no?—
Nay, we would simply praise the free goodwill
With which, though slighted, he, on naked hill
Or in warm valley, seeks his part to fill;
Cheerful alike if bare of flowers as now,
Or when his tiny gems shall deck his brow
Yet more, we wish that men by men despised,

* [illegible] known by that name.

And such as lift their foreheads overprized,
Should sometimes think, where'er they
chance to spy
This child of Nature's own humility,
What recompense is kept in store or left
For all that seem neglected or bereft;
With what nice care equivalents are given,
How just, how bountiful, the hand of
Heaven.

March 1840.

THE GLEANER.

(SUGGESTED BY A PICTURE.)

THAT happy gleam of vernal eyes,
Those locks from summer's golden skies,
That o'er thy brow are shed;
That cheek—a kindling of the morn,
That lip—a rose-bud from the thorn,
I saw; and Fancy sped
To scenes Arcadian, whispering, through
soft air,
Of bliss that grows without a care,
And happiness that never flies—
(How can it where love never dies?)
Whispering of promise, where no blight
Can reach the innocent delight;
Where pity, to the mind conveyed
In pleasure, is the darkest shade
That Time, unwrinkled grandsire, flings
From his smoothly gliding wings.

What mortal form, what earthly face
Inspired the pencil, lines to trace,
And mingled colours, that should breed
Such rapture, nor want power to feed;
For had thy charge been idle flowers,
Fair Damsel! o'er my captive mind,
To truth and sober reason blind,
'Mid that soft air, those long-lost bowers,
The sweet illusion might have hung, for
hours.

Thanks to this tell-tale sheaf of corn,
That touchingly bespeaks thee born
Life's daily tasks with them to share
Who, whether from their lowly bed
They rise, or rest the weary head,
Ponder the blessing they entreat
From Heaven, and *feel* what they repeat,
While they give utterance to the prayer
That asks for daily bread.

1828.

PRELUDE,

PREFIXED TO THE VOLUME ENTITLED "POEMS CHIEFLY OF EARLY AND LATE YEARS."

IN desultory walk through orchard grounds,
Or some deep chestnut grove, oft have I
paused
The while a Thrush, urged rather than
restrained
By gusts of vernal storm, attuned his song
To his own genial instincts; and was heard
(Though not without some plaintive tones
between)
To utter, above showers of blossom swept
From tossing boughs, the promise of a
calm,
Which the unsheltered traveller might
receive
With thankful spirit. The descant, and
the wind
That seemed to play with it in love or
scorn,
Encouraged and endeared the strain of
words
That haply flowed from me, by fits of
silence
Impelled to livelier pace. But now, my
Book!
Charged with those lays, and others of like
mood,
Or loftier pitch if higher rose the theme,
Go, single—yet aspiring to be joined
With thy Forerunners that through many
a year
Have faithfully prepared each other's way—
Go forth upon a mission best fulfilled
When and wherever, in this changeful
world,
Power hath been given to please for higher
ends
Than pleasure only; gladdening to pre-
pare
For wholesome sadness, troubling to re-
fine,
Calming to raise; and, by a sapient Art
Diffused through all the mysteries of our
Being,
Softening the toils and pains that have not
ceased
To cast their shadows on our mother Earth
Since the primeval doom. Such is the
grace
Which, though unsued for, fails not to
descend
With heavenly inspiration; such the aim
That reason dictates; and, as even the
wish

Has virtue in it, why should hope to me
Be wanting that sometimes, where fancied ills
Harass the mind and strip from off the bowers
Of private life their natural pleasantness?
A Voice—devoted to the love whose seeds
Are sown in every human breast, to beauty
Lodged within compass of the humblest sight,
To cheerful intercourse with wood and field,
And sympathy with man's substantial griefs—
Will not be heard in vain! And in those days
When unforeseen distress spreads far and wide
Among a People mournfully cast down,
Or into anger roused by venal words
In recklessness flung out to overturn
The judgment, and divert the general heart
From mutual good—some strain of thine, my Book!
Caught at propitious intervals, may win
Listeners who not unwillingly admit
Kindly emotion tending to console
And reconcile, and both with young and old
Exalt the sense of thoughtful gratitude
For benefits that still survive, by faith
In progress, under laws divine, maintained.

Rydal Mount, March 26, 1842.

GRACE DARLING

AMONG the dwellers in the silent fields
The natural heart is touched, and public way
And crowded street resound with ballad strains,
Inspired by ONE whose very name bespeaks
Favour divine, exalting human love;
Whom, since her birth on bleak Northumbria's coast,
Known unto few but prized as far as known,
A single Act endears to high and low
Through the whole land—to Manhood, moved in spite
Of the world's freezing cares—to generous Youth—
To Infancy, that lisps her praise—to Age
Whose eye reflects it, glistening through a tear
Of tremulous admiration. Such true fame
Awaits her *now*; but, verily, good deeds
Do no imperishable record find
Save in the rolls of heaven, where hers may live
A theme for angels, when they celebrate
The high-souled virtues which forgetful earth
Has witness'd. Oh! that winds and waves could speak
Of things which their united power called forth
From the pure depths of her humanity!
A Maiden gentle, yet, at duty's call,
Firm and unflinching, as the Lighthouse reared
On the Island-rock, her lonely dwelling-place;
Or like the invincible Rock itself that braves,
Age after age, the hostile elements,
As when it guarded holy Cuthbert's cell.

All night the storm had raged, nor ceased, nor paused,
When, as day broke, the Maid, through misty air,
Espies far off a Wreck, amid the surf,
Beating on one of those disastrous isles—
Half of a Vessel, half—no more, the rest
Had vanished, swallowed up with all that there
Had for the common safety striven in vain,
Or thither thronged for refuge. With quick glance
Daughter and Sire through optic-glass discern,
Clinging about the remnant of this Ship,
Creatures—how precious in the Maiden's sight!
For whom, belike, the old Man grieves still more
Than for their fellow-sufferers engulfed
Where every parting agony is hushed,
And hope and fear mix not in further strife.
"But courage, Father! let us out to sea—
A few may yet be saved." The Daughter's words,
Her earnest tone, and look beaming with faith,
Dispel the Father's doubts nor do they lack
The noble-minded Mother's helping hand
To launch the boat; and with her blessing cheered,
And inwardly sustained by silent prayer
Together they put forth, Father and Child!
Each grasps an oar, and struggling on they go—
Rivals in effort; and, alike intent

Here to elude and there surmount, they watch
The billows lengthening, mutually crossed
And shattered, and re-gathering their might;
As if the tumult, by the Almighty's will
Were, in the conscious sea, roused and prolonged,
That woman's fortitude—so tried, so proved—
May brighten more and more!

True to the mark,
They stem the current of that perilous gorge,
Their arms still strengthening with the strengthening heart,
Though danger, as the Wreck is near'd, becomes
More imminent. Not unseen do they approach,
And rapture, with varieties of fear
Incessantly conflicting, thrills the frames
Of those who, in that dauntless energy,
Foretaste deliverance; but the least perturbed
Can scarcely trust his eyes, when he perceives
That of the pair—tossed on the waves to bring
Hope to the hopeless, to the dying, life—
One is a Woman, a poor earthly sister,
Or, be the Visitant other than she seems,
A guardian Spirit sent from pitying Heaven,
In woman's shape. But why prolong the tale,
Casting weak words amid a host of thoughts
Armed to repel them? Every hazard faced
And difficulty mastered, with resolve
That no one breathing should be left to perish,
This last remainder of the crew are all
Placed in the little boat, then o'er the deep
Are safely borne, landed upon the beach,
And, in fulfilment of God's mercy, lodged
Within the sheltering Lighthouse.—Shout, ye Waves!
Send forth a song of triumph. Waves and Winds,
Exult in this deliverance wrought through faith
In Him whose Providence your rage hath served!
Ye screaming Sea-mews, in the concert join!
And would that some immortal Voice—a Voice
Fitly attuned to all that gratitude
Breathes out from floor or couch, through pallid lips
Of the survivors—to the clouds might bear—
Blended with praise of that parental love,
Beneath whose watchful eye the Maiden grew
Pious and pure, modest and yet so brave,
Though young so wise, though meek so resolute—
Might carry to the clouds and to the stars,
Yea, to celestial Choirs, GRACE DARLING'S name!

1842.

Memorials of a Tour in Italy.

1837.

TO HENRY CRABB ROBINSON.

COMPANION! by whose buoyant Spirit cheered,
In whose experience trusting, day by day
Treasures I gained with zeal that neither feared
The toils nor felt the crosses of the way,
These records take: and happy should I be
Were but the Gift a meet Return to thee
For kindnesses that never ceased to flow,
And prompt self-sacrifice to which I owe
Far more than any heart but mine can know.

RYDAL MOUNT, *Feb.* 14*th*, 1842.

W. WORDSWORTH.

THE Tour of which the following Poems are very inadequate remembrances was shortened by report, too well founded, of the prevalence of cholera at Naples. To make some amends for what was reluctantly left unseen in the South of Italy, we visited the Tuscan Sanctuaries among the Apennines, and the principal Italian Lakes among the Alps. Neither of those lakes, nor of Venice, is there any notice in these Poems, chiefly because I have touched upon them elsewhere. See, in particular, "Descriptive Sketches," "Memorials of a Tour on the Continent in 1820," and a Sonnet upon the extinction of the Venetian Republic.

I.

MUSINGS NEAR AQUAPENDENTE

APRIL, 1837

YE Apennines! with all your fertile vales
Deeply embosomed, and your winding shores
Of either sea, an Islander by birth,
A Mountaineer by habit, would resound
Your praise, in meet accordance with your claims
Bestowed by Nature, or from man's great deeds
Inherited. — presumptuous thought! — it fled
Like vapour, like a towering cloud, dissolved.
Not, therefore, shall my mind give way to sadness;—
Yon snow-white torrent-fall, plumb down it drops
Yet ever hangs or seems to hang in air,
Lulling the leisure of that high perched town,
AQUAPENDENTE, in her lofty site
Its neighbour and its namesake — town and flood
Forth flashing out of its own gloomy chasm
Bright sunbeams—the fresh verdure of this lawn
Strewn with grey rocks, and on the horizon's verge,
O'er intervenient waste, through glimmering haze,
Unquestionably kenned, that cone-shaped hill
With fractured summit, no indifferent sight
To travellers, from such comforts as are thine,
Bleak Radicofani! escaped with joy—
These are before me, and the varied scene
May well suffice, till noon-tide's sultry heat
Relax, to fix and satisfy the mind
Passive yet pleased. What! with this Broom in flower
Close at my side! She bids me fly to greet
Her sisters, soon like her to be attired
With golden blossoms opening at the feet
Of my own Fairfield. The glad greeting given,
Given with a voice and by a look returned

Of old companionship, Time counts not minutes
Ere, from accustomed paths, familiar fields,
The local Genius hurries me aloft,
Transported over that cloud-wooing hill,
Seat Sandal, a fond suitor of the clouds,
With dream-like smoothness, to Helvellyn's top,
There to alight upon crisp moss, and range
Obtaining ampler boon, at every step,
Of visual sovereignty—hills multitudinous,
(Not Apennine can boast of fairer) hills
Pride of two nations, wood and lake and plains,
And prospect right below of deep coves shaped
By skeleton arms, that, from the mountain's trunk
Extended, clasp the winds, with mutual moan
Struggling for liberty, while undismayed
The shepherd struggles with them. Onward thence
And downward by the skirt of Greenside fell,
And by Glenridding-screes, and low Glencoign,
Places forsaken now, though loving still
The muses, as they loved them in the days
Of the old minstrels and the border bards.—
But here am I fast bound; and let it pass,
The simple rapture;—who that travels far
To feed his mind with watchful eyes could share
Or wish to share it?—One there surely was,
"The Wizard of the North," with anxious hope
Brought to this genial climate, when disease
Preyed upon body and mind—yet not the less
Had his sunk eye kindled at those dear words
That spake of bards and minstrels; and his spirit
Had flown with mine to old Helvellyn's brow
Where once together, in his day of strength,
We stood rejoicing, as if earth were free
From sorrow, like the sky above our heads.

Years followed years, and when, upon the eve
Of his last going from Tweed-side, thought turned,
Or by another's sympathy was led,
To this bright land, Hope was for him no friend,
Knowledge no help: Imagination shaped
No promise. Still, in more than ear-deep seats,
Survives for me, and cannot but survive
The tone of voice which wedded borrowed words
To sadness not their own, when, with faint smile
Forced by intent to take from speech its edge,
He said, "When I am there, although 'tis fair,
'Twill be another Yarrow." Prophecy
More than fulfilled, as gay Campania's shores
Soon witnessed, and the city of seven hills,
Her sparkling fountains, and her mouldering tombs;
And more than all, that Eminence which showed
Her splendours, seen, not felt, the while he stood
A few short steps (painful they were) apart
From Tasso's Convent-haven, and retired grave.

Peace to their Spirits! why should Poesy
Yield to the lure of vain regret, and hover
In gloom on wings with confidence outspread
To move in sunshine!—Utter thanks, my Soul!
Tempered with awe, and sweetened by compassion
For them who in the shades of sorrow dwell
That I—so near the term to human life
Appointed by man's common heritage,
Frail as the frailest, one withal (if that
Deserve a thought) but little known to fame—
Am free to rove where Nature's loveliest looks,
Art's noblest relics, History's rich bequests,
Failed to reanimate and but feebly cheered
The whole world's Darling—free to rove at will
O'er high and low, and if requiring rest,
Rest from enjoyment only.
Thanks poured forth
For what thus far hath blessed my wanderings, thanks
Fervent but humble as the lips can breathe
Where gladness seems a duty—let me guard
Those seeds of expectation which the fruit
Already gathered in this favoured Land
Enfolds within its core. The faith be mine,
That He who guides and governs all, approves

When gratitude, though disciplined to look
Beyond these transient spheres, doth wear a crown
Of earthly hope put on with trembling hand;
Nor is least pleased, we trust, when golden beams,
Reflected through the mists of age, from hours
Of innocent delight, remote or recent,
Shoot but a little way—'tis all they can—
Into the doubtful future Who would keep
Power must resolve to cleave to it through life,
Else it deserts him, surely as he lives.
Saints would not grieve nor guardian angels frown
If one—while tossed, as was my lot to be,
In a frail bark urged by two slender oars
Over waves rough and deep, that, when they broke,
Dashed their white foam against the palace walls
Of Genoa the superb—should there be led
To meditate upon his own appointed tasks,
However humble in themselves, with thoughts
Raised and sustained by memory of Him
Who oftentimes within those narrow bounds
Rocked on the surge, there tried his spirit's strength
And grasp of purpose, long ere sailed his ship
To lay a new world open.
Nor less prized
By those impressions which incline the heart
To mild, to lowly, and to seeming weak,
Bend that way her desires. The dew, the storm—
The dew whose moisture fell in gentle drops
On the small hyssop destined to become,
By Hebrew ordinance devoutly kept,
A purifying instrument—the storm
That shook on Lebanon the cedar's top,
And as it shook, enabling the blind roots
Further to force their way, endowed its trunk
With magnitude and strength fit to uphold
The glorious temple—did alike proceed
From the same gracious will, were both an offspring
Of bounty infinite.
Between Powers that aim
Higher to lift their lofty heads, impelled
By no profane ambition, Powers that thrive
By conflict, and their opposites, that trust
In lowliness—a midway tract there lies
Of thoughtful sentiment for every mind
Pregnant with good. Young, Middle-aged, and Old,
From century on to century, must have known
The emotion—nay, more fitly were it said—
The blest tranquillity that sunk so deep
Into my spirit, when I paced, enclosed
In Pisa's Campo Santa, the smooth floor
Of its Arcades paved with sepulchral slabs,
And through each window's open fret-work looked
O'er the blank Area of sacred earth
Fetched from Mount Calvary, or haply delved
In precincts nearer to the Saviour's tomb,
By hands of men, humble as brave, who fought
For its deliverance—a capacious field
That to descendants of the dead it holds
And to all living mute memento breathes,
More touching far than aught which on the walls
Is pictured, or their epitaphs can speak,
Of the changed City's long-departed power,
Glory, and wealth, which, perilous as they are,
Here did not kill, but nourished, Piety
And, high above that length of cloistral roof,
Peering in air, and backed by azure sky,
To kindred contemplations ministers
The Baptistery's dome, and that which swells
From the Cathedral pile; and with the twain
Conjoined in prospect mutable or fixed
(As hurry on in eagerness the feet
Or pause) the summit of the Leaning-tower
Nor less remuneration waits on him
Who having left the Cemetery stands
In the Tower's shadow, of decline and fall
Admonished not without some sense of fear,
Fear that soon vanishes before the sight
Of splendour unextinguished, pomp unscathed,
And beauty unimpaired. Grand in itself,
And for itself, the assemblage, grand and fair
To view, and for the mind's consenting eye
A type of age in man, upon its front
Bearing the world-acknowledged evidence
Of past exploits, nor fondly after more
Struggling against the stream of destiny,
But with its peaceful majesty content.
—Oh what a spectacle at every turn
The Place unfolds, from pavement skinned with moss,
Or grass grown spaces, where the heaviest foot

Provokes no echoes, but must softly tread;
Where Solitude with Silence paired stops short
Of Desolation, and to Ruin's scythe
Decay submits not.
But where'er my steps
Shall wander, chiefly let me cull with care
Those images of genial beauty, oft
Too lovely to be pensive in themselves
But by reflection made so, which do best
And fitliest serve to crown with fragrant wreaths
Life's cup when almost filled with years, like mine.
—How lovely robed in forenoon light and shade,
Each ministering to each, didst thou appear
Savona, Queen of territory fair
As aught that marvellous coast thro' all its length
Yields to the Stranger's eye. Remembrance holds
As a selected treasure thy one cliff,
That, while it wore for melancholy crest
A shattered Convent, yet rose proud to have
Clinging to its steep sides a thousand herbs
And shrubs, whose pleasant looks gave proof how kind
The breath of air can be where earth had else
Seemed churlish. And behold, both far and near,
Garden and field all decked with orange bloom,
And peach and citron, in Spring's mildest breeze
Expanding; and, along the smooth shore curved
Into a natural port, a tideless sea,
To that mild breeze with motion and with voice
Softly responsive; and, attuned to all
Those vernal charms of sight and sound, appeared
Smooth space of turf which from the guardian fort
Sloped seaward, turf whose tender April green,
In coolest climes too fugitive, might even here
Plead with the sovereign Sun for longer stay
Than his unmitigated beams allow,
Nor plead in vain, if beauty could preserve,
From mortal change, aught that is born on earth
Or doth on time depend.
While on the brink
Of that high Convent-crested cliff I stood,
Modest Savona! over all did brood
A pure poetic Spirit—as the breeze,
Mild—as the verdure, fresh—the sunshine, bright—
Thy gentle Chiabrera!—not a stone,
Mural or level with the trodden floor,
In Church or Chapel, if my curious quest
Missed not the truth, retains a single name
Of young or old, warrior, or saint, or sage,
To whose dear memories his sepulchral verse
Paid simple tribute, such as might have flowed
From the clear spring of a plain English heart,
Say rather, one in native fellowship
With all who want not skill to couple grief
With praise, as genuine admiration prompts.
The grief, the praise, are severed from their dust,
Yet in his page the records of that worth
Survive, uninjured;—glory then to words,
Honour to word-preserving Arts, and hail
Ye kindred local influences that still,
If Hope's familiar whispers merit faith,
Await my steps when they the breezy height
Shall range of philosophic Tusculum;
Or Sabine vales explored inspire a wish
To meet the shade of Horace by the side
Of his Bandusian fount; or I invoke
His presence to point out the spot where once
He sate, and eulogised with earnest pen
Peace, leisure, freedom, moderate desires;
And all the immunities of rural life
Extolled, behind Vacuna's crumbling fane.
Or let me loiter, soothed with what is given
Nor asking more, on that delicious Bay,
Parthenope's Domain—Virgilian haunt,
Illustrated with never-dying verse,
And, by the Poet's laurel-shaded tomb,
Age after age to Pilgrims from all lands
Endeared.
And who—if not a man as cold
In heart as dull in brain—while pacing ground
Chosen by Rome's legendary Bards, high minds
Out of her early struggles well inspired
To localise heroic acts—could look
Upon the spots with undelighted eye,
Though even to their last syllable the Lays
And very names of those who gave them birth
Have perished?—Verily, to her utmost depth,

Imagination feels what Reason fears not
To recognise, the lasting virtue lodged
In those bold fictions that, by deeds assigned
To the Valerian, Fabian, Curian Race,
And others like in fame, created Powers
With attributes from History derived,
By Poesy irradiate, and yet graced,
Through marvellous felicity of skill,
With something more propitious to high aims
Than either, pent within her separate sphere,
Can oft with justice claim.
And not disdaining
Union with those primeval energies
To virtue consecrate, stoop ye from your height
Christian Traditions! at my Spirit's call
Descend, and, on the brow of ancient Rome
As she survives in ruin, manifest
Your glories mingled with the brightest hues
Of her memorial halo, fading, fading,
But never to be extinct while Earth endures.
O come, if undishonoured by the prayer,
From all her Sanctuaries!—Open for my feet,
Ye Catacombs, give to mine eyes a glimpse
Of the Devout, as, mid your glooms convened
For safety, they of yore enclasped the Cross
On knees that ceased from trembling, or intoned
Their orisons with voices half-suppressed,
But sometimes heard, or fancied to be heard,
Even at this hour.
And thou Mamertine prison,
Into that vault receive me from whose depth
Issues, revealed in no presumptuous vision,
Albeit lifting human to divine,
A Saint, the Church's Rock, the mystic Keys
Grasped in his hand; and lo! with upright sword
Prefiguring his own impendent doom,
The Apostle of the Gentiles; both prepared
To suffer pains with heathen scorn and hate
Inflicted:—blessed Men, for so to Heaven
They follow their dear Lord!
Time flows—nor winds,
Nor stagnates, nor precipitates his course,
But many a benefit borne upon his breast
For human-kind sinks out of sight, is gone,
No one knows how; nor seldom is put forth
An angry arm that snatches good away,
Never perhaps to reappear. The Stream
Has to our generation brought and brings
Innumerable gains; yet we, who now
Walk in the light of day, pertain full surely
To a chilled age, most pitiably shut out
From that which *is* and actuates, by forms,
Abstractions, and by lifeless fact to fact
Minutely linked with diligence uninspired,
Unrectified, unguided, unsustained,
By godlike insight. To this fate is doomed
Science, wide-spread and spreading still as be
Her conquests, in the world of sense made known.
So with the internal mind it fares; and so
With morals, trusting, in contempt or fear
Of vital principle's controlling law,
To her purblind guide Expediency; and so
Suffers religious faith. Elate with view
Of what is won, we overlook or scorn
The best that should keep pace with it, and must,
Else more and more the general mind will droop,
Even as if bent on perishing. There lives
No faculty within us which the Soul
Can spare, and humblest earthly Weal demands,
For dignity not placed beyond her reach,
Zealous co-operation of all means
Given or acquired, to raise us from the mire,
And liberate our hearts from low pursuits.
By gross Utilities enslaved we need
More of ennobling impulse from the past,
If to the future aught of good must come
Sounder and therefore holier than the ends
Which, in the giddiness of self-applause,
We covet as supreme Oh grant the crown
That Wisdom wears, or take his treacherous staff
From Knowledge!—If the Muse, whom I have served
This day, be mistress of a single pearl
Fit to be placed in that pure diadem;
Then, not in vain, under these chestnut boughs
Reclined, shall I have yielded up my soul
To transports from the secondary founts
Flowing of time and place, and paid to both
Due homage; nor shall fruitlessly have striven,
By love of beauty moved, to enshrine in verse
Accordant meditations, which in times
Vexed and disordered, as our own, may shed
Influence, at least among a scattered few,
To soberness of mind and peace of heart
Friendly; as here to my repose hath been
This flowering broom's dear neighbourhood. the light

And murmur issuing from yon pendent flood,
And all the varied landscape. Let us now
Rise, and to-morrow greet magnificent Rome.

II.

THE PINE OF MONTE MARIO AT ROME.

I SAW far off the dark top of a Pine
Look like a cloud—a slender stem the tie
That bound it to its native earth—poised high
'Mid evening hues, along the horizon line,
Striving in peace each other to outshine.
But when I learned the Tree was living there,
Saved from the sordid axe by Beaumont's care,
Oh, what a gush of tenderness was mine!
The rescued Pine-tree, with its sky so bright
And cloud-like beauty, rich in thoughts of home,
Death-parted friends, and days too swift in flight,
Supplanted the whole majesty of Rome
(Then first apparent from the Pincian Height)
Crowned with St. Peter's everlasting Dome.

III.

AT ROME.

Is this, ye Gods, the Capitolian Hill?
Yon petty Steep in truth the fearful Rock,
Tarpeian named of yore, and keeping still
That name—a local Phantom proud to mock
The Traveller's expectation?—Could our Will
Destroy the ideal Power within, 'twere done
Thro' what men see and touch,—slaves wandering on,
Impelled by thirst of all but Heaven-taught skill.
Full oft, our wish obtained, deeply we sigh;
Yet not unrecompensed are they who learn,
From that depression raised, to mount on high
With stronger wing, more clearly to discern
Eternal things; and, if need be, defy
Change, with a brow not insolent, though stern.

IV.

AT ROME.—REGRETS.—IN ALLUSION TO NIEBUHR AND OTHER MODERN HISTORIANS.

THOSE old credulities, to nature dear,
Shall they no longer bloom upon the stock
Of History, stript naked as a rock
Mid a dry desert? What is it we hear?
The glory of Infant Rome must disappear,
Her morning splendours vanish, and their place
Know them no more. If Truth, who veiled her face
With those bright beams yet hid it not, must steer
Henceforth a humbler course perplexed and slow;
One solace yet remains for us who came
Into this world in days when story lacked
Severe research, that in our hearts we know
How, for exciting youth's heroic flame,
Assent is power, belief the soul of fact.

V.

CONTINUED.

COMPLACENT Fictions were they, yet the same
Involved a history of no doubtful sense,
History that proves by inward evidence
From what a precious source of truth it came.
Ne'er could the boldest Eulogist have dared
Such deeds to paint, such characters to frame,
But for coeval sympathy prepared
To greet with instant faith their loftiest claim.
None but a noble people could have loved
Flattery in Ancient Rome's pure-minded style:
Not in like sort the Runic Scald was moved;
He, nursed 'mid savage passions that defile
Humanity, sang feats that well might call
For the bloodthirsty mead of Odin's riotous Hall.

VI.

PLEA FOR THE HISTORIAN.

FORBEAR to deem the Chronicler unwise,
Ungentle, or untouched by seemly ruth,

Who, gathering up all that Time's envious tooth
Has spared of sound and grave realities,
Firmly rejects those dazzling flatteries,
Dear as they are to unsuspecting Youth,
That might have drawn down Clio from the skies
To vindicate the majesty of truth.
Such was her office while she walked with men,
A Muse, who, not unmindful of her Sire,
All-ruling Jove, whate'er the theme might be
Revered her mother, sage Mnemosyne,
And taught her faithful servants how the lyre
Should animate, but not mislead, the pen.

VII.

AT ROME.

THEY—who have seen the noble Roman's scorn
Break forth at thought of laying down his head,
When the blank day is over, garreted
In his ancestral palace, where, from morn
To night, the desecrated floors are worn
By feet of purse-proud strangers, they—who have read
In one meek smile, beneath a peasant's shed,
How patiently the weight of wrong is borne,
They—who have heard some learned Patriot treat
Of freedom, with mind grasping the whole theme
From ancient Rome, downwards through that bright dream
Of Commonwealths, each city a starlike seat
Of rival glory; they—fallen Italy—
Nor must, nor will, nor can, despair of Thee!

VIII.

NEAR ROME, IN SIGHT OF ST. PETER'S

LONG has the dew been dried on tree and lawn,
O'er man and beast a not unwelcome boon
Is shed, the languor of approaching noon;
To shady rest withdrawing or withdrawn
Mute are all creatures, as this couchant fawn,
Save insect-swarms that hum in air afloat,
Save that the Cock is crowing, a shrill note,
Startling and shrill as that which roused the dawn.
—Heard in that hour, or when, as now, the nerve
Shrinks from the note as from a mis-timed thing,
Oft for a holy warning may it serve,
Charged with remembrance of *his* sudden sting,
His bitter tears, whose name the Papal Chair
And yon resplendent Church are proud to bear.

IX.

AT ALBANO.

DAYS passed—and Monte Calvo would not clear
His head from mist; and, as the wind sobbed through
Albano's dripping Ilex avenue,
My dull forebodings in a Peasant's ear
Found casual vent. She said, "Be of good cheer;
Our yesterday's procession did not sue
In vain; the sky will change to sunny blue,
Thanks to our Lady's grace." I smiled to hear,
But not in scorn:—the Matron's Faith may lack
The heavenly sanction needed to ensure
Fulfilment; but, we trust, her upward track
Stops not at this low point, nor wants the lure
Of flowers the Virgin without fear may own,
For by her Son's blest hand the seed was sown.

X

NEAR Anio's stream, I spied a gentle Dove
Perched on an olive branch, and heard her cooing
'Mid new-born blossoms that soft airs were wooing,
While all things present told of joy and love.
But restless Fancy left that olive grove
To hail the exploratory Bird renewing
Hope for the few, who, at the world's undoing,
On the great flood were spared to live and move.
O bounteous Heaven, signs true as dove and bough
Brought to the ark are coming evermore
Given though we seek them not, but, while we plough

This sea of life without a visible shore,
Do neither promise ask nor grace implore
In what alone is ours, the living Now.

XI.

FROM THE ALBAN HILLS, LOOKING TOWARDS ROME.

Forgive, illustrious Country! these deep sighs,
Heaved less for thy bright plains and hills bestrown
With monuments decayed or overthrown,
For all that tottering stands or prostrate lies,
Than for like scenes in moral vision shown,
Ruin perceived for keener sympathies;
Faith crushed, yet proud of weeds, her gaudy crown;
Virtues laid low, and mouldering energies.
Yet why prolong this mournful strain?—Fallen Power
Thy fortunes, twice exalted, might provoke
Verse to glad notes prophetic of the hour
When thou, uprisen, shalt break thy double yoke,
And enter, with prompt aid from the Most High,
On the third stage of thy great destiny.

XII.

NEAR THE LAKE OF THRASYMENE.

When here with Carthage Rome to conflict came,
An earthquake, mingling with the battle's shock,
Checked not its rage; unfelt the ground did rock,
Sword dropped not, javelin kept its deadly aim.—
Now all is sun-bright peace. Of that day's shame,
Or glory, not a vestige seems to endure,
Save in this Rill that took from blood the name*
Which yet it bears, sweet Stream! as crystal pure.
So may all trace and sign of deeds aloof
From the true guidance of humanity,
Through Time and Nature's influence, purify
Their spirit; or, unless they for reproof
Or warning serve, thus let them all, on ground
That gave them being, vanish to a sound.

XIII.

NEAR THE SAME LAKE.

For action born, existing to be tried,
Powers manifold we have that intervene
To stir the heart that would too closely screen
Her peace from images to pain allied.
What wonder if at midnight by the side
Of Sanguinetto or broad Thrasymene,
The clang of arms is heard, and phantoms glide,
Unhappy ghosts in troops by moonlight seen;
And singly thine, O vanquished Chief! whose corse,
Unburied, lay hid under heaps of slain:
But who is He?—the Conqueror. Would he force
His way to Rome? Ah, no, round hill and plain
Wandering, he haunts, at fancy's strong command,
This spot—his shadowy death-cup in his hand.

XIV.

THE CUCKOO AT LAVERNA.

MAY 25TH, 1837.

List—'twas the Cuckoo—Oh with what delight
Heard I that voice! and catch it now, though faint,
Far off and faint, and melting into air,
Yet not to be mistaken. Hark again!
Those louder cries give notice that the Bird,
Although invisible as Echo's self,
Is wheeling hitherward. Thanks, happy Creature,
For this unthought-of greeting!
While allured
From vale to hill, from hill to vale led on,
We have pursued through various lands, a long

* Sanguinetto.

And pleasant course; flower after flower has blown,
Embellishing the ground that gave them birth
With aspects novel to my sight; but still
Most fair, most welcome, when they drank the dew
In a sweet fellowship with kinds beloved,
For old remembrance sake. And oft—where Spring
Display'd her richest blossoms among files
Of orange-trees bedecked with glowing fruit
Ripe for the hand, or under a thick shade
Of Ilex, or, if better suited to the hour,
The lightsome Olive's twinkling canopy—
Oft have I heard the Nightingale and Thrush
Blending as in a common English grove
Their love-songs; but, where'er my feet might roam,
Whate'er assemblages of new and old,
Strange and familiar, might beguile the way,
A gratulation from that vagrant Voice
Was wanting,—and most happily till now.

For see, Laverna! mark the far-famed Pile,
High on the brink of that precipitous rock,
Implanted like a Fortress, as in truth
It is, a Christian Fortress, garrisoned
In faith and hope, and dutiful obedience,
By a few Monks, a stern society,
Dead to the world and scorning earth-born joys.
Nay—though the hopes that drew, the fears that drove
St. Francis, far from Man's resort, to abide
Among these sterile heights of Apennine,
Bound him, nor, since he raised yon House, have ceased
To bind his spiritual Progeny, with rules
Stringent as flesh can tolerate and live;
His milder Genius (thanks to the good God
That made us) over those severe restraints
Of mind, that dread heart-freezing discipline,
Doth sometimes here predominate, and works
By unsought means for gracious purposes;
For earth, through heaven, for heaven, by changeful earth,
Illustrated, and mutually endeared.

Rapt though He were above the power of sense,
Familiarly, yet out of the cleansed heart
Of that once sinful Being overflowed
On sun, moon, stars, the nether elements,
And every shape of creature they sustain,
Divine affections; and with beast and bird
(Stilled from afar—such marvel story tells—
By casual outbreak of his passionate words,
And from their own pursuits in field or grove
Drawn to his side by look or act of love
Humane, and virtue of his innocent life)
He wont to hold companionship so free,
So pure, so fraught with knowledge and delight,
As to be likened in his Followers' minds
To that which our first Parents, ere the fall
From their high state darkened the Earth with fear,
Held with all Kinds in Eden's blissful bowers.

Then question not that, 'mid the austere Band,
Who breathe the air he breathed, tread where he trod,
Some true Partakers of his loving spirit
Do still survive, and, with those gentle hearts
Consorted, Others, in the power, the faith,
Of a baptized imagination, prompt
To catch from Nature's humblest monitors
Whate'er they bring of impulses sublime.

Thus sensitive must be the Monk, though pale
With fasts, with vigils worn, depressed by years,
Whom in a sunny glade I chanced to see
Upon a pine-tree's storm-uprooted trunk,
Seated alone, with forehead sky-ward raised,
Hands clasped above the crucifix he wore
Appended to his bosom, and lips closed
By the joint pressure of his musing mood
And habit of his vow. That ancient Man—
Nor haply less the Brother whom I marked,
As we approached the Convent gate, aloft
Looking far forth from his aerial cell,
A young Ascetic, Poet, Hero, Sage,
He might have been, Lover belike he was—
If they received into a conscious ear
The notes whose first faint greeting startled me,
Whose sedulous iteration thrilled with joy
My heart—may have been moved like me to think,
Ah! not like me who walk in the world's ways,
On the great Prophet, styled *the Voice of One*

Crying amid the Wilderness, and given,
Now that their snows must melt, their herbs and flowers
Revive, their obstinate winter pass away,
That awful name to Thee, thee, simple Cuckoo,
Wandering in solitude, and evermore
Foretelling and proclaiming, ere thou leave
This thy last haunt beneath Italian skies
To carry thy glad tidings over heights
Still loftier, and to climes more near the Pole.

Voice of the desert, fare-thee-well; sweet Bird!
If that substantial title please thee more,
Farewell!—but go thy way, no need hast thou
Of a good wish sent after thee; from bower
To bower as green, from sky to sky as clear,
Thee gentle breezes waft—or airs that meet
Thy course and sport around thee softly fan—
Till Night, descending upon hill and vale,
Grants to thy mission a brief term of silence,
And folds thy pinions up in blest repose.

XV.

AT THE CONVENT OF CAMALDOLI.

GRIEVE for the Man who hither came bereft,
And seeking consolation from above;
Nor grieve the less that skill to him was left
To paint this picture of his lady-love:
Can she, a blessed saint, the work approve?
And O, good Brethren of the cowl, a thing
So fair, to which with peril he must cling,
Destroy in pity, or with care remove.
That bloom—those eyes—can they assist to bind
Thoughts that would stray from Heaven! The dream must cease
To be; by Faith, not sight, his soul must live
Else will the enamoured Monk too surely find
How wide a space can part from inward peace
The most profound repose his cell can give.

XVI.

CONTINUED.

THE world forsaken, all its busy cares
And stirring interests shunned with desperate flight,
All trust abandoned in the healing might
Of virtuous action; all that courage dares,
Labour accomplishes, or patience bears—
Those helps rejected, they, whose minds perceive
How subtly works man's weakness, sighs may heave
For such a One beset with cloistral snares.
Father of Mercy! rectify his view,
If with his vows this object ill agree;
Shed over it thy grace, and thus subdue
Imperious passion in a heart set free:—
That earthly love may to herself be true,
Give him a soul that cleaveth unto Thee.

XVII.

AT THE EREMITE OR UPPER CONVENT OF CAMALDOLI.

WHAT aim had they, the Pair of Monks, in size
Enormous, dragged, while side by side they sate,
By panting steers up to this convent gate?
How, with empurpled cheeks and pampered eyes,
Dare they confront the lean austerities
Of Brethren who, here fixed, on Jesu wait
In sackcloth, and God's anger deprecate
Through all that humbles flesh and mortifies?
Strange contrast!—verily the world of dreams,
Where mingle, as for mockery combined,
Things in their very essences at strife,
Shows not a sight incongruous as the extremes
That everywhere, before the thoughtful mind,
Meet on the solid ground of waking life.

XVIII.

AT VALLOMBROSA.

Thick as autumnal leaves that strew the brooks
In Vallombrosa, where Etrurian shades
High over-arch'd embower.—PARADISE LOST

"VALLOMBROSA—I longed in thy shadiest wood

To slumber, reclined on the moss-covered floor!"
Fond wish that was granted at last, and the Flood,
That lulled me asleep, bids me listen once more.
Its murmur how soft! as it falls down the steep,
Near that Cell—yon sequestered Retreat high in air—
Where our Milton was wont lonely vigils to keep
For converse with God, sought through study and prayer.

The Monks still repeat the tradition with pride,
And its truth who shall doubt? for his Spirit is here;
In the cloud-piercing rocks doth her grandeur abide,
In the pines pointing heavenward her beauty austere,
In the flower-besprent meadows his genius we trace
Turned to humbler delights, in which youth might confide,
That would yield him fit help while prefiguring that Place
Where, if Sin had not entered, Love never had died.
When with life lengthened out came a desolate time,
And darkness and danger had compassed him round,
With a thought he would flee to these haunts of his prime,
And here once again a kind shelter be found.
And let me believe that when nightly the Muse
Did waft him to Zion, the glorified hill,
Here also, on some favoured height, he would choose
To wander, and drink inspiration at will.

Vallombrosa! of thee I first heard in the page
Of that holiest of Bards, and the name for my mind
Had a musical charm, which the winter of age
And the changes it brings had no power to unbind.
And now, ye Miltonian shades! under you
I repose, nor am forced from sweet fancy to part,
While your leaves I behold and the brooks they will strew,
And the realised vision is clasped to my heart.

Even so, and unblamed, we rejoice as we may
In Forms that must perish, frail objects of sense;
Unblamed—if the Soul be intent on the day
When the Being of Beings shall summon her hence.
For he and he only with wisdom is blest
Who, gathering true pleasures wherever they grow,
Looks up in all places, for joy or for rest,
To the Fountain whence Time and Eternity flow.

XIX.

AT FLORENCE.

UNDER the shadow of a stately Pile,
The dome of Florence, pensive and alone,
Nor giving heed to aught that passed the while,
I stood, and gazed upon a marble stone,
The laurell'd Dante's favourite seat. A throne,
In just esteem, it rivals: though no style
Be there of decoration to beguile
The mind, depressed by thought of greatness flown.
As a true man, who long had served the lyre,
I gazed with earnestness, and dared no more.
But in his breast the mighty Poet bore
A Patriot's heart, warm with undying fire.
Bold with the thought, in reverence I sate down,
And, for a moment, filled that empty Throne.

XX.

BEFORE THE PICTURE OF THE BAPTIST, BY RAPHAEL, IN THE GALLERY AT FLORENCE.

THE Baptist might have been ordain'd to cry
Forth from the towers of that huge Pile, wherein
His Father served Jehovah; but how win
Due audience, how for aught but scorn defy
The obstinate pride and wanton revelry

Of the Jerusalem below, her sin
And folly, if they with united din
Drown not at once mandate and prophecy?
Therefore the Voice spake from the Desert, thence
To Her, as to her opposite in peace,
Silence, and holiness, and innocence,
To Her and to all Lands its warning sent,
Crying with earnestness that might not cease,
"Make straight a highway for the Lord—repent!"

XXI.

AT FLORENCE.—FROM MICHAEL ANGELO.

RAPT above earth by power of one fair face,
Hers in whose sway alone my heart delights,
I mingle with the blest on those pure heights
Where Man, yet mortal, rarely finds a place.
With Him who made the Work that Work accords
So well, that by its help and through his grace
I raise my thoughts, inform my deeds and words,
Clasping her beauty in my soul's embrace.
Thus, if from two fair eyes mine cannot turn,
I feel how in their presence doth abide
Light which to God is both the way and guide;
And, kindling at their lustre, if I burn,
My noble fire emits the joyful ray
That through the realms of glory shines for aye.

XXII.

AT FLORENCE.—FROM M. ANGELO.

ETERNAL Lord! eased of a cumbrous load,
And loosened from the world, I turn to Thee;
Shun, like a shattered bark, the storm, and flee
To thy protection for a safe abode.
The crown of thorns, hands pierced upon the tree,
The meek, benign, and lacerated face,
To a sincere repentance promise grace,
To the sad soul give hope of pardon free.
With justice mark not Thou, O Light divine,
My fault, nor hear it with thy sacred ear;
Neither put forth that way thy arm severe;
Wash with thy blood my sins; thereto incline
More readily the more my years require
Help, and forgiveness speedy and entire.

XXIII.

AMONG THE RUINS OF A CONVENT IN THE APENNINES.

YE Trees! whose slender roots entwine
Altars that piety neglects;
Whose infant arms enclasp the shrine
Which no devotion now respects:
If not a straggler from the herd
Here ruminate, nor shrouded bird,
Chanting her low-voiced hymn, take pride
In aught that ye would grace or hide—
How sadly is your love misplaced,
Fair Trees, your bounty run to waste!

Ye, too, wild Flowers! that no one heeds,
And ye—full often spurned as weeds—
In beauty clothed, or breathing sweetness
From fractured arch and mouldering wall—
Do but more touchingly recal
Man's headstrong violence and Time's fleetness,
Making the precincts ye adorn
Appear to sight still more forlorn.

XXIV.

IN LOMBARDY.

SEE, where his difficult way that Old Man wins
Bent by a load of Mulberry leaves!—most hard
Appears *his* lot, to the small Worm's compared,
For whom his toil with early day begins.
Acknowledging no task-master, at will
(As if her labour and her ease were twins)
She seems to work, at pleasure to lie still;—
And softly sleeps within the thread she spins.
So fare they—the Man serving as her Slave.
Ere long their fates do each to each conform:
Both pass into new being—but the Worm,
Transfigured, sinks into a hopeless grave;
His volant Spirit will, he trusts, ascend
To bliss unbounded, glory without end.

XXV

AFTER LEAVING ITALY.

FAIR Land! Thee all men greet with joy; how few,
Whose souls take pride in freedom, virtue, fame,
Part from thee without pity dyed in shame
I could not—while from Venice we withdrew,
Led on till an Alpine strait confined our view
Within its depths, and to the shore we came
Of Lago Morto, dreary sight and name,
Which o'er sad thoughts a sadder colouring threw
Italia! on the surface of thy spirit,
(Too aptly emblemed by that torpid lake)
Shall a few partial breezes only creep?—
Be its depths quickened; what thou dost inherit
Of the world's hopes, dare to fulfil; awake,
Mother of Heroes, from thy death-like sleep!

XXVI.

CONTINUED.

As indignation mastered grief, my tongue
Spake bitter words; words that did ill agree
With those rich stores of Nature's imagery,
And divine Art, that fast to memory clung—
Thy gifts, magnificent Region, ever young
In the sun's eye, and in his sister's sight
How beautiful! how worthy to be sung
In strains of rapture, or subdued delight!
I feign not; witness that unwelcome shock
That followed the first sound of German speech,
Caught the far-winding barrier Alps among.
In that announcement, greeting seemed to mock
Parting; the casual word had power to reach
My heart, and filled that heart with conflict strong.

XXVII

COMPOSED AT RYDAL ON MAY MORNING, 1838.

IF with old love of you, dear Hills! I share
New love of many a rival image brought
From far, forgive the wanderings of my thought:
Nor art thou wronged, sweet May! when I compare
Thy present birth-morn with thy last, so fair,
So rich to me in favours. For my lot
Then was, within the famed Egerian Grot
To sit and muse, fanned by its dewy air
Mingling with thy soft breath! That morning too,
Warblers I heard their joy unbosoming
Amid the sunny, shadowy Coliseum;
Heard them, unchecked by aught of saddening hue,
For victories there won by flower-crowned Spring,
Chant in full choir their innocent Te Deum

The Borderers.

A TRAGEDY. COMPOSED 1795-96.)

DRAMATIS PERSONÆ.

MARMADUKE, OSWALD, WALLACE, LACY, LENNOX, } Of the Band of Borderers.
HERBERT.
WILFRED, Servant to MARMADUKE.
Host.
Forester.
ELDRED, a Peasant.
Peasant, Pilgrims, &c
IDONEA.
Female Beggar.
ELEANOR, Wife to ELDRED.

SCENE—*Borders of England and Scotland.*

TIME.—*The Reign of Henry III.*

Readers already acquainted with my Poems will recognise, in the following composition, some eight or ten lines which I have not scrupled to retain in the places where they originally stood. It is proper, however, to add, that they would not have been used elsewhere, if I had foreseen the time when I might be induced to publish this Tragedy.

February 28, 1842.

ACT I.

SCENE.—*Road in a Wood.*

WALLACE *and* LACY.

Lacy. The Troop will be impatient; let us hie
Back to our post, and strip the Scottish Foray
Of their rich Spoil, ere they recross the Border.
—Pity that our young Chief will have no part
In this good service.
Wal. Rather let us grieve
That, in the undertaking which has caused
His absence, he hath sought, whate'er his aim,
Companionship with One of crooked ways,
From whose perverted soul can come no good
To our confiding, open-hearted, Leader.
Lacy. True; and, remembering how the Band have proved
That Oswald finds small favour in our sight,
Well may we wonder he has gained such power
Over our much-loved Captain.
Wal. I have heard
Of some dark deed to which in early life
His passion drove him—then a Voyager
Upon the midland Sea. You knew his bearing
In Palestine?
Lacy. Where he despised alike
Mohammedan and Christian. But enough,
Let us begone—The Band may else be foiled. [*Exeunt*

Enter MARMADUKE *and* WILFRED.

Wil. Be cautious, my dear Master!
Mar. I perceive
That fear is like a cloak which old men huddle
About their love, as if to keep it warm.
Wil. Nay, but I grieve that we should part. This Stranger,
For such he is——
Mar. Your busy fancies, Wilfred,

Might tempt me to a smile, but what of him?

Wil. You know that you have saved his life.

Mar. I know it.

Wil. And that he hates you!—Pardon me, perhaps
That word was hasty.

Mar. Fy! no more of it

Wil. Dear Master! gratitude's a heavy burden
To a proud soul. — Nobody loves this Oswald—
Yourself, you do not love him.

Mar. I do more,
I honour him. Strong feelings to his heart
Are natural, and from no one can be learnt
More of man's thoughts and ways than his experience
Has given him power to teach. and then for courage
And enterprise — what perils hath he shunned?
What obstacles hath he failed to overcome?
Answer these questions, from our common knowledge,
And be at rest.

Wil. Oh, Sir!

Mar. Peace, my good Wilfrid
Repair to Liddesdale, and tell the Band
I shall be with them in two days, at farthest.

Wil. May He whose eye is over all protect you! [*Exit.*

Enter OSWALD (*a bunch of plants in his hand*).

Osw. This wood is rich in plants and curious simples.

Mar (*looking at them*). The wild rose, and the poppy, and the nightshade:
Which is your favourite, Oswald?

Osw. That which, while it is
Strong to destroy, is also strong to heal.
[*Looking forward.*
Not yet in sight!—We'll saunter here awhile;
They cannot mount the hill, by us unseen.

Mar. (*a letter in his hand.*) It is no common thing when one like you
Performs these delicate services, and therefore
I feel myself much bounden to you, Oswald:
'Tis a strange letter this!—You saw her write it?

Osw. And saw the tears with which she blotted it.

Mar. And nothing less would satisfy him?

Osw. No less;
For that another in his Child's affection
Should hold a place, as if 'twere robbery,
He seemed to quarrel with the very thought.
Besides, I know not what strange prejudice
Is rooted in his mind, this Band of ours,
Which you've collected for the noblest ends,
Along the confines of the Esk and Tweed
To guard the Innocent—he calls us "Outlaws;"
And, for yourself, in plain terms he asserts
This garb was taken up that indolence
Might want no cover, and rapacity
Be better fed.

Mar. Ne'er may I own the heart
That cannot feel for one helpless as he is.

Osw. Thou know'st me for a Man not easily moved,
Yet was I grievously provoked to think
Of what I witnessed.

Mar. This day will suffice
To end her wrongs.

Osw. But if the blind Man's tale
Should *yet* be true?

Mar. Would it were possible!
Did not the Soldier tell thee that himself,
And others who survived the wreck, beheld
The Baron Herbert perish in the waves
Upon the coast of Cyprus?

Osw. Yes, even so,
And I had heard the like before: in sooth
The tale of this his quondam Barony
Is cunningly devised; and, on the back
Of his forlorn appearance, could not fail
To make the proud and vain his tributaries,
And stir the pulse of lazy charity.
The seignories of Herbert are in Devon;
We, neighbours of the Esk and Tweed: 'tis much
The Arch-impostor——

Mar. Treat him gently, Oswald;
Though I have never seen his face, methinks,
There cannot come a day when I shall cease
To love him. I remember, when a Boy
Of scarcely seven years' growth, beneath the Elm
That casts its shade over our village school,
'Twas my delight to sit and hear Idonea
Repeat her Father's terrible adventures,
Till all the band of play-mates wept together;
And that was the beginning of my love.
And, through all converse of our later years
An image of this Old Man still was present,
When I had been most happy. Pardon me
If this be idly spoken.

Osw. See, they come,
Two travellers!

Mar. (*points*). The woman is Idonea.

Osw. And leading Herbert.
Mar. We must let them pass—
This thicket will conceal us.
[*They step aside.*

Enter IDONEA, *leading* HERBERT *blind.*

Idon. Dear Father, you sigh deeply; ever since
We left the willow shade by the brook-side,
Your natural breathing has been troubled.
Her. Nay,
You are too fearful; yet must I confess,
Our march of yesterday had better suited
A firmer step than mine.
Idon. That dismal moor—
In spite of all the larks that cheered our path,
I never can forgive it: but how steadily
You paced along, when the bewildering moonlight
Mocked me with many a strange fantastic shape!—
I thought the Convent never would appear;
It seemed to move away from us: and yet,
That you are thus the fault is mine; for the air
Was soft and warm, no dew lay on the grass,
And midway on the waste ere night had fallen
I spied a Covert walled and roofed with sods—
A miniature; belike some Shepherd-boy,
Who might have found a nothing-doing hour
Heavier than work, raised it: within that hut
We might have made a kindly bed of heath,
And thankfully there rested side by side
Wrapped in our cloaks, and, with recruited strength,
Have hailed the morning sun. But cheerily, Father,—
That staff of yours, I could almost have heart
To fling't away from you: you make no use
Of me, or of my strength;—come, let me feel
That you do press upon me. There—indeed
You are quite exhausted. Let us rest awhile
On this green bank. [*He sits down.*
Her. (*after some time*). Idonea, you are silent,
And I divine the cause.
Idon. Do not reproach me:
I pondered patiently your wish and will
When I gave way to your request; and now,
When I behold the ruins of that face,
Those eyeballs dark—dark beyond hope of light,
And think that they were blasted for my sake,
The name of Marmaduke is blown away:
Father, I would not change that sacred feeling
For all this world can give.
Her. Nay, be composed:
Few minutes gone a faintness overspread
My frame, and I bethought me of two things
I ne'er had heart to separate—my grave,
And thee, my Child!
Idon. Believe me, honoured Sire!
'Tis weariness that breeds these gloomy fancies,
And you mistake the cause: you hear the woods
Resound with music; could you see the sun,
And look upon the pleasant face of Nature——
Her. I comprehend thee—I should be as cheerful
As if we two were twins: two songsters bred
In the same nest, my spring-time one with thine.
My fancies, fancies if they be, are such
As come, dear Child! from a far deeper source
Than bodily weariness. While here we sit
I feel my strength returning.—The bequest
Of thy kind Patroness, which to receive
We have thus far adventured, will suffice
To save thee from the extreme of penury;
But when thy Father must lie down and die,
How wilt thou stand alone?
Idon. Is he not strong?
Is he not valiant?
Her. Am I then so soon
Forgotten? have my warnings passed so quickly
Out of thy mind? My dear, my only, Child:
Thou wouldst be leaning on a broken reed—
This Marmaduke——
Idon. O could you hear his voice:
Alas! you do not know him. He is one
(I wot not what ill tongue has wronged him with you)
All gentleness and love. His face bespeaks
A deep and simple meekness: and that Soul,
Which with the motion of a virtuous act

Flashes a look of terror upon guilt,
Is, after conflict, quiet as the ocean,
By a miraculous finger, stilled at once.
He Unhappy woman!
Idon. Nay, it was my duty
Thus much to speak; but think not I forget—
Dear Father! how *could* I forget and live—
You and the story of that doleful night
When, Antioch blazing to her topmost towers,
You rushed into the murderous flames, returned
Blind as the grave, but, as you oft have told me,
Clasping your infant Daughter to your heart.
Her. Thy Mother too!—scarce had I gained the door,
I caught her voice; she threw herself upon me,
I felt thy infant brother in her arms,
She saw my blasted face—a tide of soldiers
That instant rushed between us, and I heard
Her last death-shriek, distinct among a thousand.
Idon. Nay, Father, stop not; let me hear it all.
Her. Dear Daughter! precious relic of that time—
For my old age, it doth remain with thee
To make it what thou wilt. Thou hast been told,
That when, on our return from Palestine,
I found how my domains had been usurped,
I took thee in my arms, and we began
Our wanderings together. Providence
At length conducted us to Rossland,—there,
Our melancholy story moved a Stranger
To take thee to her home—and for myself,
Soon after, the good Abbot of St. Cuthbert's
Supplied my helplessness with food and raiment,
And, as thou know'st, gave me that humble Cot
Where now we dwell.—For many years I bore
Thy absence, till old age and fresh infirmities
Exacted thy return, and our reunion
I did not think that, during that long absence,
My Child, forgetful of the name of Herbert,
Had given her love to a wild Freebooter,
Who here, upon the borders of the Tweed,
Doth prey alike on two distracted Countries,
Traitor to both.
Idon. Oh, could you hear his voice!
I will not call on Heaven to vouch for me,
But let this kiss speak what is in my heart.

Enter a Peasant.

Pea. Good morrow, Strangers! If you want a Guide,
Let me have leave to serve you!
Idon. My Companion
Hath need of rest, the sight of Hut or Hostel
Would be most welcome.
Pea. Yon white hawthorn gained,
You will look down into a dell, and there
Will see an ash from which a sign-board hangs,
The house is hidden by the shade. Old Man,
You seem worn out with travel—shall I support you?
Her. I thank you; but, a resting-place so near,
'Twere wrong to trouble you.
Pea. God speed you both.
[*Exit* Peasant
Her. Idonea, we must part. Be not alarmed—
'Tis but for a few days—a thought has struck me.
Idon. That I should leave you at this house, and thence
Proceed alone. It shall be so; for strength
Would fail you ere our journey's end be reached.
[*Exit* HERBERT *supported by* IDONEA

Re-enter MARMADUKE *and* OSWALD.

Mar. This instant will we stop him——
Osw. Be not hasty,
For, sometimes, in despite of my conviction,
He tempted me to think the Story true;
'Tis plain he loves the Maid, and what he said
That savoured of aversion to thy name
Appeared the genuine colour of his soul—
Anxiety lest mischief should befal her
After his death.
Mar. I have been much deceived.
Osw. But sure he loves the Maiden, and never love
Could find delight to nurse itself so strangely,
Thus to torment her with *inventions!*—death—
There must be truth in this.
Mar. Truth in his story!
He must have felt it then, known what it was,

And in such wise to rack her gentle heart
Had been a tenfold cruelty.

Osw. Strange pleasures
Do we poor mortals cater for ourselves!
To see him thus provoke her tenderness
With tales of weakness and infirmity!
I'd wager on his life for twenty years.

Mar. We will not waste an hour in such a cause.

Osw. Why, this is noble! Shake her off at once.

Mar. Her virtues are his instruments.—A Man
Who has so practised on the world's cold sense
May well deceive his Child—what! leave her thus,
A prey to a deceiver?—no—no—no—
'Tis but a word and then——

Osw. Something is here
More than we see, or whence this strong aversion?
Marmaduke! I suspect unworthy tales
Have reached his ear—you have had enemies.

Mar. Enemies!—of his own coinage.

Osw. That may be,
But wherefore slight protection such as you
Have power to yield? perhaps he looks elsewhere.—
I am perplexed.

Mar. What hast thou heard or seen?

Osw. No—no—the thing stands clear of mystery;
(As you have said) he coins himself the slander
With which he taints her ear;—for a plain reason;
He dreads the presence of a virtuous man
Like you; he knows your eye would search his heart,
Your justice stamp upon his evil deeds
The punishment they merit. All is plain:
It cannot be——

Mar. What cannot be?

Osw. Yet that a Father
Should in his love admit no rivalship,
And torture thus the heart of his own Child—

Mar. Nay, you abuse my friendship!

Osw. Heaven forbid!—
There was a circumstance, trifling indeed—
It struck me at the time—yet I believe
I never should have thought of it again
But for the scene which we by chance have witnessed.

Mar. What is your meaning?

Osw. Two days gone I saw,
Though at a distance and he was disguised,
Hovering round Herbert's door, a man whose figure
Resembled much that cold voluptuary,
The villain, Clifford. He hates you, and he knows
Where he can stab you deepest.

Mar. Clifford never
Would stoop to skulk about a Cottage door—
It could not be.

Osw. And yet I now remember,
That, when your praise was warm upon my tongue,
And the blind Man was told how you had rescued
A maiden from the ruffian violence
Of this same Clifford, he became impatient
And would not hear me.

Mar. No—it cannot be—
I dare not trust myself with such a thought—
Yet whence this strange aversion? You are a man
Not used to rash conjectures——

Osw. If you deem it
A thing worth further notice, we must act
With caution, sift the matter artfully.

[*Exeunt* MARMADUKE *and* OSWALD.

SCENE.—*The Door of the Hostel.*

HERBERT, IDONEA, *and* Host.

Her (*seated*). As I am dear to you, remember, Child!
This last request.

Idon. You know me, Sire; farewell!

Her. And are you going then? Come, come, Idonea,
We must not part,—I have measured many a league
When these old limbs had need of rest,—and now
I will not play the sluggard.

Idon. Nay, sit down.
[*Turning to* Host.
Good Host, such tendance as you would expect
From your own Children if yourself were sick,
Let this old Man find at your hands; poor Leader, [*Looking at the dog.*
We soon shall meet again. If thou neglect
This charge of thine, then ill befall thee!—Look,
The little fool is loth to stay behind.
Sir Host! by all the love you bear to courtesy,
Take care of him, and feed the truant well.

Host. Fear not, I will obey you,—but One so young,
And One so fair, it goes against my heart
That you should travel unattended, Lady!—
I have a palfrey and a groom: the lad
Shall squire you, (would it not be better, Sir?)
And for less fee than I would let him run
For any lady I have seen this twelvemonth.

Idon. You know, Sir, I have been too long your guard
Not to have learnt to laugh at little fears.
Why, if a wolf should leap from out a thicket,
A look of mine would send him scouring back,
Unless I differ from the thing I am
When you are by my side.

Her. Idonea, wolves
Are not the enemies that move my fears.

Idon. No more, I pray, of this. Three days at farthest
Will bring me back—protect him, Saints—farewell! [*Exit* IDONEA.

Host. 'Tis never drought with us—St. Cuthbert and his Pilgrims,
Thanks to them, are to us a stream of comfort:
Pity the Maiden did not wait awhile;
She could not, Sir, have failed of company.

Her. Now she is gone, I fain would call her back.

Host (*calling*). Holla!

Her. No, no, the business must be done.—
What means this riotous noise?

Host. The villagers
Are flocking in—a wedding festival—
That's all—God save you, Sir.

Enter OSWALD

Osw. Ha! as I live,
The Baron Herbert.

Host. Mercy, the Baron Herbert!

Osw. So far into your journey! on my life,
You are a lusty Traveller. But how fare you?

Her. Well as the wreck I am permits. And you, Sir?

Osw. I do not see Idonea.

Her. Dutiful Girl,
She is gone before, to spare my weariness.
But what has brought you hither?

Osw A slight affair,
That will be soon despatched.

Her. Did Marmaduke
Receive that letter?

Osw. Be at peace.—The tie
Is broken, you will hear no more of *him*

Her. This is true comfort, thanks a thousand times!—
That noise!—would I had gone with her as far
As the Lord Clifford's Castle: I have heard
That, in his milder moods, he has expressed
Compassion for me. His influence is great
With Henry, our good King!—the Baron might
Have heard my suit, and urged my plea at Court.
No matter—he's a dangerous Man.—That noise!—
'Tis too disorderly for sleep or rest.
Idonea would have fears for me,—the Convent
Will give me quiet lodging. You have a boy, good Host,
And he must lead me back.

Osw. You are most lucky;
I have been waiting in the wood hard by
For a companion—here he comes; our journey

Enter MARMADUKE.

Lies on your way; accept us as your Guides.

Her. Alas! I creep so slowly.

Osw. Never fear;
We'll not complain of that.

Her. My limbs are stiff
And need repose. Could you but wait an hour?

Osw. Most willingly!—come, let us lead you in,
And, while you take your rest, think not of us,
We'll stroll into the wood, lean on my arm.
[*Conducts* HERBERT *into the house.*
Exit MARMADUKE.

Enter Villagers.

Osw. (*to himself coming out of the Hostel*).
I have prepared a most apt Instrument—
The Vagrant must, no doubt, be loitering somewhere
About this ground, she hath a tongue well skilled,
By mingling natural matter of her own
With all the daring fictions I have taught her,
To win belief, such as my plot requires.
[*Exit* OSWALD.

Enter more Villagers, *a* Musician *among them.*

Host (*to them*). Into the Court, my Friend, and perch yourself
Aloft upon the elm-tree. Pretty Maids,
Garlands and flowers, and cakes and merry thoughts,
Are here, to send the sun into the west
More speedily than you belike would wish.

SCENE *changes to the Wood adjoining the Hostel.*—MARMADUKE *and* OSWALD *entering.*

Mar. I would fain hope that we deceive ourselves:
When first I saw him sitting there, alone,
It struck upon my heart I know not how.

Osw. To-day will clear up all.—You marked a Cottage,
That ragged Dwelling, close beneath a rock
By the brook side: it is the abode of one,
A Maiden innocent till ensnared by Clifford,
Who soon grew weary of her, but, alas!
What she had seen and suffered turned her brain.
Cast off by her Betrayer, she dwells alone,
Nor moves her hands to any needful work;
She eats her food which every day the peasants
Bring to her hut; and so the Wretch has lived
Ten years; and no one ever heard her voice;
But every night at the first stroke of twelve
She quits her house, and, in the neighbouring Churchyard
Upon the self-same spot, in rain or storm,
She paces out the hour 'twixt twelve and one—
She paces round and round an Infant's grave,
And in the Churchyard sod her feet have worn
A hollow ring; they say it is knee-deep——
Ah! what is here?

A female Beggar *rises up, rubbing her eyes as if in sleep—a Child in her arms.*

Beg. Oh! Gentlemen, I thank you;
I've had the saddest dream that ever troubled
The heart of living creature—My poor Babe
Was crying, as I thought, crying for bread
When I had none to give him; whereupon,
I put a slip of foxglove in his hand,
Which pleased him so, that he was hushed at once:
When, into one of these same spotted bells
A bee came darting, which the Child with joy
Imprisoned there, and held it to his ear,
And suddenly grew black, as he would die.

Mar. We have no time for this, my babbling Gossip;
Here's what will comfort you.
[*Gives her money.*

Beg. The saints reward you
For this good deed!—Well, Sirs, this passed away;
And afterwards I fancied, a strange dog,
Trotting alone along the beaten road,
Came to my child as by my side he slept
And, fondling, licked his face, then on a sudden
Snapped fierce to make a morsel of his head:
But here he is [*kissing the Child*], it must have been a dream.

Osw. When next inclined to sleep, take my advice,
And put your head, good Woman, under cover.

Beg. Oh, Sir, you would not talk thus, if you knew
What life is this of ours, how sleep will master
The weary-worn.—You gentlefolk have got
Warm chambers to your wish. I'd rather be
A stone than what I am.—But two nights gone,
The darkness overtook me—wind and rain
Beat hard upon my head—and yet I saw
A glow-worm, through the covert of the furze,
Shine calmly as if nothing ailed the sky.
At which I half accused the God in Heaven.—
You must forgive me.

Osw. Ay, and if you think
The Fairies are to blame, and you should chide
Your favourite saint—no matter—this good day
Has made amends.

Beg. Thanks to you both; but, Oh, Sir!
How would you like to travel on whole hours
As I have done, my eyes upon the ground,
Expecting still, I knew not how, to find
A piece of money glittering through the dust.

Mar. This woman is a prater. Pray, good Lady!
Do you tell fortunes?

Beg. Oh, Sir, you are like the rest,
This Little-one—it cuts me to the heart—
Well! they might turn a beggar from their doors,
But there are mothers who can see the Babe
Here at my breast, and ask me where I bought it:
This they can do, and look upon my face—
But you, Sir, should be kinder.
Mar. Come hither, Fathers,
And learn what Nature is from this poor Wretch!
Beg. Ay, Sir, there's nobody that feels for us.
Why now—but yesterday I overtook
A blind old Greybeard and accosted him,
I' th' name of all the Saints, and by the Mass
He should have used me better!—Charity!
If you can melt a rock, he is your man;
But I'll be even with him—here again
Have I been waiting for him.
Osw. Well, but softly,
Who is it that hath wronged you?
Beg. Mark you me;
I'll point him out;—a Maiden is his guide,
Lovely as Spring's first rose; a little dog,
Tied by a woollen cord moves on before
With look as sad as he were dumb; the cur,
I owe him no ill will, but in good sooth
He does his Master credit.
Mar. As I live,
'Tis Herbert and no other!
Beg. 'Tis a feast to see him,
Lank as a ghost and tall, his shoulders bent,
And long beard white with age—yet evermore,
As if he were the only Saint on earth,
He turns his face to heaven.
Osw. But why so violent
Against this venerable Man?
Beg. I'll tell you:
He has the very hardest heart on earth;
I had as lief turn to the Friar's school
And knock for entrance, in mid holiday.
Mar. But to your story.
Beg. I was saying, Sir—
Well!—he has often spurned me like a toad,
But yesterday was worse than all;—at last
I overtook him, Sirs, my Babe and I,
And begged a little aid for charity:
But he was snappish as a cottage cur.
Well then, says I—I'll out with it; at which
I cast a look upon the Girl, and felt
As if my heart would burst; and so I left him.
Osw. I think, good Woman, you are the very person
Whom, but some few days past, I saw in Eskdale,
At Herbert's door.
Beg. Ay; and if truth were known,
I have good business there.
Osw. I met you at the threshold,
And he seemed angry.
Beg. Angry! well he might;
And long as I can stir I'll dog him.—Yesterday,
To serve me so, and knowing that he owes
The best of all he has to me and mine.
But 'tis all over now.—That good old Lady
Has left a power of riches; and I say it,
If there's a lawyer in the land, the knave
Shall give me half.
Osw. What's this?—I fear, good Woman,
You have been insolent.
Beg. And there's the Baron,
I spied him skulking in his peasant's dress.
Osw. How say you? in disguise?—
Mar. But what's your business
With Herbert or his Daughter?
Beg. Daughter! truly—
But how's the day?—I fear, my little Boy,
We've overslept ourselves.—Sirs, have you seen him? [*Offers to go.*
Mar. I must have more of this;—you shall not stir
An inch, till I am answered. Know you aught
That doth concern this Herbert?
Beg. You are provoked,
And will misuse me, Sir!
Mar. No trifling, Woman!—
Osw. You are as safe as in a sanctuary;
Speak.
Mar. Speak!
Beg. He is a most hard-hearted Man.
Mar. Your life is at my mercy.
Beg. Do not harm me,
And I will tell you all!—You know not, Sir,
What strong temptations press upon the Poor.
Osw. Speak out.
Beg. Oh, Sir, I've been a wicked Woman.
Osw. Nay, but speak out!
Beg. He flattered me, and said
What harvest it would bring us both; and so,
I parted with the Child.
Mar. You parted with whom?
Beg. Idonea, as he calls her; but the Girl
Is mine.

Mar. Yours, Woman! are you Herbert's wife?
Beg. Wife, Sir?—his wife—not I,—my husband, Sir,
Was of Kirkoswald—many a snowy winter
We've weathered out together. My poor Gilfred!
He has been two years in his grave.
Mar. Enough.
Osw. We've solved the riddle—Miscreant!
Mar. Do you,
Good Dame, repair to Liddesdale and wait
For my return; be sure you shall have justice.
Osw. A lucky woman!—go, you have done good service. [*Aside.*
Mar. (*to himself*). Eternal praises on the power that saved her!—
Osw. (*gives her money*). Here's for your little boy, and when you christen him
I'll be his Godfather.
Beg. Oh, Sir, you are merry with me.
In grange or farm this Hundred scarcely owns
A dog that does not know me.—These good Folks,
For love of God, I must not pass their doors;
But I'll be back with my best speed: for you—
God bless and thank you both, my gentle Masters. [*Exit* Beggar.
Mar. (*to himself*). The cruel Viper!—Poor devoted Maid,
Now I *do* love thee.
Osw. I am thunderstruck.
Mar. Where is she—holla!
[*Calling to the* Beggar, *who returns; he looks at her steadfastly.*
You are Idonea's Mother?—
Nay, be not terrified—it does me good
To look upon you.
Osw. (*interrupting*). In a peasant's dress
You saw, who was it?
Beg. Nay, I dare not speak;
He is a man, if it should come to his ears
I never shall be heard of more.
Osw. Lord Clifford?
Beg. What can I do? believe me, gentle Sirs,
I love her, though I dare not call her daughter.
Osw. Lord Clifford—did you see him talk with Herbert?
Beg. Yes, to my sorrow—under the great oak
At Herbert's door—and when he stood beside
The blind Man—at the silent Girl he looked
With such a look—it makes me tremble, Sir,
To think of it.
Osw. Enough! you may depart.
Mar. (*to himself*). Father!—to God himself we cannot give
A holier name; and, under such a mask,
To lead a Spirit, spotless as the blessed,
To that abhorrèd den of brutish vice!—
Oswald, the firm foundation of my life
Is going from under me; these strange discoveries—
Looked at from every point of fear or hope,
Duty, or love—involve, I feel, my ruin.

ACT II.

SCENE, *A Chamber in the Hostel.* OSWALD *alone, rising from a Table on which he had been writing.*

Osw. They chose *him* for their Chief!—what covert part
He, in the preference, modest Youth, might take,
I neither know nor care. The insult bred
More of contempt than hatred; both are flown;
That either e'er existed is my shame:
'Twas a dull spark—a most unnatural fire
That died the moment the air breathed upon it.
—These fools of feeling are mere birds of winter
That haunt some barren island of the north,
Where, if a famishing man stretch forth his hand,
They think it is to feed them. I have left him
To solitary meditation;—now
For a few swelling phrases, and a flash
Of truth, enough to dazzle and to blind,
And he is mine for ever—here he comes.

Enter MARMADUKE.

Mar. These ten years she has moved her lips all day
And never speaks!
Osw. Who is it?
Mar. I have seen her
Osw. Oh! the poor tenant of that ragged homestead,
Her whom the Monster, Clifford, drove to madness.
Mar. I met a peasant near the spot; he told me,

These ten years she had sate all day alone
Within those empty walls.
Osw. I too have seen her;
Chancing to pass this way some six months gone,
At midnight, I betook me to the Church-yard:
The moon shone clear, the air was still, so still
The trees were silent as the graves beneath them.
Long did I watch, and saw her pacing round
Upon the self-same spot, still round and round,
Her lips for ever moving.
Mar. At her door
Rooted I stood; for, looking at the woman,
I thought I saw the skeleton of Idonea.
Osw. But the pretended Father——
Mar. Earthly law
Measures not crimes like his.
Osw. *We* rank not, happily,
With those who take the spirit of their rule
From that soft class of devotees who feel
Reverence for life so deeply that they spare
The verminous brood, and cherish what they spare
While feeding on their bodies. Would that Idonea
Were present, to the end that we might hear
What she can urge in his defence; she loves him.
Mar. Yes, loves him; 'tis a truth that multiplies
His guilt a thousand-fold.
Osw. 'Tis most perplexing:
What must be done?
Mar. We will conduct her hither;
These walls shall witness it—from first to last
He shall reveal himself.
Osw. Happy are we,
Who live in these disputed tracts, that own
No law but what each man makes for himself:
Here justice has indeed a field of triumph.
Mar. Let us begone and bring her hither;—here
The truth shall be laid open, his guilt proved
Before her face. The rest be left to me.
Osw. You will be firm: but though we well may trust
The issue to the justice of the cause,
Caution must not be flung aside; remember,
Yours is no common life. Self-stationed here
Upon these savage confines, we have seen you
Stand like an isthmus 'twixt two stormy seas
That oft have checked their fury at your bidding.
'Mid the deep holds of Solway's mossy waste,
Your single virtue has transformed a Band
Of fierce barbarians into Ministers
Of peace and order. Aged men with tears
Have blessed their steps, the fatherless retire
For shelter to their banners. But it is,
As you must needs have deeply felt, it is
In darkness and in tempest that we seek
The Majesty of Him who rules the world.
Benevolence, that has not heart to use
The wholesome ministry of pain and evil,
Becomes at last weak and contemptible.
Your generous qualities have won due praise,
But vigorous Spirits look for something more
Than Youth's spontaneous products; and to-day
You will not disappoint them; and hereafter——
Mar. You are wasting words; hear me then, once for all:
You are a man—and therefore, if compassion,
Which to our kind is natural as life,
Be known unto you, you will love this Woman,
Even as I do; but I should loathe the light,
If I could think one weak or partial feeling——
Osw. You will forgive me——
Mar. If I ever knew
My heart, could penetrate its inmost core,
'Tis at this moment.—Oswald, I have loved
To be the friend and father of the oppressed,
A comforter of sorrow;—there is something
Which looks like a transition in my soul,
And yet it is not.—Let us lead him hither.
Osw. Stoop for a moment! 'tis an act of justice;
And where's the triumph if the delegate
Must fall in the execution of his office?
The deed is done—if you will have it so—
Here where we stand—that tribe of vulgar wretches
(You saw them gathering for the festival)
Rush in—the villains seize us——
Mar. Seize!
Osw. Yes, they—
Men who are little given to sift and weigh—

Would wreak on us the passion of the moment.

Mar. The cloud will soon disperse—farewell—but stay,
Thou wilt relate the story.

Osw. Am I neither
To bear a part in this Man's punishment,
Nor be its witness?

Mar. I had many hopes
That were most dear to me, and some will bear
To be transferred to thee.

Osw. When I'm dishonoured!

Mar. I would preserve thee. How may this be done?

Osw. By showing that you look beyond the instant.
A few leagues hence we shall have open ground,
And nowhere upon earth is place so fit
To look upon the deed. Before we enter
The barren Moor, hangs from a beetling rock
The shattered Castle in which Clifford oft
Has held infernal orgies—with the gloom,
And very superstition of the place,
Seasoning his wickedness. The Debauchee
Would there perhaps have gathered the first fruits
Of this mock Father's guilt.

Enter Host *conducting* HERBERT.

Host. The Baron Herbert
Attends your pleasure.

Osw. (*to* Host). We are ready—
(*to* HERBERT) Sir!
I hope you are refreshed.—I have just written
A notice for your Daughter, that she may know
What is become of you.—You'll sit down and sign it;
'Twill glad her heart to see her father's signature.

[*Gives the letter he had written.*

Her. Thanks for your care.

[*Sits down and writes. Exit* Host.

Osw. (*aside to* MARMADUKE). Perhaps it would be useful
That you too should subscribe your name.

[MARMADUKE *overlooks* HERBERT—*then writes—examines the letter eagerly.*

Mar. I cannot leave this paper.

[*He puts it up, agitated.*

Osw. (*aside*). Dastard! Come.

[MARMADUKE *goes towards* HERBERT *and supports him*—MARMADUKE *tremblingly beckons* OSWALD *to take his place.*

Mar. (*as he quits* HERBERT). There is a palsy in his limbs—he shakes.

[*Exeunt* OSWALD *and* HERBERT—MARMADUKE *following.*

SCENE *changes to a Wood—a Group of* Pilgrims, *and* IDONEA *with them.*

First Pil. A grove of darker and more lofty shade
I never saw.

Sec. Pil. The music of the birds
Drops deadened from a roof so thick with leaves.

Old Pil. This news! It made my heart leap up with joy.

Idon. I scarcely can believe it.

Old Pil. Myself, I heard
The Sheriff read, in open Court, a letter
Which purported it was the royal pleasure
The Baron Herbert, who, as was supposed,
Had taken refuge in this neighbourhood,
Should be forthwith restored. The hearing, Lady,
Filled my dim eyes with tears.—When I returned
From Palestine, and brought with me a heart,
Though rich in heavenly, poor in earthly, comfort,
I met your Father, then a wandering Outcast:
He had a Guide, a Shepherd's boy; but grieved
He was that One so young should pass his youth
In such sad service; and he parted with him.
We joined our tales of wretchedness together,
And begged our daily bread from door to door.
I talk familiarly to you, sweet Lady!
For once you loved me.

Idon. You shall back with me
And see your Friend again. The good old Man
Will be rejoiced to greet you.

Old Pil. It seems but yesterday
That a fierce storm o'ertook us, worn with travel,
In a deep wood remote from any town.
A cave that opened to the road presented
A friendly shelter, and we entered in.

Idon. And I was with you?

Old Pil. If indeed 'twas you—
But you were then a tottering Little-one—
We sate us down. The sky grew dark and darker:

I struck my flint, and built up a small fire
With rotten boughs and leaves, such as the winds
Of many autumns in the cave had piled.
Meanwhile the storm fell heavy on the woods:
Our little fire sent forth a cheering warmth
And we were comforted, and talked of comfort;
But 'twas an angry night, and o'er our heads
The thunder rolled in peals that would have made
A sleeping man uneasy in his bed.
O Lady, you have need to love your Father
His voice—methinks I hear it now, his voice
When, after a broad flash that filled the cave,
He said to me, that he had seen his Child,
A face (no cherub's face more beautiful)
Revealed by lustre brought with it from Heaven;
And it was you, dear Lady!

Idon. God be praised,
That I have been his comforter till now!
And will be so through every change of fortune
And every sacrifice his peace requires.—
Let us be gone with speed, that he may hear
These joyful tidings from no lips but mine.

[*Exeunt* IDONEA *and* Pilgrims.

SCENE, *the Area of a half-ruined Castle—on one side the entrance to a dungeon*—OSWALD *and* MARMADUKE *pacing backwards and forwards.*

Mar. 'Tis a wild night.

Osw. I'd give my cloak and bonnet
For sight of a warm fire.

Mar. The wind blows keen;
My hands are numb.

Osw. Ha! ha! 'tis nipping cold.
[*Blowing his fingers.*
I long for news of our brave Comrades; Lacy
Would drive those Scottish Rovers to their dens
If once they blew a horn this side the Tweed.

Mar. I think I see a second range of Towers;
This castle has another Area—come,
Let us examine it.

Osw. 'Tis a bitter night;
I hope Idonea is well housed. That horseman,
Who at full speed swept by us where the wood
Roared in the tempest, was within an ace
Of sending to his grave our precious Charge:
That would have been a vile mischance.

Mar. It would.

Osw. Justice had been most cruelly defrauded.

Mar. Most cruelly.

Osw. As up the steep we clomb,
I saw a distant fire in the north-east;
I took it for the blaze of Cheviot Beacon:
With proper speed our quarters may be gained
To-morrow evening.

[*Looks restlessly towards the mouth of the dungeon.*

Mar. When, upon the plank,
I had led him 'cross the torrent, his voice blessed me:
You could not hear, for the foam beat the rocks
With deafening noise,—the benediction fell
Back on himself; but changed into a curse.

Osw. As well indeed it might.

Mar. And this you deem
The fittest place?

Osw. (*aside*). He is growing pitiful

Mar. (*listening*). What an odd moaning that is!—

Osw. Mighty odd
The wind should pipe a little, while we stand
Cooling our heels in this way!—I'll begin
And count the stars.

Mar. (*still listening*). That dog of his, you are sure,
Could not come after us—he *must* have perished;
The torrent would have dashed an oak to splinters.
You said you did not like his looks—that he
Would trouble us; if he were here again,
I swear the sight of him would quail me more
Than twenty armies.

Osw. How?

Mar. The old blind Man,
When you had told him the mischance, was troubled
Even to the shedding of some natural tears
Into the torrent over which he hung,
Listening in vain.

Osw He has a tender heart!
[OSWALD *offers to go down into the dungeon.*

Mar. How now, what mean you?

Osw. Truly, I was going
To waken our stray Baron. Were there not
A farm or dwelling-house within five leagues,

We should deserve to wear a cap and bells,
Three good round years, for playing the fool here
In such a night as this.

Mar. Stop, stop.

Osw. Perhaps,
You'd better like we should descend together,
And lie down by his side—what say you to it?
Three of us—we should keep each other warm:
I'll answer for it that our four-legged friend
Shall not disturb us; further I'll not engage;
Come, come, for manhood's sake!

Mar. These drowsy shiverings,
This mortal stupor which is creeping over me,
What do they mean? were this my single body
Opposed to armies, not a nerve would tremble:
Why do I tremble now?—Is not the depth
Of this Man's crimes beyond the reach of thought?
And yet, in plumbing the abyss for judgment,
Something I strike upon which turns my mind
Back on herself, I think, again—my breast
Concentres all the terrors of the Universe:
I look at him and tremble like a child.

Osw. Is it possible?

Mar. One thing you noticed not:
Just as we left the glen a clap of thunder
Burst on the mountains with hell-rousing force.
This is a time, said he, when guilt may shudder;
But there's a Providence for them who walk
In helplessness, when innocence is with them.
At this audacious blasphemy, I thought
The spirit of vengeance seemed to ride the air.

Osw. Why are you not the man you were that moment?

[*He draws* MARMADUKE *to the dungeon.*

Mar. You say he was asleep,—look at this arm,
And tell me if 'tis fit for such a work.
Oswald, Oswald! [*Leans upon* OSWALD.

Osw. This is some sudden seizure!

Mar. A most strange faintness,—will you hunt me out
A draught of water?

Osw. Nay, to see you thus
Moves me beyond my bearing.—I will try
To gain the torrent's brink.

[*Exit* OSWALD.

Mar. (*after a pause*). It seems an age
Since that Man left me.—No, I am not lost.

Her. (*at the mouth of the dungeon*). Give me your hand; where are you, Friends? and tell me
How goes the night.

Mar. 'Tis hard to measure time,
In such a weary night, and such a place.

Her. I do not hear the voice of my friend Oswald.

Mar. A minute past, he went to fetch a draught
Of water from the torrent. 'Tis, you'll say,
A cheerless beverage.

Her. How good it was in you
To stay behind!—Hearing at first no answer,
I was alarmed.

Mar. No wonder; this is a place
That well may put some fears into *your* heart.

Her. Why so? a roofless rock had been a comfort,
Storm-beaten and bewildered as we were;
And in a night like this, to lend your cloaks
To make a bed for me!—My Girl will weep
When she is told of it.

Mar. This Daughter of yours
Is very dear to you.

Her. Oh! but you are young;
Over your head twice twenty years must roll,
With all their natural weight of sorrow and pain,
Ere can be known to you how much a Father
May love his Child.

Mar. Thank you, old Man, for this!

[*Aside.*

Her. Fallen am I, and worn out, a useless Man;
Kindly have you protected me to-night,
And no return have I to make but prayers;
May you in age be blest with such a daughter!—
When from the Holy Land I had returned
Sightless, and from my heritage was driven,
A wretched Outcast—but this strain of thought
Would lead me to talk fondly.

Mar. Do not fear,
Your words are precious to my ears, go on.

Her. You will forgive me, but my heart runs over
When my old Leader slipped into the flood

And perished, what a piercing outcry you
Sent after him. I have loved you ever since.
You start—where are we?
Mar Oh, there is no danger;
The cold blast struck me.
Her 'Twas a foolish question.
Mar. But when you were an Outcast?—Heaven is just;
Your piety would not miss its due reward,
The little Orphan would then be your succour,
And do good service, though she knew it not.
Her. I turned me from the dwellings of my Fathers,
Where none but those who trampled on my rights
Seemed to remember me. To the wide world
I bore her, in my arms; her looks won pity;
She was my Raven in the wilderness,
And brought me food. Have I not cause to love her?
Mar. Yes.
Her. More than ever Parent loved a Child?
Mar. Yes, yes.
Her. I will not murmur, merciful God!
I will not murmur; blasted as I have been,
Thou hast left me ears to hear my Daughter's voice,
And arms to fold her to my heart. Submissively
Thee I adore, and find my rest in faith.
Enter OSWALD.
Osw Herbert! — confusion! (*aside*). Here it is, my Friend,
[*Presents the Horn.*
A charming beverage for you to carouse,
This bitter night.
Her. Ha! Oswald! ten bright crosses
I would have given, not many minutes gone,
To have heard your voice.
Osw. Your couch, I fear, good Baron,
Has been but comfortless; and yet that place
When the tempestuous wind first drove us hither,
Felt warm as a wren's nest. You'd better turn
And under covert rest till break of day,
Or till the storm abate.
(*To* MARMADUKE *aside*). He has restored you.
No doubt you have been nobly entertained?
But soft—how came he forth? The Nightmare Conscience
Has driven him out of harbour?
Mar. I believe
You have guessed right.
Her. The trees renew their murmur
Come, let us house together.
[OSWALD *conducts him to the dungeon*
Osw. (*returns*). Had I not
Esteemed you worthy to conduct the affair
To its most fit conclusion, do you think
I would so long have struggled with my Nature,
And smothered all that's man in me?—away!—
[*Looking towards the dungeon*
This man's the property of him who best
Can feel his crimes. I have resigned a privilege;
It now becomes my duty to resume it.
Mar. Touch not a finger——
Osw. What then must be done?
Mar. Which way so'er I turn, I am perplexed.
Osw. Now, on my life, I grieve for you The misery
Of doubt is insupportable. Pity, the facts
Did not admit of stronger evidence;
Twelve honest men, plain men, would set us right;
Their verdict would abolish these weak scruples.
Mar. Weak!—I am weak—there does my torment lie,
Feeding itself.
Osw. Verily, when he said
How his old heart would leap to hear her steps,
You thought his voice the echo of Idonea's.
Mar. And never heard a sound so terrible.
Osw. Perchance you think so now?
Mar. I cannot do it:
Twice did I spring to grasp his wither'd throat,
When such a sudden weakness fell upon me,
I could have dropped asleep upon his breast.
Osw. Justice—is there not thunder in the word?
Shall it be law to stab the petty robber
Who aims but at our purse; and shall this Parricide—
Worse is he far, far worse (if foul dishonour
Be worse than death) to that confiding Creature
Whom he to more than filial love and duty
Hath falsely trained—shall he fulfil his purpose?
But you are fallen.

Mar. Fallen should I be indeed—
Murder—perhaps asleep, blind, old, alone,
Betrayed, in darkness! Here to strike the blow—
Away! away!——[*Flings away his sword.*

Osw. Nay, I have done with you.
We'll lead him to the Convent. He shall live
And she shall love him. With unquestioned title
He shall be seated in his Barony,
And we too chant the praise of his good deeds.
I now perceive we do mistake our masters,
And most despise the men who best can teach us:
Henceforth it shall be said that bad men only
Are brave: Clifford is brave; and that old Man
Is brave.

[*Taking* MARMADUKE'S *sword and giving it to him.*

To Clifford's arms he would have led
His Victim—haply to this desolate house.

Mar. (*advancing to the dungeon*). It must be ended!—

Osw. Softly; do not rouse him;
He will deny it to the last. He lies
Within the Vault, a spear's length to the left.

[MARMADUKE *descends to the dungeon.*

(*Alone.*) The Villains rose in mutiny to destroy me;
I could have quelled the Cowards, but this Stripling
Must needs step in, and save my life. The look
With which he gave the boon—I see it now!
The same that tempted me to loathe the gift.—
For this old venerable Grey-beard—faith
'Tis his own fault if he hath got a face
Which doth play tricks with them that look on it:
'Twas this that put it in my thoughts—that countenance—
His staff—his figure—Murder!—what, of whom?
We kill a worn-out horse, and who but women
Sigh at the deed? Hew down a wither'd tree,
And none look grave but dotards. He may live
To thank me for this service Rainbow arches,
Highways of dreaming passion, have too long,
Young as he is, diverted wish and hope
From the unpretending ground we mortals tread;—
Then shatter the delusion, break it up
And set him free. What follows? I have learned
That things will work to ends the slaves o' the world
Do never dream of. I *have* been what he—
This Boy—when he comes forth with bloody hands—
Might envy, and am now,—but he shall know
What I am now—

[*Goes and listens at the dungeon.*

Praying or parleying?—tut!
Is he not eyeless? He has been half dead
These fifteen years——

Enter female Beggar *with two or three of her Companions.*

(*Turning abruptly*). *Ha! speak*—what Thing art thou?
(*Recognises her*). Heavens! my good friend! [*To her.*

Beg. Forgive me, gracious sir!—

Osw. (*to her companions*). Begone, ye Slaves, or I will raise a Whirlwind
And send ye dancing to the clouds, like leaves. [*They retire affrighted.*

Beg. Indeed we meant no harm; we lodge sometimes
In this deserted Castle—*I repent me.*

[OSWALD *goes to the dungeon—listens—returns to the* Beggar.

Osw. Woman, thou hast a helpless Infant—keep
Thy secret for its sake, or verily
That wretched life of thine shall be the forfeit.

Beg. I *do* repent me, Sir; I fear the curse
Of that blind Man. 'Twas not your money, sir——

Osw. Begone!

Beg. (*going*). There is some wicked deed in hand; [*Aside.*
Would I could find the old Man and his Daughter. [*Exit* Beggar.

MARMADUKE *re-enters from the dungeon.*

Osw. It is all over then;—your foolish fears
Are hushed to sleep by your own act and deed,
Made quiet as he is.

Mar. Why came you down?

And when I felt your hand upon my arm
And spake to you, why did you give no answer?
Feared you to waken him? he must have been
In a deep sleep. I whispered to him thrice.
There are the strangest echoes in that place!

Osw. Tut! let them gabble till the day of doom.

Mar. Scarcely, by groping, had I reached the Spot,
When round my wrist I felt a cord drawn tight,
As if the blind Man's dog were pulling at it.

Osw. But after that?

Mar. The features of Idonea
Lurked in his face——

Osw. Psha! never to these eyes
Will retribution show itself again
With aspect so inviting. Why forbid me
To share your triumph?

Mar. Yes, her very look,
Smiling in sleep——

Osw. A pretty feat of Fancy!

Mar. Though but a glimpse, it sent me to my prayers.

Osw. Is he alive?

Mar. What mean you? who alive?

Osw. Herbert! since you will have it, Baron Herbert;
He who will gain his Seignory when Idonea
Hath become Clifford's harlot—is *he* living?

Mar. The old Man in that dungeon *is* alive.

Osw. Henceforth, then, will I never in camp or field
Obey you more. Your weakness, to the Band,
Shall be proclaimed: brave Men, they all shall hear it.
You a protector of humanity!
Avenger you of outraged innocence!

Mar. 'Twas dark—dark as the grave; yet did I see,
Saw him—his face turned towards me; and I tell thee
Idonea's filial countenance was there
To baffle me—it put me to my prayers.
Upwards I cast my eyes, and, through a crevice,
Beheld a star twinkling above my head,
And, by the living God, I could not do it.
[*Sinks exhausted.*

Osw. (*to himself*). Now may I perish if this turn do more
Than make me change my course.
(*To* MARMADUKE.) Dear Marmaduke,
My words were rashly spoken: I recal them:
I feel my error: shedding human blood
Is a most serious thing.

Mar. Not I alone,
Thou too art deep in guilt.

Osw. We have indeed
Been most presumptuous. There *is* guilt in this,
Else could so strong a mind have ever known
These trepidations? Plain it is that Heaven
Has marked out this foul Wretch as one whose crimes
Must never come before a mortal judgment-seat,
Or be chastised by mortal instruments.

Mar. A thought that's worth a thousand worlds! [*Goes towards the dungeon*

Osw. I grieve
That, in my zeal, I have caused you so much pain.

Mar. Think not of that!—'tis over—we are safe.

Osw. (*as if to himself, yet speaking aloud*). The truth is hideous, but how stifle it? [*Turning to* MARMADUKE.
Give me your sword—nay, here are stones and fragments,
The least of which would beat out a man's brains;
Or you might drive your head against that wall.
No! this is not the place to hear the tale:
It should be told you pinioned in your bed,
Or on some vast and solitary plain
Blown to you from a trumpet.

Mar. Why talk thus?
Whate'er the monster brooding in your breast
I care not: fear I have none, and cannot fear——
[*The sound of a horn is heard.*
That horn again—'Tis some one of our Troop;
What do they here? Listen!

Osw. What! dogged like thieves!

Enter WALLACE *and* LACY, *&c.*

Lacy. You are found at last, thanks to the vagrant Troop
For not misleading us.

Osw. (*looking at* WALLACE) That subtle Greybeard—
I'd rather see my father's ghost.

Lacy (*to* MARMADUKE) My Captain,
We come by order of the Band. Belike
You have not heard that Henry has at last
Dissolved the Barons' League, and sent abroad

His Sheriffs with fit force to reinstate
The genuine owners of such Lands and Baronies
As, in these long commotions, have been seized.
His Power is this way tending. It befits us
To stand upon our guard, and with our swords
Defend the innocent.

Mar. Lacy! we look
But at the surfaces of things; we hear
Of towns in flames, fields ravaged, young and old
Driven out in troops to want and nakedness;
Then grasp our swords and rush upon a cure
That flatters us, because it asks not thought:
The deeper malady is better hid;
The world is poisoned at the heart.

Lacy. What mean you?

Wal. (*whose eye has been fixed suspiciously upon* OSWALD). Ay, what is it you mean?

Mar. Harkee, my Friends;—
[*appearing gay.*
Were there a Man who, being weak and helpless
And most forlorn, should bribe a Mother, pressed
By penury, to yield him up her Daughter,
A little Infant, and instruct the Babe,
Prattling upon his knee, to call him Father——

Lacy. Why, if his heart be tender, that offence
I could forgive him.

Mar. (*going on*). And should he make the Child
An instrument of falsehood, should he teach her
To stretch her arms, and dim the gladsome light
Of infant playfulness with piteous looks
Of misery that was not——

Lacy. Troth, 'tis hard—
But in a world like ours——

Mar. (*changing his tone*) This self-same Man—
Even while he printed kisses on the cheek
Of this poor Babe, and taught its innocent tongue
To lisp the name of Father—could he look
To the unnatural harvest of that time
When he should give her up, a Woman grown,
To him who bid the highest in the market
Of foul pollution——

Lacy. The whole visible world
Contains not such a Monster!

Mar. For this purpose
Should he resolve to taint her Soul by means
Which bathe the limbs in sweat to think of them;
Should he, by tales which would draw tear from iron,
Work on her nature, and so turn compassion
And gratitude to ministers of vice,
And make the spotless spirit of filial love
Prime mover in a plot to damn his Victim
Both soul and body——

Wal. 'Tis too horrible;
Oswald, what say you to it?

Lacy Hew him down,
And fling him to the ravens.

Mar. But his aspect
It is so meek, his countenance so venerable.

Wal. (*with an appearance of mistrust*). But how, what say you, Oswald?

Lacy. (*at the same moment*). Stab him, were it
Before the Altar.

Mar. What, if he were sick,
Tottering upon the very verge of life,
And old, and blind——

Lacy. Blind, say you?

Osw. (*coming forward*). Are we Men,
Or own we baby Spirits? Genuine courage
Is not an accidental quality,
A thing dependent for its casual birth
On opposition and impediment.
Wisdom, if Justice speak the word, beats down
The giant's strength; and, at the voice of Justice,
Spares not the worm. The giant and the worm—
She weighs them in one scale. The wiles of woman,
And craft of age, seducing reason, first
Made weakness a protection, and obscured
The moral shapes of things. His tender cries
And helpless innocence—do they protect
The infant lamb? and shall the infirmities,
Which have enabled this enormous Culprit
To perpetrate his crimes, serve as a Sanctuary
To cover him from punishment? Shame!—Justice,
Admitting no resistance, bends alike
The feeble and the strong She needs not here

Her bonds and chains, which make the mighty feeble.
—We recognise in this old Man a victim
Prepared already for the sacrifice.

Lacy. By heaven, his words are reason!

Osw. Yes, my Friends,
His countenance is meek and venerable;
And, by the Mass, to see him at his prayers!—
I am of flesh and blood, and may I perish
When my heart does not ache to think of it!—
Poor Victim! not a virtue under heaven
But what was made an engine to ensnare thee;
But yet I trust, Idonea, thou art safe.

Lacy. Idonea!

Wal. How! what? your Idonea? [*To* MARMADUKE.

Mar. *Mine*,
But now no longer mine. You know Lord Clifford;
He is the Man to whom the Maiden—pure
As beautiful, and gentle and benign,
And in her ample heart loving even me—
Was to be yielded up.

Lacy. Now, by the head
Of my own child, this Man must die; my hand,
A worthier wanting, shall itself entwine
In his grey hairs!—

Mar. (*to* LACY). I love the Father in thee,
You know me, Friends; I have a heart to feel,
And I have felt, more than perhaps becomes me
Or duty sanctions.

Lacy. We will have ample justice.
Who are we, Friends? Do we not live on ground
Where Souls are self-defended, free to grow
Like mountain oaks rocked by the stormy wind?
Mark the Almighty Wisdom, which decreed
This monstrous crime to be laid open—*here*,
Where Reason has an eye that she can use,
And Men alone are Umpires. To the Camp
He shall be led, and there, the Country round
All gathered to the spot, in open day
Shall Nature be avenged.

Osw. 'Tis nobly thought;
His death will be a monument for ages.

Mar. (*to* LACY) I thank you for that hint He shall be brought
Before the Camp, and would that best and wisest
Of every country might be present. There,
His crime shall be proclaimed; and for the rest
It shall be done as Wisdom shall decide.
Meanwhile, do you two hasten back and see
That all is well prepared.

Wal. We will obey you.
(*Aside*) But softly! we must look a little nearer.

Mar. Tell where you found us. At some future time
I will explain the cause [*Exeunt.*

ACT III.

SCENE, *the door of the Hostel, a group of* Pilgrims *as before;* IDONEA *and the* Host *among them.*

Host. Lady, you'll find your Father at the Convent
As I have told you! He left us yesterday
With two Companions; one of them, as seemed,
His most familiar friend. (*Going.*) There was a letter
Of which I heard them speak, but that I fancy
Has been forgotten.

Idon. (*to* Host). Farewell!

Host. Gentle pilgrims,
St. Cuthbert speed you on your holy errand.
[*Exeunt* IDONEA *and* Pilgrims

SCENE, *a desolate Moor.*

OSWALD (*alone*)

Osw. Carry him to the Camp! Yes, to the Camp.
Oh, Wisdom! a most wise resolve! and then,
That half a word should blow it to the winds!
This last device must end my work.—Methinks
It were a pleasant pastime to construct
A scale and table of belief—as thus—
Two columns, one for passion, one for proof;
Each rises as the other falls: and first,
Passion a unit and *against* us—proof—
Nay, we must travel in another path,
Or we're stuck fast for ever;—passion, then
Shall be a unit *for* us; proof—no, passion
We'll not insult thy majesty by time,

Person, and place—the where, the when, the how,
And all particulars that dull brains require
To constitute the spiritless shape of Fact,
They bow to, calling the idol, Demonstration.
A whipping to the Moralists who preach
That misery is a sacred thing: for me,
I know no cheaper engine to degrade a man,
Nor any half so sure. This Stripling's mind
Is shaken till the dregs float on the surface;
And, in the storm and anguish of the heart,
He talks of a transition in his Soul,
And dreams that he is happy. We dissect
The senseless body, and why not the mind?—
These are strange sights—the mind of man, upturned,
Is in all natures a strange spectacle;
In some a hideous one—hem! shall I stop?
No.—Thoughts and feelings will sink deep, but then
They have no substance. Pass but a few minutes,
And something shall be done which Memory
May touch, whene'er her Vassals are at work.

Enter MARMADUKE, *from behind.*

Osw. (*turning to meet him*). But listen, for my peace——

Mar. Why, I *believe* you.

Osw. But hear the proofs——

Mar. Ay, prove that when two peas
Lie snugly in a pod, the pod must then
Be larger than the peas—prove this—'twere matter
Worthy the hearing. Fool was I to dream
It ever could be otherwise!

Osw. Last night
When I returned with water from the brook,
I overheard the Villains—every word
Like red-hot iron burnt into my heart.
Said one, "It is agreed on. The blind Man
Shall feign a sudden illness, and the Girl,
Who on her journey must proceed alone,
Under pretence of violence, be seized.
She is," continued the detested Slave,
"She is right willing—strange if she were not!—
They say, Lord Clifford is a savage man;
But, faith, to see him in his silken tunic,
Fitting his low voice to the minstrel's harp,
There's witchery in't. I never knew a maid
That could withstand it. True," continued he,
"When we arranged the affair, she wept a little
(Not the less welcome to my Lord for that)
And said, 'My Father he will have it so.'"

Mar. I am your hearer.

Osw. This I caught, and more
That may not be retold to any ear.
The obstinate bolt of a small iron door
Detained them near the gateway of the Castle.
By a dim lantern's light I saw that wreaths
Of flowers were in their hands, as if designed
For festive decoration; and they said,
With brutal laughter and most foul allusion,
That they should share the banquet with their Lord
And his new Favourite.

Mar. Misery!—

Osw. I knew
How you would be disturbed by this dire news,
And therefore chose this solitary Moor,
Here to impart the tale, of which, last night,
I strove to ease my mind when our two Comrades,
Commissioned by the Band, burst in upon us.

Mar. Last night, when moved to lift the avenging steel,
I did believe all things were shadows—yea,
Living or dead all things were bodiless,
Or but the mutual mockeries of body,
Till that same star summoned me back again.
Now I could laugh till my ribs ached. O Fool!
To let a creed, built in the heart of things,
Dissolve before a twinkling atom!—Oswald,
I could fetch lessons out of wiser schools
Than you have entered, were it worth the pains.
Young as I am, I might go forth a teacher,
And you should see how deeply I could reason
Of love in all its shapes, beginnings, ends;
Of moral qualities in their diverse aspects;
Of actions, and their laws and tendencies.

Osw. You take it as it merits——

Mar. One a King,
General or Cham, Sultan or Emperor,
Strews twenty acres of good meadow-ground
With carcasses, in lineament and shape
And substance, nothing differing from his own,
But that they cannot stand up of themselves;
Another sits i' th' sun, and by the hour

Floats kingcups in the brook—a Hero one
We call, and scorn the other as Time's spendthrift,
But have they not a world of common ground
To occupy—both fools, or wise alike,
Each in his way?

Osw. Troth, I begin to think so.

Mar. Now for the corner-stone of my philosophy.
I would not give a denier for the man
Who, on such provocation as this earth
Yields, could not chuck his babe beneath the chin,
And send it with a fillip to its grave.

Osw. Nay, you leave me behind.

Mar. That such a One,
So pious in demeanour! in his look
So saintly and so pure!——Hark'ee, my Friend,
I'll plant myself before Lord Clifford's Castle,
A surly mastiff kennels at the gate,
And he shall howl and I will laugh, a medley
Most tunable.

Osw. In faith, a pleasant scheme;
But take your sword along with you, for that
Might in such neighbourhood find seemly use.—
But first, how wash our hands of this old Man?

Mar. Oh yes, that mole, that viper in the path;
Plague on my memory, him I had forgotten.

Osw. You know we left him sitting—see him yonder.

Mar. Ha! ha!—

Osw. As 'twill be but a moment's work,
I will stroll on, you follow when 'tis done.
[*Exeunt.*

SCENE *changes to another part of the Moor at a short distance.*—HERBERT *is discovered seated on a stone.*

Her. A sound of laughter, too!—'tis well—I feared
The Stranger had some pitiable sorrow
Pressing upon his solitary heart.
Hush!—'tis the feeble and earth-loving wind
That creeps along the bells of the crisp heather
Alas! 'tis cold—I shiver in the sunshine—
What can this mean? There is a psalm that speaks
Of God's parental mercies—with Idonea
I used to sing it—Listen!—what foot is there?

Enter MARMADUKE.

Mar. (*aside—looking at* HERBERT). And I have loved this Man! and *she* hath loved him!
And I loved her, and she loves the Lord Clifford!
And there it ends;—if this be not enough
To make mankind merry for evermore,
Then plain it is as day, that eyes were made
For a wise purpose—verily to weep with!
[*Looking round.*
A pretty prospect this, a masterpiece
Of Nature, finished with most curious skill!
(*To* HERBERT). Good Baron, have you ever practised tillage?
Pray tell me what this land is worth by the acre?

Her. How glad I am to hear your voice! I know not
Wherein I have offended you;—last night
I found in you the kindest of Protectors;
This morning, when I spoke of weariness,
You from my shoulder took my scrip and threw it
About your own; but for these two hours past
Once only have you spoken, when the lark
Whirred from among the fern beneath our feet,
And I, no coward in my better days,
Was almost terrified

Mar That's excellent!—
So, you bethought you of the many ways
In which a man may come to his end, whose crimes
Have roused all Nature up against him—pshaw!—

Her For mercy's sake, is nobody in sight?
No traveller, peasant, herdsman?

Mar. Not a soul:
Here is a tree, ragged, and bent, and bare,
That turns its goat's-beard flakes of pea-green moss
From the stern breathing of the rough sea-wind;
This have we, but no other company:
Commend me to the place. If a man should die
And leave his body here, it were all one
As he were twenty fathoms underground.

Her. Where is our common Friend?

Mar. A ghost, methinks—
The spirit of a murdered man, for instance—

Might have fine room to ramble about here,
A grand domain to squeak and gibber in.

Her. Lost Man! if thou have any close-pent guilt
Pressing upon thy heart, and this the hour
Of visitation——

Mar. A bold word from *you!*

Her. Restore him, Heaven!

Mar. The desperate Wretch!—a Flower,
Fairest of all flowers, was she once, but now
They have snapped her from the stem—Poh!—let her lie
Besoiled with mire, and let the houseless snail
Feed on her leaves. You knew her well—ay, there,
Old Man! you were a very Lynx, you knew
The worm was in her——

Her. Mercy! Sir, what mean you?

Mar. You have a Daughter!

Her. Oh that she were here!
She hath an eye that sinks into all hearts,
And if I have in aught offended you,
Soon would her gentle voice make peace between us.

Mar. (*aside*). I do believe he weeps—I could weep too—
There is a vein of her voice that runs through his:
Even such a Man my fancy bodied forth
From the first moment that I loved the Maid,
And for his sake I loved her more: these tears—
I did not think that aught was left in me
Of what I have been—yes, I thank thee, Heaven!
One happy thought has passed across my mind.
—It may not be—I am cut off from man;
No more shall I be man—no more shall I
Have human feelings!—(*To* HERBERT)—Now, for a little more
About your Daughter!

Her. Troops of armed men,
Met in the roads, would bless us; little children,
Rushing along in the full tide of play,
Stood silent as we passed them! I have heard
The boisterous carman, in the miry road,
Check his loud whip and hail us with mild voice,
And speak with milder voice to his poor beasts!

Mar. And whither were you going?

Her. Learn, young Man,
To fear the virtuous, and reverence misery,
Whether too much for patience, or, like mine,
Softened till it becomes a gift of mercy.

Mar. Now, this is as it should be!

Her. I am weak!—
My Daughter does not know how weak I am;
And, as thou see'st, under the arch of heaven
Here do I stand, alone, to helplessness,
By the good God, our common Father, doomed!—
But I had once a spirit and an arm—

Mar. Now, for a word about your Barony:
I fancy when you left the Holy Land,
And came to—what's your title—eh? your claims
Were undisputed!

Her. Like a mendicant,
Whom no one comes to meet, I stood alone;—
I murmured—but, remembering Him who feeds
The pelican and ostrich of the desert,
From my own threshold I looked up to Heaven
And did not want glimmerings of quiet hope.
So, from the Court I passed, and down the brook,
Led by its murmur, to the ancient oak
I came; and when I felt its cooling shade,
I sate me down, and cannot but believe—
While in my lap I held my little Babe
And clasped her to my heart, my heart that ached
More with delight than grief—I heard a voice
Such as by Cherith on Elijah called:
It said, "I will be with thee." A little boy,
A shepherd-lad, ere yet my trance was gone,
Hailed us as if he had been sent from heaven,
And said, with tears, that he would be our guide:
I had a better guide—that innocent Babe—
Her, who hath saved me, to this hour, from harm,
From cold, from hunger, penury, and death;
To whom I owe the best of all the good
I have, or wish for, upon earth—and more
And higher far than lies within earth's bounds:
Therefore I bless her: when I think of Man

I bless her with sad spirit,—when of God,
I bless her in the fulness of my joy!

Mar. The name of daughter in his mouth, he prays!
With nerves so steady, that the very flies
Sit unmolested on his staff.—Innocent!—
If he were innocent—then he would tremble
And be disturbed, as I am. (*Turning aside.*) I have read
In Story, what men now alive have witnessed,
How, when the people's mind was racked with doubt,
Appeal was made to the great Judge: the Accused
With naked feet walked over burning ploughshares.
Here is a Man by Nature's hand prepared
For a like trial, but more merciful.
Why else have I been led to this bleak Waste?
Bare is it, without house or track, and destitute
Of obvious shelter, as a shipless sea.
Here will I leave him—here—All-seeing God!
Such as *he* is, and sore perplexed as I am,
I will commit him to this final *Ordeal!*
He heard a voice—a shepherd-lad came to him
And was his guide; if once, why not again,
And in this desert? If never—then the whole
Of what he says, and looks, and does, and is,
Makes up one damning falsehood. Leave him here
To cold and hunger!—Pain is of the heart,
And what are a few throes of bodily suffering
If they can waken one pang of remorse?

[*Goes up to* HERBERT

Old Man! my wrath is as a flame burned out,
It cannot be rekindled. Thou art here
Led by my hand to save thee from perdition;
Thou wilt have time to breathe and think——

Her. Oh, mercy!

Mar. I know the need that all men have of mercy,
And therefore leave thee to a righteous judgment.

Her. My Child, my blessèd Child!

Mar. No more of that:
Thou wilt have many guides if thou art innocent;
Yea, from the utmost corners of the earth
That Woman will come o'er this Waste to save thee.

[*He pauses and looks at* HERBERT'S *staff.*

Ha! what is here? and carved by her own hand!

[*Reads upon the staff.*

"I am eyes to the blind, saith the Lord.
He that puts his trust in me shall not fail!"
Yes, be it so;—repent and be forgiven—
God and that staff are now thy only guides.

[*He leaves* HERBERT *on the Moor.*

SCENE, *an eminence, a Beacon on the summit.*

LACY, WALLACE, LENNOX, &c., &c.

Several of the Band (*confusedly*). But patience!

One of the Band. Curses on that Traitor, Oswald!—
Our Captain made a prey to foul device!—

Len. (*to Wal.*) His tool, the wandering Beggar, made last night
A plain confession, such as leaves no doubt,
Knowing what otherwise we know too well,
That she revealed the truth. Stand by me now;
For rather would I have a nest of vipers
Between my breast-plate and my skin, than make
Oswald my special enemy, if you
Deny me your support.

Lacy. We have been fooled—
But for the motive?

Wal. Natures such as his
Spin motives out of their own bowels, Lacy!
I learn'd this when I was a Confessor.
I know him well; there needs no other motive
Than that most strange incontinence in crime
Which haunts this Oswald. Power is life to him
And breath and being; where he cannot govern,
He will destroy.

Lacy. To have been trapped like moles!—
Yes, you are right, we need not hunt for motives:
There is no crime from which this man would shrink;
He recks not human law; and I have noticed
That often when the name of God is uttered,
A sudden blankness overspreads his face.

Len. Yet, reasoner as he is, his pride has built
Some uncouth superstition of its own.

Wal. I have seen traces of it.
Len. Once he headed
A band of Pirates in the Norway seas;
And when the King of Denmark summoned him
To the oath of fealty, I well remember,
'Twas a strange answer that he made; he said,
"I hold of Spirits, and the Sun in heaven."
Lacy. He is no madman.
Wal. A most subtle doctor
Were that man, who could draw the line that parts
Pride and her daughter, Cruelty, from Madness,
That should be scourged, not pitied. Restless Minds,
Such minds as find amid their fellow-men
No heart that loves them, none that they can love,
Will turn perforce and seek for sympathy
In dim relation to imagined Beings.
One of the Band. What if he mean to offer up our Captain
An expiation and a sacrifice
To those infernal fiends!
Wal. Now, if the event
Should be as Lennox has foretold, then swear,
My Friends, his heart shall have as many wounds
As there are daggers here.
Lacy. What need of swearing!
One of the Band. Let us away!
Another. Away!
A third. Hark! how the horns
Of those Scotch Rovers echo through the vale.
Lacy. Stay you behind; and when the sun is down,
Light up this beacon.
One of the Band. You shall be obeyed.
[*They go out together.*

SCENE, *the Wood on the edge of the Moor.*

MARMADUKE (*alone*).

Mar. Deep, deep and vast, vast beyond human thought,
Yet calm.—I could believe, that there was here
The only quiet heart on earth. In terror,
Remembered terror, there is peace and rest.

Enter OSWALD.

Osw. Ha! my dear Captain!
Mar. A later meeting, Oswald,
Would have been better timed.
Osw. Alone, I see;
You have done your duty. I had hopes, which now
I feel that you will justify.
Mar. I had fears,
From which I have freed myself—but 'tis my wish
To be alone, and therefore we must part.
Osw. Nay then—I am mistaken. There's a weakness
About you still, you talk of solitude—
I am your friend.
Mar. What need of this assurance
At any time? and why given now?
Osw. Because
You are now in truth my Master; you have taught me
What there is not another living man
Had strength to teach;—and therefore gratitude
Is bold, and would relieve itself by praise.
Mar. Wherefore press this on me?
Osw. Because I feel
That you have shown, and by a signal instance
How they who would be just must seek the rule
By diving for it into their own bosoms.
To-day you have thrown off a tyranny
That lives but in the torpid acquiescence
Of our emasculated souls, the tyranny
Of the world's masters, with the musty rules
By which they uphold their craft from age to age:
You have obeyed the only law that sense
Submits to recognise; the immediate law,
From the clear light of circumstances, flashed
Upon an independent Intellect.
Henceforth new prospects open on your path;
Your faculties should grow with the demand;
I still will be your friend, will cleave to you
Through good and evil, obloquy and scorn,
Oft as they dare to follow on your steps
Mar. I would be left alone.
Osw. (*exultingly*). I know your motives!
I am not of the world's presumptuous judges,
Who damn where they can neither see nor feel,
With a hard-hearted ignorance; your struggles
I witnessed, and now hail your victory.
Mar. Spare me awhile that greeting.
Osw. It may be.

That some there are, squeamish half-thinking cowards,
Who will turn pale upon you, call you murderer,
And you will walk in solitude among them.
A mighty evil for a strong-built mind!—
Join twenty tapers of unequal height
And light them joined, and you will see the less
How 'twill burn down the taller; and they all
Shall prey upon the tallest. Solitude!—
The Eagle lives in Solitude!

Mar. Even so,
The Sparrow so on the house-top, and I,
The weakest of God's creatures, stand resolved
To abide the issue of my act, alone.

Osw. *Now* would you? and for ever?—My young Friend,
As time advances either we become
The prey or masters of our own past deeds.
Fellowship we *must* have, willing or no;
And if good Angels fail, slack in their duty,
Substitutes, turn our faces where we may,
Are still forthcoming; some which, though they bear
Ill names, can render no ill services,
In recompense for what themselves required.
So meet extremes in this mysterious world,
And opposites thus melt into each other.

Mar. Time, since Man first drew breath, has never moved
With such a weight upon his wings as now;
But they will soon be lightened.

Osw. Ay, look up—
Cast round you your mind's eye, and you will learn
Fortitude is the child of Enterprise:
Great actions move our admiration, chiefly
Because they carry in themselves an earnest
That we can suffer greatly.

Mar. Very true.

Osw. Action is transitory—a step, a blow,
The motion of a muscle—this way or that—
'Tis done, and in the after-vacancy
We wonder at ourselves like men betrayed:
Suffering is permanent, obscure and dark,
And shares the nature of infinity.

Mar. Truth—and I feel it.

Osw. What if you had bid
Eternal farewell to unmingled joy
And the light dancing of the thoughtless heart;
It is the toy of fools, and little fit
For such a world as this. The wise abjure
All thoughts whose idle composition lives
In the entire forgetfulness of pain
—I see I have disturbed you.

Mar. By no means

Osw. Compassion!—pity!—pride can do without them,
And what if you should never know them more!—
He is a puny soul who, feeling pain,
Finds ease because another feels it too.
If e'er I open out this heart of mine
It shall be for a nobler end—to teach
And not to purchase puling sympathy.
—Nay, you are pale.

Mar It may be so.

Osw. Remorse—
It cannot live with thought; think on, think on,
And it will die. What! in this universe,
Where the least things control the greatest, where
The faintest breath that breathes can move a world;
What! feel remorse, where, if a cat had sneezed,
A leaf had fallen, the thing had never been
Whose very shadow gnaws us to the vitals.

Mar. Now, whither are you wandering? That a man
So used to suit his language to the time,
Should thus so widely differ from himself—
It is most strange.

Osw. Murder!—what's in the word!—
I have no cases by me ready made
To fit all deeds. Carry him to the Camp!—
A shallow project; you of late have seen
More deeply, taught us that the institutes
Of Nature, by a cunning usurpation
Banished from human intercourse, exist
Only in our relations to the brutes
That make the fields their dwelling. If a snake
Crawl from beneath our feet we do not ask
A licence to destroy him: our good governors
Hedge in the life of every pest and plague
That bears the shape of man; and for what purpose,
But to protect themselves from extirpation?—
This flimsy barrier you have overleaped.

Mar. My Office is fulfilled—the Man is now
Delivered to the Judge of all things.

Osw. Dead!

Mar. I have borne my burthen to its destined end.

Osw. This instant we'll return to our Companions—
Oh how I long to see their faces again!

Enter IDONEA, *with* Pilgrims *who continue their journey.*

Idon. (*after some time*) What, Marmaduke! now thou art mine for ever.
And Oswald too! (*To* MARMADUKE). On will we to my Father
With the glad tidings which this day hath brought:
We'll go together, and, such proof received
Of his own rights restored, his gratitude
To God above will make him feel for ours.
Osw. I interrupt you?
Idon. Think not so.
Mar. Idonea,
That I should ever live to see this moment!
Idon. Forgive me.—Oswald knows it all—he knows,
Each word of that unhappy letter fell
As a blood drop from my heart.
Osw. 'Twas even so.
Mar. I have much to say, but for whose ear?—not thine.
Idon. Ill can I bear that look—Plead for me, Oswald!
You are my Father's Friend.
(*To* MARMADUKE.) Alas, you know not,
And never *can* you know, how much he loved me.
Twice had he been to me a father, twice
Had given me breath, and was I not to be
His daughter, once his daughter? could I withstand
His pleading face, and feel his clasping arms,
And hear his prayer that I would not forsake him
In his old age—— [*Hides her face.*
Mar. Patience—Heaven grant me patience!—
She weeps, she weeps—*my* brain shall burn for hours
Ere *I* can shed a tear.
Idon. I was a woman;
And, balancing the hopes that are the dearest
To womankind with duty to my Father,
I yielded up those precious hopes, which nought
On earth could else have wrested from me;—if erring,
Oh let me be forgiven!
Mar. I *do* forgive thee.
Idon. But take me to your arms—this breast, alas!
It throbs, and you have a heart that does not feel it.
Mar. (*exultingly*). She is innocent.
[*He embraces her.*
Osw. (*aside*). Were I a moralist.
I should make wondrous revolution here;
It were a quaint experiment to show
The beauty of truth— [*Addressing them.*
I see I interrupt you;
I shall have business with you, Marmaduke;
Follow me to the Hostel. [*Exit* OSWALD.
Idon. Marmaduke,
This is a happy day. My father soon
Shall sun himself before his native doors;
The lame, the hungry, will be welcome there.
No more shall he complain of wasted strength,
Of thoughts that fail, and a decaying heart;
His good works will be balm and life to him.
Mar. This is most strange!—I know not what it was,
But there was something which most plainly said,
That thou wert innocent.
Idon. How innocent!
Oh Heavens! you've been deceived.
Mar. Thou art a Woman
To bring perdition on the universe.
Idon. Already I've been punished to the height
Of my offence. [*Smiling affectionately.*
I see you love me still,
The labours of my hand are still your joy;
Bethink you of the hour when on your shoulder
I hung this belt.
[*Pointing to the belt on which was suspended* HERBERT'S *scrip.*
Mar. Mercy of Heaven. [*Sinks.*
Idon. What ails you! [*Distractedly.*
Mar. The scrip that held his food, and I forgot
To give it back again!
Idon. What mean your words?
Mar. I know not what I said—all may be well.
Idon. That smile hath life in it!
Mar. This road is perilous;
I will attend you to a Hut that stands
Near the Wood's edge—rest there to-night, I pray you:
For me, I have business, as you hear, with Oswald,
But will return to you by break of day.
[*Exeunt.*

ACT IV.

SCENE, *A desolate prospect—a ridge of rocks—a Chapel on the summit of one—Moon behind the rocks—night stormy—irregular sound of a bell*—HERBERT *enters exhausted.*

Her. That Chapel-bell in mercy seemed to guide me,
But now it mocks my steps; its fitful stroke
Can scarcely be the work of human hands.
Hear me, ye Men, upon the cliffs, if such
There be who pray nightly before the Altar.
Oh that I had but strength to reach the place!
My Child—my child—dark—dark—I faint—this wind—
These stifling blasts—God help me!

Enter ELDRED.

Eld. Better this bare rock,
Though it were tottering o'er a man's head,
Than a tight case of dungeon walls for shelter
From such rough dealing.
[*A moaning voice is heard.*
Ha! what sound is that?
Trees creaking in the wind (but none are here)
Send forth such noises—and that weary bell!
Surely some evil Spirit abroad to-night
Is ringing it— twould stop a Saint in prayer,
And that—what is it? never was sound so like
A human groan. Ha! what is here? Poor Man—
Murdered! alas! speak—speak, I am your friend:
No answer—hush—lost wretch, he lifts his hand
And lays it to his heart—(*Kneels to him*).
I pray you speak!
What has befallen you?

Her. (*feebly*). A stranger has done this,
And in the arms of a stranger I must die.

Eld. Nay, think not so: come, let me raise you up: [*Raises him.*
This is a dismal place—well—that is well—
I was too fearful—take me for your guide
And your support—my hut is not far off.
[*Draws him gently off the stage.*

SCENE, *a room in the Hostel*—MARMADUKE *and* OSWALD.

Mar. But for Idonea!—I have cause to think
That she is innocent

Osw. Leave that thought awhile,
As one of those beliefs which in their hearts
Lovers lock up as pearls; though oft no better
Than feathers clinging to their points of passion.
This day's event has laid on me the duty
Of opening out my story, you must hear it,
And without further preface.—In my youth,
Except for that abatement which is paid
By envy as a tribute to desert,
I was the pleasure of all hearts, the darling
Of every tongue—as you are now. You've heard
That I embarked for Syria. On our voyage
Was hatched among the crew a foul Conspiracy
Against my honour, in which our Captain
Was, I believed, prime Agent. The wind fell;
We lay becalmed week after week, until
The water of the vessel was exhausted;
I felt a double fever in my veins,
Yet rage suppressed itself:—to a deep stillness
Did my pride tame my pride;—for many days,
On a dead sea, under a burning sky,
I brooded o'er my injuries, deserted
By man and nature;—if a breeze had blown,
It might have found its way into my heart,
And I had been—no matter—do you mark me?

Mar. Quick—to the point—if any untold crime
Doth haunt your memory.

Osw. Patience, hear me further!—
One day in silence did we drift at noon
By a bare rock, narrow, and white, and bare;
No food was there, no drink, no grass, no shade,
No tree, nor jutting eminence, nor form
Inanimate large as the body of man,
Nor any living thing whose lot of life
Might stretch beyond the measure of one moon.
To dig for water on the spot, the Captain
Landed with a small troop, myself being one:
There I reproached him with his treachery
Imperious at all times, his temper rose;
He struck me; and that instant had I killed him,

And put an end to his insolence, but my Comrades
Rushed in between us: then did I insist
(All hated him, and I was stung to madness)
That we should leave him there, alive!—we did so.

Mar. And he was famished?

Osw. Naked was the spot;
Methinks I see it now—how in the sun
Its stony surface glittered like a shield;
And in that miserable place we left him,
Alone but for a swarm of minute creatures
Not one of which could help him while alive,
Or mourn him dead.

Mar. A man by men cast off,
Left without burial! nay, not dead nor dying,
But standing, walking, stretching forth his arms,
In all things like ourselves, but in the agony
With which he called for mercy; and—even so—
He was forsaken?

Osw. There is a power in sounds:
The cries he uttered might have stopped the boat
That bore us through the water——

Mar. You returned
Upon that dismal hearing—did you not?

Osw. Some scoffed at him with hellish mockery,
And laughed so loud it seemed that the smooth sea
Did from some distant region echo us.

Mar. We all are of one blood, our veins are filled
At the same poisonous fountain!

Osw. 'Twas an island
Only by sufferance of the winds and waves,
Which with their foam could cover it at will.
I know not how he perished: but the calm,
The same dead calm, continued many days.

Mar. But his own crime had brought on him this doom,
His wickedness prepared it; these expedients
Are terrible, yet ours is not the fault.

Osw. The man was famished, and was innocent!

Mar. Impossible!

Osw. The man had never wronged me.

Mar. Banish the thought, crush it, and be at peace.
His guilt was marked—these things could never be
Were there not eyes that see, and for good ends,
Where ours are baffled.

Osw. I had been deceived.

Mar. And from that hour the miserable man
No more was heard of?

Osw. I had been betrayed.

Mar. And he found no deliverance!

Osw. The Crew
Gave me a hearty welcome; they had laid
The plot to rid themselves, at any cost,
Of a tyrannic Master whom they loathed.
So we pursued our voyage: when we landed,
The tale was spread abroad: my power at once
Shrunk from me; plans and schemes, and lofty hopes—
All vanished. I gave way—do you attend?

Mar. The Crew deceived you?

Osw. Nay, command yourself.

Mar. It is a dismal night—how the wind howls!

Osw. I hid my head within a Convent, there
Lay passive as a dormouse in mid winter.
There was no life for me—I was o'erthrown
But not destroyed.

Mar. The proofs—you ought to have seen
The guilt—have touched it—felt it at your heart—
As I have done.

Osw. A fresh tide of Crusaders
Drove by the place of my retreat: three nights
Did constant meditation dry my blood;
Three sleepless nights I passed in sounding on,
Through words and things, a dim and perilous way:
And, wheresoe'er I turned me, I beheld
A slavery compared to which the dungeon
And clanking chains are perfect liberty.
You understand me—I was comforted;
I saw that every possible shape of action
Might lead to good—I saw it and burst forth
Thirsting for some of those exploits that fill
The earth with sure redemption of lost peace.

[*Marking* MARMADUKE'S *countenance.*

Nay, you have had the worst. Ferocity
Subsided in a moment, like a wind
That drops down dead out of a sky it vexed.
And yet I had within me evermore

A salient spring of energy, I mounted
From action up to action with a mind
That never rested—without meat or drink
Have I lived many days—my sleep was bound
To purposes of reason—not a dream
But had a continuity and substance
That waking life had never power to give.
Mar. O wretched Human-kind!—Until the mystery
Of all this world is solved, well may we envy
The worm, that, underneath a stone whose weight
Would crush the lion's paw with mortal anguish,
Doth lodge, and feed, and coil, and sleep, in safety
Fell not the wrath of Heaven upon those traitors?
Osw. Give not to them a thought. From Palestine
We marched to Syria. oft I left the Camp,
When all that multitude of hearts was still,
And followed on, through woods of gloomy cedar,
Into deep chasms troubled by roaring streams;
Or from the top of Lebanon surveyed
The moonlight desert, and the moonlight sea:
In these my lonely wanderings I perceived
What mighty objects do impress their forms
To elevate our intellectual being;
And felt, if aught on earth deserves a curse,
'Tis that worst principle of ill which dooms
A thing so great to perish self-consumed
—So much for my remorse!
Mar. Unhappy man!
Osw. When from these forms I turned to contemplate
The World's opinions and her usages,
I seemed a being who had passed alone
Into a region of futurity,
Whose natural element was freedom——
Mar. Stop!
I may not, cannot, follow thee.
Osw. You must.
I had been nourished by the sickly food
Of popular applause. I now perceived
That we are praised, only as men in us
Do recognise some image of themselves,
An abject counterpart of what they are,
Or the empty thing that they would wish to be.
I felt that merit has no surer test
Than obloquy: that, if we wish to serve
The world in substance, not deceive by show,
We must become obnoxious to its hate,
Or fear disguised in simulated scorn.
Mar. I pity, can forgive you; but those wretches—
That monstrous perfidy!
Osw. Keep down your wrath
False Shame discarded, spurious Fame despised,
Twin sisters both of Ignorance, I found
Life stretched before me smooth as some broad way
Cleared for a monarch's progress Priests might spin
Their veil, but not for me—'twas in fit place
Among its kindred cobwebs. I had been,
And in that dream had left my native land,
One of Love's simple bondsmen—the soft chain
Was off for ever; and the men, from whom
This liberation came, you would destroy:
Join me in thanks for their blind services.
Mar. Tis a strange aching that, when we would curse
And cannot —You have betrayed me—I have done—
I am content—I know that he is guiltless—
That both are guiltless, without spot or stain,
Mutually consecrated Poor old man!
And I had heart for this, because thou lovedst
Her who from very infancy had been
Light to thy path, warmth to thy blood!—
Together [*Turning to* OSWALD
We propped his steps, he leaned upon us both.
Osw. Ay, we are coupled by a chain of adamant;
Let us be fellow-labourers, then, to enlarge
Man's intellectual empire. We subsist
In slavery; all is slavery; we receive
Laws, but we ask not whence those laws have come;
We need an inward sting to goad us on.
Mar. Have you betrayed me? Speak to that.
Osw. The mask,
Which for a season I have stooped to wear,
Must be cast off.—Know then that I was urged,
(For other impulse let it pass) was driven,
To seek for sympathy, because I saw
In you a mirror of my youthful self;
I would have made us equal once again,

But that was a vain hope. You have struck home,
With a few drops of blood cut short the business;
Therein for ever you must yield to me
But what is done will save you from the blank
Of living without knowledge that you live:
Now you are suffering—for the future day,
'Tis his who will command it.—Think of my story—
Herbert is *innocent*.

Mar. (*in a faint voice, and doubtingly*). You do but echo
My own wild words!

Osw. Young Man, the seed must lie
Hid in the earth, or there can be no harvest;
'Tis Nature's law. What I have done in darkness
I will avow before the face of day.
Herbert *is* innocent.

Mar. What fiend could prompt
This action? Innocent!—oh, breaking heart!—
Alive or dead, I'll find him. [*Exit.*

Osw. Alive—perdition! [*Exit.*

SCENE, *the inside of a poor Cottage.*

ELEANOR *and* IDONEA *seated.*

Idon. The storm beats hard—Mercy for poor or rich,
Whose heads are shelterless in such a night!

A Voice without. Holla! to bed, good Folks, within!

Elea. Oh save us!

Idon. What can this mean?

Elea. Alas, for my poor husband!—
We'll have a counting of our flocks to-morrow:
The wolf keeps festival these stormy nights:
Be calm, sweet Lady, they are wassailers
[*The voices die away in the distance.*
Returning from their feast—my heart beats so—
A noise at midnight does *so* frighten me.

Idon. Hush! [*Listening.*

Elea. They are gone. On such a night, my husband,
Dragged from his bed, was cast into a dungeon,
Where, hid from me, he counted many years,
A criminal in no one's eyes but theirs—
Not even in theirs—whose brutal violence
So dealt with him.

Idon. I have a noble Friend
First among youths of knightly breeding, One
Who lives but to protect the weak or injured.
There again! [*Listening.*

Elea. 'Tis my husband's foot. Good Eldred
Has a kind heart; but his imprisonment
Has made him fearful, and he'll never be
The man he was.

Idon. I will retire;—good night!
[*She goes within.*

Enter ELDRED (*hides a bundle*).

Eld. Not yet in bed, Eleanor!—there are stains in that frock which must be washed out.

Elea. What has befallen you?

Eld. I am belated, and you must know the cause—(*speaking low*) that is the blood of an unhappy Man.

Elea. Oh! we are undone for ever.

Eld. Heaven forbid that I should lift my hand against any man. Eleanor, I have shed tears to-night, and it comforts me to think of it.

Elea. Where, where is he?

Eld. I have done him no harm, but—— it will be forgiven me; it would not have been so once.

Elea. You have not *buried* anything? You are no richer than when you left me?

Eld. Be at peace; I am innocent.

Elea. Then God be thanked—
[*A short pause; she falls upon his neck.*

Eld. To-night I met with an old Man lying stretched upon the ground—a sad spectacle: I raised him up with a hope that we might shelter and restore him.

Elea. (*as if ready to run*). Where is he? You were not able to bring him *all* the way with you; let us return, I can help you.
[ELDRED *shakes his head.*

Eld. He did not seem to wish for life: as I was struggling on, by the light of the moon I saw the stains of blood upon my clothes—he waved his hand, as if it were all useless; and I let him sink again to the ground.

Elea. Oh that I had been by your side!

Eld. I tell you his hands and his body were cold,—how could I disturb his last moments? he strove to turn from me as if he wished to settle into sleep.

Elea. But, for the stains of blood—

Eld. He must have fallen, I fancy, for

his head was cut; but I think his malady was cold and hunger.

Elea. O Eldred! I shall never be able to look up at this roof in storm or fair but I shall tremble.

Eld. Is it not enough that my ill stars have kept me abroad to-night till this hour? I come home, and this is my comfort!

Elea. But did he say nothing which might have set you at ease?

Eld. I thought he grasped my hand while he was muttering something about his Child—his Daughter—(*starting as if he heard a noise*). What is that?

Elea. Eldred, you are a father.

Eld. God knows what was in my heart, and will not curse my son for my sake

Elea. But you prayed by him? you waited the hour of his release?

Eld. The night was wasting fast; I have no friend; I am spited by the world—his wound terrified me—if I had brought him along with me, and he had died in my arms!——I am sure I heard something breathing—and this chair!

Elea. O Eldred! you will die alone. You will have nobody to close your eyes—no hand to grasp your dying hand—I shall be in my grave. A curse will attend us all.

Eld. Have you forgot your own troubles when I was in the dungeon?

Elea. And you left him alive?

Eld. Alive!—the damps of death were upon him—he could not have survived an hour.

Elea. In the cold, cold night.

Eld. (*in a savage tone*). Ay, and his head was bare; I suppose you would have had me lend my bonnet to cover it.—You will never rest till I am brought to a felon s end.

Elea. In there nothing to be done? cannot we go to the Convent?

Eld. Ay, and say at once that I murdered him!

Elea. Eldred, I know that ours is the only house upon the Waste; let us take heart; this Man may be rich; and could he be saved by our means, his gratitude may reward us.

Eld. 'Tis all in vain.

Elea. But let us make the attempt. This old Man may have a wife, and he may have children—let us return to the spot; we may restore him, and his eyes may yet open upon those that love him.

Eld. He will never open them more: even when he spoke to me, he kept them firmly sealed as if he had been blind.

Idon. (*rushing out*). It is, it is, my Father—

Eld. We are betrayed (*looking at* IDONEA).

Elea. His Daughter!—God have mercy! (*turning to* IDONEA).

Idon. (*sinking down*). Oh! lift me up
and carry me to the place.
You are safe; the whole world shall not
harm you.

Elea. This Lady is his Daughter.

Eld. (*moved*). I'll lead you to the spot.

Idon. (*springing up*). Alive!—you heard him breathe? quick, quick— [*Exeunt.*

ACT V.

SCENE, *A wood on the edge of the Waste.*

Enter OSWALD *and a* Forester.

For. He leaned upon the bridge that
spans the glen,
And down into the bottom cast his eye,
That fastened there, as it would check the
current.

Osw. He listened too; did you not say
he listened?

For. As if there came such moaning
from the flood
As is heard often after stormy nights.

Osw. But did he utter nothing?

For. See him there!
[MARMADUKE *appearing.*

Mar. Buzz, buzz, ye black and winged
freebooters;
That is no substance which ye settle on!

For. His senses play him false; and
see, his arms
Outspread, as if to save himself from fall-
ing!—
Some terrible phantom I believe is now
Passing before him, such as God will not
Permit to visit any but a man
Who has been guilty of some horrid crime.
[MARMADUKE *disappears.*

Osw. The game is up!—

For. If it be needful, Sir,
I will assist you to lay hands on him.

Osw. No, no, my Friend, you may pur-
sue your business—
'Tis a poor wretch of an unsettled mind,
Who has a trick of straying from his
keepers:
We must be gentle. Leave him to my
care. [*Exit* Forester.

If his own eyes play false with him, these freaks
Of fancy shall be quickly tamed by mine;
The goal is reached. My master shall become
A shadow of myself—made by myself.

SCENE, *the edge of the Moor.*

MARMADUKE *and* ELDRED *enter from opposite sides.*

Mar. (*raising his eyes and perceiving* ELDRED). In any corner of this savage Waste,
Have you, good Peasant, seen a blind old Man?
Eld. I heard——
Mar. You heard him, where? when heard him?
Eld. As you know,
The first hours of last night were rough with storm:
I had been out in search of a stray heifer;
Returning late, I heard a moaning sound.
Then, thinking that my fancy had deceived me,
I hurried on, when straight again a moan,
A human voice distinct, struck mine ear.
So guided, distant a few steps, I saw
An aged Man, and such as you describe.
Mar. You heard!—he called you to him? Of all men
The best and kindest! but where is he? guide me,
That I may see him.
Eld. On a ridge of rocks
A lonesome Chapel stands, deserted now:
The bell is left, which no one dares remove;
And, when the stormy wind blows o'er the peak,
It rings, as if a human hand were there
To pull the cord. I guess he must have heard it;
And it had led him towards the precipice,
To climb up to the spot whence the sound came;
But he had failed through weakness. From his hand
His staff had dropped, and close upon the brink
Of a small pool of water he was laid,
As if he had stooped to drink, and so remained
Without the strength to rise.
Mar. Well, well, he lives
And all is safe: what said he?
Eld. But few words:
He only spake to me of a dear Daughter,
Who, so he feared, would never see him more;
And of a Stranger to him, One by whom
He had been sore misused; but he forgave
The wrong and the wrong-doer. You are troubled—
Perhaps you are his son?
Mar. The All-seeing knows,
I did not think he had a living Child.—
But whither did you carry him?
Eld. He was torn,
His head was bruised, and there was blood about him——
Mar. That was no work of mine.
Eld. Nor was it mine.
Mar. But had he strength to walk? I could have borne him
A thousand miles.
Eld. I am in poverty,
And know how busy are the tongues of men;
My heart was willing, Sir, but I am one
Whose good deeds will not stand by their own light;
And, though it smote me more than words can tell,
I left him.
Mar. I believe that there are phantoms,
That in the shape of man do cross our path
On evil instigation, to make sport
Of our distress—and thou art one of them!
But things substantial have so pressed on me——
Eld. My wife and children came into my mind.
Mar. O Monster! Monster! there are three of us,
And we shall howl together.
[*After a pause and in a feeble voice.*
I am deserted
At my worst need, my crimes have in a net
(*Pointing to* ELDRED) Entangled this poor man.—
Where was it? where?
[*Dragging him along.*
Eld. 'Tis needless; spare your violence.
His Daughter——
Mar. Ay, in the word a thousand scorpions lodge:
This old man *had* a Daughter.
Eld. To the spot
I hurried back with her.—Oh save me, Sir,
From such a journey!—there was a black tree,
A single tree; she thought it was her Father.—

Oh, Sir, I would not see that hour again
For twenty lives. The daylight dawned, and now—
Nay; hear my tale, 'tis fit that you should hear it—
As we approached, a solitary crow
Rose from the spot;—the Daughter clapped her hands,
And then I heard a shriek so terrible
[MARMADUKE *shrinks back.*
The startled bird quivered upon the wing.
Mar. Dead, dead!—
Eld. (*after a pause*) A dismal matter, Sir, for me,
And seems the like for you, if 'tis your wish,
I'll lead you to his Daughter; but 'twere best
That she should be prepared; I'll go before
Mar. There will be need of preparation
[ELDRED *goes off.*
Elea. (*enters*). Master!
Your limbs sink under you, shall I support you?
Mar. (*taking her arm*). Woman, I've lent my body to the service
Which now thou tak'st upon thee. God forbid
That thou shouldst ever meet a like occasion
With such a purpose in thine heart as mine was.
Elea. Oh, why have I to do with things like these? [*Exeunt*

SCENE *changes to the door of* ELDRED'S *cottage*—IDONEA *seated—enter* ELDRED.

Eld. Your Father, Lady, from a wilful hand
Has met unkindness; so indeed he told me,
And you remember such was my report:
From what has just befallen me I have cause
To fear the very worst.
Idon. My Father is dead;
Why dost thou come to me with words like these?
Eld. A wicked Man should answer for his crimes.
Idon. Thou seest me what I am.
Eld. It was most heinous,
And doth call out for vengeance
Idon. Do not add,
I prithee, to the harm thou'st done already.
Eld. Hereafter you will thank me for this service.
Hard by, a Man I met, who, from plain proofs
Of interfering Heaven, I have no doubt,
Laid hands upon your Father. Fit it were
You should prepare to meet him.
Idon. I have nothing
To do with others; help me to my Father—
[*She turns and sees* MARMADUKE *leaning on* ELEANOR—*throws herself upon his neck, and after some time,*
In joy I met thee, but a few hours past;
And thus we meet again; one human stay
Is left me still in thee. Nay, shake not so.
Mar. In such a wilderness—to see no thing,
No, not the pitying moon!
Idon. And perish so.
Mar. Without a dog to moan for him.
Idon. Think not of it,
But enter there and see him how he sleeps,
Tranquil as he had died in his own bed.
Mar. Tranquil—why not?
Idon. Oh, peace!
Mar. He is at peace,
His body is at rest: there was a plot,
A hideous plot, against the soul of man:
It took effect—and yet I baffled it,
In *some* degree.
Idon. Between us stood, I thought,
A cup of consolation, filled from Heaven
For both our needs, must I, and in thy presence,
Alone partake of it?—Beloved Marmaduke!
Mar Give me a reason why the wisest thing
That the earth owns shall never choose to die,
But some one must be near to count his groans.
The wounded deer retires to solitude,
And dies in solitude: all things but man,
All die in solitude.
[*Moving towards the cottage door*
Mysterious God,
If she had never lived I had not done it!—
Idon. Alas! the thought of such a cruel death
Has overwhelmed him.—I must follow.
Eld. Lady!
You will do well; (*she goes*) unjust suspicion may
Cleave to this Stranger: if, upon his entering,
The dead Man heave a groan, or from his side
Uplift his hand—that would be evidence.
Elea. Shame! Eldred, shame!
Mar. (*both returning*) The dead have but one face (*to himself*)

And such a Man—so meek and unoffending—
Helpless and harmless as a babe . a Man,
By obvious signal to the world's protection,
Solemnly dedicated—to decoy him!—
Idon. Oh, had you seen him living!—
Mar. I (so filled
With horror is this world) am unto thee
The thing most precious that it now contains:
Therefore through me alone must be revealed
By whom thy Parent was destroyed, Idonea!
I have the proofs!—
Idon. O miserable Father!
Thou didst command me to bless all mankind;
Nor to this moment, have I ever wished
Evil to any living thing: but hear me,
Hear me, ye Heavens!—(*kneeling*)—may vengeance haunt the fiend
For this most cruel murder: let him live
And move in terror of the elements;
The thunder send him on his knees to prayer
In the open streets, and let him think he sees,
If e'er he entereth the house of God,
The roof, self-moved, unsettling o'er his head;
And let him, when he would lie down at night,
Point to his wife the blood-drops on his pillow!
Mar. My voice was silent but my heart hath joined thee.
Idon. (*leaning on* MARMADUKE). Left to the mercy of that savage Man!
How could he call upon his Child!—O Friend! [*Turns to* MARMADUKE.
My faithful true and only Comforter.
Mar. Ay, come to me and weep. (*He kisses her.*) (*To* ELDRED.) Yes, varlet, look.
The devils at such sights do clap their hands. [ELDRED *retires alarmed.*
Idon. Thy vest is torn, thy cheek is deadly pale;
Hast thou pursued the monster?
Mar. I have found him.—
Oh! would that thou hadst perished in the flames!
Idon. Here art thou, then can I be desolate?—
Mar. There was a time, when this protecting hand
Availed against the mighty: never more
Shall blessings wait upon a deed of mine.
Idon. Wild words for me to hear, for me, an orphan,
Committed to thy guardianship by Heaven;
And, if thou hast forgiven me, let me hope,
In this deep sorrow, trust, that I am thine
For closer care,—here is no malady.
(*Taking his arm.*)
Mar. There, *is* a malady—
(*Striking his heart and forehead*). And here, and here,
A mortal madady.—I am accurst:
All nature curses me, and in my heart
Thy curse is fixed: the truth must be laid bare.
It must be told, and borne. I am the man,
(Abused, betrayed, but how it matters not)
Presumptuous above all that ever breathed,
Who, casting as I thought a guilty Person
Upon Heaven's righteous judgment, did become
An instrument of Fiends. Through me, through me
Thy Father perished.
Idon. Perished—by what mischance?
Mar. Beloved!—if I dared, so would I call thee—
Conflict must cease, and, in thy frozen heart,
The extremes of suffering meet in absolute peace. [*He gives her a letter.*
Idon. (*reads*) "Be not surprised if you hear that some signal judgment has befallen the man who calls himself your father; he is now with me, as his signature will show: abstain from conjecture till you see me.

"HERBERT.
"MARMADUKE"

The writing Oswald's; the signature my Father's:
(*Looks steadily at the paper*) And here is yours,—or do my eyes deceive me?
You have then seen my Father?
Mar. He has leaned
Upon this arm.
Idon. You led him towards the Convent?
Mar. That Convent was Stone-Arthur Castle. Thither
We were his guides. I on that night resolved
That he should wait thy coming till the day
Of resurrection.
Idon. Miserable Woman,
Too quickly moved, too easily giving way,
I put denial on thy suit, and hence,
With the disastrous issue of last night,

Thy perturbation, and these frantic words.
Be calm, I pray thee!

Mar. Oswald——

Idon. Name him not.

Enter female Beggar.

Beg. And he is dead!—that Moor—how shall I cross it?
By night, by day, never shall I be able
To travel half a mile alone.—Good Lady!
Forgive me!—Saints forgive me. Had I thought
It would have come to this!—

Idon. What brings you hither? speak!

Beg. (*pointing to* MARMADUKE). This innocent Gentleman. Sweet heavens! I told him
Such tales of your dead Father!—God is my judge,
I thought there was no harm: but that bad Man,
He bribed me with his gold, and looked so fierce.
Mercy! I said I know not what—oh pity me—
I said, sweet Lady, you were not his Daughter—
Pity me, I am haunted,—thrice this day
My conscience made me wish to be struck blind;
And then I would have prayed, and had no voice.

Idon. (*to* MARMADUKE). Was it my Father?—no, no, no, for he
Was meek and patient, feeble, old and blind,
Helpless, and loved me dearer than his life.
—But hear me. For *one* question, I have a heart
That will sustain me. Did you murder him?

Mar. No, not by stroke of arm. But learn the process:
Proof after proof was pressed upon me; guilt
Made evident, as seemed, by blacker guilt,
Whose impious folds enwrapped even thee; and truth
And innocence, embodied in his looks,
His words and tones and gestures, did but serve
With me to aggravate his crimes, and heaped
Ruin upon the cause for which they pleaded.
Then pity crossed the path of my resolve.
Confounded, I looked up to Heaven, and cast,
Idonea! thy blind Father, on the Ordeal
Of the bleak Waste—left him—and so he died!—

[IDONEA *sinks senseless;* Beggar, ELEANOR, *&c., crowd round, and bear her off.*

Why may we speak these things, and do no more;
Why should a thrust of the arm have such a power,
And words that tell these things be heard in vain?
She is not dead. Why!—if I loved this Woman,
I would take care she never woke again;
But she WILL wake, and she will weep for me,
And say, no blame was mine—and so, poor fool,
Will waste her curses on another name.

[*He walks about distractedly.*

Enter OSWALD.

Oswald (*to himself*). Strong to o'erturn, strong also to build up.

[*To* MARMADUKE.

The starts and sallies of our last encounter
Were natural enough, but that, I trust,
Is all gone by. You have cast off the chains
That fettered your nobility of mind—
Delivered heart and head!
Let us to Palestine;
This is a paltry field for enterprise.

Mar. Ay, what shall we encounter next? This issue—
'Twas nothing more than darkness deepening darkness,
And weakness crowned with the impotence of death!—
Your pupil is, you see, an apt proficient, (*ironically*).
Start not!—here is another face hard by;
Come, let us take a peep at both together,
And, with a voice at which the dead will quake,
Resound the praise of your morality—
Of this too much.

[*Drawing* OSWALD *towards the Cottage—stops short at the door.*

Men are there, millions, Oswald,
Who with bare hands would have plucked out thy heart
And flung it to the dogs: but I am raised
Above, or sunk below, all further sense
Of provocation. Leave me, with the weight
Of that old Man's forgiveness on thy heart,
Pressing as heavily as it doth on mine.

Coward I have been; know, there lies not now
Within the compass of a mortal thought,
A deed that I would shrink from;—but to endure
That is my destiny. May it be thine:
Thy office, thy ambition, be henceforth
To feed remorse, to welcome every sting
Of penitential anguish, yea with tears.
When seas and continents shall lie between us—
The wider space the better—we may find
In such a course fit links of sympathy,
An incommunicable rivalship
Maintained, for peaceful ends beyond our view.

[*Confused voices—several of the band enter—rush upon* OSWALD *and seize him.*

One of them. I would have dogged him to the jaws of Hell—

Osw. Ha! is it so!—That vagrant Hag!—this comes
Of having left a thing like her alive!
[*Aside.*

Several voices. Despatch him!

Osw. If I pass beneath a rock
And shout, and, with the echo of my voice,
Bring down a heap of rubbish, and it crush me,
I die without dishonour. Famished, starved,
A Fool and Coward blended to my wish!

[*Smiles scornfully and exultingly at* MARMADUKE.

Wal. 'Tis done! (*stabs him*).

Another of the band. The ruthless Traitor!

Mar. A rash deed!—
With that reproof I do resign a station
Of which I have been proud.

Wil. (*approaching* MARMADUKE). O my poor Master!

Mar. Discerning Monitor, my faithful Wilfred,
Why art thou here?
[*Turning to* WALLACE.
Wallace, upon these Borders,
Many there be whose eyes will not want cause
To weep that I am gone. Brothers in arms!
Raise on that dreary Waste a monument
That may record my story: nor let words—
Few must they be, and delicate in their touch
As light itself—be there withheld from Her
Who, through most wicked arts, was made an orphan
By One who would have died a thousand times,
To shield her from a moment's harm. To you,
Wallace and Wilfred, I commend the Lady,
By lowly nature reared, as if to make her
In all things worthier of that noble birth,
Whose long-suspended rights are now on the eve
Of restoration: with your tenderest care
Watch over her, I pray—sustain her——

Several of the band (*eagerly*). Captain!

Mar. No more of that; in silence hear my doom:
A hermitage has furnished fit relief
To some offenders; other penitents,
Less patient in their wretchedness, have fallen,
Like the old Roman, on their own sword's point.
They had their choice: a wanderer *must I* go,
The Spectre of that innocent Man, my guide.
No human ear shall ever hear me speak;
No human dwelling ever give me food,
Or sleep, or rest: but, over waste and wild,
In search of nothing that this earth can give,
But expiation, will I wander on—
A Man by pain and thought compelled to live,
Yet loathing life—till anger is appeased
In Heaven, and Mercy gives me leave to die.

1795–6.

Printed by BALLANTYNE, HANSON & CO
Edinburgh and London

www.ingramcontent.com/pod-product-compliance
Ingram Content Group UK Ltd.
Pitfield, Milton Keynes, MK11 3LW, UK
UKHW021034070526
12320UKWH00030B/376

9 781021 172419